A LONGMAN CRITICAL EDITION

Herman Melville
MOBY-DICK

Edited by

John Bryant
Hofstra University

Haskell Springer
University of Kansas

PEARSON
Longman

New York   Boston   San Francisco
London   Toronto   Sydney   Tokyo   Singapore   Madrid
Mexico City   Munich   Paris   Cape Town   Hong Kong   Montreal

Editor-in-Chief: Joseph Terry
Director of Development: Mary Ellen Curley
Executive Marketing Manager: Ann Stypuloski
Production Manager: Denise Phillip
Project Coordination, Text Design, and Electronic Page Makeup: Big Color
    Systems, Inc.
Cover Designer/Manager: Wendy Ann Fredericks
Cover Art: *Ahab's Boat Seemed Drawn Up Towards Heaven* by George Klauba
Senior Manufacturing Buyer: Alfred C. Dorsey
Printer and Binder: Courier Corporation
Cover Printer: Phoenix Color Corporation

Library of Congress Cataloging-in-Publication Data

Melville, Herman, 1819–1891.
  Moby-Dick / Herman Melville ; edited by John Bryant, Haskell Springer.
    p. cm. — (A Longman critical edition)
  Includes bibliographical references.
  ISBN 0-321-22800-6 (alk. paper)
  1. Melville, Herman, 1819–1891. Moby-Dick. 2. Ahab, Captain (Fictitious
character)—Fiction. 3. Whaling ships—Fiction. 4. Ship captains—Fiction.
5. Whaling—Fiction. 6. Whales—Fiction. 7. Psychological fiction. lcsh
I. Bryant, John, 1949– II. Springer, Haskell S. III. Title. IV. Series.
  PS2384.M6 2006
  813'.3—dc22

                              2006016919

Visit us at www.ablongman.com

College ISBN 0-321-22800-6
Sourcebook ISBN 0-205-51408-1

1 2 3 4 5 6 7 8 9 10—CRW—09 08 07 06

PRAISE FOR THE LONGMAN CRITICAL EDITION OF *MOBY-DICK*

"In this superb edition of *Moby-Dick*, John Bryant and Haskell Springer offer us something new. For the first time, we are able to see on the page, in a reading text, the differences between the original American and British editions of Melville's book, published a month apart in 1851. They provide a meticulously edited version of the American *Moby-Dick* and, through highlighting, notes, and learned speculation, a vivid guide to the changes made in the British text by Melville and his editors. They also offer a wealth of explanatory material for the reader, including extensive notes on Melville's references and allusions, a glossary of nautical terms, and illustrations. In the Longman Critical Edition, Bryant and Springer make palpable the distinctions between the two *Moby-Dick*s, and they encourage and equip readers to consider the meaning of those differences. It is a major achievement."

—Samuel Otter, University of California, Berkeley

"Particularly valuable for its excellent introduction and for its authoritative analysis of the often puzzling differences between the American and British editions of Melville's masterpiece."

—Lawrence Buell, Harvard University

"Many regard *Moby-Dick* as a complex, mysterious work, in which history, natural history, psychology and religious symbolism are boiled up together in what might be called a cetological bouillabaisse. John Bryant and Haskell Springer have provided a useful antidote for the kind of indigestion that often accompanies such a heavy meal. Their notes and annotations make it possible to experience Melville's great novel at the rollicking pace at which it was written, without having to stumble over unfamiliar terms, weird locutions, or enigmatic references."

—Richard Ellis, author of *Men and Whales*

"No edition of *Moby-Dick* will be more valuable and illuminating to a more diverse reading public than Longman's Critical Edition of *Moby-Dick*, edited by John Bryant and Haskell Springer. The clarity of this edition's introduction, page notes, and explanatory notes will help the newcomer with the novel's layered contexts and its allusive language, while the editors' scrupulous attention to earlier publications of the novel and their thoughtful responses to variant readings in these publications will delight the scholar. In addition, a new and accurate map of the *Pequod*'s voyage and a full glossary of nautical terms with precise explanatory drawings usefully complement the text. By reducing certain of the novel's difficulties and obscurities, the care taken by the editors in creating Longman's *Moby-Dick* provides its readers a fuller understanding of its multiple complexities. Such care assures that this edition will be the definitive *Moby-Dick* for years to come."

—Elizabeth Schultz, author of *Unpainted to the Last: Moby-Dick and Twentieth-Century American Art*

THE EDITORS

John Bryant has published numerous articles, editions, and books related to Melville, including *A Companion to Melville Studies*, *Melville & Repose: The Rhetoric of Humor in the American Renaissance*, and *Melville's Tales, Poems, and Other Writings*. As a textual scholar, he has written *The Fluid Text: A Theory of Revision and Editing for Book and Screen*, and published an online, fluid-text edition of the *Typee Manuscript*. A professor of English at Hofstra University, Bryant is also editor of *Leviathan: A Journal of Melville Studies*.

Haskell Springer has published many books and articles in American literature. He edited *America and the Sea: A Literary History* and *Studies in Billy Budd*, and co-edited *Melville and Women*. Other publications include a hypertext edition of "Bartleby, the Scrivener" and the standard scholarly edition of Washington Irving's *Sketch Book of Geoffrey Crayon*. Currently professor emeritus of English at the University of Kansas, Springer has also taught at the University of Virginia, at the Sorbonne, on sailing vessels of the Sea Education Association, and as a Fulbright Professor in Rio de Janeiro.

CONTENTS

INTRODUCTION

Mid-Atlantic. Homeward bound. January 1850. Herman Melville sat snug below deck, reading. He had spent the past two months, mostly in London, arranging the British publication of *White-Jacket*, touring the city and its environs, and taking brief excursions to France and Germany. It was to have been a longer tour, but a lack of funds and homesickness had cut it short. Now heading back to New York, he drew about him the books he had purchased in London. Already ice was forming on the rigging of the *Independence* as it cut through snow-capping waves, and in his heated cabin he began to wonder, "What next?"

Starting in 1845, he had written five books in as many years, each drawn from his life at sea. Now, it seemed, he had written out his life: his well of experience was low; the tour of Europe was to have given him new sights, ideas, and people to write about. But that adventure had been aborted. Melville was at a turning point, and the sea gave him time to focus.

Born in 1819 to a well-regarded family—his father was a prominent Bostonian; his mother, also prosperous, hailed from upstate New York; both were descendants of revolutionary heroes—Melville had enjoyed a brief spell of upward mobility as a child until his father's import business went belly up. Hard times were sharpened in 1832 when his father unexpectedly died. Herman never lacked family support—neither as a child nor as an adult—but suddenly fatherless at twelve, he found himself a kind of orphan: not abandoned or cast away, but left feeling incidental to a family that had to soldier on. No amount of travel or writing could fill this hole in him. Even so, he was always itching for remote places and was never at a loss for words.

When not working, the boy attended various private academies, but college was out of the question; like many Americans who found themselves treading water after the economic crisis of 1837, he was soon out of work. In 1839 he went to sea as a greenhorn, sailed to Liverpool and back in less than half a year, and stored up images for *Redburn* (1849). In January 1841, after a trip out west to Illinois, he signed aboard the whaling ship *Acushnet*. Eighteen months later (having touched land only twice), he had had enough, and the twenty-two-year-old jumped ship on the Pacific island of Nuku Hiva in the Marquesas. Melville's memories of hiding away with the island's Taipi tribe formed the basis of his first book, *Typee* (1846).

Making his getaway on another whaling vessel, he participated in a minor-league mutiny, ended up in a Tahitian jail, and then bummed around the Society Islands; these antics became the stuff of a second book, *Omoo* (1847), which was followed by *Mardi* (1849), a mystical, political romance. A third whaling ship took him to Hawai'i where he joined the U.S. Navy, and returned home aboard a man-of-war. That experience inspired *White-Jacket* (1850). Now a tourist on board the *Independence* and sailing home again, Melville thought that if he were to write another book, it should not be another narrative of his adventures at sea. And yet, ironically, the next thing he would write would be the greatest sea book ever written: *Moby-Dick*.

No one knows how Melville came upon the idea of writing *Moby-Dick*, whether he first conceived it as just another personal narrative, or as an ambitious fiction, like *Mardi*. No entry in his London journal hints that he would turn to whaling. In fact, his earliest intention seems to have been to write up the misadventures of Israel Potter, a Yankee prisoner of war hiding in London during the American Revolution; he had even purchased a London map of the period to help him with the biographical novel. In short, he was aiming to tell someone else's life, a departure from the first-person narrative of all five of his previous books. His mind was not on whales. But something happened aboard the *Independence*, and he put the Potter project aside. Something happened that turned him back to the sea.

Of course, given his whaling years, a whaling adventure was a natural, indeed expected, topic for him. But if so, why did Melville almost not write *Moby-Dick*?

One reason is that before Melville made whaling an engrossing topic, the subject seemed monumentally dull. Granted, nineteenth-century whaling was a dangerous business. But like war, most of the business was devoted to routine, regimentation, and boredom, until the moment of the hunt when boredom erupted into violence resulting in bloody dismemberment and death, of the whale, yourself, or both. After the hunt came more routine, but this time in butchering the whale, peeling away the blubber from the meat, and frying out its oil on deck. This involved sweat, grease, and an "unspeakable" stench. The oil was then stored in barrels so manufacturers on land could convert it into lamp oil, lubricants, and high-grade candles. Whaling was not adventure or war, it was labor: the ship, a slow-moving factory; the captain, a profit-driven capitalist; the workers, mostly society's refuse. Readers, at the time, were neither accustomed to, nor ready for, fiction based on an industry. So the first strike against a book about whaling was that readers would have to be convinced of its appeal.

The second strike, from Melville's point of view, was that, despite his closeness to the subject, the book would not "write itself" as his other books seemed to have done: it would have to be "worked up." For whaling to become entertaining, its logic and customs would have to be explained, and the story, not just the hunt but the business, would have to be either very comic, very tragic, or, as Melville eventually made it, both.

These problems had made whaling an unlikely option for Melville when he began to write professionally. But now more seasoned and now with the snow-capped waves of the Atlantic reminding him of the January day in 1841 when he first set sail on the whaling ship *Acushnet*, memories of whaling triggered the idea that his whaling life—its boredom, humor, terror, and tragedy—might fill a hole in him he needed to fill.

One approach was to "anatomize" whales and whaling life as he had just done with naval life in *White-Jacket*. That is, he would give readers an insider's view of the captains, mates, and harpooners, the carpenter, cook and cabin boys, even the whales they hunt; he would describe the ship, the hunting itself, the butchering, the "stowing down and clearing up." Interesting characters would emerge, but the hardest part—a plot—was needed.

In truth, Melville's previous books are not keenly plotted. They tend to follow the events in his life as those events had unfolded. But, with the exception of *Mardi*, whose plot is the quest for a mythic girl, most of Melville's narratives do not adhere slavishly to the Aristotelian unities of probability and necessity exhibited in the most compelling works of dramatic literature, in particular Shakespeare's. Unlike his earlier works, Melville's whaling book would have drama, and a beginning, middle, and end. But whether Melville found a plot for *Moby-Dick* aboard the *Independence*, or simply determined that he would discover his plot in the process of writing, is not known. We do know that Melville carried with him a trunk-load of books, including works by dramatists (Jonson, Davenant, Marlowe, Beaumont and Fletcher, and Shakespeare), romantics (Rousseau, Goethe, De Quincey, Lamb), and gothicists (Horace Walpole and Mary Shelley). Also in the trunk were Boswell's *Life of Johnson*, Sir Thomas Browne's *Vulgar Errors*, various guidebooks, Lavater's book on phrenology, and more. References to nearly all of these works are scattered throughout *Moby-Dick*, and it is safe to say that Melville's reading in them, either at sea or back home, helped him shape his whaling narrative, including its plot.

A year earlier, Melville had steeped himself in Shakespeare, and in a letter to his friend and editor Evert Duyckinck, he compared the "divine William" to Jesus (Melville's correspondence is collected in *Writings*, vol. 14). In London, he purchased "2 plays of Shakespeare" and other Elizabethan plays, which might have further fueled his interest in the structural elements of drama and the staging of a play. Learning the dynamics of drama—the conflicts; the tight development of act, scene, episode, and speech; the use of dialogue and soliloquy—was easy for this gifted writer. But whether he could master the dynamics of stagecraft—just how one might transform a whaling ship into a theater—remained to be seen. And by reading so much romantic and gothic fiction popular among his contemporaries, Melville was also preparing to pitch his writing to an international audience. His whaling story would nearly circumnavigate the globe, and its plot would follow the obsession of a cosmopolitan man—like Victor Frankenstein, who loses a parent in childhood, teaches himself to animate dead tissue as if this might undo his orphan status, creates a man, and vengefully and relentlessly pursues that seemingly ubiquitous, omnipotent, and symbolic monster. If the reading of Elizabethan plays and the modern novel *Frankenstein* gave Melville the structures of obsession, revenge, and transcendental being to plot his whaling fiction, then all he needed was to create a whaling world through which the plot would move: settings, conflicts, episodes, scenes, characters; but, above all, a monster to hunt: the whale itself.

THE GENESIS OF THE WHALE

The *Independence* docked in New York on February 1, 1850, and Melville spent the next year and a half writing *Moby-Dick*. Given its length and the fact that it is a remarkably tight fiction despite its apparent wanderings, readers marvel that it took Melville only eighteen months to write his masterpiece. But scholars wonder why it took him so long, given his publishing record. By June 27, 1850, he was telling his British publisher, Richard Bentley, that by late fall he would deliver the text of "a romance of adventure, founded upon certain wild legends in the Southern Sperm Whale Fisheries." Melville was on pace; however, the book did not appear until the fall of 1851, a full year later. What was the delay?

One theory is that Melville changed his mind about his book. In his letter to Bentley, Melville makes no mention of an Ishmael and Queequeg hitching up and going to sea, or of an Ahab seeking revenge, or of a symbolic white whale. Even though words like "romance" and "wild legends" might hint that he was writing something experimental like *Mardi*, Melville's further claim that the narrative would be "illustrated by the author's own experience, of two years & more as a harpooneer" signals that the proposed book would be more like *Typee* or *White-Jacket*.

If Melville was writing only a conventional narrative, what happened in the summer of 1850 to make the writer dive deeper, change his mind, and expand his "romance" into the proto-postmodern epic we know? Since the 1940s, scholars have argued that the turning point occurred in early August, 1850 when on a vacation visit to his uncle's family farm in Pittsfield, Massachusetts, Melville met Nathaniel Hawthorne.

Hawthorne had moved his growing family, temporarily, to a cottage in nearby Lenox, and Melville arranged a picnic hike up Monument Mountain that included several other literary figures: Duyckinck, Hawthorne's editor James T. Fields, the humorist and poet Oliver Wendell Holmes, and writer Cornelius Mathews. Hawthorne had just published *The Scarlet Letter*, but Melville, who had yet to read much Hawthorne, picked up instead *Mosses from an Old Manse*, a collection of short pieces, including "Young Goodman Brown" and the seriocomic sketch "Fire Worship."

Hawthorne was famously shy, but he and the more gregarious Melville (fifteen years younger) became instant friends. Melville devoured *Mosses* and immediately composed a review essay ("Hawthorne and His Mosses") for Duyckinck's journal, *Literary World*, which is now read as a manifesto for American literary originality and a national literature. In it, Melville explores Hawthorne's artful containment of dark truths within a "great intellect in repose." Hawthorne, he wrote, was a master at the "great Art of Telling the Truth" and argued that Americans like Hawthorne (Melville included) should exceed Shakespeare at this art, for, unlike the Elizabethans, who kowtowed to monarchs, Americans are free to speak the unspeakable. Of course, Melville knew that in a liberal democracy, readers are also free to complain, and that (as this edition shows) the marketplace will censor free speech.

Melville's enthusiasm for Hawthorne was irrepressible. The excitement of being back in the Berkshires—where the literati vacationed and where he had spent boyhood summers on his uncle's farm—inspired Melville to relocate his family from cramped Manhattan to a farm he called Arrowhead, adjacent to his uncle's property. Once settled, Melville visited Hawthorne, prying him out of his shell: they drank and smoked and talked; they read each other's work and wrote each other letters. Hawthorne's side of that correspondence does not survive; Melville's side provides flashes into the feverish mind that composed *Moby-Dick*.

In his April 16, 1851 letter, Melville attributes to Hawthorne "a certain tragic phase of humanity" that goes deeper than divinity. What thwarts both mankind and God, he wrote, is the secret of consciousness—how we know that we exist—and then there is the mystery of existence, itself, of "Being." In words that echo Ahab's in "The Candles" (Ch. 119), Melville places humanity on a par with God: "We mortals astonish Him as much as He us. But it is this *Being* of the matter; there lies the knot with which we choke ourselves. As soon as you say *Me*, a *God*, a *Nature*, so soon you jump from the stool and hang from the beam." Consciousness is our "tragic phase": we know that we cannot know our reason for being. Religion is just a cover-up for the rude fact that God is as clueless as we about this mystery of who we are and where we come from; and defiance is the only real response to God. Thus, Melville praises Hawthorne in his letter for being the sort who can say "NO! in thunder." Here, in these brave and defiant words—what he called in another letter his "onto-logical heroics"—is the philosophical source of Ahab's anger.

According to one theory, the encounter with Hawthorne inspired Melville to insert Ahab's tragic obsession into his heretofore conventional whaling book, and this decision, again according to theory, added months to his creative process. Others have observed the simple reality that moving from Manhattan to a Pittsfield farm seriously disrupted Melville's life and must have stalled his writing. Granted, the encounter with Hawthorne was so stimulating that Melville dedicated *Moby-Dick* to his friend, but Melville had also had other encounters predating Hawthorne that might have triggered the idea (and plot) of Ahab: the Bible's Jonah and Job, Shakespeare's Lear, Milton's Satan, Byron's heroes, Shelley's Frankenstein (as sug-gested here), and any of a number of maritime martinets. What Hawthorne did provide was a creative mind that would listen to Melville and respond. Hawthorne was Melville's best reader; no one could ask for a better friend.

A countervailing theory of delay involves the shaping of Ishmael as a character, narrator, and central consciousness. All of Melville's previous books feature a dis-tinctive first-person narrator, but none is as moody, jocular, manic, and mystical as Ishmael, and none is as bound to the tragic center of his narrative as Ishmael is to Ahab. There is an anger, a sense of being orphaned, a hole in both Ahab and Ishmael, but what distinguishes the two is how they attempt to fill their psycholog-ical vacancies: Ahab with violence, Ishmael with meditation. Ahab's vengeance drives the plot in *Moby-Dick*, but Ishmael's desire to grasp the "ungraspable" drives the novel's lyricism. The invention of Ishmael as an observer and explainer of Ahab, as a survivor and moral center, also must have added to Melville's creative delay.

Ishmael begins as an autobiographical character; looking backward, he presents himself as a comically suicidal young man who paradoxically goes to the destructive sea to avoid self-destruction and pairs up with a Polynesian harpooner, Queequeg. However, mid-book, he no longer takes part in the action and becomes a kind of stage-manager, walking us through the "play" of Ahab's dramatic interactions with the crew and himself. But he also spends much of his time, between scenes as it were, essaying on the symbolism of whales and whaling. Ishmael becomes a seriocomic voice chal-lenging the reader to find deeper meaning in the material world Ahab is out to destroy.

In all likelihood, Ishmael was part of *Moby-Dick* from the start, for it is through him (and not Ahab) that we hear the "wild legends" about whaling that

Melville had promised Bentley in late June of 1850. And Melville might have thought that his own two-year experience as a "harpooneer" (as he put it to Bentley) would be enough to fill a book. But being a whaler does not mean one knows whaling—its history, customs, and impact. To create the kind of Ishmael that this strange sort of book required—comic, mystic, encyclopedic—Melville needed to supplement personal experience with research. He needed to become a scholar, and his research into whaling sources also created delay.

MELVILLE AND HIS SOURCES
Before turning to the written sources of *Moby-Dick*, consider the sea. Melville knew the sea. His experiences in the Atlantic and Pacific inform his book's most entrancing sea passages. Ishmael goes to the sea because, for him, "meditation and water are wedded for ever"; the sea opens for him "the great flood-gates of the wonder world." He ponders its deceptive reflections, and gropes in its obscuring depths for the essence of "the ungraspable phantom of life" and of self. He is staggered by its immensity and illimitable power, embraces its serenity, fears its solitude, recoils in horror from its "universal cannibalism" and "inscrutable malice," and puzzles over its life-giving, death-dealing paradox. The sea is boundless, dark, unknown, alluring, and never still. It is the geographical equivalent of the human mind, and Melville's primary source. Second to the sea as a resource were books. Consider then Melville's reading.

Some of the wildest of whaling legends, crucial to the plotting of *Moby-Dick*, had been known to Melville even before he went to sea or saw a whale. (As "Etymology" and "Extracts" attest, the whale is as much a text as it is a beast.) First among these legends were the circumstances surrounding the *Essex*, a Nantucket whaling vessel sunk in the Pacific after repeated battering by a seemingly malicious whale. News of the disaster had electrified Americans before Owen Chase, one of the incident's few survivors, published an account in 1821. Melville knew the story and the book, and used them to remind readers of the probability of the *Pequod*'s catastrophic demise, that a whale can sink a ship. The whale that sank the *Essex* was not white, and did not have a name, but other whales had achieved legendary status in Melville's day, in particular an old white sperm whale featured in J. N. Reynolds's 1839 magazine story titled "Mocha Dick: Or The White Whale of the Pacific." Mocha is an island, not a color or a drink; and Melville obviously appropriated the name for his white whale, adapting the name "Moby," perhaps, from "mobled" (meaning "veiled") found in *Hamlet*. But more than adapting the name of his whale from popular and high-brow culture, Melville latched on to the whale's whiteness, transforming the oddity of that feature into a symbol representing the vacancy felt by both Ishmael and Ahab. For critics today, this artful transformation establishes *Moby-Dick* as a precursor of modern literature.

The oldest of "wild legends" originate in ancient myth. One fraught with meaning is the story of Jonah, the biblical prophet who tries to escape his fearful duty to God and ends up, for a spell, in the belly of a whale. Melville was far more spiritual than religious, but he knew the Bible better than any other text and felt that his contact with scripture got him closer to the writers who first confronted the problem of *Being*, *God*, and *Me*. Through Father Mapple, based on the popular seamen's preachers Enoch Mudge and Edward Taylor, Ishmael retells the Jonah legend in "The Sermon" (Ch. 9) as if Jonah's duty to the people of Nineveh to deliver his appalling message of God's destruction parallels Melville's duty to confront his own readers with the blasphemy yet logic of Ahab's anger and defiance. Equally important is the book of Job, in which "leviathan" surfaces at the end as a symbol of God; it is the tale of a man of faith and acceptance who, like Ishmael, survives affliction. Borrowing from the Greeks, Romans, and Persians, Melville also researched Hindu legend, in which creator and destroyer gods manifest themselves in human and animal forms, such as the fish-like Matsye avatar. Whales, he found, were everywhere.

But popular legend and myth were not enough to satisfy Melville's need for facts. For his book to work, it had to be believable; it had to wrap readers in the fabric of whaling's probabilities and necessities. To absorb the logic of whalemen, readers had to be exposed to the details of their work: the ship, the routine, the tools, the lines, the whale. Melville probably began his whaling research with the article on "Whales" in the *Penny Cyclopedia*, a multivolume compendium he had used in writing parts of *Redburn*. There he found references and quotations (which he cribbed) from other resources—like works by Thomas Beale and William Scoresby—which he later acquired and read more closely. He had already read, in fact reviewed, more recent publications, J. Ross Browne's *Etchings of a Whaling Cruise* (1846) and Henry Cheever's *The Whale and Its Captors* (1849). Thus, with his own invention and experiences giving him Ishmael, Queequeg, and even Ahab, and with various resources inspiring further description, commentary, and meditation, Melville was well equipped, throughout the eighteen months of writing, to "work up" various whaling legends into a modern fiction.

Melville did not write in successive chapters, beginning with "Call me Ishmael" and ending with "Epilogue." Instead, he seems to have attempted characters, scenes, and episodes in trial runs before settling on his final sequencing, and he inserted new chapters between older ones as he revised. This creative process might explain, for instance, the appearance and quick disappearance of Bulkington, a character seemingly intended to be a heroic, defiant sailor, either as a match for, or early version of, Ahab. Bulkington is simply dismissed in the brief but eloquent "The Lee Shore" (Ch. 23) shortly before Ahab is about to enter. One hint at the writing process is the tantalizing possibility that "The Town-Ho's Story" (Ch. 54) might have been a trial run for the entire novel. Here, a mutinous sailor tangles with a sadistic mate as the white whale emerges like an avenging god. The tale, narrated by Ishmael, is so tightly realized that it served as an effective pre-publication excerpt from the novel in the October, 1851 issue of *Harper's New Monthly Magazine*.

Whatever had delayed his book's completion, by April, 1851 Melville was deep into the final chapters in which Ahab breaks his quadrant, defies God and nature, and tracks down the white whale through dead reckoning. By mid-May, with planting and repairs to the farm interrupting his routine, Melville began submitting early chapters to a New York City printer for typesetting even though his text was not yet polished or even completed. By the end of June, the book was only halfway set in type. Melville found himself back home at Arrowhead "building some shanties of chapters and essays." In short, he was still composing fresh material, perhaps some of the essayistic chapters on whales for insertion into the latter half of the book, as the printer was setting and printing the first half.

At this same time, in France, the bachelor Gustave Flaubert could take six years to write his masterpiece, *Madame Bovary* (1856), while living in the country and keeping a mistress on the side. But for Melville—husband, father, farmer, and writer—it was otherwise, and he felt the pressure keenly. This hectic pace of planting, building, writing, and printing was not what he had hoped country life would be. Rushing to make ends meet, he told Hawthorne that Arrowhead was not permitting him "the calm, the coolness, the silent grass-growing mood in which a man *ought* always to compose." And spiraling down into a momentary depression, he complained: "Dollars damn me . . . and all my books are botches." But he finished *Moby-Dick*, or let's say surrendered it to publishers, so that in the fall of 1851, after eighteen months of research, writing, moving, farming, and revising, Melville's "whale" finally breached.

READING *MOBY-DICK*: EXPECTATIONS AND STRATEGIES
Today, readers of *Moby-Dick*—whether they are the general public, students and professors, or critics and artists—pick up the book as a Received Classic of American Literature, and therefore must first contend with the anxiety that such a capitalized label entails. A classic is the epitome of literary form, an object of reverence, a cultural icon. It is an obligation: we are required to like it. But *Moby-Dick* was not a classic when it first appeared; and readers then did not particularly like it. They found it irritating (for reasons still voiced today), and fifty years would pass before modern readers began to appreciate the book. When they did, it was not because *Moby-Dick* struck them as a classic, which (we assume) reinforces cultural values and does so in perfectly structured forms, but because it is defiant, iconoclastic, irreverent, and full of doubt; because it is delivered in a mingling of voices and genres; because it pulls you in and tangles you in a world of thought, feeling, and conflicted minds that both delights and terrifies, and because as some writers today attest, it gives you courage to write yourself. *Moby-Dick* is a classic because it defies classification.

The first readers of *Moby-Dick* knew that they were reading something different. Nathaniel and Sophia Hawthorne marveled at its power and symbolism, and, in Melville's mind, their response alone compensated for less enthusiastic reviews. But Melville's supporter, Evert Duyckinck, was troubled. Although he saw (better than most) that *Moby-Dick* was really three books—Ishmael's, Ahab's, and the whale's—he could not get past Melville's irreverence, and in his *Literary World* he wrote that the book was an "intellectual chowder of romance, philosophy, natural history, fine writing, good feeling, [and] bad sayings." (Reviews of Melville's works are reprinted in Higgins and Parker, *The Contemporary Reviews.*) "Chowder" was a kind way of registering what other reviewers called an "ill-compounded mixture" of genres (*Athenaeum*), an "extravaganza" (London *Examiner*), a "tangled overgrowth" (*Leader*), and "a strange and unaccountable book" (London *Morning Chronicle*). In the early nineteenth century when the words "romance" and "novel" were often interchangeable and not yet critically defined, readers expected a fictional narrative to involve family conflicts and love affairs between boy and girl, not the soliloquies of a monomaniacal captain, the allegorized and sensualized humors of a heathenish crew, and certainly not the implied "matrimonial" coupling of Presbyterian Ishmael and "savage" Queequeg, or the "amours" and birthings of whales. This was the kind of "originality" (*MR* 384) that a transcendentalist would welcome, as did George Ripley, the reviewer for the New York *Tribune*, but many found *Moby-Dick* to be wildly excessive, irreverent, and, again, a structural chowder.

Today, we embrace the experimentalism of Melville's chowder. *Moby-Dick* is both drama and meditation; it is a tragedy and comedy, a stage play and prose poem. It is essay, myth, and encyclopedia. Above all, it is language: nautical, biblical, Homeric, Shakespearean, Miltonic, cetological, alliterative, fanciful, colloquial, archaic, and unceasingly allusive. The stagy rhetoric of Ahab and mystic ruminations of Ishmael jostle with sailor lingo and the wild voices of madmen prophets. "I try all things," says Ishmael, "I achieve what I can." Most amazing are the paragraph-long sentences that defy the gravity of normal syntax, and yet stay grammatical and alive. It is as though the twisting and turning of each sentence is itself an idea conveying what William A. Butler aptly called "the sinuosities of a thought." And yet, at the same time, images are deployed in crisp bursts of language that seem all action with no philosophizing, only the sea, the whale, the man, the moment. Witness this sinuous sentence from "The Try-Works" (Ch. 96):

> As they narrated to each other their unholy adventures, their tales of terror told in words of mirth; as their uncivilized laughter forked upwards out of them, like the flames from the furnace; as to and fro, in their front, the harpooneers wildly gesticulated with their huge pronged forks and dippers; as the wind howled on, and the sea leaped, and the ship groaned and dived, and yet steadfastly shot her red hell further and further into the blackness of the sea and the night, and scornfully champed the white bone in her mouth, and viciously spat round her on all sides; then the rushing Pequod, freighted with savages, and laden with fire, and burning a corpse, and plunging into that blackness of darkness, seemed the material counterpart of her monomaniac commander's soul.

Facing such challenges to our regular notions of fiction and language, we must adjust our expectations of a narrative and also develop some new strategies for reading.

One strategy for following *Moby-Dick* is to recognize that it is a tragic play called "Ahab" within a seriocomic meditation called "Ishmael." Essentially, *Moby-Dick* is Ishmael's story. A moody, anxious landsman, Ishmael goes to sea to come to terms with the injustices of power, the violence within others and himself, the inadequacy of faith, the nothingness of existence, and yet the mystery of consciousness (what he calls the "ungraspable phantom of life"). He witnesses love and self-possession in Queequeg, anger in Ahab, abandonment and insanity in Pip, atheism and nothingness in Moby Dick. He alone survives the white whale's attack. Telling the tale is his working out of the love, abandonment, anger, and despair. To the extent that he is the central focus of Ishmael's tale, Ahab is a staged projection of Ishmael's anger and despair. Ishmael writes in order to contain the Ahab in him: defiance, narcissism, self-destruction.

By keeping in mind Ishmael's embedding of Ahab's consciousness, we recognize that Ishmael and Ahab think and speak differently. Ahab is dramatic, at times melodramatic; he struts and frets upon the deck-like stage; he delivers soliloquies: he is all Shakespeare. As with any drama, his scenes involve conflict and confrontation, and his words propel the action. He is a force of linearity in the book, and is an iron-railed thinker. He sees Moby Dick as a conscious, evil force, either a god of malice or God's willful, reasoning agent. The whale has bitten off his leg (and, it is hinted, some part of his masculinity), and he will hunt this phantom beast, and kill it. Moreover, he will manipulate and subvert the crew into following him in this crazy, but then not-so-crazy, pursuit. Ahab plots his revenge and gives the narrative its linear plot.

Ishmael, on the other hand, is far from linear. He interrupts the Ahab plot to digress on some aspect of whales and whaling. These meditative essays freeze the action but allow us to see more deeply the connections between man and nature, crew and Ahab, or Ahab and mind that make the action plausible. The digressions might examine the whale's dual vision, its warm blanket of blubber, unknowable face, feeding and mating patterns, or indomitable tail; or whaling's entangling ropes and its rendering the whale into a marketable commodity. In each of these "ceto-logical" chapters, Ishmael invariably finds a connection to you, the reader, and thus draws you into the logic of Ahab's obsession and into Ishmael's habit of grasping at the ungraspable. Ishmael confronts a thing in order to sing out the essence of that thing. He can also lose himself, as when he finds himself perched at the mast-head lost in a transcendental, pantheistic trance, becoming one with the universe. But the consequence of such self-negation—the dissolving of the "me" into the "oversoul"—is that in such a self-less state, you can "slip your hold" and suddenly, falling to your death, your identity returns to you in horror. Ishmael's transcendental digressions are compelling but as potentially disastrous as Ahab's linearity.

Since *Moby-Dick* is structured around these two consciousnesses, the book requires us to remain open to both ways of thinking. Often, though, we come to *Moby-Dick* preconditioned to favor one way and not the other. We arrive as an Ishmael or an Ahab. Thus, some readers love Ishmael and find Ahab's histrionics excessive, while some love Ahab and have no patience for Ishmael's digressions and symbolizing. One might skip the chapters one does not like, but the brilliance of *Moby-Dick* is that Ishmael and Ahab are versions of one another, and by the book's end their voices seem to blend, and this makes skipping chapters a hard choice. A better strategy is to develop both Ishmaelean and Ahabian modes of reading. If you are in an Ahabian mood, task yourself to finish an Ishmael chapter and discern its relevance to Ahab, and to you. If an Ishmaelite, notice how Ahab's certitude is only a crust concealing his fear of nothingness. In the end, both Ahab and Ishmael are orphans trying to make sense of the holes in their lives.

As a political novel, *Moby-Dick* requires us to develop strategies of interpretation that relate past and present. Conceived soon after the Mexican War and just as the laws known as the Compromise of 1850 were enacted to restore the fragile balance of power between North and South, the events on board the *Pequod* act out the problems of a democracy in conflict with capitalism, racism, and imperialism still relevant today. Ahab is not only a captain of industry but the demagogic leader of a crew representing all nations and races. The multicultural crew is easily swayed by the promise of Ahab's gold doubloon, generous portions of rum, and parlor tricks involving magnetism and static electricity. In the book's most stage-like scene, "Midnight, Forecastle" (Ch. 40), the racial harmony established by Ishmael and Queequeg's sensual friendship is shattered when the crew's equally sensual dancing erupts into racial conflict. Witnessing the mob scene's symbolic disintegration of democracy is the black cabin boy, Pip, who fifty chapters later endures a mental disintegration after incidents in which he is reminded that he is worth less than a whale and left to drown. Brutalized, commodified, and abandoned, Pip becomes the ship's conscience but speaks in riddling gibberish. His proposal to Ahab in "The Cabin" (Ch. 129) that he might stand in for his captain's lost leg and mend the fractured, angry man—and mend as well America's racial divide on the eve of Civil War—is, perhaps, the book's finest political moment.

Moby-Dick remains a lively fiction because its critique of America, beyond the problem of race and capitalism that still persists, resonates with other current events of our day. Recent readers find an affirmation of gay liberation in Ishmael and Queequeg's affection; a warning against totalitarianism, the Cold War, modern imperialism, even nuclear annihilation in Ahab's destructive obsession; and, since September 11, 2001, a debate on terrorism (the whale) and disastrous overreaction to it (Ahab) in the novel's central conflict. If, after all, *Moby-Dick is* a classic, it is because its dynamic structure and engrossing symbolism encourage readers to develop new ways of reading it, as they grow and as the nation grows.

MOBY-DICK AS FLUID TEXT

The story of how *Moby-Dick* came to be, or how one might read that text, or what, for that matter, the "text" of *Moby-Dick* actually is, is not entirely over. *Moby-Dick* is a "fluid text": it exists in multiple versions created by a process of revision involving changes to the original made by Melville, his editors, and modern scholars. This Longman Critical Edition (LCRE) of *Moby-Dick* is designed to give unprecedented access to these various kinds of revision so that readers may witness how *Moby-Dick*—its actual wording—has evolved. By reading *Moby-Dick* as a fluid text, we experience new and vibrant ways of understanding Melville's creative process, the world of his readers, and the book's meaning.

Moby-Dick exists in two historical versions—the American and British first editions—each consisting of meaningfully different wordings, each representing a different stage in Melville's creative process, and each aimed at a different audience. In 1988, textual scholars offered an edition that conflated the two historical editions, thereby providing a third *Moby-Dick*.

The two historical versions derive from nineteenth-century publishing practices. Because no international copyright law existed then, British and American publishers were not obliged to honor each other's copyrights. That is, American publishers could reprint British works, and vice versa, without paying royalties, thus depriving the writers of significant income. Charles Dickens was particularly outraged by such piracies, but American writers were doubly disadvantaged. American publishers pirated popular British works to such an extent that lesser-known American writers, who demanded and needed royalties, could not compete. But when Americans were published at home, they had no guarantee that British publishers would not pirate their works as well. To guard against piracy, writers attempted to secure copyrights simultaneously in both countries. Melville had done this for all of his books, and in the summer of 1851, even as he was inserting various "chapters and essays" to complete *Moby-Dick*, he arranged for the dual publication of his book on both sides of the Atlantic.

Melville had already contracted with Harper and Brothers to publish *Moby-Dick* in America, but he did something unusual. Typically, a writer submits a manuscript, and it is copyedited, then set in type, printed, and distributed by the publisher. But either to save money or avoid censoring in the copyediting process, Melville arranged to have his book typeset by an independent printer, Robert Craighead of New York City, who set *Moby-Dick* in type directly from the manuscript Melville was expanding and polishing in the spring and summer of 1851. In turn, Melville handed over the printed pages to Harper and Brothers for binding and distribution in America. This means that Melville served as his own copyeditor, so the American edition is free of editorial censoring and expurgations. In order to promote sales, Melville's American publisher re-set (and edited with only minor changes) one chapter of *Moby-Dick*, "The Town-Ho's Story" (Ch. 54), for the October, 1851 issue of *Harper's New Monthly Magazine*.

To secure his copyright, Melville also arranged for his book to be published in England by Richard Bentley. To do this, he sent Bentley a set of proof sheets taken from the American edition, which Bentley would then have to re-set in type. However, before he sent the American proofs to England, Melville could not resist making changes, which he entered directly onto the proof sheets. In doing so, he *corrected* misprinted words, but he also *revised* his text; that is, he changed his mind about various original wordings. Most of these changes involved single words and phrases; in one instance, he added a lengthy footnote about the word "gallied." But because Melville's American typesetter had already molded stereotyped (that is, fixed) plates from the assembled pieces of moveable type used and then recycled in typesetting *Moby-Dick*, Melville could no longer make the same revisions to his American text. Therefore, the American and British texts vary with regard to Melville's intended wording.

But more: Melville's British publisher further revised *Moby-Dick*. Once Bentley received Melville's revised proof sheets, he submitted them to a consulting reader and copyeditor with certain understandings. As early as *Mardi*, the publisher had appreciated Melville's genius, but he also knew the limits of his Victorian readers: they had little tolerance for even the hint of irreverence, coarse language, sexual innuendo, and revolutionary politics, even if the irreverence, language, and politics are delivered by characters meant to be irreverent, racy, and rebellious. To protect Melville's text from itself, Bentley and his editorial staff made scores of deletions: single words, lines, paragraphs, and one entire chapter. They also made changes for the sake of style, grammar, sentence sense, and British usage. And, of course, by having his own printer re-set the text from scratch, Bentley also introduced as many new typographical errors as he and Melville might have corrected. But even typos, if they are themselves recognizable words in context, can change meaning in seemingly intended ways. Thus, at all levels, the British edition varies significantly from the American.

We know, then, that *Moby-Dick* exists in different versions. How do we "read" the differences? How do we even know what the differences are? One way of knowing would be to inspect Melville's manuscript of *Moby-Dick* and the proof sheets he sent to England. The manuscript might show us how Melville inserted chapters and revised words; the proofs would certainly show us the revisions he made in one ink and those his British editor made in another. But these two important documents are lost. Part of Melville's *Typee* manuscript has survived, and it shows Melville to be an inveterate reviser, not only of words but of attitudes and ideas; surviving proof sheets of other works also show him tinkering with the tiniest of details. Certainly Melville revised *Moby-Dick* as intensely as he revised these other works. And regardless of the size of his revisions, each is a peep-hole into the creative process. As an artist, Melville struggled with language to make words represent the shifting of meaning in his mind. Ideas evolve; they require new wordings, which, in turn, trigger new ideas. The core of a writer and of a text is in these shiftings. If we are to read *Moby-Dick*, we need access to Melville's revisions in whatever way we might discern them.

Lacking the manuscript and proofs for *Moby-Dick*, we have only the American and British texts as evidence of revision. The British edition is what scientists call a "black box": it contains hundreds of differences, but we can only guess at who made them and why. Some are due to Melville's shifting intentions or corrections; others, to Bentley's intended and unintended changes and expurgations. All are intermingled in the black box. One might assume that any large deletion is automatically a British expurgation, but some may be attributed to Melville's change of mind or even self-censoring. The smallest of changes—simple *water* to the biblical *waters*, let's say, or even the addition of a crucial comma—might be Melville's correction, or an editor's revision, or a printer's mistake. To sort out these matters, we must read each change critically. In making our educated guesses about who did what to *Moby-Dick* and why, we see more clearly what is at stake for writer and editor; we recognize how simple changes embody the desire for meaning and the anxiety over meaning in both Melville and British culture. Our profit from such scrutiny is that we learn more about language, Melville, and his world.

The problem, of course, is that we cannot *see* Melville's revisions directly unless we hold the two texts of *Moby-Dick* together. Decades ago, scholars charted the textual differences in *Moby-Dick* by comparing (collating) the British and American editions word for word and making lists of the variants. But critical and editorial theories at the time were not open to the idea that revisions to a literary work were as aesthetically or culturally relevant as what was finally intended. In following this principle, the Northwestern-Newberry (NN) editors, first in their 1967 Norton Critical Edition and then in their revised 1988 edition, created an "eclectic" edition of *Moby-Dick* that selectively combines elements of the two versions. They based their text on the American version but altered it in scores of places so as to include some (not all) of the revisions plausibly made by Melville in the British edition. They also made changes of their own to bring their conflated text more fully into conformity with their conception of Melville's final intention. The result was the creation of a third version of *Moby-Dick*. While the NN text, with its numerous corrections of and changes to the American edition, has become a standard reading text for *Moby-Dick*, the Longman Critical Edition of *Moby-Dick* offers a significant alternative.

The LCRE *Moby-Dick* adopts a different approach. It presents the original text of the American edition, lightly edited to remove obvious typos (such as "tke" for "the") and to correct misspellings of certain words, names, and places (for instance, "Cooke" for explorer James Cook); the List of Emendations records all changes. However, in order to showcase the revisions made to *Moby-Dick*, we have printed in a gray typeface those places in the American text that were later revised or expurgated in the British and NN editions. For each of these grayed revision sites, this edition also supplies a Revision Narrative, either on the text page near the site or in the section called Making *Moby-Dick*. Each narrative provides the revised wording, discusses who might have made the revision and why, and directs readers to possible interpretations. Revision sites too numerous to discuss are indicated in Changes Not Discussed.

With this new fluid text edition in hand, readers will want to develop their own strategies of reading and interpretation. They may choose to read only the text of *Moby-Dick* and experience the book in the form in which Americans first experienced it. Or they may pause at each revision site in gray type, examine the revisions noted in the revision narrative, and consider how Melville's text evolved.

This introduction can only touch on a small sampling of the revisions discussed in this edition of *Moby-Dick*.

Some of Bentley's revisions were blunders that nevertheless have interpretive consequences. Chief among them was the failure to print the book's "Epilogue," which relates the fact that Ishmael survives the sinking of the *Pequod*. For Melville's first British readers, *The Whale*, as it was titled, was a tale told by a dead man, a point British reviewers enjoyed making, and an omission that would embarrass any craftsman, like Melville, hoping to prove himself in the literary marketplace. The changes most readily assignable are the British edition's political, sexual, and religious expurgations. The largest cut was the removal of "Postscript" (Ch. 25), probably one of Melville's late-added "chapters and essays" directly addressing British readers and comparing a king to a "head of salad." If Melville's British publisher found such flippancy objectionable, he was all the more threatened by the idea expressed in the following chapter ("Knights and Squires") that God is the "centre and circumference of all democracy": for Bentley, not only must the divine right of kings be respected, but the divinely granted rights of the people shall not be mentioned. God is not "democratic," and Melville's pronounced antimonarchical sentiments were routinely excised.

The degree to which Victorians would not abide coarse language, sexuality, and irreverence is hard for modern readers to fathom. The word "Blast" (meaning "curse") is changed to "Hang." Stubb's joke on himself and the cook—"Why, damn your eyes, you mustn't swear [while preaching]" (Ch. 64)—is a fine undoing of Victorian hypocrisy, but it was reduced to "Why, you mustn't swear [while preaching]." Still funny, though not nearly. For Victorians, explicit sexual reference was unacceptable in a literary text, where the word "sex" referred only to male and female genders. Sexuality was expunged, although not evenly and not entirely. References to "obstetrics" (Ch. 78) and the treatment of sky and sea as bride and groom (Ch. 132) were cut, as was the reference to Ishmael and Queequeg's "matrimonial" hugging and intertwined legs (Ch. 4 and 11). Ironically, more gay than heterosexual reference remains intact in the British version because homosocial love, in particular, male bonding, was not considered at the time to imply homosexual behavior, whereas heterosexuality was taken as a vulgar reality. Perhaps the most devastating expurgation is the removal of Ishmael's shocking claim in "The Whiteness of the Whale" (Ch. 42) that "deified nature paints like the harlot." This "NO! in thunder" conclusion manages to offend not simply God, but also transcendental naturalists, perhaps even secular humanists. Today, the line is read as a climactic passage in a crucial chapter; but for British readers, it simply was not there.

Many of the British expurgations tone down Melville's irreverence or, as in the sexually tinged remark about "deified nature," his downright blasphemy. Victorians treated the institutions of the church, in particular the Church of England, as if they were Faith itself, as if any flippancy or disrespect regarding the Bible, its tales and characters, the ministry and its missionaries was a blow to the hierarchies of authority and belief. These institutions were social walls erected as Britain evolved into a nation state and world power, and they were also convenient walls of the mind, preventing one from thinking too fully about things best left unexamined: God, Queen, Empire. Melville's irreverence chipped at these sacred walls. Bentley made sizable cuts to Ishmael's use of the New Testament story of Lazarus and Dives because of its critique of modern capitalism (Ch. 2), and toward the end of the novel where the *Pequod* approaches its demise, he removed a series of aptly ironic references to the archangel Gabriel and the apocalyptic doom he is to announce. Bentley not only cut words; he revised them as well, with laughable results: where Ishmael describes Ahab as having a "crucifixion in his face" (Ch. 28), Bentley gave him instead "an apparently eternal anguish in his face." In an age when doubt and scientific revolution were challenging faith in God, editors like Bentley treated Melville's iconoclasm as a corrosion of already crumbling religious institutions and conventions.

Melville too made a significant number of small changes, with big consequences. In some cases he added words to extend an already present image, such as when he revised a whale's skeleton or "hull" to "embryo hull" (Ch. 103), thus bringing gestation and death together. One set of revisions heightens stage effects. These might be as simple as the italicizing of the word "he" in Bildad's groaning retort, "What lay does *he* want?" (Ch. 16), to underscore the groaning. In other stagings, the use of "ye" to indicate informal sailor talk stands in contrast to the more gentlemanly "you." The subtle shift indicates Melville's close attention to voice and class consciousness. Other changes affect tone and meaning. The dropping of a word, for instance, can be profound. In Ch. 32, Ishmael calls the Killer and Thrasher whales outlaws "even in the lawless seas." The implication is that all seas are lawless. But in the British edition, "the" has been omitted, and the meaning intensifies, for "even in lawless seas" implies that only some seas are lawless, and these Killer and Thrasher whales, considered outlaws even in such lawless seas, are made to seem all the more lawless. A similar kind of change, this time an alteration of prepositions, occurs in the phrase "demonism in the world," which precedes the shocking claim about "deified Nature" censored in Ch. 42. Here, "in" is changed to "of": In the American version, demonism may reside in certain localized places *in* the world, but the British version turns demonism into an inherent element *of* the entire world. A printer might have made this change accidentally, but it intensifies Ishmael's sense of the ubiquity *of* the demonic, and chances are Melville intended the revision.

In some revision sites, we find changes that only an author, not an editor or printer, is likely to make. In describing the relation of chance, fate, and free will in "The Mat-Maker" (Ch. 47), Melville thought better of his first view that chance and fate are "directed" by free will, and he toned the word down to "modified," thus diminishing the human power to act. In "The Honor and Glory of Whaling" (Ch. 82), Melville first wrote that "we find the head-waters of our fraternity" in the gods. The water image articulates a familiar principle of universal brotherhood. But in the British edition, "fraternity" has been changed to "paternity." Of course, a typesetter might have simply misread one word for the other, but "paternity" also more fully resonates with Ahab's and Ishmael's orphan-like search for their origins. If not a typo, Melville's "fraternity" to "paternity" revision is emblematic of one of the book's hidden themes: we are brothers looking for fathers. A more certain Melville revision occurs in Ch. 133 when Ahab peers into the water as Moby Dick comes swimming up at him from below. At first Ahab sees nothing, and in the American version Melville writes that Ahab could "discover no sign" of the whale. "Discovery" is finding what already exists. However, *Moby-Dick* is about reading symbols (the sea, the whale), or rather "perceiving" them, and perception is a matter of shaping what exists by the way in which we see it. In the British edition, "discover" is changed to "perceive" at the moment Ahab waits for the whale. At issue is not that Ahab would "discover" the whale as a thing; but that he would "perceive" it as a symbol of his making.

If the revisions Melville made to the British text seem to give us "better" readings or reveal what Melville "finally wanted," why don't the editors of the LCRE *Moby-Dick* simply make those changes to the original text? First, "better" and "finally wanted" are highly debatable terms. But more to the point, the goal of editing a fluid text is to keep versions distinct. The NN editors chose to combine versions in their edition and added some authorial revisions (for instance, "embryo"), refrained from adding others (such as "paternity"), and made revisions of their own (discussed in our revision narratives). Rather than mixing versions, the LCRE *Moby-Dick* presents the unrevised text of the first American edition and uses distinctively-marked revision narratives either on the page or in the back to show where and what Melville and his editors revised. With this approach, readers have fuller access to Melville's first printed text and a clearer understanding of his revision process. And by seeing what is at stake in each revision, readers also have new access to the total text of *Moby-Dick*: what it might have meant for Melville, for his editors and early readers, and what it means for us today.

MOBY-DICK TODAY: SYMBOL AND ICON

In Rio de Janeiro, a driving school advertises its name on its fleet of white Volkswagen Beetles: "Auto Escola Moby Dick." As a fluid text, *Moby-Dick* has evolved beyond its historical editions and into the popular imagination. The white whale is everywhere. But that evolution was slow in coming, especially during the remainder of Melville's life.

For Melville, *Moby-Dick* was one of many books he needed to peel off his brain. He continued to publish at his furious rate throughout most of the 1850s. His psychological novel, *Pierre*, followed immediately in 1852 and shocked readers with its alleged immoralities. To regain his readership and a steadier income, he turned to magazine writing, producing for *Harper's* and *Putnam's* such stories as "Bartleby, the Scrivener," "Benito Cereno," and the serialized novel *Israel Potter*. His last published fiction was a dark comedy, *The Confidence-Man* (1857). Exhausted, Melville toured the Mediterranean and Holy Land, and the journey proved to be transformative: he returned a poet. The failure of *Battle-Pieces* (1866), a collection of craggy, unsentimental Civil War poems, signaled the end of his career as a professional writer. But he continued to write and to issue poems in limited editions. In 1876, he published his epic, *Clarel,* set in and around Jerusalem. Before his death in 1891, he put out two other volumes of selected poems, leaving behind another volume ready for publication and the unpolished manuscript of *Billy Budd.*

During these years as a poet, Melville's literary reputation vanished: he was no longer a public figure; indeed, he relished obscurity. Working as a customs official, he wrote poems and saw himself as a poet, not the author of *Moby-Dick.* Readers (many in England) remembered the whaling book, but considered *Typee* to be his major work. Shortly after his death both books were republished, but Melville's reputation did not begin to grow again until the 1920s when writers (such as D. H. Lawrence) and scholars (Raymond Weaver and Carl Van Doren among others) challenged a modern generation to examine his life and works. Soon enough *Moby-Dick* was heralded as the "best sea story ever told," and remarkably, in 1926, a film adaptation, *The Sea-Beast,* starring John Barrymore, was released (see Illustrations). It mattered not, apparently, that Barrymore's version bears no real resemblance to *Moby-Dick*—Ahab competes with a brother for the affections of a girl (played by Barrymore's then-current paramour), kills the whale, and lives happily ever after—what matters is that the iconic image of an angry embittered American slaying a mythic beast seemed to capture the popular imagination.

Modern writers and critics were captivated as well and, oddly enough, for similar reasons. Melville became recognized as an early practitioner of symbolism. In Melville's novel, the white whale does not appear until the last three chapters, but it enters our consciousness early on as a phantom, is elaborated in terms of myth, is further anatomized so that all of its parts have meaning, and eventually becomes just an "object," whose meaning is entirely a matter of our individual perception. Furthermore, in "The Whiteness of the Whale" (Ch. 42), Ishmael isolates the meaning of Moby Dick in whiteness itself, so that the mythic whale becomes a symbolic whale. But what is this whiteness? A blank—"a colorless all-color of atheism." And what, then, is this blank symbol of blankness? A word, a sound: everything and yet nothing. What intrigues modern and postmodern readers is that Melville uses symbolism to get at the heart of the whale's fearful meaning, but the discovered meaning is "there is no meaning," so that Melville's most subversive achievement is both the construction and deconstruction of symbolism.

Moby-Dick is compelling because its range of thought and emotion encompasses all and nothing, both the delight and the terror of seeking truth. But what makes it appealing is also what makes it appalling. Why, then, does such a challenging book as *Moby-Dick* have such a vibrant life in the world's popular culture: its movies, comics, and commerce? The answer may lie in popular culture's obsession with death, the unknown, and personality; or its ability to convert challenging symbols into safe icons, feeling into sentiment, and terror into something manageable, tangible, and knowable. Thus, in popular culture, the image of Moby the whale is an icon that, like the Christian cross, represents great peril and deep pain but is also the object of enormous affection.

In the 1956 John Huston film, *Moby Dick*, Melville's novel is transformed into yet another version, happily more accurate in terms of plot than the Barrymore film, but again modified, this time to reflect a postwar, cinematic age. In this adaptation, written by science fiction novelist Ray Bradbury, the "Ahab" plot prevails; and while Ishmael and Queequeg start the movie, their enduring presence and Ishmael's meditations are nonexistent. Ahab's demise, however, is altered. In Melville's book, Fedallah (Ahab's prophet) precedes Ahab in death, as predicted: the dark figure is caught in the ropes that entangle Moby Dick and is taken down, rising up a corpse the next day still attached to the whale and eyeing Ahab. In Huston's film, Fedallah does not exist. However, Ahab is given Fedallah's mode of death, so that Ahab, memorably played by Gregory Peck, is seen tangled up with Moby Dick, rising as a corpse, stretched as if crucified (for indeed he is), and beckoning the crew to follow (see Illustrations). And to a man (except one), they follow to their deaths. This revised conclusion fits a Cold War need for martyred men of action following their martyred captain to the end, in pursuit of monstrous evil. Huston's melodramatization of Ahab and the film's iconic conclusion are so compelling for postwar audiences that even readers who know better imagine Ahab as Peck strapped to Moby Dick, forgetting that in the book Ahab is caught around the neck by a flying loop of rope and immediately jerked overboard, never to be seen again.

The Barrymore and Huston films show how readers in different periods of American popular culture have re-written *Moby-Dick*. In effect, such adaptations continue the process of textual revision that makes Melville's book a fluid text. Melville's whale has been abridged for children numerous times in numerous languages, and adapted for stage, radio, and television. In his 1955 play *Moby Dick Rehearsed*, Orson Welles brilliantly explores the intersection between *King Lear* and the book. In 2004, actor Chris Moore offered up Ishmael and Ahab in a bracing, one-hour monologue. Innovative, multimedia performances combining words, music, dance, and art by JoAnne Spies (1997), Ellen Driscoll (1998), and Laurie Anderson (1999) have extended our understanding of the book in their interpretive renderings of it, while at the same time they firmly establish Melville's ardent readership among women. Actor and singer Rinde Eckert's operatic production, *And God Created Great Whales* (2000), is about a composer trying to write an opera of *Moby-Dick* while losing his short-term memory: funny and tragic, it does more justice to Melville's Ishmael and Pip than any other adaptation thus far.

Melville and his novel frequently surface in the world of art, books, film, and, of course, cartoons, either as the core inspiration for a work or tangentially through direct quotation. Renowned artist and writer Maurice Sendak frequently inserts visual references to famous artists, in particular Herman Melville, in his children's books. Among other artists, Leonard Baskin, Mark Milloff, George Klauba (see cover illustration), Aileen Callahan, and Robert Del Tredici have created sets of *Moby-Dick*-inspired graphic art. The postexpressionist sculptor Frank Stella has completed a long series of works in metal and found objects, some monumental and each taking the title of a chapter from Melville's book. Novels by Sena Jeter Naslund (*Ahab's Wife*) and Frederick Busch (*The Night Inspector*) build upon Melville's life and work. References to *Moby-Dick* invariably crop up in recent films: Woody Allen's title character in *Zelig* cannot finish the book; in *Fried Green Tomatoes*, a minister swears in court on his own Bible to tell the truth but (happily) lies, revealing later that his "Bible" was a copy of *Moby-Dick*; in the Coen brothers' *Oh Brother Where Art Thou*, our heroes are saved in a flood when a coffin rises to the surface. The postwar French film noir director Jean-Pierre Melville changed his original name to honor the author. Since the first appearance of Louis Zansky's *Moby-Dick* in the *Classic Comics* series in 1942 (see Illustrations), the book has been drawn or featured over a dozen times in comic book format. *Moby-Dick* has inspired several resilient motifs in comic strips and single-panel cartoons: Melville struggling with editors trying to change his opening line, Moby rear-ending Ahab in traffic, and so on.

Each of the artists mentioned offers a "version" of *Moby-Dick*, and, in doing so, gives us a tangible, creative interpretation. Their renderings of the whale in the fine and popular arts are a measure of the culture's fascination with Melville's challenging subjects: Ahab's anger, Ishmael's pragmatic idealism, the whale's phantom of life and death. As readers, they rewrite *Moby-Dick*. But in rewriting, they show how modern readers reconstruct the text to resemble the modern imagination. Thus, *Moby-Dick* becomes a true cultural icon, a mirror of ourselves. Rather than a frozen emblem of some lost national identity, it is a text that evolves because we need it to evolve, as we evolve. But if we are to comprehend ourselves and our own evolutions as individuals and as a culture, and if *Moby-Dick* is itself evolving, we must first read the book not only as the symbol and cultural icon it has become, but as a work created in its own time and place. This Longman Critical Edition gives readers that first text, and more. But it is the reader who in reading makes Ahab, Ishmael, and the whale happen; it is the reader who makes *Moby-Dick* evolve.

ACKNOWLEDGMENTS

The editors have worked closely together on all features of the LCRE *Moby-Dick* and throughout all phases of its development. John Bryant prepared the text, determined its emendations and revision sites, and is principal writer of the revision narratives and the introduction. Haskell Springer is principal writer of the footnotes, explanatory notes, and glossary, and he assembled the illustrations. However, both editors vetted, revised, and augmented each other's work so that each segment of the edition is the product of true collaboration.

No editorial project of a literary work as highly regarded as *Moby-Dick* can come to fruition without the benefit of the scholarship of past editors and the guidance of present colleagues. While the reading text of the LCRE *Moby-Dick* provides a distinct alternative to the Northwestern-Newberry (NN) edition, it draws (as any new edition must) upon the NN collations; the editors would also like to thank, in particular, Harrison Hayford and G. Thomas Tanselle for the encouragement they have offered scholars in pursuing critical editions of their own. In addition, we are grateful to the following individuals for their feedback and assistance: John Barrow, Virginia Blanford, Michael Dyer, Mary K. Bercaw Edwards, Richard Ellis, Leonard Finegold, Anne Fowler, Stephen Grimsley, Henry Hughes, M. Thomas Inge, Wyn Kelley, Jeffrey Levine, Dennis Marnon, Members of ISHMAIL (the Melville

Society's discussion list), James Millinger, Boyce Moses, Steven Olsen-Smith, Samuel Otter, Kathleen Piercefield, Jack Putnam, Elizabeth Schultz, Robert K. Wallace, and John Wolf.

The editors would like to thank the University of Kansas and Hofstra University for their support, as well as the National Endowment for the Humanities for providing John Bryant with released time from teaching in 2004–05.

Finally, we are grateful to Longman's staff for the support and guidance provided at every step of the editorial, development, and production process, including Roth Wilkofsky, Joseph Terry, Lai Moi, Mary Ellen Curley, and Denise Phillip, and to Lorraine Patsco for contributions to layout and design.

THE LONGMAN CRITICAL EDITION OF *MOBY-DICK*

The Longman Critical Edition Series provides general readers, instructors, and students an accessible and informed reading experience of classic literary works in a readable format with thorough and unobtrusive notes. A distinctive feature of the series is its focus on revision and the different versions (fluid texts) of a given work generated by the author's writing process, the demands of publishing, even censorship and adaptation.

THE TEXT OF *MOBY-DICK*

Moby-Dick has a fascinating textual history. Separate American and British editions appeared within a month of each other in 1851; however, the British version expurgated numerous passages while it also included other revisions sanctioned by Melville. A reliable scholarly edition of *Moby-Dick* did not appear until the Northwestern-Newberry edition (NN) of 1988. This modern edition adds to the American text certain corrections and revisions derived from the British edition as well as changes made by the editors, and it creates a third version of *Moby-Dick* that approximates the NN editors' conception of Melville's "final intentions." (See Making *Moby-Dick* for more details.)

The Longman Critical Edition (LCRE) of *Moby-Dick*, with its focus on stages of revision, does not combine American and British versions, but instead bases its text on the American edition to create an accurate representation of Melville's first printed text. The copy-text for this Longman Critical Edition is the first American edition of *Moby-Dick*, located in the Taylor Collection at the Alderman Library, University of Virginia (Taylor 1851 .M44 M6). In preparing this edition's reading text, the editors used the electronic transcription of the Taylor volume, proofed and corrected in 2002. This prepared text was proofed twice again, directly against digital images of each page of the Taylor volume: once before revision sites were indicated and revision narratives, annotations, and emendations were added (see below), and then once again just at press time. In preparing the revision sites and emendations, the LCRE editors drew upon the collations listed in the textual apparatus of the 1988 Northwestern-Newberry (NN) and 1952 Hendricks House editions, the working papers of the NN editorial project located at The Newberry Library, Chicago, and direct inspections of the American and British first editions at the Newberry Library and the Berg Collection of the New York Public Library.

REVISION SITES AND REVISION NARRATIVES

Revision Sites are places in the original text where Melville or Melville's editors (historical and modern) made changes to *Moby-Dick*. By and large, most of the revision sites are deletions of sexual, religious, or political content insisted upon by Melville's British publisher; these range in length from a sentence or paragraph to an entire chapter. But many smaller sites—a word, phrase, or sentence—may represent meaningful changes added later by Melville himself, or his modern scholarly editors.

- In the LCRE *Moby-Dick*, the words of a ***Revision Site*** are indicated in the reading text in gray type.

- In those cases in which a Revision Site demonstrates a significant critical or cultural problem, its ***Revision Narrative*** appears near the site set off distinctively from the rest of the text.

- Revision Narratives for all other revision sites appear at the back of the book in **Making *Moby-Dick***, and are keyed to the page and line numbers of the site.

For example, readers coming upon the grayed passage "**Do you think the archangel Gabriel thinks anything the less of me**" will know that these words in the American edition were later revised in some way, and as the accompanying Revision Narrative on that page explains, the sentence was cut completely, by British editors, for religious reasons. Readers coming upon "I at last came to **a dim sort of light**" in Chapter 2 but finding no Revision Narrative on the page will know that a narrative can be found in "Making *Moby-Dick*," in this case explaining that Melville revised the sentence to "I at last came to a dim sort of out-hanging light."

ANNOTATIONS AND ILLUSTRATIONS

The LCRE *Moby-Dick* also includes a full range of lively, non-interpretive annotations explaining literary allusions and the biographical, historical, and cultural aspects of each work. It includes four features: footnote, explanatory note, glossary, and graphic illustration.

- ***Footnotes*** briefly define unusual words, places, or references (such as *Battery* and *mole*) that might obstruct reading if left unexplained. Such words are indicated with a degree sign (°) in the text and appear italicized in boldface at the foot of the page.

- ***Explanatory notes*** are more discursive, explaining a full range of references and allusions. These items are indicated with a standard superscript number and appear after the text of *Moby-Dick*.

- A ***Glossary*** of nautical and whaling terms, in layman's language, focuses on the particular meanings of those words as found in *Moby-Dick*.

- ***Illustrations*** help the reader to visualize whaling objects and processes now little-known and difficult to comprehend without graphic assistance. Additional illustrations represent adaptations of *Moby-Dick* in popular culture.

MOBY-DICK;

OR,

THE WHALE.

by
Herman Melville

Author of
TYPEE, OMOO, REDBURN, MARDI, WHITE-JACKET

NEW YORK:
HARPER & BROTHERS, PUBLISHERS.
LONDON: RICHARD BENTLEY.
1851

IN TOKEN

OF MY ADMIRATION FOR HIS GENIUS,

𝔗𝔥𝔦𝔰 𝔅𝔬𝔬𝔨 𝔦𝔰 𝔍𝔫𝔰𝔠𝔯𝔦𝔟𝔢𝔡

TO

NATHANIEL HAWTHORNE.

CONTENTS

ETYMOLOGY

(SUPPLIED BY A LATE CONSUMPTIVE USHER°
TO A GRAMMAR SCHOOL.)

———◆———

The pale Usher—threadbare in coat, heart, body, and brain; I see him now. He was ever dusting his old lexicons and grammars, with a queer handkerchief, mockingly embellished with all the gay flags of all the known nations of the world. He loved to dust his old grammars; it somehow mildly reminded him of his mortality.

Consumptive Usher: assistant teacher with consumption (tuberculosis).

ETYMOLOGY.

———◆———

"While you take in hand to school others, and to teach them by what name a whale-fish is to be called in our tongue, leaving out, through ignorance, the letter H, which almost alone maketh up the signification of the word, you deliver that which is not true."

Hackluyt.

"WHALE. * * * Sw. and Dan. *hval.* This animal is named from round-ness or rolling; for in Dan. *hvalt* is arched or vaulted."

Webster's Dictionary.

"WHALE. * * * It is more immediately from the Dut. and Ger. *Wallen;* A.S. *Walw-ian,* to roll, to wallow."

Richardson's Dictionary.

וֹה,	*Hebrew.*
χητος,	*Greek.*
CETUS,	*Latin.*
WHÆL,	*Anglo-Saxon.*
HVALT,	*Danish.*
WAL,	*Dutch.*
HWAL,	*Swedish.*
WHALE,	*Icelandic.*
WHALE,	*English.*
BALEINE,	*French.*
BALLENA,	*Spanish.*
PEKEE-NUEE-NUEE,	*Fegee.*
PEHEE-NUEE-NUEE,	*Erromangoan.*

EXTRACTS

(SUPPLIED BY A SUB-SUB-LIBRARIAN.)

———◆———

It will be seen that this mere painstaking burrower and grub-worm of a poor devil of a Sub-Sub appears to have gone through the long Vaticans° and street-stalls of the earth, picking up whatever random allusions to whales he could anyways find in any book whatsoever, sacred or profane. Therefore you must not, in every case at least, take the higgledy-piggledy whale statements, however authentic, in these extracts, for veritable gospel cetology. Far from it. As touching the ancient authors generally, as well as the poets here appearing, these extracts are solely valuable or entertaining, as affording a glancing bird's eye view of what has been promiscuously° said, thought, fancied, and sung of Leviathan,° by many nations and generations, including our own.

So fare thee well, poor devil of a Sub-Sub, whose commentator I am. Thou belongest to that hopeless, sallow tribe which no wine of this world will ever warm; and for whom even Pale Sherry would be too rosy-strong; but with whom one sometimes loves to sit, and feel poor-devilish, too; and grow convivial upon tears; and say to them bluntly, with full eyes and empty glasses, and in not altogether unpleasant sadness—Give it up, Sub-Subs! For by how much the more pains ye take to please the world, by so much the more shall ye for ever go thankless! Would that I could clear out Hampton Court and the Tuileries° for ye! But gulp down your tears and hie aloft to the royal-mast° with your hearts; for your friends who have gone before are clearing out the seven-storied heavens,° and making refugees of long-pampered Gabriel, Michael, and Raphael, against your coming.° Here ye strike but splintered hearts together—there, ye shall strike unsplinterable glasses!

Vaticans: great libraries, such as the Vatican's. *promiscuously*: diversely; unsystematically. *Leviathan*: biblical sea creature, not necessarily a whale. **Hampton Court and the Tuileries**: royal residences in London and Paris. **royal-mast**: highest part of a mast. **seven-storied heavens**: in Jewish and Islamic traditions Heaven has seven levels. **Gabriel, Michael, and Raphael, against your coming**: archangels; here, against means preparing for.

EXTRACTS.

"And God created great whales."
Genesis.

"**Leviathan** maketh a path to shine after him;
One would think the deep to be hoary."
Job.

"Now the Lord had prepared a great fish to swallow up Jonah."
Jonah.

"There go the ships; there is that Leviathan whom thou hast made to play therein."
Psalms.

"In that day, the Lord with his sore, and great, and strong sword, shall punish Leviathan the piercing serpent, even Leviathan that crooked serpent; and he shall slay the dragon that is in the sea."
Isaiah.

"And what thing soever besides cometh within the chaos of this monster's mouth, be it beast, boat, or stone, down it goes all incontinently that foul great swallow of his, and perisheth in the bottomless gulf of his paunch."
Holland's Plutarch's Morals.

"The Indian Sea breedeth the most and the biggest fishes that are: among which the Whales and Whirlpooles called Balæne, take up as much in length as four acres or arpens of land."
Holland's Pliny.

"Scarcely had we proceeded two days on the sea, when about sunrise a great many Whales and other monsters of the **sea**, appeared. Among the former, one was of a most **monstrous** size. * * This came towards us, open-mouthed, raising the waves on all sides, and beating the sea before him into a foam."
Tooke's Lucian.
"The True History."

"He visited this country also with a view of catching horse-whales, which had bones of very great value for their teeth, of which he brought some to the king.
* * * The best whales were catched in his own country, of which some were forty-eight, some fifty yards long. He said that he was one of six who had killed sixty in two days."
Other or Octher's verbal narrative taken down
from his mouth by King Alfred. A. D. 890.

"And whereas all the other things, whether beast or vessel, that enter into the dreadful gulf of this monster's (whale's) mouth, are immediately lost and swallowed up, the sea-gudgeon retires into it in great security, and there sleeps."
MONTAIGNE.—*Apology for Raimond Sebond.*

"Let us fly, let us fly! Old Nick take me if it is not Leviathan described by the noble prophet Moses in the life of patient Job." *Rabelais.*

"This whale's liver was two cart-loads."
Stowe's Annals.

"The great Leviathan that maketh the seas to seethe like boiling pan."
Lord Bacon's Version of the Psalms.

"Touching that monstrous bulk of the whale or ork we have received nothing certain. They grow exceeding fat, insomuch that an incredible quantity of oil will be extracted out of one whale."
Ibid. "History of Life and Death."

"The sovereignest thing on earth is parmacetti for an inward bruise."
King Henry.

"Very like a whale."

Hamlet.

"Which to secure, no skill of leach's art
Mote him availle, but to returne againe
To his wound's worker, that with lowly dart,
Dinting his breast, had bred his restless paine,
Like as the wounded whale to shore flies thro' the maine."
The Fairie Queen.

"Immense as whales, the motion of whose vast bodies can in a peaceful calm trouble the ocean till it boil."
Sir William Davenant. Preface to Gondibert.

"What spermacetti is, men might justly doubt, since the learned Hofmannus in his work of thirty years, saith plainly, *Nescio quid sit.*"
Sir T. Browne. Of Sperma Ceti and the
Sperma Ceti Whale. Vide his V. E.

"Like Spencer's Talus with his **modern** flail
He threatens ruin with his ponderous tail.
        *   *   *   *   *

Their fixed jav'lins in **his** side he wears,
And on **his** back a grove of pikes appears."
Waller's Battle of the Summer Islands.

"By art is created that great Leviathan, called a Commonwealth or State—
(in Latin, Civitas) which is but an artificial man."
Opening sentence of Hobbes's Leviathan.

"Silly Mansoul swallowed it without chewing, as if it had been a sprat in the
mouth of a whale."   **Pilgrim's Progress.** °

"That sea beast
Leviathan, which God of all his works
Created hugest that swim the ocean stream."
Paradise Lost.

—— "There Leviathan,
Hugest of living creatures, **in** the deep
Stretched like a promontory sleeps or swims,
And seems a moving land; and at his gills
Draws in, and at his **breath** spouts out a sea."
Ibid.

"The mighty whales which swim in a sea of water, and have a sea of oil swimming in them."
Fuller's Profane and Holy State.

"So close behind some promontory lie
    The huge Leviathans to attend their prey,
And give no chace, but swallow in the fry,
    Which through their gaping jaws mistake the way."
Dryden's Annus Mirabilis.

"While the whale is floating at the stern of the ship, they cut off his head,
and tow it with a boat as near the shore as it will come; but it will be aground in
twelve or thirteen foot water."
Thomas Edge's Ten Voyages to Spitzbergen, in Purchass.

Pilgrim's Progress: the source is actually Bunyan's *The Holy War.*

"In their way they saw many whales sporting in the ocean, and in wantonness fuzzing up the water through their pipes and vents, which nature has placed on their shoulders."

Sir T. Herbert's Voyages into Asia and Africa.
Harris Coll.

"Here they saw such huge troops of whales, that they were forced to proceed with a great deal of caution for fear they should run their ship upon them."

Schouten's Sixth Circumnavigation.

"We set sail from the Elbe, wind N. E. in the ship called The Jonas-in-the-Whale. * * *

Some say the whale can't open his mouth, but that is a fable. * * *

They frequently climb up the masts to see whether they can see a whale, for the first discoverer has a ducat for his pains. * * *

I was told of a whale taken near Shetland, that had above a barrel of herrings in his belly. * * *

One of our harpooneers told me that he caught once a whale in Spitzbergen that was white all over."

A Voyage to Greenland, A.D. 1671.
Harris Coll.

"Several whales have come in upon this coast (Fife). Anno 1652, one eighty feet in length of the whale-bone kind came in, which, (as I was informed) besides a vast quantity of oil, did afford 500 weight of baleen. The jaws of it stand for a gate in the garden of Pitfirren."

Sibbald's Fife and Kinross.

"Myself have agreed to try whether I can master and kill this Sperma-ceti whale, for I could never hear of any of that sort that was killed by any man, such is his fierceness and swiftness."

Richard Stafford's Letter from the Bermudas.
Phil. Trans. A. D. 1668.

"Whales in the sea
God's voice obey."

N. E. Primer.

"We saw also abundance of large whales, there being more in those southern seas, as I may say, by a hundred to one; than we have to the northward of us."

Captain Cowley's Voyage round the Globe. A. D. 1729.

* * * * * "and the breath of the whale is frequently attended with such an **insupportable smell**, as to bring on a disorder of the brain."

Ulloa's South America.

"To fifty chosen sylphs of special note,
We trust the important charge, the petticoat.
Oft have we known that seven-fold fence to fail,
Tho' stuffed with hoops and armed with ribs of whale."

Rape of the Lock.

"If we compare land animals in respect to magnitude, with those that take up their abode in the deep, we shall find they will appear contemptible in the comparison. The whale is doubtless the largest animal in creation."

Goldsmith, Nat. His.

"If you should write a fable for little fishes, you would make them speak like great whales."

Goldsmith to Johnson.

"In the afternoon we saw what was supposed to be a rock, but it was found to be a dead whale, which some Asiatics had killed, and were then towing ashore. They seemed to endeavor to conceal themselves behind the whale, in order to avoid being seen by us."

Cook's Voyages.

"The larger whales, they seldom venture to attack. They stand in so great dread of some of them, that when out at sea they are afraid to mention even their names, and carry dung, **lime-stone**, juniper-wood, and some other articles of the same nature in their boats, in order to terrify and prevent their too near approach."

*Uno Von Troil's Letters on Banks's and
Solander's Voyage to Iceland in 1772.*

"The Spermacetti Whale found by the Nantuckois, is an active, fierce animal, and requires vast address and boldness in the fishermen."

*Thomas Jefferson's Whale Memorial
to the French minister in 1778.*

"And pray, sir, what in the world is equal to it?"

*Edmund Burke's reference in Parliament
to the Nantucket Whale-Fishery.*

"Spain—a great whale stranded on the shores of Europe."

Edmund Burke. (somewhere.)

"A tenth branch of the king's ordinary revenue, said to be grounded on the consideration of his guarding and protecting the seas from pirates and robbers, is the right to *royal* fish, which are whale and sturgeon. And these, when either thrown ashore or caught near the coast, are the property of the king."

Blackstone.

"Soon to the sport of death the crews repair:
Rodmond unerring o'er his head suspends
The barbed steel, and every turn attends."

Falconer's Shipwreck.

"Bright shone the roofs, the domes, the spires,
    And rockets blew self driven,
To hang their momentary fires
    Around the vault of heaven.

"So fire with water to compare,
    The ocean serves on high,
Up-spouted by a whale in air,
    To express unwieldy joy."

Cowper, on the Queen's Visit to London.

"Ten or fifteen gallons of blood are thrown out of the heart at a stroke, with immense velocity."

*John Hunter's account of the dissection
of a whale. (A small sized one.)*

"The aorta of a whale is larger in the bore than the main pipe of the water-works at London Bridge, and the water roaring in its passage through that pipe is inferior in impetus and velocity to the blood gushing from the whale's heart."

Paley's Theology.

"The whale is a mammiferous animal without hind feet."

Baron Cuvier.

"In 40 degrees south, we saw Spermacetti Whales, but did not take any till the first of May, the sea being then covered with them."

*Colnett's Voyage for the Purpose of Extending
the Spermacetti Whale Fishery.*

"In the free element beneath me swam,
Floundered and dived, in play, in chace, in battle,
Fishes of every color, form, and kind;
Which language cannot paint, and mariner
Had never seen; from dread Leviathan
To insect millions peopling every wave:
Gather'd in shoals immense, like floating islands,
Led by mysterious instincts through that waste
And trackless region, though on every side
Assaulted by voracious enemies,
Whales, sharks, and monsters, arm'd in front or jaw,
With swords, saws, spiral horns, or hooked fangs."

Montgomery's World before the Flood.°

World before the Flood: the source is actually Montgomery's "Pelican Island."

"Io! Pæan! Io! sing,
To the finny people's king.
Not a mightier whale than this
In the vast Atlantic is;
Not a fatter fish than he,
Flounders round the Polar Sea."
Charles Lamb's Triumph of the Whale.

"In the year 1690 some persons were on a high hill observing the whales spouting and sporting with each other, when one observed; there—pointing to the sea—is a green pasture where our children's grand-children will go for bread."
Obed Macy's History of Nantucket.

"I built a cottage for Susan and myself and made a gateway in the form of a Gothic Arch, by setting up a whale's jaw bones."
Hawthorne's Twice Told Tales.

"She came to bespeak a monument for her first love, who had been killed by a whale in the Pacific ocean, no less than forty years ago."
Ibid.

"No, Sir, 'tis a Right Whale," answered Tom; "I saw his spout; he threw up a pair of as pretty rainbows as a Christian would wish to look at. He's a raal oil-butt, that fellow!"
Cooper's Pilot.

"The papers were brought in, and we saw in the Berlin Gazette that whales had been introduced on the stage there."
Eckermann's Conversations with Goethe.

"My God! Mr. **Chace**, what is the matter?" I answered, "we have been stove by a whale."
"Narrative of the **Shipwreck** *of the Whale Ship Essex of Nantucket, which was attacked and finally destroyed by a large* **Sperm Whale** *in the Pacific Ocean." By Owen* **Chace** *of Nantucket, first mate of said vessel. New York. 1821.*

"A mariner sat **in** the shrouds one night,
The wind was piping free;
Now bright, now dimmed, was the moonlight pale,
And the phospher gleamed in the wake of the whale,
As **it** floundered in the sea."
Elizabeth Oakes Smith.

"The quantity of line withdrawn from the different boats engaged in the capture of this one whale, amounted altogether to 10,440 yards or nearly six English miles."   *   *   *

"Sometimes the whale shakes its tremendous tail in the air, which, cracking like a whip, resounds to the distance of three or four miles."

Scoresby.

"Mad with the **agonies** he endures from these fresh attacks, the infuriated **Sperm Whale** rolls over and over; he rears his enormous head, and with wide expanded **jaws** snaps at everything around **him**; he rushes at the boats with his head; they are propelled before him with vast swiftness, and sometimes utterly destroyed.

*   *   * It is a matter of great astonishment that the consideration of the habits of so interesting, and, in a commercial point of view, of so important an animal **(as the Sperm Whale)** should have been so entirely neglected, or should have excited so little curiosity among the numerous, and many of them competent observers, that of late years must have possessed the most abundant and the most convenient opportunities of witnessing their habitudes."

Thomas Beale's History of the Sperm Whale, 1839.

"The Cachalot" (Sperm Whale) "is not only better armed than the True Whale" (Greenland or Right Whale) "in possessing a formidable weapon at either extremity of its body, but also more frequently displays a disposition to employ these weapons offensively, and in a manner at once so artful, bold, and mischievous, as to lead to its being regarded as the most dangerous to attack of all the known species of the whale tribe."

Frederick Debell Bennett's Whaling
Voyage Round the Globe. 1840.

October 13. "There she blows," was sung out from the mast-head.
"Where away?" demanded the captain.
"Three points off the lee bow, sir."
"Raise up your wheel. Steady!"
"Steady, sir."
"Mast-head ahoy! Do you see that whale now?"
"Ay ay, sir! A shoal of Sperm Whales! There she blows! There she breaches!"
"Sing out! sing out every time!"
"Ay ay, sir! There she blows! there—there—*thar* she blows—bowes—bo-o-o-s!"
"How far off?"
"Two miles and a half."
"Thunder and lightning! so near! Call all hands!"

J. Ross Browne's Etchings of a Whaling Cruize. 1846.

"The Whale-ship Globe, on board of which vessel occurred the horrid trans-actions we are about to relate, belonged to the island of Nantucket."

"Narrative of the Globe Mutiny,"
by Lay and Hussey survivors. A. D. 1828.

"Being once pursued by a whale which he had wounded, he parried the assault for some time with a lance; but the furious monster at length rushed on the boat; himself and comrades only being preserved by leaping into the water when they saw the onset was inevitable."

Missionary Journal of Tyerman and Bennet.

"Nantucket itself," said Mr. Webster, "is a very striking and peculiar portion of the National interest. There is a population of eight or nine thousand persons, living here in the sea, adding largely every year to the National wealth by the bold-est and most persevering industry."

Report of Daniel Webster's Speech in the U. S. Senate, on the
application for the Erection of a Breakwater at Nantucket. 1828.

"The whale fell directly over him, and probably killed him in a moment."

"The Whale and his Captors, or The Whaleman's Adventures
and the Whale's Biography, gathered on the Homeward Cruise
of the Commodore Preble." By Rev. Henry T. Cheever.

"If you make the least damn bit of noise," replied Samuel, "I will send you to hell."

Life of Samuel Comstock (the mutineer), by his brother, William
Comstock. Another Version of the whale-ship Globe narrative.

"The voyages of the Dutch and English to the Northern Ocean, in order, if possible, to discover a passage through it to India, though they failed of their main object, laid open the haunts of the whale."

McCulloch's Commercial Dictionary.

"These things are reciprocal; the ball rebounds, only to bound forward again; for now in laying open the haunts of the whale, the whalemen seem to have indi-rectly hit upon new clews to that same mystic North-West Passage."

From "Something" unpublished.

"It is impossible to meet a whale-ship on the ocean without being struck by her mere appearance. The vessel under short sail, with look-outs at the mast-heads, eagerly scanning the wide expanse around them, has a totally different air from those engaged in a regular voyage."

Currents and Whaling. U. S. Ex. Ex.

"Pedestrians in the vicinity of London and elsewhere may recollect having seen large curved bones set upright in the earth, either to form arches over gateways, or entrances to alcoves, and they may perhaps have been told that these were the ribs of whales."

Tales of a Whale Voyager to the Arctic Ocean.

"It was not till the boats returned from the pursuit of these whales, that the whites saw their ship in bloody possession of the savages enrolled among the crew."

Newspaper Account of the Taking and Retaking of the Whale-ship **Hobomack***.*

"It is generally well known that out of the crews of Whaling vessels (American) few ever return in the ships on board of which they departed."

Cruise in a Whale Boat.

"Suddenly a mighty mass emerged from the water, and shot up perpendicularly into the air. It was the whale."

Miriam Coffin or the Whale Fisherman.

"The Whale is harpooned to be sure; but bethink you, how you would manage a powerful unbroken colt, with the mere appliance of a rope tied to the root of his tail."

A Chapter on Whaling in Ribs and Trucks.

"On one occasion I saw two of these monsters (whales) probably male and female, slowly swimming, one after the other, within less than a stone's throw of the shore" (**Tierra** Del Fuego), "over which the beech tree extended its branches."

Darwin's Voyage of a Naturalist.

"'Stern all!' exclaimed the mate, as upon turning his head, he saw the distended jaws of a large Sperm Whale close to the head of the boat, threatening it with instant destruction;—'Stern all, for your lives!'"

Wharton the Whale Killer.

"So be cheery, my lads, let your hearts never fail,
While the bold harpooneer is striking the whale!"

Nantucket Song.

"Oh, the rare old Whale, mid storm and gale
　　In his ocean home will be
A giant in might, where might is right,
　　And King of the boundless sea."

Whale Song.

CHAPTER 1

LOOMINGS

C ALL ME ISHMAEL. Some years ago—never mind how long precisely—having little or no money in my purse, and nothing particular to interest me on shore, I thought I would sail about a little and see the watery part of the world.[1] It is a way I have of driving off the spleen,° and regulating the circulation. Whenever I find myself growing grim about the mouth; whenever it is a damp, drizzly November in my soul; whenever I find myself involuntarily pausing before coffin warehouses, and bringing up the rear of every funeral I meet; and especially whenever my hypos° get such an upper hand of me, that it requires a strong moral principle to prevent me from deliberately stepping into the street, and methodically knocking people's hats off—then, I account it high time to get to sea as soon as I can. This is my substitute for pistol and ball. With a philosophical flourish Cato[2] throws himself upon his sword; I quietly take to the ship. There is nothing surprising in this. If they but knew it, almost all men in their degree, some time or other, cherish very nearly the same feelings towards the ocean with me.

There now is your insular city of the Manhattoes,[3] belted round by wharves as Indian isles by coral reefs—commerce surrounds it with her surf. Right and left, the streets take you waterward. Its extreme down-town is the Battery,° where that noble mole° is washed by waves, and cooled by breezes, which a few hours previous were out of sight of land. Look at the crowds of water-gazers there.

Circumambulate the city of a dreamy Sabbath afternoon. Go from Corlears Hook to Coenties Slip, and from thence, by Whitehall, northward.[4] What do you see?— Posted like silent sentinels all around the town, stand thousands upon thousands of mortal men fixed in ocean reveries. Some leaning against the spiles;° some seated upon the pier-heads; some looking over the bulwarks° of ships from China; some high aloft in the rigging, as if striving to get a still better seaward peep. But these are all landsmen; of week days pent up in lath and plaster—tied to counters, nailed to benches, clinched° to desks. How then is this? Are the green fields gone? What do they here?

spleen: melancholy or irritation, from the spleen's supposed fluid or "humour." *hypos*: short for "hypochondria," or depression. *Battery*: site (near Melville's birthplace) of a fort on the southern tip of Manhattan island guarding New York harbor, but already a park in Melville's day. *mole*: massive sea wall. *spiles*: foundation posts. *bulwarks*: pronounced bularks, a ship's side above the deck. *tied . . . nailed . . . clinched*: a series of increasing entrapments.

But look! here come more crowds, pacing straight for the water, and seemingly bound for a dive. Strange! Nothing will content them but the extremest limit of the land; loitering under the shady lee° of yonder warehouses will not suffice. No. They must get just as nigh the water as they possibly can without falling in. And there they stand—miles of them—leagues.° Inlanders all, they come from lanes and alleys, streets and avenues—north, east, south, and west. Yet here they all unite. Tell me, does the magnetic virtue of the needles of the compasses of all those ships attract them thither?

Once more. Say, you are in the country; in some high land of lakes. Take almost any path you please, and ten to one it carries you down in a dale, and leaves you there by a pool in the stream. There is magic in it. Let the most absent-minded of men be plunged in his deepest reveries—stand that man on his legs, set his feet a-going, and he will infallibly lead you to water, if water there be in all that region. Should you ever be athirst in the great American desert,° try this experiment, if your caravan happen to be supplied with a metaphysical professor. Yes, as every one knows, meditation and water are wedded for ever.

But here is an artist. He desires to paint you the dreamiest, shadiest, quietest, most enchanting bit of romantic landscape in all the valley of the Saco.° What is the chief element he employs? There stand his trees, each with a hollow trunk, as if a hermit and a crucifix were within; and here sleeps his meadow, and there sleep his cattle; and up from yonder cottage goes a sleepy smoke. Deep into distant woodlands winds a mazy way, reaching to overlapping spurs of mountains bathed in their hill-side blue. But though the picture lies thus tranced, and though this pine-tree shakes down its sighs like leaves upon this shepherd's head, yet all were vain, unless the shepherd's eye were fixed upon the magic stream before him. Go visit the Prairies in June, when for scores on scores of miles you wade knee-deep among Tiger-lilies—what is the one charm wanting?—Water—there is not a drop of water there! Were Niagara but a cataract of sand, would you travel your thousand miles to see it? Why did the poor poet of Tennessee,[5] upon suddenly receiving two handfuls of silver, deliberate whether to buy him a coat, which he sadly needed, or invest his money in a pedestrian trip to Rockaway Beach?[6] Why is almost every robust healthy boy with a robust healthy soul in him, at some time or other crazy to go to sea? Why upon your first voyage as a passenger, did you yourself feel such a mystical vibration, when first told that you and your ship were now out of sight of land? Why did the old Persians hold the sea holy? Why did the Greeks give it a separate deity, and **own brother of Jove?**[7] Surely all this is not without meaning. And still deeper the meaning of that story of Narcissus,[8] who because he could not grasp the tormenting, mild image he saw in the fountain, plunged into it and was drowned. But that same image, we ourselves see in all rivers and oceans. It is the image of the ungraspable phantom of life; and this is the key to it all.

Now, when I say that I am in the habit of going to sea whenever I begin to grow hazy about the eyes, and begin to be over conscious of my lungs, I do not mean to have it inferred that I ever go to sea as a passenger. For to go as a passenger you must needs have a purse, and a purse is but a rag unless you have something in it. Besides, passen-

---

lee: the side protected from the wind. **league**: three nautical miles. **great American desert**: the largely unknown semi-arid plains between the Missouri River and the Rocky Mountains. **Saco**: scenic New Hampshire valley and a common subject for painters.

gers get sea-sick—grow quarrelsome—don't sleep of nights—do not enjoy themselves much, as a general thing;—no, I never go as a passenger; nor, though I am something of a salt, do I ever go to sea as a Commodore,° or a Captain, or a Cook.[9] I abandon the glory and distinction of such offices to those who like them. For my part, I abominate all honorable respectable toils, trials, and tribulations of every kind whatsoever. It is quite as much as I can do to take care of myself, without taking care of ships, barques, brigs, schooners,° and what not. And as for going as cook,—though I confess there is considerable glory in that, a cook being a sort of officer on ship-board—yet, somehow, I never fancied broiling fowls;—though once broiled, judiciously buttered, and judgmatically salted and peppered, there is no one who will speak more respectfully, not to say reverentially, of a broiled fowl than I will. It is out of the idolatrous dotings of the old Egyptians upon broiled ibis and roasted river horse,° that you see the mummies of those creatures in their huge bake-houses the pyramids.

No, when I go to sea, I go as a simple sailor, right before the mast,[10] plumb down into the forecastle, aloft there to the royal mast-head.° True, they rather order me about some, and make me jump from spar to spar,° like a grasshopper in a May meadow. And at first, this sort of thing is unpleasant enough. It touches one's sense of honor, particularly if you come of an old established family in the land, the Van Rensselaers, or Randolphs, or Hardicanutes.[11] And more than all, if just previous to putting your hand into the tar-pot, you have been lording it as a country schoolmaster,[12] making the tallest boys stand in awe of you. The transition is a keen one, I assure you, from a schoolmaster to a sailor, and requires a strong decoction of Seneca and the Stoics[13] to enable you to grin and bear it. But even this wears off in time.

What of it, if some old hunks° of a sea-captain orders me to get a broom and sweep down the decks? What does that indignity amount to, weighed, I mean, in the scales of the New Testament? **Do you think the archangel Gabriel thinks anything the less of me, because I promptly and respectfully obey that old hunks in that particular instance? Who aint a slave?[14]** Tell me that. Well, then, however the old sea-captains may order me about—however they

---

Commodore: then the highest rank in the U.S. Navy. **ships, barques, brigs, schooners**: common sailing vessels in descending size. **river horse**: hippopotamus. **royal mast-head**: top of the highest section of a mast. **spar to spar**: from one wooden sail support to another. **hunks**: grouch.

REVISION NARRATIVE

What the Archangel Gabriel Thinks

Melville's British editor altered two passages, presumably objecting to the blasphemy and grammar of Ishmael's playful musings. The editor cut Ishmael's first question, probably because of its flippant reference to Gabriel, who in the Bible heralds the Judgment Day. The word "aint" in the second, and elsewhere, was also "corrected" to "is not."

may thump and punch me about, I have the satisfaction of knowing that it is all right; that everybody else is one way or other served in much the same way—either in a physical or metaphysical point of view, that is; and so the universal thump is passed round, and all hands should rub each other's shoulder-blades, and be content.

Again, I always go to sea as a sailor, because they make a point of paying me for my trouble, whereas they never pay passengers a single penny that I ever heard of. On the contrary, passengers themselves must pay. And there is all the difference in the world between paying and being paid. **The act of paying is perhaps the most uncomfortable infliction that the two orchard thieves entailed upon us. But *being paid*,—what will compare with it?** The urbane activity with which a man receives money is really marvellous, considering that we so earnestly believe money to be the root of all earthly ills, and that on no account can a monied man enter heaven.[15] Ah! how cheerfully we consign ourselves to perdition!

Finally, I always go to sea as a sailor, because of the wholesome exercise and pure air of the forecastle deck. For as in this world, head winds are far more prevalent than winds from astern (that is, if you never violate the Pythagorean maxim),[16] so for the most part the Commodore on the quarter-deck gets his atmosphere at second hand from the sailors on the forecastle. He thinks he breathes it first; but not so. In much the same way do the commonalty lead their leaders in many other things, at the same time that the leaders little suspect it. But wherefore it was that after having repeatedly smelt the sea as a merchant sailor, I should now take it into my head to go on a whaling voyage; this the invisible police officer of the Fates, who has the constant surveillance of me, and secretly dogs me, and influences me in some unaccountable way—he can better answer than any one else. **And, doubtless, my going on this whaling voyage, formed part of the grand programme of Providence that was drawn up a long time ago. It came in as a sort of brief interlude and solo between more extensive performances. I take it that this part of the bill must have run something like this:**

"Grand Contested Election for the Presidency of the United States.
"WHALING VOYAGE BY ONE ISHMAEL.
"BLOODY BATTLE IN AFFGHANISTAN."[17]

Though I cannot tell why it was exactly that those stage managers, the Fates,[18] put me down for this shabby part of a whaling voyage, when others were set down

---

REVISION NARRATIVE

Adam and Eve as Thieves

In the paragraph about the difference between "paying and being paid," the British removed two sentences referring to "the two orchard thieves." The "thieves" are Adam and Eve, who, because they disobeyed God by eating of the fruit of the tree of knowledge of good and evil, were punished by, among other things, having to sweat for a living.

for magnificent parts in high tragedies, and short and easy parts in genteel comedies, and jolly parts in farces—though I cannot tell why this was exactly; yet, now that I recall all the circumstances, I think I can see a little into the springs and motives which being cunningly presented to me under various disguises, induced me to set about performing the part I did, besides cajoling me into the delusion that it was a choice resulting from my own unbiased freewill and discriminating judgment.

Chief among these motives was the overwhelming idea of the great whale himself. Such a portentous and mysterious monster roused all my curiosity. Then the wild and distant seas where he rolled his island bulk; the undeliverable,° nameless perils of the whale; these, with all the attending marvels of a thousand Patagonian sights and sounds,° helped to sway me to my wish. With other men, perhaps, such things would not have been inducements; but as for me, I am tormented with an everlasting itch for things remote. I love to sail forbidden seas, and land on barbarous coasts.[19] Not ignoring what is good, I am quick to perceive a horror, and could still be social with it—would they let me—since it is but well to be on friendly terms with all the inmates of the place one lodges in.[20]

By reason of these things, then, the whaling voyage was welcome; the great flood-gates of the wonder-world swung open, and in the wild conceits° that swayed me to my purpose, two and two there floated into my inmost soul, end less processions of the whale, and, midmost of them all, one grand hooded phantom, like a snow hill in the air.[21]

undeliverable: indescribable. **Patagonian sights and sounds**: Patagonia, the southern extreme of South America, is a region of legend and mystery. **conceits**: imaginings.

REVISION NARRATIVE

Providence and Politics on Stage

Melville's British editor cut two sentences and revised a third, effectively ruining Ishmael's joke in which God places him on stage with the great political events of the day. Previous to these three sentences, Ishmael states that only the "invisible police officer of the Fates" can account for his decision to go whaling. However, in getting to his joke, he shifts, in the next two sentences, to a stage metaphor, comparing God's will to "the grand programme of Providence" and Ishmael's whaling voyage to just an "interlude and solo." But in expurgating both sentences, the editor had to revise the next sentence because its reference to "the bill" (i.e., the playbill for the "programme") would no longer make sense. Thus, words were added to refer the reader back to "the Fates," earlier in the passage. In the British edition, then, Melville's mildly blasphemous joke is gone and his original sentence—"I take it that this part of the bill must have run something like this:"—instead reads "I take it that this part of the bill **of those three mysterious ladies** must have run something like this:". Here, the "bill" is linked to "the Fates," or, more specifically in the revision, the three old women who spin, measure, and cut the thread of a person's life.

CHAPTER 2

THE CARPET-BAG

I STUFFED a shirt or two into my old carpet-bag, tucked it under my arm, and started for Cape Horn° and the Pacific. Quitting the good city of old Manhatto, I duly arrived in New Bedford.[1] It was on a Saturday night in December. Much was I disappointed upon learning that the little packet° for Nantucket[2] had already sailed, and that no way of reaching that place would offer, till the following Monday.

As most young candidates for the pains and penalties of whaling stop at this same New Bedford, thence to embark on their voyage, it may as well be related that I, for one, had no idea of so doing. For my mind was made up to sail in no other than a Nantucket craft, because there was a fine, boisterous something about everything connected with that famous old island, which amazingly pleased me. Besides though New Bedford has of late been gradually monopolizing the business of whaling, and though in this matter poor old Nantucket is now much behind her, yet Nantucket was her great original—the Tyre of this Carthage;[3]—the place where the first dead American whale was stranded. Where else but from Nantucket did those aboriginal whalemen, the Red-Men, first sally out in canoes to give chase to the Leviathan? And where but from Nantucket, too, did that first adventurous little sloop put forth, partly laden with imported cobble-stones—so goes the story—to throw at the whales, in order to discover when they were nigh enough to risk a harpoon from the bowsprit?

Now having a night, a day, and still another night following before me in New Bedford, ere I could embark for my destined port, it became a matter of concernment where I was to eat and sleep meanwhile. It was a very dubious-looking, nay, a very dark and dismal night, bitingly cold and cheerless. I knew no one in the place. With anxious grapnels° I had sounded my pocket, and only brought up a few pieces of silver,—So, wherever you go, Ishmael, said I to myself, as I stood in the middle of a dreary street shouldering my bag, and comparing the gloom towards the north with the darkness towards the south—wherever in your wisdom you may conclude to lodge for the night, my dear Ishmael, be sure to inquire the price, and don't be too particular.

Cape Horn: southern tip of South America. *packet*: mail and passenger vessel making scheduled trips between the same ports. *grapnels*: small, anchor-like devices for dragging the sea floor; here, his fingers.

With halting steps I paced the streets, and passed the sign of "The Crossed Harpoons"—but it looked too expensive and jolly there. Further on, from the bright red windows of the "Sword-Fish Inn," there came such fervent rays, that it seemed to have melted the packed snow and ice from before the house, for everywhere else the congealed frost lay ten inches thick in a hard, asphaltic pavement,—rather weary for me, when I struck my foot against the flinty projections, because from hard, remorseless service the soles of my boots were in a most miserable plight. Too expensive and jolly, again thought I, pausing one moment to watch the broad glare in the street, and hear the sounds of the tinkling glasses within. But go on, Ishmael, said I at last; don't you hear? get away from before the door; your patched boots are stopping the way. So on I went. I now by instinct followed the streets that took me waterward, for there, doubtless, were the cheapest, if not the cheeriest inns.

Such dreary streets! blocks of blackness, not houses, on either hand, and here and there a candle, like a candle moving about in a tomb. At this hour of the night, of the last day of the week, that quarter of the town proved all but deserted. But presently I came to a smoky light proceeding from a low, wide building, the door of which stood invitingly open. It had a careless look, as if it were meant for the uses of the public; so, entering, the first thing I did was to stumble over an ash-box° in the porch. Ha! thought I, ha, as the flying particles almost choked me, are these ashes from that destroyed city, Gomorrah?[4] But "The Crossed Harpoons," and "The Sword-Fish?"—this, then, must needs be the sign of "The Trap." However, I picked myself up and hearing a loud voice within, pushed on and opened a second, interior door.

It seemed the great Black Parliament[5] sitting in Tophet.° A hundred black faces turned round in their rows to peer; and beyond, a black Angel of Doom was beating a book in a pulpit. It was a negro church; and the preacher's text was about the blackness of darkness,[6] and the weeping and wailing and teeth-gnashing there. Ha, Ishmael, muttered I, backing out, Wretched entertainment at the sign of "The Trap!"

Moving on, I at last came to a **dim sort of light** not far from the docks, and heard a forlorn creaking in the air; and looking up, saw a swinging sign over the door with a white painting upon it, faintly representing a tall straight jet of misty spray, and these words underneath—"The Spouter-Inn:—Peter Coffin."

Coffin?—Spouter?—Rather ominous in that particular connexion, thought I. But it is a common name in Nantucket, they say, and I suppose this Peter here is an emigrant from there. As the light looked so dim, and the place, for the time, looked quiet enough, and the dilapidated little wooden house itself looked as if it might have been carted here from the ruins of some burnt district,[7] and as the swinging sign had a poverty-stricken sort of creak to it, I thought that here was the very spot for cheap lodgings, and the best of pea coffee.°

It was a queer sort of place—a gable-ended old house, one side palsied as it were, and leaning over sadly. It stood on a sharp bleak corner, where that tempestuous wind Euroclydon° kept up a worse howling than ever it did about **poor** Paul's tossed craft. Euroclydon, nevertheless, is a mighty pleasant zephyr to any one indoors, with his feet on the hob quietly toasting for bed. "In judging of that tempes-

---

ash-box: ashes were kept to spread on icy walkways. **Tophet**: hell. **pea coffee**: made from roasted green peas or chickpeas. **Euroclydon**: the wind that wrecked St. Paul's ship in Acts 27.

tuous wind called Euroclydon," says an old writer—of whose works I possess the only copy extant—"it maketh a marvellous difference, whether thou lookest out at it from a glass window where the frost is all on the outside, or whether thou observest it from that sashless window, where the frost is on both sides, and of which the wight Death is the only glazier."° True enough, thought I, as this passage occurred to my mind—old black-letter,° thou reasonest well. Yes, these eyes are windows, and this body of mine is the house. What a pity they didn't stop up the chinks and the crannies though, and thrust in a little lint here and there. But it's too late to make any improvements now. **The universe is finished; the copestone° is on, and the chips were carted off a million years ago. Poor Lazarus there, chattering his teeth against the curbstone for his pillow, and shaking off his tatters with his shiverings, he might plug up both ears with rags, and put a corn-cob into his mouth, and yet that would not keep out the tempestuous Euroclydon. Euroclydon! says old Dives, in his red silken wrapper—(he had a redder one afterwards) pooh, pooh!** What a fine frosty night; how Orion glitters; what northern lights! Let them talk of their oriental summer climes of everlasting conservatories; give me the privilege of making my own summer with my own coals.

But what thinks Lazarus? Can he warm his blue hands by holding them up to the grand northern lights? Would not Lazarus rather be in

wight . . . glazier: wight means any person; a glazier installs window glass; the quotation is Ishmael's invention. ***black-letter***: old book printed in a heavy typeface resembling hand-written manuscript. ***copestone***: stone placed at the top of a wall or other structure; compare Ch. 32, last paragraph.

REVISION NARRATIVE

Lazarus and Dives

In Luke 16:19–23, the homeless and sore-ridden Lazarus lies at the gates of a scornful rich man (elsewhere called Dives) begging for crumbs. When both die, Lazarus goes to heaven, and Dives burns in hell, begging Lazarus to send him water. Ishmael elaborates on the inequality of rich and poor by comparing the differences we feel between a tight window that keeps the warmth inside and a sashless or ill-framed window that lets the frost come through. He then compares this difference to the living Lazarus and Dives, the one chattering out in the cold, the other enjoying "a fine frosty night" from inside his summery room. But Melville's religiously and politically sensitive British editor expurgated all reference to the parable. He removed the last three paragraphs entirely as well as three sentences toward the end of what became the chapter's final paragraph. This latter excision inadvertently reassigns Dives's jolly words ("What a fine frosty night . . . making my own summer with my own coals") to Ishmael, thus making Ishmael conclude his previously compassionate reflections by incongruously voicing Dives's privileged point of view. In addition, the editor revised Melville's "poor Paul" at the beginning of the paragraph to "St. Paul."

Sumatra° than here? Would he not far rather lay him down lengthwise along the line of the equator; yea, ye gods! go down to the fiery pit itself, in order to keep out this frost?

Now, that Lazarus should lie stranded there on the curbstone before the door of Dives, this is more wonderful than that an iceberg should be moored to one of the Moluccas.° Yet Dives himself, he too lives like a Czar in an ice palace8 made of frozen sighs, and being a president of a temperance society,° he only drinks the tepid tears of orphans.

But no more of this blubbering now, we are going a-whaling, and there is plenty of that yet to come. Let us scrape the ice from our frosted feet, and see what sort of a place this "Spouter" may be.

Sumatra: island in the Indian Ocean, now part of Indonesia. **Moluccas**: also called the Spice Islands; presently Indonesia's Maluku. **temperance society**: organization promoting complete abstinence from alcohol.

CHAPTER 3

THE SPOUTER-INN

ENTERING that gable-ended Spouter-Inn,° you found yourself in a wide, low, straggling entry with old-fashioned wainscots,° reminding one of the bulwarks of some condemned old craft. On one side hung a very large oil-painting so thoroughly besmoked, and every way defaced, that in the unequal cross-lights by which you viewed it, it was only by diligent study and a series of systematic visits to it, and careful inquiry of the neighbors, that you could any way arrive at an understanding of its purpose. Such unaccountable masses of shades and shadows, that at first you almost thought some ambitious young artist, in the time of the New England hags,° had endeavored to delineate chaos bewitched. But by dint of much and earnest contemplation, and oft repeated ponderings, and especially by throwing open the little window towards the back of the entry, you at last **come** to the conclusion that such an idea, however wild, might not be altogether unwarranted.

But what most puzzled and confounded you was a long, limber, portentous, black mass of something hovering in the centre of the picture over three blue, dim, perpendicular lines floating in a nameless yeast. A boggy, soggy, squitchy picture truly, enough to drive a nervous man distracted. Yet was there a sort of indefinite, half-attained, unimaginable sublimity about it that fairly froze you to it, till you involuntarily took an oath with yourself to find out what that marvellous painting meant. Ever and anon a bright, but, alas, deceptive idea would dart you through.—It's the Black Sea° in a midnight gale.—It's the unnatural combat of the four primal elements.—It's a blasted heath.—It's a Hyperborean° winter scene.—It's the breaking-up of the ice-bound stream of Time. But at last all these fancies yielded to that one portentous something in the picture's midst. *That* once found out, and all the rest were plain. But stop; does it not bear a faint resemblance to a gigantic fish? even the great leviathan himself?

In fact, the artist's design seemed this: a final theory of my own, partly based upon the aggregated opinions of many aged persons with whom I conversed upon

---

Spouter-Inn: in sailor slang, a spouter is a whaleship. **wainscots**: wood paneling covering the lower part of the walls. **New England hags**: the supposed witches in 17th-century Salem, Massachusetts. **Black Sea**: in Eastern Europe, bordered by Turkey, Russia, Ukraine, and other countries. **Hyperborean**: arctic (*blasted heath* recalls *Macbeth* 1.3.73–76).

the subject. The picture represents a Cape-Horner° in a great hurricane; the half-foundered ship weltering there with its three dismantled masts alone visible; and an exasperated whale, purposing to spring clean over the craft, is in the enormous act of impaling himself upon the three mast-heads.

The opposite wall of this entry was hung all over with a heathenish array of monstrous clubs and spears. Some were thickly set with glittering teeth resembling ivory saws; others were tufted with knots of human hair; and one was sickle-shaped, with a vast handle sweeping round like the segment made in the new-mown grass by a long-armed mower. You shuddered as you gazed, and wondered what monstrous cannibal and savage could ever have gone a death-harvesting with such a hacking, horrifying implement. Mixed with these were rusty old whaling lances° and harpoons all broken and deformed. Some were storied weapons. With this once long lance, now wildly elbowed, fifty years ago did Nathan Swain° kill fifteen whales between a sunrise and a sunset. And that harpoon—so like a corkscrew now—was flung in Javan seas, and run away with by a whale, years afterwards slain off the Cape of Blanco.[1] The original iron entered nigh the tail, and, like a restless needle sojourning in the body of a man, travelled full forty feet, and at last was found imbedded in the hump.

Crossing this dusky entry, and on through yon low-arched way—cut through what in old times must have been a great central chimney with fire-places all round—you enter the public room. A still duskier place is this, with such low ponderous beams above, and such old wrinkled planks beneath, that you would almost fancy you trod some old craft's cockpits,° especially of such a howling night, when this corner-anchored old ark rocked so furiously. On one side stood a long, low, shelf-like table covered with cracked glass cases, filled with dusty rarities gathered from this wide world's remotest nooks. Projecting from the further angle of the room stands a dark-looking den—the bar—a rude attempt at a right whale's head. Be that how it may, there stands the vast arched bone of the whale's jaw, so wide, a coach might almost drive beneath it. Within are shabby shelves, ranged round with old decanters, bottles, flasks; and in those jaws of swift destruction, **like another cursed Jonah**[2] **(by which name indeed they called him)**, bustles a little withered old man, who, for their money, dearly sells the sailors deliriums and death.

Abominable are the tumblers into which he pours his poison. Though true cylinders without—within, the villanous green goggling glasses[3] deceitfully tapered downwards to a cheating bottom. Parallel meridians rudely pecked into the glass, surround these footpads'° goblets. Fill to *this* mark, and your charge is but a penny; to *this* a penny more; and so on to the full glass—the Cape Horn measure, which you may gulph° down for a shilling.

Upon entering the place I found a number of young seamen gathered about a table, examining by a dim light divers specimens of *skrimshander.*° I sought the

---

Cape-Horner: large square-rigged ship built to withstand the rigors of a Cape Horn passage. **lances**: spears for killing a whale while fastened to it by a harpoon. **Nathan Swain**: name for any whaleman. **cockpits**: low-ceilinged space below the waterline. **footpads**: highwaymen, robbers. **gulph**: obsolete form of gulp. **skrimshander**: scrimshaw; sperm whale teeth with incised designs, or items carved from whale bone; defined in Ch. 57.

landlord, and telling him I desired to be accommodated with a room, received for answer that his house was full—not a bed unoccupied. "But avast," he added, tapping his forehead, "you haint no objections to sharing a harpooneer's blanket, have ye? I s'pose you are goin' a whalin', so you'd better get used to that sort of thing."

I told him that I never liked to sleep two in a bed; that if I should ever do so, it would depend upon who the harpooneer might be, and that if he (the landlord) really had no other place for me, and the harpooneer was not decidedly objectionable, why rather than wander further about a strange town on so bitter a night, I would put up with the half of any decent man's blanket.

"I thought so. All right; take a seat. Supper?—you want supper? Supper 'll be ready directly."

I sat down on an old wooden settle, carved all over like a bench on the Battery. At one end a ruminating tar was still further adorning it with his jack-knife, stooping over and diligently working away at the space between his legs. He was trying his hand at a ship under full sail, but he didn't make much headway, I thought.

At last some four or five of us were summoned to our meal in an adjoining room. It was cold as Iceland—no fire at all—the landlord said he couldn't afford it. Nothing but two dismal tallow candles, each in a winding sheet.° We were fain to button up our monkey jackets,° and hold to our lips cups of scalding tea with our half frozen fingers. But the fare was of the most substantial kind—not only meat and potatoes, but dumplings; good heavens! dumplings for supper! One young fellow in a green box coat,° addressed himself to these dumplings in a most direful manner.

"My boy," said the landlord, "you'll have the nightmare to a dead sartainty."

"Landlord," I whispered, "that aint the harpooneer, is it?"

"Oh, no," said he, looking a sort of diabolically funny, "the harpooner is a dark complexioned chap. He never eats dumplings, he don't—he eats nothing but steaks, and likes 'em rare."

"The devil he does," says I. "Where is that harpooneer? Is he here?"

"He'll be here afore long," was the answer.

I could not help it, but I began to feel suspicious of this "dark complexioned" harpooneer. At any rate, I made up my mind that if it so turned out that we should sleep together, he must undress and get into bed before I did.

Supper over, the company went back to the bar-room, when, knowing not what else to do with myself, I resolved to spend the rest of the evening as a looker on.

Presently a rioting noise was heard without. Starting up, the landlord cried, "That's the Grampus's crew. I seed her reported in the offing° this morning; a **three** years' voyage,[4] and a full ship. Hurrah, boys; now we'll have the latest news from the Feegees."°

A tramping of sea boots was heard in the entry; the door was flung open, and in rolled a wild set of mariners enough. Enveloped in their shaggy watch coats,° and

---

winding sheet: congealed grease surrounding a candle, evoking an image of the sheet in which a corpse is wrapped. *monkey jackets*: short, tight-fitting jackets. *box coat*: loose overcoat. *offing*: that distant part of the sea visible from shore. *Feegees*: the Fiji Islands, 1,300 miles north of New Zealand. *watch coats*: heavy coats, worn while on watch.

with their heads muffled in woollen comforters,° all bedarned and ragged, and their beards stiff with icicles, they seemed an eruption of bears from Labrador.° They had just landed from their boat, and this was the first house they entered. No wonder, then, that they made a straight wake for the whale's mouth—the bar—when the wrinkled little old **Jonah**, there officiating, soon poured them out brimmers all round. One complained of a bad cold in his head, upon which **Jonah** mixed him a pitch-like potion of gin and molasses, which he swore was a sovereign cure for all colds and catarrhs whatsoever, never mind of how long standing, or whether caught off the coast of Labrador, or on the weather side° of an ice-island.

The liquor soon mounted into their heads, as it generally does even with the arrantest topers° newly landed from sea, and they began capering about most obstreperously.

I observed, however, that one of them held somewhat aloof, and though he seemed desirous not to spoil the hilarity of his shipmates by his own sober face, yet upon the whole he refrained from making as much noise as the rest. This man interested me at once; and since the sea-gods had ordained that he should soon become my shipmate (though but a sleeping-partner° one, so far as this narrative is concerned), I will here venture upon a little description of him. He stood full six feet in height, with noble shoulders, and a chest like a coffer-dam.° I have seldom seen such brawn in a man. His face was deeply brown and burnt, making his white teeth dazzling by the contrast; while in the deep shadows of his eyes floated some reminiscences that did not seem to give him much joy. His voice at once announced that he was a Southerner, and from his fine stature, I thought he must be one of those tall mountaineers from the Alleganian Ridge in Virginia. When the revelry of his companions had mounted to its height, this man slipped away unobserved, and I saw no more of him till he became my comrade on the sea. In a few minutes, however, he was missed by his shipmates, and being, it seems, for some reason a huge favorite with them, they raised a cry of "Bulkington! Bulkington! where's Bulkington?" and darted out of the house in pursuit of him.

It was now about nine o'clock, and the room seeming almost supernaturally quiet after these orgies, I began to congratulate myself upon a little plan that had occurred to me just previous to the entrance of the seamen.

No man prefers to sleep two in a bed. In fact, you would a good deal rather not sleep with your own brother. I don't know how it is, but people like to be private when they are sleeping. And when it comes to sleeping with an unknown stranger, in a strange inn, in a strange town, and that stranger a harpooneer, then your objections indefinitely multiply. Nor was there any earthly reason why I as a sailor should sleep two in a bed, more than anybody else; for sailors no more sleep two in a bed at sea, than bachelor Kings do ashore. To be sure they all sleep together in one apartment, but you have your own hammock, and cover yourself with your own blanket, and sleep in your own skin.

---

comforters: long scarves. **Labrador**: rugged, snowy peninsula of northeastern Canada. **weather side**: windy side, opposite the sheltered lee side. **arrantest topers**: most confirmed of alcoholics. **sleeping-partner**: business associate behind the scenes. **coffer-dam**: watertight structure used in repairing any structure below water level.

The more I pondered over this harpooneer, the more I abominated the thought of sleeping with him. **It was fair to presume that being a harpooneer, his linen or woollen, as the case might be, would not be of the tidiest, certainly none of the finest. I began to twitch all over.** Besides, it was getting late, and **my** decent harpooneer ought to be home and going bed-wards. Suppose now, he should tumble in upon me at midnight—how could I tell from what vile hole he had been coming?

"Landlord! I've changed my mind about that harpooneer.—I shan't sleep with him. I'll try the bench here."

"Just as you please; I'm sorry I cant spare ye a table-cloth for a mattress, and it's a plaguy° rough board here"—feeling of the knots and notches. "But wait a bit, Skrimshander;° I've got a carpenter's plane there in the bar—wait, I say, and I'll make ye snug enough." So saying he procured the plane; and with his old silk handkerchief first dusting the bench, vigorously set to planing away at my bed, the while grinning like an ape. The shavings flew right and left; till at last the plane-iron came bump against an indestructible knot. The landlord was near spraining his wrist, and I told him for heaven's sake to quit—the bed was soft enough to suit me, and I did not know how all the planing in the world could make eider down of a pine plank. So gathering up the shavings with another grin, and throwing them into the great stove in the middle of the room, he went about his business, and left me in a brown study.°

I now took the measure of the bench, and found that it was a foot too short; but that could be mended with a chair. But it was a foot too narrow, and the other bench in the room was about four inches higher than the planed one—so there was no yoking them. I then placed the first bench lengthwise along the only clear space against the wall, leaving a little interval between, for my back to settle down in. But I soon found that there came such a draught of cold air over me from under the sill of the window, that this plan would never do at all, especially as another current from the rickety door met the one from the window, and both together formed a series of small whirlwinds in the immediate vicinity of the spot where I had thought to spend the night.

The devil fetch that harpooneer, thought I, but stop, couldn't I steal a march on him—bolt his door inside, and jump into his bed, not to be wakened by the most violent knockings? It seemed no bad idea; but upon second thoughts I dismissed it. For who could tell but what the next morning, so soon as I popped out of the room, the harpooneer might be standing in the entry, all ready to knock me down!

Still, looking round me again, and seeing no possible chance of spending a sufferable night unless in some other person's bed, I began to think that after all I might be cherishing unwarrantable prejudices against this unknown harpooneer. Thinks I, I'll wait awhile; he must be dropping in before long. I'll have a good look at him then, and perhaps we may become jolly good bedfellows after all—there's no telling.

But though the other boarders kept coming in by ones, twos, and threes, and going to bed, yet no sign of my harpooneer.

"Landlord!" said I, "what sort of a chap is he—does he always keep such late hours?" It was now hard upon twelve o'clock.

---

plaguy: irritatingly. ***Skrimshander***: here, a carver of scrimshaw. ***brown study***: deep meditation.

The landlord chuckled again with his lean chuckle, and seemed to be mightily tickled at something beyond my comprehension. "No," he answered, "generally he's an early bird—airley to bed and airley to rise—yes, he's the bird what catches the worm.—But to-night he went out a peddling, you see, and I don't see what on airth keeps him so late, unless, may be, he can't sell his head."

"Can't sell his head?—What sort of a bamboozling story is this you are telling me?" getting into a towering rage. "Do you pretend to say, landlord, that this harpooneer is actually engaged this blessed Saturday night, or rather Sunday morning, in peddling his head around this town?"

"That's precisely it," said the landlord, "and I told him he couldn't sell it here, the market's overstocked."

"With what?" shouted I.

"With heads to be sure; ain't there too many heads in the world?"

"I tell you what it is, landlord," said I, quite calmly, "you'd better stop spinning that yarn to me—I'm not green."

"May be not," taking out a stick and whittling a toothpick, "but I rayther guess you'll be done *brown* if that ere harpooneer hears you a slanderin' his head."

"I'll break it for him," said I, now flying into a passion again at this unaccountable farrago° of the landlord's.

"It's broke a'ready," said he.

"Broke," said I—"*broke*, do you mean?"

"Sartain, and that's the very reason he can't sell it, I guess."

"Landlord," said I, going up to him as cool as Mt. Hecla° in a snow storm,— "landlord, stop whittling. You and I must understand one another, and that too without delay. I come to your house and want a bed; you tell me you can only give me half a one; that the other half belongs to a certain harpooneer. And about this harpooneer, whom I have not yet seen, you persist in telling me the most mystifying and exasperating stories, tending to beget in me an uncomfortable feeling towards the man whom you design for my bedfellow—a sort of connexion, landlord, which is an intimate and confidential one in the highest degree. I now demand of you to speak out and tell me who and what this harpooneer is, and whether I shall be in all respects safe to spend the night with him. And in the first place, you will be so good as to unsay that story about selling his head, which if true I take to be good evidence that this harpooneer is stark mad, and I've no idea of sleeping with a madman; and you, sir, *you* I mean, landlord, *you,* sir, by trying to induce me to do so knowingly, would thereby render yourself liable to a criminal prosecution."

"Wall," said the landlord, fetching a long breath, "that's a purty long sarmon for a chap that rips° a little now and then. But be easy, be easy, this here harpooneer I have been tellin' you of has just arrived from the south seas,° where he bought up a lot of 'balmed New Zealand heads (great curios, you know), and he's sold all on 'em but one, and that one he's trying to sell to-night, cause to-morrow's Sunday, and it would not do to be sellin' human heads about the streets when folks is goin' to

---

farrago: mixed nonsense. **Mt. Hecla**: volcano in Iceland that had erupted in 1845. **rips**: (slang) speaks hotly. **south seas**: the South Pacific.

churches. He wanted to, last Sunday, but I stopped him just as he was goin' out of the door with four heads strung on a string, for all the airth like a string of inions."

This account cleared up the otherwise unaccountable mystery, and showed that the landlord, after all, had had no idea of fooling me—but at the same time what could I think of a harpooneer who stayed out of a Saturday night clean into the holy Sabbath, engaged in such a cannibal business as selling the heads of dead idolators?

"Depend upon it, landlord, that harpooneer is a dangerous man."

"He pays reg'lar," was the rejoinder. "But come, it's getting dreadful late, you had better be turning flukes°—it's a nice bed: **Sall** and me slept in that ere bed the night we were spliced. There's plenty room for two to kick about in that bed; it's an almighty big bed that. Why, afore we give it up, Sal used to put our Sam and little Johnny in the foot of it. But I got a dreaming and sprawling about one night, and somehow, Sam got pitched on the floor, and came near breaking his arm. Arter that, Sal said it wouldn't do. Come along here, I'll give ye a glim in a jiffy;" and so saying he lighted a candle and held it towards me, offering to lead the way. But I stood irresolute; when looking at a clock in the corner, he exclaimed "I vum° it's Sunday— you won't see that harpooneer to-night; he's come to anchor somewhere—come along then; *do* come; *won't* ye come?"

I considered the matter a moment, and then up stairs we went, and I was ushered into a small room, cold as a clam, and furnished, sure enough, with a prodigious bed, almost big enough indeed for any four harpooneers to sleep abreast.

"There," said the landlord, placing the candle on a crazy old sea chest that did double duty as a wash-stand and centre table; "there, make yourself comfortable now, and good night to ye." I turned round from eyeing the bed, but he had disappeared.

Folding back the counterpane, I stooped over the bed. Though none of the most elegant, it yet stood the scrutiny tolerably well. I then glanced round the room; and besides the bedstead and centre table, could see no other furniture belonging to the place, but a rude shelf, the four walls, and a papered fireboard° representing a man striking a whale. Of things not properly belonging to the room, there was a hammock lashed up, and thrown upon the floor in one corner; also a large seaman's bag, containing the harpooneer's wardrobe, no doubt in lieu of a land trunk. Likewise, there was a parcel of outlandish bone fish hooks on the shelf over the fireplace, and a tall harpoon standing at the head of the bed.

But what is this on the chest? I took it up, and held it close to the light, and felt it, and smelt it, and tried every way possible to arrive at some satisfactory conclusion concerning it. I can compare it to nothing but a large door mat, ornamented at the edges with little tinkling tags something like the stained porcupine quills round an Indian moccasin. There was a hole or slit in the middle of this mat, as you see the same in South American ponchos. But could it be possible that any sober harpooneer would get into a door mat, and parade the streets of any Christian town in that sort of guise? I put it on, to try it, and it weighed me down like a hamper,° being

---

turning flukes: going to bed, analogous to a whale's showing its tail flukes when diving. ***vum***: vow, swear. ***fireboard***: cover for a fireplace not in use. ***hamper***: shackle or fetter.

uncommonly shaggy and thick, and I thought a little damp, as though this mysterious harpooneer had been wearing it of a rainy day. I went up in it to a bit of glass stuck against the wall, and **I never saw such a sight in my life.** I tore myself out of it in such a hurry that I gave myself a kink in the neck.

I sat down on the side of the bed, and commenced thinking about this head-peddling harpooneer, and his door mat. After thinking some time on the bed-side, I got up and took off my monkey jacket, and then stood in the middle of the room thinking. I then took off my coat, and thought a little more in my shirt sleeves. But beginning to feel very cold now, half undressed as I was, and remembering what the landlord said about the harpooneer's not coming home at all that night, it being so very late, I made no more ado, but jumped out of my pantaloons and boots, and then blowing out the light tumbled into bed, and commended myself to the care of heaven.

Whether that mattress was stuffed with corn-cobs or broken crockery, there is no telling, but I rolled about a good deal, and could not sleep for a long time. At last I slid off into a light doze, and had pretty nearly made a good offing towards the land of Nod,[5] when I heard a heavy footfall in the passage, and saw a glimmer of light come into the room from under the door.

Lord save me, thinks I, that must be the harpooneer, the infernal head-peddler. But I lay perfectly still, and resolved not to say a word till spoken to. Holding a light in one hand, and that identical New Zealand head in the other, the stranger entered the room, and without looking towards the bed, placed his candle a good way off from me on the floor in one corner, and then began working away at the knotted cords of the large bag I before spoke of as being in the room. I was all eagerness to see his face, but he kept it averted for some time while employed in unlacing the bag's mouth. This accomplished, however, he turned round—when, good heavens! what a sight! Such a face! It was of a dark, purplish, yellow color, here and there stuck over with large, blackish looking squares.[6] Yes, it's just as I thought, he's a terrible bedfellow; he's been in a fight, got dreadfully cut, and here he is, just from the surgeon. But at that moment he chanced to turn his face so towards the light, that I plainly saw they could not be sticking-plasters at all, those black squares on his cheeks. They were stains of some sort or other. At first I knew not what to make of this; but soon an inkling of the truth occurred to me. I remembered a story of a white man—a whaleman too—who, falling among the cannibals, had been tattooed by them. I concluded that this harpooneer, in the course of his distant voyages, must have met with a similar adventure. And what is it, thought I, after all! It's only his outside; a man can be honest in any sort of skin. But then, what to make of his unearthly complexion, that part of it, I mean, lying round about, and completely independent of the squares of tattooing. To be sure, it might be nothing but a good coat of tropical tanning; but I never heard of a hot sun's tanning a white man into a purplish yellow one. However, I had never been in the South Seas; and perhaps the sun there produced these extraordinary effects upon the skin. Now, while all these ideas were passing through me like lightning, this harpooneer never noticed me at all. But, after some difficulty having opened his bag, he commenced fumbling in it, and presently pulled out a sort of tomahawk, and a seal-skin wallet with the hair on. Placing these on the old chest in the middle of the room, he then took the New Zealand head—a ghastly thing enough—and crammed it down into the bag. He now took off his hat—a new beaver hat°—when I came nigh singing out with fresh surprise. There was no hair on his head—none to speak of at least—nothing but a small scalp-knot twisted up on his forehead. His bald purplish head now looked for all the world like a mildewed skull. Had not the stranger stood between me and the door, I would have bolted out of it quicker than ever I bolted a dinner.

Even as it was, I thought something of slipping out of the window, but it was the second floor back. I am no coward, but what to make of this head-peddling purple rascal altogether passed my comprehension. Ignorance is the parent of fear, and being completely nonplussed and confounded about the stranger, I confess I was now as much afraid of him as if it was the devil himself who had thus broken into my room at the dead of night. In fact, I was so afraid of him that I was not game enough just then to address him, and demand a satisfactory answer concerning what seemed inexplicable in him.

Meanwhile, he continued the business of undressing, and at last showed his chest and arms. As I live, these covered parts of him were checkered with the same squares as his face; his back, too, was all over the same dark squares; he seemed to have been in a Thirty Years' War,° and just escaped from it with a sticking-plaster° shirt. Still more, his very legs were marked, as if a parcel of dark green frogs were running up the trunks of young palms. It was now quite plain that he must be some abominable savage or other shipped aboard of a whaleman in the South Seas, and so landed in this Christian country. I quaked to think of it. A peddler of heads too—perhaps the heads of his own brothers. He might take a fancy to mine—heavens! look at that tomahawk!

But there was no time for shuddering, for now the savage went about something that completely fascinated my attention, and convinced me that he must indeed be a heathen. Going to his heavy grego, or wrapall, or dreadnaught,° which he had previously hung on a chair, he fumbled in the pockets, and produced at length a curious little deformed image with a hunch on its back, and exactly the color of a three days' old Congo baby. Remembering the embalmed head, at first I almost thought that this black manikin was a real baby preserved in some similar manner. But seeing that it was not at all limber, and that it glistened a good deal like polished ebony, I concluded that it must be nothing but a wooden idol, which indeed it proved to be. For now the savage goes up to the empty fire-place, and removing the papered fire-board, sets up this little hunchbacked image, like a ten-pin, between the andirons. The chimney jambs and all the bricks inside were very sooty, so that I thought this fire-place made a very appropriate little shrine or chapel for his Congo idol.

I now screwed my eyes hard towards the half hidden image, feeling but ill at ease meantime—to see what was next to follow. First he takes about a double handful of shavings out of his grego pocket, and places them carefully before the idol; then laying a bit of ship biscuit on top and applying the flame from the lamp, he kindled the shavings into a sacrificial blaze. Presently, after many hasty snatches into the

---

beaver hat: top hat of beaver fur. ***Thirty Years' War***: fought by various European nations, 1618–48. ***sticking-plaster***: adhesive bandage. ***grego, wrapall, dreadnaught***: types of over-coat.

fire, and still hastier withdrawals of his fingers (whereby he seemed to be scorching them badly), he at last succeeded in drawing out the biscuit; then blowing off the heat and ashes a little, he made a polite offer of it to the little negro. But the little devil did not seem to fancy such dry sort of fare at all; he never moved his lips. All these strange antics were accompanied by still stranger guttural noises from the devotee, who seemed to be praying in a sing-song or else singing some pagan psalmody or other, during which his face twitched about in the most unnatural manner. At last extinguishing the fire, he took the idol up very unceremoniously, and bagged it again in his grego pocket as carelessly as if he were a sportsman bagging a dead woodcock.

All these queer proceedings increased my uncomfortableness, and seeing him now exhibiting strong symptoms of concluding his business operations, and jumping into bed with me, I thought it was high time, now or never, before the light was put out, to break the spell in which I had so long been bound.

But the interval I spent in deliberating what to say, was a fatal one. Taking up his tomahawk from the table, he examined the head of it for an instant, and then holding it to the light, with his mouth at the handle, he puffed out great clouds of tobacco smoke.[7] The next moment the light was extinguished, and this wild cannibal, tomahawk between his teeth, sprang into bed with me. I sang out, I could not help it now; and giving a sudden grunt of astonishment he began feeling me.

Stammering out something, I knew not what, I rolled away from him against the wall, and then conjured him, whoever or whatever he might be, to keep quiet, and let me get up and light the lamp again. But his guttural responses satisfied me at once that he but ill comprehended my meaning.

"Who-e debel you?"—he at last said—"you no speak-e, dam-me, I kill-e." And so saying the lighted tomahawk began flourishing about me in the dark.

"Landlord, for God's sake, Peter Coffin!" shouted I. "Landlord! Watch!° Coffin! Angels! save me!"

"Speak-e! tell-ee me who-ee be, or dam-me, I kill-e!" again growled the cannibal, while his horrid flourishings of the tomahawk scattered the hot tobacco ashes about me till I thought my linen would get on fire. But thank heaven, at that moment the landlord came into the room light in hand, and leaping from the bed I ran up to him.

"Don't be afraid now," said he, grinning again. "Queequeg here wouldn't harm a hair of your head."

"Stop your grinning," shouted I, "and why didn't you tell me that that infernal harpooneer was a cannibal?"

"I thought ye know'd it;—didn't I tell ye, he was a peddlin' heads around town?—but turn flukes again and go to sleep. Queequeg, look here—you sabbee me, I sabbee you—this man sleepe you—you sabbee?"—

"Me sabbee plenty"—grunted Queequeg, puffing away at his pipe and sitting up in bed.

"You gettee in," he added, motioning to me with his tomahawk, and throwing the clothes to one side. He really did this in not only a civil but a really kind and charitable way. I stood looking at him a moment. For all his tattooings he was on the

Watch!: "Police!"

whole a clean, comely looking cannibal. What's all this fuss I have been making about, thought I to myself—the man's a human being just as I am: he has just as much reason to fear me, as I have to be afraid of him. Better sleep with a sober cannibal than a drunken Christian.

"Landlord," said I, "tell him to stash his tomahawk there, or pipe, or whatever you call it; tell him to stop smoking, in short, and I will turn in with him. But I don't fancy having a man smoking in bed with me. It's dangerous. Besides, I aint insured."

This being told to Queequeg, he at once complied, and again politely motioned me to get into bed—rolling over to one side as much as to say—I wont touch a leg of ye.

"Good night, landlord," said I, "you may go."

I turned in, and never slept better in my life.

CHAPTER 4

THE COUNTERPANE

U PON waking next morning about daylight, I found Queequeg's arm thrown over me in the most loving and affectionate manner. You had almost thought I had been his wife. The counterpane° was of patchwork, full of odd little parti-colored squares and triangles; and this arm of his tattooed all over with an interminable Cretan labyrinth° of a figure, no two parts of which were of one precise shade— owing I suppose to his keeping his arm at sea unmethodically in sun and shade, his shirt sleeves irregularly rolled up at various times—this same arm of his, I say, looked for all the world like a strip of that same patchwork quilt. Indeed, partly lying on it as the arm did when I first awoke, I could hardly tell it from the quilt, they so blended their hues together; and it was only by the sense of weight and pressure that I could tell that Queequeg was hugging me.

My sensations were strange. Let me try to explain them. When I was a child, I well remember a somewhat similar circumstance that befell me; whether it was a reality or a dream, I never could entirely settle. The circumstance was this. I had been cutting up some caper° or other—I think it was trying to crawl up the chimney, as I had seen a little sweep° do a few days previous; and my stepmother who, some-how or other, was all the time whipping me, or sending me to bed supperless,—my mother dragged me by the legs out of the chimney and packed me off to bed, though it was only two o'clock in the afternoon of the 21st June, the longest day in the year in our hemisphere. I felt dreadfully. But there was no help for it, so up stairs I went to my little room in the third floor, undressed myself as slowly as possible so as to kill time, and with a bitter sigh got between the sheets.

I lay there dismally calculating that sixteen entire hours must elapse before I could hope **for a resurrection**. Sixteen hours in bed! the small of my back ached to think of it. And it was so light too; the sun shining in at the window, and a great rattling of coaches in the streets, and the sound of gay voices all over the house. I felt worse and worse—at last I got up, dressed, and softly going down in my stockinged feet, sought out my stepmother, and suddenly threw myself at her feet, beseeching

counterpane: bedspread. **Cretan labyrinth**: mythical maze built by Daedalus on the island of Crete, imprisoning the Minotaur (see also Ch. 85). **caper**: prank. **little sweep**: boy who cleans chimneys.

her as a particular favor to give me a good slippering for my misbehavior; anything indeed but condemning me to lie abed such an unendurable length of time. But she was the best and most conscientious of stepmothers, and back I had to go to my room. For several hours I lay there broad awake, feeling a great deal worse than I have ever done since, even from the greatest subsequent misfortunes. At last I must have fallen into a troubled nightmare of a doze; and slowly waking from it—half steeped in dreams—I opened my eyes, and the before sun-lit room was now wrapped in outer darkness. Instantly I felt a shock running through all my frame; nothing was to be seen, and nothing was to be heard; but a supernatural hand seemed placed in mine. My arm hung over the counterpane, and the nameless, unimaginable, silent form or phantom, to which the hand belonged, seemed closely seated by my bedside. For what seemed ages piled on ages, I lay there, frozen with the most awful fears, not daring to drag away my hand; yet ever thinking that if I could but stir it one single inch, the horrid spell would be broken. I knew not how this consciousness at last glided away from me; but waking in the morning, I shudderingly remembered it all, and for days and weeks and months afterwards I lost myself in confounding attempts to explain the mystery. Nay, to this very hour, I often puzzle myself with it.

Now, take away the awful fear, and my sensations at feeling the supernatural hand in mine were very similar, in their strangeness, to those which I experienced on waking up and seeing Queequeg's pagan arm thrown round me. But at length all the past night's events soberly recurred, one by one, in fixed reality, and then I lay only alive to the comical predicament. For though I tried to move his arm—unlock his **bridegroom** clasp—yet, sleeping as he was, he still hugged me tightly, as though naught but death should part us twain. I now strove to rouse him—"Queequeg!"—but his only answer was a snore. I then rolled over, my neck feeling as if it were in a horse-collar; and suddenly felt a slight scratch. Throwing aside the counterpane, there lay the tomahawk sleeping by the savage's side, as if it were a hatchet-faced baby. A pretty pickle, truly, thought I; abed here in a strange house in the broad day, with a cannibal

REVISION NARRATIVE

Ishmael and Queequeg I

Having shared a bed with Queequeg, Ishmael wakes up with Queequeg's arm over him and recalls the strange feelings he had felt as a boy when he had been sent to bed as a punishment and had awakened with the feeling of being held by some supernatural hand. The British version of this scene makes three small revisions. Ishmael's irreverent use of "resurrection" (p. 41) is an expression for his release from punishment; the editor revised "hope for a resurrection" to simply "hope to get out of bed again." The editor also made two other excisions: he changed "unlock his **bridegroom** clasp" to "unlock his clasp," and he altered "hugging a fellow male in that **matrimonial** sort of style" (p. 43) to "hugging a fellow male in that sort of style."

and a tomahawk! "Queequeg!—in the name of goodness, Queequeg, wake!" At length, by dint of much wriggling, and loud and incessant expostulations° upon the unbecomingness of his hugging a fellow male in that **matrimonial** sort of style, I succeeded in extracting a grunt; and presently, he drew back his arm, shook himself all over like a Newfoundland dog[1] just from the water, and sat up in bed, stiff as a pike-staff,° looking at me, and rubbing his eyes as if he did not altogether remember how I came to be there, though a dim consciousness of knowing something about me seemed slowly dawning over him. Meanwhile, I lay quietly eyeing him, having no serious misgivings now, and bent upon narrowly observing so curious a creature. When, at last, his mind seemed made up touching the character of his bedfellow, and he became, as it were, reconciled to the fact; he jumped out upon the floor, and by certain signs and sounds gave me to understand that, if it pleased me, he would dress first and then leave me to dress afterwards, **leaving** the whole apartment to myself. Thinks I, Queequeg, under the circumstances, this is a very civilized overture; but, the truth is, these savages have an innate sense of delicacy, say what you will; it is marvellous how essentially polite they are. I pay this particular compliment to Queequeg, because he treated me with so much civility and consideration, while I was guilty of great rudeness; staring at him from the bed, and watching all his toilette motions; for the time my curiosity getting the better of my breeding. Nevertheless, a man like Queequeg you don't see every day, he and his ways were well worth unusual regarding.

He commenced dressing at top by donning his beaver hat, a very tall one, by the by, and then—still minus his trowsers—he hunted up his boots. What under the heavens he did it for, I cannot tell, but his next movement was to crush himself—boots in hand, and hat on—under the bed; when, from sundry° violent gaspings and strainings, I inferred he was hard at work booting himself; though by no law of propriety that I ever heard of, is any man required to be private when putting on his boots. But Queequeg, do you see, was a creature in the transition state—neither caterpillar nor butterfly.[2] He was just enough civilized to show off his outlandishness in the strangest possible manner. His education was not yet completed. He was an undergraduate. If he had not been a small degree civilized, he very probably would not have troubled himself with boots at all; but then, if he had not been still a savage, he never would have dreamt of getting under the bed to put them on. At last, he emerged with his hat very much dented and crushed down over his eyes, and began creaking and limping about the room, as if, not being much accustomed to boots, his pair of damp, wrinkled cowhide ones—probably not made to order either—rather pinched and tormented him at the first go off of a bitter cold morning.

Seeing, now, that there were no curtains to the window, and that the street being very narrow, the house opposite commanded a plain view into the room, and observing more and more the indecorous figure that Queequeg made, staving about° with little else but his hat and boots on; I begged him as well as I could, to accelerate his toilet somewhat, and particularly to get into his pantaloons as soon as possible. He complied, and then proceeded to wash himself. At that time in the morning any Christian would have washed his face; but Queequeg, to my amaze-

---

expostulations: strong explanations. ***pike-staff***: long pole of a heavy spear. ***sundry***: assorted. ***staving about***: rapidly walking back and forth.

ment, contented himself with restricting his ablutions to his chest, arms, and hands. He then donned his waistcoat,° and taking up a piece of hard soap on the wash-stand centre-table, dipped it into water and commenced lathering his face. I was watching to see where he kept his razor, when lo and behold, he takes the harpoon from the bed corner, slips out the long wooden stock, unsheathes the head, whets it a little on his boot, and striding up to the bit of mirror against the wall, begins a vigorous scraping, or rather harpooning of his cheeks. Thinks I, Queequeg, this is using Rogers's best cutlery° with a vengeance. Afterwards I wondered the less at this operation when I came to know of what fine steel the head of a harpoon is made, and how exceedingly sharp the long straight edges are always kept.

The rest of his toilet was soon achieved, and he proudly marched out of the room, wrapped up in his great pilot monkey jacket, and sporting his harpoon like a marshal's baton.

waistcoat: vest. ***Rogers's best cutlery***: well-known American tableware.

CHAPTER 5

BREAKFAST

I QUICKLY followed suit, and descending into the bar-room accosted the grinning landlord very pleasantly. I cherished no malice towards him, though he had been skylarking with me not a little in the matter of my bedfellow.

However, a good laugh is a mighty good thing, and rather too scarce a good thing; the more's the pity. So, if any one man, in his own proper person, afford stuff for a good joke to anybody, let him not be backward, but let him cheerfully allow himself to spend and be spent[1] in that way. And the man that has anything bountifully laughable about him, be sure there is more in that man than you perhaps think for.

The bar-room was now full of the boarders who had been dropping in the night previous, and whom I had not as yet had a good look at. They were nearly all whalemen; chief mates, and second mates, and third mates, and sea carpenters, and sea coopers,° and sea blacksmiths, and harpooneers, and ship keepers;° a brown and brawny company, with bosky beards; an unshorn, shaggy set, all wearing monkey jackets for morning gowns.

You could pretty plainly tell how long each one had been ashore. This young fellow's healthy cheek is like a sun-toasted pear in hue, and would seem to smell almost as musky; he cannot have been three days landed from his Indian voyage. That man next him looks a few shades lighter; you might say a touch of satin wood° is in him. In the complexion of a third still lingers a tropic tawn,° but slightly bleached withal; *he* doubtless has tarried whole weeks ashore. But who could show a cheek like Queequeg? which, barred with various tints, seemed like the Andes' western slope,[2] to show forth in one array, contrasting climates, zone by zone.

"Grub, ho!" now cried the landlord, flinging open a door, and in we went to breakfast.

They say that men who have seen the world, thereby become quite at ease in manner, quite self-possessed in company. Not always, though: Ledyard, the great New England traveller, and Mungo Park, the Scotch one;[3] of all men, they possessed the least assurance in the parlor. But perhaps the mere crossing of Siberia in a

---

coopers: barrel makers. **ship keepers**: crew members who work on board ship only (not in the whaleboats). **satin wood**: yellowish wood from southern Asia. **tawn**: tan.

sledge drawn by dogs as Ledyard did, or the taking a long solitary walk on an empty stomach, in the negro heart of Africa, which was the sum of poor Mungo's performances—this kind of travel, I say, may not be the very best mode of attaining a high social polish. Still, for the most part, that sort of thing is to be had anywhere.

These reflections just here are occasioned by the circumstance that after we were all seated at the table, and I was preparing to hear some good stories about whaling; to my no small surprise, nearly every man maintained a profound silence. And not only that, but they looked embarrassed. Yes, here were a set of sea-dogs, many of whom without the slightest bashfulness had boarded great whales on the high seas—entire strangers to them—and duelled them dead without winking; and yet, here they sat at a social breakfast table—all of the same calling, all of kindred tastes—looking round as sheepishly at each other as though they had never been out of sight of some sheepfold among the Green Mountains.° A curious sight; these bashful bears, these timid warrior whalemen!

But as for Queequeg—why, Queequeg sat there among them—at the head of the table, too, it so chanced; as cool as an icicle. To be sure I cannot say much for his breeding. His greatest admirer could not have cordially justified his bringing his harpoon into breakfast with him, and using it there without ceremony; reaching over the table with it, to the imminent jeopardy of many heads, and grappling the beefsteaks towards him. But *that* was certainly very coolly done by him, and every one knows that in most people's estimation, to do anything coolly is to do it genteelly.

We will not speak of all Queequeg's peculiarities here; how he eschewed coffee and hot rolls, and applied his undivided attention to beefsteaks, done rare. Enough, that when breakfast was over he withdrew like the rest into the public room, lighted his tomahawk-pipe, and was sitting there quietly digesting and smoking with his inseparable hat on, when I sallied out for a stroll.

Green Mountains: part of the Appalachian chain, in Vermont; here, "green" also implies "inexperienced."

CHAPTER 6

THE STREET

IF I had been astonished at first catching a glimpse of so outlandish an individual as Queequeg circulating among the polite society of a civilized town, that astonishment soon departed upon taking my first daylight stroll through the streets of New Bedford.

In thoroughfares nigh the docks, any considerable seaport will frequently offer to view the queerest looking nondescripts from foreign parts. Even in Broadway and Chestnut streets, Mediterranean mariners will sometimes jostle the affrighted ladies. Regent street is not unknown to Lascars and Malays; and at Bombay, in the Apollo Green,[1] live Yankees have often scared the natives. But New Bedford beats all Water street and Wapping. In these last-mentioned haunts you see only sailors; but in New Bedford, actual cannibals stand chatting at street corners; savages outright; many of whom yet carry on their bones unholy flesh. It makes a stranger stare.

But, besides the Feegeeans, Tongatabooans, Erromanggoans, Pannangians, and Brighggians,° and, besides the wild specimens of the whaling-craft which unheeded reel about the streets, you will see other sights still more curious, certainly more comical. There weekly arrive in this town scores of green Vermonters and New Hampshire men, all athirst for gain and glory in the fishery. They are mostly young, of stalwart frames; fellows who have felled forests, and now seek to drop the axe and snatch the whale-lance. Many are as green as the Green Mountains whence they came. In some things you would think them but a few hours old. Look there! that chap strutting round the corner. He wears a beaver hat and swallow-tailed coat,° girdled with a sailor-belt and sheath-knife. Here comes another with a sou'-wester and a bombazine cloak.°

No town-bred dandy will compare with a country-bred one—I mean a downright bumpkin dandy—a fellow that, in the dog-days,° will mow his two acres

---

Feegeeans, . . . and Brighggians: Pacific islanders; however, the last is Melville's invention. ***swallow-tailed coat***: black formal coat with split tail. ***sou'-wester and a bombazine cloak***: waterproof sailor's hat with an extra-wide brim at the back; bombazine is a fine fabric of silk and either wool or cotton. ***dog-days***: in the Northern Hemisphere, the oppressively hot days of July to September, associated with Sirius, the "dog star."

in buckskin gloves for fear of tanning his hands. Now when a country dandy like this takes it into his head to make a distinguished reputation, and joins the great whale-fishery, you should see the comical things he does upon reaching the sea-port. In bespeaking his sea-outfit, he orders bell-buttons to his waistcoats; straps° to his canvas trowsers. Ah, poor Hay-Seed! how bitterly will burst those straps in the first howling gale, when thou art driven, straps, buttons, and all, down the throat of the tempest.

But think not that this famous town has only harpooneers, cannibals, and bumpkins to show her visitors. Not at all. Still New Bedford is a queer place. Had it not been for us whalemen, that tract of land would this day perhaps have been in as howling condition as the coast of Labrador. As it is, parts of her back country are enough to frighten one, they look so bony. The town itself is perhaps the dearest place to live in, in all New England. It is a land of oil, true enough: but not like Canaan;[2] a land, also, of corn and wine. The streets do not run with milk; nor in the spring-time do they pave them with fresh eggs. Yet, in spite of this, nowhere in all America will you find more patrician-like houses; parks and gardens more opulent, than in New Bedford. Whence came they? how planted upon this once scraggy scoria° of a country?

Go and gaze upon the iron emblematical harpoons round yonder lofty mansion, and your question will be answered. Yes; all these brave houses and flowery gardens came from the Atlantic, Pacific, and Indian oceans. One and all, they were harpooned and dragged up hither from the bottom of the sea. **Can Herr Alexander**[3] **perform a feat like that?**

In New Bedford, fathers, they say, give whales for dowers° to their daughters, and portion off their nieces with a few porpoises a-piece. You must go to New Bedford to see a brilliant wedding; for, they say, they have reservoirs of oil in every house, and every night recklessly burn their lengths in spermaceti° candles.

In summer time, the town is sweet to see; full of fine maples—long avenues of green and gold. And in August, high in air, the beautiful and bountiful horse-chestnuts, candelabra-wise, proffer the passer-by their tapering upright cones of congregated blossoms. So omnipotent is art; which in many a district of New Bedford has superinduced bright terraces of flowers upon **the barren refuse rocks thrown aside at creation's final day.**

And the women of New Bedford, they bloom like their own red roses. But roses only bloom in summer; whereas the fine carnation of their cheeks is perennial as sunlight in the seventh heavens.[4] Elsewhere match that bloom of theirs, ye cannot, save in Salem,[5] where they tell me the young girls breathe such musk, their sailor sweethearts smell them miles off shore, as though they were drawing nigh the odorous Moluccas instead of the Puritanic sands.

straps: suspenders. *scoria*: slag; lava. *spermaceti*: waxy oil from the sperm whale's head, from which the finest candles were made. *dowers*: dowries; cash or property given by a bride's family to a bridegroom.

CHAPTER 7

THE CHAPEL

IN this same New Bedford there stands a Whaleman's Chapel,[1] and few are the moody fishermen, shortly bound for the Indian Ocean or Pacific, who fail to make a Sunday visit to the spot. I am sure that I did not.

Returning from my first morning stroll, I again sallied out upon this special errand. The sky had changed from clear, sunny cold, to driving sleet and mist. Wrapping myself in my shaggy jacket of the cloth called bearskin,° I fought my way against the stubborn storm. Entering, I found a small scattered congregation of sailors, and sailors' wives and widows. A muffled silence reigned, only broken at times by the shrieks of the storm. Each silent worshipper seemed purposely sitting apart from the other, as if each silent grief were insular and incommunicable. The chaplain had not yet arrived; and there these silent islands of men and women sat steadfastly eyeing several marble tablets, with black borders, masoned into the wall on either side the pulpit. Three of them ran something like the following, but I do not pretend to quote:—

SACRED

𝕮𝖔 𝖙𝖍𝖊 𝕸𝖊𝖒𝖔𝖗𝖞

O F

J O H N T A L B O T,

Who, at the age of eighteen, was lost overboard,
Near the Isle of Desolation,° off Patagonia,
November 1st, 1836.

THIS TABLET
Is erected to his Memory
BY HIS SISTER.

---

bearskin: shaggy woolen cloth. ***Isle of Desolation***: uninhabited island off the tip of South America.

SACRED

Ⓣⓞ ⓣⓗⓔ Ⓜⓔⓜⓞⓡⓨ

OF

ROBERT LONG, WILLIS ELLERY,

NATHAN COLEMAN, WALTER CANNY, SETH MACY,

AND SAMUEL GLEIG,

Forming one of the boats' crews

OF

THE SHIP ELIZA,

Who were towed out of sight by a Whale,

On the Off-shore Ground[2] in the

PACIFIC,

December 31st, 1839.

THIS MARBLE

Is here placed by their surviving

Shipmates.

SACRED

Ⓣⓞ ⓣⓗⓔ Ⓜⓔⓜⓞⓡⓨ

OF

The late

CAPTAIN EZEKIEL HARDY,

Who in the bows of his boat was killed by a

Sperm Whale on the coast of Japan,[3]

August 3d, 1833.

THIS TABLET

Is erected to his Memory

BY

HIS WIDOW.

Shaking off the sleet from my ice-glazed hat and jacket, I seated myself near the door, and turning sideways was surprised to see Queequeg near me. Affected by the solemnity of the scene, there was a wondering gaze of incredulous curiosity in his countenance. This savage was the only person present who seemed to notice my entrance; because he was the only one who could not read, and, therefore, was not reading those frigid inscriptions on the wall. Whether any of the relatives of the seamen whose names appeared there were now among the congregation, I knew not; but so many are the unrecorded accidents in the fishery, and so plainly did several women present wear the countenance if not the trappings of some unceasing grief, that I feel sure that here before me were assembled those, in whose unhealing hearts the sight of those bleak tablets sympathetically caused the old wounds to bleed afresh.

Oh! ye whose dead lie buried beneath the green grass; who standing among flowers can say—here, *here* lies my beloved; ye know not the desolation that broods in bosoms like these. What bitter blanks in those black-bordered marbles which cover no ashes! What despair in those immovable inscriptions! What deadly voids and unbidden infidelities in the lines that seem to gnaw upon all Faith, and refuse resurrections to the beings who have placelessly perished without a grave. As well might those tablets stand in the cave of Elephanta as here.°

In what census of living creatures, the dead of mankind are included; why it is that a universal proverb says of them, that they tell no tales, though containing more secrets than the Goodwin Sands;° how it is that to his name who yesterday departed for the other world, we prefix so significant and infidel a word, and yet do not thus entitle him, if he but embarks for the remotest Indies of this living earth; why the Life Insurance Companies pay death-forfeitures upon immortals; in what eternal, unstirring paralysis, and deadly, hopeless trance, yet lies antique Adam who died sixty round centuries ago;[4] how it is that we still refuse to be comforted for those who we nevertheless maintain are dwelling in unspeakable bliss; why all the living so strive to hush all the dead; wherefore but the rumor of a knocking in a tomb will terrify a whole city. All these things are not without their meanings.

But Faith, like a jackal, feeds among the tombs, and even from these dead doubts she gathers her most vital hope.

It needs scarcely to be told, with what feelings, on the eve of a Nantucket voyage, I regarded those marble tablets, and by the murky light of that darkened, doleful day read the fate of the whalemen who had gone before me. Yes, Ishmael, the same fate may be thine. But somehow I grew merry again. Delightful inducements to embark, fine chance for promotion, it seems—aye, a stove boat° will make me an immortal by brevet.° Yes, there is death in this business of whaling—a speechlessly quick chaotic bundling of a man into Eternity. But what then? Methinks we have hugely mistaken this matter of Life and Death. Methinks that what they call my shadow here on earth is my true substance.[5] Methinks that in looking at things spiritual, we are too much like oysters observing the sun through the water, and thinking that thick water the thinnest of air. Methinks my body is but the lees° of my better being. In fact take my body who will, take it I say, it is not me. And therefore three cheers for Nantucket; and come a stove boat and stove body when they will, for stave my soul, **Jove himself cannot.**

Elephanta: cave-temple to Hindu goddess Siva the Destroyer on an island in the Bay of Bombay, India. **Goodwin Sands**: treacherous shoals and graveyard of ships, off the east coast of England. **stove boat**: smashed or punctured boat (in this case by a whale); see present tense form in "stave my soul" in the last sentence. **brevet**: temporary military promotion sometimes given on the battlefield. **lees**: dregs.

CHAPTER 8

THE PULPIT

I HAD not been seated very long ere a man of a certain venerable robustness entered; immediately as the storm-pelted door flew back upon admitting him, a quick regardful eyeing of him by all the congregation, sufficiently attested that this fine old man was the chaplain. Yes, it was the famous Father Mapple,[1] so called by the whalemen, among whom he was a very great favorite. He had been a sailor and a harpooneer in his youth, but for many years past had dedicated his life to the ministry. At the time I now write of, Father Mapple was in the hardy winter of a healthy old age; that sort of old age which seems merging into a second flowering youth, for among all the fissures of his wrinkles, there shone certain mild gleams of a newly developing bloom—the spring verdure peeping forth even beneath February's snow. No one having previously heard his history, could for the first time behold Father Mapple without the utmost interest, because there were certain engrafted clerical peculiarities about him, imputable to that adventurous maritime life he had led. When he entered I observed that he carried no umbrella, and certainly had not come in his carriage, for his tarpaulin hat° ran down with melting sleet, and his great pilot cloth° jacket seemed almost to drag him to the floor with the weight of the water it had absorbed. However, hat and coat and overshoes were one by one removed, and hung up in a little space in an adjacent corner; when, arrayed in a decent suit, he quietly approached the pulpit.

Like most old fashioned pulpits, it was a very lofty one, and since a regular stairs to such a height would, by its long angle with the floor, seriously contract the already small area of the chapel, the architect, it seemed, had acted upon the hint of Father Mapple, and finished the pulpit without a stairs, substituting a perpendicu-lar side ladder, like those used in mounting a ship from a boat at sea. The wife of a whaling captain had provided the chapel with a handsome pair of red worsted man-ropes for this ladder, which, being itself nicely headed,° and stained with a mahogany color, the whole contrivance, considering what manner of chapel it was, seemed by no means in bad taste. Halting for an instant at the foot of the ladder, and with both

---

tarpaulin hat: made of waterproofed canvas. ***pilot cloth***: coarse, strong fabric. ***headed***: fin-ished at the top.

hands grasping the ornamental knobs of the man-ropes, Father Mapple cast a look upwards, and then with a truly sailor-like but still reverential dexterity, hand over hand, mounted the steps as if ascending the main-top° of his vessel.

The perpendicular parts of this side ladder, as is usually the case with swinging ones, were of cloth-covered rope, only the rounds were of wood, so that at every step there was a joint. At my first glimpse of the pulpit, it had not escaped me that however convenient for a ship, these joints in the present instance seemed unnecessary. For I was not prepared to see Father Mapple after gaining the height, slowly turn round, and stooping over the pulpit, deliberately drag up the ladder step by step, till the whole was deposited within, leaving him impregnable in his little Quebec.[2]

I pondered some time without fully comprehending the reason for this. Father Mapple enjoyed such a wide reputation for sincerity and sanctity, that I could not suspect him of courting notoriety by any mere tricks of the stage. No, thought I, there must be some sober reason for this thing; furthermore, it must symbolize something unseen. Can it be, then, that by that act of physical isolation, he signifies his spiritual withdrawal for the time, from all outward worldly ties and connexions? Yes, for replenished with the meat and wine of the word, to the faithful man of God, this pulpit, I see, is a self-containing stronghold—a lofty Ehrenbreitstein,[3] with a perennial well of water within the walls.

But the side ladder was not the only strange feature of the place, borrowed from the chaplain's former sea-farings. Between the marble cenotaphs° on either hand of the pulpit, the wall which formed its back was adorned with a large painting representing a gallant ship beating against a terrible storm off a lee coast° of black rocks and snowy breakers. But high above the flying scud° and dark-rolling clouds, there floated a little isle of sunlight, from which beamed forth an angel's face; and this bright face shed a distinct spot of radiance upon the ship's tossed deck, something like that silver plate now inserted into the Victory's plank where Nelson fell.[4] "Ah, noble ship," the angel seemed to say, "beat on, beat on, thou noble ship, and bear a hardy helm; for lo! the sun is breaking through; the clouds are rolling off—serenest azure is at hand."

Nor was the pulpit itself without a trace of the same sea-taste that had achieved the ladder and the picture. Its panelled front was in the likeness of a ship's bluff bows,° and the Holy Bible rested on a projecting piece of scroll work, fashioned after a ship's fiddle-headed beak.°

What could be more full of meaning?—for the pulpit is ever this earth's foremost part; all the rest comes in its rear; the pulpit leads the world. From thence it is the storm of God's quick wrath is first descried, and the bow must bear the earliest brunt. From thence it is the God of breezes fair or foul is first invoked for favorable winds. Yes, the world's a ship on its passage out, and not a voyage complete; and the pulpit is its prow.

---

main-top: platform at the top of the lower mainmast. *cenotaphs*: memorials to the dead whose remains are elsewhere. *lee coast*: shore toward which a ship is being blown. *flying scud*: driving mist or low, broken clouds. *bluff bows*: rounded, full front. *beak*: wood carving like the head of a violin, substituting for a ship's ornamental figurehead.

CHAPTER 9

THE SERMON

FATHER Mapple rose, and in a mild voice of unassuming authority ordered the scattered people to condense. "Starboard gangway, there![1] side away to larboard—larboard gangway to starboard! Midships! midships!"

There was a low rumbling of heavy sea-boots among the benches, and a still slighter shuffling of women's shoes, and all was quiet again, and every eye on the preacher.

He paused a little; then kneeling in the pulpit's bows, folded his large brown hands across his chest, uplifted his closed eyes, and offered a prayer so deeply devout that he seemed kneeling and praying at the bottom of the sea.

This ended, in prolonged solemn tones, like the continual tolling of a bell in a ship that is foundering° at sea in a fog—in such tones he commenced reading the following hymn; but changing his manner towards the concluding stanzas, burst forth with a pealing exultation and joy—

> "The ribs and terrors in the whale,
>   Arched over me a dismal gloom,
> While all God's sun-lit waves rolled by,
>   And **left** me deepening down to doom.
>
> "I saw the **opening maw**°of hell,
>   With endless pains and sorrows there;
> Which none but they that feel can tell—
>   Oh, I was plunging to despair.
>
> "In black distress, I called my God,
>   When I could scarce believe him mine,
> He bowed his ear to my complaints—
>   No more the whale did me confine.

foundering: sinking. ***maw***: gaping mouth.

"With speed he flew to my relief,
　　As on a radiant dolphin borne;
Awful, yet bright, as lightning shone
　　The face of my Deliverer God.

"My song for ever shall record
　　That terrible, that joyful hour;
I give the glory to my God,
　　His all the mercy and the power."[2]

　　Nearly all joined in singing this hymn, which swelled high above the howling of the storm. A brief pause ensued; the preacher slowly turned over the leaves of the Bible, and at last, folding his hand down upon the proper page, said: "Beloved shipmates, clinch° the last verse of the first chapter of Jonah—'And God had prepared a great fish to swallow up Jonah.' [3]

　　"Shipmates, this book, containing only four chapters—four yarns—is one of the smallest strands in the mighty cable of the Scriptures. Yet what depths of the soul does Jonah's deep sea-line sound! what a pregnant lesson to us is this prophet! What a noble thing is that canticle° in the fish's belly! How billow-like° and boisterously grand! We feel the floods surging over us; we sound with him to the kelpy bottom of the waters; sea-weed and all the slime of the sea is about us! But *what* is this lesson that the book of Jonah teaches? Shipmates, it is a two-stranded lesson; a lesson to us all as sinful men, and a lesson to me as a pilot of the living God.° As sinful men, it is a lesson to us all, because it is a story of the sin, hard-heartedness, suddenly awakened fears, the swift punishment, repentance, prayers, and finally the deliverance and joy of Jonah. As with all sinners among men, the sin of this son of Amittai was in his wilful disobedience of the command of God—never mind now what that command was, or how conveyed—which he found a hard command. But all the things that God would have us do are hard for us to do—remember that—and hence, he oftener commands us than endeavors to persuade. And if we obey God, we must disobey ourselves; and it is in this disobeying ourselves, wherein the hardness of obeying God consists.

　　"With this sin of disobedience in him, Jonah still further flouts at° God, by seeking to flee from Him. He thinks that a ship made by men, will carry him into countries where God does not reign, but only the Captains of this earth. He skulks about the wharves of Joppa, and seeks a ship that's bound for Tarshish.[4] There lurks, perhaps, a hitherto unheeded meaning here. By all accounts Tarshish could have been no other city than the modern Cadiz. That's the opinion of learned men. And where is Cadiz, shipmates? Cadiz is in Spain; as far by water, from Joppa, as Jonah could possibly have sailed in those ancient days, when the Atlantic was an almost unknown sea. Because Joppa, the modern Jaffa, shipmates, is on the most easterly coast of the Mediterranean, the Syrian; and Tarshish or Cadiz more than two thou-

---

clinch: seize tightly. ***canticle***: religious song or chant. ***billow-like***: wavelike. ***pilot of the living God***: spiritual guide. ***flouts at***: scorns.

sand miles to the westward from that, just outside the Straits of Gibraltar.° See ye not then, shipmates, that Jonah sought to flee world-wide from God? Miserable man! Oh! most contemptible and worthy of all scorn; with slouched hat and guilty eye, skulking from his God; prowling among the shipping like a vile burglar hastening to cross the seas. So disordered, self-condemning is his look, that had there been policemen in those days, Jonah, on the mere suspicion of something wrong, had been arrested ere he touched a deck. How plainly he's a fugitive! no baggage, not a hat box, valise, or carpet-bag,—no friends accompany him to the wharf with their adieux. At last, after much dodging search, he finds the Tarshish ship receiving the last items of her cargo; and as he steps on board to see its Captain in the cabin, all the sailors for the moment desist from hoisting in the goods, to mark the stranger's evil eye. Jonah sees this; but in vain he tries to look all ease and confidence; in vain essays his wretched smile. Strong intuitions of the man assure the mariners he can be no innocent. In their gamesome but still serious way, one whispers to the other—'Jack, he's robbed a widow;' or, 'Joe, do you mark him; he's a bigamist;' or, 'Harry lad, I guess he's the adulterer that broke jail in old Gomorrah, or belike, one of the missing murderers from Sodom.' Another runs to read the bill that's stuck against the spile upon the wharf to which the ship is moored, offering five hundred gold coins for the apprehension of a parricide,° and containing a description of his person. He reads, and looks from Jonah to the bill; while all his sympathetic shipmates now crowd round Jonah, prepared to lay their hands upon him. Frighted Jonah trembles, and summoning all his boldness to his face, only looks so much the more a coward. He will not confess himself suspected; but that itself is strong suspicion. So he makes the best of it; and when the sailors find him not to be the man that is advertised, they let him pass, and he descends into the cabin.

"'Who's there?' cries the Captain at his busy desk, hurriedly making out his papers for the Customs—'Who's there?' Oh! how that harmless question mangles Jonah! For the instant he almost turns to flee again. But he rallies. 'I seek a passage in this ship to Tarshish; how soon sail ye, sir?' Thus far the busy Captain had not looked up to Jonah, though the man now stands before him; but no sooner does he hear that hollow voice, than he darts a scrutinizing glance. 'We sail with the next coming tide,' at last he slowly answered, still intently eyeing him. 'No sooner, sir?'—'Soon enough for any honest man that goes a passenger.' Ha! Jonah, that's another stab. But he swiftly calls away the Captain from that scent. 'I'll sail with ye,'—he says,—'the passage money, how much is that?—I'll pay now.' For it is particularly written, shipmates, as if it were a thing not to be overlooked in this history, 'that he paid the fare thereof' ere the craft did sail. And taken with the context, this is full of meaning.

"Now Jonah's Captain, shipmates, was one whose discernment detects crime in any, but whose cupidity° exposes it only in the penniless. In this world, shipmates, sin that pays its way can travel freely, and without a passport; whereas Virtue, if a pauper, is stopped at all frontiers. So Jonah's Captain prepares to test the length of Jonah's purse, ere he judge him openly. He charges him thrice the usual sum; and it's assented to. Then the Captain knows that Jonah is a fugitive; but at the same time

Straits of Gibraltar: connecting the Atlantic Ocean and Mediterranean Sea. **parricide**: killer of one's parent. **cupidity**: greed.

resolves to help a flight that paves its rear with gold. Yet when Jonah fairly takes out his purse, prudent suspicions still molest the Captain. He rings every coin to find a counterfeit. Not a forger, any way, he mutters; and Jonah is put down for his passage. 'Point out my state-room, Sir,' says Jonah now, 'I'm travel-weary; I need sleep.' 'Thou look'st like it,' says the Captain, 'there's thy room.' Jonah enters, and would lock the door, but the lock contains no key. Hearing him foolishly fumbling there, the Captain laughs lowly to himself, and mutters something about the doors of convicts' cells being never allowed to be locked within. All dressed and dusty as he is, Jonah throws himself into his berth, and finds the little state-room ceiling almost resting on his forehead. The air is close, and Jonah gasps. Then, in that contracted hole, sunk, too, beneath the ship's water-line, Jonah feels the heralding presentiment of that stifling hour, when the whale shall hold him in the smallest of his bowel's wards.

"Screwed at its axis against the side, a swinging lamp slightly oscillates in Jonah's room; and the ship, heeling over towards the wharf with the weight of the last bales received, the lamp, flame and all, though in slight motion, still maintains a permanent obliquity with reference to the room; though, in truth, infallibly straight itself, it but made obvious the false, lying levels among which it hung. The lamp alarms and frightens Jonah; as lying in his berth his tormented eyes roll round the place, and this thus far successful fugitive finds no refuge for his restless glance. But that contradiction in the lamp more and more appals him. The floor, the ceiling, and the side, are all awry. 'Oh! so my conscience hangs in me!' he groans, 'straight upward, so it burns; but the chambers of my soul are all in crookedness!'

"Like one who after a night of drunken revelry hies to his bed, still reeling, but with conscience yet pricking him, as the plungings of the Roman race-horse but so much the more strike his steel tags into him; as one who in that miserable plight still turns and turns in giddy anguish, praying God for annihilation until the fit be passed; and at last amid the whirl of woe he feels, a deep stupor steals over him, as over the man who bleeds to death, for conscience is the wound, and there's naught to staunch it; so, after sore wrestlings in his berth, Jonah's prodigy° of ponderous misery drags him drowning down to sleep.

"And now the time of tide has come; the ship casts off her cables; and from the deserted wharf the uncheered ship for Tarshish, all careening, glides to sea. That ship, my friends, was the first of recorded smugglers! the contraband was Jonah. But the sea rebels; he will not bear the wicked burden. A dreadful storm comes on, the ship is like to break. But now when the boatswain° calls all hands to lighten her; when boxes, bales, and jars are **clattering** overboard; when the wind is shrieking, and the men are yelling, and every plank thunders with trampling feet right over Jonah's head; in all this raging tumult, Jonah sleeps his hideous sleep. He sees no black sky and raging sea, feels not the reeling timbers, and little hears he or heeds he the far rush of the mighty whale, which even now with open mouth is cleaving° the seas after him. Aye, shipmates, Jonah was gone down into the sides of the ship°—a berth in the cabin as I have taken it, and was fast asleep. But the frightened master

---

prodigy: something evoking awe; here, awful burden. ***boatswain***: pronounced bos'n, a subordinate ship's officer. ***cleaving***: cutting through. ***was gone down into the sides of the ship***: Jonah 1.5.

comes to him, and shrieks in his dead ear, 'What meanest thou, O sleeper! arise!' Startled from his lethargy by that direful cry, Jonah staggers to his feet, and stumbling to the deck, grasps a shroud,° to look out upon the sea. But at that moment he is sprung upon by a panther billow leaping over the bulwarks. Wave after wave thus leaps into the ship, and finding no speedy vent runs roaring fore and aft, till the mariners come nigh to drowning while yet afloat. And ever, as the white moon shows her affrighted face from the steep gullies in the blackness overhead, aghast Jonah sees the rearing bowsprit pointing high upward, but soon beat downward again towards the tormented deep.

"Terrors upon terrors run shouting through his soul. In all his cringing attitudes, the God-fugitive is now too plainly known. The sailors mark him; more and more certain grow their suspicions of him, and at last, fully to test the truth, by referring the whole matter to high Heaven, they fall to casting lots,° to see for whose cause this great tempest was upon them. The lot is Jonah's; that discovered, then how furiously they mob him with their questions. 'What is thine occupation? Whence comest thou? Thy country? What people?' But mark now, my shipmates, the behavior of poor Jonah. The eager mariners but ask him who he is, and where from; whereas, they not only receive an answer to those questions, but likewise another answer to a question not put by them, but the unsolicited answer is forced from Jonah by the hard hand of God that is upon him.

"'I am a Hebrew,' he cries—and then—'I fear the Lord the God of Heaven who hath made the sea and the dry land!' Fear him, O Jonah? Aye, well mightest thou fear the Lord God *then!* Straightway, he now goes on to make a full confession; whereupon the mariners became more and more appalled, but still are pitiful.° For when Jonah, not yet supplicating God for mercy, since he but too well knew the darkness of his deserts,°—when wretched Jonah cries out to them to take him and cast him forth into the sea, for he knew that for *his* sake this great tempest was upon them; they mercifully turn from him, and seek by other means to save the ship. But all in vain; the indignant gale howls louder; then, with one hand raised invokingly to God, with the other they not unreluctantly lay hold of Jonah.

"And now behold Jonah taken up as an anchor and dropped into the sea; when instantly an oily calmness floats out from the east, and the sea is still, as Jonah carries down the gale with him, leaving smooth water behind. He goes down in the whirling heart of such a masterless commotion that he scarce heeds the moment when he drops seething into the yawning jaws awaiting him; and the whale shoots-to° all his ivory teeth, like so many white bolts, upon his prison. Then Jonah prayed unto the Lord out of the fish's belly.° But observe his prayer, and learn a weighty lesson. For sinful as he is, Jonah does not weep and wail for direct deliverance. He feels that his dreadful punishment is just. He leaves all his deliverance to God, contenting himself with this, that spite of all his pains and pangs, he will still look towards His holy temple. And here, shipmates, is true and faithful repentance; not clamorous for pardon, but grateful for punishment. And how pleasing to God was this conduct in

---

shroud: heavy rope supporting a mast. **casting lots**: choosing by throwing dice or drawing straws. **pitiful**: pitying. **deserts**: deserved punishment. **shoots-to**: closes. **Then Jonah prayed unto the Lord out of the fish's belly**: Jonah 2.1

Jonah, is shown in the eventual deliverance of him from the sea and the whale. Shipmates, I do not place Jonah before you to be copied for his sin but I do place him before you as a model for repentance. Sin not; but if you do, take heed to repent of it like Jonah."

While he was speaking these words, the howling of the shrieking, slanting storm without seemed to add new power to the preacher, who, when describing Jonah's sea-storm, seemed tossed by a storm himself. His deep chest heaved as with a ground-swell;° his tossed arms seemed the warring elements at work; and the thunders that rolled away from off his swarthy brow, and the light leaping from his eye, made all his simple hearers look on him with a quick fear that was strange to them.

There now came a lull in his look, as he silently turned over the leaves of the Book once more; and, at last, standing motionless, with closed eyes, for the moment, seemed communing with **God and himself.**

But again he leaned over towards the people, and bowing his head lowly, with an aspect of the deepest yet manliest humility, he spake these words:

"Shipmates, God has laid but one hand upon you; both his hands press upon me. I have read ye by what murky light may be mine the lesson that Jonah teaches to all sinners; and therefore to ye, and still more to me, for I am a greater sinner than ye. And now how gladly would I come down from this mast-head and sit on the hatches° there where you sit, and listen as you listen, while some one of you reads *me* that other and more awful lesson which Jonah teaches to *me*, as a pilot of the living God. How being an anointed pilot-prophet, or speaker of true things, and bidden by the Lord to sound those unwelcome truths in the ears of a wicked Nineveh,[5] Jonah, appalled at the hostility he should raise, fled from his mission, and sought to escape his duty and his God by taking ship at Joppa. But God is everywhere; Tarshish he never reached. As we have seen, God came upon him in the whale, and swallowed him down to living gulfs of doom, and with swift slantings tore him along 'into the midst of the seas,' where the eddying depths sucked him ten thousand fathoms down,° and 'the weeds were wrapped about his head,'[6] and all the watery world of woe bowled over him. Yet even then beyond the reach of any plummet—'out of the belly of hell'—when the whale grounded upon the ocean's utmost bones, even then, God heard the engulphed, repenting prophet when he cried. Then God spake unto the fish; and from the shuddering cold and blackness of the sea, the whale came breeching up towards the warm and pleasant sun, and all the delights of air and earth; and 'vomited out Jonah upon the dry land;' when the word of the Lord came a second time; and Jonah, bruised and beaten—his ears, like two sea-shells, still multitudinously murmuring of the ocean—Jonah did the Almighty's bidding. And what was that, shipmates? To preach the Truth to the face of Falsehood! That was it!

"This, shipmates, this is that other lesson; and woe to that pilot of the living God who slights it. Woe to him whom this world charms from Gospel duty! Woe to him who seeks to pour oil upon the waters° when God has brewed them into a gale!

---

ground-swell: long, rolling waves. **hatches**: coverings for the hatchways, or openings in the deck of a ship. **ten thousand fathoms down**: a fathom is six feet; Mapple is exaggerating for effect. **pour oil upon the waters**: calm a troubled situation, from the practice of pouring oil on the surface of rough seas.

Woe to him who seeks to please rather than to appal! Woe to him whose good name is more to him than goodness! Woe to him who, in this world, courts not dishonor! Woe to him who would not be true, even though to be false were salvation! Yea, woe to him who, as the great Pilot Paul has it, while preaching to others is himself a castaway!"[7]

He drooped and fell away from himself for a moment; then lifting his face to them again, showed a deep joy in his eyes, as he cried out with a heavenly enthusiasm,—"But oh! shipmates! on the starboard hand of every woe, there is a sure delight; and higher the top of that delight, than the bottom of the woe is deep. Is not the main-truck higher than the kelson is low?[8] Delight is to him—a far, far upward, and inward delight—who against the proud gods and commodores° of this earth, ever stands forth his own inexorable° self. Delight is to him whose strong arms yet support him, when the ship of this base treacherous world has gone down beneath him. Delight is to him, who gives no quarter in the truth, and kills, burns, and destroys all sin though he pluck it out from under the robes of Senators and Judges.[9] Delight,—top-gallant° delight is to him, who acknowledges no law or lord, but the Lord his God, and is only a patriot to heaven. Delight is to him, whom all the waves of the billows of the seas of the boisterous mob can never shake from this sure Keel of the Ages.° And eternal delight and deliciousness will be his, who coming to lay him down, can say with his final breath—O Father!—chiefly known to me by Thy rod—mortal or immortal, here I die. I have striven to be Thine, more than to be this world's, or mine own. Yet this is nothing; I leave eternity to Thee; for what is man[10] that he should live out the lifetime of his God?"

He said no more, but slowly waving a benediction, covered his face with his hands, and so remained kneeling, till all the people had departed, and he was left alone[11] in the place.

---

commodores: high-ranking naval officers, used here metaphorically. **inexorable**: unyielding. **top-gallant**: highest and greatest; the top-gallant mast was then the highest of the three sections of a mast. **Keel of the Ages**: God; the keel is the backbone of a vessel.

CHAPTER 10

A BOSOM FRIEND

RETURNING to the Spouter-Inn from the Chapel, I found Queequeg there quite alone; he having left the Chapel before the benediction some time. He was sitting on a bench before the fire, with his feet on the stove hearth, and in one hand was holding close up to his face that little negro idol of his; peering hard into its face, and with a jack-knife gently whittling away at its nose, meanwhile humming to himself in his heathenish way.

But being now interrupted, he put up the image; and pretty soon, going to the table, took up a large book there, and placing it on his lap began counting the pages with deliberate regularity; at every fiftieth page—as I fancied—stopping a moment, looking vacantly around him, and giving utterance to a long-drawn gurgling whistle of astonishment. He would then begin again at the next fifty; seeming to commence at number one each time, as though he could not count more than fifty, and it was only by such a large number of fifties being found together, that his astonishment at the multitude of pages was excited.

With much interest I sat watching him. Savage though he was, and hideously marred about the face—at least to my taste—his countenance yet had a something in it which was by no means disagreeable. You cannot hide the soul. Through all his unearthly tattooings, I thought I saw the traces of a simple honest heart; and in his large, deep eyes, fiery black and bold, there seemed tokens of a spirit that would dare a thousand devils. And besides all this, there was a certain lofty bearing about the Pagan, which even his uncouthness could not altogether maim. He looked like a man who had never cringed and never had had a creditor. Whether it was, too, that his head being shaved, his forehead was drawn out in freer and brighter relief, and looked more expansive than it otherwise would, this I will not venture to decide; but certain it was his head was phrenologically° an excellent one. It may seem ridiculous,

phrenologically: the pseudo-science of phrenology links personality and mental ability to the shape of the skull.

but it reminded me of General Washington's head, as seen in the popular busts of him. It had the same long regularly graded retreating slope from above the brows, which were likewise very projecting, like two long promontories thickly wooded on top. Queequeg was George Washington cannibalistically developed.

Whilst I was thus closely scanning him, half-pretending meanwhile to be looking out at the storm from the casement, he never heeded my presence, never troubled himself with so much as a single glance; but appeared wholly occupied with counting the pages of the marvellous book. Considering how sociably we had been sleeping together the night previous, and especially considering the affectionate arm I had found thrown over me upon waking in the morning, I thought this indifference of his very strange. But savages are strange beings; at times you do not know exactly how to take them. At first they are overawing; their calm self-collectedness of simplicity seems a Socratic wisdom.° I had noticed also that Queequeg never consorted at all, or but very little, with the other seamen in the inn. He made no advances whatever; appeared to have no desire to enlarge the circle of his acquaintances. All this struck me as mighty singular; yet, upon second thoughts, there was something almost sublime in it. Here was a man some twenty thousand miles from home, by the way of Cape Horn, that is—which was the only way he could get there—thrown among people as strange to him as though he were in the planet Jupiter; and yet he seemed entirely at his ease; preserving the utmost serenity; content with his own companionship; always equal to himself. Surely this was a touch of fine philosophy; though no doubt he had never heard there was such a thing as that. But, perhaps, to be true philosophers, we mortals should not be conscious of so living or so striving. So soon as I hear that such or such a man gives himself out for a philosopher, I conclude that, like the dyspeptic° old woman, he must have "broken his digester."

As I sat there in that now lonely room; the fire burning low, in that mild stage when, after its first intensity has warmed the air, it then only glows to be looked at; the evening shades and phantoms gathering round the casements, and peering in upon us silent, solitary twain; the storm booming without in solemn swells: I began to be sensible of strange feelings. I felt a melting in me. No more my splintered heart and maddened hand were turned against the wolfish world. This soothing savage had redeemed it. There he sat, his very indifference speaking a nature in which there lurked no civilized hypocrisies and bland deceits. Wild he was; a very sight of sights to see; yet I began to feel myself mysteriously drawn towards him. And those same things that would have repelled most others, they were the very magnets that thus drew me. I'll try a pagan friend, thought I, since Christian kindness has proved but hollow courtesy. I drew my bench near him, and made some friendly signs and hints, doing my best to talk with him meanwhile. At first he little noticed these advances; but presently, upon my referring to his last night's hospitalities, he

---

Socratic wisdom: the oracle of Delphi declared Greek philosopher Socrates (470–399 BCE) to be the wisest of men. **dyspeptic**: having indigestion.

made out to ask me whether we were again to be bedfellows. I told him yes; whereat I thought he looked pleased, perhaps a little complimented.

We then turned over the book together, and I endeavored to explain to him the purpose of the printing, and the meaning of the few pictures that were in it. Thus I soon engaged his interest; and from that we went to jabbering the best we could about the various outer sights to be seen in this famous town. Soon I proposed a social smoke; and, producing his pouch and tomahawk, he quietly offered me a puff. And then we sat exchanging puffs from that wild pipe of his, and keeping it regularly passing between us.

If there yet lurked any ice of indifference towards me in the Pagan's breast, this pleasant, genial smoke we had, soon thawed it out, and left us cronies. He seemed to take to me quite as naturally and unbiddenly as I to him; and when our smoke was over, he pressed his forehead against mine, clasped me round the waist, and said that henceforth we were married; meaning, in his country's phrase, that we were bosom friends; he would gladly die for me, if need should be. In a countryman, this sudden flame of friendship would have seemed far too premature, a thing to be much distrusted; but in this simple savage those old rules would not apply.

After supper, and another social chat and smoke, we went to our room together. He made me a present of his embalmed head; took out his enormous tobacco wallet, and groping under the tobacco, drew out some thirty dollars in silver; then spreading them on the table, and mechanically dividing them into two equal portions, pushed one of them towards me, and said it was mine. I was going to remonstrate; but he silenced me by pouring them into my trowsers' pockets. I let them stay. He then went about his evening prayers, took out his idol, and removed the paper fireboard. By certain signs and symptoms, I thought he seemed anxious for me to join him; but well knowing what was to follow, I deliberated a moment whether, in case he invited me, I would comply or otherwise.

I was a good Christian; born and bred in the bosom of the infallible Presbyterian Church.[1] How then could I unite with this wild idolator in worshipping his piece of wood? But what is worship? thought I. **Do you suppose now, Ishmael, that the magnanimous God of heaven and earth—pagans and all included—can possibly be jealous of an insignificant bit of black wood? Impossible!** But what is worship?—to do the will of God—*that* is worship. And what is the will of God?—to do to my fellow man what I would have my fellow man to do to me—*that* is the will of God. Now, Queequeg is my fellow man. And what do I wish that this Queequeg would do to me? Why, unite with me in my particular Presbyterian form of worship. Consequently, I must then unite with him in his; ergo, I must turn idolator. So I kindled the shavings; helped prop up the innocent little idol; offered him burnt biscuit with Queequeg; salamed before him twice or thrice; kissed his nose; and that done, we undressed and went to bed, at peace with our own consciences and all the world. But we did not go to sleep without some little chat.

How it is I know not; but there is no place like a bed for confidential disclosures between friends. Man and wife, they say, there open the very bottom of their souls to each other; and some old couples often lie and chat over old times till nearly morning. Thus, then, **in our hearts' honeymoon**, lay I and Queequeg—a cosy, loving pair.[2]

REVISION NARRATIVE

Ishmael and Queequeg II

Here, a second set of British revisions regarding Ishmael's relation to Queequeg spans two chapters. In closing Ch. 10, Ishmael argues that to be a good Christian, he must turn idolator, but his sentence introducing this argument on p. 63 bothered the censor, who expurgated both the question asking whether God could "possibly be jealous" of a wooden idol and the emphatic answer "Impossible!" Two sexual references were also cut. The first is "in our hearts' honeymoon," which concludes Ch. 10. In the opening to Ch. 11, the editor found Ishmael and Queequeg being too "cosy," and he removed the reference to Queequeg's "affectionately throwing his brown tattooed legs over mine" as well as the less sexually charged line: "so entirely sociable and free and easy were we."

CHAPTER 11

NIGHTGOWN

W E had lain thus in bed, chatting and napping at short intervals, **and Queequeg now and then affectionately throwing his brown tattooed legs over mine, and then drawing them back; so entirely sociable and free and easy were we;** when, at last, by reason of our confabulations, what little nappishness remained in us altogether departed, and we felt like getting up again, though day-break was yet some way down the future.

Yes, we became very wakeful; so much so that our recumbent position began to grow wearisome, and by little and little we found ourselves sitting up; the clothes well tucked around us, leaning against the head-board with our four knees drawn up close together, and our two noses bending over them, as if our knee-pans were warming-pans.° We felt very nice and snug, the more so since it was so chilly out of doors; indeed out of bed-clothes too, seeing that there was no fire in the room. The more so, I say, because truly to enjoy bodily warmth, some small part of you must be cold, for there is no quality in this world that is not what it is merely by contrast. Nothing exists in itself. If you flatter yourself that you are all over comfortable, and have been so a long time, then you cannot be said to be comfortable any more. But if, like Queequeg and me in the bed, the tip of your nose or the crown of your head be slightly chilled, why then, indeed, in the general consciousness you feel most delightfully and unmistakably warm. For this reason a sleeping apartment should never be furnished with a fire, which is one of the luxurious discomforts of the rich. For the height of this sort of deliciousness is to have nothing but the blanket between you and your snugness and the cold of the outer air. Then there you lie like the one warm spark in the heart of an arctic crystal.

We had been sitting in this crouching manner for some time, when all at once I thought I would open my eyes; for when between sheets, whether by day or by night, and whether asleep or awake, I have a way of always keeping my eyes shut, in order the more to concentrate the snugness of being in bed. Because no man can ever feel his own identity aright except his eyes be closed; as if darkness were indeed the proper element of our essences, though light be more congenial to our clayey part.

---

warming-pans: long-handled, covered pans holding hot coals, for warming beds.

Upon opening my eyes then, and coming out of my own pleasant and self-created darkness into the imposed and coarse outer gloom of the unilluminated twelve-o'clock-at-night, I experienced a disagreeable revulsion. Nor did I at all object to the hint from Queequeg that perhaps it were best to strike a light, seeing that we were so wide awake; and besides he felt a strong desire to have a few quiet puffs from his Tomahawk. Be it said, that though I had felt such a strong repugnance to his smoking in the bed the night before, yet see how elastic our stiff prejudices grow when love once comes to bend them. For now I liked nothing better than to have Queequeg smoking by me, even in bed, because he seemed to be full of such serene household joy then. I no more felt unduly concerned for the landlord's policy of insurance. I was only alive to the condensed confidential comfortableness of sharing a pipe and a blanket with a real friend. With our shaggy jackets drawn about our shoulders, we now passed the Tomahawk from one to the other, till slowly there grew over us a blue hanging tester° of smoke, illuminated by the flame of the new-lit lamp.

Whether it was that this undulating tester rolled the savage away to far distant scenes, I know not, but he now spoke of his native island; and, eager to hear his history, I begged him to go on and tell it. He gladly complied. Though at the time I but ill comprehended not a few of his words, yet subsequent disclosures, when I had become more familiar with his broken phraseology, now enable me to present the whole story such as it may prove in the mere skeleton I give.

tester: bed canopy.

CHAPTER 12

BIOGRAPHICAL

QUEEQUEG was a native of Kokovoko,° an island far away to the West and South. It is not down in any map; true places never are.

When a new-hatched savage running wild about his native woodlands in a grass clout,° followed by the nibbling goats, as if he were a green sapling; even then, in Queequeg's ambitious soul, lurked a strong desire to see something more of Christendom than a specimen whaler or two. His father was a High Chief, a King; his uncle a High Priest; and on the maternal side he boasted aunts who were the wives of unconquerable warriors. There was excellent blood in his veins—royal stuff; though sadly vitiated,° I fear, by the cannibal propensity he nourished in his untutored youth.

A Sag Harbor° ship visited his father's bay, and Queequeg sought a passage to Christian lands. But the ship, having her full complement of seamen, spurned his suit; and not all the King his father's influence could prevail. But Queequeg vowed a vow. Alone in his canoe, he paddled off to a distant strait, which he knew the ship must pass through when she quitted the island. On one side was a coral reef; on the other a low tongue of land, covered with mangrove thickets that grew out into the water. Hiding his canoe, still afloat, among these thickets, with its prow seaward, he sat down in the stern, paddle low in hand; and when the ship was gliding by, like a flash he darted out; gained her side; with one backward dash of his foot capsized and sank his canoe; climbed up the chains;° and throwing himself at full length upon the deck, grappled a ring-bolt there, and swore not to let it go, though hacked in pieces.

In vain the captain threatened to throw him overboard; suspended a cutlass over his naked wrists; Queequeg was the son of a King, and Queequeg budged not. Struck by his desperate dauntlessness, and his wild desire to visit Christendom, the captain at last relented, and told him he might make himself at home. But this fine young savage—this sea Prince of Wales,[1] never saw the captain's cabin. They put him

---

Kokovoko: Queequeg's Pacific Island home is Melville's invention. ***clout***: loincloth. ***vitiated***: debased. ***Sag Harbor***: major whaling port on southeastern Long Island, NY. ***chains***: combination of rigid chains and narrow wood platforms, fastened to the sides of a ship to strengthen the rigging supporting the masts.

down among the sailors, and made a whaleman of him. But like Czar Peter[2] content to toil in the shipyards of foreign cities, Queequeg disdained no seeming ignominy, if thereby he might **happily** gain the power of enlightening his untutored country-men. For at bottom—so he told me—he was actuated by a profound desire to learn among the Christians, the arts whereby to make his people still happier than they were; and more than that, still better than they were. But, alas! the practices of whalemen soon convinced him that even Christians could be both miserable and wicked; infinitely more so, than all his father's heathens. Arrived at last in old Sag Harbor; and seeing what the sailors did there; and then going on to Nantucket, and seeing how they spent their wages in *that* place also, poor Queequeg gave it up for lost. Thought he, it's a wicked world in all meridians;° I'll die a pagan.

And thus an old idolator at heart, he yet lived among these Christians, wore their clothes, and tried to talk their gibberish. Hence the queer ways about him, though now some time from home.

By hints, I asked him whether he did not propose going back, and having a coronation; since he might now consider his father dead and gone, he being very old and feeble at the last accounts. He answered no, not yet; and added that he was fear-ful Christianity, or rather Christians, had unfitted him for ascending the pure and undefiled throne of thirty pagan Kings before him. But by and by, he said, he would return,—as soon as he felt himself baptized again. For the nonce,° however, he pro-posed to sail about, and sow his wild oats in all four oceans. They had made a har-pooneer of him, and that barbed iron was in lieu of a sceptre now.

I asked him what might be his immediate purpose, touching his future move-ments. He answered, to go to sea again, in his old vocation. Upon this, I told him that whaling was my own design,° and informed him of my intention to sail out of Nantucket, as being the most promising port for an adventurous whaleman to embark from. He at once resolved to accompany me to that island, ship aboard the same vessel, get into the same watch, the same boat, the same mess° with me, in short to share my every hap;° with both my hands in his, boldly dip into the Potluck° of both worlds. To all this I joyously assented; for besides the affection I now felt for Queequeg, he was an experienced harpooneer, and as such, could not fail to be of great usefulness to one, who, like me, was wholly ignorant of the mysteries of whal-ing, though well acquainted with the sea, as known to merchant seamen.

His story being ended with his pipe's last dying puff, Queequeg embraced me, pressed his forehead against mine, and blowing out the light, we rolled over from each other, this way and that, and very soon were sleeping.

---

meridians: longitudes. **For the nonce**: For now. **design**: objective. **mess**: group of ship-mates who eat their meals together. **hap**: chance happening. **Potluck**: whatever turns up.

CHAPTER 13

WHEELBARROW

NEXT morning, Monday, after disposing of the embalmed head to a barber, for a block,° I settled my own and comrade's bill; using, however, my comrade's money. The grinning landlord, as well as the boarders, seemed amazingly tickled at the sudden friendship which had sprung up between me and Queequeg—especially as Peter Coffin's cock and bull stories **about him had previously so much alarmed me concerning the very person whom I now companied with.**

We borrowed a wheelbarrow, and embarking our things, including my own poor carpet-bag, and Queequeg's canvas sack and hammock, away we went down to "the Moss," the little Nantucket packet schooner° moored at the wharf. As we were going along the people stared; not at Queequeg so much—for they were used to seeing cannibals like him in their streets,—but at seeing him and me upon such confidential terms. But we heeded them not, going along wheeling the barrow by turns, and Queequeg now and then stopping to adjust the sheath on his harpoon barbs. I

block: a stand for displaying a wig. *schooner*: two-masted, fore-and-aft rigged vessel.

REVISION NARRATIVE

Correcting Melville's Line

Because Melville inscribed additions and corrections on the proof sheets he sent to England, some of the British revisions are likely to have been made at his request. Equally possible is that an editor made changes that Melville would have made himself or approved. One case in point is the rambling clause at the end of the first paragraph of Ch. 13, which seems to circle back on itself. Referring to Queequeg, the phrasing states that Peter Coffin's cock and bull "stories about him had previously so much alarmed me concerning the very person whom I now companied with." Someone—either Melville or an editor—revised this to the equally clumsy "stories had previously alarmed me about him."

asked him why he carried such a troublesome thing with him ashore, and whether all whaling ships did not find° their own harpoons. To this, in substance, he replied, that though what I hinted was true enough, yet he had a particular affection for his own harpoon, because it was of assured stuff, well tried in many a mortal combat, and deeply intimate with the hearts of whales. In short, like many inland reapers and mowers, who go into the farmers' meadows armed with their own scythes—though in no wise obliged to furnish them—even so, Queequeg, for his own private reasons, preferred his own harpoon.

Shifting the barrow from my hand to his, he told me a funny story about the first wheelbarrow he had ever seen. It was in Sag Harbor. The owners of his ship, it seems, had lent him one, in which to carry his heavy chest to his boarding house. Not to seem ignorant about the thing—though in truth he was entirely so, concerning the precise way in which to manage the barrow—Queequeg puts his chest upon it; lashes it fast; and then shoulders the barrow and marches up the wharf. "Why," said I, "Queequeg, you might have known better than that, one would think. Didn't the people laugh?"

Upon this, he told me another story. The people of his island of Kokovoko, it seems, at their wedding feasts express the fragrant water of young cocoanuts into a large stained calabash° like a punchbowl; and this punchbowl always forms the great central ornament on the braided mat where the feast is held. Now a certain grand merchant ship once touched at Kokovoko, and its commander—from all accounts, a very stately punctilious° gentleman, at least for a sea captain—this commander was invited to the wedding feast of Queequeg's sister, a pretty young princess just turned of ten. Well; when all the wedding guests were assembled at the bride's bamboo cottage, this Captain marches in, and being assigned the post of honor, placed himself over against the punchbowl, and between the High Priest and his majesty the King, Queequeg's father. Grace being said,—for those people have their grace as well as we—though Queequeg told me that unlike us, who at such times look downwards to our platters, they, on the contrary, copying the ducks, glance upwards to the great Giver of all feasts—Grace, I say, being said, the High Priest opens the banquet by the immemorial ceremony of the island; that is, dipping his consecrated and consecrating fingers into the bowl before the blessed beverage circulates. Seeing himself placed next the Priest, and noting the ceremony, and thinking himself—being Captain of a ship—as having plain precedence over a mere island King, especially in the King's own house—the Captain coolly proceeds to wash his hands in the punch bowl;—taking it I suppose for a huge finger-glass.° "Now," said Queequeg, "what you tink now?—Didn't our people laugh?"

At last, passage paid, and luggage safe, we stood on board the schooner. Hoisting sail, it glided down the Acushnet river.[1] On one side, New Bedford rose in terraces of streets, their ice-covered trees all glittering in the clear, cold air. Huge hills and mountains of casks on casks were piled upon her wharves, and side by side the world-wandering whale ships lay silent and safely moored at last; while from others came a sound of carpenters and coopers, with blended noises of fires and forges

---

find: supply free of cost. **calabash**: bowl made from a gourd. **punctilious**: strictly adhering to etiquette. **finger-glass**: small bowl for washing soiled fingers at a formal dinner.

to melt the pitch, all betokening that new cruises were on the start; that one most perilous and long voyage ended, only begins a second; and a second ended, only begins a third, and so on, for ever and for aye. Such is the endlessness, yea, the intolerableness of all earthly effort.

Gaining the more open water, the bracing breeze waxed fresh; the little Moss tossed the quick foam from her bows, as a young colt his snortings. How I snuffed that Tartar° air!—how I spurned that turnpike earth!—that common highway all over dented with the marks of slavish heels and hoofs; and turned me to admire the magnanimity of the sea which will permit no records.

At the same foam-fountain, Queequeg seemed to drink and reel with me. His dusky nostrils swelled apart; he showed his filed and pointed teeth. On, on we flew; and our offing gained, the Moss did homage to the blast; ducked and dived her bows as a slave before the Sultan. Sideways leaning, we sideways darted; every rope-yarn tingling like a wire; the two tall masts buckling like Indian canes° in land tornadoes. So full of this reeling scene were we, as we stood by the plunging bowsprit, that for some time we did not notice the jeering glances of the passengers, a lubber-like° assembly, who marvelled that two fellow beings should be so companionable; as though a white man were anything more dignified than a whitewashed negro. But there were some boobies and bumpkins there, who, by their intense greenness, must have come from the heart and centre of all verdure. Queequeg caught one of these young saplings mimicking him behind his back. I thought the bumpkin's hour of doom was come. Dropping his harpoon, the brawny savage caught him in his arms, and by an almost miraculous dexterity and strength, sent him high up bodily into the air; then slightly tapping his stern in mid-somerset, the fellow landed with bursting lungs upon his feet, while Queequeg, turning his back upon him, lighted his tomahawk pipe and passed it to me for a puff.

"Capting! Capting!" yelled the bumpkin, running towards that officer; "Capting, Capting, here's the devil."

"Hallo, *you* sir," cried the Captain, a gaunt rib of the sea, stalking up to Queequeg, "what in thunder do you mean by that? Don't you know you might have killed that chap?"

"What him say?" said Queequeg, as he mildly turned to me.

"He say," said I, "that you came near kill-e that man there," pointing to the still shivering greenhorn.

"Kill-e," cried Queequeg, twisting his tattooed face into an unearthly expression of disdain, "ah! him **bevy** small-e fish-e; Queequeg no kill-e so small-e fish-e; Queequeg kill-e big whale!"

"Look you," roared the Captain, "I'll kill-e *you*, you cannibal, if you try any more of your tricks aboard here; so mind your eye."

But it so happened just then, that it was high time for the Captain to mind his own eye. The prodigious strain upon the main-sail had parted the weather-sheet,°

Tartar: wild (from the nomadic Tartars, or Tartary, a region in Siberia). ***canes***: bamboo-like grasses of India. ***lubber-like***: nautically ignorant (from land-lover). ***weather-sheet***: rope controlling the boom on the side from which the wind is blowing.

and the tremendous boom° was now flying from side to side, completely sweeping the entire after part of the deck. The poor fellow whom Queequeg had handled so roughly, was swept overboard; all hands were in a panic; and to attempt snatching at the boom to stay it, seemed madness. It flew from right to left, and back again, almost in one ticking of a watch, and every instant seemed on the point of snapping into splinters. Nothing was done, and nothing seemed capable of being done; those on deck rushed towards the bows, and stood eyeing the boom as if it were the lower jaw of an exasperated whale. In the midst of this consternation, Queequeg dropped deftly to his knees, and crawling under the path of the boom, whipped hold of a rope, secured one end to the bulwarks, and then flinging the other like a lasso, caught it round the boom as it swept over his head, and at the next jerk, the spar was that way trapped, and all was safe. The schooner was run into the wind, and while the hands were clearing away the stern boat, Queequeg, stripped to the waist, darted from the side with a long living arc of a leap. For three minutes or more he was seen swimming like a dog, throwing his long arms straight out before him, and by turns revealing his brawny shoulders through the freezing foam. I looked at the grand and glorious fellow, but saw no one to be saved. The greenhorn had gone down. Shooting himself perpendicularly from the water, Queequeg now took an instant's glance around him, and seeming to see just how matters were, dived down and disappeared. A few minutes more, and he rose again, one arm still striking out, and with the other dragging a lifeless form. The boat soon picked them up. The poor bumpkin was restored. All hands voted Queequeg a noble trump; the captain begged his pardon. From that hour I clove to Queequeg like a barnacle; yea, till poor Queequeg took his last long dive.

Was there ever such unconsciousness?° He did not seem to think that he at all deserved a medal from the Humane and Magnanimous Societies. He only asked for water—fresh water—something to wipe the brine off; that done, he put on dry clothes, lighted his pipe, and leaning against the bulwarks, and mildly eyeing those around him, seemed to be saying to himself—"It's a mutual, joint-stock° world, in all meridians. We cannibals must help these Christians."

---

boom: heavy pole extending horizontally from the mast along the foot of the mainsail. ***unconsciousness***: unself-consciousness. ***joint-stock***: owned by stockholders.

CHAPTER 14

NANTUCKET

Nothing more happened on the passage worthy the mentioning; so, after a fine run, we safely arrived in Nantucket.[1]

Nantucket! Take out your map and look at it. See what a real corner of the world it occupies; how it stands there, away off shore, more lonely than the Eddystone lighthouse.° Look at it—a mere hillock, and elbow of sand; all beach, without a background. There is more sand there than you would use in twenty years as a substitute for blotting paper. Some gamesome wights° will tell you that they have to plant weeds there, they don't grow naturally; that they import Canada this-tles; that they have to send beyond seas for a spile° to stop a leak in an oil cask; that pieces of wood in Nantucket are carried about like bits of the true cross in Rome; that people there plant toadstools before their houses, to get under the shade in summer time; that one blade of grass makes an oasis, three blades in a day's walk a prairie; that they wear quicksand shoes, something like Laplander snow-shoes; that they are so shut up, belted about, every way inclosed, surrounded, and made an utter island of by the ocean, that to their very chairs and tables small clams will sometimes be found adhering, as to the backs of sea turtles. But these extravaganzas° only show that Nantucket is no Illinois.

Look now at the wondrous traditional story of how this island was settled by the red-men. Thus goes the legend. In olden times an eagle swooped down upon the New England coast, and carried off an infant Indian in his talons. With loud lament the parents saw their child borne out of sight over the wide waters. They resolved to follow in the same direction. Setting out in their canoes, after a perilous passage they discovered the island, and there they found an empty ivory casket,—the poor little Indian's skeleton.

What wonder, then, that these Nantucketers, born on a beach, should take to the sea for a livelihood! They first caught crabs and quohogs° in the sand; grown bolder, they waded out with nets for mackerel; more experienced, they pushed off in

---

Eddystone lighthouse: on a reef fourteen miles off England's Channel Coast. **gamesome wights**: humorous people. **spile**: wooden plug. **extravanganzas**: tall tales. **quohogs**: quahog, a thick-shelled American clam.

boats and captured cod; and at last, launching a navy of great ships on the sea, explored this watery world; put an incessant belt of circumnavigations round it; peeped in at Bhering's Straits;° and in all seasons and all oceans declared everlasting war with the mightiest animated mass that has survived the flood; most monstrous and most mountainous! That Himmalehan,° salt-sea Mastodon,[2] clothed with such portentousness of unconscious power, that his very panics are more to be dreaded than his most fearless and malicious assaults!

And thus have these naked Nantucketers, these sea hermits, issuing from their ant-hill in the sea, overrun and conquered the watery world like so many Alexanders; parcelling out among them the Atlantic, Pacific, and Indian oceans, as the three pirate powers did Poland. Let America add Mexico to Texas, and pile Cuba upon Canada; let the English overswarm all India,[3] and hang out their blazing banner from the sun; two thirds of this terraqueous globe[4] are the Nantucketer's. For the sea is his; he owns it, as Emperors own empires; other seamen having but a right of way through it. Merchant ships are but extension bridges; armed ones but floating forts; even pirates and privateers, though following the sea as highwaymen the road, they but plunder other ships, other fragments of the land like themselves, without seeking to draw their living from the bottomless deep itself. The Nantucketer, he alone resides and **riots** on the sea; he alone, in Bible language, goes down to it in ships;[5] to and fro ploughing it as his own special plantation. *There* is his home; *there* lies his business, which a Noah's flood would not interrupt, though it overwhelmed all the millions in China. He lives on the sea, as prairie cocks in the prairie; he hides among the waves, he climbs them as chamois° hunters climb the Alps. For years he knows not the land; so that when he comes to it at last, it smells like another world, more strangely than the moon would to an Earthsman. With the landless gull, that at sunset folds her wings and is rocked to sleep between billows; so at nightfall, the Nantucketer, out of sight of land, furls his sails, and lays him to his rest, while under his very pillow rush herds of walruses and whales.

Bhering's Straits: Bering Strait, between Alaska and Asia. ***Himmalehan***: as huge as the Himalayas. ***chamois***: European goat-like antelope.

CHAPTER 15

CHOWDER

I T was quite late in the evening when the little Moss came snugly to anchor, and Queequeg and I went ashore; so we could attend to no business that day, at least none but a supper and a bed. The landlord of the Spouter-Inn had recommended us to his cousin Hosea Hussey of the Try Pots,° whom he asserted to be the proprietor of one of the best kept hotels in all Nantucket, and moreover he had assured us that cousin Hosea, as he called him, was famous for his chowders. In short, he plainly hinted that we could not possibly do better than try pot-luck at the Try Pots. But the directions he had given us about keeping a yellow warehouse on our starboard hand till we opened° a white church to the larboard, and then keeping that on the larboard hand till we made° a corner three points° to the starboard, and that done, then ask the first man we met where the place was: these crooked directions of his very much puzzled us at first, especially as, at the outset, Queequeg insisted that the yellow warehouse—our first point of departure—must be left on the larboard hand, whereas I had understood Peter Coffin to say it was on the starboard. However, by dint of beating about a little in the dark, and now and then knocking up° a peaceable inhabitant to inquire the way, we at last came to something which there was no mistaking.

Two enormous wooden pots painted black, and suspended by asses' ears,° swung from the cross-trees of an old top-mast, planted in front of an old doorway. The horns of the cross-trees° were sawed off on the other side, so that this old top-mast looked not a little like a gallows. Perhaps I was over sensitive to such impressions at the time, but I could not help staring at this gallows with a vague misgiving. A sort of crick was in my neck as I gazed up to the two remaining horns; yes, *two* of them, one for Queequeg, and one for me. It's ominous, thinks I. A Coffin my Innkeeper upon landing in my first whaling port; tombstones staring at me in the whalemen's chapel; and here a gallows! and a pair of prodigious black pots too! Are these last throwing out oblique hints touching Tophet?

Try Pots: the name refers to the iron vats on a whaleship's deck in which blubber was boiled to extract the oil; see Ch. 96, "The Try-Works." ***opened***: could see. ***made***: arrived at. ***three points***: a point is 1/32 of a compass circle; three points equal 33.75°. ***knocking up***: calling upon. ***asses' ears***: handles shaped like donkeys' ears. ***horns of the cross-trees***: ends of the horizontal timbers attached high up on a mast.

I was called from these reflections by the sight of a freckled woman with yellow hair and a yellow gown, standing in the porch of the inn, under a dull red lamp swinging there, that looked much like an injured eye, and carrying on a brisk scolding with a man in a purple woollen shirt.

"Get along with ye," said she to the man, "or I'll be combing° ye!"

"Come on, Queequeg," said I, "all right. There's Mrs. Hussey."

And so it turned out; Mr. Hosea Hussey being from home, but leaving Mrs. Hussey entirely competent to attend to all his affairs. Upon making known our desires for a supper and a bed, Mrs. Hussey, postponing further scolding for the present, ushered us into a little room, and seating us at a table spread with the relics of a recently concluded repast, turned round to us and said—"Clam or Cod?"

"What's that about Cods, ma'am?" said I, with much politeness.

"Clam or Cod?" she repeated.

"A clam for supper? a cold clam; is *that* what you mean, Mrs. Hussey?" says I; "but that's a rather cold and clammy reception in the winter time, ain't it, Mrs. Hussey?"

But being in a great hurry to resume scolding the man in the purple shirt, who was waiting for it in the entry, and seeming to hear nothing but the word "clam," Mrs. Hussey hurried towards an open door leading to the kitchen, and bawling out "clam for two," disappeared.

"Queequeg," said I, "do you think that we can make out a supper for us both on one clam?"

However, a warm savory steam from the kitchen served to belie the apparently cheerless prospect before us. But when that smoking chowder came in, the mystery was delightfully explained. Oh, sweet friends! hearken to me. It was made of small juicy clams, scarcely bigger than hazel nuts, mixed with pounded ship biscuit,° and salted pork cut up into little flakes; the whole enriched with butter, and plentifully seasoned with pepper and salt. Our appetites being sharpened by the frosty voyage, and in particular, Queequeg seeing his favorite fishy food before him, and the chowder being surpassingly excellent, we despatched it with great expedition: when leaning back a moment and bethinking me of Mrs. Hussey's clam and cod announcement, I thought I would try a little experiment. Stepping to the kitchen door, I uttered the word "cod" with great emphasis, and resumed my seat. In a few moments the savory steam came forth again, but with a different flavor, and in good time a fine cod-chowder was placed before us.

We resumed business; and while plying our spoons in the bowl, thinks I to myself, I wonder now if this here has any effect on the head? What's that stultifying saying about chowder-headed° people? "But look, Queequeg, ain't that a live eel in your bowl? Where's your harpoon?"

Fishiest of all fishy places was the Try Pots, which well deserved its name; for the pots there were always boiling chowders. Chowder for breakfast, and chowder for dinner, and chowder for supper, till you began to look for fish-bones coming

---

combing: giving a beating to. **ship biscuit**: hardtack; unsalted flour-and-water biscuit baked hard for preservation. **chowder-headed**: confused or stupid.

through your clothes. The area before the house was paved with clam-shells. Mrs. Hussey wore a polished necklace of codfish vertebra; and Hosea Hussey had his account books bound in superior old shark-skin. There was a fishy flavor to the milk, too, which I could not at all account for, till one morning happening to take a stroll along the beach among some fishermen's boats, I saw Hosea's brindled° cow feeding on fish remnants, and marching along the sand with each foot in a cod's decapitated head, looking very slip-shod,° I assure ye.

Supper concluded, we received a lamp, and directions from Mrs. Hussey concerning the nearest way to bed; but, as Queequeg was about to precede me up the stairs, the lady reached forth her arm, and demanded his harpoon; she allowed no harpoon in her chambers. "Why not?" said I; "every true whaleman sleeps with his harpoon—but why not?" "Because it's dangerous," says she. "Ever since young Stiggs coming from that unfort'nt v'y'ge of his, when he was gone four years and a half, with **only** three barrels of *ile,* was found dead in my first floor back, with his harpoon in his side; ever since then I allow no boarders to take sich dangerous weepons in their rooms **at night**. So, Mr. Queequeg" (for she had learned his name), "I will just take this here iron, and keep it for you till morning. But the chowder; clam or cod to-morrow for breakfast, men?"

"Both," says I; "and let's have a couple of smoked herring by way of variety."

---

brindled: light-colored with dark streaks or spots. **slip-shod**: looking sloppy (literally, wearing loose slippers).

CHAPTER 16

THE SHIP

I<small>N</small> bed we concocted our plans for the morrow. But to my surprise and no small concern, Queequeg now gave me to understand, that he had been diligently consulting Yojo—the name of his black little god—and Yojo had told him two or three times over, and strongly insisted upon it everyway, that instead of our going together among the whaling-fleet in harbor, and in concert selecting our craft; instead of this, I say, Yojo earnestly enjoined that the selection of the ship should rest wholly with me, inasmuch as Yojo purposed befriending us; and, in order to do so, had already pitched upon a vessel, which, if left to myself, I, Ishmael, should infallibly light upon, for all the world as though it had turned out by chance; and in that vessel I must immediately ship myself, for the present irrespective of Queequeg.

I have forgotten to mention that, in many things, Queequeg placed great confidence in the excellence of Yojo's judgment and surprising forecast of things; and cherished Yojo with considerable esteem, as a rather good sort of god, who perhaps meant well enough upon the whole, but in all cases did not succeed in his benevolent designs.

Now, this plan of Queequeg's, or rather Yojo's, touching the selection of our craft; I did not like that plan at all. I had not a little relied upon Queequeg's sagacity to point out the whaler best fitted to carry us and our fortunes securely. But as all my remonstrances produced no effect upon Queequeg, I was obliged to acquiesce; and accordingly prepared to set about this business with a determined rushing sort of energy and vigor, that should quickly settle that trifling little affair. Next morning early, leaving Queequeg shut up with Yojo in our little bedroom—for it seemed that it was some sort of Lent or Ramadan,[1] or day of fasting, humiliation, and prayer with Queequeg and Yojo that day; *how* it was I never could find out, for, though I applied myself to it several times, I never could master his **liturgies and XXXIX Articles°**—leaving Queequeg, then, fasting on his tomahawk pipe, and Yojo warming himself at his sacrificial fire of shavings, I sallied out among the shipping.[2] After much prolonged sauntering and many random inquiries, I learnt that there were

liturgies and XXXIX Articles: rites and the creed of the Anglican Church.

three ships up for three-years' voyages—The Devil-dam, the Tit-bit, and the Pequod. *Devil-Dam,* I do not know the origin of; *Tit-bit* is obvious; *Pequod,* you will no doubt remember, was the name of a celebrated tribe of Massachusetts Indians, now extinct as the ancient Medes.[3] I peered and pryed about the Devil-Dam; from her, hopped over to the Tit-bit; and, finally, going on board the Pequod, looked around her for a moment, and then decided that this was the very ship for us.

You may have seen many a quaint craft in your day, for aught I know;—square-toed luggers; mountainous Japanese junks; butter-box galliots,° and what not; but take my word for it, you never saw such a rare old craft as this same rare old Pequod. She was a ship of the old school, rather small if anything; with an old fashioned claw-footed look about her. Long seasoned and weather-stained in the typhoons and calms of all four oceans, her old hull's complexion was darkened like a French grenadier's, who has alike fought in Egypt and Siberia.[4] Her venerable bows looked bearded. Her masts—cut somewhere on the coast of Japan, where her original ones were lost overboard in a gale—her masts stood stiffly up like the spines of the three old kings of Cologne.[5] Her ancient decks were worn and wrinkled, like the pilgrim-worshipped flag-stone in Canterbury Cathedral where Becket bled.[6] But to all these her old antiquities, were added new and marvellous features, pertaining to the wild business that for more than half a century she had followed. Old Captain Peleg,[7] many years her chief-mate, before he commanded another vessel of his own, and now a retired seaman, and one of the principal owners of the Pequod,—this old Peleg, during the term of his chief-mateship, had built upon her original grotesqueness, and inlaid it, all over, with a quaintness both of material and device, unmatched by anything except it be Thorkill-Hake's carved buckler or bedstead.[8] She was apparelled like any barbaric Ethiopian emperor, his neck heavy with pendants of polished ivory. She was a thing of trophies. A cannibal of a craft, tricking° herself forth in the chased° bones of her enemies. All round, her unpanelled, open bulwarks° were garnished like one continuous jaw, with the long sharp teeth of the sperm whale, inserted there for pins,° to fasten her old hempen thews and tendons to. Those thews ran not through base blocks of land wood, but deftly travelled over sheaves° of sea-ivory. Scorning a turnstile wheel at her reverend helm,° she sported there a tiller;° and that tiller was in one mass, curiously carved from the long narrow lower jaw of her hereditary foe. The helmsman who steered by that tiller in a tempest, felt like the Tartar, when he holds back his fiery steed by clutching its jaw. A noble craft, but somehow a most melancholy! All noble things are touched with that.

Now when I looked about the quarter-deck, for some one having authority, in order to propose myself as a candidate for the voyage, at first I saw nobody; but I could not well overlook a strange sort of tent, or rather wigwam, pitched a little

---

square-toed luggers . . . galliots: types of old-fashioned sailing vessels. **tricking**: ornamenting. **chased**: grooved, engraved. **open bulwarks**: railings around the ship above the deck, although in Ch. 51 the bulwarks are solid walls as on most whaling vessels. **pins**: belaying pins, to which ropes are temporarily secured. **sheaves**: wheels or rollers within blocks; the combination is a pulley. **helm**: steering position. **tiller**: steering lever attached to the rudder.

behind the main-mast. It seemed only a temporary erection used in port. It was of a conical shape, some ten feet high; consisting of the long, huge slabs of limber black bone taken from the middle and highest part of the jaws of the right-whale.[9] Planted with their broad ends on the deck, a circle of these slabs laced together, mutually sloped towards each other, and at the apex united in a tufted point, where the loose hairy fibres waved to and fro like the top-knot on some old Pottowottamie Sachem's head.[10] A triangular opening faced towards the bows of the ship, so that the insider commanded a complete view forward.

And half concealed in this queer tenement, I at length found one who by his aspect seemed to have authority; and who, it being noon, and the ship's work suspended, was now enjoying respite from the burden of command. He was seated on an old-fashioned oaken chair, wriggling all over with curious carving; and the bottom of which was formed of a stout interlacing of the same elastic stuff of which the wigwam was constructed.

There was nothing so very particular, perhaps, about the appearance of the elderly man I saw; he was brown and brawny, like most old seamen, and heavily rolled up in blue pilot-cloth, cut in the Quaker style;[11] only there was a fine and almost microscopic net-work of the minutest wrinkles interlacing round his eyes, which must have arisen from his continual sailings in many hard gales, and always looking to windward;—for this causes the muscles about the eyes to become pursed together. Such eye-wrinkles are very effectual in a scowl.

"Is this the Captain of the Pequod?" said I, advancing to the door of the tent.

"Supposing it be the Captain of the Pequod, what dost thou want of him?" he demanded.

"I was thinking of shipping."

"Thou wast, wast thou? I see thou art no Nantucketer—ever been in a stove boat?"

"No, Sir, I never have"

"Dost know nothing at all about whaling, I dare say—eh?"

"Nothing, Sir; but I have no doubt I shall soon learn. I've been several voyages in the merchant service, and I think that—"

"Merchant service be damned. Talk not that lingo to me. Dost see that leg?—I'll take that leg away from thy stern, if ever thou talkest of the marchant service to me again. Marchant service indeed! I suppose now ye feel considerable proud of having served in those marchant ships. But flukes! man, what makes thee want to go a whaling, eh?—it looks a little suspicious, don't it, eh?—Hast not been a pirate, hast thou?—Didst not rob thy last Captain, didst thou?—Dost not think of murdering the officers when thou gettest to sea?"

I protested my innocence of these things. I saw that under the mask of these half humorous inuendoes, this old seaman, as an insulated Quakerish Nantucketer, was full of his insular prejudices, and rather distrustful of all aliens, unless they hailed from Cape Cod or the Vineyard.[12]

"But what takes thee a-whaling? I want to know that before I think of shipping ye."

"Well, sir, I want to see what whaling is. I want to see the world."

"Want to see what whaling is, eh? Have ye clapped eye on Captain Ahab?"

"Who is Captain Ahab, sir?"

"Aye, aye, I thought so. Captain Ahab is the Captain of this ship."

"I am mistaken then. I thought I was speaking to the Captain himself."

"Thou art speaking to Captain Peleg—that's who ye are speaking to, young man. It belongs to me and Captain Bildad[13] to see the Pequod fitted out for the voyage, and supplied with all her needs, including crew. We are part owners and agents. But as I was going to say, if thou wantest to know what whaling is, as thou tellest ye do, I can put ye in a way of finding it out before ye bind yourself to it, past backing out. Clap eye on Captain Ahab, young man, and thou wilt find that he has only one leg."

"What do you mean, sir? Was the other one lost by a whale?"

"Lost by a whale! Young man, come nearer to me: it was devoured, chewed up, crunched by the monstrousest parmacetty° that ever chipped a boat!—ah, ah!"

I was a little alarmed by his energy, perhaps also a little touched at the hearty grief in his concluding exclamation, but said as calmly as I could, "What you say is no doubt true enough, sir; but how could I know there was any peculiar ferocity in that particular whale, though indeed I might have inferred as much from the simple fact of the accident."

"Look ye now, young man, thy lungs are a sort of soft, d'ye see; thou dost not talk shark a bit.° *Sure*, ye've been to sea before now; sure of that?"

"Sir," said I, "I thought I told you that I had been four voyages in the merchant—"

"Hard down out of that!° Mind what I said about the marchant service—don't aggravate me—I won't have it. But let us understand each other. I have given thee a hint about what whaling is; do ye yet feel inclined for it?"

"I do, sir."

"Very good. Now, art thou the man to pitch a harpoon down a live whale's throat, and then jump after it? Answer, quick!"

"I am, sir, if it should be positively indispensable to do so; not to be got rid of, that is; which I don't take to be the fact."

"Good again. Now then, thou not only wantest to go a-whaling, to find out by experience what whaling is, but ye also want to go in order to see the world? Was not that what ye said? I thought so. Well then, just step forward there, and take a peep over the weather-bow,° and then back to me and tell me what ye see there."

For a moment I stood a little puzzled by this curious request, not knowing exactly how to take it, whether humorously or in earnest. But concentrating all his crow's feet into one scowl, Captain Peleg started me on the errand.

Going forward and glancing over the weather bow, I perceived that the ship swinging to her anchor with the flood-tide, was now obliquely pointing towards the open ocean. The prospect was unlimited, but exceedingly monotonous and forbidding; not the slightest variety that I could see.

---

parmacetty: sperm whale, from spermaceti. **lungs . . . talk shark a bit**: meek voice or way of speaking; not straightforward (as a shark would be). **Hard down out of that!**: "Stay away from that subject!" **weather-bow**: side of the bow on which the wind is blowing.

"Well, what's the report?" said Peleg when I came back; "what did ye see?"

"Not much," I replied—"nothing but water; considerable horizon though, and there's a squall° coming up, I think."

"Well, what dost thou think then of seeing the world? Do ye wish to go round Cape Horn to see any more of it, eh? Can't ye see the world where you stand?"

I was a little staggered, but go a-whaling I must, and I would; and the Pequod was as good a ship as any—I thought the best—and all this I now repeated to Peleg. Seeing me so determined, he expressed his willingness to ship me.

"And thou mayest as well sign the papers right off," he added—"come along with ye." And so saying, he led the way below deck into the cabin.

Seated on the transom° was what seemed to me a most uncommon and surprising figure. It turned out to be Captain Bildad, who along with Captain Peleg was one of the largest owners of the vessel; the other shares, as is sometimes the case in these ports, being held by a crowd of old annuitants; widows, fatherless children, and chancery wards;° each owning about the value of a timber head, or a foot of plank, or a nail or two in the ship. People in Nantucket invest their money in whaling vessels, the same way that you do yours in approved state stocks bringing in good interest.

Now, Bildad, like Peleg, and indeed many other Nantucketers, was a Quaker, the island having been originally settled by that sect; and to this day its inhabitants in general retain in an uncommon measure the peculiarities of the Quaker, only variously and anomalously modified by things altogether alien and heterogeneous. For some of these same Quakers are the most sanguinary° of all sailors and whale-hunters. They are fighting Quakers; they are Quakers with a vengeance.[14]

So that there are instances among them of men, who, named with Scripture names—a singularly common fashion on the island—and in childhood naturally imbibing the stately dramatic thee and thou of the Quaker idiom; still, from the audacious, daring, and boundless adventure of their subsequent lives, strangely blend with these unoutgrown peculiarities, a thousand bold dashes of character, not unworthy a Scandinavian sea-king, or a poetical Pagan Roman. And when these things unite in a man of greatly superior natural force, with a globular brain and a ponderous heart; who has also by the stillness and seclusion of many long night-watches in the remotest waters, and beneath constellations never seen here at the north, been led to think untraditionally and independently; receiving all nature's sweet or savage impressions fresh from her own virgin, voluntary, and confiding breast, and thereby chiefly, but with some help from accidental advantages, to learn a bold and nervous lofty language—that man makes one in a whole nation's census—a mighty pageant creature, formed for noble tragedies. Nor will it at all detract from him, dramatically regarded, if either by birth or other circumstances, he **have** what seems a half wilful over-ruling morbidness° at the bottom of his nature. For all men tragically great are made so through a certain morbidness. Be

---

squall: sudden storm. **transom**: crossbeam in the stern, used as a seat. **annuitants . . . chancery wards**: people living on fixed annual income; *chancery wards* are under court guardianship. **sanguinary**: bloodthirsty. **morbidness**: unhealthy preoccupation with unwholesome matters.

sure of this, O young ambition, all mortal greatness is but disease. But, as yet we have not to do with such an one, but with quite another; and still a man, who, if indeed peculiar, it only results again from another phase of the Quaker, modified by individual circumstances.

Like Captain Peleg, Captain Bildad was a well-to-do, retired whaleman. But unlike Captain Peleg—who cared not a rush° for what are called serious things, and indeed deemed those self-same serious things the veriest of all trifles—Captain Bildad had not only been originally educated according to the strictest sect of Nantucket Quakerism, but all his subsequent ocean life, and the sight of many unclad, lovely island creatures, round the Horn°—all that had not moved this native born Quaker one single jot, had not so much as altered one angle of his vest. Still, for all this immutableness, was there some lack of common consistency about worthy Captain **Bildad**. Though refusing, from conscientious scruples, to bear arms against land invaders, yet himself had illimitably invaded the Atlantic and Pacific; and though a sworn foe to human bloodshed, yet had he in his straight-bodied coat, spilled tuns upon tuns° of leviathan gore. How now in the contemplative evening of his days, the pious Bildad reconciled these things in the reminiscence, I do not know; but it did not seem to concern him much, and very probably he had long since come to the sage and sensible conclusion that a man's religion is one thing, and this practical world quite another. This world pays dividends. Rising from a little cabin-boy in short clothes of the drabbest drab, to a harpooneer in a broad shad-bellied waistcoat;° from that becoming boat-header,° chief-mate, and captain, and finally a ship-owner; Bildad, as I hinted before, had concluded his adventurous career by wholly retiring from active life at the goodly age of sixty, and dedicating his remaining days to the quiet receiving of his well-earned income.

Now Bildad, I am sorry to say, had the reputation of being an incorrigible old hunks, and in his sea-going days, a bitter, hard task-master. They told me in Nantucket, though it certainly seems a curious story, that when he sailed the old Categut whaleman,[15] his crew, upon arriving home, were mostly all carried ashore to the hospital, sore exhausted and worn out. For a pious man, especially for a Quaker, he was certainly rather hard-hearted, to say the least. He never used to swear, though, at his men, they said; but somehow he got an inordinate quantity of cruel, unmitigated hard work out of them. When Bildad was a chief-mate, to have his drab-colored eye intently looking at you, made you feel completely nervous, till you could clutch something—a hammer or a marling-spike,° and go to work like mad, at something or other, never mind what. Indolence and idleness perished from before him. His own person was the exact embodiment of his utilitarian character. On his long, gaunt body, he carried no spare flesh, no superfluous beard, his chin having a soft, economical nap to it, like the worn nap of his broad-brimmed hat.

Such, then, was the person that I saw seated on the transom when I followed Captain Peleg down into the cabin. The space between the decks was small; and

***

rush: reed; hence "cared not at all." **the Horn**: Cape Horn. **tuns**: huge barrels holding 252 gallons. **shad-bellied waistcoat**: style of vest common in Quaker dress. **boat-header**: commander of a whaleboat, usually a mate, who kills the harpooned whale. **marling-spike**: pointed steel tool used in splicing rope.

there, bolt-upright, sat old Bildad, who always sat so, and never leaned, and this to save his coat tails. His broad-brim° was placed beside him; his legs were stiffly crossed; his drab vesture was buttoned up to his chin; and spectacles on nose, he seemed absorbed in reading from a ponderous volume.

"Bildad," cried Captain Peleg, "at it again, Bildad, eh? Ye have been studying those Scriptures, now, for the last thirty years, to my certain knowledge. How far ye got, Bildad?"

As if long habituated to such profane talk from his old shipmate, Bildad, without noticing his present irreverence, quietly looked up, and seeing me, glanced again inquiringly towards Peleg.

"He says he's our man, Bildad," said Peleg, "he wants to ship."

"Dost thee?" said Bildad, in a hollow tone, and turning round to me.

"I *dost*," said I unconsciously, he was so intense a Quaker.

"What do ye think of him, Bildad?" said Peleg.

"He'll do," said Bildad, eyeing me, and then went on spelling away at° his book in a mumbling tone quite audible.

I thought him the queerest old Quaker I ever saw, especially as Peleg, his friend and old shipmate, seemed such a blusterer. But I said nothing, only looking round me sharply. Peleg now threw open a chest, and drawing forth the ship's articles, placed pen and ink before him, and seated himself at a little table. I began to think it was high time to settle with myself at what terms I would be willing to engage for the voyage. I was already aware that in the whaling business they paid no wages; but all hands, including the captain, received certain shares of the profits called *lays*, and that these lays were proportioned to the degree of importance pertaining to the respective duties of the ship's company. I was also aware that being a green hand at whaling, my own lay would not be very large; but considering that I was used to the sea, could steer a ship, splice a rope,° and all that, I made no doubt that from all I had heard I should be offered at least the 275th lay[16]—that is, the 275th part of the clear nett proceeds of the voyage, whatever that might eventually amount to. And though the 275th lay was what they call a rather *long lay*, yet it was better than nothing; and if we had a lucky voyage, might pretty nearly pay for the clothing I would wear out on it, not to speak of my three years' beef and board, for which I would not have to pay one stiver.°

It might be thought that this was a poor way to accumulate a princely fortune—and so it was, a very poor way indeed. But I am one of those that never take on about princely fortunes, and am quite content if the world is ready to board and lodge me, while I am putting up at this grim sign of the Thunder Cloud.° Upon the whole, I thought that the 275th lay would be about the fair thing, but would not have been surprised had I been offered the 200th, considering I was of a broad-shouldered make.

But one thing, nevertheless, that made me a little distrustful about receiving a generous share of the profits was this: Ashore, I had heard something of both

---

broad-brim: hat generally worn by Quaker men. **spelling away at**: reading. **splice a rope**: weaving together the ends of two ropes. **stiver**: small Dutch coin. **putting up at this grim sign of the Thunder Cloud**: living at this threatening inn called the Earth.

Captain Peleg and his unaccountable old crony Bildad; how that they being the principal proprietors of the Pequod, therefore the other and more inconsiderable and scattered owners, left nearly the whole management of the ship's affairs to these two. And I did not know but what the stingy old Bildad might have a mighty deal to say about shipping hands, especially as I now found him on board the Pequod, quite at home there in the cabin, and reading his Bible as if at his own fireside. Now while Peleg was vainly trying to mend a pen with his jack-knife, old Bildad, to my no small surprise, considering that he was such an interested party in these proceedings; Bildad never heeded us, but went on mumbling to himself out of his book, "*Lay* not up for yourselves treasures upon earth, where moth—"[17]

"Well, Captain Bildad," interrupted Peleg, "what d'ye say, what lay shall we give this young man?"

"Thou knowest best," was the sepulchral reply, "the seven hundred and seventy-seventh[18] wouldn't be too much, would it?—'where moth and rust do corrupt, but *lay*—'"

Lay, indeed, thought I, and such a lay! the seven hundred and seventy-seventh! Well, old Bildad, you are determined that I, for one, shall not *lay* up many *lays* here below, where moth and rust do corrupt. It was an exceedingly *long lay* that, indeed; and though from the magnitude of the figure it might at first deceive a landsman, yet the slightest consideration will show that though seven hundred and seventy-seven is a pretty large number, yet, when you come to make a *teenth* of it, you will then see, I say, that the seven hundred and seventy-seventh part of a farthing° is a good deal less than seven hundred and seventy-seven gold doubloons;° and so I thought at the time.

"Why, blast your eyes, Bildad," cried Peleg, "thou dost not want to swindle this young man! he must have more than that."

"Seven hundred and seventy-seventh," again said Bildad, without lifting his eyes; and then went on mumbling—"for where your treasure is, there will your heart be also."

"I am going to put him down for the three hundredth," said Peleg, "do ye hear that, Bildad! The three hundredth lay, I say."

Bildad laid down his book, and turning solemnly towards him said, "Captain Peleg, thou hast a generous heart; but thou must consider the duty thou owest to the other owners of this ship—widows and orphans, many of them—and that if we too abundantly reward the labors of this young man, we may be taking the bread from those widows and those orphans. The seven hundred and seventy-seventh lay, Captain Peleg."

"Thou Bildad!" roared Peleg, starting up and clattering about the cabin. "Blast ye, Captain Bildad, if I had followed thy advice in these matters, I would afore now had a conscience to lug about that would be heavy enough to founder the largest ship that ever sailed round Cape Horn."

"Captain Peleg," said Bildad steadily, "thy conscience may be drawing ten inches of water, or ten fathoms, I can't tell; but as thou art still an impenitent man,[19]

---

farthing: British coin worth one-fourth of a penny. **doubloons**: Spanish gold coins weighing one ounce and worth 16 silver dollars.

Captain Peleg, I greatly fear lest thy conscience be but a leaky one; and will in the end sink thee foundering down to the fiery pit, Captain Peleg."

"Fiery pit! fiery pit! ye insult me, man; past all natural bearing, ye insult me. It's an all-fired outrage to tell any human creature that he's bound to hell. Flukes and flames! Bildad, say that again to me, and start my soul-bolts,° but I'll—I'll—yes, I'll swallow a live goat with all his hair and horns on. Out of the cabin, ye canting,° drab-colored son of a wooden gun—a straight wake with ye!"°

As he thundered out this he made a rush at Bildad, but with a marvellous oblique, sliding celerity, Bildad for that time eluded him.

Alarmed at this terrible outburst between the two principal and responsible owners of the ship, and feeling half a mind to give up all idea of sailing in a vessel so questionably owned and temporarily commanded, I stepped aside from the door to give egress to Bildad, who, I made no doubt, was all eagerness to vanish from before the awakened wrath of Peleg. But to my astonishment, he sat down again on the transom very quietly, and seemed to have not the slightest intention of withdrawing. He seemed quite used to impenitent Peleg and his ways. As for Peleg, after letting off his rage as he had, there seemed no more left in him, and he, too, sat down like a lamb, though he twitched a little as if still nervously agitated. "Whew!" he whistled at last—"the squall's gone off to leeward,° I think. Bildad, thou used to be good at sharpening a lance, mend that pen, will ye. My jack-knife here needs the grindstone. That's he; thank ye, Bildad. Now then, my young man, Ishmael's thy name, didn't ye say? Well then, down ye go here, Ishmael, for the three hundredth lay."

"Captain Peleg," said I, "I have a friend with me who wants to ship too—shall I bring him down to-morrow?"

"To be sure," said Peleg. "Fetch him along, and we'll look at him."

"What lay does **he** want?" groaned Bildad, glancing up from the book in which he had again been burying himself.

"Oh! never thee mind about that, Bildad," said Peleg. "Has he ever whaled it any?" turning to me.

"Killed more whales than I can count, Captain Peleg."

"Well, bring him along then."

And, after signing the papers, off I went; nothing doubting but that I had done a good morning's work, and that the Pequod was the identical ship that Yojo had provided to carry Queequeg and me round the Cape.

But I had not proceeded far, when I began to bethink me that the captain with whom I was to sail yet remained unseen by me; though indeed, in many cases, a whale-ship will be completely fitted out, and receive all her crew on board, ere the captain makes himself visible by arriving to take command; for sometimes these voyages are so prolonged, and the shore intervals at home so exceedingly brief, that if the captain have a family, or any absorbing concernment of that sort, he does not trouble himself much about his ship in port, but leaves her to the owners till all is ready for sea. However, it is always as well to have a look at him before irrevocably

---

start my soul-bolts: "upon my soul," or "I'll be damned," without blasphemy. ***canting***: using religious jargon. ***a straight wake with ye!***: "Get out of here!" ***to leeward***: downwind; that is, "I'm calm again."

committing yourself into his hands. Turning back I accosted Captain Peleg, inquiring where Captain Ahab was to be found.

"And what dost thou want of Captain Ahab? It's all right enough; thou art shipped."

"Yes, but I should like to see him."

"But I don't think thou wilt be able to at present. I don't know exactly what's the matter with him; but he keeps close inside the house; a sort of sick, and yet he don't look so. In fact, he ain't sick; but no, he isn't well either. Any how, young man, he won't always see me, so I don't suppose he will thee. He's a queer man, Captain Ahab—so some think—but a good one. Oh, thou'lt like him well enough; no fear, no fear. He's a grand, ungodly, god-like man, Captain Ahab; doesn't speak much; but, when he does speak, then you may well listen. Mark ye, be forewarned; Ahab's above the common; Ahab's been in colleges, as well as 'mong the cannibals; been used to deeper wonders than the waves; fixed his fiery lance in mightier, stranger foes than whales. His lance! aye, the keenest and the surest that, out of all our isle! Oh! he ain't Captain Bildad; no, and he ain't Captain Peleg; *he's Ahab*, boy; and Ahab of old, thou knowest, was a crowned king!"

"And a very vile one. When that wicked king was slain, the dogs, did they not lick his blood?"[20]

"Come hither to me—hither, hither," said Peleg, with a significance in his eye that almost startled me. "Look ye, lad; never say that on board the Pequod. Never say it anywhere. Captain Ahab did not name himself. 'Twas a foolish, ignorant whim of his crazy, widowed mother, who died when he was only a twelvemonth old. And yet the old squaw Tistig, at Gay-head,° said that the name would somehow prove prophetic. And, perhaps, other fools like her may tell thee the same. I wish to warn thee. It's a lie. I know Captain Ahab well; I've sailed with him as mate years ago; I know what he is—a good man—not a pious, good man, like Bildad, but a swearing good man—something like me—only there's a good deal more of him. Aye, aye, I know that he was never very jolly; and I know that on the passage home, he was a little out of his mind for a spell; but it was the sharp shooting pains in his bleeding stump that brought that about, as any one might see. I know, too, that ever since he lost his leg last voyage by that accursed whale, he's been a kind of moody—desperate moody, and savage sometimes; but that will all pass off. And once for all, let me tell thee and assure thee, young man, it's better to sail with a moody good captain than a laughing bad one. So good-bye to thee—and wrong not Captain Ahab, because he happens to have a wicked name. Besides, my boy, he has a wife—not three voyages wedded—a sweet, resigned girl. Think of that; by that sweet girl that old man has a child: hold ye then there can be any utter, hopeless harm in Ahab? No, no, my lad; stricken, blasted, if he be, Ahab has his humanities!"°

As I walked away, I was full of thoughtfulness; what had been incidentally revealed to me of Captain Ahab, filled me with a certain wild vagueness of painfulness concerning him. And somehow, at the time, I felt a sympathy and a sorrow for

Gay-head: western tip of Martha's Vineyard, also home to Tashtego. **humanities**: humane characteristics.

him, but for I don't know what, unless it was the cruel loss of his leg. And yet I also felt a strange awe of him; but that sort of awe, which I cannot at all describe, was not exactly awe; I do not know what it was. But I felt it; and it did not disincline me towards him; though I felt impatience at what seemed like mystery in him, so imperfectly as he was known to me then.[21] However, my thoughts were at length carried in other directions, so that for the present dark Ahab slipped my mind.

CHAPTER 17

THE RAMADAN

As Queequeg's Ramadan, **or Fasting and Humiliation**, was to continue all day, I did not choose to disturb him till towards night-fall; for I cherish the greatest respect towards everybody's religious obligations, never mind how comical, and could not find it in my heart to undervalue even a congregation of ants worshipping a toad-stool; or those other creatures in certain parts of our earth, who with a degree of footmanism° quite unprecedented in other planets, bow down before the torso of a deceased landed proprietor merely on account of the inordinate possessions yet owned and rented in his name.

I say, we good Presbyterian Christians should be charitable in these things, and not fancy ourselves so vastly superior to other mortals, pagans and what not, because of their half-crazy conceits on these subjects. There was Queequeg, now, certainly entertaining the most absurd notions about Yojo and his Ramadan;—but what of that? Queequeg thought he knew what he was about, I suppose; he seemed to be content; and there let him rest. All our arguing with him would not avail; let him be, I say: and Heaven have mercy on us all—Presbyterians and Pagans alike—for we are all somehow dreadfully cracked about the head, and sadly need mending.

Towards evening, when I felt assured that all his performances and rituals must be over, I went up to his room and knocked at the door; but no answer. I tried to open it, but it was fastened inside. "Queequeg," said I softly through the key-hole:—all silent. "I say, Queequeg! why don't you speak? It's I—Ishmael." But all remained still as before. I began to grow alarmed. I had allowed him such abundant time; I thought he might have had an apoplectic fit.° I looked through the key-hole; but the door opening into an odd corner of the room, the key-hole prospect was but a crooked and sinister° one. I could only see part of the foot-board of the bed and a line of the wall, but nothing more. I was surprised to behold resting against the wall the wooden shaft of Queequeg's harpoon, which the landlady the evening previous had taken from him, before our mounting to the chamber. That's strange, thought I; but at any rate, since the harpoon stands yonder, and he seldom or never goes abroad without it, therefore he must be inside here, and no possible mistake.

footmanism: servile obedience. *apoplectic fit*: stroke. *sinister*: leftward, but implying ominous.

"Queequeg!—Queequeg!"—all still. Something must have happened. Apoplexy! I tried to burst open the door; but it stubbornly resisted. Running down stairs, I quickly stated my suspicions to the first person I met—the chamber-maid. "La! La!" she cried, "I thought something must be the matter. I went to make the bed after breakfast, and the door was locked; and not a mouse to be heard; and it's been just so silent ever since. But I thought, may be, you had both gone off and locked your baggage in for safe keeping. La! La, ma'am!—Mistress! murder! Mrs. Hussey! apoplexy!"—and with these cries, she ran towards the kitchen, I following.

Mrs. Hussey soon appeared, with a mustard-pot in one hand and a vinegar-cruet in the other, having just broken away from the occupation of attending to the castors,° and scolding her little black boy meantime.

"Wood-house!" cried I, "which way to it? Run for God's sake, and fetch something to pry open the door—the axe!—the axe!—he's had a stroke; depend upon it!"—and so saying I was unmethodically rushing up stairs again empty-handed, when Mrs. Hussey interposed the mustard-pot and vinegar-cruet, and the entire castor of her countenance.

"What's the matter with you, young man?"

"Get the axe! For God's sake, run for the doctor, some one, while I pry it open!"

"Look here," said the landlady, quickly putting down the vinegar-cruet, so as to have one hand free; "look here; are you talking about prying open any of my doors?"—and with that she seized my arm. "What's the matter with you? What's the matter with you, shipmate?"

In as calm, but rapid a manner as possible, I gave her to understand the whole case. Unconsciously clapping the **vinegar-cruet** to one side of her nose, she ruminated for an instant; then exclaimed—"No! I haven't seen it since I put it there." Running to a little closet under the landing of the stairs, she glanced in, and returning, told me that Queequeg's harpoon was missing. "He's killed himself," she cried. "It's unfort'nate Stiggs done over again—there goes another counterpane—God pity his poor mother!—it will be the ruin of my house. Has the poor lad a sister? Where's that girl?—there, Betty, go to Snarles the Painter, and tell him to paint me a sign, with—'no suicides permitted here, and no smoking in the parlor;'—might as well kill both birds at once. Kill? The Lord be merciful to his ghost! What's that noise there? You, young man, avast there!"

And running up after me, she caught me as I was again trying to force open the door.

"I won't allow it; I won't have my premises spoiled. Go for the locksmith, there's one about a mile from here. But avast!" putting her hand in her side-pocket, "here's a key that'll fit, I guess; let's see." And with that, she turned it in the lock; but, alas! Queequeg's supplemental bolt remained unwithdrawn within.

"Have to burst it open," said I, and was running down the entry a little, for a good start, when the landlady caught at me, again vowing I should not break down her premises; but I tore from her, and with a sudden bodily rush dashed myself full against the mark.

---

castors: holders for condiment containers such as the pot and cruet.

With a prodigious noise the door flew open, and the knob slamming against the wall, sent the plaster to the ceiling; and there, good heavens! there sat Queequeg, altogether cool and self-collected; right in the middle of the room; squatting on his hams, and holding Yojo on top of his head. He looked neither one way nor the other way, but sat like a carved image with scarce a sign of active life.

"Queequeg," said I, going up to him, "Queequeg, what's the matter with you?"

"He hain't been a sittin' so all day, has he?" said the landlady.

But all we said, not a word could we drag out of him; I almost felt like pushing him over, so as to change his position, for it was almost intolerable, it seemed so painfully and unnaturally constrained; especially, as in all probability he had been sitting so for upwards of eight or ten hours, going too without his regular meals.

"Mrs. Hussey," said I, "he's *alive* at all events; so leave us, if you please, and I will see to this strange affair myself."

Closing the door upon the landlady, I endeavored to prevail upon Queequeg to take a chair; but in vain. There he sat; and all I could do—for all my polite arts and blandishments°—he would not move a peg, nor say a single word, nor even look at me, nor notice my presence in any the slightest way.

I wonder, thought I, if this can possibly be a part of his Ramadan; do they fast on their hams that way in his native island. It must be so; yes, it's part of his creed, I suppose; well, then, let him rest; he'll get up sooner or later, no doubt. It can't last for ever, thank God, and his Ramadan only comes once a year; and I don't believe it's very punctual then.

I went down to supper. After sitting a long time listening to the long stories of some sailors who had just come from a plum-pudding voyage, as they called it (that is, a short whaling-voyage in a schooner or brig, confined to the north of the line,° in the Atlantic Ocean only); after listening to these plum-puddingers till nearly eleven o'clock, I went up stairs to go to bed, feeling quite sure by this time Queequeg must certainly have brought his Ramadan to a termination. But no; there he was just where I had left him; he had not stirred an inch. I began to grow vexed with him; it seemed so downright senseless and insane to be sitting there all day and half the night on his hams in a cold room, holding a piece of wood on his head.

"For heaven's sake, Queequeg, get up and shake yourself; get up and have some supper. You'll starve; you'll kill yourself, Queequeg." But not a word did he reply.

Despairing of him, therefore, I determined to go to bed and to sleep; and no doubt, before a great while, he would follow me. But previous to turning in, I took my heavy bearskin jacket, and threw it over him, as it promised to be a very cold night; and he had nothing but his ordinary round jacket° on. For some time, do all I would, I could not get into the faintest doze. I had blown out the candle; and the mere thought of Queequeg—not four feet off—sitting there in that uneasy position, stark alone in the cold and dark; this made me really wretched. Think of it; sleeping all night in the same room with a wide awake pagan on his hams in this dreary, unaccountable Ramadan!

---

blandishments: kind words of persuasion. **line**: equator. **round jacket**: short, tight jacket.

But somehow I dropped off at last, and knew nothing more till break of day; when, looking over the bedside, there squatted Queequeg, as if he had been screwed down to the floor. But as soon as the first glimpse of sun entered the window, up he got, with stiff and grating joints, but with a cheerful look; limped towards me where I lay; pressed his forehead again against mine; and said his Ramadan was over.

Now, as I before hinted, I have no objection to any person's religion, be it what it may, so long as that person does not kill or insult any other person, because that other person don't believe it also. But when a man's religion becomes really frantic; when it is a positive torment to him; and, in fine, makes this earth of ours an uncomfortable inn to lodge in; then I think it high time to take that individual aside and argue the point with him.

And just so I now did with Queequeg. "Queequeg," said I, "get into bed now, and lie and listen to me." I then went on, beginning with the rise and progress of the primitive religions, and coming down to the various religions of the present time, during which time I labored to show Queequeg that all **these Lents, Ramadans, and prolonged ham-squattings in cold, cheerless rooms were stark nonsense; bad for the health; useless for the soul; opposed, in short, to the obvious laws of Hygiene and common sense. I told him, too, that he being in other things such an extremely sensible and sagacious savage, it pained me, very badly pained me, to see him now so deplorably foolish about this ridiculous Ramadan of his. Besides, argued I, fasting makes the body cave in; hence the spirit caves in; and all thoughts born of a fast must necessarily be half-starved. This is the reason why most dyspeptic religionists cherish such melancholy notions about their hereafters. In one word, Queequeg, said I, rather**

REVISION NARRATIVE

Lents and Ramadans

Seeing Queequeg as an excessive "religionist" whose devotion to fasting runs counter to common sense and good health, Ishmael argues facetiously that Christian Lent and Islamic Ramadan are "useless for the soul" and that "hell is an idea first born on an undigested apple-dumpling." Melville's British editor—no doubt finding the argument both disrespectful of Christian practice (Lent) and dogma (hell) as well as blasphemous in its reduction of Adam and Eve's eating of the apple and mankind's consequent damnation to mere indigestion—cut most of this paragraph, revising the final line to read:

> during which time I labored to show Queequeg that all these fasts, voluntary or otherwise, were excessively bad for the digestion.

The editor's reason for inserting "voluntary or otherwise" is unclear, suggesting perhaps an invidious contrast between Lent and Ramadan or variations in Christian practice.

digressively; hell is an idea first born on an undigested apple-dumpling;° and since then perpetuated through the hereditary dyspepsias° nurtured by Ramadans.

I then asked Queequeg whether he himself was ever troubled with dyspepsia; expressing the idea very plainly, so that he could take it in. He said no; only upon one memorable occasion. It was after a great feast given by his father the king, on the gaining of a great battle wherein fifty of the enemy had been killed by about two o'clock in the afternoon, and all cooked and eaten that very evening.

"No more, Queequeg," said I, shuddering; "that will do;" for I knew the inferences without his further hinting them. I had seen a sailor who had visited that very island,[1] and he told me that it was the custom, when a great battle had been gained there, to barbecue all the slain in the yard or garden of the victor; and then, one by one, they were placed in great wooden trenchers, and garnished round like a pilau,° with breadfruit and cocoanuts; and with some parsley in their mouths, were sent round with the victor's compliments to all his friends, just as though these presents were so many Christmas turkeys.

After all, I do not think that my remarks about religion made much impression upon Queequeg. Because, in the first place, he somehow seemed dull of hearing on that important subject, unless considered from his own point of view; and, in the second place, he did not more than one third understand me, couch my ideas simply as I would; and, finally, he no doubt thought he knew a good deal more about the true religion than I did. He looked at me with a sort of condescending concern and compassion, as though he thought it a great pity that such a sensible young man should be so hopelessly lost to evangelical° pagan piety.

At last we rose and dressed; and Queequeg, taking a prodigiously hearty breakfast of chowders of all sorts, so that the landlady should not make much profit by reason of his Ramadan, we sallied out to board the Pequod, sauntering along, and picking our teeth with halibut bones.

---

undigested apple-dumpling: the fruit of the forbidden tree in Eden (Genesis 3). **dyspepsias**: bouts of indigestion. **pilau**: pilaf; rice with meat and spices. **evangelical**: here, faithful to the pagan religion.

CHAPTER 18

HIS MARK

As we were walking down the end of the wharf[1] towards the ship, Queequeg carrying his harpoon, Captain Peleg in his gruff voice loudly hailed us from his wigwam, saying he had not suspected my friend was a cannibal, and furthermore announcing that he let no cannibals on board that craft, unless they previously produced their papers.[2]

"What do you mean by that, Captain Peleg?" said I, now jumping on the bulwarks, and leaving my comrade standing on the wharf.

"I mean," he replied, "he must show his papers."

"Yea," said Captain Bildad in his hollow voice, sticking his head from behind Peleg's, out of the wigwam. "He must show that he's converted. Son of darkness," he added, turning to Queequeg, "art thou at present in communion with any christian church?"

"Why," said I, "he's a member of the first Congregational Church." Here be it said, that many tattooed savages sailing in Nantucket ships at last come to be converted into the churches.

"First Congregational Church," cried Bildad, "what! that worships in Deacon Deuteronomy Coleman's meeting-house?" and so saying, taking out his spectacles, he rubbed them with his great yellow bandana handkerchief, and putting them on very carefully, came out of the wigwam, and leaning stiffly over the bulwarks, took a good long look at Queequeg.

"How long hath he been a member?" he then said, turning to me; "not very long, I rather guess, young man."

"No," said Peleg, "and he hasn't been baptized right either, or it would have washed some of that devil's blue off his face."

"Do tell, now," cried Bildad, "is this Philistine° a regular member of Deacon Deuteronomy's meeting? I never saw him going there, and I pass it every Lord's day."

"I don't know anything about Deacon Deuteronomy or his meet-

Philistine: unbeliever, pagan; from the idol-worshipping enemies of the biblical Hebrews. "Hittite," just below, has the same implication. Both appear often in Genesis.

ing," said I, "all I know is, that Queequeg here is a born member of the First Congregational Church. He is a deacon himself, Queequeg is."

"Young man," said Bildad sternly, "thou art skylarking with me— explain thyself, thou young Hittite. What church dost thee mean? answer me."

Finding myself thus hard pushed, I replied. "I mean, sir, the same ancient Catholic Church to which you and I, and Captain Peleg there, and Queequeg here, and all of us, and every mother's son and soul of us belong; the great and everlasting First Congregation of this whole worshipping world; we all belong to that; only some of us cher-

REVISION NARRATIVE

Converting Queequeg

When Bildad insists that Queequeg must "show that he's converted" to Christianity in order to join the *Pequod*, Ishmael claims Queequeg is a member of the "first Congregational Church." His point in the highlighted passage is that all people belong to one spiritual community—humanity itself—which constitutes a "Catholic" (that is, "universal") church, distinct from Roman Catholicism. Melville's reference to the (lower-case) "first" Church underscores this argument. But Bildad thinks Ishmael is referring to an actual, local Protestant church: the (upper-case) First Congregational Church, down the road, run by a Deacon Deuteronomy Coleman. When Ishmael further claims that Queequeg is himself a "deacon" (a lay assistant to a minister), Bildad and Peleg know that he has been "skylarking" with them. Ishmael then explains his larger meaning: all of us are united in one "grand belief," and some (like Bildad) adhere to "crotchets" (that is, certain peculiarities, in this case, Bildad's exclusionary views) that undermine Ishmael's all-accepting, universalist "church." The more tolerant Peleg is delighted by the joke, shakes Ishmael's hand, and brings Queequeg on board.

Melville's British editors removed this comic moment entirely, reducing its eight paragraphs to one significantly revised paragraph, the first in the highlighted revision site. The revision eliminates Ishmael's universalism and comic irreverence. Moreover, it inverts Queequeg's religious condition. Whereas throughout the American version, Queequeg remains true to his religion, never converting to either Ishmael's universalism or Bildad's fundamentalism; in the British version, Queequeg is a convert to Christianity. The revised and only surviving paragraph reads:

> "Why," said I, "he's a member of the First Congregational Church;" and I entered upon a long rigmarole story, touching the conversion of Queequeg, and concluded by saying that in the grand belief we all joined hands.

Ishmael's "first" is now "First," making Queequeg a member of an actual, local church; and Ishmael's explanation of Queequeg's conversion to Christianity is merely a "long rigmarole story." (Here, "rigmarole" means tedious and complicated but not facetious.) In addition, Ishmael's original wording, "grand belief" (meaning "universalism"), in revision means Christianity exclusively.

**ish some queer crotchets noways touching the grand belief; in that we
all join hands.**"[3]

"Splice, thou mean'st *splice* hands," cried Peleg, drawing nearer. "Young man,
you'd better ship for a missionary, instead of a fore-mast hand; I never heard a better sermon. Deacon Deuteronomy—why Father Mapple himself couldn't beat it,
and he's reckoned something. Come aboard, come aboard; never mind about the
papers. I say, tell Quohog° there—what's that you call him? tell Quohog to step
along. By the great anchor, what a harpoon he's got there! looks like good stuff that;
and he handles it about right. I say, Quohog, or whatever your name is, did you
ever stand in the head of a whale-boat? did you ever strike a fish?"

Without saying a word, Queequeg, in his wild sort of way, jumped upon the
bulwarks, from thence into the bows of one of the whale-boats hanging to the side;
and then bracing his left knee, and poising his harpoon, cried out in some such way
as this:—

"Cap'ain, you see him small drop tar on water dere? You see him? well, spose
him one whale eye, well, den!" and taking sharp aim at it, he darted the iron right
over old Bildad's broad brim, clean across the ship's decks, and struck the glistening
tar spot out of sight.

"Now," said Queequeg, quietly hauling in the line, "spos-ee him whale-e eye;
why, dad whale dead."

"Quick, Bildad," **said Peleg, his partner**, who, aghast at the close vicinity
of the flying harpoon, had retreated towards the cabin gangway.° "Quick, I say, you
Bildad, and get the ship's papers. We must have Hedgehog there, I mean Quohog,
in one of our boats. Look ye, Quohog, we'll give ye the ninetieth lay, and that's more
than ever was given a harpooneer yet out of Nantucket."

So down we went into the cabin, and to my great joy Queequeg was soon
enrolled among the same ship's company to which I myself belonged.

When all preliminaries were over and Peleg had got everything ready for signing, he turned to me and said, "I guess, Quohog there don't know how to write, does
he? I say, Quohog, blast ye! dost thou sign thy name or make thy mark?"

But at this question, Queequeg, who had twice or thrice before taken part in
similar ceremonies, looked no ways abashed; but taking the offered pen, copied
upon the paper, in the proper place, an exact counterpart of a queer round figure
which was tattooed upon his arm; so that through Captain Peleg's obstinate mistake
touching his appellative, it stood something like this:—

Quohog.
his ✚ mark.

Meanwhile Captain Bildad sat earnestly and steadfastly eyeing Queequeg,
and at last rising solemnly and fumbling in the huge pockets of his broad-skirted
drab coat, took out a bundle of tracts, and selecting one entitled "The Latter Day

---

Quohog: type of clam. **cabin gangway**: stairway down to the cabin.

Coming; or No Time to Lose," placed it in Queequeg's hands, and then grasping them and the book with both his, looked earnestly into his eyes, and said, "Son of darkness, I must do my duty by thee; I am part owner of this ship, and feel concerned for the souls of all its crew; if thou still clingest to thy Pagan ways, which I sadly fear, I beseech thee, remain not for aye a Belial bondsman. Spurn the idol Bel, and the hideous dragon;[4] turn from the wrath to come; mind thine eye, I say; oh! goodness gracious! steer clear of the fiery pit!"

Something of the salt sea yet lingered in old Bildad's language, heterogeneously mixed with Scriptural and domestic phrases.

"Avast there, avast there, Bildad, avast now spoiling our harpooneer," cried Peleg. "Pious harpooneers never make good voyagers—it takes the shark out of 'em; no harpooneer is worth a straw who aint pretty sharkish. There was young Nat Swaine, once the bravest boat-header out of all Nantucket and the Vineyard; he joined the meeting, and never came to good. He got so frightened about his plaguy soul, that he shrinked and sheered away from whales, for fear of after-claps,° in case he got stove and went to Davy Jones."°

"Peleg! Peleg!" said Bildad, lifting his eyes and hands, "thou thyself, as I myself, hast seen many a perilous time; thou knowest, Peleg, what it is to have the fear of death; how, then, can'st thou prate° in this ungodly guise. Thou beliest thine own heart, Peleg. Tell me, when this same Pequod here had her three masts overboard in that typhoon on Japan, that same voyage when thou went mate with Captain Ahab, did'st thou not think of Death and the Judgment then?"

"Hear him, hear him now," cried Peleg, marching across the cabin, and thrusting his hands far down into his pockets,—"hear him, all of ye. Think of that! When every moment we thought the ship would sink! Death and the Judgment then? What? With all three masts making such an everlasting thundering against the side; and every sea breaking over us, fore and aft. Think of Death and the Judgment then? No! no time to think about Death then. Life was what Captain Ahab and I was thinking of; and how to save all hands—how to rig jury-masts°—how to get into the nearest port; that was what I was thinking of."

Bildad said no more, but buttoning up his coat, stalked on deck, where we followed him. There he stood, very quietly overlooking some sail-makers who were mending a top-sail in the waist.° Now and then he stooped to pick up a patch, or save an end of the tarred twine, which otherwise might have been wasted.

---

after-claps: unexpected results; here, damnation. *went to Davy Jones*: Davy Jones's locker, the bottom of the sea in sailor folklore. *prate*: speak foolishly. *rig jury-masts*: set up temporary replacements for lost masts. *waist*: midsection of the deck.

CHAPTER 19

THE PROPHET

"SHIPMATES, have ye shipped in that ship?"

Queequeg and I had just left the Pequod, and were sauntering away from the water, for the moment each occupied with his own thoughts, when the above words were put to us by a stranger, who, pausing before us, levelled his massive fore-finger at the vessel in question. He was but shabbily apparelled in faded jacket and patched trowsers; a rag of a black handkerchief investing his neck. A confluent small-pox had in all directions flowed over his face, and left it like the complicated ribbed bed of a torrent, when the rushing waters have been dried up.

"Have ye shipped in her?" he repeated.

"You mean the ship Pequod, I suppose," said I, trying to gain a little more time for an uninterrupted look at him.

"Aye, the Pequod—that ship there," he said, drawing back his whole arm, and then rapidly shoving it straight out from him, with the fixed bayonet of his pointed finger darted full at the object.

"Yes," said I, "we have just signed the articles."°

"Anything down there about your souls?"

"About what?"

"Oh, perhaps you hav'n't got any," he said quickly. "No matter though, I know many chaps that hav'n't got any,—good luck to 'em; and they are all the better off for it. A soul's a sort of a fifth wheel to a wagon."

"What are you jabbering about, shipmate?" said I.

"*He's* got enough, though, to make up for all deficiencies of that sort in other chaps," abruptly said the stranger, placing a nervous emphasis upon the word *he*.

"Queequeg," said I, "let's go; this fellow has broken loose from somewhere; he's talking about something and somebody we don't know."

"Stop!" cried the stranger. "Ye said true—ye hav'n't seen Old Thunder yet, have ye?"

"Who's Old Thunder?" said I, again riveted with the insane earnestness of his manner.

the articles: seaman's contract.

"Captain Ahab."

"What! the captain of our ship, the Pequod?"

"Aye, among some of us old sailor chaps, he goes by that name. Ye hav'n't seen him yet, have ye?"

"No, we hav'n't. He's sick they say, but is getting better, and will be all right again before long."

"All right again before long!" laughed the stranger, with a solemnly derisive sort of laugh. "Look ye; when captain Ahab is all right, then this left arm of mine will be all right; not before."

"What do you know about him?"

"What did they *tell* you about him? Say that!"

"They didn't tell much of anything about him; only I've heard that he's a good whale-hunter, and a good captain to his crew."

"That's true, that's true—yes, both true enough. But you must jump when he gives an order. Step and growl; growl and go—that's the word with Captain Ahab. But nothing about that thing that happened to him off Cape Horn, long ago, when he lay like dead for three days and nights; nothing about that deadly skrimmage with the Spaniard afore the altar in Santa?°—heard nothing about that, eh? Nothing about the silver calabash he spat into? And nothing about his losing his leg last voyage, according to the **prophecy**. Didn't ye hear a word about them matters and something more, eh? No, I don't think ye did; how could ye? Who knows it? Not all Nantucket, I guess. But hows'ever, mayhap, ye've heard tell about the leg, and how he lost it; aye, ye have heard of that, I dare say. Oh yes, *that* every one knows a'most—I mean they know he's only one leg; and that a parmacetti took the other off."

"My friend," said I, "what all this gibberish of yours is about, I don't know, and I don't much care; for it seems to me that you must be a little damaged in the head. But if you are speaking of Captain Ahab, of that ship there, the Pequod, then let me tell you, that I know all about the loss of his leg."

"*All* about it, eh—sure you do?—all?"

"Pretty sure."

With finger pointed and eye levelled at the Pequod, the beggar-like stranger stood a moment, as if in a troubled reverie; then starting a little, turned and said:— "Ye've shipped, have ye? Names down on the papers? Well, well, what's signed, is signed; and what's to be, will be; and then again, perhaps it wont be, after all. Any how, it's all fixed and arranged a'ready;° and some sailors or other must go with him, I suppose; as well these as any other men, God pity 'em! Morning to ye, shipmates, morning; the ineffable heavens bless ye; I'm sorry I stopped ye."

"Look here, friend," said I, "if you have anything important to tell us, out with it; but if you are only trying to bamboozle us, you are mistaken in your game; that's all I have to say."

"And it's said very well, and I like to hear a chap talk up that way; you are just the man for him—the likes of ye. Morning to ye, shipmates, morning! Oh! when ye

Santa: Peruvian seaport often used by whalemen. ***fixed and arranged a'ready***: fated, as Ahab also claims in Ch. 132.

get there, tell 'em I've concluded not to make one of 'em."

"Ah, my dear fellow, you can't fool us that way—you can't fool us. It is the easiest thing in the world for a man to look as if he had a great secret in him."

"Morning to ye, shipmates, morning."

"Morning it is," said I. "Come along, Queequeg, let's leave this crazy man. But stop, tell me your name, will you?"

"Elijah."[1]

Elijah! thought I, and we walked away, both commenting, after each other's fashion, upon this ragged old sailor; and agreed that he was nothing but a humbug, trying to be a bugbear.° But we had not gone perhaps above a hundred yards, when chancing to turn a corner, and looking back as I did so, who should be seen but Elijah following us, though at a distance. Somehow, the sight of him struck me so, that I said nothing to Queequeg of his being behind, but passed on with my comrade, anxious to see whether the stranger would turn the same corner that we did. He did; and then it seemed to me that he was dogging us, but with what intent I could not for the life of me imagine. This circumstance, coupled with his ambiguous, half-hinting, half-revealing, shrouded sort of talk, now begat in me all kinds of vague wonderments and half-apprehensions, and all connected with the Pequod; and Captain Ahab; and the leg he had lost; and the Cape Horn fit; and the silver calabash; and what Captain Peleg had said of him, when I left the ship the day previous; and the prediction of the squaw Tistig; and the voyage we had bound ourselves to sail; and a hundred other shadowy things.

I was resolved to satisfy myself whether this ragged Elijah was really dogging us or not, and with that intent crossed the way with Queequeg, and on that side of it retraced our steps. But Elijah passed on, without seeming to notice us. This relieved me; and once more, and finally as it seemed to me, I pronounced him in my heart, a humbug.

humbug . . . bugbear: a fake trying to be frightening.

CHAPTER 20

ALL ASTIR

A DAY or two passed, and there was great activity aboard the Pequod. Not only were the old sails being mended, but new sails were coming on board, and bolts of canvas, and coils of rigging; in short, everything betokened that the ship's preparations were hurrying to a close. Captain Peleg seldom or never went ashore, but sat in his wigwam keeping a sharp look-out upon the hands: Bildad did all the purchasing and providing at the stores; and the men employed in the hold and on the rigging were working till long after night-fall.

On the day following Queequeg's signing the articles, word was given at all the inns where the ship's company were stopping, that their chests must be on board before night, for there was no telling how soon the vessel might be sailing. So Queequeg and I got down our traps,° resolving, however, to sleep ashore till the last. But it seems they always give very long notice in these cases, and the ship did not sail for several days. But no wonder; there was a good deal to be done, and there is no telling how many things to be thought of, before the Pequod was fully equipped.

Every one knows what a multitude of things—beds, sauce-pans, knives and forks, shovels and tongs, napkins, nut-crackers, and what not, are indispensable to the business of housekeeping. Just so with whaling, which necessitates a three-years' housekeeping upon the wide ocean, far from all grocers, coster-mongers,° doctors, bakers, and bankers. And though this also holds true of merchant vessels, yet not by any means to the same extent as with whalemen.° For besides the great length of the whaling voyage, the numerous articles peculiar to the prosecution of the fishery, and the impossibility of replacing them at the remote harbors usually frequented, it must be remembered, that of all ships, whaling vessels are the most exposed to accidents of all kinds, and especially to the destruction and loss of the very things upon which the success of the voyage most depends. Hence, the spare boats, spare spars, and spare lines and harpoons, and spare everythings, almost, but a spare Captain and duplicate ship.

At the period of our arrival at the Island, the heaviest **stowage** of the Pequod had been almost completed; comprising her beef, bread, water, fuel, and iron hoops

***got down our traps**: put our belongings on board. **coster-mongers**: street venders, mainly of fruits and vegetables. **whalemen**: here, whaling vessels.

and staves.° But, as before hinted, for some time there was a continual fetching and carrying on board of divers° odds and ends of things, both large and small.

Chief among those who did this fetching and carrying was Captain Bildad's sister, a lean old lady of a most determined and indefatigable spirit, but withal very kindhearted, who seemed resolved that, if *she* could help it, nothing should be found wanting in the Pequod, after once fairly getting to sea. At one time she would come on board with a jar of pickles for the steward's pantry; another time with a bunch of quills for the chief mate's desk, where he kept his log;[1] a third time with a roll of flannel for the small of some one's rheumatic back. Never did any woman better deserve her name, which was Charity—Aunt Charity, as everybody called her. And like a sister of charity did this charitable Aunt Charity bustle about hither and thither, ready to turn her hand and heart to anything that promised to yield safety, comfort, and consolation to all on board a ship in which her beloved brother Bildad was concerned, and in which she herself owned a score or two of well-saved dollars.

But it was startling to see this excellent hearted Quakeress coming on board, as she did the last day, with a long oil-ladle in one hand, and a still longer whaling lance in the other. Nor was Bildad himself nor Captain Peleg at all backward. As for Bildad, he carried about with him a long list of the articles needed, and at every fresh arrival, down went his mark opposite that article upon the paper. Every once and a while Peleg came **hobbling** out of his whalebone den, roaring at the men down the hatchways, roaring up to the riggers° at the mast-head, and then concluded by roaring back into his wigwam.

During these days of preparation, Queequeg and I often visited the craft, and as often I asked about Captain Ahab, and how he was, and when he was going to come on board his ship. To these questions they would answer, that he was getting better and better, and was expected aboard every day; meantime, the two Captains, Peleg and Bildad, could attend to everything necessary to fit the vessel for the voyage. If I had been downright honest with myself, I would have seen very plainly in my heart that I did but half fancy being committed this way to so long a voyage, without once laying my eyes on the man who was to be the absolute dictator of it, so soon as the ship sailed out upon the open sea. But when a man suspects any wrong, it sometimes happens that if he be already involved in the matter, he insensibly strives to cover up his suspicions even from himself. And much this way it was with me. I said nothing, and tried to think nothing.

At last it was given out that some time next day the ship would certainly sail. So next morning, Queequeg and I took a very early start.

---

hoops and staves: used in making barrels; staves are narrow strips of wood. *divers*: various, diverse. *riggers*: workers setting up the ship's rigging.

CHAPTER 21

GOING ABOARD

IT was nearly six o'clock, but only grey imperfect misty dawn, when we drew nigh the wharf.

"There are some sailors running ahead there, if I see right," said I to Queequeg, "it can't be shadows; she's off by sunrise, I guess; come on!"

"Avast!" cried a voice, whose owner at the same time coming close behind us, laid a hand upon both our shoulders,[1] and then insinuating himself between us, stood stooping forward a little, in the uncertain twilight, strangely peering from Queequeg to me. It was Elijah.

"Going aboard?"

"Hands off, will you," said I.

"Lookee here," said Queequeg, shaking himself, "go 'way!"

"Aint going aboard, then?"

"Yes, we are," said I, "but what business is that of yours? Do you know, Mr. Elijah, that I consider you a little impertinent?"

"No, no, no; I wasn't aware of that," said Elijah, slowly and wonderingly looking from me to Queequeg, with the most unaccountable glances.

"Elijah," said I, "you will oblige my friends and me by withdrawing. We are going to the Indian and Pacific Oceans,[2] and would prefer not to be detained."

"Ye be, be ye? Coming back afore breakfast?"

"He's cracked, Queequeg," said I, "come on."

"Holloa!" cried stationary Elijah, hailing us when we had removed a few paces.

"Never mind him," said I, "Queequeg, come on."

But he stole up to us again, and suddenly clapping his hand on my shoulder, said—"Did ye see anything looking like men going towards that ship a while ago?"

Struck by this plain matter-of-fact question, I answered, saying "Yes, I thought I did see four or five men; but it was too dim to be sure."

"Very dim, very dim," said Elijah. "Morning to ye."

Once more we quitted him; but once more he came softly after us; and touching my shoulder again, said, "See if you can find 'em now, will ye?"

"Find who?"

"Morning to ye! morning to ye!" he rejoined, again moving off. "Oh! I was going to warn ye against—but never mind, never mind—it's all one, all in the family too;—sharp frost this morning, ain't it? Good bye to ye. Shan't see ye again very soon, I guess; unless it's before the Grand Jury."° And with these cracked words he finally departed, leaving me, for the moment, in no small wonderment at his frantic impudence.

At last, stepping on board the Pequod, we found everything in profound quiet, not a soul moving. The cabin entrance was locked within; the hatches were all on, and lumbered with coils of rigging. Going forward to the forecastle, we found the slide of the scuttle° open. Seeing a light, we went down, and found only an old rigger there, wrapped in a tattered pea-jacket. He was thrown at whole length upon two chests, his face downwards and inclosed in his folded arms. The profoundest slumber **slept** upon him.

"Those sailors we saw, Queequeg, where can they have gone to?" said I, looking dubiously at the sleeper. But it seemed that, when on the wharf, Queequeg had not at all noticed what I now alluded to; hence I would have thought myself to have been optically deceived in that matter, were it not for Elijah's otherwise inexplicable question. But I beat the thing down; and again marking the sleeper, jocularly hinted to Queequeg that perhaps we had best sit up with the body;[3] telling him to establish himself accordingly. He put his hand upon the sleeper's rear, as though feeling if it was soft enough; and then, without more ado, sat quietly down there.

"Gracious! Queequeg, don't sit there," said I.

"Oh! perry dood seat," said Queequeg, "my country way;[4] won't hurt him face."

"Face!" said I, "call that his face? very benevolent countenance then; but how hard he breathes, he's heaving himself; get off, Queequeg, you are heavy, it's grinding the face of the poor.[5] Get off, Queequeg! Look, he'll twitch you off soon. I wonder he don't wake."

Queequeg removed himself to just beyond the head of the sleeper, and lighted his tomahawk pipe. I sat at the feet. We kept the pipe passing over the sleeper, from one to the other. Meanwhile, upon questioning him **in his broken fashion,** Queequeg gave me to understand that, in his land, owing to the absence of settees and sofas of all sorts, the king, chiefs, and great people generally, were in the custom of fattening some of the lower orders for ottomans; and to furnish a house comfortably in that respect, you had only to buy up eight or ten lazy fellows, and lay them round in the piers° and alcoves. Besides, it was very convenient on an excursion; much better than those garden-chairs which are convertible into walking-sticks; upon occasion, a chief calling his attendant, and desiring him to make a settee of himself under a spreading tree, perhaps in some damp marshy place.

While narrating these things, every time Queequeg received the tomahawk from me, he flourished the hatchet-side of it over the sleeper's head.

"What's that for, Queequeg?"

"Perry easy, kill-e; oh! perry easy!"

---

before the Grand Jury: at the Last Judgment. **scuttle**: entrance to a stairway leading below. **piers**: parts of walls between doors or windows.

He was going on with some wild reminiscences about his tomahawk-pipe, which, it seemed, had in its two uses both brained his foes and soothed his soul, when we were directly attracted to the sleeping rigger. The strong vapor now completely filling the contracted hole, it began to tell upon him. He breathed with a sort of muffledness; then seemed troubled in the nose; then revolved over once or twice; then sat up and rubbed his eyes.

"Holloa!" he breathed at last, "who be ye smokers?"

"Shipped men,"° answered I, "when does she sail?"

"Aye, aye, ye are going in her, be ye? She sails to-day. The Captain came aboard last night."

"What Captain?—Ahab?"

"Who but him indeed?"

I was going to ask him some further questions concerning Ahab, when we heard a noise on deck.

"Holloa! Starbuck's astir," said the rigger. "He's a lively chief mate, that; good man, and a pious; but all alive now, I must turn to." And so saying he went on deck, and we followed.

It was now clear sunrise. Soon the crew came on board in twos and threes; the riggers bestirred themselves; the mates were actively engaged; and several of the shore people were busy in bringing various last things on board. Meanwhile Captain Ahab remained invisibly enshrined within his cabin.

Shipped men: those signed up for the voyage.

CHAPTER 22

MERRY CHRISTMAS

A T length, towards noon, upon the final dismissal of the ship's riggers, and after the Pequod had been hauled out[1] from the wharf, and after the ever-thoughtful Charity had come off in a whaleboat, with her last **gift**—a night-cap for Stubb, the second mate, her brother-in-law, and a spare Bible for the steward—after all this, the two captains, Peleg and Bildad, issued from the cabin, and turning to the chief mate, Peleg said:

"Now, Mr. Starbuck, are you sure everything is right? Captain Ahab is all ready—just spoke to him—nothing more to be got from shore, eh? Well, call all hands, then. Muster 'em aft here—blast 'em!"

"No need of profane words, however great the hurry, Peleg," said Bildad, "but away with thee, friend Starbuck, and do our bidding."

How now! Here upon the very point of starting for the voyage, Captain Peleg and Captain Bildad were going it with a high hand on the quarter-deck, just as if they were to be joint-commanders at sea, as well as to all appearances in port. And, as for Captain Ahab, no sign of him was yet to be seen; only, they said he was in the cabin. But then, the idea was, that his presence was by no means necessary in getting the ship under weigh,° and steering her well out to sea. Indeed, as that was not at all his proper business, but the pilot's; and as he was not yet completely recovered—so they said—therefore, Captain Ahab stayed below. And all this seemed natural enough; especially as in the merchant service many captains never show themselves on deck for a considerable time after heaving up the anchor, but remain over the cabin table, having a farewell merry-making with their shore friends, before they quit the ship for good with the pilot.

But there was not much chance to think over the matter, for Captain Peleg was now all alive. He seemed to do most of the talking and commanding, and not Bildad.

"Aft here, ye sons of bachelors," he cried, as the sailors lingered at the main-mast. "Mr. Starbuck, drive 'em aft."

"Strike the tent there!"—was the next order. As I hinted before, this whale-bone marquee° was never pitched except in port; and on board the Pequod, for

getting the ship under weigh: raising (weighing) the anchor. **marquee**: tent for someone of high rank.

thirty years, the order to strike the tent was well known to be the next thing to heaving up the anchor.

"Man the capstan!° Blood and thunder!—jump!"—was the next command, and the crew sprang for the handspikes.

Now, in getting under weigh, the station generally occupied by the pilot is the forward part of the ship. And here Bildad, who, with Peleg, be it known, in addition to his other offices, was one of the licensed pilots of the port—he being suspected to have got himself made a pilot in order to save the Nantucket pilot-fee to all the ships he was concerned in, for he never piloted any other craft—Bildad, I say, might now be seen actively engaged in looking over the bows for the approaching anchor, and at intervals singing what seemed a dismal stave of psalmody, to cheer the hands at the windlass,° who roared forth some sort of a chorus about the girls in Booble Alley,[2] with hearty good will. Nevertheless, not three days previous, Bildad had told them that no profane songs would be allowed on board the Pequod, particularly in getting under weigh; and Charity, his sister, had placed a small choice copy of Watts[3] in each seaman's berth.

Meantime, overseeing the other part of the ship, Captain Peleg ripped and swore astern in the most frightful manner. I almost thought he would sink the ship before the anchor could be got up; involuntarily I paused on my handspike, and told Queequeg to do the same, thinking of the perils we both ran, in starting on the voyage with such a devil for a pilot. I was comforting myself, however, with the thought that in pious Bildad might be found some salvation, spite of his seven hundred and seventy-seventh lay; when I felt a sudden sharp poke in my rear, and turning round, was horrified at the apparition of Captain Peleg in the act of withdrawing his leg from my immediate vicinity. That was my first kick.

"Is that the way they heave in the marchant service?" he roared. "Spring, thou sheep-head; spring, and break thy backbone! Why don't ye spring, I say, all of ye— **spring! Quohag!** spring, thou chap with the red whiskers; spring there, Scotch-cap;° spring, thou green pants. Spring, I say, all of ye, and spring your eyes out!" And so saying, he moved along the windlass, here and there using his leg very freely, while imperturbable Bildad kept leading off with his psalmody. Thinks I, Captain Peleg must have been drinking something to-day.

At last the anchor was up, the sails were set, and off we glided. It was a short, cold Christmas; and as the short northern day merged into night, we found ourselves almost broad upon the wintry ocean, whose freezing spray cased us in ice, as in polished armor. The long rows of teeth on the bulwarks glistened in the moonlight; and like the white ivory tusks of some huge elephant, vast curving icicles depended from the bows.

Lank Bildad, as pilot, headed the first watch, and ever and anon, as the old craft deep dived into the green seas, and sent the shivering frost all over her, and the winds howled, and the cordage rang, his steady notes were heard,—

---

capstan: upright cylindrical device turned with spoke-like wooden bars, and used for heavy tasks; it becomes a windlass in the next paragraph. ***windlass***: horizontal cylindrical machine near the bow, turned with levers ("handspikes"); not to be confused with a capstan, although Melville uses both almost interchangeably. ***Scotch-cap***: referring to a sailor wearing a brim-less cap with two streamers.

"Sweet fields beyond the swelling flood,
    Stand dressed in living green.
So to the Jews old Canaan stood,
    While Jordan rolled between."[4]

Never did those sweet words sound more sweetly to me than then. They were full of hope and fruition. Spite of this frigid winter night in the boisterous Atlantic, spite of my wet feet and wetter jacket, there was yet, it then seemed to me, many a pleasant haven in store; and meads and glades so eternally vernal, that the grass shot up by the spring, untrodden, unwilted, remains at midsummer.

At last we gained such an offing, that the two pilots were needed no longer. The stout sail-boat that had accompanied us began ranging alongside.

It was curious and not unpleasing, how Peleg and Bildad were affected at this juncture, especially Captain Bildad. For loath to depart, yet; very loath to leave, for good, a ship bound on so long and perilous a voyage—beyond both stormy Capes;° a ship in which some thousands of his hard earned dollars were invested; a ship, in which an old shipmate sailed as captain; a man almost as old as he, once more starting to encounter all the terrors of the pitiless jaw; loath to say good-bye to a thing so every way brimful of every interest to him,—poor old Bildad lingered long; paced the deck with anxious strides; ran down into the cabin to speak another farewell word there; again came on deck, and looked to windward; looked towards the wide and endless waters, only bounded by the far-off unseen Eastern Continents; looked towards the land; looked aloft; looked right and left; looked everywhere and nowhere; and at last, mechanically coiling a rope upon its pin,° convulsively grasped stout Peleg by the hand, and holding up a lantern, for a moment stood gazing heroically in his face, as much as to say, "Nevertheless, friend Peleg, I can stand it; yes, I can."

As for Peleg himself, he took it more like a philosopher; but for all his philosophy, there was a tear twinkling in his eye, when the lantern came too near. And he, too, did not a little run from cabin to deck—now a word below, and now a word with Starbuck, the chief mate.

But, at last, he turned to his comrade, with a final sort of look about him,— "Captain Bildad—come, old shipmate, we must go. Back the main-yard° there! Boat ahoy! Stand by to come close alongside, now! Careful, careful!—come, Bildad, boy—say your last. Luck to ye, Starbuck—luck to ye, Mr. Stubb—luck to ye, Mr. Flask—good-bye, and good luck to ye all—and this day three years I'll have a hot supper smoking for ye in old Nantucket. Hurrah and away!"

"God bless ye, and have ye in His holy keeping, men," murmured old Bildad, almost incoherently. "I hope ye'll have fine weather now, so that Captain Ahab may soon be moving among ye—a pleasant sun is all he needs, and ye'll have plenty of them in the tropic voyage ye go. Be careful in the hunt, ye mates. Don't stave° the

---

both stormy Capes: Cape Horn and the Cape of Good Hope. **pin**: belaying pin. **back the main-yard**: turn the mainsail so the wind strikes the front of the sail (and slows the ship). **stave**: smash; past tense is stove.

boats needlessly, ye harpooneers; good white cedar plank is raised full three per cent. within the year. Don't forget your prayers, either. Mr. Starbuck, mind that cooper don't waste the spare staves. Oh! the sail-needles are in the green locker! Don't whale it too much a' Lord's days, men; but don't miss a fair chance either, that's rejecting Heaven's good gifts. Have an eye to the molasses tierce,° Mr. Stubb; it was a little leaky, I thought. **If ye touch at the islands, Mr. Flask, beware of fornication.** Good-bye, good-bye! Don't keep that cheese too long down in the hold, Mr. Starbuck; it'll spoil. Be careful with the butter—twenty cents the pound it was, and mind ye, if—"

"Come, come, Captain Bildad; stop palavering,—away!" and with that, Peleg hurried him over the side, and both dropt into the boat.

Ship and boat diverged; the cold, damp night breeze blew between; a screaming gull flew overhead; the two hulls wildly rolled; we gave three heavy-hearted cheers, and blindly plunged like fate into the lone Atlantic.

tierce: 42-gallon barrel.

CHAPTER 23

THE LEE SHORE

S OME chapters back,° one Bulkington was spoken of, a tall, new-landed mariner, encountered in New Bedford at the inn.

When on that shivering winter's night, the Pequod thrust her vindictive bows into the cold malicious waves, who should I see standing at her helm but Bulkington! I looked with sympathetic awe and fearfulness upon the man, who in midwinter just landed from a four years' dangerous voyage, could so unrestingly push off again for still another tempestuous term. The land seemed scorching to his feet. Wonderfullest things are ever the unmentionable; deep memories yield no epitaphs; this six-inch chapter is the stoneless grave of Bulkington. Let me only say that it fared with him as with the storm-tossed ship, that miserably drives along the leeward land.[1] The port would fain give succor; the port is pitiful; in the port is safety, comfort, hearthstone, supper, warm blankets, friends, all that's kind to our mortalities.° But in that gale, the port, the land, is that ship's direst jeopardy; she must fly all hospitality; one touch of land, though it but graze the keel, would make her shudder through and through. With all her might she crowds all sail° off shore; in so doing, fights 'gainst the very winds that fain would blow her homeward; seeks all the lashed sea's landlessness again; for refuge's sake forlornly rushing into peril; her only friend her bitterest foe!

Know ye, now, Bulkington?[2] Glimpses do ye seem to see of that mortally intolerable truth; that all deep, earnest thinking is but the intrepid effort of the soul to keep the open independence of her sea; while the wildest winds of heaven and earth conspire to cast her on the treacherous, slavish shore?

But as in landlessness alone resides the highest truth, shoreless, indefinite as **God**—so, better is it to perish in that howling infinite, than be ingloriously dashed upon the lee, even if that were safety! For worm-like, then, oh! who would craven crawl to land! Terrors of the terrible! is all this agony so vain? Take heart, take heart, O Bulkington! Bear thee grimly, demigod! Up from the spray of thy ocean-perishing—straight up, leaps thy apotheosis!°

Some chapters back: See Ch. 3. ***would fain give succor . . . pitiful . . . our mortalities***: would like to help; has pity; our human needs and weaknesses. ***crowds all sail***: sets all possible sails. ***apotheosis***: transformation into an immortal spirit.

110

CHAPTER 24

THE ADVOCATE[1]

As Queequeg and I are now fairly embarked in this business of whaling; and as this business of whaling has somehow come to be regarded among landsmen as a rather unpoetical and disreputable pursuit; therefore, I am all anxiety to convince ye, ye landsmen, of the injustice hereby done to us hunters of whales.

In the first place, it may be deemed almost superfluous to establish the fact, that among people at large, the business of whaling is not accounted on a level with what are called the liberal professions. If a stranger were introduced into any miscellaneous metropolitan society, it would but slightly advance the general opinion of his merits, were he presented to the company as a harpooneer, say; and if in emulation of the naval officers he should append the initials S. W. F. (Sperm Whale Fishery) to his visiting card, such a procedure would be deemed pre-eminently presuming and ridiculous.

Doubtless one leading reason why the world declines honoring us whalemen, is this: they think that, at best, our vocation amounts to a butchering sort of business; and that when actively engaged therein, we are surrounded by all manner of defilements. Butchers we are, that is true. But butchers, also, and butchers of the bloodiest badge have been all Martial Commanders whom the world invariably delights to honor. And as for the matter of the alleged uncleanliness of our business, ye shall soon be initiated into certain facts hitherto pretty generally unknown, and which, upon the whole, will triumphantly plant the sperm whale-ship at least among the cleanliest things of this tidy earth. But even granting the charge in question to be true; what disordered slippery decks of a whale-ship are comparable to the unspeakable carrion of those battle-fields from which so many soldiers return to drink in all ladies' plaudits? And if the idea of peril so much enhances the popular conceit of the soldier's profession; let me assure ye that many a veteran who has freely marched up to a battery, would quickly recoil at the apparition of the sperm whale's vast tail, fanning into eddies the air over his head. For what are the comprehensible terrors of man compared with the interlinked terrors and wonders of God!

But, though the world scouts at° us whale hunters, yet does it unwittingly pay us the profoundest homage; yea, an all-abounding adoration! for almost all the

scouts at: scorns; derides.

tapers, lamps, and candles° that burn round the globe, burn, as before so many shrines, to our glory!

But look at this matter in other lights; weigh it in all sorts of scales; see what we whalemen are, and have been.

Why did the Dutch in De Witt's time[2] have admirals of their whaling fleets? Why did Louis XVI. of France, at his own personal expense, fit out whaling ships from Dunkirk,° and politely invite to that town some score or two of families from our own island of Nantucket? Why did Britain between the years 1750 and 1788 pay to her whalemen in bounties upwards of £1,000,000?[3] And lastly, how comes it that we whalemen of America now outnumber all the rest of the banded whalemen in the world; sail a navy of upwards of seven hundred vessels; manned by eighteen thousand men; yearly consuming 4,000,000 of dollars; the ships worth, at the time of sailing, $20,000,000; and every year importing into our harbors a well reaped harvest of $7,000,000. How comes all this, if there be not something puissant° in whaling?

But this is not the half; look again.

I freely assert,[4] that the cosmopolite philosopher[5] cannot, for his life, point out one single peaceful influence, which within the last sixty years has operated more potentially upon the whole broad world, taken in one aggregate, than the high and mighty business of whaling. One way and another, it has begotten events so remarkable in themselves, and so continuously momentous in their sequential issues, that whaling may well be regarded as that Egyptian mother, who bore offspring themselves pregnant from her womb.[6] It would be a hopeless, endless task to catalogue all these things. Let a handful suffice. For many years past the whale-ship has been the pioneer in ferreting out the remotest and least known parts of the earth. She has explored seas and archipelagoes which had no chart, where no Cook or Vancouver had ever sailed. If American and European men-of-war now peacefully ride in once savage harbors, let them fire salutes to the honor and the glory of the whale-ship, which originally showed them the way, and first interpreted between them and the savages. They may celebrate as they will the heroes of Exploring Expeditions, your Cooks, your Krusensterns; but I say that scores of anonymous Captains have sailed out of Nantucket, that were as great, and greater than your Cook and your Krusenstern.[7] For in their succorless empty-handedness, they, in the heathenish sharked waters, and by the beaches of unrecorded, javelin° islands, battled with virgin wonders and terrors that Cook with all his marines and muskets would not willingly have dared. All that is made such a flourish of in the old South Sea Voyages,° those things were but the life-time commonplaces of our heroic Nantucketers. Often, adventures which Vancouver dedicates three chapters to, these men accounted unworthy of being set down in the ship's common log. Ah, the world! Oh, the world!

Until the whale fishery rounded Cape Horn, no commerce but colonial, scarcely any intercourse but colonial, was carried on between Europe and the long line of the opulent Spanish provinces on the Pacific coast. It was the whaleman who

---

tapers, lamps, and candles: tapers were long, waxed, candlelighting wicks; lamps burned whale oil; the best candles were made of spermaceti. **Dunkirk**: French port on the Strait of Dover (North Sea). **puissant**: powerful. **javelin**: here, spear-filled. **South Sea Voyages**: that is, the written accounts of such voyages.

first broke through **the jealous policy of the Spanish crown**, touching those colonies; and, if space permitted, it might be distinctly shown how from those whale-men at last eventuated the liberation of Peru, Chili, and Bolivia from the yoke of Old Spain,[8] and the establishment of the eternal democracy in those parts.

That great America on the other side of the sphere, Australia, was given to the enlightened world by the whaleman. After its first blunder-born discovery by a Dutchman, all other ships long shunned those shores as pestiferously barbarous; but the whale-ship touched there. The whale-ship is the true mother of that now mighty colony. Moreover, in the infancy of the first Australian settlement, the emigrants were several times saved from starvation by the **benevolent biscuit** of the whale-ship luckily dropping an anchor in their waters. The uncounted isles of all Polynesia confess the same truth, and do commercial homage to the whale-ship, that cleared the way for the missionary and the merchant, and in many cases carried the **primitive** missionaries to their first destinations. If that double-bolted land, Japan, is ever to become hospitable, it is the whale-ship alone to whom the credit will be due; for already she is on the threshold.[9]

REVISION NARRATIVE

Beale and Melville's Beale

Thomas Beale's *Natural History of the Sperm Whale* was a major source of information for Melville, and on occasion he borrowed Beale's wording without acknowledgment—a common practice among writers at the time. This can be seen in Melville's phrase, "the jealous policy of the Spanish crown," which is lifted from Beale's phrase, "so meanly jealous was Spain of the interference of foreigners." Generally speaking, Melville would paraphrase the borrowed text, putting the passage so fully into his own words as to make it as much his own text as Beale's. In this regard, the appropriation of a source is a form of revision, and the unacknowledged borrowing may be taken as one author's version of another author. In the paragraph beginning "That great America," Melville lifts three closely positioned passages (quoted below) from Beale's discussion of whaling's advancement of Pacific imperialism. But Melville's version of Beale adds a subtle critique. (See 1 and 3 below.) For instance, Mellville's phrase "benevolent biscuit" seems a comic undercutting of the scenes of "starvation" found in passage 2. And his re-positioning of Beale's word "primitive" suggests a snubbing of the "missionaries."

1. But our whaling vessels, cruising for whales, examined their shores and brought home information respecting their value, and . . . they carried out people to reside upon them, and established a regular communication between them and our own country—by which the wants of the **primitive** settlers could be supplied. . . .

2. It is a fact, that the original settlers at Botany Bay were more than once saved from **starvation** by the timely arrival of some whaling vessels.

3. missionaries . . . have been preceded by the whaler, who has opened a barter with the savage, and brought about a friendly regard towards us, by which he has secured a ready welcome to the **missionaries**.

But if, in the face of all this, you still declare that whaling has no æsthetically noble associations connected with it, then am I ready to shiver° fifty lances with you there, and unhorse you with a split helmet every time.

The whale has no famous author, and whaling no famous chronicler, you will say.

The whale no famous author, and whaling no famous chronicler? Who wrote the first account of our Leviathan? Who but mighty Job!° And who composed the first narrative of a whaling-voyage? Who, but no less a prince than Alfred the Great, who, with his own royal pen, took down the words from Other, the Norwegian whale-hunter of those times![10] And who pronounced our glowing eulogy in Parliament? Who, but Edmund Burke![11]

True enough, but then whalemen themselves are poor devils; they have no good blood in their veins.

No good blood in their veins? They have something better than royal blood there. The grandmother of Benjamin Franklin was Mary Morrel;[12] afterwards, by marriage, Mary Folger, one of the old settlers of Nantucket, and the ancestress to a long line of Folgers and harpooneers—all kith and kin to noble Benjamin—this day darting the barbed iron from one side of the world to the other.

Good again; but then all confess that somehow whaling is not respectable.

Whaling not respectable? Whaling is imperial! By old English statutory law, the whale is declared "a royal fish."*[13]

Oh, that's only nominal! The whale himself has never figured in any grand imposing way.

The whale never figured in any grand imposing way? In one of the mighty triumphs given to a Roman general upon his entering the world's capital, the bones of a whale, brought all the way from the Syrian coast, were the most conspicuous object in the cymballed procession.*

Grant it, since you cite it; but, say what you will, there is no real dignity in whaling.

No dignity in whaling? The dignity of our calling the very heavens attest. Cetus° is a constellation in the South! No more! Drive down your hat in presence of the Czar, and take it off to Queequeg! No more! I know a man that, in his lifetime, has taken three hundred and fifty whales. I account that man more honorable than that great captain of antiquity who boasted of taking as many walled towns.[14]

And, as for me, if, by any possibility, there be any as yet undiscovered prime thing in me; if I shall ever deserve any real repute in that small but high hushed world which I might not be unreasonably ambitious of; if hereafter I shall do anything that, upon the whole, a man might rather have done than to have left undone; if, at my death, my executors, or more properly my creditors, find any precious MSS. in my desk, then here I prospectively ascribe all the honor and the glory to whaling; for a whale-ship was my Yale College and my Harvard.[15]

---

*See subsequent chapters for something more on this head.

---

shiver: break into bits (in a medieval joust). **mighty Job**: Job 41 describes "Leviathan" at length. **Cetus**: constellation visible in the Southern Hemisphere.

CHAPTER 25

POSTSCRIPT

IN behalf of the dignity of whaling, I would fain advance naught but substantiated facts. But after embattling his facts, an advocate who should wholly suppress a not unreasonable surmise, which might tell eloquently upon his cause—such an advocate, would he not be blame-worthy?

It is well known that at the coronation of kings and queens, even modern ones, a certain curious process of seasoning them for their functions is gone through. There is a saltcellar of state,° so called, and there may be a caster of state. How they use the salt, precisely—who knows? Certain I am, however, that a king's head is solemnly oiled at his coronation, even as a head of salad. Can it be, though, that they anoint it with a view of making its interior run well, as they anoint machinery? Much might be ruminated here, concerning the

---

saltcellar of state: container for table salt at state banquets.

REVISION NARRATIVE

Addressing Britain

If *Moby-Dick* is to work as a narrative, readers must sympathize with its working-class characters and understand, even admire, the particular world of work in which they live. In the preceding chapter, Ishmael adopts the role of an "advocate" (lawyer) arguing, as if in court, for the nobility and dignity of whalers and whaling. In his "Postscript," Melville extends the argument, with British readers in mind. (Melville may have added this four-paragraph chapter as an afterthought late in the composition process.) But Ishmael's flippancies—in one instance, he compares the royal head of state to a "head of salad"—doomed the little chapter, for it was cut entirely from the British edition.

essential dignity of this regal process, because in common life we esteem but meanly and contemptibly a fellow who anoints his hair, and palpably smells of that anointing. In truth, a mature man who uses hair-oil, unless medicinally, that man has probably got a quoggy° spot in him somewhere. As a general rule, he can't amount to much in his totality.

But the only thing to be considered here, is this—what kind of oil is used at coronations? Certainly it cannot be olive oil, nor macassar oil, nor castor oil, nor bear's oil, nor train oil, nor cod-liver oil.1 What then can it possibly be, but sperm oil in its unmanufactured, unpolluted state, the sweetest of all oils?

Think of that, ye loyal Britons! we whalemen supply your kings and queens with coronation stuff!

quoggy: boggy, swampy.

CHAPTER 26

KNIGHTS AND SQUIRES

THE chief mate of the Pequod was Starbuck,° a native of Nantucket, and a Quaker by descent. He was a long, earnest man, and though born on an icy coast, seemed well adapted to endure hot latitudes, his flesh being hard as twice-baked biscuit. Transported to the Indies,° his live blood would not spoil like bottled ale. He must have been born in some time of general drought and famine, or upon one of those fast days for which his state is famous. Only some thirty arid summers had he seen; those summers had dried up all his physical superfluousness. But this, his thinness, so to speak, seemed no more the token of wasting anxieties and cares, than it seemed the indication of any bodily blight. It was merely the condensation of the man. He was by no means ill-looking; quite the contrary. His pure tight skin was an excellent fit; and closely wrapped up in it, and embalmed with inner health and strength, like a revivified Egyptian, this Starbuck seemed prepared to endure for long ages to come, and to endure always, as now; for be it Polar snow or torrid sun, like a patent chronometer,° his interior vitality was warranted to do well in all climates. Looking into his eyes, you seemed to see there the yet lingering images of those thousand-fold perils he had calmly confronted through life. A staid, steadfast man, whose life for the most part was a telling pantomime of action, and not a tame chapter of **sounds**. Yet, for all his hardy sobriety and fortitude, there were certain qualities in him which at times affected, and in some cases seemed well nigh to overbalance all the rest. Uncommonly conscientious for a seaman, and endued with a deep natural reverence, the wild watery loneliness of his life did therefore strongly incline him to superstition; but to that sort of superstition, which in some organizations° seems rather to spring, somehow, from intelligence than from ignorance. Outward portents and inward presentiments were his. And if at times these things bent the welded iron of his soul, much more did his far-away domestic memories of his young Cape° wife and child, tend to bend him still more from the original ruggedness of his nature, and open him still further to those latent influences which,

Starbuck: common Nantucket Quaker name. **the Indies**: India. **patent chronometer**: exceptionally precise timepiece used in navigation; a major metaphor in *Pierre*. **organizations**: personalities. **Cape**: Cape Cod.

in some honest-hearted men, restrain the gush of dare-devil daring, so often evinced by others in the more perilous vicissitudes of the fishery. "I will have no man in my boat," said Starbuck, "who is not afraid of a whale." By this, he seemed to mean, not only that the most reliable and useful courage was that which arises from the fair estimation of the encountered peril, but that an utterly fearless man is a far more dangerous comrade than a coward.

"Aye, aye," said Stubb, the second mate, "Starbuck, there, is as careful a man as you'll find anywhere in this fishery." But we shall ere long see what that word "careful" precisely means when used by a man like Stubb, or almost any other whale hunter.

Starbuck was no crusader after perils; in him courage was not a sentiment; but a thing simply useful to him, and always at hand upon all **mortally** practical occasions. Besides, he thought, perhaps, that in this business of whaling, courage was one of the great staple outfits of the ship, like her beef and her bread, and not to be foolishly wasted. Wherefore he had no fancy for lowering for whales after sun down; nor for persisting in fighting a fish that too much persisted in fighting him. For, thought Starbuck, I am here in this critical° ocean to kill whales for my living, and not to be killed by them for theirs; and that hundreds of men had been so killed Starbuck well knew. What doom was his own father's? Where, in the bottomless deeps, could he find the torn limbs of his brother?

With memories like these in him, and, moreover, given to a certain superstitiousness, as has been said; the courage of this Starbuck which could, nevertheless, still flourish, must indeed have been extreme. But it was not in reasonable nature that a man so organized, and with such terrible experiences and remembrances as he had; it was not in nature that these things should fail in latently engendering an element in him, which, under suitable circumstances, would break out from its confinement, and burn all his courage up. And brave as he might be, it was that sort of **bravery chiefly, visible** in some intrepid men, which, while generally abiding firm in the conflict with seas, or winds, or whales, or any of the ordinary irrational horrors of the world, yet cannot withstand those more terrific, because more spiritual terrors, which sometimes menace you from the concentrating brow of an enraged and mighty man.

But were the coming narrative to reveal, in any instance, the complete abasement of poor Starbuck's fortitude, scarce might I have the heart to write it; for it is a thing most sorrowful, nay shocking, to expose the fall of valor in the soul. Men may seem detestable as joint stock-companies and nations; knaves, fools, and murderers there may be; men may have mean and meagre faces; but man, in the ideal, is so noble and so sparkling, such a grand and glowing creature, that over any ignominious blemish in him all his fellows should run to throw their costliest robes. That immaculate manliness we feel within ourselves, so far within us, that it remains intact though all the outer character seem gone; bleeds with keenest anguish at the undraped spectacle of a valor-ruined man. Nor can piety itself, at such a shameful sight, completely stifle her upbraidings against the permitting stars. But this august dignity I treat of, is not the dignity of kings and robes, but that abounding dignity which has no robed investiture. Thou shalt see it shining in the arm that wields a pick

critical: dangerous, risky.

or drives a spike; that democratic dignity which, on all hands, radiates without end from God; Himself! **The great God absolute! The centre and circumference of all democracy! His omnipresence, our divine equality!**

If, then, to meanest mariners, and renegades and castaways, I shall hereafter ascribe high qualities, though dark; weave round them tragic graces; if even the most mournful, perchance the most abased, among them all, shall at times lift himself to the exalted mounts; if I shall touch that workman's arm with some ethereal light; if I shall spread a rainbow over his disastrous set of sun; then against all mortal critics bear me out in it, thou just Spirit of Equality, which hast spread one royal mantle° of humanity over all my kind! Bear me out in it, thou great **democratic** God! who didst not refuse to the swart convict, Bunyan, the pale, poetic pearl; Thou who didst clothe with doubly hammered leaves of finest gold, the stumped and paupered arm of old Cervantes; Thou who didst pick up Andrew Jackson from the pebbles; who didst hurl him upon a war-horse; who didst thunder him higher than a throne! Thou who, in all Thy mighty, earthly marchings,[1] ever cullest Thy selectest champions from the kingly commons; bear me out in it, O God!

mantle: cloak.

REVISION NARRATIVE

God and Democracy

On the heels of describing Starbuck's courage, but also the possible limits of that courage, Ishmael argues that our admiration for such individuals stems from our recognition of an "immaculate manliness" within humankind that underpins each and all individuals' strengths and weaknesses. However, where he pushes the argument to encompass kings, democracy, and God, British editors began to cut. Although the phrase "democratic dignity" remains in the British version, the three sentences concluding that paragraph and linking human equality to divine order were expurgated in deference to the monarchy. In the next paragraph, the word "democratic" is also removed, reducing "thou great democratic God" to "thou great God!"

CHAPTER 27

KNIGHTS AND SQUIRES

STUBB was the second mate. He was a native of Cape Cod; and hence, according to local usage, was called a Cape-Cod-man. A happy-go-lucky; neither craven nor valiant; taking perils as they came with an indifferent air; and while engaged in the most imminent crisis of the chase, toiling away, calm and collected as a journeyman joiner° engaged for the year. Good-humored, easy, and careless, he presided over his whale-boat as if the most deadly encounter were but a dinner, and his crew all invited guests. He was as particular about the comfortable arrangement of his part of the boat, as an old stage-driver is about the snugness of his box. When close to the whale, in the very death-lock of the fight, he handled his unpitying lance coolly and off-handedly, as a whistling tinker° his hammer. He would hum over his old rigadig° tunes while flank and flank with the most exasperated monster. Long usage had, for this Stubb, converted the jaws of death into an easy chair. What he thought of death itself, there is no telling. Whether he ever thought of it at all, might be a question; but, if he ever did chance to cast his mind that way after a comfortable dinner, no doubt, like a good sailor, he took it to be a sort of call of the watch° to tumble aloft, and bestir themselves there, about something which he would find out when he obeyed the order, and not sooner.

What, perhaps, with other things, made Stubb such an easy-going, unfearing man, so cheerily trudging off with the burden of life in a world full of grave peddlers, all bowed to the ground with their packs; what helped to bring about that almost impious good-humor of his; that thing must have been his pipe. For, like his nose, his short, black little pipe was one of the regular features of his face. You would almost as soon have expected him to turn out of his bunk without his nose as without his pipe. He kept a whole row of pipes there ready loaded, stuck in a rack, within easy reach of his hand; and, whenever he turned in, he smoked them all out in succession, lighting one from the other to the end of the chapter; then loading them again to be in readiness anew. For, when Stubb dressed, instead of first putting his legs into his trowsers, he put his pipe into his mouth.

journeyman joiner: carpenter working for wages, not self-employed. **tinker**: traveling mender of pots and pans. **rigadig**: word imitating the tune's lyrics. **watch**: those men on duty at the time.

I say this continual smoking must have been one cause, at least, of his peculiar disposition; for every one knows that this earthly air, whether ashore or afloat, is terribly infected with the nameless miseries of the numberless mortals who have died exhaling it; and as in time of the cholera, some people go about with a camphorated handkerchief to their mouths; so, likewise, against all mortal tribulations, Stubb's tobacco smoke might have operated as a sort of disinfecting agent.

The third mate was Flask, a native of Tisbury, in Martha's Vineyard. A short, stout, ruddy young fellow, very pugnacious concerning whales, who somehow seemed to think that the great Leviathans had personally and hereditarily affronted him; and therefore it was a sort of point of honor with him, to destroy them whenever encountered. So utterly lost was he to all sense of reverence for the many marvels of their majestic bulk and mystic ways; and so dead to anything like an apprehension of any possible danger from encountering them; that in his poor opinion, the wondrous whale was but a species of magnified mouse, or at least water-rat, requiring only a little circumvention and some small application of time and trouble in order to kill and boil. This ignorant, unconscious fearlessness of his made him a little waggish in the matter of whales; he followed these fish for the fun of it; and a three years' voyage round Cape Horn was only a jolly joke that lasted that length of time. As a carpenter's nails are divided into wrought nails and cut nails;° so mankind may be similarly divided. Little Flask was one of the wrought ones; made to clinch tight and last long. They called him King-Post on board of the Pequod; because, in form, he could be well likened to the short, square timber known by that name in Arctic whalers; and which by the means of many radiating side timbers inserted into it, serves to brace the ship against the icy concussions of those battering seas.

Now these three mates—Starbuck, Stubb, and Flask, were momentous men. They it was who by universal **prescription** commanded three of the Pequod's boats as headsmen. In that grand order of battle in which Captain Ahab would **probably** marshal his forces to descend on the whales, these three headsmen were as captains of companies. Or, being armed with their long keen whaling spears, they were as a picked trio of lancers; even as the harpooneers were flingers of javelins.

And since in this famous fishery, each mate or headsman, like a Gothic° Knight of old, is always accompanied by his boat-steerer or harpooneer, who in certain conjunctures provides him with a fresh lance, when the former one has been badly twisted, or elbowed in the assault; and moreover, as there generally subsists between the two, a close intimacy and friendliness; it is therefore but meet,° that in this place we set down who the Pequod's harpooneers were, and to what headsman each of them belonged.

First of all was Queequeg, whom Starbuck, the chief mate, had selected for his squire.° But Queequeg is already known.

Next was Tashtego, an unmixed Indian from Gay Head, the most westerly promontory of Martha's Vineyard, where there still exists the last remnant of a village

---

wrought nails and cut nails: the first are forged by a blacksmith; a machine chops iron wire into cheaper *cut nails*. **Gothic**: medieval. ***but meet***: (archaic) only proper. ***squire***: knight's attendant.

of red men, which has long supplied the neighboring island of Nantucket with many of her most daring harpooneers. In the fishery, they usually go by the generic name of Gay-Headers. Tashtego's long, lean, sable° hair, his high cheek bones, and black rounding eyes—for an Indian, Oriental in their largeness, but Antarctic in their glittering expression—all this sufficiently proclaimed him an inheritor of the unvitiated blood of those proud warrior hunters, who, in quest of the great New England moose, had scoured, bow in hand, the aboriginal forests of the main.° But no longer snuffing in the trail of the wild beasts of the woodland, Tashtego now hunted in the wake of the great whales of the sea; the unerring harpoon of the son fitly replacing the infallible arrow of the sires. To look at the tawny brawn of his lithe snaky limbs, you would almost have credited the superstitions of some of the earlier Puritans, and half believed this wild Indian to be a son of the Prince of the Powers of the Air.° Tashtego was Stubb the second mate's squire.

Third among the harpooneers was Daggoo, a gigantic, coal-black negro-savage, with a lion-like tread—an Ahasuerus° to behold. Suspended from his ears were two golden hoops, so large that the sailors called them ring-bolts,° and would talk of securing the top-sail halyards° to them. In his youth Daggoo had voluntarily shipped on board of a whaler, lying in a lonely bay on his native coast. And never having been anywhere in the world but in Africa, Nantucket, and the pagan harbors most frequented by whalemen; and having now led for many years the bold life of the fishery in the ships of owners uncommonly heedful of what manner of men they shipped; Daggoo retained all his barbaric virtues, and erect as a giraffe, moved about the decks in all the pomp of six feet five in his socks. There was a corporeal humility in looking up at him; and a white man standing before him seemed a white flag come to beg truce of a fortress. Curious to tell, this imperial negro, Ahasuerus Daggoo, was the Squire of little Flask, who looked like a chess-man beside him. As for the residue of the Pequod's company, be it said, that at the present day not one in two of the many thousand men before the mast employed in the American whale fishery, are Americans born, though pretty nearly all the officers are. Herein it is the same with the American whale fishery as with the American army and military and merchant navies, and the engineering forces employed in the construction of the American Canals and Railroads. The same, I say, because in all these cases the native American liberally provides the brains, the rest of the world as generously supplying the muscles. No small number of these whaling seamen belong to the Azores,° where the outward bound Nantucket whalers frequently touch to augment their crews from the hardy peasants of those rocky shores. In like manner, the Greenland whalers sailing out of Hull or London, put in at the Shetland Islands,[1] to receive the full complement of their crew. Upon the passage homewards, they drop them there again. How it is, there is no telling, but Islanders seem to make the best whalemen. They were nearly all Islanders in the Pequod, *Isolatoes*° too, I call such,

---

sable: heraldic term for black. *main*: mainland. **Prince of the Powers of the Air**: Satan (see Ephesians 2.2), thought by some American Puritans to possess Native Americans. **Ahasuerus**: mighty king of Persia in the book of Esther. **ring-bolts**: large iron rings bolted through the deck. **halyards**: ropes for raising and lowering sails. **Azores**: Portuguese islands 700 miles west of the mainland. **Isolatoes**: Melville's word.

not acknowledging the common continent of men, but each *Isolato* living on a separate continent of his own. Yet now, federated along one keel, what a set these Isolatoes were! An Anacharsis Clootz deputation from all the isles of the sea,[2] and all the ends of the earth, accompanying Old Ahab in the Pequod to lay the world's grievances before that bar° from which not very many of them ever come back. Black Little Pip°—he never did—**oh, no! he went before.** Poor Alabama boy! On the grim Pequod's forecastle, ye shall ere long see him, beating his tambourine; prelusive of the eternal time, when sent for, to the great quarter-deck on high, he was bid strike in° with angels, and beat his tambourine in glory; called a coward here, hailed a hero there!

that bar: God's courtroom. ***Pip***: the cabin boy, not seen until Ch. 40. ***strike in***: join in.

CHAPTER 28

AHAB

For several days after leaving Nantucket, nothing above hatches was seen of Captain Ahab. The mates regularly relieved each other at the watches, and for aught that could be seen to the contrary, they seemed to be the only commanders of the ship; only they sometimes issued from the cabin with orders so sudden and peremptory, that after all it was plain they but commanded vicariously. Yes, their supreme lord and dictator was there, though hitherto unseen by any eyes not permitted to penetrate into the now sacred retreat of the cabin.

Every time I ascended to the deck from my watches below, I instantly gazed aft to mark if any strange face were visible; for my first vague disquietude touching the unknown captain, now in the seclusion of the sea, became almost a perturbation. This was strangely heightened at times by the ragged Elijah's diabolical incoherences uninvitedly recurring to me, with a subtle energy I could not have before conceived of. But poorly could I withstand them, much as in other moods I was almost ready to smile at the solemn whimsicalities of that outlandish prophet of the wharves. But whatever it was of apprehensiveness or uneasiness—to call it so—which I felt, yet whenever I came to look about me in the ship, it seemed against all warranty° to cherish such emotions. For though the harpooneers, with the great body of the crew, were a far more barbaric, heathenish, and motley set than any of the tame merchant-ship companies which my previous experiences had made me acquainted with, still I ascribed this—and rightly ascribed it—to the fierce uniqueness of the very nature of that wild Scandinavian° vocation in which I had so abandonedly embarked. But it was especially the aspect of the three chief officers of the ship, the mates, which was most forcibly calculated to allay these colorless misgivings, and induce confidence and cheerfulness in every presentment° of the voyage. Three better, more likely sea-officers and men, each in his own different way, could not readily be found, and they were every one of them Americans; a Nantucketer, a Vineyarder, a Cape man. Now, it being Christmas when the ship shot from out her harbor, for a space we had biting Polar weather, though all the time running away from it to the southward; and by

against all warranty: without justification. *Scandinavian*: here implying Viking-like, dangerous. *presentment*: appearance.

every degree and minute of latitude which we sailed, gradually leaving that merciless winter, and all its intolerable weather behind us. It was one of those less lowering,° but still grey and gloomy enough mornings of the transition, when with a fair wind the ship was rushing through the water with a vindictive sort of leaping and melancholy rapidity, that as I mounted to the deck at the call of the forenoon watch, so soon as I levelled my glance towards the taffrail,° foreboding shivers ran over me. Reality outran apprehension; Captain Ahab stood upon his quarter-deck.

There seemed no sign of common bodily illness about him, nor of the recovery from any. He looked like a man cut away from the stake, when the fire has overrunningly wasted all the limbs without consuming them, or taking away one particle from their compacted aged robustness. His whole high, broad form, seemed made of solid bronze, and shaped in an unalterable mould, like Cellini's cast Perseus.[1] Threading its way out from among his grey hairs, and continuing right down one side of his tawny scorched face and neck, till it disappeared in his clothing, you saw a slender rod-like mark, lividly whitish. It resembled that perpendicular seam sometimes made in the straight, lofty trunk of a great tree, when the upper lightning tearingly darts down it, and without wrenching a single twig, peels and grooves out the bark from top to bottom, ere running off into the soil, leaving the tree still greenly alive, but branded. Whether that mark was born with him, or whether it was the scar left by some desperate wound, no one could certainly say. By some tacit consent, throughout the voyage little or no allusion was made to it, especially by the mates. But once Tashtego's senior, an old Gay-Head Indian among the crew, superstitiously asserted that not till he was full forty years old did Ahab become that way branded, and then it came upon him, not in the fury of any mortal fray, but in an elemental strife at sea. Yet, this wild hint seemed inferentially negatived, by what a grey Manxman° insinuated, an old sepulchral man, who, having never before sailed out of Nantucket, had never ere this laid eye upon wild Ahab. Nevertheless, the old sea-traditions, the immemorial credulities, popularly invested this old Manxman with preternatural powers of discernment. So that no white sailor seriously contradicted him when he said that if ever Captain Ahab should be tranquilly laid out—which might hardly come to pass, so he muttered—then, whoever should do that last office for the dead, would find a birth-mark on him from crown to sole.

So powerfully did the whole grim aspect of Ahab affect me, and the livid brand which streaked it, that for the first few moments I hardly noted that not a little of this overbearing grimness was owing to the barbaric white leg upon which he partly stood. It had previously come to me that this ivory leg had at sea been fashioned from the polished bone of the sperm whale's jaw. "Aye, he was dismasted off Japan," said the old Gay-Head Indian once; "but like his dismasted craft, he shipped another mast without coming home for it. He has a quiver of 'em."

I was struck with the singular posture he maintained. Upon each side of the Pequod's quarter deck, and pretty close to the mizen shrouds,° there was an auger

---

lowering: dark; threatening. *taffrail*: curved deck-railing at the ship's stern. **Manxman**: from the Isle of Man, in the Irish Sea; in sailor superstition, Manxmen have supernatural powers. **mizen shrouds**: fixed rigging supporting the rearmost mast.

hole, bored about half an inch or so, into the plank. His bone leg steadied in that hole; one arm elevated, and holding by a shroud; Captain Ahab stood erect, looking straight out beyond the ship's ever-pitching prow. There was an infinity of firmest fortitude, a determinate, unsurrenderable wilfulness, in the fixed and fearless, forward dedication of that glance. Not a word he spoke; nor did his officers say aught to him; though by all their minutest gestures and expressions, they plainly showed the uneasy, if not painful, consciousness of being under a troubled master-eye. And not only that, but moody stricken Ahab stood before them with a **crucifixion** in his face; in all the nameless regal overbearing dignity of some mighty woe.

Ere long, from his first visit in the air, he withdrew into his cabin. But after that morning, he was every day visible to the crew; either standing in his pivot-hole, or seated upon an ivory stool he had; or heavily walking the deck. As the sky grew less gloomy; indeed, began to grow a little genial, he became still less and less a recluse; as if, when the ship had sailed from home, nothing but the dead wintry bleakness of the sea had then kept him so secluded. And, by and by, it came to pass, that he was almost continually in the air; but, as yet, for all that he said, or perceptibly did, on the at last sunny deck, he seemed as unnecessary there as another mast. But the Pequod was only making a passage now; not regularly cruising; nearly all whaling preparatives needing supervision the mates were fully competent to, so that there was little or nothing, out of himself, to employ or excite Ahab, now; and thus chase away, for that one interval, the clouds that layer upon layer were piled upon his brow, as ever all clouds choose the loftiest peaks to pile themselves upon.

Nevertheless, ere long, the warm, warbling persuasiveness of the pleasant, holiday weather we came to, seemed gradually to charm him from his mood. For, as when the red-cheeked, dancing girls, April and May, trip home to the wintry, misanthropic woods; even the barest, ruggedest, most thunder-cloven old oak will at least send forth some few green sprouts, to welcome such glad-hearted visitants; so Ahab did, in the end, a little respond to the playful allurings of that girlish air. More than once did he put forth the faint blossom of a look, which, in any other man, would have soon flowered out in a smile.

CHAPTER 29

ENTER AHAB; TO HIM, STUBB[1]

S OME days elapsed, and ice and icebergs all astern, the Pequod now went rolling through the bright Quito° spring, which, at sea, almost perpetually reigns on the threshold of the eternal August of the Tropic. The warmly cool, clear, ringing, perfumed, overflowing, redundant days, were as crystal goblets of Persian sherbet, heaped up—flaked up, with rose-water snow. The starred and stately nights seemed haughty dames in jewelled velvets, nursing at home in lonely pride, the memory of their absent conquering Earls, the golden helmeted suns! For sleeping man, 'twas hard to choose between such winsome days and such seducing nights. But all the witcheries of that unwaning weather did not merely lend new spells and potencies to the outward world. Inward they turned upon the soul, especially when the still mild hours of eve came on; then, memory shot her crystals as the clear ice most forms of noiseless twilights. And all these subtle agencies, more and more they wrought on Ahab's texture.

Old age is always wakeful; as if, the longer linked with life, the less man has to do with aught that looks like death. Among sea-commanders, the old greybeards will oftenest leave their berths to visit the night-cloaked deck. It was so with Ahab; only that now, of late, he seemed so much to live in the open air, that truly speaking, his visits were more to the cabin, than from the cabin to the planks. "It feels like going down into one's tomb,"—he would mutter to himself,—"for an old captain like me to be descending this narrow scuttle, to go to my grave-dug berth."

So, almost every twenty-four hours, when the watches of the night were set, and the band on deck sentinelled° the slumbers of the band below; and when if a rope was to be hauled upon the forecastle, the sailors flung it not rudely down, as by day, but with some cautiousness dropt it to its place, for fear of disturbing their slumbering shipmates; when this sort of steady quietude would begin to prevail, habitually, the silent steersman would watch the cabin-scuttle; and ere long the old man would emerge, griping at° the iron banister, to help his crippled way. Some considerating touch of humanity was in him; for at times like these, he usually abstained

---

Quito: capital of Ecuador, near the equator but high in the Andes, with a year-round temperate climate. **sentinelled**: guarded. **griping at**: grasping.

from patrolling the quarter-deck; because to his wearied mates, seeking repose within six inches of his ivory heel, such would have been the reverberating crack and din of that bony step, that their dreams would have been of the crunching teeth of sharks. But once, the mood was on him too deep for common regardings; and as with heavy, lumber-like° pace he was measuring the ship from taffrail to mainmast, Stubb, the odd second mate, came up from below, and with a certain unassured, deprecating humorousness, hinted that if Captain Ahab was pleased to walk the planks, then, no one could say nay; but there might be some way of muffling the noise; hinting something indistinctly and hesitatingly about a globe of tow,° and the insertion into it, of the ivory heel. Ah! Stubb, thou did'st not know Ahab then.

"Am I a cannon-ball, Stubb," said Ahab, "that thou wouldst wad me that fashion? But go thy ways; I had forgot. Below to thy nightly grave; where such as ye sleep between shrouds, to use ye to the filling one at last.°—Down, dog, and kennel!"[2]

Starting at the unforeseen concluding exclamation of the so suddenly scornful old man, Stubb was speechless a moment; then said excitedly, "I am not used to be spoken to that way, sir; I do but less than half like it, sir."

"Avast!" gritted Ahab between his set teeth, and violently moving away, as if to avoid some passionate temptation.

"No, sir; not yet," said Stubb, emboldened, "I will not tamely be called a dog, sir."

"Then be called ten times a donkey, and a mule, and an ass, and begone, or I'll clear the world of thee!"

As he said this, Ahab advanced upon him with such overbearing terrors in his aspect, that Stubb involuntarily retreated.

"I was never served so before without giving a hard blow for it," muttered Stubb, as he found himself descending the cabin-scuttle. "It's very queer. Stop, Stubb; somehow, now, I don't well know whether to go back and strike him, or—what's that?—down here on my knees and pray for him? Yes, that was the thought coming up in me; but it would be the first time I ever *did* pray. It's queer; very queer; and he's queer too; aye, take him fore and aft, he's about the queerest old man Stubb ever sailed with. How he flashed at me!—his eyes like powder-pans!° is he mad? Anyway there's something on his mind, as sure as there must be something on a deck when it cracks. He aint in his bed now, either, more than three hours out of the twenty-four; and he don't sleep then. Didn't that Dough-Boy,° the steward, tell me that of a morning he always finds the old man's hammock clothes all rumpled and tumbled, and the sheets down at the foot, and the coverlid almost tied into knots, and the pillow a sort of frightful hot, as though a baked brick had been on it? A hot old man! I guess he's got what some folks ashore call a conscience; it's a kind of Tic-Dolly-row° they say—worse nor a toothache. Well, well; I don't know what it is, but the Lord keep me from catching it. He's full of riddles; I wonder what he goes into the after hold for, every night, as Dough-Boy tells me he suspects; what's that

---

lumber-like: heavily lurching. **globe of tow**: wad of flax or hemp fiber. **use ye to the filling one at last**: "accustom you to your eventual grave." **powder-pans**: like powder in the priming-pan of a musket. **Dough-Boy**: his name means boiled dumpling. **Tic-Dolly-row**: from French, *tic douloureux*, painful facial twitching.

for, I should like to know? Who's made appointments with him in the hold? Ain't that queer, now? But there's no telling, it's the old game—Here goes for a snooze. Damn me, it's worth a fellow's while to be born into the world, if only to fall right asleep. And now that I think of it, that's about the first thing babies do, and that's a sort of queer, too. Damn me, but all things are queer, come to think of 'em. But that's against my principles. Think not, is my eleventh commandment; and sleep when you can, is my twelfth—So here goes again. But how's that? didn't he call me a dog? blazes! he called me ten times a donkey, and piled a lot of jackasses on top of *that!* He might as well have kicked me, and done with it. Maybe he *did* kick me, and I didn't observe it, I was so taken all aback with his brow, somehow. It flashed like a bleached bone. What the devil's the matter with me? I don't stand right on my legs. Coming afoul of° that old man has a sort of turned me wrong side out. By the Lord, I must have been dreaming, though—How? how? how?—but the only way's to stash it; so here goes to hammock again; and in the morning, I'll see how this plaguey juggling thinks over by daylight."

coming afoul of: coming dangerously in contact, or getting tangled with.

CHAPTER 30

THE PIPE

WHEN Stubb had departed, Ahab stood for a while leaning over the bulwarks; and then, as had been usual with him of late, calling a sailor of the watch, he sent him below for his ivory stool, and also his pipe. Lighting the pipe at the binnacle lamp and planting the stool on the weather side of the deck, he sat and smoked.

In old Norse times, the thrones of the sea-loving Danish kings were fabricated, saith tradition, of the tusks of the narwhale. How could one look at Ahab then, seated on that tripod of bones, without bethinking him of the royalty it symbolized? For a Khan° of the plank, and a king of the sea, and a great lord of Leviathans was Ahab.

Some moments passed, during which the thick vapor came from his mouth in quick and constant puffs, which blew back again into his face. "How now," he soliloquized at last, withdrawing the tube, "this smoking no longer soothes. Oh, my pipe! hard must it go with me if thy charm be gone! Here have I been unconsciously toiling, not pleasuring,—aye, and ignorantly smoking to windward all the while; to windward, and with such nervous whiffs, as if, like the dying whale, my final jets were the strongest and fullest of trouble. What business have I with this pipe? This thing that is meant for sereneness, to send up mild white vapors among mild white hairs, not among torn iron grey locks like mine. I'll smoke no more—"

He tossed the still lighted pipe into the sea. The fire hissed in the waves; the same instant the ship shot by the bubble the sinking pipe made. With slouched hat, Ahab lurchingly paced the planks.

Khan: Tartar king, an absolute ruler.

CHAPTER 31

QUEEN MAB°

Next morning Stubb accosted Flask.

"Such a queer dream, King-Post, I never had. You know the old man's ivory leg, well I dreamed he kicked me with it; and when I tried to kick back, upon my soul, my little man, I kicked my leg right off! And then, presto! Ahab seemed a pyramid, and I, like a blazing fool, kept kicking at it. But what was still more curious, Flask—you know how curious all dreams are—through all this rage that I was in, I somehow seemed to be thinking to myself, that after all, it was not much of an insult, that kick from Ahab. 'Why,' thinks I, 'what's the row? It's not a real leg, only a false leg.' And there's a mighty difference between a living thump and a dead thump. That's what makes a blow from the hand, Flask, fifty times more savage to bear than a blow from a cane. The living member—that makes the living insult, my little man. And thinks I to myself all the while, mind, while I was stubbing my silly toes against that cursed pyramid—so confoundedly contradictory was it all, all the while, I say, I was thinking to myself, 'what's his leg now, but a cane—a whalebone cane. Yes,' thinks I, 'it was only a playful cudgelling—in fact, only a whaleboning that he gave me—not a base kick. Besides,' thinks I, 'look at it once; why, the end of it—the foot part—what a small sort of end it is; whereas, if a broad footed farmer kicked me, *there's* a devilish broad insult. But this insult is whittled down to a point only.' But now comes the greatest joke of the dream, Flask. While I was battering away at the pyramid, a sort of badger-haired old merman,[1] with a hump on his back, takes me by the shoulders, and slews me round. 'What are you 'bout?' says he. Slid! man, but I was frightened. Such a phiz!° But, somehow, next moment I was over the fright. 'What am I about?' says I at last. 'And what business is that of yours, I should like to know, Mr. Humpback? Do *you* want a kick?' By the lord, Flask, I had no sooner said that, than he turned round his stern to me, bent over, and dragging up a lot of seaweed he had for a clout°—what do you think, I saw?—why thunder alive, man, his stern was stuck full of marlinspikes, with the points out. Says I, on second thoughts,

Queen Mab: in *Romeo and Juliet* I.4, the fairy midwife who brings dreams. ***slews me . . . Slid! . . . phiz***: turns me; *Slid* is short for God's [eye]lid, an archaic oath; *phiz* is short for physiognomy, face. ***clout***: loincloth.

131

'I guess I won't kick you, old fellow.' 'Wise Stubb,' said he, 'wise Stubb;' and kept muttering it all the time, a sort of eating of his own gums like a chimney hag.° Seeing he wasn't going to stop saying over his 'wise Stubb, wise Stubb,' I thought I might as well fall to kicking the pyramid again. But I had only just lifted my foot for it, when he roared out, 'Stop that kicking!' 'Halloa,' says I, 'what's the matter now, old fellow?' 'Look ye here,' says he; 'let's argue the insult. Captain Ahab kicked ye, didn't he?' 'Yes, he did,' says I—'right *here* it was.' 'Very good,' says he—'he used his ivory leg, didn't he?' 'Yes, he did,' says I. 'Well then,' says he, 'wise Stubb, what have you to complain of? Didn't he kick with right good will? it wasn't a common pitch pine leg he kicked with, was it? No, you were kicked by a great man, and with a beautiful ivory leg, Stubb. It's an honor; I consider it an honor. Listen, wise Stubb. In old England the greatest lords think it great glory to be slapped by a queen, and made garter-knights² of; but, be *your* boast, Stubb, that ye were kicked by old Ahab, and made a wise man of. Remember what I say; *be* kicked by him; account his kicks honors; and on no account kick back; for you can't help yourself, wise Stubb. Don't you see that pyramid?' With that, he all of a sudden seemed somehow, in some queer fashion, to swim off into the air. I snored; rolled over; and there I was in my hammock! Now, what do you think of that dream, Flask?"

"I don't know; it seems a sort of foolish to me, tho'."

"May be; may be. But it's made a wise man of me, Flask. D'ye see Ahab standing there, sideways looking over the stern? Well, the best thing you can do, Flask, is to let that old man alone; never speak **quick** to him,° whatever he says. Halloa! what's that he shouts? Hark!"

"Mast-head, there! Look sharp, all of ye! There are whales hereabouts! If ye see a white one, split your lungs for him!"

"What d'ye think of that now, Flask? ain't there a small drop of something queer about that, eh? A white whale—did ye mark that, man? Look ye—there's something special in the wind. Stand by for it, Flask. Ahab has that that's bloody on his mind. But, mum; he comes this way."

---

chimney hag: old woman, keeping warm by the fire. ***speak quick***: talk back; defy.

CHAPTER 32

CETOLOGY

Aᴌʀᴇᴀᴅʏ we are boldly launched upon the deep; but soon we shall be lost in its unshored, harborless immensities. Ere that come to pass; ere the Pequod's weedy hull rolls side by side with the barnacled hulls° of the leviathan; at the outset it is but well to attend to a matter almost indispensable to a thorough appreciative understanding of the more special leviathanic revelations and allusions of all sorts which are to follow.[1]

It is some systematized exhibition of the whale in his broad genera, that I would now fain put before you. Yet is it no easy task. The classification of the constituents of a chaos, nothing less is here essayed.[2] Listen to what the best and latest authorities have laid down.

"No branch of Zoology is so much involved as that which is entitled Cetology," says Captain Scoresby, A. D. 1820.[3]

"It is not my intention, were it in my power, to enter into the inquiry as to the true method of dividing the cetacea into groups and families. * * * Utter confusion exists among the historians of this animal" (sperm whale), says Surgeon Beale, A. D. 1839.

"Unfitness to pursue our research in the unfathomable waters." "Impenetrable veil covering our knowledge of the cetacea." "A field strewn with thorns." "All these incomplete indications but serve to torture us naturalists."

Thus speak of the whale, the great Cuvier, and John Hunter, and Lesson,[4] those lights of zoology and anatomy. Nevertheless, though of real knowledge there be little, yet of books there are a plenty; and so in some small degree, with cetology, or the science of whales. Many are the men, small and great, old and new, landsmen and seamen, who have at large or in little, written of the whale. Run over a few:— The Authors of the Bible; Aristotle; Pliny; Aldrovandi; Sir Thomas Browne; Gesner; Ray; Linnæus; Rondeletius; Willoughby; Green; Artedi; Sibbald; Brisson; Marten; Lacépède; Bonnaterre; Desmarest; Baron Cuvier; Frederick Cuvier; John Hunter; Owen; Scoresby; Beale; Bennett; J. Ross Browne; the Author of Miriam Coffin; Olmsted; and the Rev. **Henry** T. Cheever.[5] But to what ultimate generalizing purpose all these have written, the above cited extracts will show.

barnacled hulls: barnacles live on the bodies of some whales.

Of the names in this list of whale authors, only those following Owen ever saw living whales; and but one of them was a real professional harpooneer and whaleman. I mean Captain Scoresby. On the separate subject of the Greenland or right-whale,[6] he is the best existing authority. But Scoresby knew nothing and says nothing of the great sperm whale, compared with which the Greenland whale is almost unworthy mentioning. And here be it said, that the Greenland whale is an usurper upon the throne of the seas. He is not even by any means the largest of the whales. Yet, owing to the long priority of his claims, and the profound ignorance which, till some seventy years back, invested the then fabulous or utterly unknown sperm-whale, and which ignorance to this present day still reigns in all but some few scientific retreats and whale-ports; this usurpation has been every way complete. Reference to nearly all the leviathanic allusions in the great poets of past days, will satisfy you that the Greenland whale, without one rival, was to them the monarch of the seas. But the time has at last come for a new proclamation. This is Charing Cross;° hear ye! good people all,—the Greenland whale is deposed,—the great sperm whale now reigneth!

There are only two books in being which at all pretend to put the living sperm whale before you, and at the same time, in the remotest degree succeed in the attempt. Those books are Beale's and Bennett's; both in their time surgeons to English South-Sea whale-ships, and both exact and reliable men. The original matter touching the sperm whale to be found in their volumes is necessarily small; but so far as it goes, it is of excellent quality, though mostly confined to scientific description. As yet, however, the sperm whale, scientific or poetic, lives not complete in any literature. Far above all other hunted whales, his is an unwritten life.

Now the various species of whales need some sort of popular comprehensive classification, if only an easy outline one for the present, hereafter to be filled in all its departments by subsequent laborers. As no better man advances to take this matter in hand, I hereupon offer my own poor endeavors. I promise nothing complete; because any human thing supposed to be complete, must for that very reason infallibly be faulty. I shall not pretend to a minute anatomical description of the various species, or—in this place at least—to much of any **description. My object here is simply to project the draught° of a** systematization of cetology. I am the architect, not the builder.

But it is a ponderous task; no ordinary letter-sorter in the Post-office is equal to it. To grope down into the bottom of the sea after them; to have one's hands among the unspeakable foundations, ribs, and very pelvis of the world;[7] this is a fearful thing. What am I that I should essay to hook the nose of this leviathan! The awful tauntings in Job might well appal me. "Will he (the leviathan) make a covenant with thee? Behold the hope of him is vain!"[8] But I have swam through libraries and sailed through oceans; I have had to do with whales with these visible hands; I am in earnest; and I will try. There are some preliminaries to settle.

First: The uncertain, unsettled condition of this science of Cetology is in the very vestibule attested by the fact, that in some quarters it still remains a moot point whether a whale be a fish. In his System of Nature, A. D. **1776,** Linnæus declares,

---

Charing Cross: old London city center where new monarchs were proclaimed. ***draught***: sketch.

"I hereby separate the whales from the fish."[9] But of my own knowledge, I know that down to the year 1850, sharks and shad, alewives and herring, against Linnæus's express edict, were still found dividing the possession of the same seas with the Leviathan.

The grounds upon which Linnæus would fain have banished the whales from the waters, he states as follows: "On account of their warm bilocular heart, their lungs, their movable eyelids, their hollow ears, penem intrantem feminam mammis lactantem," and finally, "ex lege naturæ jure meritoque."° I submitted all this to my friends Simeon Macey and Charley Coffin,° of Nantucket, both messmates of mine in a certain voyage, and they united in the opinion that the reasons set forth were altogether insufficient. Charley profanely hinted they were humbug.

Be it known that, waiving all argument, I take the good old fashioned ground that the whale is a fish, and call upon holy Jonah to back me.° This fundamental thing settled, the next point is, in what internal respect does the whale differ from other fish. Above, Linnæus has given you those items. But in brief, they are these: lungs and warm blood; whereas, all other fish are lungless and cold blooded.

Next: how shall we define the whale, by his obvious externals, so as conspicuously to label him for all time to come? To be short, then, a whale is *a spouting fish with a horizontal tail*. There you have him. However contracted, that definition is the result of expanded meditation. A walrus spouts much like a whale, but the walrus is not a fish, because he is amphibious. But the last term of the definition is still more cogent, as coupled with the first. Almost any one must have noticed that all the fish familiar to landsmen have not a flat, but a vertical, or up-and-down tail. Whereas, among spouting fish the tail, though it may be similarly shaped, invariably assumes a horizontal position.

By the above definition of what a whale is, I do by no means exclude from the leviathanic brotherhood any sea creature hitherto identified with the whale by the best informed Nantucketers; nor, on the other hand, link with it any fish hitherto authoritatively regarded as alien.* Hence, all the smaller, spouting, and horizontal tailed fish must be included in this ground-plan of Cetology. Now, then, come the grand divisions of the entire whale host.

---

* I am aware that down to the present time, the fish styled Lamantins and Dugongs° (Pig-fish and Sow-fish of the Coffins of Nantucket) are included by many naturalists among the whales. But as these pig-fish are a nosy, contemptible set, mostly lurking in the mouths of rivers, and feeding on wet hay, and especially as they do not spout, I deny their credentials as whales; and have presented them with their passports to quit the Kingdom of Cetology.

". . . *their warm bilocular heart*, . . . *penem intrantem feminam mammis lactantem*," . . . "*ex lege naturæ jure meritoque*.": as quoted in the *Penny Cyclopaedia*; *bilocular* means two-chambered; the Latin reads, "a penis that enters the female, who gives milk from teats," and, "by the law of nature, justly and deservedly." **Simeon Macey and Charley Coffin**: invented men with typical Nantucket names. **call upon holy Jonah to back me**: see Father Mapple's sermon, Ch. 9. **Lamantins and Dugongs**: manatees; Bennett, for one, included them.

First: According to magnitude I divide the whales into three primary BOOKS (subdivisible into CHAPTERS), and these shall comprehend them all, both small and large.

I. The FOLIO WHALE; II. the OCTAVO WHALE; III. the DUODECIMO[10] WHALE.

As the type° of the FOLIO I present the *Sperm Whale;* of the OCTAVO, the *Grampus;* of the DUODECIMO, the *Porpoise.*

FOLIOS. Among these I here include the following chapters:—I. The *Sperm Whale;* II. the *Right Whale;* III. the *Fin Back Whale;* IV. the *Hump-backed Whale;* V. the *Razor Back Whale;* VI. the *Sulphur Bottom Whale.*

BOOK I. (*Folio*), CHAPTER I. (*Sperm Whale*).—This whale, among the English of old vaguely known as the Trumpa whale, and the Physeter whale, and the Anvil Headed whale, is the present Cachalot of the French, and the Pottfisch of the Germans, and the Macrocephalus of the Long Words.[11] He is, without doubt, the largest inhabitant of the globe;[12] the most formidable of all whales to encounter; the most majestic in aspect; and lastly, by far the most valuable in commerce; he being the only creature from which that valuable substance, spermaceti, is obtained. All his peculiarities will, in many other places, be enlarged upon. It is chiefly with his name that I now have to do. Philosophically considered, it is absurd. Some centuries ago, when the Sperm whale was almost wholly unknown in his own proper individuality, and when his oil was only accidentally obtained from the stranded fish; in those days spermaceti, it would seem, was popularly supposed to be derived from a creature identical with the one then known in England as the Greenland or Right Whale. It was the idea also, that this same spermaceti was that quickening humor° of the Greenland Whale which the first syllable of the word literally expresses. In those times, also, spermaceti was exceedingly scarce, not being used for light, but only as an ointment and medicament. It was only to be had from the druggists as you nowadays buy an ounce of rhubarb.° When, as I opine, in the course of time, the true nature of spermaceti became known, its original name was still retained by the dealers; no doubt to enhance its value by a notion so strangely significant of its scarcity. And so the appellation must at last have come to be bestowed upon the whale from which this spermaceti was really derived.

BOOK I. (*Folio*), CHAPTER II. (*Right Whale*).—In one respect this is the most venerable of the leviathans, being the one first regularly hunted by man. It yields the article commonly known as whalebone or baleen;[13] and the oil specially known as "whale oil," an inferior article in commerce. Among the fishermen, he is indiscriminately designated by all the following titles: The Whale; the Greenland Whale; the Black Whale; the Great Whale; the True Whale; the Right Whale. There is a deal of obscurity concerning the identity of the species thus multitudinously baptized. What then is the whale, which I include in the second species of my Folios? It is the Great Mysticetus[14] of the English naturalists; the Greenland Whale of the English whalemen; the Baleine Ordinaire° of the French whalemen; the Gronlands Walfisk of the Swedes. It is the whale which for more than two centuries past has been hunted by the Dutch and English in the Arctic seas; it is the whale which the American fishermen have long pursued in the Indian ocean, on the Brazil Banks, on

---

type: model or epitome. ***quickening humor***: life-giving fluid; here, whale semen. ***rhubarb***: a laxative. ***Baleine Ordinaire***: common whale.

the Nor' West Coast,[15] and various other parts of the world, designated by them Right Whale Cruising Grounds.

Some pretend to see a difference between the Greenland whale of the English and the right whale of the Americans. But they precisely agree in all their grand features; nor has there yet been presented a single determinate fact upon which to ground a radical distinction. It is by endless subdivisions based upon the most inconclusive differences, that some departments of natural history become so repellingly intricate. The right whale will be elsewhere treated° of at some length, with reference to elucidating the sperm whale.

BOOK I. (*Folio*), CHAPTER III. (*Fin-Back*).—Under this head I reckon a monster which, by the various names of Fin-Back, Tall-Spout, and Long-John, has been seen almost in every sea and is commonly the whale whose distant jet is so often descried by passengers crossing the Atlantic, in the New York packet-tracks.° In the length he attains, and in his baleen, the Fin-back resembles the right whale, but is of a less portly girth, and a lighter color, approaching to olive. His great lips present a cable-like aspect, formed by the intertwisting, slanting folds of large wrinkles. His grand distinguishing feature, the fin, from which he derives his name, is often a conspicuous object. This fin is some three or four feet long, growing vertically from the hinder part of the back, of an angular shape, and with a very sharp pointed end. Even if not the slightest other part of the creature be visible, this isolated fin will, at times, be seen plainly projecting from the surface. When the sea is moderately calm, and slightly marked with spherical ripples, and this gnomon-like° fin stands up and casts shadows upon the wrinkled surface, it may well be supposed that the watery circle surrounding it somewhat resembles a dial, with its style and wavy hour-lines graved° on it. On that Ahaz-dial[16] the shadow often goes back. The Fin-Back is not gregarious. He seems a whale-hater, as some men are man-haters. Very shy; always going solitary; unexpectedly rising to the surface in the remotest and most sullen waters; his straight and single lofty jet rising like a tall misanthropic spear upon a barren plain; gifted with such wondrous power and velocity in swimming, as to defy all present pursuit from man; this leviathan seems the banished and unconquerable Cain of his race, bearing for his mark[17] that style° upon his back. From having the baleen in his mouth, the Fin-Back is sometimes included with the right whale, among a theoretic species denominated *Whalebone whales*, that is, whales with baleen. Of these so called Whalebone whales, there would seem to be several varieties, most of which, however, are little known. Broad-nosed whales and beaked whales; pike-headed whales; bunched whales; under-jawed whales and rostrated whales,° are the fishermen's names for a few sorts.

In connexion with this appellative° of "Whalebone whales," it is of great importance to mention, that however such a nomenclature may be convenient in facilitating allusions to some kind of whales, yet it is in vain to attempt a clear clas-

---

The right whale will be elsewhere treated: see Ch. 75. **packet-tracks**: routes sailed by the New York packet ships. **gnomon-like**: like the vertical part of a sundial; same as "style," below. **graved**: engraved. **style**: see "gnomon," above. **pike-headed whales; bunched whales; under-jawed whales and rostrated whales**: in order: pointed like the weapon called a pike; humped; with a protruding lower jaw; and with a long beak or snout. **appellative**: name.

sification of the Leviathan, founded upon either his baleen, or hump, or fin, or teeth; notwithstanding that those marked parts or features very obviously seem better adapted to afford the basis for a regular system of Cetology than any other detached bodily distinctions, which the whale, in his kinds, presents. How then? The baleen, hump, back-fin, and teeth; these are things whose peculiarities are indiscriminately dispersed among all sorts of whales, without any regard to what may be the nature of their structure in other and more essential particulars. Thus, the sperm whale and the humpbacked whale, each has a hump; but there the similitude ceases. Then, this same humpbacked whale and the Greenland whale, each of these has baleen; but there again the similitude ceases. And it is just the same with the other parts above mentioned. In various sorts of whales, they form such irregular combinations; or, in the case of any one of them detached, such an irregular isolation; as utterly to defy all general methodization formed upon such a basis. On this rock every one of the whale-naturalists has split.

But it may possibly be conceived that, in the internal parts of the whale, in his anatomy—there, at least, we shall be able to hit the right classification. Nay; what thing, for example, is there in the Greenland whale's anatomy more striking than his baleen? Yet we have seen that by his baleen it is impossible correctly to classify the Greenland whale. And if you descend into the bowels of the various leviathans, why there you will not find distinctions a fiftieth part as available to the systematizer as those external ones already enumerated. What then remains? nothing but to take hold of the whales bodily, in their entire liberal volume, and boldly sort them that way. And this is the Bibliographical system[18] here adopted; and it is the only one that can possibly succeed, for it alone is practicable. To proceed.

BOOK I. (*Folio*), Chapter IV. (*Hump Back*).—This whale is often seen on the northern American coast. He has been frequently captured there, and towed into harbor. He has a great pack on him like a peddler; or you might call him the Elephant and Castle[19] whale. At any rate, the popular name for him does not sufficiently distinguish him, since the sperm whale also has a hump, though a smaller one. His oil is not very valuable. He has baleen. He is the most gamesome and light-hearted of all the whales, making more gay foam and white water generally than any other of them.

BOOK I. (*Folio*), Chapter V. (*Razor Back*).—Of this whale little is known but his name. I have seen him at a distance off Cape Horn. Of a retiring nature, he eludes both hunters and philosophers. Though no coward, he has never yet shown any part of him but his back, which rises in a long sharp ridge. Let him go. I know little more of him, nor does anybody else.

BOOK I. (*Folio*), Chapter VI. (*Sulphur Bottom*).—Another retiring gentleman, with a brimstone belly, doubtless got by scraping along the Tartarian tiles[20] in some of his profounder divings. He is seldom seen; at least I have never seen him except in the remoter southern seas, and then always at too great a distance to study his countenance. He is never chased; he would run away with rope-walks of line.° Prodigies° are told of him. Adieu, Sulphur Bottom! I can say nothing more that is true of ye, nor can the oldest Nantucketer.

---

rope-walks of line: rope was manufactured in very long buildings called *rope-walks*.
Prodigies: wondrous acts.

Thus ends BOOK I. (*Folio*), and now begins BOOK II. (*Octavo*).

OCTAVOES.* These embrace the whales of middling magnitude, among which at present may be numbered:—I., the *Grampus;* II., the *Black Fish;* III., the *Narwhale;* IV., the *Thrasher;* V., the *Killer.*

BOOK II. (*Octavo*), CHAPTER I. (*Grampus*).—Though this fish, whose loud sonorous breathing, or rather blowing, has furnished a proverb to landsmen,[21] is so well known a denizen of the deep, yet is he not popularly classed among whales. But possessing all the grand distinctive features of the leviathan, most naturalists have recognised him for one. He is of moderate octavo size, varying from fifteen to twenty-five feet in length, and of corresponding dimensions round the waist. He swims in herds; he is never regularly hunted, though his oil is considerable in quantity, and pretty good for light. By some fishermen his approach is regarded as premonitory of the advance of the great sperm whale.

BOOK II. (*Octavo*), CHAPTER II. (*Black Fish*).—I give the popular fishermen's names for all these fish, for generally they are the best. Where any name happens to be vague or inexpressive, I shall say so, and suggest another. I do so now, touching the Black Fish, so called, because blackness is the rule among almost all whales. So, call him the Hyena Whale, if you please.° His voracity is well known, and from the circumstance that the inner angles of his lips are curved upwards, he carries an everlasting Mephistophelean[22] grin on his face. This whale averages some sixteen or eighteen feet in length. He is found in almost all latitudes. He has a peculiar way of showing his dorsal° hooked fin in swimming, which looks something like a Roman nose. When not more profitably employed, the sperm whale hunters sometimes capture the Hyena whale, to keep up the supply of cheap oil for domestic employment— as some frugal housekeepers, in the absence of company, and quite alone by themselves, burn unsavory tallow instead of odorous wax.° Though their blubber is very thin, some of these whales will yield you upwards of thirty gallons of oil.

BOOK II. (*Octavo*), CHAPTER III. (*Narwhale*), that is, *Nostril whale*.[23]— Another instance of a curiously named whale, so named I suppose from his peculiar horn being originally mistaken for a peaked nose. The creature is some sixteen feet in length, while its horn averages five feet, though some exceed ten, and even attain to fifteen feet. Strictly speaking, this horn is but a lengthened tusk, growing out from the jaw in a line a little depressed from the horizontal. But it is only found on the sinister side, which has an ill effect, giving its owner something analogous to the aspect of a clumsy left-handed man. What precise purpose this ivory horn or lance answers, it would be hard to say. It does not seem to be used like the blade of the

---

* Why this book of whales is not denominated the Quarto is very plain. Because, while the whales of this order, though smaller than those of the former order, nevertheless retain a proportionate likeness to them in figure, yet the bookbinder's Quarto volume in its diminished form does not preserve the shape of the Folio volume, but the Octavo volume does.

Hyena Whale, *if you please*: from the supposed grin of the "laughing" Hyena; see also Ch. 49. **dorsal**: on the back. **unsavory tallow . . . odorous wax**: animal fat smells bad, but wax is fragrant.

sword-fish and bill-fish;[24] though some sailors tell me that the Narwhale employs it for a rake in turning over the bottom of the sea for food. Charley Coffin said it was used for an ice-piercer; for the Narwhale, rising to the surface of the Polar Sea, and finding it sheeted with ice, thrusts his horn up, and so breaks through. But you cannot prove either of these surmises to be correct. My own opinion is, that however this one-sided horn may really be used by the Narwhale—however that may be—it would certainly be very convenient to him for a folder[25] in reading pamphlets. The Narwhale I have heard called the Tusked whale, the Horned whale, and the Unicorn whale. He is certainly a curious example of the Unicornism to be found in almost every kingdom of animated nature. From certain cloistered old authors I have gathered that this same sea-unicorn's horn was in ancient days regarded as the great antidote against poison, and as such, preparations of it brought immense prices. It was also distilled to a volatile salts for fainting ladies, the same way that the horns of the male deer are manufactured into hartshorn.° Originally it was in itself accounted an object of great curiosity. Black Letter tells me that Sir Martin Frobisher[26] on his return from that voyage, when Queen Bess did gallantly wave her jewelled hand to him from a window of Greenwich Palace, as his bold ship sailed down the Thames; "when Sir Martin returned from that voyage," saith Black Letter, "on bended knees he presented to her highness a prodigious long horn of the Narwhale, which for a long period after hung in the castle at Windsor." An Irish author avers that the Earl of Leicester, on bended knees, did likewise present to her highness another horn, pertaining to a land beast of the unicorn nature.[27]

The Narwhale has a very picturesque, leopard-like look, being of a milk-white ground color, dotted with round and oblong spots of black. His oil is very superior, clear and fine; but there is little of it, and he is seldom hunted. He is mostly found in the circumpolar seas.

BOOK II. (*Octavo*), CHAPTER IV. (*Killer*).—Of this whale little is precisely known to the Nantucketer, and nothing at all to the professed naturalist. From what I have seen of him at a distance, I should say that he was about the bigness of a grampus. He is very savage—a sort of Feegee fish.° He sometimes takes the great Folio whales by the lip, and hangs there like a leech, till the mighty brute is worried to death. The Killer is never hunted. I never heard what sort of oil he has. Exception might be taken to the name bestowed upon this whale, on the ground of its indistinctness. For we are all killers, on land and on sea; Bonapartes and Sharks included.[28]

BOOK II. (*Octavo*), CHAPTER V. (*Thrasher*).—This gentleman is famous for his tail, which he uses for a ferule° in thrashing his foes. He mounts the Folio whale's back, and as he swims, he works his passage by flogging him; as some schoolmasters get along in the world by a similar process. Still less is known of the Thrasher than of the Killer. Both are outlaws, even in **the** lawless seas.

Thus ends BOOK II. (*Octavo*), and begins BOOK III. (*Duodecimo.*)

DUODECIMOES.—These include the smaller whales. I. The Huzza Porpoise. II. The Algerine Porpoise. III. The Mealy-mouthed Porpoise.

---

hartshorn: ammonia-based "smelling salts." **Feegee fish**: Fiji Islanders were proverbially fierce. **ferule**: cane or stick used for punishment.

To those who have not chanced specially to study the subject, it may possibly seem strange, that fishes not commonly exceeding four or five feet should be marshalled among WHALES—a word, which, in the popular sense, always conveys an idea of hugeness. But the creatures set down above as Duodecimoes are infallibly whales, by the terms of my definition of what a whale is—i.e. a spouting fish, with a horizontal tail.

BOOK III. (*Duodecimo*), CHAPTER I. (*Huzza Porpoise*).—This is the common porpoise found almost all over the globe. The name is of my own bestowal; for there are more than one sort of porpoises, and something must be done to distinguish them. I call him thus, because he always swims in hilarious shoals, which upon the broad sea keep tossing themselves to heaven like caps in a Fourth-of-July crowd. Their appearance is generally hailed with delight by the mariner. Full of fine spirits, they invariably come from the breezy billows to windward. They are the lads that always live before the wind. They are accounted a lucky omen. If you yourself can withstand three cheers at beholding these vivacious fish, then heaven help ye; the spirit of godly gamesomeness is not in ye. A well-fed, plump Huzza Porpoise will yield you one good gallon of good oil. But the fine and delicate fluid extracted from his jaws is exceedingly valuable. It is in request among jewellers and watchmakers. Sailors put it on their hones.° Porpoise meat is good eating, you know. It may never have occurred to you that a porpoise spouts. Indeed, his spout is so small that it is not very readily discernible. But the next time you have a chance, watch him; and you will then see the great Sperm whale himself in miniature.

BOOK III. (*Duodecimo*), CHAPTER II. (*Algerine Porpoise*). A pirate.[29] Very savage. He is only found, I think, in the Pacific. He is somewhat larger than the Huzza Porpoise, but much of the same general make. Provoke him, and he will buckle to° a shark. I have lowered for him many times, but never yet saw him captured.

BOOK III. (*Duodecimo*), CHAPTER III. (*Mealy-mouthed Porpoise*).—The largest kind of Porpoise; and only found in the Pacific, so far as it is known. The only English name, by which he has hitherto been designated, is that of the fishers—Right-Whale Porpoise, from the circumstance that he is chiefly found in the vicinity of that Folio. In shape, he differs in some degree from the Huzza Porpoise, being of a less rotund and jolly girth; indeed, he is of quite a neat and gentlemanlike figure. He has no fins on his back (most other porpoises have), he has a lovely tail, and sentimental Indian eyes[30] of a hazel hue. But his mealy-mouth spoils all. Though his entire back down to his side fins is of a deep sable, yet a boundary line, distinct as the mark in a ship's hull, called the "bright waist,"[31] that line streaks him from stem to stern, with two separate colors, black above and white below. The white comprises part of his head, and the whole of his mouth, which makes him look as if he had just escaped from a felonious visit to a meal-bag. A most mean and mealy aspect! His oil is much like that of the common porpoise.

*   *   *   *   *   *

Beyond the DUODECIMO, this system does not proceed, inasmuch as the Porpoise is the smallest of the whales. Above, you have all the Leviathans of note.

---

hones: sharpening stones. **buckle to**: attack.

But there are a rabble of uncertain, fugitive, half-fabulous whales, which as an American whaleman, I know by reputation, but not personally. I shall enumerate them by their forecastle appellations; for possibly such a list may be valuable to future investigators, who may complete what I have here but begun. If any of the following whales, shall hereafter be caught and marked, then he can readily be incorporated into this System, according to his Folio, Octavo, or Duodecimo magnitude:—The Bottle-Nose Whale; the Junk Whale; the Pudding-Headed Whale; the Cape Whale; the Leading Whale; the Cannon Whale; the Scragg Whale; the Coppered Whale; the Elephant Whale; the Iceberg Whale; the Quog Whale; the Blue Whale; &c. From Icelandic, Dutch, and old English authorities, there might be quoted other lists of uncertain whales, blessed with all manner of uncouth names. But I omit them as altogether obsolete; and can hardly help suspecting them for mere sounds, full of Leviathanism, but signifying nothing.[32]

Finally: It was stated at the outset, that this system would not be here, and at once, perfected. You cannot but plainly see that I have kept my word. But I now leave my cetological System standing thus unfinished, even as the great Cathedral of Cologne[33] was left, with the crane still standing upon the top of the uncompleted tower. For small erections may be finished by their first architects; grand ones, true ones, ever leave the copestone to posterity. God keep me from ever completing anything. This whole book is but a draught—nay, but the draught of a draught. Oh, Time, Strength, Cash, and Patience!

CHAPTER 33

THE SPECKSYNDER

CONCERNING the officers of the whale-craft, this seems as good a place as any to set down a little domestic peculiarity on ship-board, arising from the existence of the harpooneer class of officers, a class unknown of course in any other marine than the whale-fleet.

The large importance attached to the harpooneer's vocation is evinced by the fact, that originally in the old Dutch Fishery, two centuries and more ago, the command of a whale ship was not wholly lodged in the person now called the captain, but was divided between him and an officer called the Specksynder.[1] Literally this word means Fat-Cutter; usage, however, in time made it equivalent to Chief Harpooneer. In those days, the captain's authority was restricted to the navigation and general management of the vessel: while over the whale-hunting department and all its concerns, the Specksynder or Chief Harpooneer reigned supreme. In the British Greenland Fishery, under the corrupted title of Specksioneer, this old Dutch official is still retained, but his former dignity is sadly abridged. At present he ranks simply as senior Harpooneer; and as such, is but one of the captain's more inferior subalterns.° Nevertheless, as upon the good conduct of the harpooneers the success of a whaling voyage largely depends, and since in the American Fishery he is not only an important officer in the boat, but under certain circumstances (night watches on a whaling ground) the command of the ship's deck is also his; therefore the grand political maxim of the sea demands, that he should nominally live apart from the men before the mast, and be in some way distinguished as their professional superior; though always, by them, familiarly regarded as their social equal.

Now, **the** grand distinction drawn between officer and man at sea, is this—the first lives aft, the last forward. Hence, in whale-ships and merchantmen alike, the mates have their quarters with the captain; and so, too, in most of the American whalers the harpooneers are lodged in the after part of the ship. That is to say, they take their meals in the captain's cabin, and sleep in a place indirectly communicating with it.

Though the long period of a Southern whaling voyage (by far the longest of all voyages now or ever made by man), the peculiar perils of it, and the community of

subalterns: subordinates.

interest prevailing among a company, all of whom, high or low, depend for their profits, not upon fixed wages, but upon their common luck, together with their common
vigilance, intrepidity, and hard work; though all these things do in some cases tend
to beget a less rigorous discipline than in merchantmen generally; yet, never mind
how much like an old Mesopotamian family° these whalemen may, in some primitive
instances, live together; for all that, the punctilious externals,° at least, of the quarter-deck are seldom materially relaxed, and in no instance done away. Indeed, many
are the Nantucket ships in which you will see the skipper parading his quarter-deck
with an elated grandeur not surpassed in any military navy; nay, extorting almost as
much outward homage as if he wore the imperial purple,° and not the shabbiest of
pilot-cloth.

And though of all men the moody captain of the Pequod was the least given to
that sort of shallowest assumption; and though the only homage he ever exacted, was
implicit, instantaneous obedience; though he required no man to remove the shoes
from his feet ere stepping upon the quarter-deck; and though there were times
when, owing to peculiar circumstances connected with events hereafter to be
detailed, he addressed them in unusual terms, whether of condescension or *in terrorem,*° or otherwise; yet even Captain Ahab was by no means unobservant of the
paramount forms and usages° of the sea.

Nor, perhaps, will it fail to be eventually perceived, that behind those forms
and usages, as it were, he sometimes masked himself; incidentally making use of
them for other and more private ends than they were legitimately intended to sub-
serve. That certain sultanism° of his brain, which had otherwise in a good degree
remained unmanifested; through those forms that same sultanism became incarnate in an irresistible dictatorship. For be a man's intellectual superiority what it
will, it can never assume the practical, available supremacy over other men, without
the aid of some sort of external arts and entrenchments,° always, in themselves,
more or less paltry and base. This it is, that for ever keeps God's true princes of the
Empire from the world's hustings;° and leaves the highest **honors** that this air
can give, to those men who become famous more through their infinite inferiority
to the choice hidden handful of the Divine Inert, than through their undoubted
superiority over the dead level of the mass. Such large virtue lurks in these small
things when extreme political superstitions invest them, that in some royal instances
even to idiot imbecility they have imparted potency. But when, as in the case of
Nicholas the Czar,[2] the ringed crown of geographical empire encircles an imperial
brain; then, the plebeian herds crouch abased before the tremendous centraliza-
tion. Nor, will the tragic dramatist who would depict mortal indomitableness in its
fullest sweep and **direst** swing, ever forget a hint, incidentally so important in his
art, as the one now alluded to.

---

*an old **Mesopotamian** family*: referring to the ancient patriarchy of the Middle East. ***punctilious externals***: precise formalities. ***imperial purple***: color of a Roman emperor's toga. ***in
terrorem***: to create fear. ***forms and usages***: procedures and customs. ***sultanism*** abso-
lutism. ***entrenchments***: concealments, as in fortifications. ***Empire . . . hustings***: Holy
Roman Empire (800–1806); *hustings* are sites of political campaigning.

But Ahab, my Captain, still moves before me in all his Nantucket grimness and shagginess; and in this episode touching Emperors and Kings, I must not conceal that I have only to do with a poor old whale-hunter like him; and, therefore, all outward majestical trappings and housings are denied me. Oh, Ahab! what shall be grand in thee, it must needs be plucked at from the skies, and dived for in the deep,[3] and featured in the unbodied air!

CHAPTER 34

THE CABIN-TABLE

IT is noon; and Dough-Boy, the steward, thrusting his pale loaf-of-bread face from the cabin-scuttle, announces dinner to his lord and master; who, sitting in the lee quarter-boat, has just been taking an observation of the sun; and is now mutely reckoning the latitude on the smooth, medallion-shaped tablet, reserved for that daily purpose on the upper part of his ivory leg.[1] From his complete inattention to the tidings, you would think that moody Ahab had not heard his menial. But presently, catching hold of the mizen shrouds, he swings himself to the deck, and in an even, unexhilarated voice, saying, "Dinner, Mr. Starbuck," disappears into the cabin.

When the last echo of his sultan's step has died away, and Starbuck, the first Emir,° has every reason to suppose that he is seated, then Starbuck rouses from his quietude, takes a few turns along the planks, and, after a grave peep into the binnacle, says, with some touch of pleasantness, "Dinner, Mr. Stubb," and descends the scuttle. The second Emir lounges about the rigging awhile, and then slightly shaking the main brace,° to see whether it be all right with that important rope, he likewise takes up the old burden,° and with a rapid "Dinner, Mr. Flask," follows after his predecessors.

But the third Emir, now seeing himself all alone on the quarter-deck, seems to feel relieved from some curious restraint; for, tipping all sorts of knowing winks in all sorts of directions, and kicking off his shoes, he strikes into a sharp but noiseless squall of a hornpipe right over the Grand Turk's head;° and then, by a dexterous sleight, pitching his cap up into the mizen-top° for a shelf, he goes down rollicking, so far at least as he remains visible from the deck, reversing all other processions, by bringing up the rear with music. But ere stepping into the cabin doorway below, he pauses, ships° a new face altogether, and, then, independent, hilarious little Flask enters King Ahab's presence, in the character of Abjectus, or the Slave.[2]

It is not the least among the strange things bred by the intense artificialness of sea-usages, that while in the open air of the deck some officers will, upon provocation, bear themselves boldly and defyingly enough towards their commander; yet,

---

Emir: Turkish ruler subordinate to a sultan. **main brace**: rope controlling the angle of the mainsail to the wind. **burden**: refrain of a song. **hornpipe . . . Grand Turk's head**: lively folk dance, popular among sailors; the Grand Turk was the sultan of Turkey. **mizen-top**: small platform at the top of the lower mizzenmast, the third and rearmost mast. **ships**: puts on.

ten to one, let those very officers the next moment go down to their customary dinner in that same commander's cabin, and straightway their inoffensive, not to say deprecatory and humble air towards him, as he sits at the head of the table; this is marvellous, sometimes most comical. Wherefore this difference? A problem? Perhaps not. To have been Belshazzar, King of Babylon;[3] and to have been Belshazzar, not haughtily but courteously, therein certainly must have been some touch of mundane grandeur. But he who in the rightly regal and intelligent spirit presides over his own private dinner-table of invited guests, that man's unchallenged power and dominion of individual influence for the time; that man's royalty of state transcends Belshazzar's, for Belshazzar was not the greatest. Who has but once dined his friends, has tasted what it is to be Cæsar. It is a witchery of social czarship which there is no withstanding. Now, if to this consideration you superadd the official supremacy of a ship-master, then, by inference, you will derive the cause of that peculiarity of sea-life just mentioned.

Over his ivory-inlaid table, Ahab presided like a mute, maned sea-lion on the white coral beach, surrounded by his war-like but still deferential cubs. In his own proper turn, each officer waited to be served. They were as little children before Ahab; and yet, in Ahab, there seemed not to lurk the smallest social arrogance. With one mind, their intent eyes all fastened upon the old man's knife, as he carved the chief dish before him. I do not suppose that for the world they would have profaned that moment with the slightest observation, even upon so neutral a topic as the weather. No! And when reaching out his knife and fork, between which the slice of beef was locked, Ahab thereby motioned Starbuck's plate towards him, the mate received his meat as though receiving alms; and cut it tenderly; and a little started if, perchance, the knife grazed against the plate; and chewed it noiselessly; and swallowed it, not without circumspection. For, like the Coronation banquet at Frankfort,[4] where the German Emperor profoundly dines with the seven Imperial Electors, so these cabin meals were somehow solemn meals, eaten in awful silence; and yet at table old Ahab forbade not conversation; only he himself was dumb. What a relief it was to choking Stubb, when a rat made a sudden racket in the hold below. And poor little Flask, he was the youngest son, and little boy of this weary family party. His were the shinbones of the saline beef; his would have been the drumsticks. For Flask to have presumed to help himself, this must have seemed to him tantamount to larceny in the first degree. Had he helped himself at that table, doubtless, never more would he have been able to hold his head up in this honest world; nevertheless, strange to say, Ahab never forbade him. And had Flask helped himself, the chances were Ahab had never so much as noticed it. Least of all, did Flask presume to help himself to butter. Whether he thought the owners of the ship denied it to him, on account of its clotting his clear, sunny complexion; or whether he deemed that, on so long a voyage in such marketless waters, butter was at a premium, and therefore was not for him, a subaltern; however it was, Flask, alas! was a butterless man!

Another thing. Flask was the last person down at the dinner, and Flask is the first man up. Consider! For hereby Flask's dinner was badly jammed in point of time. Starbuck and Stubb both had the start of him; and yet they also have the privilege of lounging in the rear. If Stubb even, who is but a peg higher than Flask, happens to have but a small appetite, and soon shows symptoms of concluding his repast, then

Flask must bestir himself, he will not get more than three mouthfuls that day; for it is against holy usage for Stubb to precede Flask to the deck. Therefore it was that Flask once admitted in private, that ever since he had arisen to the dignity of an officer, from that moment he had never known what it was to be otherwise than hungry, more or less. For what he ate did not so much relieve his hunger, as keep it immortal in him. Peace and satisfaction, thought Flask, have for ever departed from my stomach.[5] I am an officer; but, how I wish I could fist a bit of old-fashioned beef in the forecastle, as I used to when I was before the mast. There's the fruits of promotion now; there's the vanity of glory: there's the insanity of life! Besides, if it were so that any mere sailor of the Pequod had a grudge against Flask in Flask's official capacity, all that sailor had to do, in order to obtain ample vengeance, was to go aft at dinner-time, and get a peep at Flask through the cabin sky-light, sitting silly and dumfoundered before awful Ahab.

Now, Ahab and his three mates formed what may be called the first table in the Pequod's cabin. After their departure, taking place in inverted order to their arrival, the canvas cloth was cleared, or rather was restored to some hurried **order** by the pallid steward. And then the three harpooneers were bidden to the feast, they being its residuary legatees.° They made a sort of temporary servants' hall of the high and mighty cabin.

In strange contrast to the hardly tolerable constraint and nameless invisible domineerings of the captain's table, was the entire care-free license and ease, the almost frantic democracy of those inferior fellows the harpooneers. While their masters, the mates, seemed afraid of the sound of the hinges of their own jaws, the harpooneers chewed their food with such a relish that there was a report° to it. They dined like lords; they filled their bellies like Indian ships all day loading with spices. Such portentous° appetites had Queequeg and Tashtego, that to fill out the vacancies made by the previous repast, often the pale Dough-Boy was fain to bring on a great baron of salt-junk,° seemingly quarried out of the solid ox. And if he were not lively about it, if he did not go with a nimble hop-skip-and-jump, then Tashtego had an ungentlemanly way of accelerating him by darting a fork at his back, harpoonwise. And once Daggoo, seized with a sudden humor, assisted Dough-Boy's memory by snatching him up bodily, and thrusting his head into a great empty wooden trencher, while Tashtego, knife in hand, began laying out the circle preliminary to scalping him. He was naturally a very nervous, shuddering sort of little fellow, this bread-faced steward; the progeny of a bankrupt baker and a hospital nurse. And what with the standing spectacle of the black terrific Ahab, and the periodical tumultuous visitations of these three savages, Dough-Boy's whole life was one continual lip-quiver. Commonly, after seeing the harpooneers furnished with all things they demanded, he would escape from their clutches into his little pantry adjoining, and fearfully peep out at them through the blinds of **its** door, till all was over.

It was a sight to see Queequeg seated over against Tashtego, opposing his filed teeth to the Indian's: crosswise to them, Daggoo seated on the floor, for a

residuary legatees: those who divide whatever is left after the specific bequests of a will have been paid. ***report***: loud noise. ***portentous***: huge, prodigious. ***fain . . . baron of salt-junk***: obliged . . . undivided loin of hard salt beef.

bench would have brought his hearse-plumed head to the low carlines;° at every motion of his colossal limbs, making the low cabin framework to shake, as when an African elephant goes passenger in a ship. But for all this, the great negro was wonderfully abstemious, not to say dainty. It seemed hardly possible that by such comparatively small mouthfuls he could keep up the vitality diffused through so broad, baronial, and superb a person. But, doubtless, this noble savage fed strong and drank deep of the abounding element of air; and through his dilated nostrils snuffed in the sublime life of the worlds. Not by beef or by bread, are giants made or nourished. But Queequeg, he had a mortal, barbaric smack of the lip in eating—an ugly sound enough—so much so, that the trembling Dough-Boy almost looked to see whether any marks of teeth lurked in his own lean arms. And when he would hear Tashtego singing out for him to produce himself, that his bones might be picked, the simple-witted Steward all but shattered the crockery hanging round him in the pantry, by his sudden fits of the palsy. Nor did the whetstone which the harpooneers carried in their pockets, for their lances and other weapons; and with which whetstones, at dinner, they would ostentatiously sharpen their knives; that grating sound did not at all tend to tranquillize poor Dough-Boy. How could he forget that in his Island days, Queequeg, for one, must certainly have been guilty of some murderous, convivial indiscretions. Alas! Dough-Boy! hard fares the white waiter who waits upon cannibals. Not a napkin should he carry on his arm, but a buckler.° In good time, though, to his great delight, the three salt-sea warriors would rise and depart; to his credulous, fable-mongering ears, all their martial bones jingling in them at every step, like Moorish scimetars in scabbards.

But, though these barbarians dined in the cabin, and nominally lived there; still, being anything but sedentary in their habits, they were scarcely ever in it except at meal-times, and just before sleeping-time, when they passed through it to their own peculiar° quarters.

In this one matter, Ahab seemed no exception to most American whale captains, who, as a set, rather incline to the opinion that by rights the ship's cabin belongs to them; and that it is by courtesy alone that anybody else is, at any time, permitted there. So that, in real truth, the mates and harpooneers of the Pequod might more properly be said to have lived out of the cabin than in it. For when they did enter it, it was something as a street-door enters a house; turning inwards for a moment, only to be turned out the next; and, as a permanent thing, residing in the open air. Nor did they lose much hereby; in the cabin was no companionship; socially, Ahab was inaccessible. Though nominally included in the census of Christendom, he was still an alien to it. He lived in the world, as the last of the Grisly Bears lived in settled Missouri. And as when Spring and Summer had departed, that wild Logan of the woods, burying himself in the hollow of a tree, lived out the winter there, sucking his own paws;[6] so, in his inclement, howling old age, Ahab's soul, shut up in the caved trunk of his body, there fed upon the sullen paws of its gloom!

---

hearse-plumed . . . carlines: like the black plumes placed on hearses; *carlines* are timbers between the ceiling beams. **buckler**: shield. **peculiar**: particular; separate.

CHAPTER 35

THE MAST-HEAD

IT was during the more pleasant weather, that in due rotation with the other seamen my first mast-head¹ came round.

In most American whalemen the mast-heads are manned almost simultaneously with the vessel's leaving her port; even though she may have fifteen thousand miles, and more, to sail ere reaching her proper cruising ground.° And if, after a three, four, or five years' voyage she is drawing nigh home with anything empty in her—say, an empty vial even—then, her mast-heads are kept manned to the last; and not till her skysail-poles° sail in among the spires of the port, does she altogether relinquish the hope of capturing one whale more.

Now, as the business of standing mast-heads, ashore or afloat, is a very ancient and interesting one, let us in some measure expatiate here. I take it, that the earliest standers of mast-heads were the old Egyptians; because, in all my researches, I find none prior to them. For though their progenitors, the builders of Babel, must doubtless, by their tower, have intended to rear the loftiest mast-head in all Asia, or Africa either; yet (ere the final truck was put to it) as that great stone mast of theirs may be said to have gone by the board,² in the dread gale of God's wrath; therefore, we cannot give these Babel builders priority over the Egyptians. And that the Egyptians were a nation of mast-head standers, is an assertion based upon the general belief among archæologists, that the first pyramids³ were founded for astronomical purposes: a theory singularly supported by the peculiar stair-like formation of all four sides of those edifices; whereby, with prodigious long upliftings of their legs, those old astronomers were wont to mount to the apex, and sing out for new stars; even as the look-outs of a modern ship sing out for a sail, or a whale just bearing in sight. In Saint Stylites,⁴ the famous Christian hermit of old times, who built him a lofty stone pillar in the desert and spent the whole latter portion of his life on its summit, hoisting his food from the ground with a tackle; in him we have a remarkable instance of a dauntless stander-of-mast-heads; who was not to be driven from his place by fogs

---

cruising ground: an area of the sea where, expecting to find whales, a whaler will slowly sail back and forth. ***skysail-poles***: highest parts of masts, supporting the highest yards and sails (skysails), and added only under fine sailing conditions.

150

or frosts, rain, hail, or sleet; but valiantly facing everything out to the last, literally died at his post. Of modern standers-of-mast-heads we have but a lifeless set; mere stone, iron, and bronze men; who, though well capable of facing out a stiff gale, are still entirely incompetent to the business of singing out upon discovering any strange sight. There is Napoleon; who, upon the top of the column of Vendome,[5] stands with arms folded, some one hundred and fifty feet in the air; careless, now, who rules the decks below; whether Louis Philippe, Louis Blanc, or Louis **the Devil**.[6] Great Washington, too, stands high aloft on his towering main-mast in Baltimore, and like one of Hercules' pillars,[7] his column marks that point of human grandeur beyond which few mortals will go. Admiral Nelson, also, on a capstan of gun-metal, stands his mast-head in Trafalgar Square; and ever when most obscured by that London smoke, token is yet given that a hidden hero is there; for where there is smoke, must be fire. But neither great Washington, nor Napoleon, nor Nelson, will answer a single hail from below, however madly invoked to befriend by their counsels the distracted decks upon which they gaze; however, it may be surmised, that their spirits penetrate through the thick haze of the future, and descry what shoals and what rocks must be shunned.

It may seem unwarrantable to couple in any respect the mast-head standers of the land with those of the sea; but that in truth it is not so, is plainly evinced by an item for which Obed Macy, the sole historian of Nantucket, stands accountable. The worthy Obed tells us, that in the early times of the whale fishery, ere ships were regularly launched in pursuit of the game, the people of that island erected lofty spars along the sea-coast, to which the look-outs ascended by means of nailed cleats, something as fowls go upstairs in a hen-house. A few years ago this same plan was adopted by the Bay whalemen of New Zealand,[8] who, upon descrying the game, gave notice to the ready-manned boats nigh the beach. But this custom has now become obsolete; turn we then to the one proper mast-head, that of a whale-ship at sea. The three mast-heads are kept manned from sun-rise to sun-set; the seamen taking their regular turns (as at the helm), and relieving each other every two hours. In the serene weather of the tropics it is exceedingly pleasant—the mast-head; nay, to a dreamy meditative man it is delightful. There you stand, a hundred feet above the silent decks, striding along the deep, as if the masts were gigantic stilts, while beneath you and between your legs, as it were, swim the hugest monsters of the sea, even as ships once sailed between the boots of the famous Colossus at old Rhodes.[9] There you stand, lost in the infinite series of the sea, with nothing ruffled but the waves. The tranced ship indolently rolls; the drowsy trade winds blow; everything resolves you into languor. For the most part, in this tropic whaling life, a sublime uneventfulness invests you; you hear no news; read no gazettes; extras° with startling accounts of commonplaces never delude you into unnecessary excitements; you hear of no domestic afflictions; bankrupt securities; fall of stocks; are never troubled with the thought of what you shall have for dinner—for all your meals for three years and more are snugly stowed in casks, and your bill of fare is immutable.

In one of those southern whalemen, on a long three or four years' voyage, as often happens, the sum of the various hours you spend at the mast-head would

gazettes; extras: newspapers; special editions providing late-breaking news.

amount to several entire months. And it is much to be deplored that the place to which you devote so considerable a portion of the whole term of your natural life, should be so sadly destitute of anything approaching to a cosy inhabitiveness, or adapted to breed a comfortable localness of feeling, such as pertains to a bed, a hammock, a hearse, a sentry box, a pulpit, a coach, or any other of those small and snug contrivances in which men temporarily isolate themselves. Your most usual point of perch is the head of the t' gallant-mast, where you stand upon two thin parallel sticks (almost peculiar to whalemen) called the t' gallant cross-trees.° Here, tossed about by the sea, the beginner feels about as cosy as he would standing on a bull's horns. To be sure, in **cold** weather you may carry your house aloft with you, in the shape of a watch-coat; but properly speaking the thickest watch-coat is no more of a house than the unclad body; for as the soul is glued inside of its fleshly tabernacle,[10] and cannot freely move about in it, nor even move out of it, without running great risk of perishing (like an ignorant pilgrim crossing the snowy Alps in winter); so a watch-coat is not so much of a house as it is a mere envelope, or additional skin encasing you. You cannot put a shelf or chest of drawers in your body, and no more can you make a convenient closet of your watch-coat.

Concerning all this, it is much to be deplored that the mast-heads of a southern whale ship are unprovided with those enviable little tents or pulpits, called *crow's-nests,* in which the look-outs of a Greenland whaler are protected from the inclement weather of the frozen seas. In the fire-side narrative of Captain Sleet, entitled "A Voyage among the Icebergs, in quest of the Greenland Whale, and incidentally for the re-discovery of the Lost Icelandic Colonies of Old Greenland;" in this admirable volume, all standers of mast-heads are furnished with a charmingly circumstantial account of the then recently invented *crow's-nest* of the Glacier, which was the name of Captain Sleet's[11] good craft. He called it the *Sleet's crow's-nest,* in honor of himself; he being the original inventor and patentee, and free from all ridiculous false delicacy, and holding that if we call our own children after our own names (we fathers being the original inventors and patentees), so likewise should we denominate after ourselves any other apparatus we may beget. In shape, the Sleet's crow's-nest is something like a large tierce or pipe;° it is open above, however, where it is furnished with a movable side-screen to keep to windward of your head in a hard gale. Being fixed on the summit of the mast, you ascend into it through a little traphatch in the bottom. On the after side, or side next the stern of the ship, is a comfortable seat, with a locker underneath for umbrellas, comforters, and coats. In front is a leather rack, in which to keep your speaking trumpet, pipe, telescope, and other nautical conveniences. When Captain Sleet in person stood his mast-head in this crow's nest of his, he tells us that he always had a rifle with him (also fixed in the rack), together with a powder flask and shot, for the purpose of popping off the stray narwhales, or vagrant sea unicorns infesting those waters; for you cannot successfully shoot at them from the deck owing to the resistance of the water, but to shoot down upon them is a very different thing. Now, it was plainly a labor of love for Captain Sleet to describe, as he does, all the little detailed conveniences of his

---

t' gallant-mast . . . t' gallant cross-trees: third section of the mast; *cross-trees*: light, horizontal timbers. **tierce or pipe**: 40- and 120-gallon wine casks, respectively.

crow's-nest; but though he so enlarges upon many of these, and though he treats us to a very scientific account of his experiments in this crow's-nest, with a small compass he kept there for the purpose of counter-acting the errors resulting from what is called the "local attraction" of all binnacle magnets; an error ascribable to the horizontal vicinity of the iron in the ship's planks, and in the Glacier's case, perhaps, to there having been so many broken-down blacksmiths among her crew; I say, that though the Captain is very discreet and scientific here, yet, for all his learned "binnacle deviations," "azimuth compass observations," and "approximate errors,"° he knows very well, Captain Sleet, that he was not so much immersed in those profound magnetic meditations, as to fail being attracted occasionally towards that well replenished little case-bottle,° so nicely tucked in on one side of his crow's nest, within easy reach of his hand. Though, upon the whole, I greatly admire and even love the brave, the honest, and learned Captain; yet I take it very ill of him that he should so utterly ignore that case-bottle, seeing what a faithful friend and comforter it must have been, while with mittened fingers and hooded head he was studying the mathematics aloft there in that bird's nest within three or four perches of the pole.°

But if we Southern whale-fishers are not so snugly housed aloft as Captain Sleet and his Greenland-men were; yet that disadvantage is greatly counterbalanced by the widely contrasting serenity of those seductive seas in which we Southern fishers mostly float. For one, I used to lounge up the rigging very leisurely, resting in the top to have a chat with Queequeg, or any one else off duty whom I might find there; then ascending a little way further, and throwing a lazy leg over the top-sail yard,° take a preliminary view of the watery pastures, and so at last mount to my ultimate destination.

Let me make a clean breast of it here, and frankly admit that I kept but sorry guard. With the problem of the universe revolving in me, how could I—being left completely to myself at such a thought-engendering altitude,—how could I but lightly hold my obligations to observe all whale-ships' standing orders, "Keep your weather eye open, and sing out° every time."

And let me in this place movingly admonish you, ye ship-owners of Nantucket! Beware of enlisting in your vigilant fisheries any lad with lean brow and hollow eye; given to unseasonable meditativeness; and who offers to ship with the Phædon instead of Bowditch[12] in his head. Beware of such an one, I say: your whales must be seen before they **can be** killed; and this sunken-eyed **young** Platonist will tow you ten wakes round the world, and never make you one pint of sperm the richer. Nor are these monitions at all unneeded. For nowadays, the whale-fishery furnishes an asylum for many romantic, melancholy, and absent-minded young men, disgusted with the carking cares of earth,[13] and seeking sentiment in tar and blubber. Childe Harold not unfrequently perches himself upon the mast-head of some luckless disappointed whale-ship, and in moody phrase ejaculates:—

"binnacle deviations," . . . "approximate errors,": navigational terms. *case-bottle*: small, square flask. *perches of the pole*: a perch (also called a pole) is 5.5 yards, but perches are also birds' resting places; hence a triple pun. *top-sail yard*: long, heavy pole, crossing the mast, from which the topsail hung. *weather eye open . . . sing out*: be on guard; shout out.

> "Roll on, thou deep and dark blue ocean, roll!
> Ten thousand blubber-hunters sweep over thee in vain."[14]

Very often do the captains of such ships take those absent-minded young philosophers to task, upbraiding them with not feeling sufficient "interest" in the voyage; half-hinting that they are so hopelessly lost to all honorable ambition, as that in their secret souls they would rather not see whales than otherwise. But all in vain; those young Platonists have a notion that their vision is imperfect; they are short-sighted; what use, then, to strain the visual nerve? They have left their opera-glasses at home.

"Why, thou monkey," said a harpooneer to one of these lads, "we've been cruising now hard upon three years, and thou hast not raised a whale yet. Whales are scarce as hen's teeth whenever thou art up here." Perhaps they were; or perhaps there might have been shoals° of them in the far horizon; but lulled into such an opium-like listlessness of vacant, unconscious reverie is this absent-minded youth by the blending cadence of waves with thoughts, that at last he loses his identity; takes the mystic ocean at his feet for the visible image of that deep, blue, bottomless soul, pervading mankind and nature; and every strange, half-seen, gliding, beautiful thing that eludes him; every dimly-discovered, uprising fin of some undiscernible form,

shoals: large groups.

REVISION NARRATIVE

Pantheism

In the British edition several small revisions were made to the conclusion of Ch. 35. In the sentence, "your whales must be seen before they can be killed," probably Melville (and not an editor) changed "can be" to "are" (p. 153). The tinkering sharpens the tone, but in the following sentence, the removal of the word "young" from "this sunken-eyed young Platonist" (probably, again, by the author) indicates a modification of Melville's argument, for with the revision Ishmael speaks of any Platonist, not just young ones. Different changes occur in the last sentence of the next paragraph (p. 155). For instance, the British edition alters the phrase "Cranmer's sprinkled Pantheistic ashes," to "Wickliff's sprinkled ashes." Both Thomas Cranmer (Henry VIII's Archbishop of Canterbury, later deposed) and William Wycliffe (early anti-papist and translator of the Bible) were reduced to ashes, but only Wycliffe's ashes were spread (famously) over water, on the river Swift, a tributary of the Avon, which leads to the sea. Either an editor or Melville himself may have made the correction from "Cranmer's" to "Wickliff's." But an editor was not likely to have removed "Pantheistic," from the phrase since Ishmael is cautioning against Pantheism. Melville probably cut the word, for while Wickliff's ashes were spread everywhere, they are not strictly speaking pantheistic (nor was Wycliffe a pantheist). Moreover, since Ishmael uses the word in his last line—"Heed it well, ye Pantheists!"—Melville might also have cut the dubious reference regarding Wycliffe's ashes so as not to undermine its more effective use in the chapter's ending.

seems to him the embodiment of those elusive thoughts that only people the soul by continually flitting through it. In this enchanted mood, thy spirit ebbs away to whence it came; becomes diffused through time and space; like **Cranmer's** sprinkled **Pantheistic** ashes, forming at last a part of every shore the round globe over.

There is no life in thee, now, except that rocking life imparted by a gently rolling ship; by her, borrowed from the sea; by the sea, from the inscrutable tides of God. But while this sleep, this dream is on ye, move your foot or hand an inch; slip your hold at all; and your identity comes back in horror. Over Descartian vortices[15] you hover. And perhaps, at mid-day, in the fairest weather, with one half-throttled shriek you drop through that transparent air into the summer sea, no more to rise for ever. Heed it well, ye Pantheists![16]

CHAPTER 36

THE QUARTER-DECK

(Enter Ahab: Then, all.)[1]

IT was not a great while after the affair of the pipe, that one morning shortly after breakfast, Ahab, as was his wont, ascended the cabin-gangway to the deck. There most sea-captains usually walk at that hour, as country gentlemen, after the same meal, take a few turns in the garden.

Soon his steady, ivory stride was heard, as to and fro he paced his old rounds, upon planks so familiar to his tread, that they were all over dented, like geological stones, with the peculiar mark of his walk. Did you fixedly gaze, too, upon that ribbed and dented brow; there also, you would see still stranger foot-prints—the foot-prints of his one unsleeping, ever-pacing thought.

But on the occasion in question, those dents looked deeper, even as his nervous step that morning left a deeper mark. And, so full of his thought was Ahab, that at every uniform turn that he made, now at the main-mast and now at the binnacle, you could almost see that thought turn in him as he turned, and pace in him as he paced; so completely possessing him, indeed, that it all but seemed the inward mould of every outer movement.

"D'ye mark him, Flask?" whispered Stubb; "the chick that's in him pecks the shell. T'will soon be out."

The hours wore on;—Ahab now shut up within his cabin; anon, pacing the deck, with the same intense bigotry of purpose° in his aspect.

It drew near the close of day. Suddenly he came to a halt by the bulwarks, and inserting his bone leg into the auger-hole there, and with one hand grasping a shroud, he ordered Starbuck to send everybody aft.

"Sir!" said the mate, astonished at an order seldom or never given on shipboard except in some extraordinary case.

"Send everybody aft," repeated Ahab. "Mast-heads, there! come down!"

When the entire ship's company were assembled, and with curious and not wholly unapprehensive faces, were eyeing him, for he looked not unlike the weather horizon when a storm is coming up, Ahab, after rapidly glancing over the bulwarks, and then darting his eyes among the crew, started from his stand-point; and as

bigotry of purpose: obstinate, selfish intent.

though not a soul were nigh him resumed his heavy turns upon the deck. With bent head and half-slouched hat he continued to pace, unmindful of the wondering whispering among the men; till Stubb cautiously whispered to Flask, that Ahab must have summoned them there for the purpose of witnessing a pedestrian feat. But this did not last long. Vehemently pausing, he cried:—

"What do ye do when ye see a whale, men?"

"Sing out for him!" was the impulsive rejoinder from a score of clubbed° voices.

"Good!" cried Ahab, with a wild approval in his tones; observing the hearty animation into which his unexpected question had so magnetically thrown them.

"And what do ye next, men?"

"Lower away, and after him!"

"And what tune is it ye pull to, men?"

"A dead whale or a stove boat!"[2]

More and more strangely and fiercely glad and approving, grew the countenance of the old man at every shout; while the mariners began to gaze curiously at each other, as if marvelling how it was that they themselves became so excited at such seemingly purposeless questions.

But, they were all eagerness again, as Ahab, now half-revolving in his pivot-hole, with one hand reaching high up a shroud, and tightly, almost convulsively grasping it, addressed them thus:—

"All ye mast-headers have before now heard me give orders about a white whale. Look ye! d'ye see this Spanish ounce of gold?"—holding up a broad bright coin to the sun—"it is **a sixteen dollar piece, men.** D'ye see it? Mr. Starbuck, hand me yon top-maul."

While the mate was getting the hammer, Ahab, without speaking, was slowly rubbing the gold piece against the skirts of his jacket, as if to heighten its lustre, and without using any words was meanwhile lowly humming to himself, producing a sound so strangely muffled and inarticulate that it seemed the mechanical humming of the wheels of his vitality in him.

Receiving the top-maul from Starbuck, he advanced towards the main-mast with the hammer uplifted in one hand, exhibiting the gold with the other, and with a high raised voice exclaiming: "Whosoever of ye raises° me a white-headed whale with a wrinkled brow and a crooked jaw; whosoever of ye raises me that white-headed whale, with three holes punctured in his starboard fluke—look ye, whosoever of ye raises me that same white whale, he shall have this gold ounce, my boys!"

"Huzza! huzza!" cried the seamen, as with swinging tarpaulins they hailed the act of nailing the gold to the mast.

"It's a white whale, I say," resumed Ahab, as he threw down the top-maul; "a white whale. Skin your eyes for him, men; look sharp for white water;° if ye see but a bubble, sing out."

All this while Tashtego, Daggoo, and Queequeg had looked on with even more intense interest and surprise than the rest, and at the mention of the wrinkled brow

---

clubbed: joined. ***raises***: sees and shouts out for. ***white water***: foam created when a whale falls back into the sea after flinging itself out of the water ("breaching").

and crooked jaw they had started as if each was separately touched by some specific recollection.

"Captain Ahab," said Tashtego, "that white whale must be the same that some call Moby Dick."

"Moby Dick?" shouted Ahab. "Do ye know the white whale then, Tash?"

"Does he fan-tail a little curious, sir, before he goes down?" said the Gay-Header deliberately.

"And has he a curious spout, too," said Daggoo, "very bushy, even for a par-macetty,° and mighty quick, Captain Ahab?"

"And he have one, two, tree—oh! good many iron in him hide, too, Captain," cried Queequeg disjointedly, "all twiske-tee be-twisk, like him—him—" faltering hard for a word, and screwing his hand round and round as though uncorking a bot-tle—"like him—him—"

"Corkscrew!" cried Ahab, "aye, Queequeg, the harpoons lie all twisted and wrenched in him; aye, Daggoo, his spout is a big one, like a whole shock of wheat, and white as a pile of our Nantucket wool after the great annual sheep-shearing; aye, Tashtego, and he fan-tails like a split jib in a squall.° Death and devils! men, it is Moby Dick ye have seen—Moby Dick—Moby Dick!"

"Captain Ahab," said Starbuck, who, with Stubb and Flask, had thus far been eyeing his superior with increasing surprise, but at last seemed struck with a thought which somewhat explained all the wonder. "Captain Ahab, I have heard of Moby Dick—but it was not Moby Dick that took off thy leg?"

"Who told thee that?" cried Ahab; then pausing, "Aye, Starbuck; aye, my hearties all round; it was Moby Dick that dismasted me; Moby Dick that brought me to this dead stump I stand on now. Aye, aye," he shouted with a terrific, loud, animal **sob**, like that of a heart-stricken moose; "Aye, aye! it was that accursed white whale that razeed me;° made a poor pegging lubber of me for ever and a day!" Then toss-ing both arms, with measureless imprecations he shouted out: "Aye, aye! and I'll chase him round Good Hope, and round the Horn, and round the Norway Maelstrom,[3] and round perdition's flames before I give him up. And this is what ye have shipped for, men! to chase that white whale on both sides of land,° and over all sides of earth, till he spouts black blood and rolls fin out.° What say ye, men, will ye splice hands on it, now? I think ye do look brave."

"Aye, aye!" shouted the harpooneers and seamen, running closer to the excited old man: "A sharp eye for the White Whale; a sharp lance for Moby Dick!"

"God bless ye," he seemed to half sob and half shout. "God bless ye, men. Steward! go draw the great measure of grog.° But what's this long face about, Mr. Starbuck; wilt thou not chase the white whale? art not game for Moby Dick?"

"I am game for his crooked jaw, and for the jaws of Death too, Captain Ahab, if it fairly comes in the way of the business we follow; but I came here to hunt whales, not my commander's vengeance. How many barrels will thy vengeance yield

---

parmacetty: sperm whale. **split jib in a squall**: ripped triangular headsail in a storm. **razeed me**: "cut away part of me." **on both sides of land**: in the Atlantic and Pacific. **fin out**: a dead whale rolls to one side, revealing its fin. **great measure of grog**: large, measured pitcher of watered rum.

thee even if thou gettest it, Captain Ahab? it will not fetch thee much in our Nantucket market."

"Nantucket market! Hoot!° But come closer, Starbuck; thou requirest a little lower layer.[4] If money's to be the measurer, man, and the accountants have computed their great counting-house the globe, by girdling it with guineas,° one to every three parts of an inch; then, let me tell thee, that my vengeance will fetch a great premium *here!*"

"He smites his chest," whispered Stubb, "what's that for? methinks it rings most vast, but hollow."

"Vengeance on a dumb brute!" cried Starbuck, "that simply smote thee from blindest instinct! Madness! To be enraged with a dumb thing, Captain Ahab, seems blasphemous."

"Hark ye yet again,—the little lower layer. All visible objects, man, are but as pasteboard masks.[5] But in each event—in the living act, the undoubted deed—there, some unknown but still reasoning thing puts forth the mouldings of its features from behind the unreasoning mask. If man will strike, strike through the mask! How can the prisoner reach outside except by thrusting through the wall? To me, the white whale is that wall, shoved near to me. Sometimes I think there's naught beyond. But 'tis enough. He tasks me; he heaps° me; I see in him outrageous strength, with an inscrutable malice sinewing it. That inscrutable thing is chiefly what I hate; and be the white whale agent, or be the white whale principal, I will wreak that hate upon him. Talk not to me of blasphemy, man; I'd strike the sun if it insulted me. For could the sun do that, then could I do the other; since there is ever a sort of fair play herein, jealousy presiding over all creations. But not my master, man, is even that fair play. Who's over me? Truth hath no confines. Take off thine eye! more intolerable than fiends' glarings is a doltish stare! So, so; thou reddenest and palest; my heat has melted thee to anger-glow. But look ye, Starbuck, what is said in heat, that thing unsays itself. There are men from whom warm words are small indignity. I meant not to incense thee. Let it go. Look! see yonder Turkish cheeks of spotted tawn°—living, breathing pictures painted by the sun. The Pagan leopards—the unrecking and unworshipping things, that live; and seek, and give no reasons for the torrid life they feel! The crew, man, the crew! Are they not one and all with Ahab, in this matter of the whale? See Stubb! he laughs! See yonder Chilian! he snorts to think of it. Stand up amid the general hurricane, thy one tost sapling cannot, Starbuck! And what is it? Reckon it. 'Tis but to help strike a fin; no wondrous feat for Starbuck. What is it more? From this one poor hunt, then, the best lance out of all Nantucket, surely he will not hang back, when every foremast-hand has clutched a whetstone? Ah! constrainings° seize thee; I see! the billow lifts thee! Speak, but speak!—Aye, aye! thy silence, **then,** *that* voices thee. (*Aside*) Something shot from my dilated nostrils, he has inhaled it in his lungs. Starbuck now is mine, cannot oppose me **now,** without rebellion."

Hoot! scornfully, "Hah!" ***guineas***: British gold coins equal to one pound plus one shilling. ***heaps***: imposes on (Melville's invention). **Turkish cheeks of spotted tawn**: savage, tanned, dirty cheeks of the crew, like a Turk's (a Western stereotype). ***constrainings***: compunctions, doubts.

"God keep me!—keep us all!" murmured Starbuck, lowly.

But in his joy at the enchanted, tacit acquiescence of the mate, Ahab did not hear his foreboding invocation; nor yet the low laugh from the hold; nor yet the presaging vibrations of the winds in the cordage; nor yet the hollow flap of the sails against the masts, as for a moment their hearts sank in. For again Starbuck's downcast eyes lighted up with the stubbornness of life; the subterranean laugh died away; the winds blew on; the sails filled out; the ship heaved and rolled as before. Ah, ye admonitions and warnings! why stay ye not when ye come? But rather are ye predictions than warnings, ye shadows! Yet not so much predictions from without, as verifications of the foregoing things within. For with little external to constrain us, the innermost necessities in our being, these still drive us on.

"The measure! the measure!" cried Ahab.

Receiving the brimming pewter, and turning to the harpooneers, he ordered them to produce their weapons. Then ranging them before him near the capstan, with their harpoons in their hands, while his three mates stood at his side with their lances, and the rest of the ship's company formed a circle round the group; he stood for an instant searchingly eyeing every man of his crew. But those wild eyes met his, as the bloodshot eyes of the prairie wolves meet the eye of their leader, ere he rushes on at their head in the trail of the bison; but, alas! only to fall into the hidden snare of the Indian.

"Drink and pass!" he cried, handing the heavy charged flagon to the nearest seaman. "The crew alone now drink. Round with it, round! Short draughts—long swallows, men; 'tis hot as Satan's hoof. So, so; it goes round excellently. It spiralizes in ye; forks out at the serpent-snapping eye. Well done; almost drained. That way it went, this way it comes. Hand it me—here's a hollow! Men, ye seem the years; so brimming life is gulped and gone. Steward, refill!

"Attend now, my braves. I have mustered ye all round this capstan; and ye mates, flank me with your lances; and ye harpooneers, stand there with your irons; and ye, stout mariners, ring me in, that I may in some sort revive **a noble** custom[6] of my fisherman fathers before me. O men, you will yet see that——Ha! boy, come back? bad pennies[7] come not sooner. Hand it me. Why, now, this pewter had run brimming again, wert not thou St. Vitus' imp—away, thou ague![8]

"Advance, ye mates! Cross your lances full before me. Well done! Let me touch the axis." So saying, with extended arm, he grasped the three level, radiating lances at their crossed centre; while so doing, suddenly and nervously twitched them; meanwhile, glancing intently from Starbuck to Stubb; from Stubb to Flask. It seemed as though, by some nameless, interior volition, he would fain have shocked **into them** the same fiery emotion accumulated within the Leyden jar of his own magnetic life.[9] The three mates quailed before his strong, sustained, and mystic aspect. Stubb and Flask looked sideways from him; the honest eye of Starbuck fell downright.

"In vain!" cried Ahab; "but, maybe, 'tis well. For did ye three but once take the fall-forced shock, then mine own electric thing, *that* had perhaps expired from out me. Perchance, too, it would have dropped ye dead. Perchance ye need it not. Down lances! And now, ye mates, I do appoint ye three cup-bearers to my three pagan kinsmen there—yon three most honorable gentlemen and noblemen, my valiant harpooneers. Disdain the task? What, when the great Pope washes the feet of beggars, using his tiara for ewer?[10] Oh, my sweet cardinals! your own condescension, *that* shall bend ye to it. I do not order ye; ye will it. Cut your seizings° and draw the poles, ye harpooners!"

Silently obeying the order, the three harpooneers now stood with the detached iron part of their harpoons, some three feet long, held, barbs up, before him.

"Stab me not with that keen steel! Cant them; cant them over! know ye not the goblet end? Turn up the socket! So, so; now, ye cup-bearers, advance. The irons! take them; hold them while I fill!" Forthwith, slowly going from one officer to the other, he brimmed the harpoon sockets with the fiery waters from the pewter.

"Now, three to three, ye stand. Commend° the murderous chalices! Bestow them, ye who are now made parties to this indissoluble league. Ha! Starbuck! but the deed is done! Yon ratifying sun now waits to sit upon it. Drink, ye harpooneers! drink and swear, ye men that man the deathful whaleboat's bow—Death to Moby Dick! God hunt us all, if we do not hunt Moby Dick to his death!" The long, barbed steel goblets were lifted; and to cries and maledictions against the white whale, the spirits were simultaneously quaffed down with a hiss. Starbuck paled, and turned, and shivered. Once more, and finally, the replenished pewter went the rounds among the frantic crew; when, waving his free hand to them, they all dispersed; and Ahab retired within his cabin.

---

seizings: bindings of cord holding together the steel heads and wooden poles of the harpoons.
Commend: Entrust; as in *Macbeth* 1.7.10–12, "this . . . / Commends the ingredients of our poison'd chalice / To our own lips."

CHAPTER 37

SUNSET

The cabin; by the stern windows; Ahab sitting alone, and gazing out.

I LEAVE a white and turbid wake; pale waters, paler cheeks, where'er I sail. The envious billows sidelong swell to whelm my track; let them; but first I pass.

Yonder, by the ever-brimming goblet's rim, the warm waves blush like wine. The gold brow plumbs the blue. The diver sun—slow dived from noon,—goes down; my soul mounts up! she wearies with her endless hill. Is, then, the crown too heavy that I wear? this Iron Crown of Lombardy.[1] Yet is it bright with many a gem; I, the wearer, see not its far flashings; but darkly feel that I wear that, that dazzlingly confounds. 'Tis iron—that I know—not gold. 'Tis split, too—that I feel; the jagged edge galls me so, my brain seems to beat against the solid metal; **aye, steel skull, mine; the sort that needs no helmet in the most brain-battering fight!**

Dry heat upon my brow? Oh! time was, when as the sunrise nobly spurred me, so the sunset soothed. No more. This lovely light, it lights not me; all loveliness is anguish to me, since I can ne'er enjoy. Gifted with the high perception, I lack the low, enjoying power; damned, most subtly and most malignantly! damned in the midst of Paradise![2] Good night—good night! (*waving his hand, he moves from the window.*)

'Twas not so hard a task. I thought to find one stubborn, at the least; but my one cogged circle fits into all their various wheels, and they revolve. Or, if you will, like so many ant-hills of powder, they all stand before me; and I their match. Oh, hard! that to fire others, the match itself must needs be wasting! What I've dared, I've willed; and what I've willed, I'll do! They think me mad—Starbuck does; but I'm demoniac,[3] I am madness maddened! That wild madness that's only calm to comprehend itself! The prophecy° was that I should be dismembered; and—Aye! I lost this leg. I now prophesy that I will dismember my dismemberer. Now, then, be the prophet and the fulfiller one. That's more than ye, ye great gods, ever were. I laugh and hoot at ye, ye cricket-players, ye pugilists, ye deaf Burkes and blinded Bendigoes![4] I will not say as schoolboys do to bullies,—Take some one of your own size; don't pommel *me!* No, ye've knocked me down, and I am up again; but *ye* have run and hidden. Come forth from behind your cotton bags![5] I have no long gun to reach ye. Come, Ahab's compliments to ye; come and see if ye can swerve me.

prophecy: See Ch. 19.

Swerve me? ye cannot swerve me, else ye swerve yourselves! man has ye there. Swerve me? The path to my fixed purpose is laid with iron rails, whereon my soul is grooved to run. Over unsounded gorges, through the rifled hearts of mountains, under torrents' beds, unerringly I rush! Naught's an obstacle, naught's an angle° to the iron way!

angle: remote place.

CHAPTER 38

DUSK

By the Mainmast; Starbuck leaning against it.

MY soul is more than matched; she's overmanned; and by a madman! Insufferable sting, that sanity should ground arms on such a field! But he drilled deep down, and blasted all my reason out of me! I think I see his impious end; but feel that I must help him to it. Will I, nill I,° the ineffable thing has tied me to him; tows me with a cable I have no knife to cut. Horrible old man! Who's over him, he cries;—aye, he would be a democrat to all above; look, how he lords it over all below! Oh! I plainly see my miserable office,—to obey, rebelling; and worse yet, to hate with touch of pity! For in his eyes I read some lurid woe would shrivel me up, had I it. Yet is there hope. Time and tide flow wide.[1] The hated whale has the round watery world to swim in, as the small gold-fish has its glassy globe. His heaven-insulting purpose, God may wedge aside. I would up heart, were it not like lead. But my whole clock's run down; my heart the all-controlling weight, I have no key to lift again.[2]

[*A burst of revelry from the forecastle.*

Oh, God! to sail with such a heathen crew that have small touch of human mothers in them! Whelped° somewhere by the sharkish sea. The white whale is their demogorgon.[3] Hark! the infernal orgies! that revelry is forward! mark the unfaltering silence aft! Methinks it pictures life. Foremost through the sparkling sea shoots on the gay, embattled, bantering bow, but only to drag dark Ahab after it, where he broods within his sternward cabin, builded over the dead water of the wake, and further on,° hunted by its wolfish gurglings. The long howl thrills me through! Peace! ye revellers, and set the watch! Oh, life! 'tis in an hour like this, with soul beat down and held to knowledge,—as wild, untutored things are forced to feed—Oh, life! 'tis now that I do feel the latent horror in thee! but 'tis not me! that horror's out of me! and with the soft feeling of the human in me, yet will I try to fight ye, ye grim, phantom futures! Stand by me, hold me, bind me, O ye blessed influences!

Will I, nill I: willy-nilly, or whether I want to or not. **Whelped**: given birth to. ***further on***: further back in the wake.

CHAPTER 39

FIRST NIGHT-WATCH.
FORE-TOP.

(Stubb solus,° and mending a brace.)

Ha! ha! ha! ha! hem! clear my throat!—I've been thinking over it ever since, and that ha, ha's the final consequence. Why so? Because a laugh's the wisest, easiest answer to all that's queer; and come what will, one comfort's always left—that unfailing comfort is, it's all predestinated. I heard not all his talk with Starbuck; but to my poor eye Starbuck then looked something as I the other evening felt. Be sure the old Mogul° has fixed him, too. I twigged it, knew it; had had the gift, might readily have prophesied it—for when I clapped my eye upon his skull I saw it. Well, Stubb, *wise* Stubb—that's my title—well, Stubb, what of it, Stubb? Here's a carcase.[1] I know not all that may be coming, but be it what it will, I'll go to it laughing. Such a waggish leering as lurks in all your horribles! I feel funny. Fa, la! lirra, skirra! What's my juicy little pear at home doing now? Crying its eyes out?—Giving a party to the last arrived harpooneers, I dare say, gay as a frigate's pennant, and so am I— fa, la! lirra, skirra! Oh—

> We'll drink to-night with hearts as light,
> To **love,** as gay and fleeting
> As bubbles that swim, on the beaker's brim,
> And break on the lips while meeting.[2]

A brave stave that—who calls? Mr. Starbuck? Aye, aye, sir—(*Aside*) he's my superior, he has his too, if I'm not mistaken.—Aye, aye, sir, just through with this job—coming.

---

solus: Latin, alone. **Mogul**: Mongol ruler.

MIDNIGHT, FORECASTLE.

HARPOONEERS AND SAILORS.
(*Foresail rises and discovers the watch standing, lounging, leaning, and lying in various attitudes, all singing in chorus.*)[1]
Farewell and adieu to you, Spanish ladies![2]
Farewell and adieu to you, ladies of Spain!
Our captain's **commanded**—

1ST NANTUCKET SAILOR.
Oh, boys, don't be sentimental; it's bad for the digestion! Take a tonic, follow me!
(*Sings, and all follow.*)
Our captain stood upon the deck,[3]
    A spy-glass in his hand,
A viewing of those gallant whales
    That blew at every strand.°
Oh, your tubs in your boats, my boys,
    And by your braces stand,
And we'll have one of those fine whales,
    Hand, boys, over hand!
So, be cheery, my lads! may your hearts never fail!
While the bold harpooneer is striking the whale!

strand: wave.

MATE'S VOICE FROM THE QUARTER-DECK.

Eight bells° there, forward!

2D NANTUCKET SAILOR.

Avast the chorus! Eight bells there! d'ye hear, bell-boy? Strike the bell eight, thou Pip! thou blackling! and let me call the watch. I've the sort of mouth for that— the hogshead° mouth. So, so, (*thrusts his head down the scuttle,*) Star—bo-l-e-e-n-s, a-h-o-y!⁴ Eight bells there below! Tumble up!

DUTCH SAILOR.

Grand snoozing to-night, maty; fat night for that. I mark this in our old Mogul's wine; it's quite as deadening to some as filliping° to others. We sing; they sleep—aye, lie down there, like ground-tier butts. At 'em again! There, take this copper-pump, and hail 'em through it. Tell 'em to avast dreaming of their lasses. **Tell 'em it's the resurrection; they must kiss their last, and come to judgment.** That's the way—*that's* it; thy throat ain't spoiled with eating Amsterdam butter.⁵

FRENCH SAILOR.

Hist, boys! let's have a jig or two before we ride to anchor in Blanket Bay. What say ye? There comes the other watch. Stand by all legs! Pip! little Pip! hurrah with your tambourine!

PIP.

(*Sulky and sleepy.*)

Don't know where it is.

FRENCH SAILOR.

Beat thy belly, then, and wag thy ears. Jig it, men, I say; merry's the word; hurrah! Damn me, won't you dance? Form, now, Indian-file, and gallop into the double-shuffle?° Throw yourselves! Legs! legs!

ICELAND SAILOR.

I don't like your floor, maty; it's too springy to my taste. I'm used to ice-floors. I'm sorry to throw cold water on the subject; but excuse me.

MALTESE SAILOR.

Me too; where's your girls? Who but a fool would take his left hand by his right, and say to himself, how d'ye do? Partners! I must have partners!

SICILIAN SAILOR.

Aye; girls and a green!°—then I'll hop with ye; yea, turn grasshopper!

LONG-ISLAND SAILOR.

Well, well, ye sulkies, there's plenty more of us. Hoe corn° when you may, say I. All legs go to harvest soon. Ah! here comes the music; now for it!

Eight bells: midnight. **hogshead**: large barrel. **filliping**: stimulating. **double-shuffle**: Charles Dickens called it "a low, noisy dance." **green**: village commons, or grassy lawn. **Hoe corn**: do a hoe-down, a wild country dance.

AZORE SAILOR.
(Ascending, and pitching the tambourine up the scuttle.)
Here you are, Pip; and there's the windlass-bitts;° up you mount! Now, boys!

(The half of them dance to the tambourine; some go below; some sleep or lie among the coils of rigging. Oaths a-plenty.)

AZORE SAILOR.
(Dancing.)
Go it, Pip! Bang it, bell-boy! Rig it, dig it, stig it, quig it, bell-boy! Make fire-flies; break the **jinglers**!

PIP.
Jinglers, you say?—there goes another, dropped off; I pound it so.

CHINA SAILOR.
Rattle thy teeth, then, and pound away; make a pagoda of thyself.°

FRENCH SAILOR.
Merry-mad! Hold up thy hoop, Pip, till I jump through it! Split jibs!° tear yourselves!

TASHTEGO.
(Quietly smoking.)
That's a white man; he calls that fun: humph! I save my sweat.

OLD MANX SAILOR.
I wonder whether those jolly lads bethink them of what they are dancing over. I'll dance over your grave, I will—that's the bitterest threat of your night-women, that beat° head-winds round corners. O **Christ!** to think of the green navies and the green-skulled crews! Well, well; belike the whole world's **a** ball, as **you** scholars have it;[6] and so 'tis right to make one ball-room of it. Dance on, lads, you're young; I was once.

3D NANTUCKET SAILOR.
Spell oh!—whew! this is worse than pulling after whales in a calm—give us a whiff, Tash.

(They cease dancing, and gather in clusters. Meantime the sky darkens—the wind rises.)

LASCAR° SAILOR.
By Brahma! boys, it'll be douse sail soon. The sky-born, high-tide Ganges turned to wind! Thou showest thy black brow, Seeva!

---

windlass-bitts: two strong vertical timbers supporting the ends of the windlass. **make a pagoda of thyself**: bells were often hung on Chinese pagodas. **Split jibs!**: split yourselves like sails torn in a violent storm. **night-women . . . beat**: either witches, who can supposedly make such maneuvers in the air, or, perhaps, prostitutes; *beat* means to sail closely into the wind. **Lascar**: from Lashkar, India; here, an Indian sailor. *Brahma* and *Seeva* are the Hindu gods of creation and destruction, respectively; the *Ganges* is India's holy river.

MALTESE SAILOR.

(Reclining and shaking his cap.)

It's the **waves**—the **snow's caps** turn to jig it now. They'll shake their tassels soon. Now would all the waves were women, then I'd go drown, and chassee° with them evermore! There's naught so sweet on earth—heaven may not match it!—as those swift glances of warm, wild bosoms in the dance, when the over-arboring arms hide such ripe, bursting grapes.

SICILIAN SAILOR.

(Reclining.)

Tell me not of it! Hark ye, lad—fleet interlacings of the limbs—lithe swayings—coyings—flutterings! lip! heart! hip! all graze: unceasing touch and go! **not taste, observe ye, else come satiety.** Eh, Pagan? *(Nudging.)*

TAHITIAN SAILOR.

(Reclining on a mat.)

Hail, holy nakedness of our dancing girls!—the Heeva-Heeva!° Ah! low veiled, high palmed Tahiti![7] I still rest me on thy mat, but the soft soil has slid! I saw thee woven in the wood, my mat! green the first day I brought ye thence; now worn and wilted quite. Ah me!—not thou nor I can bear the change! How then, if so be transplanted to yon sky? Hear I the roaring streams from Pirohitee's peak of spears,[8] when they leap down the crags and drown the villages?—The blast! the blast! Up, spine, and meet it! *(Leaps to his feet.)*

PORTUGUESE SAILOR.

How the sea rolls swashing 'gainst the side! Stand by for reefing, hearties! the winds are just crossing swords, pell-mell they'll go lunging presently.

DANISH SAILOR.

Crack, crack, old ship![9] so long as thou crackest, thou holdest! Well done! The mate there holds ye to it stiffly. He's no more afraid than the isle fort at Cattegat,[10] put there to fight the Baltic with storm-lashed guns, on which the sea-salt cakes!

4TH NANTUCKET SAILOR.

He has his orders, mind ye that. I heard old Ahab tell him he must always kill a squall, something as they burst a water-spout with a pistol—fire your ship right into it!

ENGLISH SAILOR.

Blood! but that old man's a grand old cove!° We are the lads to hunt him up his whale!

ALL.

Aye! aye!

---

chassee: dance. **Heeva-Heeva**: Tahitian dance of peace. **cove**: fellow.

OLD MANX SAILOR.

How the three pines° shake! Pines are the hardest sort of tree to live when shifted to any other soil, and here there's none but the crew's cursed clay. Steady, helmsman! steady. This is the sort of weather when brave hearts snap ashore, and keeled hulls split at sea. Our captain has his birth-mark; look yonder, boys, there's another in the sky—lurid-like, ye see, all else pitch black.

DAGGOO.

What of that? Who's afraid of black's afraid of me! I'm quarried out of it!

SPANISH SAILOR.

(*Aside.*) He wants to bully, ah!—the old grudge[11] makes me touchy. (*Advancing.*) Aye, harpooneer, thy race is the undeniable dark side of mankind—devilish dark at that. No offence.

DAGGOO (*grimly*).

None.

ST. JAGO'S SAILOR.[12]

That Spaniard's mad or drunk. But that can't be, or else in his one case our old Mogul's fire-waters are somewhat long in working.

5TH NANTUCKET SAILOR.

What's that I saw—lightning? Yes.

SPANISH SAILOR.

No; Daggoo showing his teeth.

DAGGOO (*springing*).

Swallow thine, mannikin!° White skin, white liver!

SPANISH SAILOR (*meeting him*).

Knife thee heartily! big frame, small spirit!

ALL.

A row! a row! a row!

TASHTEGO (*with a whiff*).

A row a'low, and a row aloft—Gods and men—both brawlers! Humph!

BELFAST SAILOR.

A row! arrah° a row! The Virgin be blessed, a row! Plunge in with ye!

ENGLISH SAILOR.

Fair play! Snatch the Spaniard's knife! A ring, a ring!

---

pines: ship's masts. **mannikin**: little one. **arrah**: Anglo-Irish, really.

OLD MANX SAILOR.

Ready formed. There! the ringed horizon. In that ring Cain struck Abel. Sweet work, right work! No? **Why then, God, mad'st thou the ring?**

MATE'S VOICE FROM THE QUARTER DECK.

Hands by the halyards! in top-gallant sails! Stand by to reef topsails![13]

ALL.

The squall! the squall! jump, my jollies! (*They scatter.*)

PIP (*shrinking under the windlass*).

Jollies? Lord help such jollies! Crish, crash! there goes the jib-stay! Blang-whang! **God!** Duck lower, Pip, here comes the royal yard![14] It's worse than being in the whirled woods, the last day of the year! Who'd go climbing after chestnuts now? But there they go, all cursing, and here I don't. Fine prospects to 'em; they're on the road to heaven.° Hold on hard! Jimmini, what a squall! But those chaps there are worse yet—they are your white squalls, they. White squalls? white whale, shirr! shirr! Here have I heard all their chat just now, and the white whale—shirr! shirr!— but spoken of once! and only this evening—it makes me jingle all over like my tambourine—that anaconda of an old man swore 'em in to hunt him! Oh, thou big white God aloft there somewhere in yon darkness, have mercy on this small black boy down here; preserve him from all men that have no bowels° to feel fear!

   *   *   *   *   *   *

road to heaven: to reach the sails, the sailors are climbing the rigging. **bowels**: in scripture, the seat of pity or kindness; the supposed bodily source of compassion.

CHAPTER 41

MOBY DICK

I, ISHMAEL, was one of that crew; my shouts had gone up with the rest; my oath had been welded with theirs; and stronger I shouted, and more did I hammer and clinch my oath, because of the dread in my soul. A wild, mystical, sympathetical feeling was in me; Ahab's quenchless feud seemed mine. With greedy ears I learned the history of that murderous monster against whom I and all the others had taken our oaths of violence and revenge.

For some time past, though at intervals only, the unaccompanied, secluded White Whale had haunted those uncivilized seas mostly frequented by the Sperm Whale fishermen. But not all of them knew of his existence; only a few of them, comparatively, had knowingly seen him; while the number who as yet had actually and knowingly given battle to him, was small indeed. For, owing to the large number of whale-cruisers; the disorderly way they were sprinkled over the entire watery circumference, many of them adventurously pushing their quest along solitary latitudes, so as seldom or never for a whole twelvemonth or more on a stretch, to encounter a single news-telling sail of any sort; the inordinate length of each separate voyage; the irregularity of the times of sailing from home; all these, with other circumstances, direct and indirect, long obstructed the spread through the whole world-wide whaling-fleet of the special individualizing tidings concerning Moby Dick. It was hardly to be doubted, that several vessels reported to have encountered, at such or such a time, or on such or such a meridian, a Sperm Whale of uncommon magnitude and malignity, which whale, after doing great mischief to his assailants, had completely escaped them; to some minds it was not an unfair presumption, I say, that the whale in question must have been no other than Moby Dick. Yet as of late the Sperm Whale fishery had been marked by various and not unfrequent instances of great ferocity, cunning, and malice in the monster attacked; therefore it was, that those who by accident ignorantly gave battle to Moby Dick; such hunters, perhaps, for the most part, were content to ascribe the peculiar terror he bred, more, as it were, to the perils of the Sperm Whale fishery at large, than to the individual cause. In that way, mostly, the disastrous encounter between Ahab and the whale had hitherto been popularly regarded.[1]

And as for those who, previously hearing of the White Whale, by chance caught sight of him; in the beginning of the thing they had every one of them, almost, as boldly and fearlessly lowered for him, as for any other whale of that species. But at length, such calamities did ensue in these assaults—not restricted to sprained wrists and ancles, broken limbs, or devouring amputations—but fatal to the last degree of fatality; those repeated disastrous repulses, all accumulating and piling their terrors upon Moby Dick; those things had gone far to shake the fortitude of many brave hunters, to whom the story of the White Whale had eventually come.

Nor did wild rumors of all sorts fail to exaggerate, and still the more horrify° the true histories of these deadly encounters. For not only do fabulous rumors naturally grow out of the very body of all surprising terrible events,—as the smitten tree gives birth to its fungi; but, in maritime life, far more than in that of terra firma, wild rumors abound, wherever there is any adequate reality for them to cling to. And as the sea surpasses the land in this matter, so the whale fishery surpasses every other sort of maritime life, in the wonderfulness and fearfulness of the rumors which sometimes circulate there. For not only are whalemen as a body unexempt from that ignorance and superstitiousness hereditary to all sailors; but of all sailors, they are by all odds the most directly brought into contact with whatever is appallingly astonishing in the sea; face to face they not only eye its greatest marvels, but, hand to jaw, give battle to them. Alone, in such remotest waters, that though you sailed a thousand miles, and passed a thousand shores, you would not come to any chiselled hearthstone, or aught hospitable beneath that part of the sun; in such latitudes and longitudes, pursuing too such a calling as he does, the whaleman is wrapped by influences all tending to make his fancy pregnant with many a mighty birth.

No wonder, then, that ever gathering volume from the mere transit over the widest watery spaces, the outblown rumors of the White Whale did in the end incorporate with themselves all manner of morbid hints, and half-formed fœtal suggestions of supernatural agencies, which eventually invested Moby Dick with new terrors unborrowed from anything that visibly appears. So that in many cases such a panic did he finally strike, that few who by those rumors, at least, had heard of the White Whale, few of those hunters were willing to encounter the perils of his jaw.

But there were still other and more vital practical influences at work. Not even at the present day has the original prestige of the Sperm Whale, as fearfully distinguished from all other species of the leviathan, died out of the minds of the whalemen as a body. There are those this day among them, who, though intelligent and courageous enough in offering battle to the Greenland or Right whale, would perhaps—either from professional inexperience, or incompetency, or timidity, decline a contest with the Sperm Whale; at any rate, there are plenty of whalemen, especially among those whaling nations not sailing under the American flag, who have never hostilely encountered the Sperm Whale, but whose sole knowledge of the leviathan is restricted to the ignoble monster primitively pursued in the North; seated on their hatches, these men will hearken with a childish fire-side interest and awe, to the wild, strange tales of Southern whaling. Nor is the pre-eminent tremendousness of the great Sperm Whale anywhere more feelingly comprehended, than on board of those prows which stem him.°

horrify: make more horrific. ***prows which stem him***: ships that stop him.

And as if the now tested reality of his might had in former legendary times thrown its shadow before it; we find some book naturalists—Olassen and Povelsen[2]—declaring the Sperm Whale not only to be a consternation to every other creature in the sea, but also to be so incredibly ferocious as continually to be athirst for human blood. Nor even down to so late a time as Cuvier's, were these or almost similar impressions effaced. For in his Natural History, the Baron himself affirms that at sight of the Sperm Whale, all fish (sharks included) are "struck with the most lively **terrors**," and "often in the precipitancy of their flight dash themselves against the rocks with such violence as to cause instantaneous death." And however the general experiences in the fishery may amend such reports as these; yet in their full terribleness, even to the bloodthirsty item of Povelsen, the superstitious belief in them is, in some vicissitudes of their vocation, revived in the minds of the hunters.

So that overawed by the rumors and portents concerning him, not a few of the fishermen recalled, in reference to Moby Dick, the earlier days of the Sperm Whale fishery, when it was oftentimes hard to induce long practised Right whalemen to embark in the perils of this new and daring warfare; such men protesting that although other leviathans might be hopefully pursued, yet to chase and point lance at such an apparition as the Sperm Whale was not for mortal man. That to attempt it, would be inevitably to be torn into a quick eternity. On this head, there are some remarkable documents that may be consulted.

Nevertheless, some there were, who even in the face of these things were ready to give chase to Moby Dick; and a still greater number who, chancing only to hear of him distantly and vaguely, without the specific details of any certain calamity, and without superstitious accompaniments, were sufficiently hardy not to flee from the battle if offered.

One of the wild suggestings referred to, as at last coming to be linked with the White Whale in the minds of the superstitiously inclined, was the unearthly conceit that Moby Dick was ubiquitous; that he had actually been encountered in opposite latitudes at one and the same instant of time.

Nor, credulous as such minds must have been, was this conceit altogether without some faint show of superstitious probability. For as the secrets of the currents in the seas have never yet been divulged, even to the most erudite research; so the hidden ways of the Sperm Whale when beneath the surface remain, in great part, unaccountable to his pursuers; and from time to time have originated the most curious and contradictory speculations regarding them, especially concerning the mystic modes whereby, after sounding to a great depth, he transports himself with such vast swiftness to the most widely distant points.

It is a thing well known to both American and English whale-ships, and as well a thing placed upon authoritative record years ago by Scoresby, that some whales have been captured far north in the Pacific, in whose bodies have been found the barbs of harpoons darted in the Greenland seas. Nor is it to be gainsaid,° that in some of these instances it has been declared that the interval of time between the two assaults could not have exceeded very many days. Hence, by inference, it has been believed by some whalemen, that the Nor' West Passage,[3] so long a problem to

gainsaid: denied.

man, was never a problem to the whale. So that here, in the real living experience of living men, the prodigies related in old times of the inland Strella mountain[4] in Portugal (near whose top there was said to be a lake in which the wrecks of ships floated up to the surface); and that still more wonderful story of the Arethusa fountain[5] near Syracuse (whose waters were believed to have come from the Holy Land by an underground passage); these fabulous narrations are almost fully equalled by the realities of the whaleman.

Forced into familiarity, then, with such prodigies as these; and knowing that after repeated, intrepid assaults, the White Whale had escaped alive; it cannot be much matter of surprise that some whalemen should go still further in their superstitions; declaring Moby Dick not only ubiquitous, but immortal (for immortality is but ubiquity in time); that though groves of spears should be planted in his flanks, he would still swim away unharmed; or if indeed he should ever be made to spout thick blood, such a sight would be but a ghastly deception; for again in unensanguined billows° hundreds of leagues away, his unsullied jet would once more be seen.

But even stripped of these supernatural surmisings, there was enough in the earthly make and incontestable character of the monster to strike the imagination with unwonted power. For, it was not so much his uncommon bulk that so much distinguished him from other sperm whales, but, as was elsewhere thrown out°—a peculiar snow-white wrinkled forehead, and a high, pyramidical white hump. These were his prominent features; the tokens whereby, even in the limitless, uncharted seas, he revealed his identity, at a long distance, to those who knew him.

The rest of his body was so streaked, and spotted, and marbled with the same shrouded hue, that, in the end, he had gained his distinctive appellation of the White Whale; a name, indeed, literally justified by his vivid aspect, when seen gliding at high noon through a dark blue sea, leaving a milky-way wake of creamy foam, all spangled with golden gleamings.

Nor was it his unwonted magnitude, nor his remarkable hue, nor yet his deformed lower jaw, that so much invested the whale with natural terror, as that unexampled, intelligent malignity which, according to specific accounts, he had over and over again evinced in his assaults. More than all, his treacherous retreats struck more of dismay than perhaps aught else. For, when swimming before his exulting pursuers, with every apparent symptom of alarm, he had several times been known to turn round suddenly, and, bearing down upon them, either stave their boats to splinters, or drive them back in consternation to their ship.

Already several fatalities had attended his chase. But though similar disasters however little bruited ashore, were by no means unusual in the fishery; yet, in most instances, such seemed the White Whale's infernal aforethought of ferocity, that every dismembering or death that he caused, was not wholly regarded as having been inflicted by an unintelligent agent.

Judge, then, to what pitches of inflamed, distracted fury the minds of his more desperate hunters were impelled, when amid the chips of chewed boats, and the sinking limbs of torn comrades, they swam out of the white curds of the whale's direful wrath into the serene, exasperating sunlight, that smiled on, as if at a birth or a bridal.

---

unensanguined billows: unbloodied waves. **thrown out**: alluded to; see Ch. 36.

His three boats stove around him, and oars and men both whirling in the eddies; one captain, seizing the line-knife° from his broken prow, had dashed at the whale, as an Arkansas duellist[6] at his foe, blindly seeking with a six inch blade to reach the fathom-deep life of the whale. That captain was Ahab. And then it was that suddenly sweeping his sickle-shaped lower jaw beneath him, Moby Dick had reaped away Ahab's leg, as a mower a blade of grass in the field. No turbaned Turk, no hired Venetian or Malay, could have smote him with more seeming malice. Small reason was there to doubt, then, that ever since that almost fatal encounter, Ahab had cherished a wild vindictiveness against the whale, all the more fell° for that in his frantic morbidness he at last came to identify with him, not only all his bodily woes, but all his intellectual and spiritual exasperations. The White Whale swam before him as the monomaniac incarnation of all those malicious agencies which some deep men feel eating in them, till they are left living on with half a heart and half a lung. That intangible malignity which has been from the beginning; **to whose dominion even the modern Christians ascribe one-half of the worlds**; which the ancient Ophites[7] of the east reverenced in their statue devil;—Ahab did not fall down and worship it like them; but deliriously transferring its idea to the abhorred white whale, he pitted himself, all mutilated, against it. All that most maddens and torments; all that stirs up the lees of things; all truth with malice in it; all that cracks the sinews and cakes the brain; all the subtle demonisms of life and thought; all evil, to crazy Ahab, were visibly personified, and made practically assailable in Moby Dick. He piled upon the whale's white hump the sum of all the general rage and hate felt by his whole race from Adam down; and then, as if his chest had been a mortar, he burst his hot heart's shell upon it.

It is not probable that this monomania° in him took its instant rise at the precise time of his bodily dismemberment. Then, in darting at the monster, knife in hand, he had but given loose to a sudden, passionate, corporal animosity; and when he received the stroke that tore him, he probably but felt the agonizing bodily laceration, but nothing more. Yet, when by this collision forced to turn towards home, and for long months of days and weeks, Ahab and anguish lay stretched together in one hammock, rounding in mid winter that dreary, howling Patagonian Cape;° then it was, that his torn body and gashed soul bled into one another; and so interfusing, made him mad. That it was only then, on the homeward voyage, after the encounter, that the final monomania seized him, seems all but certain from the fact that, at intervals during the passage, he was a raving lunatic; and, though unlimbed of a leg, yet such vital strength yet lurked in his Egyptian chest,[8] and was moreover intensified by his delirium, that his mates were forced to lace him fast, even there, as he sailed, raving in his hammock. In a strait-jacket, he swung to the mad rockings of the gales. And, when running into more sufferable latitudes, the ship, with mild stun'-sails° spread, floated across the tranquil tropics, and, to all appearances, the old man's delirium seemed left behind him with the Cape Horn swells, and he came forth from his dark den into the blessed light and air; even then, when he bore that

---

line-knife: for cutting the whale line in an emergency. **fell**: fierce; cruel. **monomania**: obsession with one subject. **Patagonian Cape**: Cape Horn. **stun'sails**: light sails hung from extensions to both yardarms, used in gentle winds.

firm, collected front, however pale, and issued his calm orders once again; and his mates thanked God the direful madness was now gone; even then, Ahab, in his hidden self, raved on. Human madness is oftentimes a cunning and most feline thing. When you think it fled, it may have but become transfigured into some still subtler form. Ahab's full lunacy subsided not, but deepeningly contracted; like the unabated Hudson, when that noble Northman flows narrowly, but unfathomably through the Highland gorge. But, as in his narrow-flowing monomania, not one jot of Ahab's broad madness had been left behind; so in that broad madness, not one jot of his great natural intellect had perished. That before living agent, now became the living instrument. If such a furious trope° may stand, his special lunacy stormed his general sanity, and carried it, and turned all its concentred cannon upon its own mad mark; so that far from having lost his strength, Ahab, to that one end, did now possess a thousand fold more potency than ever he had sanely brought to bear upon any one reasonable object.

This is much; yet Ahab's larger, darker, deeper part remains unhinted. But vain to popularize profundities, and all truth is profound. Winding far down from within the very heart of this spiked Hotel de Cluny[9] where we here stand—however grand and wonderful, now quit it;—and take your way, ye **nobler, sadder** souls, to those vast Roman halls of Thermes; where far beneath the fantastic towers of man's upper earth, his root of grandeur, his whole awful essence sits in bearded state; an antique buried beneath antiquities, and throned on torsoes!° So with a broken throne, the great gods mock that captive king; so like a Caryatid,[10] he patient sits, upholding on his frozen brow the piled entablatures of ages. Wind ye down there, ye prouder, sadder souls! question that proud, sad king! A family likeness! aye, he did beget ye, ye young exiled royalties; and from your grim sire only will the old State-secret come.

Now, in his heart, Ahab had some glimpse of this, namely: all my means are sane, my motive and my object mad. Yet without power to kill, or change, or shun the fact; he likewise knew that to mankind he did long dissemble; in some sort, did still. But that thing of his dissembling was only subject to his perceptibility, not to his will determinate.° Nevertheless, so well did he succeed in that dissembling, that when with ivory leg he stepped ashore at last, no Nantucketer thought him otherwise than but naturally grieved, and that to the quick, with the terrible casualty which had overtaken him.

The report of his undeniable delirium at sea was likewise popularly ascribed to a kindred cause. And so too, all the added moodiness which always afterwards, to the very day of sailing in the Pequod on the present voyage, sat brooding on his brow. Nor is it so very unlikely, that far from distrusting his fitness for another whaling voyage, on account of such dark symptoms, the calculating people of that prudent isle were inclined to harbor the conceit, that for those very reasons he was all the better qualified and set on edge, for a pursuit so full of rage and wildness as the bloody hunt of whales. Gnawed within and scorched without, with the infixed, unrelenting fangs of some incurable idea; such an one, could he be found, would seem the very man

---

trope: figure of speech. **torsoes**: broken statuary. **to his perceptibility, not to his will determinate**: that is, he could see his deception but not control it.

to dart his iron and lift his lance against the most appalling of all brutes. Or, if for any reason thought to be corporeally incapacitated for that, yet such an one would seem superlatively competent to cheer and howl on his underlings to the attack. But be all this as it may, certain it is, that with the mad secret of his unabated rage bolted up and keyed° in him, Ahab had purposely sailed upon the present voyage with the one only and all-engrossing object of hunting the White Whale. Had any one of his old acquaintances on shore but half dreamed of what was lurking in him then, how soon would their aghast and righteous souls have wrenched the ship from such a fiendish man! They were bent on profitable cruises, the profit to be counted down in dollars from the mint. He was intent on an audacious, immitigable, and super-natural revenge.

Here, then, was this grey-headed, ungodly old man, chasing with curses a Job's whale[11] round the world, at the head of a crew, too, chiefly made up of mongrel renegades, and castaways, and cannibals—morally enfeebled also, by the incompe-tence of mere unaided virtue or right-mindedness in Starbuck, the invulnerable jol-lity of indifference and recklessness in Stubb, and the pervading mediocrity in Flask. Such a crew, so officered, seemed specially picked and packed by some infernal fatality to help him to his monomaniac revenge. How it was that they so aboundingly responded to the old man's ire—by what evil magic their souls were possessed, that at times his hate seemed almost theirs; the White Whale as much their insufferable foe as his; how all this came to be—what the White Whale was to them, or how to their unconscious understandings, also, in some dim, unsuspected way, he might have seemed the gliding great demon of the seas of life,—all this to explain, would be to dive deeper than Ishmael can go. The subterranean miner that works in us all, how can one tell whither leads his shaft by the ever shifting, muffled sound of his pick? Who does not feel the irresistible arm drag? What skiff in tow of a seventy-four° can stand still? For one, I gave myself up to the abandonment of the time and the place; but while yet all a-rush to encounter the whale, could see naught in that brute but the deadliest ill.

keyed: locked. **skiff in tow of a seventy-four**: row boat pulled by a battleship.

CHAPTER 42

THE WHITENESS OF THE WHALE

W HAT the white whale was to Ahab, has been hinted; what, at times, he was to me, as yet remains unsaid.

Aside from those more obvious considerations touching Moby Dick, which could not but occasionally awaken in any man's soul some alarm, there was another thought, or rather vague, nameless horror concerning him, which at times by its intensity completely overpowered all the rest; and yet so mystical and well nigh ineffable was it, that I almost despair of putting it in a comprehensible form. It was the whiteness of the whale[1] that above all things appalled me. But how can I hope to explain myself here; and yet, in some dim, random way, explain myself I must, else all these chapters might be naught.

Though in many natural objects, whiteness refiningly enhances beauty, as if imparting some special virtue of its own, as in marbles, japonicas,° and pearls; and though various nations have in some way recognised a certain royal pre-eminence in this hue; even the barbaric, grand old kings of Pegu[2] placing the title "Lord of the White Elephants" above all their other magniloquent ascriptions of dominion; and the modern kings of Siam° unfurling the same snow-white quadruped in the royal standard; and the Hanoverian° flag bearing the one figure of a snow-white charger; and the great Austrian Empire, Cæsarian heir to overlording Rome,[3] having for the imperial color the same imperial hue; and though this pre-eminence in it applies to the human race itself, giving the white man ideal mastership over every dusky tribe; and though, besides all this, whiteness has been even made significant of gladness, for among the Romans a white stone[4] marked a joyful day; and though in other mortal sympathies and symbolizings, this same hue is made the emblem of many touching, noble things—the innocence of brides, the benignity of age; though among the Red Men of America the giving of the white belt of wampum was the deepest pledge of honor; though in many climes, whiteness typifies the majesty of Justice in the ermine of the Judge, and contributes to the daily state of kings and queens drawn by milk-white steeds; though even in the higher mysteries of the most august religions it has been made the symbol of the divine spotlessness and

japonicas: white camelias (*Camelia japonica*). **Siam**: Thailand. **Hanoverian**: of Hanover, a German state.

179

power, by the Persian fire worshippers,[5] the white forked flame being held the holiest on the altar; and in the Greek mythologies, Great Jove himself being made incarnate in a snow-white bull;[6] and though to the noble Iroquois, the midwinter sacrifice of the sacred White Dog[7] was by far the holiest festival of their theology, that spotless, faithful creature being held the purest envoy they could send to the Great Spirit with the annual tidings of their own fidelity; and though directly from the Latin word for white, all Christian priests derive the name of one part of their sacred vesture, the alb or tunic, worn beneath the cassock;[8] and though among the holy pomps of the Romish faith, white is specially employed in the celebration of the Passion of our Lord; though in the Vision of St. John, white robes are given to the redeemed, and the four-and-twenty elders stand clothed in white before the great white throne, and the Holy One that sitteth there white like wool;[9] yet for all these accumulated associations, with whatever is sweet, and honorable, and sublime, there yet lurks an elusive something in the innermost idea of this hue, which strikes more of panic to the soul than that redness which affrights in blood.

This elusive quality it is, which causes the thought of whiteness, when divorced from more kindly associations, and coupled with any object terrible in itself, to heighten that terror to the furthest bounds. Witness the white bear of the poles, and the white shark of the tropics; what but their smooth, flaky whiteness makes them the transcendent horrors they are? That ghastly whiteness it is which imparts such an abhorrent mildness, even more loathsome than terrific, to the dumb gloating of their aspect. So that not the fierce-fanged tiger in his heraldic coat° can so stagger courage as the white-shrouded bear or shark.*

Bethink thee of the albatross: whence come those clouds of spiritual wonderment and pale dread, in which that white phantom sails in all imaginations? Not Coleridge first threw that spell;[10] but God's great, unflattering laureate, Nature.*

---

* With reference to the Polar bear, it may possibly be urged by him who would fain go still deeper into this matter, that it is not the whiteness, separately regarded, which heightens the intolerable hideousness of that brute; for, analysed, that heightened hideousness, it might be said, only arises from the circumstance, that the irresponsible ferociousness of the creature stands invested in the fleece of celestial innocence and love; and hence, by bringing together two such opposite emotions in our minds, the Polar bear frightens us with so unnatural a contrast. But even assuming all this to be true; yet, were it not for the whiteness, you would not have that intensified terror.

As for the white shark, the white gliding ghostliness of repose in that creature, when beheld in his ordinary moods, strangely tallies with the same quality in the Polar quadruped. This peculiarity is most vividly hit by the French in the name they bestow upon that fish. The Romish mass for the dead begins with "Requiem eternam" (eternal rest), whence *Requiem* denominating the mass itself, and any other funereal music. Now, in allusion to the white, silent stillness of death in this shark, and the mild deadliness of his habits, the French call him *Requin*.

* I remember the first albatross I ever saw. It was during a prolonged gale, in waters hard upon the Antarctic seas. From my forenoon watch below, I ascended to the overclouded deck; and there, dashed upon the main hatches, I saw a regal, feathery thing of unspotted whiteness, and with a hooked, Roman bill sublime. At intervals, it arched forth its vast archangel wings, as if to embrace some holy ark. Wondrous flutterings and throbbings shook it. Though bodily unharmed, it uttered cries, as some king's ghost in supernatural distress. Through its inexpressible, strange eyes, methought I peeped to secrets

---

heraldic coat: striped, as in a coat of arms.

Most famous in our Western annals and Indian traditions is that of the White Steed of the Praries;[13] a magnificent milk-white charger, large-eyed, small-headed, bluff-chested, and with the dignity of a thousand monarchs in his lofty, overscorning carriage. He was the elected Xerxes[14] of vast herds of wild horses, whose pastures in those days were only fenced by the Rocky Mountains and the Alleghanies. At their flaming head he westward trooped it like that chosen star[15] which every evening leads on the hosts of light. The flashing cascade of his mane, the curving comet of his tail, invested him with housings more resplendent than gold and silver-beaters could have furnished him. A most imperial and archangelical apparition of that unfallen, western world, which to the eyes of the old trappers and hunters revived the glories of those primeval times when Adam walked majestic as a god, bluff-bowed° and fearless as this mighty steed. Whether marching amid his aides and marshals in the van° of countless cohorts that endlessly streamed it over the plains, like an Ohio;° or whether with his circumambient° subjects browsing all around at the horizon, the White Steed gallopingly reviewed them with warm nostrils reddening through his cool milkiness; in whatever aspect he presented himself, always to the bravest Indians he was the object of trembling reverence and awe. Nor can it be questioned from what stands on legendary record of this noble horse, that it was his spiritual whiteness chiefly, which so clothed him with divineness; and that this divineness had that in it which, though commanding worship, at the same time enforced a certain nameless terror.

But there are other instances where this whiteness loses all that accessory and strange glory which invests it in the White Steed and Albatross.

What is it that in the Albino man so peculiarly repels and often shocks the eye, as that sometimes he is loathed by his own kith and kin! It is that whiteness which invests him, a thing expressed by the name he bears. The Albino is as well made as

---

which took hold of God. As Abraham before the angels,[11] I bowed myself; the white thing was so white, its wings so wide, and in those for ever exiled waters, I had lost the miserable warping memories of traditions and of towns. Long I gazed at that prodigy of plumage. I cannot tell, can only hint, the things that darted through me then. But at last I awoke; and turning, asked a sailor what bird was this. A goney, he replied. Goney! I never had heard that name before; is it conceivable that this glorious thing is utterly unknown to men ashore! never! But some time after, I learned that goney was some seaman's name for albatross. So that by no possibility could Coleridge's wild Rhyme have had aught to do with those mystical impressions which were mine, when I saw that bird upon our deck. For neither had I then read the Rhyme, nor knew the bird to be an albatross. Yet, in saying this, I do but indirectly burnish a little brighter the noble merit of the poem and the poet.

I assert, then, that in the wondrous bodily whiteness of the bird chiefly lurks the secret of the spell; a truth the more evinced in this, that by a solecism of terms there are birds called grey albatrosses; and these I have frequently seen, but never with such emotions as when I beheld the Antarctic fowl.

But how had the mystic thing been caught? Whisper it not, and I will tell; with a treacherous hook and line, as the fowl floated on the sea. At last the Captain made a postman of it;[12] tying a lettered, leathern tally round its neck, with the ship's time and place; and then letting it escape. **But I doubt not, that leathern tally, meant for man, was taken off in Heaven, when the white fowl flew to join the wing-folding, the invoking, and adoring cherubim!**

---

bluff-bowed: here, broad-chested. *van*: short for vanguard. *an Ohio*: like the wide Ohio River. *circumambient*: surrounding.

other men—has no substantive deformity—and yet this mere aspect of all-pervading whiteness makes him more strangely hideous than the ugliest abortion. Why should this be so?

Nor, in quite other aspects, does Nature in her least palpable but not the less malicious agencies, fail to enlist among her forces this crowning attribute of the terrible. From its snowy aspect, the gauntleted ghost of the Southern Seas has been denominated the White Squall.° Nor, in some historic instances, has the art of human malice omitted so potent an auxiliary. How wildly it heightens the effect of that passage in Froissart, when, masked in the snowy symbol of their faction, the desperate White Hoods of Ghent murder their bailiff in the market-place![16]

Nor, in some things, does the common, hereditary experience of all mankind fail to bear witness to the supernaturalism of this hue. It cannot well be doubted, that the one visible quality in the aspect of the dead which most appals the gazer, is the marble pallor lingering there; as if indeed that pallor were as much like the badge of consternation in the other world, as of mortal trepidation here. And from that pallor of the dead, we borrow the expressive hue of the shroud in which we wrap them. Nor even in our superstitions do we fail to throw the same snowy mantle round our phantoms; all ghosts rising in a milk-white fog—Yea, while these terrors seize us, let us add, that even the king of terrors, when personified by the evangelist, rides on his pallid horse.[17]

Therefore, in his other moods, symbolize whatever grand or gracious thing he will by whiteness, no man can deny that in its profoundest idealized significance it calls up a peculiar apparition to the soul.

But though without dissent this point be fixed, how is mortal man to account for it? To analyse it, would seem impossible. Can we, then, by the citation of some of those instances wherein this thing of whiteness—though for the time either wholly or in great part stripped of all direct associations calculated to impart to it aught fearful, but, nevertheless, is found to exert over us the same sorcery, however modified;—can we thus hope to light upon some chance clue to conduct us to the hidden cause we seek?

Let us try. But in a matter like this, subtlety appeals to subtlety, and without imagination no man can follow another into these halls. And though, doubtless, some at least of the imaginative impressions about to be presented may have been shared by most men, yet few perhaps were entirely conscious of them at the time, and therefore may not be able to recall them now.

Why to the man of untutored ideality, who happens to be but loosely acquainted with the peculiar character of the day, does the bare mention of Whitsuntide[18] marshal in the fancy such long, dreary, speechless processions of slow-pacing pilgrims, down-cast and hooded with new-fallen snow? Or, to the unread, unsophisticated Protestant of the Middle American States, why does the passing mention of a White Friar or a White Nun,[19] evoke such an eyeless statue in the soul?

Or what is there apart from the traditions of dungeoned warriors and kings (which will not wholly account for it) that makes the White Tower of London tell so

White Squall: sudden, violent tropical storm with a characteristic white cloud.

much more strongly on the imagination of an untravelled American,[20] than those other storied structures, its neighbors—the Byward Tower, or even the Bloody? And those sublimer towers, the White Mountains of New Hampshire,[21] whence, in peculiar moods, comes that gigantic ghostliness over the soul at the bare mention of that name, while the thought of Virginia's Blue Ridge is full of a soft, dewy, distant dreaminess? Or why, irrespective of all latitudes and longitudes, does the name of the White Sea exert such a spectralness over the fancy, while that of the Yellow Sea[22] lulls us with mortal thoughts of long lacquered mild afternoons on the waves, followed by the gaudiest and yet sleepiest of sunsets? Or, to choose a wholly unsubstantial instance, purely addressed to the fancy, why, in reading the old fairy tales of Central Europe, does "the tall pale man" of the Hartz forests, whose changeless pallor unrustlingly glides through the green of the groves—why is this phantom more terrible than all the whooping imps of the Blocksburg?[23]

Nor is it, altogether, the remembrance of her cathedral-toppling earthquakes; nor the stampedoes of her frantic seas; nor the tearlessness of arid skies that never rain; nor the sight of her wide field of leaning spires, wrenched cope-stones, and crosses all adroop (like canted° yards of anchored fleets); and her suburban avenues of house-walls lying over upon each other, as a tossed pack of cards;—it is not these things alone which make tearless Lima,[24] the strangest, saddest city thou can'st see. For Lima has taken the white veil; and there is a higher horror in this whiteness of her woe. Old as Pizarro,[25] this whiteness keeps her ruins for ever new; admits not the cheerful greenness of complete decay; spreads over her broken ramparts the rigid pallor of an apoplexy that fixes its own distortions.

I know that, to the common apprehension, this phenomenon of whiteness is not confessed to be the prime agent in exaggerating the terror of objects otherwise terrible; nor to the unimaginative mind is there aught of terror in those appearances whose awfulness to another mind almost solely consists in this one phenomenon, especially when exhibited under any form at all approaching to muteness or universality.° What I mean by these two statements may perhaps be respectively elucidated by the following examples.

First: The mariner, when drawing nigh the coasts of foreign lands, if by night he hear the roar of breakers, starts to vigilance, and feels just enough of trepidation to sharpen all his faculties; but under precisely similar circumstances, let him be called from his hammock to view his ship sailing through a midnight sea of milky whiteness—as if from encircling headlands shoals° of combed white bears were swimming round him, then he feels a silent, superstitious dread;[26] the shrouded phantom of the whitened waters is horrible to him as a real ghost; in vain the lead° assures him he is still off soundings; heart and helm they both go down;[27] he never rests till blue water is under him again. Yet where is the mariner who will tell thee, "Sir, it was not so much the fear of striking hidden rocks, as the fear of that hideous whiteness that so stirred me?"

---

canted: tilted from the horizontal as a sign of mourning on naval vessels. **universality**: completeness; uncontrastedness. **shoals**: large numbers (usually of sea-creatures). **lead**: lead weight attached to a marked line, used for measuring water depth.

Second: To the native Indian of Peru, the continual sight of the snow-howdahed Andes[28] conveys naught of dread, except, perhaps, in the mere fancying of the eternal frosted desolateness reigning at such vast altitudes, and the natural conceit of what a fearfulness it would be to lose oneself in such inhuman solitudes. Much the same is it with the backwoodsman of the West, who with comparative indifference views an unbounded prairie sheeted with driven snow, no shadow of tree or twig to break the fixed trance of whiteness. Not so the sailor, beholding the scenery of the Antarctic seas; where at times, by some infernal trick of legerdemain in the powers of frost and air, he, shivering and half shipwrecked, instead of rainbows speaking hope and solace to his misery, views what seems a boundless church-yard grinning upon him with its lean ice monuments and splintered crosses.

But thou sayest, methinks this white-lead chapter about whiteness is but a white flag hung out from a craven soul; thou surrenderest to a hypo, Ishmael.

Tell me, why this strong young colt, foaled in some peaceful valley of Vermont, far removed from all beasts of prey—why is it that upon the sunniest day, if you but shake a fresh buffalo robe behind him, so that he cannot even see it, but only smells its wild animal muskiness—why will he start, snort, and with bursting eyes paw the ground in phrensies of affright? There is no remembrance in him of any gorings of wild creatures in his green northern home, so that the strange muskiness he smells cannot recall to him anything associated with the experience of former perils; for what knows he, this New England colt, of the black bisons of distant Oregon?[29]

No: but here thou beholdest even in a dumb brute, the instinct of the knowledge of the demonism **in** the world. Though thousands of miles from Oregon, still when he smells that savage musk, the rending, goring bison herds are as present as to the deserted wild foal of the prairies, which this instant they may be trampling into dust.

Thus, then, the muffled rollings of a milky sea; the bleak rustlings of the festooned frosts of mountains; the desolate shiftings of the windrowed snows of prairies; all these, to Ishmael, are as the shaking of that buffalo robe to the frightened colt!

Though neither knows where lie the nameless things of which the mystic sign gives forth such hints; yet with me, as with the colt, somewhere those things must exist. Though in many of its aspects this visible world seems formed in love, the invisible spheres were formed in fright.

But not yet have we solved the incantation° of this whiteness, and learned why it appeals with such power to the soul; and more strange and far more portentous—why, as we have seen, it is at once the most meaning symbol of spiritual things, nay, the very veil of the Christian's Deity; and yet should be as it is, the intensifying agent in things the most appalling to mankind.

Is it that by its indefiniteness it shadows forth the heartless voids and immensities of the universe, and thus stabs us from behind with the thought of annihilation, when beholding the white depths of the milky way? Or is it, that as in essence whiteness is not so much a color[30] as the visible absence of color, and at the same time the concrete of all colors; is it for these reasons that there is such a dumb blankness, full of meaning, in a wide landscape of snows—a colorless, all-color of atheism from

incantation: spell, enchantment.

which we shrink? And when we consider that other theory of the natural philosophers,[31] that all other earthly hues—every stately or lovely emblazoning—the sweet tinges of sunset skies and woods; yea, and the gilded velvets of butterflies, and the butterfly cheeks of young girls; all these are but subtile deceits, not actually inherent in substances, but only laid on from without; **so that all deified Nature absolutely paints like the harlot, whose allurements cover nothing but the charnel-house within**; and when we proceed further, and consider that the mystical cosmetic which produces every one of her hues, the great principle of light, for ever remains white or colorless in itself, and if operating without medium upon matter, would touch all objects, even tulips and roses, with its own blank tinge—pondering all this, the palsied universe lies before us a leper; and like wilful travellers in Lapland,[32] who refuse to wear colored and coloring glasses upon their eyes, so the wretched infidel gazes himself blind at the monumental white shroud that wraps all the prospect around him. And of all these things the Albino whale was the symbol. Wonder ye then at the fiery hunt?

REVISION NARRATIVE

Nature as Harlot

One of the most crippling British expurgations to *Moby-Dick* occurs in the final paragraph of "The Whiteness of the Whale." Ishmael calls the chapter an attempt to "explain myself," and by essaying on "whiteness," he hopes to get to the heart of what appalls him about the idea of Moby Dick. His "dim, random way" is, in fact, quite methodical; and here, he explains that whiteness instills fear because it symbolizes the "dumb blankness," or nothingness, of the world. But the consequence of this deep, metaphysical view is that given this nothingness, nature—with all its color—is itself not real, or worse, just so many "subtile deceits." Ishmael's intensity mounts as he reaches for the concluding line: "Wonder ye then at the fiery hunt?" But before he poses this question, his dismay at the physical world's deceptiveness achieves its most forceful expression: "so that all deified Nature absolutely paints like the harlot, whose allurements cover nothing but the charnel-house within." The British edition expurgates the line not only for its graphic image of a painted prostitute and a warehouse for dead bodies but also for its equating "deified Nature," that is, God's creation, with prostitution and death.

CHAPTER 43

HARK!

"Hist! Did you hear that noise, Cabaco?"

It was the middle-watch: a fair moonlight; the seamen were standing in a cordon, extending from one of the fresh-water butts in the waist, to the scuttle-butt[1] near the taffrail. In this manner, they passed the buckets to fill the scuttle-butt. Standing, for the most part, on the hallowed precincts of the quarter-deck, they were careful not to speak or rustle their feet. From hand to hand, the buckets went in the deepest silence, only broken by the occasional flap of a sail, and the steady hum of the unceasingly advancing keel.

It was in the midst of this repose, that Archy, one of the cordon, whose post was near the after-hatches, whispered to his neighbor, a Cholo,° the words above.

"Hist! did you hear that noise, Cabaco?"

"Take the bucket, will ye, Archy? what noise d'ye mean?"

"There it is again—under the hatches—don't you hear it—a cough—it sounded like a cough."

"Cough be damned! Pass along that return bucket."

"There again—there it is!—it sounds like two or three sleepers turning over, now!"

"Caramba! have done, shipmate, will ye? It's the three soaked biscuits ye eat for supper turning over inside of ye—nothing else. Look to the bucket!"

"Say what ye will, shipmate; I've sharp ears."

"Aye, you are the chap, ain't ye, that heard the hum of the old Quakeress's knitting-needles[2] fifty miles at sea from Nantucket; you're the chap."

"Grin away; we'll see what turns up. Hark ye, Cabaco, there is somebody down in the after-hold that has not yet been seen on deck; and I suspect our old Mogul knows something of it too. I heard Stubb tell Flask, one morning watch, that there was something of that sort in the wind."

"Tish! the bucket!"

Cholo: Peruvian of Indian and Spanish lineage.

CHAPTER 44

THE CHART

Had you followed Captain Ahab down into his cabin after the squall that took place on the night succeeding that wild ratification of his purpose with his crew, you would have seen him go to a locker in the transom, and bringing out a large wrinkled roll of yellowish sea charts, spread them before him on his screwed-down table. Then seating himself before it, you would have seen him intently study the various lines and shadings which there met his eye; and with slow but steady pencil trace additional courses over spaces that before were blank. At intervals, he would refer to piles of old log-books beside him, wherein were set down the seasons and places in which, on various former voyages of various ships, sperm whales had been captured or seen.[1]

While thus employed, the heavy pewter lamp suspended in chains over his head, continually rocked with the motion of the ship, and for ever threw shifting gleams and shadows of lines upon his wrinkled brow, till it almost seemed that while he himself was marking out lines and courses on the wrinkled charts, some invisible pencil was also tracing lines and courses upon the deeply marked chart of his forehead.

But it was not this night in particular that, in the solitude of his cabin, Ahab thus pondered over his charts. Almost every night they were brought out; almost every night some pencil marks were effaced, and others were substituted. For with the charts of all four oceans before him, Ahab was threading a maze of currents and eddies, with a view to the more certain accomplishment of that monomaniac thought of his soul.

Now, to any one not fully acquainted with the ways of the leviathans, it might seem an absurdly hopeless task thus to seek out one solitary creature in the unhooped° oceans of this planet. But not so did it seem to Ahab, who knew the sets of all tides and currents; and thereby calculating the driftings of the sperm whale's food;° and, also, calling to mind the regular, ascertained seasons for hunting him in particular latitudes; could arrive at reasonable surmises, almost approaching to certainties, concerning the timeliest day to be upon this or that ground in search of his prey.

unhooped: Uncontained, by analogy to the hoops on barrels. ***sperm whale's food***: large deep-water squid.

So assured, indeed, is the fact concerning the periodicalness of the sperm whale's resorting to given waters, that many hunters believe that, could he be closely observed and studied throughout the world; were the logs for one voyage of the entire whale fleet carefully collated, then the migrations of the sperm whale would be found to correspond in invariability to those of the herring-shoals or the flights of swallows. On this hint, attempts have been made to construct elaborate migratory charts of the sperm whale.*

Besides, when making a passage from one feeding-ground to another, the sperm whales, guided by some infallible instinct—say, rather, secret intelligence from the Deity—mostly swim in *veins,* as they are called; continuing their way along a given ocean-line with such undeviating exactitude, that no ship ever sailed her course, by any chart, with one tithe° of such marvellous precision. Though, in these cases, the direction taken by any one whale be straight as a surveyor's parallel, and though the line of advance be strictly confined to its own unavoidable, straight wake, yet the arbitrary *vein* in which at these times he is said to swim, generally embraces some few miles in width (more or less, as the vein is presumed to expand or contract); but never exceeds the visual sweep from the whale-ship's mast-heads, when circumspectly gliding along this magic zone. The sum is, that at particular seasons within that breadth and along that path, migrating whales may with great confidence be looked for.

And hence not only at substantiated times, upon well known separate feeding-grounds, could Ahab hope to encounter his prey; but in crossing the widest expanses of water between those grounds he could, by his art, so place and time himself on his way, as even then not to be wholly without prospect of a meeting.

There was a circumstance which at first sight seemed to entangle his delirious but still methodical scheme. But not so in the reality, perhaps. Though the gregarious sperm whales have their regular seasons for particular grounds, yet in general you cannot conclude that the herds which haunted such and such a latitude or longitude this year, say, will turn out to be identically the same with those that were found there the preceding season; though there are peculiar and unquestionable instances where the contrary of this has proved true. In general, the same remark, only within a less wide limit, applies to the solitaries and hermits among the matured, aged sperm whales. So that though Moby Dick had in a former year been seen, for example, on what is called the Seychelle ground° in the Indian ocean, or

---

* Since the above was written, the statement is happily borne out by an official circular, issued by Lieutenant Maury,[2] of the National Observatory, Washington, April 16th, 1851. By that circular, it appears that precisely such a chart is in course of completion; and portions of it are presented in the circular. "This chart divides the ocean into districts of five degrees of latitude by five degrees of longitude; perpendicularly through each of which districts are twelve columns for the twelve months; and horizontally through each of which districts are three lines; one to show the number of days that have been spent in each month in every district, and the two others to show the number of days in which whales, sperm or right, have been seen."

---

tithe: typically a ten-percent religious tax or pledge, but here simply one-tenth. ***Seychelle ground***: the whaling waters near the Seychelle Islands, northeast of Madagascar.

Volcano Bay[3] on the Japanese Coast; yet it did not follow, that were the Pequod to visit either of those spots at any subsequent corresponding season, she would infallibly encounter him there. So, too, with some other feeding grounds, where he had at times revealed himself. But all these seemed only his casual stopping-places and ocean-inns, so to speak, not his places of prolonged abode. And where Ahab's chances of accomplishing his object have hitherto been spoken of, allusion has only been made to whatever way-side, antecedent, extra prospects were his, ere a particular set time or place were attained, when all possibilities would become probabilities, and, as Ahab fondly° thought, every **possibility** the next thing to a certainty. That particular set time and place were conjoined in the one technical phrase—the Season-on-the-Line.° For there and then, for several consecutive years, Moby Dick had been periodically descried, lingering in those waters for awhile, as the sun, in its annual round, loiters for a predicted interval in any one sign of the Zodiac.[4] There it was, too, that most of the deadly encounters with the white whale had taken place; there the waves were storied with his deeds; there also was that tragic spot where the monomaniac old man had found the awful motive to his vengeance. But in the cautious comprehensiveness and unloitering vigilance with which Ahab threw his brooding soul into this unfaltering hunt, he would not permit himself to rest all his hopes upon the one crowning fact above mentioned, however flattering it might be to those hopes; nor in the sleeplessness of his vow could he so tranquillize his unquiet heart as to postpone all intervening quest.

Now, the Pequod had sailed from Nantucket at the very beginning of the Season-on-the-Line. No possible endeavor then could enable her commander to make the great passage southwards, double Cape Horn, and then running down sixty degrees of latitude° arrive in the equatorial Pacific in time to cruise there. Therefore, he must wait for the next ensuing season. Yet the premature hour of the Pequod's sailing had, perhaps, been covertly selected by Ahab, with a view to this very complexion of things. Because, an interval of three hundred and sixty-five days and nights was before him; an interval which, instead of impatiently enduring ashore, he would spend in a miscellaneous hunt; if by chance the White Whale, spending his vacation in seas far remote from his periodical feeding-grounds, should turn up his wrinkled brow off the Persian Gulf, or in the Bengal Bay,[5] or China Seas, or in any other waters haunted by his race. So that Monsoons, Pampas, Nor-Westers, Harmattans, Trades; any wind but the Levanter and Simoom,[6] might blow Moby Dick into the devious zig-zag world-circle of the Pequod's circumnavigating wake.

But granting all this; yet, regarded discreetly and coolly, seems it not but a mad idea, this; that in the broad boundless ocean, one solitary whale, even if encountered, should be thought capable of individual recognition from his hunter, even as a white-bearded Mufti in the thronged thoroughfares of Constantinople?° **Yes.** For the peculiar snow-white brow of Moby Dick, and his snow-white hump, could not but

---

fondly: foolishly. *Season-on-the-Line*: the best time for whaling along the Equator ("the Line") in the Pacific. *running down sixty degrees of latitude*: sailing north in the Pacific for 60 degrees from Cape Horn toward the equator. *Mufti . . . Constantinople*: official interpreter of Islamic law; *Constantinople* now Istanbul, capital of Turkey.

be unmistakable. And have I not tallied° the whale, Ahab would mutter to himself, as after poring over his charts till long after midnight he would throw himself back in reveries—tallied him, and shall he escape? His broad fins are bored, and scalloped out° like a lost sheep's ear! And here, his mad mind would run on in a breathless race; till a weariness and faintness of pondering came over him; and in the open air of the deck he would seek to recover his strength. Ah, God! what trances of torments does that man endure who is consumed with one unachieved revengeful desire. He sleeps with clenched hands; and wakes with his own bloody nails in his palms.

Often, when forced from his hammock by exhausting and intolerably vivid dreams of the night, which, resuming his own intense thoughts through the day, carried them on amid a clashing of phrensies, and whirled them round and round in his blazing brain, till the very throbbing of his life-spot became insufferable anguish; and when, as was sometimes the case, these spiritual throes in him heaved his being up from its base, and a chasm seemed opening in him, from which forked flames and lightnings shot up, and accursed fiends beckoned him to leap down among them; when this hell in himself[7] yawned beneath him, a wild cry would be heard through the ship; and with glaring eyes Ahab would burst from his state room, as though escaping from a bed that was on fire. Yet these, perhaps, instead of being the unsuppressable symptoms of some latent weakness, or fright at his own resolve, were but the plainest tokens of its intensity. For, at such times, crazy Ahab, the scheming, unappeasedly steadfast hunter of the white whale; this Ahab that had gone to his hammock, was not the agent that so caused him to burst from it in horror again. The

REVISION NARRATIVE

Yes or No

In the paragraph on the previous page beginning "But granting all this," Ishmael asks a question, answers it with one word and a follow-up sentence, and then slips into Ahab's interior monologue. With the sentence beginning "And here," Ishmael returns to his point of view, but with his invocation beginning "Ah, God!" he provides an interior monologue of his own. Thus, the narration seems to navigate through two minds. But Melville's opening question, or rather Ishmael's answer to his own question, poses problems. The question asks whether trying to find "one solitary whale" in the ocean is madness. In the American edition, Ishmael answers "Yes!" However, the follow-up sentence, beginning with "For," tells us that Moby Dick's whiteness is "unmistakable," and the implication is that it is not madness to assume one can find this one unmistakable white whale at sea. Either Melville intended to have Ishmael say "Yes! However . . ." or "No! For . . ." But neither he nor his editor caught the inadequate "Yes! For . . ." combination. The NN edition changes the "yes" to "no"; but LCRE makes no change.

---

tallied: added up; a method of recording debts. ***scalloped out***: where the identity tag was torn off.

latter was the eternal, living principle or soul in him; and in sleep, being for the time dissociated from the characterizing mind, which at other times employed it for its outer vehicle or agent, it spontaneously sought escape from the scorching contiguity of the frantic thing, of which, for the time, it was no longer an integral. But as the mind does not exist unless leagued with the soul, therefore it must have been that, in Ahab's case, yielding up all his thoughts and fancies to his one supreme purpose; that purpose, by its own sheer inveteracy of will, forced itself against gods and devils into a kind of self-assumed, independent being of its own. Nay, could grimly live and burn, while the common vitality to which it was conjoined, fled horror-stricken from the unbidden and **unfathered** birth. Therefore, the tormented spirit that glared out of bodily eyes, when what seemed Ahab rushed from his room, was for the time but a vacated thing, a formless somnambulistic° being, a ray of living light, to be sure, but without an object to color, and therefore a blankness in itself. God help thee, old man, thy thoughts have created a creature in thee; and he whose intense thinking thus makes him a Prometheus; a vulture feeds upon that heart for ever;[8] that vulture the very creature he creates.

somnambulistic: sleep-walking.

CHAPTER 45

THE AFFIDAVIT

So far as what there may be of a narrative in this book; and, indeed, as indirectly touching one or two very interesting and curious particulars in the habits of sperm whales, the foregoing chapter, in its earlier part, is as important a one as will be found in this volume; but the leading matter of it requires to be still further and more familiarly enlarged upon, in order to be adequately understood, and moreover to take away any incredulity which a profound ignorance of the entire subject may induce in some minds, as to the natural verity of the main points of this affair.

I care not to perform this part of my task methodically; but shall be content to produce the desired impression by separate citations of items, practically or reliably known to me as a whaleman; and from these citations, I take it—the conclusion aimed at will naturally follow of itself.

First: I have personally known three instances where a whale, after receiving a harpoon, has effected a complete escape; and, after an interval (in one instance of three years), has been again struck by the same hand, and slain; when the two irons, both marked by the same private cypher, have been taken from the body. In the instance where three years intervened between the flinging of the two harpoons; and I think it may have been something more than that; the man who darted them happening, in the interval, to go in a trading ship on a voyage to Africa, went ashore there, joined a discovery party, and penetrated far into the interior, where he travelled for a period of nearly two years, often endangered by serpents, savages, tigers, poisonous miasmas, with all the other common perils incident to wandering in the heart of unknown regions. Meanwhile, the whale he had struck must also have been on its travels; no doubt it had thrice circumnavigated the globe, brushing with its flanks all the coasts of Africa; but to no purpose. This man and this whale again came together, and the one vanquished the other. I say I, myself, have known three instances similar to this; that is in two of them I saw the whales struck; and, upon the second attack, saw the two irons with the respective marks cut in them, afterwards taken from the dead fish. In the three-year instance, it so fell out that I was in the boat both times, first and last, and the last time distinctly recognized a peculiar sort of huge mole under the whale's eye, which I had observed there three years previous. I say three years, but I am pretty sure it was more than that. Here are three instances, then, which I personally know the truth of; but I have heard of many other instances from persons whose veracity in the matter there is no good ground to impeach.

Secondly: It is well known in the Sperm Whale Fishery, however ignorant the world ashore may be of it, that there have been several memorable historical instances where a particular whale in the ocean has been at distant times and places popularly cognisable. Why such a whale became thus marked was not altogether and originally owing to his bodily peculiarities as distinguished from other whales; for however peculiar in that respect any chance whale may be, they soon put an end to his peculiarities by killing him, and boiling him down into a peculiarly valuable oil. No: the reason was this: that from the fatal experiences of the fishery there hung a terrible prestige of perilousness about such a whale as there did about Rinaldo Rinaldini,[1] insomuch that most fishermen were content to recognise him by merely touching their tarpaulins when he would be discovered lounging by them on the sea, without seeking to cultivate a more intimate acquaintance. Like some poor devils ashore that happen to know an irascible great man, they make distant unobtrusive salutations to him in the street, lest if they pursued the acquaintance further, they might receive a summary thump for their presumption.

But not only did each of these famous whales enjoy great individual celebrity—nay, you may call it an ocean-wide renown; not only was he famous in life and now is immortal in forecastle stories after death, but he was admitted into all the rights, privileges, and distinctions of a name; had as much a name indeed as Cambyses or Cæsar.[2] Was it not so, O Timor Jack! thou famed leviathan, scarred like an iceberg, who so long did'st lurk in the Oriental straits of that name, whose spout was oft seen from the palmy beach of Ombay?[3] Was it not so, O New Zealand Tom! thou terror of all cruisers that crossed their wakes in the vicinity of the Tattoo Land?[4] Was it not so, O Morquan! King of Japan, whose lofty jet they say at times assumed the semblance of a snow-white cross against the sky? Was it not so, O Don Miguel![5] thou Chilian whale, marked like an old tortoise with mystic hieroglyphics upon the back! In plain prose, here are four whales as well known to the students of Cetacean History as Marius or Sylla[6] to the classic scholar.

But this is not all. New Zealand Tom and Don Miguel, after at various times creating great havoc among the boats of different vessels, were finally gone in quest of, systematically hunted out, chased and killed by valiant whaling captains, who heaved up their anchors with that express object as much in view, as in setting out through the Narragansett Woods, Captain **Butler** of old had it in his mind to capture that notorious murderous savage Annawon,[7] the headmost warrior of the Indian King Philip.

I do not know where I can find a better place than just here, to make mention of one or two other things, which to me seem important, as in printed form establishing in all respects the reasonableness of the whole story of the White Whale, more especially the catastrophe. For this is one of those disheartening instances where truth requires full as much bolstering as error. So ignorant are most landsmen of some of the plainest and most palpable wonders of the world, that without some hints touching the plain facts, historical and otherwise, of the fishery, they might scout° at Moby Dick as a monstrous fable, or still worse and more detestable, a hideous and intolerable allegory.[8]

scout: scoff.

First: Though most men have some vague flitting ideas of the general perils of the grand fishery, yet they have nothing like a fixed, vivid conception of those perils, and the frequency with which they recur. One reason perhaps is, that not one in fifty of the actual disasters and deaths by casualties in the fishery, ever finds a public record at home, however transient and immediately forgotten that record. Do you suppose that that poor fellow there, who this moment perhaps caught by the whale-line off the coast of New Guinea,[9] is being carried down to the bottom of the sea by the sounding leviathan—do you suppose that that poor fellow's name will appear in the newspaper obituary you will read to-morrow at your breakfast? No: because the mails are very irregular between here and New Guinea. In fact, did you ever hear what might be called regular news direct or indirect from New Guinea? Yet I tell you that upon one particular voyage which I made to the Pacific, among many **others,** we spoke° thirty different ships, every one of which had had a death by a whale, some of them more than one, and three that had each lost a boat's crew. For God's sake, be economical with your lamps and candles! not a gallon you burn, but at least one drop of man's blood was spilled for it.

Secondly: People ashore have indeed some indefinite idea that a whale is an enormous creature of enormous power; but I have ever found that when narrating to them some specific example of this two-fold enormousness, they have significantly complimented me upon my facetiousness; when, I declare upon my soul, I had no more idea of being facetious than Moses, when he wrote the history of the plagues of Egypt.[10]

But fortunately the special point I here seek can be established upon testimony entirely independent of my own. That point is this: The Sperm Whale is in some cases sufficiently powerful, knowing, and judiciously malicious, as with direct aforethought to stave in, utterly destroy, and sink a large ship; and what is more, the Sperm Whale *has* done it.

First: In the year 1820 the ship Essex, Captain Pollard, of Nantucket, was cruising in the Pacific Ocean. One day she saw spouts, lowered her boats, and gave chase to a shoal of sperm whales. Ere long, several of the whales were wounded; when, suddenly, a very large whale escaping from the boats, issued from the shoal, and bore directly down upon the ship. Dashing his forehead against her hull, he so stove her in, that in less than "ten minutes" she settled down and fell over. Not a surviving plank of her has been seen since. After the severest exposure, part of the crew reached the land in their boats. Being returned home at last, Captain Pollard once more sailed for the Pacific in command of another ship, but the gods shipwrecked him again upon unknown rocks and breakers; for the second time his ship was utterly lost, and forthwith forswearing the sea, he has never tempted it since. At this day Captain Pollard is a resident of Nantucket. I have seen Owen Chace, who was chief mate of the Essex at the time of the tragedy; I have read his plain and faithful narrative; I have conversed with his son;[11] and all this within a few miles of the scene of the catastrophe.*

---

* The following are extracts from Chace's narrative: "Every fact seemed to warrant me in concluding that it was anything but chance which directed his operations; he made two several attacks upon the ship, at

---

spoke: to "speak" a ship at sea is to communicate with it.

Secondly: The ship Union,[12] also of Nantucket, was in the year 1807 totally lost off the Azores by a similar onset, but the authentic particulars of this catastrophe I have never chanced to encounter, though from the whale hunters I have now and then heard casual allusions to it.

Thirdly: Some eighteen or twenty years ago Commodore J—then commanding an American sloop-of-war of the first class, happened to be dining with a party of whaling captains, on board a Nantucket ship in the harbor of Oahu, Sandwich Islands.[13] Conversation turning upon whales, the Commodore was pleased to be sceptical touching the amazing strength ascribed to them by the professional gentlemen present. He peremptorily denied for example, that any whale could so smite his stout sloop-of-war as to cause her to leak so much as a thimbleful. Very good; but there is more coming. Some weeks after, the commodore set sail in this impregnable craft for Valparaiso.° But he was stopped on the way by a portly sperm whale, that begged a few moments' confidential business with him. That business consisted in fetching the Commodore's craft such a thwack, that with all his pumps going he made straight for the nearest port to heave down and repair. I am not superstitious, but I consider the Commodore's interview with that whale as providential. **Was not Saul of Tarsus**[14] **converted from unbelief by a similar fright?** I tell you, the sperm whale will stand no nonsense.

I will now refer you to Langsdorff's Voyages for a little circumstance in point, peculiarly interesting to the writer hereof. Langsdorff, you must know by the way, was attached to the Russian Admiral Krusenstern's famous Discovery Expedition in the beginning of the present century. Captain Langsdorff thus begins his seventeenth chapter.

"By the thirteenth of May our ship was ready to sail, and the next day we were out in the open sea, on our way to Ochotsk.[15] The weather was very clear and fine, but so intolerably cold that we were obliged to keep on our fur clothing. For some

---

a short interval between them, both of which, according to their direction, were calculated to do us the most injury, by being made ahead, and thereby combining the speed of the two objects for the shock; to effect which, the exact manœuvres which he made were necessary. His aspect was most horrible, and such as indicated resentment and fury. He came directly from the shoal which we had just before entered, and in which we had struck three of his companions, as if fired with revenge for their sufferings." Again: "At all events, the whole circumstances taken together, all happening before my own eyes, and producing, at the time, impressions in my mind of decided, calculating mischief, on the part of the whale (many of which impressions I cannot now recall), induce me to be satisfied that I am correct in my opinion."

Here are his reflections some time after quitting the ship, during a black night in an open boat, when almost despairing of reaching any hospitable shore. "The dark ocean and swelling waters were nothing; the fears of being swallowed up by some dreadful tempest, or dashed upon hidden rocks, with all the other ordinary subjects of fearful contemplation, seemed scarcely entitled to a moment's thought; the dismal looking wreck, and *the horrid aspect and revenge of the whale,* wholly engrossed my reflections, until day again made its appearance."

In another place—p. 45,—he speaks of *"the mysterious and mortal attack of the animal."*

*　　*　　*　　*　　*　　*　　*　　*　　*　　*　　*

*　　*　　*　　*　　*　　*　　*　　*　　*　　*　　*

Valparaiso: Chilean port.

days we had very little wind; it was not till the nineteenth that a brisk gale from the northwest sprang up. An uncommon large whale, the body of which was larger than the ship itself, lay almost at the surface of the water, but was not perceived by any one on board till the moment when the ship, which was in full sail, was almost upon him, so that it was impossible to prevent its striking against him. We were thus placed in the most imminent danger, as this gigantic creature, setting up its back, raised the ship three feet at least out of the water. The masts reeled, and the sails fell altogether, while we who were below all sprang instantly upon the deck, concluding that we had struck upon some rock; instead of this we saw the monster sailing off with the utmost gravity and solemnity. Captain D'Wolf applied immediately to the pumps to examine whether or not the vessel had received any damage from the shock, but we found that very happily it had escaped entirely uninjured."

Now, the Captain D'Wolf here alluded to as commanding the ship in question, is a New Englander, who, after a long life of unusual adventures as a sea-captain, this day resides in the village of Dorchester near Boston. I have the honor of being a nephew of his. I have particularly questioned him concerning this passage in Langsdorff. He substantiates every word. The ship, however, was by no means a large one: a Russian craft built on the Siberian coast, and purchased by my uncle after bartering away the vessel in which he sailed from home.

In that up and down manly book of old-fashioned adventure, so full, too, of honest wonders—the voyage of Lionel Wafer, one of ancient Dampier's old chums[16]—I found a little matter set down so like that just quoted from Langsdorff, that I cannot forbear inserting it here for a corroborative example, if such be needed.

Lionel, it seems, was on his way to "John Ferdinando," as he calls the modern Juan Fernandes.[17] "In our way thither," he says, "about four o'clock in the morning, when we were about one hundred and fifty leagues from the Main of America,[18] our ship felt a terrible shock, which put our men in such consternation that they could hardly tell where they were or what to think; but every one began to prepare for death. And, indeed, the shock was so sudden and violent, that we took it for granted the ship had struck against a rock; but when the amazement was a little over, we cast the lead, and sounded, but found no ground.   *   *   *   *   *
The suddenness of the shock made the guns leap in their carriages, and several of the men were shaken out of their hammocks. Captain Davis, who lay with his head on a gun, was thrown out of his cabin!" Lionel then goes on to impute the shock to an earthquake, and seems to substantiate the imputation by stating that a great earthquake, somewhere about that time, did actually do great mischief along the Spanish land. But I should not much wonder if, in the darkness of that early hour of the morning, the shock was after all caused by an unseen whale vertically bumping the hull from beneath.

I might proceed with several more examples, one way or another known to me, of the great power and malice at times of the sperm whale. In more than one instance, he has been known, not only to chase the assailing boats back to their ships, but to pursue the ship itself, and long withstand all the lances hurled at him from its decks. The English ship Pusie Hall[19] can tell a story on that head; and, as for his strength, let me say, that there have been examples where the lines attached to a running sperm whale have, in a calm, been transferred to the ship, and secured there; the whale towing her great hull through the water, as a horse walks off with a cart. Again, it is very often observed that, if the sperm whale, once struck, is allowed time to rally, he then acts, not so often with blind rage, as with wilful, deliberate designs of destruction to his pursuers; nor is it without conveying some eloquent indication of his character, that upon being attacked he will frequently open his mouth, and retain it in that dread expansion for several consecutive minutes. But I must be content with only one more and a concluding illustration; a remarkable and most significant one, by which you will not fail to see, that not only is the most marvellous event in this book corroborated by plain facts of the present day, but that these marvels (like all marvels) are mere repetitions of the ages; so that for the millionth time we say amen with Solomon—Verily there is nothing new under the sun.[20]

In the sixth Christian century lived Procopius, a Christian magistrate of Constantinople, in the days when Justinian was Emperor and Belisarius[21] general. As many know, he wrote the history of his own times, a work every way of uncommon value. By the best authorities, he has always been considered a most trustworthy and unexaggerating historian, except in some one or two particulars, not at all affecting the matter presently to be mentioned.

Now, in this history of his, Procopius mentions that, during the term of his prefecture at Constantinople, a great sea-monster was captured in the neighboring Propontis, or Sea of Marmora,[22] after having destroyed vessels at intervals in those waters for a period of more than fifty years. A fact thus set down in substantial history cannot easily be gainsaid. Nor is there any reason it should be. Of what precise species this sea-monster was, is not mentioned. But as he destroyed ships, as well as for other reasons, he must have been a whale; and I am strongly inclined to think a sperm whale. And I will tell you why. For a long time I fancied that the sperm whale had been always unknown in the Mediterranean and the deep waters connecting with it. Even now I am certain that those seas are not, and perhaps never can be, in the present constitution of things, a place for his habitual gregarious resort. But further investigations have recently proved to me, that in modern times there have been isolated instances of the presence of the sperm whale in the Mediterranean. I am told, on good authority, that on the Barbary coast, a **Commodore Davis**[23] of the British navy found the skeleton of a sperm whale. Now, as a vessel of war readily passes through the Dardanelles, hence a sperm whale could, by the same route, pass out of the Mediterranean into the Propontis.

In the Propontis, as far as I can learn, none of that peculiar substance called *brit°* is to be found, the aliment of the right whale. But I have every reason to believe that the food of the sperm whale—squid or cuttle-fish—lurks at the bottom of that sea, because large creatures, but by no means the largest of that sort, have been found at its surface. If, then, you properly put these statements together, and reason upon them a bit, you will clearly perceive that, according to all human reasoning, Procopius's sea-monster, that for half a century stove the ships of a Roman Emperor, must in all probability have been a sperm whale.

---

brit: tiny, floating crustaceans; see Ch. 58.

CHAPTER 46

SURMISES

Though, consumed with the hot fire of his purpose, Ahab in all his thoughts and actions ever had in view the ultimate capture of Moby Dick; though he seemed ready to sacrifice all mortal interests to that one passion; nevertheless it may have been that he was by nature and long habituation far too wedded to a fiery whaleman's ways, altogether to abandon the collateral prosecution of the voyage. Or at least if this were otherwise, there were not wanting other motives much more influential with him. It would be refining too much, perhaps, even considering his monomania, to hint that his vindictiveness towards the White Whale might have possibly extended itself in some degree to all sperm whales, and that the more monsters he slew by so much the more he multiplied the chances that each subsequently encountered whale would prove to be the hated one he hunted. But if such an hypothesis be indeed exceptionable, there were still additional considerations which, though not so strictly according with the wildness of his ruling passion, yet were by no means incapable of swaying him.

To accomplish his object Ahab must use tools; and of all tools used in the shadow of the moon,[1] men are most apt to get out of order. He knew, for example, that however magnetic his ascendency in some respects was over Starbuck, yet that ascendency did not cover the complete spiritual man any more than mere corporeal superiority involves intellectual mastership; for to the purely spiritual, the intellectual but stand in a sort of corporeal relation. Starbuck's body and Starbuck's coerced will were Ahab's, so long as Ahab kept his magnet at Starbuck's brain; still he knew that for all this the chief mate, in his soul, abhorred his captain's quest, and could he, would joyfully disintegrate himself from it, or even frustrate it. It might be that a long interval would elapse ere the White Whale was seen. During that long interval Starbuck would ever be apt to fall into open relapses of rebellion against his captain's leadership, unless some ordinary, prudential, circumstantial influences were brought to bear upon him. Not only that, but the subtle insanity of Ahab respecting Moby Dick was noways more significantly manifested than in his superlative sense and shrewdness in foreseeing that, for the present, the hunt should in some way be stripped of that strange imaginative impiousness which naturally invested it; that the full terror of the voyage must be kept withdrawn into the obscure background (for few men's courage is proof against protracted meditation unrelieved by action); that when they stood their long night watches, his officers and men must have some nearer things to think of than Moby Dick. For however eagerly and impetuously the savage crew had hailed the announcement of his quest; yet all sailors of all sorts are more or less capricious and unreliable—they live in the varying outer weather, and they inhale its fickleness—and when retained for any object remote and blank in the pursuit, however promissory of life and passion in the end, it is above all things requisite that temporary interests and employments should intervene and hold them healthily suspended for the final dash.

Nor was Ahab unmindful of another thing. In times of strong emotion mankind disdain all base considerations; but such times are evanescent. The permanent constitutional condition of the manufactured man, thought Ahab, is sordidness. Granting that the White Whale fully incites the hearts of this my savage crew, and playing round their savageness even breeds a certain generous knight-errantism[2] in them, still, while for the love of it they give chase to Moby Dick, they must also have food for their more common, daily appetites. For even the high lifted and chivalric Crusaders of old times were not content to traverse two thousand miles of land to fight for their holy sepulchre, without committing burglaries, picking pockets, and gaining other pious perquisites by the way. Had they been strictly held to their one final and romantic object—that final and romantic object, too many would have turned from in disgust. I will not strip these men, thought Ahab, of all hopes of cash—aye, cash. They may scorn cash now; but let some months go by, and no perspective° promise of it to them, and then this same quiescent cash all at once mutinying in them, this same cash would soon cashier° Ahab.

Nor was there wanting still another precautionary motive more related to Ahab personally. Having impulsively, it is probable, and perhaps somewhat prematurely revealed the prime but private purpose of the Pequod's voyage, Ahab was now entirely conscious that, in so doing, he had indirectly laid himself open to the unanswerable charge of usurpation; and with perfect impunity, both moral and legal, his crew if so disposed, and to that end competent, could refuse all further obedience to him, and even violently wrest from him the command. From even the barely hinted imputation of usurpation, and the possible consequences of such a suppressed impression gaining ground, Ahab must of course have been most anxious to protect himself. That protection could only consist in his own predominating brain and heart and hand, backed by a heedful, closely calculating attention to every minute atmospheric influence which it was possible for his crew to be subjected to.

For all these reasons then, and others perhaps too analytic to be verbally developed here, Ahab plainly saw that he must still in a good degree continue true to the natural, nominal purpose of the Pequod's voyage; observe all customary usages; and not only that, but force himself to evince all his well known passionate interest in the general pursuit of his profession.

Be all this as it may, his voice was now often heard hailing the three mast-heads and admonishing them to keep a bright look-out, and not omit reporting even a porpoise. This vigilance was not long without reward.

perspective: prospective, anticipated. ***cashier***: remove from authority.

CHAPTER 47

THE MAT-MAKER

I was a cloudy, sultry afternoon; the seamen were lazily lounging about the decks, or vacantly gazing over into the lead-colored waters. Queequeg and I were mildly employed weaving what is called a sword-mat, for an additional lashing° to our boat. So still and subdued and yet somehow preluding was all the scene, and such an incantation of revery lurked in the air, that each silent sailor seemed resolved into his own invisible self.

I was the attendant or page of Queequeg, while busy at the mat. As I kept passing and repassing the filling or woof of marline between the long yarns of the warp, using my own hand for the shuttle, and as Queequeg, standing sideways, ever and anon slid his heavy oaken sword between the threads,[1] and idly looking off upon the water, carelessly and unthinkingly drove home every yarn: I say so strange a dreaminess did there then reign all over the ship and all over the sea, only broken by the intermitting dull sound of the sword, that it seemed as if this were the Loom of Time,[2] and I myself were a shuttle mechanically weaving and weaving away at the Fates. There lay the fixed threads of the warp subject to but one single, ever return- ing, unchanging vibration, and that vibration merely enough to admit of the cross- wise interblending of other threads with its own. This warp seemed necessity; and here, thought I, with my own hand I ply my own shuttle and weave my own destiny into these unalterable threads. Meantime, Queequeg's impulsive, indifferent sword, sometimes hitting the woof slantingly, or crookedly, or strongly, or weakly, as the case might be; and by this difference in the concluding blow producing a corresponding contrast in the final aspect of the completed fabric; this savage's sword, thought I, which thus finally shapes and fashions both warp and woof; this easy, indifferent sword must be chance—aye, chance, free will, and necessity—no wise incompati- ble—all interweavingly working together. The straight warp of necessity, not to be swerved from its ultimate course—its every alternating vibration, indeed, only tend- ing to that; free will still free to ply her shuttle between given threads; and chance, though restrained in its play within the right° lines of necessity, and sideways in its motions **directed** by free will, though thus prescribed to by both, chance by turns

lashing: tie-down used to secure a whaleboat when suspended in its place over the ship's side.
right: straight, rigid.

rules either, and has the last featuring blow at events.

      *   *   *   *   *   *

Thus we were weaving and weaving away when I started at a sound so strange, long drawn, and musically wild and unearthly, that the ball of free will dropped from my hand, and I stood gazing up at the clouds whence that voice dropped like a wing. High aloft in the cross-trees was that mad Gay-Header, Tashtego. His body was reaching eagerly forward, his hand stretched out like a wand, and at brief sudden intervals he continued his cries. To be sure the same sound was that very moment perhaps being heard all over the seas, from hundreds of whalemen's lookouts perched as high in the air; but from few of those lungs could that accustomed old cry have derived such a marvellous cadence as from Tashtego the Indian's.

As he stood hovering over you half suspended in air, so wildly and eagerly peering towards the horizon, you would have thought him some prophet or seer beholding the shadows of Fate, and by those wild cries announcing their coming.

"There she blows! there! there! there! she blows! she blows!"

"Where-away?"

"On the lee-beam,° about two miles off! a school of them!"

Instantly all was commotion.

The Sperm Whale blows as a clock ticks, with the same undeviating and reliable uniformity. And thereby whalemen distinguish this fish from other tribes of his genus.

"There go flukes!"° was now the cry from Tashtego; and the whales disappeared.

"Quick, steward!" cried Ahab. "Time! time!"

Dough-Boy hurried below, glanced at the watch, and reported the exact minute to Ahab.

The ship was now kept away from the wind,° and she went gently rolling before it. Tashtego reporting that the whales had gone down heading to leeward, we confidently looked to see them again directly in advance of our bows. For that singular craft at times evinced by the Sperm Whale when, sounding with his head in one direction, he nevertheless, while concealed beneath the surface, mills round, and **swiftly swims** off in the opposite quarter—this deceitfulness of his could not now be in action; for there was no reason to suppose that the fish seen by Tashtego had been in any way alarmed, or indeed knew at all of our vicinity. One of the men selected for shipkeepers—that is, those not appointed to the boats, by this time relieved the Indian at the main-mast head. The sailors at the fore and mizzen had come down; the line tubs were fixed in their places; the cranes were thrust out; the mainyard was backed,[3] and the three boats swung over the sea like three samphire baskets over high cliffs.[4] Outside of the bulwarks their eager crews with one hand clung to the rail, while one foot was expectantly poised on the gunwale.[5] So look the long line of man-of-war's men about to throw themselves on board an enemy's ship.

But at this critical instant a sudden exclamation was heard that took every eye from the whale. With a start all glared at dark Ahab, who was surrounded by five dusky phantoms that seemed fresh formed out of air.

On the lee-beam: at a right angle to the middle of the ship on the side away from the wind. **"There go flukes!"**: "The whale is diving!" (showing its tail). **kept away from the wind**: steered so the wind blows directly from behind.

CHAPTER 48

THE FIRST LOWERING

THE phantoms, for so they then seemed, were flitting on the other side of the deck, and, with a noiseless celerity, were casting loose the tackles and bands° of the boat which swung there. This boat had always been deemed one of the spare boats, though technically called the captain's, on account of its hanging from the starboard quarter. The figure that now stood by its bows was tall and swart, with one white tooth evilly protruding from its steel-like lips. A rumpled Chinese jacket of black cotton funereally invested him, with wide **black** trowsers of the same dark stuff. But strangely crowning this ebonness was a glistening white plaited turban, the living hair braided and coiled round and round upon his head. Less swart in aspect, the companions of this figure were of that vivid, tiger-yellow complexion peculiar to some of the aboriginal natives of the Manillas;[1]—a race notorious for a certain diabolism of subtilty, and by some honest white mariners supposed to be the paid spies and secret confidential agents on the water of the devil, their lord, whose counting-room° they suppose to be elsewhere.

While yet the wondering ship's company were gazing upon these strangers, Ahab cried out to the white-turbaned old man at their head, "All ready there, Fedallah?"[2]

"Ready," was the half-hissed reply.

"Lower away then; d'ye hear?" shouting across the deck. "Lower away there, I say."

Such was the thunder of his voice, that spite of their amazement the men sprang over the rail; the sheaves whirled round in the blocks; with a wallow, the three boats dropped into the sea; while, with a dexterous, off-handed daring, unknown in any other vocation, the sailors, goat-like, leaped down the rolling ship's side into the tossed boats below.

Hardly had they pulled out from under the ship's lee, when a fourth keel, coming from the windward side, pulled round under the stern, and showed the five strangers rowing Ahab, who, standing erect in the stern, loudly hailed Starbuck,

---

bands: ties, fastenings. **counting-room**: U.S. term for the British "counting-house," an office where accounts are kept.

Stubb, and Flask, to spread themselves widely, so as to cover a large expanse of water. But with all their eyes again riveted upon the swart Fedallah and his crew, the inmates of the other boats obeyed not the command.

"Captain Ahab?—" said Starbuck.

"Spread yourselves," cried Ahab; "give way,° all four boats. Thou, Flask, pull out more to leeward!"

"Aye, aye, sir," cheerily cried little King-Post, sweeping round his great steering oar. "Lay back!" addressing his crew. "There!—there!—there again! There she blows right ahead, boys!—lay back!—Never heed yonder yellow boys, Archy."

"Oh, I don't mind 'em, sir," said Archy; "I knew it all before now. Didn't I hear 'em in the hold? And didn't I tell Cabaco here of it? What say ye, Cabaco? They are stowaways, Mr. Flask."

"Pull, pull, my fine hearts-alive; pull, my children; pull, my little ones," drawlingly and soothingly sighed Stubb to his crew, some of whom still showed signs of uneasiness. "Why don't you break your backbones, my boys? What is it you stare at? Those chaps in yonder boat? Tut! They are only five more hands come to help us—never mind from where—the more the merrier. Pull, then, do pull; never mind the brimstone—devils are good fellows enough. So, so; there you are now; that's the stroke for a thousand pounds; that's the stroke to sweep the stakes! Hurrah for the gold cup of sperm oil, my heroes! Three cheers, men—all hearts alive! Easy, easy; don't be in a hurry—don't be in a hurry. Why don't you snap your oars, you rascals? Bite something, you dogs! So, so, so, then;—softly, softly! That's it—that's it! long and strong. Give way there, give way! The devil fetch ye, ye ragamuffin rapscallions; ye are all asleep. Stop snoring, ye sleepers, and pull. Pull, will ye? pull, can't ye? pull, won't ye? Why in the name of gudgeons[3] and ginger-cakes don't ye pull?—pull and break something! pull, and start your eyes out! Here!" whipping out the sharp knife from his girdle; "every mother's son of ye draw his knife, and pull with the blade between his teeth. That's it—that's it. Now ye do something; that looks like it, my steel-bits. Start her—start her, my silver-spoons! Start her, marling-spikes!"[4]

Stubb's exordium to his crew is given here at large, because he had rather a peculiar way of talking to them in general, and especially in inculcating the religion of rowing. But you must not suppose from this specimen of his sermonizings that he ever flew into downright passions with his congregation. Not at all; and therein consisted his chief peculiarity. He would say the most terrific things to his crew, in a tone so strangely compounded of fun and fury, and the fury seemed so calculated merely as a spice to the fun, that no oarsman could hear such queer invocations without pulling for dear life, and yet pulling for the mere joke of the thing. Besides he all the time looked so easy and indolent himself, so loungingly managed his steering-oar, and so broadly gaped—open-mouthed at times—that the mere sight of such a yawning commander, by sheer force of contrast, acted like a charm upon the crew. Then again, Stubb was one of those odd sort of humorists, whose jollity is sometimes so curiously ambiguous, as to put all inferiors on their guard in the matter of obeying them.

In obedience to a sign from Ahab, Starbuck was now pulling obliquely across Stubb's bow; and when for a minute or so the two boats were pretty near to each

give way: begin rowing.

other, Stubb hailed the mate.

"Mr. Starbuck! larboard boat there, ahoy! a word with ye, sir, if ye please!"

"Halloa!" returned Starbuck, turning round not a single inch as he spoke; still earnestly but whisperingly urging his crew; his face set like a flint[5] from Stubb's.

"What think ye of those yellow boys, sir!"

"Smuggled on board, somehow, before the ship sailed. (Strong, strong, boys!)" in a whisper to his crew, then speaking out loud again: "A sad business, Mr. Stubb! (seethe her, seethe her, my lads!) but never mind, Mr. Stubb, all for the best. Let all your crew pull strong, come what will. (Spring, my men, spring!) There's hogsheads of sperm ahead, Mr. Stubb, and that's what ye came for. (Pull, my boys!) Sperm, sperm's the play! This at least is duty; duty and profit hand in hand!"

"Aye, aye, I thought as much," soliloquized Stubb, when the boats diverged, "as soon as I clapt eye on 'em, I thought so. Aye, and that's what he went into the after hold for, so often, as Dough-Boy long suspected. They were hidden down there. The White Whale's at the bottom of it. Well, well, so be it! Can't be helped! All right! Give way, men! It ain't the White Whale to-day! Give way!"

Now the advent of these outlandish strangers at such a critical instant as the lowering of the boats from the deck, this had not unreasonably awakened a sort of superstitious amazement in some of the ship's company; but Archy's fancied discovery having some time previous got abroad among them, though indeed not credited then, this had in some small measure prepared them for the event. It took off the extreme edge of their wonder; and so what with all this and Stubb's confident way of accounting for their appearance, they were for the time freed from superstitious surmisings; though the affair still left abundant room for all manner of wild conjectures as to dark Ahab's precise agency in the matter from the beginning. For me, I silently recalled the mysterious shadows I had seen creeping on board the Pequod during the dim Nantucket dawn, as well as the enigmatical hintings of the unaccountable Elijah.

Meantime, Ahab, out of hearing of his officers, having sided the furthest to windward, was still ranging ahead of the other boats; a circumstance bespeaking how potent a crew was pulling him. Those tiger yellow creatures of his seemed all steel and whalebone; like five trip-hammers they rose and fell with regular strokes of strength, which periodically started the boat along the water like a horizontal burst boiler out of a Mississippi steamer. As for Fedallah, who was seen pulling the harpooneer oar,° he had thrown aside his black jacket, and displayed his naked chest with the whole part of his body above the gunwale, clearly cut against the alternating depressions of the watery horizon; while at the other end of the boat Ahab, with one arm, like a fencer's, thrown half backward into the air, as if to counterbalance any tendency to trip; Ahab was seen steadily managing his steering oar as in a thousand boat lowerings ere the White Whale had torn him. All at once the outstretched arm gave a peculiar motion and then remained fixed, while the boat's five oars were seen simultaneously peaked.[6] Boat and crew sat motionless on the sea. Instantly the three spread boats in the rear paused on their way. The whales had irregularly settled bodily down into the blue, thus giving no distantly discernible token of the movement, though from his closer vicinity Ahab had observed it.

---

harpooneer oar: the first oar, in the bow of the boat.

"Every man look out along his oar!" cried Starbuck. "Thou, Queequeg, stand up!"

Nimbly springing up on the triangular raised box in the bow, the savage stood erect there, and with intensely eager eyes gazed off towards the spot where the chase had last been descried. Likewise upon the extreme stern of the boat where it was also triangularly platformed level with the gunwale, Starbuck himself was seen coolly and adroitly balancing himself to the jerking tossings of his chip of a craft, and silently eyeing the vast blue eye of the sea.

Not very far distant Flask's boat was also lying breathlessly still; its commander recklessly standing upon the top of the loggerhead, a stout sort of post rooted in the keel, and rising some two feet above the level of the stern platform. It is used for catching turns with the whale line. Its top is not more spacious than the palm of a man's hand, and standing upon such a base as that, Flask seemed perched at the mast-head of some ship which had sunk to all but her trucks. But little King-Post was small and short, and at the same time little King-Post was full of a large and tall ambition, so that this loggerhead stand-point of his did by no means satisfy King-Post.

"I can't see three seas off; tip us up an oar there, and let me on to that."

Upon this, Daggoo, with either hand upon the gunwale to steady his way, swiftly slid aft, and then erecting himself volunteered his lofty shoulders for a pedestal.

"Good a mast-head as any, sir. Will you mount?"

"That I will, and thank ye very much, my fine fellow; only I wish you fifty feet taller."

Whereupon planting his feet firmly against two opposite planks of the boat, the gigantic negro, stooping a little, presented his flat palm to Flask's foot, and then putting Flask's hand on his hearse-plumed head and bidding him spring as he himself should toss, with one dexterous fling landed the little man high and dry on his shoulders. And here was Flask now standing, Daggoo with one lifted arm furnishing him with a breast-band to lean against and steady himself by.

At any time it is a strange sight to the tyro° to see with what wondrous habitude of unconscious skill the whaleman will maintain an erect posture in his boat, even when pitched about by the most riotously perverse and cross-running seas. Still more strange to see him giddily perched upon the loggerhead itself, under such circumstances. But the sight of little Flask mounted upon gigantic Daggoo was yet more curious; for sustaining himself with a cool, indifferent, easy, unthought of, barbaric majesty, the noble negro to every roll of the sea harmoniously rolled his fine form. On his broad back, flaxen-haired Flask seemed a snow-flake. The bearer looked nobler than the rider. Though truly vivacious, tumultuous, ostentatious little Flask would now and then stamp with impatience; but not one added heave did he thereby give to the negro's lordly chest. So have I seen Passion and Vanity stamping the living magnanimous earth,[7] but the earth did not alter her tides and her seasons for that.

Meanwhile Stubb, the third mate, betrayed no such far-gazing solicitudes. The whales might have made one of their regular soundings, not a temporary dive

tyro: inexperienced person.

from mere fright; and if that were the case, Stubb, as his wont in such cases, it seems, was resolved to solace the languishing interval with his pipe. He withdrew it from his hatband, where he always wore it aslant like a feather. He loaded it, and rammed home the loading with his thumb-end; but hardly had he ignited his match across the rough sand-paper of his hand, when Tashtego, his harpooneer, whose eyes had been setting to windward like two fixed stars, suddenly dropped like light from his erect attitude to his seat, crying out in a quick phrensy of hurry, "Down, down all, and give way!—there they are!"

To a landsman, no whale, nor any sign of a herring, would have been visible at that moment; nothing but a troubled bit of greenish white water, and thin scattered puffs of vapor hovering over it, and suffusingly blowing off to leeward, like the confused scud from white rolling billows. The air around suddenly vibrated and tingled, as it were, like the air over intensely heated plates of iron. Beneath this atmospheric waving and curling, and partially beneath a thin layer of water, also, the whales were swimming. Seen in advance of all the other indications, the puffs of vapor they spouted, seemed their forerunning couriers and detached flying outriders.

All four boats were now in keen pursuit of that one spot of troubled water and air. But it bade far to outstrip them; it flew on and on, as a mass of interblending bubbles borne down a rapid stream from the hills.

"Pull, pull, my good boys," said Starbuck, in the lowest possible but intensest concentrated whisper to his men; while the sharp fixed glance from his eyes darted straight ahead of the bow, almost seemed as two visible needles in two unerring binnacle compasses. He did not say much to his crew, though, nor did his crew say anything to him. Only the silence of the boat was at intervals startlingly pierced by one of his peculiar whispers, now harsh with command, now soft with entreaty.

How different the loud little King-Post. "Sing out and say something, my hearties. Roar and pull, my thunderbolts! Beach me, beach me on their black backs, boys; only do that for me, and I'll sign over to you my Martha's Vineyard plantation, boys; including wife and children, boys. Lay me on—lay me on! O Lord, Lord! but I shall go stark, staring mad: See! see that white water!" And so shouting, he pulled his hat from his head, and stamped up and down on it; then picking it up, flirted it far off upon the sea; and finally fell to rearing and plunging in the boat's stern like a crazed colt from the prairie.

"Look at that chap now," philosophically drawled Stubb, who, with his unlighted short pipe, mechanically retained between his teeth, at a short distance, followed after—"He's got fits, that Flask has. Fits? yes, give him fits—that's the very word—pitch fits into 'em. Merrily, merrily, hearts-alive. Pudding for supper, you know;—merry's the word. Pull, babes—pull, sucklings—pull, all. But what the devil are you hurrying about? Softly, softly, and steadily, my men. Only pull, and keep pulling; nothing more. Crack all your backbones, and bite your knives in two—that's all. Take it easy—why don't ye take it easy, I say, and burst all your livers and lungs!"

But what it was that inscrutable Ahab said to that tiger-yellow crew of his— these were words best omitted here; for you live under the blessed light of the evangelical land. Only the infidel sharks[8] in the audacious seas may give ear to such words, when, with tornado brow, and eyes of red murder, and foam-glued lips, Ahab leaped after his prey.

Meanwhile, all the boats tore on. The repeated specific allusions of Flask to "that whale," as he called the fictitious monster which he declared to be incessantly tantalizing his boat's bow with its tail—these allusions of his were at times so vivid and life-like, that they would cause some one or two of his men to snatch a fearful look over the shoulder. But this was against all rule; for the oarsmen must put out their eyes, and ram a skewer through their necks; usage pronouncing that they must have no organs but ears, and no limbs but arms, in these critical moments.

It was a sight full of quick wonder and awe! The vast swells of the omnipotent sea; the surging, hollow roar they made, as they rolled along the eight gunwales, like gigantic bowls in a boundless bowling-green; the brief suspended agony of the boat, as it would tip for an instant on the knife-like edge of the sharper waves, that almost seemed threatening to cut it in two; the sudden profound dip into the watery glens and hollows; the keen spurrings and goadings to gain the top of the opposite hill; the headlong, sled-like slide down its other side;—all these, with the cries of the heads-men and harpooneers, and the shuddering gasps of the oarsmen, with the won-drous sight of the ivory Pequod bearing down upon her boats with outstretched sails, like a wild hen after her screaming brood;—all this was thrilling. Not the raw recruit, marching from the bosom of his wife into the fever heat of his first battle; not the dead man's ghost encountering the first unknown phantom in the other world;— neither of these can feel stranger and stronger emotions than that man does, who for the first time finds himself pulling into the charmed, churned circle of the hunted sperm whale.

The dancing white water made by the chase was now becoming more and more visible, owing to the increasing darkness of the dun cloud-shadows flung upon the sea. The jets of vapor no longer blended, but tilted everywhere to right and left; the whales seemed separating their wakes. The boats were pulled more apart; Starbuck giving chase to three whales running dead to leeward. Our sail was now set, and, with the still rising wind, we rushed along; the boat going with such madness through the water, that the lee oars could scarcely be worked rapidly enough to escape being torn from the row-locks.

Soon we were running through a suffusing wide veil of mist; neither ship nor boat to be seen.

"Give way, men," whispered Starbuck, drawing still further aft the sheet of his sail; "there is time to kill a fish yet before the squall comes. There's white water again!—close to! Spring!"

Soon after, two cries in quick succession on each side of us denoted that the other boats had got fast; but hardly were they overheard, when with a lightning-like hurtling whisper Starbuck said: "Stand up!" and Queequeg, harpoon in hand, sprang to his feet.

Though not one of the oarsmen was then facing the life and death peril so close to them ahead, yet with their eyes on the intense countenance of the mate in the stern of the boat, they knew that the imminent instant had come; they heard, too, an enormous wallowing sound as of fifty elephants stirring in their litter. Meanwhile the boat was still booming through the mist, the waves curling and hiss-ing around us like the erected crests of enraged serpents.

"That's his hump. *There, there,* give it to him!" whispered Starbuck.

A short rushing sound leaped out of the boat; it was the darted iron of Queequeg. Then all in one welded commotion came an invisible push from astern, while forward the boat seemed striking on a ledge; the sail collapsed and exploded; a gush of scalding vapor shot up near by; something rolled and tumbled like an earthquake beneath us. The whole crew were half suffocated as they were tossed helter-skelter into the white curdling cream of the squall. Squall, whale, and harpoon had all blended together; and the whale, merely grazed by the iron, escaped.

Though completely swamped, the boat was nearly unharmed. Swimming round it we picked up the floating oars, and lashing them across the gunwale, tumbled back to our places. There we sat up to our knees in the sea, the water covering every rib and plank, so that to our downward gazing eyes the suspended craft seemed a coral boat grown up to us from the bottom of the ocean.

The wind increased to a howl; the waves dashed their bucklers° together; the whole squall roared, forked, and crackled around us like a white fire upon the prairie, in which, unconsumed, we were burning;[9] immortal in these jaws of death! In vain we hailed the other boats; as well roar to the live coals down the chimney of a flaming furnace as hail those boats in that storm. Meanwhile the driving scud, rack,° and mist, grew darker with the shadows of night; no sign of the ship could be seen. The rising sea forbade all attempts to bale out the boat. The oars were useless as propellers, performing now the office of life-preservers. So, cutting the lashing of the waterproof match keg, after many failures Starbuck contrived to ignite the lamp in the lantern; then stretching it on a waif pole,[10] handed it to Queequeg as the standard-bearer of this forlorn hope. There, then, he sat, holding up that imbecile candle in the heart of that almighty forlornness. There, then, he sat, the sign and symbol of a man without faith, hopelessly holding up hope in the midst of despair.

Wet, drenched through, and shivering cold, despairing of ship or boat, we lifted up our eyes as the dawn came on. The mist still spread over the sea, the empty lantern lay crushed in the bottom of the boat. Suddenly Queequeg started to his feet, hollowing his hand to his ear. We all heard a faint creaking, as of ropes and yards hitherto muffled by the storm. The sound came nearer and nearer; the thick mists were dimly parted by a huge, vague form. Affrighted, we all sprang into the sea as the ship at last loomed into view, bearing right down upon us within a distance of not much more than its length.

Floating on the waves we saw the abandoned boat, as for one instant it tossed and gaped beneath the ship's bows like a chip at the base of a cataract; and then the vast hull rolled over it, and it was seen no more till it came up weltering astern. Again we swam for it, were dashed against it by the seas, and were at last taken up and safely landed on board. Ere the squall came close to, the other boats had cut loose from their fish and returned to the ship in good time. The ship had given us up, but was still cruising, if haply° it might light upon some token of our perishing,—an oar or a lance pole.

---

bucklers: shields. **scud, rack**: fast-moving, broken clouds, respectively low and high. **haply**: by chance.

CHAPTER 49

THE HYENA

THERE are certain queer times and occasions in this strange mixed affair we call life when a man takes this whole universe for a vast practical joke, though the wit thereof he but dimly discerns, and more than suspects that the joke is at nobody's expense but his own. However, nothing dispirits, and nothing seems worth while disputing. He bolts down all events, all creeds, and beliefs, and persuasions, all hard things visible and invisible, never mind how knobby; as an ostrich of potent digestion gobbles down bullets and gun flints. And as for small difficulties and worryings, prospects of sudden disaster, peril of life and limb; all these, and death itself, seem to him only sly, good-natured hits, and jolly punches in the side bestowed by the unseen and unaccountable old joker. That odd sort of wayward mood I am speaking of, comes over a man only in some time of extreme tribulation; it comes in the very midst of his earnestness, so that what just before might have seemed to him a thing most momentous, now seems but a part of the general joke. There is nothing like the perils of whaling to breed this free and easy sort of genial, desperado philosophy; and with it I now regarded this whole voyage of the Pequod, and the great While Whale its object.

"Queequeg," said I, when they had dragged me, the last man, to the deck, and I was still shaking myself in my jacket to fling off the water; "Queequeg, my fine friend, does this sort of thing often happen?" Without much emotion, though soaked through just like me, he gave me to understand that such things did often happen.

"Mr. Stubb," said I, turning to that worthy, who, buttoned up in his oil-jacket, was now calmly smoking his pipe in the rain; "Mr. Stubb, I think I have heard you say that of all whalemen you ever met, our chief mate, Mr. Starbuck, is by far the most careful and prudent. I suppose then, that going plump on a flying whale with your sail set in a foggy squall is the height of a whaleman's discretion?"

"Certain. I've lowered for whales from a leaking ship in a gale off Cape Horn."

"Mr. Flask," said I, turning to little King-Post, who was standing close by; "you are experienced in these things, and I am not. Will you tell me whether it is an unalterable law in this fishery, Mr. Flask, for an oarsman to break his own back pulling himself back-foremost into death's jaws?"

"Can't you twist that smaller?" said Flask. "Yes, that's the law. I should like to see a boat's crew backing water up to a whale face foremost. Ha, ha! the whale would give them squint for squint, mind that!"

Here then, from three impartial witnesses, I had a deliberate statement of the entire case. Considering, therefore, that squalls and capsizings in the water and consequent bivouacks on the deep, were matters of common occurrence in this kind of life; considering that at the superlatively critical instant of going on to the whale I must resign my life into the hands of him who steered the boat—oftentimes a fellow who at that very moment is in his impetuousness upon the point of scuttling the craft with his own frantic stampings; considering that the particular disaster to our own particular boat was chiefly to be imputed to Starbuck's driving on to his whale almost in the teeth of a squall, and considering that Starbuck, notwithstanding, was famous for his great heedfulness in the fishery; considering that I belonged to this uncommonly prudent Starbuck's boat; and finally considering in what a devil's chase I was implicated, touching the White Whale: taking all things together, I say, I thought I might as well go below and make a rough draft of my will. "Queequeg," said I, "come along, you shall be my lawyer, executor, and legatee."

It may seem strange that of all men sailors should be tinkering at their last wills and testaments, but there are no people in the world more fond of the diversion. This was the fourth time in my nautical life that I had done the same thing. After the ceremony was concluded upon the present occasion, I felt all the easier; a stone was rolled away from my heart. Besides, all the days I should now live would be **as good as the days that Lazarus lived after his resurrection;** a supplementary clean gain of so many months or weeks as the case might be. I survived myself; my death and burial were locked up in my chest. I looked round me tranquilly and contentedly, like a quiet ghost with a clean conscience sitting inside the bars of a snug family vault.

Now then, thought I, unconsciously rolling up the sleeves of my frock, here goes for a cool, collected dive at death and destruction, and the devil fetch the hindmost.

REVISION NARRATIVE

The Other Lazarus

After the near-death experience of the first lowering in Ch. 48, Ishmael revises his will and feels as though "a stone was rolled away from my heart." The image echoes the resurrection of Jesus and the rolling away of the stone that had sealed his sepulcher (Matthew 28, Mark 16, Luke 24). In the next sentence, Ishmael makes additional reference to Lazarus of Bethany, whom Jesus raised from the dead (John 11.39–41) only a week or so before he was crucified and was himself resurrected. This Lazarus is presumed to be the brother of Mary Magdalene, not the homeless Lazarus of Luke 16 featured in Ch. 2 (but expurgated by a British editor). In claiming that his survival is a "clean gain of so many months or weeks," Ishmael also compares himself to both the resurrected Lazarus and Jesus. But finding it presumptuous, Melville's British editor removed the comparison by expurgating "as good as the days that Lazarus lived after his resurrection;".

CHAPTER 50

AHAB'S BOAT AND CREW. FEDALLAH

"**W**HO would have thought it, Flask!" cried Stubb; "if I had but one leg you would not catch me in a boat, unless maybe to stop the plug-hole° with my timber toe. Oh! he's a wonderful old man!"

"I don't think it so strange, after all, on that account," said Flask. "If his leg were off at the hip, now, it would be a different thing. That would disable him; but he has one knee, and good part of the other left, you know."

"I don't know that, my little man; I never yet saw him kneel."

*   *   *   *   *   *

Among whale-wise people it has often been argued whether, considering the paramount importance of his life to the success of the voyage, it is right for a whaling captain to jeopardize that life in the active perils of the chase. So Tamerlane's soldiers often argued with tears in their eyes,[1] whether that invaluable life of his ought to be carried into the thickest of the fight.

But with Ahab the question assumed a modified aspect. Considering that with two legs man is but a hobbling wight in all times of danger; considering that the pursuit of whales is always under great and extraordinary difficulties; that every individual moment, indeed, then comprises a peril; under these circumstances is it wise for any maimed man to enter a whale-boat in the hunt? As a general thing, the joint-owners of the Pequod must have plainly thought not.

Ahab well knew that although his friends at home would think little of his entering a boat in certain comparatively harmless vicissitudes of the chase, for the sake of being near the scene of action and giving his orders in person, yet for Captain Ahab to have a boat actually apportioned to him as a regular headsman in the hunt—above all for Captain Ahab to be supplied with five extra men, as that same boat's crew, he well knew that such generous conceits never entered the heads of the owners of the Pequod. Therefore he had not solicited a boat's crew from them, nor had he in any way hinted his desires on that head. Nevertheless he had taken private measures of his own touching all that matter. Until **Archy's** published discovery, the sailors had little foreseen it, though to be sure when, after being a little while out of

plug-hole: drain hole in the bottom of a boat.

port, all hands had concluded the customary business of fitting the whaleboats for service; when some time after this Ahab was now and then found bestirring himself in the matter of making thole-pins° with his own hands for what was thought to be one of the spare boats, and even solicitously cutting the small wooden skewers, which when the line is running out are pinned over the groove in the bow: when all this was observed in him, and particularly his solicitude in having an extra coat of sheathing° in the bottom of the boat, as if to make it better withstand the pointed pressure of his ivory limb; and also the anxiety he evinced in exactly shaping the thigh board, or clumsy cleat, as it is sometimes called, the horizontal piece in the boat's bow for bracing the knee **against** in darting or stabbing at the whale; when it was observed how often he stood up in that boat with his solitary knee fixed in the semi-circular depression **in** the cleat, and with the carpenter's chisel gouged out a little here and straightened **it** a little there; all these things, I say, had awakened much interest and curiosity at the time. But almost everybody supposed that this particular preparative heedfulness in Ahab must only be with a view to the ultimate chase of Moby Dick; for he had already revealed his intention to hunt that mortal monster

REVISION NARRATIVE

Melville Tinkers

Four small stylistic changes appear in two paragraphs of the British edition. Since these tinkerings do not involve corrections of grammar or usage, they are probably not the work of an editor and may be Melville's attempt (sometimes unsuccessful) to render his images more precisely.

- In describing the "clumsy cleat," a board in the whaleboat's bow against which one can lean a thigh or knee for balance, Melville originally wrote that the board is "for bracing the knee against in darting or stabbing at the whale," but in the British edition, "it" has been inserted to give "for bracing the knee against it in darting." Here, the insertion, though not ungrammatical, sends readers unnecessarily back to "clumsy cleat," and makes the phrase sound more odd than it was.

- In a second, seemingly unneeded "correction," Melville changed "depression in the cleat" to "depression of the cleat," reducing the repetition of "in" in his sentence.

- A third revision drops "it" from "gouged out a little here and straightened it a little there" and thereby enhances parallel structure and sentence rhythm.

- Finally, Melville revised "waned away" in "what wonder remained soon waned away" to "went away." This change gives finality to the departure of wonder and avoids a repetition of "wane" when later in the sentence Ishmael intones: "for in a whaler wonders soon wane."

Taken together, Melville's tinkerings suggest the writer continued to struggle with his whale even at the level of pronouns and prepositions.

---

thole-pins: pegs that keep the oars in place while rowing. ***sheathing***: planking.

in person. But such a supposition did by no means involve the remotest suspicion as to any boat's crew being assigned to that boat.

Now, with the subordinate phantoms, what wonder remained soon **waned** away; for in a whaler wonders soon wane. Besides, now and then such unaccountable odds and ends of strange nations come up from the unknown nooks and ash-holes of the earth to man these floating outlaws of whalers; and the ships themselves often pick up such queer castaway creatures found tossing about the open sea on planks, bits of wreck, oars, whale-boats, canoes, blown-off Japanese junks, and what not; that Beelzebub[2] himself might climb up the side and step down into the cabin to chat with the captain, and it would not create any unsubduable excitement in the forecastle.

But be all this as it may, certain it is that while the subordinate phantoms soon found their place among the crew, though still as it were somehow distinct from them, yet that hair-turbaned Fedallah remained a muffled mystery to the last. Whence he came in a mannerly world like this, by what sort of unaccountable tie he soon evinced himself to be linked with Ahab's peculiar fortunes; nay, so far as to have some sort of a half-hinted influence; Heaven knows, but it might have been even authority over him; all this none knew. But one cannot sustain an indifferent air concerning Fedallah. He was such a creature as civilized, domestic people in the temperate zone only see in their dreams, and that but dimly; but the like of whom now and then glide among the unchanging Asiatic communities, especially the Oriental isles to the east of the continent—those insulated, immemorial, unalterable countries, which even in these modern days still preserve much of the ghostly aboriginalness of earth's primal generations, when the memory of the first man was a distinct recollection, and all men his descendants, unknowing whence he came, eyed each other as real phantoms, and asked of the sun and the moon why they were created and to what end; when though, according to Genesis, the angels indeed consorted with the daughters of men, the devils also, add the uncanonical Rabbins, indulged in mundane amours.[3]

CHAPTER 51

THE SPIRIT-SPOUT[1]

Dᴀʏꜱ, weeks passed, and under easy sail, the ivory Pequod had slowly swept across four several cruising-grounds; that off the Azores; off the Cape de Verdes; on the Plate (so called), being off the mouth of the Rio de la Plata; and the Carrol Ground, an unstaked, watery locality, southerly from St. Helena.[2]

It was while gliding through these latter waters that one serene and moonlight night, when all the waves rolled by like scrolls of silver; and, by their soft, suffusing seethings, made what seemed a silvery silence, not a solitude: on such a silent night[3] a silvery jet was seen far in advance of the white bubbles at the bow. Lit up by the moon, it looked celestial; seemed some plumed and glittering god uprising from the sea. Fedallah first descried this jet. For of these moonlight nights, it was his wont to mount to the main-mast head, and stand a look-out there, with the same precision as if it had been day. And yet, though herds of whales were seen by night, not one whaleman in a hundred would venture a lowering for them. You may think with what emotions, then, the seamen beheld this old Oriental perched aloft at such unusual hours; his turban and the moon, companions in one sky. But when, after spending his uniform interval there for several successive nights without uttering a single sound; when, after all this silence, his unearthly voice was heard announcing that silvery, moon-lit jet, every reclining mariner started to his feet as if some winged spirit had lighted in the rigging, and hailed the mortal crew. "There she blows!" Had the trump of judgment blown, they could not have quivered more; yet still they felt no terror; rather pleasure. For though it was a most unwonted hour, yet so impressive was the cry, and so deliriously exciting, that almost every soul on board instinctively desired a lowering.

Walking the deck with quick, side-lunging strides, Ahab commanded the t'gallant sails and royals° to be set, and every stunsail° spread. The best man in the ship must take the helm. Then, with every mast-head manned, the piled-up craft rolled down before the wind. The strange, upheaving, lifting tendency of the taffrail breeze filling the hollows of so many sails, made the buoyant, hovering deck to feel like air beneath the feet; while still she rushed along, as if two antagonistic influences were

---

t'gallant sails and royals: third and fourth level of sails from the deck. **stunsail**: light sail set in fair weather to increase speed.

struggling in her—one to mount direct to heaven, the other to drive yawingly° to some horizontal goal. And had you watched Ahab's face that night, you would have thought that in him also two different things were warring. While his one live leg made lively echoes along the deck, every stroke of his dead limb sounded like a coffin-tap. On life and death this old man walked. But though the ship so swiftly sped, and though from every eye, like arrows, the eager glances shot, yet the silvery jet was no more seen that night. Every sailor swore he saw it once, but not a second time.

This midnight-spout had almost grown a forgotten thing, when, some days after, lo! at the same silent hour, it was again announced: again it was descried by all; but upon making sail to overtake it, once more it disappeared as if it had never been. And so it served us night after night, till no one heeded it but to wonder at it. Mysteriously jetted into the clear moonlight, or starlight, as the case might be; disappearing again for one whole day, or two days, or three; and somehow seeming at every distinct repetition to be advancing, still further and further in our van, this solitary jet seemed for ever alluring us on.

Nor with the immemorial superstition of their race, and in accordance with the preternaturalness, as it seemed, which in many things invested the Pequod, were there wanting some of the seamen who swore that whenever and wherever descried; at however remote times, or in however far apart latitudes and longitudes, that unnearable spout was cast by one self-same whale; and that whale, Moby Dick. For a time, there reigned, too, a sense of peculiar dread at this flitting apparition, as if it were treacherously beckoning us on and on, in order that the monster might turn round upon us, and rend us[4] at last in the remotest and most savage seas.

These temporary apprehensions, so vague but so awful, derived a wondrous potency from the contrasting serenity of the weather, in which, beneath all its blue blandness, some thought there lurked a devilish charm, as for days and days we voyaged along, through seas so wearily, lonesomely mild, that all space, in repugnance to our vengeful errand, seemed vacating itself of life before our urn-like° prow.

But, at last, when turning to the eastward,° the Cape winds began howling around us, and we rose and fell upon the long, troubled seas that are there; when the ivory-tusked Pequod sharply bowed to the blast, and gored the dark waves in her madness, till, like showers of silver chips, the foam-flakes flew over her bulwarks; then all this desolate vacuity of life went away, but gave place to sights more dismal than before.

Close to our bows, strange forms in the water darted hither and thither before us; while thick in our rear flew the inscrutable sea-ravens.[5] And every morning, perched on our stays,° rows of these birds were seen; and spite of our hootings, for a long time obstinately clung to the hemp, as though they deemed our ship some drifting, uninhabited craft; a thing appointed to desolation, and therefore fit roosting-place for their homeless selves. And heaved and heaved, still unrestingly heaved the black sea, as if its vast tides were a conscience; and the great mundane soul were in anguish and remorse for the long sin and suffering it had bred.

---

yawingly: veering from one side to the other of an intended course. *urn-like*: rounded. *turning to the eastward*: heading round the Cape of Good Hope, from the Atlantic into the Indian Ocean. *stays*: ropes supporting the masts.

Cape of Good Hope, do they call ye? Rather Cape **Tormentoto**,[6] as called of yore; for long allured by the perfidious silences that before had attended us, we found ourselves launched into this tormented sea, where guilty beings transformed into those fowls and these fish, seemed condemned to swim on everlastingly without any haven in store, or beat that black air without any horizon. But calm, snow-white, and unvarying; still directing its fountain of feathers to the sky; still beckoning us on from before, the solitary jet would at times be descried.

During all this blackness of the elements, Ahab, though assuming for the time the almost continual command of the drenched and dangerous deck, manifested the gloomiest reserve; and more seldom than ever addressed his mates. In tempestuous times like these, after everything above and aloft has been secured, nothing more can be done but passively to await the issue of the gale. Then Captain and crew become practical fatalists. So, with his ivory leg inserted into its accustomed hole, and with one hand firmly grasping a shroud, Ahab for hours and hours would stand gazing dead to windward, while an occasional squall of sleet or snow would all but congeal his very eyelashes together. Meantime, the crew driven from the forward part of the ship by the perilous seas that burstingly broke over its bows, stood in a line along the bulwarks in the waist; and the better to guard against the leaping waves, each man had slipped himself into a sort of bowline° secured to the rail, in which he swung as in a loosened belt. Few or no words were spoken; and the silent ship, as if manned by painted sailors in wax, day after day tore on through all the swift madness and gladness of the demoniac waves. By night the same muteness of humanity before the shrieks of the ocean prevailed; still in silence the men swung in the bowlines; still wordless Ahab stood up to the blast. Even when wearied nature seemed demanding repose he would not seek that repose in his hammock. Never could Starbuck forget the old man's aspect, when one night going down into the cabin to mark how the barometer stood, he saw him with closed eyes sitting straight in his floor-screwed chair; the rain and half-melted sleet of the storm from which he had some time before emerged, still slowly dripping from the unremoved hat and coat. On the table beside him lay unrolled one of those charts of tides and currents which have previously been spoken of. His lantern swung from his tightly clenched hand. Though the body was erect, the head was thrown back so that the closed eyes were pointed towards the needle of the tell-tale that swung from a beam in the ceiling.*

Terrible old man! thought Starbuck with a shudder, sleeping in this gale, still thou steadfastly eyest thy purpose.

---

* The cabin-compass is called the tell-tale, because without going to the compass at the helm, the Captain, while below, can inform himself of the course of the ship.

---

sort of bowline: fixed loop of rope.

CHAPTER 52

THE ALBATROSS

SOUTH-EASTWARD from the Cape, off the distant Crozetts,[1] a good cruising ground for Right Whalemen, a sail loomed ahead, the Goney (Albatross) by name. As she slowly drew nigh, from my lofty perch at the fore-mast-head, I had a good view of that sight so remarkable to a tyro in the far ocean fisheries—a whaler at sea, and long absent from home.

As if the waves had been fullers,° this craft was bleached like the skeleton of a stranded walrus. All down her sides, this spectral appearance was traced with long channels of reddened rust, while all her spars and her rigging were like the thick branches of trees furred over with hoar-frost. Only her lower sails were set. A wild sight it was to see her long-bearded look-outs at those three mast-heads. They seemed clad in the skins of beasts, so torn and bepatched the raiment that had survived nearly four years of cruising. Standing in iron hoops nailed to the mast, they swayed and swung over a fathomless sea; and though, when the ship slowly glided close under our stern, we six men in the air came so nigh to each other that we might almost have leaped from the mast-heads of one ship to those of the other; yet, those forlorn-looking fishermen, mildly eyeing us as they passed, said not one word to our own look-outs, while the quarter-deck hail was being heard from below.

"Ship ahoy! Have ye seen the White Whale?"

But as the strange captain, leaning over the pallid bulwarks, was in the act of putting his trumpet to his mouth, it somehow fell from his hand into the sea; and the wind now rising amain,° he in vain strove to make himself heard without it. Meantime his ship was still increasing the distance between. While in various silent ways the seamen of the Pequod were evincing their observance of this ominous incident at the first mere mention of the White Whale's name to another ship, Ahab for a moment paused; it almost seemed as though he would have lowered a boat to board the stranger, had not the threatening wind forbade. But taking advantage of his windward position, he again seized his trumpet, and knowing by her aspect that the stranger vessel[2] was a Nantucketer and shortly bound home, he loudly hailed— "Ahoy there! This is the Pequod, bound round the world! Tell them to address all

fullers: people who scour cloth during its manufacture. ***amain***: suddenly; strongly.

future letters to the Pacific ocean! and this time three years, if I am not at home, tell them to address them to——"

At that moment the two wakes were fairly crossed, and instantly, then, in accordance with their singular ways, shoals of small harmless fish, that for some days before had been placidly swimming by our side, darted away with what seemed shuddering fins, and ranged themselves fore and aft with the stranger's flanks. Though in the course of his continual voyagings Ahab must often before have noticed a similar sight, yet, to any monomaniac man, the veriest trifles capriciously carry meanings.

"Swim away from me, do ye?" murmured Ahab, gazing over into the water. There seemed but little in the words, but the tone conveyed more of deep helpless sadness than the insane old man had ever before evinced. But turning to the steersman, who thus far had been holding the ship in the wind to diminish her headway, he cried out in his old lion voice,—"Up helm!° Keep her off round the world!"

Round the world! There is much in that sound to inspire proud feelings; but whereto does all that circumnavigation conduct? Only through numberless perils to the very point whence we started, where those that we left behind secure, were all the time before us.

Were this world an endless plain, and by sailing eastward we could for ever reach new distances, and discover sights more sweet and strange than any Cyclades or Islands of King Solomon,[3] then there were promise in the voyage. But in pursuit of those far mysteries we dream of, or in tormented chase of that demon phantom that, some time or other, swims before all human hearts; while chasing such over this round globe, they either lead us on in barren mazes or midway leave us whelmed.

Up helm!: move the tiller toward the "upper," or windward side of the vessel to turn the ship so the wind blows from behind.

CHAPTER 53

THE GAM

THE ostensible reason why Ahab did not go on board of the whaler we had spoken was this: the wind and sea betokened storms. But even had this not been the case, he would not after all, perhaps, have boarded her—judging by his subsequent conduct on similar occasions—if so it had been that, by the process of hailing, he had obtained a negative answer to the question he put. For, as it eventually turned out, he cared not to consort, even for five minutes, with any stranger captain,° except he could contribute some of that information he so absorbingly sought. But all this might remain inadequately estimated, were not something said here of the peculiar usages of whaling-vessels when meeting each other in foreign seas, and especially on a common cruising-ground.

If two strangers crossing the Pine Barrens in New York State, or the equally desolate Salisbury Plain[1] in England; if casually encountering each other in such inhospitable wilds, these twain, for the life of them, cannot well avoid a mutual salutation; and stopping for a moment to interchange the news; and, perhaps, sitting down for a while and resting in concert: then, how much more natural that upon the illimitable Pine Barrens and Salisbury Plains of the sea, two whaling vessels descrying each other at the ends of the earth—off lone Fanning's Island, or the far away King's Mills;° how much more natural, I say, that under such circumstances these ships should not only interchange hails, but come into still closer, more friendly and sociable contact. And especially would this seem to be a matter of course, in the case of vessels owned in one seaport, and whose captains, officers, and not a few of the men are personally known to each other; and consequently, have all sorts of dear domestic things to talk about.

For the long absent ship, the outward-bounder, perhaps, has letters on board; at any rate, she will be sure to let her have some papers of a date a year or two later than the last one on her blurred and thumb-worn files. And in return for that courtesy, the outward-bound ship would receive the latest whaling intelligence from the cruising-ground to which she may be destined, a thing of the utmost importance to her. And in degree, all this will hold true concerning whaling vessels crossing each

any stranger captain: the captain of any other vessel. ***Fanning's Island . . . King's Mills***: mid-Pacific islands near the equator, now part of Kiribati.

other's track on the cruising-ground itself, even though they are equally long absent from home. For one of them may have received a transfer of letters from some third, and now far remote vessel; and some of those letters may be for the people of the ship she now meets. Besides, they would exchange the whaling news, and have an agreeable chat. For not only would they meet with all the sympathies of sailors, but likewise with all the peculiar congenialities arising from a common pursuit and mutually shared privations and perils.

Nor would difference of country make any very essential difference; that is, so long as both parties speak one language, as is the case with Americans and English. Though, to be sure, from the small number of English whalers, such meetings do not very often occur, and when they do occur there is too apt to be a sort of shyness between them; for your Englishman is rather reserved, and your Yankee, he does not fancy that sort of thing in anybody but himself. Besides, the English whalers sometimes affect a kind of metropolitan superiority over the American whalers; regarding the long, lean Nantucketer, with his nondescript provincialisms, as a sort of sea-peasant. But where this superiority in the English whalemen does really consist, it would be hard to say, seeing that the Yankees in one day, collectively, kill more whales than all the English, collectively, in ten years. But this is a harmless little foible in the English whale-hunters, which the Nantucketer does not take much to heart; probably, because he knows that he has a few foibles himself.

So, then, we see that of all ships separately sailing the sea, the whalers have most reason to be sociable—and they are so. Whereas, some merchant ships crossing each other's wake in the mid-Atlantic, will oftentimes pass on without so much as a single word of recognition, mutually cutting° each other on the high seas, like a brace of dandies in Broadway; and all the time indulging, perhaps, in finical criticism upon each other's rig. As for Men-of-War, when they chance to meet at sea, they first go through such a string of silly bowings and scrapings, such a ducking of ensigns,° that there does not seem to be much right-down hearty good-will and brotherly love about it at all. As touching Slave-ships meeting, why, they are in such a prodigious hurry, they run away from each other as soon as possible. And as for Pirates, when they chance to cross each other's cross-bones, the first hail is—"How many skulls?"—the same way that whalers hail—"How many barrels?" And that question once answered, pirates straightway steer apart, for they are infernal villains on both sides, and don't like to see overmuch of each other's villanous likenesses.

But look at the godly, honest, unostentatious, hospitable, sociable, free-and-easy whaler! What does the whaler do when she meets another whaler in any sort of decent weather? She has a *"Gam,"* a thing so utterly unknown to all other ships that they never heard of the name even; and if by chance they should hear of it, they only grin at it, and repeat gamesome stuff about "spouters" and "blubber-boilers," and such like pretty exclamations. Why it is that all Merchant-seamen, and also all Pirates and Man-of-War's men, and Slave-ship sailors, cherish such a scornful feeling towards Whale-ships; this is a question it would be hard to answer. Because, in the case of pirates, say, I should like to know whether that profession of their has any peculiar glory about it. It sometimes ends in uncommon elevation, indeed; but only at the gallows. And

---

cutting: snubbing. ***ducking of ensigns***: ceremonial dipping of their national flags.

besides, when a man is elevated in that odd fashion, he has no proper foundation for his superior altitude. Hence, I conclude, that in boasting himself to be high lifted above a whaleman, in that assertion the pirate has no solid basis to stand on.

But what is a *Gam*?[2] You might wear out your index-finger running up and down the columns of dictionaries, and never find the word. Dr. Johnson never attained to that erudition; Noah Webster's ark[3] does not hold it. Nevertheless, this same expressive word has now for many years been in constant use among some fifteen thousand true born Yankees. Certainly, it needs a definition, and should be incorporated into the Lexicon. With that view, let me learnedly define it.

GAM. NOUN—*A social meeting of two (or more) Whale-ships, generally on a cruising-ground; when, after exchanging hails, they exchange visits by boats' crews: the two captains remaining, for the time, on board of one ship, and the two chief mates on the other.*

There is another little item about Gamming which must not be forgotten here. All professions have their own little peculiarities of detail; so has the whale fishery. In a pirate, man-of-war, or slave ship, when the captain is rowed anywhere in his boat, he always sits in the stern sheets° on a comfortable, sometimes cushioned seat there, and often steers himself with a pretty little milliner's tiller° decorated with gay cords and ribbons. But the whale-boat has no seat astern, no sofa of that sort whatever, and no tiller at all. High times indeed, if whaling captains were wheeled about the water on castors like gouty old aldermen in patent chairs. And as for a tiller, the whale-boat never admits of any such effeminacy; and therefore as in gamming a complete boat's crew must leave the ship, and hence as the boat steerer or harpooneer is of the number, that subordinate is the steersman upon the occasion, and the captain, having no place to sit in, is pulled off to his visit all standing like a pine tree. And often you will notice that being conscious of the eyes of the whole visible world resting on him from the sides of the two ships, this standing captain is all alive to the importance of sustaining his dignity by maintaining his legs. Nor is this any very easy matter; for in his rear is the immense projecting steering oar hitting him now and then in the small of his back, the after-oar reciprocating by rapping his knees in front. He is thus completely wedged before and behind, and can only expand himself sideways by settling down on his stretched legs; but a sudden, violent pitch of the boat will often go far to topple him, because length of foundation is nothing without corresponding breadth. Merely make a spread angle of two poles, and you cannot stand them up. Then, again, it would never do in plain sight of the world's riveted eyes, it would never do, I say, for this straddling captain to be seen steadying himself the slightest particle by catching hold of anything with his hands; indeed, as token of his entire, buoyant self-command, he generally carries his hands in his trowsers' pockets; but perhaps being generally very large, heavy hands, he carries them there for ballast. Nevertheless there have occurred instances, well authenticated ones too, where the captain has been known for an uncommonly critical moment or two, in a sudden squall say—to seize hold of the nearest oarsman's hair, and hold on there like grim death.

---

stern sheets: space to the rear of the seats in a rowboat. **milliner's tiller**: used disparagingly, a little steering handle decorated as if by a ladies' hat maker.

CHAPTER 54

THE TOWN-HO'S STORY[1]

(As told at the Golden Inn.)

THE Cape of Good Hope, and all the watery region round about there, is much like some noted four corners of a great highway, where you meet more travellers than in any other part.

It was not very long after speaking the Goney that another homeward-bound whaleman, the Town-Ho,* was encountered. She was manned almost wholly by Polynesians. In the short gam that ensued she gave us strong news of Moby Dick. To some the general interest in the White Whale was now wildly heightened by a circumstance of the Town-Ho's story, which seemed obscurely to involve with the whale a certain wondrous, inverted visitation of one of those so called judgments of God which at times are said to overtake some men. This latter circumstance, with its own particular accompaniments, forming what may be called the secret part of the tragedy about to be narrated, never reached the ears of Captain Ahab or his mates. For that secret part of the story was unknown to the captain of the Town-Ho himself. It was the private property of three confederate white seamen of that ship, one of whom, it seems, communicated it to Tashtego with Romish° injunctions of secrecy, but the following night Tashtego rambled in his sleep, and revealed so much of it in that way, that when he was wakened he could not well withhold the rest. Nevertheless, so potent an influence did this thing have on those seamen in the Pequod who came to the full knowledge of it, and by such a strange delicacy, to call it so, were they governed in this matter, that they kept the secret among themselves so that it never transpired abaft the Pequod's main-mast.[4] Interweaving in its proper place this darker thread with the story as publicly narrated on the ship, the whole of this strange affair I now proceed to put on lasting record.

For my humor's sake, I shall preserve the style in which I once narrated it at Lima, to a lounging circle of my Spanish friends, one saint's eve, smoking upon the thick-gilt tiled piazza of the Golden Inn. Of those fine cavaliers, the young Dons,

---

* The ancient whale-cry[2] upon first sighting a whale from the mast-head, still used by whalemen in hunting the famous Gallipagos terrapin.[3]

Romish: Roman Catholic.

Pedro and Sebastian, were on the closer terms with me; and hence the interluding questions they occasionally put, and which are duly answered at the time.

"Some two years prior to my first learning the events which I am about rehearsing to you, gentlemen, the Town-Ho, Sperm Whaler of Nantucket, was cruising in your Pacific here, not very many days' sail **eastward** from the eaves of this good Golden Inn. She was somewhere to the northward of the Line. One morning upon handling the pumps, according to daily usage, it was observed that she made more water° in her hold than common. They supposed a sword-fish had stabbed her,[5] gentlemen. But the captain, having some unusual reason for believing that rare good luck awaited him in those latitudes; and therefore being very averse to quit them, and the leak not being then considered at all dangerous, though, indeed, they could not find it after searching the hold as low down as was possible in rather heavy weather, the ship still continued her cruisings, the mariners working at the pumps at wide and easy intervals; but no good luck came; more days went by, and not only was the leak yet undiscovered, but it sensibly increased. So much so, that now taking some alarm, the captain, making all sail, stood away for the nearest harbor among the islands, there to have his hull hove out° and repaired.

"Though no small passage was before her, yet, if the commonest chance favored, he did not at all fear that his ship would founder by the way, because his pumps were of the best, and being periodically relieved at them, those six-and-thirty men of his could easily keep the ship free; never mind if the leak should double on her. In truth, well nigh the whole of this passage being attended by very prosperous breezes, the Town-Ho had all but certainly arrived in perfect safety at her port without the occurrence of the least fatality, had it not been for the brutal overbearing of Radney, the mate, a **Vineyarder**, and the bitterly provoked vengeance of Steelkilt, a Lakeman and desperado from Buffalo."

"'**Lakeman!**—Buffalo! Pray, what is a Lakeman, and where is **Buffalo?**'[6] said Don Sebastian, rising in his swinging mat of grass.

"On the eastern shore of our Lake Erie, Don; but—I crave your courtesy—may be, you shall soon hear further of all that. Now, gentlemen, in square-sail brigs and three-masted ships, well nigh as large and stout as any that ever sailed out of your old Callao to far Manilla;[7] this Lakeman, in the land-locked heart of our America, had yet been nurtured by all those agrarian freebooting impressions° popularly connected with the open ocean. For in their interflowing aggregate, those grand fresh-water seas of ours,—Erie, and Ontario, and Huron, and Superior, and Michigan,—possess an ocean-like expansiveness, with many of the ocean's noblest traits; with many of its rimmed varieties of races and of climes. They contain round archipelagoes of romantic isles, even as the Polynesian waters do; in large part, are shored by two great contrasting nations, as the Atlantic is; they furnish long maritime approaches to our numerous territorial colonies from the East, dotted all round their banks; here and there are frowned upon by batteries, and by the goat-like

---

made more water: leaked more. *stood away . . . hove out*: steered a course . . . tipped to one side. *yet been nurtured by all those agrarian freebooting impressions*: already accustomed to inland conceptions of the piratical high seas.

craggy guns of lofty Mackinaw; they have heard the fleet thunderings of naval victories;[8] at intervals, they yield their beaches to wild barbarians, whose red painted faces flash from out their peltry° wigwams; for leagues and leagues are flanked by ancient and unentered forests, where the gaunt pines stand like serried lines of kings in Gothic genealogies;[9] those same woods harboring wild Afric beasts of prey, and silken creatures whose exported furs give robes to Tartar Emperors;[10] they mirror the paved capitals of Buffalo and Cleveland, as well as Winnebago villages;[11] they float alike the full-rigged merchant ship, the armed cruiser of the State, the steamer, and the beech canoe; they are swept by Borean[12] and dismasting blasts as direful as any that lash the salted wave; they know what shipwrecks are, for out of sight of land, however inland, they have drowned full many a midnight ship with all its shrieking crew. Thus, gentlemen, though an inlander, Steelkilt was wild-ocean born, and wild-ocean nurtured; as much of an audacious mariner as any. And for Radney, though in his infancy he may have laid him down on the lone Nantucket beach, to nurse at his maternal sea; though in after life he had long followed our austere Atlantic and your contemplative Pacific; yet was he quite as vengeful and full of social quarrel as the backwoods seaman, fresh from the latitudes of buck-horn handled Bowie-knives.[13] Yet was this Nantucketer a man with some good-hearted traits; and this Lakeman, a mariner, who though a sort of devil indeed, might yet by inflexible firmness, only tempered by that common decency of human recognition which is the meanest slave's right; thus treated, this Steelkilt had long been retained harmless and docile. At all events, he had proved so thus far; but Radney was doomed and made mad, and Steelkilt—but, gentlemen, you shall hear.

"It was not more than a day or two at the furthest after pointing her prow for her island haven, that the Town-Ho's leak seemed again increasing, but only so as to require an hour or more at the pumps every day. You must know that in a settled and civilized ocean like our Atlantic, for example, some skippers think little of pumping their whole way across it; though of a still, sleepy night, should the officer of the deck happen to forget his duty in that respect, the probability would be that he and his shipmates would never again remember it, on account of all hands gently subsiding to the bottom. Nor in the solitary and savage seas far from you to the westward, gentlemen, is it altogether unusual for ships to keep clanging at their pump-handles in full chorus even for a voyage of considerable length; that is, if it lie along a tolerably accessible coast, or if any other reasonable retreat is afforded them. It is only when a leaky vessel is in some very out of the way part of those waters, some really landless latitude, that her captain begins to feel a little anxious.

"Much this way had it been with the Town-Ho; so when her leak was found gaining once more, there was in truth some small concern manifested by several of her company; especially by Radney the mate. He commanded the upper sails to be well hoisted, sheeted home° anew, and every way expanded to the breeze. Now this Radney, I suppose, was as little of a coward, and as little inclined to any sort of nervous apprehensiveness touching his own person as any fearless, unthinking creature on land or on sea that you can conveniently imagine, gentlemen. Therefore when he

peltry: made of animal pelts. **sheeted home**: extended horizontally as far as possible by hauling on the sheets (ropes attached to the sails' lower corners).

betrayed this solicitude about the safety of the ship, some of the seamen declared that it was only on account of his being a part owner in her. So when they were working that evening at the pumps, there was on this head no small gamesomeness slily going on among them, as they stood with their feet continually overflowed by the rippling clear water; clear as any mountain spring, gentlemen—that bubbling from the pumps ran across the deck, and poured itself out in steady spouts at the lee scupper-holes.°

"Now, as you well know, it is not seldom the case in this conventional world of ours—watery or otherwise; that when a person placed in command over his fellow-men finds one of them to be very significantly his superior in general pride of manhood, straightway against that man he conceives an unconquerable dislike and bitterness; and if he have a chance he will pull down and pulverize that subaltern's tower, and make a little heap of dust of it. Be this conceit of mine as it may, gentlemen, at all events Steelkilt was a tall and noble animal with a head like a Roman,° and a flowing golden beard like the tasseled housings of your last viceroy's snorting charger;[14] and a brain, and a heart, and a soul in him, gentlemen, which had made Steelkilt Charlemagne,[15] had he been born son to Charlemagne's father. But Radney, the mate, was ugly as a mule; yet as hardy, as stubborn, as malicious. He did not love Steelkilt, and Steelkilt knew it.

"Espying the mate drawing near as he was toiling at the pump with the rest, the Lakeman affected not to notice him, but unawed, went on with his gay banterings.

"'Aye, aye, my merry lads, it's a lively leak this; hold a cannikin,° one of ye, and let's have a taste. By the Lord, it's worth bottling! I tell ye what, men, old Rad's investment must go for it! he had best cut away his part of the hull and tow it home. The fact is, boys, that sword-fish only began the job; he's come back again with a gang of ship-carpenters, saw-fish, and file-fish, and what not; and the whole posse of 'em are now hard at work cutting and slashing at the bottom; making improvements, I suppose. If old Rad were here now, I'd tell him to jump overboard and scatter 'em. They're playing the devil with his estate, I can tell him. But he's a simple old soul,—Rad, and a beauty too. Boys, they say the rest of his property is invested in looking-glasses. I wonder if he'd give a poor devil like me the model of his nose.'

"'Damn your eyes! what's that pump stopping for?' roared Radney, pretending not to have heard the sailor's talk. 'Thunder away at it!'

"'Aye, aye, sir,' said Steelkilt, merry as a cricket. 'Lively, boys, lively, now!' And with that the pump clanged like fifty fire-engines; the men tossed their hats off to it, and ere long that peculiar gasping of the lungs was heard which denotes the fullest tension of life's utmost energies.

"Quitting the pump at last, with the rest of his band, the Lakeman went forward all panting, and sat himself down on the windlass; his face fiery red, his eyes bloodshot, and wiping the profuse sweat from his brow. Now what cozening° fiend it was, gentlemen, that possessed Radney to meddle with such a man in that corporeally exasperated state, I know not; but so it happened. Intolerably striding along

scupper-holes: drain holes where the deck meets the sides of the ship. **head like a Roman**: like the idealized heads on Roman statuary or coins. **cannikin**: small drinking vessel. **cozening**: beguiling, seductive.

the deck, the mate commanded him to get a broom and sweep down the planks, and also a shovel, and remove some offensive matters consequent upon allowing a pig to run at large.

"Now, gentlemen, sweeping a ship's deck at sea is a piece of household work which in all times but raging gales is regularly attended to every evening; it has been known to be done in the case of ships actually foundering at the time. Such, gentlemen, is the inflexibility of sea-usages and the instinctive love of neatness in seamen; some of whom would not willingly drown without first washing their faces. But in all vessels this broom business is the prescriptive province of the boys, if boys there be aboard. Besides, it was the stronger men in the Town-Ho that had been divided into gangs, taking turns at the pumps; and being the most athletic seaman of them all, Steelkilt had been regularly assigned captain of one of the gangs; consequently he should have been freed from any trivial business not connected with truly nautical duties, such being the case with his comrades. I mention all these particulars so that you may understand exactly how this affair stood between the two men.

"But there was more than this: the order about the shovel was almost as plainly meant to sting and insult Steelkilt, as though Radney had spat in his face. Any man who has gone sailor in a whale-ship will understand this; and all this and doubtless much more, the Lakeman fully comprehended when the mate uttered his command. But as he sat still for a moment, and as he steadfastly looked into the mate's malignant eye and perceived the stacks of powder-casks heaped up in him and the slow-match° silently burning along towards them; as he instinctively saw all this, that strange forbearance and unwillingness to stir up the deeper passionateness in any already ireful being—a repugnance most felt, when felt at all, by really valiant men even when aggrieved—this nameless phantom feeling, gentlemen, stole over Steelkilt.

"Therefore, in his ordinary tone, only a little broken by the bodily exhaustion he was temporarily in, he answered him saying that sweeping the deck was not his business, and he would not do it. And then, without at all alluding to the shovel, he pointed to three lads as the customary sweepers; who, not being billeted at° the pumps, had done little or nothing all day. To this, Radney replied with an oath, in a most domineering and outrageous manner unconditionally reiterating his command; meanwhile advancing upon the still seated Lakeman, with an uplifted cooper's club hammer° which he had snatched from a cask near by.

"Heated and irritated as he was by his spasmodic toil at the pumps, for all his first nameless feeling of forbearance the sweating Steelkilt could but ill brook this bearing in the mate; but somehow still smothering the conflagration within him, without speaking he remained doggedly rooted to his seat, till at last the incensed Radney shook the hammer within a few inches of his face, furiously commanding him to do his bidding.

"Steelkilt rose, and slowly retreating round the windlass, steadily followed by the mate with his menacing hammer, deliberately repeated his intention not to obey. Seeing, however, that his forbearance had not the slightest effect, by an awful and unspeakable intimation with his twisted hand he warned off the foolish and infatu-

---

slow-match: fuse. ***billeted at***: assigned to. ***cooper's club hammer***: barrel-maker's axe-like hammer.

ated man; but it was to no purpose. And in this way the two went once slowly round the windlass; when, resolved at last no longer to retreat, bethinking him that he had now forborne as much as comported with his humor, the Lakeman paused on the hatches and thus spoke to the officer:

"'Mr. Radney, I will not obey you. Take that hammer away, or look to yourself.' But the predestinated mate coming still closer to him, where the Lakeman stood fixed, now shook the heavy hammer within an inch of his teeth; meanwhile repeating a string of insufferable maledictions. Retreating not the thousandth part of an inch; stabbing him in the eye with the unflinching poniard of his glance, Steelkilt, clenching his right hand behind him and creepingly drawing it back, told his persecutor that if the hammer but grazed his cheek he (Steelkilt) would murder him. But, gentlemen, the fool had been branded for the slaughter by the gods. Immediately the hammer touched the cheek; the next instant the lower jaw of the mate was stove in his head; he fell on the hatch spouting blood like a whale.

"Ere the cry could go aft Steelkilt was shaking one of the backstays° leading far aloft to where two of his comrades were standing their mast-heads. They were both Canallers."

"'Canallers!' cried Don Pedro. 'We have seen many whale-ships in our harbors, but never heard of your Canallers. Pardon: who and what are they?'

"'Canallers, Don, are the boatmen belonging to our grand Erie Canal.[16] You must have heard of it.'

"'Nay, Senor; hereabouts in this dull, warm, most lazy, and hereditary land, we know but little of your vigorous North.'

"'Aye? Well then, Don, refill my cup. Your chicha's very fine;[17] and ere proceeding further I will tell **ye** what our Canallers are; for such information may throw side-light upon my story.'

"For three hundred and sixty miles, gentlemen, through the entire breadth of the state of New York; through numerous populous cities and most thriving villages; through long, dismal, uninhabited swamps, and affluent, cultivated fields, unrivalled for fertility; by billiard-room and bar-room; through **the holy-of-holies of** great forests; on Roman arches over Indian rivers;[18] through sun and shade; by happy hearts or broken; through all the wide contrasting scenery of those noble Mohawk counties;[19] and especially, by rows of snow-white chapels, whose spires stand almost like milestones, flows one continual stream of Venetianly corrupt and often lawless life. There's your true Ashantee,[20] gentlemen; there howl your pagans; where you ever find them, next door to you; under the long-flung shadow, and the snug patronizing lee of churches. For by some curious fatality, as it is often noted of your metropolitan freebooters° that they ever encamp around the halls of justice, so sinners, gentlemen, most abound in holiest vicinities."

"'Is that a friar passing?' said Don Pedro, looking downwards into the crowded piazza, with humorous concern.

"'Well for our northern friend, Dame Isabella's Inquisition wanes in Lima,'[21] laughed Don Sebastian. 'Proceed, Senor.'

---

backstays: ropes supporting a mast to the rear, connected to the sides of the vessel. **freebooters**: pirates.

"'A moment! Pardon!' cried another of the company. 'In the name of all us Limeese, I but desire to express to you, sir sailor, that we have by no means overlooked your delicacy in not substituting present Lima for distant Venice in your corrupt comparison. Oh! do not bow and look surprised; you know the proverb all along this coast—"Corrupt as Lima."[22] It but bears out your saying, too; churches more plentiful than billiard-tables, and for ever open—and "Corrupt as Lima." So, too, Venice; I have been there; the holy city of the blessed evangelist, St. Mark!—St. Dominic, purge it![23] Your cup! Thanks: here I refill; now, you pour out again.'

"Freely depicted in his own vocation, gentlemen, the Canaller would make a fine dramatic hero, so abundantly and picturesquely wicked is he. Like Mark Antony, for days and days along his green-turfed, flowery Nile, he indolently floats, openly toying with his red-cheeked Cleopatra,[24] **ripening his apricot thigh upon the sunny deck**. But ashore, all this effeminacy is dashed. The brigandish guise which the Canaller so proudly sports; his slouched and gaily-ribboned hat betoken his grand features. A terror to the smiling innocence of the villages through which he floats; his swart visage and bold swagger are not unshunned in cities. Once a vagabond on his own canal, I have received good turns from one of these Canallers; I thank him heartily; would fain be not ungrateful; but it is often one of the prime redeeming qualities of your man of violence, that at times he has as stiff an arm to back a poor stranger in a strait, as to plunder a wealthy one. In sum, gentlemen, what the wildness of this canal life is, is emphatically evinced by this; that our wild whale-fishery contains so many of its most finished graduates, and that scarce any race of mankind, except Sydney men,[25] are so much distrusted by our whaling captains. Nor does it at all diminish the curiousness of this matter, that to many thousands of our rural boys and young men born along its line, the probationary life of the Grand Canal furnishes the sole transition between quietly reaping in a Christian corn-field, and recklessly ploughing the waters of the most barbaric seas."

"'I see! I see!' impetuously exclaimed Don Pedro, spilling his chicha upon his silvery ruffles. 'No need to travel! The world's one Lima. I had thought, now, that at your temperate North the generations were cold and holy as the hills.—But the story.'

"I left off, gentlemen, where the Lakeman shook the backstay. Hardly had he done so, when he was surrounded by the three junior mates and the four harpooneers, who all crowded him to the deck. But sliding down the ropes like baleful comets, the two Canallers rushed into the uproar, and sought to drag their man out of it towards the forecastle. Others of the sailors joined with them in this attempt, and a twisted turmoil ensued; while standing out of harm's way, the valiant captain danced up and down with a whale-pike,° calling upon his officers to manhandle that atrocious scoundrel, and smoke him along° to the quarter-deck. At intervals, he ran close up to the revolving border of the confusion, and prying into the heart of it with his pike, sought to prick out the object of his resentment. But Steelkilt and his desperadoes were too much for them all; they succeeded in gaining the forecastle deck, where, hastily slewing about three or four large casks in a line with the windlass, these sea-Parisians entrenched themselves behind the barricade.[26]

---

whale-pike: single-pronged pole used for moving pieces of blubber. **smoke him along**: drive or drag him swiftly.

"'Come out of that, ye pirates!' roared the captain, now menacing them with a pistol in each hand, just brought to him by the steward. 'Come out of that, ye cut-throats!'

"Steelkilt leaped on the barricade, and striding up and down there, defied the worst the pistols could do; but gave the captain to understand distinctly, that his (Steelkilt's) death would be the signal for a murderous mutiny on the part of all hands. Fearing in his heart lest this might prove but too true, the captain a little desisted, but still commanded the insurgents instantly to return to their duty.

"'Will you promise not to touch us, if we do?' demanded their ringleader.

"'Turn to! turn to!°—I make no promise;—to your duty! Do you want to sink the ship, by knocking off at a time like this? Turn to!' and he once more raised a pistol.

"'Sink the ship?' cried Steelkilt. 'Aye, let her sink. Not a man of us turns to, unless you swear not to raise a rope-yarn against us. What say ye, men?' turning to his comrades. A fierce cheer was their response.

"The Lakeman now patrolled the barricade, all the while keeping his eye on the Captain, and jerking out such sentences as these:—'It's not our fault; we didn't want it; I told him to take his hammer away; it was boy's business; he might have known me before this; I told him not to prick the buffalo; I believe I have broken a finger here against his cursed jaw; ain't those mincing knives° down in the forecastle there, men? look to those handspikes, my hearties. Captain, **by God,** look to yourself; say the word; don't be a fool; forget it all; we are ready to turn to; treat us decently, and we're your men; but we won't be flogged.'

"'Turn to! I make no promises, turn to, I say!'

"'Look ye, now,' cried the Lakeman, flinging out his arm towards him, 'there are a few of us here (and I am one of them) who have shipped for the cruise, d'ye see; now as you well know, sir, we can claim our discharge as soon as the anchor is down; so we don't want a row; it's not our interest; we want to be peaceable; we are ready to work, but we won't be flogged.'

"'Turn to!' roared the Captain.

"Steelkilt glanced round him a moment, and then said:—'I tell you what it is now, Captain, rather than kill ye, and be hung for such a shabby rascal, we won't lift a hand against ye unless ye attack us; but till you say the word about not flogging us, we don't do a hand's turn.'

"'Down into the forecastle then, down with ye, I'll keep ye there till ye're sick of it. Down ye go.'

"'Shall we?' cried the ringleader to his men. Most of them were against it; but at length, in obedience to Steelkilt, they preceded him down into their dark den, growlingly disappearing, like bears into a cave.

"As the Lakeman's bare head was just level with the planks, the Captain and his posse leaped the barricade, and rapidly drawing over the slide of the scuttle, planted their group of hands upon it, and loudly called for the steward to bring the heavy brass padlock belonging to the companion-way. Then opening the slide a little, the Captain whispered something down the crack, closed it, and turned the key upon them—ten in number—leaving on deck some twenty or more, who thus far had remained neutral.

---

turn to!: get to work! **mincing knives**: long, two-handled blubber-slicing knives.

"All night a wide-awake watch was kept by all the officers, forward and aft, especially about the forecastle scuttle and fore hatchway;° at which last place it was feared the insurgents might emerge, after breaking through the bulkhead° below. But the hours of darkness passed in peace; the men who still remained at their duty toiling hard at the pumps, whose clinking and clanking at intervals through the dreary night dismally resounded through the ship.

"At sunrise the Captain went forward, and knocking on the deck, summoned the prisoners to work; but with a yell they refused. Water was then lowered down to them, and a couple of handfuls of biscuit were tossed after it; when again turning the key upon them and pocketing it, the Captain returned to the quarter-deck. Twice every day for three days this was repeated; but on the fourth morning a confused wrangling, and then a scuffling was heard, as the customary summons was delivered; and suddenly four men burst up from the forecastle, saying they were ready to turn to. The fetid closeness of the air, and a famishing diet, united perhaps to some fears of ultimate retribution, had constrained them to surrender at discretion. Emboldened by this, the Captain reiterated his demand to the rest, but Steelkilt shouted up to him a terrific hint to stop his babbling and betake himself where he belonged. On the fifth morning three others of the mutineers bolted up into the air from the desperate arms below that sought to restrain them. Only three were left.

"'Better turn to, now!' said the Captain with a heartless jeer.

"'Shut us up again, will ye!' cried Steelkilt.

"'Oh! certainly,' said the Captain, and the key clicked.

"It was at this point, gentlemen, that enraged by the defection of seven of his former associates, and stung by the mocking voice that had last hailed him, and maddened by his long entombment in a place as black as the bowels of despair; it was then that Steelkilt proposed to the two Canallers, thus far apparently of one mind with him, to burst out of their hole at the next summoning of the garrison; and armed with their keen mincing knives (long, crescentic, heavy implements with a handle at each end) run a muck from the bowsprit to the taffrail; and if by any devilishness of desperation possible, seize the ship. For himself, he would do this, he said, whether they joined him or not. That was the last night he should spend in that den. But the scheme met with no opposition on the part of the other two; they swore they were ready for that, or for any other mad thing, for anything in short but a surrender. And what was more, they each insisted upon being the first man on deck, when the time to make the rush should come. But to this their leader as fiercely objected, reserving that priority for himself; particularly as his two comrades would not yield, the one to the other, in the matter; and both of them could not be first, for the ladder would but admit one man at a time. And here, gentlemen, the foul play of these miscreants must come out.

"Upon hearing the frantic project of their leader, each in his own separate soul had suddenly lighted, it would seem, upon the same piece of treachery, namely: to be foremost in breaking out, in order to be the first of the three, though the last of the ten, to surrender; and thereby secure whatever small chance of pardon such

fore hatchway: opening in the deck to the forward hold. *bulkhead*: partition wall below deck.

conduct might merit. But when Steelkilt made known his determination still to lead them to the last, they in some way, by some subtle chemistry of villany, mixed their before secret treacheries together; and when their leader fell into a doze, verbally opened their souls to each other in three sentences; and bound the sleeper with cords, and gagged him with cords; and shrieked out for the Captain at midnight.

"Thinking murder at hand, and smelling in the dark for the blood, he and all his armed mates and harpooneers rushed for the forecastle. In a few minutes the scuttle° was opened, and, bound hand and foot, the still struggling ringleader was shoved up into the air by his perfidious allies, who at once claimed the honor of securing a man who had been fully ripe for murder. But all three were collared, and dragged along the deck like dead cattle; and, side by side, were seized up into the mizen rigging,° like three quarters of meat, and there they hung till morning. 'Damn ye,' cried the Captain, pacing to and fro before them, 'the vultures would not touch ye, ye villains!'

"At sunrise he summoned all hands; and separating those who had rebelled from those who had taken no part in the mutiny, he told the former that he had a good mind to flog them all round—thought, upon the whole, he would do so—he ought to—justice demanded it; but for the present, considering their timely surrender; he would let them go with a reprimand, which he accordingly administered in the vernacular.

"'But as for you, ye carrion rogues,' turning to the three men in the rigging—'for you, I mean to mince ye up for the try-pots;' and, seizing a rope, he applied it with all his might to the backs of the two traitors, till they yelled no more, but lifelessly hung their heads sideways, as the two crucified thieves are drawn.

"'My wrist is sprained with ye!' he cried, at last; 'but there is still rope enough left for you, my fine bantam, that wouldn't give up. Take that gag from his mouth, and let us hear what he can say for himself.'

"For a moment the exhausted mutineer made a tremulous motion of his cramped jaws, and then painfully twisting round his head, said in a sort of hiss, 'What I say is this—and mind it well—if you flog me, I murder you!'

"'Say ye so? then see how ye frighten me'—and the Captain drew off with the rope to strike.

"'Best not,' hissed the Lakeman.

"'But I must,'—and the rope was once more drawn back for the stroke.

"Steelkilt here hissed out something, inaudible to all but the Captain; who, to the amazement of all hands, started back, paced the deck rapidly two or three times, and then suddenly throwing down his rope, said, 'I won't do it—let him go—cut him down: d'ye hear?'

"But as the junior mates were hurrying to execute the order, a pale man, with a bandaged head, arrested them—Radney the chief mate. Ever since the blow, he had lain in his berth; but that morning, hearing the tumult on the deck, he had crept out, and thus far had watched the whole scene. Such was the state of his mouth, that he could hardly speak; but mumbling something about *his* being willing

scuttle: stairway. **seized up into the mizen rigging**: lifted up and tied to the fixed ropes ("shrouds") supporting the mizzenmast.

and able to do what the captain dared not attempt, he snatched the rope and advanced to his pinioned foe.

"'You are a coward!' hissed the Lakeman.

"'So I am, but take that.' The mate was in the very act of striking, when another hiss stayed his uplifted arm. He paused: and then pausing no more, made good his word, spite of Steelkilt's threat, whatever that might have been. The three men were then cut down, all hands were turned to, and, sullenly worked by the moody seamen, the iron pumps clanged as before.

"Just after dark that day, when one watch had retired below, a clamor was heard in the forecastle; and the two trembling traitors running up, besieged the cabin door, saying they durst not consort with the crew. Entreaties, cuffs, and kicks could not drive them back, so at their own instance they were put down in the ship's run° for **salvation**. Still, no sign of mutiny reappeared among the rest. On the contrary, it seemed, that mainly at Steelkilt's instigation, they had resolved to maintain the strictest peacefulness, obey all orders to the last, and, when the ship reached port, desert her in a body. But in order to insure the speediest end to the voyage, they all agreed to another thing—namely, not to sing out for whales, in case any should be discovered. For, spite of her leak, and spite of all her other perils, the Town-Ho still maintained her mast-heads, and her captain was just as willing to lower for a fish that moment, as on the day his craft first struck the cruising ground; and Radney the mate was quite as ready to change his berth for a boat, and with his bandaged mouth seek to gag in death the vital jaw of the whale.

"But though the Lakeman had induced the seamen to adopt this sort of passiveness in their conduct, he kept his own counsel (at least till all was over) concerning his own proper and private revenge upon the man who had stung him in the ventricles of his heart. He was in Radney the chief mate's watch; and as if the infatuated man sought to run more than half way to meet his doom, after the scene at the rigging, he insisted, against the express counsel of the captain, upon resuming the head of his watch at night. Upon this, and one or two other circumstances, Steelkilt systematically built the plan of his revenge.

"During the night, Radney had an unseamanlike way of sitting on the bulwarks of the quarter-deck, and leaning his arm upon the gunwale of the boat which was hoisted up there, a little above the ship's side. In this attitude, it was well known, he sometimes dozed. There was a considerable vacancy between the boat and the ship, and down between this was the sea. Steelkilt calculated his time, and found that his next trick° at the helm would come round at two o'clock, in the morning of the third day from that in which he had been betrayed.[27] At his leisure, he employed the interval in braiding something very carefully in his watches below.

"'What are you making there?' said a shipmate.

"'What do you think? what does it look like?'

"'Like a lanyard° for your bag; but it's an odd one, seems to me.'

"'Yes, rather oddish,' said the Lakeman, holding it at arm's length before him; 'but I think it will answer. Shipmate, I haven't enough twine,—have you any?'

ship's run: space below decks where a ship begins to narrow and curve upward toward the stern. ***trick***: "time allotted to a man" at the tiller (Dana). ***lanyard***: handle.

"But there was none in the forecastle.

"'Then I must get some from old Rad;' and he rose to go aft.

"'You don't mean to go a begging to *him!*' said a sailor.

"'Why not? Do you think he won't do me a turn, when it's to help himself in the end, shipmate?' and going to the mate, he looked at him quietly, and asked him for some twine to mend his hammock. It was given him—neither twine nor lanyard were seen again; but the next night an iron ball, closely netted, partly rolled from the pocket of the Lakeman's monkey jacket, as he was tucking the coat into his hammock for a pillow. Twenty-four hours after, his trick at the silent helm—nigh to the man who was apt to doze over the grave always ready dug to the seaman's hand—that fatal hour was then to come; and in the fore-ordaining soul of Steelkilt, the mate was already stark and stretched as a corpse, with his forehead crushed in.

"But, gentlemen, a fool saved the would-be murderer from the bloody deed he had planned. Yet complete revenge he had, and without being the avenger. For by a mysterious fatality, Heaven itself seemed to step in to take out of his hands into its own the damning thing he would have done.

"It was just between daybreak and sunrise of the morning of the second day, when they were washing down the decks, that a stupid Teneriffe[28] man, drawing water in the main-chains, all at once shouted out, 'There she rolls! there she rolls! Jesu, what a whale!' It was Moby Dick."

"'Moby Dick!' cried Don Sebastian; 'St. Dominic! Sir sailor, but do whales have christenings? Whom call you Moby Dick?'

"'A very white, and famous, and most deadly immortal monster, Don;—but that would be too long a story.'

"'How? how?' cried all the young Spaniards, crowding.

"'Nay, Dons, Dons—nay, nay! I cannot rehearse that now. Let me get more into the air, Sirs.'

"'The chicha! the chicha!' cried Don Pedro; 'our vigorous friend looks faint;—fill up his empty glass!'

"No need, gentlemen; one moment, and I proceed.—Now, gentlemen, so suddenly perceiving the snowy whale within fifty yards of the ship—forgetful of the compact among the crew—in the excitement of the moment, the Teneriffe man had instinctively and involuntarily lifted his voice for the monster, though for some little time past it had been plainly beheld from the three sullen mast-heads. All was now a phrensy. 'The White Whale—the White Whale!' was the cry from captain, mates, and harpooneers, who, undeterred by fearful rumors, were all anxious to capture so famous and precious a fish; while the dogged crew eyed askance, and with curses, the appalling beauty of the vast milky mass, that lit up by a horizontal spangling sun, shifted and glistened like a living opal in the blue morning sea. Gentlemen, a strange fatality pervades the whole career of these events, as if verily mapped out before the world itself was charted. The mutineer was the bowsman° of the mate, and when fast to a fish, it was his duty to sit next him, while Radney stood up with his lance in the prow, and haul in or slacken the line, at the word of command. Moreover, when the four boats were lowered, the mate's got the start; and none howled more fiercely with

bowsman: man who pulls the second oar, next to the harpooneer.

delight than did Steelkilt, as he strained at his oar. After a stiff pull, their harpooneer got fast, and, spear in hand, Radney sprang to the bow. He was always a furious man, it seems, in a boat. And now his bandaged cry was, to beach him on the whale's topmost back. Nothing loath, his bowsman hauled him up and up, through a blinding foam that blent two whitenesses together; till of a sudden the boat struck as against a sunken ledge, and keeling over, spilled out the standing mate. That instant, as he fell on the whale's slippery back, the boat righted, and was dashed aside by the swell, while Radney was tossed over into the sea, on the other flank of the whale. He struck out through the spray, and, for an instant, was dimly seen through that veil, wildly seeking to remove himself from the eye of Moby Dick. But the whale rushed round in a sudden maelstrom; seized the swimmer between his jaws; and rearing high up with him, plunged headlong again, and went down.

"Meantime, at the first tap of the boat's bottom, the Lakeman had slackened the line, so as to drop astern from the whirlpool; calmly looking on, he thought his own thoughts. But a sudden, terrific, downward jerking of the boat, quickly brought his knife to the line. He cut it; and the whale was free. But, at some distance, Moby Dick rose again, with some tatters of Radney's red woollen shirt, caught in the teeth that had destroyed him. All four boats gave chase again; but the whale eluded them, and finally wholly disappeared.

"In good time, the Town-Ho reached her port—a savage, solitary place—where no civilized creature resided. There, headed by the Lakeman, all but five or six of the foremast-men deliberately deserted among the palms; eventually, as it turned out, seizing a large double war-canoe of the savages, and setting sail for some other harbor.

"The ship's company being reduced to but a handful, the captain called upon the Islanders to assist him in the laborious business of heaving down the ship to stop the leak. But to such unresting vigilance over their dangerous allies was this small band of whites necessitated, both by night and by day, and so extreme was the hard work they underwent, that upon the vessel being ready again for sea, they were in such a weakened condition that the captain durst not put off with them in so heavy a vessel. After taking counsel with his officers, he anchored the ship as far off shore as possible; loaded and ran out his two cannon from the bows; stacked his muskets on the poop;° and warning the Islanders not to approach the ship at their peril, took one man with him, and setting the sail of his best whaleboat, steered straight before the wind for Tahiti, five hundred miles distant, to procure a reinforcement to his crew.

"On the fourth day of the sail, a large canoe was descried, which seemed to have touched at a low isle of corals. He steered away from it; but the savage craft bore down on him; and soon the voice of Steelkilt hailed him to heave to,° or he would run him under water. The captain presented a pistol. With one foot on each prow of the yoked war-canoes, the Lakeman laughed him to scorn; assuring him that if the pistol so much as clicked in the lock, he would bury him in bubbles and foam.

"'What do you want of me?' cried the captain.

"'Where are you bound? and for what are you bound?' demanded Steelkilt; 'no lies.'

"'I am bound to Tahiti for more men.'

poop: raised section of the deck at the stern. **heave to**: stop.

"'Very good. Let me board you a moment—I come in peace.' With that he leaped from the canoe, swam to the boat; and climbing the gunwale, stood face to face with the captain.

"'Cross your arms, sir; throw back your head. Now, repeat after me. 'As soon as Steelkilt leaves me, I swear to beach this boat on yonder island, and remain there six days. If I do not, may lightnings strike me!''

"'A pretty scholar,' laughed the Lakeman. 'Adios, Senor!' and leaping into the sea, he swam back to his comrades.

"Watching the boat till it was fairly beached, and drawn up to the roots of the cocoa-nut trees, Steelkilt made sail again, and in due time arrived at Tahiti, his own place of destination. There, luck befriended him; two ships were about to sail for France, and were providentially in want of precisely that number of men which the sailor headed. They embarked; and so for ever got the start of their former captain, had he been at all minded to work them legal retribution.

"Some ten days after the French ships sailed, the whale-boat arrived, and the captain was forced to enlist some of the more civilized Tahitians, who had been somewhat used to the sea. Chartering a small native schooner, he returned with them to his vessel; and finding all right there, again resumed his cruisings.

"Where Steelkilt now is, gentlemen, none know; but upon the island of Nantucket, the widow of Radney still turns to the sea which refuses to give up its dead; still in dreams sees the awful white whale that destroyed him." *   *   *   *

"'Are you through?' said Don Sebastian, quietly.

"'I am, Don.'

"'Then I entreat **you, tell** me if to the best of your own convictions, this your story is in substance really true? It is so passing wonderful! Did you get it from an unquestionable source? Bear with me if I seem to press.'

"'Also bear with all of us, sir sailor; for we all join in Don Sebastian's suit,' cried the company, with exceeding interest.

"'Is there a copy of the Holy Evangelists° in the Golden Inn, gentlemen?'

"'Nay,' said Don Sebastian; 'but I know a worthy priest near by, who will quickly procure one for me. I go for it; but are you well advised? this may grow too serious.'

"'Will you be so good as to bring the priest also, Don?'

"'Though there are no Auto-da-Fés[29] in Lima now,' said one of the company to another; 'I fear our sailor friend runs risk of the archiepiscopacy. Let us withdraw more out of the moonlight. I see no need of this.'

"'**Excuse me for running after you, Don Sebastian; but may I also beg that you will be particular in procuring the largest sized Evangelists you can.**'"

*   *   *   *   *   *

"'This is the priest, he brings you the Evangelists,' said Don Sebastian, gravely, returning with a tall and solemn figure.

"'Let me remove my hat. Now, venerable priest, further into the light, and hold the Holy Book before me that I may touch it.'

Holy Evangelists: Gospels.

"'So help me Heaven, and on my honor, the story I have told ye, gentlemen, is in substance and its great items, true. I know it to be true; it happened on this ball; I trod the ship; I knew the **crew; I** have seen and talked with Steelkilt since the death of Radney.'"

REVISION NARRATIVE

Procuring the Evangelists

The reason for the removal of the sentence on p. 235 from the British edition is not entirely clear. The evangelists are Matthew, Mark, Luke, and John, the disciples of Jesus who wrote the four Gospels; and the book called The Evangelists that Ishmael is requesting is a New Testament containing these four scriptures and perhaps some other New Testament writings. (Such short-version Bibles are commonly found in English.) Ishmael is proposing to swear on such a Bible that he is telling the truth, and since there is no blasphemy in doing so, it is unlikely that an editor would cut the line for that reason. However, in this sentence, Ishmael insists upon procuring the largest Bible available, thus comically suggesting that the truth of his tale and his sincerity in telling it will be sanctioned by the size of the book he swears by. This is precisely the kind of audacity a con man might use to perpetrate a big lie. An editor might have found Ishmael's flippancy to be irreverent, if not blasphemous, and therefore removed the line. On the other hand, the line's humor also undercuts the serious tone of the swearing scene to come, and its implications of insincerity undercut Ishmael's credibility. With these problems in mind, Melville is just as likely to have removed the line as is an editor.

CHAPTER 55

OF THE MONSTROUS PICTURES OF WHALES[1]

I SHALL ere long paint to you[2] as well as one can without canvas, something like the true form of the whale as he actually appears to the eye of the whaleman when in his own absolute° body the whale is moored alongside the whale-ship so that he can be fairly stepped upon there. It may be worth while, therefore, previously to advert to those curious imaginary portraits of him which even down to the present day confidently challenge the faith of the landsman. It is time to set the world right in this matter, by proving such pictures of the whale all wrong.

It may be that the primal source of all those pictorial delusions will be found among the oldest Hindoo, Egyptian, and Grecian sculptures. For ever since those inventive but unscrupulous times when on the marble panellings of temples, the pedestals of statues, and on shields, medallions, cups, and coins, the dolphin was drawn in scales of chain-armor like Saladin's, and a helmeted head like St. George's;[3] ever since then has something of the same sort of license prevailed, not only in most popular pictures of the whale, but in many scientific presentations of him.

Now, by all odds, the most ancient extant portrait anyways purporting to be the whale's, is to be found in the famous cavern-pagoda of Elephanta,[4] in India. The Brahmins maintain that in the almost endless sculptures of that immemorial pagoda, all the trades and pursuits, every conceivable avocation of man, were prefigured ages before any of them actually came into being. No wonder then, that in some sort our noble profession of whaling should have been there shadowed forth. The Hindoo whale referred to, occurs in a separate department of the wall, depicting the incarnation of Vishnu in the form of leviatan, learnedly known as the Matse Avatar.[5] But though this sculpture is half man and half whale, so as only to give the tail of the latter, yet that small section of him is all wrong. It looks more like the tapering tail of an anaconda, than the broad palms of the true whale's majestic flukes.

But go to the old Galleries, and look now at a great Christian painter's portrait of this fish; for he succeeds no better than the antediluvian Hindoo. It is Guido's picture of Perseus rescuing Andromeda from the sea-monster or whale.[6] Where did Guido get the model of such a strange creature as that? Nor does Hogarth, in paint-

absolute: actual, certain.

ing the same scene in his own "Perseus Descending,"[7] make out one whit better. The huge corpulence of that Hogarthian monster undulates on the surface, scarcely drawing one inch of water. It has a sort of howdah on its back, and its distended tusked mouth into which the billows are rolling, might be taken for the Traitors' Gate leading from the Thames by water into the Tower.[8] Then, there are the Prodromus whales of old Scotch Sibbald,[9] and Jonah's whale, as depicted in the prints of old Bibles and the cuts of old primers.[10] What shall be said of these? As for the book-binder's whale winding like a vine-stalk round the stock of a descending anchor—as stamped and gilded on the backs and title-pages of many books both old and new— that is a very picturesque but purely fabulous creature, imitated, I take it, from the like figures on antique vases. Though universally denominated a dolphin, I never-theless call this book-binder's fish an attempt at a whale; because it was so intended when the device was first introduced. It was introduced by an old Italian publisher somewhere about the 15th century, during the Revival of Learning; and in those days, and even down to a comparatively late period, dolphins were popularly sup-posed to be a species of the Leviathan.[11]

In the vignettes and other embellishments of some ancient books you will at times meet with very curious touches at the whale, where all manner of spouts, jets d'eau,° hot springs and cold, Saratoga and Baden-Baden,[12] come bubbling up from his unexhausted brain. In the title-page of the original edition of the "Advancement of Learning"[13] you will find some curious whales.

But quitting all these unprofessional attempts, let us glance at those pictures of leviathan purporting to be sober, scientific delineations, by those who know. In old Harris's collection of voyages there are some plates of whales extracted from a Dutch book of voyages, A. D. 1671, entitled "A Whaling Voyage to Spitzbergen in the ship Jonas in the Whale, Peter Peterson of Friesland, master." In one of those plates the whales, like great rafts of logs, are represented lying among ice-isles, with white bears running over their living backs. In another plate, the prodigious blunder is made of representing the whale with perpendicular flukes.[14]

Then again, there is an imposing quarto, written by one Captain Colnett,[15] a Post Captain in the English navy, entitled "A Voyage round Cape Horn into the South Seas, for the purpose of extending the Spermaceti Whale Fisheries." In this book is an outline purporting to be a "Picture of a Physeter or Spermaceti whale, drawn by scale from one killed on the coast of Mexico, August, 1793, and hoisted on deck." I doubt not the captain had this veracious picture taken for the benefit of his marines.[16] To mention but one thing about it, let me say that it has an eye which applied, according to the accompanying scale, to a full grown sperm whale, would make the eye of that whale a bow-window some five feet long. Ah, my gallant cap-tain, why did ye not give us Jonah looking out of that eye!

Nor are the most conscientious compilations of Natural History for the bene-fit of the young and tender, free from the same heinousness of mistake. Look at that popular work "Goldsmith's Animated Nature."[17] In the abridged London edition of 1807, there are plates of an alleged "whale" and a "narwhale." I do not wish to seem

---

jets d'eau: French for fountains.

inelegant, but this unsightly whale looks much like an amputated sow; and, as for the narwhale, one glimpse at it is enough to amaze one, that in this nineteenth century such a hippogriff° could be palmed for genuine upon any intelligent public of schoolboys.

Then, again, in 1825, Bernard Germain, Count de Lacépède,[18] a great naturalist, published a scientific systemized whale book, wherein are several pictures of the different species of the Leviathan. All these are not only incorrect, but the picture of the Mysticetus or Greenland whale (that is to say, the Right whale), even Scoresby, a long experienced man as touching that species, declares not to have its counterpart in nature.

But the placing of the cap-sheaf° to all this blundering business was reserved for the scientific Frederick Cuvier, brother to the famous Baron. In 1836, he published a Natural History of Whales, in which he gives what he calls a picture of the Sperm Whale. Before showing that picture to any Nantucketer, you had best provide for your summary retreat from Nantucket. In a word, Frederick Cuvier's Sperm Whale is not a Sperm Whale, but a squash.[19] Of course, he never had the benefit of a whaling voyage (such men seldom have), but whence he derived that picture, who can tell? Perhaps he got it as his scientific predecessor in the same field, Desmarest, got one of his authentic abortions; that is, from a Chinese drawing.[20] And what sort of lively lads with the pencil those Chinese are, many queer cups and saucers inform us.

As for the sign-painters' whales seen in the streets hanging over the shops of oil-dealers, what shall be said of them? They are generally Richard III. whales, with dromedary humps,[21] and very savage; breakfasting on three or four sailor tarts, that is whaleboats full of mariners: their deformities floundering in seas of blood and blue paint.

But these manifold mistakes in depicting the whale are not so very surprising after all. Consider! Most of the scientific drawings have been taken from the stranded fish;[22] and these are about as correct as a drawing of a wrecked ship, with broken back, would correctly represent the noble animal itself in all its undashed pride of hull and spars. Though elephants have stood for their full-lengths, the living Leviathan has never yet fairly floated himself for his portrait. The living whale, in his full majesty and significance, is only to be seen at sea in unfathomable waters; and afloat the vast bulk of him is out of sight, like a launched line-of-battle ship; and out of that element it is a thing eternally impossible for mortal man to hoist him bodily into the air, so as to preserve all his mighty swells and undulations. And, not to speak of the highly presumable difference of contour between a young sucking whale and a full-grown Platonian Leviathan;[23] yet, even in the case of one of those young sucking whales hoisted to a ship's deck, such is then the outlandish, eel-like, limbered, varying shape of him, that his precise expression the devil himself could not catch.

But it may be fancied, that from the naked skeleton of the stranded whale,[24] accurate hints may be derived touching his true form. Not at all. For it is one of the more curious things about this Leviathan, that his skeleton gives very little idea of his general shape. Though Jeremy Bentham's skeleton, which **hangs for candelabra**

---

hippogriff: legendary animal, half horse and half griffin (which is itself part lion and part eagle). **cap-sheaf**: topmost of a stack of sheaves; hence, the final touch.

in the library of one of his executors,[25] correctly conveys the idea of a burly-browed utilitarian old gentleman, with all Jeremy's other leading personal characteristics; yet nothing of this kind could be inferred from any leviathan's articulated bones. In fact, as the great Hunter[26] says, the mere skeleton of the whale bears the same relation to the fully invested and padded animal as the insect does to the chrysalis that so roundingly envelopes it. This peculiarity is strikingly evinced in the head, as in some part of this book will be incidentally shown.° It is also very curiously displayed in the side fin, the bones of which almost exactly answer to the bones of the human hand, minus only the thumb. This fin has four regular bone-fingers, the index, middle, ring, and little finger. But all these are permanently lodged in their fleshy covering, as the human fingers in an artificial covering. "However recklessly the whale may sometimes serve us," said humorous Stubb one day, "he can never be truly said to handle us without mittens."

For all these reasons, then, any way you may look at it, you must needs conclude that the great Leviathan is that one creature in the world which must remain unpainted to the last. True, one portrait may hit the mark much nearer than another, but none can hit it with any very considerable degree of exactness. So there is no earthly way of finding out precisely what the whale really looks like. And the only mode in which you can derive even a tolerable idea of his living contour, is by going a whaling yourself; but by so doing, you run no small risk of being eternally stove and sunk by him. Wherefore, it seems to me you had best not be too fastidious in your curiosity touching this Leviathan.

will be incidentally shown: see Chs. 74–80.

CHAPTER 56

OF THE LESS ERRONEOUS PICTURES OF WHALES, AND THE TRUE PICTURES OF WHALING SCENES

IN connexion with the monstrous pictures of whales, I am strongly tempted here to enter upon those still more monstrous stories of them which are to be found in certain books, both ancient and modern, especially in Pliny, Purchas, Hackluyt, Harris, Cuvier,[1] &c. But I pass that matter by.

I know of only four published outlines° of the great Sperm Whale; Colnett's, Huggins's, Frederick Cuvier's, and Beale's. In the previous chapter Colnett and Cuvier have been referred to. Huggins's is far better than theirs; but, by great odds, Beale's is the best.[2] All Beale's drawings of this whale are good, excepting the middle figure[3] in the picture of three whales in various attitudes, capping his second chapter. His frontispiece, boats attacking Sperm Whales, though no doubt calculated to excite the civil scepticism of some parlor men, is admirably correct and life-like in its general effect. Some of the Sperm Whale drawings in J. Ross Browne[4] are pretty correct in contour; but they are wretchedly engraved. That is not his fault though.

Of the Right Whale, the best outline pictures are in Scoresby; but they are drawn on too small a scale to convey a desirable impression. He has but one picture of whaling scenes, and this is a sad deficiency,[5] because it is by such pictures only, when at all well done, that you can derive anything like a truthful idea of the living whale as seen by his living hunters.

outlines: schematic drawings.

But, taken for all in all, by far the finest, though in some details not the most correct, presentations of whales and whaling scenes to be anywhere found, are two large French engravings, well executed, and taken from paintings by one Garnery.[6] Respectively, they represent attacks on the Sperm and Right Whale. In the first engraving a noble Sperm Whale is depicted in full majesty of might, just risen beneath the boat from the profundities of the ocean, and bearing high in the air upon his back the terrific wreck of the stoven planks. The prow of the boat is partially unbroken, and is drawn just balancing upon the monster's spine; and standing in that prow, for that one single incomputable flash of time, you behold an oarsman, half shrouded by the incensed boiling spout of the whale, and in the act of leaping, as if from a precipice. The action of the whole thing is wonderfully good and true. The half-emptied line-tub floats on the whitened sea; the wooden poles of the spilled harpoons obliquely bob in it; the heads of the swimming crew are scattered about the whale in contrasting expressions of affright; while in the black stormy distance the ship is bearing down upon the scene. Serious fault might be found with the anatomical details of this whale, but let that pass; since, for the life of me, I could not draw so good a one.

In the second engraving, the boat is in the act of drawing alongside the barnacled flank of a large running Right Whale, that rolls his black weedy bulk in the sea like some mossy rock-slide from the Patagonian cliffs. His jets are erect, full, and black like soot; so that from so abounding a smoke in the chimney, you would think there must be a brave supper cooking in the great bowels below. Sea fowls are pecking at the small crabs, shell-fish, and other sea candies and maccaroni, which the Right Whale sometimes carries on his pestilent back. And all the while the thick-lipped leviathan is rushing through the deep, leaving tons of tumultuous white curds in his wake, and causing the slight boat to rock in the swells like a skiff caught nigh the paddle-wheels of an ocean steamer. Thus, the foreground is all raging commotion; but behind, in admirable artistic contrast, is the glassy level of a sea becalmed, the drooping unstarched° sails of the powerless ship, and the inert mass of a dead whale, a conquered fortress, with the flag of capture lazily hanging from the whale-pole° inserted into his spout-hole.

Who Garnery the painter is, or was, I know not. But my life for it he was either practically conversant with his subject, or else marvellously tutored by some experienced whaleman. The French are the lads for painting action. Go and gaze upon all the paintings of Europe, and where will you find such a gallery of living and breathing commotion on canvas, as in that triumphal hall at Versailles[7]; where the beholder fights his way, pell-mell, through the consecutive great battles of France; where every sword seems a flash of the Northern Lights, and the successive armed kings and Emperors dash by, like a charge of crowned centaurs? Not wholly unworthy of a place in that gallery, are these sea battle-pieces of Garnery.

The natural aptitude of the French for seizing the picturesqueness of things seems to be peculiarly evinced in what paintings and engravings they have of their

---

unstarched: not smoothed by wind pressure. **whale-pole**: pole with small flag to mark ownership of a floating whale carcass; also waif-pole; see Ch. 89.

whaling scenes. With not one tenth of England's experience in the fishery, and not the thousandth part of that of the Americans, they have nevertheless furnished both nations with the only finished sketches at all capable of conveying the real spirit of the whale hunt. For the most part, the English and American whale draughtsmen seem entirely content with presenting the mechanical outline of things, such as the vacant profile of the whale; which, so far as picturesqueness of effect is concerned, is about tantamount to sketching the profile of a pyramid. Even Scoresby, the justly renowned Right whaleman, after giving us a stiff full length of the Greenland whale, and three or four delicate miniatures of narwhales and porpoises, treats us to a series of classical engravings of boat hooks, chopping knives, and grapnels; and with the microscopic diligence of a Leuwenhoeck[8] submits to the inspection of a shivering world ninety-six fac-similes of magnified Arctic snow crystals. I mean no disparagement to the excellent voyager (I honor him for a veteran), but in so important a matter it was certainly an oversight not to have procured for every crystal a sworn affidavit taken before a Greenland Justice of the Peace.

In addition to those fine engravings from Garnery, there are two other French engravings worthy of note, by some one who subscribes himself "H. Durand."[9] One of them, though not precisely adapted to our present purpose, nevertheless deserves mention on other accounts. It is a quiet noon-scene among the isles of the Pacific; a French whaler anchored, inshore, in a calm, and lazily taking water on board; the loosened sails of the ship, and the long leaves of the palms in the background, both drooping together in the breezeless air. The effect is very fine, when considered with reference to its presenting the hardy fishermen under one of their few aspects of oriental repose. The other engraving is quite a different affair: the ship hove-to upon the open sea, and in the very heart of the Leviathanic life, with a Right Whale alongside; the vessel (in the act of cutting-in) hove over to the monster as if to a quay; and a boat, hurriedly pushing off from this scene of activity, is about giving° chase to whales in the distance. The harpoons and lances lie levelled for use; three oarsmen are just setting the mast in its hole; while from a sudden roll of the sea, the little craft stands half-erect out of the water, like a rearing horse. From the ship, the smoke of the torments of the boiling whale is going up like the smoke over a village of smithies;° and to windward, a black cloud, rising up with earnest of squalls° and rains, seems to quicken the activity of the excited seamen.

---

about giving: starting to. ***smithies***: blacksmith shops. ***with earnest of squalls***: indicating approaching storms.

OF WHALES IN PAINT; IN TEETH; IN WOOD; IN SHEET-IRON; IN STONE; IN MOUNTAINS; IN STARS

O N Tower-hill, as you go down to the London docks, you may have seen a crippled beggar (or *kedger,* as the sailors say) holding a painted board before him, representing the tragic scene in which he lost his leg.[1] There are three whales and three boats; and one of the boats (presumed to contain the missing leg in all its original integrity) is being crunched by the jaws of the foremost whale. Any time these ten years, they tell me, has that man held up that picture, and exhibited that stump to an incredulous world. But the time of his justification has now come. His three whales are as good whales as were ever published in Wapping,° at any rate; and his stump as unquestionable a stump as any you will find in the western clearings. But, though for ever mounted on that stump, never a stump-speech does the poor whaleman make; but, with downcast eyes, stands ruefully contemplating his own amputation.

Throughout the Pacific, and also in Nantucket, and New Bedford, and Sag Harbor,° you will come across lively sketches of whales and whaling-scenes, graven by the fishermen themselves on Sperm Whale-teeth, or ladies' busks° wrought out of the Right Whale-bone, and other like skrimshander articles, as the whalemen call the numerous little ingenious contrivances they elaborately carve out of the

Wapping: area frequented by sailors, near the Tower of London docks. **Sag Harbor**: important whaling port on eastern Long Island, New York. **busks**: corset stays.

rough material, in their hours of ocean leisure. Some of them have little boxes of dentistical-looking implements, specially intended for the skrimshandering business. But, in general, they toil with their jack-knives alone; and, with that almost omnipotent tool of the sailor, they will turn you out anything you please, in the way of a mariner's fancy.

Long exile from Christendom and civilization inevitably restores a man to that condition in which God placed him, *i.e.* what is called savagery. Your true whale-hunter is as much a savage as an Iroquois. I myself am a savage, owning no allegiance but to the King of the Cannibals; and ready at any moment to rebel against him.

Now, one of the peculiar characteristics of the savage in his domestic hours, is his wonderful patience of industry. An ancient Hawaiian war-club or spear-paddle, in its full multiplicity and elaboration of carving, is as great a trophy of human perseverance as a Latin lexicon. For, with but a bit of broken sea-shell or a shark's tooth, that miraculous intricacy of wooden net-work has been achieved; and it has cost steady years of steady application.

As with the Hawaiian savage, so with the white sailor-savage. With the same marvellous patience, and with the same single shark's tooth, of his one poor jack-knife, he will carve you a bit of bone sculpture, not quite as workmanlike, but as close packed in its maziness of design, as the Greek savage, Achilles's shield;[2] and full of barbaric spirit and suggestiveness, as the prints of that fine old Dutch savage, Albert Durer.[3]

Wooden whales, or whales cut in profile out of the small dark slabs of the noble South Sea war-wood, are frequently met with in the forecastles of American whalers. Some of them are done with much accuracy.

At some old gable-roofed country houses you will see brass whales hung by the tail for knockers to the road-side door. When the porter is sleepy, the anvil-headed whale would be best. But these knocking whales are seldom remarkable as faithful essays. On the spires of some old-fashioned churches you will see sheet-iron whales placed there for weather-cocks; but they are so elevated, and besides that are to all intents and purposes so labelled with "*Hands off!*" you cannot examine them closely enough to decide upon their merit.

In bony, ribby regions of the earth, where at the base of high broken cliffs masses of rock lie strewn in fantastic groupings upon the plain, you will often discover images as of the petrified forms of the Leviathan partly merged in grass, which of a windy day breaks against them in a surf of green surges.

Then, again, in mountainous countries where the traveller is continually girdled by amphitheatrical heights; here and there from some lucky point of view you will catch passing glimpses of the profiles of whales defined along the undulating ridges. But you must be a thorough whaleman, to see these sights; and not only that, but if you wish to return to such a sight again, you must be sure and take the exact intersecting latitude and longitude of your first stand-point, else so chance-like are such observations of the hills, that your precise, previous stand-point would require a laborious re-discovery; like the Solomon islands, which still remain incognita, though once high-ruffed Mendanna trod them and old Figueroa chronicled them.[4]

Nor when expandingly lifted by your subject, can you fail to trace out great whales in the starry heavens, and boats in pursuit of them; as when long filled with thoughts of war the Eastern nations saw armies locked in battle among the clouds. Thus at the North have I chased Leviathan round and round the Pole[5] with the revolutions of the bright points that first defined him to me. And beneath the effulgent Antarctic skies I have boarded the Argo-Navis, and joined the chase against the starry Cetus far beyond the utmost stretch of Hydrus and the Flying Fish.[6]

With a frigate's anchors for my bridle-bits and fasces° of harpoons for spurs, would I could mount that whale and leap the topmost skies, to see whether the fabled heavens with all their countless tents really lie encamped beyond my mortal sight!

fasces: distinctive bundle of rods and ax symbolizing Roman authority.

CHAPTER 58

BRIT

S TEERING north-eastward from the Crozetts, we fell in with vast meadows of brit,[1] the minute, yellow substance, upon which the Right Whale largely feeds. For leagues and leagues it undulated round us, so that we seemed to be sailing through boundless fields of ripe and golden wheat.

On the second day, numbers of Right Whales were seen, who, secure from the attack of a Sperm Whaler like the Pequod, with open jaws sluggishly swam through the brit, which, adhering to the fringing fibres of that wondrous Venetian blind in their mouths, was in that manner separated from the water that escaped at the lip.

As morning mowers, who side by side slowly and seethingly advance their scythes through the long wet grass of marshy meads; even so these monsters swam, making a strange, grassy, cutting sound; and leaving behind them endless swaths of blue upon the yellow sea.*

But it was only the sound they made as they parted the brit which at all reminded one of mowers. Seen from the mast-heads, especially when they paused and were stationary for a while, their vast black forms looked more like lifeless masses of rock than anything else. And as in the great hunting countries of India, the stranger at a distance will sometimes pass on the plains recumbent elephants without knowing them to be such, taking them for bare, blackened elevations of the soil; even so, often, with him, who for the first time beholds this species of the leviathans of the sea. And even when recognised at last, their immense magnitude renders it very hard really to believe that such bulky masses of overgrowth can possibly be instinct, in all parts, with the same sort of life that lives in a dog or a horse.

Indeed, in other respects, you can hardly regard any creatures of the deep with the same feelings that you do those of the shore. For though some old naturalists have maintained that all creatures of the land are of their kind° in the sea; and

---

* That part of the sea known among whalemen as the "Brazil Banks" does not bear that name as the Banks of Newfoundland[2] do, because of there being shallows and soundings there, but because of this remarkable meadow-like appearance, caused by the vast drifts of brit continually floating in those latitudes, where the Right Whale is often chased.

---

are of their kind: have equivalents.

though taking a broad general view of the thing, this may very well be; yet coming to specialities, where, for example, does the ocean furnish any fish that in disposition answers to the sagacious kindness of the dog? The accursed shark alone can in any generic respect be said to bear comparative analogy to him.

But though, to landsmen in general, the native inhabitants of the seas have ever been regarded with emotions unspeakably unsocial and repelling; though we know the sea to be an everlasting terra incognita, so that Columbus sailed over numberless unknown worlds to discover his one superficial western one; though, by vast odds, the most terrific of all mortal disasters have immemorially and indiscriminately befallen tens and hundreds of thousands of those who have gone upon the **waters**; though but a moment's consideration will teach, that however baby man may brag of his science and skill, and however much, in a flattering future, that science and skill may augment; yet for ever and for ever, to the crack of doom, the sea will insult and murder him, and pulverize the stateliest, stiffest frigate he can make; nevertheless, by the continual repetition of these very impressions, man has lost that sense of the full awfulness of the sea which aboriginally belongs to it.

The first boat we read of, floated on an ocean, that with Portuguese vengeance[3] had whelmed a whole world without leaving so much as a widow. That same ocean rolls now; that same ocean destroyed the wrecked ships of last year. Yea, foolish mortals, Noah's flood is not yet subsided; two thirds of the fair world it yet covers.

Wherein differ the sea and the land, that a miracle upon one is not a miracle upon the other? Preternatural terrors rested upon the Hebrews, when under the feet of Korah and his company the live ground opened and swallowed them up for ever;[4] yet not a modern sun ever sets, but in precisely the same manner the live sea swallows up ships and crews.

But not only is the sea such a foe to man who is an alien to it, but it is also a fiend to its own offspring; worse than the Persian host[5] who murdered his own guests; sparing not the creatures which itself hath spawned. Like a savage tigress that tossing in the jungle overlays her own cubs, so the sea dashes even the mightiest whales against the rocks, and leaves them there side by side with the split wrecks of ships. No mercy, no power but its own controls it. Panting and snorting like a mad battle steed that has lost its rider, the masterless ocean overruns the globe.

Consider the subtleness of the sea; how its most dreaded creatures glide under water, unapparent for the most part, and treacherously hidden beneath the loveliest tints of azure. Consider also the devilish brilliance and beauty of many of its most remorseless tribes, as the dainty embellished shape of many species of sharks. Consider, once more, the universal cannibalism of the sea; all whose creatures prey upon each other, carrying on eternal war since the world began.

Consider all this; and then turn to this green, gentle, and most docile earth; consider them both, the sea and the land; and do you not find a strange analogy to something in yourself? For as this appalling ocean surrounds the verdant land, so in the soul of man there lies one insular Tahiti, full of peace and joy, but encompassed by all the horrors of the half known life. God keep thee! Push not off from that isle, thou canst never return!

CHAPTER 59

SQUID

Slowly wading through the meadows of brit, the Pequod still held on her way north-eastward towards the island of Java;[1] a gentle air impelling her keel, so that in the surrounding serenity her three tall tapering masts mildly waved to that languid breeze, as three mild palms on a plain. And still, at wide intervals in the silvery night, the lonely, alluring jet would be seen.

But one transparent blue morning, when a stillness almost preternatural spread over the sea, however unattended with any stagnant calm; when the long burnished sun-glade on the waters seemed a golden finger laid across them, enjoining some secrecy; when the slippered waves whispered together as they softly ran on; in this profound hush of the visible sphere a strange spectre was seen by Daggoo from the main-mast-head.

In the distance, a great white mass lazily rose, and rising higher and higher, and disentangling itself from the azure, at last gleamed before our prow like a snow-slide, new slid from the hills. Thus glistening for a moment, as slowly it subsided, and sank. Then once more arose; and silently gleamed. It seemed not a whale; and yet is this Moby Dick? thought Daggoo. Again the phantom went down, but on re-appearing once more, with a stiletto-like cry that startled every man from his nod, the negro yelled out—"There! there again! there she breaches! right ahead! The White Whale, the White Whale!"

Upon this, the seamen rushed to the yard-arms, as in swarming-time the bees rush to the boughs. Bare-headed in the sultry sun, Ahab stood on the bowsprit, and with one hand pushed far behind in readiness to wave his orders to the helmsman, cast his eager glance in the direction indicated aloft by the outstretched motionless arm of Daggoo.

Whether the flitting attendance of the one still and solitary jet had gradually worked upon Ahab, so that he was now prepared to connect the ideas of mildness and repose with the first sight of the particular whale he pursued; however this was, or whether his eagerness betrayed him; whichever way it might have been, no sooner did he distinctly perceive the white mass, than with a quick intensity he instantly gave orders for lowering.

The four boats were soon on the water; Ahab's in advance, and all swiftly pulling towards their prey. Soon it went down, and while, with oars suspended, we were awaiting its reappearance, lo! in the same spot where it sank, once more it slowly rose. Almost forgetting for the moment all thoughts of Moby Dick, we now gazed at the most wondrous phenomenon which the secret seas have hitherto revealed to mankind. A vast pulpy mass, furlongs in length and breadth, of a glancing cream-color, lay floating on the water, innumerable long arms[2] radiating from its centre, and curling and twisting like a nest of anacondas, as if blindly to clutch at any hapless object within reach. No perceptible face or front did it have; no conceivable token of either sensation or instinct; but undulated there on the billows, an unearthly, formless, chance-like apparition of life.

As with a low sucking sound it slowly disappeared again, Starbuck still gazing at the agitated waters where it had sunk, with a wild voice exclaimed—"Almost rather had I seen Moby Dick and fought him, than to have seen thee, thou white ghost!"

"What was it, Sir?" said Flask.

"The great live squid, which, they say, few whale-ships ever beheld, and returned to their ports to tell of it."

But Ahab said nothing; turning his boat, he sailed back to the vessel; the rest as silently following.

Whatever superstitions the sperm whalemen in general have connected with the sight of this object, certain it is, that a glimpse of it being so very unusual, that circumstance has gone far to invest it with portentousness. So rarely is it beheld, that though one and all of them declare it to be the largest animated thing in the ocean, yet very few of them have any but the most vague ideas concerning its true nature and form; notwithstanding, they believe it to furnish to the sperm whale his only food.[3] For though other species of whales find their food above water, and may be seen by man in the act of feeding, the spermaceti whale obtains his whole food in unknown zones below the surface; and only by inference is it that any one can tell of what, precisely, that food consists. At times, when closely pursued, he will disgorge what are supposed to be the detached arms of the squid; some of them thus exhibited exceeding twenty and thirty feet in length. They fancy that the monster to which these arms belonged ordinarily clings by them to the bed of the ocean; and that the sperm whale, unlike other species, is supplied with teeth in order to attack and tear it.

There seems some ground to imagine that the great Kraken of Bishop Pontoppidan[4] may ultimately resolve itself into Squid. The manner in which the Bishop describes it, as alternately rising and sinking, with some other particulars he narrates, in all this the two correspond. But much abatement is necessary with respect to the incredible bulk he assigns it.

By some naturalists who have vaguely heard rumors of the mysterious creature, here spoken of, it is included among the class of cuttle-fish, to which, indeed, in certain external respects it would seem to belong, but only as the Anak of the tribe.[5]

CHAPTER 60

THE LINE

WITH reference to the whaling scene shortly to be described, as well as for the better understanding of all similar scenes elsewhere presented, I have here to speak of the magical, sometimes horrible whale-line.

The line originally used in the fishery was of the best hemp, slightly vapored with tar, not impregnated with it, as in the case of ordinary ropes; for while tar, as ordinarily used, makes the hemp more pliable to the rope-maker, and also renders the rope itself more convenient to the sailor for common ship use; yet, not only would the ordinary quantity too much stiffen the whale-line for the close coiling to which it must be subjected; but as most seamen are beginning to learn, tar in general by no means adds to the rope's durability or strength, however much it may give it compactness and gloss.

Of late years the Manilla rope[1] has in the American fishery almost entirely superseded hemp as a material for whale-lines; for, though not so durable as hemp, it is stronger, and far more soft and elastic; and I will add (since there is an æsthetics in all things), is much more handsome and becoming to the boat, than hemp. Hemp is a dusky, dark fellow, a sort of Indian; but Manilla is as a golden-haired Circassian[2] to behold.

The whale line is only two thirds of an inch in thickness. At first sight, you would not think it so strong as it really is. By experiment its one and fifty yarns will each suspend a weight of one hundred and twenty pounds; so that the whole rope will bear a strain nearly equal to three tons. In length, the common sperm whale-line measures something over two hundred fathoms. Towards the stern of the boat it is spirally coiled away in the tub, not like the worm-pipe of a still though, but so as to form one round, cheese-shaped mass of densely bedded "sheaves," or layers of concentric spiralizations, without any hollow but the "heart," or minute vertical tube formed at the axis of the cheese.[3] As the least tangle or kink in the coiling would, in running out, infallibly take somebody's arm, leg, or entire body off, the utmost precaution is used in stowing the line in its tub. Some harpooneers will consume almost an entire morning in this business, carrying the line high aloft and then reeving it downwards through a block° towards

reeving it . . . through a block: passing it over the wheel of a pulley.

the tub, so as in the act of coiling to free it from all possible wrinkles and twists.

In the English boats two tubs are used instead of one; the same line being continuously coiled in both tubs. There is some advantage in this; because these twin-tubs being so small they fit more readily into the boat, and do not strain it so much; whereas, the American tub, nearly three feet in diameter and of proportionate depth, makes a rather bulky freight for a craft whose planks are but one half-inch in thickness; for the bottom of the whale-boat is like critical ice, which will bear up a considerable distributed weight, but not very much of a concentrated one. When the painted canvas cover is clapped on the American line-tub, the boat looks as if it were pulling off with a prodigious great wedding-cake to present to the whales.

Both ends of the line are exposed; the lower end terminating in an eye-splice or loop coming up from the bottom against the side of the tub, and hanging over its edge completely disengaged from everything. This arrangement of the lower end is necessary on two accounts. First: In order to facilitate the fastening to it of an additional line from a neighboring boat, in case the stricken whale should sound so deep as to threaten to carry off the entire line originally attached to the harpoon. In these instances, the whale of course is shifted like a mug of ale, as it were, from the one boat to the other; though the first boat always hovers at hand to assist its consort. Second: This arrangement is indispensable for common safety's sake; for were the lower end of the line in any way attached to the boat, and were the whale then to run the line out to the end almost in a single, smoking minute as he sometimes does, he would not stop there, for the doomed boat would infallibly be dragged down after him into the profundity of the sea; and in that case no town-crier would ever find her again.

Before lowering the boat for the chase, the upper end of the line is taken aft from the tub, and passing round the loggerhead there, is again carried forward the entire length of the boat, resting crosswise upon the loom or handle of every man's oar, so that it jogs against his wrist in rowing; and also passing between the men, as they alternately sit at the opposite gunwales, to the leaded° chocks or grooves in the extreme pointed prow of the boat, where a wooden pin or skewer the size of a common quill, prevents it from slipping out. From the chocks it hangs in a slight festoon over the bows, and is then passed inside the boat again; and some ten or twenty fathoms (called box-line) being coiled upon the box in the bows, it continues its way to the gunwale still a little further aft, and is then attached to the short-warp—the rope which is immediately connected with the harpoon; but previous to that connexion, the short-warp goes through sundry mystifications too tedious to detail.

Thus the whale-line folds the whole boat in its complicated coils, twisting and writhing around it in almost every direction.[4] All the oarsmen are involved in its perilous contortions; so that to the timid eye of the landsman, they seem as Indian jugglers,[5] with the deadliest snakes sportively festooning their limbs. Nor can any son of mortal woman, for the first time, seat himself amid those hempen intricacies, and while straining his utmost at the oar, bethink him that at any unknown instant the harpoon may be darted, and all these horrible contortions be put in play like ringed lightnings; he cannot be thus circumstanced without a shudder that makes the very marrow in his bones to quiver in him like a shaken jelly. Yet habit—strange thing!

leaded: lined with lead.

what cannot habit accomplish?—Gayer sallies, more merry mirth, better jokes, and brighter repartees, you never heard over your mahogany,° than you will hear over the half-inch white cedar of the whale-boat, when thus hung in hangman's nooses; and, like the six burghers of Calais before King Edward,[6] the six men composing the crew pull into the jaws of death, with a halter around every neck, as you may say.

Perhaps a very little thought will now enable you to account for those repeated whaling disasters—some few of which are casually chronicled—of this man or that man being taken out of the boat by the line, and lost. For, when the line is darting out, to be seated then in the boat, is like being seated in the midst of the manifold whizzings of a steam-engine in full play, when every flying beam, and shaft, and wheel, is grazing you. It is worse; for you cannot sit motionless in the heart of these perils, because the boat is rocking like a cradle, and you are pitched one way and the other, without the slightest warning; and only by a certain self-adjusting buoyancy and simultaneousness of volition and action, can you escape being made a Mazeppa[7] of, and run away with where the all-seeing sun himself could never pierce you out.

Again: as the profound calm which only apparently precedes and prophesies of the storm, is perhaps more awful than the storm itself; for, indeed, the calm is but the wrapper and envelope of the storm; and contains it in itself, as the seemingly harmless rifle holds the fatal powder, and the ball, and the explosion; so the graceful repose of the line, as it silently serpentines about the oarsmen before being brought into actual play—this is a thing which carries more of true terror than any other aspect of this dangerous affair. But why say more? All men live enveloped in whale-lines. All are born with halters round their necks; but it is only when caught in the swift, sudden turn of death, that mortals realize the silent, subtle, ever-present perils of life. And if you be a philosopher, though seated in the whale-boat, you would not at heart feel one whit more of terror, than though seated before your evening fire with a poker, and not a harpoon, by your side.

mahogany: fine dinner table (Melville's usage).

CHAPTER 61

STUBB KILLS A WHALE

Iᶠ to Starbuck the apparition of the Squid was a thing of portents, to Queequeg it was quite a different object.

"When you see him 'quid," said the savage, honing his harpoon in the bow of his hoisted boat, "then you quick see him 'parm whale."

The next day was exceedingly still and sultry, and with nothing special to engage them, the Pequod's crew could hardly resist the spell of sleep induced by such a vacant sea. For this part of the Indian Ocean through which we **then were** voyaging is not what whalemen call a lively ground; that is, it affords fewer glimpses of porpoises, dolphins, flying-fish, and other vivacious denizens of more stirring waters, than those off the Rio de la Plata, or the in-shore ground off Peru.[1]

It was my turn to stand at the foremast-head; and with my shoulders leaning against the slackened royal shrouds,[2] to and fro I idly swayed in what seemed an enchanted air. No resolution could withstand it; in that dreamy mood losing all consciousness, at last my soul went out of my body; though my body still continued to sway as a pendulum will, long after the power which first moved it is withdrawn.

Ere forgetfulness altogether came over me, I had noticed that the seamen at the main and mizen mast-heads were already drowsy. So that at last all three of us lifelessly swung from the spars, and for every swing that we made there was a nod from below from the slumbering helmsman. The waves, too, nodded their indolent crests; and across the wide trance of the sea, east nodded to west, and the sun over all.

Suddenly bubbles seemed bursting beneath my closed eyes; like vices my hands grasped the shrouds; some invisible, gracious agency preserved me; with a shock I came back to life. And lo! close under our lee, not forty fathoms off, a gigantic Sperm Whale lay rolling in the water like the capsized hull of a frigate, his broad, glossy back, of an Ethiopian° hue, glistening in the sun's rays like a mirror. But lazily undulating in the trough of the sea, and ever and anon tranquilly spouting his vapory jet, the whale looked like a portly burgher° smoking his pipe of a warm afternoon. But that pipe, poor whale, was thy last. As if struck by some enchanter's wand, the sleepy ship and every sleeper in it all at once started into wakefulness; and more than

Ethiopian: African, dark. ***burgher***: middle-class citizen of a town (Dutch).

a score of voices from all parts of the vessel, simultaneously with the three notes from aloft, shouted forth the accustomed cry, as the great fish slowly and regularly spouted the sparkling brine into the air.

"Clear away the boats! Luff!"° cried Ahab. And obeying his own order, he dashed the helm down before the helmsman could handle the spokes.[3]

The sudden exclamations of the crew must have alarmed the whale; and ere the boats were down, majestically turning, he swam away to the leeward, but with such a steady tranquillity, and making so few ripples as he swam, that thinking after all he might not as yet be alarmed, Ahab gave orders that not an oar should be used, and no man must speak but in whispers. So seated like Ontario Indians on the gunwales of the boats, we swiftly but silently paddled[4] along; the calm not admitting of the noiseless sails being set. Presently, as we thus glided in chase, the monster perpendicularly flitted his tail forty feet into the air, and then sank out of sight like a tower swallowed up.

"There go flukes!" was the cry, an announcement immediately followed by Stubb's producing his match and igniting his pipe, for now a respite was granted. After the full interval of his sounding had elapsed, the whale rose again, and being now in advance of the smoker's boat, and much nearer to it than to any of the others, Stubb counted upon the honor of the capture. It was obvious, now, that the whale had at length become aware of his pursuers. All silence of cautiousness was therefore no longer of use. Paddles were dropped, and oars came loudly into play. And still puffing at his pipe, Stubb cheered on his crew to the assault.

Yes, a mighty change had come over the fish. All alive to his jeopardy, he was going "head out;" that part obliquely projecting from the mad yeast which he brewed.*

"Start her, start her, my men![6] Don't hurry yourselves; take plenty of time— but start her; start her like thunder-claps, that's all," cried Stubb, spluttering out the smoke as he spoke. "Start her, now; give 'em the long and strong stroke, Tashtego. Start her, Tash, my boy—start her, all; but keep cool, keep cool—cucumbers is the word—easy, easy—only start her like grim death and grinning devils, and raise the buried dead perpendicular out of their graves, boys—that's all. Start her!"

"Woo-hoo! Wa-hee!" screamed the Gay-Header in reply, raising some old war-whoop to the skies; as every oarsman in the strained boat involuntarily bounced forward with the one tremendous leading stroke which the eager Indian gave.

But his wild screams were answered by others quite as wild. "Kee-hee! Kee-hee!" yelled Daggoo, straining forwards and backwards on his seat, like a pacing tiger in his cage.

---

* It will be seen in some other place° of what a very light substance the entire interior of the sperm whale's enormous head consists. Though apparently the most massive, it is by far the most buoyant part about him. So that with ease he elevates it in the air, and invariably does so when going at his utmost speed. Besides, such is the breadth of the upper part of the front of his head, and such the tapering cut-water formation of the lower part, that by obliquely elevating his head, he thereby may be said to transform himself from a bluff-bowed sluggish galliot into a sharp-pointed New York pilot-boat.[5]

Luff!: "Slow down!" ***some other place***: see Ch. 76.

"Ka-la! Koo-loo!" howled Queequeg, as if smacking his lips over a mouthful of Grenadier's steak.[7] And thus with oars and yells the keels cut the sea. Meanwhile, Stubb retaining his place in the van, still encouraged his men to the onset, all the while puffing the smoke from his mouth. Like desperadoes they tugged and they strained, till the welcome cry was heard—"Stand up, Tashtego!—give it to him!" The harpoon was hurled. "Stern all!" The oarsmen backed water;° the same moment something went hot and hissing along every one of their wrists. It was the magical line. An instant before, Stubb had swiftly caught two additional turns with it round the loggerhead, whence, by reason of its increased rapid circlings, a hempen blue smoke now jetted up and mingled with the steady fumes from his pipe. As the line passed round and round the loggerhead; so also, just before reaching that point, it blisteringly passed through and through both of Stubb's hands, from which the hand-cloths, or squares of quilted canvas sometimes worn at these times, had accidentally dropped. It was like holding an enemy's sharp two-edged sword by the blade, and that enemy all the time striving to wrest it out of your clutch.

"Wet the line! wet the line!" cried Stubb to the tub oarsman (him seated by the tub) who, snatching off his hat, dashed the sea-water into it.* More turns were taken, so that the line began holding its place. The boat now flew through the boiling water like a shark all fins. Stubb and Tashtego here changed places—stem for stern—a staggering business truly in that rocking commotion.

From the vibrating line extending the entire length of the upper part of the boat, and from its now being more tight than a harpstring, you would have thought the craft had two keels—one cleaving the water, the other the air—as the boat churned on through both opposing elements at once. A continual cascade played at the bows; a ceaseless whirling eddy in her wake; and, at the slightest motion from within, even but of a little finger, the vibrating, cracking craft canted over her spasmodic gunwale into the sea. Thus they rushed; each man with might and main clinging to his seat, to prevent being tossed to the foam; and the tall form of Tashtego at the steering oar crouching almost double, in order to bring down his centre of gravity. Whole Atlantics and Pacifics seemed passed as they shot on their way, till at length the whale somewhat slackened his flight.

"Haul in—haul in!" cried Stubb to the bowsman; and, facing round towards the whale, all hands began pulling the boat up to him, while yet the boat was being towed on. Soon ranging up by his flank, Stubb, firmly planting his knee in the clumsy cleat, darted dart after dart into the flying fish; at the word of command, the boat alternately sterning out of the way of the whale's horrible wallow, and then ranging up for another fling.

The red tide now poured from all sides of the monster like brooks down a hill. His tormented body rolled not in brine but in blood, which bubbled and seethed for

---

* Partly to show the indispensableness of this act, it may here be stated, that, in the old Dutch fishery, a mop was used to dash the running line with water; in many other ships, a wooden piggin, or bailer, is set apart for that purpose. Your hat, however, is the most convenient.

---

backed water: rowed backward.

furlongs behind in their wake. The slanting sun playing upon this crimson pond in the sea, sent back its reflection into every face, so that they all glowed to each other like red men. And all the while, jet after jet of white smoke was agonizingly shot from the spiracle of the whale, and vehement puff after puff from the mouth of the excited headsman; as at every dart, hauling in upon his crooked lance (by the line attached to it), Stubb straightened it again and again, by a few rapid blows against the gunwale, then again and again sent it into the whale.

"Pull up—pull up!" he now cried to the bowsman, as the waning whale relaxed in his wrath. "Pull up!—close to!" and the boat ranged along the fish's flank. When reaching far over the bow, Stubb slowly churned his long sharp lance into the fish, and kept it there, carefully churning and churning, as if cautiously seeking to feel after some gold watch that the whale might have swallowed, and which he was fearful of breaking ere he could hook it out. But that gold watch he sought was the innermost life of the fish. And now it is struck; for, starting from his trance into that unspeakable thing called his "flurry," the monster horribly wallowed in his blood, overwrapped himself in impenetrable, mad, boiling spray, so that the imperilled craft, instantly dropping astern, had much ado blindly to struggle out from that phrensied twilight into the clear air of the day.

And now abating in his flurry, the whale once more rolled out into view; surging from side to side; spasmodically dilating and contracting his spout-hole, with sharp, cracking, agonized respirations. At last, gush after gush of clotted red gore, as if it had been the purple lees of red wine, shot into the frighted air; and falling back again, ran dripping down his motionless flanks into the sea. His heart had burst!

"He's dead, Mr. Stubb," said **Daggoo**.

"Yes; both pipes smoked out!" and withdrawing his own from his mouth, Stubb scattered the dead ashes over the water; and, for a moment, stood thoughtfully eyeing the vast corpse he had made.

CHAPTER 62

THE DART

A WORD concerning an incident in the last chapter.

According to the invariable usage of the fishery, the whaleboat pushes off from the ship, with the headsman or whale-killer as temporary steersman, and the harpooneer or whale-fastener pulling the foremost oar, the one known as the harpooneer-oar. Now it needs a strong, nervous° arm to strike the first iron into the fish; for often, in what is called a long dart, the heavy implement has to be flung to the distance of twenty or thirty feet. But however prolonged and exhausting the chase, the harpooneer is expected to pull his oar meanwhile to the uttermost; indeed, he is expected to set an example of superhuman activity to the rest, not only by incredible rowing, but by repeated loud and intrepid exclamations; and what it is to keep shouting at the top of one's compass,° while all the other muscles are strained and half started—what that is none know but those who have tried it. For one, I cannot bawl very heartily and work very recklessly at one and the same time. In this straining, bawling state, then, with his back to the fish, all at once the exhausted harpooneer hears the exciting cry—"Stand up, and give it to him!" He now has to drop and secure his oar, turn round on his centre half way, seize his harpoon from the crotch, and with what little strength may remain, he essays to pitch it somehow into the whale. No wonder, taking the whole fleet of whalemen in a body, that out of fifty fair chances for a dart, not five are successful; no wonder that so many hapless harpooneers are madly cursed and disrated;° no wonder that some of them actually burst their blood-vessels in the boat; no wonder that some sperm whalemen are absent four years with four barrels; no wonder that to many ship owners, whaling is but a losing concern; for it is the harpooneer that makes the voyage, and if you take the breath out of his body how can you expect to find it there when most wanted!

Again, if the dart be successful, then at the second critical instant, that is, when the whale starts to run, the boat-header and harpooneer likewise start to running fore and aft, to the imminent jeopardy of themselves and every one else. It is then they change places; and the headsman, the chief officer of the little craft, takes his proper station in the bows of the boat.

nervous: powerful, sinewy. ***top of one's compass***: top volume. ***disrated***: demoted.

Now, I care not who maintains the contrary, but all this is both foolish and unnecessary. The headsman should stay in the bows from first to last; he should both dart the harpoon and the lance, and no rowing whatever should be expected of him, except under circumstances obvious to any fisherman. I know that this would sometimes involve a slight loss of speed in the chase; but long experience in various whalemen of more than one nation[1] has convinced me that in the vast majority of failures in the fishery, it has not by any means been so much the speed of the whale as the before described exhaustion of the harpooneer that has caused them.

To insure the greatest efficiency in the dart, the harpooneers of this world must start to their feet from out of idleness, and not from out of toil.

CHAPTER 63

THE CROTCH

O UT of the trunk, the branches grow; out of them, the twigs. So, in productive
subjects, grow the chapters.

The crotch alluded to on a previous page deserves independent mention. It is
a notched stick of a peculiar form, some two feet in length, which is perpendicularly
inserted into the starboard gunwale near the bow, for the purpose of furnishing a rest
for the wooden extremity of the harpoon, whose other naked, barbed end slopingly
projects from the prow. Thereby the weapon is instantly at hand to its hurler, who
snatches it up as readily from its rest as a backwoodsman swings his rifle from the
wall. It is customary to have two harpoons reposing in the crotch, respectively called
the first and second irons.

But these two harpoons, each by its own cord, are both connected with the
line; the object being this: to dart them both, if possible, one instantly after the
other into the same whale; so that if, in the coming drag, one should draw out, the
other may still retain a hold. It is a doubling of the chances. But it very often happens
that owing to the instantaneous, violent, convulsive running of the whale upon
receiving the first iron, it becomes impossible for the harpooneer, however lightning-
like in his movements, to pitch the second iron into him. Nevertheless, as the second
iron is already connected with the line, and the line is running, hence that weapon
must, at all events, be anticipatingly tossed out of the boat, somehow and somewhere; else the most terrible jeopardy would involve all hands. Tumbled into the
water, it accordingly is in such cases; the spare coils of box line (mentioned in a preceding chapter°) making this feat, in most instances, prudently practicable. But this
critical act is not always unattended with the saddest and most fatal casualties.

Furthermore: you must know that when the second iron is thrown overboard,
it thenceforth becomes a dangling, sharp-edged terror, skittishly curvetting° about
both boat and whale, entangling the lines, or cutting them, and making a prodigious sensation in all directions. Nor, in general, is it possible to secure it again until
the whale is fairly captured and a corpse.

a preceding chapter: "The Line" (Ch. 60). **curvetting**: prancing like a horse.

Consider, now, how it must be in the case of four boats all engaging one unusually strong, active, and knowing whale; when owing to these qualities in him, as well as to the thousand concurring accidents of such an audacious enterprise, eight or ten loose second irons may be simultaneously dangling about him. For, of course, each boat is supplied with several harpoons to bend on to the line should the first one be ineffectually darted without recovery. All these particulars are faithfully narrated here, as they will not fail to elucidate several most important, however intricate passages, in scenes hereafter to be painted.

CHAPTER 64

STUBB'S SUPPER

STUBB'S whale had been killed some distance from the ship. It was a calm; so, forming a tandem of three boats, we commenced the slow business of towing the trophy to the Pequod. And now, as we eighteen men with our thirty-six arms, and one hundred and eighty thumbs and fingers, slowly toiled hour after hour upon that inert, sluggish corpse in the sea; and it seemed hardly to budge at all, except at long intervals; good evidence was hereby furnished of the enormousness of the mass we moved. For, upon the great canal of Hang-Ho,[1] or whatever they call it, in China, four or five laborers on the foot-path will draw a bulky freighted junk at the rate of a mile an hour; but this grand argosy° we towed heavily forged along, as if laden with pig-lead° in bulk.

Darkness came on; but three lights up and down in the Pequod's main-rigging dimly guided our way; till drawing nearer we saw Ahab dropping one of several more lanterns over the bulwarks. Vacantly eyeing the heaving whale for a moment, he issued the usual orders for securing it for the night, and then handing his lantern to a seaman, went his way into the cabin, and did not come forward again until morning.

Though, in overseeing the pursuit of this whale, Captain Ahab had evinced his customary activity, to call it so; yet now that the creature was dead, some vague dissatisfaction, or impatience, or despair, seemed working in him; as if the sight of that dead body reminded him that Moby Dick was yet to be slain; and though a thousand other whales were brought to his ship, all that would not one jot advance his grand, monomaniac object. Very soon you would have thought from the sound on the Pequod's decks, that all hands were preparing to cast anchor in the deep; for heavy chains are being dragged along the deck, and thrust rattling out of the port-holes. But by those clanking links, the vast corpse itself, not the ship, is to be moored. Tied by the head to the stern, and by the tail to the bows, the whale now lies with its black hull close to the vessel's, and seen through the darkness of the night, which obscured the spars and rigging aloft, the two—ship and whale, seemed yoked together like colossal bullocks,° whereof one reclines while the other remains standing.*

---

* A little item may as well be related here. The strongest and most reliable hold which the ship has upon the whale when moored alongside, is by the flukes or tail; and as from its greater density that part is rel-

---

argosy: large merchant vessel. ***pig-lead***: small cast-lead bars. ***bullocks***: steers.

If moody Ahab was now all quiescence, at least so far as could be known on deck, Stubb, his second mate, flushed with conquest, betrayed an unusual but still good-natured excitement. Such an unwonted bustle was he in that the staid Starbuck, his official superior, quietly resigned to him for the time the sole management of affairs. One small, helping cause of all this liveliness in Stubb, was soon made strangely manifest. Stubb was a high liver; he was somewhat intemperately fond of the whale as a flavorish thing to his palate.

"A steak, a steak, ere I sleep! You, Daggoo! overboard you go, and cut me one from his small!"°

Here be it known, that though these wild fishermen do not, as a general thing, and according to the great military maxim, make the enemy defray the current expenses of the war (at least before realizing the proceeds of the voyage), yet now and then you find some of these Nantucketers who have a genuine relish for that particular part of the Sperm Whale designated by Stubb; comprising the tapering extremity of the body.

About midnight that steak was cut and cooked; and lighted by two lanterns of sperm oil, Stubb stoutly stood up to his spermaceti supper at the capstan-head,° as if that capstan were a sideboard. Nor was Stubb the only banqueter on whale's flesh that night. Mingling their mumblings[2] with his own mastications, thousands on thousands of sharks, swarming round the dead leviathan, smackingly feasted on its fatness.[3] The few sleepers below in their bunks were often startled by the sharp slapping of their tails against the hull, within a few inches of the sleepers' hearts. Peering over the side you could just see them (as before you heard them) wallowing in the sullen, black waters, and turning over on their backs as they scooped out huge globular pieces of the whale of the bigness of a human head. This particular feat of the shark seems all but miraculous. How, at such an apparently unassailable surface, they contrive to gouge out such symmetrical mouthfuls, remains a part of the universal problem of all things. The mark they thus leave on the whale, may best be likened to the hollow made by a carpenter in countersinking for a screw.

Though amid all the smoking horror and diabolism of a sea-fight, sharks will be seen longingly gazing up to the ship's decks, like hungry dogs round a table where red meat is being carved, ready to bolt down every killed man that is tossed to them; and though, while the valiant butchers over the deck-table are thus cannibally carving each other's live meat with carving-knives all gilded and tasselled, the sharks, also, with their jewel-hilted mouths, are quarrelsomely carving away under the table at the dead meat; and though, were you to turn the whole affair upside down, it

atively heavier than any other (excepting the side-fins), its flexibility even in death, causes it to sink low beneath the surface; so that with the hand you cannot get at it from the boat, in order to put the chain round it. But this difficulty is ingeniously overcome: a small, strong line is prepared with a wooden float at its outer end, and a weight in its middle, while the other end is secured to the ship. By adroit management the wooden float is made to rise on the other side of the mass, so that now having girdled the whale, the chain is readily made to follow suit; and being slipped along the body, is at last locked fast round the smallest part of the tail, at the point of junction with its broad flukes or lobes.

small: "the narrow part of the tail of the whale, in front of the flukes" (Smyth). **capstan-head**: the top of the upright, cylindrical capstan, used to move heavy objects.

would still be pretty much the same thing, that is to say, a shocking sharkish business enough for all parties; and though sharks also are the invariable outriders of all slave ships crossing the Atlantic, systematically trotting alongside, to be handy in case a parcel is to be carried anywhere, or a dead slave to be decently buried;[4] and though one or two other like instances might be set down, touching the set terms, places, and occasions, when sharks do most socially congregate, and most hilariously feast; yet is there no conceivable time or occasion when you will find them in such countless numbers, and in gayer or more jovial spirits, than around a dead sperm whale, moored by night to a whale-ship at sea. If you have never seen that sight, then suspend your decision about the propriety **of devil-worship,** and **the** expediency of conciliating the devil.

But, as yet, Stubb heeded not the mumblings of the banquet that was going on so nigh him, no more than the sharks heeded the smacking of his own epicurean lips.

"Cook, cook!—where's that old Fleece?" he cried at length, widening his legs still further, as if to form a more secure base for his supper; and, at the same time darting his fork into the dish, as if stabbing with his lance; "cook, you cook!—sail this way, cook!"

The old black, not in any very high glee at having been previously roused from his warm hammock at a most unseasonable hour, came shambling along from his galley, for, like many old blacks, there was something the matter with his knee-pans,° which he did not keep well scoured like his other pans; this old Fleece, as they called him, came shuffling and limping along, assisting his step with his tongs, which, after a clumsy fashion, were made of straightened iron hoops; this old Ebony floundered along, and in obedience to the word of command, came to a dead stop on the opposite side of Stubb's sideboard; when, with both hands folded before him, and resting on his two-legged cane, he bowed his arched back still further over, at the same time sideways inclining his head, so as to bring his best ear into play.

"Cook," said Stubb, rapidly lifting a rather reddish morsel to his mouth, "don't you think this steak is rather overdone? You've been beating this steak too much, cook; it's too tender. Don't I always say that to be good, a whale-steak must be tough? There are those sharks now over the side, don't you see they prefer it tough and rare? What a shindy they are kicking up! Cook, go and talk to 'em; tell 'em they are welcome to help themselves civilly, and in moderation, but they must keep quiet. **Blast** me, if I can hear my own voice. Away, cook, and deliver my message. Here, take this lantern," snatching one from his sideboard; "now then, go and preach to 'em!"

Sullenly taking the offered lantern, old Fleece limped across the deck to the bulwarks; and then, with one hand dropping his light low over the sea, so as to get a good view of his congregation, with the other hand he solemnly flourished his tongs, and leaning far over the side in a mumbling voice began addressing the sharks, while Stubb, softly crawling behind, overheard all that was said.

"Fellow-critters: I'se ordered here to say dat you must stop dat dam noise dare. You hear? Stop dat dam smackin' ob de lip! Massa Stubb say dat you can fill your dam bellies up to de hatchings,° but by Gor! you must stop dat dam racket!"

---

knee-pans: kneecaps. **hatchings**: hatch covers; hence, the limit.

"Cook," here interposed Stubb, accompanying the word with a sudden slap on the shoulder,—"Cook! why, **damn your eyes**, you mustn't swear that way when you're preaching. That's no way to convert sinners, Cook!"

"Who dat? Den preach to him yourself," sullenly turning to go.

"No, Cook; go on, go on."

"Well, den, Belubed fellow-critters:"—

"Right!" exclaimed Stubb, approvingly, "coax 'em to it; try that," and Fleece continued.

"**Do** you is all sharks, and by natur wery woracious, yet I zay to you, fellow-critters, dat dat woraciousness—'top dat dam slappin' ob de tail! How you tink to hear, 'spose you keep up such a dam slappin' and bitin' dare?"

"Cook," cried Stubb, collaring him, "I wont have that swearing. Talk to 'em gentlemanly."

REVISION NARRATIVE

Black Diction

By 1850 minstrel shows, in which white entertainers in burnt-cork makeup performed black stereotypes, were highly popular, reflecting a peculiar blend of guilt, affection, and disdain among white audiences for black slaves. Melville's attempts to render African-American dialect with Fleece echo that tradition, and his and his editors' revisions of Fleece's sermon to the sharks reveal the difficulties in such racializations. To begin with, the spelling of black dialect was a problem. The expression "Do you is all sharks"—with "Do" pronounced *doe* (not *doo*) to mean "Though"—was confusing enough, and either Melville or his British editor changed the word to "Dough" to suggest the intended word. (The NN edition also adopts "Dough," but since this word is also confusing, LCRE retains "Do.") Even a typo might look like dialect. The American reading, "helping yoursebls" for "helping yourselbs" (on p. 246) is conceivable, perhaps, as a parody of dialect inversions, although both NN and LCRE assume it is a printing error and correct it accordingly. A third problem is that modern editors have emended the sermon on the basis of a possible misreading. Thinking that "dood" in "Is not one shark dood right as toder to dat whale" is a typo for "good," the NN editors altered "dood" to "good" to give the meaning *Does not one shark have as a good a right as the other to that whale?* But "dood" may be a form of *to do* so the meaning registers something more like *Does not one shark do right by that whale as the other?*—a possible ironic echoing of the golden rule. In addition, both Melville and his British editor altered nondialect expressions spoken by Stubb. For instance, when Fleece explains that the adult sharks should let their young ("small fry") have the smaller bits of flesh, Stubb irreverently responds, "that's Christianity"; however, the British editor revised the phrase to "that's the right sort," thus eliminating any elevation of bestial sharing to Christian charity. On the other hand, where in the American edition Stubb asks Fleece to end his sermon and "give the benediction," in the British text the phrasing is "give them a blessing." Chances are Melville changed the wording to make Stubb less pretentious.

"Your woraciousness, fellow-critters, I don't blame ye so much for; dat is natur, and can't be helped; but to gobern dat wicked natur, dat is de pint. You is sharks, sartin; but if you gobern de shark in you, why den you be angel; for all angel is not'ing more dan de shark well goberned. Now, look here, bred'ren, just try wonst to be cibil, a helping **yourselbs** from dat whale. Don't be tearin' de blubber out your neighbour's mout, I say. Is not one shark **dood** right as toder to dat whale? And, by Gor, none on you has de right to dat whale; dat whale belong to some one else. I know some o' you has berry brig mout, brigger dan oders; but den de brig mouts sometimes has de small bellies; so dat de brigness ob de mout is not to swallar wid, but to bite off de blubber for de small fry ob sharks, dat can't get into de scrouge° to help demselves."

"Well done, old Fleece!" cried Stubb, "that's **Christianity**; go on."

"No use goin' on; de dam willains will keep a scrougin' and slappin' each oder, Massa Stubb; dey don't hear one word; no use a-preachin' to such dam g'uttons as you call 'em, till dare bellies is full, and dare bellies is bottomless; and when dey do get em full, dey wont hear you den; for den dey sink in de sea, go fast to sleep on de coral, and can't hear not'ing at all, no more, for eber and eber."

"Upon my soul, I am about of the same opinion; so give the **benediction**, Fleece, and I'll away to my supper."

Upon this, Fleece, holding both hands over the fishy mob, raised his shrill voice, and cried—

"Cussed fellow-critters! Kick up de damndest row as ever you can; fill your dam' bellies 'till dey bust—and den die."

"Now, cook," said Stubb, resuming his supper at the capstan; "Stand just where you stood before, there, over against me, and pay particular attention."

"All dention," said Fleece, again stooping over upon his tongs in the desired position.

"Well," said Stubb, helping himself freely meanwhile; "I shall now go back to the subject of this steak. In the first place, how old are you, cook?"

"What dat do wid de 'teak," said the old black, testily.

"Silence! How old are you, cook?"

"'Bout ninety, dey say," he gloomily muttered.

"And have you lived in this world hard upon one hundred years, cook, and don't know yet how to cook a whale-steak?" rapidly bolting another mouthful at the last word, so that that morsel seemed a continuation of the question. "Where were you born, cook?"

"'Hind de hatchway, in ferry-boat, goin' ober de Roanoke."°

"Born in a ferry-boat! That's queer, too. But I want to know what country you were born in, cook?"

"Didn't I say de Roanoke country?" he cried, sharply.

"No, you didn't, cook; but I'll tell you what I'm coming to, cook. You must go home and be born over again; you don't know how to cook a whale-steak yet."

"Bress my soul, if I cook noder one," he growled, angrily, turning round to depart.

scrouge: crowd; crush. **Roanoke**: river in Virginia and North Carolina.

"Come back, cook;—here, hand me those tongs;—now take that bit of steak there, and tell me if you think that steak cooked as it should be? Take it, I say"— holding the tongs towards him—"take it, and taste it."

Faintly smacking his withered lips over it for a moment, the old negro muttered, "Best cooked 'teak I eber taste; joosy, berry joosy."

"Cook," said Stubb, squaring himself once more; "do you belong to the church?"

"Passed one once in Cape-Down," said the old man sullenly.

"And you have once in your life passed a holy church in Cape-Town, where you doubtless overheard a holy parson addressing his hearers as his beloved fellow-creatures, have you, cook! And yet you come here, and tell me such a dreadful lie as you did just now, eh?" said Stubb. "Where do you expect to go to, cook?"

"Go to bed berry soon," he mumbled, half-turning as he spoke.

"Avast! heave to! I mean when you die, cook. It's an awful question. Now what's your answer?"

"When dis old brack man dies," said the negro slowly, changing his whole air and demeanor, "he hisself won't go nowhere; but some bressed angel will come and fetch him."

"Fetch him? **How? In a coach and four, as they fetched Elijah?**[5] And fetch him where?"

"Up dere," said Fleece, holding his tongs straight over his head and keeping it there very solemnly.

"So, then, you expect to go up into our main-top, do you, cook, when you are dead? **But don't you know the higher you climb, the colder it gets? Main-top eh?**"

"Didn't say dat t'all," said Fleece, again in the sulks.

"You said up there, didn't you? and now look yourself, and see where your tongs are pointing. **But, perhaps you expect to get into heaven by crawling through the lubber's hole,**[6] **cook; but, no, no, cook, you don't get there, except you go the regular way, round by the rigging. It's a ticklish business, but must be done, or else it's no go. But none of us are in heaven yet.** Drop your tongs, cook, and hear my orders. Do ye hear? Hold your hat in one hand, and clap t'other a'top of your heart, when I'm giving my orders, cook. What! that your heart, there?—that's your gizzard! Aloft! aloft!—that's it—now you have it. Hold it there now, and pay attention."

"All 'dention," said the old black, with both hands placed as desired, vainly wriggling his grizzled head, as if to get both ears in front at one and the same time.

"Well then, cook, you see this whale-steak of yours was so very bad, that I have put it out of sight as soon as possible; you see that, don't you? Well, for the future, when you cook another whale-steak for my private table here, the capstan, I'll tell you what to do so as not to spoil it by overdoing. Hold the steak in one hand, and show a live coal to it with the other; that done, dish it; d'ye hear? And now to-morrow, cook, when we are cutting in the fish, be sure you stand by to get the tips of his fins; have them put in pickle. As for the ends of the flukes, have them soused,° cook. There, now **ye** may go."

soused: pickled in brine.

But Fleece had hardly got three paces off, when he was recalled.

"Cook, give me cutlets for supper to-morrow night in the mid-watch. D'ye hear? away you sail, then.—Halloa! stop! make a bow before you go.—Avast heaving° again! Whale-balls for breakfast—don't forget."

"Wish, by gor! whale eat him, 'stead of him eat whale. I'm bressed if he ain't more **of** shark dan Massa Shark hisself," muttered the old man, limping away; with which sage ejaculation he went to his hammock.

Avast heaving: stop pulling (on the ropes); here, facetiously, "Stop."

CHAPTER 65

THE WHALE AS A DISH

THAT mortal man should feed upon the creature that feeds his lamp, and, like Stubb, eat him by his own light, as you may say; this seems so outlandish a thing that one must needs go a little into the history and philosophy of it.

It is upon record, that three centuries ago the tongue of the Right Whale was esteemed a great delicacy in France, and commanded large prices there. Also, that in Henry VIIIth's time, a certain cook of the court obtained a handsome reward for inventing an admirable sauce to be eaten with barbacued porpoises, which, you remember, are a species of whale. Porpoises, indeed, are to this day considered fine eating. The meat is made into balls about the size of billiard balls, and being well seasoned and spiced might be taken for turtle-balls or veal balls. The old monks of Dunfermline[1] were very fond of them. They had a great porpoise grant from the crown.

The fact is, that among his hunters at least, the whale would by all hands be considered a noble dish, were there not so much of him; but when you come to sit down before a meat-pie nearly one hundred feet long, it takes away your appetite. Only the most unprejudiced of men like Stubb, nowadays partake of cooked whales; but the Esquimaux are not so fastidious. We all know how they live upon whales, and have rare old vintages of prime old train oil. Zogranda,[2] one of their most famous doctors, recommends strips of blubber for infants, as being exceedingly juicy and nourishing. And this reminds me that certain Englishmen, who long ago were accidentally left in Greenland by a whaling vessel—that these men actually lived for several months on the mouldy scraps of whales which had been left ashore after trying out the blubber. Among the Dutch whalemen these scraps are called "fritters;" which, indeed, they greatly resemble, being brown and crisp, and smelling something like old Amsterdam housewives' dough-nuts or oly-cooks, when fresh. They have such an eatable look that the most self-denying stranger can hardly keep his hands off.

But what further depreciates the whale as a civilized dish, is his exceeding richness. He is the great prize ox of the sea, too fat to be delicately good. Look at his hump, which would be as fine eating as the buffalo's (which is esteemed a rare dish), were it not such a solid pyramid of fat. But the spermaceti itself, how bland and creamy that is; like the transparent, half-jellied, white meat of a cocoanut in the third month of its growth, yet far too rich to supply a substitute for butter.

Nevertheless, many whalemen have a method of absorbing it into some other substance, and then partaking of it. In the long try watches° of the night it is a common thing for the seamen to dip their ship-biscuit into the huge oil-pots and let them fry there awhile. Many a good supper have I thus made.[3]

In the case of a small Sperm Whale the brains are accounted a fine dish. The casket of the skull is broken into with an axe, and the two plump, whitish lobes being withdrawn (precisely resembling two large puddings), they are then mixed with flour, and cooked into a most delectable mess, in flavor somewhat resembling calves' head, which is quite a dish among some epicures; and every one knows that some young bucks° among the epicures, by continually dining upon calves' brains, by and by get to have a little brains of their own, so as to be able to tell a calf's head from their own heads; which, indeed, requires uncommon discrimination. And that is the reason why a young buck with an intelligent looking calf's head before him, is somehow one of the saddest sights you can see. The head looks a sort of reproachfully at him, with an "Et tu Brute!"[4] expression.

It is not, perhaps, entirely because the whale is so excessively unctuous that landsmen seem to regard the eating of him with abhorrence; that appears to result, in some way, from the consideration before mentioned: i. e. that a man should eat a newly murdered thing of the sea, and eat it too by its own light. But no doubt the first man that ever murdered an ox was regarded as a murderer; perhaps he was

REVISION NARRATIVE

Pâté de Foie

In "The Whale as a Dish," Ishmael considers the "history and philosophy" of eating whale meat and extends his pantheism, or belief that divinity resides in all things, to the comic but not necessarily illogical conclusion that eating whale is a form of cannibalism. The question "who is not a cannibal?" (p. 271) echoes the query "Who ain't a slave?" in Ch. 1, "Loomings," and recalls the image of "the universal cannibalism of the sea" in Ch. 58, "Brit"; it also anticipates the more frightful scene of "The Shark Massacre" in the following chapter. Here, however, Ishmael brings cannibalism to the dinner table and with a religious zeal that prompted his British editor to expurgate. It would have been one thing to let stand Ishmael's stereotype of the Feejee Islander salting down a missionary, but Melville pushes the image, calling the Feejee "provident" (which here means nothing more than economical, but also suggests God's providential favor), and he pushes further when he finds the "provident Feejee" in better standing at "the day of judgment" than the "civilized and enlightened gourmand" who feasts on pâté de foie gras, a delicacy made from the livers of geese who are force fed until their livers nearly burst. Melville makes a good case for vegetarianism.

---

try watches: turns of duty at the tryworks. ***bucks***: stylish fellows, dandies.

hung; and if he had been put on his trial by oxen, he certainly would have been; and he certainly deserved it if any murderer does. Go to the meat-market of a Saturday night and see the crowds of live bipeds staring up at the long rows of dead quadrupeds. Does not that sight take a tooth out of the cannibal's jaw? Cannibals? who is not a cannibal? **I tell you it will be more tolerable for the Fejee that salted down a lean missionary in his cellar against a coming famine; it will be more tolerable for that provident Fejee, I say, in the day of judgment, than for thee,[5] civilized and enlightened gourmand, who nailest geese to the ground and feastest on their bloated livers in thy paté-de-foie-gras.**

But Stubb, he eats the whale by its own light, does he? and that is adding insult to injury, is it? Look at your knife-handle, there, my civilized and enlightened gourmand dining off that roast beef, what is that handle made of?—what but the bones of the brother of the very ox you are eating? And what do you pick your teeth with, after devouring that fat goose? With a feather of the same fowl. And with what quill did the Secretary of the Society for the Suppression of Cruelty to Ganders **formally** indite his circulars? It is only within the last month or two that that society passed a resolution to patronize nothing but steel pens.

CHAPTER 66

THE SHARK MASSACRE

W HEN in the Southern Fishery, a captured Sperm Whale, after long and weary toil, is brought alongside late at night, it is not, as a general thing at least, customary to proceed at once to the business of cutting him in. For that business is an exceedingly laborious one; is not very soon completed; and requires all hands to set about it. Therefore, the common usage is to take in all sail; lash the helm a'lee;° and then send every one below to his hammock till daylight, with the reservation that, until that time, anchor-watches[1] shall be kept; that is, two and two, for an hour each couple, the crew in rotation shall mount the deck to see that all goes well.

But sometimes, especially upon the Line° in the Pacific, this plan will not answer at all; because such incalculable hosts of sharks gather round the moored carcase, that were he left so for six hours, say, on a stretch, little more than the skeleton would be visible by morning. In most other parts of the ocean, however, where these fish do not so largely abound, their wondrous voracity can be at times considerably diminished, by vigorously stirring them up with sharp whaling-spades, a procedure notwithstanding, which, in some instances, only seems to tickle them into still greater activity. But it was not thus in the present case with the Pequod's sharks; though, to be sure, any man unaccustomed to such sights, to have looked over her side that night, would have almost thought the whole round sea was one huge cheese, and those sharks the maggots in it.

Nevertheless, upon Stubb setting the anchor-watch after his supper was concluded; and when, accordingly, Queequeg and a forecastle seaman came on deck, no small excitement was created among the sharks; for immediately suspending the cutting stages° over the side, and lowering three lanterns, so that they cast long gleams of light over the turbid sea, these two mariners, darting their long whaling-spades,

---

lash the helm a'lee: tie the tiller so as to point the ship into the wind and keep it relatively still. **the Line**: the equator. **cutting stages**: narrow platforms hung over the side for men to stand on while cutting into the whale.

kept up an incessant murdering of the sharks,* by striking the keen steel deep into their skulls, seemingly their only vital part. But in the foamy confusion of their mixed and struggling hosts, the marksmen could not always hit their mark; and this brought about new revelations of the incredible ferocity of the foe. They viciously snapped, not only at each other's disembowelments, but like flexible bows, bent round, and bit their own; till those entrails seemed swallowed over and over again by the same mouth, to be oppositely voided by the gaping wound. Nor was this all. It was unsafe to meddle with the corpses and ghosts of these creatures. A sort of generic or Pantheistic vitality[2] seemed to lurk in their very joints and bones, after what might be called the individual life had departed. Killed and hoisted on deck for the sake of his skin, one of these sharks almost took poor Queequeg's hand off, when he tried to shut down the dead lid of his murderous jaw.

"Queequeg no care what god made him shark," said the savage, agonizingly lifting his hand up and down; "wedder Fejee god or Nantucket god; but de god wat made shark must be one dam Ingin."[3]

---

* The whaling-spade used for cutting-in is made of the very best steel; is about the bigness of a man's spread hand; and in general shape, corresponds to the garden implement after which it is named; only its sides are perfectly flat, and its upper end considerably narrower than the lower. This weapon is always kept as sharp as possible; and when being used is occasionally honed, just like a razor. In its socket, a stiff pole, from twenty to thirty feet long, is inserted for a handle.

CHAPTER 67

CUTTING IN

IT was a Saturday night, and such a Sabbath as followed! Ex officio professors of Sabbath breaking[1] are all whalemen. The ivory Pequod was turned into what seemed a shamble;° every sailor a butcher. You would have thought we were offering up ten thousand red oxen to the sea gods.[2]

In the first place, the enormous cutting tackles,° among other ponderous things comprising a cluster of blocks generally painted green, and which no single man can possibly lift—this vast bunch of grapes was swayed up° to the main-top and firmly lashed to the lower mast-head, the strongest point anywhere above a ship's deck. The end of the hawser-like° rope winding through these intricacies, was then conducted to the windlass, and the huge lower block of the tackles was swung over the whale; to this block the great blubber hook, weighing some one hundred pounds, was attached. And now suspended in stages over the side, Starbuck and Stubb, the mates, armed with their long spades, began cutting a hole in the body for the insertion of the hook just above the nearest of the two side-fins. This done, a broad, semicircular line is cut round the hole, the hook is inserted, and the main body of the crew striking up a wild chorus, now commence heaving in one dense crowd at the windlass. When instantly, the entire ship careens over on her side; every bolt in her starts like the nail-heads of an old house in frosty weather; she trembles, quivers, and nods her frighted mast-heads to the sky. More and more she leans over to the whale, while every gasping heave of the windlass is answered by a helping heave from the billows; till at last, a swift, startling snap is heard; with a great swash the ship rolls upwards and backwards from the whale, and the triumphant tackle rises into sight dragging after it the disengaged semicircular end of the first strip of blubber. Now as the blubber envelopes the whale precisely as the rind does an orange, so is it stripped off from the body precisely as an orange is sometimes stripped by spiralizing it. For the strain constantly kept up by the windlass continually keeps the whale rolling over and over in the water, and as the blubber in one strip uniformly peels off along the line called the "scarf," simultaneously cut by the spades of Starbuck and

shamble: slaughterhouse. ***cutting tackles***: multiple rope and pulley arrangement with large hooks. ***swayed up***: hoisted. ***hawser-like***: very thick, like the rope used to tow a vessel.

Stubb, the mates; and just as fast as it is thus peeled off, and indeed by that very act itself, it is all the time being hoisted higher and higher aloft till its upper end grazes the main-top; the men at the windlass then cease heaving, and for a moment or two the prodigious blood-dripping mass sways to and fro as if let down from the sky, and every one present must take good heed to dodge it when it swings, else it may box his ears and pitch him headlong overboard.

One of the attending harpooneers now advances with a long, keen weapon called a boarding-sword, and watching his chance he dexterously slices out a considerable hole in the lower part of the swaying mass. Into this hole, the end of the second alternating great tackle is then hooked so as to retain a hold upon the blubber, in order to prepare for what follows. Whereupon, this accomplished swordsman, warning all hands to stand off, once more makes a scientific dash at the mass, and with a few sidelong, desperate, lunging slicings, severs it completely in twain; so that while the short lower part is still fast, the long upper strip, called a blanket-piece, swings clear, and is all ready for lowering. The heavers forward now resume their song, and while the one tackle is peeling and hoisting a second strip from the whale, the other is slowly slackened away, and down goes the first strip through the main hatchway right beneath, into an unfurnished parlor called the blubber-room. Into this twilight apartment sundry nimble hands keep coiling away the long blanket-piece as if it were a great live mass of plaited serpents. And thus the work proceeds; the two tackles hoisting and lowering simultaneously; both whale and windlass heaving, the heavers singing, the blubber-room gentlemen coiling, the mates scarfing, the ship straining, and all hands swearing occasionally, by way of assuaging the general friction.

CHAPTER 68

THE BLANKET

I HAVE given no small attention to that not unvexed subject, the skin of the whale. I have had controversies about it with experienced whalemen afloat, and learned naturalists ashore. My original opinion remains unchanged; but it is only an opinion.

The question is, what and where is the skin of the whale? Already you know what his blubber is. That blubber is something of the consistence of firm, close-grained beef, but tougher, more elastic and compact, and ranges from eight or ten to twelve and fifteen inches in thickness.

Now, however preposterous it may at first seem to talk of any creature's skin as being of that sort of consistence and thickness, yet in point of fact these are no arguments against such a presumption; because you cannot raise any other dense enveloping layer from the whale's body but that same blubber; and the outermost enveloping layer of any animal, if reasonably dense, what can that be but the skin? True, from the unmarred dead body of the whale, you may scrape off with your hand an infinitely thin, transparent substance, somewhat resembling the thinnest shreds of isinglass,° only it is almost as flexible and soft as satin; that is, previous to being dried, when it not only contracts and thickens, but becomes rather hard and brittle. I have several such dried bits, which I use for marks in my whale-books. It is transparent, as I said before; and being laid upon the printed page, I have sometimes pleased myself with fancying it exerted a magnifying influence. At any rate, it is pleasant to read about whales through their own spectacles, as you may say. But what I am driving at here is this. That same infinitely thin, isinglass substance, which, I admit, invests the entire body of the whale, is not so much to be regarded as the skin of the creature, as the skin of the skin, so to speak; for it were simply ridiculous to say, that the proper skin of the tremendous whale is thinner and more tender than the skin of a new-born child. But no more of this.

Assuming the blubber to be the skin of the whale; then, when this skin, as in the case of a very large Sperm Whale, will yield the bulk of one hundred barrels of oil; and, when it is considered that, in quantity, or rather weight, that oil, in its expressed state, is only three fourths, and not the entire substance of the coat; some

isinglass: mica, a flaky mineral.

276

idea may hence be had of the enormousness of that animated mass, a mere part of whose mere integument yields such a lake of liquid as that. Reckoning ten barrels to the ton, you have ten tons for the net weight of only three quarters of the stuff of the whale's skin.

In life, the visible surface of the Sperm Whale is not the least among the many marvels he presents. Almost invariably it is all over obliquely crossed and re-crossed with numberless straight marks in thick array, something like those in the finest Italian line engravings. But these marks do not seem to be impressed upon the isin-glass substance above mentioned, but seem to be seen through it, as if they were engraved upon the body itself. Nor is this all. In some instances, to the quick, obser-vant eye, those linear marks, as in a veritable engraving, but afford the ground for far other delineations. These are hieroglyphical;° that is, if you call those mysterious cyphers on the walls of pyramids hieroglyphics, then that is the proper word to use in the present connexion. By my retentive memory of the hieroglyphics upon one Sperm Whale in particular, I was much struck with a plate representing the old Indian characters chiselled on the famous hieroglyphic palisades on the banks of the Upper Mississippi.[1] Like those mystic rocks, too, the mystic-marked whale remains undecipherable. This allusion to the Indian rocks reminds me of another thing. Besides all the other phenomena which the exterior of the Sperm Whale presents, he not seldom displays the back, and more especially his flanks, effaced in great part of the regular linear appearance, by reason of numerous rude scratches, altogether of an irregular, random aspect. I should say that those New England rocks on the sea-coast, which Agassiz imagines to bear the marks of violent scraping contact with vast floating icebergs[2]—I should say, that those rocks must not a little resemble the Sperm Whale in this particular. It also seems to me that such scratches in the whale are probably made by hostile contact with other whales; for I have most remarked them in the large, full-grown bulls of the species.

A word or two more concerning this matter of the skin or blubber of the whale. It has already been said, that it is stript from him in long pieces, called blan-ket-pieces. Like most sea-terms, this one is very happy° and significant. For the whale is indeed wrapt up in his blubber as in a real blanket or counterpane; or, still better, an Indian poncho slipt over his head, and skirting his extremity. It is by rea-son of this cosy blanketing of his body, that the whale is enabled to keep himself comfortable in all weathers, in all seas, times, and tides. What would become of a Greenland whale, say, in those shuddering, icy seas of the North, if unsupplied with his cosy surtout?°° True, other fish are found exceedingly brisk in those Hyperborean° waters; but these, be it observed, are your cold-blooded, lungless fish, whose very bellies are refrigerators; creatures, that warm themselves under the lee of an iceberg, as a traveller in winter would bask before an inn fire; whereas, like man, the whale has lungs and warm blood. Freeze his blood, and he dies. How wonderful is it then—except after explanation—that this great monster, to whom corporeal warmth is as indispensable as it is to man; how wonderful that he should

---

hieroglyphical: hard to decipher. **happy**: appropriate. **surtout**: overcoat (French). **Hyperborean**: far northern.

be found at home, immersed to his lips for life in those Arctic waters! where, when seamen fall overboard, they are sometimes found, months afterwards, perpendicularly frozen into the hearts of fields of ice, as a fly is found glued in amber. But more surprising is it to know, as has been proved by experiment, that the blood of a Polar whale is warmer than that of a Borneo negro in summer.

It does seem to me, that herein we see the rare virtue of a strong individual vitality, and the rare virtue of thick walls, and the rare virtue of interior spaciousness. Oh, man! admire and model thyself after the whale! Do thou, too, remain warm among ice. Do thou, too, live in this world without being of it.[3] Be cool at the equator; keep thy blood fluid at the Pole. Like the great dome of St. Peter's, and like the great whale, retain, O man! in all seasons a temperature[4] of thine own.

But how easy and how hopeless to teach these fine things! Of erections, how few are domed like St. Peter's! of creatures, how few vast as the whale!

CHAPTER 69

THE FUNERAL

"Haul in the chains! Let the carcase go astern!"

The vast tackles have now done their duty. The peeled white body of the beheaded whale flashes like a marble sepulchre; though changed in hue, it has not perceptibly lost anything in bulk. It is still colossal. Slowly it floats more and more away, the water round it torn and splashed by the insatiate sharks, and the air above vexed with rapacious flights of screaming fowls, whose beaks are like so many insulting poniards[1] in the whale. The vast white headless phantom floats further and further from the ship, and every rod that it so floats, what seem square roods° of sharks and cubic roods of fowls, augment the murderous din. For hours and hours from the almost stationary ship that hideous sight is seen. Beneath the unclouded and mild azure sky, upon the fair face of the pleasant sea, wafted by the joyous breezes, that great mass of death floats on and on, till lost in infinite perspectives.

There's a most doleful and most mocking funeral! The sea-vultures all in pious mourning, the air-sharks all punctiliously in black or speckled. In life but few of them would have helped the whale, I ween, if peradventure° he had needed it; but upon the banquet of his funeral they most piously do pounce. Oh, horrible vultureism of earth! from which not the mightiest whale is free.

Nor is this the end. Desecrated as the body is, a vengeful ghost survives and hovers over it to scare. Espied by some timid man-of-war or blundering discovery-vessel from afar, when the distance obscuring the swarming fowls, nevertheless still shows the white mass floating in the sun, and the white spray heaving high against it; straightway the whale's unharming corpse, with trembling fingers is set down in the log—*shoals, rocks, and breakers hereabouts: beware!* And for years afterwards, perhaps, ships shun the place; leaping over it as silly sheep leap over a vacuum, because their leader originally leaped there when a stick was held. There's your law of precedents; there's your utility of traditions; there's the story of your obstinate survival of old beliefs never bottomed on the earth, and now not even hovering in the air! **There's orthodoxy!**

---

square roods: a rood is one-fourth of an acre, but here means huge numbers occupying a lot of space. **I ween, if peradventure**: "I think, if by chance" (obsolete).

Thus, while in life the great whale's body may have been a real terror to his foes, in his death his ghost becomes a **powerful** panic to a world.

Are you a believer in ghosts, my friend? There are other ghosts than the Cock-Lane one, and far deeper men than Doctor Johnson[2] who believe in them.

CHAPTER 70

THE SPHYNX

IT should not have been omitted that previous to completely stripping the body of the leviathan, he was beheaded. Now, the beheading of the Sperm Whale is a scientific anatomical feat, upon which experienced whale surgeons very much pride themselves: and not without reason.

Consider that the whale has nothing that can properly be called a neck; on the contrary, where his head and body seem to join, there, in that very place, is the thickest part of him. Remember, also, that the surgeon must operate from above, some eight or ten feet intervening between him and his subject, and that subject almost hidden in a discolored, rolling, and oftentimes tumultuous and bursting sea. Bear in mind, too, that under these untoward circumstances he has to cut many feet deep in the flesh; and in that subterraneous manner, without so much as getting one single peep into the ever-contracting gash thus made, he must skilfully steer clear of all adjacent, interdicted parts, and exactly divide the spine at a critical point hard by its insertion into the skull. Do you not marvel, then, at Stubb's boast, that he demanded but ten minutes to behead a sperm whale?

When first severed, the head is dropped astern and held there by a cable till the body is stripped. That done, if it belong to a small whale it is hoisted on deck to be deliberately disposed of. But, with a full grown leviathan this is impossible; for the sperm whale's head embraces nearly one third of his entire bulk, and completely to suspend such a burden as that, even by the immense tackles of a whaler, this were as vain a thing as to attempt weighing a Dutch barn¹ in jewellers' scales.

The Pequod's whale being decapitated and the body stripped, the head was hoisted against the ship's side—about half way out of the sea, so that it might yet in great part be buoyed up by its native element. And there with the strained craft steeply leaning over to it, by reason of the enormous downward drag from the lower mast-head, and every yard-arm on that side projecting like a crane over the waves; there, that blood-dripping head hung to the Pequod's waist like the giant Holofernes's from the girdle of Judith.²

When this last task was accomplished it was noon, and the seamen went below to their dinner. Silence reigned over the before tumultuous but now deserted deck.

An intense copper calm, like a universal yellow lotus,[3] was more and more unfolding its noiseless measureless leaves upon the sea.

A short space elapsed, and up into this noiselessness came Ahab alone from his cabin. Taking a few turns on the quarterdeck, he paused to gaze over the side, then slowly getting into the main-chains he took Stubb's long spade—still remaining there after the whale's decapitation—and striking it into the lower part of the half-suspended mass, placed its other end crutch-wise under one arm, and so stood leaning over with eyes attentively fixed on this head.

It was a black and hooded head; and hanging there in the midst of so intense a calm, it seemed the Sphynx's in the desert.[4] "Speak, thou vast and venerable head," muttered Ahab, "which, though ungarnished with a beard, yet here and there lookest hoary° with mosses; speak, mighty head, and tell us the secret thing that is in thee. Of all divers, thou hast dived the deepest. That head upon which the upper sun now gleams, has moved amid this world's foundations. Where unrecorded names and navies rust, and untold hopes and anchors rot; where in her murderous hold this frigate earth is ballasted with bones of millions of the drowned; there, in that awful water-land, there was thy most familiar home. Thou hast been where bell° or diver never went; hast slept by many a sailor's side, where sleepless mothers would give their lives to lay them down. Thou saw'st the locked lovers when leaping from their flaming ship; heart to heart they sank beneath the exulting wave; true to each other, when heaven seemed false to them. Thou saw'st the murdered mate when tossed by pirates from the midnight deck; for hours he fell into the deeper midnight of the insatiate maw;° and his murderers still sailed on unharmed—while swift lightnings shivered the neighboring ship that would have borne a righteous husband to outstretched, longing arms. **O head! thou hast seen enough to split the planets and make an infidel of Abraham,[5] and not one syllable is thine!**"

"Sail ho!" cried a triumphant voice from the main-mast-head.

"Aye? Well, now, that's cheering," cried Ahab, suddenly erecting himself, while whole thunder-clouds swept aside from his brow. "That lively cry upon this deadly calm might almost convert a better man.—Where away?"

"Three points on the starboard bow, sir, and bringing down her breeze to us!"

"Better and better, man. Would now St. Paul would come along that way, and to my breezelessness bring his breeze! O Nature, and O soul of man! how far beyond all utterance are your linked analogies! not the smallest atom stirs or lives in matter, but has its cunning duplicate in mind."[6]

---

hoary: ancient. **bell**: device holding air, used for underwater work and observation. **insatiate maw**: ever-hungry mouth (of the sea).

CHAPTER 71

THE JEROBOAM'S STORY

H AND in hand, ship and breeze blew on; but the breeze came faster than the ship, and soon the Pequod began to rock.

By and by, through the glass° the stranger's boats and manned mast-heads proved her a whale-ship. But as she was so far to windward, and shooting by, apparently making a passage to some other ground,° the Pequod could not hope to reach her. So the signal was set to see what response would be made.

Here be it said, that like the vessels of military marines, the ships of the American Whale Fleet have each a private signal;° all which signals being collected in a book with the names of the respective vessels attached, every captain is provided with it. Thereby, the whale commanders are enabled to recognise each other upon the ocean, even at considerable distances, and with no small facility.

The Pequod's signal was at last responded to by the stranger's setting her own; which proved the ship to be the Jeroboam[1] of Nantucket. Squaring her yards, she bore down, ranged abeam under the Pequod's lee,° and lowered a boat; it soon drew nigh; but, as the side-ladder was being rigged by Starbuck's order to accommodate the visiting captain, the stranger in question waved his hand from his boat's stern in token of that proceeding being entirely unnecessary. It turned out that the Jeroboam had a malignant epidemic on board, and that Mayhew, her captain, was fearful of infecting the Pequod's company. For, though himself and boat's crew remained untainted, and though his ship was half a rifle-shot off, and an incorruptible sea and air rolling and flowing between; yet conscientiously adhering to the timid quarantine of the land, he peremptorily refused to come into direct contact with the Pequod.

But this did by no means prevent all communication. Preserving an interval of some few yards between itself and the ship, the Jeroboam's boat by the occasional use of its oars contrived to keep parallel to the Pequod, as she heavily forged through the sea (for by this time it blew very fresh), with her main-top-sail aback;° though,

---

glass: telescope. **ground**: cruising ground, an area of the sea where whale sightings are likely. **private signal**: unique flag or pennant. **squaring her yards . . . ranged abeam . . . lee**: turning the yards, with their sails, to right angles with its hull, the Jeroboam positions itself parallel to and downwind of the *Pequod*. **aback**: turned so the wind strikes its front.

indeed, at times by the sudden onset of a large rolling wave, the boat would be pushed some way ahead; but would be soon skilfully brought to her proper bearings again. Subject to this, and other the like interruptions now and then, a conversation was sustained between the two parties; but at intervals not without still another interruption of a very different sort.

Pulling an oar in the Jeroboam's boat, was a man of a singular appearance, even in that wild whaling life where individual notabilities make up all totalities. He was a small, short, youngish man, sprinkled all over his face with freckles, and wearing redundant yellow hair. A long-skirted, cabalistically-cut° coat of a faded walnut tinge enveloped him; the overlapping sleeves of which were rolled up on his wrists. A deep, settled, fanatic delirium was in his eyes.

So soon as this figure had been first descried, Stubb had exclaimed—"That's he! that's he!—the long-togged scaramouch[2] the Town-Ho's company told us of!" Stubb here alluded to a strange story told of the Jeroboam, and a certain man among her crew, some time previous when the Pequod spoke the Town-Ho. According to this account and what was subsequently learned, it seemed that the scaramouch in question had gained a wonderful ascendency over almost everybody in the Jeroboam. His story was this:

He had been originally nurtured among the crazy society of Neskyeuna Shakers,[3] where he had been a great prophet; in their cracked, secret meetings having several times descended from heaven by the way of a trap-door, announcing the speedy opening of the seventh vial,[4] which he carried in his vest-pocket; but, which, instead of containing gunpowder, was supposed to be charged with laudanum.[5] A strange, apostolic whim having seized him, he had left Neskyeuna for Nantucket, where, with that cunning peculiar to craziness, he assumed a steady, common sense exterior, and offered himself as a green-hand candidate for the Jeroboam's whaling voyage. They engaged him; but straightway upon the ship's getting out of sight of land, his insanity broke out in a freshet. He announced himself as the archangel Gabriel,[6] and commanded the captain to jump overboard. He published his manifesto, whereby he set himself forth as the deliverer of the isles of the sea and vicar-general of all Oceanica.[7] The unflinching earnestness with which he declared these things;—the dark, daring play of his sleepless, excited imagination, and all the preternatural terrors of real delirium, united to invest this Gabriel in the minds of the majority of the ignorant crew, with an atmosphere of sacredness. Moreover, they were afraid of him. As such a man, however, was not of much practical use in the ship, especially as he refused to work except when he pleased, the incredulous captain would fain have been rid of him; but apprised that that individual's intention was to land him in the first convenient port, the **archangel** forthwith opened all his seals and vials[8]—devoting the ship and all hands to unconditional perdition, in case this intention was carried out. So strongly did he work upon his disciples among the crew, that at last in a body they went to the captain and told him if Gabriel was sent from the ship, not a man of them would remain. He was therefore forced to relinquish his plan. Nor would they permit Gabriel to be any way maltreated, say or do what he would; so that it came to pass that Gabriel had the complete freedom of the

---

cabalistically-cut: oddly styled, suggesting secret meanings.

ship. The consequence of all this was, that **the archangel** cared little or nothing for the captain and mates; and since the epidemic had broken out, he carried a higher hand than ever; declaring that the plague, as he called it, was at his sole command; nor should it be stayed but according to his good pleasure. The sailors, mostly poor devils, cringed, and some of them fawned before him; in obedience to his instructions, sometimes rendering him personal homage, as to a god. Such things may seem incredible; but, however wondrous, they are true. Nor is the history of fanatics half so striking in respect to the measureless self-deception of the fanatic himself, as his measureless power of deceiving and bedevilling so many others. But it is time to return to the Pequod.

"I fear not thy epidemic, man," said Ahab from the bulwarks, to Captain Mayhew, who stood in the boat's stern; "come on board."

But now Gabriel started to his feet.

"Think, think of the fevers, yellow and bilious! Beware of the horrible plague!"

"Gabriel, Gabriel!" cried Captain Mayhew; "thou must either—" But that instant a headlong wave shot the boat far ahead, and its seethings drowned all speech.

"Hast thou seen the White Whale?" demanded Ahab, when the boat drifted back.

"Think, think of thy whale-boat, stoven and sunk! Beware of the horrible tail!"

"I tell thee again, Gabriel, that—" But again the boat tore ahead as if dragged by fiends. Nothing was said for some moments, while a succession of riotous waves rolled by, which by one of those occasional caprices of the seas were tumbling, not heaving it. Meantime, the hoisted sperm whale's head jogged about very violently, and Gabriel was seen eyeing it with rather more apprehensiveness than **his archangel nature** seemed to warrant.

When this interlude was over, Captain Mayhew began a dark story concerning Moby Dick; not, however, without frequent interruptions from Gabriel, whenever his name was mentioned, and the crazy sea that seemed leagued with him.

It seemed that the Jeroboam had not long left home, when upon speaking a whale-ship, her people were reliably apprised of the existence of Moby Dick, and the havoc he had made. Greedily sucking in this intelligence, Gabriel solemnly warned the captain against attacking the White Whale, in case the monster should be seen; in his gibbering insanity, pronouncing the White Whale to be no less a being than the Shaker God incarnated; the Shakers receiving the Bible.[9] But when, some year or two afterwards, Moby Dick was fairly sighted from the mast-heads, Macey, the chief mate, burned with ardor to encounter him; and the captain himself being not unwilling to let him have the opportunity, despite all the archangel's denunciations and forewarnings, Macey succeeded in persuading five men to man his boat. With them he pushed off; and, after much weary pulling, and many perilous, unsuccessful onsets, he at last succeeded in getting one iron fast. Meantime, Gabriel, ascending to the main-royal mast-head, was tossing one arm in frantic gestures, and hurling forth prophecies of speedy doom to the sacrilegious assailants of his divinity. Now, while Macey, the mate, was standing up in his boat's bow, and with all the reckless energy of his tribe was venting his wild exclamations upon the whale, and essaying to get a fair chance for his poised lance, lo! a broad white shadow rose from the sea; by its quick, fanning motion, temporarily taking the breath out of the bodies of the oarsmen. Next instant, the luckless mate, so full of furious life, was smitten bodily into the air, and making a long arc in his descent, fell into the sea at the distance of about fifty yards. Not a chip of the boat was harmed, nor a hair of any oarsman's head; but the mate for ever sank.

It is well to parenthesize here, that of the fatal accidents in the Sperm-Whale Fishery, this kind is perhaps almost as frequent as any. Sometimes, nothing is injured but the man who is thus annihilated; oftener the boat's bow is knocked off, or the thigh-board, in which the headsman stands, is torn from its place and accompanies the body. But strangest of all is the circumstance, that in more instances than one, when the body has been recovered, not a single mark of violence is discernible; the man being stark dead.[10]

The whole calamity, with the falling form of Macey, was plainly descried from the ship. Raising a piercing shriek—"The vial! the vial!" Gabriel called off the terror-stricken crew from the further hunting of the whale. This **terrible** event clothed the archangel with added influence; because his credulous disciples believed that he had specifically fore-announced it, instead of only making a general prophecy, which any one might have done, and so have chanced to hit one of many marks in the wide margin allowed. He became a nameless terror to the ship.

Mayhew having concluded his narration, Ahab put such questions to him, that the stranger captain could not forbear inquiring whether he intended to hunt the White Whale, if opportunity should offer. To which Ahab answered—"Aye." Straightway, then, Gabriel once more started to his feet, glaring upon the old man, and vehemently exclaimed, with downward pointed finger—"Think, think of the blasphemer—dead, and down there!—beware of the blasphemer's end!"

Ahab stolidly turned aside; then said to Mayhew, "Captain, I have just bethought me of my letter-bag; there is a letter for one of thy officers, if I mistake not. Starbuck, look over the bag."

Every whale-ship takes out a goodly number of letters for various ships, whose delivery to the persons to whom they may be addressed, depends upon the mere chance of encountering them in the four oceans. Thus, most letters never reach their mark; and many are only received after attaining an age of two or three years or more.

Soon Starbuck returned with a letter in his hand. It was sorely tumbled, damp, and covered with a dull, spotted, green mould, in consequence of being kept in a dark locker of the cabin. Of such a letter, Death himself might well have been the post-boy.

"Can'st not read it?" cried Ahab. "Give it me, man. Aye, aye, it's but a dim scrawl;—what's this?" As he was studying it out, Starbuck took a long cutting-spade pole, and with his knife slightly split the end, to insert the letter there, and in that way, hand it to the boat, without its coming any closer to the ship.

Meantime, Ahab holding the letter, muttered, "Mr. Har—yes, Mr. Harry—(a woman's pinny° hand,—the man's wife, I'll wager)—Aye—Mr. Harry Macey, Ship Jeroboam;—why it's Macey, and he's dead!"

---

pinny: from "pinafore," here meaning "feminine."

"Poor fellow! poor fellow! and from his wife," sighed Mayhew; "but let me have it."

"Nay, keep it thyself," cried Gabriel to Ahab; "thou art soon going that way."

"Curses throttle thee!" yelled Ahab. "Captain Mayhew, stand by now to receive it;" and taking the fatal missive from Starbuck's hands, he caught it in the slit of the pole, and reached it over towards the boat. But as he did so, the oarsmen expectantly desisted from rowing; the boat drifted a little towards the ship's stern; so that, as if by magic, the letter suddenly ranged along with Gabriel's eager hand. He clutched it in an instant, seized the boat-knife,° and impaling the letter on it, sent it thus loaded back into the ship. It fell at Ahab's feet. Then Gabriel shrieked out to his comrades to give way with their oars, and in that manner the mutinous boat rapidly shot away from the Pequod.

As, after this interlude, the seamen resumed their work upon the jacket of the whale, many strange things were hinted in reference to this wild affair.

boat-knife: kept at the bow of a whaleboat for cutting the whale line in an emergency; also "line-knife."

CHAPTER 72

THE MONKEY-ROPE

I N the tumultuous business of cutting-in and attending to a whale, there is much running backwards and forwards among the crew. Now hands are wanted here, and then again hands are wanted there. There is no staying in any one place; for at one and the same time everything has to be done everywhere. It is much the same with him who endeavors the description of the scene.[1] We must now retrace our way a little. It was mentioned that upon first breaking ground in the whale's back, the blubber-hook was inserted into the original hole there cut by the spades of the mates. But how did so clumsy and weighty a mass as that same hook get fixed in that hole? It was inserted there by my particular friend Queequeg, whose duty it was, as harpooneer, to descend upon the monster's back for the special purpose referred to. But in very many cases, circumstances require that the harpooneer shall remain on the whale till the whole flensing or stripping operation is concluded. The whale, be it observed, lies almost entirely submerged, excepting the immediate parts operated upon. So down there, some ten feet below the level of the deck, the poor harpooneer flounders about, half on the whale and half in the water, as the vast mass revolves like a tread-mill beneath him. On the occasion in question, Queequeg figured in the Highland costume—a **shirt** and socks—in which to my eyes, at least, he appeared to uncommon advantage; and no one had a better chance to observe him, as will presently be seen.

Being the savage's bowsman, that is, the person who pulled the bow-oar in his boat (the second one from forward), it was my cheerful duty to attend upon him while taking that hard-scrabble° scramble upon the dead whale's back. You have seen Italian organ-boys holding a dancing-ape by a long cord. Just so, from the ship's steep side, did I hold Queequeg down there in the sea, by what is technically called in the fishery a monkey-rope, attached to a strong strip of canvas belted round his waist.

It was a humorously perilous business for both of us. For, before we proceed further, it must be said that the monkey-rope was fast at both ends; fast to Queequeg's broad canvas belt, and fast to my narrow leather one. So that for better or for worse, we two, for the time, were wedded; and should poor Queequeg sink to

hard-scrabble: barely managing; from subsistence on bad land.

rise no more, then both usage and honor demanded, that instead of cutting the cord, it should drag me down in his wake. So, then, an elongated Siamese ligature[2] united us. Queequeg was my own inseparable twin brother; nor could I any way get rid of the dangerous liabilities which the hempen bond entailed.

So strongly and metaphysically did I conceive of my situation then, that while earnestly watching his motions, I seemed distinctly to perceive that my own individuality was now merged in a joint stock company of two: that my free will had received a mortal wound; and that another's mistake or misfortune might plunge innocent me into unmerited disaster and death. Therefore, I saw that here was a sort of interregnum° in Providence; for its even-handed equity never could have sanctioned so gross an injustice. And yet still further pondering—while I jerked him now and then from between the whale and the ship, which would threaten to jam him—still further pondering, I say, I saw that this situation of mine was the precise situation of every mortal that breathes; only, in most cases, he, one way or other, has this Siamese connexion with a plurality of other mortals. If your banker breaks, you snap; if your apothecary by mistake sends you poison in your pills, you die. True, you may say that, by exceeding caution, you may possibly escape these and the multitudinous other evil chances of life. But handle Queequeg's monkey-rope heedfully as I would, sometimes he jerked it so, that I came very near sliding overboard. Nor could I possibly forget that, do what I would, I only had the management of one end of it.*

I have hinted that I would often jerk poor Queequeg from between the whale and the ship—where he would occasionally fall, from the incessant rolling and swaying of both. But this was not the only jamming jeopardy he was exposed to. Unappalled by the massacre made upon them during the night, the sharks now freshly and more keenly allured by the before pent° blood which began to flow from the carcase—the rabid creatures swarmed round it like bees in a beehive.

And right in among those sharks was Queequeg; who often pushed them aside with his floundering feet. A thing altogether incredible were it not that attracted by such prey as a dead whale, the otherwise miscellaneously carnivorous shark will seldom touch a man.

Nevertheless, it may well be believed that since they have such a ravenous finger in the pie, it is deemed but wise to look sharp to them. Accordingly, besides the monkey-rope, with which I now and then jerked the poor fellow from too close a vicinity to the maw of what seemed a peculiarly ferocious shark—he was provided with still another protection. Suspended over the side in one of the stages, Tashtego and Daggoo continually flourished over his head a couple of keen whale-spades,

---

* The monkey-rope is found in all whalers; but it was only in the *Pequod* that the monkey and his holder were ever tied together. This improvement upon the original usage was introduced by no less a man than Stubb, in order to afford to the imperilled harpooneer the strongest possible guarantee for the faithfulness and vigilance of his monkey-rope holder.

---

interregnum: gap in continuity of rule. **pent**: shut in.

wherewith they slaughtered as many sharks as they could reach. This procedure of theirs, to be sure, was very disinterested and benevolent of them. They meant Queequeg's best happiness, I admit; but in their hasty zeal to befriend him, and from the circumstance that both he and the sharks were at times half hidden by the blood-mudded water, those indiscreet spades of theirs would come nearer amputating a leg than a tail. But poor Queequeg, I suppose, straining and gasping there with that great iron hook—poor Queequeg, I suppose, only prayed to his Yojo, and gave up his life into the hands of his gods.

Well, well, my dear comrade and twin-brother, thought I, as I drew in and then slacked off the rope to every swell of the sea—what matters it, after all? Are you not the precious image of each and all of us **men** in this whaling world? That unsounded ocean you gasp in, is Life; those sharks, your foes; those spades, your friends; and what between sharks and spades you are in a sad pickle and peril, poor lad.

But courage! there is good cheer in store for you, Queequeg. For now, as with blue lips and bloodshot eyes the exhausted savage at last climbs up the chains and stands all dripping and involuntarily trembling over the side; the steward advances, and with a benevolent, consolatory glance hands him—what? Some hot Cogniac? No! hands him, ye gods! hands him a cup of tepid ginger and water!

"Ginger? Do I smell ginger?" suspiciously asked Stubb, coming near. "Yes, this must be ginger," peering into the as yet untasted cup. Then standing as if incredulous for a while, he calmly walked towards the astonished steward slowly saying, "Ginger? ginger? and will you have the goodness to tell me, Mr. Dough-Boy, where lies the virtue of ginger? Ginger! is ginger the sort of fuel you use, Dough-Boy, to kindle a fire in this shivering cannibal? Ginger!—what the devil is ginger?—seacoal?—fire-wood?—lucifer matches?°—tinder?—gun-powder?—what the devil is ginger, I say, that you offer this cup to our poor Queequeg here?"

"There is some sneaking Temperance Society movement about this business," he suddenly added, now approaching Starbuck, who had just come from forward. "Will you look at that kannakin,° sir: smell of it, if you please." Then watching the mate's countenance, he added: "The steward, Mr. Starbuck, had the face to offer that calomel and jalap° to Queequeg, there, this instant off the whale. Is the steward an apothecary, sir? and may I ask whether this is the sort of **bitters** by which he blows back the **life** into a half-drowned man?"

"I trust not," said Starbuck, "it is poor stuff enough."

"Aye, aye, steward," cried Stubb, "we'll teach you to drug a harpooneer; none of your apothecary's medicine here; you want to poison us, do ye? You have got out insurances on our lives and want to murder us all, and pocket the proceeds, do ye?"

"It was not me," cried Dough-Boy, "it was Aunt Charity that brought the ginger on board; and bade me never give the harpooneers any spirits, but only this ginger-jub—so she called it."

"Ginger-jub! you gingerly rascal! take that! and run along with ye to the lockers, and get something better. I hope I do no wrong, Mr. Starbuck. It is the captain's orders—grog for the harpooneer on a whale."

sea-coal . . . lucifer matches: mined coal . . . wooden friction matches. ***kannakin***: small drinking vessel; "cannikin" in Ch. 54. ***calomel and jalap***: laxatives, commonly given together.

"Enough," replied Starbuck, "only don't **hit** him again, but—"

"Oh, I never hurt when I hit, except when I hit a whale or something of that sort; and this fellow's a weazel. What were you about saying, sir?"

"Only this: go down with him, and get what thou wantest thyself."

When Stubb reappeared, he came with a dark flask in one hand, and a sort of tea-caddy° in the other. The first contained strong spirits, and was handed to Queequeg; the second was Aunt Charity's gift, and that was freely given to the waves.

tea-caddy: small box for loose tea.

CHAPTER 73

STUBB AND FLASK KILL A RIGHT WHALE; AND THEN HAVE A TALK OVER HIM

IT must be borne in mind that all this time we have a Sperm Whale's prodigious head hanging to the Pequod's side. But we must let it continue hanging there a while till we can get a chance to attend to it. For the present other matters press, and the best we can do now for the head, is to pray heaven the tackles may hold.

Now, during the past night and forenoon, the Pequod had gradually drifted into a sea, which, by its occasional patches of yellow brit, gave unusual tokens of the vicinity of Right Whales, a species of the Leviathan that but few supposed to be at this particular time lurking anywhere near. And though all hands commonly disdained the capture of those inferior creatures; and though the Pequod was not commissioned to cruise for them at all, and though she had passed numbers of them near the Crozetts without lowering a boat; yet now that a Sperm Whale had been brought alongside and beheaded, to the surprise of all, the announcement was made that a Right Whale should be captured that day, if opportunity offered.

Nor was this long wanting. Tall spouts were seen to leeward; and two boats, Stubb's and Flask's, were detached in pursuit. Pulling further and further away, they at last became almost invisible to the men at the mast-head. But suddenly in the distance, they saw a great heap of tumultuous white water, and soon after news came from aloft that one or both the boats must be fast. An interval passed and the boats were in plain sight, in the act of being dragged right towards the ship by the towing whale. So close did the monster come to the hull, that at first it seemed as if he meant it malice; but suddenly going down in a maelstrom, within three rods of the planks, he wholly disappeared from view, as if diving under the keel. "Cut, cut!" was the cry from the ship to the boats, which, for one instant, seemed on the point of being brought with a deadly dash against the vessel's side. But having plenty of line yet in the tubs, and the whale not sounding very rapidly, they paid out abundance of rope, and at the same time pulled with all their might so as to get ahead of the ship. For a few minutes the struggle was intensely critical; for while they still slacked out the tightened line in one direction, and still plied their oars in another, the contending strain threatened to take them under. But it was only a few feet advance they sought to gain. And they stuck to it till they did gain it; when instantly, a swift tremor was felt running like lightning along the keel, as the strained line, scraping beneath the ship, suddenly rose to view under her bows, snapping and quivering; and so flinging off its drippings, that the drops fell like bits of broken glass on the water, while the whale beyond also rose to sight, and once more the boats were free to fly. But the fagged° whale abated his speed, and blindly altering his course, went round the stern of the ship towing the two boats after him, so that they performed a complete circuit.

Meantime, they hauled more and more upon their lines, till close flanking him on both sides, Stubb answered Flask with lance for lance; and thus round and round the Pequod the battle went, while the multitudes of sharks that had before swum round the Sperm Whale's body, rushed to the fresh blood that was spilled, thirstily drinking at every new gash, as the eager Israelites did at the new bursting fountains that poured from the smitten rock.[1]

At last his spout grew thick, and with a frightful roll and vomit, he turned upon his back a corpse.

While the two headsmen were engaged in making fast cords to his flukes, and in other ways getting the mass in readiness for towing, some conversation ensued between them.

"I wonder what the old man wants with this lump of foul lard," said Stubb, not without some disgust at the thought of having to do with so ignoble a leviathan.

"Wants with it?" said Flask, coiling some spare line in the boat's bow, "did you never hear that the ship which but once has a Sperm Whale's head hoisted on her starboard side, and at the same time a Right Whale's on the larboard; did you never hear, Stubb, that that ship can never afterwards capsize?"

"Why not?"

"I don't know, but I heard that gamboge° ghost of a Fedallah saying so, and he seems to know all about ships' charms. But I sometimes think he'll charm the ship to no good at last. I don't half like that chap, Stubb. Did you ever notice how that tusk of his° is a sort of carved into a snake's head, Stubb?"

"Sink him! I never look at him at all; but if ever I get a chance of a dark night, and he standing hard by the bulwarks, and no one by; look down there, Flask"— pointing into the sea with a peculiar motion of both hands—"Aye, will I! Flask, I take that Fedallah to be the devil in disguise. Do you believe that cock and bull story about his having been stowed away on board ship? He's the devil, I say. The reason why you don't see his tail, is because he tucks it up out of sight; he carries it coiled

---

fagged: tired. ***gamboge***: reddish- or brownish-yellow pigment; a corruption of "Cambodia" and the color of a resin from that area. ***that tusk of his***: Fedallah's protruding tooth.

away in his pocket, I guess. **Blast him!** now that I think of it, he's always wanting oakum to stuff into the toes of his boots."[2]

"He sleeps in his boots, don't he? He hasn't got any hammock; but I've seen him lay of nights in a coil of rigging."

"No doubt, and it's because of his cursed tail; he coils it down, do ye see, in the eye of the rigging."

"What's the old man have so much to do with him for?"

"Striking up a swap or a bargain, I suppose."[3]

"Bargain?—about what?"

"Why, do ye see, the old man is hard bent after that White Whale, and the devil there is trying to come round him, and get him to swap away his silver watch, or his soul, or something of that sort, and then he'll surrender Moby Dick."

"Pooh! Stubb, you are skylarking; how can Fedallah do that?"

"I don't know, Flask, but the devil is a curious chap, and a wicked one, I tell ye. Why, they say as how he went a sauntering into the old flag-ship once, switching his tail about devilish easy and gentlemanlike, and inquiring if the old governor was at home.[4] Well, he was at home, and asked the devil what he wanted. The devil, switching his hoofs, up and says, 'I want John.' 'What for?' says the old governor. 'What business is that of yours,' says the devil, getting mad,—'I want to use him.' 'Take him,' says the governor—and by the Lord, Flask, if the devil didn't give John the Asiatic cholera[5] before he got through with him, I'll eat this whale in one mouthful. But look sharp—aint you all ready there? Well, then, pull ahead, and let's get the whale alongside."

"I think I remember some such story as you were telling," said Flask, when at last the two boats were slowly advancing with their burden towards the ship, "but I can't remember where."

"Three Spaniards?[6] Adventures of those three bloody-minded soldadoes?° Did ye read it there, Flask? I guess ye did?"

"No: never saw such a book; heard of it, though. But now, tell me, Stubb, do you suppose that that devil you was speaking of just now, was the same you say is now on board the Pequod?"

"Am I the same man that helped kill this whale? Doesn't the devil live for ever; who ever heard that the devil was dead? Did you ever see any parson a wearing mourning for the devil? And if the devil has a latch-key to get into the admiral's cabin, don't you suppose he can crawl into a port-hole? Tell me that, Mr. Flask?"

"How old do you suppose Fedallah is, Stubb?"

"Do you see that mainmast there?" pointing to the ship; "well, that's the figure one; now take all the hoops in the Pequod's hold, and string 'em along in a row with that mast, for oughts, do you see; well, that wouldn't begin to be Fedallah's age. Nor all the coopers in creation couldn't show hoops enough to make oughts enough."

"But see here, Stubb, I thought you a little boasted just now, that you meant to give Fedallah a sea-toss, if you got a good chance. Now, if he's so old as all those hoops of yours come to, and if he is going to live for ever, what good will it do to pitch him overboard—tell me that?"

soldadoes: soldiers.

"Give him a good ducking, anyhow."

"But he'd crawl back."

"Duck him again; and keep ducking him."

"Suppose he should take it into his head to duck you, though—yes, and drown you—what then?"

"I should like to see him try it; I'd give him such a pair of black eyes that he wouldn't dare to show his face in the admiral's cabin again for a long while, let alone down in the orlop° there, where he lives, and hereabouts on the upper decks where he sneaks so much. Damn the devil, Flask; do you suppose I'm afraid of the devil? Who's afraid of him, except the old governor who daresn't catch him and put him in double-darbies,° as he deserves, but lets him go about kidnapping people; aye, and signed a bond with him, that all the people the devil kidnapped, he'd roast for him? There's a governor!"

"Do you suppose Fedallah wants to kidnap Captain Ahab?"

"Do I suppose it? You'll know it before long, Flask. But I am going now to keep a sharp look-out on him; and if I see anything very suspicious going on, I'll just take him by the nape of his neck, and say—Look here, Beelzebub, you don't do it; and if he makes any fuss, by the Lord I'll make a grab into his pocket for his tail, take it to the capstan, and give him such a wrenching and heaving, that his tail will come short off at the stump—do you see; and then, I rather guess when he finds himself docked in that queer fashion, he'll sneak off without the poor satisfaction of feeling his tail between his legs."

"And what will you do with the tail, Stubb?"

"Do with it? Sell it for an ox whip when we get home;—what else?"

"Now, do you mean what you say, and have been saying all along, Stubb?"

"Mean or not mean, here we are at the ship."

The boats were here hailed, to tow the whale on the larboard side, where fluke chains and other necessaries were already prepared for securing him.

"Didn't I tell you so?" said Flask; "yes, you'll soon see this right whale's head hoisted up opposite that parmacetti's."

In good time, Flask's saying proved true. As before, the Pequod steeply leaned over towards the sperm whale's head, now, by the counterpoise of both heads, she regained her even keel; though sorely strained, you may well believe. So, when on one side you hoist in Locke's head, you go over that way; but now, on the other side, hoist in Kant's and you come back again; but in very poor plight.[7] Thus, some minds for ever keep trimming boat.° Oh, ye foolish! throw all these thunder-heads° overboard, and then you will float light and right.

In disposing of the body of a right whale, when brought alongside the ship, the same preliminary proceedings commonly take place as in the case of a sperm whale; only, in the latter instance, the head is cut off whole, but in the former the lips and tongue are separately removed and hoisted on deck, with all the well known black bone° attached to what is called the crown-piece. But nothing like this, in the present

---

orlop: the lowest deck. **double-darbies**: shackles. **trimming boat**: literally, keeping a vessel level ("on an even keel"). **thunder-heads**: heavy storm clouds, and a pun on "dunderheads," fools (Parker). **black bone**: baleen

case, had been done. The carcases of both whales had dropped astern; and the head-laden ship not a little resembled a mule carrying a pair of overburdening panniers.°

Meantime, Fedallah was calmly eyeing the right whale's head, and ever and anon glancing from the deep wrinkles there to the lines in his own hand. And Ahab chanced so to stand, that the Parsee[8] occupied his shadow; while, if the Parsee's shadow was there at all it seemed only to blend with, and lengthen Ahab's. As the crew toiled on, Laplandish[9] speculations were bandied among them, concerning all these passing things.

panniers: baskets for carrying goods.

CHAPTER 74

THE SPERM WHALE'S HEAD — CONTRASTED VIEW

HERE, now, are two great whales, laying their heads together; let us join them, and lay together our own.

Of the grand order of folio leviathans,[1] the Sperm Whale and the Right Whale are by far the most noteworthy. They are the only whales regularly hunted by man. To the Nantucketer, they present the two extremes of all the known varieties of the whale. As the external difference between them is mainly observable in their heads; and as a head of each is this moment hanging from the Pequod's side; and as we may freely go from one to the other, by merely stepping across the deck:—where, I should like to know, will you obtain a better chance to study practical cetology than here?

In the first place, you are struck by the general contrast between these heads. Both are massive enough in all conscience; but there is a certain mathematical symmetry in the Sperm Whale's which the Right Whale's sadly lacks. There is more character in the Sperm Whale's head. As you behold it, you involuntarily yield the immense superiority to him, in point of pervading dignity. In the present instance, too, this dignity is heightened by the pepper and salt color of his head at the summit, giving token of advanced age and large experience. In short, he is what the fishermen technically call a "greyheaded whale."

Let us now note what is least dissimilar in these heads—namely, the two most important organs, the eye and the ear. Far back on the side of the head, and low down, near the angle of either whale's jaw, if you narrowly search, you will at last see a lashless eye, which you would fancy to be a young colt's eye; so out of all proportion is it to the magnitude of the head.

Now, from this peculiar sideway position of the whale's eyes, it is plain that he can never see an object which is exactly ahead, no more than he can one exactly astern. In a word, the position of the whale's eyes corresponds to that of a man's ears; and you may fancy, for yourself, how it would fare with you, did you sideways survey objects through your ears. You would find that you could only command some thirty degrees of vision in advance of the straight side-line of sight; and about thirty more behind it. If your bitterest foe were walking straight towards you, with dagger uplifted in broad day, you would not be able to see him, any more than if he were stealing upon you from behind. In a word, you would have two backs, so to speak; but, at the same time, also, two fronts (side fronts): for what is it that makes the front of a man—what, indeed, but his eyes?

Moreover, while in most other animals that I can now think of, the eyes are so planted as imperceptibly to blend their visual power, so as to produce one picture and not two to the brain; the peculiar position of the whale's eyes, effectually divided as they are by many cubic feet of solid head, which towers between them like a great mountain separating two lakes in valleys; this, of course, must wholly separate the impressions which each independent organ imparts. The whale, therefore, must see one distinct picture on this side, and another distinct picture on that side; while all between must be profound darkness and nothingness to him. Man may, in effect, be said to look out on the world from a sentry-box with two joined sashes for his window. But with the whale, these two sashes are separately inserted, making two distinct windows, but sadly impairing the view. This peculiarity of the whale's eyes is a thing always to be borne in mind in the fishery; and to be remembered by the reader in some subsequent scenes.[2]

A curious and most puzzling question might be started concerning this visual matter as touching the Leviathan. But I must be content with a hint. So long as a man's eyes are open in the light, the act of seeing is involuntary; that is, he cannot then help mechanically seeing whatever objects are before him. Nevertheless, any one's experience will teach him, that though he can take in an undiscriminating sweep of things at one glance, it is quite impossible for him, attentively, and completely, to examine any two things—however large or however small—at one and the same instant of time; never mind if they lie side by side and touch each other. But if you now come to separate these two objects, and surround each by a circle of profound darkness; then, in order to see one of them, in such a manner as to bring your mind to bear on it, the other will be utterly excluded from your contemporary consciousness. How is it, then, with the whale? True, both his eyes, in themselves, must simultaneously act; but is his brain so much more comprehensive, combining, and subtle than man's, that he can at the same moment of time attentively examine two distinct prospects, one on one side of him, and the other in an exactly opposite direction? If he can, then is it as marvellous a thing in him, as if a man were able simultaneously to go through the demonstrations of two distinct problems in Euclid.[3] Nor, strictly investigated, is there any incongruity in this comparison.

It may be but an idle whim, but it has always seemed to me, that the extraordinary vacillations of movement displayed by some whales when beset by three or four boats; the timidity and liability to queer frights, so common to such whales; I think that all this indirectly proceeds from the helpless perplexity of volition, in which their divided and diametrically opposite powers of vision must involve them.

But the ear of the whale is full as curious as the eye.[4] If you are an entire stranger to their race, you might hunt over these two heads for hours, and never discover that organ. The ear has no external leaf whatever; and into the hole itself you can hardly insert a quill, so wondrously minute is it. It is lodged a little behind the eye. With respect to their ears, this important difference is to be observed between the sperm whale and the right. While the ear of the former has an external opening, that of the latter is entirely and evenly covered over with a membrane, so as to be quite imperceptible from without.

Is it not curious, that so vast a being as the whale should see the world through so small an eye, and hear the thunder through an ear which is smaller than a hare's? But if his eyes were broad as the lens of Herschel's great telescope;[5] and his ears capacious as the porches of cathedrals; would that make him any longer of sight, or sharper of hearing? Not at all.—Why then do you try to "enlarge" your mind? Subtilize it.

Let us now with whatever levers and steam-engines we have at hand, cant over the sperm whale's head, so that it may lie bottom up; then, ascending by a ladder to the summit, have a peep down the mouth; and were it not that the body is now completely separated from it, with a lantern we might descend into the great Kentucky Mammoth Cave[6] of his stomach. But let us hold on here by this tooth, and look about us where we are. What a really beautiful and chaste-looking mouth! from floor to ceiling, lined, or rather papered with a glistening white membrane, glossy as bridal satins.

But come out now, and look at this portentous lower jaw, which seems like the long narrow lid of an immense snuff-box, with the hinge at one end, instead of one side. If you pry it up, so as to get it overhead, and expose its rows of teeth, it seems a terrific portcullis; and such, alas! it proves to many a poor wight in the fishery, upon whom these spikes fall with impaling force. But far more terrible is it to behold, when fathoms down in the sea, you see some sulky whale, floating there suspended, with his prodigious jaw, some fifteen feet long, hanging straight down at right-angles with his body, for all the world like a ship's jib-boom.° This whale is not dead; he is only dispirited; out of sorts, perhaps; hypochondriac;° and so supine, that the hinges of his jaw have relaxed, leaving him there in that ungainly sort of plight, a reproach to all his tribe, who must, no doubt, imprecate° lock-jaws upon him.

In most cases this lower jaw—being easily unhinged by a practised artist—is disengaged and hoisted on deck for the purpose of extracting the ivory teeth, and furnishing a supply of that hard white whalebone with which the fishermen fashion all sorts of curious articles, including canes, umbrella-stocks, and handles to riding-whips.

With a long, weary hoist the jaw is dragged on board, as if it were an anchor; and when the proper time comes—some few days after the other work—Queequeg, Daggoo, and Tashtego, being all accomplished dentists, are set to drawing teeth. With a keen cutting-spade, Queequeg lances the gums; then the jaw is lashed down to ringbolts, and a tackle being rigged from aloft, they drag out these teeth, as Michigan oxen drag stumps of old oaks out of wild wood-lands. There are generally forty-two teeth in all; in old whales, much worn down, but undecayed; nor filled after our artificial fashion. The jaw is afterwards sawn into slabs, and piled away like joists for building houses.

---

jib-boom: spar extending forward beyond the bowsprit. **hypochondriac**: depressed. **imprecate**: invoke a curse

CHAPTER 75

THE RIGHT WHALE'S HEAD — CONTRASTED VIEW

CROSSING the deck, let us now have a good long look at the Right Whale's head.

As in general shape the noble Sperm Whale's head may be compared to a Roman war-chariot[1] (especially in front, where it is so broadly rounded); so, at a broad view, the Right Whale's head bears a rather inelegant resemblance to a gigantic galliot-toed shoe. Two hundred years ago an old Dutch voyager likened its shape to that of a shoemaker's last.[2] And in this same last or shoe, that old woman of the nursery tale, with the swarming brood, might very comfortably be lodged, she and all her progeny.

But as you come nearer to this great head it begins to assume different aspects, according to your point of view. If you stand on its summit and look at these two *f*-shaped spout-holes, you would take the whole head for an enormous bass-viol, and these spiracles, the apertures in its sounding-board. Then, again, if you fix your eye upon this strange, crested, comb-like incrustation on the top of the mass—this green, barnacled thing, which the Greenlanders call the "crown," and the Southern fishers the "bonnet" of the Right Whale; fixing your eyes solely on this, you would take the head for the trunk of some huge oak, with a bird's nest in its crotch. At any rate, when you watch those live crabs that nestle here on this bonnet, such an idea will be almost sure to occur to you; unless, indeed, your fancy has been fixed by the technical term "crown" also bestowed upon it; in which case you will take great interest in thinking how this mighty monster is actually a diademed king of the sea, whose green crown has been put together for him in this marvellous manner. But if this whale be a king, he is a very sulky looking fellow to grace a diadem. Look at that hanging lower lip! what a huge sulk and pout is there! a sulk and pout, by carpenter's measurement, about twenty feet long and five feet deep; a sulk and pout that will yield you some 500 gallons of oil and more.

A great pity, now, that this unfortunate whale should be hare-lipped. The fissure is about a foot across. Probably the mother during an important interval[3] was sailing down the Peruvian coast, when earthquakes caused the beach to gape. Over this lip, as over a slippery threshold, we now slide into the mouth. Upon my word were I at Mackinaw, I should take this to be the inside of an Indian wigwam. Good Lord! is this the road that Jonah went? The roof is about twelve feet high, and runs to a pretty sharp angle, as if there were a regular ridge-pole[4] there; while these ribbed, arched, hairy sides, present us with those wondrous, half vertical, scimetar-shaped slats of whalebone, say three hundred on a side, which depending from the upper part of the head or crown bone, form those Venetian blinds which have elsewhere been cursorily mentioned.° The edges of these bones are fringed with hairy fibres, through which the Right Whale strains the water, and in whose intricacies he retains the small fish, when open-mouthed he goes through the seas of brit in feeding time. In the central blinds of bone, as they stand in their natural order, there are certain curious marks, curves, hollows, and ridges, whereby some whalemen calculate the creature's age, as the age of an oak by its circular rings. Though the certainty of this criterion is far from demonstrable, yet it has the savor of analogical probability. At any rate, if we yield to it, we must grant a far greater age to the Right Whale than at first glance will seem reasonable.

In old times, there seem to have prevailed the most curious fancies concerning these blinds. One voyager in Purchas calls them the wondrous "whiskers" inside of the whale's mouth;* another, "hogs' bristles;" a third old gentleman in Hackluyt[5] uses the following elegant language: "There are about two hundred and fifty fins growing on each side of his upper *chop*, which arch over his tongue on each side of his mouth."

As every one knows, these same "hogs' bristles," "fins," "whiskers," "blinds," or whatever you please, furnish to the ladies their busks° and other stiffening contrivances. But in this particular, the demand has long been on the decline. It was in Queen Anne's time that the bone was in its glory, the farthingale[6] being then all the fashion. And as those ancient dames moved about gaily, though in the jaws of the whale, as you may say; even so, in a shower, with the like thoughtlessness, do we nowadays fly under the same jaws for protection; the umbrella being a tent spread over thes same bone.

But now forget all about blinds and whiskers for a moment, and, standing in the Right Whale's mouth, look around you afresh. Seeing all these colonnades of bone so methodically ranged about, would you not think you were inside of the great Haarlem organ,[7] and gazing upon its thousand pipes? For a carpet to the organ we have a rug of the softest Turkey[8]—the tongue, which is glued, as it were, to the floor of the mouth. It is very fat and tender, and apt to tear in pieces in hoisting it on deck. This particular tongue now before us; at a passing glance I should say it was a six-barreler; that is, it will yield you about that amount of oil.

---

* This reminds us that the Right Whale really has a sort of whisker, or rather a moustache, consisting of a few scattered white hairs on the upper part of the outer end of the lower jaw. Sometimes these tufts impart a rather brigandish expression to his otherwise solemn countenance.

---

cursorily mentioned: see Ch. 58. **busks**: corset stays.

Ere this, you must have plainly seen the truth of what I started with—that the Sperm Whale and the Right Whale have almost entirely different heads. To sum up, then: in the Right Whale's there is no great well of sperm; no ivory teeth at all; no long, slender mandible of a lower jaw, like the Sperm Whale's. Nor in the Sperm Whale are there any of those blinds of bone; no huge lower lip; and scarcely anything of a tongue. Again, the Right Whale has two external spout-holes, the Sperm Whale only one.

Look your last, now, on these venerable hooded heads, while they yet lie together; for one will soon sink, unrecorded, in the sea; the other will not be very long in following.

Can you catch the expression of the Sperm Whale's there? It is the same he died with, only some of the longer wrinkles in the forehead seem now faded away. I think his broad brow to be full of a prairie-like placidity, born of a speculative indifference as to death. But mark the other head's expression. See that amazing lower lip, pressed by accident against the vessel's side, so as firmly to embrace the jaw. Does not this whole head seem to speak of an enormous practical resolution in facing death? This Right Whale I take to have been a Stoic; the Sperm Whale, a Platonian, who might have taken up Spinoza[9] in his latter years.

CHAPTER 76

THE BATTERING-RAM[1]

E RE quitting, for the nonce, the Sperm Whale's head, I would have you, as a sensi-ble physiologist, simply—particularly remark its front aspect, in all its compacted collectedness. I would have you investigate it now with the sole view of forming to yourself some unexaggerated, intelligent estimate of whatever battering-ram power may be lodged there. Here is a vital point; for you must either satisfactorily settle this matter with yourself, or for ever remain an infidel as to one of the most appalling, but not the less true events,[2] perhaps anywhere to be found in all recorded history.

You observe that in the ordinary swimming position of the Sperm Whale, the front of his head presents an almost wholly vertical plane to the water; you observe that the lower part of that front slopes considerably backwards, so as to furnish more of a retreat for the long socket which receives the boom-like lower jaw; you observe that the mouth is entirely under the head, much in the same way, indeed, as though your own mouth **were** entirely under your chin. Moreover you observe that the whale has no external nose; and that what nose he has—his spout hole—is on the top of his head; you observe that his eyes and ears are at the sides of his head, nearly one third of his entire length from the front. Wherefore, you must now have per-ceived that the front of the Sperm Whale's head is a dead, blind wall,[3] without a sin-gle organ or tender prominence of any sort whatsoever. Furthermore, you are now to consider that only in the extreme, lower, backward sloping part of the front of the head, is there the slightest vestige of bone; and not till you get near twenty feet from the forehead do you come to the full cranial development. So that this whole enormous boneless mass is as one wad. Finally, though, as will soon be revealed, its contents partly comprise the most delicate oil; yet, you are now to be apprised of the nature of the substance which so impregnably invests all that apparent effeminacy.° In some previous place° I have described to you how the blubber wraps the body of the whale, as the rind wraps an orange. Just so with the head; but with this differ-ence: about the head this envelope, though not so thick, is of a boneless toughness, inestimable by any man who has not handled it. The severest pointed harpoon, the

effeminacy: delicacy within masculinity, pertaining to "the most delicate oil" earlier in the sentence. *previous place*: Ch. 67.

sharpest lance darted by the strongest human arm, impotently rebounds from it. It is as though the forehead of the Sperm Whale were paved with horses' hoofs. I do not think that any sensation lurks in it.[4]

Bethink yourself also of another thing. When two large, loaded Indiamen° chance to crowd and crush towards each other in the docks, what do the sailors do? They do not suspend between them, at the point of coming contact, any merely hard substance, like iron or wood. No, they hold there a large, round wad of tow° and cork, enveloped in the thickest and toughest of ox-hide. That bravely and uninjured takes the jam which would have snapped all their oaken handspikes and iron crowbars. By itself this sufficiently illustrates the obvious fact I drive at. But supplementary to this, it has hypothetically occurred to me, that as ordinary fish possess what is called a swimming bladder in them, capable, at will, of distension or contraction; and as the Sperm Whale, as far as I know, has no such provision in him; considering, too, the otherwise inexplicable manner in which he now depresses his head altogether beneath the surface, and anon swims with it high elevated out of the water; considering the unobstructed elasticity of its envelop; considering the unique interior of his head; it has hypothetically occurred to me, I say, that those mystical lung-celled honeycombs° there may possibly have some hitherto unknown and unsuspected connexion with the outer air, so as to be susceptible to atmospheric distension and contraction. If this be so, fancy the irresistibleness of that might, to which the most impalpable and destructive of all elements contributes.[5]

Now, mark. Unerringly impelling this dead, impregnable, uninjurable wall, and this most buoyant thing within; there swims behind it all a mass of tremendous life, only to be adequately estimated as piled wood is—by the cord; and all obedient to one volition, as the smallest insect. So that when I shall hereafter detail to you all the specialities and concentrations of potency everywhere lurking in this expansive monster; when I shall show you some of his more inconsiderable braining feats;[6] I trust you will have renounced all ignorant incredulity, and be ready to abide by this; that though the Sperm Whale stove a passage through the Isthmus of Darien,[7] and mixed the Atlantic with the Pacific, you would not elevate one hair of your eyebrow. For unless you own the whale,° you are but a provincial and sentimentalist in Truth. But clear Truth is a thing for salamander giants[8] only to encounter; how small the chances for the provincials then? What befel the weakling youth lifting the dread goddess's veil at **Lais**?[9]

Indiamen: large cargo vessels trading with the East Indies. *tow*: broken hemp or flax fiber. *lung-celled honeycombs*: described in Ch. 77. *own the whale*: acknowledge the whale's greatness.

CHAPTER 77

THE GREAT HEIDELBURGH TUN

N ow comes the Baling of the Case.[1] But to comprehend it aright, you must know something of the curious internal structure of the thing operated upon.

Regarding the Sperm Whale's head as a solid oblong, you may, on an inclined plane, sideways divide it into two quoins,* whereof the lower is the bony structure, forming the cranium and jaws, and the upper an unctuous mass wholly free from bones; its broad forward end forming the expanded vertical apparent forehead of the whale. At the middle of the forehead horizontally subdivide this upper quoin, and then you have two almost equal parts, which before were naturally divided by an internal wall of a thick tendinous substance.

The lower subdivided part, called the junk, is one immense honeycomb of oil, formed by the crossing and re-crossing, into ten thousand infiltrated cells, of tough elastic white fibres throughout its whole extent. The upper part, known as the Case, may be regarded as the great Heidelburgh Tun of the Sperm Whale. And as that famous great tierce is mystically carved in front,[2] so the whale's vast plaited forehead forms innumerable strange devices for the emblematical adornment of his wondrous tun. Moreover, as that of Heidelburgh was always replenished with the most excellent of the wines of the Rhenish valleys,[3] so the tun of the whale contains by far the most precious of all his oily vintages; namely, the highly-prized spermaceti, in its absolutely pure, limpid, and odoriferous state. Nor is this precious substance found unalloyed in any other part of the creature. Though in life it remains perfectly fluid, yet, upon exposure to the air, after death, it soon begins to concrete; sending forth beautiful crystalline shoots, as when the first thin delicate ice is just forming in water. A large whale's case generally yields about five hundred gallons of sperm, though from unavoidable circumstances, considerable of it is spilled, leaks, and dribbles away, or is otherwise irrevocably lost in the ticklish business of securing what you can.

I know not with what fine and costly material the Heidelburgh Tun was coated within, but in superlative richness that coating could not possibly have compared

---

* Quoin is not a Euclidean term. It belongs to the pure nautical mathematics. I know not that it has been defined before. A quoin is a solid which differs from a wedge in having its sharp end formed by the steep inclination of one side, instead of the mutual tapering of both sides.

with the silken pearl-colored membrane, like the lining of a fine pelisse,° forming the inner surface of the Sperm Whale's case.

It will have been seen that the Heidelburgh Tun of the Sperm Whale embraces the entire length of the entire top of the head; and since—as has been elsewhere set forth—the head embraces one third of the whole length of the creature, then setting that length down at eighty feet for a good sized whale, you have more than twenty-six feet for the depth of the tun, when it is lengthwise hoisted up and down against a ship's side.

As in decapitating the whale, the operator's instrument is brought close to the spot where an entrance is subsequently forced into the spermaceti magazine;° he has, therefore, to be uncommonly heedful, lest a careless, untimely stroke should invade the sanctuary and wastingly let out its invaluable contents. It is this decapitated end of the head, also, which is at last elevated out of the water, and retained in that position by the enormous cutting tackles, whose hempen combinations, on one side, make quite a wilderness of ropes in that quarter.

Thus much being said, attend now, I pray you, to that marvellous and—in this particular instance—almost fatal operation whereby the Sperm Whale's great Heidelburgh Tun is tapped.

---

pelisse: long coat or cloak. *magazine*: storage compartment.

CHAPTER 78

CISTERN AND BUCKETS

NIMBLE as a cat, Tashtego mounts aloft; and without altering his erect posture, runs straight out upon the overhanging main-yard-arm, to the part where it exactly projects over the hoisted Tun. He has carried with him a light tackle called a whip, consisting of only two parts, travelling through a single-sheaved block.° Securing this block, so that it hangs down from the yard-arm, he swings one end of the rope, till it is caught and firmly held by a hand on deck. Then, hand-over-hand, down the other part, the Indian drops through the air, till dexterously he lands on the summit of the head. There—still high elevated above the rest of the company, to whom he vivaciously cries—he seems some Turkish Muezzin calling the good people to prayers from the top of a tower. A short-handled sharp spade being sent up to him, he diligently searches for the proper place to begin breaking into the Tun. In this business he proceeds very heedfully, like a treasure-hunter in some old house, sounding the walls to find where the gold is masoned in. By the time this cautious search is over, a stout iron-bound bucket, precisely like a well-bucket, has been attached to one end of the whip; while the other end, being stretched across the deck, is there held by two or three alert hands. These last now hoist the bucket within grasp of the Indian, to whom another person has reached up a very long pole. Inserting this pole into the bucket, Tashtego downward guides the bucket into the Tun, till it entirely disappears; then giving the word to the seamen at the whip, up comes the bucket again, all bubbling like a dairy-maid's pail of new milk. Carefully lowered from its height, the full-freighted° vessel is caught by an appointed hand, and quickly emptied into a large tub. Then re-mounting aloft, it again goes through the same round until the deep cistern will yield no more. Towards the end, Tashtego has to ram his long pole harder and harder, and deeper and deeper into the Tun, until some twenty feet of the pole have gone down.

Now, the people of the Pequod had been baling some time in this way; several tubs had been filled with the fragrant sperm; when all at once a queer accident happened. Whether it was that Tashtego, that wild Indian, was so heedless and reck-

---

tackle . . . single-sheaved block: rope running through a one-pulley device. **full-freighted**: brim-full.

less as to let go for a moment his one-handed hold on the great cabled tackles suspending the head; or whether the place where he stood was so treacherous and
oozy; or whether the Evil One himself would have it to fall out so, without stating his
particular reasons; how it was exactly, there is no telling now; but, on a sudden, as the
eightieth or ninetieth bucket came suckingly up—my God! poor Tashtego—like the
twin reciprocating bucket in a veritable well, dropped head-foremost down into this
great Tun of Heidelburgh, and with a horrible oily gurgling, went clean out of sight!

"Man overboard!" cried Daggoo, who amid the general consternation first came
to his senses. "Swing the bucket this way!" and putting one foot into it, so as the better to secure his slippery hand-hold on the whip itself, the hoisters ran him high up to
the top of the head, almost before Tashtego could have reached its interior bottom.
Meantime, there was a terrible tumult. Looking over the side, they saw the before
lifeless head throbbing and heaving just below the surface of the sea, as if that
moment seized with some momentous idea; whereas it was only the poor Indian
unconsciously revealing by those struggles the perilous depth to which he had sunk.

At this instant, while Daggoo, on the summit of the head, was clearing the
whip—which had somehow got foul° of the great cutting tackles—a sharp cracking
noise was heard; and to the unspeakable horror of all, one of the two enormous
hooks suspending the head tore out, and with a vast vibration the enormous mass
sideways swung, till the drunk ship reeled and shook as if smitten by an iceberg. The
one remaining hook, upon which the entire strain now depended, seemed every
instant to be on the point of giving way; an event still more likely from the violent
motions of the head.

"Come down, come down!" yelled the seamen to Daggoo, but with one hand
holding on to the heavy tackles, so that if the head should drop, he would still remain
suspended; the negro having cleared the foul line, rammed down the bucket into the
now collapsed well, meaning that the buried harpooneer should grasp it, and so be
hoisted out.

"In heaven's name, man," cried Stubb, "are you ramming home a cartridge°
there?—Avast! How will that help him; jamming that iron-bound bucket on top of
his head? Avast, will ye!"

"Stand clear of the tackle!" cried a voice like the bursting of a rocket.

Almost in the same instant, with a thunder-boom, the enormous mass dropped
into the sea, like Niagara's Table-Rock into the whirlpool;[1] the suddenly relieved hull
rolled away from it, to far down her glittering copper;° and all caught their breath, as
half swinging—now over the sailors' heads, and now over the water—Daggoo, through
a thick mist of spray, was dimly beheld clinging to the pendulous tackles, while poor,
buried-alive Tashtego was sinking utterly down to the bottom of the sea! But hardly
had the blinding vapor cleared away, when a naked figure with a boarding-sword in its
hand, was for one swift moment seen hovering over the bulwarks. The next, a loud
splash announced that my brave Queequeg had dived to the rescue. One packed rush

---

got foul: became entangled. **ramming home a cartridge**: pushing a packet of gunpowder
into the muzzle of a musket or cannon. **copper**: sheathing on the wooden hull, protecting it
from worms.

was made to the side, and every eye counted every ripple, as moment followed moment, and no sign of either the sinker or the diver could be seen. Some hands now jumped into a boat alongside, and pushed a little off from the ship.

"Ha! ha!" cried Daggoo, all at once, from his now quiet, swinging perch overhead; and looking further off from the side, we saw an arm thrust upright from the blue waves; a sight strange to see, as an arm thrust forth from the grass over a grave.

"Both! both!—it is both!"—cried Daggoo again with a joyful shout; and soon after, Queequeg was seen boldly striking out with one hand, and with the other clutching the long hair of the Indian. Drawn into the waiting boat, they were quickly brought to the deck; but Tashtego was long in coming to, and Queequeg did not look very brisk.

Now, how had this noble rescue been accomplished? Why, diving after the slowly descending head, Queequeg with his keen sword had made side lunges near its bottom, so as to scuttle° a large hole there; then dropping his sword, had thrust his long arm far inwards and upwards, and so hauled out our poor Tash by the head. He averred, that upon first thrusting in for him, a leg was presented; but well knowing that that was not as it ought to be, and might occasion great trouble;—he had thrust back the leg, and by a dexterous heave and toss, had wrought a somerset upon the Indian; so that with the next trial, he came forth in the good old way—head foremost. As for the great head itself, that was doing as well as could be expected.[2]

And thus, through the courage and great skill **in obstetrics** of Queequeg, the deliverance, or rather, delivery of Tashtego, was successfully accomplished, in the teeth, too, of the most untoward and apparently hopeless impediments; which is a lesson by no means to be forgotten. **Midwifery should be taught in the same course with fencing and boxing, riding and rowing.**

I know that this queer adventure of the Gay-Header's will be sure to seem incredible to some landsmen, though they themselves may have either seen or heard of some one's falling into a cistern ashore; an accident which not seldom happens, and with much less reason too than the Indian's, considering the exceeding slipperiness of the curb of the Sperm Whale's well.

But, peradventure, it may be sagaciously urged, how is this? We thought the tissued, infiltrated head of the Sperm Whale, was the lightest and most corky part about him; and yet thou makest it sink in an element of a far greater specific gravity than itself. We have thee there. Not at all, but I have ye; for at the time poor Tash fell in, the case had been nearly emptied of its lighter contents, leaving little but the dense tendinous wall of the well—a double welded, hammered substance, as I have before said, much heavier than the sea water, and a lump of which sinks in it like lead almost. But the tendency to rapid sinking in this substance was in the present instance materially counteracted by the other parts of the head remaining unde-

---

scuttle: to make a hole in the hull to sink a vessel, but here, simply to cut.

tached from it, so that it sank very slowly and deliberately indeed, affording Queequeg a fair chance for performing his agile **obstetrics** on the run, as you may say. **Yes, it was a running delivery, so it was.**

Now, had Tashtego perished in that head, it had been a very precious perishing; smothered in the very whitest and daintiest of fragrant spermaceti; coffined, hearsed, and tombed in the secret inner chamber and sanctum sanctorum[3] of the whale. Only one sweeter end can readily be recalled—the delicious death of an Ohio honey-hunter, who seeking honey in the crotch of a hollow tree, found such exceeding store of it, that leaning too far over, it sucked him in, so that he died embalmed. How many, think ye, have likewise fallen into Plato's honey head, and sweetly perished there?[4]

REVISION NARRATIVE

Queequeg's Obstetrics

Melville's second son, Stanwix, was born on about the same day that *The Whale* was published in England; therefore, obstetrics (a word for midwifery first appearing in print in 1813) was on the writer's mind in the preceding months as he was preparing his text for publication. Ishmael describes Queequeg's rescue of Tashtego as if it were the delivery of a baby. But British editors found Melville's exuberance over this natural process to be unseemly. They deleted "in obstetrics" in one sentence and revised "obstetrics" to "dexterities" in the second. They also expurgated two sentences: one calling for the teaching of obstetrics as if it were a gentlemanly sport like fencing, boxing, riding, and rowing; and the other punning on Queequeg's "running delivery," as though he were a letter carrier.

CHAPTER 79

THE PRAIRIE

To scan the lines of his face, or feel the bumps on the head of this Leviathan; this is a thing which no Physiognomist or Phrenologist has as yet undertaken. Such an enterprise would seem almost as hopeful as for Lavater to have scrutinized the wrinkles on the Rock of Gibraltar, or for Gall to have mounted a ladder and manipulated the Dome of the Pantheon.[1] Still, in that famous work of his, Lavater not only treats of the various faces of men, but also attentively studies the faces of horses, birds, serpents, and fish; and dwells in detail upon the modifications of expression discernible therein. Nor have Gall and his disciple Spurzheim[2] failed to throw out some hints touching the phrenological characteristics of other beings than man. Therefore, though I am but ill qualified for a pioneer, in the application of these two semi-sciences to the whale, I will do my endeavor. I try all things; I achieve what I can.

Physiognomically regarded, the Sperm Whale is an anomalous creature. He has no proper nose. And since the nose is the central and most conspicuous of the features; and since it perhaps most modifies and finally controls their combined expression; hence it would seem that its entire absence, as an external appendage, must very largely affect the countenance of the whale. For as in landscape gardening, a spire, cupola, monument, or tower of some sort, is deemed almost indispensable to the completion of the scene; so no face can be physiognomically in keeping without the elevated open-work belfry of the nose. Dash the nose from Phidias's marble Jove,[3] and what a sorry remainder! Nevertheless, Leviathan is of so mighty a magnitude, all his proportions are so stately, that the same deficiency which in the sculptured Jove were hideous, in him is no blemish at all. Nay, it is an added grandeur. A nose to the whale would have been impertinent. As on your physiognomical voyage you sail round his vast head in your jolly-boat,° your noble conceptions of him are never insulted by the reflection that he has a nose to be pulled.[4] A pestilent conceit, which so often will insist upon obtruding even when beholding the mightiest **royal beadle**° on his throne.

In some particulars, perhaps the most imposing physiognomical view to be had of the Sperm Whale, is that of the full front of his head. This aspect is sublime.

jolly-boat: small, wide work boat. ***beadle***: minor church, court, or academic official.

In thought, a fine human brow is like the East when troubled with the morning. In the repose of the pasture, the curled brow of the bull has a touch of the grand in it. Pushing heavy cannon up mountain defiles, the elephant's brow is majestic. Human or animal, the mystical brow is as that great golden seal affixed by the German emperors[5] to their decrees. It signifies—"God: done this day by my hand." But in most creatures, nay in man himself, very often the brow is but a mere strip of alpine land lying along the snow line. Few are the foreheads which like Shakspeare's or Melancthon's rise so high,[6] and descend so low, that the eyes themselves seem clear, eternal, tideless mountain lakes; and all above them in the forehead's wrinkles, you seem to track the antlered thoughts descending there to drink, as the Highland hunters track the snow prints of the deer. But in the great Sperm Whale, this high and mighty **god-like** dignity inherent in the brow is so immensely amplified, that gazing on it, in that full front view, you feel the Deity and the dread powers more forcibly than in beholding any other object in living nature. For you see no one point precisely; not one distinct feature is revealed; no nose, eyes, ears, or mouth; no face; he has none, proper; nothing but that one broad firmament of a forehead, pleated with riddles; dumbly lowering with° the doom of boats, and ships, and men. Nor, in profile, does this wondrous brow diminish; though that way viewed, its grandeur does not domineer upon you so. In profile, you plainly perceive that horizontal, semi-crescentic depression in the forehead's middle, which, in man, is Lavater's mark of genius.

But how? Genius in the Sperm Whale? Has the Sperm Whale ever written a book, spoken a speech? No, his great genius is declared in his doing nothing particular to prove it. It is moreover declared in his pyramidical silence.[7] And this reminds me that had the great Sperm Whale been known to the young Orient World, he would have been deified by their child-magian thoughts.[8] They deified the crocodile of the Nile, because the crocodile is tongueless;[9] and the Sperm Whale has no tongue, or at least it is so exceedingly small, as to be incapable of protrusion. If hereafter any highly cultured, poetical nation shall lure back to their birth-right, the merry May-day gods of old; and livingly enthrone them again in the now egotistical sky; in the now unhaunted hill; then be sure, exalted to Jove's high seat,[10] the great Sperm Whale shall lord it.

Champollion deciphered the wrinkled granite hieroglyphics. But there is no Champollion to decipher the Egypt of every man's and every being's face. Physiognomy, like every other human science, is but a passing fable. If then, Sir William Jones, who read in thirty languages, could not read the simplest peasant's face in its profounder and more subtle meanings, how may unlettered Ishmael hope to read the awful Chaldee[11] of the Sperm Whale's brow? I but put that brow before you. Read it if you can.

dumbly lowering with: silently, angrily threatening.

CHAPTER 80

THE NUT

Iᶠ the Sperm Whale be physiognomically a Sphinx, to the phrenologist his brain seems that geometrical circle which it is impossible to square.[1]

In the full-grown creature the skull will measure at least twenty feet in length.[2] Unhinge the lower jaw, and the side view of this skull is as the side view of a moderately inclined plane resting throughout on a level base. But in life—as we have elsewhere seen°—this inclined plane is angularly filled up, and almost squared by the enormous superincumbent° mass of the junk and sperm. At the high end the skull forms a crater to bed that part of the mass; while under the long floor of this crater—in another cavity seldom exceeding ten inches in length and as many in depth—reposes the mere handful of this monster's brain. The brain is at least twenty feet from his apparent forehead in life; it is hidden away behind its vast outworks, like the innermost citadel within the amplified fortifications of Quebec. So like a choice casket is it secreted in him, that I have known some whalemen who peremptorily deny that the Sperm Whale has any other brain than that palpable semblance of one formed by the cubic-yards of his sperm magazine. Lying in strange folds, courses, and convolutions, to their apprehensions, it seems more in keeping with the idea of his general might to regard that mystic part of him as the seat of his intelligence.

It is plain, then, that phrenologically the head of this Leviathan, in the creature's living intact state, is an entire delusion. As for his true brain, you can then see no indications of it, nor feel any. The whale, like all things that are mighty, wears a false **bow**° to the common world.

If you unload his skull of its spermy heaps and then take a rear view of its rear end, which is the high end, you will be struck by its resemblance to the human skull, beheld in the same situation, and from the same point of view. Indeed, place this reversed skull (scaled down to the human magnitude) among a plate° of men's skulls, and you would involuntarily confound it with them; and remarking the depressions on one part of its summit, in phrenological phrase you would say—This

---

elsewhere seen: at the beginning of Ch. 57. ***superincumbent***: lying on top. ***false bow***: wood or metal structure to repair a bow or deceive enemies. ***plate***: page of illustrations.

man had no self-esteem, and no veneration. And by those negations, considered along with the affirmative fact of his prodigious bulk and power, you can best form to yourself the truest, though not the most exhilarating conception of what the most exalted potency is.

But if from the comparative dimensions of the whale's proper brain, you deem it incapable of being adequately charted, then I have another idea for you. If you attentively regard almost any quadruped's spine, you will be struck with the resemblance of its vertebræ to a strung necklace of dwarfed skulls, all bearing rudimental resemblance to the skull proper. It is a German conceit, that the vertebræ are absolutely undeveloped skulls.[3] But the curious external resemblance, I take it the Germans were not the first men to perceive. A foreign friend once pointed it out to me, in the skeleton of a foe he had slain, and with the vertebræ of which he was inlaying, in a sort of basso-relievo,° the beaked prow of his canoe. Now, I consider that the phrenologists have omitted an important thing in not pushing their investigations from the cerebellum through the spinal canal. For I believe that much of a man's character will be found betokened in his backbone. I would rather feel your spine than your skull, whoever you are. A thin joist of a spine never yet upheld a full and noble soul. I rejoice in my spine, as in the firm audacious staff of that flag which I fling half out to the world.

Apply this spinal branch of phrenology to the Sperm Whale. His cranial cavity is continuous with the first neck-vertebra; and in that vertebra the bottom of the spinal canal will measure ten inches across, being eight in height, and of a triangular figure with the base downwards. As it passes through the remaining vertebræ the canal tapers in size, but for a considerable distance remains of large capacity. Now, of course, this canal is filled with much the same strangely fibrous substance—the spinal cord—as the brain; and directly communicates with the brain. And what is still more, for many feet after emerging from the brain's cavity, the spinal cord remains of an undecreasing girth, almost equal to that of the brain. Under all these circumstances, would it be unreasonable to survey and map out the whale's spine phrenologically? For, viewed in this light, the wonderful comparative smallness of his brain proper is more than compensated by the wonderful comparative magnitude of his spinal cord.

But leaving this hint to operate as it may with the phrenologists, I would merely assume the spinal theory for a moment, in reference to the Sperm Whale's hump. This august hump, if I mistake not, rises over one of the larger vertebræ, and is, therefore, in some sort, the outer convex mould of it. From its relative situation then, I should call this high hump the organ of firmness or indomitableness in the Sperm Whale. And that the great monster is indomitable, you will yet have reason to know.

---

basso-relievo: sculpted design projecting slightly from a flat surface.

CHAPTER 81

THE PEQUOD
MEETS THE VIRGIN

THE predestinated day arrived, and we duly met the ship Jungfrau, Derick De Deer, master, of Bremen.°

At one time the greatest whaling people in the world, the Dutch and Germans are now among the least; but here and there at very wide intervals of latitude and longitude, you still occasionally meet with their flag in the Pacific.

For some reason, the Jungfrau seemed quite eager to pay her respects. While yet some distance from the Pequod, she rounded to, and dropping a boat, her captain was impelled towards us, impatiently standing in the bows instead of the stern.

"What has he in his hand there?" cried Starbuck, pointing to something wavingly held by the German. "Impossible!—a lamp-feeder!"°

"Not that," said Stubb, "no, no, it's a coffee-pot, Mr. Starbuck; he's coming off to make us our coffee, is the Yarman;° don't you see that big tin can there alongside of him?—that's his boiling water. Oh! he's all right, is the Yarman."

"Go along with you," cried Flask, "it's a lamp-feeder and an oil-can. He's out of oil, and has come a-begging."

However curious it may seem for an oil-ship to be borrowing oil on the whale-ground, and however much it may invertedly contradict the old proverb about carrying coals to Newcastle,[1] yet sometimes such a thing really happens; and in the present case Captain Derick De Deer did indubitably conduct a lamp-feeder as Flask did declare.

As he mounted the deck, Ahab abruptly accosted him, without at all heeding what he had in his hand; but in his broken lingo, the German soon evinced his complete ignorance of the White Whale; immediately turning the conversation to his lamp-feeder and oil can, with some remarks touching his having to turn into his hammock at night in profound darkness—his last drop of Bremen oil being gone, and not a single flying-fish yet captured to supply the deficiency; concluding by hinting that his ship was indeed what in the Fishery is technically called a *clean* one (that is, an empty one), well deserving the name of Jungfrau or the Virgin.

Jungfrau . . . Bremen: virgin (German) . . . German port. ***lamp-feeder***: spouted can for filling oil lamps. ***Yarman***: dialect for "German."

His necessities supplied, Derick departed; but he had not gained his ship's side, when whales were almost simultaneously raised from the mast-heads of both vessels; and so eager for the chase was Derick, that without pausing to put his oil-can and lamp-feeder aboard, he slewed round his boat and made after the leviathan lamp-feeders.

Now, the game having risen to leeward, he and the other three German boats that soon followed him, had considerably the start of the Pequod's keels. There were eight whales, an average pod.° Aware of their danger, they were going all abreast with great speed straight before the wind, rubbing their flanks as closely as so many spans of horses in harness. They left a great, wide wake, as though continually unrolling a great wide parchment upon the sea.

Full in this rapid wake, and many fathoms in the rear, swam a huge, humped old bull, which by his comparatively slow progress, as well as by the unusual yellowish incrustations overgrowing him, seemed afflicted with the jaundice, or some other infirmity. Whether this whale belonged to the pod in advance, seemed questionable; for it is not customary for such venerable leviathans to be at all social. Nevertheless, he stuck to their wake, though indeed their back water must have retarded him, because the white-bone or swell at his broad muzzle was a dashed one, like the swell formed when two hostile currents meet. His spout was short, slow, and laborious; coming forth with a choking sort of gush, and spending itself in torn shreds, followed by strange subterranean commotions in him, which seemed to have egress at his other buried extremity, causing the waters behind him to upbubble.

"Who's got some paregoric?"° said Stubb, "he has the stomach-ache, I'm afraid. Lord, think of having half an acre of stomach-ache! Adverse winds are holding mad Christmas in him, boys. It's the first foul wind° I ever knew to blow from astern; but look, did ever whale yaw so before? it must be, he's lost his tiller."

As an overladen Indiaman bearing down the Hindostan° coast with a deck load of frightened horses, careens, buries,° rolls, and wallows on her way; so did this old whale heave his aged bulk, and now and then partly turning over on his cumbrous rib-ends, expose the cause of his devious wake in the unnatural stump of his starboard fin. Whether he had lost that fin in battle, or had been born without it, it were hard to say.

"Only wait a bit, old chap, and I'll give ye a sling for that wounded arm," cried cruel Flask, pointing to the whale-line near him.

"Mind he don't sling thee with it," cried Starbuck. "Give way, or the German will have him."

With one intent all the combined rival boats were pointed for this one fish, because not only was he the largest, and therefore the most valuable whale, but he was nearest to them, and the other whales were going with such great velocity, moreover, as almost to defy pursuit for the time. At this juncture, the Pequod's keels had shot by the three German boats last lowered; but from the great start he had had, Derick's boat still led the chase, though every moment neared by his foreign

pod: group of whales. *paregoric*: tincture of opium, taken for intestinal pain and diarrhea. *foul wind*: ominous "ill-wind," but, here, fart. **Hindostan**: India. *buries*: that is, "buries its bow in the waves."

rivals. The only thing they feared, was, that from being already so nigh to his mark, he would be enabled to dart his iron before they could completely overtake and pass him. As for Derick, he seemed quite confident that this would be the case, and occasionally with a deriding gesture shook his lamp-feeder at the other boats.

"The ungracious and ungrateful dog!" cried Starbuck; "he mocks and dares me with the very poor-box I filled for him not five minutes ago!"—then in his old intense whisper—"give way, greyhounds! Dog to it!"°

"I tell **ye** what it is, men"—cried Stubb to his crew—"It's against my religion to get mad; but I'd like to eat that villanous Yarman—Pull—wont ye? Are ye going to let that rascal beat ye? Do ye love brandy? A hogshead of brandy, then, to the best man. Come, why don't some of ye burst a blood-vessel? Who's that been dropping an anchor overboard—we don't budge an inch—we're becalmed. Halloo, here's grass growing in the boat's bottom—and by the Lord, the mast there's budding. This won't do, boys. Look at that Yarman! The short and **long** of it is, men, will ye spit fire or not?"

"Oh! see the suds he makes!" cried Flask, dancing up and down—"What a hump—Oh, *do* pile on the beef°—lays like a log! Oh! my lads, *do* spring—slap-jacks and quohogs for supper, you know, my lads—baked clams and muffins—oh, *do, do,* spring—he's a hundred barreler—don't lose him now—don't, oh, *don't!*—see that Yarman—Oh! won't ye pull for your duff,° my lads—such a sog! such a sogger!° Don't ye love sperm? There goes three thousand dollars, men!—a bank!—a whole bank! The bank of England!—Oh, *do, do, do!*—What's that Yarman about now?"

At this moment Derick was in the act of pitching his lamp-feeder at the advancing boats, and also his oil-can; perhaps with the double view of retarding his rivals' way, and at the same time economically accelerating his own by the momentary impetus of the backward toss.

"The unmannerly Dutch dogger!"° cried Stubb. "Pull now, men, like fifty thousand line-of-battle-ship loads of red-haired devils. What d'ye say, Tashtego; are you the man to snap your spine in two-and-twenty pieces for the honor of old Gay-head? What d'ye say?"

"I say, pull like god-dam,"—cried the Indian.

Fiercely, but evenly incited by the taunts of the German, the Pequod's three boats now began ranging almost abreast; and, so disposed, momentarily neared him. In that fine, loose, chivalrous attitude of the headsman when drawing near to his prey, the three mates stood up proudly, occasionally backing the after oarsman° with an exhilarating cry of, "There she slides, now! Hurrah for the white-ash breeze!° Down with the Yarman! Sail over him!"

But so decided an original start had Derick had, that spite of all their gallantry, he would have proved the victor in this race, had not a righteous judgment

---

Dog to it!*:** "Stick to the chase!" (as would a hunting dog). ***pile on the beef: That is, "There's good eating tonight if we get this whale." ***duff***: pudding made of flour and cooking grease. **sog . . . sogger**: large whale . . . something large and heavy. ***dogger***: two-masted Dutch fishing vessel and, here, its captain. ***backing the after oarsman***: assisting the oarsman closest to the mate by pushing on the oar. ***white-ash breeze***: facetiously, wind caused by the fast-moving oars, made of white-ash wood.

descended upon him in a crab which caught the blade° of his midship oarsman. While this clumsy lubber was striving to free his white-ash, and while, in consequence, Derick's boat was nigh to capsizing, and he thundering away at his men in a mighty rage;—that was a good time for Starbuck, Stubb, and Flask. With a shout, they took a mortal start forwards, and slantingly ranged up on the German's quarter.° An instant more, and all four boats were diagonically in the whale's immediate wake, while stretching from them, on both sides, was the foaming swell that he made.

It was a terrific, most pitiable, and maddening sight. The whale was now going head out, and sending his spout before him in a continual tormented jet; while his one poor fin beat his side in an agony of fright. Now to this hand, now to that, he yawed in his faltering flight, and still at every billow that he broke, he spasmodically sank in the sea, or sideways rolled towards the sky his one beating fin. So have I seen a bird with clipped wing, making affrighted broken circles in the air, vainly striving to escape the piratical hawks. But the bird has a voice, and with plaintive cries will make known her fear; but the fear of this vast dumb brute of the sea, was chained up and enchanted in him; he had no voice, save that choking respiration through his spiracle, and this made the sight of him unspeakably pitiable; while still, in his amazing bulk, portcullis jaw, and omnipotent tail, there was enough to appal the stoutest man who so pitied.

Seeing now that but a very few moments more would give the Pequod's boats the advantage, and rather than be thus foiled of his game, Derick chose to hazard what to him must have seemed a most unusually long dart, ere the last chance would for ever escape.

But no sooner did his harpooneer stand up for the stroke, than all three tigers—Queequeg, Tashtego, Daggoo—instinctively sprang to their feet, and standing in a diagonal row, simultaneously pointed their barbs; and darted over the head of the German harpooneer, their three Nantucket irons entered the whale. Blinding vapors of foam and white-fire! The three boats, in the first fury of the whale's headlong rush, bumped the German's aside with such force, that both Derick and his baffled harpooneer were spilled out, and sailed over by the three flying keels.

"Don't be afraid, my butter-boxes,"° cried Stubb, casting a passing glance upon them as he shot by; "ye'll be picked up presently—all right—I saw some sharks astern—St. Bernard's dogs, you know—relieve distressed travellers. Hurrah! this is the way to sail now. Every keel a sun-beam! Hurrah!—Here we go like three tin kettles at the tail of a mad cougar! This puts me in mind of fastening to an elephant in a tilbury° on a plain—makes the wheel-spokes fly, boys, when you fasten to him that way; and there's danger of being pitched out too, when you strike a hill. Hurrah! this is the way a fellow feels when he's going to Davy Jones—all a rush down an endless inclined plane! Hurrah! this whale carries the everlasting mail!"

But the monster's run was a brief one. Giving a sudden gasp, he tumultuously sounded. With a grating rush, the three lines flew round the loggerheads with such

---

crab which caught the blade: the rower has clumsily dipped his oar into the water on the backstroke. **ranged up on the German's quarter**: closed in alongside the rear of the German boat. **butter-boxes**: scornful term for Dutchmen. **tilbury**: light, two-wheeled open carriage.

a force as to gouge deep grooves in them; while so fearful were the harpooneers that this rapid sounding would soon exhaust the lines, that using all their dexterous might, they caught repeated smoking turns with the rope to hold on; till at last— owing to the perpendicular strain from the lead-lined chocks of the boats, whence the three ropes went straight down into the blue—the gunwales of the bows were almost even with the water, while the three sterns tilted high in the air. And the whale soon ceasing to sound, for some time they remained in that attitude, fearful of expending more line, though the position was a little ticklish. But though boats have been taken down and lost in this way, yet it is this "holding on," as it is called; this hooking up by the **sharp** barbs of his live flesh from the back; this it is that often torments the Leviathan into soon rising again to meet the sharp lance of his foes. Yet not to speak of the peril of the thing, it is to be doubted whether this course is always the best; for it is but reasonable to presume, that the longer the stricken whale stays under water, the more he is exhausted. Because, owing to the enor- mous surface of him—in a full grown sperm whale something less than 2000 square feet—the pressure of the water is immense. We all know what an astonishing atmos- pheric weight we ourselves stand up under; even here, above-ground, in the air; how vast, then, the burden of a whale, bearing on his back a column of two hundred fath- oms of ocean! It must at least equal the weight of fifty atmospheres. One whaleman has estimated it at the weight of twenty line-of-battle ships,° with all their guns, and stores, and men on board.

As the three boats lay there on that gently rolling sea, gazing down into its eter- nal blue noon; and as not a single groan or cry of any sort, nay, not so much as a rip- ple or a bubble came up from its depths; what landsman would have thought, that beneath all that silence and placidity, the utmost monster of the seas was writhing and wrenching in agony! Not eight inches of perpendicular rope were visible at the bows. Seems it credible that by three such thin threads the great Leviathan was suspended like the big weight to an eight day clock. Suspended? and to what? To three bits of board. Is this the creature of whom it was once so triumphantly said— "Canst thou fill his skin with barbed irons? or his head with fish-spears? The sword of him that layeth at him cannot hold, the spear, the dart, nor the habergeon:° he esteemeth iron as straw; the arrow cannot make him flee; darts are counted as stub- ble; he laugheth at the shaking of a spear!" This the creature? this he? **Oh! that unfulfilments should follow the prophets. For** with the strength of a thou- sand thighs in his tail, Leviathan **had** run his head under the mountains of the sea, to hide him from the Pequod's fish-spears!

In that sloping afternoon sunlight, the shadows that the three boats sent down beneath the surface, must have been long enough and broad enough to shade half Xerxes' army.[2] Who can tell how appalling to the wounded whale must have been such huge phantoms flitting over his head!

"Stand by, men; he stirs," cried Starbuck, as the three lines suddenly vibrated in the water, distinctly conducting upwards to them, as by magnetic wires,[3] the life

---

fifty atmospheres. . . . line-of-battle ships: Fifty times the air pressure at sea level . . . largest contemporary warships. **habergeon**: chain mail jacket (but also "javelin" in some translations).

and death throbs of the whale, so that every oarsman felt them in his seat. The next moment, relieved in great part from the downward strain at the bows, the boats gave a sudden bounce upwards, as a small ice-field will, when a dense herd of white bears are scared from it into the sea.

"Haul in! Haul in!" cried Starbuck again; "he's rising."

The lines, of which, hardly an instant before, not one hand's breadth could have been gained, were now in long quick coils flung back all dripping into the boats, and soon the whale broke water within two ships' lengths of the hunters.

His motions plainly denoted his extreme exhaustion. In most land animals there are certain valves or flood-gates in many of their veins, whereby when wounded, the blood is in some degree at least instantly shut off in certain directions. Not so with the whale; one of whose peculiarities it is, to have an entire non-valvular structure of the blood-vessels, so that when pierced even by so small a point as a harpoon, a deadly drain is at once begun upon his whole arterial system; and when this is heightened by the extraordinary pressure of water at a great distance below

REVISION NARRATIVE

Melville and Job

In the book of Job, God tests Job's faith by allowing Satan to inflict upon him a series of misfortunes. Job withstands the afflictions (although not without some periods of doubt), and in the book's penultimate Chapter 41, God challenges the presumption that prideful humans can ever capture the uncapturable (and crocodilian) monster, "leviathan." In describing the capture of a harpooned whale that has plunged deep into the sea to escape its human predators, Ishmael quotes accurately from five verses of Job 41, with some excisions, noted here in brackets. The full text of those verses from the King James Version is as follows:

> 7   Canst thou fill his skin with barbed irons? or his head with fish spears? . . .
>
> 26   The sword of him that layeth at him cannot hold: the spear, the dart, nor the habergeon.
>
> 27   He esteemeth iron as straw, [and brass as rotten wood.]
>
> 28   The arrow cannot make him flee: [sling-stones are turned with him into stubble.]
>
> 29   Darts are counted as stubble: he laugheth at the shaking of a spear.

And yet, the whalemen have in fact captured "Leviathan," and Ishmael's hubristic "This the creature? this he?" introduces a more subversive remark, "Oh! that unfulfilments should follow the prophets." Chances are an editor expurgated this blasphemous line in the British edition. But it is also possible that, sensing he might have gone too far, Melville cut the line in the proof sheets he sent to England. In doing so, he also converted "For" in the following sentence to "Why," and "had" to the present tense in "Leviathan has run."

the surface, his life may be said to pour from him in incessant streams.[4] Yet so vast is the quantity of blood in him, and so distant and numerous its interior fountains, that he will keep thus bleeding and bleeding for a considerable period; even as in a drought a river will flow, whose source is in the well-springs of far-off and undiscernible hills. Even now, when the boats pulled upon this whale, and perilously drew over his swaying flukes, and the lances were darted into him, they were followed by steady jets from the new made wound, which kept continually playing, while the natural spout-hole in his head was only at intervals, however rapid, sending its affrighted moisture into the air. From this last vent no blood yet came, because no vital part of him had thus far been struck. His life,° as they significantly call it, was untouched.

As the boats now more closely surrounded him, the whole upper part of his form, with much of it that is ordinarily submerged, was plainly revealed. His eyes, or rather the places where his eyes had been, were beheld.[5] As strange misgrown masses gather in the knot-holes of the noblest oaks when prostrate, so from the points which the whale's eyes had once occupied, now protruded blind bulbs, horribly pitiable to see. But pity there was none. For all his old age, and his one arm, and his blind eyes, he must die the death and be murdered, in order to light the gay bridals and other merry-makings of men, and also to illuminate the solemn churches that preach unconditional inoffensiveness by all to all. Still rolling in his blood, at last he partially disclosed a strangely discolored bunch or protuberance, the size of a bushel, low down on the flank.

"A nice spot," cried Flask; "just let me prick him there once."

"Avast!" cried Starbuck, "there's no need of that!"

But humane Starbuck was too late. At the instant of the dart an ulcerous jet shot from this cruel wound, and goaded by it into more than sufferable anguish, the whale now spouting thick blood, with swift fury blindly darted at the craft, bespattering them and their glorying crews all over with showers of gore, capsizing Flask's boat and marring the bows. It was his death stroke. For, by this time, so spent was he by loss of blood, that he helplessly rolled away from the wreck he had made; lay panting on his side, impotently flapped with his stumped fin, then over and over slowly revolved like a waning world; turned up the white secrets of his belly; lay like a log, and died. It was most piteous, that last expiring spout. As when by unseen hands the water is gradually drawn off from some mighty fountain, and with half-stifled melancholy gurglings the spray-column lowers and lowers to the ground—so the last long dying spout of the whale.[6]

Soon, while the crews were awaiting the arrival of the ship, the body showed symptoms of sinking with all its treasures unrifled.° Immediately, by Starbuck's orders, lines were secured to it at different points, so that ere long every boat was a buoy; the sunken whale being suspended a few inches beneath them by the cords. By very heedful management, when the ship drew nigh, the whale was transferred to her side, and was strongly secured there by the stiffest fluke-chains, for it was plain that unless artificially upheld, the body would at once sink to the bottom.

---

life: lungs; also "life spot" on p. 330. **unrifled**: unstolen.

It so chanced that almost upon first cutting into him with the spade, the entire length of a corroded harpoon was found imbedded in his flesh, on the lower part of the bunch before described. But as the stumps of harpoons are frequently found in the dead bodies of captured whales, with the flesh perfectly healed around them, and no prominence of any kind to denote their place; therefore, there must needs have been some other unknown reason in the present case fully to account for the ulceration alluded to. But still more curious was the fact of a lance-head of stone being found in him, not far from the buried iron, the flesh perfectly firm about it. Who had darted that stone lance?[7] And when? It might have been darted by some Nor' West Indian long before America was discovered.

What other marvels might have been rummaged out of this monstrous cabinet there is no telling. But a sudden stop was put to further discoveries, by the ship's being unprecedentedly dragged over sideways to the sea, owing to the body's immensely increasing tendency to sink. However, Starbuck, who had the ordering of affairs, hung on to it to the last; hung on to it so resolutely, indeed, that when at length the ship would have been capsized, if still persisting in locking arms with the body; then, when the command was given to break clear from it, such was the immovable strain upon the timber-heads to which the fluke-chains and cables were fastened, that it was impossible to cast them off. Meantime everything in the Pequod was aslant. To cross to the other side of the deck was like walking up the steep gabled roof of a house. The ship groaned and gasped. Many of the ivory inlayings of her bulwarks and cabins were started from their places, by the unnatural dislocation. In vain handspikes and crows° were brought to bear upon the immovable fluke-chains, to pry them adrift from the timber-heads; and so low had the whale now settled that the submerged ends could not be at all approached, while every moment whole tons of ponderosity seemed added to the sinking bulk, and the ship seemed on the point of going over.

"Hold on, hold on, won't ye?" cried Stubb to the body, "don't be in such a devil of a hurry to sink! By thunder, men, we must do something or go for it. No use prying there; avast, I say with your handspikes, and run one of ye for a prayer book and a pen-knife, and cut the big chains."

"Knife? Aye, aye," cried Queequeg, and seizing the carpenter's heavy hatchet, he leaned out of a porthole, and steel to iron, began slashing at the largest fluke-chains. But a few strokes, full of sparks, were given, when the exceeding strain effected the rest. With a terrific snap, every fastening went adrift; the ship righted, the carcase sank.[8]

Now, this occasional inevitable sinking of the recently killed Sperm Whale is a very curious thing; nor has any fisherman yet adequately accounted for it. Usually the dead Sperm Whale floats with great buoyancy, with its side or belly considerably elevated above the surface. If the only whales that thus sank were old, meagre, and broken-hearted creatures, their pads of lard diminished and all their bones heavy and rheumatic; then you might with some reason assert that this sinking is caused by an uncommon specific gravity in the fish so sinking, consequent upon this absence

---

handspikes and crows: levers used for turning a windlass, and crowbars.

of buoyant matter in him. But it is not so. For young whales, in the highest health, and swelling with noble aspirations, prematurely cut off in the warm flush and May of life, with all their panting lard about them; even these brawny, buoyant heroes do sometimes sink.

Be it said, however, that the Sperm Whale is far less liable to this accident than any other species. Where one of that sort go down, twenty Right Whales do. This difference in the species is no doubt imputable in no small degree to the greater quantity of bone in the Right Whale; his Venetian blinds alone sometimes weighing more than a ton; from this incumbrance the Sperm Whale is wholly free. But there are instances where, after the lapse of many hours or several days, the sunken whale again rises, more buoyant than in life. But the reason of this is obvious. Gases are generated in him; he swells to a prodigious magnitude; becomes a sort of animal balloon. A line-of-battle ship could hardly keep him under then. In the Shore Whaling, on soundings,° among the Bays of New Zealand, when a Right Whale gives token of sinking, they fasten buoys to him, with plenty of rope; so that when the body has gone down, they know where to look for it when it shall have ascended again.

It was not long after the sinking of the body that a cry was heard from the Pequod's mast-heads, announcing that the Jungfrau was again lowering her boats; though the only spout in sight was that of a Fin-Back, belonging to the species of uncapturable whales, because of its incredible power of swimming. Nevertheless, the Fin-Back's spout is so similar to the Sperm Whale's, that by unskilful fishermen it is often mistaken for it. And consequently Derick and all his host were now in valiant chase of this unnearable brute. The Virgin crowding all sail, made after her four young keels, and thus they all disappeared far to leeward, still in bold, hopeful chase.

Oh! many are the Fin-Backs, and many are the Dericks, my friend.

on soundings: in water shallow enough to be measured.

CHAPTER 82

THE HONOR AND GLORY OF WHALING¹

T HERE are some enterprises in which a careful disorderliness is the true method.

The more I dive into this matter of whaling, and push my researches up to the very spring-head of it, so much the more am I impressed with its great honorableness and antiquity; and especially when I find so many great demi-gods and heroes, prophets of all sorts, who one way or other have shed distinction upon it, I am transported with the reflection that I myself belong, though but subordinately, to so emblazoned° a fraternity.

The gallant Perseus, a son of Jupiter,² was the first whaleman; and to the eternal honor of our calling be it said, that the first whale attacked by our brotherhood was not killed with any sordid intent. Those were the knightly days of our profession, when we only bore arms to succor the distressed, and not to fill men's lamp-feeders. Every one knows the fine story of Perseus and Andromeda; how the lovely Andromeda, the daughter of a king, was tied to a rock on the sea-coast, and as Leviathan was in the very act of carrying her off, Perseus, the prince of whalemen, intrepidly advancing, harpooned the monster, and delivered and married the maid. It was an admirable artistic exploit, rarely achieved by the best harpooneers of the present day; inasmuch as this Leviathan was slain at the very first dart. And let no man doubt this Arkite story;³ for in the ancient Joppa, now Jaffa, on the Syrian coast, in one of the Pagan temples, there stood for many ages the vast skeleton of a whale, which the city's legends and all the inhabitants asserted to be the identical bones of the monster that Perseus slew. When the Romans took Joppa, the same skeleton was carried to Italy in triumph.⁴ What seems most singular and suggestively important in this story, is this: it was from Joppa that Jonah set sail.

Akin to the adventure of Perseus and Andromeda—indeed, by some supposed to be indirectly derived from it—is that famous story of St. George and the Dragon;⁵ which dragon I maintain to have been a whale; for in many old chronicles whales and dragons are strangely jumbled together, and often stand for each other. "Thou art as a lion of the waters, and as a dragon of the sea," saith Ezekiel;⁶ hereby,

emblazoned: illustrious.

324

plainly meaning a whale; in truth, some versions of the Bible use that word itself. Besides, it would much subtract from the glory of the exploit had St. George but encountered a crawling reptile of the land, instead of doing battle with the great monster of the deep. Any man may kill a snake, but only a Perseus, a St. George, a Coffin,° have the heart in them to march boldly up to a whale.

Let not the modern paintings of this scene mislead us; for though the creature encountered by that valiant whaleman of old is vaguely represented of a griffin-like shape,[7] and though the battle is depicted on land and the saint on horseback, yet considering the great ignorance of those times, when the true form of the whale was unknown to artists; and considering that as in Perseus' case, St. George's whale might have crawled up out of the sea on the beach; and considering that the animal ridden by St. George might have been only a large seal, or sea-horse;° bearing all this in mind, it will not appear altogether incompatible with the sacred legend and the ancientest draughts of the scene, to hold this so-called dragon no other than the great Leviathan himself. In fact, placed before the strict and piercing truth, this whole story will fare like that fish, flesh, and fowl idol of the Philistines, Dagon by name; who being planted before the ark of Israel, his horse's head and both the palms of his hands fell off from him, and only the stump or fishy part of him remained.[8] Thus, then, one of our own noble stamp, even a whaleman, is the tutelary guardian of England; and by good rights, we harpooneers of Nantucket should be enrolled in the most noble order of St. George.[9] And therefore, let not the knights of that honorable company (none of whom, I venture to say, have ever had to do with a whale like their great patron), let them never eye a Nantucketer with disdain, since even in our woollen frocks and tarred trowsers we are much better entitled to St. George's decoration than they.

Whether to admit Hercules among us or not, concerning this I long remained dubious: for though according to the Greek mythologies, that antique Crockett and Kit Carson[10]—that brawny doer of rejoicing good deeds, was swallowed down and thrown up by a whale; still, whether that strictly makes a whaleman of him, that might be mooted. It nowhere appears that he ever actually harpooned his fish, unless, indeed, from the inside. Nevertheless, he may be deemed a sort of involuntary whaleman; at any rate the whale caught him, if he did not the whale. I claim him for one of our clan.[11]

But, by the best contradictory authorities, this Grecian story of Hercules and the whale is considered to be derived from the still more ancient Hebrew story of Jonah and the whale; and vice versâ; certainly they are very similar. If I claim the demi-god then, why not the prophet?

Nor do heroes, saints, demigods, and prophets alone comprise the whole roll of our order. Our grand master° is still to be named; for like royal kings of old times, we find the head-waters of our **fraternity** in nothing short of the great gods themselves. That wondrous oriental story is now to be rehearsed from the Shaster, which gives us the dread Vishnoo, one of the three persons **in** the godhead of the Hindoos;

---

a Coffin: member of the well-known Nantucket whaling family. *sea-horse*: walrus. *grand master*: elected leader of a Masonic Grand Lodge.

gives us this divine Vishnoo himself for our Lord;—Vishnoo, who, by the first of his ten earthly incarnations, has for ever set apart and sanctified the whale. When Bramha, or the God of Gods, saith the Shaster, resolved to recreate the world after one of its periodical dissolutions, he gave birth to Vishnoo, to preside over the work; but the Vedas, or mystical books, whose perusal would seem to have been indispensable to Vishnoo before beginning the creation, and which therefore must have contained something in the shape of practical hints to young architects, these Vedas were lying at the bottom of the waters; so Vishnoo became incarnate in a whale, and sounding down in him to the uttermost depths, rescued the sacred volumes.[12] Was not this Vishnoo a whaleman, then? even as a man who rides a horse is called a horseman?

Perseus, St. George, Hercules, Jonah, and Vishnoo! there's a member-roll for you! What club but the whaleman's can head off like that?

CHAPTER 83

JONAH HISTORICALLY REGARDED

R EFERENCE was made to the historical story of Jonah and the whale in the preceding chapter. Now some Nantucketers rather distrust this historical story of Jonah and the whale. But then there were some sceptical Greeks and Romans, who, standing out from the orthodox pagans of their times, equally doubted the story of Hercules and the whale, and Arion and the dolphin;[1] and yet their doubting those traditions did not make those traditions one whit the less facts, for all that.

One old Sag-Harbor whaleman's chief reason for questioning the Hebrew story was this:—He had one of those quaint old-fashioned Bibles, embellished with curious, unscientific plates; one of which represented Jonah's whale with two spouts in his head—a peculiarity only true with respect to a species of the Leviathan (the Right Whale, and the varieties of that order), concerning which the fishermen have this saying, "A penny roll° would choke him;" his swallow is so very small. But, to this, Bishop Jebb's anticipative answer is ready.[2] It is not necessary, hints the Bishop, that we consider Jonah as tombed in the whale's belly, but as temporarily lodged in some part of his mouth. And this seems reasonable enough in the good Bishop. For truly, the Right Whale's mouth would accommodate a couple of whist-tables,° and comfortably seat all the players. Possibly, too, Jonah might have ensconced himself in a hollow tooth; but, on second thoughts, the Right Whale is toothless.[3]

Another reason which Sag-Harbor (he went by that name) urged for his want of faith in this matter of the prophet, was something obscurely in reference to his incarcerated body and the whale's gastric juices. But this objection likewise falls to the ground, because a German exegetist supposes that Jonah must have taken refuge in the floating body of a *dead* whale—even as the French soldiers in the Russian campaign turned their dead horses into tents, and crawled into them.[4] Besides, it has been divined by other continental commentators, that when Jonah was thrown overboard from the Joppa ship, he straightway effected his escape to another vessel near by, some vessel with a whale for a figure-head; and, I would add, possibly called "The Whale," as some craft are nowadays christened the "Shark," the "Gull," the "Eagle." Nor have there been wanting learned exegetists who have opined that the whale

penny roll: bread roll costing one cent. ***whist-tables***: card tables.

mentioned in the book of Jonah merely meant a life-preserver—an inflated bag of wind—which the endangered prophet swam to, and so was saved from a watery doom. Poor Sag-Harbor, therefore, seems worsted all round. But he had still another reason for his want of faith. It was this, if I remember right: Jonah was swallowed by the whale in the Mediterranean Sea, and after three days he was vomited up somewhere within three days' journey of Nineveh, a city on the Tigris, very much more than three days' journey across from the nearest point of the Mediterranean coast. How is that?

But was there no other way for the whale to land the prophet within that short distance of Nineveh? Yes. He might have carried him round by the way of the Cape of Good Hope. But not to speak of the passage through the whole length of the Mediterranean, and another passage up the Persian Gulf and Red Sea, such a supposition would involve the complete circumnavigation of all Africa in three days, not to speak of the Tigris waters, near the site of Nineveh, being too shallow for any whale to swim in. Besides, this idea of Jonah's weathering the Cape of Good Hope at so early a day would wrest the honor of the discovery of that great headland from Bartholomew Diaz, its reputed discoverer, and so make modern history a liar.

But all these foolish arguments of old Sag-Harbor only evinced his foolish pride of reason—a thing still more reprehensible in him, seeing that he had but little learning except what he had picked up from the sun and the sea. I say it only shows his foolish, impious pride, and abominable, devilish rebellion against the reverend clergy. For by a Portuguese Catholic priest,[5] this very idea of Jonah's going to Nineveh viâ the Cape of Good Hope was advanced as a signal magnification of the general miracle. And so it was. Besides, to this day, the highly enlightened Turks devoutly believe in the historical story of Jonah. And some three centuries ago, an English traveller in old Harris's Voyages,[6] speaks of a Turkish Mosque built in honor of Jonah, in which mosque was a miraculous lamp that burnt without any oil.

CHAPTER 84

PITCHPOLING

To make them run easily and swiftly, the axles of carriages are anointed; and for much the same purpose, some whalers perform an analogous operation upon their boat; they grease the bottom. Nor is it to be doubted that as such a procedure can do no harm, it may possibly be of no contemptible advantage; considering that oil and water are hostile; that oil is a sliding thing, and that the object in view is to make the boat slide bravely. Queequeg believed strongly in anointing his boat, and one morning not long after the German ship Jungfrau disappeared, took more than customary pains in that occupation; crawling under its bottom, where it hung over the side, and rubbing in the unctuousness as though diligently seeking to insure a crop of hair from the craft's bald keel. He seemed to be working in obedience to some particular presentiment. Nor did it remain unwarranted by the event.

Towards noon whales were raised; but so soon as the ship sailed down to them, they turned and fled with swift precipitancy; a disordered flight, as of Cleopatra's barges from Actium.[1]

Nevertheless, the boats pursued, and Stubb's was foremost. By great exertion, Tashtego at last succeeded in planting one iron; but the stricken whale, without at all sounding, still continued his horizontal flight, with added fleetness. Such unintermitted strainings upon the planted iron must sooner or later inevitably extract it. It became imperative to lance the flying whale, or be content to lose him. But to haul the boat up to his flank was impossible, he swam so fast and furious. What then remained?

Of all the wondrous devices and dexterities, the sleights of hand and countless subtleties, to which the veteran whaleman is so often forced, none exceed that fine manœuvre with the lance called pitchpoling. Small sword, or broad sword,° in all its exercises boasts nothing like it. It is only indispensable with an inveterate running whale; its grand fact and feature is the wonderful distance to which the long lance is accurately darted from a violently rocking, jerking boat, under extreme headway. Steel and wood included, the entire spear is some ten or twelve feet in length; the staff is much slighter than that of the harpoon, and also of a lighter material—pine.

Small sword, or broad sword: kinds of swordplay.

It is furnished with a small rope called a warp, of considerable length, by which it can be hauled back to the hand after darting.

But before going further, it is important to mention here, that though the harpoon may be pitchpoled in the same way with the lance, yet it is seldom done; and when done, is still less frequently successful, on account of the greater weight and inferior length of the harpoon as compared with the lance, which in effect become serious drawbacks. As a general thing, therefore, you must first get fast to a whale, before any pitchpoling comes into play.

Look now at Stubb; a man who from his humorous, deliberate coolness and equanimity in the direst emergencies, was specially qualified to excel in pitchpoling. Look at him; he stands upright in the tossed bow of the flying boat; wrapt in fleecy foam, the towing whale is forty feet ahead. Handling the long lance lightly, glancing twice or thrice along its length to see if it be exactly straight, Stubb whistlingly gathers up the coil of the warp in one hand, so as to secure its free end in his grasp, leaving the rest unobstructed. Then holding the lance full before his waistband's middle, he levels it at the whale; when, covering him with it, he steadily depresses the butt-end in his hand, thereby elevating the point till the weapon stands fairly balanced upon his palm, fifteen feet in the air. He minds you somewhat of a juggler, balancing a long staff on his chin. Next moment with a rapid, nameless impulse, in a superb lofty arch the bright steel spans the foaming distance, and quivers in the life spot° of the whale. Instead of sparkling water, he now spouts red blood.

"That drove the spigot° out of him!" cries Stubb. "'Tis July's immortal Fourth; all fountains must run wine to-day! Would now, it were old Orleans whiskey, or old Ohio, or unspeakable old Monongahela![2] Then, Tashtego, lad, I'd have ye hold a canakin to the jet, and we'd drink round it! Yea, verily, hearts alive, we'd brew choice punch in the spread of his spout-hole there, and from that live punch-bowl quaff the living stuff!"

Again and again to such gamesome talk, the dexterous dart is repeated, the spear returning to its master like a greyhound held in skilful leash. The agonized whale goes into **his** flurry; the tow-line is slackened, and the pitchpoler dropping astern, folds his hands, and mutely watches the monster die.

---

life spot: lungs. **spigot**: plug for the hole in a cask.

CHAPTER 85

THE FOUNTAIN

THAT for six thousand years—and no one knows how many millions of ages before—the great whales should have been spouting all over the sea, and sprinkling and mistifying the gardens of the deep, as with so many sprinkling or mistifying pots; and that for some centuries back, thousands of hunters should have been close by the fountain of the whale, watching these sprinklings and spoutings—that all this should be, and yet, that down to this blessed minute (fifteen and a quarter minutes past one o'clock P.M. of this sixteenth day of December, A.D. 1851), it should still remain a problem, whether these spoutings are, after all, really water, or nothing but vapor—this is surely a noteworthy thing.[1]

Let us, then, look at this matter, along with some interesting items contingent. Every one knows that by the peculiar cunning of their gills, the finny tribes in general breathe the air which at all times is combined with the element in which they swim; hence, a herring or a cod might live a century, and never once raise its head above the surface. But owing to his marked internal structure which gives him regular lungs, like a human being's, the whale can only live by inhaling the disengaged air in the open atmosphere. Wherefore the necessity for his periodical visits to the upper world. But he cannot in any degree breathe through his mouth, for, in his ordinary attitude, the Sperm Whale's mouth is buried at least eight feet beneath the surface; and what is still more, his windpipe has no connexion with his mouth.[2] No, he breathes through his spiracle alone; and this is on the top of his head.

If I say, that in any creature breathing is only a function indispensable to vitality, inasmuch as it withdraws from the air a certain element, which being subsequently brought into contact with the blood imparts to the blood its vivifying principle, I do not think I shall err; though I may possibly use some superfluous scientific words. Assume it, and it follows that if all the blood in a man could be aerated with one breath, he might then seal up his nostrils and not fetch another for a considerable time. That is to say, he would then live without breathing. Anomalous as it may seem, this is precisely the case with the whale, who systematically lives, by intervals, his full hour and more (when at the bottom) without drawing a single breath, or so much as in any way inhaling a particle of air; for, remember, he has no gills. How is this? Between his ribs and on each side of his spine he is supplied with a remarkable

331

involved Cretan labyrinth of vermicelli-like vessels,[3] which vessels, when he quits the surface, are completely distended with oxygenated blood. So that for an hour or more, a thousand fathoms in the sea, he carries a surplus stock of vitality in him, just as the camel crossing the waterless desert carries a surplus supply of drink for future use in its four supplementary stomachs.[4] The anatomical fact of this labyrinth is indisputable; and that the supposition founded upon it is reasonable and true, seems the more cogent to me, when I consider the otherwise inexplicable obstinacy of that leviathan in *having his spoutings out,* as the fishermen phrase it. This is what I mean. If unmolested, upon rising to the surface, the Sperm Whale will continue there for a period of time exactly uniform with all his other unmolested risings. Say he stays eleven minutes, and jets seventy times, that is, respires seventy breaths; then whenever he rises again, he will be sure to have his seventy breaths over again, to a minute. Now, if after he fetches a few breaths you alarm him, so that he sounds, he will be always dodging up again to make good his regular allowance of air. And not till those seventy breaths are told, will he finally go down to stay out his full term below. Remark, however, that in different individuals these rates are different; but in any one they are alike. Now, why should the whale thus insist upon having his spoutings out, unless it be to replenish his reservoir of air, ere descending for good? How obvious is it, too, that this necessity for the whale's rising exposes him to all the fatal hazards of the chase. For not by hook or by net could this vast leviathan be caught, when sailing a thousand fathoms beneath the sunlight. Not so much thy skill, then, O hunter, as the great necessities that strike the victory to thee!

In man, breathing is incessantly going on—one breath only serving for two or three pulsations; so that whatever other business he has to attend to, waking or sleeping, breathe he must, or die he will. But the Sperm Whale only breathes about one seventh or Sunday of his time.

It has been said that the whale only breathes through his spout-hole; if it could truthfully be added that his spouts are mixed with water, then I opine we should be furnished with the reason why his sense of smell seems obliterated in him; for the only thing about him that at all answers to his nose is that identical spout-hole; and being so clogged with two elements, it could not be expected to have the power of smelling. But owing to the mystery of the spout—whether it be water or whether it be vapor—no absolute certainty can as yet be arrived at on this head. Sure it is, nevertheless, that the Sperm Whale has no proper olfactories. But what does he want of them? No roses, no violets, no Cologne-water in the sea.

Furthermore, as his windpipe solely opens into the tube of his spouting canal, and as that long canal—like the grand Erie Canal—is furnished with a sort of locks (that open and shut) for the downward retention of air or the upward exclusion of water, therefore the whale has no voice; unless you insult him by saying, that when he so strangely rumbles, he talks through his nose.[5] But then again, what has the whale to say? Seldom have I known any profound being that had anything to say to this world, unless forced to stammer out something by way of getting a living. Oh! happy that the world is such an excellent listener!

Now, the spouting canal of the Sperm Whale, chiefly intended as it is for the conveyance of air, and for several feet laid along, horizontally, just beneath the upper surface of his head, and a little to one side; this curious canal is very much like a gas-pipe laid down in a city on one side of a street. But the question returns whether this gas-pipe is also a water-pipe; in other words, whether the spout of the Sperm Whale is the mere vapor of the exhaled breath, or whether that exhaled breath is mixed with water taken in at the mouth, and discharged through the spiracle. It is certain that the mouth indirectly communicates with the spouting canal; but it cannot be proved that this is for the purpose of discharging water through the spiracle. Because the greatest necessity for so doing would seem to be, when in feeding he accidentally takes in water. But the Sperm Whale's food is far beneath the surface, and there he cannot spout even if he would. Besides, if you regard him very closely, and time him with your watch, you will find that when unmolested, there is an undeviating rhyme° between the periods of his jets and the ordinary periods of respiration.

But why pester one with all this reasoning on the subject? Speak out! You have seen him spout; then declare what the spout is; can you not tell water from air? My dear sir, in this world it is not so easy to settle these plain things. I have ever found your plain things the knottiest of all. And as for this whale spout, you might almost stand in it, and yet be undecided as to what it is precisely.

The central body of it is hidden in the snowy sparkling mist enveloping it; and how can you certainly tell whether any water falls from it, when, always, when you are close enough to a whale to get a close view of his spout, he is in a prodigious commotion, the water cascading all around him. And if at such times you should think that you really perceived drops of moisture in the spout, how do you know that they are not merely condensed from its vapor; or how do you know that they are not those identical drops superficially lodged in the spout-hole fissure, which is countersunk into the summit of the whale's head? For even when tranquilly swimming through the mid-day sea in a calm, with his elevated hump sun-dried as a dromedary's in the desert; even then, the whale always carries a small basin of water on his head, as under a blazing sun you will sometimes see a cavity in a rock filled up with rain.

Nor is it at all prudent for the hunter to be over curious touching the precise nature of the whale spout. It will not do for him to be peering into it, and putting his face in it. You cannot go with your pitcher to this fountain and fill it, and bring it away. For even when coming into slight contact with the outer, vapory shreds of the jet, which will often happen, your skin will feverishly smart, from the acridness of the thing so touching it. And I know one, who coming into still closer contact with the spout, whether with some scientific object in view, or otherwise, I cannot say, the skin peeled off from his cheek and arm. Wherefore, among whalemen, the spout is deemed poisonous; they try to evade it. Another thing; I have heard it said, and I do not much doubt it, that if the jet is fairly spouted into your eyes, it will blind you. The wisest thing the investigator can do then, it seems to me, is to let this deadly spout alone.

Still, we can hypothesize, even if we cannot prove and establish. My hypothesis is this: that the spout is nothing but mist. And besides other reasons, to this conclusion I am impelled, by considerations touching the great inherent dignity and sublimity of the Sperm Whale; I account him no common, shallow being, inasmuch as it is an undisputed fact that he is never found on soundings, or near shores; all other whales sometimes are. He is both ponderous and profound. And I am con-

rhyme: correspondence.

vinced that from the heads of all ponderous profound beings, such as Plato, Pyrrho,[6] **the Devil,** Jupiter, Dante, and so on, there always goes up a certain semi-visible steam, while in the act of thinking deep thoughts. While composing a little treatise on Eternity, I had the curiosity to place a mirror before me; and ere long saw reflected there, a curious involved worming and undulation in the atmosphere over my head. The invariable moisture of my hair, while plunged in deep thought, after six cups of hot tea in my thin shingled attic, of an August noon; this seems an additional argument for the above supposition.

And how nobly it raises our conceit of the mighty, misty monster, to behold him solemnly sailing through a calm tropical sea; his vast, mild head overhung by a canopy of vapor, engendered by his incommunicable contemplations, and that vapor—as you will sometimes see it—glorified by a rainbow, as if Heaven itself had put its seal upon his thoughts. For, d'ye see, rainbows do not visit the clear air; they only irradiate vapor. And so, through all the thick mists of the dim doubts in my mind, divine intuitions now and then shoot, enkindling my fog with a heavenly ray. And for this I thank God; for all have doubts; many deny; but doubts or denials, few along with them, have intuitions. Doubts of all things earthly, and intuitions of some things heavenly; this combination makes neither believer nor infidel, but makes a man who regards them both with equal eye.

CHAPTER 86

THE TAIL

OTHER poets have warbled the praises of the soft eye of the antelope, and the lovely plumage of the bird that never alights; less celestial, I celebrate a tail.

Reckoning the largest sized Sperm Whale's tail to begin at that point of the trunk where it tapers to about the girth of a man, it comprises upon its upper surface alone, an area of at least fifty square feet. The compact round body of its root expands into two broad, firm, flat palms or flukes, gradually shoaling away to less than an inch in thickness. At the crotch or junction, these flukes slightly overlap, then sideways recede from each other like wings, leaving a wide vacancy between. In no living thing are the lines of beauty more exquisitely defined than in the crescentic borders of these flukes. At its utmost expansion in the full grown whale, the tail will considerably exceed twenty feet across.

The entire member seems a dense webbed bed of welded sinews; but cut into it, and you find that three distinct strata compose it:—upper, middle, and lower. The fibres in the upper and lower layers, are long and horizontal; those of the middle one, very short, and running crosswise between the outside layers. This triune° structure, as much as anything else, imparts power to the tail. To the student of old Roman walls, the middle layer will furnish a curious parallel to the thin course of tiles always alternating with the stone in those wonderful relics of the antique, and which undoubtedly contribute so much to the great strength of the masonry.

But as if this vast local power in the tendinous tail were not enough, the whole bulk of the leviathan is knit over with a warp and woof of muscular fibres and filaments, which passing on either side the loins and running down into the flukes, insensibly blend with them, and largely contribute to their might; so that in the tail the confluent measureless force of the whole whale seems concentrated to a point. Could annihilation occur to matter, this were the thing to do it.

Nor does this—its amazing strength, at all tend to cripple the graceful flexion of its motions; where infantileness of ease undulates through a Titanism of power.[1] On the contrary, those motions derive their most appalling beauty from it. Real strength never impairs beauty or harmony, but it often bestows it; and in everything imposingly beau-

triune: three in one, typically in reference to the Holy Trinity.

tiful, strength has much to do with the magic. Take away the tied tendons that all over seem bursting from the marble in the carved Hercules,[2] and its charm would be gone. As devout Eckermann lifted the linen sheet from the naked corpse of Goethe,[3] he was overwhelmed with the massive chest of the man, that seemed as a Roman triumphal arch. When Angelo paints even God the Father in human form, mark what robustness is there.[4] And whatever they may reveal of the divine love in the Son, the soft, curled, **hermaphroditical** Italian pictures,[5] in which his idea has been most successfully embodied; these pictures, so destitute as they are of all brawniness, hint nothing of any power, but the mere negative, feminine one of submission and endurance, which on all hands it is conceded, form the peculiar practical virtues of his teachings.

Such is the subtle elasticity of the organ I treat of, that whether wielded in sport, or in earnest, or in anger, whatever be the mood it be in, its flexions are invariably marked by exceeding grace. Therein no fairy's arm can transcend it.

Five great motions are peculiar to it. First, when used as a fin for progression; Second, when used as a mace in battle; Third, in sweeping; Fourth, in lobtailing; Fifth, in peaking flukes.

First: Being horizontal in its position, the Leviathan's tail acts in a different manner from the tails of all other sea creatures. It never wriggles. In man or fish, wriggling is a sign of inferiority. To the whale, his tail is the sole means of propulsion. Scroll-wise coiled forwards beneath the body, and then rapidly sprung backwards, it is this which gives that singular darting, leaping motion to the monster when furiously swimming. His side-fins only serve to steer by.

Second: It is a little significant, that while one sperm whale only fights another sperm whale with his head and jaw, nevertheless, in his conflicts with man, he chiefly and contemptuously uses his tail. In striking at a boat, he swiftly curves away his flukes from it, and the blow is only inflicted by the recoil. If it be made in the unobstructed air, especially if it descend to its mark, the stroke is then simply irresistible. No ribs of man or boat can withstand it. Your only salvation lies in eluding it; but if it comes sideways through the opposing **water**, then partly owing to the light buoyancy of the whale-boat, and the elasticity of its materials, a cracked rib or a dashed plank or two, a sort of stitch in the side, is generally the most serious result. These submerged side blows are so often received in the fishery, that they are accounted mere child's play. Some one strips off a frock, and the hole is stopped.

Third: I cannot demonstrate it, but it seems to me, that in the whale the sense of touch is concentrated in the tail; for in this respect there is a delicacy in it only equalled by the daintiness of the elephant's trunk. This delicacy is chiefly evinced in the action of sweeping, when in maidenly gentleness the whale with a certain soft slowness moves his immense flukes from side to side upon the surface of the sea; and if he feel but a sailor's whisker, woe to that sailor, whiskers and all. What tenderness there is in that preliminary touch! Had this tail any prehensile° power, I should straightway bethink me of Darmonodes' elephant that so frequented the flower-market, and with low salutations presented nosegays to damsels, and then caressed their zones.[6] On more accounts than one, a pity it is that the whale does not

prehensile: able to grasp.

possess this prehensile virtue in his tail; for I have heard of yet another elephant, that when wounded in the fight, curved round his trunk and extracted the dart.

Fourth: Stealing unawares upon the whale in the fancied security of the middle of **solitary** seas, you find him unbent° from the vast corpulence of his dignity, and kitten-like, he plays on the ocean as if it were a hearth. But still you see his power in his play. The broad palms of his tail are flirted high into the air; then smiting the surface, the thunderous concussion resounds for miles. You would **almost** think a great gun had been discharged; and if you noticed the light wreath of vapor from the spiracle at his other extremity, you would think that that was the smoke from the touch-hole.°

Fifth: As in the ordinary floating posture of the leviathan the flukes lie considerably below the level of his back, they are then completely out of sight beneath the surface; but when he is about to plunge into the deeps, his entire flukes with at least thirty feet of his body are tossed erect in the air, and so remain vibrating a moment, till they downwards shoot out of view. Excepting the sublime *breach*— somewhere else to be described°—this peaking of the whale's flukes is perhaps the grandest sight to be seen in all animated nature. Out of the bottomless profundities the gigantic tail seems spasmodically snatching at the highest **heaven**. So in dreams, have I seen majestic Satan thrusting forth his tormented colossal claw from the flame Baltic of Hell.[7] But in gazing at such scenes, it is all in all what mood you are in; if in the Dantean, the devils will occur to you; if in that of Isaiah, the archangels.[8] Standing at the mast-head **of my ship** during a sunrise that crimsoned sky and sea, I once saw a large herd of whales in the east, all heading towards the sun, and for a moment vibrating in concert with peaked flukes. As it seemed to me at the time, such a grand embodiment of adoration of the gods was never beheld, even in Persia, the home of the fire worshippers. As Ptolemy Philopater testified of the African elephant, I then testified of the whale, pronouncing him the most devout of all beings. For according to King Juba,[9] the military elephants of antiquity often hailed the morning with their trunks uplifted in the profoundest silence.

The chance comparison in this chapter, between the whale and the elephant, so far as some aspects of the tail of the one and the trunk of the other are concerned, should not tend to place those two opposite organs on an equality, much less the creatures to which they respectively belong. For as the mightiest elephant is but a terrier to Leviathan, so, compared with Leviathan's tail, his trunk is but the stalk of a lily. The most direful blow from the elephant's trunk were as the playful tap of a fan, compared with the measureless crush and crash of the sperm whale's ponderous flukes, which in repeated instances have one after the other hurled entire boats with all their oars and crews into the air, very much as an Indian juggler tosses his balls.*

---

* Though all comparison in the way of general bulk between the whale and the elephant is preposterous, inasmuch as in that particular the elephant stands in much the same respect to the whale that a dog does to the elephant; nevertheless, there are not wanting some points of curious similitude; among these is the spout. It is well known that the elephant will often draw up water or dust in his trunk, and then elevating it, jet it forth in a stream.

---

unbent: relaxed; untied (naut.). **touch-hole**: hole in a cannon through which gunpowder is ignited. **somewhere else to be described**: see Ch. 134.

The more I consider this mighty tail, the more do I deplore my inability to express it. At times there are gestures in it, which, though they would well grace the hand of man, remain wholly inexplicable. In an extensive herd, so remarkable, occasionally, are these mystic gestures, that I have heard hunters who have declared them akin to Free-Mason signs and symbols;[10] that the whale, indeed, by these methods intelligently conversed with the world. Nor are there wanting other motions of the whale in his general body, full of strangeness, and unaccountable to his most experienced assailant. Dissect him how I may, then, I **but go** skin deep; I know him not, and never **will**. But if I know not even the tail of this whale, how understand his head? much more, how comprehend his face, when face he has none? **Thou shalt see my back parts, my tail, he seems to say, but my face shall not be seen. But I cannot completely make out his back parts; and hint what he will about his face, I say again he has no face.**

REVISION NARRATIVE

Biblical Joking

In Exodus 33.13, Moses says to God, "shew me now thy way, that I may know thee," but God responds that no one can see his glory or face without perishing. God arranges to meet Moses at a rock where he will cover Moses' eyes and then "take away mine hand, and thou shalt see my back parts: but my face shall not be seen" (33.23). In the final two sentences of Ch. 86, Melville accurately quotes the King James Version of the Bible as he humorously compares the whale's tail to God's "back parts." The punch line to Melville's joke is that unlike Moses, Ishmael cannot even "make out his back parts," much less his face. Melville has already said as much in the preceding sentence, but in using the Bible comically here, he raises the intellectual stakes by implying that Ishmael cannot make sense of even what God allows us to know. Not surprisingly, the two sentences were removed from the British edition. The likely culprit is a British editor, but Melville, who in writing *Typee* learned early on to curb his humor, might have thought better of this biblical joke, and made the cut himself.

CHAPTER 87

THE GRAND ARMADA

THE long and narrow peninsula of Malacca, extending south-eastward from the territories of Birmah, forms the most southerly point of all Asia. In a continuous line from that peninsula stretch the long islands of Sumatra, Java, Bally, and Timor;[1] which, with many others, form a vast mole, or rampart, lengthwise connecting Asia with Australia, and dividing the long unbroken Indian ocean from the thickly studded oriental archipelagoes. This rampart is pierced by several sally-ports° for the convenience of ships and whales; conspicuous among which are the straits of Sunda and Malacca. By the straits of Sunda, chiefly, vessels bound to China from the west, emerge into the China seas.

Those narrow straits of Sunda divide Sumatra from Java; and standing midway in that vast rampart of islands, buttressed by that bold green promontory, known to seamen as Java Head; they not a little correspond to the central gateway opening into some vast walled empire: and considering the inexhaustible wealth of spices, and silks, and jewels, and gold, and ivory, with which the thousand islands of that oriental sea are enriched, it seems a significant provision of nature, that such treasures, by the very formation of the land, should at least bear the appearance, however ineffectual, of being guarded from the all-grasping western world. The shores of the Straits of Sunda are unsupplied with those domineering fortresses which guard the entrances to the Mediterranean, the Baltic, and the Propontis.[2] Unlike the Danes, these Orientals do not demand the obsequious homage of lowered top-sails from the endless procession of ships before the wind, which for centuries past, by night and by day, have passed between the islands of Sumatra and Java, freighted with the costliest cargoes of the east. But while they freely waive a ceremonial like this, they do by no means renounce their claim to more solid tribute.

Time out of mind the piratical proas° of the Malays, lurking among the low shaded coves and islets of Sumatra, have sallied out upon the vessels sailing through the straits, fiercely demanding tribute at the point of their spears. Though by the repeated bloody chastisements they have received at the hands of European cruis-

---

sally-ports: openings in a fortification through which troops may pass. **proas**: large, fast vessels with outriggers and triangular sails.

ers, the audacity of these corsairs° has of late been somewhat repressed; yet, even at the present day, we occasionally hear of English and American vessels, which, in those waters, have been remorselessly boarded and pillaged.

With a fair, fresh wind, the Pequod was now drawing nigh to these straits; Ahab purposing to pass through them into the Javan sea, and thence, cruising northwards, over waters known to be frequented here and there by the Sperm Whale, sweep inshore by the Philippine Islands, and gain the far coast of Japan, in time for the great whaling season there.° By these means, the circumnavigating Pequod would sweep almost all the known Sperm Whale cruising grounds of the world, previous to descending upon the Line in the Pacific; where Ahab, though everywhere else foiled in his pursuit, firmly counted upon giving battle to Moby Dick, in the sea he was most known to frequent; and at a season when he might most reasonably be presumed to be haunting it.

But how now? in this zoned° quest, does Ahab touch no land? does his crew drink air? Surely, he will stop for water. Nay. For a long time, now, the circus-running sun has raced within his fiery ring, and needs no sustenance but what's in himself. So Ahab. Mark this, too, in the whaler. While other hulls are loaded down with alien stuff, to be transferred to foreign wharves; the world-wandering whale-ship carries no cargo but herself and crew, their weapons and their wants. She has a whole lake's contents bottled in her ample hold. She is ballasted with utilities; not altogether with unusable pig-lead and kentledge.° She carries years' water in her. Clear old prime Nantucket water; which, when three years afloat, the Nantucketer, in the Pacific, prefers to drink before the brackish fluid, but yesterday rafted off in casks, from the Peruvian or Indian streams.[3] Hence it is, that, while other ships may have gone to China from New York, and back again, touching at a score of ports, the whale-ship, in all that interval, may not have sighted one grain of soil; her crew having seen no man but floating seamen like themselves. So that did you carry them the news that another flood had come; they would only answer—"Well, boys, here's the ark!"

Now, as many Sperm Whales had been captured off the western coast of Java, in the near vicinity of the Straits of Sunda; indeed, as most of the ground, roundabout, was generally recognised by the fishermen as an excellent spot for cruising; therefore, as the Pequod gained more and more upon Java Head, the look-outs were repeatedly hailed, and admonished to keep wide awake. But though the green palmy cliffs of the land soon loomed on the starboard bow, and with delighted nostrils the fresh cinnamon was snuffed in the air, yet not a single jet was descried. Almost renouncing all thought of falling in with any game hereabouts, the ship had well nigh entered the straits, when the customary cheering cry was heard from aloft, and ere long a spectacle of singular magnificence saluted us.

But here be it premised, that owing to the unwearied activity with which of late they have been hunted over all four oceans, the Sperm Whales, instead of almost invariably sailing in small detached companies, as in former times, are now frequently met with in extensive herds, sometimes embracing so great a multitude, that it would almost seem as if numerous nations of them had sworn solemn league

corsairs: pirates. **whaling season there**: May to September. **zoned**: organized by regions. **kentledge**: pig-iron ballast.

and covenant for mutual assistance and protection. To this aggregation of the Sperm Whale into such immense caravans, may be imputed the circumstance that even in the best cruising grounds, you may now sometimes sail for weeks and months together, without being greeted by a single spout; and then be suddenly saluted by what sometimes seems thousands on thousands.

Broad on both bows, at the distance of some two or three miles, and forming a great semicircle, embracing one half of the level horizon, a continuous chain of whale-jets were up-playing and sparkling in the noon-day air. Unlike the straight perpendicular twin-jets of the Right Whale, which, dividing at top, fall over in two branches, like the cleft drooping boughs of a willow, the single forward-slanting spout of the Sperm Whale presents a thick curled bush of white mist, continually rising and falling away to leeward.

Seen from the Pequod's deck, then, as she would rise on a high hill of the sea, this host of vapory spouts, individually curling up into the air, and beheld through a blending atmosphere of bluish haze, showed like the thousand cheerful chimneys of some dense metropolis, descried of a balmy autumnal morning, by some horseman on a height.

As marching armies approaching an unfriendly defile in the mountains, accelerate their march, all eagerness to place that perilous passage in their rear, and once more expand in comparative security upon the plain; even so did this vast fleet of whales now seem hurrying forward through the straits; gradually contracting the wings of their semicircle, and swimming on, in one solid, but still crescentic centre.

Crowding all sail the Pequod pressed after them; the harpooneers handling their weapons, and loudly cheering from the heads of their yet suspended boats. If the wind only held, little doubt had they, that chased through these Straits of Sunda, the vast host would only deploy into the Oriental seas to witness the capture of not a few of their number. And who could tell whether, in that congregated caravan, Moby Dick himself might not temporarily be swimming, like the worshipped white-elephant[4] in the coronation procession of the Siamese! So with stun-sail piled on stun-sail, we sailed along, driving these leviathans before us; when, of a sudden, the voice of Tashtego was heard, loudly directing attention to something in our wake.

Corresponding to the crescent in our van,° we beheld another in our rear. It seemed formed of detached white vapors, rising and falling something like the spouts of the whales; only they did not so completely come and go; for they constantly hovered, without finally disappearing. Levelling his glass at this sight, Ahab quickly revolved in his pivot-hole, crying, "Aloft there, and rig whips and buckets to wet the sails;°—Malays, sir, and after us!"

As if too long lurking behind the headlands, till the Pequod should fairly have entered the straits, these rascally Asiatics were now in hot pursuit, to make up for their over-cautious delay. But when the swift Pequod, with a fresh leading wind, was herself in hot chase; how very kind of these tawny philanthropists to assist in speeding her on to her own chosen pursuit,—mere riding-whips and rowels° to her, that they were. As with glass under arm, Ahab to-and-fro paced the deck; in his forward

---

in our van: ahead of us. **wet the sails**: to make them less porous, more efficient. **rowels**: toothed wheels of spurs.

turn beholding the monsters he chased, and in the after one the bloodthirsty pirates chasing *him;* some such fancy as the above seemed his. And when he glanced upon the green walls of the watery defile in which the ship was then sailing, and bethought him that through that gate lay the route to his vengeance, and beheld, how that through that same gate he was now both chasing and being chased to his deadly end; and not only that, but a herd of remorseless wild pirates and inhuman atheistical devils were infernally cheering him on with their curses;—when all these conceits had passed through his brain, Ahab's brow was left gaunt and ribbed, like the black sand beach after some stormy tide has been gnawing it, without being able to drag the firm thing from its place.

But thoughts like these troubled very few of the reckless crew; and when, after steadily dropping and dropping the pirates astern, the Pequod at last shot by the vivid green Cockatoo Point[5] on the Sumatra side, emerging at last upon the broad waters beyond; then, the harpooneers seemed more to grieve that the swift whales had been gaining upon the ship, than to rejoice that the ship had so victoriously gained upon the Malays. But still driving on in the wake of the whales, at length they seemed abating their speed; gradually the ship neared them; and the wind now dying away, word was passed to spring to the boats. But no sooner did the herd, by some presumed wonderful instinct of the Sperm Whale, become notified of the three keels that were after them,—though as yet a mile in their rear,—than they rallied again, and forming in close ranks and battalions, so that their spouts all looked like flashing lines of stacked bayonets, moved on with redoubled velocity.

Stripped to our shirts and drawers, we sprang to the white-ash, and after several hours' pulling were almost disposed to renounce the chase, when a general pausing commotion among the whales gave animating token that they were now at last under the influence of that strange perplexity of inert irresolution, which, when the fishermen perceive it in the whale, they say he is **gallied**. The compact martial columns in which they had been hitherto rapidly and steadily swimming, were now broken up in one measureless rout; and like King Porus' elephants in the Indian battle with Alexander,[6] they seemed going mad with consternation. In all directions expanding in vast irregular circles, and aimlessly swimming hither and thither, by their short thick spoutings, they plainly betrayed their distraction of panic. This was still more strangely evinced by those of their number, who, completely paralysed as it were, helplessly floated like water-logged dismantled ships on the sea. Had these leviathans been but a flock of simple sheep, pursued over the pasture by three fierce wolves, they could not possibly have evinced such excessive dismay. But this occasional timidity is characteristic of almost all herding creatures. Though banding together in tens of thousands, the lion-maned buffaloes of the West have fled before a solitary horseman. Witness, too, all human beings, how when herded together in the sheepfold of a theatre's pit, they will, at the slightest alarm of fire, rush helter-skelter for the outlets, crowding, trampling, jamming, and remorselessly dashing each other to death. Best, therefore, withhold any amazement at the strangely gallied whales before us, for there is no folly of the beasts of the earth[7] which is not infinitely outdone by the madness of men.

Though many of the whales, as has been said, were in violent motion, yet it is to be observed that as a whole the herd neither advanced nor retreated, but collectively remained in one place. As is customary in those cases, the boats at once separated, each making for some one lone whale on the outskirts of the shoal. In about three minutes' time, Queequeg's harpoon was flung; the stricken fish darted blinding spray in our faces, and then running away with us like light, steered straight for the heart of the herd. Though such a movement on the part of the whale struck under such circumstances, is in no wise unprecedented; and indeed is almost always more or less anticipated; yet does it present one of the more perilous vicissitudes of the fishery. For as the swift monster drags you deeper and deeper into the frantic shoal, you bid adieu to circumspect life and only exist in a delirious throb.[8]

As, blind and deaf, the whale plunged forward, as if by sheer power of speed to rid himself of the iron leech that had fastened to him; as we thus tore a white gash in the sea, on all sides menaced as we flew, by the crazed creatures to and fro rush-

REVISION NARRATIVE

Melville Adds a Footnote

The largest revision Melville made to the American version of *Moby-Dick* was the addition of a footnote explaining the derivation of "gallied," which he attached to the corrected proof sheets he sent to England. The note is directed at two distinct audiences: the "landsman" and British readers. Because *gallied* is obsolete (according to Ishmael) and no longer in parlance, landsmen are inclined to think a Nantucketer's use of the word is a recent nautical invention. In fact, as Melville claims, "it is an old Saxon word," which since "the time of the Commonwealth" (the English Republic under Cromwell, 1649–1660), has been kept alive in the democratic New World, a point Melville makes with special emphasis for British readers. Some indication of the word's return from obscurity is that *gally* appears in Webster's 1828 Dictionary and in Cheever's glossary (1840), and it is also defined in *Poor Jack*, the popular 1840 sea novel by Frederick Marryat, whose work Melville knew. The following is the full text of Melville's British edition note:

> * To *gally*, or *gallow*, is to frighten excessively,—to confound with fright. It is an old Saxon word. It occurs once in Shakspere:—
>
> > "The wrathful skies
> > *Gallow* the very wanderers of the dark,
> > And make them keep their caves."
> >
> > *Lear*, Act iii, sc. II.

> To common land usages, the word is now completely obsolete. When the polite landsman first hears it from the gaunt Nantucketer, he is apt to set it down as one of the whaleman's self-derived savageries. Much the same is it with many other sinewy Saxonisms of this sort, which emigrated to the New-England rocks with the noble brawn of the old English emigrants in the time of the Commonwealth. Thus, some of the best and furthest-descended English words—the etymological Howards and Percys—are now democratised, nay, plebeianised—so to speak—in the New World.

ing about us; our beset boat was like a ship mobbed by ice-isles in a tempest, and striving to steer through their complicated channels and straits, knowing not at what moment it may be locked in and crushed.

But not a bit daunted, Queequeg steered us manfully; now sheering off from this monster directly across our route in advance; now edging away from that, whose colossal flukes were suspended overhead, while all the time, Starbuck stood up in the bows, lance in hand, pricking out of our way whatever whales he could reach by short darts, for there was no time to make long ones. Nor were the oarsmen quite idle, though their wonted duty was now altogether dispensed with. They chiefly attended to the shouting part of the business. "Out of the way, Commodore!" cried one, to a great dromedary that of a sudden rose bodily to the surface, and for an instant threatened to swamp us. "Hard down with your tail, there!" cried a second to another, which, close to our gunwale, seemed calmly cooling himself with his own fan-like extremity.

All whaleboats carry certain curious contrivances, originally invented by the Nantucket Indians, called druggs. Two thick squares of wood of equal size are stoutly clenched together, so that they cross each other's grain at right angles; a line of considerable length is then attached to the middle of this block, and the other end of the line being looped, it can in a moment be fastened to a harpoon. It is chiefly among gallied whales that this drugg is used. For then, more whales are close round you than you can possibly chase at one time. But sperm whales are not every day encountered; while you may, then, you must kill all you can. And if you cannot kill them all at once, you must wing them, so that they can be afterwards killed at your leisure. Hence it is, that at times like these the drugg comes into requisition. Our boat was furnished with three of them. The first and second were successfully darted, and we saw the whales staggeringly running off, fettered by the enormous sidelong resistance of the towing drugg. They were cramped like malefactors with the chain and ball. But upon flinging the third, in the act of tossing overboard the clumsy wooden block, it caught under one of the seats of the boat, and in an instant tore it out and carried it away, dropping the oarsman in the boat's bottom as the seat slid from under him. On both sides the sea came in at the wounded planks, but we stuffed two or three drawers and shirts in, and so stopped the leaks for the time.

It had been next to impossible to dart these drugged-harpoons, were it not that as we advanced into the herd, our whale's way greatly diminished; moreover, that as we went still further and further from the circumference of commotion, the direful disorders seemed waning. So that when at last the jerking harpoon drew out, and the towing whale sideways vanished; then, with the tapering force of his parting momentum, we glided between two whales into the innermost heart of the shoal, as if from some mountain torrent we had slid into a serene valley lake. Here the storms in the roaring glens between the outermost whales, were heard but not felt. In this central expanse the sea presented that smooth satin-like surface, called a sleek, produced by the subtle moisture thrown off by the whale in his more quiet moods. Yes, we were now in that enchanted calm which they say lurks at the heart of every commotion. And still in the distracted distance we beheld the tumults of the outer concentric circles, and saw successive pods of whales, eight or ten in each, swiftly going round and round, like multiplied spans of horses in a ring; and so closely shoulder to shoulder, that a Titanic circus-rider might easily have overarched the middle ones, and so have gone round on their backs. Owing to the density of the crowd of reposing whales, more immediately surrounding the embayed axis of the herd, no possible chance of escape was at present afforded us. We must watch for a breach in the living wall that hemmed us in; the wall that had only admitted us in order to shut us up. Keeping at the centre of the lake, we were occasionally visited by small tame cows and calves; the women and children of this routed host.°

Now, inclusive of the occasional wide intervals between the revolving outer circles, and inclusive of the spaces between the various pods in any one of those circles, the entire area at this juncture, embraced by the whole multitude, must have contained at least two or three square miles. At any rate—though indeed such a test at such a time might be deceptive—spoutings might be discovered from our low boat that seemed playing up almost from the rim of the horizon. I mention this circumstance, because, as if the cows and calves had been purposely locked up in this innermost fold; and as if the wide extent of the herd had hitherto prevented them from learning the precise cause of its stopping; or, possibly, being so young, unsophisticated, and every way innocent and inexperienced; however it may have been, these smaller whales—now and then visiting our becalmed boat from the margin of the lake—evinced a wondrous fearlessness and confidence, or else a **still becharmed panic** which it was impossible not to marvel at. Like household dogs they came snuffling round us, right up to our gunwales, and touching them; till it almost seemed that some spell had suddenly domesticated them. Queequeg patted their foreheads; Starbuck scratched their backs with his lance; but fearful of the consequences, for the time refrained from darting it.

But far beneath this wondrous world upon the surface, another and still stranger world met our eyes as we gazed over the side.[9] For, suspended in those watery vaults, floated the forms of the nursing mothers of the whales, and those that by their enormous girth seemed shortly to become mothers. The lake, as I have hinted, was to a considerable depth exceedingly transparent; and as human infants while suckling will calmly and fixedly gaze away from the breast, as if leading two different lives at the time; and while yet drawing mortal nourishment, be still spiritually feasting upon some unearthly reminiscence;—even so did the young of these whales seem looking up towards us, but not at us, as if we were but a bit of Gulf-weed[10] in their new-born sight. Floating on their sides, the mothers also seemed quietly eyeing us. One of these little infants, that from certain queer tokens seemed hardly a day old, might have measured some fourteen feet in length, and some six feet in girth. He was a little frisky; though as yet his body seemed scarce yet recovered from that irksome position it had so lately occupied in the maternal reticule;° where, tail to head, and all ready for the final spring, the unborn whale lies bent like a Tartar's bow.° The delicate side-fins, and the palms of his flukes, still freshly retained the plaited crumpled appearance of a baby's ears newly arrived from foreign parts.

"Line! line!" cried Queequeg, looking over the gunwale; "him fast! him fast!— Who line him! Who struck?—Two whale; one big, one little!"

"What ails ye, man?" cried Starbuck.

___

routed host: fleeing army. **reticule**: woman's drawstring purse, but here, womb. **Tartar's bow**: short, deeply-curved bow used by horsemen of Mongolia.

"Look-e here," said Queequeg pointing down.

As when the stricken whale, that from the tub has reeled out hundreds of fathoms of rope; as, after deep sounding, he floats up again, and shows the slackened curling line buoyantly rising and spiralling towards the air; so now, Starbuck saw long coils of the umbilical cord of Madame Leviathan, by which the young cub seemed still tethered to its dam. Not seldom in the rapid vicissitudes of the chase, this natural line, with the maternal end loose, becomes entangled with the hempen one, so that the cub is thereby trapped. Some of the subtlest secrets of the seas seemed divulged to us in this enchanted pond. **We saw young Leviathan amours in the deep.***

And thus, though surrounded by circle upon circle of consternations and affrights, did these inscrutable creatures at the centre freely and fearlessly indulge in all peaceful concernments; yea, serenely revelled in dalliance and delight. But even so, amid the tornadoed Atlantic of my being, do I myself still for ever centrally disport in mute calm; and while ponderous planets of unwaning woe revolve round me, deep down and deep inland there I still bathe me in eternal mildness of joy.

Meanwhile, as we thus lay entranced, the occasional sudden frantic spectacles in the distance evinced the activity of the other boats, still engaged in drugging the whales on the frontier of the host; or possibly carrying on the war within the first circle, where abundance of room and some convenient retreats were afforded them. But the sight of the enraged drugged whales now and then blindly darting to and fro across the circles, was nothing to what at last met our eyes. It is sometimes the custom when fast to a whale more than commonly powerful and alert, to seek to hamstring him, as it were, by sundering or maiming his gigantic tail-tendon. It is done by darting a short-handled cutting-spade, to which is attached a rope for hauling it back again. A whale wounded (as we afterwards learned) in this part, but not effectually, as it seemed, had broken away from the boat, carrying along with him half of the harpoon line; and in the extraordinary agony of the wound, he was now dashing among the revolving circles like the lone mounted desperado Arnold, at the battle of Saratoga, carrying dismay wherever he went.[12]

But agonizing as was the wound of this whale, and an appalling spectacle enough, any way; yet the peculiar horror with which he seemed to inspire the rest of the herd, was owing to a cause which at first the intervening distance obscured from us. But at length we perceived that by one of the unimaginable accidents of the fishery, this whale had become entangled in the harpoon-line that he towed; he had also

---

* The sperm whale, as with all other species of the Leviathan, but unlike most other fish, breeds indifferently at all seasons; after a gestation which may probably be set down at nine months, producing but one at a time; though in some few known instances giving birth to an Esau and Jacob:°—a contingency provided for in suckling by two teats, curiously situated, one on each side of the anus; but the breasts themselves extend upwards from that. When by chance these precious parts in a nursing whale are cut by the hunter's lance, the mother's pouring milk and blood rivallingly discolor the sea for rods. The milk is very sweet and rich; it has been tasted by man; **it might do well with strawberries. When overflowing with mutual esteem, the whales salute *more hominum.***[11]

---

an Esau and Jacob: twins; sons of Isaac and Rebecca (Genesis 25.24–26).

run away with the cutting-spade in him; and while the free end of the rope attached to that weapon, had permanently caught in the coils of the harpoon-line round his tail, the cutting-spade itself had worked loose from his flesh. So that tormented to madness, he was now churning through the water, violently flailing with his flexible tail, and tossing the keen spade about him, wounding and murdering his own comrades.

This terrific object seemed to recall the whole herd from their stationary fright. First, the whales forming the margin of our lake began to crowd a little, and tumble against each other, as if lifted by half spent billows from afar; then the lake itself began faintly to heave and swell; the submarine bridal-chambers and nurseries vanished; in more and more contracting orbits the whales in the more central circles began to swim in thickening clusters. Yes, the long calm was departing. A low advancing hum was soon heard; and then like to the tumultuous masses of block-ice when the great river Hudson breaks up in Spring, the entire host of whales came tumbling upon their inner centre, as if to pile themselves up in one common mountain. Instantly Starbuck and Queequeg changed places; Starbuck taking the stern.

"Oars! Oars!" he intensely whispered, seizing the helm—"gripe your oars, and clutch your souls, now! My God, men, stand by! Shove him off, you Queequeg—the whale there!—prick him!—hit him! Stand up—stand up, and stay so! Spring, men—pull, men; never mind their backs—scrape them!—scrape away!"

The boat was now all but jammed between two vast black bulks, leaving a narrow Dardanelles between their long lengths. But by desperate endeavor we at last shot into a temporary opening; then giving way rapidly, and at the same time earnestly watching for another outlet. After many similar hair-breadth escapes, we at last swiftly glided into what had just been one of the outer circles, but now crossed by random whales, all violently making for one centre. This lucky salvation was cheaply purchased by the loss of Queequeg's hat, who, while standing in the bows to prick the fugitive whales, had his hat taken clean from his head by the air-eddy made by the sudden tossing of a pair of broad flukes close by.

Riotous and disordered as the universal commotion now was, it soon resolved itself into what seemed a systematic movement; for having clumped together at last in one dense body, they then renewed their onward flight with augmented fleetness. Further pursuit was useless; but the boats still lingered in their wake to pick up what drugged whales might be dropped astern, and likewise to secure one which Flask had killed and waifed. The waif is a pennoned pole,° two or three of which are carried by every boat; and which, when additional game is at hand, are inserted upright into the floating body of a dead whale, both to mark its place on the sea, and also as token of prior possession, should the boats of any other ship draw near.

The result of this lowering was somewhat illustrative of that sagacious saying in the Fishery,—the more whales the less fish. Of all the drugged whales only one was captured. The rest contrived to escape for the time, but only to be taken, as will hereafter be seen, by some other craft than the Pequod.

---

pennoned pole: pole with a pennant bearing a ship's symbol.

CHAPTER 88

SCHOOLS AND SCHOOLMASTERS

THE previous chapter gave account of an immense body or herd of Sperm Whales, and there was also then given the probable cause° inducing those vast aggregations.

Now, though such great bodies are at times encountered, yet, as must have been seen, even at the present day, small detached bands are occasionally observed, embracing from twenty to fifty individuals each. Such bands are known as schools. They generally are of two sorts; those composed almost entirely of females, and those mustering none but young vigorous males, or bulls, as they are familiarly designated.

In cavalier attendance upon the school of females, you invariably see a male of full grown magnitude, but not old; who, upon any alarm, evinces his gallantry by falling in the rear and covering the flight of his ladies. In truth, this gentleman is a luxurious Ottoman,° swimming about over the watery world, surroundingly accompanied by all the solaces and endearments of the harem. The contrast between this Ottoman and his concubines is striking; because, while he is always of the largest leviathanic proportions, the ladies, even at full growth, are not more than one third of the bulk of an average-sized male. They are comparatively delicate, indeed; I dare say, not to exceed half a dozen yards round the waist. Nevertheless, it cannot be denied, that upon the whole they are hereditarily entitled to *en bon point.*°

It is very curious to watch this harem and its lord in their indolent ramblings. Like fashionables, they are for ever on the move in leisurely search of variety. You meet them on the Line in time for the full flower of the Equatorial feeding season, having just returned, perhaps, from spending the summer in the Northern seas, and so cheating summer of all unpleasant weariness and warmth. By the time they have lounged up and down the promenade of the Equator awhile, they start for the Oriental waters in anticipation of the cool season there, and so evade the other excessive temperature of the year.

When serenely advancing on one of these journeys, if any strange suspicious sights are seen, my lord whale keeps a wary eye on his interesting family. Should any

probable cause: mutual protection against constant hunting. **Ottoman**: Turk. **en bon point**: enbonpoint (French), plumpness.

unwarrantably pert young Leviathan coming that way, presume to draw confidentially close to one of the ladies, with what prodigious fury the Bashaw° assails him, and chases him away! High times, indeed, if unprincipled young rakes like him are to be permitted to invade the sanctity of domestic bliss; though do what the Bashaw will, he cannot **keep** the most notorious Lothario **out of his bed**; for, alas! all fish **bed in common**. As ashore, the ladies often cause the most terrible duels among their rival admirers; just so with the whales, who sometimes come to deadly battle, and all for love. They fence with their long lower jaws, sometimes locking them together, and so striving for the supremacy like elks that warringly interweave their antlers. Not a few are captured having the deep scars of these encounters,—furrowed heads, broken teeth, scolloped fins; and in some instances, wrenched and dislocated mouths.

But supposing the invader of domestic bliss to betake himself away at the first rush of the harem's lord, then is it very diverting to watch that lord. Gently he insin-

REVISION NARRATIVE

Lotharios and Whales

Lothario is the "haughty, gallant, gay [carefree]" male lover in Nicholas Rowe's highly popular play "The Fair Penitent" (1703), and well before the nineteenth century, a "Lothario" had become any adventurous, usually heartless, "love-'em-and-leave-'em" libertine. Melville uses the word to describe young male whales challenging the dominance of any larger bull who, like an Ottoman or Turkish ruler (Bashaw or Pasha), is the protective, sexual master of a group of females, or harem. At the same time, he compares these encounters to the amorous courting of humans. Melville was on precarious ground, and knew it, because in writing *Typee* five years earlier, he (and his editors) had in successive stages pared down (in manuscript and print) various sexual jokes that also compared Polynesian male and female groupings to Roman and Turkish practice. Wary of further censorings by the British, Melville may have censored himself in his depiction of the antics of the Lothario and Bashaw whales. For instance, Melville, rather than an editor, was probably responsible for the revisions of the highlighted words in the text bracketed here in this sentence: "though do what the Bashaw will, he cannot [always frustrate] the most notorious Lothario [. . .]; for, alas! all fish [have very vague notions of the connubial tie]." In the following paragraph, he may have also deleted the comparison of Lothario to "pious Solomon devoutly worshipping among his thousand concubines." The joke in his next sentence is cleverly concealed, but Melville may have decided to dispense with it as well, although an editor may have caught on and cut it. The joke—that a Grand Turk whale is not worth hunting because he uses up his "unctuousness" (oiliness) among the ladies of his harem—plays on the facetious assumption (introduced in Ch. 32) that spermaceti is actually semen.

Bashaw: also Pasha; honorific Turkish title, implying, for western readers, a proud, overbearing man.

uates his vast bulk among them again and revels there awhile, still in tantalizing vicinity to young Lothario, **like pious Solomon devoutly worshipping among his thousand concubines.**[1] Granting other whales to be in sight, the fishermen will seldom give chase to one of these Grand Turks; **for these Grand Turks are too lavish of their strength, and hence their unctuousness is small**. As for the sons and the daughters they beget, why, those sons and daughters must take care of themselves; at least, with only the maternal help. For like certain other omnivorous roving lovers that might be named, my Lord Whale has no taste for the nursery, however much for the bower;° and so, being a great traveller, he leaves his anonymous babies all over the world; every baby an exotic. In good time, nevertheless, as the ardor of youth declines; as years and dumps increase; as reflection lends her solemn pauses; in short, as a general lassitude overtakes the sated Turk; then a love of ease and virtue supplants the love for maidens; our Ottoman enters upon the **impotent,** repentant, admonitory stage of life, forswears, disbands the harem, and grown to an exemplary, sulky old soul, goes about all alone among the meridians and parallels saying his prayers, and warning each young Leviathan from his **amorous** errors.

Now, as the harem of whales is called by the fishermen a school, so is the lord and master of that school technically known as the schoolmaster. It is therefore not in strict character, however admirably satirical, that after going to school himself, he should then go abroad inculcating not what he learned there, but the folly of it. His title, schoolmaster, would very naturally seem derived from the name bestowed upon the harem itself, but some have surmised that the man who first thus entitled this sort of Ottoman whale, must have read the memoirs of Vidocq, and informed himself what sort of a country-schoolmaster that famous Frenchman was in his younger days, and what was the nature of those occult lessons he inculcated into some of his pupils.[2]

The same secludedness and isolation to which the schoolmaster whale betakes himself in his advancing years, is true of all aged Sperm Whales. Almost universally, a lone whale—as a solitary Leviathan is called—proves an ancient one. Like venerable moss-bearded Daniel Boone, he will have no one near him but Nature herself;[3] and her he takes to wife in the wilderness of waters, and the best of wives she is, though she keeps so many moody secrets.

The schools composing none but young and vigorous males, previously mentioned, offer a strong contrast to the harem schools. For while those female whales are characteristically timid, the young males, or forty-barrel-bulls, as they call them, are by far the most pugnacious of all Leviathans, and proverbially the most dangerous to encounter; excepting those wondrous greyheaded, grizzled whales, sometimes met, and these will fight you like grim fiends exasperated by a penal gout.°

The Forty-barrel-bull schools are larger than the harem schools. Like a mob of young collegians, they are full of fight, fun, and wickedness, tumbling round the world at such a reckless, rollicking rate, that no prudent underwriter would insure

---

bower: woman's bedroom. **penal gout**: painful inflammation of the joints, typically affecting older men; in this case a punitive ailment caused by rich food, and drink.

them any more than he would a riotous lad at Yale or Harvard. They soon relinquish this turbulence though, and when about three fourths grown, break up, and separately go about in quest of settlements,° that is, harems.[4]

Another point of difference between the male and female schools is still more characteristic of the sexes. Say you strike a Forty-barrel-bull—poor devil! all his comrades quit him. But strike a member of the harem school, and her companions swim around her with every token of concern, sometimes lingering so near her and so long, as themselves to fall a prey.

settlements: matrimony; settling down.

CHAPTER 89

FAST-FISH AND LOOSE-FISH

T HE allusion to the waifs and waif-poles in the last chapter but one, necessitates some account of the laws and regulations of the whale fishery, of which the waif may be deemed the grand symbol and badge.

It frequently happens that when several ships are cruising in company, a whale may be struck by one vessel, then escape, and be finally killed and captured by another vessel; and herein are indirectly comprised many minor contingencies, all partaking of this one grand feature. For example,—after a weary and perilous chase and capture of a whale, the body may get loose from the ship by reason of a violent storm; and drifting far away to leeward, be retaken by a second whaler, who, in a calm, snugly tows it alongside, without risk of life or line. Thus the most vexatious and violent disputes would often arise between the fishermen, were there not some written or unwritten, universal, undisputed law applicable to all cases.

Perhaps the only formal whaling code authorized by legislative enactment, was that of Holland. It was decreed by the States-General in A.D. 1695. But though no other nation has ever had any written whaling law, yet the American fishermen have been their own legislators and lawyers in this matter. They have provided a system which for terse comprehensiveness surpasses Justinian's Pandects[1] and the By-laws of the Chinese Society for the Suppression of Meddling with other People's Business. Yes; these laws might be engraven on a Queen Anne's farthing,[2] or the barb of a harpoon, and worn round the neck, so small are they.

I. A Fast-Fish belongs to the party fast to it.

II. A Loose-Fish is fair game for anybody who can soonest catch it.

But what plays the mischief with this masterly code is the admirable brevity of it, which necessitates a vast volume of commentaries to expound it.

First: What is a Fast-Fish? Alive or dead a fish is technically fast, when it is connected with an occupied ship or boat, by any medium at all controllable by the occupant or occupants,—a mast, an oar, a nine-inch cable, a telegraph wire, or a strand of cobweb, it is all the same. Likewise a fish is technically fast when it bears a waif, or any other recognised symbol of possession; so long as the party waifing it plainly evince their ability at any time to take it alongside, as well as their intention so to do.

These are scientific commentaries; but the commentaries of the whalemen themselves sometimes consist in hard words and harder knocks—the Coke-upon-Littleton[3] of the fist. True, among the more upright and honorable whalemen allowances are always made for peculiar cases, where it would be an outrageous moral injustice for one party to claim possession of a whale previously chased or killed by another party. But others are by no means so scrupulous.

Some fifty years ago there was a curious case of whale-trover° litigated in England, wherein the plaintiffs set forth that after a hard chase of a whale in the Northern seas; and when indeed they (the plaintiffs) had succeeded in harpooning the fish; they were at last, through peril of their lives, obliged to forsake not only their lines, but their boat itself. Ultimately the defendants (the crew of another ship) came up with the whale, struck, killed, seized, and finally appropriated it before the very eyes of the plaintiffs. And when those defendants were remonstrated with, their captain snapped his fingers in the plaintiffs' teeth, and assured them that by **way** of doxology° to the deed he had done, he would now retain their line, harpoons, and boat, which had remained attached to the whale at the time of the seizure. Wherefore the plaintiffs now sued for the recovery of the value of their whale, line, harpoons, and boat.

Mr. Erskine was counsel for the defendants; Lord Ellenborough was the judge.[4] In the course of the defence, the witty Erskine went on to illustrate his position, by alluding to a recent crim. con.° case, wherein a gentleman, after in vain trying to bridle his wife's viciousness, had at last abandoned her upon the seas of life; but in the course of years, repenting of that step, he instituted an action to recover possession of her. **Erskine was on the other side; and he then supported it by saying,** that though the gentleman had originally harpooned the lady, and had once had her fast, and only by reason of the great stress of her plunging viciousness, had at last abandoned her; yet abandon her he did, so that she became a loose-fish; and therefore when a subsequent gentleman re-harpooned her, the lady then became that subsequent gentleman's property, along with whatever harpoon might have been found sticking in her.

Now in the present case Erskine contended that the examples of the whale and the lady were reciprocally illustrative of each other.

These pleadings, and the counter pleadings, being duly heard, the very learned judge in set terms decided, to wit,—That as for the boat, he awarded it to the plaintiffs, because they had merely abandoned it to save their lives; but that with regard to the controverted whale, harpoons, and line, they belonged to the defendants; the whale, because it was a Loose-Fish at the time of the final capture; and the harpoons and line because when the fish made off with them, it (the fish) acquired a property in those articles; and hence anybody who afterwards took the fish had a right to them. Now the defendants afterwards took the fish; ergo, the aforesaid articles were theirs.

---

trover: legal term for an attempt to recover damages for personal property held or used by another. ***by way of doxology***: in the manner of a song of praise to God affirming church doctrine that concludes a religious service. ***crim. con.***: "criminal conversation," legalese for adultery.

A common man looking at this decision of the very learned Judge, might possibly object to it. But ploughed up to the primary rock of the matter, the two great principles laid down in the twin whaling laws previously quoted, and applied and elucidated by Lord Ellenborough in the above cited case; these two laws touching Fast-Fish and Loose-Fish, I say, will, on reflection, be found the fundamentals of all human jurisprudence; for notwithstanding its complicated tracery of sculpture, the Temple of the Law, like the Temple of the Philistines, has but two props to stand on.[5]

Is it not a saying in every one's mouth, Possession is half of the law: that is, regardless of how the thing came into possession? But often possession is the whole of the law. What are the sinews and souls of Russian serfs and Republican° slaves but Fast-Fish, whereof possession is the whole of the law? What to the rapacious landlord is the widow's last mite but a Fast-Fish?[6] What is yonder undetected villain's marble mansion with a door-plate for a waif; what is that but a Fast-Fish? What is the ruinous discount which Mordecai, the broker,[7] gets from poor Woebegone, the bankrupt, on a loan to keep Woebegone's family from starvation; what is that ruinous discount but a Fast-Fish? What is the Archbishop of Savesoul's income of £100,000 seized from the scant bread and cheese of hundreds of thousands of broken-backed laborers (**all sure of heaven without any of Savesoul's help**) what is that globular 100,000 but a Fast-Fish? What are the Duke of Dunder's hereditary towns and hamlets but Fast-Fish? What to that redoubted harpooneer, John Bull, is poor Ireland, but a Fast-Fish? What to that apostolic lancer, Brother Jonathan, is Texas but a Fast-Fish?[8] And concerning all these, is not Possession the whole of the law?

But if the doctrine of Fast-Fish be pretty generally applicable, the kindred doctrine of Loose-Fish is still more widely so. That is internationally and universally applicable.

What was America in 1492 but a Loose-Fish, in which Columbus struck the Spanish standard by way of waifing it for his royal master and mistress? What was Poland to the Czar? What Greece to the Turk? What India to England? What at last will Mexico be to the United States? All Loose-Fish.[9]

What are the Rights of Man and the Liberties of the World but Loose-Fish? What all men's minds and opinions but Loose-Fish? What is the principle of religious belief in **them** but a Loose-Fish? What to the ostentatious smuggling verbalists are the thoughts of thinkers but Loose-Fish? What is the great globe itself but a Loose-Fish? And what are you, reader, but a Loose-Fish and a Fast-Fish, too?

Republican: American.

CHAPTER 90

HEADS OR TAILS

"De balena vero sufficit, si rex habeat caput, et regina caudam."
Bracton, l. 3, c. 3.[1]

LATIN from the books of the Laws of England, which taken along with the context, means, that of all whales captured by anybody on the coast of that land, the King, as Honorary Grand Harpooneer, must have the head, and the Queen be respectfully presented with the tail. A division which, in the whale, is much like halving an apple; there is no intermediate remainder. Now as this law, under a modified form, is to this day in force in England; and as it offers in various respects a strange anomaly touching the general law of Fast and Loose-Fish, it is here treated of in a separate chapter, on the same courteous principle that prompts the English railways to be at the expense of a separate car, specially reserved for the accommodation of royalty. In the first place, in curious proof of the fact that the above-mentioned law is still in force, I proceed to lay before you a circumstance that happened within the last two years.

It seems that some honest mariners of Dover, or Sandwich, or some one of the Cinque Ports,[2] had after a hard chase succeeded in killing and beaching a fine whale which they had originally descried afar off from the shore. Now the Cinque Ports are partially or somehow under the jurisdiction of a sort of policeman or beadle, called a Lord Warden. Holding the office directly from the crown, I believe, all the royal emoluments° incident to the Cinque Port territories become by assignment his. By some writers this office is called a sinecure.° But not so. Because the Lord Warden is busily employed at times in fobbing his perquisites;° which are his chiefly by virtue of that same fobbing of them.

Now when these poor sun-burnt mariners, bare-footed, and with their trowsers rolled high up on their eely legs, had wearily hauled their fat fish high and dry, promising themselves a good £150 from the precious oil and bone, and in fantasy sipping rare tea with their wives, and good ale with their cronies, upon the

---

emoluments: compensation, benefits. **sinecure**: paid position requiring little or no work.
fobbing his perquisites: pocketing his profits.

strength of their respective shares; up steps a very learned and most Christian and charitable gentleman, with a copy of Blackstone[3] under his arm; and laying it upon the whale's head, he says—"Hands off! this fish, my masters, is a Fast-Fish. I seize it as the Lord Warden's." Upon this the poor mariners in their respectful consternation—so truly English—knowing not what to say, fall to vigorously scratching their heads all round; meanwhile ruefully glancing from the whale to the stranger. But that did in nowise mend the matter, or at all soften the hard heart of the learned gentleman with the copy of Blackstone. At length one of them, after long scratching about for his ideas, made bold to speak.

"Please, sir, who is the Lord Warden?"

"The Duke."

"But the duke had nothing to do with taking this fish?"

"It is his."

"We have been at great trouble, and peril, and some expense, and is all that to go to the Duke's benefit; we getting nothing at all for our pains but our blisters?"

"It is his."

"Is the Duke so very poor as to be forced to this desperate mode of getting a livelihood?"

"It is his."

"I thought to relieve my old bed-ridden mother by part of my share of this whale."

"It is his."

"Won't the Duke be content with a quarter or a half?"

"It is his."

In a word, the whale was seized and sold, and his Grace the Duke of Wellington received the money. Thinking that viewed in some particular lights, the case might by a bare possibility in some small degree be deemed, under the circumstances, a rather hard one, an honest clergyman of the town respectfully addressed a note to his Grace, begging him to take the case of those unfortunate mariners into full consideration. To which my Lord Duke in substance replied (both letters were published) that he had already done so, and received the money, and would be obliged to the reverend gentleman if for the future he (the reverend gentleman) would decline meddling with other people's business. **Is this the still militant old man, standing at the corners of the three kingdoms, on all hands coercing alms of beggars?**[4]

It will readily be seen that in this case the alleged right of the Duke to the whale was a delegated one from the Sovereign. We must needs inquire then on what principle the Sovereign is originally invested with that right. The law itself has already been set forth. But Plowden[5] gives us the reason for it. Says Plowden, the whale so caught belongs to the King and Queen, "because of its superior excellence." And by the soundest commentators this has ever been held a cogent argument in such matters.

But why should the King have the head, and the Queen the tail? A reason for that, ye lawyers!

In his treatise on "Queen-Gold," or Queen-pinmoney, an old King's Bench author, one William Prynne,[6] thus discourseth: "**Ye** tail is **ye** Queen's, that **ye**

Queen's wardrobe may be supplied with **ye** whalebone." Now this was written at a time when the black limber bone of the Greenland or Right whale was largely used in ladies' bodices. But this same bone is not in the tail; it is in the head, which is a sad mistake for a sagacious lawyer like Prynne. But is the Queen a mermaid, to be presented with a tail? An allegorical meaning may lurk here.

There are two royal fish so styled by the English law writers—the whale and the sturgeon; both royal property under certain limitations, and nominally supplying the tenth branch of the crown's ordinary revenue. I know not that any other author has hinted of the matter; but by inference it seems to me that the sturgeon must be divided in the same way as the whale, the King receiving the highly dense and elastic head peculiar to that fish, which, symbolically regarded, may possibly be humorously grounded upon some presumed congeniality. And thus there seems a reason in all things, even in law.

CHAPTER 91

THE PEQUOD MEETS THE ROSE-BUD[1]

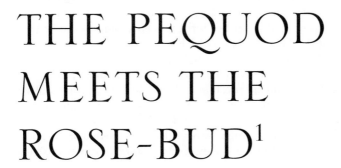

> "In vain it was to rake for Ambergriese in the paunch of this Leviathan, insufferable fetor° denying that inquiry."
>
> *Sir T. Browne, V. E.*[2]

IT was a week or two after the last whaling scene recounted, and when we were slowly sailing over a sleepy, vapory, mid-day sea, that the many noses on the Pequod's deck proved more vigilant discoverers than the three pairs of eyes aloft. A peculiar and not very pleasant smell was smelt in the sea.

"I will bet something now," said Stubb, "that somewhere hereabouts are some of those drugged whales we tickled the other day. I thought they would keel up° before long."

Presently, the vapors in advance slid aside; and there in the distance lay a ship, whose furled sails betokened that some sort of whale must be alongside. As we glided nearer, the stranger showed French colors from his peak; and by the eddying cloud of vulture sea-fowl that circled, and hovered, and swooped around him, it was plain that the whale alongside must be what the fishermen call a blasted whale, that is, a whale that has died unmolested on the sea, and so floated an unappropriated corpse. It may well be conceived, what an unsavory odor such a mass must exhale; worse than an Assyrian city in the plague,[3] when the living are incompetent to bury the departed. So intolerable indeed is it regarded by some, that no cupidity could persuade them to moor alongside of it. Yet are there those who will still do it; notwithstanding the fact that the oil obtained from such subjects is of a very inferior quality, and by no means of the nature of attar-of-rose.°

Coming still nearer with the expiring breeze, we saw that the Frenchman had a second whale alongside; and this second whale seemed even more of a nosegay° than the first. In truth, it turned out to be one of those problematical whales that seem to dry up and die with a sort of prodigious dyspepsia, or indigestion; leaving

---

fetor: stench. ***keel up***: capsize; but here, die. ***attar-of-rose***: aromatic oil from rose petals. ***nosegay***: small bunch of flowers, and its aroma.

358

their defunct bodies almost entirely bankrupt of anything like oil. Nevertheless, in the proper place we shall see that no knowing fisherman will ever turn up his nose at such a whale as this, however much he may shun blasted whales in general.

The Pequod had now swept so nigh to the stranger, that Stubb vowed he recognised his cutting spade-pole entangled in the lines that were knotted round the tail of one of these whales.

"There's a pretty fellow, now," he banteringly laughed, standing in the ship's bows, "there's a jackal for ye! I well know that these Crappoes° of Frenchmen are but poor devils in the fishery; sometimes lowering their boats for breakers, mistaking them for Sperm Whale spouts; yes, and sometimes sailing from their port with their hold full of boxes of tallow candles, and cases of snuffers, foreseeing that all the oil they will get won't be enough to dip the Captain's wick into;° aye, we all know these things; but look ye, here's a Crappo that is content with our leavings, the drugged whale there, I mean; aye, and is content too with scraping the dry bones of that other precious fish he has there. Poor devil! I say, pass round a hat, some one, and let's make him a present of a little oil for dear charity's sake. For what oil he'll get from that drugged whale there, wouldn't be fit to burn in a jail; no, not in a condemned cell. And as for the other whale, why, I'll agree to get more oil by chopping up and trying out these three masts of ours, than he'll get from that bundle of bones; though, now that I think of it, it may contain something worth a good deal more than oil; yes, ambergris.[4] I wonder now if our old man has thought of that. It's worth trying. Yes, I'm in for it;" and so saying he started for the quarter-deck.

By this time the faint air had become a complete calm; so that whether or no, the Pequod was now fairly entrapped in the smell, with no hope of escaping except by its breezing up again. Issuing from the cabin, Stubb now called his boat's crew, and pulled off for the stranger. Drawing across her bow, he perceived that in accordance with the fanciful French taste, the upper part of her stem-piece was carved in the likeness of a huge drooping stalk, was painted green, and for thorns had copper spikes projecting from it here and there; the whole terminating in a symmetrical folded bulb of a bright red color. Upon her head boards,[5] in large gilt letters, he read "Bouton de Rose,"—Rose-button, or Rose-bud; and this was the romantic name of this aromatic ship.

Though Stubb did not understand the *Bouton* part of the inscription, yet the word *rose,* and the bulbous figure-head put together, sufficiently explained the whole to him.

"A wooden rose-bud, eh?" he cried with his hand to his nose, "that will do very well; but how like all creation it smells!"

Now in order to hold direct communication with the people on deck, he had to pull round the bows to the starboard side, and thus come close to the blasted whale; and so talk over it.

Arrived then at this spot, with one hand still to his nose, he bawled—"Bouton-de-Rose, ahoy! are there any of you Bouton-de-Roses that speak English?"

Crappoes: slur on Frenchmen, from crapaud (French), meaning toad; here, also a pun on "crap." ***dip the captain's wick into***: jocular sexual expression.

"Yes," rejoined a Guernsey-man° from the bulwarks, who turned out to be the chief-mate.

"Well, then, my Bouton-de-Rose-bud, have you seen the White Whale?"

"*What* whale?"

"The *White* Whale—a Sperm Whale—Moby Dick, have ye seen him?"

"Never heard of such a whale. Cachalot Blanche! White Whale—no."

"Very good, then; good bye now, and I'll call again in a minute."

Then rapidly pulling back towards the Pequod, and seeing Ahab leaning over the quarter-deck rail awaiting his report, he moulded his two hands into a trumpet and shouted—"No, Sir! No!" Upon which Ahab retired, and Stubb returned to the Frenchman.

He now perceived that the Guernsey-man, who had just got into the chains, and was using a cutting-spade, had slung his nose in a sort of bag.

"What's the matter with your nose, there?" said Stubb. "Broke it?"

"I wish it was broken, or that I didn't have any nose at all!" answered the Guernsey-man, who did not seem to relish the job he was at very much. "But what are you holding *yours* for?"

"Oh, nothing! It's a wax nose; I have to hold it on. Fine day, aint it? Air rather gardenny, I should say; throw us a bunch of posies, will ye, Bouton-de-Rose?"

"What in the devil's name do you want here?" roared the Guernsey-man, flying into a sudden passion.

"Oh! keep cool—cool? yes, that's the word; why don't you pack those whales in ice while you're working at 'em? But joking aside, though; do you know, Rose-bud, that it's all nonsense trying to get any oil out of such whales? As for that dried up one, there, he hasn't a gill° in his whole carcase."

"I know that well enough; but, d'ye see, the Captain here won't believe it; this is his first voyage; he was a Cologne manufacturer[6] before. But come aboard, and mayhap he'll believe you, if he won't me; and so I'll get out of this dirty scrape."

"Anything to oblige ye, my sweet and pleasant fellow," rejoined Stubb, and with that he soon mounted to the deck. There a queer scene presented itself. The sailors, in tasselled caps of red worsted, were getting the heavy tackles in readiness for the whales. But they worked rather slow and talked very fast, and seemed in anything but a good humor. All their noses upwardly projected from their faces like so many jib-booms. Now and then pairs of them would drop their work, and run up to the mast-head to get some fresh air. Some thinking they would catch the plague, dipped oakum in coal-tar,° and at intervals held it to their nostrils. Others having broken the stems of their pipes almost short off at the bowl, were vigorously puffing tobacco-smoke, so that it constantly filled their olfactories.

Stubb was struck by a shower of outcries and anathemas proceeding from the Captain's round-house abaft;[7] and looking in that direction saw a fiery face thrust from behind the door, which was held ajar from within. This was the tormented surgeon, who, after in vain remonstrating against the proceedings of the day, had

---

Guernsey-man: from the French-speaking, British island of Guernsey in the English Channel. **gill**: half a cup. **coal-tar**: viscous black liquid obtained from coal.

betaken himself to the Captain's round-house (*cabinet*° he called it) to avoid the pest;° but still, could not help yelling out his entreaties and indignations at times.

Marking all this, Stubb argued well for his scheme, and turning to the Guernsey-man had a little chat with him, during which the stranger mate° expressed his detestation of his Captain as a conceited ignoramus, who had brought them all into so unsavory and unprofitable a pickle. Sounding him carefully, Stubb further perceived that the Guernsey-man had not the slightest suspicion concerning the ambergris. He therefore held his peace on that head, but otherwise was quite frank and confidential with him, so that the two quickly concocted a little plan for both circumventing and satirizing the Captain, without his at all dreaming of distrusting their sincerity. According to this little plan of theirs, the Guernsey-man, under cover of an interpreter's office, was to tell the Captain what he pleased, but as coming from Stubb; and as for Stubb, he was to utter any nonsense that should come uppermost in him during the interview.

By this time their destined victim appeared from his cabin. He was a small and dark, but rather delicate looking man for a sea-captain, with large whiskers and moustache, however; and wore a red cotton velvet vest with watch-seals° at his side. To this gentleman, Stubb was now politely introduced by the Guernsey-man, who at once ostentatiously put on the aspect of interpreting between them.

"What shall I say to him first?" said he.

"Why," said Stubb, eyeing the velvet vest and the watch and seals, "you may as well begin by telling him that he looks a sort of babyish to me, though I don't pretend to be a judge."

"He says, Monsieur," said the Guernsey-man, in French, turning to his captain, "that only yesterday his ship spoke a vessel, whose captain and chief-mate, with six sailors, had all died of a fever caught from a blasted whale they had brought alongside."

Upon this the captain started, and eagerly desired to know more.

"What now?" said the Guernsey-man to Stubb.

"Why, since he takes it so easy, tell him that now I have eyed him carefully, I'm quite certain that he's no more fit to command a whale-ship than a St. Jago monkey.[8] In fact, tell him from me he's a baboon."

"He vows and declares, Monsieur, that the other whale, the dried one, is far more deadly than the blasted one; in fine, Monsieur, he conjures us, as we value our lives, to cut loose from these fish."

Instantly the captain ran forward, and in a loud voice commanded his crew to desist from hoisting the cutting-tackles, and at once cast loose the cables and chains confining the whales to the ship.

"What now?" said the Guernsey-man, when the captain had returned to them.

"Why, let me see; yes, you may as well tell him now that—that—in fact, tell him I've diddled° him, and (aside to himself) perhaps somebody else."

---

cabinet: cabinet d'aisance (French), privy. **pest**: plague or pestilence (French and English); supposed contagion from the carcass. **stranger mate**: the mate of the "stranger vessel," *Rose-bud*. **watch-seals**: ornaments (usually gold) on a pocket-watch chain. **diddled**: cheated (with the sexual innuendo of "screwed").

"He says, Monsieur, that he's very happy to have been of any service to us."

Hearing this, the captain vowed that they were the grateful parties (meaning himself and mate) and concluded by inviting Stubb down into his cabin to drink a bottle of Bordeaux.

"He wants you to take a glass of wine with him," said the interpreter.

"Thank him heartily; but tell him it's against my principles to drink with the man I've diddled. In fact, tell him I must go."

"He says, Monsieur, that his principles won't admit of his drinking; but that if Monsieur wants to live another day to drink, then Monsieur had best drop all four boats, and pull the ship away from these whales, for it's so calm they won't drift."

By this time Stubb was over the side, and getting into his boat, hailed the Guernsey-man to this effect,—that having a long tow-line in his boat, he would do what he could to help them, by pulling out the lighter whale of the two from the ship's side. While the Frenchman's boats, then, were engaged in towing the ship one way, Stubb benevolently towed away at his whale the other way, ostentatiously slacking out a most unusually long tow-line.

Presently a breeze sprang up; Stubb feigned to cast off from the whale; hoisting his boats, the Frenchman soon increased his distance, while the Pequod slid in between him and Stubb's whale. Whereupon Stubb quickly pulled to the floating body, and hailing the Pequod to give notice of his intentions, at once proceeded to reap the fruit of his unrighteous cunning. Seizing his sharp boat-spade, he commenced an excavation in the body, a little behind the side fin. You would almost have thought he was digging a cellar there in the sea; and when at length his spade struck against the gaunt ribs, it was like turning up old Roman tiles and pottery buried in fat English loam. His boat's crew were all in high excitement, eagerly helping their chief, and looking as anxious as gold-hunters.

And all the time numberless fowls were diving, and ducking, and screaming, and yelling, and fighting around them. Stubb was beginning to look disappointed, especially as the horrible nosegay increased, when suddenly from out the very heart of this plague, there stole a faint stream of perfume,[9] which flowed through the tide of bad smells without being absorbed by it, as one river will flow into and then along with another, without at all blending with it for a time.

"I have it, I have it," cried Stubb, with delight, striking something in the subterranean regions, "a purse!° a purse!"

Dropping his spade, he thrust both hands in, and drew out handfuls of something that looked like ripe Windsor soap,° or rich mottled old cheese; very unctuous and savory withal. You might easily dent it with your thumb; it is of a hue between yellow and ash color. And this, good friends, is ambergris, worth a gold guinea an ounce to any druggist. Some six handfuls were obtained; but more was unavoidably lost in the sea, and still more, perhaps, might have been secured were it not for impatient Ahab's loud command to Stubb to desist, and come on board, else the ship would bid them good bye.

---

purse: prize of money. **Windsor soap**: scented toilet soap.

CHAPTER 92

AMBERGRIS

Now this ambergris is a very curious substance, and so important as an article of commerce, that in 1791 a certain Nantucket-born Captain Coffin was examined at the bar of the English House of Commons on that subject.[1] For at that time, and indeed until a comparatively late day, the precise origin of ambergris remained, like amber° itself, a problem to the learned. Though the word ambergris is but the French compound for grey amber, yet the two substances are quite distinct. For amber, though at times found on the sea-coast, is also dug up in some far inland soils, whereas ambergris is never found except upon the sea. Besides, amber is a hard, transparent, brittle, odorless substance, used for mouth-pieces to pipes, for beads and ornaments; but ambergris is soft, waxy, and so highly fragrant and spicy, that it is largely used in perfumery, in pastiles,° precious candles, hair-powders, and pomatum.° The Turks use it in cooking, and also carry it to Mecca, for the same purpose that frankincense is carried to St. Peter's in Rome. Some wine merchants drop a few grains into claret, to flavor it.

Who would think, then, that such fine ladies and gentlemen should regale themselves with an essence found in the inglorious bowels of a sick whale! Yet so it is. By some, ambergris is supposed to be the cause, and by others the effect, of the dyspepsia in the whale. How to cure such a dyspepsia it were hard to say, unless by administering three or four boat loads of Brandreth's pills,° and then running out of harm's way, as laborers do in blasting rocks.

I have forgotten to say that there were found in this ambergris, certain hard, round, bony plates, which at first Stubb thought might be sailors' trousers buttons; but it afterwards turned out that they were nothing more than pieces of small squid bones embalmed in that manner.

Now that the incorruption of this most fragrant ambergris should be found in the heart of such decay; is this nothing? Bethink thee of that saying of St. Paul in Corinthians, about corruption and incorruption; how that we are sown in dishonor, but raised in glory.[2] And likewise call to mind that saying of Paracelsus about what it

---

amber: translucent, yellow-brown, fossilized sap. **pastiles**: deodorizing tablets. **pomatum**: pomade, hair ointment. **Brandreth's pills**: a brand of laxative.

is that maketh the best musk.[3] Also forget not the strange fact that of all things of ill-savor, Cologne-water, in its rudimental manufacturing stages, is the worst.

I should like to conclude the chapter with the above appeal, but cannot, owing to my anxiety to repel a charge often made against whalemen, and which, in the estimation of some already biased minds, might be considered as indirectly substantiated by what has been said of the Frenchman's two whales. Elsewhere in this volume° the slanderous aspersion has been disproved, that the vocation of whaling is throughout a slatternly, untidy business. But there is another thing to rebut. They hint that all whales always smell bad. Now how did this odious stigma originate?

I opine, that it is plainly traceable to the first arrival of the Greenland whaling ships in London, more than two centuries ago. Because those whalemen did not then, and do not now, try out° their oil at sea as the Southern ships have always done; but cutting up the fresh blubber in small bits, thrust it through the bung holes of large casks, and carry it home in that manner; the shortness of the season in those Icy Seas, and the sudden and violent storms to which they are exposed, forbidding any other course. The consequence is, that upon breaking into the hold, and unloading one of these whale cemeteries, in the Greenland dock, a savor is given forth somewhat similar to that arising from excavating an old city grave-yard, for the foundations of a Lying-in° Hospital.

I partly surmise also, that this wicked charge against whalers may be likewise imputed to the existence on the coast of Greenland, in former times, of a Dutch village called Schmerenburgh or Smeerenberg, which latter name is the one used by the learned Fogo Von Slack, in his great work on Smells,[4] a text-book on that subject. As its name imports (smeer, fat; berg, to put up), this village was founded in order to afford a place for the blubber of the Dutch whale fleet to be tried out, without being taken home to Holland for that purpose. It was a collection of furnaces, fat-kettles, and oil sheds; and when the works were in full operation certainly gave forth no very pleasant savor. But all this is quite different with a South Sea Sperm Whaler; which in a voyage of four years perhaps, after completely filling her hold with oil, does not, perhaps, consume fifty days in the business of boiling out; and in the state that it is casked, the oil is nearly scentless. The truth is, that living or dead, if but decently treated, whales as a species are by no means creatures of ill odor; nor can whalemen be recognised, as the people of the middle ages affected to detect a Jew in the company, by the nose.[5] Nor indeed can the whale possibly be otherwise than fragrant, when, as a general thing, he enjoys such high health; taking abundance of exercise; always out of doors; though, it is true, seldom in the open air. I say, that the motion of a Sperm Whale's flukes above water dispenses a perfume, as when a musk-scented lady rustles her dress in a warm parlor. What then shall I liken the Sperm Whale to for fragrance, considering his magnitude? Must it not be to that famous elephant, with jewelled tusks, and redolent with myrrh, which was led out of an Indian town to do honor to Alexander the Great?[6]

Elsewhere in this volume: see Ch. 98. *try out*: extract oil from blubber by heating. *Lying-in*: maternity.

THE CASTAWAY

I T was but some few days after encountering the Frenchman, that a most significant event befell the most insignificant of the Pequod's crew; an event most lamentable; and which ended in providing the sometimes madly merry and predestinated craft with a living and ever accompanying prophecy of whatever shattered sequel might prove her own.

Now, in the whale ship, it is not every one that goes in the boats. Some few hands are reserved called ship-keepers, whose province it is to work the vessel while the boats are pursuing the whale. As a general thing, these ship-keepers are as hardy fellows as the men comprising the boats' crews. But if there happen to be an unduly slender, clumsy, or timorous wight in the ship, that wight is certain to be made a ship-keeper. It was so in the Pequod with the little negro Pippin by nick-name, Pip by abbreviation. Poor Pip! ye have heard of him before;° ye must remember his tambourine on that dramatic midnight, so gloomy-jolly.

In outer aspect, Pip and Dough-Boy made a match, like a black pony and a white one, of equal developments, though of dissimilar color, driven in one eccentric span. But while hapless Dough-Boy was by nature dull and torpid in his intellects, Pip, though over tender-hearted, was at bottom very bright, with that pleasant, genial, jolly brightness peculiar to his tribe; a tribe, which ever enjoy all holidays and festivities with finer, freer relish than any other race. For blacks, the year's calendar should show naught but three hundred and sixty-five Fourth of Julys and New Year's Days. Nor smile so, while I write that this little black was brilliant, for even blackness has its brilliancy; behold yon lustrous ebony, panelled in king's cabinets. But Pip loved life, and all life's peaceable securities; so that the panic-striking business in which he had somehow unaccountably become entrapped, had most sadly blurred his brightness; though, as ere long will be seen, what was thus temporarily subdued in him, in the end was destined to be luridly illumined by strange wild fires, that fictitiously showed him off to ten times the natural lustre with which in his native Tolland County in Connecticut,[1] he had once enlivened many a fiddler's frolic on the green; and at melodious even-tide, with his gay ha-ha! had turned the round horizon

ye have heard of him before: in Ch. 40.

into one star-belled tambourine. So, though in the clear air of day, suspended against a blue-veined neck, the pure-watered diamond drop will healthful glow; yet, when the cunning jeweller would show you the diamond in its most impressive lustre, he lays it against a gloomy ground, and then lights it up, not by the sun, but by some unnatural gases. Then come out those fiery effulgences, infernally superb; then the evil-blazing diamond, once the divinest symbol of the crystal skies, looks like some crown-jewel stolen from the King of Hell. But let us to the story.

It came to pass, that in the ambergris affair Stubb's after-oarsman chanced so to sprain his hand, as for a time to become quite maimed; and, temporarily, Pip was put into his place.

The first time Stubb lowered with him, Pip evinced much nervousness; but happily, for that time, escaped close contact with the whale; and therefore came off not altogether discreditably; though Stubb observing him, took care, afterwards, to exhort him to cherish his courageousness to the utmost, for he might often find it needful.

Now upon the second lowering, the boat paddled upon the whale; and as the fish received the darted iron, it gave its customary rap,° which happened, in this instance, to be right under poor Pip's seat. The involuntary consternation of the moment caused him to leap, paddle in hand, out of the boat; and in such a way, that part of the slack whale line coming against his chest, he breasted it overboard with him, so as to become entangled in it, when at last plumping into the water. That instant the stricken whale started on a fierce run, the line swiftly straightened; and presto! poor Pip came all foaming up to the chocks of the boat, remorselessly dragged there by the line, which had taken several turns around his chest and neck.

Tashtego stood in the bows. He was full of the fire of the hunt. He hated Pip for a poltroon.° Snatching the boat-knife from its sheath, he suspended its sharp edge over the line, and turning towards Stubb, exclaimed interrogatively, "Cut?" Meantime Pip's blue, choked face plainly looked, Do, for God's sake! All passed in a flash. In less than half a minute, this entire thing happened.

"Damn him, cut!" roared Stubb; and so the whale was lost and Pip was saved.

So soon as he recovered himself, the poor little negro was assailed by yells and execrations from the crew. Tranquilly permitting these irregular cursings to evaporate, Stubb then in a plain, business-like, but still half humorous manner, cursed Pip officially; and that done, unofficially gave him much wholesome advice. The substance was, Never jump from a boat, Pip, except—but all the rest was indefinite, as the soundest advice ever is. Now, in general, *Stick to the boat,* is your true motto in whaling; but cases will sometimes happen when *Leap from the boat,* is still better. Moreover, as if perceiving at last that if he should give undiluted conscientious advice to Pip, he would be leaving him too wide a margin to jump in for the future; Stubb suddenly dropped all advice, and concluded with a peremptory command, "Stick to the boat, Pip, or by the Lord, I won't pick you up if you jump; mind that. We can't afford to lose whales by the likes of you; a whale would sell for thirty times what you would, Pip, in Alabama. Bear that in mind, and don't jump any more." Hereby perhaps Stubb indirectly hinted, that though man loved his fellow, yet man is a money-making animal, which propensity too often interferes with his benevolence.

---

rap: convulsive blow with its tail. **poltroon**: coward.

But we are all in the hands of the Gods; and Pip jumped again. It was under very similar circumstances to the first performance; but this time he did not breast out the line; and hence, when the whale started to run, Pip was left behind on the sea, like a hurried traveller's trunk. Alas! Stubb was but too true to his word. It was a beautiful, bounteous, blue day; the spangled sea calm and cool, and flatly stretching away, all round, to the horizon, like gold-beater's skin° hammered out to the extremest. Bobbing up and down in that sea, Pip's ebon head showed like a head of cloves. No boat-knife was lifted when he fell so rapidly astern. Stubb's inexorable back was turned upon him; and the whale was winged. In three minutes, a whole mile of shoreless ocean was between Pip and Stubb. Out from the centre of the sea, poor Pip turned his crisp, curling, black head to the sun, another lonely castaway, though the loftiest and the brightest.

Now, in calm weather, to swim in the open ocean is as easy to the practised swimmer as to ride in a spring-carriage ashore. But the awful lonesomeness is intolerable. The intense concentration of self in the middle of such a heartless immensity, my God! who can tell it? Mark, how when sailors in a dead calm bathe in the open sea—mark how closely they hug their ship and only coast along her sides.

But had Stubb really abandoned the poor little negro to his fate? No; he did not mean to, at least. Because there were two boats in his wake, and he supposed, no doubt, that they would of course come up to Pip very quickly, and pick him up; though, indeed, such **considerations** towards oarsmen jeopardized through their own timidity, is not always manifested by the hunters in all similar instances; and such instances not unfrequently occur; almost invariably in the fishery, a coward, so called, is marked with the same ruthless detestation peculiar to military navies and armies.

But it so happened, that those boats, without seeing Pip, suddenly spying whales close to them on one side, turned, and gave chase; and Stubb's boat was now so far away, and he and all his crew so intent upon his fish, that Pip's ringed horizon began to expand around him miserably. By the merest chance the ship itself at last rescued him; but from that hour the little negro went about the deck an idiot; such, at least, they said he was. The sea had jeeringly kept his finite body up, but drowned the infinite of his soul. Not drowned entirely, though. Rather carried down alive to wondrous depths,[2] where strange shapes of the unwarped primal world glided to and fro before his passive eyes; and the miser-merman, Wisdom,[3] revealed his hoarded heaps; and among the joyous, heartless, ever-juvenile eternities, Pip saw the multitudinous, God-omnipresent, coral insects, that out of the firmament of waters heaved the colossal orbs. He saw God's foot upon the treadle° of the loom, and spoke it; and therefore his shipmates called him mad. So man's insanity is heaven's sense;[4] and wandering from all mortal reason, man comes at last to that celestial thought, which, to reason, is absurd and frantic; and weal or woe, feels then uncompromised**, indifferent as his God**.

For the rest, blame not Stubb too hardly. The thing is common in that fishery; and in the sequel of the narrative, it will then be seen what like abandonment befell myself.[5]

---

gold-beater's skin: animal membrane used in beating gold; but here confused with gold-leaf.
treadle: pedal or lever.

CHAPTER 94

A SQUEEZE OF THE HAND

THAT whale of Stubb's, so dearly purchased, was duly brought to the Pequod's side, where all those cutting and hoisting operations previously detailed, were regularly gone through, even to the baling of the Heidelburgh Tun, or Case.

While some were occupied with this latter duty, others were employed in dragging away the larger tubs, so soon as filled with the sperm; and when the proper time arrived, this same sperm was carefully manipulated ere going to the try-works,° of which anon.

It had cooled and crystallized to such a degree, that when, with several others, I sat down before a large Constantine's bath[1] of it, I found it strangely concreted into lumps, here and there rolling about in the liquid part. It was our business to squeeze these lumps back into fluid. A sweet and unctuous duty! No wonder that in old times this sperm was such a favorite cosmetic. Such a clearer! such a sweetener! such a softener! such a delicious mollifier! After having my hands in it for only a few minutes, my fingers felt like eels, and began, as it were, to serpentine and spiralize.

As I sat there at my ease, cross-legged on the deck; after the bitter exertion at the windlass; under a blue tranquil sky; the ship under indolent sail, and gliding so serenely along; as I bathed my hands among those soft, gentle globules of infiltrated tissues, woven almost within the hour; as they richly broke to my fingers, and discharged all their opulence, like fully ripe grapes their wine; as I snuffed up that uncontaminated aroma,—literally and truly, like the smell of spring violets; I declare to you, that for the time I lived as in a musky meadow; I forgot all about our horrible oath; in that inexpressible sperm, I washed my hands and my heart of it; I almost began to credit the old Paracelsan superstition that sperm is of rare virtue in allaying the heat of anger:[2] while bathing in that bath, I felt divinely free from all ill-will, or petulance, or malice, of any sort whatsoever.

Squeeze! squeeze! squeeze! all the morning long; I squeezed that sperm till I myself almost melted into it; I squeezed that sperm till a strange sort of insanity came over me; and I found myself unwittingly squeezing my co-laborers' hands in it, mistaking their hands for the gentle globules. Such an abounding, affectionate,

try-works: brick furnace with iron cauldrons in which oil is boiled out of blubber.

friendly, loving feeling did this avocation beget; that at last I was continually squeezing their hands, and looking up into their eyes sentimentally; as much as to say,—Oh! my dear fellow beings, why should we longer cherish any social acerbities, or know the slightest ill-humor or envy! Come; let us squeeze hands all round; nay, let us all squeeze ourselves into each other; let us squeeze ourselves universally into the very milk and sperm of kindness.

Would that I could keep squeezing that sperm for ever! For now, since by many prolonged, repeated experiences, I have perceived that in all cases man must eventually lower, or at least shift, his conceit of attainable felicity; not placing it anywhere in the intellect or the fancy; but in the wife, the heart, the bed, the table, the saddle, the fire-side, the country; now that I have perceived all this, I am ready to squeeze case eternally. In thoughts of the visions of the night, I saw long rows of angels in paradise, each with his hands in a jar of spermaceti.[3]

*　　*　　*　　*　　*　　*　　*　　*　　*

Now, while discoursing of sperm, it behooves to speak of other things akin to it, in the business of preparing the sperm whale for the try-works.

First comes white-horse, so called, which is obtained from the tapering part of the fish, and also from the thicker portions of his flukes. It is tough with congealed tendons—a wad of muscle—but still contains some oil. After being severed from the whale, the white-horse is first cut into portable oblongs ere going to the mincer. They look much like blocks of Berkshire marble.

Plum-pudding is the term bestowed upon certain fragmentary parts of the whale's flesh, here and there adhering to the blanket of blubber, and often participating to a considerable degree in its unctuousness. It is a most refreshing, convivial, beautiful object to behold. As its name imports, it is of an exceedingly rich, mottled tint, with a bestreaked snowy and golden ground, dotted with spots of the deepest crimson and purple.[4] It is plums of rubies, in pictures of citron.° Spite of reason, it is hard to keep yourself from eating it. I confess, that once I stole behind the foremast to try it. It tasted something as I should conceive a royal cutlet from the thigh of Louis le Gros[5] might have tasted, supposing him to have been killed the first day after the venison season, and that particular venison season contemporary with an unusually fine vintage of the vineyards of Champagne.

There is another substance, and a very singular one, which turns up in the course of this business, but which I feel it to be very puzzling adequately to describe. It is called slobgollion; an appellation original with the whalemen, and even so is the nature of the substance. It is an ineffably oozy, stringy affair, most frequently found in the tubs of sperm, after a prolonged squeezing, and subsequent decanting. I hold it to be the wondrously thin, ruptured membranes of the case, coalescing.

Gurry, so called, is a term properly belonging to right whalemen, but sometimes incidentally used by the sperm fishermen. It designates the dark, glutinous substance which is scraped off the back of the Greenland or right whale, and much of which covers the decks of those inferior souls who hunt that ignoble Leviathan.

---

citron: yellowish fruit.

Nippers. Strictly this word is not indigenous to the whale's vocabulary. But as applied by whalemen, it becomes so. A whaleman's nipper is a short firm strip of tendinous stuff cut from the tapering part of Leviathan's tail: it averages an inch in thickness, and for the rest, is about the size of the iron part of a hoe. Edgewise moved along the oily deck, it operates like a leathern squilgee;° and by nameless blandishments, as of magic, allures along with it all impurities.

But to learn all about these recondite matters, your best way is at once to descend into the blubber-room, and have a long talk with its inmates. This place has previously been mentioned° as the receptacle for the blanket-pieces, when stript and hoisted from the whale. When the proper time arrives for cutting up its contents, this apartment is a scene of terror to all tyros, especially by night. On one side, lit by a dull lantern, a space has been left clear for the workmen. They generally go in pairs,—a pike-and-gaff-man and a spade-man. The whaling-pike is similar to a frigate's boarding-weapon of the same name. The gaff is something like a boat-hook. With his gaff, the gaffman hooks on to a sheet of blubber, and strives to hold it from slipping, as the ship pitches and lurches about. Meanwhile, the spade-man stands on the sheet itself, perpendicularly chopping it into the portable horse-pieces.° This spade is sharp as hone can make it; the spademan's feet are shoeless; the thing he stands on will sometimes irresistibly slide away from him, like a sledge. If he cuts off one of his own toes, or one of his assistant's, would you be very much astonished? Toes are scarce among veteran blubber-room men.

squilgee: squeegee. **previously been mentioned**: see Ch. 67. **horse-pieces**: blocks of blubber about 10 inches wide and 2 feet long.

CHAPTER 95

THE CASSOCK

H AD you stepped on board the Pequod at a certain juncture of this post-mortem-izing of the whale; and had you strolled forward nigh the windlass, pretty sure am I that you would have scanned with no small curiosity a very strange, enigmatical object, which you would have seen there, lying along lengthwise in the lee scuppers. Not the wondrous cistern in the whale's huge head; not the prodigy of his unhinged lower jaw; not the miracle of his symmetrical tail; none of these would so surprise you, as half a glimpse of that unaccountable cone,°—longer than a Kentuckian is tall, nigh a foot in diameter at the base, and jet-black as Yojo, the ebony idol of Queequeg. And an idol, indeed, it is; or, rather, in old times, its likeness was. Such an idol as that found in the secret groves of Queen Maachah in Judea; and for worshipping which, king Asa, her son, did depose her, and destroyed the idol, and burnt it for an abomination at the brook Kedron, as darkly set forth in the 15th chapter of the first book of Kings.[1]

Look at the sailor, called the mincer, who now comes along, and assisted by two allies, heavily backs the grandissimus,° as the mariners call it, and with bowed shoulders, staggers off with it as if he were a grenadier carrying a dead comrade from the field. Extending it upon the forecastle deck, he now proceeds cylindrically to remove its dark pelt, as an African hunter the pelt of a boa. This done he turns the pelt inside out, like a pantaloon leg; gives it a good stretching, so as almost to double its diameter; and at last hangs it, well spread, in the rigging, to dry. Ere long, it is taken down; when removing some three feet of it, towards the pointed extremity, and then cutting two slits for arm-holes at the other end, he lengthwise slips himself bodily into it. The mincer now stands before you invested in the full canonicals° of his calling. Immemorial to all his order, this investiture alone will adequately protect him, while employed in the peculiar functions of his office.

That office consists in mincing the horse-pieces of blubber for the pots; an operation which is conducted at a curious wooden horse, planted endwise against the bulwarks, and with a capacious tub beneath it, into which the minced pieces

---

unaccountable cone: the whale's penis. **grandissimus**: big one; here the whale's penis. **canonicals**: clerical garments, but here the whale's foreskin.

drop, fast as the sheets from a rapt orator's desk. Arrayed in decent black; occupying a conspicuous pulpit; intent on bible leaves;° what a candidate for an archbish-oprick,[2] what a lad for a Pope were this mincer!*

* Bible leaves! Bible leaves! This is the invariable cry from the mates to the mincer. It enjoins him to be careful, and cut his work into as thin slices as possible, inasmuch as by so doing the business of boiling **out** the oil is much accelerated, and its quantity considerably increased, besides perhaps improving it in quality.

---

bible leaves: thin slices (like pages in a Bible) into which the mincer cuts the horse-pieces.

CHAPTER 96

THE TRY-WORKS

BESIDES her hoisted boats, an American whaler is outwardly distinguished by her try-works. She presents the curious anomaly of the most solid masonry joining with oak and hemp in constituting the completed ship. It is as if from the open field a brick-kiln were transported to her planks.

The try-works are planted between the foremast and main-mast, the most roomy part of the deck. The timbers beneath are of a peculiar strength, fitted to sustain the weight of an almost solid mass of brick and mortar, some ten feet by eight square, and five in height. The foundation does not penetrate the deck, but the masonry is firmly secured to the surface by ponderous knees of iron bracing it on all sides, and screwing it down to the timbers. On the flanks it is cased with wood, and at top completely covered by a large, sloping, battened° hatchway. Removing this hatch we expose the great try-pots, two in number, and each of several barrels' capacity. When not in use, they are kept remarkably clean. Sometimes they are polished with soapstone and sand, till they shine within like silver punch-bowls. During the night-watches some cynical old sailors will crawl into them and coil themselves away there for a nap. While employed in polishing them—one man in each pot, side by side— many confidential communications are carried on, over the iron lips. It is a place also for profound mathematical meditation. It was in the left hand try-pot of the Pequod, with the soapstone diligently circling round me, that I was first indirectly struck by the remarkable fact, that in geometry all bodies gliding along the cycloid,[1] my soapstone for example, will descend from any point in precisely the same time.

Removing the fire-board from the front of the try-works, the bare masonry of that side is exposed, penetrated by the two iron mouths of the furnaces, directly underneath the pots. These mouths are fitted with heavy doors of iron. The intense heat of the fire is prevented from communicating itself to the deck, by means of a shallow reservoir extending under the entire inclosed surface of the works. By a tunnel inserted at the rear, this reservoir is kept replenished with water as fast as it evaporates. There are no external chimneys; they open direct from the rear wall. And here let us go back for a moment.

battened: tightly covered.

It was about nine o'clock at night that the Pequod's try-works were first started on this present voyage. It belonged to Stubb to oversee the business.

"All ready there? Off hatch, then, and start her. You cook, fire the works." This was an easy thing, for the carpenter had been thrusting his shavings into the furnace throughout the passage. Here be it said that in a whaling voyage the first fire in the try-works has to be fed for a time with wood. After that no wood is used, except as a means of quick ignition to the staple fuel. In a word, after being tried out, the crisp, shrivelled blubber, now called scraps or fritters, still contains considerable of its unctuous properties. These fritters feed the flames. Like **a plethoric burning martyr, or** a self-consuming misanthrope, once ignited, the whale supplies his own fuel and burns by his own body. Would that he consumed his own smoke! for his smoke is horrible to inhale, and inhale it you must, and not only that, but you must live in it for the time. It has an unspeakable, wild, Hindoo odor about it, such as may lurk in the vicinity of funereal pyres. **It smells like the left wing of the day of judgment; it is an argument for the pit.**[2]

By midnight the works were in full operation. We were clear from the **carcase**; sail had been made; the wind was freshening; the wild ocean darkness was intense. But that darkness was licked up by the fierce flames, which at intervals forked forth from the sooty flues, and illuminated every lofty rope in the rigging, as with the famed Greek fire.[3] The burning ship drove on, as if remorselessly commissioned to some vengeful deed. So the pitch and sulphur-freighted brigs of the bold Hydriote, Canaris, issuing from their midnight harbors, with broad sheets of flame for sails, bore down upon the Turkish frigates, and folded them in conflagrations.[4]

The hatch, removed from the top of the works, now afforded a wide hearth in front of them. Standing on this were the Tartarean shapes of the pagan harpooneers, always the whale-ship's stokers. With huge pronged poles they pitched hissing masses of blubber into the scalding pots, or stirred up the fires beneath, till the

REVISION NARRATIVE

Burning Martyrs

The British edition made two expurgations in Melville's seemingly innocuous explanation of how to fire up the try-works furnace. According to Ishmael, once the fire is started with wood, and once pieces of blubber have been rendered like crisp bacon, these remnant fritters are used to fuel the fire. Thus, the whale can be said to burn itself. But calling the whale in this condition "a plethoric burning martyr" verged on blasphemy and was cut, if not for the reference to victims such as Wycliffe and Cranmer (both burned at the stake for their religious views and mentioned in Ch. 35) then for the word "plethoric" (which means a superabundance of blood and implies a pathological excessiveness). The last sentence of the paragraph was also cut, probably not for its irreverence, but for its presumed crudeness in evoking the "unspeakable" smell of damnation and hell.

snaky flames darted, curling, out of the doors to catch them by the feet. The smoke rolled away in sullen heaps. To every pitch of the ship there was a pitch of the boiling oil, which seemed all eagerness to leap into their faces. Opposite the mouth of the works, on the further side of the wide wooden hearth, was the windlass. This served for a sea-sofa. Here lounged the watch, when not otherwise employed, looking into the red heat of the fire, till their eyes felt scorched in their heads. Their tawny features, now all begrimed with smoke and sweat, their matted beards, and the contrasting barbaric brilliancy of their teeth, all these were strangely revealed in the capricious emblazonings of the works. As they narrated to each other their unholy adventures, their tales of terror told in words of mirth; as their uncivilized laughter forked upwards out of them, like the flames from the furnace; as to and fro, in their front, the harpooneers wildly gesticulated with their huge pronged forks and dippers; as the wind howled on, and the sea leaped, and the ship groaned and dived, and yet steadfastly shot her red hell further and further into the blackness of the sea and the night, and scornfully champed the white bone in her mouth,° and viciously spat round her on all sides; then the rushing Pequod, freighted with savages, and laden with fire, and burning a corpse, and plunging into that blackness of darkness,[5] seemed the material counterpart of her monomaniac commander's soul.

So seemed it to me, as I stood at her helm, and for long hours silently guided the way of this fire-ship on the sea. Wrapped, for that interval, in darkness myself, I but the better saw the redness, the madness, the ghastliness of others. The continual sight of the fiend shapes before me, capering half in smoke and half in fire, these at last begat kindred visions in my soul, so soon as I began to yield to that unaccountable drowsiness which ever would come over me at a midnight helm.

But that night, in particular, a strange (and ever since inexplicable) thing occurred to me. Starting from a brief standing sleep, I was horribly conscious of something fatally wrong. The jaw-bone tiller smote my side, which leaned against it; in my ears was the low hum of sails, just beginning to shake in the wind; I thought my eyes were open; I was half conscious of putting my fingers to the lids and mechanically stretching them still further apart. But, spite of all this, I could see no compass before me to steer by; though it seemed but a minute since I had been watching the card,° by the steady binnacle lamp illuminating it. Nothing seemed before me but a jet gloom, now and then made ghastly by flashes of redness. Uppermost was the impression, that whatever swift, rushing thing I stood on was not so much bound to any haven ahead as rushing from all havens astern. A stark, bewildered feeling, as of death, came over me. Convulsively my hands grasped the tiller, but with the crazy conceit that the tiller was, somehow, in some enchanted way, inverted. My God! what is the matter with me? thought I. Lo! in my brief sleep I had turned myself about, and was fronting the ship's stern, with my back to her prow and the compass. In an instant I faced back, just in time to prevent the vessel from flying up into the wind, and very probably capsizing her. How glad and how grateful the relief from this unnatural hallucination of the night, and the fatal contingency of being brought by the lee![6]

white bone in her mouth: foamy wave at the bow.   **card**: short for "compass card," flat surface on which the directional points are marked.

Look not too long in the face of the fire, O man! Never dream with thy hand on the helm! Turn not thy back to the compass; accept the first hint of the hitching tiller; believe not the artificial fire, when its redness makes all things look ghastly. To-morrow, in the natural sun, the skies will be bright; those who glared like devils in the forking flames, the morn will show in far other, at least gentler, relief; the glori-ous, golden, glad sun, the only true lamp—all others but liars!

Nevertheless the sun hides not Virginia's Dismal Swamp, nor Rome's accursed Campagna, nor wide Sahara,[7] nor all the millions of miles of deserts and of griefs beneath the moon. The sun hides not the ocean, which is the dark side of this earth, and which is two thirds of this earth.[8] So, therefore, that mortal man who hath more of joy than sorrow in him, that mortal man cannot be true—not true, or undevel-oped.° With books the same. The truest of all men was the Man of Sorrows, and the truest of all books is Solomon's, and Ecclesiastes is the fine hammered steel of woe. "All is vanity."[9] ALL. This wilful world hath not got hold of unchristian Solomon's wis-dom yet. But he who dodges hospitals and jails, and walks fast crossing grave-yards, and would rather talk of operas than hell; calls Cowper, Young, Pascal, Rousseau, poor devils all of sick men;[10] and throughout a care-free lifetime swears by Rabelais[11] as passing wise, and therefore jolly;—not that man is fitted to sit down on tomb-stones, and break the green damp mould with unfathomably wondrous Solomon.

But even Solomon, he says, "the man that wandereth out of the way of under-standing shall remain" (*i. e.* even while living) "in the congregation of the dead."[12] Give not thyself up, then, to fire, lest it invert thee, deaden thee; as for the time it did me. There is a wisdom that is woe; but there is a woe that is madness. And there is a Catskill eagle in some souls that can alike dive down into the blackest gorges, and soar out of them again and become invisible in the sunny spaces. And even if he for ever flies within the gorge, that gorge is in the mountains; so that even in his lowest swoop the mountain eagle is still higher than other birds upon the plain, even though they soar.

*or **undeveloped***: or else immature.

CHAPTER 97

THE LAMP

H AD you descended from the Pequod's try-works to the Pequod's forecastle, where the off duty watch were sleeping, for one single moment you would have almost thought you were standing in some illuminated shrine of canonized kings and counsellors.[1] There they lay in their triangular oaken vaults, each mariner a chiselled muteness; a score of lamps flashing upon his hooded eyes.

In merchantmen,° oil for the sailor is more scarce than the milk of queens. To dress in the dark, and eat in the dark, and stumble in darkness to his pallet,° this is his usual lot. But the whaleman, as he seeks the food of light, so he lives in light. He makes his berth an Aladdin's lamp, and lays him down in it; so that in the pitchiest night the ship's black hull still houses an illumination.

See with what entire freedom the whaleman takes his handful of lamps— often but old bottles and vials, though—to the copper cooler at the try-works, and replenishes them there, as mugs of ale at a vat. He burns, too, the purest of oil, in its unmanufactured, and, therefore, unvitiated° state; a fluid unknown to solar, lunar, or astral° contrivances ashore. It is sweet as early grass butter in April. He goes and hunts for his oil, so as to be sure of its freshness and genuineness, even as the traveller on the prairie hunts up his own supper of game.

---

merchantmen: vessels carrying merchandise. **pallet**: uncomfortable makeshift bed. **unvitiated**: pure; uncorrupted. **solar, lunar, or astral**: names of contemporary oil lamps.

CHAPTER 98

STOWING DOWN AND CLEARING UP

Already has it been related how the great leviathan is afar off descried from the mast-head; how he is chased over the watery moors, and slaughtered in the valleys of the deep; how he is then towed alongside and beheaded; and how (on the principle which entitled the headsman of old to the garments in which the beheaded was killed) his great padded surtout° becomes the property of his executioner; how, in due time, he is condemned to the pots, **and, like Shadrach, Meshach, and Abednego,**[1] his spermaceti, oil, and bone pass unscathed through the fire;—but now it remains to conclude the last chapter of this part of the description by rehearsing—singing, if I may—the romantic proceeding of decanting off his oil into the casks and striking them down° into the hold, where once again leviathan returns to his native profundities, sliding along beneath the surface as before; but, alas! never more to rise and blow.

While still warm, the oil, like hot punch, is received into the six-barrel casks; and while, perhaps, the ship is pitching and rolling this way and that in the midnight sea, the enormous casks are slewed round and headed over, end for end, and sometimes perilously scoot across the slippery deck, like so many land slides, till at last man-handled and stayed in their course; and all round the hoops, rap, rap, go as many hammers as can play upon them, for now, *ex officio*, every sailor is a cooper.

At length, when the last pint is casked, and all is cool, then the great hatchways are unsealed, the bowels of the ship are thrown open, and down go the casks to their final rest in the sea. This done, the hatches are replaced, and hermetically closed, like a closet walled up.

In the sperm fishery, this is perhaps one of the most remarkable incidents in all the business of whaling. One day the planks stream with freshets of blood and oil; on the sacred quarter-deck enormous masses of the whale's head are profanely piled; great rusty casks lie about, as in a brewery yard; the smoke from the try-works has besooted all the bulwarks; the mariners go about suffused with unctuousness; the entire ship seems great leviathan himself; while on all hands the din is deafening.

---

surtout: overcoat (French). ***striking them down***: lowering them.

But a day or two after, you look about you, and prick your ears in this self-same ship; and were it not for the tell-tale boats and try-works, you would all but swear you trod some silent merchant vessel, with a most scrupulously neat commander. The unmanufactured sperm oil possesses a singularly cleansing virtue. This is the reason why the decks never look so white as just after what they call an affair of oil. Besides, from the ashes of the burned scraps of the whale, a potent ley° is readily made; and whenever any adhesiveness from the back of the whale remains clinging to the side, that ley quickly exterminates it. Hands go diligently along the bulwarks, and with buckets of water and rags restore them to their full tidiness. The soot is brushed from the lower rigging. All the numerous implements which have been in use are likewise faithfully cleansed and put away. The great hatch is scrubbed and placed upon the try-works, completely hiding the pots; every cask is out of sight; all tackles are coiled in unseen nooks; and when by the combined and simultaneous industry of almost the entire ship's company, the whole of this conscientious duty is at last concluded, then the crew themselves proceed to their own ablutions; shift themselves from top to toe; and finally issue to the immaculate deck, fresh and all aglow**, as bridegrooms new-leaped from out the daintiest Holland**.

Now, with elated step, they pace the planks in twos and threes, and humorously discourse of parlors, sofas, carpets, and fine cambrics; propose to mat the deck; think of having hangings to the top; object not to taking tea by moonlight on the piazza of the forecastle. To hint to such musked mariners of oil, and bone, and blubber, were little short of audacity. They know not the thing you distantly allude to. Away, and bring us napkins!

ley: lye.

REVISION NARRATIVE

Bridegrooms Aglow

"The daintiest Holland" is fine, imported bed sheets, and the arresting comparison of the freshly scrubbed, formerly begrimed crew to "bridegrooms" leaping all "aglow" from their bridal beds, is as unexpected as it is amusing. All the more intriguing is the linking of sexuality to cleanliness: the paragraph opens with the observation that "sperm oil" spilled on the decks has a "singularly cleansing virtue," which in turn leads to the censored observation that the sexualized bridegroom crew is as fresh and glowing as the deck is "immaculate." As with other references to homosexual and heterosexual masculinity regarding Queequeg, Ishmael, whalemen squeezing sperm, and bull whales (in previous chapters), Melville's sexualizing here is put in context by a subsequent scene of domesticity: young, wedded men seeking parlors and requesting napkins. Nevertheless, Ishmael's bridegroom comparison was expurgated in the British edition.

But mark: aloft there, at the three mast heads, stand three men intent on spying out more whales, which, if caught, infallibly will again soil the old oaken furniture, and drop at least one small grease-spot somewhere. Yes; and many is the time, when, after the severest uninterrupted labors, which know no night; continuing straight through for ninety-six hours; when from the boat, where they have swelled their wrists with all day rowing on the Line,—they only step to the deck to carry vast chains, and heave the heavy windlass, and cut and slash, yea, and in their very sweatings to be smoked and burned anew by the combined fires of the equatorial sun and the equatorial try-works; when, on the heel of all this, they have finally bestirred themselves to cleanse the ship, and make a spotless dairy room of it; many is the time the poor fellows, just buttoning the necks of their clean frocks, are startled by the cry of "There she blows!" and away they fly to fight another whale, and go through the whole weary thing again. Oh! my friends, but this is man-killing! Yet this is life. For hardly have we mortals by long toilings extracted from this world's vast bulk its small but valuable sperm; and then, with weary patience, cleansed ourselves from its defilements, and learned to live here in clean tabernacles of the soul; hardly is this done, when—*There she blows!*—the ghost is spouted up, and away we sail to fight some other world, and go through young life's old routine again.

Oh! the metempsychosis! Oh! Pythagoras,[2] that in bright Greece, two thousand years ago, did die, so good, so wise, so mild; I sailed with thee along the Peruvian coast last voyage—and, foolish as I am, taught thee, a green simple boy, how to splice a rope!

CHAPTER 99

THE DOUBLOON

E RE now it has been related how Ahab was wont to pace his quarter-deck, taking regular turns at either limit, the binnacle and mainmast; but in the multiplicity of other things requiring narration it has not been added how that sometimes in these walks, when most plunged in his mood, he was wont to pause in turn at each spot, and stand there strangely eyeing the particular object before him. When he halted before the binnacle, with his glance fastened on the pointed needle in the compass, that glance shot like a javelin with the pointed intensity of his purpose; and when resuming his walk he again paused before the mainmast, then, as the same riveted glance fastened upon the riveted gold coin there, he still wore the same aspect of nailed firmness, only dashed with a certain wild longing, if not hopefulness.

But one morning, turning to pass the doubloon, he seemed to be newly attracted by the strange figures and inscriptions stamped on it, as though now for the first time beginning to interpret for himself in some monomaniac way whatever significance might lurk in them. And some certain significance lurks in all things, else all things are little worth, and the round world itself but an empty cipher, except to sell by the cartload, as they do hills about Boston,[1] to fill up some morass in the Milky Way.

Now this doubloon was of purest, virgin gold, raked somewhere out of the heart of gorgeous hills, whence, east and west, over golden sands, the head-waters of many a Pactolus[2] flow. And though now nailed amidst all the rustiness of iron bolts and the verdigris° of copper spikes, yet, untouchable and immaculate to any foulness, it still preserved its Quito glow. Nor, though placed amongst a ruthless crew and every hour passed by ruthless hands, and through the livelong nights shrouded with thick darkness which might cover any pilfering approach, nevertheless every sunrise found the doubloon where the sunset left it last. For it was set apart and sanctified to one awe-striking end; and however wanton in their sailor ways, one and all, the mariners revered it as the white whale's talisman.° Sometimes they talked it over in the weary watch by night, wondering whose it was to be at last, and whether he would ever live to spend it.

verdigris: greenish crust formed on copper exposed to seawater. ***talisman***: object marked with mystic signs to avert evil.

Now those noble golden coins of South America are as medals of the sun and tropic token-pieces. Here palms, alpacas, and volcanoes; sun's disks and stars; ecliptics,° horns-of-plenty, and rich banners waving, are in luxuriant profusion stamped; so that the precious gold seems almost to derive an added preciousness and enhancing glories, by passing through those fancy mints, so Spanishly poetic.

It so chanced that the doubloon of the Pequod[3] was a most wealthy example of these things. On its round border it bore the letters, REPUBLICA DEL ECUADOR: QUITO. So this bright coin came from a country planted in the middle of the world, and beneath the great equator, and named after it; and it had been cast midway up the Andes, in the unwaning clime that knows no autumn. Zoned by those letters you saw the likeness of three Andes' summits; from one a flame; a tower on another; on the third a crowing cock; while arching over all was a segment of the partitioned zodiac, the signs all marked with their usual cabalistics,° and the keystone sun entering the equinoctial point at Libra.[4]

Before this equatorial coin, Ahab, not unobserved by others, was now pausing. "There's something ever egotistical in mountain-tops and towers, and all other grand and lofty things; look here,—three peaks as proud as Lucifer.[5] The firm tower, that is Ahab; the volcano, that is Ahab; the courageous, the undaunted, and victorious fowl, that, too, is Ahab; all are Ahab; and this round gold is but the image of the rounder globe, which, like a magician's glass, to each and every man in turn but mirrors back his own mysterious self. Great pains, small gains for those who ask the world to solve them; it cannot solve itself. Methinks now this coined sun wears a ruddy face; but see! aye, he enters the sign of storms, the equinox! and but six months before he wheeled out of a former equinox at Aries! From storm to storm![6] So be it, then. Born in throes, 'tis fit that man should live in pains and die in pangs! So be it, then! Here's stout stuff for woe to work on. So be it, then."

"No fairy fingers can have pressed the gold, but devil's claws must have left their mouldings there since yesterday," murmured Starbuck to himself, leaning against the bulwarks. "The old man seems to read Belshazzar's awful writing.[7] I have never marked the coin inspectingly. He goes below; let me read. A dark valley between three mighty, heaven-abiding peaks, that almost seem the Trinity, in some faint earthly symbol. So in this vale of Death,[8] God girds us round; and over all our gloom, the sun of Righteousness still shines a beacon and a hope. If we bend down our eyes, the dark vale shows her mouldy soil; but if we lift them, the bright sun meets our glance half way, to cheer. Yet, oh, the great sun is no fixture; and if, at midnight, we would fain snatch some sweet solace from him, we gaze for him in vain! This coin speaks wisely, mildly, truly, but still sadly to me. I will quit it, lest Truth shake me falsely."

"There now's the old Mogul," soliloquized Stubb by the try-works, "he's been twigging° it; and there goes Starbuck from the same, and both with faces which I should say might be somewhere within nine fathoms long. And all from looking at a

---

ecliptics: the ecliptic is the apparent yearly path of the sun as observed from Earth. *cabalistics*: hidden meanings, but here the symbols associated with of the signs of the zodiac. *twigging*: observing (sailor slang).

piece of gold, which did I have it now on Negro Hill or in Corlaer's Hook,[9] I'd not look at it very long ere spending it. Humph! in my poor, insignificant opinion, I regard this as queer. I have seen doubloons before now in my voyagings; your doubloons of old Spain, your doubloons of Peru, your doubloons of Chili, your doubloons of Bolivia, your doubloons of Popayan;° with plenty of gold moidores and pistoles, and joes, and half joes, and quarter joes.° What then should there be in this doubloon of the Equator that is so killing wonderful? By Golconda![10] let me read it once. Halloa! here's signs and wonders[11] truly! That, now, is what old Bowditch in his Epitome calls the zodiac, and what my almanack below calls ditto. I'll get the almanack; and as **I have** heard devils can be raised with Daboll's arithmetic,[12] I'll try my hand at raising a meaning out of these queer curvicues here with the Massachusetts calendar.[13] Here's the book. Let's see now. Signs and wonders; and the sun, he's always among 'em. Hem, hem, hem; here they are—here they go—all alive:—Aries, or the Ram; Taurus, or the Bull and Jimini! here's Gemini himself, or the Twins. Well; the sun he wheels among 'em. Aye, here on the coin he's just crossing the threshold between two of twelve sitting-rooms all in a ring. Book! you lie there; the fact is, you books must know your places. You'll do to give us the bare words and facts, but we come in to supply the thoughts. That's my small experience, so far as the Massachusetts calendar, and Bowditch's navigator, and Daboll's arithmetic go. Signs and wonders, eh? Pity if there is nothing wonderful in signs, and significant in wonders! There's a clue somewhere; wait a bit; hist—hark! By Jove, I have it! Look you, Doubloon, your zodiac here is the life of man in one round° chapter; and now I'll read it off, straight out of the book. Come, Almanack! To begin: there's Aries, or the Ram—**lecherous dog,** he begets us; then, Taurus, or the Bull—he bumps us the first thing; then Gemini, or the Twins—that is, Virtue and Vice; we try to reach Virtue, when lo! comes Cancer the Crab, and drags us back; and here, going from Virtue, Leo, a roaring Lion,[14] lies in the path—he gives a few fierce bites and surly dabs with his paw; we escape, and hail Virgo, the Virgin! that's our first love; we marry and think to be happy for aye,° when pop comes Libra, or the Scales—happiness weighed and found wanting; and while we are very sad about that, Lord! how we suddenly jump, as Scorpio, or the Scorpion, stings us in the rear; we are curing the wound, when whang come the arrows all round; Sagittarius, or the Archer, is amusing himself. As we pluck out the shafts, stand aside! here's the battering-ram, Capricornus, or the Goat; full tilt, he comes rushing, and headlong we are tossed; when Aquarius, or the Water-bearer, pours out his whole deluge and drowns us; **and to wind up** with Pisces, or the Fishes, we sleep. There's a sermon now, writ in high heaven, and the sun goes through it every year, and yet comes out of it all alive and hearty. Jollily he, aloft there, wheels through toil and trouble;[15] and so, alow here,° does jolly Stubb. Oh, jolly's the word for aye! Adieu, Doubloon! But stop; here comes little King-Post; dodge round the try-works, now, and let's hear what he'll have to say. There; he's before it; he'll out with something presently. So, so; he's beginning."

Popayan: site of a famous mint in Colombia. **moidores and pistoles, and . . . joes**: Spanish and Portuguese coins. **round**: like the coin, but also meaning whole or complete. **for aye**: forever. **alow here**: down here.

"I see nothing here, but a round thing made of gold, and whoever raises a certain whale, this round thing belongs to him. So, what's all this staring been about? It is worth sixteen dollars, that's true; and at two cents the cigar, that's nine hundred and sixty cigars.[16] I won't smoke dirty pipes like Stubb, but I like cigars, and here's nine hundred and sixty of them; so here goes Flask aloft to spy 'em out."

"Shall I call that wise or foolish, now; if it be really wise it has a foolish look to it; yet, if it be really foolish, then has it a sort of wiseish look to it. But, avast; here comes our old Manxman—the old hearse-driver,[17] he must have been, that is, before he took to the sea. He luffs up° before the doubloon; halloa, and goes round on the other side of the mast; why, there's a horse-shoe nailed on that side; and now he's back again; what does that mean? Hark! he's muttering—voice like an old worn-out coffee-mill. Prick ears, and listen!"

"If the White Whale be raised, it must be in a month and a day, when the sun stands in some one of these signs. I've studied signs, and know their marks; they were taught me two score years ago, by the old witch in Copenhagen. Now, in what sign will the sun then be? The horse-shoe sign; for there it is, right opposite the gold. And what's the horse-shoe sign? The lion is the horse-shoe sign—the roaring and devouring lion. Ship, old ship! my old head shakes to think of thee."

"There's another rendering now; but still one text. All sorts of men in one kind of world, you see. Dodge again! here comes Queequeg—all tattooing—looks like the signs of the Zodiac himself. What says the Cannibal? As I live he's comparing notes; looking at his thigh bone; thinks the sun is in the thigh, or in the calf, or in the bowels, I suppose, as the old women talk Surgeon's Astronomy in the back country.[18] And by Jove, he's found something there in the vicinity of his thigh—I guess it's Sagittarius, or the Archer. No: he don't know what to make of the doubloon; he takes it for an old button off some king's trowsers. But, aside again! here comes that **ghost-devil**, Fedallah; tail coiled out of sight as usual, oakum in the toes of his pumps as usual.[19] What does he say, with that look of his? Ah, only makes a sign to the sign and bows himself; there is a sun on the coin—fire worshipper,[20] depend upon it. Ho! more and more. This way comes Pip—poor boy! would he had died, or I; he's half horrible to me. He too has been watching all of these interpreters— myself included—and look now, he comes to read, with that unearthly idiot face. Stand away again and hear him. Hark!"

"I look, you look, he looks; we look, ye look, they look."

"Upon my soul, he's been studying Murray's Grammar![21] Improving his mind, poor fellow! But what's that he says now—hist!"

"I look, you look, he looks; we look, ye look, they look."

"Why, he's getting it by heart—hist! again."

"I look, you look, he looks; we look, ye look, they look."

"Well, that's funny."

"And I, you, and he; and we, ye, and they, are all bats; and I'm a crow,[22] especially when I stand a'top of this pine tree here. Caw! caw! caw! caw! caw! caw! Ain't I a crow? And where's the scare-crow? There he stands; two bones stuck into a pair of old trowsers, and two more poked into the sleeves of an old jacket."

luffs up: stops.

"Wonder if he means me?—complimentary!—poor lad!—I could go hang myself. Any way, for the present, I'll quit Pip's vicinity. I can stand the rest, for they have plain wits; but he's too crazy-witty for my sanity. So, so, I leave him muttering."

"Here's the ship's navel, this doubloon here, and they are all on fire to unscrew it. But, unscrew your navel, and what's the consequence?[23] Then again, if it stays here, that is ugly, too, for when aught's nailed to the mast it's a sign that things grow desperate.[24] Ha, ha! old Ahab! the White Whale; he'll nail ye! This is a pine tree. My father, in old Tolland county, cut down a pine tree once, and found a silver ring grown over in it; some old darkey's wedding ring. How did it get there? And so they'll say **in the resurrection**, when they come to fish up this old mast, and find a doubloon lodged in it, with bedded oysters for the shaggy bark. Oh, the gold! the precious, precious gold!—the green miser° 'll hoard ye soon! **Hish! hish! God goes 'mong the worlds blackberrying. Cook! ho, cook! and cook us! Jenny! hey, hey, hey, hey, hey, Jenny, Jenny! and get your hoe-cake done!**"[25]

green miser: Davy Jones, also mentioned in Chs. 18 and 81.

REVISION NARRATIVE

Hushing Pip

Some of Pip's mutterings were taken to be mildly irreverent. His phrase, "in the resurrection," referring to the so-called Last Day or Judgment Day, when all souls are sent either to heaven or hell (see Revelation 20), was revised by British editors to simply "one day." And Pip's last lines—when he hushes himself, sees God picking blackberries, greets the cook, and breaks into song—were cut entirely, even though only the image of God going berry picking might have been taken as objectionable. Perhaps Melville made this cut to end on Pip's more ominous prediction: "the green miser'll hoard ye soon!"

LEG AND ARM

The Pequod, of Nantucket, Meets the Samuel Enderby, of London

"SHIP, ahoy! Hast seen the White Whale?"

So cried Ahab, once more hailing a ship showing English colors, bearing down under the stern.° Trumpet to mouth, the old man was standing in his hoisted quarter-boat, his ivory leg plainly revealed to the stranger captain, who was carelessly reclining in his own boat's bow. He was a darkly-tanned, burly, good-natured, fine-looking man, of sixty or thereabouts, dressed in a spacious roundabout,° that hung round him in festoons of blue pilot-cloth; and one empty arm of this jacket streamed behind him like the broidered arm of a huzzar's surcoat.

"Hast seen the White Whale?"

"See you this?" and withdrawing it from the folds that had hidden it, he held up a white arm of sperm whale bone, terminating in a wooden head like a mallet.

"Man my boat!" cried Ahab, impetuously, and tossing about the oars near him—"Stand by to lower!"

In less than a minute, without quitting his little craft, he and his crew were dropped to the water, and were soon alongside of the stranger. But here a curious difficulty presented itself. In the excitement of the moment, Ahab had forgotten that since the loss of his leg he had never once stepped on board of any vessel at sea but his own, and then it was always by an ingenious and very handy mechanical contrivance peculiar to the Pequod, and a thing not to be rigged and shipped in any other vessel at a moment's warning. Now, it is no very easy matter for anybody—except those who are almost hourly used to it, like whalemen—to clamber up a ship's side from a boat on the open sea; for the great swells now lift the boat high up towards the bulwarks, and then instantaneously drop it half way down to the kelson. So, deprived of one leg, and the strange ship of course being altogether unsupplied with the kindly invention, Ahab now found himself abjectly reduced to a clumsy landsman again; hopelessly eyeing the uncertain changeful height he could hardly hope to attain.

It has before been hinted, perhaps, that every little untoward circumstance that befel him, and which indirectly sprang from his luckless mishap, almost invari-

---

under the stern: from behind. **roundabout**: large, unfitted coat.

ably irritated or exasperated Ahab. And in the present instance, all this was heightened by the sight of the two officers of the strange ship, leaning over the side, by the perpendicular ladder of nailed cleets there, and swinging towards him a pair of tastefully-ornamented man-ropes; for at first they did not seem to bethink them that a one-legged man must be too much of a cripple to use their sea bannisters. But this awkwardness only lasted a minute, because the strange captain, observing at a glance how affairs stood, cried out, "I see, I see!—avast heaving there! Jump, boys, and swing over the cutting-tackle."

As good luck would have it, they had had a whale alongside a day or two previous, and the great tackles were still aloft, and the massive curved blubber-hook, now clean and dry, was still attached to the end. This was quickly lowered to Ahab, who at once comprehending it all, slid his solitary thigh[1] into the curve of the hook (it was like sitting in the fluke of an anchor, or the crotch of an apple tree), and then giving the word, held himself fast, and at the same time also helped to hoist his own weight, by pulling hand-over-hand upon one of the running parts of the tackle. Soon he was carefully swung inside the high bulwarks, and gently landed upon the capstan head. With his ivory arm frankly thrust forth in welcome, the other captain advanced, and Ahab, putting out his ivory leg, and crossing the ivory arm (like two sword-fish blades) cried out in his walrus way, "Aye, aye, hearty! let us shake bones together!—an arm and a leg!—an arm that never can shrink, d'ye see; and a leg that never can run. Where did'st thou see the White Whale?—how long ago?"

"The White Whale," said the Englishman, pointing his ivory arm towards the East, and taking a rueful sight along it, as if it had been a telescope; "There I saw him, on the Line, last season."

"And he took that arm off, did he?" asked Ahab, now sliding down from the capstan, and resting on the Englishman's shoulder, as he did so.

"Aye, he was the cause of it, at least; and that leg, too?"

"Spin me the yarn," said Ahab; "how was it?"

"It was the first time in my life that I ever cruised on the Line," began the Englishman. "I was ignorant of the White Whale at that time. Well, one day we lowered for a pod of four or five whales, and my boat fastened to one of them; a regular circus horse he was, too, that went milling and milling round so, that my boat's crew could only trim dish, by sitting all their sterns on the outer gunwale.[2] Presently up breaches from the bottom of the sea a bouncing great whale, with a milky-white head and hump, all crows' feet and wrinkles."

"It was he, it was he!" cried Ahab, suddenly letting out his suspended breath.

"And harpoons sticking in near his starboard fin."

"Aye, aye—they **were** mine—*my* irons," cried Ahab, exultingly—"but on!"

"Give me a chance, then," said the Englishman, good-humoredly. "Well, this old great-grandfather, with the white head and hump, runs all afoam into the pod, and goes to snapping furiously at my fast-line."

"Aye, I see!—wanted to part it; free the fast-fish—an old trick—I know him."

"How it was exactly," continued the one-armed commander, "I do not know; but in biting the line, it got foul of his teeth, caught there somehow; but we didn't know it then; so that when we afterwards pulled on the line, bounce we came plump on to his hump! instead of the other whale's that went off to windward, all fluking. Seeing how matters stood, and what a noble great whale it was—the noblest and biggest I ever saw, sir, in my life—I resolved to capture him, spite of the boiling rage he seemed to be in. And thinking the hap-hazard line would get loose, or the tooth it was tangled to might draw (for I have a devil of a boat's crew for a pull on a whale-line); seeing all this, I say, I jumped into my first mate's boat—Mr. Mounttop's here (by the way, Captain—Mounttop; Mounttop—the captain);—as I was saying, I jumped into Mounttop's boat, which, d'ye see, was gunwale and gunwale with mine, then; and snatching the first harpoon, let this old great-grandfather have it. But, Lord, look you, sir—hearts and souls alive, man—the next instant, in a jiff, I was blind as a bat—both eyes out—all befogged and bedeadened with black foam—the whale's tail looming straight up out of it, perpendicular in the air, like a marble steeple. No use sterning all, then; but as I was groping at midday, with a blinding sun, all crown-jewels; as I was groping, I say, after the second iron, to toss it over-board—down comes the tail like a Lima tower,[3] cutting my boat in two, leaving each half in splinters; and, flukes first, the white hump backed through the wreck, as though it was all chips. We all struck out. To escape his terrible flailings, I seized hold of my harpoon-pole sticking in him, and for a moment clung to that like a sucking fish. But a combing sea dashed me off, and at the same instant, the fish, taking one good dart forwards, went down like a flash; and the barb of that cursed second iron towing along near me caught me here" (clapping his hand just below his shoulder); "yes, caught me just here, I say, and bore me down to Hell's flames, I was thinking; when, when, all of a sudden, thank the good God, the barb ript its way along the flesh—clear along the whole length of my arm—came out nigh my wrist, and up I floated;—and that gentleman there will tell you the rest (by the way, captain—Dr. Bunger, ship's surgeon: Bunger, my lad,—the captain). Now, Bunger boy, spin your part of the yarn."

The professional gentleman thus familiarly pointed out, had been all the time standing near them, with nothing specific visible, to denote his gentlemanly rank on board. His face was an exceedingly round but sober one; he was dressed in a faded blue woollen frock or shirt, and patched trowsers; and had thus far been dividing his attention between a marlingspike he held in one hand, and a pill-box held in the other, occasionally casting a critical glance at the ivory limbs of the two crippled captains. But, at his superior's introduction of him to Ahab, he politely bowed, and straightway went on to do his captain's bidding.

"It was a shocking had wound," began the whale-surgeon; "and, taking my advice, Captain Boomer here, stood our old Sammy—"

"Samuel Enderby is the name of my ship," interrupted the one-armed captain, addressing Ahab; "go on, boy."

"Stood our old Sammy off to the northward, to get out of the blazing hot weather there on the Line. But it was no use—I did all I could; sat up with him nights; was very severe with him in the matter of diet—"

"Oh, very severe!" chimed in the patient himself; then suddenly altering his voice, "Drinking hot rum toddies with me every night, till he couldn't see to put on the bandages; and sending me to bed, half seas over, about three o'clock in the morning. Oh, ye stars! he sat up with me indeed, and was very severe in my diet. Oh!

a great watcher, and very dietetically severe, is Dr. Bunger. (Bunger, you dog, laugh out! why don't ye? You know **you're** a precious jolly rascal.) But, heave ahead, boy, I'd rather be killed by you than kept alive by any other man."

"My captain, you must have ere this perceived, respected sir"—said the imperturbable godly-looking Bunger, slightly bowing to Ahab—"is apt to be facetious at times; he spins us many clever things of that sort. But I may as well say—en passant,° as the French remark—that I myself—that is to say, Jack Bunger, late of the reverend clergy—am a strict total abstinence man; I never drink—"

"Water!" cried the captain; "he never drinks it; it's a sort of fits to him; fresh water throws him into the hydrophobia;[4] but go on—go on with the arm story."

"Yes, I may as well," said the surgeon, coolly. "I was about observing, sir, before Captain Boomer's facetious interruption, that spite of my best and severest endeavors, the wound kept getting worse and worse; the truth was, sir, it was as ugly gaping a wound as surgeon ever saw; more than two feet and several inches long. I measured it with the lead line.° In short, it grew black; I knew what was threatened, and off it came. But I had no hand in shipping that ivory arm there; that thing is against all rule"—pointing at it with the marlingspike—"that is the captain's work, not mine; he ordered the carpenter to make it; he had that club-hammer there put to the end, to knock some one's brains out with, I suppose, as he tried mine once. He flies into diabolical passions sometimes. Do ye see this dent, sir"—removing his hat, and brushing aside his hair, and exposing a bowl-like cavity in his skull, but which bore not the slightest scarry trace, or any token of ever having been a wound—"Well, the captain there will tell you how that came here; he knows."

"No, I don't," said the captain, "but his mother did; he was born with it. Oh, you solemn rogue, you—you Bunger! was there ever such another Bunger in the watery world? Bunger, when you die, you ought to die in pickle, you dog; you should be preserved to future ages, you rascal."

"What became of the White Whale?" now cried Ahab, who thus far had been impatiently listening to this bye-play between the two Englishmen.

"Oh!" cried the one-armed captain, "Oh, yes! Well; after he sounded, we didn't see him again for some time; in fact, as I before hinted, I didn't then know what whale it was that had served me such a trick, till some time afterwards, when coming back to the Line, we heard about Moby Dick—as some call him—and then I knew it was he."

"Did'st thou cross his wake again?"

"Twice."

"But could not fasten?"

"Didn't want to try to: ain't one limb enough? What should I do without this other arm? And I'm thinking Moby Dick doesn't bite so much as he swallows."

"Well, then," interrupted Bunger, "give him your left arm for bait to get the right. Do you know, gentlemen"—very gravely and mathematically bowing to each Captain in succession—"Do you know, gentlemen, that the digestive organs of the whale are so inscrutably constructed by Divine Providence, that it is quite impossi-

---

en passant: in passing (French); by the way. **lead line**: marked rope with a lead weight, for measuring water depth.

ble for him to completely digest even a man's arm?[5] And he knows it too. So that what you take for the White Whale's malice is only his awkwardness. For he never means to swallow a single limb; he only thinks to terrify by feints. But sometimes he is like the old juggling fellow, formerly a patient of mine in Ceylon, that making believe to swallow jack-knives, once upon a time let one drop into him in good earnest, and there it stayed for a twelvemonth or more; when I gave him an emetic, and he heaved it up in small tacks, d'ye see. No possible way for him to digest that jack-knife, and fully incorporate it into his general bodily system. Yes, Captain Boomer, if you are quick enough about it, and have a mind to pawn one arm for the sake of the privilege of giving decent burial to the other, why in that case the arm is yours; only let the whale have another chance at you shortly, that's all."

"No, thank ye, Bunger," said the English Captain, "he's welcome to the arm he has, since I can't help it, and didn't know him then; but not to another one. No more White Whales for me; I've lowered for him once, and that has satisfied me. There would be great glory in killing him, I know that; and there is a ship-load of precious sperm in him, but, hark ye, he's best let alone; don't you think so, Captain?"—glancing at the ivory leg.

"He is. But he will still be hunted, for all that. What is best let alone, that accursed thing is not always what least allures. He's all a magnet! How long since **thou saw'st** him last? Which way heading?"

"Bless my soul, and curse the foul fiend's," cried Bunger, stoopingly walking round Ahab, and like a dog, strangely snuffing; "this man's blood—bring the thermometer!—it's at the boiling point!—his pulse makes these planks beat!—sir!"—taking a lancet from his pocket, and drawing near to Ahab's arm.

"Avast!" roared Ahab, dashing him against the bulwarks—"Man the boat! Which way heading?"

"Good God!" cried the English Captain, to whom the question was put. "What's the matter? He was heading east, I think.—Is your Captain crazy?" whispering Fedallah.

But Fedallah, putting a finger on his lip, slid over the bulwarks to take the boat's steering oar, and Ahab, swinging the cutting-tackle towards him, commanded the ship's sailors to stand by to lower.

In a moment he was standing in the boat's stern, and the Manilla men were springing to their oars. In vain the English Captain hailed him. With back to the stranger ship, and face set like a flint to his own, Ahab stood upright till alongside of the Pequod.

CHAPTER 101

THE DECANTER

ERE the English ship fades from sight, be it set down here, that she hailed from London, and was named after the late Samuel Enderby, merchant of that city, the original of the famous whaling house of Enderby & Sons;[1] a house which in my poor whaleman's opinion, comes not far behind the united royal houses of the Tudors and Bourbons,[2] in point of real historical interest. How long, prior to the year of our Lord 1775, this great whaling house was in existence, my numerous fish-documents° do not make plain; but in that year (1775) it fitted out the first English ships that ever regularly hunted the Sperm Whale; though for some score of years previous (ever since 1726) our valiant Coffins and Maceys of Nantucket and the Vineyard had in large fleets pursued that Leviathan, but only in the North and South Atlantic: not elsewhere. Be it distinctly recorded here, that the Nantucketers were the first among mankind to harpoon with civilized steel the great Sperm Whale; and that for half a century they were the only people of the whole globe who so harpooned him.

In 1778, a fine ship, the Amelia, fitted out for the express purpose, and at the sole charge of the vigorous Enderbys, boldly rounded Cape Horn, and was the first among the nations to lower a whale-boat of any sort in the great South Sea. The voyage was a skilful and lucky one; and returning to her berth with her hold full of the precious sperm, the Amelia's example was soon followed by other ships, English and American, and thus the vast Sperm Whale grounds of the Pacific were thrown open. But not content with this good deed, the indefatigable house again bestirred itself: Samuel and all his Sons—**how many, their mother only knows**—and under their immediate auspices, and partly, I think, at their expense, the British government was induced to send the sloop-of-war Rattler on a whaling voyage of discovery into the South Sea. Commanded by a naval Post-Captain,° the Rattler made a rattling voyage of it,[3] and did some service;[4] how much does not appear. But this is not all. In 1819, the same house fitted out a discovery whale ship of their own, to go on a **tasting** cruise to the remote waters of Japan. That ship—well called the "Syren"—made a noble experimental cruise; and it was thus that the great Japanese Whaling Ground[5] first became generally known. The Syren in this famous voyage was commanded by a Captain Coffin, a Nantucketer.

fish-documents: Ishmael's whaling sources. *Post-Captain*: commanding officer of a vessel who has the naval rank of captain.

All honor to the Enderbies, therefore, whose house, I think, exists to the present day; though doubtless the original Samuel must long ago have slipped his cable° for the great South Sea of the other world.

The ship named after him was worthy of the honor, being a very fast sailer and a noble craft every way. I boarded her once at midnight somewhere off the Patagonian coast, and drank good flip° down in the forecastle. It was a fine gam we had, and they were all trumps°—every soul on board. A short life to them, and a jolly death. And that fine gam I had—long, very long after old Ahab touched her planks with his ivory heel—it minds me of the noble, solid, Saxon hospitality of that ship; and may my parson forget me, and the devil remember me, if I ever lose sight of it. Flip? Did I say we had flip? Yes, and we flipped it at the rate of ten gallons the hour; and when the squall came (for it's squally off there by Patagonia), and all hands—visitors and all—were called to reef topsails, we were so top-heavy[6] that we had to swing each other aloft in bowlines; and we ignorantly furled the skirts of our jackets into the sails, so that we hung there, reefed fast in the howling gale, a warning example to all drunken tars. However, the masts did not go overboard; and by and bye we scrambled down, so sober, that we had to pass the flip again, though the savage salt spray bursting down the forecastle scuttle, rather too much diluted and pickled it to my taste.

The beef was fine—tough, but with body in it. They said it was bull-beef; others, that it was dromedary beef; but I do not know, for certain, how that was. They had dumplings too; small, but substantial, symmetrically globular, and indestructible dumplings. I fancied that you could feel them, and roll them about in you after they were swallowed. If you stooped over too far forward, you risked their pitching out of you like billiard-balls. The bread—but that couldn't be helped; besides, it was an anti-scorbutic;[7] in short, the bread contained the only fresh fare they had. But the forecastle was not very light, and it was very easy to step over into a dark corner when you ate it. But all in all, taking her from truck to helm, considering the dimensions of the cook's boilers, including his own live parchment boilers;° fore and aft, I say, the Samuel Enderby was a jolly ship; of good fare and plenty; fine flip and strong; crack fellows all, and capital° from boot heels to hat-band.

But why was it, think ye, that the Samuel Enderby, and some other English whalers I know of—not all though—were such famous, hospitable ships; that passed round the beef, and the bread, and the can, and the joke; and were not soon weary of eating, and drinking, and laughing? I will tell you. The abounding good cheer of these English whalers is matter for historical research. Nor have I been at all sparing of historical whale research, when it has seemed needed.

The English were preceded in the whale fishery by the Hollanders, Zealanders,[8] and Danes; from whom they derived many terms still extant in the fishery; and what is yet more, their fat old fashions, touching plenty to eat and drink. For, as a general thing, the English merchant-ship scrimps her crew; but not so the English whaler. Hence, in the English, this thing of whaling good cheer is not nor-

---

slipped his cable: departed; but here, died. **flip**: heated, sweetened mixture of beer and liquor. **trumps**: "first-rate guys." **live parchment boilers**: that is, his big belly, covered by his skin. **crack . . . capital**: both mean excellent.

mal and natural, but incidental and particular; and, therefore, must have some special origin, which is here pointed out, and will be still further elucidated.

During my researches in the Leviathanic histories, I stumbled upon an ancient Dutch volume,[9] which, by the musty whaling smell of it, I knew must be about whalers. The title was, "Dan Coopman," wherefore I concluded that this must be the invaluable memoirs of some Amsterdam cooper in the fishery, as every whale ship must carry its cooper. I was reinforced in this opinion by seeing that it was the production of one "Fitz Swackhammer." But my friend Dr. Snodhead, a very learned man, professor of Low Dutch and High German[10] in the college of Santa Claus and St. Pott's, to whom I handed the work for translation, giving him a box of sperm candles for his trouble—this same Dr. Snodhead, so soon as he spied the book, assured me that "Dan Coopman" did not mean "The Cooper," but "The Merchant." In short, this ancient and learned Low Dutch book treated of the commerce of Holland; and, among other subjects, contained a very interesting account of its whale fishery. And in this chapter it was, headed "Smeer," or "Fat," that I found a long detailed list of the outfits for the larders and cellars of 180 sail of Dutch whalemen;° from which list, as translated by Dr. Snodhead, I transcribe the following:

> 400,000 lbs. of beef.
> 60,000 lbs. Friesland° pork.
> 150,000 lbs. of stock fish.°
> 550,000 lbs. of biscuit.
> 72,000 lbs. of soft bread.
>   2,800 firkins° of butter.
> 20,000 lbs. Texel & Leyden° cheese.
> 144,000 lbs. cheese (probably an inferior article).
>   550 ankers of Geneva.°
> 10,800 barrels of beer.

Most statistical tables are parchingly dry in the reading; not so in the present case, however, where the reader is flooded with whole pipes, barrels, quarts, and gills° of good gin and good cheer.

At the time, I devoted three days to the studious digesting of all this beer, beef, and bread, during which many profound thoughts were incidentally suggested to me, capable of a transcendental and Platonic application; and, furthermore, I compiled supplementary tables of my own, touching the probable quantity of stock-fish, &c., consumed by every Low Dutch[11] harpooneer in that ancient Greenland and Spitzbergen whale fishery.[12] In the first place, the amount of butter, and Texel and Leyden cheese consumed, seems amazing. I impute it, though, to their naturally unctuous natures, being rendered still more unctuous by the nature of their vocation, and especially by their pursuing their game in those frigid Polar Seas, on the very coasts of that Esquimaux country where the convivial natives pledge each other in bumpers of train oil.

---

sail of Dutch whalemen: *sail* is a figure of speech for ship or ships, while *whalemen* means whaleships. **Friesland**: Dutch agricultural province. **stock fish**: dried fish. **firkins**: small wooden kegs. **Texel & Leyden**: Dutch island (pronounced tessel) and city. **ankers of Geneva**: 10-gallon casks of gin. **pipes . . . and gills**: 120-gallon barrels; a gill is half a cup.

The quantity of beer, too, is very large, 10,800 barrels. Now, as those polar fisheries could only be prosecuted in the short summer of that climate, so that the whole cruise of one of these Dutch whalemen, including the short voyage to and from the Spitzbergen sea, did not much exceed three months, say, and reckoning 30 men to each of their fleet of 180 sail, we have 5,400 Low Dutch seamen in all; therefore, I say, we have precisely two barrels of beer per man, for a twelve weeks' allowance, exclusive of his fair proportion of that 550 ankers of gin. Now, whether these gin and beer harpooneers, so fuddled as one might fancy them to have been, were the right sort of men to stand up in a boat's head, and take good aim at flying whales; this would seem somewhat improbable. Yet they did aim at them, and hit them too. But this was very far North, be it remembered, where beer agrees well with the constitution; upon the Equator, in our southern fishery, beer would be apt to make the harpooneer sleepy at the mast-head and boozy in his boat; and grievous loss might ensue to Nantucket and New Bedford.

But no more; enough has been said to show that the old Dutch whalers of two or three centuries ago were high livers; and that the English whalers have not neglected so excellent an example. For, say they, when cruising in an empty ship, if you can get nothing better out of the world, get a good dinner out of it, at least. And this empties the decanter.

CHAPTER 102

A BOWER IN THE ARSACIDES[1]

HITHERTO, in descriptively treating of the Sperm Whale, I have chiefly dwelt upon the marvels of his outer aspect; or separately and in detail upon some few interior structural features. But to a large and thorough sweeping comprehension of him, it behoves me now to unbutton him still further, and **untagging** the points of his hose,° unbuckling his garters, and casting loose the hooks and the eyes of the joints of his innermost bones, set him before you in his ultimatum; that is to say, in his unconditional skeleton.

But how now, Ishmael? How is it, that you, a mere oarsman in the fishery, pretend to know aught about the subterranean parts of the whale? Did erudite Stubb, mounted upon your capstan, deliver lectures on the anatomy of the Cetacea; and by help of the windlass, hold up a specimen rib for exhibition? Explain thyself, Ishmael. Can you land a full-grown whale on your deck for examination, as a cook dishes a roast-pig? Surely not. A veritable witness have you hitherto been, Ishmael; but have a care how you seize the privilege of Jonah alone; the privilege of discoursing upon **the** joists and beams; the rafters, ridge-pole, sleepers, and under-pinnings, making up the frame-work of leviathan; and belike of the tallow-vats, dairy-rooms, butteries, and cheeseries in his bowels.

I confess, that since Jonah, few whalemen have penetrated very far beneath the skin of the adult whale; nevertheless, I have been blessed with an opportunity to dissect him in miniature. In a ship I belonged to, a small cub Sperm Whale was once bodily hoisted to the deck for his poke or bag,° to make sheaths for the barbs of the harpoons, and for the heads of the lances. Think you I let that chance go, without using my boat-hatchet and jack-knife, and breaking the seal[2] and reading all the contents of that young cub?

And as for my exact knowledge of the bones of the leviathan in their gigantic, full grown development, for that rare knowledge I am indebted to my late royal friend Tranquo, king of Tranque, one of the Arsacides. For being at Tranque, years ago, when attached to the trading-ship Dey of Algiers,[3] I was invited to spend part of the Arsacidean holidays with the lord of Tranque, at his retired palm villa at Pupella; a seaside glen not very far distant from what our sailors called Bamboo-Town, his capital.

points of his hose: laces of his stockings. *poke or bag*: stomach.

Among many other fine qualities, my royal friend Tranquo, being gifted with a devout love for all matters of barbaric vertù,° had brought together in Pupella whatever rare things the more ingenious of his people could invent; chiefly carved woods of wonderful devices, chiselled shells, inlaid spears, costly paddles, aromatic canoes; and all these distributed among whatever natural wonders, the wonder-freighted, tribute-rendering waves had cast upon his shores.

Chief among these latter was a great Sperm Whale, which, after an unusually long raging gale, had been found dead and stranded, with his head against a cocoa-nut tree, whose plumage-like, tufted droopings seemed his verdant jet. When the vast body had at last been stripped of its fathom-deep enfoldings, and the bones become dust dry in the sun, then the skeleton was carefully transported up the Pupella glen, where a grand temple of lordly palms now sheltered it.

The ribs were hung with trophies; the vertebræ were carved with Arsacidean annals, in strange hieroglyphics; in the skull, the priests kept up an unextinguished aromatic flame, so that the mystic head again sent forth its vapory spout; while, suspended from a bough, the terrific lower jaw vibrated over all the devotees, like the hair-hung sword that so affrighted Damocles.[4]

It was a wondrous sight. The wood was green as mosses of the Icy Glen;[5] the trees stood high and haughty, feeling their living sap; the industrious earth beneath was as a weaver's loom, with a gorgeous carpet on it, whereof the ground-vine ten-drils formed the warp and woof, and the living flowers the figures. All the trees, with all their laden branches; all the shrubs, and ferns, and grasses; the message-carrying air; all these unceasingly were active. Through the lacings of the leaves, the great sun seemed a flying shuttle weaving the unwearied verdure. Oh, busy weaver! unseen weaver!—pause!—one word!—whither flows the fabric? what palace may it deck? wherefore all these ceaseless toilings? Speak, weaver!—stay thy hand!—but one single word with thee! Nay—the shuttle flies—the figures float from forth the loom; the freshet-rushing carpet° for ever slides away. The weaver-god, he weaves; and by that weaving **is he** deafened, that he hears no mortal voice; and by that humming, we, too, who look on the loom are deafened; and only when we escape it shall we hear the thousand voices that speak through it. For even so it is in all material fac-tories. The spoken words that are inaudible among the flying spindles; those same words are plainly heard without the walls, bursting from the opened casements. Thereby have villanies been detected. Ah, mortal! then, be heedful; for so, in all this din of the great world's loom, thy subtlest thinkings may be overheard afar.

Now, amid the green, life-restless loom of that Arsacidean wood, the great, white, worshipped skeleton lay lounging—a gigantic idler! Yet, as the ever-woven ver-dant warp and woof intermixed and hummed around him, the mighty idler seemed the cunning weaver; himself all woven over with the vines; every month assuming greener, fresher verdure; but himself a skeleton. Life folded Death; Death trellised Life; the grim god wived with youthful Life, and begat him curly-headed glories.

Now, when with royal Tranquo I visited this wondrous whale, and saw the skull an altar, and the artificial smoke ascending from where the real jet had issued,

---

vertù: art objects and curios. ***freshet-rushing carpet***: images in the carpet flow like a sud-denly flooding stream.

I marvelled that the king should regard a chapel as an object of vertù. He laughed. But more I marvelled that the priests should swear that smoky jet of his was genuine. To and fro I paced before this skeleton—brushed the vines aside—broke through the ribs—and with a ball of Arsacidean twine,[6] wandered, eddied long amid its many winding, shaded colonnades and arbors. But soon my line was out; and following it back, I emerged from the opening where I entered. I saw no living thing within; naught was there but bones.

Cutting me a green measuring-rod, I once more dived within the skeleton. From their arrow-slit in the skull, the priests perceived me taking the altitude of the final rib. "How now!" they shouted; "Dar'st thou measure this our god! That's for us." "Aye, priests—well, how long do ye make him, then?" But hereupon a fierce contest rose among them, concerning feet and inches; they cracked each other's sconces° with their yard-sticks—the great skull echoed—and seizing that lucky chance, I quickly concluded my own admeasurements.

These admeasurements I now propose to set before you. But first, be it recorded, that, in this matter, I am not free to utter any fancied measurement I please. Because there are skeleton authorities you can refer to, to test my accuracy. There is a Leviathanic Museum, they tell me, in Hull, England, one of the whaling ports of that country, where they have some fine specimens of fin-backs and other whales. Likewise, I have heard that in the museum of Manchester, in New Hampshire, they have what the proprietors call "the only perfect specimen of a Greenland or River Whale in the United States." Moreover, at a place in Yorkshire, England, Burton Constable by name, a certain Sir Clifford Constable has in his possession the skeleton of a Sperm Whale,[7] but of moderate size, by no means of the full-grown magnitude of my friend King Tranquo's.

In both cases, the stranded whales to which these two skeletons belonged, were originally claimed by their proprietors upon similar grounds. King Tranquo seizing his because he wanted it; and Sir Clifford, because he was lord of the seignories° of those parts. Sir Clifford's whale has been articulated throughout; so that, like a great chest of drawers, you can open and shut him, in all his bony cavities—spread out his ribs like a gigantic fan—and swing all day upon his lower jaw. Locks are to be put upon some of his trap-doors and shutters; and a footman will show round future visitors with a bunch of keys at his side. **Sir Clifford thinks of charging twopence for a peep at the whispering gallery in the spinal column; threepence to hear the echo in the hollow of his cerebellum; and sixpence for the unrivalled view from his forehead.**

The skeleton dimensions I shall now proceed to set down are copied verbatim from my right arm, where I had them tattooed; as in my wild wanderings at that period, there was no other secure way of preserving such valuable statistics. But as I was crowded for space, and wished the other parts of my body to remain a blank page for a poem I was then composing—at least, what untattooed parts might remain—I did not trouble myself with the odd inches; nor, indeed, should inches at all enter into a congenial admeasurement of the whale.

---

sconces: heads (slang). **seignories**: feudal domains.

CHAPTER 103

MEASUREMENT OF THE WHALE'S SKELETON

IN the first place, I wish to lay before you a particular, plain statement, touching the living bulk of this leviathan, whose skeleton we are briefly to exhibit. Such a statement may prove useful here.

According to a careful calculation I have made, and which I partly base upon Captain Scoresby's estimate, of seventy tons for the largest sized Greenland whale of sixty feet in length; according to my careful calculation, I say, a Sperm Whale of the largest magnitude, between eighty-five and ninety feet in length, and something less than forty feet in its fullest circumference, such a whale will weigh at least ninety tons; so that, reckoning thirteen men to a ton, he would considerably outweigh the combined population of a whole village of one thousand one hundred inhabitants.

Think you not then that brains, like yoked cattle, should be put to this leviathan, to make him at all budge to any landsman's imagination?

Having already in various ways put before you his skull, spout-hole, jaw, teeth, tail, forehead, fins, and divers other parts, I shall now simply point out what is most interesting in the general bulk of his unobstructed bones. But as the colossal skull embraces so very large a proportion of the entire extent of the skeleton; as it is by far the most complicated part; and as nothing is to be repeated concerning it in this chapter, you must not fail to carry it in your mind, or under your arm, as we proceed, otherwise you will not gain a complete notion of the general structure we are about to view.

In length, the Sperm Whale's skeleton at Tranque measured seventy-two feet; so that when fully invested and extended in life, he must have been ninety feet long; for in the whale, the skeleton loses about one fifth in length compared with the living body. Of this seventy-two feet, his skull and jaw comprised some twenty feet, leaving some fifty feet of plain back-bone. Attached to this back-bone, for something less than a third of its length, was the mighty circular basket of ribs which once enclosed his vitals.

To me this vast ivory-ribbed chest, with the long, unrelieved spine, extending far away from it in a straight line, not a little resembled the **hull** of a great ship new-laid upon the stocks, when only some twenty of her naked bow-ribs are inserted, and the keel is otherwise, for the time, but a long, disconnected timber.

The ribs were ten on a side. The first, to begin from the neck, was nearly six feet long; the second, third, and fourth were each successively longer, till you came to the climax of the fifth, or one of the middle ribs, which measured eight feet and some inches. From that part, the remaining ribs diminished, till the tenth and last only spanned five feet and some inches. In general thickness, they all bore a seemly correspondence to their length. The middle ribs were the most arched. In some of the Arsacides they are used for beams whereon to lay foot-path bridges over small streams.

In considering these ribs, I could not but be struck anew with the circumstance, so variously repeated in this book, that the skeleton of the whale is by no means the mould of his invested form. The largest of the Tranque ribs, one of the middle ones, occupied that part of the fish which, in life, is greatest in depth. Now, the greatest depth of the invested body of this particular whale must have been at least sixteen feet; whereas, the corresponding rib measured but little more than eight feet. So that this rib only conveyed half of the true notion of the living magnitude of that part. Besides, for some way, where I now saw but a naked spine, all that had been once wrapped round with tons of added bulk in flesh, muscle, blood, and bowels. Still more, for the ample fins, I here saw but a few disordered joints; and in place of the **weighty** and majestic, but boneless flukes, an utter blank!

How vain and foolish, then, thought I, for timid untravelled man to try to comprehend aright this wondrous whale, by merely poring over his dead attenuated skeleton, stretched in this peaceful wood. No. Only in the heart of quickest° perils; only when within the eddyings of his angry flukes; only on the profound unbounded sea, can the fully invested whale be truly and livingly found out.

But the spine. For that, the best way we can consider it is, with a crane, to pile its bones high up on end. No speedy enterprise. But now it's done, it looks much like Pompey's Pillar.[1]

There are forty and odd vertebræ in all, which in the skeleton are not locked together. They mostly lie like the great **knobbed** blocks on a Gothic spire, forming solid courses of heavy masonry. The largest, a middle one, is in width something less than three feet, and in depth more than four. The smallest, where the spine tapers away into the tail, is only two inches in width, and looks something like a white billiard-ball. I was told that there were still smaller ones, but they had been lost by some little cannibal urchins, **the priest's children,** who had stolen them to play marbles with. Thus we see how that the spine of even the hugest of living things tapers off at last into simple child's play.

---

quickest: liveliest; most life-threatening.

CHAPTER 104

THE FOSSIL WHALE

Fʀᴏᴍ his mighty bulk the whale affords a most congenial theme whereon to enlarge, amplify, and generally expatiate. Would you, you could not compress him. By good rights he should only be treated of in imperial folio.[1] Not to tell over again his furlongs from spiracle to tail, and the yards he measures about the waist; only think of the gigantic involutions of his intestines, where they lie in him like great cables and hausers coiled away in the subterranean orlop-deck of a line-of-battle-ship.

Since I have undertaken to manhandle this Leviathan, it behoves me to approve° myself omnisciently exhaustive in the enterprise; not overlooking the minutest seminal germs° of his blood, and spinning him out to the uttermost coil of his bowels. Having already described him in most of his present habitatory and anatomical peculiarities, it now remains to magnify him in an archæological, fossiliferous, and antediluvian° point of view. Applied to any other creature than the Leviathan—to an ant or a flea—such portly terms might justly be deemed unwarrantably grandiloquent. But when Leviathan is the text, the case is altered. Fain am I to stagger to this emprise° under the weightiest words of the dictionary. And here be it said, that whenever it has been convenient to consult one in the course of these dissertations, I have invariably used a huge quarto **edition** of Johnson,[2] expressly purchased for that purpose; because that famous lexicographer's uncommon personal bulk more fitted him to compile a lexicon to be used by a whale author like me.

One often hears of writers that rise and swell with their subject, though it may seem but an ordinary one. How, then, with me, writing of this Leviathan? Unconsciously my chirography° expands into placard capitals. Give me a condor's quill! Give me Vesuvius' crater[3] for an inkstand! Friends, hold my arms! For in the mere act of penning my thoughts of this Leviathan, they weary me, and make me faint with their outreaching comprehensiveness of sweep, as if to include the whole circle of the sciences, and all the generations of whales, and men, and mastodons, past, present, and to come, with all the revolving panoramas of empire on earth, and

approve: prove. *germs*: cells. *antediluvian*: before the biblical flood. *Fain . . . emprise*: eager to undertake the enterprise. *chirography*: penmanship.

throughout the whole universe, **not excluding its suburbs**. Such, and so magnifying, is the virtue of a large and liberal theme! We expand to its bulk. To produce a mighty book, you must choose a mighty theme. No great and enduring volume can ever be written on the flea, though many there be who have tried it.[4]

Ere entering upon the subject of Fossil Whales, I present my credentials as a geologist, by stating that in my miscellaneous time I have been a stone-mason, and also a great digger of ditches, canals and wells, wine-vaults, cellars, and cisterns of all sorts.[5] Likewise, by way of preliminary, I desire to remind the reader, that while in the earlier geological strata there are found the fossils of monsters now almost completely extinct; the subsequent relics discovered in what are called the Tertiary formations seem the connecting, or at any rate intercepted links, between the ante-chronical° creatures, and those whose remote posterity are said to have entered the Ark; all the Fossil Whales hitherto discovered belong to the Tertiary period, which is the last preceding the superficial formations.[6] And though none of them precisely answer to any known species of the present time, they are yet sufficiently akin to them in general respects, to justify their taking rank as Cetacean fossils.

Detached broken fossils of pre-adamite° whales, fragments of their bones and skeletons, have within thirty years past, at various intervals, been found at the base of the Alps, in Lombardy, in France, in England, in Scotland, and in the States of Louisiana, Mississippi, and Alabama. Among the more curious of such remains is part of a skull, which in the year 1779 was disinterred in the Rue Dauphiné in Paris, a short street opening almost directly upon the palace of the Tuileries;[7] and bones disinterred in excavating the great docks of Antwerp, in Napoleon's time. Cuvier pronounced these fragments to have belonged to some utterly unknown Leviathanic species.[8]

But by far the most wonderful of all cetacean relics was the almost complete vast skeleton of an extinct monster, found in the year 1842, on the plantation of Judge Creagh, in Alabama. The awe-stricken credulous slaves in the vicinity took it for the bones of one of the fallen angels. The Alabama doctors declared it a huge reptile, and bestowed upon it the name of Basilosaurus. But some specimen bones of it being taken across the sea to Owen, the English Anatomist, it turned out that this alleged reptile was a whale, though of a departed species. A significant illustration of the fact, again and again repeated in this book, that the skeleton of the whale furnishes but little clue to the shape of his fully invested body. So Owen rechristened the monster Zeuglodon; and in his paper read before the London Geological Society, pronounced it, in substance, one of the most extraordinary creatures which the mutations of the globe have blotted out of existence.[9]

When I stand among these mighty Leviathan skeletons, skulls, tusks, jaws, ribs, and vertebræ, all characterized by partial resemblances to the existing breeds of sea monsters; but at the same time bearing on the other hand similar affinities to the annihilated ante-chronical Leviathans, their incalculable seniors; I am, by a flood, borne back to that wondrous period, ere time itself can be said to have begun; for time began with man. Here Saturn's grey chaos[10] rolls over me, and I obtain dim, shuddering glimpses into those Polar eternities; when wedged bastions of ice

ante-chronical: before recorded time. ***pre-adamite***: before Adam.

pressed hard upon what are now the Tropics; and in all the 25,000 miles of this world's circumference, not an inhabitable hand's breadth of land was visible. Then the whole world was the whale's; and, king of creation, he left his wake along the present lines of the Andes and the Himmalehs. Who can show a pedigree like **Leviathan**? Ahab's harpoon had shed older blood than the Pharaohs'. Methuselah seems a schoolboy. I look round to shake hands with Shem.[11] I am horror-struck at this antemosaic,° unsourced existence of the unspeakable terrors of the whale, which, having been before all time, must needs exist after all **humane** ages are over.

But not alone has this Leviathan left his pre-adamite traces in the stereotype plates of nature, and in limestone and marl[12] bequeathed his ancient bust; but upon Egyptian tablets, whose antiquity seems to claim for them an almost fossiliferous character, we find the unmistakable print of his fin. In an apartment of the great temple of Denderah,[13] some fifty years ago, there was discovered upon the granite ceiling a sculptured and painted planisphere, abounding in centaurs, griffins, and dolphins, similar to the grotesque figures on the celestial globe of the moderns. Gliding among them, old Leviathan swam as of yore; was there swimming in that planisphere, centuries before Solomon was cradled.

Nor must there be omitted another strange attestation of the antiquity of the whale, in his own osseous° post-diluvian reality, as set down by the venerable John Leo, the old Barbary traveller.[14]

"Not far from the Sea-side, they have a Temple, the Rafters and Beams of which are made of Whale-Bones; for Whales of a monstrous size are oftentimes cast up dead upon that shore. The Common People imagine, that by a secret Power bestowed by God upon the Temple, no Whale can pass it without immediate death. But the truth of the Matter is, that on either side of the Temple, there are Rocks that shoot two Miles into the Sea, and wound the Whales when they light upon 'em. They keep a Whale's Rib of an incredible length for a Miracle, which lying upon the Ground with its convex part uppermost, makes an Arch, the Head of which cannot be reached by a Man upon a Camel's Back. This Rib (says John Leo) is said to have layn there a hundred Years before I saw it. Their Historians affirm, that a Prophet who prophesy'd of Mahomet,[15] came from this Temple, and some do not stand° to assert, that the Prophet Jonas° was cast forth by the Whale at the Base of the Temple."

In this Afric Temple of the Whale I leave you, reader, and if you be a Nantucketer, and a whaleman, you will silently worship there.

---

antemosaic: before Moses. ***osseous***: skeletal. ***stand***: hesitate. ***Jonas***: Jonah.

CHAPTER 105

DOES THE WHALE'S MAGNITUDE DIMINISH?—WILL HE PERISH?

INASMUCH, then, as this Leviathan comes floundering down upon us from the head-waters of the Eternities, it may be fitly inquired, whether, in the long course of his generations, he has not degenerated from the original bulk of his sires.[1]

But upon investigation we find, that not only are the whales of the present day superior in magnitude to those whose fossil remains are found in the Tertiary system (embracing a distinct geological period prior to man), but of the whales found in that Tertiary system, those belonging to its latter formations exceed in size those of its earlier ones.

Of all the pre-adamite whales yet exhumed, by far the largest is the Alabama one mentioned in the last chapter, and that was less than seventy feet in length in the skeleton. Whereas, we have already seen, that the tape-measure gives seventy-two feet for the skeleton of a large sized modern whale. And I have heard, on whalemen's authority, that Sperm Whales have been captured near a hundred feet long at the time of capture.

But may it not be, that while the whales of the present hour are an advance in magnitude upon those of all previous geological periods; may it not be, that since Adam's time they have degenerated?

Assuredly, we must conclude so, if we are to credit the accounts of such gentlemen as Pliny, and the ancient naturalists generally. For Pliny tells us of whales that embraced acres of living bulk, and Aldrovandus[2] of others which measured eight hundred feet in length—Rope Walks and Thames Tunnels of Whales![3] And even in the days of Banks and Solander, Cook's naturalists,[4] we find a Danish member of the Academy of Sciences[5] setting down certain Iceland Whales (reydar-fiskur, or Wrinkled Bellies) at one hundred and twenty yards; that is, three hundred and sixty feet. And Lacépède, the French naturalist, in his elaborate history of whales, in the very beginning of his work (page 3), sets down the Right Whale at one hundred metres, three hundred and twenty-eight feet. And this work was published so late as A. D. 1825.[6]

But will any whaleman believe these stories? No. The whale of to-day is as big as his ancestors in Pliny's time. And if ever I go where Pliny is, I, a whaleman (more than he was), will make bold to tell him so. Because I cannot understand how it is, that while the Egyptian mummies that were buried thousands of years before even Pliny was born, do not measure so much in their coffins as a modern Kentuckian in his socks; and while the cattle and other animals sculptured on the oldest Egyptian and Nineveh tablets, by the relative proportions in which they are drawn, just as plainly prove that the high-bred, stall-fed, prize cattle of Smithfield, not only equal, but far exceed in magnitude the fattest of Pharaoh's fat kine;[7] in the face of all this, I will not admit that of all animals the whale alone should have degenerated.

But still another inquiry remains; one often agitated by the more recondite Nantucketers. Whether owing to the almost omniscient look-outs at the mast-heads of the whale-ships, now penetrating even through Behring's straits, and into the remotest secret drawers and lockers of the world; and the thousand harpoons and lances darted along all continental coasts; the moot point° is, whether Leviathan can long endure so wide a chase, and so remorseless a havoc; whether he must not at last be exterminated from the waters, and the last whale, like the last man, smoke his last pipe, and then himself evaporate in the final puff.

Comparing the humped herds of whales with the humped herds of buffalo, which, not forty years ago, overspread by tens of thousands the prairies of Illinois and Missouri, and shook their iron manes and scowled with their thunder-clotted brows upon the sites of populous river-capitals, where now the polite broker sells you land at a dollar an inch; in such a comparison an irresistible argument would seem furnished, to show that the hunted whale cannot now escape speedy extinction.

But you must look at this matter in every light. Though so short a period ago—not a good life-time—the census of the buffalo in Illinois exceeded the census of men now in London,[8] and though at the present day not one horn or hoof of them remains in all that region; and though the cause of this wondrous extermination was the spear of man; yet the far different nature of the whale-hunt peremptorily forbids so inglorious an end to the Leviathan. Forty men in one ship hunting the Sperm Whale for forty-eight months think they have done extremely well, and thank God, if at last they carry home the oil of forty fish. Whereas, in the days of the old Canadian and Indian hunters and trappers of the West, when the far west (in whose sunset suns still rise) was a wilderness and a virgin, the same number of moccasined men, for the same number of months, mounted on horse instead of sailing in ships, would have slain not forty, but forty thousand and more buffaloes; a fact that, if need were, could be statistically stated.

Nor, considered aright, does it seem any argument in favor of the gradual extinction of the Sperm Whale, for example, that in former years (the latter part of the last century, say) these Leviathans, in small pods, were encountered much oftener than at present, and, in consequence, the voyages were not so prolonged, and were also much more remunerative. Because, as has been elsewhere noticed, those whales, influenced by some views to safety, now swim the seas in immense caravans, so that to a large degree the scattered solitaries, yokes,° and pods, and schools of other days

moot point: issue for debate. **yokes**: pairs.

are now aggregated into vast but widely separated, unfrequent armies. That is all. And equally fallacious seems the conceit, that because the so-called whale-bone whales no longer haunt many grounds in former years abounding with them, hence that species also is declining. For they are only being driven from promontory to cape;[9] and if one coast is no longer enlivened with their jets, then, be sure, some other and remoter strand has been very recently startled by the unfamiliar spectacle.

Furthermore: concerning these last mentioned Leviathans, they have two firm fortresses, which, in all human probability, will for ever remain impregnable. And as upon the invasion of their valleys, the frosty Swiss have retreated to their mountains; so, hunted from the savannas and glades of the middle seas, the whale-bone whales can at last resort to their Polar citadels, and diving under the ultimate glassy barriers and walls there, come up among icy fields and floes; and in a charmed circle of everlasting December, bid defiance to all pursuit from man.

But as perhaps fifty of these whale-bone whales are harpooned for one cachalot,° some philosophers of the forecastle have concluded that this positive havoc has already very seriously diminished their battalions. But though for some time past a number of these whales, not less than 13,000, have been annually slain on the nor' west coast by the Americans alone; yet there are considerations which render even this circumstance of little or no account as an opposing argument in this matter.

Natural as it is to be somewhat incredulous concerning the populousness of the more enormous creatures of the globe, yet what shall we say to Horto, the historian of Goa,[10] when he tells us that at one hunting the King of Siam took 4000 elephants; that in those regions elephants are numerous as droves of cattle in the temperate climes. And there seems no reason to doubt that if these elephants, which have now been hunted for thousands of years, by Semiramis, by Porus, by Hannibal,[11] and by all the successive monarchs of the East—if they still survive there in great numbers, much more may the great whale outlast all hunting, since he has a pasture to expatiate in, which is precisely twice as large as all Asia, both Americas, Europe and Africa, New Holland,[12] and all the Isles of the sea combined.

Moreover: we are to consider, that from the presumed great longevity of whales, their probably attaining the age of a century and more, therefore at any one period of time, several distinct adult generations must be contemporary. And what that is, we may soon gain some idea of, by imagining all the grave-yards, cemeteries, and family vaults of creation yielding up the live bodies of all the men, women, and children who were alive seventy-five years ago; and adding this countless host to the present human population of the globe.

Wherefore, for all these things, we account the whale immortal in his species, however perishable in his individuality. He swam the seas before the continents broke water; he once swam over the site of the Tuileries, and Windsor Castle, and the Kremlin. In Noah's flood he despised Noah's Ark; and if ever the world is to be again flooded, like the Netherlands, to kill off its rats, then the eternal whale will still survive, and rearing upon the topmost crest of the equatorial flood, spout his frothed defiance to the skies.

---

cachalot: sperm whale (French).

CHAPTER 106

AHAB'S LEG

THE precipitating manner in which Captain Ahab had quitted the Samuel Enderby of London, had not been unattended with some small violence to his own person. He had lighted with such energy upon a thwart° of his boat that his ivory leg had received a half-splintering shock. And when after gaining his own deck, and his own pivot-hole there, he so vehemently wheeled round with an urgent command to the steersman (it was, as ever, something about his not steering inflexibly enough); then, the already shaken ivory received such an additional twist and wrench, that though it still remained entire, and to all appearances lusty, yet Ahab did not deem it entirely trustworthy.

And, indeed, it seemed small matter for wonder, that for all his pervading, mad recklessness, Ahab did at times give careful heed to the condition of that dead bone upon which he partly stood. For it had not been very long prior to the Pequod's sailing from Nantucket, that he had been found one night lying prone upon the ground, and insensible; by some unknown, and seemingly inexplicable, unimaginable casualty, his ivory limb having been so violently displaced, that it had stake-wise smitten, and all but pierced his groin; nor was it without extreme difficulty that the agonizing wound was entirely cured.

Nor, at the time, had it failed to enter his monomaniac mind, that all the anguish of that then present suffering was but the direct issue of a former woe; and he too plainly seemed to see, that as the most poisonous reptile of the marsh perpetuates his kind as inevitably as the sweetest songster of the grove; so, equally with every felicity, all miserable events do naturally beget their like. Yea, more than equally, thought Ahab; since both the ancestry and posterity of Grief go further than the ancestry and posterity of Joy. For, not to hint of this: that it is an inference from certain canonic teachings,° that while some natural enjoyments here shall have no children born to them for the other world, but, on the contrary, shall be followed by the joy-childlessness of all hell's despair; whereas, some guilty mortal miseries shall still fertilely beget to themselves an eternally progressive progeny of griefs beyond the grave; not at all to hint of this, there still seems an inequality in the

---

thwart: rowing seat. **canonic teachings**: standard church doctrines.

deeper analysis of the thing. For, thought Ahab, while even the highest earthly felicities ever have a certain unsignifying pettiness lurking in them, but, at bottom, all heart-woes, a mystic significance, and, in some men, an archangelic grandeur; so do their diligent tracings-out not belie the obvious deduction. To trail the genealogies of these high mortal miseries, carries us at last among the sourceless primogenitures° of the gods; so that, in the face of all the glad, hay-making suns, and soft-cymballing, round harvest-moons, we must needs give in to this: that the gods themselves are not for ever glad. The ineffaceable, sad birth-mark in the brow of man,[1] is but the stamp of sorrow in the signers.

Unwittingly here a secret has been divulged, which perhaps might more properly, in set way, have been disclosed before. With many other particulars concerning Ahab, always had it remained a mystery to some, why it was, that for a certain period, both before and after the sailing of the Pequod, he had hidden himself away with such Grand-Lama-like exclusiveness;[2] and, for that one interval, sought speechless refuge, as it were, among the marble senate of the dead. Captain Peleg's bruited reason° for this thing appeared by no means adequate;[3] though, indeed, as touching all Ahab's deeper part, every revelation partook more of significant darkness than of explanatory light. But, in the end, it all came out; this one matter did, at least. That direful mishap° was at the bottom of his temporary recluseness. And not only this, but to that ever-contracting, dropping circle ashore, who, for any reason, possessed the privilege of a less banned approach to him; to that timid circle the above hinted casualty—remaining, as it did, moodily unaccounted for by Ahab—invested itself with terrors, not entirely underived from the land of spirits and of wails. So that, through their zeal for him, they had all conspired, so far as in them lay, to muffle up the knowledge of this thing from others; and hence it was, that not till a considerable interval had elapsed, did it transpire upon the Pequod's decks.

But be all this as it may; let the unseen, ambiguous synod in the air, or the vindictive princes and potentates of fire,[4] have to do or not with earthly Ahab, yet, in this present matter of his leg, he took plain practical procedures;—he called the carpenter.

And when that functionary appeared before him, he bade him without delay set about making a new leg, and directed the mates to see him supplied with all the studs and joists of jaw-ivory (Sperm Whale) which had thus far been accumulated on the voyage, in order that a careful selection of the stoutest, clearest-grained stuff might be secured. This done, the carpenter received orders to have the leg completed that night; and to provide all the fittings for it, independent of those pertaining to the distrusted one in use. Moreover, the ship's forge was ordered to be hoisted out of its temporary idleness in the hold; and, to accelerate the affair, the blacksmith was commanded to proceed at once to the forging of whatever iron contrivances might be needed.

---

sourceless primogenitures: parentless first generation of the gods. **bruited reason**: reported explanation. **direful mishap**: his groin injury.

CHAPTER 107

THE CARPENTER

S EAT thyself sultanically among the moons of Saturn, and take high abstracted man alone; and he seems a wonder, a grandeur, and a woe. But from the same point, take mankind in mass, and for the most part, they seem a mob of unnecessary duplicates, both contemporary and hereditary. But most humble though he was, and far from furnishing an example of the high, humane abstraction; the Pequod's carpenter was no duplicate; hence, he now comes in person on this stage.

Like all sea-going ship carpenters, and more especially those belonging to whaling vessels, he was, to a certain off-handed, practical extent, alike experienced in numerous trades and callings collateral to his own; the carpenter's pursuit being the ancient and outbranching trunk of all those numerous handicrafts which more or less have to do with wood as an auxiliary material. But, besides the application to him of the generic remark above, this carpenter of the Pequod was singularly efficient in those thousand nameless mechanical emergencies continually recurring in a large ship, upon a three or four years' voyage, in uncivilized and far-distant seas. For not to speak of his readiness in ordinary duties:—repairing stove boats, sprung spars, reforming the shape of clumsy-bladed oars, inserting bull's eyes in the deck, or new tree-nails[1] in the side planks, and other miscellaneous matters more directly pertaining to his special business; he was moreover unhesitatingly expert in all manner of conflicting aptitudes, both useful and capricious.°

The one grand stage where he enacted all his various parts so manifold, was his vice-bench; a long rude ponderous table furnished with several vices, of different sizes, and both of iron and of wood. At all times except when whales were alongside, this bench was securely lashed athwartships° against the rear of the Try-works.

A belaying pin° is found too large to be easily inserted into its hole: the carpenter claps it into one of his ever-ready vices, and straightway files it smaller. A lost land-bird of strange plumage strays on board, and is made a captive: out of clean shaved rods of right-whale bone, and cross-beams of sperm whale ivory, the carpenter makes a pagoda-looking cage for it. An oarsman sprains his wrist: the car-

---

capricious: responsive to others' whims. **athwartships**: sideways, crosswise. **belaying pin**: large peg in the rail, to which ropes are secured.

408

penter concocts a soothing lotion. Stubb longed for vermillion stars to be painted upon the blade of his every oar; screwing each oar in his big vice of wood, the carpenter symmetrically supplies the constellation. A sailor takes a fancy to wear shark-bone ear-rings: the carpenter drills his ears. Another has the toothache: the carpenter out pincers, and clapping one hand upon his bench bids him be seated there; but the poor fellow unmanageably winces under the unconcluded operation; whirling round the handle of his wooden vice, the carpenter signs him to clap his jaw in that, if he would have him draw the tooth.

Thus, this carpenter was prepared at all points, and alike indifferent and without respect in all. Teeth he accounted bits of ivory; heads he deemed but top-blocks;° men themselves he lightly held for capstans. But while now upon so wide a field thus variously accomplished, and with such liveliness of expertness in him, too; all this would seem to argue some uncommon vivacity of intelligence. But not precisely so. For nothing was this man more remarkable, than for a certain impersonal stolidity as it were; impersonal, I say; for it so shaded off into the surrounding infinite of things, that it seemed one with the general stolidity discernible in the whole visible world; which while pauselessly active in uncounted modes, still eternally holds its peace, and ignores you, though you dig foundations for cathedrals. Yet was this half-horrible stolidity in him, involving, too, as it appeared, an all-ramifying heartlessness;—yet was it oddly dashed at times, with an old, crutch-like, antediluvian, wheezing humorousness, not unstreaked now and then with a certain grizzled wittiness; such as might have served to pass the time during the midnight watch on the bearded forecastle of Noah's ark. Was it that this old carpenter had been a life-long wanderer, whose much rolling, to and fro, not only had gathered no moss; but what is more, had rubbed off whatever small outward clingings might have originally pertained to him? He was a stript abstract;° an unfractioned integral; uncompromised as a new-born babe; living without premeditated reference to this world or the next. You might almost say, that this strange uncompromisedness in him involved a sort of unintelligence; for in his numerous trades, he did not seem to work so much by reason or by instinct, or simply because he had been tutored to it, or by any intermixture of all these, even or uneven; but merely by a kind of deaf and dumb, spontaneous literal process. He was a pure manipulator; his brain, if he had ever had one, must have early oozed along into the muscles of his fingers. He was like one of those unreasoning but still highly useful, *multum in parvo,* Sheffield contrivances,° assuming the exterior—though a little swelled—of a common pocket knife; but containing, not only blades of various sizes, but also screw-drivers, cork-screws, tweezers, awls, pens, rulers, nail-filers, countersinkers. So, if his superiors wanted to use the carpenter for a screw-driver, all they had to do was to open that part of him, and the screw was fast: or if for tweezers, take him up by the legs, and there they were.

Yet, as previously hinted, this omnitooled, open-and-shut carpenter, was, after all, no mere machine of an automaton.[2] If he **did not have** a common soul in him,

---

top-blocks: large block-and-pulley for raising and lowering a topmast. **abstract**: epitome. **multum in parvo, Sheffield contrivances**: an all-in-one knife (the Latin means "much in little"); *Sheffield*, England, was known for its cutlery.

he had a subtle something that somehow anomalously did its duty. What that was, whether essence of quicksilver, or a few drops of hartshorn,° there is no telling. But there it was; and there it had abided for now some sixty years or more. And this it was, this same unaccountable, cunning life-principle in him; this it was, that kept him a great part of the time soliloquizing; but only like an unreasoning wheel, which also hummingly soliloquizes; or rather, his body was a sentry-box and this soliloquizer on guard there, and talking all the time to keep himself awake.

quicksilver . . . hartshorn: mercury and ammonia, both used in extracting metals from ore.

CHAPTER 108

AHAB AND
THE CARPENTER

THE DECK—FIRST NIGHT WATCH.

(Carpenter standing before his vice-bench, and by the light of two lanterns busily filing the ivory joist for the leg, which joist is firmly fixed in the vice. Slabs of ivory, leather straps, pads, screws, and various tools of all sorts lying about the bench. Forward, the red flame of the forge is seen, where the blacksmith is at work.)

D RAT the file, and drat the bone! That is hard which should be soft, and that is soft which should be hard. So we go, who file old jaws and shinbones. Let's try another. Aye, now, this works better (*sneezes*). Halloa, this bone dust is (*sneezes*)— why it's (*sneezes*)—yes it's (*sneezes*)—bless my soul, it won't let me speak! This is what an old fellow gets now for working in dead lumber. Saw a live tree, and you don't get this dust; amputate a live bone, and you don't get it (*sneezes*). Come, come, you old Smut,° there, bear a hand, and let's have that ferule and buckle-screw;° I'll be ready for them presently. Lucky now (*sneezes*) there's no knee-joint to make; that might puzzle a little; but a mere shinbone—why it's easy as making hop-poles;° only I should like to put a good finish on. Time, time; if I but only had the time, I could turn him out as neat a leg now as ever (*sneezes*) scraped° to a lady in a parlor. Those buckskin legs and calves of legs I've seen in shop windows wouldn't compare at all. They soak water, they do; and of course get rheumatic, and have to be doctored (*sneezes*) with washes and lotions, just like live legs. There; before I saw it off, now, I must call his old Mogulship, and see whether the length will be all right; too short, if anything, I guess. Ha! that's the heel; we are in luck; here he comes, or it's somebody else, that's certain.

AHAB (*advancing*).
(During the ensuing scene, the carpenter continues sneezing at times.)

Well, manmaker!

Just in time, sir. If the captain pleases, I will now mark the length. Let me measure, sir.

Smut: nickname for Perth, the blacksmith. ***ferule and buckle-screw***: iron ring or band, and buckle-fastener. ***hop-poles***: used in growing hops. ***scraped***: bowed ceremoniously.

Measured for a leg! good. Well, it's not the first time. About it! There; keep thy finger on it. This is a cogent vice thou hast here, carpenter; let me feel its grip once. So, so; it does pinch some.

Oh, sir, it will break bones—beware, beware!

No fear; I like a good grip; I like to feel something in this slippery world that can hold, man. What's Prometheus about there?—the blacksmith, I mean—what's he about?

He must be forging the buckle-screw, sir, now.

Right. It's a partnership; he supplies the muscle part. He makes a fierce red flame there!

Aye, sir; he must have the white heat for this kind of fine work.

Um-m. So he must. I do deem it now a most meaning thing, that that old Greek, Prometheus, who made men, they say, should have been a blacksmith, and animated them with fire; for what's made in fire must properly belong to fire; and so hell's probable. How the soot flies! This must be the remainder the Greek made the Africans of. Carpenter, when he's through with that buckle, tell him to forge a pair of steel shoulder-blades; there's a pedlar aboard with a crushing pack.

Sir?

Hold; while Prometheus is about it, I'll order a complete man[1] after a desirable pattern. Imprimis,° fifty feet high in his socks; then, chest modelled after the Thames Tunnel; then, legs with roots to 'em, to stay in one place; then, arms three feet through the wrist; no heart at all, brass forehead, and about a quarter of an acre of fine brains; and let me see—shall I order eyes to see outwards? No, but put a sky-light on top of his head to illuminate inwards.[2] There, take the order, and away.

Now, what's he speaking about, and who's he speaking to, I should like to know? Shall I keep standing here? (*aside.*)

'Tis but indifferent architecture to make a blind dome; here's one. No, no, no; I must have a lantern.

Ho, ho! That's it, hey? Here are two, sir; one will serve my turn.

What art thou thrusting that thief-catcher into my face for, man? Thrusted light is worse than presented pistols.

I thought, sir, that you spoke to carpenter.

Carpenter?[3] why that's—but no;—a very tidy, and, I may say, an extremely gentlemanlike sort of business thou art in here, carpenter;—or would'st thou rather work in clay?

Sir?—Clay? clay, sir? That's mud; we leave clay to ditchers, sir.

The fellow's impious![4] What art thou sneezing about?

Bone is rather dusty, sir.

Take the hint, then; and when thou art dead, never bury thyself under living people's noses.

Sir?—oh! ah!—I guess so;—yes—oh, dear!

Look ye, carpenter, I dare say thou callest thyself a right good workmanlike workman, eh? Well, then, will it speak thoroughly well for thy work, if, when I come to mount this leg thou makest, I shall nevertheless feel another leg in the same

---

Imprimis: first (Latin).

identical place with it; that is, carpenter, my old lost leg; the flesh and blood one, I mean. Canst thou not drive that old Adam° away?

Truly, sir, I begin to understand somewhat now. Yes, I have heard something curious on that score, sir; how that a dismasted man never entirely loses the feeling of his old spar, but it will be still pricking him at times. May I humbly ask if it be really so, sir?

It is, man. Look, put thy live leg here in the place where mine once was; so, now, here is only one distinct leg to the eye, yet two to the soul. Where thou feelest tingling life; there, exactly there, there to a hair, do I. Is't a riddle?

I should humbly call it a poser, sir.

Hist, then. How dost thou know that some entire, living, thinking thing may not be invisibly and uninterpenetratingly standing precisely where thou now standest; aye, and standing there in thy spite? In thy most solitary hours, then, dost thou not fear eavesdroppers? Hold, don't speak! And if I still feel the smart of my crushed leg, though it be now so long dissolved; then, why mayst not thou, carpenter, feel the fiery pains of hell for ever, and without a body? Hah!

Good Lord! Truly, sir, if it comes to that, I must calculate over again; I think I didn't carry a small figure, sir.

Look ye, pudding-heads should never grant premises.—How long before the leg is done?

Perhaps an hour, sir.

Bungle away at it then, and bring it to me (*turns to go*). Oh, Life! Here I am, proud as a Greek god, and yet standing debtor to this blockhead for a bone to stand on! Cursed be that mortal inter-indebtedness which will not do away with ledgers. I would be free as air; and I'm down in the whole world's books.° I am so rich, I could have given bid for bid with the wealthiest Prætorians[5] at the auction of the Roman empire (which was the world's); and yet I owe for the flesh in the tongue I brag with. By heavens! I'll get a crucible, and into it, and dissolve myself down to one small, compendious vertebra. So.

CARPENTER (*resuming his work*).

Well, well, well! Stubb knows him best of all, and Stubb always says he's queer; says nothing but that one sufficient little word queer; he's queer, says Stubb; he's queer—queer, queer; and keeps dinning it into Mr. Starbuck all the time—queer, sir—queer, queer, very queer. And here's his leg! Yes, now that I think of it, here's his bedfellow! has a stick of whale's jaw-bone for a wife! And this is his leg; he'll stand on this. What was that now about one leg standing in three places, and all three places standing in one hell—how was that? Oh! I don't wonder he looked so scornful at me! I'm a sort of strange-thoughted sometimes, they say; but that's only haphazard-like. Then, a short, little old body like me, should never undertake to wade out into deep waters with tall, heron-built captains; the water chucks you under the chin pretty quick, and there's a great cry for life-boats. And here's the heron's leg! long and slim, sure enough! Now, for most folks one pair of legs lasts a lifetime, and that

---

old Adam: traditional Christian term for the flesh. **down in the whole world's books**: listed in all financial ledgers as a debtor.

must be because they use them mercifully, as a tender-hearted old lady uses her roly-poly old coach-horses. But Ahab; oh he's a hard driver. Look, driven one leg to death, and spavined° the other for life, and now wears out bone legs by the cord. Halloa, there, you Smut! bear a hand there with those screws, and let's finish it **before the resurrection fellow**[6] **comes a-calling with his horn for all legs, true or false, as brewery-men go round collecting old beer barrels, to fill 'em up again.** What a leg this is! It looks like a real live leg, filed down to nothing but the core; he'll be standing on this to-morrow; he'll be taking altitudes on it.[7] Halloa! I almost forgot the little oval slate, smoothed ivory, where he figures up the latitude. So, so; chisel, file, and sand-paper, now!

spavined: crippled, normally said of horses.

REVISION NARRATIVE

Resurrection Fellow

The carpenter recognizes that Ahab's obsessive spirit outlasts the captain's natural and prosthetic legs, and he hurries along the replacement of Ahab's new leg, noting that the "resurrection fellow" will soon enough signal the demise of all legs (that is, bodies) come Judgment Day. In Islamic, Jewish, and Christian traditions that final day is announced by the blowing of a horn. The good and the evil are divided, and the good are reborn or resurrected into eternal life. Melville alludes to this apocalyptic event throughout *Moby-Dick*, and here, as the novel approaches its own cataclysmic conclusion, the carpenter's commentary underscores the image as it prefigures the *Pequod*'s demise. But British editors found the playful reference to the horn-blowing Gabriel as a "fellow," and one likened to a "brewery-man," to be irreverent; they cut the entire passage.

CHAPTER 109

AHAB AND STARBUCK IN THE CABIN

ACCORDING to usage they were pumping the ship next morning; and lo! no inconsiderable oil came up with the water; the casks below must have sprung a bad leak. Much concern was shown; and Starbuck went down into the cabin to report this unfavorable affair.*

Now, from the South and West the Pequod was drawing nigh to Formosa and the Bashee Isles, between which lies one of the tropical outlets from the China waters into the Pacific.[1] And so Starbuck found Ahab with a general chart of the oriental archipelagoes spread before him; and another separate one representing the long eastern coasts of the Japanese islands—Niphon, Matsmai, and Sikoke.[2] With his snow-white new ivory leg braced against the screwed leg of his table, and with a long pruning-hook of a jack-knife in his hand, the wondrous old man, with his back to the gangway door, was wrinkling his brow, and tracing his old courses again.

"Who's there?" hearing the footstep at the door, but not turning round to it. "On deck! Begone!"

"Captain Ahab mistakes; it is I. The oil in the hold is leaking, sir. We must up Burtons and break out."°

"Up Burtons and break out? Now that we are nearing Japan; heave-to here for a week to tinker a parcel of old hoops?"

"Either do that, sir, or waste in one day more oil than we may make good in a year. What we come twenty thousand miles to get is worth saving, sir."

"So it is, so it is; if we get it."

"I was speaking of the oil in the hold, sir."

"And I was not speaking or thinking of that at all. Begone! Let it leak! I'm all

---

* In Sperm-whalemen with any considerable quantity of oil on board, it is a regular semi-weekly duty to conduct a hose into the hold, and drench the casks with sea-water; which afterwards, at varying intervals, is removed by the ship's pumps. Hereby the casks are sought to be kept damply tight; while by the changed character of the withdrawn water, the mariners readily detect any serious leakage in the precious cargo.

---

up Burtons and break out: prepare the hoisting tackle and lift casks from the hold.

aleak myself. Aye! leaks in leaks! not only full of leaky casks, but those leaky casks are in a leaky ship; and that's a far worse plight than the Pequod's, man. Yet I don't stop to plug my leak; for who can find it in the deep-loaded hull; or how hope to plug it, even if found, in this life's howling gale? Starbuck! I'll not have the Burtons hoisted."

"What will the owners say, sir?"

"Let the owners stand on Nantucket beach and outyell the Typhoons. What cares Ahab? Owners, owners? Thou art always prating to me, Starbuck, about those miserly owners, as if the owners were my conscience. But look ye, the only real owner of anything is its commander; and hark ye, my conscience is in this ship's keel.—On deck!"

"Captain Ahab," said the reddening mate, moving further into the cabin, with a daring so strangely respectful and cautious that it almost seemed not only every way seeking to avoid the slightest outward manifestation of itself, but within also seemed more than half distrustful of itself; "A better man than I might well pass over in thee what he would quickly enough resent in a younger man; aye, and in a happier, Captain Ahab."

"Devils! Dost thou then so much as dare to critically think of me?—On deck!"

"Nay, sir, not yet; I do entreat. And I do dare, sir—to be forbearing! Shall we not understand each other better than hitherto, Captain Ahab?"

Ahab seized a loaded musket from the rack (forming part of most South-Sea-men's cabin furniture°), and pointing it towards Starbuck, exclaimed: "There is one God that is Lord over the earth,[3] and one Captain that is lord over the Pequod.—On deck!"

For an instant in the flashing eyes of the mate, and his fiery cheeks, you would have almost thought that he had really received the blaze of the levelled tube. But, mastering his emotion, he half calmly rose, and as he quitted the cabin, paused for an instant and said: "Thou hast outraged, not insulted me, sir; but for that I ask thee not to beware of Starbuck; thou wouldst but laugh; but let Ahab beware of Ahab; beware of thyself, old man."

"He waxes brave, but nevertheless obeys; most careful bravery that!" murmured Ahab, as Starbuck disappeared. "What's that he said—Ahab beware of Ahab—there's something there!" Then unconsciously using the musket for a staff, with an iron brow he paced to and fro in the little cabin; but presently the thick plaits of his forehead relaxed, and returning the gun to the rack, he went to the deck.

"Thou art but too good a fellow, Starbuck," he said lowly to the mate; then raising his voice to the crew: "Furl the t'gallant-sails, and close-reef° the top-sails, fore and aft; back the main-yard;° up Burtons, and break out in the main-hold."

It were perhaps vain to surmise exactly why it was, that as respecting Starbuck, Ahab thus acted. It may have been a flash of honesty in him; or mere prudential policy which, under the circumstance, imperiously forbade the slightest symptom of open disaffection, however transient, in the important chief officer of his ship. However it was, his orders were executed; and the Burtons were hoisted.

---

furniture: equipment. ***close-reef***: tie up a sail so that only a fraction is exposed to the wind. ***Furl the t'gallant-sails . . . back the main-yard***: actions meant to halt the ship.

CHAPTER 110

QUEEQUEG IN HIS COFFIN

U PON searching, it was found that the casks last struck into the hold were per-fectly sound, and that the leak must be further off. So, it being calm weather, they broke out deeper and deeper, disturbing the slumbers of the huge ground-tier butts; and from that black midnight sending those gigantic moles into the daylight above. So deep did they go; and so ancient, and corroded, and weedy the aspect of the lowermost puncheons,° that you almost looked next for some mouldy corner-stone cask containing coins of Captain Noah, with copies of the posted placards, vainly warning the infatuated old world from the flood.[1] Tierce after tierce, too, of water, and bread, and beef, and shooks of staves,° and iron bundles of hoops, were hoisted out, till at last the piled decks were hard to get about; and the hollow hull echoed under foot, as if you were treading over empty catacombs, and reeled and rolled in the sea like an air-freighted demijohn.° Top-heavy was the ship as a din-nerless student with all Aristotle in his head. Well was it that the Typhoons did not visit them then.

Now, at this time it was that my poor pagan companion, and fast bosom-friend, Queequeg, was seized with a fever, which brought him nigh to his endless end.

Be it said, that in this vocation of whaling, sinecures are unknown; dignity and danger go hand in hand; till you get to be Captain, the higher you rise the harder you toil. So with poor Queequeg, who, as harpooneer, must not only face all the rage of the living whale, but—as we have elsewhere seen—mount his dead back in a rolling sea; and finally descend into the gloom of the hold, and bitterly sweating all day in that subterraneous confinement, resolutely manhandle the clumsiest casks and see to their stowage. To be short, among whalemen, the harpooneers are the holders, so called.

Poor Queequeg! when the ship was about half disembowelled, you should have stooped over the hatchway, and peered down upon him there; where, stripped to his woollen drawers, the tattooed savage was crawling about amid that dampness and slime, like a green spotted lizard at the bottom of a well. And a well, or an ice-house, it somehow proved to him, poor pagan; where, strange to say, for all the heat

puncheons: large casks. ***shooks of staves***: bundles of wooden strips for making barrels.
demijohn: large glass or clay bottle.

of his sweatings, he caught a terrible chill which lapsed into a fever; and at last, after some days' suffering, laid him in his hammock, close to the very sill of the door of death. How he wasted and wasted away in those few long-lingering days, till there seemed but little left of him but his frame and tattooing. But as all else in him thinned, and his cheek-bones grew sharper, his eyes, nevertheless, seemed growing fuller and fuller; they became of a strange softness of lustre; and mildly but deeply looked out at you there from his sickness, a wondrous testimony to that immortal health in him which could not die, or be weakened. And like circles on the water, which, as they grow fainter, expand; so his eyes seemed rounding and rounding, like the rings of Eternity. An awe that cannot be named would steal over you as you sat by the side of this waning savage, and saw as strange things in his face, as any beheld who were bystanders when Zoroaster[2] died. For whatever is truly wondrous and fearful in man, never yet was put into words or books. And the drawing near of Death, which alike levels all, **alike** impresses all with a last revelation, which only an author from the dead could adequately tell. So that—let us say it again—no dying Chaldee or Greek[3] had higher and holier thoughts than those, whose mysterious shades you saw creeping over the face of poor Queequeg, as he quietly lay in his swaying hammock, and the rolling sea seemed gently rocking him to his final rest, and the ocean's invisible flood-tide lifted him higher and higher towards his destined heaven.

Not a man of the crew but gave him up; and, as for Queequeg himself, what he thought of his case was forcibly shown by a curious favor he asked. He called one to him in the grey morning watch,[4] when the day was just breaking, and taking his hand, said that while in Nantucket he had chanced to see certain little canoes of dark wood, like the rich war-wood of his native isle; and upon inquiry, he had learned that all whalemen who died in Nantucket, were laid in those same dark canoes, and that the fancy of being so laid had much pleased him; for it was not unlike the custom of his own race, who, after embalming a dead warrior, stretched him out in his canoe, and so left him to be floated away to the starry archipelagoes; for not only do they believe that the stars are isles, but that far beyond all visible horizons, their own mild, uncontinented seas, interflow with the blue heavens; and so form the white breakers of the milky way. He added, that he shuddered at the thought of being buried in his hammock, according to the usual sea-custom, tossed like something vile to the death-devouring sharks. No: he desired a canoe like those of Nantucket, all the more congenial to him, being a whaleman, that like a whale-boat these coffin-canoes were without a keel; though that involved but uncertain steering, and much lee-way adown the dim ages.

Now, when this strange circumstance was made known aft, the carpenter was at once commanded to do Queequeg's bidding, whatever it might include. There was some heathenish, coffin-colored old lumber aboard, which, upon a long previous voyage, had been cut from the aboriginal groves of the Lackaday islands,[5] and from these dark planks the coffin was recommended to be made. No sooner was the carpenter apprised of the order, than taking his rule, he forthwith with all the indifferent promptitude of his character, proceeded into the forecastle and took Queequeg's measure with great accuracy, regularly chalking Queequeg's person as he shifted the rule.

"Ah! poor fellow! he'll have to die now," ejaculated the Long Island sailor.

Going to his vice-bench, the carpenter for convenience' sake and general reference, now transferringly measured on it the exact length the coffin was to be, and then made the transfer permanent by cutting two notches at its extremities. This done, he marshalled the planks and his tools, and to work.

When the last nail was driven, and the lid duly planed and fitted, he lightly shouldered the coffin and went forward with it, inquiring whether they were ready for it yet in that direction.

Overhearing the indignant but half-humorous cries with which the people on deck began to drive the coffin away, Queequeg, to every one's consternation, commanded that the thing should be instantly brought to him, nor was there any denying him; seeing that, of all mortals, some dying men are the most tyrannical; and certainly, since they will shortly trouble us so little for evermore, the poor fellows ought to be indulged.

Leaning over in his hammock, Queequeg long regarded the coffin with an attentive eye. He then called for his harpoon, had the wooden stock drawn from it, and then had the iron part placed in the coffin along with one of the paddles of his boat. All by his own request, also, biscuits were then ranged round the sides within: a flask of fresh water was placed at the head, and a small bag of woody earth scraped up in the hold at the foot; and a piece of sail-cloth being rolled up for a pillow, Queequeg now entreated to be lifted into his final bed, that he might make trial of its comforts, if any it had. He lay without moving a few minutes, then told one to go to his bag and bring out his little god, Yojo. Then crossing his arms on his breast with Yojo between, he called for the coffin lid (hatch he called it) to be placed over him. The head part turned over with a leather hinge, and there lay Queequeg in his coffin with little but his composed countenance in view. "Rarmai" (it will do; it is easy), he murmured at last, and signed to be replaced in his hammock.

But ere this was done, Pip, who had been slily hovering near by all this while, drew nigh to him where he lay, and with soft sobbings, took him by the hand; in the other, holding his tambourine.

"Poor rover! will ye never have done with all this weary roving? where go ye now? But if the currents carry ye to those sweet Antilles where the beaches are only beat with water-lilies, will ye do one little errand for me? Seek out one Pip, who's now been missing long: I think he's in those far Antilles. If ye find him, then comfort him; for he must be very sad; for look! he's left his tambourine behind;—I found it. Rig-a-dig, dig, dig! Now, Queequeg, die; and I'll beat ye your dying march."

"I have heard," murmured Starbuck, gazing down the scuttle, "that in violent fevers, men, all ignorance, have talked in ancient tongues; and that when the mystery is probed, it turns out always that in their wholly forgotten childhood those ancient tongues had been really spoken in their hearing by some lofty scholars. So, to my fond faith, poor Pip, in this strange sweetness of his lunacy, brings heavenly vouchers of all our heavenly homes. Where learned he that, but there?—Hark! he speaks again: but more wildly now."

"Form two and two! Let's make a General of him! Ho, where's his harpoon? Lay it across here,—Rig-a-dig, dig, dig! huzza! Oh for a game cock now to sit upon his head and crow! Queequeg dies game!—mind ye that; Queequeg dies game!—

take ye good heed of that; Queequeg dies game! I say; game, game, game! but base little Pip, he died a coward; died all a'shiver;—out upon Pip! Hark ye; if ye find Pip, tell all the Antilles he's a runaway; a coward, a coward, a coward! Tell them he jumped from a whale-boat! I'd never beat my tambourine over base Pip, and hail him General, if he were **once more** dying here. No, no! shame upon all cowards—shame upon **them**! Let 'em go **drown** like Pip, that jumped from a whale-boat. Shame! shame!"

During all this, Queequeg lay with closed eyes, as if in a dream. Pip was led away, and the sick man was replaced in his hammock.

But now that he had apparently made every preparation for death; now that his coffin was proved a good fit, Queequeg suddenly rallied; soon there seemed no need of the carpenter's box: and thereupon, when some expressed their delighted surprise, he, in substance, said, that the cause of his sudden convalescence was this;—at a critical moment, he had just recalled a little duty ashore, which he was leaving undone; and therefore had changed his mind about dying: he could not die yet, he averred. They asked him, then, whether to live or die was a matter of his own sovereign will and pleasure. He answered, certainly. In a word, it was Queequeg's conceit, that if a man made up his mind to live, mere sickness could not kill him: nothing but a whale, or a gale, or some violent, ungovernable, unintelligent destroyer of that sort.

Now, there is this noteworthy difference between savage and civilized; that while a sick, civilized man may be six months convalescing, generally speaking, a sick savage is almost half-well again in a day. So, in good time my Queequeg gained strength; and at length after sitting on the windlass for a few indolent days (but eating with a vigorous appetite) he suddenly leaped to his feet, threw out arms and legs, gave himself a good stretching, yawned a little bit, and then springing into the head of his hoisted boat, and poising a harpoon, pronounced himself fit for a fight.

REVISION NARRATIVE

Pip Going Down

Three changes in the British edition, certainly made by Melville, alter the tone of the concluding lines in Pip's elegy for Queequeg. Imagining Queequeg to be a valiant "General," the mad cabin boy considers himself unworthy of anything but shame; he is "drowned" and has already "died" (spiritually) because of what he takes to have been his cowardice in jumping from the whaleboat in Ch. 93, "The Castaway." In revising this passage, Melville made the routine dialect alteration of "them" to "'em." But he also removed "once more" to give simply "if he were dying here," and he altered "go drown" to "go down." Rather than reiterating Pip's self-deprecating notion that he is effectively dead and drowned, these two revisions build a nuanced link between Pip's madness and his having gone "down," that is, dived deep to the core of human consciousness.

With a wild whimsiness, he now used his coffin for a sea-chest; and emptying into it his canvas bag of clothes, set them in order there. Many spare hours he spent, in carving the lid with all manner of grotesque figures and drawings; and it seemed that hereby he was striving, in his rude way, to copy parts of the twisted tattooing on his body. And this tattooing, had been the work of a departed prophet and seer of his island, who, by those hieroglyphic marks, had written out on his body a complete theory of the heavens and the earth, and a mystical treatise on the art of attaining truth;[6] so that Queequeg in his own proper person was a riddle to unfold; a wondrous work in one volume; but whose mysteries not even himself could read, though his own live heart beat against them; and these mysteries were therefore destined in the end to moulder away with the living parchment whereon they were inscribed, and so be unsolved to the last. And this thought it must have been which suggested to Ahab that wild exclamation of his, when one morning turning away from surveying poor Queequeg—"Oh, devilish tantalization of the gods!"

THE PACIFIC

W HEN gliding by the Bashee isles we emerged at last upon the great South Sea; were it not for other things, I could have greeted my dear Pacific with uncounted thanks, for now the long supplication of my youth was answered; that serene ocean rolled eastwards from me a thousand leagues of blue.

There is, one knows not what sweet mystery about this sea, whose **gently** awful stirrings seem to speak of some hidden soul beneath; like those fabled undulations of the Ephesian sod over the buried Evangelist St. John.[1] And meet it is, that over these sea-pastures, wide-rolling **watery** prairies **and Potters' Fields**[2] of all four continents, the waves should rise and fall, and ebb and flow unceasingly; for here, millions of mixed shades and shadows, drowned dreams, somnambulisms,° reveries; all that we call lives and souls, lie dreaming, dreaming, still; tossing like slumberers in their beds; the ever-rolling waves but made so by their restlessness.

To any meditative Magian[3] rover, this serene Pacific, once beheld, must ever after be the sea of his adoption. It rolls the midmost waters of the world, the Indian ocean and Atlantic being but its arms. The same waves wash the moles of the new-built Californian towns, but yesterday planted by the recentest race of men, and lave the faded but still gorgeous skirts of Asiatic lands, older than Abraham;[4] while all between float milky-ways of coral isles, and low-lying, endless, unknown Archipelagoes, and impenetrable Japans.[5] Thus this mysterious, divine Pacific zones the world's **whole** bulk about; makes all coasts one bay to it; seems the tide-beating heart of earth. Lifted by those eternal swells, you needs must own the seductive god, bowing your head to Pan.[6]

But few thoughts of Pan stirred Ahab's brain, as standing like an iron statue at his accustomed place beside the mizen rigging, with one nostril he unthinkingly snuffed the sugary musk from the Bashee isles (in whose sweet woods mild lovers must be walking), and with the other consciously inhaled the salt breath of the new found sea; that sea in which the hated White Whale must even then be swimming. Launched at length upon these almost final waters, and gliding towards the Japanese cruising-ground, the old man's purpose intensified itself. His firm lips met like the

somnambulisms: sleepwalking.

lips of a vice; the Delta of his forehead's veins swelled like overladen brooks; in his very sleep, his ringing cry ran through the vaulted hull, "Stern all! the White Whale spouts thick blood!"

CHAPTER 112

THE BLACKSMITH

AVAILING himself of the mild, summer-cool weather that now reigned in these latitudes, and in preparation for the peculiarly active pursuits shortly to be anticipated, Perth, the begrimed, blistered old blacksmith, had not removed his portable forge to the hold again, after concluding his contributory work for Ahab's leg, but still retained it on deck, fast lashed to ringbolts by the foremast; being now almost incessantly invoked by the headsmen, and harpooneers, and bowsmen to do some little job for them; altering, or repairing, or new shaping their various weapons and boat furniture. Often he would be surrounded by an eager circle, all waiting to be served; holding boat-spades, pike-heads, harpoons, and lances, and jealously watching his every sooty movement, as he toiled. Nevertheless, this old man's was a patient hammer wielded by a patient arm. No murmur, no impatience, no petulance did come from him. Silent, slow, and solemn; bowing over still further his chronically broken back, he toiled away, as if toil were life itself, and the heavy beating of his hammer the heavy beating of his heart. And so it was.—Most miserable!

A peculiar walk in this old man, a certain slight but painful appearing yawing° in his gait, had at an early period of the voyage excited the curiosity of the mariners. And to the importunity of their persisted questionings he had finally given in; and so it came to pass that every one now knew the shameful story of his wretched fate.

Belated, and not innocently, one bitter winter's midnight, on the road running between two country towns, the blacksmith half-stupidly felt the deadly numbness stealing over him, and sought refuge in a leaning, dilapidated barn. The issue was, the loss of the extremities of both feet. Out of this revelation, part by part, at last came out the four acts of the gladness, and the one long, and as yet uncatastrophied fifth act of the grief of his life's drama.

He was an old man, who, at the age of nearly sixty, had postponedly encountered that thing in sorrow's technicals° called ruin. He had been an artisan of famed excellence, and with plenty to do; owned a house and garden; embraced a youthful, daughter-like, loving wife, and three blithe, ruddy children; every Sunday went to a cheerful-looking church, planted in a grove. But one night, under cover of darkness,

yawing: lurch. *technicals*: minor details; here an ironic understatement.

424

and further concealed in a most cunning disguisement, a desperate burglar slid into his happy home, and robbed them all of everything. And darker yet to tell, the blacksmith himself did ignorantly conduct this burglar into his family's heart. It was the Bottle Conjuror![1] Upon the opening of that fatal cork, forth flew the fiend, and shrivelled up his home. Now, for prudent, most wise, and economic reasons, the blacksmith's shop was in the basement of his dwelling, but with a separate entrance to it; so that always had the young and loving healthy wife listened with no unhappy nervousness, but with vigorous pleasure, to the stout ringing of her young-armed old husband's hammer; whose reverberations, muffled by passing through the floors and walls, came up to her, not unsweetly, in her nursery; and so, to stout Labor's iron lullaby, the blacksmith's infants were rocked to slumber.

Oh, woe on woe! Oh, Death, why canst thou not sometimes be timely? Hadst thou taken this old blacksmith to thyself ere his full ruin came upon him, then had the young widow had a delicious grief, and her orphans a truly venerable, legendary sire to dream of in their after years; and all of them a care-killing competency.° But Death plucked down some virtuous elder brother, on whose whistling daily toil solely hung the responsibilities of some other family, and left the worse than useless old man standing, till the hideous rot of life should make him easier to harvest.

Why tell the whole? The blows of the basement hammer every day grew more and more between; and each blow every day grew fainter than the last; the wife sat frozen at the window, with tearless eyes, glitteringly gazing into the weeping faces of her children; the bellows fell; the forge choked up with cinders; the house was sold; the mother dived down into the long church-yard grass; her children twice followed her thither; and the houseless, familyless old man staggered off a vagabond in crape; his every woe unreverenced; his grey head a scorn to flaxen curls!

Death seems the only desirable sequel for a career like this; but Death is only a launching into the region of the strange Untried; it is but the first salutation to the possibilities of the immense Remote, the Wild, the Watery, the Unshored; therefore, to the death-longing eyes of such men, who still have left in them some interior compunctions against suicide, does the all-contributed and all-receptive ocean alluringly spread forth his whole plain of unimaginable, taking° terrors, and wonderful, new-life adventures; and from the hearts of infinite Pacifics, the thousand mermaids sing to them—"Come hither, broken-hearted; here is another life without the guilt of intermediate death; here are wonders supernatural, without dying for them. Come hither! bury thyself in a life which, to your now equally abhorred and abhorring, landed world, is more oblivious than death. Come hither! put up *thy* gravestone, too, within the churchyard, and come hither, till we marry thee!"

Hearkening to these voices, East and West, by early sun-rise, and by fall of eve, the blacksmith's soul responded, Aye, I come! And so Perth went a-whaling.

---

all of them a care-killing competency: the family would have had enough money to live on.
taking: gripping.

CHAPTER 113

THE FORGE

WITH matted beard, and swathed in a bristling shark-skin apron, about mid-day, Perth was standing between his forge and anvil, the latter placed upon an iron-wood log, with one hand holding a pike-head in the coals, and with the other at his forge's lungs, when Captain Ahab came along, carrying in his hand a small rusty-looking leathern bag. While yet a little distance from the forge, moody Ahab paused; till at last, Perth, withdrawing his iron from the fire, began hammering it upon the anvil—the red mass sending off the sparks in thick hovering flights, some of which flew close to Ahab.

"Are these thy Mother Carey's chickens,[1] Perth? they are always flying in thy wake; birds of good omen, too, but not to all;—look here, they burn; but thou—thou liv'st among them without a scorch."

"Because I am scorched all over, Captain Ahab," answered Perth, resting for a moment on his hammer; "I am past scorching; not easily can'st thou scorch a scar."

"Well, well; no more. Thy shrunk voice sounds too calmly, sanely woful to me. In no Paradise myself, I am impatient of all misery in others that is not mad. Thou should'st go mad, blacksmith; say, why dost thou not go mad? How can'st thou endure without being mad? Do the heavens yet hate thee, that thou can'st not go mad?—What wert thou making there?"

"Welding an old pike-head, sir; there were seams and dents in it."

"And can'st thou make it all smooth again, blacksmith, after such hard usage as it had?"

"I think so, sir."

"And I suppose thou can'st smoothe almost any seams and dents; never mind how hard the metal, blacksmith?"

"Aye, sir, I think I can; all seams and dents but one."

"Look ye here, then," cried Ahab, passionately advancing, and leaning with both hands on Perth's shoulders; "look ye here—*here*—can ye smoothe out a seam like this, blacksmith," sweeping one hand across his ribbed brow; "if thou could'st, blacksmith, glad enough would I lay my head upon thy anvil, and feel thy heaviest hammer between my eyes. Answer! Can'st thou smoothe this seam?"

"Oh! that is the one, sir! Said I not all seams and dents but one?"

"Aye, blacksmith, it is the one; aye, man, it is unsmoothable; for though thou only see'st it here in my flesh, it has worked down into the bone of my skull—*that* is all wrinkles! But, away with child's play; no more gaffs and pikes to-day. Look ye here!" jingling the leathern bag, as if it were full of gold coins. "I, too, want a harpoon made;[2] one that a thousand yoke of fiends could not part, Perth; something that will stick in a whale like his own fin-bone. There's the stuff," flinging the pouch upon the anvil. "Look ye, blacksmith, these are the gathered nail-stubs of the steel shoes of racing horses."

"Horse-shoe stubs, sir? Why, Captain Ahab, thou hast here, then, the best and stubbornest stuff we blacksmiths ever work."

"I know it, old man; these stubs will weld together like glue from the melted bones of murderers. Quick! forge me the harpoon. And forge me first, twelve rods for its shank; then wind, and twist, and hammer these twelve together like the yarns and strands of a tow-line. Quick! I'll blow the fire."

When at last the twelve rods were made, Ahab tried them, one by one, by spiralling them, with his own hand, round a long, heavy iron bolt. "A flaw!" rejecting the last one. "Work that over again, Perth."

This done, Perth was about to begin welding the twelve into one, when Ahab stayed his hand, and said he would weld his own iron. As, then, with regular, gasping hems, he hammered on the anvil, Perth passing to him the glowing rods, one after the other, and the hard pressed forge shooting up its intense straight flame, the Parsee passed silently, and bowing over his head towards the fire, seemed invoking some curse or some blessing on the toil. But, as Ahab looked up, he slid aside.

"What's that bunch of lucifers dodging about there for?" muttered Stubb, looking on from the forecastle. "That Parsee smells fire like a fusee; and smells of it himself,[3] like a hot musket's powder-pan."

At last the shank, in one complete rod, received its final heat; and as Perth, to temper it, plunged it all hissing into the cask of water near by, the scalding steam shot up into Ahab's bent face.

"Would'st thou brand me, Perth?" wincing for a moment with the pain; "have I been but forging my own branding-iron, then?"

"Pray God, not that; yet I fear something, Captain Ahab. Is not this harpoon for the White Whale?"

"For the white fiend! But now for the barbs; thou must make them thyself, man. Here are my razors—the best of steel; here, and make the barbs sharp as the needle-sleet of the Icy Sea."[4]

For a moment, the old blacksmith eyed the razors as though he would fain not use them.

"Take them, man, I have no need for them; for I now neither shave, sup, nor pray till——but here—to work!"

Fashioned at last into an arrowy shape, and welded by Perth to the shank, the steel soon pointed the end of the iron; and as the blacksmith was about giving the barbs their final heat, prior to tempering them, he cried to Ahab to place the water-cask near.

"No, no—no water for that; I want it of the true death-temper. Ahoy, there! Tashtego, Queequeg, Daggoo! What say ye, pagans! Will ye give me as much blood as will cover this barb?" holding it high up. A cluster of dark **nods** replied, Yes. Three punctures were made in the heathen flesh, and the White Whale's barbs were then tempered.

"Ego non baptizo te in nomine patris, sed in nomine diaboli!"[5] deliriously howled Ahab, as the malignant iron scorchingly devoured the baptismal blood.

Now, mustering the spare poles from below, and selecting one of hickory, with the bark still investing it, Ahab fitted the end to the socket of the iron. A coil of new tow-line was then unwound, and some fathoms of it taken to the windlass, and stretched to a great tension. Pressing his foot upon it, till the rope hummed like a harp-string, then eagerly bending over it, and seeing no strandings, Ahab exclaimed, "Good! and now for the seizings."°

At one extremity the rope was unstranded, and the separate spread yarns were all braided and woven round the socket of the harpoon; the pole was then driven hard up into the socket; from the lower end the rope was traced half way along the pole's length, and firmly secured so, with intertwistings of twine. This done, pole, iron, and rope—like the Three Fates—remained inseparable, and Ahab moodily stalked away with the weapon; the sound of his ivory leg, and the sound of the hickory pole, both hollowly ringing along every plank. But ere he entered his cabin, a light, unnatural, half-bantering, yet most piteous sound was heard. Oh, Pip! thy wretched laugh, thy idle but unresting eye; all thy strange mummeries° not unmeaningly blended with the black tragedy of the melancholy ship, and mocked it!

---

strandings . . . seizings: broken strands . . . bindings of cord. **mummeries**: impertinent, mocking displays, including Pip's laugh and "unresting eye."

CHAPTER 114

THE GILDER

Penetrating further and further into the heart of the Japanese cruising ground, the Pequod was soon all astir in the fishery. Often, in mild, pleasant weather, for twelve, fifteen, eighteen, and twenty hours on the stretch, they were engaged in the boats, steadily pulling, or sailing, or paddling after the whales, or for an interlude of sixty or seventy minutes calmly awaiting their uprising; though with but small success for their pains.

At such times, under an abated sun; afloat all day upon smooth, slow heaving swells; seated in his boat, light as a birch canoe; and so sociably mixing with the soft waves themselves, that like hearth-stone cats they purr against the gunwale; these are the times of dreamy quietude, when beholding the tranquil beauty and brilliancy of the ocean's skin, one forgets the tiger heart that pants beneath it; and would not willingly remember, that this velvet paw but conceals a remorseless fang.

These are the times, when in his whale-boat the rover softly feels a certain filial, confident, land-like feeling towards the sea; that he regards it as so much flowery earth; and the distant ship revealing only the tops of her masts, seems struggling forward, not through high rolling waves, but through the tall grass of a rolling prairie: as when the western emigrants' horses only show their erected ears, while their hidden bodies widely wade through the amazing verdure.

The long-drawn virgin vales; the mild blue hill-sides; as over these there steals the hush, the hum; you almost swear that play-wearied children lie sleeping in these solitudes, in some glad May-time, when the flowers of the woods are plucked. And all this mixes with your most mystic mood; so that fact and fancy, half-way meeting, interpenetrate, and form one seamless whole.

Nor did such soothing scenes, however temporary, fail of at least as temporary an effect on Ahab. But if these secret golden keys did seem to open in him his own secret golden treasuries, yet did his breath upon them prove but tarnishing.

Oh, grassy glades! oh, ever vernal endless landscapes in the soul; in ye,—though long parched by the dead drought of the earthy life,— in ye, men yet may roll, like young horses in new morning clover; and for some few fleeting moments, feel the cool dew of the life immortal on them. Would to God these blessed calms would last. But

the mingled, mingling threads of life are woven by warp and woof: calms crossed by storms, a storm for every calm. There is no steady unretracing progress in this life; we do not advance through fixed gradations, and at the last one pause:—through infancy's unconscious spell, boyhood's thoughtless faith, adolescence' doubt (the common doom), then scepticism, then disbelief, resting at last in manhood's pondering repose of If.[1] But once gone through, we trace the round again; and are infants, boys, and men, and Ifs eternally. Where lies the final harbor, whence we unmoor no more? In what rapt ether sails the world, of which the weariest will never weary? Where is the foundling's father hidden? Our souls are like those orphans whose unwedded mothers die in bearing them: the secret of our paternity lies in their grave, and we must there to learn it.

And that same day, too, gazing far down from his boat's side into that same golden sea, Starbuck lowly murmured:—

"Loveliness unfathomable, as ever lover saw in his young bride's eye!—Tell me not of thy teeth-tiered sharks, and thy kidnapping cannibal ways. Let faith oust fact; let fancy oust memory; I look deep down and do believe."

REVISION NARRATIVE

Ahab or Ishmael

Ishmael opens this chapter with an ocean reverie—a contemplation of the mildness of the sea that puts one in a "mystic mood." Not so with Ahab, whose very breath seems to tarnish the soothing scene. Despite Ahab's tarnishing effect, some readers take the "gilder" in the chapter title to refer to that craftsman who gilds or applies gold leaf to an object. But a more plausible suggestion is that "The Gilder" refers to the Dutch gold coin of that name. The chapter concludes with three crewmembers, each soliloquizing on the "same golden sea," and the first speaker, presumably Ahab, takes the scene to be a "golden key" to unlock the "golden treasury" of his mind and offer us a meditation, as if it were a gilder. Structurally, the chapter is a replay of Ch. 99, "The Doubloon," which also involves a series of individuals addressing what in that case is an actual not metaphoric gold coin. But the structure of "The Gilder" is made ambiguous by its punctuation, for while Ishmael brings Ahab forward to speak first, the ensuing monolog ("Oh, grassy glades!") in both the American and British editions has no quotation marks to indicate that he is speaking. Without this punctuation, the speech appears to belong to Ishmael, and readers often attribute the lines to the narrator, not Ahab. In 1988, the Northwestern-Newberry edition emended the text by adding quotation marks at the beginning and end of the paragraph, thereby assigning it unambiguously to Ahab; however, the present edition makes no change.

And Stubb, fish-like, with sparkling scales, leaped up in that same golden light:—

"I am Stubb, and Stubb has his history; but here Stubb takes oaths that he has always been jolly!"

CHAPTER 115

THE PEQUOD MEETS THE BACHELOR

A<small>ND</small> jolly enough were the sights and the sounds that came bearing down before the wind, some few weeks after Ahab's harpoon had been welded.°

It was a Nantucket ship, the Bachelor, which had just wedged in her last cask of oil, and bolted down her bursting hatches; and now, in glad holiday apparel, was joyously, though somewhat vain-gloriously, sailing round among the widely-separated ships on the ground, previous to pointing her prow for home.

The three men at her mast-head wore long streamers of narrow red bunting at their hats; from the stern, a whale-boat was suspended, bottom down; and hanging captive from the bowsprit was seen the long lower jaw of the last whale they had slain. Signals, ensigns, and jacks° of all colors were flying from her rigging, on every side. Sideways lashed in each of her three basketed tops were two barrels of sperm; above which, in her top-mast cross-trees, you saw slender breakers° of the same precious fluid; and nailed to her main truck was a brazen lamp.

As was afterwards learned, the Bachelor had met with the most surprising success; all the more wonderful, for that while cruising in the same seas numerous other vessels had gone entire months without securing a single fish. Not only had barrels of beef and bread been given away to make room for the far more valuable sperm, but additional supplemental casks had been bartered for, from the ships she had met; and these were stowed along the deck, and in the captain's and officers' state-rooms. Even the cabin table itself had been knocked into kindling-wood; and the cabin mess° dined off the broad head of an oil-butt, lashed down to the floor for a centrepiece. In the forecastle, the sailors had actually caulked and pitched their chests, and filled them; it was humorously added, that the cook had clapped a head on his largest boiler, and filled it; that the steward had plugged his spare coffee-pot and filled it; that the harpooneers had headed the sockets of their irons and filled them; that indeed everything was filled with sperm, except the captain's pantaloons pockets, and those he reserved to thrust his hands into, in self-complacent testimony of his entire satisfaction.

welded: see Ch. 113. ***ensigns, and jacks***: banners and small flags, respectively, showing a ship's nationality. ***breakers***: small barrels. ***cabin mess***: those who eat in the captain's cabin.

As this glad ship of good luck bore down upon the moody Pequod, the barbarian sound of enormous drums came from her forecastle; and drawing still nearer, a crowd of her men were seen standing round her huge try-pots, which, covered with the parchment-like *poke* or stomach skin of the black fish,° gave forth a loud roar to every stroke of the clenched hands of the crew. On the quarter-deck, the mates and harpooneers were dancing with the olive-hued girls who had eloped with them from the Polynesian Isles; while suspended in an ornamented boat, firmly secured aloft between the foremast and mainmast, three Long Island negroes, with glittering fiddle-bows of whale ivory, were presiding over the hilarious jig. Meanwhile, others of the ship's company were tumultuously busy at the masonry of the try-works, from which the huge pots had been removed. You would have almost thought they were pulling down the cursed Bastile,[1] such wild cries they raised, as the now useless brick and mortar were being hurled into the sea.

Lord and master over all this scene, the captain stood erect on the ship's elevated quarter-deck, so that the whole rejoicing drama was full before him, and seemed merely contrived for his own individual diversion.

And Ahab, he too was standing on his quarter-deck, shaggy and black, with a stubborn gloom; and as the two ships crossed each other's wakes—one all jubilations for things passed, the other all forebodings as to things to come—their two captains in themselves impersonated the whole striking contrast of the scene.

"Come aboard, come aboard!" cried the gay Bachelor's commander, lifting a glass and a bottle in the air.

"Hast seen the White Whale?" gritted Ahab in reply.

"No; only heard of him; but don't believe in him at all," said the other good-humoredly. "Come aboard!"

"Thou art too damned jolly. Sail on. Hast lost any men?"

"Not enough to speak of—two islanders, that's all;—but come aboard, old hearty, come along. I'll soon take that black from your brow. Come along, will ye (merry's the play); a full ship and homeward-bound."

"How wondrous familiar is a fool!" muttered Ahab; then aloud, "Thou art a full ship and homeward bound, thou sayst; well, then, call me an empty ship, and outward-bound. So go thy ways, and I will mine. Forward there! Set all sail, and keep her to the wind!"

And thus, while the one ship went cheerily before the breeze, the other stubbornly fought against it; and so the two vessels parted; the crew of the Pequod looking with grave, lingering glances towards the receding Bachelor; but the Bachelor's men never heeding their gaze for the lively revelry they were in. And as Ahab, leaning over the taffrail, eyed the homeward-bound craft, he took from his pocket a small vial of sand, and then looking from the ship to the vial, seemed thereby bringing two remote associations together, for that vial was filled with Nantucket soundings.[2]

black fish: pilot whale.

CHAPTER 116

THE DYING WHALE

NOT seldom in this life, when, on the right side, fortune's favorites sail close by us, we, though all adroop before, catch somewhat of the rushing breeze, and joyfully feel our bagging sails fill out. So seemed it with the Pequod. For next day after encountering the gay Bachelor, whales were seen and four were slain; and one of them by Ahab.

It was far down the afternoon; and when all the spearings of the crimson fight were done: and floating in the lovely sunset sea and sky, sun and whale both stilly° died together; then, such a sweetness and such plaintiveness, such inwreathing orisons° curled up in that rosy air, that it almost seemed as if far over from the deep green convent valleys of the Manilla isles,° the Spanish land-breeze, wantonly turned sailor, had gone to sea, freighted with these vesper hymns.

Soothed again, but only soothed to deeper gloom, Ahab, who had sterned off from the whale, sat intently watching his final wanings from the now tranquil boat. For that strange spectacle observable in all sperm whales dying—the turning sunwards of the head,[1] and so expiring—that strange spectacle, beheld of such a placid evening, somehow to Ahab conveyed a wondrousness unknown before.

"He turns and turns him to it,—how slowly, but how steadfastly, his homage-rendering and invoking brow, with his last dying motions. He too worships fire; most faithful, broad, baronial vassal of the sun!—Oh that these too-favoring eyes should see these too-favoring sights. Look! here, far water-locked; beyond all hum of human weal or woe; in these most candid and impartial seas; where to traditions no rocks furnish tablets; where for long Chinese ages, the billows have still rolled on speechless and unspoken to, as stars that shine upon the Niger's unknown source;[2] here, too, life dies sunwards full of faith; but see! no sooner dead, than death whirls round the corpse, and it heads some other way.—

"Oh, thou dark Hindoo half of nature,[3] who of drowned bones hast built thy separate throne somewhere in the heart of these unverdured seas; thou art an infidel, thou queen, and too truly speakest to me in the wide-slaughtering Typhoon, and the hushed burial of its after calm. Nor has this thy whale sunwards turned his dying head, and then gone round again, without a lesson to me.

stilly: quietly. *orisons*: prayers. ***Manilla isles***: The Philippines.

"Oh, trebly hooped and welded hip of power! Oh, high aspiring, rainbowed jet!—that one strivest, this one jettest all in vain! In vain, oh whale, dost thou seek intercedings with yon all-quickening sun, that only calls forth life, but gives it not again. Yet dost thou, darker half, rock me with a prouder, if a darker faith. All thy **unnamable** imminglings float beneath me here; I am buoyed by breaths of once living things, exhaled as air, but water now.

"Then hail, for ever hail, O sea, in whose eternal tossings the wild fowl finds his only rest. Born of earth, yet suckled by the sea; though hill and valley mothered me, ye billows are my foster-brothers!"

CHAPTER 117

THE WHALE WATCH

THE four whales slain that evening had died wide apart; one, far to windward; one, less distant, to leeward; one ahead; one astern. These last three were brought alongside ere nightfall; but the windward one could not be reached till morning; and the boat that had killed it lay by its side all night; and that boat was Ahab's.

The waif-pole was thrust upright into the dead whale's spout-hole; and the lantern hanging from its top, cast a troubled flickering glare upon the black, glossy back, and far out upon the midnight waves, which gently chafed the whale's broad flank, like soft surf upon a beach.

Ahab and all his boat's crew seemed asleep but the Parsee; who crouching in the bow, sat watching the sharks, that spectrally played round the whale, and tapped the light cedar planks with their tails. A sound like the moaning in squadrons over Asphaltites of unforgiven ghosts of Gomorrah,[1] ran shuddering through the air.

Started from his slumbers, Ahab, face to face, saw the Parsee; and hooped round by the gloom of the night they seemed the last men in a flooded world. "I have dreamed it again," said he.

"Of the hearses? Have I not said, old man, that neither hearse nor coffin can be thine?"

"And who are hearsed that die on the sea?"

"But I said, old man, that ere thou couldst die on this voyage, two hearses must verily be seen by thee on the sea; the first not made by mortal hands; and the visible wood of the last one must be grown in America."

"Aye, aye! a strange sight that, Parsee:—a hearse and its plumes floating over the ocean with the waves for the pall-bearers. Ha! Such a sight we shall not soon see."

"Believe it or not, thou canst not die till it be seen, old man."

"And what was that saying about thyself?"

"Though it come to the last, I shall still go before thee thy pilot."

"And when thou art so gone before—if that ever befall—then ere I can follow, thou must still appear to me, to pilot me still?—Was it not so? Well, then, did I believe all ye say, oh my pilot! I have here two pledges that I shall yet slay Moby Dick and survive it."

"Take another pledge, old man," said the Parsee, as his eyes lighted up like fire-flies in the gloom—"Hemp only can kill thee."

"The gallows, ye mean.—I am immortal then, on land and on sea," cried Ahab, with a laugh of derision;—"Immortal on land and on sea!"

Both were silent again, as one man. The grey dawn came on, and the slumbering crew arose from the boat's bottom, and ere noon the dead whale was brought to the ship.

CHAPTER 118

THE QUADRANT

THE season for the Line[1] at length drew near; and every day when Ahab, coming from his cabin, cast his eyes aloft, the vigilant helmsman would ostentatiously handle his spokes,[2] and **the** eager mariners quickly run to the braces,° and would stand there with all their eyes centrally fixed on the nailed doubloon; impatient for the order to point the ship's prow for the equator. In good time the order came. It was hard upon high noon; and Ahab, seated in the bows of his high-hoisted boat, was about taking his wonted daily observation of the sun to determine his latitude.

Now, in that Japanese sea, the days in summer are as freshets of effulgences.° That unblinkingly vivid Japanese sun seems the blazing focus of the glassy ocean's immeasurable burning-glass. The sky looks lacquered; clouds there are none; the horizon floats; and this nakedness of unrelieved radiance is as the insufferable splendors of God's throne. Well that Ahab's quadrant[3] was furnished with colored glasses, through which to take sight of that solar fire. So, swinging his seated form to the roll of the ship, and with his astrological-looking instrument placed to his eye, he remained in that posture for some moments to catch the precise instant when the sun should gain its precise meridian.° Meantime while his whole attention was absorbed, the Parsee was kneeling beneath him on the ship's deck, and with face thrown up like Ahab's, was eyeing the same sun with him; only the lids of his eyes half hooded their orbs, and his wild face was subdued to an **earthly** passionlessness. At length the desired observation was taken; and with his pencil upon his ivory leg, Ahab soon calculated what his latitude must be at that precise instant. Then falling into a moment's revery, he again looked up towards the sun and murmured to himself: "Thou sea-mark! thou high and mighty Pilot! thou tellest me truly where I *am*—but canst thou cast the least hint where I *shall* be? Or canst thou tell where some other thing besides me is this moment living? Where is Moby Dick? This instant thou must be eyeing him. These eyes of mine look into the very eye that is even now beholding him; aye, and into the eye that is even now equally beholding the objects on the unknown, thither side of thee, thou sun!"

braces: ropes leading from the yardarm ends to the deck, used to pivot the yards. **freshets of effulgences**: overflowing streams of brilliant light. **meridian**: highest point in the sky; local noon.

Then gazing at his quadrant, and handling, one after the other, its numerous cabalistical contrivances, he pondered again, and muttered: "Foolish toy! babies' plaything of haughty Admirals, and Commodores, and Captains; the world brags of thee, of thy cunning and might; but what after all canst thou do, but tell the poor, pitiful point, where thou thyself happenest to be on this wide planet, and the hand that holds thee: no! not one jot more! Thou canst not tell where one drop of water or one grain of sand will be to-morrow noon; and yet with thy impotence thou insultest the sun! Science! Curse thee, thou vain toy; and cursed be all the things that cast man's eyes aloft to that heaven, whose live vividness but scorches him, as these old eyes are even now scorched with thy light, O sun! Level by nature to this earth's horizon are the glances of man's eyes; not shot from the crown of his head, as if God had meant him to gaze on his firmament. Curse thee, thou quadrant!" dashing it to the deck, "no longer will I guide my earthly way by thee; the level ship's compass, and the level dead-reckoning, by log and by line;[4] *these* shall conduct me, and show me my place on the sea. Aye," lighting from the boat to the deck, "thus I trample on thee, thou paltry thing that feebly pointest on high; thus I split and destroy thee!"

As the frantic old man thus spoke and thus trampled with his live and dead feet, a sneering triumph that seemed meant for Ahab, and a fatalistic despair that seemed meant for himself—these passed over the mute, motionless Parsee's face. Unobserved he rose and glided away; while, awestruck by the aspect of their commander, the seamen clustered together on the forecastle, till Ahab, troubledly pacing the deck, shouted out—"To the braces! Up helm!—square in!"°

In an instant the yards swung round; and as the ship half-wheeled upon her heel, her three firm-seated graceful masts erectly poised upon her long, ribbed hull, seemed as the three Horatii[5] pirouetting on one sufficient steed.

Standing between the knight-heads,° Starbuck watched the Pequod's tumultuous way, and Ahab's also, as he went lurching along the deck.

"I have sat before the dense coal fire and watched it all aglow, full of its tormented flaming life; and I have seen it wane at last, down, down, to dumbest dust. Old man of oceans! of all this fiery life of thine, what will at length remain but one little heap of ashes!"

"Aye," cried Stubb, "but sea-coal ashes—mind ye that, Mr. Starbuck—sea-coal, not your common charcoal. Well, well; I heard Ahab mutter, 'Here some one thrusts these cards into these old hands of mine; swears that I must play them, and no others.' And damn me, Ahab, but thou actest right; live in the game, **and die it!**"

---

square in: turn the yards (and their sails) at right angles to the vessel, in order to sail directly before the wind. **knight-heads**: vertical timbers in the bow that support the bowsprit.

CHAPTER 119

THE CANDLES

WARMEST climes but nurse the cruellest fangs: the tiger of Bengal crouches in spiced groves of ceaseless verdure. Skies the most effulgent but basket the deadliest thunders: gorgeous Cuba knows tornadoes that never swept tame northern lands. So, too, it is, that in these resplendent Japanese seas the mariner encounters the direst of all storms, the Typhoon. It will sometimes burst from out that cloudless sky, like an exploding bomb upon a dazed and sleepy town.

Towards evening of that day, the Pequod was torn of her canvas, and bare-poled was left to fight a Typhoon which had struck her directly ahead. When darkness came on, sky and sea roared and split with the thunder, and blazed with the lightning, that showed the disabled masts fluttering here and there with the rags which the first fury of the tempest had left for its after sport.

Holding by a shroud, Starbuck was standing on the quarter-deck; at every flash of the lightning glancing aloft, to see what additional disaster might have befallen the intricate hamper° there; while Stubb and Flask were directing the men in the higher hoisting and firmer lashing of the boats. But all their pains seemed naught. Though lifted to the very top of the cranes, the windward quarter boat (Ahab's) did not escape. A great rolling sea, dashing high up against the reeling ship's high tetering side, stove in the boat's bottom at the stern, and left it again, all dripping through like a sieve.

"Bad work, bad work! Mr. Starbuck," said Stubb, regarding the wreck, "but the sea will have its way. Stubb, for one, can't fight it. You see, Mr. Starbuck, a wave has such a great long start before it leaps, all round the world it runs, and then comes the spring! But as for me, all the start I have to meet it, is just across the deck here. But never mind; it's all in fun: so the old song says;"—(*sings.*)

> Oh! jolly is the gale,[1]
> And a joker is the whale,
> A' flourishin' his tail,—
Such a funny, sporty, gamy, jesty, joky, hoky-poky lad, is the Ocean, oh!

hamper: spars and rigging.

> The scud° all a flyin',
> That's his flip only foamin';
> When he stirs in the spicin',—
> Such a funny, sporty, gamy, jesty, joky, hoky-poky lad, is the Ocean, oh!
>
> Thunder splits the ships,
> But he only smacks his lips,
> A tastin' of this flip,—
> Such a funny, sporty, gamy, jesty, joky, hoky-poky lad, is the Ocean, oh!

"Avast Stubb," cried Starbuck, "let the Typhoon sing, and strike his harp here in our rigging; but if thou art a brave man thou wilt hold thy peace."

"But I am not a brave man; never said I was a brave man; I am a coward; and I sing to keep up my spirits. And I tell you what it is, Mr. Starbuck, there's no way to stop my singing in this world but to cut my throat. And when that's done, ten to one I sing ye the doxology² for a wind-up."

"Madman! look through my eyes if thou hast none of thine own."

"What! how can you see better of a dark night than anybody else, never mind how foolish?"

"Here!" cried Starbuck, seizing Stubb by the shoulder, and pointing his hand towards the weather bow, "markest thou not that the gale comes from the eastward, the very course Ahab is to run for Moby Dick? the very course he swung to this day noon? now mark his boat there; where is that stove? In the stern-sheets, man; where he is wont to stand—his stand-point is stove, man! Now jump overboard, and sing away, if thou must!"

"I don't half understand ye: what's in the wind?"

"Yes, yes, round the Cape of Good Hope is the shortest way to Nantucket," soliloquized Starbuck suddenly, heedless of Stubb's question. "The gale that now hammers at us to stave us, we can turn it into a fair wind that will drive us towards home. Yonder, to windward, all is blackness of doom; but to leeward, homeward—I see it lightens up there; but not with the lightning."

At that moment in one of the intervals of profound darkness, following the flashes, a voice was heard at his side; and almost at the same instant a volley of thunder peals rolled overhead.

"Who's there?"

"Old Thunder!" said Ahab, groping his way along the bulwarks to his pivot-hole; but suddenly finding his path made plain to him by elbowed lances of fire.

Now, as the lightning rod to a spire on shore is intended to carry off the perilous fluid into the soil; so the kindred rod which at sea some ships carry to each mast, is intended to conduct it into the water. But as this conductor must descend to considerable depth, that its end may avoid all contact with the hull; and as moreover, if kept constantly towing there, it would be liable to many mishaps, besides interfering not a little with some of the rigging, and more or less impeding the vessel's

---

scud: mist or low, broken clouds.

way in the water; because of all this, the lower parts of a ship's lightning-rods are not always overboard; but are generally made in long slender links, so as to be the more readily hauled up into the chains outside, or thrown down into the sea, as occasion may require.

"The rods! the rods!" cried Starbuck to the crew, suddenly admonished to vigilance by the vivid lightning that had just been darting flambeaux,° to light Ahab to his post. "Are they overboard? drop them over, fore and aft. Quick!"

"Avast!" cried Ahab; "let's have fair play here, though we be the weaker side. Yet I'll contribute to raise rods on the Himmalehs and Andes, that all the world may be secured; but out on privileges!° Let them be, sir."

"Look aloft!" cried Starbuck. "The corpusants!³ the corpusants!"

All the yard-arms were tipped with a pallid fire; and touched at each tri-pointed lightning-rod-end with three tapering white flames, each of the three tall masts was silently burning in that sulphurous air, like three gigantic wax tapers before an altar.

"Blast the boat! let it go!" cried Stubb at this instant, as a swashing sea heaved up under his own little craft, so that its gunwale violently jammed his hand, as he was passing a lashing. "Blast it!"—but slipping backward on the deck, his uplifted eyes caught the flames; and immediately shifting his tone, he cried—"The corpusants have mercy on us all!"

To sailors, oaths are household words; they will swear in the trance of the calm, and in the teeth of the tempest; they will imprecate curses from the topsail-yard-arms, when most they teter over to a seething sea; but in all my voyagings, seldom have I heard a common oath when God's burning finger has been laid on the ship; when His "Mene, Mene, Tekel, Upharsin"⁴ has been woven into the shrouds and the cordage.

While this pallidness was burning aloft, few words were heard from the enchanted crew; who in one thick cluster stood on the forecastle, all their eyes gleaming in that pale phosphorescence, like a far away constellation of stars. Relieved against the ghostly light, the gigantic jet negro, Daggoo, loomed up to thrice his real stature, and seemed the black cloud from which the thunder had come. The parted mouth of Tashtego revealed his shark-white teeth, which strangely gleamed as if they too had been tipped by corpusants; while lit up by the preternatural light, Queequeg's tattooing burned like Satanic blue flames on his body.

The tableau all waned at last with the pallidness aloft; and once more the Pequod and every soul on her decks were wrapped in a pall. A moment or two passed, when Starbuck, going forward, pushed against some one. It was Stubb. "What thinkest thou now, man; I heard thy cry; it was not the same in the song."

"No, no, it wasn't; I said the corpusants have mercy on us all; and I hope they will, still. But do they only have mercy on long faces?—have they no bowels for a laugh? And look ye, Mr. Starbuck—but it's too dark to look. Hear me, then: I take that mast-head flame we saw for a sign of good luck; for those masts are rooted in a hold that is going to be chock a' block with sperm-oil, d'ye see; and so, all that sperm

---

flambeaux: torches (French). ***but out on privileges!***: "be done with human protections against nature!"

will work up into the masts, like sap in a tree. Yes, our three masts will yet be as three spermaceti candles—that's the good promise we saw."

At that moment Starbuck caught sight of Stubb's face slowly beginning to glimmer into sight. Glancing upwards, he cried: "See! see!" and once more the high tapering flames were beheld with what seemed redoubled supernaturalness in their pallor.

"The corpusants have mercy on us all," cried Stubb, again.

At the base of the mainmast, full beneath the doubloon and the flame, the Parsee was kneeling in Ahab's front, but with his head bowed away from him; while near by, from the arched and overhanging rigging, where they had just been engaged securing a spar, a number of the seamen, arrested by the glare, now cohered together, and hung pendulous, like a knot of numbed wasps from a drooping, orchard twig. In various enchanted attitudes, like the standing, or stepping, or running skeletons in Herculaneum,[5] others remained rooted to the deck; but all their eyes upcast.

"Aye, aye, men!" cried Ahab. "Look up at it; mark it well; the white flame but lights the way to the White Whale! Hand me those main-mast links° there; I would fain feel this pulse, and let mine beat against it; blood against fire! So."

Then turning—the last link held fast in his left hand, he put his foot upon the Parsee; and with fixed upward eye, and high-flung right arm, he stood erect before the lofty **tri-pointed trinity of** flames.

"Oh! thou clear spirit of clear fire, whom on these seas I as Persian once did worship, till in the sacramental act so burned by thee, that to this hour I bear the scar;[6] I now know thee, thou clear spirit, and I now know that thy right worship is defiance. To neither love nor reverence wilt thou be kind; and e'en for hate thou canst but kill; and all are killed. No fearless fool now fronts thee. I own° thy speechless, placeless power; but to the last gasp of my earthquake life will dispute its unconditional, unintegral mastery in me. In the midst of the personified impersonal, a personality stands here. Though but a point at best; whencesoe'er I came; wheresoe'er I go; yet while I earthly live, the queenly personality[7] lives in me, and feels her royal rights. But war is pain, and hate is woe. Come in thy lowest form of love, and I will kneel and kiss thee; but at thy highest, come as mere supernal power; and though thou launchest navies of full-freighted worlds, there's that in here that still remains indifferent. Oh, thou clear spirit, of thy fire thou madest me, and like a true child of fire, I breathe it back to thee."

[*Sudden, repeated flashes of lightning; the nine flames leap lengthwise to thrice their previous height; Ahab, with the rest, closes his eyes, his right hand pressed hard upon them.*]

"I own thy speechless, placeless power; said I not so? Nor was it wrung from me; nor do I now drop these links. Thou canst blind; but I can then grope. Thou canst consume; but I can then be ashes. Take the homage of these poor eyes, and shutter-hands. I would not take it. The lightning flashes through my skull; mine eye-balls ache and ache; my whole beaten brain seems as beheaded, and rolling on some stunning ground. Oh, oh! Yet blindfold, yet will I talk to thee. Light though

links: the lightning rod's grounding chain. **own**: admit.

thou be, thou leapest out of darkness; but I am darkness leaping out of light, leaping out of thee! The javelins cease; open eyes; see, or not? There burn the flames! Oh, thou magnanimous! now I do glory in my genealogy. But thou art but my fiery father; my sweet mother, I know not. Oh, cruel! what hast thou done with her? There lies my puzzle; but thine is greater. Thou knowest not how came ye, hence callest thyself unbegotten; certainly knowest not thy beginning, hence callest thyself unbegun. I know that of me, which thou knowest not of thyself, oh, thou **omnipotent**. There is some unsuffusing thing beyond thee, thou clear spirit, to whom all thy eternity is but time, all thy creativeness mechanical. Through thee, thy flaming self, my scorched eyes do dimly see it. Oh, thou foundling fire, thou hermit immemorial, thou too hast thy incommunicable riddle, thy unparticipated° grief. Here again with haughty agony, I read my sire. Leap! leap up, and lick the sky! I leap with thee; I burn with thee; would fain be welded with thee; defyingly I worship thee!"

"The boat! the boat!" cried Starbuck, "look at thy boat, old man!"

Ahab's harpoon, the one forged at Perth's fire, remained firmly lashed in its conspicuous crotch, so that it projected beyond his whale-boat's bow; but the sea that had stove its bottom had caused the loose leather sheath to drop off; and from the keen steel barb there now came a levelled flame of pale, forked fire. As the silent harpoon burned there like a serpent's tongue, Starbuck grasped Ahab by the arm—"God, God is against thee, old man; forbear! t'is an ill voyage! ill begun, ill continued; let me square the yards, while we may, old man, and make a fair wind of it homewards, to go on a better voyage than this."

Overhearing Starbuck, the panic-stricken crew instantly ran to the braces—though not a sail was left aloft. For the moment all the aghast mate's thoughts seemed theirs; they raised a half mutinous cry. But dashing the rattling lightning links to the deck, and snatching the burning harpoon, Ahab waved it like a torch among them; swearing to transfix with it the first sailor that but cast loose a rope's end. Petrified by his aspect, and still more shrinking from the fiery dart[8] that he held, the men fell back in dismay, and Ahab again spoke:—

"All your oaths to hunt the White Whale are as binding as mine; and heart, soul, and body, lungs and life, old Ahab is bound. And that ye may know to what tune this heart beats; look ye here; thus I blow out the last fear!" And with one blast of his breath he extinguished the flame.

As in the hurricane that sweeps the plain, men fly the neighborhood of some lone, gigantic elm,[9] whose very height and strength but render it so much the more unsafe, because so much the more a mark for thunderbolts; so at those last words of Ahab's many of the mariners did run from him in a terror of dismay.

---

unparticipated: unshared.

CHAPTER 120

THE DECK TOWARDS THE END OF THE FIRST NIGHT WATCH

Ahab standing by the helm. Starbuck approaching him.

"WE must send down the main-top-sail yard, sir. The band is working loose, and the lee lift is half-stranded. Shall I strike it,[1] sir?"

"Strike nothing; lash it. If I had sky-sail poles,° I'd sway them up now."

"Sir?—in God's name!—sir?"

"Well."

"The anchors are working, sir. Shall I get them inboard?"

"Strike nothing, and stir nothing, but lash everything. The wind rises, but it has not got up to my table-lands° yet. Quick, and see to it.—By masts and keels! he takes me for the hunchbacked skipper of some coasting smack.° Send down my main-top-sail yard! Ho, gluepots!° Loftiest trucks were made for wildest winds, and this brain-truck of mine now sails amid the cloud-scud. Shall I strike that? Oh, none but cowards send down their brain-trucks in tempest time. What a hooroosh° aloft there! I would e'en take it for sublime, did I not know that the colic is a noisy malady. Oh, take medicine, take medicine!"[2]

---

sky-sail poles: the highest parts of masts, supporting the light, fair-weather skysails and their yards. ***table-lands***: high plateaus. ***coasting smack***: small fishing boat that stays close to shore. ***gluepots***: slang for parson, addressed to Starbuck. ***hooroosh***: wild uproar.

CHAPTER 121

MIDNIGHT—
THE FORECASTLE
BULWARKS

*Stubb and Flask mounted on them, and passing additional lashings
over the anchors there hanging.*

"No, Stubb; you may pound that knot there as much as you please, but you will never pound into me what you were just now saying. And how long ago is it since you said the very contrary? Didn't you once say that whatever ship Ahab sails in, that ship should pay something extra on its insurance policy, just as though it were loaded with powder barrels aft and boxes of lucifers forward? Stop, now; didn't you say so?"

"Well, suppose I did? What then? I've part changed my flesh since that time, why not my mind? Besides, supposing we *are* loaded with powder barrels aft and lucifers forward; how the devil could the lucifers get afire in this drenching spray here? Why, my little man, you have pretty red hair, but you couldn't get afire now. Shake yourself; you're Aquarius, or the water-bearer, Flask; might fill pitchers at your coat collar. Don't you see, then, that for these extra risks the Marine Insurance companies have extra guarantees? Here are hydrants, Flask. But hark, again, and I'll answer ye the other thing. First take your leg off from the crown° of the anchor here, though, so I can pass the rope; now listen. What's the mighty difference between holding a mast's lightning-rod in the storm, and standing close by a mast that hasn't got any lightning-rod at all in a storm? Don't you see, you timber-head, that no harm can come to the holder of the rod, unless the mast is first struck? What are you talking about, then? Not one ship in a hundred carries rods, and Ahab,—aye, man, and all of us,—were in no more danger then, in my poor opinion, than all the crews in ten thousand ships now sailing the seas. Why, you King-Post, you, I suppose you

crown: "that part of an anchor where the shank and arms meet" (Russell).

would have every man in the world go about with a small lightning-rod running up the corner of his hat, like a militia officer's skewered feather, and trailing behind like his sash. Why don't ye be sensible, Flask? it's easy to be sensible; why don't ye, then? any man with half an eye can be sensible."

"I don't know that, Stubb. You sometimes find it rather hard."

"Yes, when a fellow's soaked through, it's hard to be sensible, that's a fact. And I am about drenched with this spray. Never mind; catch the turn there, and pass it. Seems to me we are lashing down these anchors now as if they were never going to be used again. Tying these two anchors here, Flask, seems like tying a man's hands behind him. And what big generous hands they are, to be sure. These are your iron fists, hey? What a hold they have, too! I wonder, Flask, whether the world is anchored anywhere; if she is, she swings with an uncommon long cable, though. There, hammer that knot down, and we've done. So; next to touching land, lighting on deck is the most satisfactory. I say, just wring out my jacket skirts, will ye? Thank ye. They laugh at long-togs° so, Flask; but seems to me, a long tailed coat ought always to be worn in all storms afloat. The tails tapering down that way, serve to carry off the water, d'ye see. Same with cocked hats; the cocks form gable-end eave-troughs. Flask. No more monkey-jackets and tarpaulins for me; I must mount a swallow-tail, and drive down a beaver;° so. Halloa! whew! there goes my tarpaulin overboard; Lord, Lord, that the winds that come from heaven should be so unmannerly! This is a nasty night, lad."

---

long-togs: landsmen's clothes (Smyth). ***mount a swallow-tail . . . drive down a beaver***: put on a swallow-tail coat; wear a tall beaver hat.

CHAPTER 122

MIDNIGHT ALOFT —THUNDER AND LIGHTNING

The Main-top-sail yard.—Tashtego passing new lashings around it.[1]

"UM, um, um. Stop that thunder! Plenty too much thunder up here. What's the use of thunder? Um, um, um. We don't want thunder; we want rum; give us a glass of rum. Um, um, um!"

CHAPTER 123

THE MUSKET

Dᴜʀɪɴɢ the most violent shocks of the Typhoon, the man at the Pequod's jaw-bone tiller had several times been reelingly hurled to the deck by its spasmodic motions, even though preventer tackles° had been attached to it—for they were slack—because some play to the tiller was indispensable.

In a severe gale like this, while the ship is but a tossed shuttle-cock to the blast, it is by no means uncommon to see the needles in the compasses, at intervals, go round and round. It was thus with the Pequod's; at almost every shock the helmsman had not failed to notice the whirling velocity with which they revolved upon the cards; it is a sight that hardly any one can behold without some sort of unwonted emotion.

Some hours after midnight, the Typhoon abated so much, that through the strenuous exertions of Starbuck and Stubb—one engaged forward and the other aft—the shivered remnants of the jib and fore and main-top-sails were cut adrift from the spars,[1] and went eddying away to leeward, like the feathers of an albatross, which sometimes are cast to the winds when that storm-tossed bird is on the wing.

The three corresponding new sails were now bent and reefed,° and a storm-try-sail° was set further aft; so that the ship soon went through the water with some precision again; and the course—for the present, East-south-east—which he was to steer, if practicable, was once more given to the helmsman. For during the violence of the gale, he had only steered according to its vicissitudes. But as he was now bringing the ship as near her course as possible, watching the compass meanwhile, lo! a good sign! the wind seemed coming round astern; aye, the foul breeze became fair!

Instantly the yards were squared, to the lively song of "*Ho! the fair wind! oh-he-yo, cheerly, men!*"[2] the crew singing for joy, that so promising an event should so soon have falsified the evil portents preceding it.

In compliance with the standing order of his commander—to report immediately, and at any one of the twenty-four hours, any decided change in the affairs of the deck,—Starbuck had no sooner trimmed the yards to the breeze—however reluctantly and gloomily,—than he mechanically went below to apprise Captain Ahab of the circumstance.

preventer tackles: additional control ropes. ***bent and reefed***: attached and shortened. ***storm-trysail***: strong triangular sail.

449

Ere knocking at his state-room, he involuntarily paused before it a moment. The cabin lamp—taking long swings this way and that—was burning fitfully, and casting fitful shadows upon the old man's bolted door,—a thin one, with fixed blinds inserted, in place of upper panels. The isolated subterraneousness of the cabin made a certain humming silence to reign there, though it was hooped round by all the roar of the elements. The loaded muskets in the rack were shiningly revealed, as they stood upright against the forward bulkhead. Starbuck was an honest, upright man; but out of Starbuck's heart, at that instant when he saw the muskets, there strangely evolved an evil thought; but so blent with its neutral or good accompaniments that for the instant he hardly knew it for itself.

"He would have shot me once,"° he murmured, "yes, there's the very musket that he pointed at me;—that one with the studded stock; let me touch it—lift it. Strange, that I, who have handled so many deadly lances, strange, that I should shake so now. Loaded? I must see. Aye, aye; and powder in the pan;—that's not good. Best spill it?—wait. I'll cure myself of this. I'll hold the musket boldly while I think.—I come to report a fair wind to him. But how fair? Fair for death and doom,—*that's* fair for Moby Dick. It's a fair wind that's only fair for that accursed fish.—The very tube he pointed at me!—the very one; *this* one—I hold it here; he would have killed me with the very thing I handle now.—Aye and he would fain kill all his crew. Does he not say he will not strike his spars to any gale? Has he not dashed his heavenly quadrant? and in these same perilous seas, gropes he not his way by mere dead reckoning of the error-abounding log? and in this very Typhoon, did he not swear that he would have no lightning-rods? But shall this crazed old man be tamely suffered to drag a whole ship's company down to doom with him?—Yes, it would make him the wilful murderer of thirty men and more, if this ship **come** to any deadly harm; and come to deadly harm, my soul swears this ship will, if Ahab have his way. If, then, he were this instant—put aside, that crime would not be his. Ha! is he muttering in his sleep? Yes, just there,—in there, he's sleeping. Sleeping? aye, but still alive, and soon awake again. I can't withstand thee, then, old man. Not reasoning; not remonstrance; not entreaty wilt thou hearken to; all this thou scornest. Flat obedience to thy own flat commands, this is all thou breathest. Aye, and say'st the men have vow'd thy vow; say'st all of us are Ahabs. Great God forbid!—But is there no other way? no lawful way?—Make him a prisoner to be taken home? What! hope to wrest this old man's living power from his own living hands? Only a fool would try it. Say he were pinioned even; knotted all over with ropes and hawsers; chained down to ring-bolts on this cabin floor; he would be more hideous than a caged tiger, then. I could not endure the sight; could not possibly fly his howlings; all comfort, sleep itself, inestimable reason would leave me on the long intolerable voyage. What, then, remains? The land is hundreds of leagues away, and locked Japan the nearest. I stand alone here upon an open sea, with two oceans and a whole continent between me and law.—Aye, aye, 'tis so.—Is heaven a murderer when its lightning strikes a would-be murderer in his bed, tindering sheets and skin together?—And would I be a murderer, then, if"[3]————and slowly, **stealthily**, and half sideways looking, he placed the loaded musket's end against the door.

"He would have shot me once": see Ch. 109.

"On this level, Ahab's hammock swings within; his head this way. A touch, and Starbuck may survive to hug his wife and child again.—Oh Mary! Mary!—boy! boy! boy!—But if I wake thee not to death, old man, who can tell to what unsounded deeps Starbuck's body this day week° may sink, with all the crew! Great God, where art thou? Shall I? shall I?——— The wind has gone down and shifted, sir; the fore and main topsails are reefed and set; she heads her course."

"Stern all! Oh Moby Dick, I clutch thy heart at last!"

Such were the sounds that now came hurtling from out the old man's tormented sleep, as if Starbuck's voice had caused the long dumb dream to speak.

The yet levelled musket shook like a drunkard's arm against the panel; Starbuck seemed wrestling with an angel;[4] but turning from the door, he placed the death-tube in its rack, and left the place.

"He's too sound asleep, Mr. Stubb; go thou down, and wake him, and tell him. I must see to the deck here. Thou know'st what to say."

---

this day week: one week from today.

CHAPTER 124

THE NEEDLE

NEXT morning the not-yet-subsided sea rolled in long slow billows of mighty bulk, and striving in the Pequod's gurgling track, pushed her on like giants' palms outspread. The strong, unstaggering breeze abounded so, that sky and air seemed vast outbellying sails; the whole world boomed before the wind. Muffled in the full morning light, the invisible sun was only known by the spread intensity of his place; where his bayonet rays moved on in stacks. Emblazonings, as of crowned Babylonian kings and queens, reigned over everything. The sea was as a crucible° of molten gold, that bubblingly leaps with light and heat.

Long maintaining an enchanted silence, Ahab stood apart; and every time the tetering ship loweringly pitched down her bowsprit, he turned to eye the bright sun's rays produced ahead; and when she profoundly settled by the stern, he turned behind, and saw the sun's rearward place, and how the same yellow rays were blending with his undeviating wake.

"Ha, ha, my ship! thou mightest well be taken now for the sea-chariot of the sun. Ho, ho! all ye nations before my prow, I bring the sun to ye! Yoke on the further billows; hallo! a tandem, I drive the sea!"[1]

But suddenly reined back by some counter thought, he hurried towards the helm, huskily demanding how the ship was heading.

"East-sou-east, sir," said the frightened steersman.

"Thou liest!" smiting him with his clenched fist. "Heading East at this hour in the morning, and the sun astern?"

Upon this every soul was confounded; for the phenomenon just then observed by Ahab had unaccountably escaped every one else; but its very blinding palpableness must have been the cause.

Thrusting his head half way into the binnacle, Ahab caught one glimpse of the compasses; his uplifted arm slowly fell; for a moment he almost seemed to stagger. Standing behind him Starbuck looked, and lo! the two compasses pointed East, and the Pequod was as infallibly going West.

crucible: melting pot.

But ere the first wild alarm could get out abroad among the crew, the old man with a rigid laugh exclaimed, "I have it! It has happened before. Mr. Starbuck, last night's thunder turned our compasses—that's all. Thou hast before now heard of such a thing, I take it."

"Aye; but never before has it happened to me, sir," said the pale mate, gloomily.

Here, it must needs be said, that accidents like this have in more than one case occurred to ships in violent storms. The magnetic energy, as developed in the mariner's needle, is, as all know, essentially one with the electricity beheld in heaven; hence it is not to be much marvelled at, that such things should be.[2] In instances where the lightning has actually struck the vessel, so as to smite down some of the spars and rigging, the effect upon the needle has at times been still more fatal; all its loadstone virtue° being annihilated, so that the before magnetic steel was of no more use than an old wife's knitting needle. But in either case, the needle never again, of itself, recovers the original virtue thus marred or lost; and if the binnacle compasses be affected, the same fate reaches all the others that may be in the ship; even were the lowermost one inserted into the kelson.

Deliberately standing before the binnacle, and eyeing the transpointed compasses, the old man, with the sharp of his extended hand, now took the precise bearing of the sun, and satisfied that the needles were exactly inverted, shouted out his orders for the ship's course to be changed accordingly. The yards were **braced** hard up;° and once more the Pequod thrust her undaunted bows into the opposing wind, for the supposed fair one had only been juggling° her.

Meanwhile, whatever were his own secret thoughts, Starbuck said nothing, but quietly he issued all requisite orders; while Stubb and Flask—who in some small degree seemed then to be sharing his feelings—likewise unmurmuringly acquiesced. As for the men, though some of them lowly rumbled, their fear of Ahab was greater than their fear of Fate. But as ever before, the pagan harpooneers remained almost wholly unimpressed; or if impressed, it was only with a certain magnetism shot into their congenial hearts from inflexible Ahab's.

For a space the old man walked the deck in rolling reveries. But chancing to slip with his ivory heel, he saw the crushed copper sight-tubes of the quadrant he had the day before dashed to the deck.

"Thou poor, proud heaven-gazer and sun's pilot! yesterday I wrecked thee, and to-day the compasses would **fain** have wrecked me. So, so. But Ahab is lord over the level loadstone yet. Mr. Starbuck—a lance without the pole; a top-maul,° and the smallest of the sail-maker's needles. Quick!"

Accessory, perhaps, to the impulse dictating the thing he was now about to do, were certain prudential motives, whose object might have been to revive the spirits of his crew by a stroke of his subtile skill, in a matter so wondrous as that of the inverted compasses. Besides, the old man well knew that to steer by transpointed needles, though clumsily practicable, was not a thing to be passed over by superstitious sailors, without some shudderings and evil portents.

---

loadstone virtue: magnetism naturally occurring in "lodestone," a magnetic iron ore. **braced hard up**: pointing as directly into the wind as possible. **juggling**: deceiving. **top-maul**: heavy hammer.

"Men," said he, steadily turning upon the crew, as the mate handed him the things he had demanded, "my men, the thunder turned old Ahab's needles; but out of this bit of steel Ahab can make one of his own,[3] that will point as true as any."

Abashed glances of servile wonder were exchanged by the sailors, as this was said; and with fascinated eyes they awaited whatever magic might follow. But Starbuck looked away.

With a blow from the top-maul Ahab knocked off the steel head of the lance, and then handing to the mate the long iron rod remaining, bade him hold it upright, without its touching the deck. Then, with the maul, after repeatedly smiting the upper end of this iron rod, he placed the blunted needle endwise on the top of it, and less strongly hammered that, several times, the mate still holding the rod as before. Then going through some small strange motions with it—whether indispensable to the magnetizing of the steel, or merely intended to augment the awe of the crew, is uncertain—he called for linen thread; and moving to the binnacle, slipped out the two reversed needles there, and horizontally suspended the sail-needle by its middle, over one of the compass-cards. At first, the steel went round and round, quivering and vibrating at either end; but at last it settled to its place, when Ahab, who had been intently watching for this result, stepped frankly back from the binnacle, and pointing his stretched arm towards it, exclaimed,—"Look ye, for yourselves, if Ahab be not lord of the level loadstone! The sun is East, and that compass swears it!"

One after another they peered in, for nothing but their own eyes could persuade such ignorance as theirs, and one after another they slunk away.

In his fiery eyes of scorn and triumph, you then saw Ahab in all his fatal pride.

CHAPTER 125

THE LOG
AND LINE

W HILE now the fated Pequod had been so long afloat this voyage, the log and
line had but very seldom been in use. Owing to a confident reliance upon
other means of determining the vessel's place, some merchantmen, and many
whalemen, especially when cruising, wholly neglect to heave the log;° though at the
same time, and frequently more for form's sake than anything else, regularly putting
down upon the customary slate the course steered by the ship, as well as the presumed average rate of progression every hour. It had been thus with the Pequod.
The wooden reel and angular log attached hung, long untouched, just beneath the
railing of the after bulwarks. Rains and spray had damped it; sun and wind had
warped it; all the elements had combined to rot a thing that hung so idly. But heedless of all this, his mood seized Ahab, as he happened to glance upon the reel, not
many hours after the magnet scene, and he remembered how his quadrant was no
more, and recalled his frantic oath° about the level log and line. The ship was sailing
plungingly; astern the billows rolled in riots.

"Forward, there! Heave the log!"

Two seamen came. The golden-hued Tahitian and the grizzly Manxman. "Take
the reel, one of ye, I'll heave."

They went towards the extreme stern, on the ship's lee side, where the deck,
with the oblique energy of the wind, was now almost dipping into the creamy, side-
long-rushing sea.

The Manxman took the reel, and holding it high up, by the projecting handle-
ends of the spindle, round which the spool of line revolved, so stood with the angular log hanging downwards, till Ahab advanced to him.

Ahab stood before him, and was lightly unwinding some thirty or forty turns to
form a preliminary hand-coil to toss overboard, when the old Manxman, who was
intently eyeing both him and the line, made bold to speak.

"Sir, I mistrust it; this line looks far gone, long heat and wet have spoiled it."

"'Twill hold, old gentleman. Long heat and wet, have they spoiled thee? Thou
seem'st to hold. Or, truer perhaps, life holds thee; not thou it."

heave the log: see Ch. 118, note 4. *frantic oath*: in Ch. 118.

"I hold the spool, sir. But just as my captain says. With these grey hairs of mine 'tis not worth while disputing, 'specially with a superior, who'll ne'er confess."

"What's that? There now's a patched professor in Queen Nature's granite-founded College; but methinks he's too subservient. Where wert thou born?"

"In the little rocky Isle of Man, sir."

"Excellent! Thou'st hit the world by that."

"I know not, sir, but I was born there."

"In the Isle of Man, hey? Well, the other way, it's good. Here's a man from Man; a man born in once independent Man,[1] and now unmanned of Man; which is sucked in—by what? Up with the reel! The dead, blind wall butts all inquiring heads at last. Up with it! So."

The log was heaved. The loose coils rapidly straightened out in a long dragging line astern, and then, instantly, the reel began to whirl. In turn, jerkingly raised and lowered by the rolling billows, the towing resistance of the log caused the old reel-man to stagger strangely.

"Hold hard!"

Snap! the overstrained line sagged down in one long festoon; the tugging log was gone.

"I crush the quadrant, the thunder turns the needles, and now the mad sea parts the log-line. But Ahab can mend all. Haul in here, Tahitian; reel up, Manxman. And look ye, let the carpenter make another log, and mend thou the line. See to it."

"There he goes now; to him **nothing's** happened; but to me, the skewer seems loosening out of the middle of the world. Haul in, haul in, Tahitian! These lines run whole, and whirling out: come in broken, and dragging slow. Ha, Pip? come to help; eh, Pip?"

"Pip? whom call ye Pip? Pip jumped from the whale-boat. Pip's missing. Let's see now if ye haven't fished him up here, fisherman. It drags hard; I guess he's holding on. Jerk him, Tahiti! Jerk him off; we haul in no cowards here. Ho! there's his arm just breaking water. A hatchet! a hatchet! cut it off—we haul in no cowards here. Captain Ahab! sir, sir! here's Pip, trying to get on board again."

"Peace, thou crazy loon," cried the Manxman, seizing him by the arm. "Away from the quarter-deck!"

"The greater idiot ever scolds the lesser," muttered Ahab, advancing. "Hands off from that holiness! Where sayest thou Pip was, boy?"

"Astern there, sir, astern! Lo, lo!"

"And who art thou, boy? I see not my reflection in the vacant pupils of thy eyes. Oh God! that man should be a thing for immortal souls to sieve through! Who art thou, boy?"

"Bell-boy, sir; ship's-crier; ding, dong, ding! Pip! Pip! Pip! **One hundred pounds of clay reward for Pip;** five feet high—looks cowardly—quickest known by that! Ding, dong, ding! Who's seen Pip the coward?"

"There can be no hearts above the snow-line. Oh, ye frozen heavens! look down here. Ye did beget this luckless child, and have abandoned him, ye creative libertines. Here, boy; Ahab's cabin shall be Pip's home henceforth, while Ahab lives. Thou touchest my inmost centre, boy; thou art tied to me by cords woven of my heart-strings. Come, let's down."

"**What's** this? here's velvet shark-skin," intently gazing at Ahab's hand, and feeling it. "Ah, now, had poor Pip but felt so kind a thing as this, perhaps he had ne'er been lost! This seems to me, sir, as a man-rope; something that weak souls may hold by. Oh, sir, let old Perth now come and rivet these two hands together; the black one with the white, for I will not let this go."

"Oh, boy, nor will I thee, unless I should thereby drag thee to worse horrors than are here. Come, then, to my cabin. Lo! ye believers in gods all goodness,° and in man all ill, lo you! see the omniscient gods oblivious of suffering man; and man, though idiotic, and knowing not what he does, yet full of the sweet things of love and gratitude. Come! I feel prouder leading thee by thy black hand, than though I grasped an Emperor's!"

"There go two daft ones now," muttered the old Manxman. "One daft with strength, the other daft with weakness. But here's the end of the rotten line—all dripping, too. Mend it, eh? I think we had best have a new line altogether. I'll see Mr. Stubb about it."

gods all goodness: gods who are nothing but good.

CHAPTER 126

THE LIFE-BUOY

S TEERING now south-eastward by Ahab's levelled steel, and her progress solely
determined by Ahab's level log and line; the Pequod held on her path towards
the Equator. Making so long a passage through such unfrequented waters, descrying
no ships, and ere long, sideways impelled by unvarying trade winds,[1] over waves
monotonously mild; all these seemed the strange calm things preluding some riotous
and desperate scene.

At last, when the ship drew near to the outskirts, as it were, of the Equatorial
fishing-ground, and in the deep darkness that goes before the dawn, was sailing by
a cluster of rocky islets; the watch—then headed by Flask—was startled by a cry so
plaintively wild and unearthly[2]—like half-articulated wailings of the ghosts of all
Herod's murdered Innocents[3]—that one and all, they started from their reveries,
and for the space of some moments stood, or sat, or leaned all transfixedly listening,
like the carved Roman slave,[4] while that wild cry remained within hearing. The
Christian or civilized part of the crew said it was mermaids, and shuddered; but the
pagan harpooneers remained unappalled. Yet the grey Manxman—the oldest
mariner of all—declared that the wild thrilling sounds that were heard, were the
voices of newly drowned men in the sea.

Below in his hammock, Ahab did not hear of this till grey dawn, when he
came to the deck; it was then recounted to him by Flask, not unaccompanied with
hinted dark meanings. He hollowly laughed, and thus explained the wonder.

Those rocky islands the ship had passed were the resort of great numbers of
seals, and some young seals that had lost their dams, or some dams that had lost their
cubs, must have risen nigh the ship and kept company with her, crying and sobbing
with their human sort of wail. But this only the more affected some of them, because
most mariners cherish a very superstitious feeling about seals, arising not only from
their peculiar tones when in distress, but also from the human look of their round
heads and semi-intelligent faces, seen peeringly uprising from the water alongside.
In the sea, under certain circumstances, seals have more than once been mistaken
for men.

But the bodings of the crew were destined to receive a most plausible confirmation in the fate of one of their number that morning. At sun-rise this man went

from his hammock to his mast-head at the fore; and whether it was that he was not yet half waked from his sleep (for sailors sometimes go aloft in a transition state), whether it was thus with the man, there is now no telling; but, be that as it may, he had not been long at his perch, when a cry was heard—a cry and a rushing—and looking up, they saw a falling phantom in the air; and looking down, a little tossed heap of white bubbles in the blue of the sea.[5]

The life-buoy—a long slender cask—was dropped from the stern, where it always hung obedient to a cunning spring; but no hand rose to seize it, and the sun having long beat upon this cask it had shrunken, so that it slowly filled, and the parched wood also filled at its every pore; and the studded iron-bound cask followed the sailor to the bottom, as if to yield him his pillow, though in sooth but a hard one.

And thus the first man of the Pequod that mounted the mast to look out for the White Whale, on the White Whale's own peculiar ground; that man was swallowed up in the deep. But few, perhaps, thought of that at the time. Indeed, in some sort, they were not grieved at this event, at least as a portent; for they regarded it, not as a foreshadowing of evil in the future, but as the fulfilment of an evil already presaged. They declared that now they knew the reason of those wild shrieks they had heard the night before. But again the old Manxman said nay.

The lost life-buoy was now to be replaced; Starbuck was directed to see to it; but as no cask of sufficient lightness could be found, and as in the feverish eagerness of what seemed the approaching crisis of the voyage, all hands were impatient of any toil but what was directly connected with its final end, whatever that might prove to be; therefore, they were going to leave the ship's stern unprovided with a buoy, when by certain strange signs and inuendoes Queequeg hinted a hint concerning his coffin.

"A life-buoy of a coffin!" cried Starbuck, starting.

"Rather queer, that, I should say," said Stubb.

"It will make a good enough one," said Flask, "the carpenter here can arrange it easily."

"Bring it up; there's nothing else for it," said Starbuck, after a melancholy pause. "Rig it, carpenter; do not look at me so—the coffin, I mean. Dost thou hear me? Rig it."

"And shall I nail down the lid, sir?" moving his hand as with a hammer.

"Aye."

"And shall I caulk the seams, sir?" moving his hand as with a caulking-iron.

"Aye."

"And shall I then pay over° the same with pitch, sir?" moving his hand as with a pitch-pot.

"Away! what possesses thee to this? Make a life-buoy of the coffin, and no more.—Mr. Stubb, Mr. Flask, come forward with me."

"He goes off in a huff. The whole he can endure; at the parts he baulks. Now I don't like this. I make a leg for Captain Ahab, and he wears it like a gentleman; but I make a bandbox for Queequeg, and he won't put his head into it. Are all my pains

---

pay over: coat.

to go for nothing with that coffin? And now I'm ordered to make a life-buoy of it. It's like turning an old coat; going to bring the flesh on the other side now. I don't like this cobbling sort of business—I don't like it at all; it's undignified; it's not my place. Let tinkers' brats do tinkerings; we are their betters. I like to take in hand none but clean, virgin, fair-and-square mathematical jobs, something that regularly begins at the beginning, and is at the middle when midway, and comes to an end at the conclusion; not a cobbler's job, that's at an end in the middle, and at the beginning at the end. It's the old woman's tricks to be giving cobbling jobs. Lord! what an affection all old women have for tinkers.[6] I know an old woman of sixty-five who ran away with a bald-headed young tinker once. And that's the reason I never would work for lonely widow old women ashore, when I kept my job-shop in the Vineyard; they might have taken it into their lonely old heads to run off with me. But heigh-ho! there are no caps at sea but snow-caps.[7] Let me see. Nail down the lid; caulk the seams; pay over the same with pitch; batten them down tight, and hang it with the snap-spring over the ship's stern. Were ever such things done before with a coffin? Some superstitious old carpenters, now, would be tied up in the rigging, ere they would do the job. But I'm made of knotty Aroostook° hemlock; I don't budge. Cruppered° with a coffin! Sailing about with a grave-yard tray! But never mind. We workers in woods make bridal-bedsteads and card-tables, as well as coffins and hearses. We work by the month, or by the job, or by the profit; not for us to ask the why and wherefore of our work, unless it be too confounded cobbling, and then we stash it if we can. Hem! I'll do the job, now, tenderly. I'll have me—let's see—how many in the ship's company, all told? But I've forgotten. Any way, I'll have me thirty separate, Turk's-headed life-lines,[8] each three feet long hanging all round to the coffin. Then, if the hull go down, there'll be thirty lively fellows all fighting for one coffin, a sight not seen very often beneath the sun! Come hammer, calking-iron, pitch-pot, and marling-spike! Let's to it."

Aroostook: northernmost county in Maine. ***Cruppered***: equipped at the stern; referring to the "crupper," or strap passing under a horse's tail.

CHAPTER 127

THE DECK

*The coffin laid upon two line-tubs, between the vice-bench and the open hatchway;
the Carpenter calking its seams; the string of twisted oakum slowly unwinding
from a large roll of it placed in the bosom of his frock.—Ahab comes slowly from
the cabin-gangway, and hears Pip following him.*

"**B**ACK, lad; **I will** be with ye again presently. He goes! Not this hand complies
with my humor more genially than that boy.—Middle aisle of a church!°
What's here?"

"Life-buoy, sir. Mr. Starbuck's orders. Oh, look, sir! Beware the hatchway!"

"Thank ye, man. Thy coffin lies handy to the vault."

"Sir? The hatchway? oh! So it does, sir, so it does."

"Art not thou the leg-maker? Look, did not this stump come from thy shop?"

"I believe it did, sir; does the ferrule° stand, sir?"

"Well enough. But art thou not also the undertaker?"

"Aye, sir; I patched up this thing here as a coffin for Queequeg; but they've set
me now to turning it into something else."

"Then tell me; art thou not an arrant, all-grasping, intermeddling, monopolizing, heathenish old scamp, to be one day making legs, and the next day coffins to
clap them in, and yet again life-buoys out of those same coffins? Thou art as unprincipled as the gods, and as much of a jack-of-all-trades."

"But I do not mean anything, sir. I do as I do."

"The gods again. Hark ye, dost thou not ever sing working about a coffin?
The Titans, they say, hummed snatches when chipping out the craters for volcanoes;
and the grave-digger in the play sings, spade in hand.[1] Dost thou never?"

"Sing, sir? Do I sing? Oh, I'm indifferent enough, sir, for that; but the reason
why the grave-digger made music must have been because there was none in his
spade, sir. But the calking mallet is full of it. Hark to it."

"Aye, and that's because the lid there's a sounding-board; and what in all things
makes the sounding-board is this—there's naught beneath. And yet, a coffin with a

Middle aisle of a church: location for the coffin at a funeral. **ferrule**: strengthening metal
band.

461

body in it rings pretty much the same, Carpenter. Hast thou ever helped carry a bier, and heard the coffin knock against the church-yard gate, going in?"

"Faith, sir, I've———"

"Faith? What's that?"

"Why, faith, sir, it's only a sort of exclamation-like—that's all, sir."

"Um, um; go on."

"I was about to say, sir, that———"

"Art thou a silk-worm? Dost thou spin thy own shroud out of thyself? Look at thy bosom![2] Despatch! and get these traps out of **sight**."

"He goes aft. That was sudden, now; but squalls come sudden in hot latitudes. I've heard that the Isle of Albemarle,[3] one of the Gallipagos, is cut by the Equator right in the middle. Seems to me some sort of Equator cuts yon old man, too, right in his middle. He's always under the Line—fiery hot, I tell ye! He's looking this way—come, oakum; quick. Here we go again. This wooden mallet is the cork, and I'm the professor of musical glasses[4]—tap, tap!"

(Ahab to himself.)

"There's a sight! There's a sound! The greyheaded woodpecker tapping the hollow tree! Blind and **dumb** might well be envied now. See! that thing rests on two line-tubs, full of tow-lines. A most malicious wag, that fellow. Rat-tat! So man's seconds tick! Oh! how immaterial are all materials! What things real are there, but imponderable thoughts? Here now's the very dreaded symbol of grim death, by a mere hap, made the expressive sign of the help and hope of most endangered life. A life-buoy of a coffin! Does it go further? Can it be that in some spiritual sense the coffin is, after all, but an immortality-preserver! I'll think of that. But no. So far gone am I in the dark side of **earth**, that its other side, the theoretic bright one, seems but uncertain twilight to me. Will ye never have done, Carpenter, with that accursed sound? I go below; let me not see that thing here when I return again. Now, then, Pip, we'll talk this over; I do suck most wondrous philosophies from thee! Some unknown conduits from the unknown worlds must empty into thee!"

CHAPTER 128

THE PEQUOD
MEETS THE RACHEL

N EXT day, a large ship, the Rachel, was descried, bearing directly down upon the Pequod, all her spars thickly clustering with men. At the time the Pequod was making good speed through the water; but as the broad-winged windward stranger shot nigh to her, the boastful sails all fell together[1] as blank bladders that are burst, and all life fled from the smitten hull.

"Bad news; she brings bad news," muttered the old Manxman. But ere her commander, who, with trumpet to mouth, stood up in his boat; ere he could hopefully hail, Ahab's voice was heard.

"Hast seen the White Whale?"

"Aye, yesterday. Have ye seen a whale-boat adrift?"

Throttling his joy, Ahab negatively answered this unexpected question; and would then have fain boarded the stranger, when the stranger captain himself, having stopped his vessel's way, was seen descending her side. A few keen pulls, and his boat-hook soon clinched the Pequod's main-chains, and he sprang to the deck. Immediately he was recognised by Ahab for a Nantucketer he knew. But no formal salutation was exchanged.

"Where was he?—not killed!—not killed!" cried Ahab, closely advancing. "How was it?"

It seemed that somewhat late on the afternoon of the day previous, while three of the stranger's boats were engaged with a shoal of whales, which had led them some four or five miles from the ship; and while they were yet in swift chase to windward, the white hump and head of Moby Dick had suddenly loomed up out of the blue water, not very far to leeward; whereupon, the fourth rigged boat—a reserved one—had been instantly lowered in chase. After a keen sail before the wind, this fourth boat—the swiftest keeled of all—seemed to have succeeded in fastening—at least, as well as the man at the mast-head could tell anything about it. In the distance he saw the diminished dotted boat; and then a swift gleam of bubbling white water; and after that nothing more; whence it was concluded that the stricken whale must have indefinitely run away with his pursuers, as often happens. There was some apprehension, but no positive alarm, as yet. The recall signals were placed in the rigging; darkness came on; and forced to pick up her three far to windward boats—ere going in quest of the fourth one in the precisely opposite direction—the ship had not only been necessitated to leave that boat to its fate till near midnight, but, for the time, to increase her distance from it. But the rest of her crew being at last safe aboard, she crowded all sail—stunsail on stunsail—after the missing boat; kindling a fire in her try-pots for a beacon; and every other man aloft on the look-out. But though when she had thus sailed a sufficient distance to gain the presumed place of the absent ones when last seen; though she then paused to lower her spare boats to pull all around her; and not finding anything, had again dashed on; again paused, and lowered her boats; and though she had thus continued doing till day light; yet not the least glimpse of the missing keel had been seen.

The story told, the stranger Captain immediately went on to reveal his object in boarding the Pequod. He desired that ship to unite with his own in the search; by sailing over the sea some four or five miles apart, on parallel lines, and so sweeping a double horizon, as it were.

"I will wager something now," whispered Stubb to Flask, "that some one in that missing boat wore off that Captain's best coat; mayhap, his watch—he's so cursed anxious to get it back. Who ever heard of two pious whale-ships cruising after one missing whale-boat in the height of the whaling season? See, Flask, only see how pale he looks—pale in the very buttons of his eyes—look—it wasn't the coat—it must have been the—"

"My boy, my own boy is among them. For God's sake—I beg, I conjure"—here exclaimed the stranger Captain to Ahab, who thus far had but icily received his petition. "For eight-and-forty hours let me charter your ship—I will gladly pay for it, and roundly pay for it—if there be no other way—for eight-and-forty hours only—only that—you must, oh, you must, and you *shall* do this thing."

"His son!" cried Stubb, "oh, it's his son he's lost! I take back the coat and watch—what says Ahab? We must save that boy."

"He's drowned with the rest on 'em, last night," said the old Manx sailor standing behind them; "I heard; all of ye heard their spirits."

Now, as it shortly turned out, what made this incident of the Rachel's the more melancholy, was the circumstance, that not only was one of the Captain's sons among the number of the missing boat's crew; but among the number of the other boats' crews, at the same time, but on the other hand, separated from the ship during the dark vicissitudes of the chase, there had been still another son; as that for a time, the wretched father was plunged to the bottom of the cruellest perplexity; which was only solved for him by his chief mate's instinctively adopting the ordinary procedure of a whale-ship in such emergencies, that is, when placed between jeopardized but divided boats, always to pick up the majority first. But the captain, for some unknown constitutional reason, had refrained from mentioning all this, and not till forced to it by Ahab's iciness did he allude to his one yet missing boy; a little lad, but twelve years old, whose father with the earnest but unmisgiving hardihood of a Nantucketer's paternal love, had thus early sought to initiate him in the perils and wonders of a vocation almost immemorially the destiny of all his race. Nor does it unfrequently occur, that Nantucket captains will send a son of such tender age away from them, for a protracted three or four years' voyage in some other ship than their own; so that their first knowledge of a whaleman's career shall be unenervated° by any chance display of a father's natural but untimely partiality, or undue apprehensiveness and concern.

Meantime, now the stranger was still beseeching his poor boon of Ahab; and Ahab still stood like an anvil, receiving every shock, but without the least quivering of his own.

"I will not go," said the stranger, "till you say *aye* to me. Do to me as you would have me do to you in the like case.[2] For *you* too have a boy, Captain Ahab—though but a child, and nestling safely at home now—a child of your old age too[3]—Yes, yes, you relent; I see it—run, run, men, now, and stand by to square in the yards."

"Avast," cried Ahab—"touch not a rope-yarn;" then in a voice that prolongingly moulded every word—"Captain Gardiner, I will not do it. Even now I lose time. Good bye, good bye. God bless ye, man, and may I forgive myself, but I must go. Mr. Starbuck, look at the binnacle watch,° and in three minutes from this present instant warn off all strangers: then brace forward again, and let the ship sail as before."

Hurriedly turning, with averted face, he descended into his cabin, leaving the strange captain transfixed at this unconditional and utter rejection of his so earnest suit. But starting from his enchantment, Gardiner silently hurried to the side; more fell than stepped into his boat, and returned to his ship.

Soon the two ships diverged their wakes; and long as the strange vessel was in view, she was seen to yaw hither and thither at every dark spot, however small, on the sea. This way and that her yards were swung round; starboard and larboard, she continued to tack; now she beat against a head sea;° and again it pushed her before it; while all the while, her masts and yards were thickly clustered with men, as three tall cherry trees, when the boys are cherrying among the boughs.

But by her still halting course and winding, woful way, you plainly saw that this ship that so wept with spray, still remained without comfort. She was Rachel, weeping for her children, because they were not.[4]

---

unenervated: not weakened. **binnacle watch**: timepiece at the helm. **head sea**: waves running directly against the course of the ship.

CHAPTER 129

THE CABIN

(Ahab moving to go on deck; Pip catches him by the hand to follow.)

"Lad, lad, I tell thee thou must not follow Ahab now. The hour is coming[1] when Ahab would not scare thee from him, yet would not have thee by him. There is that in thee, poor lad, which I feel too curing to my malady. Like cures like;[2] and for this hunt, my malady becomes my most desired health. Do thou abide below here, where they shall serve thee, as if thou wert the captain. Aye, lad, thou shalt sit here in my own screwed chair; another screw to it, thou must be."

"No, no, no! ye have not a whole body, sir; do ye but use poor me for your one lost leg; only tread upon me, sir; I ask no more, so I remain a part of ye."

"Oh! spite of million villains, this makes me a bigot in the fadeless fidelity of man!—and a black! and crazy!—but methinks like-cures-like applies to him too; he grows so sane again."

"They tell me, sir, that Stubb did once desert poor little Pip, whose drowned bones now show white, for all the blackness of his **living** skin. But I will never desert ye, sir, as Stubb did him. Sir, I must go with ye."

"If thou speakest thus to me much more, Ahab's purpose keels up in him. I tell thee no; it cannot be."

"Oh good master, master, master!"[3]

"Weep so, and I will murder thee! have a care, for Ahab too is mad. Listen, and thou wilt often hear my ivory foot upon the deck, and still know that I am there. And now I quit thee. Thy hand!—Met! True art thou, lad, as the circumference to its centre. So: God for ever bless thee; and if it come to that,—God for ever save thee, let what will befall."

(Ahab goes; Pip steps one step forward.)

"Here he this instant stood; I stand in his air,—but I'm alone. Now were even poor Pip here I could endure it, but he's missing. Pip! Pip! Ding, dong, ding! Who's seen Pip? He must be up here; let's try the door. What? neither lock, nor bolt, nor bar; and yet there's no opening it. It must be the spell; he told me to stay here: Aye, and told me this screwed chair was mine. Here, then, I'll seat me, against the transom, in the ship's full middle, all her keel and her three masts before me. Here, our old sailors say, in their black seventy-fours great admirals sometimes sit at table, and lord it over rows of captains and lieutenants. Ha! what's this? epaulets! epaulets! the epaulets all come crowding! Pass round the decanters; glad to see ye; fill up, monsieurs! What an odd feeling, now, when a black boy's host to white men with gold lace upon their coats!—Monsieurs, have ye seen one Pip?—a little negro lad, five feet high, hang-dog look, and cowardly! Jumped from a whale-boat once;—seen him? No! Well then, fill up again, captains, and let's drink shame upon all cowards! I name no names. Shame upon them! Put one foot upon the table. Shame upon all cowards.—Hist! above there, I hear ivory—Oh, master! master! I am indeed down-hearted when you walk over me. But here I'll stay, though this stern strikes rocks; and they bulge through; and oysters come to join me."

CHAPTER 130

THE HAT

AND now that at the proper time and place, after so long and wide a preliminary cruise, Ahab,—all other whaling waters swept—seemed to have chased
his foe into an ocean-fold, to slay him the more securely there; now, that he
found himself hard by the very latitude and longitude where his tormenting
wound had been inflicted; now that a vessel had been spoken which on the very
day preceding had actually encountered Moby Dick;—and now that all his successive meetings with various ships contrastingly concurred to show the demoniac
indifference with which the white whale tore his hunters, whether sinning or
sinned against; now it was that there lurked a something in the old man's eyes,
which it was hardly sufferable for feeble souls to see. As the unsetting polar star,
which through the livelong, arctic, six months' night sustains its piercing, steady,
central gaze; so Ahab's purpose now fixedly gleamed down upon the constant
midnight of the gloomy crew. It domineered above them so, that all their bodings,
doubts, misgivings, fears, were fain to hide beneath their souls, and not sprout
forth a single spear or leaf.

In this foreshadowing interval too, all humor, forced or natural, vanished.
Stubb no more strove to raise a smile; Starbuck no more strove to check one. Alike,
joy and sorrow, hope and fear, seemed ground to finest dust, and powdered, for the
time, in the clamped mortar of Ahab's iron soul. Like machines, they dumbly moved
about the deck, ever conscious that the old man's despot eye was on them.

But did you deeply scan him in his more secret confidential hours; when he
thought no glance but one was on him; then you would have seen that even as
Ahab's eyes so awed the crew's, the inscrutable Parsee's glance awed his; or somehow, at least, in some wild way, at times affected it. Such an added, gliding strangeness began to invest the thin Fedallah now; such ceaseless shudderings shook him;
that the men looked dubious at him; half uncertain, as it seemed, whether indeed he
were a mortal substance, or else a tremulous shadow cast upon the deck by some
unseen being's body. And that shadow was always hovering there. For not by night,
even, had Fedallah ever certainly been known to slumber, or go below. He would
stand still for hours: but never sat or leaned; his wan but wondrous eyes **did plainly
say**—We two watchmen never rest.

Nor, at any time, by night or day could the mariners now step upon the deck, unless Ahab was before them;° either standing in his pivot-hole, or exactly pacing the planks between two undeviating limits,—the main-mast and the mizen; or else they saw him standing in the cabin-scuttle,—his living foot advanced upon the deck, as if to step; his hat slouched heavily over his eyes; so that however motionless he stood, however the days and nights were added on, that he had not swung in his hammock; yet hidden beneath that slouching hat, they could never tell unerringly whether, for all this, his eyes were really closed at times: or whether he was still intently scanning them; no matter, though he stood so in the scuttle for a whole hour on the stretch, and the unheeded night-damp gathered in beads of dew upon that stone-carved coat and hat. The clothes that the night had wet, the next day's sunshine dried upon him; and so, day after day, and night after night; he went no more beneath the planks; whatever he wanted from the cabin that thing he sent for.

He ate in the same open air; that is, his two only meals,—breakfast and dinner: supper he never touched; nor reaped his beard; which darkly grew all gnarled, as unearthed roots of trees blown over, which still grow idly on at naked base, though perished in the upper verdure. But though his whole life was now become one watch on deck; and though the Parsee's mystic watch was without intermission as his own; yet these two never seemed to speak—one man to the other—unless at long intervals some passing unmomentous matter made it necessary. Though such a potent spell seemed secretly to join the twain; openly, and to the awe-struck crew, they seemed pole-like asunder. If by day they chanced to speak one word; by night, dumb men were both, so far as concerned the slightest verbal interchange. At times, for longest hours, without a single hail, they stood far parted in the starlight; Ahab in his scuttle, the Parsee by the mainmast; but still fixedly gazing upon each other; as if in the Parsee Ahab saw his forethrown shadow, in Ahab the Parsee his abandoned substance.

And yet, somehow, did Ahab—in his own proper self, as daily, hourly, and every instant, commandingly revealed to his subordinates,—Ahab seemed an independent lord; the Parsee but his slave. Still again both seemed yoked together, and an unseen tyrant driving them; the lean shade siding the solid rib. For be this Parsee what he may, all rib and keel was solid Ahab.

At the first faintest glimmering of the dawn, his iron voice was heard from aft—"Man the mast-heads!"—and all through the day, till after sunset and after twilight, the same voice every hour, at the striking of the helmsman's bell, was heard— "What d'ye see?—sharp! sharp!"

But when three or four days had slided by, after meeting the children-seeking Rachel; and no spout had yet been seen; the monomaniac old man seemed distrustful of his crew's fidelity; at least, of nearly all except the Pagan harpooneers; he seemed to doubt, even, whether Stubb and Flask might not willingly overlook the sight he sought. But if these suspicions were really his, he sagaciously refrained from verbally expressing them, however his actions might seem to hint them.

"I will have the first sight of the whale myself,"—he said. "Aye! Ahab must have the doubloon!" and with his own hands he rigged a nest of basketed bowlines;

unless Ahab was before them: without Ahab's already being there.

and sending a hand aloft, with a single sheaved block, to secure to the mainmast head, he received the two ends of the downward-reeved rope; and attaching one to his basket prepared a pin for the other end,° in order to fasten it at the rail. This done, with that end yet in his hand and standing beside the pin, he looked round upon his crew, sweeping from one to the other; pausing his glance long upon Daggoo, Queequeg, Tashtego; but shunning Fedallah; and then settling his firm relying eye upon the chief mate, **he** said,—"Take the rope, sir—I give it into thy hands, Starbuck." Then arranging his person in the basket, he gave the word for them to hoist him to his perch, Starbuck being the one who secured the rope at last; and afterwards stood near it. And thus, with one hand clinging round the royal mast, Ahab gazed abroad upon the sea for miles and miles,—ahead, astern, this side, and that,—within the wide expanded circle commanded at so great a height.

When in working with his hands at some lofty almost isolated place in the rigging, which chances to afford no foothold, the sailor at sea is hoisted up to that spot, and sustained there by the rope; under these circumstances, its fastened end on deck is always given in strict charge to some one man who has the special watch of it. Because in such a wilderness of running rigging, whose various different relations aloft cannot always be infallibly discerned by what is seen of them at the deck; and when the deck-ends of these ropes are being every few minutes cast down from the fastenings, it would be but a natural fatality, if, unprovided with a constant watchman, the hoisted sailor should by some carelessness of the crew be cast adrift and fall all swooping to the sea. So Ahab's proceedings in this matter were not unusual; the only strange thing about them seemed to be, that Starbuck, almost the one only man who had ever ventured to oppose him with anything in the slightest degree approaching to decision—one of those too, whose faithfulness on the look-out he had seemed to doubt somewhat;—it was strange, that this was the very man he should select for his watchman; freely giving his whole life into such an otherwise distrusted person's hands.

Now, the first time Ahab was perched aloft; ere he had been there ten minutes; one of those red-billed savage sea-hawks which so often fly incommodiously close round the manned mast-heads of whalemen in these latitudes; one of these birds came wheeling and screaming round his head in a maze of untrackably swift circlings. Then it darted a thousand feet straight up into the air; then spiralized downwards, and went eddying again round his head.

But with his gaze fixed upon the dim and distant horizon, Ahab seemed not to mark this wild bird; nor, indeed, would any one else have marked it much, it being no uncommon circumstance; only now almost the least heedful eye seemed to see some sort of cunning meaning in almost every sight.

"Your hat, your hat, sir!" suddenly cried the Sicilian seaman, who being posted at the mizen-mast-head, stood directly behind Ahab, though somewhat lower than his level, and with a deep gulf of air dividing them.

---

nest of basketed bowlines . . . downward-reeved rope . . . pin for the other end: basket-net made of knotted ropes, attached to a rope running up through a pulley at the mainmast head and back down to the deck, where it is secured to a belaying pin.

But already the sable wing was before the old man's eyes; the long hooked bill at his head: with a scream, the black hawk darted away with his prize.

An eagle flew thrice round Tarquin's head, removing his cap to replace it, and thereupon Tanaquil, his wife, declared that Tarquin would be king of Rome.[1] But only by the replacing of the cap was that omen accounted good. Ahab's hat was never restored; the wild hawk flew on and on with it; far in advance of the prow: and at last disappeared; while from the point of that disappearance, a minute black spot was dimly discerned, falling from that vast height into the sea.

REVISION NARRATIVE

Ahab's Hat

The British edition omitted the last paragraph of this chapter. An editor is not likely to have made such a cut simply for the sake of Britain's monarchical sensibilities, for, indeed, the point of comparing Ahab to Rome's early king Tarquin is that Ahab is not destined for further leadership. Nor is the passage sexually or religiously offensive. One likely explanation is that a careless printer might have skipped the paragraph while composing text. But Melville might have removed the paragraph himself, thinking that yet another bad omen for Ahab was superfluous.

CHAPTER 131

THE PEQUOD
MEETS THE DELIGHT

T HE intense Pequod sailed on; the rolling waves and days went by; the life-buoy-coffin still lightly swung; and another ship, most miserably misnamed the Delight, was descried. As she drew nigh, all eyes were fixed upon her broad beams, called shears, which, in some whaling-ships, cross the quarter-deck at the height of eight or nine feet; serving to carry the spare, unrigged, or disabled boats.

Upon the stranger's shears were beheld the shattered, white ribs, and some few splintered planks, of what had once been a whale-boat; but you now saw through this wreck, as plainly as you see through the peeled, half-unhinged, and bleaching skeleton of a horse.

"Hast seen the White Whale?"

"Look!" replied the hollow-cheeked captain from his taffrail; and with his trumpet he pointed to the wreck.

"Hast killed him?"

"The harpoon is not yet forged that will ever do that," answered the other, sadly glancing upon a rounded hammock on the deck, whose gathered sides some noiseless sailors were busy in sewing together.

"Not forged!" and snatching Perth's levelled iron° from the crotch, Ahab held it out, exclaiming—"Look ye, Nantucketer; here in this hand I hold his death! Tempered in blood, and tempered by lightning are these barbs; and I swear to temper them triply in that hot place behind the fin, where the White Whale most feels his accursed life!"

"Then God keep thee, old man—see'st thou that"—pointing to the hammock—"I bury but one of five stout men, who were alive only yesterday; but were dead ere night. Only *that* one I bury; the rest were buried before they died; you sail upon their tomb." Then turning to his crew—"Are ye ready there? place the plank then on the rail, and lift the body; so, then—Oh! God"—advancing towards the hammock with uplifted hands—"may the resurrection and the life——"[1]

"Brace forward! Up helm!" cried Ahab like lightning to his men.

Perth's levelled iron: Ahab's harpoon; see Ch. 113.

472

But the suddenly started Pequod was not quick enough to escape the sound of the splash that the corpse soon made as it struck the sea; not so quick, indeed, but that some of the flying bubbles might have sprinkled her hull with their ghostly baptism.

As Ahab now glided from the dejected Delight, the strange life-buoy hanging at the Pequod's stern came into conspicuous relief.

"Ha! yonder! look yonder, men!" cried a foreboding voice in her wake. "In vain, oh, ye strangers, ye fly our sad burial; ye but turn us your taffrail to show us your coffin!"

CHAPTER 132

THE SYMPHONY

Iᴛ was a clear steel-blue day. The firmaments of air and sea were hardly separable in that all-pervading azure;[1] only, the pensive air was transparently pure and soft, with a woman's look, and the robust and man-like sea heaved with long, strong, lingering swells, as Samson's chest in his sleep.[2]

Hither, and thither, on high, glided the snow-white wings of small, unspeckled birds; these were the gentle thoughts of the feminine air; but to and fro in the deeps, far down in the bottomless blue, rushed mighty leviathans, sword-fish, and sharks; and these were the strong, troubled, murderous thinkings of the masculine sea.

But though thus contrasting within, the contrast was only in shades and shadows without; those two seemed one; it was only the sex, as it were, that distinguished them.

REVISION NARRATIVE

Sexuality and Drama

As its title suggests, this chapter (a prelude to the book's three-chapter chase and climax) is one of Melville's more musical and dramatic scenes, with several voices speaking. Two paragraphs (on p. 475) were removed in the British edition for different reasons. In the first deleted paragraph, sky and sea are female and male elements meeting at the horizon, with the sky-bride surrendering with "throbbing trust" to the sea-groom. But the second paragraph lacks any censorable sexual content. It depicts the sky's blithe and playful indifference to Ahab's pain, and describes how air and sky are like children playing with the gray locks encircling a grandfather's "burnt-out crater" of a brain. The passage (which lacks quotation marks) may be either Ishmael or Ahab speaking, and it recalls the tone, word choice, and uncertain speaker of the "Oh, grassy glades" speech in Ch. 114, "The Gilder." Because the image is not offensive, Melville rather than an editor might have cut the paragraph to eliminate the apparent interior monologue that too closely echoes Ch. 114 and to move more quickly to Ahab's dramatic duet with Starbuck.

Aloft, like a royal czar and king, the sun seemed giving this gentle air to this bold and rolling sea; even as bride to groom. And at the girdling line of the horizon, a soft and tremulous motion—most seen here at the equator—denoted the fond, throbbing trust, the loving alarms,° with which the poor bride gave her bosom away.

Tied up and twisted; gnarled and knotted with wrinkles; haggardly firm and unyielding; his eyes glowing like coals, that still glow in the ashes of ruin; untottering Ahab stood forth in the clearness of the morn; lifting his splintered helmet of a brow to the fair girl's forehead of heaven.

Oh, immortal infancy, and innocency of the azure! Invisible winged creatures that frolic all round us! Sweet childhood of air and sky! how oblivious were ye of old Ahab's close-coiled woe! But so have I seen little Miriam and Martha,[3] laughing-eyed elves, heedlessly gambol around their old sire; sporting with the circle of singed locks which grew on the marge° of that burnt-out crater of his brain.

Slowly crossing the deck from the scuttle, Ahab leaned over the side, and watched how his shadow in the water sank and sank to his gaze, the more and the more that he strove to pierce the profundity.[4] But the lovely aromas in that enchanted air did at last seem to dispel, for a moment, the cankerous thing in his soul. That glad, happy air, that winsome sky, did at last stroke and caress him; the step-mother world,[5] so long cruel—forbidding—now threw affectionate arms round his stubborn neck, and did seem to joyously sob over him, as if over one, that however **wilful and** erring, she could yet find it in her heart to save and to bless. From beneath his slouched hat Ahab dropped a tear into the sea; nor did all the Pacific contain such wealth as that one wee drop.

Starbuck saw the old man; saw him, how he heavily leaned over the side; and he seemed to hear in his own true heart the measureless sobbing that stole out of the centre of the serenity around. Careful not to touch him, or be noticed by him, he yet drew near to him, and stood there.

Ahab turned.

"Starbuck!"

"Sir."

"Oh, Starbuck! it is a mild, mild wind, and a mild looking sky. On such a day—very much such a sweetness as this—I struck my first whale—a boy-harpooneer of eighteen! Forty—forty—forty years ago!—ago! Forty years[6] of continual whaling! forty years of privation, and peril, and storm-time! forty years on the pitiless sea! for forty years has Ahab forsaken the peaceful land, for forty years to make war on the horrors of the deep! Aye and yes, Starbuck, out of those forty years I have not spent three ashore. When I think of this life I have led; the desolation of solitude it has been; the masoned, walled-town of a Captain's exclusiveness, which admits but small entrance to any sympathy from the green country without—oh, weariness! heaviness! Guinea-coast slavery of solitary command![7]—when I think of all this; only half-suspected, not so keenly known to me before—and how for forty

alarms: apprehensions, here sexual. *marge*: margin, or edge (poetic).

years I have fed upon dry salted fare—fit emblem of the dry nourishment of my soul!—when the poorest landsman has had fresh fruit to his daily hand, and broken the world's fresh bread to my mouldy crusts—away, whole oceans away, from that young girl-wife I wedded past fifty, and sailed for Cape Horn the next day, leaving but one dent in my marriage pillow—wife? wife?—rather a widow with her husband alive! Aye, I widowed that poor girl when I married her, Starbuck; and then, the madness, the frenzy, the boiling blood and the smoking brow, with which, for a thousand lowerings old Ahab has furiously, foamingly chased his prey—more a demon than a man!—aye, aye! what a forty years' fool—fool—old fool, has old Ahab been! Why this strife of the chase? why weary, and palsy the arm at the oar, and the iron, and the lance? how the richer or better is Ahab now? Behold. Oh, Starbuck! is it not hard, that with this weary load I bear, one poor leg should have been snatched from under me? Here, brush this old hair aside; it blinds me, that I seem to weep. Locks so grey did never grow but from out some ashes! But do I look very old, so very, very old, Starbuck? I feel deadly faint, bowed, and humped, as though I were Adam, staggering beneath the piled centuries since Paradise. God! God! God!—crack my heart!—stave my brain!—mockery! mockery! bitter, biting mockery of grey hairs, have I lived enough joy to wear ye; and seem and feel thus intolerably old? Close! stand close to me, Starbuck; let me look into a human eye; it is better than to gaze into **sea** or sky; better than to **gaze** upon God. By the green land; by the bright hearth-stone! this is the magic glass, man; I see my wife and my child in thine eye. No, no; stay on board, on board!—lower not when I do; when branded Ahab gives chase to Moby Dick. That hazard shall not be thine. No, no! not with the far away home I see in that eye!"

"Oh, my Captain! my Captain! noble soul! grand old heart, after all! why should any one give chase to that hated fish! Away with me! let us fly these deadly waters! let us home! Wife and child, too, are Starbuck's—wife and child of his brotherly, sisterly, play-fellow youth; even as thine, sir, are the wife and child of thy loving, longing, paternal old age! Away! let us away!—this instant let me alter the course! How cheerily, how hilariously, O my Captain, would we bowl on our way to see old Nantucket again! I think, sir, they have some such mild blue days, even as this, in Nantucket."

"They have, they have. I have seen them—some summer days in the morning. About this time—yes, it is his noon nap now—the boy vivaciously wakes; sits up in bed; and his mother tells him of me, of cannibal old me; how I am abroad upon the deep, but will yet come back to dance him again."

"'Tis my Mary, my Mary herself! She promised that my boy, every morning, should be carried to the hill to catch the first glimpse of his father's sail! Yes, yes! no more! it is done! we head for Nantucket! Come, my Captain, study out the course, and let us away! See, see! the boy's face from the window! the boy's hand on the hill!"

But Ahab's glance was averted; like a blighted fruit tree he shook, and cast his last, cindered apple[8] to the soil.

"What is it, what nameless, inscrutable, unearthly thing is it; what cozening,° hidden lord and master, and cruel, remorseless emperor commands me; that against

---

cozening: deceiving.

all natural lovings and longings, I so keep pushing, and crowding, and jamming myself on all the time; recklessly making me ready to do what in my own proper, natural heart, I durst not so much as dare? Is **Ahab**, Ahab? Is it I, God, or who, that lifts this arm? But if the great sun move not of himself; but is as an errand-boy in heaven; nor one single star can revolve, but by some invisible power; how then can this one small heart beat; this one small brain think thoughts; unless God does that beating, does that thinking, does that living, and not I. By heaven, man, we are turned round and round in this world, like yonder windlass, and Fate is the handspike. And all the time, lo! that smiling sky, and this unsounded sea! Look! see yon Albicore! who put it into him to chase and fang that flying-fish? Where do murderers go, man! Who's to doom, when the judge himself is dragged to the bar?[9] But it is a mild, mild wind, and a mild looking sky; and the air smells now, as if it blew from a far-away meadow; they have been making hay somewhere under the slopes of the Andes, Starbuck, and the mowers are sleeping among the new-mown hay. Sleeping? Aye, toil we how we may, we all sleep at last on the field. Sleep? Aye, and rust amid greenness; as last year's scythes flung down, and left in the half-cut swaths—Starbuck!"

But blanched to a corpse's hue with despair, the Mate had stolen away.

Ahab crossed the deck to gaze over on the other side; but started at two reflected, fixed eyes in the water there. Fedallah was motionlessly leaning over the same rail.

REVISION NARRATIVE

Who Adds an It?

A famous textual puzzle involves the change in Ahab's self-searching question from its American version ("Is Ahab, Ahab?") to the British ("Is it Ahab, Ahab?"). The American reading has Ahab question his entire identity at this crucial moment before he then asks the more specific set of questions regarding who motivates his actions: "Is it I, God, or who, that lifts this arm?" The British reading, with the inserted "it," creates a more direct link between the two sets of questions. But its repetition of "Ahab" seems superfluous and may be taken as Ahab either directly addressing himself or dramatically stressing himself (perhaps with a gesture of disbelief) as his own motivator. One possible explanation for the British version is that Melville intended the British reading all along, but that the "it" was inadvertently omitted in the American edition and then replaced by Melville in the proofs he sent to England. Another possibility is that Melville intended the American reading, then changed his mind for the British. Also possible is that a British editor, not comprehending the American reading, added "it" to make Ahab's self-questioning parallel with the second question. Whether the result of a correction or revision, and whether authorial or editorial, the separate readings have their own logics and are equally meaningful.

CHAPTER 133

THE CHASE—
FIRST DAY

T HAT night, in the mid-watch, when the old man—as his wont at intervals—
stepped forth from the scuttle in which he leaned, and went to his pivot-hole, he
suddenly thrust out his face fiercely, snuffing up the sea air as a sagacious ship's dog
will, in drawing nigh to some barbarous isle. He declared that a whale must be near.
Soon that peculiar odor, sometimes to a great distance given forth by the living
sperm whale, was palpable to all the watch; nor was any mariner surprised when,
after inspecting the compass, and then the dog-vane,° and then ascertaining the
precise bearing of the odor as nearly as possible, Ahab rapidly ordered the ship's
course to be slightly altered, and the sail to be shortened.°

The acute policy dictating these movements was sufficiently vindicated at day-
break, by the sight of a long sleek on the sea directly and lengthwise ahead, smooth
as oil, and resembling in the pleated watery wrinkles bordering it, the polished
metallic-like marks of some swift tide-rip,° at the mouth of a deep, rapid stream.

"Man the mast-heads! Call all hands!"

Thundering with the butts of three clubbed handspikes on the forecastle deck,
Daggoo roused the sleepers with such judgment claps[1] that they seemed to exhale
from the scuttle, so instantaneously did they appear with their clothes in their hands.

"What d'ye see?" cried Ahab, flattening his face to the sky.

"Nothing, nothing, sir!" was the sound hailing down in reply.

"T'gallant sails!—stunsails! alow and aloft, and on both sides!"[2]

All sail being set, he now cast loose the life-line, reserved for swaying him to the
main royal-mast head; and in a few moments they were hoisting him thither, when,
while but two thirds of the way aloft, and while peering ahead through the horizontal
vacancy between the main-top-sail and top-gallant-sail, he raised a gull-like cry in the
air, "There she blows!—there she blows! A hump like a snow-hill! It is Moby Dick!"

Fired by the cry which seemed simultaneously taken up by the three look-
outs, the men on deck rushed to the rigging to behold the famous whale they had so

---

dog-vane: small streamer showing wind direction. ***sail to be shortened***: the entire sail area
to be reduced. ***tide-rip***: water made rough by the meeting of opposing currents, especially in
tidal waters.

long been pursuing. Ahab had now gained his final perch, some feet above the other look-outs, Tashtego standing just beneath him on the cap of the top-gallant-mast, so that the Indian's head was almost on a level with Ahab's heel.[3] From this height the whale was now seen some mile or so ahead, at every roll of the sea revealing his high sparkling hump, and regularly jetting his silent spout into the air. To the credulous mariners it seemed the same silent spout they had so long ago beheld in the moon-lit Atlantic and Indian Oceans.[4]

"And did none of ye see it before?" cried Ahab, hailing the perched men all around him.

"I saw him almost that same instant, sir, that Captain Ahab did, and I cried out," said Tashtego.

"Not the same instant; not the same—no, the doubloon is mine, Fate reserved the doubloon for me. *I* only; none of ye could have raised the White Whale first. There she blows! there she blows!—there she blows! There again!—there again!" he cried, in long-drawn, lingering, methodic tones, attuned to the gradual prolongings of the whale's visible jets. "He's going to sound! In stunsails! Down top-gallant-sails! Stand by three boats. Mr. Starbuck, remember, stay on board, and keep the ship. Helm there! Luff, luff a point!° So; steady, man, steady! There go flukes! No, no; only black water! All ready the boats there? Stand by, stand by! Lower me, Mr. Starbuck; lower, lower,—quick, quicker!" and he slid through the air to the deck.

"He is heading straight to leeward, sir," cried Stubb, "right away from us; cannot have seen the ship yet."

"Be dumb, man! Stand by the braces! Hard down the helm!—brace up! Shiver her!—shiver her! So; well that!° Boats, boats!"

Soon all the boats but Starbuck's were dropped; all the boat-sails set—all the paddles plying; with rippling swiftness, shooting to leeward; and Ahab heading the onset. A pale, death-glimmer lit up Fedallah's sunken eyes; a hideous motion gnawed his mouth.

Like noiseless nautilus shells,[5] their light prows sped through the sea; but only slowly they neared the foe. As they neared him, the ocean grew still more smooth; seemed drawing a carpet over its waves; seemed a noon-meadow, so serenely it spread. At length the breathless hunter came so nigh his seemingly unsuspecting prey, that his entire dazzling hump was distinctly visible, sliding along the sea as if an isolated thing, and continually set in a revolving ring of finest, fleecy, greenish foam. He saw the vast, involved wrinkles of the slightly projecting head beyond. Before it, far out on the soft Turkish-rugged waters, went the glistening white shadow from his broad, milky forehead, a musical rippling playfully accompanying the shade; and behind, the blue waters interchangeably flowed over into the moving valley of his steady wake; and on either hand bright bubbles arose and danced by his side. But these were broken again by the light toes of hundreds of gay fowl softly feathering

---

luff a point: steer closer to the wind by one compass *point* (about 11 degrees). ***Hard down the helm!—brace up! . . . shiver her! . . . So; well that!***: "Steer directly into the wind! Swing the yards around toward fore-and-aft position! Make the sails flap [because they've lost their wind]! Stop pulling; that will do."

the sea, alternate with their fitful flight; and like to some flag-staff rising from the painted hull of an argosy, the tall but shattered pole of a recent lance projected from the white whale's back; and at intervals one of the cloud of soft-toed fowls hovering, and to and fro skimming like a canopy over the fish, silently perched and rocked on this pole, the long tail feathers streaming like pennons.

A gentle joyousness—a mighty mildness of repose in swiftness, invested the gliding whale. Not the white bull Jupiter swimming away with ravished Europa clinging to his graceful horns; his lovely, leering eyes sideways intent upon the maid; with smooth bewitching fleetness, rippling straight for the nuptial bower in Crete;[6] not Jove, **not that great majesty Supreme**! did surpass the glorified White Whale as he so divinely swam.

On each soft side—coincident with the parted swell, that but once **leaving** him, then flowed so wide away—on each bright side, the whale shed off enticings.[7] No wonder there had been some among the hunters who namelessly transported and allured by all this serenity, had ventured to assail it; but had fatally found that quietude but the vesture of tornadoes. Yet calm, enticing calm, oh, whale! thou glidest on, to all who for the first time eye thee, no matter how many in that same way thou may'st have bejuggled° and destroyed before.

And thus, through the serene tranquillities of the tropical sea, among waves whose hand-clappings were suspended by exceeding rapture, Moby Dick moved on, still withholding from sight the full terrors of his submerged trunk, entirely hiding the wrenched hideousness of his jaw. But soon the fore part of him slowly rose from the water; for an instant his whole marbleized body formed a high arch, like Virginia's Natural Bridge,[8] and warningly waving his bannered flukes in the air, the grand god revealed himself, sounded, and went out of sight. Hoveringly halting, and dipping on the wing, the white sea-fowls longingly lingered over the agitated pool that he left.

With oars apeak, and paddles down, the sheets of their sails adrift,° the three boats now stilly floated, awaiting Moby Dick's reappearance.

"An hour," said Ahab, standing rooted in his boat's stern; and he gazed beyond the whale's place, towards the dim blue spaces and wide wooing vacancies to lee-ward. It was only an instant; for again his eyes seemed whirling round in his head as he swept the watery circle. The breeze now freshened; the sea began to swell.

"The birds!—the birds!" cried Tashtego.

In long Indian file, as when herons take wing, the white birds were now all fly-ing towards Ahab's boat; and when within a few yards began fluttering over the water there, wheeling round and round, with joyous, expectant cries. Their vision was keener than man's; Ahab could **discover** no sign in the sea. But suddenly as he peered down and down into its depths, he profoundly saw a white living spot no big-ger than a white weasel, with wonderful celerity uprising, and magnifying as it rose, till it turned, and then there were plainly revealed two long crooked rows of white, glistening teeth, floating up from the undiscoverable bottom. It was Moby Dick's

---

bejuggled: fooled. **apeak, ... sheets of their sails adrift**: pointed upward ... control ropes left slack.

open mouth and scrolled jaw; his vast, shadowed bulk still half blending with the blue of the sea. The glittering mouth yawned beneath the boat like an open-doored marble tomb; and giving one sidelong sweep with his steering oar, Ahab whirled the craft aside from this tremendous apparition. Then, calling upon Fedallah to change places with him, went forward to the bows, and seizing Perth's harpoon, commanded his crew to grasp their oars and stand by to stern.°

Now, by reason of this timely spinning round the boat upon its axis, its bow, by anticipation, was made to face the whale's head while yet under water. But as if perceiving this stratagem, Moby Dick, with that malicious intelligence ascribed to him, sidelingly transplanted himself, as it were, in an instant, shooting his pleated head lengthwise beneath the boat.

Through and through; through every plank and each rib, it thrilled for an instant, the whale obliquely lying on his back, in the manner of a biting shark, slowly and feelingly taking its bows full within his mouth, so that the long, narrow, scrolled lower jaw curled high up into the open air, and one of the teeth caught in a row-lock. The bluish pearl-white of the inside of the jaw was within six inches of Ahab's head, and reached higher than that. In this attitude the White Whale now shook the slight cedar as a mildly cruel cat her mouse. With unastonished eyes Fedallah gazed, and crossed his arms; but the tiger-yellow crew were tumbling over each other's heads to gain the uttermost stern.

And now, while both elastic gunwales were springing in and out, as the whale dallied with the doomed craft in this devilish way; and from his body being submerged beneath the boat, he could not be darted at from the bows, for the bows were almost inside of him, as it were; and while the other boats involuntarily paused, as before a quick crisis impossible to withstand, then it was that monomaniac Ahab, furious with this tantalizing vicinity of his foe, which placed him all alive and helpless in the very jaws he hated; frenzied with all this, he seized the long bone with his naked hands, and wildly strove to wrench it from **its** gripe. As now he thus vainly strove, the jaw slipped from him; the frail gunwales bent in, collapsed, and snapped, as both jaws, like an enormous shears, sliding further aft, bit the craft completely in twain, and locked themselves fast again in the sea, midway between the two floating wrecks. These floated aside, the broken ends drooping, the crew at the stern-wreck clinging to the gunwales, and striving to hold fast to the oars to lash them across.

At that preluding moment, ere the boat was yet snapped, Ahab, the first to perceive the whale's intent, by the crafty upraising of his head, a movement that loosed his hold for the time; at that moment his hand had made one final effort to push the boat out of the bite. But only slipping further into the whale's mouth, and tilting over sideways as it slipped, the boat had shaken off his hold on the jaw; spilled him out of it, as he leaned to the push; and so he fell flat-faced upon the sea.

Ripplingly withdrawing from his prey, Moby Dick now lay at a little distance, vertically thrusting his oblong white head up and down in the billows; and at the same time slowly revolving his whole spindled body; so that when his vast wrinkled forehead rose—some twenty or more feet out of the water—the now rising swells,

stern: row backwards.

with all their confluent waves, dazzlingly broke against it; vindictively tossing their shivered spray still higher into the air.* So, in a gale, the but half baffled Channel billows only recoil from the base of the Eddystone,[9] triumphantly to overleap its summit with their scud.

But soon resuming his horizontal attitude, Moby Dick swam swiftly round and round the wrecked crew; sideways churning the water in his vengeful wake, as if lashing himself up to still another and more deadly assault. The sight of the splintered boat seemed to madden him, as the blood of grapes and mulberries cast before Antiochus's elephants in the book of Maccabees.[10] Meanwhile Ahab half smothered in the foam of the whale's insolent tail, and too much of a cripple to swim,—though he could still keep afloat, even in the heart of such a whirlpool as that; helpless Ahab's head was seen, like a tossed bubble which the least chance shock might burst. From the boat's fragmentary stern, Fedallah incuriously and mildly eyed him; the clinging crew, at the other drifting end, could not succor him; more than enough was it for them to look to themselves. For so revolvingly appalling was the White Whale's aspect, and so planetarily swift the ever-contracting circles he made, that he seemed horizontally swooping upon them. And though the other boats, unharmed, still hovered hard by; still they dared not pull into the eddy to strike, lest that should be the signal for the instant destruction of the jeopardized castaways, Ahab and all; nor in that case could they themselves hope to escape. With straining eyes, then, they remained on the outer edge of the direful zone, whose centre had now become the old man's head.

Meantime, from the beginning all this had been descried from the ship's mast heads; and squaring her yards, she had borne down upon the scene; and was now so nigh, that Ahab in the water hailed her;—"Sail on the"—but that moment a breaking sea dashed on him from Moby Dick, and whelmed him for the time. But struggling out of it again, and chancing to rise on a towering crest, he shouted,—"Sail on the whale!—Drive him off!"

The Pequod's prow was pointed; and breaking up the charmed circle, she effectually parted the white whale from his victim. As he sullenly swam off, the boats flew to the rescue.

Dragged into Stubb's boat with blood-shot, blinded eyes, the white brine caking in his wrinkles; the long tension of Ahab's bodily strength did crack, and helplessly he yielded to his body's doom: for a time, lying all crushed in the bottom of Stubb's boat, like one trodden under foot of herds of elephants. Far inland, nameless wails came from him, as desolate sounds from out ravines.

But this intensity of his physical prostration did but so much the more abbreviate it. In an instant's compass, great hearts sometimes condense to one deep pang, the sum total of those shallow pains kindly diffused through feebler men's whole

---

* This motion is peculiar to the sperm whale. It receives its designation (pitchpoling) from its being likened to that preliminary up-and-down poise of the whale-lance, in the exercise called pitchpoling, previously described.° By this motion the whale must best and most comprehensively view whatever objects may be encircling him.

---

previously described: in Ch. 84.

lives. And so, such hearts, though summary in each one suffering; still, if the gods decree it, in their life-time aggregate a whole age of woe, wholly made up of instantaneous intensities; for even in their pointless centres, those noble natures contain the entire circumferences of inferior souls.

"The harpoon," said Ahab, half way rising, and draggingly leaning on one bended arm—"is it safe?"

"Aye, sir, for it was not darted; this is it," said Stubb, showing it.

"Lay it before me;—any missing men?"

"One, two, three, four, five;—there were five oars, sir, and here are five men."

"That's good.—Help me, man; I wish to stand. So, so, I see him! there! there! going to leeward still; what a leaping spout!—Hands off from me! The eternal sap runs up in Ahab's bones again! Set the sail; out oars; the helm!"

It is often the case that when a boat is stove, its crew, being picked up by another boat, help to work that second boat; and the chase is thus continued with what is called double-banked oars. It was thus now. But the added power of the boat did not equal the added power of the whale, for he seemed to have treble-banked his every fin; swimming with a velocity which plainly showed, that if now, under these circumstances, pushed on, the chase would prove an indefinitely prolonged, if not a hopeless one; nor could any crew endure for so long a period, such an unintermitted, intense straining at the oar; a thing barely tolerable only in some one brief vicissitude. The ship itself, then, as it sometimes happens, offered the most promising intermediate means of overtaking the chase. Accordingly, the boats now made for her, and were soon swayed up to their cranes—the two parts of the wrecked boat having been previously secured by her—and then hoisting everything to her side, and stacking her canvas high up, and sideways outstretching it with stun-sails, like the double-jointed wings of an albatross; the Pequod bore down in the leeward wake of **Moby Dick**. At the well known, methodic intervals, the whale's glittering spout was regularly announced from the manned mast-heads; and when he would be reported as just gone down, Ahab would take the time, and then pacing the deck, binnacle-watch in hand, so soon as the last second of the allotted hour expired, his voice was heard.—"Whose is the doubloon now? D'ye see him?" and if the reply was, No, sir! straightway he commanded them to lift him to his perch. In this way the day wore on; Ahab, now aloft and motionless; anon, unrestingly pacing the planks.

As he was thus walking, uttering no sound, except to hail the men aloft, or to bid them hoist a sail still higher, or to spread one to a still greater breadth—thus to and fro pacing, beneath his slouched hat, at every turn he passed his own wrecked boat, which had been dropped upon the quarter-deck, and lay there reversed; broken bow to shattered stern. At last he paused before it; and as in an already overclouded sky fresh troops of clouds will sometimes sail across, so over the old man's face there now stole some such added gloom as this.

Stubb saw him pause; and perhaps intending, not vainly, though, to evince his own unabated fortitude, and thus keep up a valiant place in his Captain's mind, he advanced, and eyeing the wreck exclaimed—"The thistle the ass refused; it pricked his mouth too keenly, sir; ha! ha!"

"What soulless thing is this that laughs before a wreck? Man, man! did I not know thee brave as fearless fire (and as mechanical)[11] I could swear thou wert a poltroon.° Groan nor laugh should be heard before a wreck."

"Aye, sir," said Starbuck drawing near, "'tis a solemn sight; an omen, and an ill one."

"Omen? omen?—the dictionary! If the gods think to speak outright to man, they will honorably speak outright; not shake their heads, and give an old wives' darkling° hint.—Begone! Ye two are the opposite poles of one thing; Starbuck is Stubb reversed, and Stubb is Starbuck; and ye two are all mankind; and Ahab stands alone among the millions of the peopled earth, nor gods nor men his neighbors! Cold, cold—I shiver!—How now? Aloft there! D'ye see him? Sing out for every spout, though he spout ten times a second!"

The day was nearly done; only the hem of his golden robe was rustling. Soon, it was almost dark, but the look-out men still remained unset.

"Can't see the spout now, sir;—too dark"—cried a voice from the air.

"How heading when last seen?"

"As before, sir,—straight to leeward."

"Good! he will travel slower now 'tis night. Down royals and top-gallant stun-sails, Mr. Starbuck. We must not run over him before morning; he's making a passage now, and may heave-to a while. Helm there! keep her full before the wind!—Aloft! come down!—Mr. Stubb, send a fresh hand to the fore-mast head, and see it manned till morning."—Then advancing towards the doubloon in the main-mast—"Men, this gold is mine, for I earned it; but I shall let it abide here till the White Whale is dead; and then, whosoever of ye first raises him, upon the day he shall be killed, this gold is that man's; and if on that day I shall again raise him, then, ten times its sum shall be divided among all of ye! Away now!—the deck is thine, sir."

And so saying, he placed himself half way within the scuttle, and slouching his hat, stood there till dawn, except when at intervals rousing himself to see how the night wore on.

poltroon: coward. *darkling*: obscure.

CHAPTER 134

THE CHASE —
SECOND DAY

AT day-break, the three mast-heads were punctually manned afresh.

"D'ye see him?" cried Ahab, after allowing a little space for the light to spread.

"See nothing, sir."

"Turn up all hands° and make sail! he travels faster than I thought for;—the top-gallant sails!—aye, they should have been kept on her all night. But no matter—'tis but resting for the rush."

Here be it said, that this pertinacious pursuit of one particular whale, continued through day into night, and through night into day, is a thing by no means unprecedented in the South sea fishery. For such is the wonderful skill, prescience of experience, and invincible confidence acquired by some great natural geniuses among the Nantucket commanders; that from the simple observation of a whale when last descried, they will, under certain given circumstances, pretty accurately foretell both the direction in which he will continue to swim for a time, while out of sight, as well as his probable rate of progression during that period. And, in these cases, somewhat as a pilot, when about losing sight of a coast, whose general trending he well knows, and which he desires shortly to return to again, but at some further point; like as this pilot stands by his compass, and takes the precise bearing of the cape at present visible, in order the more certainly to hit aright the remote, unseen headland, eventually to be visited: so does the fisherman, at his compass, with the whale; for after being chased, and diligently marked, through several hours of daylight, then, when night obscures the fish, the creature's future wake through the darkness is almost as established to the sagacious mind of the hunter, as the pilot's coast is to him. So that to this hunter's wondrous skill, the proverbial evanescence of a thing writ in water,[1] a wake, is to all desired purposes well nigh as reliable as the steadfast land. And as the mighty iron Leviathan of the modern railway is so familiarly known in its every pace, that, with watches in their hands, men time his rate as doctors that of a baby's pulse; and lightly say of it, the up train or the down train will reach such or such a spot, at such or such an hour; even so, almost, there are occasions when these Nantucketers time that other Leviathan of the deep,

Turn up all hands: call all the men below decks.

according to the observed humor of his speed; and say to themselves, so many hours hence this whale will have gone two hundred miles, will have about reached this or that degree of latitude or longitude. But to render this acuteness at all successful in the end, the wind and the sea must be the whaleman's allies; for of what present avail to the becalmed or windbound mariner is the skill that assures him he is exactly ninety-three leagues° and a quarter from his port? Inferable from these statements, are many collateral subtile matters touching the chase of whales.

The ship tore on; leaving such a furrow in the sea as when a cannon-ball, mis-sent, becomes a plough-share and turns up the level field.

"By salt and hemp!" cried Stubb, "but this swift motion of the deck creeps up one's legs and tingles at the heart. This ship and I are two brave fellows!—Ha! ha! Some one take me up, and launch me, spine-wise, on the sea,—for by live-oaks! my spine's a keel. Ha, ha! we go the gait that leaves no dust behind!"

"There she blows—she blows!—she blows!—right ahead!" was now the mast-head cry.

"Aye, aye!" cried Stubb, "I knew it—ye can't escape—blow on and split your spout, O whale! the mad fiend himself is after ye! blow your trump—blister your lungs!—Ahab will dam off your blood, as a miller shuts his water-gate upon the stream!"

And Stubb did but speak out for well nigh all that crew. The frenzies of the chase had by this time worked them bubblingly up, like old wine worked anew.[2] Whatever pale fears and forebodings some of them might have felt before; these were not only now kept out of sight through the growing awe of Ahab, but they were broken up, and on all sides routed, as timid prairie hares that scatter before the bounding bison. The hand of Fate had snatched all their souls; and by the stirring perils of the previous day; the rack of the past night's suspense; the fixed, unfearing, blind, reckless way in which their wild craft went plunging towards its flying mark; by all these things, their hearts were bowled along. The wind that made great bellies of their sails, and rushed the vessel on by arms invisible as irresistible; this seemed the symbol of that unseen agency which so enslaved them to the race.

They were one man, not thirty. For as the one ship that held them all; though it was put together of all contrasting things—oak, and maple, and pine wood; iron, and pitch, and hemp—yet all these ran into each other in the one concrete° hull, which shot on its way, both balanced and directed by the long central keel; even so, all the individualities of the crew, this man's valor, that man's fear; guilt and **guilti-ness**, all varieties were welded into oneness, and were all directed to that fatal goal which Ahab their one lord and keel did point to.

The rigging lived. The mast-heads, like the tops of tall palms, were out-spreadingly tufted with arms and legs. Clinging to a spar with one hand, some reached forth the other with impatient wavings; others, shading their eyes from the vivid sunlight, sat far out on the rocking yards; all the spars in full bearing of mortals, ready and ripe for their fate. Ah! how they still strove through that infinite blueness to seek out the thing that might destroy them!

---

leagues: a league is three nautical miles. ***concrete***: compound.

"Why sing ye not out for him, if ye see him?" cried Ahab, when, after the lapse of some minutes since the first cry, no more had been heard. "Sway me up, men; ye have been deceived; not Moby Dick casts one odd jet that way, and then disappears."

It was even so; in their headlong eagerness, the men had mistaken some other thing for the whale-spout, as the event itself soon proved; for hardly had Ahab reached his perch; hardly was the rope belayed° to its pin on deck, when he struck the key-note to an orchestra, that made the air vibrate as with the combined discharges of rifles. The triumphant halloo of thirty buckskin lungs was heard, as— much nearer to the ship than the place of the imaginary jet, less than a mile ahead— Moby Dick bodily burst into view! For not by any calm and indolent spoutings; not by the peaceable gush of that mystic fountain in his head, did the White Whale now reveal his vicinity; but by the far more wondrous phenomenon of breaching. Rising with his utmost velocity from the furthest depths, the Sperm Whale thus booms his entire bulk into the pure element of air, and piling up a mountain of dazzling foam, shows his place to the distance of seven miles and more. In those moments, the torn, enraged waves he shakes off, seem his mane; in some cases, this breaching is his act of defiance.

"There she breaches! there she breaches!" was the cry, as in his immeasurable bravadoes the White Whale tossed himself salmon-like to Heaven. So suddenly seen in the blue plain of the sea, and relieved against the still bluer margin of the sky, the spray that he raised, for the moment, intolerably glittered and glared like a glacier; and stood there gradually fading and fading away from its first sparkling intensity, to the dim mistiness of an advancing shower in a vale.

"Aye, breach your last to the sun, Moby Dick!" cried Ahab, "thy hour and thy harpoon are at hand!—Down! down all of ye, but one man at the fore.° The boats!— stand by!"

Unmindful of the tedious rope-ladders of the shrouds, the men, like shooting stars, slid to the deck, by the isolated backstays and halyards; while Ahab, less dartingly, but still rapidly was dropped from his perch.

"Lower away," he cried, so soon as he had reached his boat—a spare one, rigged the afternoon previous. "Mr. Starbuck, the ship is thine—keep away from the boats, but keep near them. Lower, all!"

As if to strike a quick terror into them, by this time being the first assailant himself, Moby Dick had turned, and was now coming for the three crews. Ahab's boat was central; and cheering his men, he told them he would take the whale head-and-head,—that is, pull straight up to his forehead,—a not uncommon thing; for when within a certain limit, such a course excludes the coming onset from the whale's sidelong vision. But ere that close limit was gained, and while yet all three boats were plain as the ship's three masts to his eye; the White Whale churning himself into furious speed, almost in an instant as it were, rushing among the boats with open jaws, and a lashing tail, offered appalling battle on every side; and heedless of the irons darted at him from every boat, seemed only intent on annihilating

belayed: secured. **the fore**: fore-masthead.

each separate plank of which those boats were made. But skilfully manœuvred, incessantly wheeling like trained chargers in the field; the boats for a while eluded him; though, at times, but by a plank's breadth; while all the time, Ahab's unearthly slogan° tore every other cry but his to shreds.

But at last in his untraceable evolutions, the White Whale so crossed and recrossed, and in a thousand ways entangled the slack of the three lines now fast to him, that they foreshortened, and, of themselves, warped the devoted° boats towards the planted irons in him; though now for a moment the whale drew aside a little, as if to rally for a more tremendous charge. Seizing that opportunity, Ahab first paid out more line: and then was rapidly hauling and jerking in upon it again—hoping that way to disencumber it of some snarls—when lo!—a sight more savage than the embattled teeth of sharks!

Caught and twisted—corkscrewed in the mazes of the line, loose harpoons and lances, with all their bristling barbs and points, came flashing and dripping up to the chocks in the bows of Ahab's boat. Only one thing could be done. Seizing the boat-knife, he critically reached within—through—and then, without—the rays of steel; dragged in the line beyond, passed it, inboard, to the bowsman, and then, twice sundering the rope near the chocks—dropped the intercepted fagot of steel into the sea; and was all fast again. That instant, the White Whale made a sudden rush among the remaining tangles of the other lines; by so doing, irresistibly dragged the more involved boats of Stubb and Flask towards his flukes; dashed them together like two rolling husks on a surf-beaten beach, and then, diving down into the sea, disappeared in a boiling maelstrom, in which, for a space, the odorous cedar chips of the wrecks danced round and round, like the grated nutmeg in a swiftly stirred bowl of punch.

While the two crews were yet circling in the waters, reaching out after the revolving line-tubs, oars, and other floating furniture, while aslope little Flask bobbed up and down like an empty vial, twitching his legs upwards to escape the dreaded jaws of sharks; and Stubb was lustily singing out for some one to ladle him up; and while the old man's line—now parting—admitted of his pulling into the creamy pool to rescue whom he could;—in that wild simultaneousness of a thousand concreted perils,—Ahab's yet unstricken boat seemed drawn up towards Heaven[3] by invisible wires,—as, arrow-like, shooting perpendicularly from the sea, the White Whale dashed his broad forehead against its bottom, and sent it, turning over and over, into the air; till it fell again—gunwale downwards—and Ahab and his men struggled out from under it, like seals from a sea-side cave.

The first uprising momentum of the whale—modifying its direction as he struck the surface—involuntarily launched him along it, to a little distance from the centre of the destruction he had made; and with his back to it, he now lay for a moment slowly feeling with his flukes from side to side; and whenever a stray oar, bit of plank, the least chip or crumb of the boats touched his skin, his tail swiftly drew back, and came sideways smiting the sea. But soon, as if satisfied that his work for that time was done, he pushed his pleated forehead through the ocean, and trailing after him the intertangled lines, continued his leeward way at a traveller's methodic pace.

slogan: battle cry. **devoted**: doomed.

As before, the attentive ship having descried the whole fight, again came bearing down to the rescue, and dropping a boat, picked up the floating mariners, tubs, oars, and whatever else could be caught at, and safely landed them on her decks. Some sprained shoulders, wrists, and ankles; livid contusions; wrenched harpoons and lances; inextricable intricacies of rope; shattered oars and planks; all these were there; but no fatal or even serious ill seemed to have befallen any one. As with Fedallah the day before, so Ahab was now found **grimly** clinging to his boat's broken half, which afforded a comparatively easy float; nor did it so exhaust him as the previous day's mishap.

But when he was helped to the deck, all eyes were fastened upon him; as instead of standing by himself he still half-hung upon the shoulder of Starbuck, who had thus far been the foremost to assist him. His ivory leg had been snapped off, leaving but one short sharp splinter.

"Aye aye, Starbuck, 'tis sweet to lean sometimes, be the leaner who he will; and would old Ahab had leaned oftener than he has."

"The ferrule has not stood, sir," said the carpenter, now coming up; "I put good work into that leg."

"But no bones broken, sir, I hope," said Stubb with true concern.

"Aye! and all splintered to pieces, Stubb!—d'ye see it.—But even with a broken bone, old Ahab is untouched; and I account no living bone of mine one jot more me, than this dead one that's lost. Nor white whale, nor man, nor fiend, can so much as graze old Ahab in his own proper and inaccessible being. Can any lead touch yonder floor, any mast scrape yonder roof?°—Aloft there! which way?"

"Dead to leeward, sir."

"Up helm, then; pile on the sail again, ship keepers! down the rest of the spare boats and rig them—Mr. Starbuck away, and muster the boats' crews."

"Let me first help thee towards the bulwarks, sir."

"Oh, oh, oh! how this splinter gores me now! Accursed fate! that the unconquerable captain in the soul should have such a craven mate!"

"Sir?"

"My body, man, not thee. Give me something for a cane—there, that shivered lance will do. Muster the men. Surely I have not seen him yet. By heaven it cannot be!—missing?—quick! call them all."

The old man's hinted thought was true. Upon mustering the company, the Parsee was not there.

"The Parsee!" cried Stubb—"he must have been caught in——"

"The black vomit° wrench thee!—run all of ye above, alow, cabin, forecastle—find him—not gone—not gone!"

But quickly they returned to him with the tidings that the Parsee was nowhere to be found.

"Aye, sir," said Stubb—"caught among the tangles of your line—I thought I saw him dragging under."

Can any lead touch yonder floor, any mast scrape yonder roof?: Can any measuring line reach the bottom of the sea; can any mast reach heaven? ***black vomit***: yellow fever.

"*My* line! *my* line? Gone?—gone? What means that little word?—What death-knell rings in it, that old Ahab shakes as if he were the belfry. The harpoon, too!—toss over the litter there,—d'ye see it?—the forged iron, men, the white whale's—no, no, no,—blistered° fool! this hand did dart it!—'tis in the fish!—Aloft there! Keep him nailed—Quick!—all hands to the rigging of the boats—collect the oars—har-pooneers! the irons, the irons!—hoist the royals higher—a pull on all the sheets!—helm there! steady, steady for your life! I'll ten times girdle the unmeasured globe; yea and dive straight through it, but I'll slay him yet!"

"Great God! but for one single instant show thyself," cried Starbuck; "never, never wilt thou capture him, old man—In Jesus' name no more of this, that's worse than devil's madness. Two days chased; twice stove to splinters; thy very leg once more snatched from under thee; thy evil shadow gone—all good angels mobbing thee with warnings:—what more wouldst thou have?—Shall we keep chasing this murderous fish till he swamps the last man? Shall we be dragged by him to the bot-tom of the sea? Shall we be towed by him to the infernal world? Oh, oh,—Impiety and blasphemy to hunt him more!"

"Starbuck, of late I've felt strangely moved to thee; ever since that hour we both saw—thou know'st what, in one another's eyes.° But in this matter of the whale, be the front of thy face to me as the palm of this hand—a lipless, unfeatured blank. Ahab is for ever Ahab, man. This whole act's immutably decreed. 'Twas rehearsed by thee and me a billion years before this ocean rolled. Fool! I am the Fates' lieutenant;[4] I act under orders. Look thou, underling! that thou obeyest mine.—Stand round me, men. Ye see an old man cut down to the stump; leaning on a shivered lance; propped up on a lonely foot. 'Tis Ahab—his body's part; but Ahab's soul's a centipede, that moves upon a hundred legs. I feel strained, half stranded, as ropes that tow dismasted frigates in a gale; and I may look so. But ere I break, ye'll hear me crack; and till ye hear *that,* know that Ahab's hawser tows his purpose yet. Believe ye, men, in the things called omens? Then laugh aloud, and cry encore! For ere they drown, drowning things will twice rise to the surface; then rise again, to sink for evermore. So with Moby Dick—two days he's floated—to-morrow will be the third. Aye, men, he'll rise once more,—but only to spout his last! D'ye feel brave, men, brave?"

"As fearless fire," cried Stubb.

"And as mechanical,"[5] muttered Ahab. Then as the men went forward, he muttered on:—"The things called omens! And yesterday I talked the same to Starbuck there, concerning my broken boat. Oh! how valiantly I seek to drive out of others' hearts what's clinched so fast in mine!—The Parsee—the Parsee!—gone, gone? and he was to go before:—but still was to be seen again ere I could perish°—How's that?—There's a riddle now might baffle all the lawyers backed by the ghosts of the whole line of judges:—like a hawk's beak it pecks my brain. *I'll, I'll* solve it, though!"

When dusk descended, the whale was still in sight to leeward.

---

blistered: cursed with blisters. ***that hour we both saw . . . in one another's eyes***: see Ch. 132. **seen again ere I could perish**: see Fedallah's prophecy, Ch. 117.

So once more the sail was shortened, and everything passed nearly as on the previous night; only, the sound of hammers, and the hum of the grindstone was heard till nearly daylight, as the men toiled by lanterns in the complete and careful rigging of the spare boats and sharpening their fresh weapons for the morrow. Meantime, of the broken keel of Ahab's wrecked craft the carpenter made him another leg; while still as on the night before, slouched Ahab stood fixed within his scuttle; his hid, heliotrope glance anticipatingly gone backward on its dial; set due eastward for the earliest sun.

CHAPTER 135

THE CHASE— THIRD DAY

THE morning of the third day dawned fair and fresh, and once more the solitary night-man at the fore-mast-head was relieved by crowds of the daylight look-outs, who dotted every mast and almost every spar.

"D'ye see him?" cried Ahab; but the whale was not yet in sight.

"In his infallible wake, though; but follow that wake, that's all. Helm there; steady, as thou goest, and hast been going. What a lovely day again! were it a new-made world, and made for a summer-house to the angels, and this morning the first of its throwing open to them, a fairer day could not dawn upon that world. Here's food for thought, had Ahab time to think; but Ahab never thinks; he only feels, feels, feels; *that's* tingling enough for mortal man! to think's audacity. God only has that right and privilege. Thinking is, or ought to be, a coolness and a calmness;[1] and our poor hearts throb, and our poor brains beat too much for that. And yet, I've sometimes thought my brain was very calm—frozen calm, this old skull cracks so, like a glass in which the contents turn to ice, and shiver it. And still this hair is grow-ing now; this moment growing, and heat must breed it; but no, it's like that sort of common grass that will grow anywhere, between the earthy clefts of Greenland ice or in Vesuvius lava. How the wild winds blow it; they whip it about me as the torn shreds of split sails lash the tossed ship they cling to. A vile wind that has no doubt blown ere this through prison corridors and cells, and wards of hospitals, and venti-lated them, and now comes blowing hither as innocent as fleeces. Out upon it!—it's tainted. Were I the wind, I'd blow no more on such a wicked, miserable world. I'd crawl somewhere to a cave, and slink there. And yet, 'tis a noble and heroic thing, the wind! who ever conquered it? In every fight it has the last and bitterest blow. Run tilting at it, and you but run through it. Ha! a coward wind that strikes stark naked men, but will not stand to receive a single blow. Even Ahab is a braver thing—a nobler thing than *that*. Would now the wind but had a body; but all the things that most exasperate and outrage mortal man, all these things are bodiless, but only bod-iless as objects, not as agents. There's a most special, a most cunning, oh, a most malicious difference![2] And yet, I say again, and swear it now, that there's something all glorious and gracious in the wind. These warm Trade Winds, at least, that in the clear heavens blow straight on, in strong and steadfast, vigorous mildness; and veer

492

not from their mark, however the baser currents of the sea may turn and tack, and mightiest Mississippies of the land **swift** and swerve about, uncertain where to go at last. And by the eternal Poles! these same Trades that so directly blow my good ship on; these Trades, or something like them—something so unchangeable, and full as strong, blow my keeled soul along! To it! Aloft there! What d'ye see?"

"Nothing, sir."

"Nothing! and noon at hand! The doubloon goes a-begging! See the sun! Aye, aye, it must be so. I've oversailed him. How, got the start? Aye, he's chasing *me* now; not I, *him*—that's bad; I might have known it, too. Fool! the lines—the harpoons he's towing. Aye, aye, I have run him by last night. About! about!° Come down, all of ye, but the regular look outs! Man the braces!"

Steering as she had done, the wind had been somewhat on the Pequod's quarter,° so that now being pointed in the reverse direction, the braced ship sailed hard upon the breeze as she rechurned the cream in her own white wake.

"Against the wind he now steers for the open jaw," murmured Starbuck to himself, as he coiled the new-hauled main-brace upon the rail. "God keep us, but already my bones feel damp within me, and from the inside wet my flesh. I misdoubt me° that I disobey my God in obeying him!"

"Stand by to sway me up!" cried Ahab, advancing to the hempen basket. "We should meet him soon."

"Aye, aye, sir," and straightway Starbuck did Ahab's bidding, and once more Ahab swung on high.

A whole hour now passed; gold-beaten out to ages.[3] Time itself now held long breaths with keen suspense. But at last, some three points off the weather bow,° Ahab descried the spout again, and instantly from the three mast-heads three shrieks went up as if the tongues of fire had voiced it.[4]

"Forehead to forehead I meet thee, this third time, Moby Dick! On deck there!—brace sharper up; crowd her into the wind's eye. He's too far off to lower yet, Mr. Starbuck. The sails shake! Stand over that helmsman with a top-maul! So, so; he travels fast, and I must down. But let me have one more good round look aloft here at the sea; there's time for that. An old, old sight, and yet somehow so young; aye, and not changed a wink since I first saw it, a boy, from the sand-hills of Nantucket! The same!—the same!—the same to Noah as to me. There's a soft shower to leeward. Such lovely leewardings! They must lead somewhere—to something else than common land, more palmy than the palms. Leeward! the white whale goes that way; look to windward, then; the better if the bitterer quarter. But good bye, good bye, old mast-head! What's this?—green? aye, tiny mosses in these warped cracks. No such green weather stains on Ahab's head! There's the difference now between man's old age and matter's. But aye, old mast, we both grow old together; sound in our hulls, though, are we not, my ship? Aye, minus a leg, that's all. By heaven this dead wood has the better of my live flesh every way. I can't compare with it; and I've

---

About! about!: in this case, "reverse direction." ***on the Pequod's quarter***: blowing from behind, at about a 45° angle. ***misdoubt me***: suspect. ***some three points off the weather bow***: at about a 33° angle to the bow, on the windy side.

known some ships made of dead trees outlast the lives of men made of the most vital stuff of vital fathers. What's that he said? he should still go before me, my pilot; and yet to be seen again? But where? Will I have eyes at the bottom of the sea, supposing I descend those endless stairs? and all night I've been sailing from him, wherever he did sink to. Aye, aye, like many more thou told'st direful truth as touching thyself, O Parsee; but, Ahab, there thy shot fell short. Good by, mast-head—keep a good eye upon the whale, the while I'm gone. We'll talk to-morrow, nay, to-night, when the white whale lies down there, tied by head and tail."

He gave the word; and still gazing round him, was steadily lowered through the cloven blue air to the deck.

In due time the boats were lowered; but as standing in his shallop's stern,° Ahab just hovered upon the point of the descent, he waved to the mate,—who held one of the tackle-ropes on deck—and bade him pause.

"Starbuck!"

"Sir?"

"For the third time my soul's ship starts upon this voyage, Starbuck."

"Aye, sir, thou wilt have it so."

"Some ships sail from their ports, and ever afterwards are missing, Starbuck!"

"Truth, sir: saddest truth."

"Some men die at ebb tide; some at low water; some at the full of the flood;— and I feel now like a billow that's all one crested comb,° Starbuck. I am old;—shake hands with me, man."

Their hands met; their eyes fastened; Starbuck's tears the glue.

"Oh, my captain, my captain!—noble heart—go not—go not!—see, it's a brave man that weeps; how great the agony of the persuasion then!"

"Lower away!"—cried Ahab, tossing the mate's arm from him. "Stand by the crew!"

In an instant the boat was pulling round close under the stern.

"The sharks! the sharks!" cried a voice from the low cabin-window there; "O master, my master, come back!"

But Ahab heard nothing; for his own voice was high-lifted then; and the boat leaped on.

Yet the voice spake true; for scarce had he pushed from the ship, when numbers of sharks, seemingly rising from out the dark waters beneath the hull, maliciously snapped at the blades of the oars, every time they dipped in the water; and in this way accompanied the boat with their bites. It is a thing not uncommonly happening to the whale-boats in those swarming seas; the sharks at times apparently following them in the same prescient way that vultures hover over the banners of marching regiments in the east. But these were the first sharks that had been observed by the Pequod since the White Whale had been first descried; and whether it was that Ahab's crew were all such tiger-yellow barbarians, and therefore their flesh more musky to the senses of the sharks—a matter sometimes well known to affect them,— however it was, they seemed to follow that one boat without molesting the others.

shallop's stern: rear of a small boat; here the whaleboat. **crested comb**: also comber, or breaking wave.

"Heart of wrought steel!" murmured Starbuck gazing over the side, and following with his eyes the receding boat—"canst thou yet ring boldly to that sight?—lowering thy keel among ravening sharks, and followed by them, open-mouthed to the chase; and this the critical third day?—For when three days flow together in one continuous intense pursuit; be sure the first is the morning, the second the noon, and the third the evening and the end of that thing—be that end what it may. Oh! my God! what is this that shoots through me, and leaves me so deadly calm, yet expectant,—fixed at the top of a shudder! Future things swim before me, as in empty outlines and skeletons; all the past is somehow grown dim. Mary, girl! thou fadest in pale glories behind me; boy! I seem to see but thy eyes grown wondrous blue. Strangest problems of life seem clearing; but clouds **sweep** between—Is my journey's end coming? My legs feel faint; like his who has footed it all day. Feel thy heart,—beats it yet?—Stir thyself, Starbuck!—stave it off—move, move! speak aloud!—Masthead there! See ye my boy's hand on the hill?—Crazed;—aloft there!—keep thy keenest eye upon the boats:—mark well the whale!—Ho! again!—drive off that hawk! see! he pecks—he tears the vane"—pointing to the red flag flying at the maintruck—"Ha! he soars away with it!—Where's the old man now? sees't thou that sight, oh Ahab!—shudder, shudder!"

The boats had not gone very far, when by a signal from the mast-heads—a downward pointed arm, Ahab knew that the whale had sounded; but intending to be near him at the next rising, he held on his way a little sideways from the vessel; the becharmed crew maintaining the profoundest silence, as the head-beat° waves hammered and hammered against the opposing bow.

"Drive, drive in your nails, oh ye waves! to their uttermost heads drive them in! ye but strike a thing without a lid; and no coffin and no hearse can be mine:—and hemp only can kill me! Ha! ha!"

Suddenly the **waters** around them slowly swelled in broad circles; then quickly upheaved, as if sideways sliding from a submerged berg of ice, swiftly rising to the surface. A low rumbling sound was heard; a subterraneous hum; and then all held their breaths; as bedraggled with trailing ropes, and harpoons, and lances, a vast form shot lengthwise, but obliquely from the sea. Shrouded in a thin drooping veil of mist, it hovered for a moment in the rainbowed air; and then fell swamping back into the deep. Crushed thirty feet upwards, the waters flashed for an instant like heaps of fountains, then brokenly sank in a shower of flakes, leaving the circling surface creamed like new milk round the marble trunk of the whale.

"Give way!" cried Ahab to the oarsmen, and the boats darted forward to the attack; but maddened by yesterday's fresh irons that corroded in him, Moby Dick seemed combinedly possessed by all the angels that fell from heaven.[5] The wide tiers of welded tendons overspreading his broad white forehead, beneath the transparent skin, looked knitted together; as head on, he came churning his tail among the boats; and once more flailed them apart; spilling out the irons and lances from the two mates' boats, and dashing in one side of the upper part of their bows, but leaving Ahab's almost without a scar.

---

head-beat: striking the boat from directly ahead.

While Daggoo and **Queequeg** were stopping the strained planks; and as the whale swimming out from them, turned, and showed one entire flank as he shot by them again; at that moment a quick cry went up. Lashed round and round to the fish's back; pinioned in the turns upon turns in which, during the past night, the whale had reeled the involutions of the lines around him, the half torn body of the Parsee was seen; his sable raiment frayed to shreds; his distended eyes turned full upon old Ahab.

The harpoon dropped from his hand.

"Befooled, befooled!"—drawing in a long lean breath—"Aye, Parsee! I see thee again.—Aye, and thou goest before; and this, *this* then is the hearse that thou didst promise. But I hold thee to the last letter of thy word. Where is the second hearse? Away, mates, to the ship! those boats are useless now; repair them if ye can in time, and return to me; if not, Ahab is enough to die—Down, men! the first thing that but offers to jump from this boat I stand in, that thing I harpoon. Ye are not other men, but my arms and my legs; and so obey me.—Where's the whale? gone down again?"

But he looked too nigh the boat; for as if bent upon escaping with the corpse he bore, and as if the particular place of the last encounter had been but a stage in his leeward voyage, Moby Dick was now again steadily swimming forward; and had almost passed the ship,—which thus far had been sailing in the contrary direction to him, though for the present her headway had been stopped. He seemed swimming with his utmost velocity, and now only intent upon pursuing his own straight path in the sea.

"Oh! Ahab," cried Starbuck, "not too late is it, even now, the third day, to desist. See! Moby Dick seeks thee not. It is thou, thou, that madly seekest him!"

Setting sail to the rising wind, the lonely boat was swiftly impelled to leeward, by both oars and canvas. And at last when Ahab was sliding by the vessel, so near as plainly to distinguish Starbuck's face as he leaned over the rail, he hailed him to turn the vessel about, and follow him, not too swiftly, at a judicious interval. Glancing upwards, he saw Tashtego, Queequeg, and Daggoo, eagerly mounting to the three mast-heads; while the oarsmen were rocking in the two staved boats which had but just been hoisted to the side, and were busily at work in repairing them. One after the other, through the port-holes, as he sped, he also caught flying glimpses of Stubb and Flask, busying themselves on deck among bundles of new irons and lances. As he saw all this; as he heard the hammers in the broken boats; far other hammers seemed driving a nail into his heart. But he rallied. And now marking that the vane or flag was gone from the main-mast-head, he shouted to Tashtego, who had just gained that perch, to descend again for another flag, and a hammer and nails, and so nail it to the mast.

Whether fagged by the three days' running chase, and the resistance to his swimming in the knotted hamper° he bore; or whether it was some latent deceitfulness and malice in him: whichever was true, the White Whale's way now began to abate, as it seemed, from the boat so rapidly nearing him once more; though indeed the whale's last start had not been so long a one as before. And still as Ahab glided

---

knotted hamper: snarled ropes.

over the waves the unpitying sharks accompanied him; and so pertinaciously stuck to the boat; and so continually bit at the plying oars, that the blades became jagged and crunched, and left small splinters in the sea, at almost every dip.

"Heed them not! those teeth but give new rowlocks to your oars. Pull on! 'tis the better rest, the shark's jaw than the yielding water."

"But at every bite, sir, the thin blades grow smaller and smaller!"

"They will last long enough! pull on!—But who can tell"—he muttered—"whether these sharks swim to feast on the whale or on Ahab?—But pull on! Aye, all alive, now—we near him. The helm! take the helm; let me pass,"—and so saying, two of the oarsmen helped him forward to the bows of the still flying boat.

At length as the craft was cast to one side, and ran ranging along with the White Whale's flank, he seemed strangely oblivious of its advance—as the whale sometimes will—and Ahab was fairly within the smoky mountain mist, which, thrown off from the whale's spout, curled round his great, Monadnock[6] hump; he was even thus close to him; when, with body arched back, and both arms lengthwise high-lifted to the poise, he darted his fierce iron, and his far fiercer curse into the hated whale. As both steel and curse sank to the socket, as if sucked into a morass, Moby Dick sideways writhed; spasmodically rolled his nigh flank against the bow, and, without staving a hole in it, so suddenly canted the boat over, that had it not been for the elevated part of the gunwale to which he then clung, Ahab would once more have been tossed into the sea. As it was, three of the oarsmen—who foreknew not the precise instant of the dart, and were therefore unprepared for its effects—these were flung out; but so fell, that, in an instant two of them clutched the gunwale again, and rising to its level on a combing wave, hurled themselves bodily inboard again; the third man helplessly dropping astern, but still afloat and swimming.

Almost **simultaneously**, with a mighty volition of ungraduated, instantaneous swiftness, the White Whale darted through the weltering sea.° But when Ahab cried out to the steersman to take new turns with the line, and hold it so; and commanded the crew to turn round on their seats, and tow the boat up to the mark; the moment the treacherous line felt that double strain and tug, it snapped in the empty air!

"What breaks in me? Some sinew cracks!—'tis whole again; oars! oars! Burst in upon him!"

Hearing the tremendous rush of the sea-crashing boat, the whale wheeled round to present his blank forehead at bay; but in that evolution, catching sight of the nearing black hull of the ship; seemingly seeing in it the source of all his persecutions; bethinking it—it may be—a larger and nobler foe; of a sudden, he bore down upon its advancing prow, smiting his jaws amid fiery showers of foam.

Ahab staggered; his hand smote his forehead. "I grow blind; hands! stretch out before me that I may yet grope my way. Is't night?"

"The whale! The ship!" cried the cringing oarsmen.

"Oars! oars! Slope downwards to thy depths, O sea, that ere it be for ever too late, Ahab may slide this last, last time upon his mark! I see: the ship! the ship! Dash on, my men! Will ye not save my ship?"

---

weltering sea: poetic commonplace for rolling and tossing waves.

But as the oarsmen violently forced their boat through the sledge-hammering seas, the before whale-smitten bow-ends of two planks burst through, and in an instant almost, the temporarily disabled boat lay nearly level with the waves; its half-wading, splashing crew, trying hard to stop the gap and bale out the pouring water.

Meantime, for that one beholding instant, Tashtego's mast-head hammer remained suspended in his hand; and the red flag, half-wrapping him as with a plaid,° then streamed itself straight out from him, as his own forward-flowing heart; while Starbuck and Stubb, standing upon the bowsprit beneath, caught sight of the down-coming monster just as soon as he.

"The whale, the whale! Up helm, up helm![7] Oh, all ye sweet powers of air, now hug me close! Let not Starbuck die, if die he must, in a woman's fainting fit. Up helm, I say—ye fools, the jaw! the jaw! Is this the end of all my bursting prayers? all my life-long fidelities? Oh, Ahab, Ahab, lo, thy work. Steady! helmsman, steady. Nay, nay! Up helm again! He turns to meet us! Oh, his unappeasable brow drives on towards one, whose duty tells him he cannot depart. My God, stand by me now!"

"Stand not by me, but stand under me, whoever you are that will now help Stubb; for Stubb, too, sticks here. I grin at thee, thou grinning whale! Who ever helped Stubb, or kept Stubb awake, but Stubb's own unwinking eye? And now poor Stubb goes to bed upon a mattrass that is all too soft; would it were stuffed with brushwood! I grin at thee, thou grinning whale! Look ye, sun, moon, and stars! I call ye assassins of as good a fellow as ever spouted up his ghost. For all that, I would yet ring glasses with **ye**, would ye but hand the cup! Oh, oh! **oh, oh!** thou grinning whale, but there'll be plenty of gulping soon! Why fly ye not, O Ahab! For me, off shoes and jacket to it; let Stubb die in his drawers! A most mouldy and over salted death, though;—cherries! cherries! cherries! Oh, Flask, for one red cherry ere we die!"

"Cherries? I only wish that we were where they grow. Oh, Stubb, I hope my poor mother's drawn my part-pay ere this; if not, few coppers will now come to her, for the voyage is up."

From the ship's bows, nearly all the seamen now hung inactive; hammers, bits of plank, lances, and harpoons, mechanically retained in their hands, just as they had darted from their various employments; all their enchanted eyes intent upon the whale, which from side to side strangely vibrating his predestinating head, sent a broad band of overspreading semicircular foam before him as he rushed. Retribution, swift vengeance, eternal malice[8] were in his whole aspect, and spite of all that mortal man could do, the solid white buttress of his forehead smote the ship's starboard bow, till men and timbers reeled. Some fell flat upon their faces. Like dislodged trucks, the heads of the harpooneers aloft shook on their bull-like necks. Through the breach, they heard the waters pour, as mountain torrents down a flume.

"The ship! The hearse!—the second hearse!" cried Ahab from the boat; "its wood could only be American!"

Diving beneath the settling ship, the whale ran quivering along its keel; but turning under water, swiftly shot to the surface again, far off the other bow, but within a few yards of Ahab's boat, where, for a time, he lay quiescent.

plaid: long, woolen, Scottish cloak.

"I turn my body from the sun. What ho, Tashtego! let me hear thy hammer. Oh! ye three unsurrendered spires of mine; thou uncracked keel; **and only god-bullied hull**; thou firm deck, and haughty helm, and Pole-pointed prow,—death-glorious ship! must ye then perish, and without me? Am I cut off from the last fond pride of meanest shipwrecked captains? Oh, lonely death on lonely life! Oh, now I feel my topmost greatness lies in my topmost grief.[9] Ho, ho! from all your furthest bounds, pour ye now in, ye bold billows of my whole foregone life, and top this one piled comber of my death! Towards thee I roll, thou all-destroying but unconquering whale; to the last I grapple with thee; from hell's heart I stab at thee; for hate's sake I spit my last breath at thee. Sink all coffins and all hearses to one common pool! and since neither can be mine, let me then tow to pieces,[10] while still chasing thee, though tied to thee, thou damned whale! *Thus*, I give up the spear!"

The harpoon was darted; the stricken whale flew forward; with igniting velocity the line ran through the groove;—ran foul. Ahab stooped to clear it; he did clear it; but the flying turn caught him round the neck, and voicelessly as Turkish mutes bowstring their victim, he was shot out of the boat,[11] ere the crew knew he was gone. Next instant, the heavy eye-splice in the rope's final end flew out of the stark-empty tub, knocked down an oarsman, and smiting the sea, disappeared in its depths.

For an instant, the tranced boat's crew stood still; then turned. "The ship? Great God, where is the ship?" Soon they through dim, bewildering mediums saw her sidelong fading phantom, as in the gaseous Fata Morgana;° only the uppermost masts out of water; while fixed by infatuation, or fidelity, or fate, to their once lofty perches, the pagan harpooneers still maintained their sinking lookouts on the sea. And now, concentric circles seized the lone boat itself, and all its crew, and each floating oar, and every lance-pole, and spinning, animate and inanimate, all round and round in one vortex, carried the smallest chip of the Pequod out of sight.

But as the last whelmings intermixingly poured themselves over the sunken head of the Indian at the mainmast, leaving a few inches of the erect spar yet visible, together with long streaming yards of the flag, which calmly undulated, with ironical coincidings, over the destroying billows they almost touched;—at that instant, a red arm and a hammer hovered backwardly uplifted in the open air, in the act of nailing the flag faster and yet faster to the subsiding spar. A sky-hawk that tauntingly had followed the main-truck downwards from its natural home among the stars, pecking at the flag,[12] and incommoding Tashtego there; this bird now chanced to intercept its broad fluttering wing between the hammer and the wood; and simultaneously feeling that etherial thrill, the submerged savage beneath, in his death-grasp, kept his hammer frozen there; and so the bird of heaven, with **archangelic** shrieks, and his imperial beak thrust upwards, and his whole captive form folded in the flag of Ahab, went down with his ship, which, like Satan, would not sink to hell till she had dragged a living part of heaven along with her,[13] and helmeted herself with it.

Now small fowls flew screaming over the yet yawning gulf; a sullen white surf beat against its steep sides; then all collapsed, and the great shroud of the sea rolled on as it rolled five thousand years ago.[14]

Fata Morgana: Italian for Fairy Morgan, that is, Morgan le Fay, the Arthurian enchantress; but here a mirage in which objects appear partly above the water and partly in it.

EPILOGUE

The drama's done. Why then here does any one step forth?—Because one did survive the wreck.

It so chanced, that after the Parsee's disappearance, I was he whom the Fates ordained to take the place of Ahab's bowsman, when that bowsman assumed the vacant post; the same, who, when on the last day the three men were tossed from out the rocking boat, was dropped astern. So, floating on the margin of the ensuing scene, and in full sight of it, when the half-spent suction of the sunk ship reached me, I was then, but slowly, drawn towards the closing vortex. When I reached it, it had subsided to a creamy pool. Round and round, then, and ever contracting towards the button-like black bubble at the axis of that slowly wheeling circle, like another Ixion I did revolve.[2] Till, gaining that vital centre, the black bubble upward burst; and now, liberated by reason of its cunning spring, and, owing to its great buoyancy, rising with great force, the coffin life-buoy shot lengthwise from the sea, fell over, and floated by my side. Buoyed up by that coffin, for almost one whole day and night, I floated on a soft and dirge-like main. The unharming sharks, they glided by as if with padlocks on their mouths; the savage sea-hawks sailed with sheathed beaks. On the second day, a sail drew near, nearer, and picked me up at last. It was the devious-cruising Rachel,[3] that in her retracing search after her missing children, only found another orphan.

FINIS.

EXPLANATORY NOTES

Works mentioned in these notes are referred to by the author's last name; full citations are found in Melville's Sources and Further Reading.

Chapter 1. Loomings.

1. *Ishmael . . . sail about a little and see the watery part of the world*: In Genesis 16 and 21, Ishmael is the son of Abraham and his servant Hagar; but when Abraham's wife, Sarah, gives birth to Isaac in her old age, he casts out Ishmael and Hagar. In Melville's day an "Ishmael" was an outcast and wanderer in conflict with others, while in Jewish and Islamic tradition Ismail is the progenitor of the Arabs. Modern writers have played with the novel's famous first line: Ray Bradbury, for example, quotes it in his radio drama *Leviathan 99* (1966); Philip Roth's baseball saga, *The Great American Novel* (1973), begins "Call me Smitty"; an unsettled Native American in Louise Erdrich's *Love Medicine* (1984) applies the line to himself; and in *Democracy* (1984), Joan Didion teases with "Call me the author." Melville wandered a good deal himself; he had been a merchant seaman in 1839, sailing from New York to Liverpool and back, and in 1841 he went whaling in the Pacific on the *Acushnet*, returning in 1844 as a sailor on the U.S. frigate *United States*.

2. *pistol and ball . . . Cato*: Ishmael may resort to pistol and ball either to commit suicide or fight a duel. Roman Republican hero *Cato* the Younger committed suicide in 46 BCE rather than submit to Julius Caesar.

3. *Manhattoes*: Residents of Manhattan, in Washington Irving's *A History of New York* (1809). In form, tone, and detail, the prefatory matter and some later chapters of *Moby-Dick* show the influence of Irving, although Melville is generally understood as disparaging him in "Hawthorne and His Mosses." (See Keil.)

4. *from Corlears Hook to Coenties Slip, and thence, by Whitehall northward*: Ishmael's proposed walk begins at the disreputable Lower East Side tenement area called Corlears Hook (just south of the present-day Williamsburg Bridge) and proceeds down Water Street to the city's southern-most wharf, Coenties Slip, then back up Whitehall Street on the west side to Bowling Green Park and what is now the terminus of fashionable Broadway.

5. *poor poet of Tennessee*: not identified and probably Melville's invention.

6. *Rockaway Beach*: On Long Island's southwestern shore, a popular resort for New Yorkers.

7. *Persians . . . brother of Jove?*: According to Greek historian Herodotus, the ancient Persians sacrificed to the earth, sun, and moon as well as to wind, fire, and water. Poseidon is the Greek god of the sea and brother of Zeus (the Roman Jove).

8. *Narcissus*: Modern readers assume that in Greek myth, Narcissus, after falling in love with his image in a fountain, drowned himself because he could not embrace it. Classical sources, however, generally depict Narcissus either wasting away or killing himself on land—turning into the flower named for him. But Melville was familiar with authors who allude to a watery death, including Plotinus (201–270 C.E.) in the *Enneads*, and Shakespeare in "The Rape of Lucrece."

9. *Cook*: The capitalization of "cook" allows Melville to pun on the name of well-known British explorer Captain James Cook (1728–1779).

10. *before the mast*: Living in the forecastle, the common sailors' dormitory in the bows, in front of the first mast. Melville greatly admired his friend Richard Henry Dana Jr.'s *Two Years Before the Mast* (1840), whose popularity made this sailor term generally known. In his May 1, 1850 letter to Dana, Melville indicated that he was "half way in the work" and that when completed, "it will be a strange sort of a book" (NN Correspondence, 162).

11. *van Rensselaers, or Randolphs, or Hardicanutes*: both of Melville's grandfathers were high-ranking officers in the Revolutionary War, and an uncle was a prominent Albany lawyer. The wealthy New York Van Rensselaer family, from whom Melville's mother claimed descent, dates back to Dutch colonial days; the Randolphs were southern aristocrats. Hardicanute, facetiously included here, was an early Danish king of England.

12. *country schoolmaster*: before he was twenty, Melville taught school briefly in 1837 and 1839.

13. *Seneca and the Stoics*: Roman philosopher, tragic poet, and adviser to Nero, Lucius Annaeus Seneca (d. CE 65) advocated emotional restraint and indifference to suffering; when asked by his emperor to kill himself, he did so, stoically.

14. *Who ain't a slave?*: Ishmael's rhetorical question reflects the frequently-heard argument of the 1840s that compared northern "wage slaves" to the chattel slaves of the South, and alludes in general to the slavery controversy, which, with the passage of laws known as the Compromise of 1850, was growing ever more heated.

15. *the root of all earthly ills . . . monied man enter heaven*: A conflation of *New Testament* passages: "For the love of money is the root of all evil" (1 Timothy: 6.10) and "It is easier for a camel to go through the eye of a needle, than for a rich man to enter the kingdom of God" (Matthew 19.24, Mark 10.25; and almost verbatim in Luke 18.25).

16. *Pythagorean maxim*: sixth century BCE philosopher Pythagoras advised against eating beans to avoid flatulence (or "winds from astern").

17. *Grand Contested Election for the Presidency . . . Bloody Battle in Affghanistan*: In 1848, Whig candidate Zachary Taylor lost the popular vote but won the presidency in the Electoral College because of a split between Free Soilers (the anti-slavery party) and the Democratic party. A revolt in 1841–42 against British colonial rule in Kabul, Afghanistan led to the destruction of a retreating British battalion; only one man survived.

18. *those stage managers, the Fates*: In *The Big Sleep* (1939), novelist Raymond Chandler has his hard-boiled detective Philip Marlowe say "Fate stage-managed the whole thing." Compare Ch. 134, note 4; see also Revision Narrative, p. 25.

19. *I love to sail forbidden seas, and land on barbarous coasts*: Ishmael sounds like a moderate version of Poe's Arthur Gordon Pym: "My visions were of shipwreck and famine; of death or captivity among barbarian hordes; of a lifetime dragged out in sorrow and tears . . . in an ocean unapproachable and unknown" (Ch. 2). Melville's brother Gansevoort owned a copy of Poe's 1838 novel, which begins in Nantucket and opens with the words "My name is Arthur Gordon Pym."

20. *I am quick to perceive a horror, and could still be social with it—would they let me—since it is but well to be on friendly terms with all the inmates of the place one lodges in*: This sentiment seems to have a source in Hope, Vol. 2, Ch. 4, bought by Melville in 1849 and marked by him, referring to an Arab sect's being respectful to the Devil: "they think it wise to make friends everywhere—not knowing where their destiny may ultimately fix them. . . ."

21. *snow hill in the air*: In actuality, a surfaced whale shows only a small fraction of its bulk. Even so, for centuries writers had exaggerated the whale's appearance, making it a land mass. Melville's Ishmael plays with this trope.

Chapter 2. The Carpet-Bag.

1. *New Bedford*: Located on the Acushnet River in Massachusetts and founded by Nantucket Quakers in the whaling trade, *New Bedford* was the world's foremost whaling port in the early 19th century.

2. *Nantucket*: The island, twenty-five miles south of Cape Cod, was indeed superseded by New Bedford in the whaling trade.

3. *Tyre . . . Carthage*: Ancient cities on the Mediterranean Sea, now in Syria and Tunisia, respectively. By tradition, Phoenicians from Tyre founded Carthage.

4. *Gomorrah*: In Genesis 19, God destroys the wicked cities Sodom and Gomorrah with fire and brimstone (sulfur).

5. *Black Parliament*: In 1320, the so-called Black Parliament gathered in judgment on conspirators against Scotland's King Robert I.

6. *a negro church . . . the blackness of darkness*: Jude 13, also qtd. by Carlyle in *Sartor Resartus* (Book 2, Ch. 4), refers to *the blackness of darkness*. Fugitive slave and famed orator Frederick Douglass (1818–1895) lived in New Bedford at the time Melville arrived there and shipped out from neighboring Fairhaven on the *Acushnet*. Douglass sometimes preached at a small *negro church* that might be the model for the church into which Ishmael stumbles. See Wallace, *Douglass and Melville*, 20.

7. *burnt district*: Common expression for any urban area destroyed by fire, but also refers to western New York State's "burned-over district," scene of heated revivalism in the 1830s.

8. *Czar in an ice palace*: Building an ice palace was an annual event in St. Petersburg.

Chapter 3. The Spouter-Inn.

1. *flung in Javan seas . . . slain off the Cape of Blanco*: from Indonesia to the coast of Peru.

2. *Jonah*: Sailor slang for someone cursed or jinxed, derived from the biblical prophet who, in trying to escape God, was swallowed by a "great fish" in the Book of Jonah. See also Ch. 9, "The Sermon."

3. *goggling glasses*: Suggesting "goggles," spectacles with colored glass.

4. *three years' voyage*: Sperm whaling voyages at this time often lasted three to four years. See also Making *Moby-Dick*.

5. *land of Nod*: metaphorically, sleep—from the refuge of Cain in Genesis 4:16.

6. *blackish looking squares*: Facial tattoos of the Marquesans, with whom Melville spent a month in 1842, typically include large geometric areas of black inking on the cheeks and across the eyes.

7. *Taking up his tomahawk . . . tobacco smoke*: That Queequeg's *tomahawk* pipe is Native American, not Polynesian, probably derives from Alexander Bradford's anthropological speculations on the connections between Indians and Polynesians. (See Melville's Sources and Hanson in Further Reading.)

Chapter 4. The Counterpane.

1. *Newfoundland dog*: Melville owned a Newfoundland on his farm, Arrowhead, in Pittsfield, MA.

2. *neither caterpillar nor butterfly*: Melville draws upon the same metaphor in discussing the transformation of young boys into con men in *The Confidence-Man*, Ch. 22.

Chapter 5. Breakfast.

1. *spend and be spent*: St. Paul states: "And I will very gladly spend and be spent for you" (2 Corinthians 12.15).

2. *Andes' western slope*: As a seaman on the U.S. frigate *United States*, Melville walked about Lima, Peru while on liberty in 1843, in sight of the Andes mountains. References to Lima and the Andes recur throughout Melville's work, as early as *Omoo* and as late as his poem "Pebbles," in *John Marr*.

3. *Ledyard . . . Mungo Park*: John Ledyard (1751–1789) sailed the Pacific with Captain James Cook, traveled across Siberia, and died on the Nile. Scottish explorer Mungo Park (1771–1806) wrote *Travels in the Interior Districts of Africa* (1799).

Chapter 6. The Street.

1. *Broadway and Chestnut streets . . . Lascars and Malays . . . Bombay, in the Apollo Green*: *Broadway* is in New York City, *Chestnut* Street in Philadelphia, "Regent Street" in London. "Water street and Wapping," below, are in Liverpool and London, respectively. *Lascars and Malays* are sailors from India and present-day Malaysia. *Apollo Green* is a gathering place in *Bombay*, the Indian seaport now known as Mumbai.

2. *Canaan*: Biblical Promised Land rich in agricultural products, Canaan was "flowing with milk and honey"; but its oil was olive, not whale.

3. *Herr Alexander*: German magician who performed in the United States in the 1840s. As reported in a Boston newspaper for the day in November 1846 on which Melville arrived in the city for a visit, "the latest trick is an apparent suicide, wherein, like Cato, the magician falls upon a sword. . . ." Compare Ishmael's first paragraph, Ch. 1. (See Abbott, "Ishmael," and Making *Moby-Dick*.)

4. *seventh heavens*: In Jewish and Islamic tradition, the highest level of Heaven. This concept of heavenly levels, conflated with medieval notions of the firmament ("the heavens"), made the plural, "seventh heavens," a common term.

5. *Salem*: Famous Massachusetts port city, home of Nathaniel Hawthorne. The humorous comparison with the Moluccas, or "Spice Islands" of Indonesia, echoes Milton's *Paradise Lost*, and Camões's *The Lusiads*.

Chapter 7. The Chapel.

1. *Whaleman's Chapel*: Melville attended a service there before sailing in January 1841. The rebuilt "Seaman's Bethel," on the walls of which the memorial tablets Ishmael mentions can still be seen, is in the same spot on Johnny-Cake Hill.

2. *Off-shore Ground*: Large area of the Pacific Ocean west of Peru, from approximately 5 to 10 degrees south latitude and 90 to 125 degrees west longitude. In 1820 the Nantucket whaler *Essex* (whose story is briefly told in Ch. 45) sank there after being struck by a bull sperm whale, 3,000 miles from the Peruvian coast.

3. *Japan*: The first of 21 references to Japan distributed throughout *Moby-Dick*. The Japanese Cruising (Whaling) Ground is cited by name four times and otherwise alluded to, as it is here on the memorial tablet. It is said that near Japan Ahab lost his leg (Ch. 28)

and the *Pequod* her masts (Ch. 18), while, remarkably, the vessel's new masts came from Japan (Ch. 16) despite the fact that it forbade foreigners to touch there, as emphasized in "That double-bolted land, Japan" (Ch. 24), "impenetrable Japans" (Ch. 111), and "locked Japan" (Ch. 123). Characteristic, high-pooped Japanese junks are alluded to in Chs. 16 and 50, while the Japanese seas are glorious and "resplendent" (Chs. 118 and 199), with their own fabulous whale, named Morquan (Ch. 45).

4. *Adam . . . sixty round centuries ago*: One of the then-current calculations from biblical chronology.

5. *my shadow here on earth is my true substance*: Ishmael speaks in contrast to the allegory of the cave in Plato's *Republic,* in which shadows are only appearances and sunlight is true being. For false and true lights, see also Chs. 96 and 119.

Chapter 8. The Pulpit.

1. *Father Mapple*: Mapple is a composite portrait of Reverend Enoch Mudge, pastor at the Seaman's Bethel in New Bedford, and the well-known "Father" Edward Taylor of Boston, who had been a sailor. Melville attended one of Mudge's sermons just before sailing on the *Acushnet.*

2. *drag up the ladder . . . Quebec*: Mansfield and Vincent suggest an allusion here to Emerson's comment in "Shakespeare," in *Representative Men,* that "the Genius draws up the ladder after him." Quebec's imposing fortress overlooks the St. Lawrence River; it was besieged and taken from the French by the British in 1759.

3. *Ehrenbreitstein*: Melville had visited this fortified castle on the Rhine in 1849, and refers to it again in *Pierre,* IV, 2.

4. *Victory's plank where Nelson fell*: Admiral Horatio Nelson (b. 1758) died on his flagship, *Victory,* at the Battle of Trafalgar, 1805. Melville discusses this hero of the Napoleonic wars in more detail in *Billy Budd, Sailor.*

Chapter 9. The Sermon.

1. *Starboard gangway, there!*: Like an officer at sea, Mapple commands his parishioners on the right to move left, those on the left to move right, all toward the middle.

2. *"The ribs and terrors in the whale, . . . His all the mercy and the power."*: Melville's adaptation of a rhymed version of Psalm 18. One of his revisions was to substitute *"black distress"* for the original "my distress." See Battenfield, and Wallace, *Douglass and Melville,* 100. See also Making *Moby-Dick.*

3. *Jonah*: Mapple retells the familiar biblical story in the Book of Jonah, Chs. 1–2, and quotes scripture with only minor variations, such as "And God had prepared" instead of "Now the Lord had prepared" in the passage quoted here (Jonah 1.17). On two occasions (cited below in footnotes), Melville draws from Jonah without using quotation marks.

4. *Joppa . . . Tarshish*: Joppa is now Jaffa, a district of Tel Aviv, Israel; Tarshish or Cadiz is on the Atlantic coast of Spain.

5. *Nineveh*: Capital of the ancient Assyrian empire (ca. 705–612 BCE), on the Tigris River at the site of present-day Mosul, Iraq; God has chosen Jonah to deliver the news to the city of Nineveh that it will be destroyed.

6. *'the weeds were wrapped about his head,'*: The wording is "wrapped about my head" in Jonah 2:5; Melville uses the image of weeds in "Billy in the Darbies," the poem that concludes *Billy Budd,* written forty years after *Moby-Dick* at the end of Melville's life.

7. *Pilot Paul . . . while preaching to others is himself a castaway!*: St. Paul, the Roman who dramatically converted to Christianity, sailed throughout the eastern Mediterranean pro-

moting his new religion. His letters constitute a major portion of the New Testament, and Melville refers to him throughout *Moby-Dick* and other works, most notably *The Confidence-Man*. Mapple's references to Paul in nautical terms as both a "Pilot" and "castaway" acknowledge his role as a spiritual guide. In 1 Corinthians 9:27, Paul states: "But I keep under my body, and bring it into subjection: lest that by any means, when I have preached to others, I myself should be a castaway." Compare Ch. 26 ("meanest mariners, and renegades and castaways"), and Ch. 93, "The Castaway."

8. *Is not the main-truck higher than the kelson is low?*: The round cap on the mainmast (*main-truck*) is higher above the ship's deck than the kelson (a reinforcement bolted to the keel) is lower than the deck.

9. *Senators and Judges*: Abolitionists attacked Senator Daniel Webster and Chief Justice Lemuel Shaw (Melville's father-in-law), both of Massachusetts, for legislating and upholding the notorious Fugitive Slave Law of 1850. See also Ch. 135, note 9.

10. *what is man*: The phrase "what is man" occurs twice in Job, but Mapple's application of it is Melville's invention. See Ch. 41, note 11 for Melville's use of Job.

11. *and he was left alone*: Echoing two biblical phrases, "and Jesus was left alone" (John 8.9), "and I am left alone" (Romans 11.3).

Chapter 10. A Bosom Friend.

1. *infallible Presbyterian Church*: Raised in the Dutch Reformed Church and later affiliated with the Episcopal Church while writing *Moby-Dick* in Pittsfield, Melville often humorously suggests the failings of doctrine and practice shared by these churches and Presbyterianism. In later years, Melville affiliated with New York City's All-Souls Unitarian Church.

2. *I and Queequeg—a cosy, loving pair*: The physical relationship between Ishmael and Queequeg is not clear. While men often shared beds for convenience, then and later, these two also have a "homosocial" bond of affection that, though typical in western cultures, may specifically reflect the Polynesian idea and practice of *aikāne*. According to Henry Hughes of Western Oregon University, although the word *ai* (sexual intercourse) + *kāne* (man) originally connoted male-male sexuality, its meaning evolved, and even Polynesians used it to mean close, non-sexual male-male friendships. With reference to Ishmael and Queequeg (the son and heir of a chief), during his years in the Pacific, Melville may have learned that *aikāne* meant not only an intimate friend of the same sex, but the male lover of a chief. Dana explains the term in *Two Years Before the Mast* (1840) in passages reflected in *Moby-Dick*, including Queequeg's sharing his money and "marrying" Ishmael, and Ishmael's explaining the printing and pictures in a book. Like Queequeg in Ch. 110, Dana's *aikāne*, Hope, falls dangerously ill and recovers. Dana tells us that "every Kanaka [Polynesian man] has one particular friend, whom he considers himself bound to do everything for, and with whom he has a sort of contract—an alliance offensive and defensive,—and for whom he will often make the greatest sacrifices. This friend they call *aikane;* and for such did Hope adopt me. I do not believe I could have wanted anything which he had, that he would not have given me. In return for this, I was always his friend among the Americans, and used to teach him letters and numbers. . . ."

Chapter 12. Biographical.

1. *Prince of Wales*: Title of the male heir to the British throne; hence an acknowledgment of Queequeg's royal rights, as well as a pun.

2. *Czar Peter*: As a youth, Russia's Peter the Great (1672–1725) learned shipbuilding in Dutch and English navy yards.

Chapter 13. Wheelbarrow.

1. *Acushnet river*: Melville sailed on the whaleship *Acushnet*, named for this river flowing between New Bedford and Fairhaven.

Chapter 14. Nantucket.

1. *Nantucket*: Melville did not visit Nantucket until after the publication of *Moby-Dick*; his main sources for this chapter were Hart and Macy.

2. *salt-sea Mastodon*: Fossilized remains of mastodons had been found as far west as Missouri (1840) and along the Hudson River (1844–45). The skeleton called "Missourium" and the "Missouri Leviathan" appears in *Representative Men* (1847), where Emerson refers to Swedenborg as "one of the Missouriums and mastodons of literature." The discovery of three mastodons in upstate New York in 1845 made news just as Melville returned from sea. In his first draft of *Typee*, he described the fatherly Marheyo as having a "heart like a mastodon's" but removed the reference, saving it for *Moby-Dick*, five years later.

3. *as the three pirate powers did Poland. . . . Let America add Mexico to Texas, and pile Cuba upon Canada; let the English overswarm all India*: The three pirate powers invading Poland were Russia, Prussia, and Austria. The United States annexed Texas (an independent republic since 1836) in 1845, and acquired all or parts of New Mexico, Arizona, Nevada, California, Oklahoma, Colorado, Wyoming and Utah at the end of the Mexican War (1848). For decades, some in the U.S. advocated expanding into Cuba and Canada as well. By 1850, the British Empire controlled most of India. Compare the conclusion to Ch. 89.

4. *terraqueous globe*: Meaning "world of earth and water," the phrase is in both Carlyle and Thomas Browne. The rest of the paragraph reflects Mayo and Weld.

5. *goes down to it in ships*: "They that go down to the sea in ships, that do business in great waters; These see the works of the Lord, and his wonders in the deep" (Psalms 107:23–24).

Chapter 16. The Ship.

1. *Lent or Ramadan*: Similar religious observances resembling Quequeg's. Lent, the forty weekdays from Ash Wednesday to Easter, is for Christians a time of prayer and dietary restrictions; during Ramadan, ninth month of the Islamic calendar, Muslims fast each day until sundown.

2. *the shipping*: The ships in port and belonging to that port. These ships are apparently docked, but later in the chapter the *Pequod* is swinging to her anchor.

3. *Pequod . . . Medes*: Although the Pequod (or Pequot) tribe, whose name means "destroyer," was nearly annihilated in the seventeenth century, it survives today. The Median kingdom, in Persia, lasted from about 728 to 550 BCE.

4. *Egypt and Siberia*: Napoleon and his army never reached Siberia; however, he invaded Egypt in 1798 and Russia in 1812. A grenadier is a grenade-carrying foot soldier.

5. *three old kings of Cologne*: The Magi, who brought gifts to the newborn Jesus. According to tradition, their bones are enshrined at the Cologne Cathedral in Prussia, which Melville visited in 1849.

6. *Becket*: Thomas Becket, Archbishop of Canterbury, murdered in Canterbury Cathedral in 1170 and later canonized. Melville visited there in 1849.

7. *Peleg*: Since the name means "division" or "part" (see Genesis 10.25, 11.16), his involvement in determining the lays is appropriate.

8. *Thorkill-Hake's carved buckler or bedstead*: Properly "Thorkell-Hákr," eleventh-century

fighter in the Icelandic *Njalssaga*, whose deeds were carved on his bed and footstool. Melville's source for Thorkell's story in the then-untranslated saga is unknown.

9. *limber black bone . . . right-whale*: Baleen, also called "whalebone," the fibrous plates with which this toothless whale strains its food from sea water.

10. *top-knot on some old Pottowottamie Sachem's head*: distinctive scalp-lock on a chief of the Potawotomi tribe, originally from New York State, but removed to a Kansas reservation by the 1840s.

11. *Quaker style*: Plain and square-cut. Blue was a common color for seamen, though Quakers usually wore brown.

12. *Cape Cod or the Vineyard*: Fishhook shaped, Cape Cod, MA, named for the once-plentiful codfish, extends into the Atlantic Ocean from the U.S. mainland; Martha's Vineyard, an island south of the base of the Cape.

13. *Bildad*: One of Job's pious friends chastised by God in the book of Job.

14. *Quakers with a vengeance*: A play on words: members of the Religious Society of Friends, known as Quakers because they were said to tremble in awe of God's word, are pacifists by creed, and thus should not be given to fighting or revenge.

15. *old Categut whaleman*: A whaleship apparently named for the Kattegat Strait between Denmark and Sweden.

16. *275th lay*: Ishmael's share would be 0.36 percent of the voyage's profit.

17. *"Lay not up . . . where moth—"*: "Stingy" Bildad's selective muttering of scripture reveals him to be perhaps stingy, perhaps conscientious, perhaps self-serving, and Melville's comic treatment of the stern figure brings out his apparent hypocrisies. The full passage from which he draws is "Lay not up for yourselves treasures upon earth, where moth and rust doth corrupt, and where thieves break through and steal: But lay up for yourselves treasures in heaven, where neither moth nor rust doth corrupt, and where thieves do not break through nor steal: For where your treasure is, there will your heart be also" (Matthew 6:19–21). In quoting Jesus, Bildad deletes the biblical passage's reference to "thieves," perhaps avoiding allusion to his own thievery in offering Ishmael the absurd 777th lay; his subsequent focus on widows, orphans, and Peleg's "conscience" might also be self-serving.

18. *seven hundred and seventy-seventh*: Punning biblical allusion to Lamech, who lived 777 years (Genesis 5.31).

19. *drawing ten inches of water, or ten fathoms . . . impenitent man*: "Drawing" refers to how much water a vessel needs to float; here, 10 inches implies innocence, while 60 feet implies a guilty conscience. Impenitent means unrepentant, and more generally, resistant to God's will. Revivalist preachers of the day urged listeners to renounce their "impenitent state" and seek salvation. Although Quakerism, like other Protestant denominations, had its own range of adherents, some of them fundamentalist, they did not require public announcements of faith. Documents on faith and practice in the New York and the New England Yearly Meetings of the Society of Friends (Quakers) do not mention "impenitence" as a barrier to membership in a meeting, although members might be "disowned" if their unspiritual behavior persisted. By calling Peleg an "impenitent man," Bildad is asserting his opinion that as a Quaker, Peleg is excessively secular and profane.

20. *Ahab of old . . . blood*: Ishmael is correct. Melville took many hints for his Ahab from the story of the wicked king of Israel in 1 Kings 16–22.

21. *so imperfectly as he was known to me then*: Ishmael narrates his tale retrospectively, growing in understanding as he tells it. Thus, his use of the word "then" reminds him and us that, at least as far as his understanding of Ahab is concerned, he has come to know this mysterious man less *imperfectly*.

Chapter 17. The Ramadan.

1. *that very island*: If Queequeg's island (named Kokovoko in Ch. 12) is based on Nuku Hiva, the Marquesan island where Melville spent a month in 1842 after jumping ship, then a reasonable supposition is that the "sailor" Ishmael alludes to as a witness to cannibalism would be Melville himself. While Melville wrote of the threat of cannibalism in *Typee*, which recounts his Marquesan adventure, there is no evidence that he actually witnessed a cannibal feast; in fact, while Polynesians did practice cannibalism, it was only an occasional ritual.

Chapter 18. His Mark.

1. *As we were walking down the end of the wharf*: Here the Pequod is not at anchor as in Ch. 16, but is once again tied to a dock.
2. *papers*: Presumably certificates of baptism or other such documents.
3. *the . . . first Congregation of this whole worshipping world; we all belong to that; . . . ; in that we all join hands*: In the same vein and repeating *join hands*, Melville had earlier written, "we are all of us—Anglo-Saxons, Dyaks, and Indians—sprung from one head, and made in one image. And if we regret this brotherhood now we shall be forced to join hands hereafter." *Literary World* (March 31, 1849: 292).
4. *Belial . . . Bel, and the hideous dragon*: In the Bible, Belial and Bel refer to the pagan god called Baal; Bildad warns an uncomprehending Queequeg against devil worship; *Bel and the Dragon* is an apocryphal text once part of the book of Daniel.

Chapter 19. The Prophet.

1. *Elijah*: The biblical prophet who denounced King Ahab.

Chapter 20. All Astir.

1. *kept his log*: Made entries in the ship's log book, a daily record of navigational and meteorological data, whales seen, chased, and caught, other vessels sighted or met, and shipboard events. See Ahab's use of log books in Ch. 44.

Chapter 21. Going Aboard.

1. *laid a hand upon both our shoulders*: But on p. 99 Elijah implies that his left arm is crippled.
2. *to the Indian and Pacific Oceans*: That is, around Africa's Cape of Good Hope, not Cape Horn.
3. *sit up with the body*: Joking that the sleeper is dead, Ishmael suggests the then-current ritual of sitting awake with the body through the night.
4. *my country way*: As reported in *Omoo*, one custom of island monarchs was to use people as sofas.
5. *grinding the face of the poor*: Joking for his own benefit, Ishmael quotes Isaiah 3.15, "What mean ye that ye beat my people to pieces and grind the faces of the poor?"

Chapter 22. Merry Christmas.

1. *hauled out*: Typically, to get under way, a ship was pulled away from the dock by a rowboat, far enough to catch a breeze; it then dropped anchor to make final preparations, raised her anchor, set sail, and departed. The text compresses the time needed for these activities and omits some details. Although Melville would have participated in this procedure when he left New Bedford/Fairhaven on his first whaling vessel, the *Acushnet*, he did not visit Nantucket until 1852, and seems not to have known, at the time of writing,

that a ship could not have been loaded at the Nantucket wharf as described in *Moby-Dick*. Because a shallow sandbar had built up across the mouth of Nantucket's harbor, unloaded vessels had to be towed over the bar, anchored, and then loaded there.

2. *some sort of a chorus about the girls in Booble Alley*: In contrast to Bildad's "dismal" New England church version of a biblical psalm, this "profane" song is probably the shanty "Haul Away Joe," with its line, "The gals o' Booble Alley," referring to a sordid, red-light district street by that name in Liverpool that also appears in *Redburn*. (See Frank, "Cheer'ly Man," in Further Reading.)

3. *Watts*: popular hymnist Isaac Watts (1674–1748) composed rhymed versions of biblical psalms.

4. *"Sweet fields beyond the swelling flood . . . While Jordan rolled between."*: Stanza 3 of Watts's "A Prospect of Heaven Makes Death Easy," also known as "There is a Land of Pure Delight."

Chapter 23. The Lee Shore.

1. *drives along the leeward land*: A ship struggles against strong storm winds, with land dangerously close on its downwind side. Although with ordinary winds the vessel could sail into port, in the gale it struggles to avoid being wrecked on that shore.

2. *Know ye, now, Bulkington?*: In Ch. 3, Melville introduces Bulkington in such detail that the character seems destined to play an important role in the narrative, but here, Bulkington is abruptly, though gloriously, dismissed by means of "apotheosis." That is, he is transformed from a character into a god-like example of human independence. Bulkington may have been part of an early conception of the narrative, eventually abandoned in the course of writing. If so, Melville might have noticed the vestigial Bulkington perhaps while proofreading his early chapters later on in his compositional process. In this line of thinking, Melville's solution to the problem of what then to do with Bulkington was to insert Ch. 23 as a retrospective erasure of him. While the chapter creates a structural problem, it also underscores Ishmael's philosophizing. Whatever compositional events may have transpired, Melville's address to his reader—"Know ye, now, Bulkington?"—initiates a pattern of rhetorical questioning, particularly evident in the concluding line of one of *Moby-Dick*'s deepest philosophical chapters, "The Whiteness of the Whale" (Ch. 42): "Wonder ye then at the fiery hunt?"

Chapter 24. The Advocate.

1. *The Advocate*: Much of this chapter is heavily indebted to Beale, Ch. 11, while minor sources are Scoresby and J. Ross Browne (see Mansfield and Vincent). An *advocate* is a lawyer.

2. *the Dutch in De Witt's time*: Jan de Witt was the leading Dutch statesman of the mid-seventeenth century. Beale supplied the information about France and Britain, and the rest of the paragraph comes from J. Ross Browne.

3. *Louis XVI. . . . Britain . . . £1,000,000?*: Beale provided this information, and Browne the rest of the paragraph.

4. *I freely assert*: The following three paragraphs echo Beale, quoting from an unnamed authority (see Vincent).

5. *cosmopolite philosopher*: The notion of the cosmopolite as a citizen of the world goes back to the fifth-century BCE gadfly-philosopher Diogenes; however, American and European *philosophes* of the eighteenth-century enlightenment adopted a cosmopolitan view that foresaw all nations, languages, arts, and sciences united under one rational governance. Melville announces this liberal perspective in "Etymology" when he has his pale Usher using "a queer handkerchief, mockingly embellished with all the gay flags of all the known

nations of the world" to dust his books. Because certain adventurers, at least one famous itinerant preacher (Lorenzo Dow), and various shady business men adopted the pose of "Cosmopolite" in their dealings, the word acquired additional, more ambiguous meanings in Melville's day, a fact he exploits by calling Frank Goodman, the main character of *The Confidence-Man*, a "cosmopolitan."

6. *Egyptian mother . . . womb*: In Egyptian mythology, Nut is the mother of the twins Osiris and Isis; as told by Plutarch (*Morals*, Book 5), Osiris impregnates his twin sister before their birth.

7. *Exploring Expeditions . . . your Cook and your Krusenstern*: The famous United States Exploring Expedition (1838–1842), under Lt. Charles Wilkes; Captain James Cook (1728–1779) and Captain George Vancouver (1758–1798) were the most famous eighteenth-century explorers of the Pacific; Adam Johann Krusenstern (1770–1846) was the first Russian circumnavigator.

8. *liberation of Peru, Chili, and Bolivia from the yoke of Old Spain*: Chile became independent in 1818, Peru in 1824, and Bolivia in 1825. As Melville knew, internal conflicts had prevented these republics from achieving the claimed "eternal democracy."

9. *discovery by a Dutchman . . . threshold*: Australia was sighted earlier by other Europeans, but a Dutch ship charted part of the coast in 1606; English whaleships preceded American ones in Polynesia (the central Pacific islands south of Hawai'i) and Japan; by treaty, Commodore Matthew Perry opened Japan to Western commerce in 1854.

10. *Alfred the Great . . . Other, the Norwegian whale-hunter of those times!*: Anglo-Saxon king of England and scholar, *Alfred* (849–899) inserted the story of *Other* (Octhere) into his translation of Orosius's *History of the World*; Other is cited in "Extracts."

11. *Edmund Burke*: In 1775 the famous British statesman (1729–1797) spoke on "Conciliation with the American Colonies," quoted in "Extracts."

12. *Mary Morrel*: With her husband, Peter Folger, and their family, she settled on Nantucket in 1663.

13. *"a royal fish."**: Melville's asterisk here and two paragraphs below refer the reader to Chs. 90 and 82, respectively; his source for the first was Scoresby, for the second, Kitto (see Mansfield and Vincent, 661).

14. *that great captain of antiquity . . . many walled towns*: Possibly Demetrius Poliorcetes ("Besieger of Cities") in Plutarch's *Lives*.

15. *if, at my death . . . precious MSS . . . Harvard*: Melville died leaving in his writing desk, among many other manuscripts of poetry and prose, the almost-completed *Billy Budd, Sailor*; like Ishmael, he never went to college, but did read books he found on the ships on which he sailed and was a voracious reader throughout life, leaving a library of over one thousand volumes.

Chapter 25. Postscript.

1. *macassar . . . train oil . . . cod-liver oil*: Macassar oil (a hairdressing) and the medicinal castor oil come from plants; train oil, from the right whale; cod-liver oil is a health supplement.

Chapter 26. Knights and Squires.

1. *swart convict, Bunyan . . . old Cervantes . . . Andrew Jackson . . . higher than a throne! . . . mighty, earthly marchings*: Swart or swarthy means dark; *John Bunyan* (1628–1688), outstanding Protestant author, wrote *The Pilgrim's Progress* (1678) and spent more than twelve years in jail. One hand of *Miguel de Cervantes Saavedra* (1547–1616), author of *Don Quixote* (1605), was maimed in war, and his later life was impoverished. *Andrew*

Jackson (1767–1845), U.S. president during Melville's youth and hero of the Battle of New Orleans (1815), had begun life in great poverty. This passage partly quotes from *Tristram Shandy* (1760–1766) by Laurence Sterne (1713–1768), while transforming Sterne's passage, in which the spirit of sweet humor "didst cast [its] mystic mantle o'er [Cervantes'] withered stump . . ." into the more serious line found here. According to Parker, *"mighty earthly marchings"* may be an allusion to the November, 1844 nighttime pre-election Democratic parade in New York City, witnessed by Melville.

Chapter 27. Knights and Squires.

1. *Greenland whalers . . . Shetland Islands*: British ships hunting for whales near Greenland, across the North Atlantic Ocean, stopped at these islands north of the Scottish mainland. Hull and London were major British whaling ports.

2. *Anacharsis Clootz . . . isles of the sea*: In 1790, Prussian Jean-Baptiste du Val-de-Grace, Baron Cloots (1755–1794), self-named *Anacharsis*, led a delegation of foreigners representing mankind into the new French National Assembly, a scene dramatically presented in Melville's source, Carlyle's *The French Revolution*. The phrase *isles of the sea* occurs in Isaiah 24.15, Esther 10.1, and three times in Maccabees (Apocrypha).

Chapter 28. Ahab.

1. *Cellini's cast Perseus*: Bronze statue of the mythical Greek hero Perseus holding the severed head of Medusa, by Benvenuto Cellini (1500–1571). Perseus appears again in Chs. 55 and 82.

Chapter 29. Enter Ahab; To Him, Stubb.

1. *Enter Ahab; to him, Stubb*: A stage-direction. Compare Chs. 38, 39, 40, 108, and 109.

2. *Down, dog, and kennel!*: Ironic echoing of the Fool in Shakespeare's *King Lear* who says, "Truth's a dog must to kennel."

Chapter 31. Queen Mab.

1. *merman*: Stories about mermen and mermaids are widespread in world folklore; the humpback is a feature of some traditional merman tales.

2. *slapped by a queen, and made garter-knights*: Touched on the shoulder with the flat of a sword in the knighthood ceremony; Knight of the Garter is the highest order conferred by the British monarchy.

Chapter 32. Cetology.

1. *leviathanic revelations and allusions of all sorts which are to follow*: Cetology is the zoological study of whales (*Cetacea*). Although Melville gives the impression of being deeply learned in this "leviathanic" subject, he actually reworked factual material from the long scholarly entry on "Whales" in the *Penny Cyclopaedia*, which gave him the names of his whaling authorities and provided other details essential to Ch. 32, as well as to his other literary explorations of the whale throughout *Moby-Dick*. He also read or consulted primary sources, as explained in Vincent, 135–42, and Mansfield and Vincent, 672–74.

2. *essayed*: Attempted; from the French *essayer* to try; compare to the whaling term "try out," which means to boil down or extract. In "essaying," Ishmael is not only trying to find meaning, he is writing an essay or writing essayistically in order to extract the essential meaning of whales. Ch. 32 is the first of many such chapters that are essentially essays rather than narratives.

3. *Captain Scoresby, A.D. 1820*: William Scoresby Jr. published *An Account of the Arctic Regions* in 1820. However, Melville found this and the three following quotations in Beale.

4. *Cuvier . . . Hunter . . . Lesson*: French zoologist, paleontologist, and statesman Georges Dagobert, Baron Cuvier (1769–1832); English anatomist John Hunter (1728–1793); and French zoologist René-Primevère Lesson (1794–1849).

5. *Aristotle . . . the Author of Miriam Coffin . . . Cheever*: Joseph C. Hart wrote *Miriam Coffin; or, The Whale-Fishermen* (1834). Melville found some of the authors in this long list under "Whales" in the *Penny Cyclopaedia*, his source for much of the information and some of the language in Ch. 32. See Melville's Sources for full citations. Those not listed in there are Italian naturalist Ulisse Aldrovandi (1522–1605); seventeenth-century English naturalist John Ray; sixteenth-century French naturalist Rondeletius (Guillaume Rondelet); Francis Willoughby, who collaborated with Ray; eighteenth-century Swedish icthyologist Peter Artedi; eighteenth-century French zoologist Mathurin Jacques Brisson; eighteenth-century French cetologist Joseph-Pierre Bonnaterre; French naturalist and cetologist Frédéric Cuvier (1773–1838); and contemporary English anatomist Sir Richard Owen. (For Marten, see Frederich Martens.)

6. *Greenland or right-whale*: so-called because it was the "right one" to hunt.

7. *foundations . . . of the world*: This phrase and "foundations of the earth" occur frequently in the Bible, as, for example, in Psalms 18, 82, and 104. The phrase "this world's foundations" also appears in Ch. 70.

8. *"Will he (the leviathan) make a covenant with thee? Behold the hope of him is vain!"*: Job 41:4, and slightly variant in 41:9. The first fourteen verses in Job 41 contain the "awful tauntings" mentioned in the preceding sentence. At the end of *Moby-Dick*'s Ch. 41, Ahab's quarry is called a "Job's whale."

9. *Linnæus declares, "I hereby separate the whales from the fish."*: Carl von Linné (1707–1778), pioneering Swedish botanist, who developed the system of binomial nomenclature (genus, species) for the classification of plants and animals, wrote under the Latinized name *Linnæus*, and published *Systema Naturae* from 1735 to 1758.

10. *Folio . . . Octavo . . . Duodecimo*: Printers' terms for sizes of books, in descending order omitting the "Quarto." Melville's footnote on this tongue-in-cheek system (p. 139) explains the omission.

11. *Trumpa whale . . . Physeter whale . . . Macrocephalus of the Long Words*: *Trumpa* is from the French for "spout"; *Physeter* (Linnæus's term) is Greek for "blower"; the German *Pottfisch* is literally "pot fish"; *Macrocephalus* is Greek for "large head"; *the Long Words* are scientific pedants, satirized here and in other chapters.

12. *largest inhabitant of the globe*: The blue whale and fin whale are actually larger than the sperm whale, but Ishmael's facetious classification system allows him to make the sperm whale more mythic.

13. *whalebone or baleen*: See Ch. 75 for a description of these fringed plates in the mouth with which the whale strains its food from seawater; they are not bone but are made of keratin, the main component of teeth and hair.

14. *Mysticetus*: Used by Linnæus, derived from Aristotle, and meaning "moustached sea-monster."

15. *on the Brazil Banks, on the Nor' West Coast*: "Banks" normally denotes a large elevated area of the sea floor, usually rich in fish and other marine life. Melville explains these atypical *Brazil Banks* of tiny floating sea-creatures in a footnote in Ch. 58. *Nor' West Coast* is the northwestern coast of North America.

16. *Ahaz-dial*: In Isaiah 38.8, the shadow on the sundial of Ahaz, idol-worshipping king of Judah, goes backward. Ishmael is saying that the whale's motions make the shadow move erratically.

17. *Cain . . . his mark*: placing a protective mark on *Cain* to indicate that vengeance is His alone, God banished him for killing his brother, Abel (Genesis 4.15–16).

18. *Bibliographical system*: Explicitly (as if the joke might not already be clear) Ishmael says that he is classifying whales by a system properly used for books.

19. *Elephant and Castle*: An elephant carrying a large howdah in the shape of a castle, a popular image that appears, for example, on the sign of the old pub that gave its name to a section of London.

20. *Tartarian tiles*: The so-called Sulphur Bottom whale gets its sulfur-yellow belly from scraping the roof tiles of Tartarus, hell in Greek myth.

21. *a proverb to landsmen*: "Snores like a grampus" was a common expression.

22. *Mephistophelean*: Devilish; Mephistopheles is a satanic spirit in Christopher Marlowe's *The Tragical History of Dr. Faustus* (1604) and Johann von Goethe's *Faust* (1808, 1832).

23. *Nostril whale*: A fanciful etymology; "nar" is from the Old Norse for corpse (alluding to the whale's whiteness or white spots). However, assuming that the narwhale's single tusk had been confused for its nose, Ishmael traces the root to "nares," Latin for nostrils.

24. *bill-fish*: Any of several species, such as marlin and sailfish, whose snout is elongated into a bill, or spear.

25. *folder*: Paper folder, a smooth bone or ivory desk tool, eight or nine inches long, used for neatly folding sheets of paper, for example, letters.

26. *Black Letter tells me that Sir Martin Frobisher*: "Black Letter" is a distinctive gothic typeface in the earliest of print books, but here refers to Richard Hakluyt, whose *Principal Navigations* (1598) reprints, among others, the voyage accounts by the sixteenth-century English navigator and explorer of Canada's Atlantic coast, Martin Frobisher.

27. *An Irish author . . . land beast of the unicorn nature*: Here, the *unicorn* is sexually suggestive. Melville no doubt invented the *Irish author*, who implies that the Earl of Leicester, a favorite of Queen Elizabeth, was also her lover.

28. *Bonapartes and Sharks included*: Napoleon had been finally defeated at Waterloo in 1815, but the legend of his cunning and greatness grew in the following years. After his death, other *Bonapartes* continued to seize power in Europe, including Louis Bonaparte (Melville's "Louis the Devil"), president, then emperor of France during Melville's publishing years. Pairing Napoleon's family name with the capitalized *Sharks*, Melville hints at the betrayal of democracy, suggesting that greatness is sharkishness in disguise. In Ch. 94, Fleece, the cook, delivers a similar message about humans as sharks.

29. *(Algerine Porpoise). A pirate*: The fierce, state-supported Algerian and Tunisian pirates of the North African coast, against whom the United States fought the Tripolitan War of 1801–1805, were finally suppressed by the French in 1830.

30. *sentimental Indian eyes*: A romantic cliché combining India and sentimental love, as in Shelley's "Indian Serenade."

31. *"bright waist"*: Broad band of white paint around the hull. On it black squares resembling gun-ports were sometimes painted to deter pirate attack.

32. *mere sounds, full of Leviathanism, but signifying nothing*: Echoing *Macbeth* 5.5, "Life's but a walking shadow, . . . a tale / Told by an idiot, full of sound and fury, / Signifying nothing."

33. *great Cathedral of Cologne*: Melville visited this famously unfinished Prussian church in 1849, and may have read that the crane had been there for two centuries. As sources for the ideas in this passage, Mansfield and Vincent suggest Goethe, and Parker cites a review of Wordsworth's *The Prelude*.

Chapter 33. The Specksynder.

1. *Specksynder*: Melville got from Scoresby, his source for the information in this chapter, this misspelling of the Dutch "Specksnyder."

2. *Nicholas the Czar*: Absolute ruler of Russia from 1825–1855, Nicholas I (1796–1855).

3. *plucked at from the skies, and dived for in the deep*: Echoing Shakespeare's *Henry the Fourth, Part 1*, 1.3.202–203: "To pluck bright honor from the pale-faced moon, / Or dive into the bottom of the deep. . . ."

Chapter 34. The Cabin-Table.

1. *lee quarter-boat . . . ivory leg*: Two whaleboats, one on each side, hang from the ship's quarters (the section of the sides near the stern). Ahab sits in the one that is at the time on the lee side, using a sextant to take the standard noon sighting of the sun, which allows him to calculate the ship's latitude. He writes his notes on a prepared surface of his *ivory leg*.

2. *Abjectus, or the Slave*: This seeming allusion has no source in classical literature.

3. *Belshazzar, King of Babylon*: As told in Daniel 5.1, he gave a great feast for a thousand; see also Ch. 119.

4. *Coronation banquet at Frankfort*: Feast prepared at Frankfurt am Main, Germany, after the election of the Holy Roman Emperor by the "princes of the Empire."

5. *have for ever departed from my stomach*: Not sounding at all like Flask, the phrase instead reflects Melville's having absorbed a locution in the King James Bible, as in "their defence is departed from them" (Numbers 14.9), or "God is departed from me" (Samuel 10.2 and 28.15).

6. *Logan . . . sucking his own paws*: Ahab is as alien to the rest of humanity as a grizzly bear is among people; the grizzly in turn is a "wild Logan," the eighteenth-century Mingo chief famous for a speech in which he refused to sign a peace treaty with colonists. Bears do suck or lick their paws during hibernation, leading to the common (but false) belief that they get nourishment from doing so.

Chapter 35. The Mast-Head.

1. *my first mast-head*: Ishmael's first turn to stand lookout at the top of one of the masts, within a barrel hoop attached there for a railing. Compare the opening of Ch. 19 of *White-Jacket*. Macy, Scoresby, J. Ross Browne, and personal experience are all sources for this chapter.

2. *Babel . . . final truck . . . gone by the board*: The Tower of *Babel* in Genesis 11.1, intended to reach heaven, was brought down by God. A *truck* is a small circle of wood topping a mast—metaphorically, the finishing piece; *gone by the board* means fallen overboard, but here, "collapsed." As in biblical illustrations showing the fall of the Tower, with people plunging through the air, this chapter ends with the image of a falling masthead-stander.

3. *pyramids*: The best-known Egyptian pyramids (at Giza, near Cairo) were originally smooth-faced, and their "steps" are at least five feet high. Melville did not visit the pyramids until his 1857 trip to the Holy Land; however, the image recurs throughout *Moby-Dick* and later writings. In particular, Moby Dick's hump is like a pyramid, and Stubb dreams in Ch. 31 of futilely kicking at a pyramid.

4. *Saint Stylites*: Fifth-century Syrian hermit who lived at the top of a pillar (stylite) for forty years; as Ishmael quips, he died "at his post."

5. *Napoleon . . . Vendome*: Melville saw the column and statue in the Place Vendôme, Paris, in 1849.

6. *Louis Philippe, Louis Blanc, or Louis the Devil*: In order, king of France (1830–1848); nineteenth-century French socialist politician and journalist (1811–1882); and Ishmael's satirical name for French president Louis Napoleon Bonaparte (1848–1852), later Emperor Napoleon III. See also Making *Moby-Dick*.

7. *Great Washington . . . Hercules' pillars*: The Baltimore statue is on a column erected in 1829; the "Pillars of Hercules" are promontories in Spain and Africa, at the entrance to the Straits of Gibraltar from the Atlantic Ocean. On his 1849 trip, Melville also saw the statue of Admiral Nelson on its 185-foot column in London's Trafalgar Square, decorated at the base with bronze scenes cast from captured cannons.

8. *Bay whalemen of New Zealand*: New Zealand had several bay-whaling stations, where whales killed close to shore were processed.

9. *Colossus at old Rhodes*: huge bronze statue of the sun god Helios, the legs of which allegedly spanned the harbor entrance on the Greek island of Rhodes.

10. *fleshly tabernacle*: For this sense of *tabernacle*, see 2 Peter 1.13–14. As 1 Corinthians 6.19 explains, "your body is the temple of the Holy Ghost which is in you."

11. *Captain Sleet*: One of Melville's nicknames for William Scoresby Jr., son of William Scoresby, perhaps the most successful of Arctic whalemen. This parody of the pompous Scoresby Jr. has him exalting his father's invention as his own.

12. *Phædon . . . Bowditch*: Plato's metaphysical dialogue *Phaedo* (overcorrected to *Phaedon* in an 1849 translation) argues that the soul is immortal; Nathaniel Bowditch's *New American Practical Navigator* (1802, and many later editions) was the standard guide to navigation in *this* world.

13. *carking cares of earth*: Echoing "the cares of this world" (Mark 4.19), and "cares of this life" (Luke 21.34). Carking means burdensome and distressing.

14. *"Roll on, thou deep and dark blue ocean, roll! Ten thousand blubber-hunters sweep over thee in vain."*: Substituting *blubber-hunters* for "fleets," Melville parodies Byron's "Childe Harold's Pilgrimage" (1812–18; canto 4, stanza 179), a poem he had criticized in his 1847 review of J. Ross Browne. Whatever his opinion of the poem, *Roll on* anticipates the concluding line of Ch. 135.

15. *Descartian vortices*: René Descartes (1596–1650) theorized that all physical motion is circular.

16. *Heed it well, ye Pantheists!*: Pantheism, a view held by thinkers including Plato, Spinoza, and Emerson, is the belief that a universal spirit (or God) suffuses all existence. But here Ishmael warns that integration with the whole can also mean loss of individual life. Paraphrasing Carlyle's rendering of Goethe, Melville objected to the idea that we can always "live in the all" but added: "there is some truth in it."

Chapter 36. The Quarter-Deck.

1. *(Enter Ahab: Then, all.)*: Beginning with this stage-direction, Chs. 36–40 increasingly use dramatic form. Chs. 37–39 are soliloquies, while Ch. 40 is a full-fledged drama staged on the forecastle and opening with a rising curtain (the foresail). Similarly, see the title of Ch. 29: "Enter Ahab; To Him, Stubb."

2. *"A dead whale or a stove boat!"*: traditional whaleman's cry.

3. *Norway Maelstrom*: Famous powerful tidal flow in the Lofoten Islands of Norway, mentioned in *Redburn* and central to Poe's 1841 tale "A Descent into the Maelström," where it is exaggerated to a gigantic whirlpool.

4. *a little lower layer*: a deeper layer of meaning.

5. *All visible objects, man, are but as pasteboard masks*: Ahab explains to Starbuck, the only officer aboard capable of understanding him, the deeper meaning of his quest—to assault the physical whale is to attack the hidden malicious force either within it or metaphysically beyond. Pasteboard (papier-mâché) is the common material of the *masks* of Egyptian mummies. As a possible source for "pasteboard mask," Mansfield and Vincent suggest Don Quixote's "Pasteboard Visor" (1.1.1) and the same book's "Paste-board-Nose" (2.3.15). In his review essay "Hawthorne and His Mosses," Melville writes: "Tormented into desperation, Lear, the frantic king, tears off the mask, and speaks the sane madness of vital truth." In *Pierre*, Pierre vows to strike through the mask of the unknown.

6. *noble custom*: Melville learned about this ceremony in Gillies; see Mansfield and Vincent, 687–88. See also Making *Moby-Dick*.

7. *bad pennies*: Proverbially, if you pay with a counterfeit coin, it will sooner or later come back to you.

8. *St. Vitus' imp . . . ague!*: Ahab is saying that the pewter cup would be full if the fearful Steward's trembling had not spilled some of the grog. *St. Vitus's dance* or chorea is a neurological disorder causing muscle spasms; *ague* is a fever or fit of shivering.

9. *Leyden jar of his own magnetic life*: Ahab attempts to transmit to the others a shock from his highly-charged self, as some scientists and showmen had used the stored static electricity of the *Leyden jar* since the eighteenth century. See also Making *Moby-Dick*.

10. *Pope washes . . . tiara for ewer?*: A ceremony conducted before Easter, evoking Jesus in John, 13.1–15. The Pope's beehive-shaped triple crown is called a tiara; *ewer* means pitcher.

Chapter 37. Sunset.

1. *Iron Crown of Lombardy*: Ancient crown used at coronations of the Holy Roman emperors, and supposed to contain a nail from the True Cross. According to Dennis Berthold, a gold band and precious stones were added to the crown.

2. *damned in the midst of Paradise!*: Echoing Eve's words "midst of" to the serpent in Genesis and evoking Milton's Satan in *Paradise Lost*, "Me miserable! which way shall I fly / Infinite wrath, and infinite despair? / Which way I fly is Hell; myself am Hell" (IV.73–75).

3. *demoniac*: Because he is aware of his madness, Ahab claims he is therefore not crazy; it is as if an internal demon or "dæmon" controls and uses his insanity. In Plato's *Symposium* and in Romantic poetry, a "dæmon" mediates between heaven and earth or gives human form to ideal truths. In this sense, Ahab's demonism is more spiritual than supernatural.

4. *deaf Burkes and blinded Bendigoes!*: William Thompson (a triplet whose childhood nickname, Abednego, was mispronounced Bendigo) won the heavyweight boxing championship of England in 1839 against James ("The Deaf 'Un") Burke.

5. *Come forth from behind your cotton bags!*: In the Battle of New Orleans (1815), Andrew Jackson's troops, including frontiersmen with their long rifles, protected in part by cotton bales, defeated a British attack force.

Chapter 38. Dusk.

1. *Time and tide flow wide*: Proverbially, "Time and tide wait for no man," but this optimistic, rhymed version is Starbuck's invention.

2. *no key to lift again*: Starbuck would lift his spirits if he could, but his heavy heart, the clock-weight that keeps him going, has hit bottom and he has no clock key to wind himself up again.

3. *demogorgon*: Derived from classical mythology, a demonic, primeval god in Spenser, Milton, Shelley, and others.

Chapter 39. First Night-Watch.

1. *carcase*: Variant of carcass, corpse; also "the decaying skeleton of a vessel . . . a ruin" (*OED*). Evoking the gravedigger scene in which Hamlet contemplates a skull, Stubb, who has just mentioned a skull, calls himself in a dismissively witty tone just a *carcase*, or anything (according to the *OED*) "from which the life, soul or essence is gone."

2. *We'll drink to-night . . . And break on the lips while meeting*: From "Sparkling and Bright" by Melville's friend, Charles Fenno Hoffman (1806–1884). See also Making *Moby-Dick*.

Chapter 40. Midnight, Forecastle.

1. *(Foresail rises . . . all singing in chorus.)*: In Melville's forecastle drama, the rising sail is a curtain that "discovers" (reveals) the on-duty crewmen.

2. *Farewell and adieu to you, Spanish ladies!*: From the popular nautical song, "Spanish Ladies." Most versions read, "For we've received orders" to sail homeward, rather than Melville's "Our captain's commanded—". See also Making *Moby-Dick*.

3. *Our captain stood upon the deck . . . :* Melville found this sailor song in J. Ross Browne, where it is called "Captain Bunker." See Frank, "'King of the Southern Sea.'"

4. *Star—bo-l-e-e-n-s, a-h-o-y!* : The men in the starboard watch ("starbowlines" or "starboleens" in sailor speech) are being called to the deck from their off-duty sleep to relieve the larboard (port) watch, but they are slow to appear. In the following speeches, the Dutch sailor compares their reluctance to leave their beds to the difficulty of hauling up the lowest level of oil barrels in the hold, and he facetiously advises using the copper pump (meant for pumping whale oil from one barrel to another) as a megaphone. As their shipmates appear from below, the French sailor calls for a dance before he and his mates in the larboard watch go to sleep.

5. *Amsterdam butter*: The joke is that the common sailors were not fed butter, with its supposedly voice-smoothing properties, much less highly-esteemed and expensive Dutch butter; see Bildad's concern over the price of butter, and Flask's avoidance of it (Chs. 21, 35).

6. *belike the whole world's a ball, as you scholars have it*: An echo of "All the world's a stage," from Shakespeare's *As You Like It*, 2.7. The Manx sailor's pun transforms the scholars' view that the world is probably ("belike") a globe into the sailor view that it is a ballroom, and a place for sexual encounter as well. See also Making *Moby-Dick*.

7. *Tahiti!*: Now part of French Polynesia and a major tourist destination, in the early nineteenth century the beautiful island was virtually synonymous with Paradise. Refusing to work on the whaler *Lucy Ann*, in 1842, Melville and several mates were imprisoned on Tahiti for a month. He and a companion escaped to its neighboring island, Eimeo (Moorea). *Omoo* is based on those adventures. See also Making *Moby-Dick*.

8. *Pirohitee's peak of spears*: Melville apparently made up this jagged mountain's name, also used in *Omoo*.

9. *Crack, crack, old ship!*: Wooden ships make such noises adjusting themselves to the sea and wind; a noisy ship was said to be a safe one. Also an echo of words uttered during a storm in *King Lear*, 3.2.1, "Blow, winds, and crack your cheeks! rage! blow!"

10. *the isle fort at Cattegat*: The Kattegat is the part of the North Sea between Denmark and Sweden. No island fort there has been identified.

11. *the old grudge*: Racial antipathy, exacerbated in this case by Daggoo's legitimate grudge against whites for enslaving black Africans while associating them with the devil, as the Spaniard says. Perhaps, too, the Spanish sailor is "touchy" because his nation was a leader in that slave trade.

12. *ST. JAGO'S SAILOR*: St. Jago is a corruption of Sao Tiago, in the Cape Verde Islands off the west coast of Africa.

13. *Hands by the halyards! in top-gallant sails! Stand by to reef topsails!*: The mate orders the men to reduce the ship's sail area, first by mustering them to handle the ropes, then by ordering them to furl (roll up) the third or top level top-gallant sails to their yards, and last to make the second-level topsails smaller.

14. *jib-stay . . . royal yard!*: According to Pip, the support rope leading from the foremast to the jib-boom (on which the triangular jib is strung) has snapped, and the royal yard, four levels above the deck, is crashing down; if true, these would amount to a serious accident. In the absence of other evidence of damage, though, it seems that Pip's fear is already running away with him, long before his disastrous leap in Ch. 93.

Chapter 41. Moby Dick.

1. *disastrous encounter . . . popularly regarded*: Details of ferocity and other characteristics in this paragraph and elsewhere in *Moby-Dick* point to J. N. Reynolds's "Mocha Dick"; see Mansfield and Vincent, 691–95.

2. *Olassen and Povelsen*: Olafsen and Povelson wrote *Travels in Iceland* (1805), about which Melville read in Beale, also his source for the Cuvier reference that follows—though it was Frédéric Cuvier who wrote *Of the Natural History of Whales* (1836), and not Baron Georges, his brother.

3. *Scoresby . . . Nor' West Passage*: William Scoresby Jr. cites accounts of whales crossing from the Atlantic to the Pacific in the Arctic region. A navigable surface connection between the oceans, though often sought for, does not exist.

4. *prodigies related . . . Strella mountain*: Serra da Estrella, Portuguese mountain range; the *prodigies* or wonders were recounted in the 1692 English translation of Madame D'Aulnoy's *Relation du Voyage d'Espagne*.

5. *story of the Arethusa fountain*: Christianized form of a classic Greek legend in which the water from the transformed nymph Arethusa flows from Greece under the sea to Syracuse, in Italy.

6. *Arkansas duellist*: Frontier knife-fighter; Melville alludes to the predominantly southern "tall tale" tradition of early American humor (1830–1860) featuring such real and imaginary frontier braggarts and belligerents as Davy Crockett and T. B. Thorpe's Jim Doggett in "The Big Bear of Arkansas."

7. *Ophites*: Early dualistic Christian sect that reverenced the liberating serpent, enemy of the Hebrew Bible's God. See also Making *Moby-Dick*.

8. *Egyptian chest*: Like the large chests of ancient Egyptian statues.

9. *Hotel de Cluny*: Gothic, fifteenth-century Parisian abbey built over the ruins of ancient Roman baths known as Palais des Thermes; in 1844 it became a museum, which Melville visited in 1849.

10. *Caryatid*: Support column sculpted in female form. The correct term for the male figure column that Melville describes is "telemon" or "atlas."

11. *a Job's whale*: In Job 41 "leviathan" is unconquerable, fearful to look upon, and "a king over all the children of pride." Job is the most heavily marked book in Melville's Bible, and throughout his long literary life he frequently used its phraseology and its story of unmerited suffering. Earlier allusions and echoes appear in *Redburn* and *White-Jacket*, while in *Moby-Dick* the references begin in "Extracts" (twice) and reappear in "what is man" (Ch. 9), Captain Bildad's name (Ch. 16), in the whale's great authors (Ch. 24), in the discussion of Cetology (Ch. 32), in Stubb's travesty of the biblical story (Ch. 73), in

the phrase "kings and counselors" (Ch. 97), and in the closing quotation in "Epilogue." Later allusions to the Book of Job appear in *Pierre*, "The Encantadas," "Bartleby," *The Confidence-Man, Clarel,* and in unpublished manuscripts.

Chapter 42. The Whiteness of the Whale.

1. *the whiteness of the whale*: Mansfield and Vincent (704–6) list many of the possible sources for Melville's exposition on whiteness, including some of his favorite authors and an 1836 article in a magazine edited by Hawthorne.

2. *Pegu*: Sixteenth-century capital (now named Bago) of the kingdom of Burma, now Myanmar.

3. *Austrian Empire . . . Rome*: The Holy Roman Empire (ca. 800–1806) claimed to be the successor of the Roman empire.

4. *among the Romans a white stone marked a joyful day*: This use of a *white stone* appears in Pliny, but Melville might have seen it in Rabelais (1.10).

5. *Persian fire worshippers*: Zoroastrians, followers of the sixth-century BCE Iranian Zoroaster or Zarathustra, venerate fire but do not worship it. Fedallah, first appearing in Ch. 48, is a Parsi, or Zoroastrian.

6. *snow-white bull*: Zeus charmed and carried off Europa by taking on this form; mentioned again in Ch. 133.

7. *sacred White Dog*: Melville's source for this ceremony, and probably for the white wampum, above, was Lewis H. Morgan.

8. *Latin word for white . . . the alb or tunic, worn beneath the cassock*: The long linen *alb* (from Latin *albus* for white) is actually an outer garment.

9. *white robes . . . elders . . . white throne . . . white like wool*: These references occur in Revelation 1.14, 4.4, 7.9, and 20.11.

10. *Not Coleridge first threw that spell*: In Samuel Taylor Coleridge's "The Rime of the Ancient Mariner" (1798), a seaman is cursed for wantonly killing an albatross believed to have brought good luck, and in penance wanders the world teaching reverence for life.

11. *As Abraham before the angels*: That is, recognizing their otherworldliness (Genesis 18.2). See also Making *Moby-Dick*.

12. *the Captain made a postman of it*: Melville's passage derives from J. Ross Browne: "The mate set him adrift with a tally around his neck, dated, and marked with the name of the vessel."

13. *White Steed of the Praries*: Probably from James Hall's *The Wilderness and the Warpath* (1846). See Mansfield and Vincent, 711. "Praries" was an acceptable, alternative spelling in Melville's copy of Webster's dictionary.

14. *Xerxes*: Fifth-century BCE Persian king who invaded Greece with a huge army and fleet.

15. *chosen star*: The planet Venus, called Vesper or Hesperus, the evening star.

16. *that passage in Froissart . . . White Hoods of Ghent murder . . . in the market-place!*: Sir John [Jean] Froissart (ca. 1337–1410) wrote *Chronicles of England, France and Spain*, trans. Lord Berners (1523–25). The original title contained *"and the Adjoining Countries"*; *Ghent*, where the described *murder* in a local war took place, is in Belgium.

17. *pallid horse*: Revelation 6.8: "and I looked, and behold a pale horse and his name that sat on him was Death." John the Evangelist (meaning gospel writer) is credited with the book of Revelation.

18. *Whitsuntide*: The week beginning with Whitsunday (Pentecost), seventh Sunday after Easter; formerly a time of baptism of new converts, robed in white.

19. *White Friar or a White Nun*: Mendicant orders of Carmelite friars and nuns, dressed in white.

20. *the White Tower of London . . . an untravelled American*: Built in 1078 and later whitewashed, surrounded by thirteen buildings including the infamous Byward and Bloody towers, it is the oldest structure in the Tower of London. Melville, not quite "an untravelled American," visited it in 1849.

21. *White Mountains of New Hampshire*: This section of the Appalachian Mountains has the highest peaks in the northeastern United States.

22. *White Sea . . . Yellow Sea*: Respectively, on Russia's northern coast, and between China and the Korean Peninsula.

23. *Hartz forests . . . imps of the Blocksburg?*: Known as Brocken, highest peak of the Hartz Mountains in Germany and reputed location of witches' ceremonies on May Day eve, described in Goethe's *Faust*, and alluded to in *Redburn*. In German folklore, supernatural beings inhabited these dense mountain forests.

24. *tearless Lima*: Capital of Peru. The results of an earthquake that destroyed the city in 1746 and of another in 1828 were still visible in 1844 when Melville visited as a sailor on the frigate *United States*. The emphasis in this passage on Lima's sad physical whiteness, though, is apparently exaggerated; Mansfield and Vincent (714–15) point to its being a symbol for Melville of Lima's proverbial moral corruption, as expressed in Ch. 54.

25. *Pizarro*: Spanish conquistador Francisco Pizarro (ca. 1475–1541), conqueror of the Incas and founder of Lima.

26. *superstitious dread*: Mansfield and Vincent cite Bennett (I, 290) as a possible source for this passage.

27. *heart and helm they both go down*: The sailors' hearts sink in dread, while the officer on deck commands, "down helm," that is, steering the ship into the wind and thereby slowing it as much as possible.

28. *snow-howdahed Andes*: The Andes mountains of South America include the highest peaks in the Western Hemisphere; many are perpetually snow-covered. A *howdah* is a sometimes canopied seat for elephant riders.

29. *black bisons of distant Oregon?*: Melville had reviewed Francis Parkman's *The Oregon Trail*, with its buffalo-hunting account, in *Literary World*, 31 March 1849. Mansfield and Vincent (716) note passages in Parkman about Indians flapping buffalo robes and a horse's fear on seeing buffalo, but Ishmael's explanation of instinct and sense perception combining to reveal hidden demonism to him as well as to the Vermont colt goes far beyond these hints.

30. *not so much a color . . . absence of color . . . all colors*: To our perception, white is an absence of color, while at the same time sunlight, which we take to be white, contains all colors.

31. *that other theory of the natural philosophers*: Enlightenment philosopher-scientists such as John Locke (1632–1704), argued that differences between qualities inherent in objects and those "secondary" ones, such as color, are products of human perception.

32. *Lapland*: Region of northern Scandinavia, Finland, and Russia, with rugged mountains, swamps and meadowlands; home of the Sami people, often called Lapps.

Chapter 43. Hark!

1. *the middle-watch . . . scuttle-butt*: Sometime during the midnight to 4 AM watch, the men stand in a line to convey buckets of water from the large barrels of drinking water in the

middle of the ship to the small cask of water for daily use, kept on deck near the rail around the stern.

2. *the old Quakeress's knitting-needles*: The reference is probably to Aunt Charity, Bildad's sister (see Ch. 20).

Chapter 44. The Chart.

1. *captured or seen*: Vincent shows that Wilkes was Melville's source for most of this chapter.

2. *an official circular, issued by Lieutenant Maury*: Oceanographer, and Director of the Naval Observatory Matthew Fontaine Maury (1806–1873); the *circular* has not been found, but a version of its contents appears in Maury.

3. *Volcano Bay*: Most likely Kagoshima Bay, below Mt. Sakurajima, a volcano active in the nineteenth century, as it is today.

4. *loiters . . . in any one sign of the Zodiac*: A narrow belt in the sky in which the sun, moon, and planets seem to rise and set, the *zodiac* is traditionally divided into twelve sectors, each related to a constellation and an astrological sign. As the earth moves around the sun, the line of constellations also appear to move every night, so that over the course of a month one constellation rises along the zodiacal belt (visible in the night sky), and another sets (becoming invisible because of daylight). From this daytime perspective, it may be said, astronomically, that during each month the sun obscures a particular constellation, or, astrologically, that the sun inhabits the "house" of that constellation's "sign"; or, in Ishmael's terms, the sun "loiters for a predicted interval in any one sign of the Zodiac." In Ch. 99, Stubb uses the zodiac in his reading of the doubloon.

5. *Persian Gulf . . . Bengal Bay*: The large Bay of Bengal on the northern Indian Ocean is bordered by India, Sri Lanka, Bangladesh, Myanmar, and Indonesia. The *Persian Gulf*, also called the Arabian Gulf and accessed from the Indian Ocean, is a 615-mile long sea bordered by Iran, Iraq, Kuwait, Quatar, Bahrain, Saudi Arabia, and the United Arab Emirates.

6. *Monsoons, Pampas, . . . Harmattans, Trades; . . . Levanter and Simoom*: The *Monsoon* is a rainy, periodic wind of the Indian Ocean; *Pampa* is the cold wind of Argentina's pampas (prairies); and *Harmattan*, the dusty wind on the northwest coast of Africa. The *Trades* are continuous tropic winds toward the equator from the northeast in the Northern Hemisphere and southeast in the Southern Hemisphere. *Levanter* is the strong, easterly wind of the Mediterranean; and *Simoom*, a hot, sandy wind from the Sahara and Arabian deserts.

7. *hell in himself*: Compare Sir Thomas Browne, *Religio Medici* (1643) Part 1, Sec. 51, "the heart of man is the place the devils dwell in: I feel sometimes a hell within myself." See also Satan's words in *Paradise Lost* IV, 75, "myself am Hell," and Ch. 37, note 2.

8. *Prometheus; a vulture feeds upon that heart for ever*: The titan in Greek mythology who stole fire from the gods and gave it to humans. As punishment, Zeus chained him to a rock for eternity: each day, an eagle or vulture ate his liver, and each day his liver grew back. Compare Ahab in Ch. 134: "like a hawk's beak it pecks my brain." See also Ch. 108 for Prometheus as man-maker, another of his roles in Greek myth. Just before writing *Moby-Dick*, Melville read Mary Shelley's *Frankenstein*, subtitled *The Modern Prometheus*, in whose introduction, "Jupiter punished the temerity of the Titan by chaining him to a rock . . . and causing a vulture to devour his still-renewed heart."

Chapter 45. The Affidavit.

1. *Rinaldo Rinaldini*: A violent knight in Italian chivalric poems, particularly Ariosto's *Orlando Furioso* (revised ed. 1532), and Tasso's *Rinaldo* (1562). Rinaldini is a robber

chief in *Rinaldo Rinaldini, der Räuberhauptmann* (1799–1801), by Christian Vulpius, which became very popular in English translation as a novel and play in the early nineteenth century.

2. *Cambyses or Cæsar*: Cambyses II, sixth-century BCE Persian king and conqueror of Egypt; the *Cæsar* here is Julius Caesar (100?–48 BCE), dictator of Rome.

3. *Oriental straits of that name . . . Ombay*: Actually the Ombai Strait, on which Ombay (now called Alor) and Timor, in the Lesser Sunda Islands, Indonesia, are located.

4. *Tattoo Land*: New Zealand's indigenous Maoris were elaborately tattooed.

5. *Timor Jack . . . New Zealand Tom . . . Morquan . . . Don Miguel*: Tom and Jack appear in Melville's major sources Beale and Bennett, but the last two may be his own contributions to whaling legend; see Mansfield and Vincent (720) for other source information and citations of famous whales.

6. *Marius or Sylla*: The rivalry of generals Marius and Sulla caused a major civil war in second-century BCE Rome.

7. *Captain Butler . . . Annawon*: Melville confused Col. William Butler, who pursued Mohawk leader Joseph Brant (Thayendanegeya), with the much earlier Capt. Benjamin Church, commissioned by Plymouth Colony, who captured Annawon, a Wampanoag chief loyal to King Philip (Pometacom or Metacomet). Brant appears again in *Pierre*, and Philip in *The Confidence-Man*. See also Making *Moby-Dick*.

8. *Moby Dick as a monstrous fable, or . . . a hideous and intolerable allegory*: Having registered the white whale's mythic features in Ch. 41 and essayed the symbol of its whiteness in Ch. 42, Ishmael here worries that readers will lose sight of the white whale as a living fact, and take Moby Dick to be fictional, or more specifically a *fable* or *allegory*, which if poorly executed might tie fantasy to a set of fixed meanings. Melville probably added Ch. 45, or this section of it which underscores the "reasonableness" of the book's "catastrophe" (i.e., the whale's sinking of the ship), as he was nearing the end of the compositional process. See also note 11 below.

9. *New Guinea*: Large island north of Australia, in the vicinity of the islands mentioned above.

10. *Moses, . . . the plagues of Egypt*: Moses, traditional author of the Pentateuch, the first five books of the Hebrew Bible, relates the seven plagues of Egypt in Exodus 7–12.

11. *the ship Essex, Captain Pollard . . . Owen Chace . . . his son*: Ishmael's story of the *Essex* and of Captain Pollard's later history is factual. Melville met Chase's son as narrated at the end of this paragraph, and he believed that a Captain Chase whom he later encountered was the veritable Owen Chase; he met Pollard on Nantucket in 1852. Melville procured a copy of Chase's narrative in April, 1851, as he was completing *Moby-Dick*, and he prepared notes, titled "What I know of Owen Chace," reproduced in the NN edition. Melville either inserted or expanded Ch. 45 probably after reading Chase's "plain and faithful narrative."

12. *The ship Union*: Macy has a full account of the sinking; Ishmael's statement of ignorance may be due to forgetfulness, or might imply that Melville did not use Macy directly while writing *Moby-Dick*.

13. *Commodore J— . . . Sandwich Islands*: Probably Commodore Thomas ap Catesby Jones (1789–1858), who was aboard the frigate *United States* along with Melville in 1843, and is also alluded to in *White-Jacket*. (See Anderson.) British explorer Capt. James Cook named present-day Hawai'i for the Earl of Sandwich.

14. *Saul of Tarsus*: Saul, born in Jerusalem to Roman and Jewish parents, was headed for

Damascus to suppress Christians there when a vision of Jesus temporarily blinded him, and he subsequently converted to Christianity (Acts 9.3–18). Changing his name to Paul, he became the religion's principal apostle and ultimately St. Paul. See also Making *Moby-Dick*.

15. *Langsdorff's . . . Krusenstern's . . . Ochotsk . . . Captain D'Wolf*: George H. von *Langsdorff* (1774–1852) and Adam Johann von *Krusenstern* (1770–1846) are cited in Melville's Sources. *Ochotsk* is the small Russian seaport on the Northern Pacific Sea of Okhotsk. John *D'Wolf* (1779–1872), mentioned in the following paragraph (and in *Redburn*), spent two years with Langsdorff and much later wrote his own account of the voyage. He was married to Melville's paternal aunt, Mary.

16. *Lionel Wafer, one of ancient Dampier's old chums*: Both men were seventeenth-century buccaneers, attacking Spanish shipping. See Melville's Sources.

17. *Juan Fernandes*: Islas Juan Fernández, small cluster of Chilean Pacific islands about 400 miles from the coast. Isla Más Afuera and Isla Más a Tierra are also called Isla Alejandro Selkirk and Isla Robinson Crusoe, recognizing the abandoned man on whose adventures Daniel Defoe based *Robinson Crusoe* (1719).

18. *the Main of America*: The Spanish colonies in Central and South America (known as the Spanish *Main*).

19. *The English ship Pusie Hall*: The story is told in Bennett.

20. *Solomon—Verily there is nothing new under the sun*: Paraphrase of Ecclesiastes 1.9: "and there is no new thing under the sun."

21. *Procopius . . . Justinian . . . Belisarius*: Melville's source here was the article "Whale" in Kitto; see Vincent (271–74).

22. *Propontis, or Sea of Marmora*: Properly "Marmara," the inland sea in Turkey that is connected to the north with the Black Sea and to the south (by the narrow Dardanelles strait) with the Aegean Sea.

23. *the Barbary coast . . . a Commodore Davis*: Famously infested with pirates, the Barbary Coast stretched along the shores of Algeria, Libya, Morocco and Tunisia. Melville's source for Davis was Kitto, who cites a Commander Davies. See also Making *Moby-Dick*.

Chapter 46. Surmises.

1. *the shadow of the moon*: "And on the bay the moonlight lay, And the shadow of the Moon" (Coleridge, "Rime of the Ancient Mariner," 6.66). The "Rime" is also cited in Ch. 42.

2. *knight-errantism*: Unselfish pursuit of an idealistic goal. The medieval tradition of the "errant" or wandering knight, in which a gallant warrior on horseback performing noble deeds, appears, for example, in Thomas Mallory's *Le Morte D'Arthur* (1470). Cervantes (a frequent source in *Moby-Dick* and elsewhere in Melville) genially satirized the already lost tradition in *Don Quixote* (1601).

Chapter 47. The Mat-Maker.

1. *lashing . . . page of Queequeg . . . woof of marline . . . warp . . . sword between the threads*: In this scene, partly derived from Olmsted, Ishmael, as Queequeg's *page* (a boy attending a knight), uses his hand rather than a wooden shuttle, a device employed by weavers, to carry the *woof* (crosswise thread) of a two-stranded, tarred rope called *marline* between the fixed, perpendicular strands of the *warp*, while Queequeg compresses the woof with a flat wooden *sword*, in order to weave a "mat" on a makeshift loom. The mat is also a *lashing* because it will help secure their whaleboat when it is suspended

over the ship's side. See *Mardi*, Ch. 5: "A broad, braided, hempen band . . . is also passed round both gunwales; and secured to the ship's bulwarks, firmly lashes the [whaleboat] to its place.

2. *Loom of Time*: According to Mansfield and Vincent (725), the phrase is from Carlyle's translated quotation in *Sartor Resartus* (1.8) from Goethe's *Faust* (1.1): "'Tis thus at the roaring Loom of Time I ply, / And weave for God the Garment thou seest Him by."

3. *fore and mizzen . . . tubs . . . cranes . . . mainyard was backed*: The lookouts climb down the rigging from the foremast and mizzenmast; the *tubs*, in which the harpoon line is coiled, are placed one to a boat; the *cranes*, hinged wooden supports on which whaleboats rest in their usual position at the ship's side, are swung back against the ship (out of the way, not "out"); and the *mainyard* is swung so the wind strikes the front of its sail, slowing the ship.

4. *samphire baskets over high cliffs*: An herb used in pickling; when growing on high rocks, *samphire* was harvested by men lowered in baskets. The image derives from *King Lear*, 4.6.18–19: "half way down" a cliff "Hangs one that gathers samphire, dreadful trade!"

5. *Outside of the bulwarks . . . gunwale*: Standing on one foot while grasping with one hand the top of the ship's side, or *bulwarks* (pronounced bularks), the men, leaning over the sea, rest the other foot on the strip of wood along the top of a whaleboat's side, the *gunwale* (pronounced gun'l).

Chapter 48. The First Lowering.

1. *Manillas*: The Philippines, Pacific nation of many islands, and producer of the manila hemp praised by Ishmael in Ch. 60.

2. *Fedallah?*: Later referred to as the Parsee, because he belongs to that Indian Zoroastrian group descended from Persia, this dark and demonic figure leads the special crew Ahab has assembled to help him capture Moby Dick. These stowaways are first mentioned by Elijah (the mad "prophet") in Ch. 19 and alluded to by the seaman Archy in Ch. 20. Eleanor Melville Melcalf suggests the Malay in De Quincey as a model for Fedallah. According to Mansfield and Vincent, Fedallah's name may derive from Fadlallah, a character in a Persian tale featured in *Spectator* 578 (August 9, 1714). Finkelstein argues that it may be an Arabic name meaning "the devoted one" or "he who offers up his life" (223–39).

3. *gudgeons*: Small fish, but also metal fittings for the rudder, and people who are easily duped. Each definition is appropriate for the sailors, who are small though necessary elements in the underpaid enterprise.

4. *steel-bits . . . silver-spoons . . . marling-spikes!*: These terms in Stubb's "exordium" (literally the introduction to a speech or essay) pun on the knives in the sailors' mouths. A *steel-bit* is both the cutting edge of a tool and the steel part of a bridle between a horse's teeth; *silver-spoons* suggests that these hard-working, low-paid sailors are men of high-class leisure, as in the saying "born with a silver spoon in his mouth"; *marling-spikes* are both the steel tools used in splicing rope, and, in nautical slang, experienced sailors—ironic in the case of those men, such as Ishmael, who are new to whaling.

5. *face set like a flint*: "therefore have I set my face like a flint" (Isaiah 50.7); repeated in Ch. 100.

6. *peaked*: The oar handles are placed in notches in the flooring on the opposite side of the boat, leaving the oars pointing upward, together making a V-shape.

7. *magnanimous earth*: Daggoo is the *earth*, with Flask perched on his "gigantic" back. The other harpooneers are also associated with the classical elements: Tashtego with air; Fedallah, fire; and Queequeg, water.

8. *evangelical land . . . infidel sharks*: Ishmael suggests the disparity between his readers from the presumably devout Christian *land* (Europe and the Americas) and the *infidel* Asian men whom an infidel Ahab has hired.

9. *fire . . . in which, unconsumed, we were burning*: Allusion to the Hebrew men Shadrach, Meshach, and Abednego who emerged unscathed from Nebuchadnezzar's "burning fiery furnace" (Daniel 3.20–27).

10. *waif pole*: Defined in Ch. 87, a pole with a small flag, inserted in a dead whale to indicate possession and show its location. The lantern would normally hang from an oar, but *waif* (also meaning forsaken child) enhances the scene's sense of abandonment.

Chapter 50. Ahab's Boat and Crew. Fedallah.

1. *Tamerlane's soldiers often argued with tears in their eyes*: English name of the Great Khan Timur-i-Leng (Timur the Lame, 1336–1405), Mongol conqueror, and subject of *Tamburlaine the Great* by Shakespeare's contemporary, Christopher Marlowe. (In Ch. 30, lame Ahab is a "Khan of the plank.") Melville purchased Marlowe's works just before writing *Moby-Dick*; however, the reference to tearful soldiers, which may be folk legend, does not appear in *Tamburlaine*. Nor is it found in Poe's poem "Tamerlane" (1827, 1845).

2. *castaway creatures . . . blown-off Japanese junks . . . Beelzebub*: Melville apparently knew at least some of the stories about *Japanese* castaways saved by American whalers, perhaps including the 14-year old Nakahama Manjiro, rescued in 1841, who was educated in Massachusetts and returned to Japan in 1851. (See Blish.) *Beelzebub* is Hebrew, meaning "Lord of the Flies," a traditional name of the devil. Originally the pagan god of the Philistine city Ekron in 2 Kings 1.2, he is also called prince or chief of the devils in Matthew, Mark, and Luke, and is Satan's lieutenant in Milton's *Paradise Lost*.

3. *when though, according to Genesis, the angels indeed consorted with the daughters of men, the devils also, add the uncanonical Rabbins, indulged in mundane amours*: In Genesis 6.4, "the sons of God came in unto the daughters of men, and they bare children to them, the same became mighty men which were of old, men of renown." The *Rabbins* (an obsolete form of rabbi, or Jewish scholar) are, in this case, *uncanonical* because their writings are not included in the canon of accepted scripture in either the Bible or Apocrypha. In two such books, the "sons of God" who "came in unto" women are lustful, fallen angels, that is, devils. The references to unconventional scripture reveal the breadth of Melville's reading in esoteric texts.

Chapter 51. The Spirit-Spout.

1. *The Spirit Spout*: In his January 8, 1852 letter to Nathaniel Hawthorne's wife, Sophia, Melville responds to her earlier letter praising *Moby-Dick* and offering, among other insights, her interpretation of the *spirit spout*. The interpretation is not known because Sophia's letter is lost, but Melville acknowledges her finding "a subtile significance" in the spirit spout, although he "did not, in that case, *mean* it." For Melville's further ruminations on the "allegoricalness of the whole" of *Moby-Dick*, see NN *Correspondence* 219.

2. *Cape de Verdes; on the Plate . . . Carroll . . . St. Helena*: Now a country, but at the time Portuguese, the Cabo Verde islands (Cape Verde in English), are located off the west coast of present-day Senegal; *the Plate*, Rio de la Plata (*silver* in Spanish), flows into the Atlantic between Argentina and Uruguay; the *Carroll Ground* is actually off the coast of Angola, not south, but east and north of *St. Helena*, the British island colony famous for Napoleon's final exile, situated 1,200 miles west of Africa's South Atlantic coast.

3. *on such a silent night*: According to F. O. Matthiessen, this phrase echoes the refrain, "in

such a night as this," by two lovers at the end of *The Merchant of Venice* (5.1.1–25); see Mansfield and Vincent (738). The reference to the moon and Melville's repeated *s*-sounds in the passage also mimic Shakespeare.

4. *the monster might turn round upon us, and rend us*: According to Parker, Ishmael's language echoes in part Matthew 7.6: "neither cast ye your pearls before swine, lest they trample them under their feet, and turn again and rend you."

5. *sea-ravens*: Cormorants (from medieval Latin *corvus marinus*, ravens of the sea).

6. *Cape Tormentoto*: Bartholomeu Dias, first European to round the tip of Africa, named it "Cabo Tormentoso" (Tempestuous Cape) in 1486, but King João II of Portugal, with an eye on future commerce with India, renamed it Cape of Good Hope ("Cabo da Boa Esperança"). From here on, the *Pequod* sails into the Indian and Western Pacific Oceans, waters that Melville never saw. See also Making *Moby-Dick*.

Chapter 52. The Albatross.

1. *Crozetts*: the Crozet Islands, five small, uninhabited islands 1,500 miles southeast of Africa in the Indian Ocean, now a natural conservation area administered by France.

2. *strange captain . . . board the stranger . . . the stranger vessel*: In nautical usage, *stranger* or *stranger vessel* refers to any unmarked, unknown, or previously unmet craft. Beginning with Ch. 52, Melville uses the words in regard to the ships that the *Pequod* meets and their officers. Thus, although the captain of the *Albatross* may look "strange" because his long-sailing ship and crew have a "spectral appearance," he is the *strange captain* here because he commands an unfamiliar ship.

3. *Cyclades or Islands of King Solomon*: The *Cyclades* are the group of about thirty Greek islands in the Aegean Sea. Spanish explorer Alvaro de Mendaña de Neyra (see also Ch. 57) named what is now the Solomon Islands, northwest of Australia, the *Islands of King Solomon* because he found some gold there in his search for the biblical Ophir, the fabled source of Solomon's gold.

Chapter 53. The Gam.

1. *Pine Barrens . . . Salisbury Plain*: New York's *Pine Barrens* are located in eastern Long Island's Suffolk County; *Salisbury Plain* is a mostly barren chalk plateau in southern England.

2. *Gam*: According to Mansfield and Vincent (739), Melville borrowed from Cheever's definition: "the meeting, exchanging visits, and keeping company of two or more whale ships, or a sociable family of whales." Ahab makes most of the *Pequod*'s encounters with other vessels too brief and unsocial to be called gams by this definition. Melville uses them structurally and dramatically throughout the remaining eighty chapters to bring the outside world onto the stage-like deck, to increase tension regarding the pursuit of Moby Dick, to inject humor, and to facilitate Ishmael's meditations and eventually his rescue. For the nine gams, see Chs. 52, 54, 71, 81, 91, 100, 115, 128, and 131.

3. *Dr. Johnson . . . Noah Webster's ark*: Samuel Johnson (1709–1784) compiled the first major dictionary of the English Language (1755); Noah Webster (1758–1843) wrote the first dictionary of American English (1806), then jokingly referred to as "Noah's Ark."

Chapter 54. The Town-Ho's Story.

1. *The Town Ho's Story*: To promote Melville's forthcoming novel, this chapter was published separately in *Harper's New Monthly Magazine* (October 1851), just as the novel was reaching readers in England, and six weeks before Harper & Brothers published *Moby-Dick* in America. See also Making *Moby-Dick*.

2. **The ancient whale-cry*: "Town-ho" derives from the Wampanoag Indian whaling cry, "townor," indicating, despite Ishmael's note, the second, not the first, sighting of a whale.

3. *Gallipagos terrapin*: The Galápagos Islands, 600 miles west of Ecuador in the Pacific Ocean, home of the giant tortoise (*terrapin*), site of Charles Darwin's early researches in biological evolution (1835), and the setting for Melville's sketches, "The Encantadas."

4. *never transpired abaft the Pequod's main-mast*: that is, the secret never reached the officers, whose quarters are at the rear of the ship.

5. *sword-fish had stabbed her*: Although this sounds like a tall tale, such stabbings have actually occurred, as with the *London Packet*, seen by Melville in Nuka Hiva in 1842. See Heflin (Ch. 20) for such historical parallels to and possible sources of the *Town Ho's* story.

6. *where is Buffalo?*: Situated on Lake Erie and New York's western border, Buffalo was made the western terminus of the Erie Canal in 1822. Its harbor received grain from Chicago via the Great Lakes and sent it on to New York City by canal and river. In the 1840s it also became a railroad center. In Melville's day, this western boom town had more than its share of rowdiness and corruption.

7. *old Callao to far Manilla*: From the sixteenth through the eighteenth century, colonial authorities sent Peruvian silver from *Callao*, Peru's major seaport, to Spain, while from Acapulco, Mexico, they shipped silver across the Pacific to Manila, capital of their Philippine Islands colony, where it was used to buy goods from India, China, Japan, and elsewhere on the Pacific Rim. Melville saw Callao in 1843–44 while stationed there on the U.S. frigate *United States*.

8. *Mackinaw . . . naval victories*: On his trip to Illinois in 1840, Melville passed the fort on the high cliffs of Mackinac (pronounced *mackinaw*) Island in Lake Huron, near the Straits of Mackinac connecting Lake Huron and Lake Michigan. Built by the French and having changed hands several times, it became American by treaty after the War of 1812. The Great Lakes were the scene of such *naval victories* as Oliver Hazard Perry's defeat of a British fleet on Lake Erie in 1813.

9. *gaunt pines stand like serried lines of kings in Gothic genealogies*: Perhaps the *gaunt pines* are crowded together like the lines drawn in royal family trees (hence a remote pun), or perhaps, as Feidelson (324) suggests, they resemble the clustered, elongated human figures of *Gothic* statuary, seen on the facades of churches.

10. *Afric beasts . . . Tartar Emperors*: Just as there are no *Afric beasts* in North America, there had not been a *Tartar Emperor* anywhere for centuries; Ishmael seems to be pulling the legs of his Spanish listeners.

11. *capitals of Buffalo and Cleveland, as well as Winnebago villages*: The two cities were capitals in the sense of being the region's largest municipalities. The *Winnebago* Indian culture was centered on Lake Winnebago, Wisconsin.

12. *Borean*: Boreas was the Greek god of the north wind.

13. *the latitudes of . . . Bowie-knives*: The sword-like knife alluded to was designed and named for Arkansas rowdy James Bowie (who died at the Alamo). With blades up to 15-inches long and double-edged near the point, they were used on what was then called the southwestern frontier for hunting and brawling, and are therefore associated with those *latitudes*, or region.

14. *tasseled housings of your last viceroy's snorting charger*: Decorated saddle-coverings (*housings*) for the war-horse of the most recent ruler (*viceroy*) of Peru and most of Spanish America under the King of Spain, whose colonial rule ended in 1821.

15. *Charlemagne*: King of the Franks and the first Holy Roman Emperor, Charlemagne, or

Charles the Great (742–814), united most of Europe. A legendary leader and model of knighthood, he lives on in the cycle of literary works known as *The Matter of France*.

16. *Erie Canal*: Completed in 1825 and running between Buffalo on Lake Erie in upstate New York, and Albany on the Hudson River, it was originally forty feet wide and four deep, with eighteen aqueducts and eighty-three locks. This engineering accomplishment, which in *Moby-Dick* is twice described as "grand," was called America's Grand Canal, evoking Venice's main thoroughfare. As a teenager, Melville lived in Lansingburgh, near Troy, New York, across from the canal system's entrance into the Hudson River, and in 1838 he studied surveying, hoping to get one of the many jobs related to the canal. That job did not materialize; instead, Melville and a friend took the canal in their trip to Illinois in 1840.

17. *chicha*: Fermented South American drink made from a variety of grains, mainly corn.

18. *Roman arches over Indian rivers*: Engineers employed the Roman arch design to create elevated waterways so that the canal could cross over swamps and unnavigable sections of *rivers* such as the Mohawk.

19. *Mohawk counties*: The canal follows the course of the Mohawk River, originally the territory of the Mohawk Indians, through central and western New York State.

20. *Ashantee*: West African warrior tribe (also Asante, Ashanti) in what is now Ghana, known for their splendor and ferocious courage. Ashantees also appear in "Benito Cereno."

21. *Dame Isabella's Inquisition wanes in Lima*: The Spanish Inquisition, established under King Ferdinand and Queen Isabella in 1478 to identify, torture, kill, or expel heretics and Jews, lasted officially until 1820 and triggered emigration to South America, where heretics and Jews were also persecuted. The Spanish gentlemen are teasing Ishmael, saying that he is lucky the Inquisition has diminished because his impious remarks would have gotten him in trouble.

22. *"Corrupt as Lima."*: The "proverb" has yet to be found elsewhere, and it is probably Melville's invention, based, no doubt, on time spent in Lima while his ship, the *United States*, was stationed in the city's port, Callao, in 1843–44. The corruption may be political, moral, or sexual. Allusions to the seductive dress and demeanor of the veiled Peruvian women recur throughout Melville's work, but more with an air of mystery or allure as in *Typee*, where the beautiful Fayaway is compared to a Peruvian lady smoking a cigar. Lima also appears in *White-Jacket*, *Mardi*, and "Benito Cereno" (the latter two of which include hints of sexual intrigue), as well as in Chs. 42 and 100 of *Moby-Dick*.

23. *St. Mark!—St. Dominic, purge it!*: *St. Mark*, the author of the second gospel, is the patron saint of Venice. *St. Dominic*, founder of the Roman Catholic Dominican order of friars in 1215, is the patron saint of the Cathedral of Lima. In the fifteenth century, the Dominicans in Spain were responsible for organizing the Inquisition; hence, their role in "purging" corruption.

24. *Mark Antony . . . Cleopatra*: Roman and Egyptian rulers, respectively, and legendary lovers. Ishmael's sensual description derives from Shakespeare's *Antony and Cleopatra*, 2.2. See also Making *Moby-Dick*.

25. *Sydney men*: The first settlers of Sydney, Australia (1788) were British convicts who exchanged prison for exile on the other side of the world. Seventy years later their name still carried a stain.

26. *sea-Parisians . . . barricade*: Parisian workers rebelling in 1848 barricaded many streets. Melville's friend George Duyckinck, brother of editor Evert Duyckinck, witnessed the rebellion firsthand and wrote home of the experience.

27. *third day from that in which he had been betrayed*: The language evokes the betrayal of

Jesus and his resurrection on the third day after the Crucifixion, which, according to Beaver, is itself suggested by the "tableau" of the three sailors tied in the rigging.

28. *Teneriffe*: Largest of the Canary Islands, close to Morocco but part of Spain.

29. *Auto-da-Fés*: Literally, "acts of the faith," but actually, formal pronouncements of heresy by the Inquisition, followed by burnings of heretics at the stake.

Chapter 55. Of the Monstrous Pictures of Whales.

1. *Of the Monstrous Pictures of Whales*: According to Mansfield and Vincent, the chapter title draws from two sources: English physician and writer Sir Thomas Browne (1605–1682), whose *Pseudodoxia Epidemica* (1646), popularly called *Vulgar Errors*, includes "Of Many Things Questionable as They are Commonly Described in Pictures" (Book 5); and William Scoresby Jr. who, in *An Account of the Arctic Regions* (1820), distinguishes between true and false pictures of whales.

2. *I shall . . . paint to you*: Melville's expression, instead of the expected "describe for you," stresses not only the substitution of painting for verbal description, but also the attempt to communicate "to you" the reality of an otherwise inaccessible objective world. Chs. 55–57 discuss the depictions of whales (in art, illustration, popular culture, and myth) from gross error to reasonable approximation, although Ishmael concludes that the whale itself "must remain unpainted to the last." See Stuart M. Frank's *Herman Melville's Picture Gallery*, which reproduces sources and analogues for all visual references in these chapters. Melville sustained his life-long study of art by collecting more than three hundred prints and engravings.

3. *Saladin's . . . St. George's*: The Sunni Muslim Salah al Din (1138–1193) from Tikrit (in what is now Iraq) defeated the Shi'ites of Egypt and became the renowned sultan and knight who expelled the Christian occupiers of Jerusalem in the Second Crusade, only to be defeated in the Third. Melville may have read about Saladin in Sir Walter Scott's chivalric novel *The Talisman* (1825). *St. George* was the late third-century Roman soldier and Christian from Capodoccia (present-day Turkey) who defied Emperor Diocletian's order to persecute Christians and was himself tortured and martyred. The patron saint of England and Portugal, St. George is most often depicted in medieval armor slaying a dragon. (In this regard, see Perseus and Andromeda in note 6 below.)

4. *cavern-pagoda of Elephanta, in India*: This temple to the Hindu destroyer-god Siva is carved into caves on the island of Elephanta, near Mombai (Bombay), India. Unlike the multistoried, tower-like Buddhist *pagoda*, its entrance consists of a row of massive stone pillars. Melville's source is Maurice's *Indian Antiquities* (1790–1800).

5. *Matse Avatar*: An avatar is the physical incarnation of a Hindu deity, and *Matse Avatar* is the half-man, half-fish manifestation of the preserver-god, Vishnu. Usually depicted with scales, it is not half whale, as Melville claims. Nor does the image of Matse appear in the caves of Elephanta, devoted to Siva. According to Mansfield and Vincent, Melville's misconception derives from his misreading of his source, Maurice.

6. *Guido's picture of Perseus rescuing Andromeda from the sea-monster or whale*: In the famous painting by Renaissance Italian, *Guido* Reni (1575–1642), Greek hero *Perseus*, riding Pegasus, slays the sea-dragon that is about to devour the sacrificial *Andromeda*, chained to the rocks by her father. Other references to the Perseus myth occur in Chs. 28 and 82. Melville would have seen Guido's painting in one of several visits he made to London's National Gallery in 1849; however, he does not list it in his journal of that trip.

7. *Hogarth . . . "Perseus Descending"*: English painter and engraver William *Hogarth* (1679–1764) is known for his satirical prints. His somewhat comic rendering of the rescue

of Andromeda, accurately described by Melville, appears as an illustration for Lewis Theobald's verse drama *Perseus and Andromeda* (London, 1730).

8. *Traitors' Gate . . . Tower*: The *Tower* of London, a walled compound of several buildings on the north bank of the Thames, was for centuries the State Prison of England. Prisoners arrived by boat, often at night, through the low-arched, gated inlet called *Traitors' Gate*.

9. *Prodromus whales of old Scotch Sibbald*: Scots physician Sir Robert *Sibbald* (1641–1722) wrote numerous works on Scottish history and natural history, including his *Scotia Illustrata; Sive Prodromus Naturalis in quo Regionis Natura* (1683), informally called Sibbald's *Prodromus* (i.e. his Introduction). However, Sibbald does not include pictures of whales in this volume; such illustrations are found in Melville's actual source, *Phalainologia Nova; Sive Observationes de Rarioribus quibusdam Balaenis in Scotiae Littus Nuper Ejectus* (1692). Thus, "Prodromus whales" combines two Sibbald references. Given Melville's Scots heritage and his father's interest in pursuing that lineage, any number of Sibbald books may have been collected in the family library, especially Sibbald's 1710 history of counties Fife and Kinross (quoted in "Extracts") where Melville's grandfather was raised. Even so, according to Frank's *Picture Gallery*, other more accessible sources used by Melville (Bonnaterre, Lacépède, Desmarest) copied Sibbald's plates, and Melville could have known Sibbald's whales through them.

10. *Jonah's whale, as depicted in the prints of old Bibles and the cuts of old primers*: Like most children of his day, Melville's first acquaintance with depictions of the whale was through antiquated illustrations from the book of Jonah, appearing in Bibles well into the nineteenth century, and through similar pictures in children's primers such as the *New England Primer*, quoted in "Extracts."

11. *book-binder's fish . . . device . . . old Italian publisher . . . species of the Leviathan*: The emblem of a dolphin wound around an anchor, first appearing in 1502, was the printer's *device* (logo) for the sixteenth-century *Italian publisher* Aldus Manutius of Venice. Sir Thomas Browne alludes to the figure in Melville's source, *Pseudodoxia Epidemica*, but Ishmael takes issue with Browne and all others by facetiously claiming that the creature represented was intended to be a whale. Ishmael's conclusion that dolphins are "popularly supposed to be a *species of the Leviathan*" also implies, contrary to fact, that dolphins are not cetaceans (whales). But as the NN editors suggest, this distinction is in keeping with Ishmael's "cetology." Whereas "dolphin" and "porpoise" are words used for the same cetacean creature related to all whales, Ishmael reserves the word "porpoise" in Ch. 32, exclusively for these smaller cetaceans, and may have taken the word "dolphin" to indicate the fish of the same name, noted among sailors and poets for changing color when dying.

12. *Saratoga and Baden-Baden*: Fashionable mineral-water resorts in northern New York and southern Germany, respectively. Melville had often visited relatives in Gansevoort, New York, a few miles from Saratoga Springs, but did not tour *Baden* until 1857.

13. *title-page of the original edition of the "Advancement of Learning"*: Sir Francis Bacon's *Of the Proficience and Advancement of Learning* (1605) is the first great book of philosophy written in English. However, the original and many subsequent editions do not, in fact, have whale decorations. Melville may have had in mind the *title-page* of the 1840 London edition, which depicts a dolphin-like "whale" on either side of a reproduction of Manutius's dolphin and whale emblem. See Ishmael's "book-binder's fish" in note 11 above, and Frank, *Picture Gallery*.

14. *Harris's collection of voyages . . . Dutch book . . . bears running . . . perpendicular flukes*: The *Dutch book* that Melville cites is by Friedrich Martens, or Marten, also cited in "Extracts"; it and the two plates mentioned are found in the 1705 edition of *Harris's col-*

lection of travel narratives. (For both texts, see Melville's Sources.) Mansfield and Vincent consulted a later edition of Harris that lacks the Martens text and plates, and erred in suggesting two other sources. Frank reproduces two plates from a later edition of Harris: one depicting a whale with erroneous *perpendicular flukes*, but also another with bears and whales, which does not fit Melville's description. Only the 1705 Harris has both plates described, including one in which a *bear* appears to be *running* on the back of a whale.

15. *Captain Colnett*: British explorer of the Pacific James Colnett (1753–1806); his *Voyage* is also cited in "Extracts." Colnett's diagram, with its misplaced and oversized eye, was reproduced in Beale.

16. *for the benefit of his marines*: *Marines*, placed on naval vessels mainly to keep the peace, were considered by sailors to be ill-informed seamen and therefore gullible; hence, the expression "Tell it to the marines," meaning "You can't fool me."

17. *Goldsmith's Animated Nature*: British writer Oliver Goldsmith (1730–1774) made ends meet by publishing semi-reliable non-fiction, including *History of the Earth and Animated Nature* (1774), which is noted for certain amusing lapses. However, the illustrations added to the posthumous 1807 abridged edition, especially the rightly named "amputated sow" and "hippogriff" to which Melville objects, were never approved by Goldsmith. See Frank, *Picture Gallery*.

18. *Bernard Germain, Count de Lacépède*: The erudite French naturalist born in 1756 published his *Histoire Naturelle des Cétacés* in 1804, not 1825 (the year of his death), and according to Mansfield and Vincent, Melville probably took this disparaging reference from the similar one found in Scoresby.

19. *Frederick Cuvier, brother to the famous Baron . . . squash*: Naturalist Frédéric Cuvier (1773–1838) wrote *De l'Histoire Naturelle des Cétacés, ou Receuil et Examen des Faits dont se Compose l'Histoire Naturelle de ces Animaux* (1836). His brother Georges, the *Baron*, was also a noted naturalist. Melville draws this paragraph directly from Beale, echoing his identification of Cuvier as "the brother of the illustrious Baron." To demonstrate the inaccuracy of what Ishmael calls Cuvier's *squash*-like whale, Beale placed his own accurate outline drawing of a sperm whale, based on works by Colnett (see note 15 above), British painter William John Huggins (1781–1845), and his own observation, next to the distorted depiction by Frédéric Cuvier. See Frank, *Picture Gallery*.

20. *Desmarest, got one of his authentic abortions . . . from a Chinese drawing*: Naturalist Anselme Desmarest (1784–1838) published an expanded, annotated version of Lacépède's *Histoire Naturelle des Cétacés*, but Mansfield and Vincent note that, once again, Melville drew upon Beale's critique of other naturalists, including his disparaging reference to a Chinese drawing, for this paragraph. Frank adds that Beale misreads Desmarest, whose original commentary refers to Japanese, not Chinese, whaling.

21. *Richard III . . . humps*: According to tradition, and as portrayed in Shakespeare's *The Tragedy of Richard the Third* (1597), the villainous fifteenth-century King Richard III was hunchbacked. In Melville's day, *Richard III* was the Shakespearean play most often staged in the United States.

22. *stranded fish*: *Stranded* whales are a common enough sight, and an occasion for profit-making as well as scientific study. Frank reprints an 1828 French lithograph depicting the celebrated "Ostend Whale," stranded on the coast of Belgium in 1827, which is being "visited" by a line of top-hatted individuals, elegant civilians and military officers, all placed in juxtaposition to an elephant (ridden by four Osage Indians then on European tour) and giraffe to contrast the largest creatures on land and sea.

23. *young sucking whale and . . . Platonian Leviathan*: The contrast drawn between infant and

adult whales is comically diverted to a metaphysical level, evoking the Platonic view—expressed in the chapter's first sentence with the words "true form" and "absolute body"—that reality exists in the ideal conceptual form of an object and not in its actual physical state. To know an object, then, one must "see" it as an idea rather than an actual thing.

24. *the naked skeleton of the stranded whale*: Articulated whale skeletons were on display in U.S. and European museums from the early 1800s. In Ch. 102, "A Bower in the Arsacides," Ishmael reports having only heard of such displays in New Hampshire and in Hull and Yorkshire, England, which suggests that Melville had not viewed such exhibits in person.

25. *Bentham's skeleton . . . one of his executors*: In his will, British utilitarian philosopher Jeremy Bentham (1748–1832) requested that his mummified head and clothed skeleton be preserved and put on display as an "Auto-Icon" to encourage others to strive for greatness. His executor, the physician Southwood Smith, followed his instructions but mangled the head; a wax head was fashioned, and the auto-icon was seated in a glass and mahogany case with the original head in a hat box at Jeremy's feet. The display remained at Smith's lodgings until it was transferred in 1850 to the University of London, where it remains on view. Melville does not mention visiting Smith's library in his journal of his trip to London in 1849, but the story of Bentham's auto-icon was common knowledge. Ishmael's remark that the skeleton was used as a candelabra is facetious, but may owe something to Poe's story "King Pest" (1835), in which, at a banquet, a fire is kindled in the skull of a skeleton hanging overhead (Pollin). See also Making *Moby-Dick*.

26. *Hunter*: Melville derived from Beale his understanding of the renowned Scots anatomist John Hunter (1728–1793), who wrote his "Observations on the Structure and Oeconomy of Whales" in 1787. According to Parker, Melville also transcribed into his copy of Bennett the essayist William Hazlitt's comparison of Hunter's "cutting up" a whale to Michelangelo's chiseling marble.

Chapter 56. Of the Less Erroneous Pictures of Whales, and the True Pictures of Whaling Scenes.

1. *Pliny, Purchas, Hackluyt, Harris, Cuvier, &c.*: Richard Hakluyt (1552–1616) was not himself an explorer but compiled important collections of travel writing by British explorers; his associate, Samuel Purchas, published *Hakluytus Posthumus; or, Purchas His Pilgrims* (1625) with additional works of the navigators found in Hakluyt's papers at his death. John Harris (1667–1719) is noted for his 1705 collection of voyage narratives. (For Pliny, see Ch. 32; for both Cuviers, see Chs. 32 and 55.) All are cited in "Extracts."

2. *Colnett's, Huggins's, Frederick Cuvier's, and Beale's . . . Huggins's is far better . . . Beale's is the best*: Melville treats Beale's outline renderings of whale depictions by Colnett, Huggins, and Cuvier in Ch. 55. Here, according to Frank, he also alludes to the well-known 1834 engraving of Huggins's colored aquatint "South Sea Whale Fishery." Melville's assertion that *Beale's is the best* refers to Beale's outline of a whale showing the pattern that whalers follow in peeling away the blubber.

3. *excepting the middle figure*: In his copy of Beale, Melville noted of this drawing depicting three whales in various poses that the second figure, a leaping whale, is "wretchedly cropped & dwarfed."

4. *Sperm Whale drawings in J. Ross Browne*: In his otherwise favorable review of Browne's book, *Etchings of a Whaling Cruise* (1846), in *Literary World* (March 6, 1847), Melville remarks that its illustrations are "coarsely or harshly drawn." Browne is cited in "Extracts."

5. *one picture of whaling scenes . . . is a sad deficiency*: Scoresby's inaccurate frontispiece is taken from James Waddel's widely reprinted "Dangers of the Whale Fishery."

6. *paintings by one Garnery*: Engravings of pictures by French marine painter Ambroise-Louis Garneray (1783–1857) were widely known in the mid-nineteenth century.

7. *Versailles . . . the consecutive great battles of France*: Melville toured Paris and its environs in December, 1849, as part of his trip to England. During his visit to the Palace of Versailles (formerly King Louis XIV's residence, now and in Melville's day a museum), he observed "splendid paintings of battles" (NN *Journals* 33) from all periods, including the Revolution and Napoleonic wars.

8. *Leuwenhoeck*: Dutch naturalist Anton van Leeuwenhoek (1632–1723), renowned for his work in microscopy.

9. *"H. Durand"*: Although "Durand" was a pseudonym used by French engravers, Frank identifies French marine artist Henri Durand-Brager (1814–1879) as the painter of the two pictures Melville describes, entitled "Whaler at Anchor" and "French Whaler Fishing."

Chapter 57. Of Whales In Paint; In Teeth; In Wood; In Sheet-Iron; In Stone; In Mountains; In Stars.

1. *Tower-hill . . . beggar . . . painted board . . . lost his leg*: According to Leyda, a book illustration very much like this scene was published in London in 1837. A similar set of images including a crippled beggar, a mute with a sign board, and a one-legged man open Melville's last novel, *The Confidence-Man. Tower-hill* is an elevation outside the Tower of London.

2. *Greek savage, Achilles's shield*: Book 18 of the *Iliad* describes this magnificent pictorial shield crafted by the god Hephaestus for the indeed savage warrior, Achilles. On it are depicted two cities—one of peace, the other war—a microcosm of Greek life. Melville was surely aware of British artist John Flaxman's celebrated rendering of the shield.

3. *Albert Durer*: German painter and engraver Albrecht Dürer (1471–1528); here *Dutch* means "Deutsch" (German).

4. *Solomon islands . . . Mendanna . . . Figueroa chronicled them*: Although Alvaro de Mendaña de Neyra (1541–1595) named the Solomons in 1568, Westerners did not come upon them again until the nineteenth century. Cristóbal Suarez de Figueroa recorded Mendaña's discovery in a document cited in *Typee* as "History of Mendanna's Voyage . . . 1613." See also Ch. 52.

5. *I chased Leviathan round and round the Pole*: Perhaps referring to the northern constellation Draco, the Dragon, which partly wraps around Polaris, the pole star, in the Little Dipper. The brightest circumpolar constellation is the Big Dipper, which to the patient observer appears to revolve around Polaris during the night.

6. *Argo-Navis . . . Cetus . . . Hydrus . . . Flying Fish*: All four are southern constellations. The first three are also known as The Ship, The Whale, and The Water-Snake. The scientific name for the fourth is Piscis Volans.

Chapter 58. Brit.

1. *brit*: Minute marine organisms, including crustaceans; see also Ch. 45.

2. *Banks of Newfoundland*: Also called the Grand Banks and stretching about 450 miles along the south coast of Newfoundland, they were, until recently, one of the richest fishing grounds in the world.

3. *Portuguese vengeance*: A Protestant stereotype held that the Catholic Portuguese were vengefully violent.

4. *Korah . . . the live ground opened and swallowed them up for ever*: In Numbers

16.32–33, the divine punishment of Korah, his family, and followers for opposing Moses.

5. *Persian host*: Melville alludes in several works to this unidentified Persian, who, as in a story told by Herodotus, may be Oroetus, deceiver and murderer of Polycrates of Samos.

Chapter 59. Squid.

1. *Java*: Most populous island in Indonesia, containing its capital, Jakarta.

2. *furlongs in length . . . innumerable long arms*: A furlong is 220 yards; but the "giant squid" (*Architeuthis dux*), which Ishmael is describing, actually reaches only 60 feet in length and has ten arms. The exaggeration suggests Melville may not have seen the rarely viewed creature.

3. *his only food*: The sperm whale does feed on large, deep-water squid, but not exclusively on the giant squid.

4. *great Kraken of Bishop Pontoppidan*: Eighteenth-century Norwegian Bishop Erik Pontoppidan described a creature he called a *kraken* (Norwegian dialect for sea-monster) one and one-half miles in circumference; Alfred Lord Tennyson's 1830 poem by that name made the word known to English readers. Thinking about the book that would follow *Moby-Dick*, Melville wrote to Hawthorne (November 17,1851), "Leviathan is not the biggest fish;—I have heard of Krakens." Melville's Kraken was *Pierre* (1852).

5. *Anak of the tribe*: Giant; Melville's usage derives from the Bible: "There we saw the giants, the sons of Anak" (Numbers 13.33).

Chapter 60. The Line.

1. *Manilla rope*: Made of abaca fiber, also called *Manila* hemp.

2. *hemp . . . Circassian*: Ishmael is saying that Yellow Manila rope evokes the proverbially blond and beautiful Cherkess people who lived mainly in Russia's Black Sea region, a part of which is called Karachay-Cherkessia; *hemp* suggests the generally dark complexion of the people of India.

3. *worm-pipe of a still . . . the axis of the cheese*: Distilled liquids are produced in a condensing unit or "worm," a lengthy coil like a spiral staircase, but the whale line is coiled in a flattened, round, tightly-layered shape resembling a wheel of cheese, with a tiny shaft of space at its center.

4. *in almost every direction*: Many of Melville's facts here come from Bennett.

5. *Indian jugglers*: Street magicians in India juggled, performed magic tricks, and charmed snakes. In an 1828 essay in *Table-Talk*, a copy of which Melville owned, William Hazlett marveled at the skill of one such performer.

6. *six burghers of Calais before King Edward*: After capturing Calais in 1347, England's Edward III offered to spare the town if six prominent citizens sacrificed themselves. The mayor and five others appeared, with nooses around their necks, but were released.

7. *Mazeppa*: Title character of Byron's 1819 poem; he was dragged behind a wild horse but survived.

Chapter 61. Stubb Kills a Whale.

1. *still and sultry . . . Rio de la Plata . . . in-shore ground off Peru*: Ishmael's description echoes similar ocean "calms" inducing sleep, as in *Typee* (Ch. 2), or anxiety, as in *Mardi* (Ch. 2). See also the repeated "calm" introducing Ahab's soliloquies in "The Sphynx" (Ch. 70) and "The Gilder" (Ch. 114). For *Plata*, see Ch. 51, note 2. The *in-shore ground* is the area of the Pacific 60 to 225 miles off the Peruvian coast, so called by whalemen to distinguish it from the "off-shore ground" further west.

2. *slackened royal shrouds*: These ropes are *slackened* either because the *Pequod* is now in warm weather, and the *shrouds*, made tight in a Massachusetts December, have relaxed, or because, as was often done on the whaling grounds, the *royal* yard (with its sail) has been taken down, and the shrouds, no longer needing to be tight to handle the royal sail's stress on the mast, have been eased to minimize wear and tear.

3. *helm . . . spokes*: To put the helm down is to push the tiller away from the wind (thereby turning the vessel itself toward the wind; to achieve the same end, a ship's wheel is turned toward the wind). Ishmael's memorable description of the *Pequod*'s whalebone tiller in Ch. 16, its striking his side in Ch. 96, and its appearance once again in Ch. 123, are inconsistent with the spoked wheel here and in Ch. 118. The variance is likely the result of error, or possibly of incomplete revision. Melville's first whaling ship, the *Acushnet*, probably had a wheel mounted on its tiller, as does the *Acushnet*'s sister ship, the *Charles W. Morgan* of Mystic, Connecticut, the only surviving American wooden whaleship.

4. *Ontario Indians . . . paddled*: Melville no doubt saw Algonquins canoeing in Ontario during his trip to Galena, Illinois in 1840 or on his honeymoon in Canada in 1847; depictions of paddling Algonquins were also common. To approach a whale more quietly, whalers switched from oars to paddles.

5. *galliot . . . pilot-boat*: Melville's footnote borrows freely from Beale. A *galliot* is a slow, old-fashioned Dutch or Flemish cargo vessel that resembles the whale in its blunt bow, rounded sides, and flattened bottom.

6. *Start her, start her, my men!*: A call to make the boat spring forward, perhaps implying (in Stubb's facetious fashion) that it is still stationary and the men must *start* it as one might pop a cork. In his "Horoscope" column appearing in *Frederick Douglass's Paper* in March 1856, noted African American activist James McCune Smith (writing under the name "Communipaw") praises New York editor Horace Greeley for his stirring leadership against slavery, calling him a "'boatsteerer' of the Whig party" and comparing him to "Stubb in Moby Dick." Smith quotes Stubb's speech to his boat crew in its entirety, with Stubb's refrain, "Start her, start her," as a rallying cry for abolition. The use of *Moby-Dick* suggests that Melville's work had penetrated African American intellectual spheres. See Stauffer, and also revision narrative for p. 257 in Making *Moby-Dick*.

7. *Grenadier's steak*: Apparently, a large steak for a hearty, elite foot soldier. However, in his 1849 London journal Melville reports eating beef several times at various restaurants. The Grenadier, located off Belgrave Square not far from publisher John Murray's office on Albemarle Street, which Melville visited frequently, specialized in (and still serves) Beef Wellington. So, Melville may also be alluding to this restaurant's dish—a filet mignon wrapped in pastry—as the *Grenadier's steak*.

Chapter 62. The Dart.

1. *long experience in various whalemen of more than one nation*: Ishmael alludes to this experience in Ch. 45. Melville himself sailed on three different whaling vessels, two American, one Australian.

Chapter 64. Stubb's Supper.

1. *canal of Hang-Ho*: Huang-ho is the Yellow River. Yun-ho or Chah-ho, the Grand Canal, follows in part the river's former bed.

2. *mumblings*: Chewing of food with difficulty, as if without teeth. Sharks do not chew their food, but bolt down large pieces gouged out with their many teeth. The word is close to literal with reference to sharks, and no doubt chosen for its alliteration with "mingling" and "mastication." In an early draft of his late poem "The Maldive Shark," Melville speaks

of the shark as "Pale mumbler of horrible meat," which he later revised to "Pale ravener."

3. *the dead leviathan, smackingly feasted on its fatness*: Here, *fatness*, frequently used in the Bible, is both corpulence and wealth, as in "the fatness of the earth" (Genesis 27.39) and "the fatness of his flesh shall wax lean" (Isaiah 17.4). This usage, along with the mention of "leviathan" adds an unexpected biblical tone to the sharkish feasting.

4. *slave ships crossing the Atlantic . . . a dead slave to be decently buried*: From a variety of causes, an estimated 10 to 15 percent of African slaves died on these infamous "Middle Passage" voyages in the early nineteenth century. Dead slaves, and some of the living, were tossed over the side in a burial anything but "decent."

5. *as they fetched Elijah?*: "behold, there appeared a chariot of fire, and horses of fire, . . . and Elijah went up by a whirlwind into heaven" (2 Kings 2.11). See also Making *Moby-Dick*.

6. *lubber's hole*: Sailors can reach the "top" (a platform where the lower mast and topmast meet, and a base for the topmast's "shrouds," or support rigging) by climbing the shrouds of the lower mast and then, by means of holding on to other rigging, scrambling over the edge of the top. They can also take the scorned, easy way—squeezing through the *lubber's hole* in the top, a space around the mast.

Chapter 65. The Whale as a Dish.

1. *It is upon record . . . France . . . Henry VIIIth's time . . . Dunfermline*: Mansfield and Vincent (757) show that in this paragraph the *record* for *France* is Scoresby, while the information about *Henry VIII* (b. 1491), king of England (1502–1547), and *Dunfermline* (a Benedictine abbey founded in 1072 near Edinburgh, Scotland) comes from Sibbald, *History . . . of Fife and Kinross*, also cited in "Extracts."

2. *Zogranda*: A corruption of Dr. Sangrado in Alain Le Sage's novel *Gil Blas* (1715–1735), suggesting "So grand" for the pompous Scoresby, whom Melville elsewhere mocks as "Snoghead," "Fogo von Slack," and "Captain Sleet."

3. *Many a good supper have I thus made*: According to Mansfield and Vincent (757), the source for the description of frying ship biscuit and whale brains in this paragraph and the next is J. Ross Browne.

4. *"Et tu Brute!"*: Caesar's famous dying words, meaning "And you too, Brutus!" to his friend and assassin, in Shakespeare's *Julius Caesar* 3.1.77.

5. *it will be more tolerable . . . in the day of judgment, than for thee*: Ishmael's warning to the reader. Parker cites its echo of Matthew 10.15, "It shall be more tolerable for the land of Sodom and Gomorrah in the day of judgment than for that city," repeated in Mark 6.11.

Chapter 66. The Shark Massacre.

1. *anchor-watches*: Named by analogy to the practice on non-whaling vessels, which assign such reduced guard duties when at anchor.

2. *Pantheistic vitality*: Universal life force separate from a specific life.

3. *one dam Ingin."*: The dark-skinned Queequeg, though himself called a "devil" in Ch. 13, uses this derogatory American term implying evil.

Chapter 67. Cutting In.

1. *Ex officio professors of Sabbath breaking*: Because of their occupation (*ex officio*), whalemen usually worked a seven-day week, violating the commandment to keep the *Sabbath* day holy. Here, *professors* are those who profess or publicly acknowledge a belief; thus, to profess Sabbath breaking is ironic. The uneasy negotiation between work and religion for Quaker whalers appears in Bildad's "Don't whale it too much a' Lord's days, men; but don't miss a fair chance either, that's rejecting Heaven's good gifts" (Ch. 22).

2. *offering up ten thousand red oxen to the sea gods*: In their religious observances, ancient Egyptians sacrificed *red oxen*.

Chapter 68. The Blanket.

1. *Indian characters chiselled . . . Upper Mississippi*: This now-destroyed petroglyph, a bird-like monster on the high bluffs along the Mississippi River near Alton, Illinois, was first described in writing in 1673, by Father Jacques Marquette. Its Illini (Hileni) Indian name, "Piasa" (pronounced pie-a-saw), means "a bird that devours men." Although Ishmael sees the image in a "plate" (book illustration), Melville may have seen it personally on his trip to Illinois in 1840.

2. *Agassiz . . . icebergs*: Harvard geologist Louis Agassiz (1807–1873) supported Cuvier's theory of successive world-wide catastrophes to explain the fossil record, and proposed glaciers, not the biblical Flood, as the last such global event.

3. *live in this world without being of it*: Echoing New Testament rhetoric, as in "be not conformed to this world: but be ye transformed by the renewing of your mind" (Romans 12.2).

4. *dome of St. Peter's . . . temperature*: Mansfield and Vincent suggest as a source Madame de Staël's novel *Corinne; or, Italy* (1807), which Melville had bought in 1849.

Chapter 69. The Funeral.

1. *insulting poniards*: A *poniard* is a concealable, sometimes bejeweled, dagger frequently associated in literary treatments with assassination and tragedy, and its use here is of a piece with the "Et tu Brute" look of a calf's head, referred to in Ch. 65. A specific source for an *insulting* or insolent poniard has not been identified.

2. *other ghosts . . . Dr. Johnson*: Samuel Johnson, the lexicographer, who sought proof that ghosts existed, helped expose London's fraudulent Cock-Lane ghost in 1762, although he was later thought to have believed in it. Melville's journal entry for November 10, 1849 records his going "through Cock-Lane (Dr. Johnson's Ghost)."

Chapter 70. The Sphynx.

1. *Dutch barn*: The barns of Dutch American farmers, who had a reputation for careful husbandry, would presumably be heavy with produce. Melville, a New Yorker of Dutch descent, might have had in mind the literary embodiment of such a barn and such a farmer in Washington Irving's well-known story "The Legend of Sleepy Hollow" (1820).

2. *like the giant Holofernes's from the girdle of Judith*: In the story told in the apocryphal book of Judith, Holofernes, the Assyrian general besieging the Hebrew city Bethulia, is a giant only in power. The pretty widow Judith charms her way into the enemy camp and the general's tent, gets him drunk, and cuts off his head with his sword. In the many works of art based on the story, Holofernes is sometimes depicted as a giant, perhaps to magnify Judith's bravery by analogy to David and Goliath. No known painting or etching depicts the scene as described here; perhaps Melville misremembered one that shows Judith holding the head by the hair, at the level of her waist, such as by Christoforo Allori (1615) or Peter Paul Rubens (1620–22).

3. *copper calm, like a universal yellow lotus*: "Copper" is common in meteorological descriptions, and the noontime *copper calm* enveloping the *Pequod* also echoes Coleridge's "Rime of the Ancient Mariner": "All in a hot and copper sky/ The bloody sun at noon,/ Right up above the mast did stand." The *lotus* flower, a symbol of the sun common to Buddist, Hindu, and ancient Egyptian beliefs, signifies universal enlightenment, and is an ironic introduction to Ahab's ensuing dark address to the whale's head.

4. *the Sphynx's in the desert*: The Egyptian *Sphinx* here is conflated with the one in Greek

myth, whose riddle was the curse of Thebes until Oedipus solved it, bringing about her death and Theban liberation. The story is one analogue of Ahab's quest to solve the riddle of existence and at the same time destroy the enigmatic Moby Dick.

5. *make an infidel of Abraham*: Even Abraham, an epitome of faith for his willingness to sacrifice his only son, Isaac, at God's command (Genesis 22), would be turned atheist by the horrors the whale had seen. See also Making *Moby-Dick*.

6. *O Nature, and O soul of man! . . . linked analogies . . . cunning duplicate in mind.*": Ahab echoes Emersonian transcendental thinking in which material nature is a symbol or *analogy* of a universal spiritual reality that suffuses all things and thereby *links* them. Similarly, all things material and spiritual have their symbolic equivalent (or *duplicate*) in the mind. While Ahab can articulate these views, he cannot himself discover the links and duplicates of nature, soul, and mind; nor is the symbolic dead whale's head divulging the secret.

Chapter 71. The Jeroboam's Story.

1. *Jeroboam*: Idol-worshiping king of Israel whom God punished for impiousness by withering his hand. His disastrous reign is narrated in 1 Kings 11–22, and his impiety is frequently alluded to elsewhere in the Hebrew Bible. He is in some ways analogous to the biblical Ahab, against whom Elijah prophesied (1 Kings). The prophet Ahijah correctly foresaw Jeroboam's ultimate defeat, making him analogous to the other true prophets in *Moby-Dick*, such as Jonah (Ch. 9), Elijah (19, 21), Tistig (16), and Fedallah (117), and contrasted with the false prophets "Gabriel" (71) and Ahab (37).

2. *scaramouch*: Rascal (from the self-important cowardly clown in Italian *commedia dell'arte*).

3. *Neskyeuna Shakers*: Originally an eighteenth-century Quaker offshoot in England, the celibate, communitarian *Shakers* (so-called because of their movements while dancing in religious ceremonies) settled at Niskayuna, north of Albany, New York, led by Mother Ann Lee, regarded as the incarnation of Christ. Melville owned a book on the sect's history and practices, and had visited Shaker villages near his home at Pittsfield, Massachusetts.

4. *seventh vial*: The last of the "vials of wrath" poured out by the seven angels in the prophetic book of Revelation (16.17), and generally taken to mean an approaching calamity. Gabriel's language would have been familiar to Melville's readers, who had lived through the revivalist ferment of the early nineteenth century, marked by a growing belief in the imminent Apocalypse, the return of the Christ, and the judgment of the wicked before the start of the great Millennium. Particularly influential was the preacher William Miller, whose warnings of the approaching end of this world drew many adherents; his prediction (the third, after two previous failures) that the Second Coming of the Christ would be on October 22, 1844, led thousands to abandon their work and homes. Despite these repeated failures of prophecy, many still believed in Adventism, whose preachers held sway over their followers as Gabriel does over the credulous sailors of the *Jeroboam*.

5. *gunpowder . . . laudanum*: In theatrical performances *gunpowder* was used for pyrotechnic effect—as might be expected from the dramatically self-aggrandizing Gabriel; *laudanum* was a popular, addictive tincture of opium in alcohol, used in nineteenth-century patent medicines for many complaints. Gabriel might be an addict.

6. *archangel Gabriel*: The mad sailor has chosen for himself an identity of power, one of the highest angels in Christian, Jewish, and Islamic belief. Biblically, he is one of only three named angels, and is God's messenger for matters of great importance, announcing, among other events, the coming of John the Baptist, the miraculous birth of Jesus, and as "Gabriel" does here, the end of the world. See also Making *Moby-Dick*.

7. *vicar-general of all Oceanica*: Specifically, a *vicar-general* is a representative of a bishop;

it is also a title for the pope, Christ's agent on earth. Here, Gabriel claims to be God's officer over all the Pacific islands, usually called Oceania.

8. *seals and vials*: In addition to the opened vials, above, Revelation 6 tells of the Lamb's opening seven seals, revealing the coming wrath of God.

9. *the Shakers receiving the Bible*: That is, the Shakers accepted the authority of the Bible. Christians have long debated whether to take the Bible literally, and which interpretation or translation to trust. Shakers believed that Jesus was one manifestation of the Christ, and their founder, Mother Ann, another. Here, Gabriel seems to take Moby Dick as a similar incarnation. See note 3, above.

10. *stark dead*: Mansfield and Vincent (763) compare this story's events and language to an incident in Bennett.

Chapter 72. The Monkey-Rope.

1. *description of the scene*: Mansfield and Vincent (764) trace the following *description* to Olmsted.

2. *Siamese ligature*: Connected by a band of flesh at the chest, Chang and Eng, the conjoined Chinese twins born in Siam (now Thailand), were such sensations when exhibited as "the Siamese Twins" in Europe and the Americas beginning in 1829, that the name for their condition has persisted.

Chapter 73. Stubb and Flask Kill a Right Whale; and Then Have a Talk over Him.

1. *fountains that poured from the smitten rock*: In Exodus 17.6 God says to Moses, "Behold, I will stand before thee there upon the rock in Horeb; and thou shalt smite the rock, and there shall come water out of it, that the people may drink."

2. *devil in disguise . . . oakum . . . toes of his boots*: In folklore the devil can change his appearance. *Oakum* is tarred caulking fiber made from unraveled old ropes; Fedallah would need it to stuff into his shoes because the devil is supposed to have cloven hooves, not feet.

3. *a swap or a bargain, I suppose*: In Christopher Marlowe's *The Tragical History of Dr. Faustus* (1604) and Johann von Goethe's *Faust* (1808, 1832), occult knowledge is obtained at the price of a human soul. Stubb is implying that Ahab has made a similar Faustian bargain for the death of Moby Dick. See Ch. 32, note 22.

4. *old flag-ship . . . old governor was at home*: Heaven and God. In this paragraph Stubb parodies the framing narrative of the book of Job, in which God tests Job's faith by allowing Satan to do anything to afflict Job, but not kill him. See also Ch. 41, note 11.

5. *Asiatic cholera*: There had been nationwide cholera epidemics in 1831–32 and 1848–49. Although brought by European immigrants, the disease was known as "Asiatic" cholera.

6. *Three Spaniards?*: Probably George Walker's novel *The Three Spaniards* (London, 1800). Several American editions had also been published by the 1830s.

7. *hoist in Locke's head . . . hoist in Kant's . . . very poor plight*: The arguments of English empiricist John Locke (1632–1704), who held that human knowledge is produced by sense experience, were challenged by German idealist Immanuel Kant (1724–1804), who emphasized the innate form of the mind. One cannot comfortably subscribe to both concepts. At the end of the following chapter, the opposition is changed to Stoicism versus Spinoza's Platonism. Melville had read these philosophers and had discussed contemporary philosophy in depth with experts during his 1849–50 tour of England, Germany, and France (see NN *Journals*).

8. *Parsee*: The first of many uses of this term for Fedallah, meaning a Zoroastrian from India. See also Ch. 48, note 2.

9. *Laplandish*: Pertaining to the supernatural. Although the culture of the nomadic Lapps (Sami) of far northern Europe was little-known, they were thought of as extraordinarily superstitious.

Chapter 74. The Sperm Whale's Head—Contrasted View.

1. *grand order of folio leviathans*: In Ishmael's facetious bibliographical taxonomy of Ch. 32, "Cetology," these are labeled the largest whales.

2. *subsequent scenes*: Chs. 76 and 79 return to the subject of the whale's widely-separated eyes, and what they can and cannot see, but no later whaling scene makes use of this detail.

3. *Euclid*: Greco-Roman mathematician (ca. 300 BCE), renowned for his treatise in geometry, *Elements*.

4. *the ear of the whale . . . as curious as the eye*: Melville probably read these details in Beale, who quotes Hunter. Other passages in this chapter also suggest Beale as their source; see Mansfield and Vincent (766–69).

5. *Herschel's great telescope*: German-born English astronomer William Herschel (1738–1822) discovered Uranus. The telescopes he and his astronomer sister, Caroline, made, the largest of which had a 4-foot mirror, were more powerful than those at the Royal Observatory at Greenwich.

6. *Mammoth Cave*: Discovered in 1799, it was known as the largest and longest cave in the world.

Chapter 75. The Right Whale's Head—Contrasted View.

1. *Roman war-chariot*: According to Mansfield and Vincent (769), this comparison derives from Bennett.

2. *galliot-toed . . . shoemaker's last*: Resembling the "bluff-bowed" cargo vessel of that name (see Melville's note, Ch. 61); a *last* is the foot-shaped form around which the maker builds the shoe. (The "Dutch voyager" has not been identified).

3. *important interval*: Pregnancy; Ishmael refers to the superstition that if a woman saw something horrible or ugly while pregnant, the sight could deform her child.

4. *roof . . . ridge-pole*: According to Mansfield and Vincent (769–70) this comparison is from Cheever, while subsequent ones in Ch. 75 come from Cheever and Scoresby.

5. *Purchas . . . Hackluyt*: See Ch. 56, note 1.

6. *Queen Anne's time . . . farthingale*: Anne reigned in Great Britain from 1702 to 1714; a *farthingale* is a frame for a hoop skirt of that period.

7. *the great Haarlem organ*: Built in the mid-eighteenth century in Haarlem, The Netherlands, it actually has five thousand pipes.

8. *softest Turkey*: Traditional Turkish rugs have a deep pile of pure wool.

9. *a Stoic . . . a Platonian . . . Spinoza*: Ancient Greek and Roman Stoics, counseling engagement in civic and military affairs, preached and practiced rationalism, mental tranquility, and a belief in moral worth. By contrast, Plato's philosophy is metaphysical, building on a search for underlying universal concepts or ideals. The Dutch Jewish philosopher Baruch Spinoza (1632–1677) similarly argued that all things are expressions of the eternal, universal order. In *Pierre* (Bk. 14, Ch. 2), Melville is more critical of Spinoza and other neo-Platonists who explain away God's silence despite the sordid facts of this world.

Chapter 76. The Battering-Ram.

1. *The Battering-Ram*: The metaphor comes from Cheever.

2. *most appalling, but not the less true events*: That is, whales ramming and sinking ships, a rare but actual event. See Ch. 45 for reference to the sensational *Essex* story, one of Melville's sources. See also Melville's November 7, 1851 letter to Evert Duyckinck, sent just a week before *Moby-Dick*'s American publication, that mentions news reports of a whale's attack on the *Ann Alexander*; the whaler sank, but the crew was saved (NN *Correspondence* 208–10).

3. *dead, blind wall*: Here, Ahab equates the whale's head with a blank wall that has no doors, and he uses the same words in Ch. 125 to describe the intellectual impediments to "all inquiring heads." Earlier, in Ch. 36, Ahab compares Moby Dick to a prisoner's wall. Melville also uses the "dead, blind wall" metaphor to convey Bartleby's condition in his 1853 story "Bartleby, the Scrivener."

4. *lurks in it*: Mansfield and Vincent (770) trace this whole paragraph to two sentences in Chase.

5. *the most impalpable and destructive of all elements contributes*: Air, *the most impalpable* of the *elements*, is elsewhere called "unbodied" and "transparent"; nowhere else in *Moby-Dick* is it seen as destructive, but is instead called "girlish," "enchanted," "rosy," "gentle," "pure," and "soft."

6. *more inconsiderable braining feats*: Trivial head buttings, but since "mighty" is the intended meaning, "more" is a likely error for "not."

7. *Isthmus of Darien*: Now known as the Isthmus of Panama. The feat imagined for the whale was accomplished by the 40-mile long Panama Canal, completed in 1914.

8. *salamander giants*: Melville had read Sir Thomas Browne's *Pseudodoxia Epidemica*, which debunks the false notion that salamanders could live in fire, but here he puts the folk belief to use. This unusual phrase echoes other allusions to giants or titans, such as to Daggoo's sublimity (Ch. 34), the biblical Anak (Ch. 59), the whale's "Titanism of power," and Goethe's massive chest (Ch. 86); it suggests that in order to encounter truth, one must be a giant in spirit and strength, able to endure fire without being consumed.

9. *What befel the weakling youth lifting the dread goddess's veil at Lais*: The correct placename is "Sais;" however, see Making *Moby-Dick*. In 1849 Melville bought *The Poems and Ballads* of Friedrich von Schiller, translated by Edward Bulwer Lytton, which he later annotated. It includes "The Veiled Statue at Sais" in which a young man goes to Sais, in Egypt, and there secretly lifts the veil before the image of Isis, said to be Truth itself. He is found unconscious the next morning, and then lives a short life of silent melancholy.

Chapter 77. The Great Heidelburgh Tun.

1. *the Case*: According to Mansfield and Vincent (772), Melville's description in this chapter echoes Beale.

2. *the great Heidelburgh Tun . . . that famous great tierce is mystically carved in front*: A huge wine cask, or *tun*, in Germany's Heidelberg Castle that held 49,000 gallons—obviously an exaggerated comparison to the whale's spermaceti case. By strict definition, a *tierce* holds 42 gallons, but here it means simply a large barrel. The front of the Tun was carved with depictions of wine-drinking.

3. *Rhenish valleys*: Valleys in the Rhine River region, famous for their wine.

Chapter 78. Cistern and Buckets.

1. *like Niagra's Table-Rock into the whirlpool*: At one time, Niagara Falls's best-known view-

ing point, located on the Canadian side, Table-Rock is the subject of several paintings from the early nineteenth century. A substantial portion of the ledge broke off and fell into the *whirlpool* at the base of the falls in June, 1850 while Melville was writing *Moby-Dick*.

2. *doing as well as could be expected*: In this extended and ironic joke about birthing and salvation, Tashtego's delivery from death is performed like a Caesarian section, by cutting into the head of the dead whale. The midwife, Queequeg, delivers the baby, Tashtego, from the mother-head. In Ch. 87, an entirely different, sympathetic tone is struck as Ishmael and his boat-mates see mother whales and their newborns in the clear water beneath them.

3. *sanctum sanctorum*: Latin: "holy of holies," referring to the most sacred chamber of Solomon's Temple in Jerusalem.

4. *the delicious death of an Ohio honey-hunter . . . Plato's honey head . . . perished there?*: Hunting for wild *honey* was common on the American frontier, and the subject of fanciful and humorous fictions in the 1830s. Here it provides a metaphor for the seductions of Plato's idealism, which can be deadly, as seen in the analogy to Narcissus in Ch. 1, and with the masthead-stander in Ch. 35. To focus on the "sweet" but "ungraspable" ideality of Platonic conceptual forms can be to lose touch with one's own physical life.

Chapter 79. The Prairie.

1. *manipulated the Dome of the Pantheon*: Built in the second century BCE, this temple, with a dome larger than that of the world's largest cathedral, St. Peter's, still stands in Rome. In phrenology, to manipulate was to feel the contours of the skull.

2. *Physiognomist or Phrenologist . . . as for Lavater . . . or for Gall . . . his disciple Spurzheim*: The Swiss *Physiognomist* Johann Kaspar *Lavater* (1741–1801) studied facial contours as a key to character. The English title of his foundational work, referred to later in the chapter, is *Essays on Physiognomy* (1789–98), bought by Melville in 1849. The second pseudo-science, phrenology—briefly espoused by Poe and more fully by Whitman, though not Melville—presumed that skull contour reveals mental and emotional characteristics. The claim was originated by the German Franz Joseph *Gall* (1758–1828) and promoted by his long-term assistant, Johann Gaspar *Spurzheim* (1776–1832). Melville had referred to all three men in *Mardi*, and in Ch. 10 of *Moby-Dick*, Ishmael compares Queequeg "phrenologically" to George Washington.

3. *Phidias's marble Jove*: Melville apparently means the statue of Zeus at Olympia by the great fifth-century BCE Greek sculptor *Phidias*. The huge sculpture, destroyed in antiquity, was in fact not made of marble. It is also alluded to in *Mardi*.

4. *a nose to be pulled*: Literally or metaphorically, nose-pulling was a sign of disrespect for an official.

5. *the German emperors*: The Holy Roman emperors, also referred to in Ch. 34.

6. *foreheads . . . like Shakspeare's or Melancthon's rise so high*: A drawing of the head of Philipp Melanchthon (1497–1560), follower of Martin Luther, with its high, bold forehead, appears in the article on phrenology in *Chambers' Information for the People* (Edinburgh, 1842; Philadelphia, 1847) as an example of the highest intellectual development. The famous First Folio engraving of Shakespeare has the same feature.

7. *his pyramidical silence*: Both Ahab and the whale are previously described as pyramid-like (Chs. 31, 41). Melville visited the pyramids on his 1857 tour of the Holy Land; in his journal, he remarked, "It was in these pyramids that was conceived the idea of Jehovah. Terrible mixture of the cunning and awful" (NN *Journals* 76). See also Melville's late poem "The Great Pyramid."

8. *child-magian thoughts*: Both childlike and wise; the Magi, Persian Zoroastrian priests, were renowned for their mysticism and wisdom. See also Melville's late poem "Magian Wine."

9. *the crocodile is tongueless*: A folk belief; the crocodile's tongue is, however, immobile. The Sperm Whale's tongue is small and limited in movement.

10. *May-day gods of old . . . the now egotistical sky . . . now unhaunted hill . . . Jove's high seat the great Sperm Whale shall lord it*: The sentence claims that if the ancient pagan gods whose presence once hovered in the hills of the natural world were to be reinstalled, they would replace the monotheistic (and therefore *egotistical*) God of Judeo-Christianity, and would again be revered in the constellations—while the Sperm Whale would replace *Jove* (Zeus), king of the gods.

11. *Champollion . . . Jones . . . Chaldee*: Jean François *Champollion* (1790–1832) deciphered the multilingual Rosetta Stone, making possible an understanding of Egyptian hieroglyphics. English orientalist, translator, and jurist Sir William *Jones* (1746–1794) learned 28 languages, many self-taught. *Chaldee* was the common term for the ancient Babylonian language inscribed in cuneiform; biblical Aramaic, also called *Chaldee*, is a separate language. Melville may also be alluding to the lost original language supposedly spoken by Adam and Eve, as explained by Noah Webster in *An American Dictionary of the English Language* (1846). See Scherting.

Chapter 80. The Nut.

1. *that geometrical circle which it is impossible to square*: Ancient Greeks first posed the problem of constructing a square whose area equals that of a given circle. In fact, the puzzle cannot be solved because *pi* (used to determine the area of a circle) is a transcendent number.

2. *the skull will measure at least twenty feet in length*: Beale is the main source for this chapter's anatomical details.

3. *strung necklace of dwarfed skulls . . . a German conceit . . . undeveloped skulls*: Some editions of Maurice, one of Melville's sources, show the goddess Kali wearing a *necklace of dwarfed skulls*. Analogies between the skull and vertebrae had been proposed by several German naturalists including Lorenz Oken (1779–1851), from whom the great German writer and natural philosopher Wolfgang von Goethe (1749–1832) borrowed the idea.

Chapter 81. The Pequod Meets the Virgin.

1. *carrying coals to Newcastle*: That is, doing something pointless; coal was mined near *Newcastle*, in northeast England.

2. *half Xerxes' army*: This king of Persia invaded Greece in 480 BCE with several hundred thousand men.

3. *as by magnetic wires*: The electro-magnetic telegraph was introduced at the 1845 Democratic Convention, attended by Melville's brother Gansevoort.

4. *heightened by the extraordinary pressure . . . his life may be said to pour from him in incessant streams*: In this case, Melville is physiologically incorrect; the bleeding rate is actually the same at any depth.

5. *His eyes . . . were beheld*: Mansfield and Vincent (777) suggest that the following description probably derives from Beale. The same is true for other passages in this episode.

6. *As when by unseen hands . . . so the last long dying spout of the whale*: According to Olsen-Smith, Melville composed a version of this passage (now partially erased) in the margins of his copy of Beale, purchased on July 10, 1850.

7. *that stone lance?*: Mansfield and Vincent (777–78) cite Scoresby as the source of this

speculation in which Ishmael adds to the legend of the whale's longevity; though some whales have long lifespans, none lives much longer than 60 years.

8. *"Knife? Aye, aye," cried Queequeg . . . With a terrific snap, every fastening went adrift; the ship righted, the carcase sank*: Queequeg's desperate attempt to cut the strong chain with a hatchet derives from Bennett: "it has been found requisite to chop asunder an iron chain, which held a large and sinking whale, to save a ship from the destructive effects of so ponderous a body" (2.208).

Chapter 82. The Honor and Glory of Whaling.

1. *The Honor and Glory of Whaling*: Most of this chapter and Ch. 83 comes from three sources: the article on "Jonas" in Bayle, the articles on "Jonah" and "Whale" in Kitto, and passages in Sir Thomas Browne (Mansfield and Vincent, 778–79).

2. *Perseus, a son of Jupiter*: Also mentioned in Chs. 28 and 55, in Greek mythology *Perseus*, slayer of Medusa and savior of Andromeda (a princess of Ethiopia who was chained to a rock to appease a rampaging sea monster) is the son of Zeus (Roman *Jupiter*). Zeus turned himself into a shower of gold to impregnate Perseus's mother, Danaë. To bring Perseus into the fraternity of whalemen, Ishmael departs significantly from the myth.

3. *this Arkite story*: From an ancient Syrian tribe that, according to Kitto, also had a myth of Perseus and Andromeda.

4. *the same skeleton was carried to Italy in triumph*: In Ch. 24, we learn that the bones of a whale were featured in "one of the mighty triumphs given to a Roman general."

5. *Perseus and Andromeda derived . . . St. George and the Dragon*: Sir Thomas Browne comments in *Vulgar Errors* that some take the *Perseus and Andromeda* story to be "the father" of the *St. George* tale, in which the future saint slays a dragon ready to devour a sacrificial princess.

6. *"Thou art as a lion of the waters, and as a dragon of the sea," saith Ezekiel*: Melville alters scripture. In Ezekiel 32.2, God commands the prophet, "Son of man, take up a lamentation for Pharaoh king of Egypt, and say unto him, Thou art like a young lion of the nations, and thou art as a whale in the seas: and thou camest forth with thy rivers, and troubledst the waters with thy feet, and fouledst their rivers."

7. *Let not the modern paintings of this scene mislead us . . . a griffin-like shape*: Raphael painted two such renderings in the early 1500s, and Tintoretto painted one sometime around 1560, all of which Melville may have seen on view during his 1849 visit to the National Gallery in London. A *griffin* has the body of a lion and the head and wings of an eagle.

8. *that fish, flesh, and fowl idol . . . Dagon . . . only the stump or fishy part of him remained*: Mentioned several times in the Bible, *Dagon* is thought by some scholars to have been represented as part *fish*, an idea that Melville combines with the proverbial expression "neither fish, flesh, nor fowl." See, in particular, 1 Samuel 5.4: "behold, Dagon was fallen upon his face to the ground before the ark of the LORD; and the head of Dagon and both the palms of his hands were cut off upon the threshold; only the stump of Dagon was left to him." According to Kitto, the Hebrew root for Dagon ("dag") is the same word for the sea beast that swallowed Jonah.

9. *the most noble order of St. George*: St. George is the patron of the British Order of the Garter, the highest of knighthood.

10. *antique Crockett and Kit Carson*: Stories told about the exploits of frontiersmen Davy Crockett (1786–1836), who died at the Alamo, and Kit Carson (1809–1868), who helped seize California in the Mexican War, are American analogues of the mythical adventures of Hercules.

11. *Hercules . . . one of our clan*: In one Greek myth, Hercules allows a sea monster to swallow him and then kills it from within. As for his being "thrown up" by the "whale," Mansfield and Vincent (799) note that three of Melville's sources—Thomas Browne, Bayle, and Kitto—associate Hercules with Jonah, a connection Ishmael also accepts in the following paragraph.

12. *ten earthly incarnations . . . Bramha . . . Shaster . . . Vishnoo . . . sacred volumes*: With Brahma (misspelled in the American edition) and Shiva, Vishnu (here, *Vishnoo*, known as the Preserver) heads the Hindu pantheon. The first of his *ten incarnations* was as a fish (matsya), which Melville makes a whale. See note on the "Matse Avatar," Ch. 55, note 5. A *Shaster* (properly "shastra") is one type of Hindu scripture. Melville closely modeled this passage on Ward (see Gretchko, "William Ward," and Melville's Sources).

Chapter 83. Jonah Historically Regarded.

1. *Arion and the dolphin*: Legendary Greek poet and musician *Arion* was forced by greedy sailors to jump overboard from his ship, but his lyre music had so charmed the dolphins that one of them carried him to shore. His lyre and the dolphin became the constellations Lyra and Delphinus. In *The Shipwreck* (1762), quoted in "Extracts," William Falconer uses Arion as a name for himself, while both Bayle and Kitto also allude to Arion in their remarks on Jonah.

2. *Bishop Jebb's anticipative answer is ready*: John Jebb (1775–1833), Protestant bishop of Limerick, Ireland, wrote a well-known biblical commentary.

3. *the Right Whale is toothless*: This paragraph and the next are adapted from Kitto (Mansfield and Vincent 780).

4. *French soldiers in the Russian campaign . . . dead horses . . . crawled into them*: During Napoleon's retreat from his disastrous invasion of Russia in 1812, some of his troops attempted to survive the bitter winter weather by killing their *horses*, cutting them open, and crawling inside the still warm carcasses.

5. *Portuguese Catholic priest*: Cited in Bayle but unidentified.

6. *English traveller in old Harris's Voyages*: According to Vincent (285), Melville read the Englishman's report not in *Harris's* collection of voyages (cited in "Extracts" and Ch. 77) but in Bayle.

Chapter 84. Pitchpoling.

1. *disordered flight, as of Cleopatra's barges from Actium*: In 31 BCE, Cleopatra and her ships fled this Roman battle on the western coast of Greece, in which Octavius defeated a combined fleet of her ships and Antony's. Melville's main source was Shakespeare's *Antony and Cleopatra*, to which he also alludes in Ch. 54.

2. *unspeakable old Monongahela*: Incomparable aged whiskey from the *Monongahela* River region in western Pennsylvania, scene of the Whiskey Rebellion of 1794.

Chapter 85. The Fountain.

1. *noteworthy thing*: This discussion of the whale's spout closely follows Beale's. (See Vincent 286–92.)

2. *his windpipe has no connexion with his mouth*: Ishmael's anatomical statement is correct; however, some paragraphs later, he seems to contradict himself by saying, "It is certain that the mouth indirectly communicates with the spouting canal."

3. *Cretan labyrinth of vermicelli-like vessels*: In Greek mythology the first *labyrinth*, or maze, was built by Daedalus on the island of Crete to house the half-man half-bull Minotaur. *Vermicelli* is thin spaghetti.

4. *four supplementary stomachs*: Camels have three stomachs and do not store water in them, nor in their humps.

5. *the whale has no voice; . . . when he so strangely rumbles, he talks through his nose*: Although whales have no larynx, they do make sounds, a fact known to whalemen in Melville's day. Sperm whales are unique in that they do not "sing" (as do Humpback whales) but generate audible and tangible pulses of sound for echolocation, communication, and stunning prey when deeply submerged. Modern cetologists speculate that these sounds (or what Melville, who hunted Sperm whales only, calls "strange rumbles") are caused by vibrations in the whale's "case" or fluid-filled compartment above the mouth and in front of the spiracle—essentially the whale's counterpart of our nose. Thus, Ishmael's amusing remark that the Sperm whale *"talks through his nose"* is, in a way, correct.

6. *Pyrrho*: Greek philosopher (ca. 360–272 BCE) who professed that truth was unknowable, and therefore taught skepticism.

Chapter 86. The Tail.

1. *Titanism of power*: The huge and powerful Titans of Greek mythology revolted unsuccessfully against their father, Uranus, who preceded the gods of Olympus. Here, Melville's *Titanism* links strength and beauty; however, in *Pierre*, "Enceladus the Titan" is associated with a writer's "appetite for God."

2. *the carved Hercules*: Probably referring to the Farnese *Hercules* in Naples, the well-known ancient statue of the muscular hero of myth leaning on his club.

3. *devout Eckermann . . . Goethe*: In the last entry of his *Conversations with Goethe* (1836–1848), Johann Peter Eckermann wrote, "The body lay naked, only wrapped in a white sheet. . . . Frederick drew aside the sheet, and I was astonished at the divine magnificence of the limbs. The breast was powerful, broad, and arched. . . ."

4. *When Angelo paints . . . what robustness is there*: Michelangelo's frescoes on the Sistine Chapel ceiling were completed in 1512. Melville saw them in 1857.

5. *soft, curled, hermaphroditical Italian pictures*: Melville had seen Italian Renaissance paintings in the Louvre and London's National Gallery, during his visit to Europe in 1849. See also Making *Moby-Dick*.

6. *Darmonodes' elephant . . . nosegays . . . zones*: Versions of this story appear in several classical sources such as Plutarch and Pliny, both of whom are quoted in "Extracts," and in Montaigne; *nosegays* are bouquets, and *zones* is a poetic term for waists. The name *Darmonodes* may be either Melville's error or invention.

7. *flame Baltic of Hell*: Melville's meaning is obscure, but perhaps the image suggests that Hell's flames resemble the turbulent waves of a cold and stormy Baltic Sea.

8. *if in the Dantean, the devils . . . if in that of Isaiah, the archangels*: The *Dantean* mood refers to Dante's *Inferno*, with its gigantic Satan in Hell. In the book of *Isaiah* (6.2–3) the prophet sees a vision of seraphim, the highest order of angels: "each one had six wings; with twain he covered his face, and with twain he covered his feet, and with twain he did fly. And one cried unto another, and said, Holy, holy, holy, is the LORD of hosts: the whole earth is full of his glory."

9. *Ptolemy Philopater . . . King Juba*: Respectively, a third-century BCE king of Egypt whose name means "loving father," and a North African king of the first century BCE. Melville's closely-followed source was Plutarch's *Morals* (Mansfield and Vincent 786).

10. *Free-Mason signs and symbols*: Gestures and objects with secret meanings in the Masonic fraternal orders. See Cohen.

Chapter 87. The Grand Armada.

1. *peninsula of Malacca . . . Birmah . . . Sumatra, Java, Bally, and Timor*: The *peninsula* is separated from Sumatra by the Straits of Malacca; it comprises the southern section of Thailand, the western landmass of Malaysia, and Singapore. *Burma* is now Myanmar; *Sumatra, Java, Bali* and *Timor* are parts of Indonesia.

2. *fortresses which guard the entrances to the Mediterranean, the Baltic, and the Propontis*: The first fortress is Gibraltar; the *Baltic* is protected by fortifications near Copenhagen, on the Øresund Strait separating Denmark from Sweden (see the "isle fort at Cattegat," Ch. 40); the *Propontis* is the inland Sea of Marmara, connected to the Black Sea on the east by the Bosporus strait at Istanbul and to the Aegean Sea on the west by the Dardenelles strait, both fortified. See also Ch. 45, note 22.

3. *Peruvian or Indian streams*: Whaleships frequently replenished their supply of water on the coast of Peru. *Indian streams* may refer to watering spots in the East Indies or Malay Archipelago, or perhaps Polynesia.

4. *the worshipped white-elephant*: The light-colored beasts, symbols of purity, fertility and knowledge, were thought essential to the success of a king's reign. Compare "Lord of the White Elephants" in Ch. 42.

5. *Cockatoo Point*: Perhaps a common sailor designation or an invention by Melville. It is not down in any map.

6. *King Porus' elephants in the Indian battle with Alexander*: During his invasion of India, Alexander the Great defeated *Porus*, one of India's most powerful rulers, in 326 BCE.

7. *the beasts of the earth*: Frequent phrase in the Hebrew Bible and the New Testament.

8. *delirious throb*: Melville used the same expression in *Redburn*, Ch. 12, in which the narrator is "lost in one delirious throb at the center of the All." "Love's delirious throb" also appears in British poet Laura Sophia Temple's 1805 book, *Poems*.

9. *as we gazed over the side*: A source for this underwater nursery scene and some of its particular details is Bennett, Vol. 2 (Mansfield and Vincent 787–88).

10. *Gulf-weed*: South Atlantic seaweed kept afloat by small air bladders.

11. *salute more hominum*: Copulate as humans do. This footnote derives entirely from passages in Beale, Scoresby, and Bennett; the Latin is Bennett's (Mansfield and Vincent 789); Melville's *salute* (meaning to kiss) replaces Bennett's word "couple." See also Making *Moby-Dick*.

12. *Arnold at the battle of Saratoga, carrying dismay wherever he went*: Although American General Benedict *Arnold* (1741–1801) was not placed in command of troops at the crucial battle in 1777 won by the Americans, he galloped into the thick of it and led soldiers into the British fortifications, where he was wounded. Also at the battle was Melville's grandfather, Major Peter Gansevoort, who had already been successful against the British at Fort Stanwix. Melville had read about Arnold's conduct in Stone.

Chapter 88. Schools and Schoolmasters.

1. *Solomon devoutly worshipping among his thousand concubines*: The biblical king had seven hundred wives and three hundred concubines, "and his wives turned away his heart" from God (1 Kings 11.3–4).

2. *the memoirs of Vidocq . . . some of his pupils*: In his ghost-written autobiography (1828–29), Eugène François *Vidocq* (1775–1857), first a criminal and later chief of detectives in Paris, claims that disguised as a friar, he taught at a country school where he seduced his female students.

3. *Daniel Boone . . . Nature herself*: The legendary American pioneer (1734–1820) whom

James Fenimore Cooper called "the patriarch of Kentucky" moved farther west as the frontier advanced, and died in Missouri. A similar reference appears in *The Confidence-Man*.

4. *harems*: This paragraph and the next closely follow Beale (Mansfield and Vincent 790–791).

Chapter 89. Fast-Fish and Loose-Fish.

1. *Justinian's Pandects*: The Roman emperor *Justinian* (483–565) was responsible for this 50-volume digest of Roman law that resolved previous legal contradictions.

2. *Queen Anne's farthing*: This small commemorative British coin, worth one-fourth of a penny, was minted in the eighteenth century.

3. *Coke-upon-Littleton*: Common title for Sir Edward Coke's (pronounced cooks) commentaries (1628–44) on Sir Thomas Littleton's authoritative fifteenth-century treatise on property law.

4. *Mr. Erskine was counsel . . . Lord Ellenborough was the judge*: Melville took this story from an appendix to Scoresby, Vol. 2 (Mansfield and Vincent 791–92). Thomas *Erskine* (1750–1823), also defense attorney for Thomas Paine, was a Whig lawyer and witty defender of civil liberties. Edward Law *Ellenborough* (1750–1818), Chief Justice of England from 1802 until the year of his death, favored governmental authority.

5. *the Temple of the Philistines, has but two props to stand on*: The building that the blinded Samson brought crashing down had "two middle pillars upon which the house stood" (Judges 16.29–30).

6. *What to the rapacious landlord is the widow's last mite but a Fast-Fish?*: The phrase *widow's last mite* combines two allusions to Mark 12.38–44. In one instance, Jesus condemns the scribes who "devour widows' houses"; in another, he judges that a widow who gives to the public treasury her last "two mites" makes a greater gift than all the wealth contributed by the rich.

7. *What is the ruinous discount which Mordecai, the broker, gets*: High interest deducted from a loan in advance. By choosing a generically Jewish name, Melville uses the demeaning, centuries-old stereotype of the Jewish moneylender.

8. *John Bull . . . Ireland . . . Brother Jonathan . . . Texas . . . Fast-Fish?*: *John Bull* is the figure introduced in the early eighteenth century as a personification of England, which had for centuries controlled and suppressed *Ireland*. The United States, similarly represented by *Brother Jonathan* (precursor of Uncle Sam), had annexed *Texas* in 1845. "Jonathan" is sarcastically "apostolic" because, despite the United States' ideological rejection of British imperialism, it follows English acquisitive precedent just as the biblical apostles followed Jesus in renouncing worldly wealth.

9. *What was Poland to the Czar? . . . Greece . . . Mexico . . . to the United States? All Loose-Fish*: Russia annexed *Poland* in 1815; Turkey held all or part of *Greece* from the fifteenth century to 1833. See also Ch. 14, note 3. Melville disapproved of the expansionism of the Mexican War of 1846–48, in which the United States seized more than half of Mexico's territory, and which, many felt, opened the West to the possibility of slavery. In explaining the international dimension of his "doctrine of Loose-Fish" (which ironically echoes the United States's Monroe Doctrine announced in 1823, warning Europe not to intervene in the Americas), Ishmael says that *Poland* and Greece were once seen by the more powerful Russia and Turkey as "loose-fish" ready to be seized, and they proceeded to annex those neighbors, making them "fast-fish." He predicts that the United States, similarly, will come to regard the rest of Mexico as a "loose-fish," and seize it. That is, Mexico, like "*All Loose-Fish*," is there for the taking.

Chapter 90. Heads or Tails.

1. *Bracton, l. 3, c. 3*: From the thirteenth-century compilation of English law and customs, *De Legibus et Consuetudinibus Angliae*, by Henry de Bracton, not printed until 1569; the Latin means "Concerning the whale, it truly suffices if the king have the head and the queen the tail." Melville's source here is Blackstone.

2. *Dover, or Sandwich, or some one of the Cinque Ports*: Both cities were among the original five (French "cinque") ports, on England's southern coast, organized in medieval times to provide ships and men to the King's navy. Melville's source for the anecdote that makes up most of Ch. 90 appeared in the *Literary World* (Mansfield and Vincent 793).

3. *Blackstone*: *Commentaries on the Laws of England* (1765–1769) by Sir William *Blackstone* (1723–1780), the most highly respected compendium of English law in Melville's time.

4. *Duke of Wellington . . . the corners of the three kingdoms . . . alms of beggars?*: Renowned for defeating Napoleon at Waterloo in 1815, the *Duke* (1769–1852) was later prime minister of England (1828–1830). His rigid conservativism appears here in the cartoon-like image of his forcing *alms* (which are by definition voluntary) from the poorest people, typically found begging on street *corners*, in the *three kingdoms*—England, Scotland and Ireland—of the United Kingdom.

5. *Plowden*: Edmund *Plowden* (1518–1585), eminent Elizabethan lawyer.

6. *old King's Bench author, one William Prynne*: The *King's Bench* is part of the British superior court system; *Prynne* (1600–1669) wrote *Aurum Reginae, or . . . Concerning Queen-Gold* (1668); "Queen-pinmoney" is Melville's joke.

Chapter 91. The Pequod Meets the Rose-Bud.

1. *Rose-bud*: Stubb's tricking of the *Rose-bud's* French captain involves numerous sexual and excremental jokes, not the least of which is the ship's name. As Poole notes, *rosebud* is slang for anus.

2. *Sir T. Browne, V. E.*: Abbreviation for Renaissance physician and philosopher Thomas Browne's *Vulgar Errors*, the common title for *Pseudodoxia Epidemica* (1646). In writing this chapter, Melville repeatedly used Beale's Ch. 10, which quotes the passage accurately. See Mansfield and Vincent (793–94).

3. *Assyrian city in the plague*: In about 765 BCE, a plague struck the Assyrian capital, Nineveh, in what is now northern Iraq.

4. *ambergris*: Soft, black, smelly substance found in the intestines of sperm whales, which after exposure gradually lightens in color and develops a pleasant aroma. It was highly valued for its use in making fine perfumes.

5. *head boards*: Planks with carved lettering, attached to both sides of the bow.

6. *Cologne manufacturer*: The captain is not from the German city Köln, generally known by its French name, *Cologne*, but had previously been a manufacturer of Cologne water (*eau de Cologne*) made from aromatic oils of fruits and flowers. Given the French captain's former trade, Stubb's swindling him out of the ambergris, which is used in perfume, is all the more amusing.

7. *Captain's round-house abaft*: Normally the round-house is a cabin at the stern or *abaft*, large enough to walk around in (hence its name). Here, though, in keeping with the excremental humor, Melville makes it the French Captain's privy, or "cabinet."

8. *St. Jago monkey*: Primate from São Tiago, off the coast of Senegal.

9. *faint stream of perfume*: Beale says that ambergris stinks when taken directly from the whale's intestines; however, Bennett, a second source, refers to only a "slight and pecu-

liar" odor. Melville used literary license in concluding with this sweet "perfume." See note 4, above.

Chapter 92. Ambergris.

1. *in 1791 a certain Nantucket-born Captain Coffin was examined at the bar of the English House of Commons on that subject*: Directly quoted from Beale, although Melville added *Nantucket-born*. Beale was the main source for Ch. 92, with added details from Cheever.

2. *saying of St. Paul . . . corruption and incorruption . . . glory*: "So also is the resurrection of the dead. It is sown in corruption; it is raised in incorruption: It is sown in dishonour; it is raised in glory: it is sown in weakness; it is raised in power" (1 Corinthians 15.42–43).

3. *that saying of Paracelsus about what it is that maketh the best musk*: Paracelsus, six-teenth-century Swiss alchemist, physician and astrologer, is quoted in Sir Thomas Browne as saying that the best musk (odorous substance used in making perfumes) comes from "ordure" (excrement). Melville likely got this passage, his quotation from Browne in "Extracts," and the epigraph for Ch. 91 from Beale, who quotes all three on one page. See also Ch. 94, note 2.

4. *Smeerenberg . . . Fogo Von Slack, in his great work on Smells*: *Fogo* is another teasing name for, and jab at, Scoresby, whose *Account of the Arctic Regions* comments on the smell of whale oil and also defines *Smeerenberg* exactly as Melville does here. See Mansfield and Vincent (795).

5. *to detect a Jew in the company, by the nose*: Among the many medieval libels about Jews is the myth of a "foetor judaicus" (Jewish smell).

6. *that famous elephant . . . myrrh . . . Alexander the Great?*: Indian princes gave many such elephants to Greek conqueror Alexander; *myrrh* is an aromatic resin from certain trees and shrubs.

Chapter 93. The Castaway.

1. *Tolland County in Connecticut*: An actual place, and verified by Pip in Ch. 99; but in Ch. 27 Pip is said to be from Alabama.

2. *wondrous depths*: "They that go down to the sea in ships, that do business in great waters; These see the works of the Lord, and his wonders in the deep" (Psalms 107.23–24).

3. *miser-merman, Wisdom*: Not Triton, the Greek sea god commonly depicted as half human, half fish, or another figure from myth or legend, but Melville's invented person-ification implying the difficulty of obtaining wisdom. Compare the "salamander giants" of Ch. 76, note 8.

4. *man's insanity is heaven's sense*: Compare *Pierre*, "though the earthly wisdom of man be heavenly folly to God, so also, conversely, is the heavenly wisdom of God an earthly folly to man" (Book 14, Part 1).

5. *sequel of the narrative . . . what like abandonment befell myselfs*: Ishmael hints at what will happen as though he has already written the book's climactic conclusion and *sequel*, the "Epilogue." One possibility is that Melville may have added this foreshadowing of Ishmael's *abandonment*—he is bumped from his boat—after writing the novel's conclu-sion, while he was revising galleys of earlier chapters already set in type by his American printer in the summer of 1851. See revision narrative for Ch. 36, p. 157 in Making *Moby-Dick* for a similar proof revision.

Chapter 94. A Squeeze of the Hand.

1. *Constantine's bath*: Possibly a baptismal font in Rome. Constantine the Great (272–337) was the first Christian emperor of Rome. See Mansfield and Vincent (531–32).

2. *Paracelsan superstition that sperm is of rare virtue in allaying the heat of anger*: The Swiss alchemist Paracelsus (1493–1541) practiced magic and medicine throughout Europe, was considered a quack, but is also credited as the founder of chemistry. Melville's source for this *superstition* is unknown. See Ch. 92, note 4.

3. *In thoughts of the visions of the night, I saw long rows of angels in paradise, each with his hands in a jar of spermaceti*: Melville revises a biblical passage, "In thoughts from the visions of the night, when deep sleep falleth on men, Fear came upon me, and trembling, which made all my bones to shake" (Job 4.13). The revision creates a mixture of peace, joy, and implicit sexuality.

4. *snowy and golden ground, dotted with spots of the deepest crimson and purple*: The phrase suggests the technique of British painter J.M.W. Turner, who applied such a *ground* (base coat) to his canvases, later adding strokes of color. (See Wallace, *Melville and Turner*.)

5. *Louis le Gros*: Louis VI of France (1081–1137), known as *le Gros* (the Fat).

Chapter 95. The Cassock.

1. *as darkly set forth in . . . Kings*: "And Asa did that which was right in the eyes of the Lord, as did David his father. And he took away the sodomites out of the land, and removed all the idols that his fathers had made. And also Maachah his mother, even her he removed from being queen, because she had made an idol in a grove; and Asa destroyed her idol, and burnt it by the brook Kidron" (1 Kings 15.11–13). Ishmael points to and imitates the biblical handling of the subject *darkly* (obscurely) by not saying that the idols were phalluses.

2. *archbishoprick*: This seemingly scandalous pun probably escaped the censors because the spelling was sanctioned by the authoritative *Murray's Grammar* (see Ch. 99, note 21). Dennis Berthold, noting the whole sentence—"What a candidate for an *archbishoprick*, what a lad for a Pope were this mincer!"—sees an allusion to the "cassock"-wearing Archbishop John Hughes of New York, who minced words in supporting both the Irish rebellion against England and the return of the Pope to Rome in May, 1850 after he had been driven out by Italian republican revolutionaries the previous year.

Chapter 96. The Try-Works.

1. *cycloid*: Melville is correct in this mathematical observation about a *cycloid*, which is a geometrical curve created by a point on the circumference of a circle that rolls in a straight line.

2. *left wing of the day of judgment . . . the pit*: According to Matthew 25.41, on Judgment Day the condemned stand to God's left; "Then shall he say also unto them on the left hand, Depart from me, ye cursed, into everlasting fire, prepared for the devil and his angels." Whaling writers often treated a night scene of trying-out as an image of *the pit*, as if it were from Dante's *Inferno*. J. Ross Browne's description, including the awful smell of the smoke, seems the image Melville had in mind. Bennett's *Ribs and Trucks*, and the anonymous "The Whale and Whale Catching," all made the comparison. See Mansfield and Vincent (797); see also Making *Moby-Dick*.

3. *famed Greek fire*: This petroleum-based substance, whose exact composition is still unknown, was introduced by the Byzantine Greeks in the seventh century. Launched at the enemy, it caught fire spontaneously and could not be extinguished with water.

4. *Hydriote, Canaris . . . Turkish frigates . . . conflagrations*: Konstantínos Kanáris (1790–1877) was not himself a *Hydriote*, or native of Hydra, a Greek island, but in June, 1822, during the Greek war of independence from Turkey (1821–29), he led the Greek fleet based at Hydra and used a fire-ship to destroy the enemy's flagship.

5. *blackness of darkness*: From Jude 13, referring to the punishment of the wicked, and quoted in "The Carpet-Bag" (see Ch. 2, note 5).

6. *brought by the lee*: Unexpectedly turned so that the wind hits the lee side of the sails, a situation that might capsize the vessel. Ishmael, steering the *Pequod*, has fallen asleep or into a trance, during which he has turned 180 degrees: once facing forward as usual with the tiller at one side, he is now facing astern with the tiller on his other side.

7. *Virginia's Dismal Swamp . . . accursed Campagna . . . wide Sahara*: The heavily forested Great *Dismal Swamp*, on the coastal plain of southern Virginia and northern North Carolina, once covered 2,000 square miles; the *Campagna*, infamous for its malaria, is the once marshy plain surrounding Rome; the *Sahara* Desert, covering more than three million square miles in northern Africa, is the largest on Earth.

8. *the ocean, which is the dark side of this earth, and which is two thirds of this earth*: Mansfield and Vincent (800) find an echo here of Emerson's essay "The Tragic" (1844): "As the salt sea covers more than two-thirds of the surface of the globe, so sorrow encroaches in man on felicity."

9. *Man of Sorrows . . . the truest of all books is Solomon's . . . Ecclesiastes is the fine hammered steel of woe . . . "All is vanity."*: Jesus, as prefigured in Isaiah 53.3, is the *Man of sorrows*. The book of *Ecclesiastes* is attributed to King Solomon. *Steel*, hard yet flexible, can be hammered into a fine sword that will bend without breaking. The famous passage on *Vanity* is from Ecclesiastes 1.2.

10. *Cowper, Young, Pascal, Rousseau . . . sick men*: English poet William *Cowper* (pronounced cooper;1731–1800); Edward Young (1683–1765), who wrote the well-known *Night Thoughts*, a poem on death; French mathematician and philosopher of religion Blaise *Pascal* (1623–1662); and revolutionary political philosopher Jean-Jacques *Rousseau* (1712–1778), all exemplify a melancholy view of individual life or of humanity as a whole.

11. *Rabelais*: François *Rabelais* (1494–1553), priest, physician, and author of the comic, satiric, scatological *Gargantua and Pantagruel* (1532–34).

12. *"the man that wandereth . . . congregation of the dead."*: Exact quotation from Proverbs 21.16, another book attributed to Solomon.

Chapter 97. The Lamp.

1. *kings and counsellors*: Job 14; Melville used the phrase again in his 1853 tale "Bartleby, the Scrivener."

Chapter 98. Stowing Down and Clearing Up.

1. *Shadrach, Meshach, and Abednego*: Refusing to bow down to the golden idol of the Babylonian king, Nebuchadnezzar, these faithful Jews were thrown into a furnace but were miraculously untouched by the fire (Daniel 3). See also Making *Moby-Dick*.

2. *Oh! the metempsychosis! Oh! Pythagoras*: The sixth-century BCE Greek philosopher *Pythagoras* taught that the spirits of the dead pass into new bodies. Having ended the toils of one life, a soul or "ghost" moves on to the labors of another life in a new body. This transmigration of the soul (*metempsychosis*), taken humorously, accounts for the story of Ishmael's teaching a basic skill to the wise *Pythagoras*, reborn as an ignorant young sailor.

Chapter 99. The Doubloon.

1. *as they do hills about Boston*: From 1807 to 1835, Boston's steep Mount Vernon, Beacon Hill, and Pemberton Hill were leveled and their earth used for landfill to expand and connect the city's buildable landmasses.

2. *Pactolus*: In Greek myth, this river in western Turkey became laden with gold after King Midas washed in it to remove the unanticipated curse of his touch, the ability to turn anything to gold, from which comes the expression "Midas touch."

3. *doubloon of the Pequod*: In describing the coin, Melville omitted some of the symbols that appear on an actual Ecuadorian doubloon, and apparently misperceived others; editors of *Moby-Dick* have misidentified some of the symbols as well. An official decree of 1836 specifies the details of the eight escudo coin, also called a *doubloon*, issued in 1838: "on the obverse it will have . . . the zodiac or the ecliptic. . . . To the right will be the two principal mountains that make up the Pichincha mountain chain; on the first point the Guagua Pichincha on which will rest a condor [not a cock as in *Moby-Dick*] and on the second the Ruco Pichincha volcano [smoking, not flame-topped]. To the left of the shield will be engraved a cliff [not a mountain summit], on it a tower and on this will be placed another condor [not mentioned in the text] that will face the one that is on the peak to the right. The inscription will be REPUBLIC OF ECUADOR—QUITO, placed perpendicularly below the sun . . ." (trans. Stephen Grimsley). Not specified by the decree are the signs of the zodiac Melville describes, two on each side of the central, "keystone" sun. From left to right they are Leo, Virgo, Libra, and Scorpio.

4. *equinoctial point at Libra*: Astrologically, the autumnal equinox in the Northern Hemisphere occurs as the sun is entering the constellation *Libra*, the Scales.

5. *proud as Lucifer*: In Christian tradition the prideful Satan was named *Lucifer*, meaning "light bearer," before he led certain angels in rebellion against God and was cast out of heaven to rule in hell. "Proud as Lucifer" is proverbial.

6. *former equinox at Aries! From storm to storm!*: In astrology, the spring or vernal equinox occurs in the Northern Hemisphere when the sun is in the constellation *Aries*, the Ram. Ahab is subscribing to the popular belief (probably derived from sailors' experience of fall hurricanes in the West Indies) that severe storms in North America occur most frequently at the vernal and autumnal equinoxes.

7. *Belshazzar's awful writing*: During a banquet held by King Belshazzar of Babylon, a disembodied hand writes mysterious, awe-inducing words on a wall (see Ch. 119, note 4), which the prophet Daniel correctly interprets as predicting the prideful king's death and the downfall of his kingdom (Daniel 4).

8. *dark valley . . . vale of Death . . . sun of Righteousness*: Briefly sermonizing before losing hope in religious solace, the Quaker Starbuck, steeped in the Bible, echoes "the valley of the shadow of death" (Psalm 23), and quotes "Sun of righteousness" (Malachi 4.2).

9. *on Negro Hill or in Corlaer's Hook*: Like Boston's infamous *Negro Hill*, Corlear's Hook was a red-light district in New York City, frequented by sailors, and referred to early in Ch. 1.

10. *Golconda*: Ruined city near Hyderabad, India, famed for its diamonds; its name implies great wealth.

11. *signs and wonders*: Frequent biblical phrase pertaining to the actions of God in the Hebrew Bible, and those of Jesus and the apostles in the New Testament.

12. *Bowditch in his Epitome . . . Daboll's arithmetic*: Nathaniel *Bowditch* (1773–1838) wrote the *New American Practical Navigator, Being an Epitome of Navigation* (1802), which became the standard American navigational handbook; Nathan *Daboll's Complete Schoolmaster's Assistant* (1799) was for many years a common American arithmetic textbook.

13. *Massachusetts calendar*: An almanac containing a diagram entitled "the Man of the Signs," showing a man surrounded by the signs of the zodiac (see Feidelson, *Moby-Dick*, 553).

14. *Leo, a roaring Lion*: For Leo, Stubb quotes part of the familiar biblical phrase, "your adversary the devil, as a roaring lion, walketh about, seeking whom he may devour" (1 Peter 5.8).

15. *toil and trouble*: From the refrain in the witches' spell in *Macbeth* 4.1. According to his sister, Helen, Melville as a teenager playfully quoted from this scene (Parker, *Herman Melville* 1, 363).

16. *nine hundred and sixty cigars*: Since 16 dollars will buy only eight-hundred cigars at 2 cents each, either Flask is egregiously bad at arithmetic or he is assuming a quantity price of twelve cigars for 20 cents on a Spanish American dollar (as noted in the NN edition).

17. *Manxman—the old hearse-driver*: In sailor folklore a *Manxman* (a native of the Isle of Man) is a soothsayer, particularly a predictor of doom and gloom as is the one on the *Pequod*, introduced in Ch. 40.

18. *Surgeon's Astronomy in the back country*: Stubb presumes Queequeg's ignorance, comparing it to the old belief still current today that surgery should be performed in accordance with astrological influences on parts of the body.

19. *tail coiled . . . oakum in the toes of his pumps as usual*: As in Ch. 73 (see note 2), Stubb presumes that Fedallah has cloven hooves and a tail, physical attributes of the devil.

20. *fire worshipper*: Melville cites Hawthorne's genial sketch "Fire-Worship," in his review essay "Hawthorne and his Mosses."

21. *Murray's Grammar!*: Lindley Murray (1745–1826) wrote *English Grammar* (1795), widely used in England and the United States.

22. *I'm a crow*: Acutely conscious of his blackness and small size, Pip may be expressing his sense of inferiority by alluding to the minstrel show stereotype called Jim Crow.

23. *But, unscrew your navel, and what's the consequence?*: Though the doubloon is central to the ship's symbolism, analogous to other metaphorical "navels" such as the Kaaba in Mecca for Islam, and the Omphalos of early Greek religion in Delphi, Melville is alluding to a very old joke: unscrew your navel and your buttocks fall off.

24. *nailed to the mast . . . things grow desperate*: In naval battle under *desperate* conditions, the colors (flag) were sometimes nailed to the mast so no one aboard could lower them in surrender. Compare Ahab's order to nail a replacement flag to the mast of the *Pequod* in Ch. 135.

25. *blackberrying . . . Jenny! and get your hoe-cake done!"*: Feidelson (557) suggests that this may be Pip's variant of "blackbirding," kidnapping black people into slavery. A blackface minstrel song with African roots, "Jenny Get Your Hoe Cake Done" was popularized by Joel Walker Sweeney and sung by him in New York City in 1840. See also *Making Moby-Dick*.

Chapter 100. Leg and Arm.

1. *his solitary thigh*: In Ch. 50, Flask believes, but Stubb doubts, that Ahab still has both knees; here, Ahab has indeed lost most of his leg, though in Ch. 108 the carpenter, fashioning a new prosthesis, says it is simply a shinbone.

2. *could only trim dish, by sitting all their sterns on the outer gunwale*: In nautical slang, *trim dish* means balance the boat. The whale, swimming in tight circles, makes the whaleboat tip dangerously to one side. The men sit on the edge (*gunwale*) of the opposite side to try to level it and reduce the danger of capsizing.

3. *like a Lima tower*: Allusion to the 1746 and 1828 earthquakes in Lima, Peru, also referred to in Ch. 42.

4. *hydrophobia*: A morbid fear of water and a term for rabies, the victims of which abhor water because drinking is painful. According to Captain Boomer, his friend Bunger is hydrophobic because he drinks only alcohol.

5. *impossible for him to completely digest even a man's arm?*: Although the sperm whale cannot digest bone, it has swallowed people whole.

Chapter 101. The Decanter.

1. *named after the late Samuel Enderby . . . Enderby & Sons*: This and the next two paragraphs actually refer to two different Samuel Enderbies. The "original Samuel" founded the firm and died in 1797; his son, Samuel Jr., who inherited the firm, died in 1829. This passage about the Enderby accomplishments very closely follows Beale. See Mansfield and Vincent (807), and Making *Moby-Dick*.

2. *united royal houses of the Tudors and Bourbons*: Ishmael imagines the combined stature of royal families of England and France. The *Tudor* line ended with the death of Queen Elizabeth I in 1603, but the *Bourbons* held power until Louis XVI was overthrown in 1792, and then sporadically in the nineteenth century.

3. *the Rattler made a rattling voyage of it*: Melville's information is from Beale, who says nothing of the *Rattler*'s accomplishments; rather, it was the preceding *Amelia* that had made a *rattling* (remarkably good) voyage. Melville's comment, then, seems made for the sake of its appealing word-play. The *Syren*, sailing two days after Melville's birth, was even more successful than the *Rattler* (whose captain was James Colnett, castigated in Ch. 55 for publishing one of the "monstrous pictures of whales").

4. *did some service*: According to Parker, a possible echo of *Othello* 5.2.339, "I have done the state some service."

5. *Japanese Whaling Ground*: The historically famous "Japan Ground," where only sperm whales were hunted—by up to one-hundred vessels per year in the 1840s. Generally speaking, it covered the area from 25 to 40 degrees north latitude, and 125 to 150 degrees east longitude. See Heflin.

6. *reef topsails . . . top-heavy*: A vessel with too many sails aloft for the weather conditions is *top-heavy*, a pun appropriate for the condition of the drunken sailors.

7. *anti-scorbutic*: Something that prevents scurvy, a vitamin C deficiency. The crippling disease, caused by eating only preserved foods, is treated by adding citrus juice and fresh, leafy greens to the diet. The worms or weevils in the old, barreled bread would, humorously, not be a very effective *anti-scorbutic*, though they would indeed be "fresh fare."

8. *Zealanders*: Zeeland, once a separate country, is a province of the Netherlands.

9. *ancient Dutch volume*: According to Mansfield and Vincent, the following passage parodies the pedantic Scoresby (807).

10. *Fitz Swackhammer . . . Dr. Snodhead . . . Low Dutch and High German*: The first name is impossible in Dutch, but humorously descriptive of what a cooper does with his hammer; *Snodhead* is another mocking name for Scoresby (see Vincent 345–46). *Dutch* was and is a frequent English rendering of "Deutsch" (German). Plattdeutsch (Low German) is a dialect, while the standard language is Hochdeutsch (High German).

11. *Low Dutch*: Seemingly redundant here, since it means from the Netherlands (literally, lowlands), home of the Dutch; but it was common usage: until the end of the nineteenth century "High Dutch" (from "Deutsch," German for the German language and people) was an English term for Germans living in the higher elevations of Germany, while Germanic peoples of the low-lying seacoast, including Flanders and Holland, were distinguished as "Low Dutch."

12. *Greenland and Spitzbergen whale fishery*: Beginning in the seventeenth century, several countries hunted Right and Bowhead whales in far northern waters between Europe and *Greenland*. *Spitzbergen* is a Norwegian island in the Arctic Ocean.

Chapter 102. A Bower in the Arsacides.

1. *Arsacides*: Part of the Solomon Islands, near the Philippines. Inhabitants of the Solomons resisted European incursion so fiercely that in 1769 the French navigator Jean François de Surville named the islands "Terre des Arsacides" ("land of the assassins") after an ancient dynasty in the Near East. Ishmael's non-eurocentric depiction of life on "Tranque" (actually the name of a little-known Chilean island) contradicts that reputation.

2. *breaking the seal*: Of a letter sealed with wax, revealing something previously secret, as with the book having "seven seals" in Revelation 5.

3. *when attached to the trading-ship Dey of Algiers*: Because the *Dey* (ruler) protected piracy, thus supporting the kidnapping and enslavement of sailors, the vessel's name is unlikely in reality but may point ironically to contemporary American slavery and the repression of seamen, about which Melville had written in *Redburn* and *White-Jacket*. He himself had shipped on one merchant vessel, the *St. Lawrence*, in 1839.

4. *the hair-hung sword that so affrighted Damocles*: In his *Tusculan Disputations*, the Roman orator and writer Marcus Tullius Cicero (106–43 BCE) tells of the tyrant Dionysius the Elder of Syracuse, Italy, who teaches his courtier *Damocles* a lesson about the precariousness of life for those in power, by seating him at a banquet under a sword hanging by a single thread.

5. *Icy Glen*: Not far from Melville's home, "Arrowhead," near Pittsfield, MA, this cold, mossy grotto near Stockbridge was on the itinerary of a social occasion at which Melville met Hawthorne on August 5, 1850. It is also mentioned in *Pierre*.

6. *ball of Arsacidean twine*: Third use of the myth of the Cretan Labyrinth, previously found in Chs. 4 and 85.

7. *Leviathanic Museum . . . in Hull . . . Manchester . . . Burton Constable . . . skeleton of a Sperm Whale*: According to Mansfield and Vincent (808–809), Melville drew on Beale for most of the British information on whale skeletons. The skeleton in *Manchester*, also mentioned by Thoreau, has disappeared. *Burton Constable* is an aristocratic house located at *Hull*, but Sir Clifford's plans are Melville's playful invention, suggesting the practices of New York showman P. T. Barnum. See also Making *Moby-Dick*.

Chapter 103. Measurement of the Whale's Skeleton.

1. *Pompey's Pillar*: Ancient granite column near Alexandria, Egypt.

Chapter 104. The Fossil Whale.

1. *imperial folio*: The largest of books, the *folio* is made of single sheets of paper (typically 17 x 22 inches) folded once. Larger folios, such as the *imperial* and "Elephant," derive from even larger sheets of paper.

2. *quarto edition of Johnson*: The large-format *quarto* edition of Johnson's *Dictionary of the English Language* (1755) and the lexicographer's legendary portliness are both wittily appropriate for research using the "weightiest" words on the enormous whale. A quarto is one of several book sizes based on the number of times a large single sheet of paper is folded to make pages: it consists of sheets folded twice to give pages one-fourth the size of single sheets. Although smaller than the single-fold folio book, the quarto is still larger than the standard octavo. Johnson's dictionary was originally published in folio format (1755), but appeared in quarto editions as early as 1808. Johnson also appears in Chs. 53 and 69; see also Making *Moby-Dick*.

3. *Vesuvius' crater*: Images of the famous volcano with its huge crater, looming above Naples, were frequently published well before and throughout Melville's day. According to Dennis Berthold, Vesuvius (which had recently erupted but was dormant by 1850)

was a metaphor of revolution as well as of size. As such, combined with the preceding South American "condor's quill," it signals Melville's attention to worldwide revolutionary explosiveness, repeatedly evoked elsewhere in *Moby-Dick*. (See, for example, Ch. 24, note 8; Ch. 54, note 26, and Ch. 96, note 4.)

4. *written on the flea, though many there be who have tried it*: Perhaps a reference to Robert Southey's novel *The Doctor* (1834–47), which gives twenty-three pages to discussing the flea (Mansfield and Vincent 810).

5. *a great digger of ditches, canals . . . of all sorts*: In 1839, after some study of engineering and surveying, Melville applied for employment on the Erie Canal improvement project. Despite support from a well-placed uncle, he failed, and instead went to sea for the first time, on a merchant vessel.

6. *Tertiary formations . . . superficial formations*: The first term refers to the evidence of geological strata formed about 26 to 66 million years ago; the *superficial formations* were then also called Quaternary. This chapter shows Melville's familiarity with geologic time, in terms used both in the *Penny Cyclopedia* article "Whales" and Robert Chambers' *Vestiges of the Natural History of Creation* (1846), though he employs biblical time when useful, as in "pre-Adamite" in the following paragraph, "Adam's time" in Ch. 105, and the supposed date of the Flood in "Epilogue."

7. *the Rue Dauphiné . . . Tuileries*: The royal palace called the *Tuilleries* (destroyed in 1871) was far from the Rue Dauphine (no accent mark), across the Seine. Melville is referring to the Rue du Dauphin, but may have confused the name with the *Dauphiné* region of the French Alps.

8. *Detached broken fossils . . . unknown Leviathanic species*: With the exception of Napoleon and the Tuilleries, all the details in this paragraph are mentioned in the *Penny Cyclopedia* article "Whales," Melville's apparent source here, in the following paragraph, and in Ch. 105.

9. *Judge Creagh, in Alabama . . . fallen angels . . . Basilosaurus . . . Owen, the English Anatomist . . . Zeuglodon . . . of existence*: Melville's generally correct description is laced with minor inaccuracies. As early as the 1830s, plantation owners in Mississippi, Alabama, and Louisiana had unearthed fossil remains of what one Judge Jonathan *Creagh* took to be a sea monster. In 1835 (not 1842) Creagh sent the relics to Richard Harlan in Philadelphia, who mistakenly identified the "monster" as a prehistoric reptile, naming it *Basilosaurus* (regal lizard). Four years later, the eminent English paleontologist Sir Richard *Owen* (1804–1892) determined that Basilosaurus was actually a mammalian relative of the whale, which he christened *Zeuglodon* (a term no longer applied). Creagh's further discovery in 1842 of an almost complete set of fossilized remains fully substantiated the identity of the prehistoric whale. Soon after, amateur paleontologist and showman Albert Koch (discoverer of the mastodon called Missourium) displayed full skeletons throughout the United States and Europe. Melville may have seen his exhibits in Albany or New York City, or read an 1845 review of the spectacle in the New York *Evangelist* (the journal that later attacked *Typee*) proclaiming: "Perhaps when we touch his ribs, we are touching the residuum of some of Cain's descendants that perished in the Deluge" (as quoted in Zimmer). Perhaps it is this absurd speculation of urban religionists that Melville, in his rendition, converts into the naïve wonderment of plantation slaves who think they have seen the remnants of *fallen angels*. See also Mansfield and Vincent (810); Vincent (346).

10. *Saturn's grey chaos*: *Saturn* is the Roman equivalent of the Greek god, Kronos, and was also associated with Chronos (Time). He was one of the Titans, who preceded the Olympian gods. Astrologically, the planet Saturn is associated with ashy colors.

11. *Methuselah . . . Shem*: Grandson of Cain, *Methuselah* lived to be 969; *Shem* was Noah's first son (Genesis 5.27; 5.32).

12. *stereotype plates of nature . . . limestone and marl*: Ishmael compares the geological strata containing fossils that one finds in nature to the stereotyping process of printing in which a solid plate is created from a molded imprint of pages set in movable type; *marl* is a crumbly, earthy material heavy in calcium. Melville's *Penny Cyclopedia* source refers to "marly limestone."

13. *the great temple of Denderah*: A first-century BCE temple at Tentyra, near Dendera, Egypt, whose interior is drawn and discussed at length by the French scholar Vivant Denon in *Travels in Upper and Lower Egypt* (English trans. 1803; see Mansfield and Vincent 810–11). Melville echoes Denon in "great temple," "ceiling," and "plani-sphere." Contrary to Ishmael's belief expressed later in the paragraph, the temple postdates Solomon.

14. *John Leo, the old Barbary traveller*: Sixteenth-century Arab commercial and diplomatic *traveller* captured and renamed by Christians, whose *Description of Africa* (1550; English trans., 1600) was long valued in Europe for its account of the Islamic world. Melville's quotation is from Harris, cited in "Extracts" and in Chs. 55, 56, and 83.

15. *a Prophet . . . Mahomet*: The first is unidentified; the second is the Prophet Muhammad, founder of Islam (ca. 570–632 CE).

Chapter 105. Does the Whale's Magnitude Diminish?—Will He Perish?

1. *bulk of his sires*: Scoresby and Wilkes had both considered whether the size of whales and their numbers had diminished over time. See Mansfield and Vincent 811.

2. *Pliny . . . Aldrovandus*: *Pliny* is the Roman naturalist mentioned in Chs. 32 and 56; Ulise Aldrovandi, sixteenth-century Italian naturalist and physician.

3. *Rope Walks and Thames Tunnels of Whales!*: Rope was manufactured in buildings called *rope-walks*, which could be 1,000 feet long or more. Opened in 1843 and visited by Melville six years later, the 1,200-foot-long, high-arched London tunnel under the Thames River also provides Ahab with a model for the chest of his "complete man" in Ch. 108.

4. *Banks and Solander, Cook's naturalists*: On his first voyage around the world (1768–1771), Captain James *Cook*, the greatest explorer of the eighteenth century, was accompanied by naturalists Joseph *Banks* (later Sir Joseph, and president of the Royal Society), and Daniel Charles *Solander*.

5. *A Danish member of the Academy of Sciences*: Uno von Troil, Archbishop of Upsala, Sweden, wrote *Letters on Iceland* (1780), cited in "Extracts," but was not a Dane.

6. *Lacépède, . . . elaborate history of whales . . . 1825*: Melville repeats his error of Ch. 55, confusing the death date of Etienne de Lacépède (1756–1825) with the 1804 publication date of his *Histoire Naturelle des Cétacées*. His source for Lacépède's words is Scoresby (Mansfield and Vincent 811–12).

7. *Smithfield . . . Pharaoh's fat kine*: Melville visited London's *Smithfield* cattle market in 1849 (NN *Journals* 15). For *Pharaoh's* cattle, see Genesis 41.

8. *the census of men now in London*: London's 1851 population was about 2.3 million, making the city the Western hemisphere's greatest metropolis.

9. *driven from promontory to cape*: Geographical play on "driven from pillar to post," that is, forced from one predicament to another.

10. *Horto, the historian of Goa*: Sir Thomas Browne's *Pseudodoxia Epidemica* cites this report by Garcias ab *Horto*, latinized name of Garcia de Orta, sixteenth-century Portuguese physician and pharmacologist in Goa, India.

11. *by Semiramis, by Porus, by Hannibal*: In Assyrian legend, Queen *Semiramis* founded Babylon and Nineveh; the powerful Indian ruler *Porus* is mentioned in Ch. 87; and Carthaginian general *Hannibal* (ca. 247–183 BCE) most famously took elephants across the Alps to battle the Roman Empire.

12. *New Holland*: Early name for Australia, discovered by Dutch seamen.

Chapter 106. Ahab's Leg.

1. *sad birth-mark in the brow of man*: Suggesting the "mark of Cain" (Genesis 4.15).

2. *Grand-Lama-like exclusiveness*: Like the isolation of the Dalai Lama of Tibet, who was at that time both cloistered and an absolute ruler.

3. *bruited reason . . . appeared by no means adequate*: In Ch. 16 Peleg makes it widely known that Ahab's moody isolation is due to grief for the loss of his leg.

4. *synod in the air, or . . . princes and potentates of fire*: The powers in heaven or in hell; a *synod* is a church council.

Chapter 107. The Carpenter.

1. *sprung spars . . . bull's eyes . . . tree-nails*: *Sprung spars* have been strained enough to injure the wood fibers; *bull's eyes* are thick pieces of glass, embedded in the deck to allow light below, or strong wooden fittings through which a rope may pass; *tree-nails* (pronounced trunnels) are long wooden pegs used to fasten the ship's planking to its timber skeleton.

2. *automaton*: A machine that appears to move on its own. The most widely-known *automaton* in Melville's day was the chess-playing contraption known as "The Turk," created in 1769 by Baron Wolfgang von Kempelen of Hungary. Purchased by Johann Maelzel, who toured the U.S. with it during the 1820s and 1830s, it concealed a person, and was exposed as a fraud by Edgar Allan Poe in his essay "Maelzel's Chess-Player" (1836). Nevertheless, it attracted crowds until its demise in a Philadelphia fire in 1854. Melville also incorporated an automaton in the deadly clock mechanism featured in his 1856 story "The Bell-Tower."

Chapter 108. Ahab and the Carpenter.

1. *while Prometheus is about it, I'll order a complete man*: In Greek myth, *Prometheus* created humankind out of clay. During his 1849–50 visit to England, Melville purchased a copy of Mary Shelley's *Frankenstein*, subtitled *The Modern Prometheus*; he probably read it on the voyage home or with family members upon his return, around the time that he was composing *Moby-Dick*. While the Promethean blacksmith makes his new leg, Ahab calls for specialized body parts in his *order* for a *complete man* in a speech echoing Shelley's novel, in which an alienated student animates a man created from body parts taken from corpses.

2. *sky-light . . . to illuminate inwards*: Perhaps an allusion to *Paradise Lost*, Book 3: "So much the rather thou, celestial Light, / Shine inward and the mind and all her powers / Irradiate. There plant eyes."

3. *Carpenter?*: Ahab seems to be thinking of Jesus.

4. *we leave clay to ditchers . . . The fellow's impious!*: Since God made man out of clay, or "dust of the earth" (Genesis 2.7), the *impious* implication of the Carpenter's remark is that God is a ditch digger.

5. *Prætorians*: Elite Roman imperial guard so powerful that it often chose the emperor, and once even put the emperorship up for auction. Ahab (or Melville) confuses them with the wealthy bidders.

6. *the resurrection fellow*: A reference to the Last Judgment or Apocalypse, when the good are resurrected into eternal life. The *fellow* may be either "the Son of man" (Jesus) who "shall send his angels with a great sound of a trumpet" (Matthew 24.30–31) or the archangel Gabriel who, in Judeo-Christian tradition (though not in the Bible) will announce the *resurrection* of the dead: "for the trumpet shall sound, and the dead shall be raised incorruptible, and we shall be changed" (1 Corinthians 15.52). Earlier references in *Moby-Dick* to the Last Judgment are: "did'st thou not think of Death and the Judgment then?" (Ch. 18); "Tell 'em it's the resurrection; they must . . . come to judgment" (Ch. 40); "Had the trump of judgment blown, they could not have quivered more" (Ch. 51); "it will be more tolerable for that provident Fejee, I say, in the day of judgment, than for thee" (Ch. 65); "It smells like the left wing of the day of judgment" (Ch. 96); "Daggoo roused the sleepers with . . . judgment claps" (Ch. 133). In addition, Ishmael refers to the angel Gabriel in Ch. 1 and again with the prophet-sailor Gabriel in Ch. 71. See also *Making Moby-Dick*.

7. *taking altitudes on it*: Ahab inscribes quadrant measurements (of the apparent height of the sun above the horizon) on a smoothed portion of his whalebone leg (see Ch. 34, note 1) as he does in Ch. 118.

Chapter 109. Ahab and Starbuck in the Cabin.

1. *Formosa and the Bashee Isles . . . one of the tropical outlets from the China waters into the Pacific*: Once called *Formosa*, Taiwan lies across the 50-mile wide Bashi Channel, connecting the China Sea to the Pacific, from the Bashi (Batan) Islands of the northern Philippines.

2. *Niphon, Matsmai, and Sikoke*: *Niphon* is an early English name (from Japanese Nihon) for Honshu, Japan's largest island; *Matsmai* is the old name for Hokkaido, the northernmost island; Shikoku is the smallest of Japan's four main islands.

3. *Lord over the earth*: Echoing "Lord of all the earth" (Joshua 3.11, Zechariah 6.5).

Chapter 110. Queequeg in his Coffin.

1. *corner-stone cask . . . coins . . . placards . . . flood*: Facetiously alluding to the practice of placing a time capsule in a building's masonry, here containing a facetious poster announcing Noah's *flood*.

2. *Zoroaster*: Persian founder of the Zoroastrian, or Parsi, religion, who lived ca. 628–551 BCE.

3. *Chaldee or Greek*: Chaldean (Babylonian) astronomers and astrologers were revered as wise men, being called on, for example, by King Nebuchadnezzar (Daniel 2.5); similarly, ancient Greek philosophers, in particular Socrates, were acclaimed for their wisdom.

4. *He called one to him in the grey morning watch*: The oddly mysterious, biblical-sounding *one* (presumably meaning Ishmael) echoes "Then said one unto him" (Luke 17.23); the sentence also evokes such biblical phrasings as "And he called them unto him" (Mark 3.23), or "Jesus called them unto him" (Luke 18.16). More specifically, "in the morning watch" occurs three times in the Bible (Exodus 14.24, 1 Samuel 11.11, Judith [Apocrypha] 12.5).

5. *Lackaday islands*: The Laccadive Islands, now called Lakshadweep, in the Arabian Sea off southern India. Ishmael is playing on *lackaday*, an archaic expression of regret or dismay, or, perhaps, "lackadaisical," meaning without energy.

6. *treatise on the art of attaining truth*: Ishmael's phrasing echoes Melville's essay "Hawthorne and His Mosses," with its discussion of "the great Art of Telling the Truth."

Chapter 111. The Pacific.

1. *fabled undulations of the Ephesian sod over the buried Evangelist St. John*: Bayle, Hawthorne, and Southey all report a fable told by St. Augustine, about Ephesus, a Greek city in Turkey, where the ground moved over the grave of *St. John the Evangelist* because, though buried, he was not dead. See Mansfield and Vincent 814–15.

2. *Potters' Fields*: Public burial grounds for paupers, unknown persons, and criminals. As told in Matthew 27.5–7, the original such field, owned by a potter, was bought for that purpose by the Jewish chief priests with the thirty pieces of silver Judas returned to them after repenting his betrayal of Jesus. See also Making *Moby-Dick*.

3. *Magian*: Profoundly spiritual; from Magi, wise men of ancient Persia, one of whom may have been Zoroaster (see Ch. 110, note 2). Compare "child-magian" (Ch. 79, note 24).

4. *Abraham*: The first Jewish patriarch (Genesis 11–50), with whose life the Judeo-Christian era begins.

5. *impenetrable Japans*: By its own laws, Japan was closed to virtually all foreigners until U.S. Commodore Matthew Perry forced a limited opening in 1854.

6. *Pan*: Greek god normally associated with fertility, but here also related to the oneness of God and nature, coincidentally called pantheism. (see Ch. 35, note 16).

Chapter 112. The Blacksmith.

1. *Bottle Conjuror!*: Refers to the 1749 London fraud of that name in which a performer promised to disappear into a bottle, but tricked the credulous theater audience by disappearing with their fees and the contents of the checkroom. Here, Ishmael adapts the popular image to his story of the "temperance" (anti-drinking) genre by connecting the *Bottle Conjuror* to alcohol.

Chapter 113. The Forge.

1. *Mother Carey's chickens*: These storm petrels, swallow-sized sea birds that often follow ships, feed where the sea is rough, leading to the belief that they bring bad weather.

2. *I, too, want a harpoon made*: Scoresby is the source for the making of the harpoon shaft (Vincent 373).

3. *lucifers . . . That Parsee smells fire like a fusee; and smells of it himself*: Friction matches, and also a name for the angel of light who became Satan. To Stubb, Perth, Ahab and Fedallah are *lucifers* in that they are associated with light and fire; the latter two characters seem ready, in fact, to ignite. The *Parsee*, Fedallah, previously identified by Stubb as the devil, appropriately *smells of* gunpowder, which is made with hell-associated sulfur; he *smells* [sniffs out] *fire* like a human fuse, in that a fuse seems to seek an encounter with fire.

4. *Icy Sea*: Body of water on Russia's western Arctic coast.

5. *"Ego non baptizo te in nomine patris, sed in nomine diaboli!"*: "I baptize you not in the name of the father but in the name of the devil" (Latin). Melville found this blasphemous invocation quoted in an 1823 review essay on witchcraft, titled "Superstition and Knowledge" (see Sanborn, "Name of the Devil"). In his June 29, 1851 letter to Hawthorne, Melville called it his "book's motto (the secret one)."

Chapter 114. The Gilder.

1. *infancy's unconscious spell . . . mankind's pondering repose of If*: In its structure the passage (like Stubb's comical zodiac speech in Ch. 99) is modeled on Jaques's "seven ages" of life speech in Shakespeare's *As You Like It* 2.7, and also echoes a speech by Touchstone from the same play, ending, "your If is the only peace-maker; much virtue in it" (5.4). For

the philosophical If, compare Plinlimmon's pamphlet in *Pierre*, Book 14, part 3. See Wendel; see also Making *Moby-Dick*.

Chapter 115. The Pequod Meets the Bachelor.

1. *Bastile*: The Bastille, a prison in Paris and symbol of repressive monarchy, was captured by a mob in 1789 during the French Revolution and later demolished.

2. *Nantucket soundings*: Samplings from the sea bottom near Nantucket Island, Ahab's home.

Chapter 116. The Dying Whale.

1. *turning sunwards of the head*: Melville affirms this belief of whalemen, though he had read Beale's doubts of the phenomenon. See Mansfield and Vincent 818.

2. *the Niger's unknown source*: European explorers had long tried to find the source of the Niger River, the most important in western Africa, and had succeeded in locating it in northern Cameroon in 1822, when Melville was 3 years old.

3. *dark Hindoo half of nature*: Called a "queen" later in the speech, this darker half in Ahab's personality alludes to female Hindu deities such as Kali and Durga, known as destroyers. Later, in Ch. 119, Ahab once again invokes his "queenly personality" in his address to fire where he also defines himself as darkness.

Chapter 117. The Whale Watch.

1. *Asphaltites . . . Gomorrah*: The Romanized Jewish historian Flavius Josephus (Joseph Ben Matthias, ca. 37–100 CE) used the Latin name *Asphaltites* for the Dead Sea, the traditional location of the biblical cities of Sodom and *Gomorrah*, destroyed by God for their wickedness. Sir Thomas Browne repeated the Latin word in *Pseudodoxia Epidemica*, where Melville likely saw it.

Chapter 118. The Quadrant.

1. *season for the Line*: In Ch. 44, "the Pequod had sailed from Nantucket [at Christmas] at the very beginning of the Season-on-the-Line," whaleman's jargon for the best time to hunt sperm whales in the Pacific along the equator (usually from November or December to April). The expression appears capitalized and hyphenated throughout *Moby-Dick*, but here the variant phrasing *season for the Line* may simply mean "the time for hunting whales near the equator was approaching."

2. *spokes*: As in Ch. 61, a wheel replaces the *Pequod*'s whalebone tiller.

3. *quadrant*: "A reflecting instrument used to [measure] the altitude above the horizon of the sun, moon, or stars at sea, and thereby to determine the latitude and longitude [of a ship's position]" (Smyth).

4. *dead-reckoning, by log and by line*: "Dead," here, is a corruption of the abbreviation "ded.," meaning "deduced"; thus, *dead-reckoning* is a deduction of a ship's approximate position relative to its previous position, achieved by multiplying speed by time elapsed to give distance covered, by observing the compass courses steered, and by estimating the effects of drift and currents on the intended course. Speed is measured by the "log line," a marked rope with a piece of wood at the end that is thrown overboard. The line unreels for a set time, and the length unreeled by then indicates the speed. It is described and used in Ch. 125.

5. *the three Horatii*: Legendary Roman triplets who fought another set of triplets, the Curiatii from Alba Longa, to decide a conflict between the cities. Although two of the *Horatii* died, the survivor was victorious. (They have sometimes been confused with Horatius Cocles who, aided by two other Romans, successfully defended a bridge over the

Tiber.) The three are depicted in a famous painting of 1784, "The Oath of the Horatii," by Jacques-Louis David.

Chapter 119. The Candles.

1. *Oh! jolly is the gale . . .*: Song probably written by Melville.

2. *the doxology*: The word means a hymn of praise to God, but had become associated with a specific one, the paraphrase of Psalm 100 in the New England standard, *Hymns and Spiritual Songs* by Isaac Watts (1707), beginning, "All people that on earth do dwell." In Ch. 22 Aunt Charity gives a copy of Watts to each member of the crew.

3. *corpusants!*: Sometimes called St. Elmo's Fire and usually spelled "corposants" (from *corpo santo*, Portuguese and Spanish for "Holy Body"), these balls of static electricity, described in Dana and witnessed by Melville in 1849, were objects of superstition among sailors.

4. *"Mene, Mene, Tekel, Upharsin"*: These mysterious words, written on a wall by a spirit hand during King Belshazzar's feast, are interpreted by the prophet Daniel as predicting the king's downfall (Daniel 5.25–28). Starbuck alludes to "Belshazzar's awful writing" (see Ch. 99, note 7).

5. *skeletons in Herculaneum*: Remains of people buried in this Roman city near Pompeii, caught by falling ash while fleeing during the eruption of Mt. Vesuvius in 79 CE.

6. *I as Persian once did worship . . . I bear the scar*: Ahab projects an earlier life as a Zoroastrian, who in worshiping the principle of light was burned. Compare Ch. 42, "by the Persian fire worshippers, the white forked flame being held the holiest on the altar"; and for *scar*, compare the white mark on Ahab's body described in Ch. 28.

7. *queenly personality*: Compare the "queen" who is the "dark Hindoo half of nature" (see Ch. 116, note 4), and Ahab's defining himself as darkness in the two following paragraphs.

8. *fiery dart*: Pommer finds an echo here of *Paradise Lost* 12.491–92, where Adam is promised "spiritual armor, able to resist / Satan's assaults, and quench his fiery darts." See also "the fiery darts of the wicked" (Ephesians 6.16).

9. *lone, gigantic elm*: The image recalls the description in Ch. 28 of Ahab as a "great tree" that attracts lightning and is "branded" by it.

Chapter 120. The Deck Towards the End of the First Night Watch.

1. *send down the main-top-sail yard . . . band . . . is half-stranded . . . strike it*: Starbuck advises lowering (striking) the *main-top-sail yard*, a heavy spar, which is in danger of falling (and doing much damage) because the unraveling lee-lift (the rope leading from the mast to an iron *band* around the yardarm, supporting its weight) may let go. Making things worse, the band itself may break loose.

2. *take medicine!"*: Recalling *King Lear* 3.4.33, "take physic, pomp."

Chapter 122. Midnight Aloft—Thunder and Lightning.

1. *Tashtego passing new lashings around it*: Tashtego is executing Ahab's order in Ch. 120, lashing the main-top-sail-yard to the mast to prevent its falling.

Chapter 123. The Musket.

1. *shivered remnants of the jib and fore and main-top-sails were cut adrift from the spars*: Though the fore-top-sail and main-top-sail are fastened ("bent") to spars, as the passage implies, the sail called a jib is instead bent to a rope, the jib-stay, not mentioned. As the storm abates, the sailors cut the fastenings still holding the remnants of these three sails to their stay and spars, respectively.

2. *"Ho! the fair wind! oh-he-yo, cheerly, men!"*: Cheerly, men and the preceding nonsense

syllables are from the chorus of a British-American sea shanty (also "chantey") or work song known by that name; it is mentioned by Dana and also in *Omoo* and *Redburn*. "*Ho! the fair wind!*" may be from another shanty; it refers to the fact that the men are squaring the yards to sail with a *fair wind* rather than battling the typhoon. See also Making *Moby-Dick*.

3. *if*: Compare the "pondering repose of If" near the end of Ch. 114 (see note 1).

4. *Starbuck seemed wrestling with an angel*: In Genesis 32.24–32, Jacob wrestles all night with a "man" (*Ish* in Hebrew) traditionally understood to be an *angel*, though by the end of the passage Jacob appears to believe that he has wrestled with the Divine, saying, "I have seen God face to face." Jacob's wrestling is richly interpretable and variously interpreted; it appears in *Moby-Dick* and other works by Melville. For instance, both Jacob and Ahab (who wrestles with his concept of divinity) have a wounded leg, and the image of Jacob and the angel is central to Melville's late poem "Art." But in the comparison of Starbuck to Jacob, we find the common dilemma of a man struggling with his own nature.

Chapter 124. The Needle.

1. "*. . . a tandem, I drive the sea!*": Ahab imagines the *Pequod* as "the sea-chariot of the sun," analogous to the sun's sky chariot driven by Apollo in Greek myth. The vessel's wave-horses are hitched "in tandem," one behind the other.

2. *marvelled at, that such things should be*: In the New Testament and Apocrypha, *marveled at* is a repeated locution, while the latter phrase echoes "such things must needs be" (Mark 13.7).

3. *Ahab can make one of his own*: Melville adapted this magnetizing procedure from Scoresby. See Mansfield and Vincent 823–24.

Chapter 125. The Log and Line.

1. *the other way, it's good . . . once independent Man*: That is, whether an island or the world of man, the name is symbolically apt. *Man* was never an independent country, but always a dependency or possession of Norway, Scotland or England.

Chapter 126. The Life-Buoy.

1. *sideways impelled by unvarying trade winds*: In the Pacific, the northern trade winds, beginning at about 30° north latitude, blow toward the equator from the northeast. The *Pequod*, steering a southeasterly course from Japan toward the equator, is being blown to the west of its intended course.

2. *startled by a cry so plaintively wild and unearthly*: Mansfield and Vincent (824) trace the incident described in this paragraph to Colnett.

3. *Herod's murdered Innocents*: All male children born in Bethlehem at about the same time as Jesus were ordered slain by King Herod of Judea, who was trying to kill the prophesied "king of the Jews" (Matthew 2.1–16).

4. *the carved Roman slave*: The most likely referent is the "Dying Gaul" (commonly known as the "Dying Gladiator"), a marble statue of an intently gazing man in a reclining position, at the Capitoline Museum, Rome, a close facsimile of which is P. Scheemakers's "Dying Gladiator" (c. 1740), at Rousham House, Oxfordshire. Another is the differently-posed 1779 statuette by Pierre Julien at the Louvre. The popular "Dying Gladiator" image, used by Byron in *Don Juan* (1821) and by Wordsworth in "Love Lies Bleeding" (1845), is mentioned in both *Mardi* and *White-Jacket*. According to Dennis Marnon (Houghton Library), Melville's first granddaughter, Eleanor Melville Metcalf, in the margins of these books, noted that her grandfather had owned a terra-cotta replica of the "Dying Gladiator."

5. *falling phantom . . . in the blue of the sea*: Compare Ishmael's imagined fall from the masthead at the end of Ch. 35.

6. *what an affection all old women have for tinkers*: Alluding to a bawdy song tradition in which *tinkers*, itinerant menders of pots and pans, irresistibly attract women.

7. *no caps at sea but snow-caps*: Thinking of the old women ashore supposedly wanting to seduce him, the carpenter alludes to an expression for such pursuit, "set their caps for him," while consoling himself that the only *caps* at sea are the whitecaps of the waves. Compare the Maltese Sailor's bawdy speech in Ch. 40.

8. *Turk's-headed life-lines*: Ropes ending in ornamental knots resembling turbans.

Chapter 127. The Deck.

1. *the grave-digger in the play sings, spade in hand*: In *Hamlet*, 5.1.

2. *Look at thy bosom!*: According to the stage directions that open the chapter, the carpenter is sealing Queequeg's coffin and stashes his supply of caulking so that it dangles out of his shirtfront and over his chest. Ahab points to the carpenter's *bosom* and likens him to a silkworm weaving its own shroud.

3. *Isle of Albemarle*: The largest of the Galápagos group and now known as Isabela Island, it is featured in Melville's "The Encantadas, or Enchanted Isles."

4. *musical glasses*: Using its common name, the carpenter imagines himself tuning the glass harmonica, a popular instrument from the mid-eighteenth to early nineteenth century, whose tuned glasses, filled with different amounts of liquid, were played with moistened fingers. Benjamin Franklin invented an improved version, with revolving glass bowls and no liquid.

Chapter 128. The Pequod Meets the Rachel.

1. *sails all fell together*: The approaching *Rachel*, to windward of the *Pequod*, literally "takes the wind out of its sails."

2. *Do to me as you would have me do to you in the like case*: Echoing the biblical injunction, "as ye would that men should do to you, do ye also unto them likewise (Luke 6.31).

3. *a child of your old age too*: In Genesis 21.7, Abraham's wife Sarah declares, "I have borne him a son in his old age." Starbuck appeals to Ahab in Ch. 132 with similar wording, reminding him of "the wife and child of thy loving, longing, paternal old age."

4. *Rachel, weeping for her children, because they were not*: The allusion is to Matthew 2.18: "In Rama was there a voice heard, lamentation, and weeping, and great mourning, Rachel weeping for her children, and would not be comforted, because they are not." Matthew closely quotes the promise in Jeremiah 31.15–17 that Rachel's children will return from the enemy's land, applying it to King Herod's slaughter of the innocents, also mentioned by Ishmael in Ch. 126 (see note 3).

Chapter 129. The Cabin.

1. *The hour is coming*: "The hour is coming, and now is, when the dead shall hear the voice of the Son of God" (John 5.25, and echoed in 5.28).

2. *Like cures like*: To bring about a cure, homeopathic physicians give small doses of medications that produce symptoms like those of the disease being treated.

3. *good master, master, master!*: The phrase quotes a thrice-repeated address to Jesus as "good master" (Matthew 19.16, Mark 10.17, Luke 18.18), and combines it with the pleading language of an American slave.

Chapter 130. The Hat.

1. *eagle . . . Tarquin's head . . . king of Rome*: Livy's first-century BCE history of Rome tells this story of the legendary, benign king. See also revision narrative on p. 471.

Chapter 131. The Pequod Meets the Delight.

1. *"may the resurrection and the life——"*: Approximate wording of the burial service in the Episcopal *Book of Common Prayer*, alluding to John 11.25, "Jesus said unto her, I am the resurrection, and the life."

Chapter 132. The Symphony.

1. *The firmaments of air and sea were hardly separable in that all-pervading azure*: "And God said, Let there be a firmament in the midst of the waters, and let it divide the waters from the waters" (Genesis 1.6).

2. *Samson's chest in his sleep*: While the mighty Samson sleeps with his head in Delilah's lap, she betrays him by having someone shave his uncut hair, the source of his strength (Judges 16.19).

3. *Miriam and Martha*: Although the names are biblical—Miriam is the sister of Moses; Martha, of Mary Magdalene and Lazarus—no biblical story places these girls alongside an aging father. See also Making *Moby-Dick*.

4. *watched how his shadow in the water sank and . . . strove to pierce the profundity*: Compare this passage to the story of Narcissus, drowned trying to grasp "the image of the ungraspable phantom of life" (Ch. 1), to Ahab's seeing the reflected eyes of Fedallah in this chapter's last lines, and to Moby Dick's rising from the depths below Ahab's peering eyes (p. 480).

5. *step-mother world*: Compare to Ahab's experience here, Ishmael's cruel stepmother and the phantom hand grasping his in Ch. 4.

6. *Forty years*: The length of time the biblical Israelites wandered in the desert.

7. *Guinea-coast slavery of solitary command!*: On the *Guinea Coast* of central West Africa, European and American vessels loaded cargoes of slaves for the New World. By rigid custom a whaling captain was forbidden any friendly intimacy with his officers.

8. *cindered apple*: Referring to the deceptively attractive "Apples of Sodom," the inedible fruit of a plant growing near the Dead Sea, legendary site of the city destroyed by fire (Genesis 19.24). "If you pluck them with your hands they dissolve into smoke and ashes" (Josephus, *The Jewish Wars*, Book 4). Melville's source may have been Milton's *Paradise Lost* (1674 version) 10.560–70.

9. *Who's to doom, when the judge himself is dragged to the bar?*: Who is left to condemn anyone for murder if the *judge himself* is on trial? As Melville was composing *Moby-Dick*, the infamous Webster-Parkman murder case was being tried in Boston by Melville's father-in-law, Lemuel Shaw, whose ruling against the defendant made him the focus of considerable controversy to the public and among legal scholars. The *judge* in this line may be a reference to Shaw (Quirk).

Chapter 133. The Chase—First Day.

1. *judgment claps*: Thunder announcing the biblical Day of Judgment. See revision narrative for "resurrection fellow" in Ch. 108, p. 414.

2. *alow and aloft, and on both sides!"*: "Carrying all sail alow and aloft is when the reefs [in the sails] are shaken out [untied], and all the studding sails set" (Smyth).

3. *the Indian's head was almost on a level with Ahab's heel*: Compare to Ahab's standing with his foot on Fedallah in Ch. 119.

4. *Atlantic and Indian Oceans*: The spirit-spout actually appears only in the Atlantic, in Ch. 51.

5. *nautilus shells*: The paper *nautilus*, a mollusk, was thought to use two tentacles as a sail.

6. *white bull Jupiter . . . ravished Europa . . . Crete*: As told in Ovid's *Metamorphoses*, *Jupiter*, king of the gods, seductively taking on the form of a *white bull* (see also Ch. 42), carried off the princess *Europa* to the island of *Crete*. A *Rape of Europa* by Veronese hung in London's National Gallery during Melville's visit in 1849, but it does not at all fit Melville's description. A canvas by Titian, in which Europa is indeed clinging to a horn of the bull, was owned by the Earl of Darnley at Cobham Hall in Kent. Although Melville toured Kent, his journal makes no mention of the painting, now in the Isabella Stewart Gardner Museum, Boston.

7. *the whale shed off enticings*: Compare 2 Chronicles 18.19: "Who shall entice Ahab king of Israel, that he may go up and fall . . . ?"

8. *Virginia's Natural Bridge*: The famed 215-foot-tall limestone arch in the Shenandoah Valley of Virginia was a tourist attraction in Melville's day.

9. *Channel . . . Eddystone*: Mentioned in Ch. 14, the *Eddystone* Lighthouse, famous in folksong and sea lore, stands on a dangerous rock in the English *Channel*, fourteen miles off Plymouth.

10. *blood of grapes and mulberries . . . Antiochus's elephants . . . Maccabees*: From the first book of *Maccabees* (in the Apocrypha), telling of the second-century BCE Jewish rebellion for independence led by Judas Maccabeus against Antiochus IV of Syria: "And to the end [the Syrians] might provoke the elephants to fight, they shewed them the blood of grapes and mulberries" (6.34).

11. *brave as fearless fire (and as mechanical)*: Ahab's aside sarcastically rejects Stubb's seemingly thoughtless humor: Stubb is as fearless as fire, but fire in this case is without soul or intelligence. The insult is replayed in Ch. 134; see note 5. Melville gives special attention to various types of fire and the values they represent for Ahab and Ishmael. Compare Ishmael's warning not to be mesmerized by the "artificial fire" of the try-works in Ch. 96, where the sun is called our "only true lamp." See also Ahab's calling the static electricity of St. Elmo's Fire "mechanical" in Ch. 99.

Chapter 134. The Chase—Second Day.

1. *writ in water*: Echoing the epitaph of John Keats (1795–1821), "Here lies one whose name is writ in water."

2. *old wine worked anew*: Yeast is added to an old still wine to create a sparkling wine.

3. *Ahab's yet unstricken boat seemed drawn up towards Heaven*: Echoing "all were drawn up again into heaven" (Acts 11.10).

4. *I am the Fates' lieutenant*: Compare Ahab's speech at the end of Ch. 132, and Ishmael's reflection on his own fate-assigned role in Ch. 1.

5. *As fearless fire . . . And as mechanical*: In Ch. 133, in response to Stubb's attempts at humor over Moby Dick's wrecking of Ahab's whaleboat, Ahab acknowledges that Stubb is "brave as fearless fire," but adds an aside, "(and as mechanical)." Here, in this chapter, Stubb spiritedly repeats Ahab's epithet, mistaking it for praise, and cries out that he is as brave "As fearless fire," to which Ahab again mutters his withering qualification, "And as mechanical."

Chapter 135. The Chase—Third Day.

1. *Thinking is, or ought to be, a coolness and a calmness*: Ahab echoes Melville's complaint in a June [?], 1851 letter to Hawthorne: "The calm, the coolness, the silent grass-growing mood in which a man *ought* always to compose,—that, I fear, can seldom be mine. Dollars damn me."

2. *Would now the wind but had a body; but all the things that most exasperate and outrage mortal man . . . are . . . only bodiless as objects, not as agents. There's a most special, a most cunning, oh, a most malicious difference!*: In this complicated speech, Ahab seems to argue that if the wind had a *body*, a visible presence, he could strike it. But he abandons this fancy to consider worse things than the wind. In doing so, he recurs to the philosophical distinction between principle (concept) and agent (manifestation of concept) he has made before, but here with a slight change in wording. In this case, *agents* are the material manifestations (that is, bodies) of *objects*, which are *bodiless* (conceptual like Platonic "forms" that are objective in the sense that they are the fundamental reality). In stressing his idea of the *malicious difference* between principle and agent, Ahab reminds us of earlier speeches concerning Moby Dick that draw upon the same distinction. See, for instance, Ahab's "be the white whale agent, or be the white whale principal, I will wreak [my] hate upon him" (Ch. 36), and "All that most maddens and torments . . . were visibly personified, and made practically assailable in Moby Dick" (Ch. 41). See also Ch. 55, note 23.

3. *gold-beaten out to ages*: Stretched out endlessly, as a small piece of gold is hammered into a large sheet of gold leaf.

4. *as if the tongues of fire had voiced it*: Compare "And there appeared unto them cloven tongues like as of fire, and it sat upon each of them. And they were all filled with the Holy Ghost, and began to speak with other tongues" (Acts 2.3–4).

5. *all the angels that fell from heaven*: The followers of Satan in his rebellion against God, listed in *Paradise Lost*, Book 1.

6. *Monadnock*: Dominant rocky dome in the White Mountains of New Hampshire, about which Emerson had published a poem in 1847.

7. *Up helm, up helm!*: With this command, to turn the ship so as to have the wind in its sails, Starbuck is attempting—though futilely, because the *Pequod* could not have moved fast enough to avoid the swift whale—to escape Moby Dick's attack. His words echo Chase's *Narrative*, a text Melville knew well: "while I stood watching his movements, and observing him but a ship's length off, coming down for us with great celerity, I involuntarily ordered the boy at the helm to put it hard up; intending to sheer off and avoid him."

8. *Retribution, swift vengeance, eternal malice*: Compare the quotation from Owen Chase in Ch. 45, p. 194–95.

9. *topmost greatness . . . topmost grief*: Mansfield and Vincent (828–29) find parallels in Carlyle's *Sartor Resartus* (Book 2, ch. 9) and De Quincey's *Suspira de Profundis* (part 2). Ahab's language also recalls, by contrast, Father Mapple's sermon (Ch. 9): "top-gallant delight is to him, who acknowledges no law or lord, but the Lord his God, and is only a patriot to heaven."

10. *tow to pieces*: Ahab's defiant phrase is an ironic reversal of his earlier claim: "Ahab's hawser tows his purpose yet" (Ch. 134).

11. *flying turn caught him round the neck, and voicelessly as Turkish mutes bowstring their victim, he was shot out of the boat*: Mansfield and Vincent (829) suggest Cheever and Bennett as sources for Ahab's demise. In Ottoman Turkey, mute slaves sometimes strangled their masters' political rivals with a *bowstring*.

12. *sky-hawk . . . pecking at the flag*: Confirmation of the sky-hawk's behavior in this scene appears in Bennett. See Mansfield and Vincent 830.

13. *which, like Satan, would not sink to hell till she had dragged a living part of heaven along with her*: Invoking *Satan*, Melville signals a connection to Milton's Satan in *Paradise Lost* and anticipates Miltonic echoes here and in the book's final paragraph (with its words "yawning" and "rolled"). Compare "Hell at last / Yawning received them whole, and on them clos'd . . . / Disburd'n'd Heav'n rejoic'd, and soon repair'd / Her mural breach, returning whence it roll'd" (*Paradise Lost* VI.874–79). See Sheldon.

14. *five thousand years ago*: The approximate time of Noah's flood according to a nineteenth-century biblical chronology by William Hales, based on the Greek Septuagint version of the Hebrew Bible.

Epilogue.

1. *"And I only am escaped alone to tell thee." Job*: Repeated phrase used by messengers who tell Job of his terrible losses, brought about by Satan and culminating in the deaths of his children (Job 1.14–19).

2. *like another Ixion I did revolve*: King in Greek mythology punished by being bound for eternity to a revolving fiery wheel; also mentioned in *Redburn* (Ch. 25). Ishmael's surviving to tell the tale after being spun around the whirlpool resembles the protagonist-narrator's survival in Poe's "Descent into the Maelström" (1841).

3. *devious-cruising Rachel*: See Ch. 128, note 4.

MAKING *MOBY-DICK*

REVISION NARRATIVES

In the summer of 1851, HM had *Moby-Dick* typeset for publication by Harper & Brothers, and sent proof sheets of that American edition to England so that his British publisher, Richard Bentley, could re-set his own edition based on the American text. (The British edition, called *The Whale*, appeared in October; the American *Moby-Dick* in November.) The British and American versions vary substantially, and for a variety of reasons. To begin with, HM revised the proof sheets he sent to England by adding new material, rewording certain passages, and correcting errors—making changes to the British edition that were not necessarily made to the American. Secondly, Bentley had his copy-editor make corrections and bring certain wordings in the American text closer to British usage. Moreover, he expurgated sexual, political, and religious passages presumably offensive to Victorian readers. *Moby-Dick* existed in these two versions for over a century.

Before either edition of *Moby-Dick* was published, a version of "The Town-Ho's Story" (Ch. 54) appeared as an excerpt from "The Whale," in the October, 1851 issue of *Harper's New Monthly Magazine*. The *Harper's* version varies from the British and American editions in several places but does not constitute a substantive revision of the text.

In 1988, the Northwestern-Newberry (NN) version of *Moby-Dick* was published. Its editors designed their text to represent their conception of HM's "final intentions." To do this, they combined elements of the American and British versions, thus mixing stages of revision, and they made changes of their own. With the American version as their base, they automatically retained all passages that the British had expurgated, but they adopted some of the changes found in the British text that might be taken as HM's intended revisions. They also changed words in the American text that did not seem to them to be HM's intended wording, either due to the author's apparent oversight or a transcriber's probable misreading of HM's handwriting. As a consequence of these editorial procedures, the NN *Moby-Dick* varies substantially from both the American and the British versions.

The Longman Critical Edition (LCRE) of *Moby-Dick* adopts a different editorial policy. Its aim is to keep the American and British versions distinct so that readers may have more direct access to the earliest printed text of *Moby-Dick* and a clearer understanding of how it was revised by its author as well as by his editors (both historical and modern). To do this, the editors follow the American edition, changing that text only to correct its typographical errors and any mistakes that would otherwise confuse or mislead the modern reader. (See List of Textual Emendations.) Accordingly, changes in the British text attributed to HM that correct errors in the American are included in the LCRE reading text; however, substantive revisions are not. Instead, places where such revisions occur are highlighted as Revision Sites in the reading text and discussed in Revision Narratives either on the page, or in this section. (See Changes Not Discussed for all other substantive changes.)

The intent of this editorial approach is to establish a text that represents the American version as a distinct creative moment and to register the revisions of the British version through highlighting and annotation so that readers can more readily distinguish the two versions and thus recognize more clearly how HM's first printed text was modified over time by historical editors and modern scholars.

In the Revision Narratives below, page numbers preceding each annotation direct readers to the referenced Revision Sites highlighted in the text. References to sources or studies are cited by the author's last name; full citations for these works may be found in Melville's Sources or Further Reading.

Title: Originally, HM called his novel *The Whale; or, Moby Dick*, and this is the title for the British edition. However, for the American edition, he reversed title and subtitle, thus giving us *Moby-Dick; or, The Whale*. The hyphenated title, retained in the NN edition, follows a common practice among publishers of the day, and the hyphenation has now become a convenient way of distinguishing *Moby-Dick*, the novel, from Moby Dick, the whale.

Epigraph: The American edition of *Moby-Dick* does not include an epigraph, whereas the British edition does; the reason for this difference is not entirely clear. For their epigraph, which appears at the beginning of each of the British edition's three volumes, the editors selected HM's slightly revised passage from Milton's *Paradise Lost* (VII. 412–16) that also serves, in both editions, as the twenty-fourth quotation in "Extracts" (see below). Oddly enough, the British edition also places "Etymology" and "Extracts" not at the beginning, as in the American edition, but at the end of the book as a kind of appendix. The NN editors speculate that publisher Richard Bentley might have reprinted the Milton epigraph up front in his British edition "as a compensation" for moving "Etymology" and "Extracts" to the back.

Etymology: HM's list of non-English language words for "whale" is not entirely correct. The Hebrew word is particularly garbled. Both American and British editions print the letters הן (*he* and *nun*, as read from right to left), or "hen," which has a number of meanings, none of which is "whale" or "leviathan." HM's source was no doubt Kitto's *Cyclopaedia of Biblical Literature*, which gives the letters תן (*tav* and *nun*, again read right to left), or "tan," as "whale," even though the Hebrew word for whale is "tanin" or "tanim." Chances are HM intended Kitto's erroneous word "tan," but his printer gave him "hen." The NN edition corrects the text to "tan"; however, LCRE retains the original. (See also Metlitzki, Schleifer, and Dreisinger.) The Greek in both American and British versions is rendered in a non-standard typeface and seems to begin with the letter *chi*; however, it is, in fact, a *kappa*, which is proper. LCRE emulates this original Greek transcription. It corrects the typo "Whœl" to "Whæl" for the Anglo-Saxon entry. However, it does not correct "Hvalt" (Danish for "arched") to "Hval" ("whale"), nor HM's confusion of Dutch for German, nor the repetition of "Whale" for the Icelandic (instead of "Hvalur"); all of which are revised in the NN edition. The Fegee and Erromangoan words are either sailor talk or HM's invention; the Polynesian for whale is actually "pahua" or "palaoa."

Extracts: HM assembled this collection of quotations from works he consulted while writing *Moby-Dick*. The British edition places both "Etymology" and "Extracts" as an appendix at the end of *The Whale*; it also omits the epilogue (in which Ishmael tells of his survival), and scholars speculate that the epilogue may have been inadvertently dropped when "Etymology" and "Extracts" were appended (see NN *Moby-Dick*, 677–80). According to NN editor G. Thomas Tanselle, HM fashioned "Extracts" by borrowing directly from sources, but also indirectly by quoting source quotations as they appeared in other books, in particular Beale, J. Ross Browne, Harris, and Richardson (813–30). (See Melville's Sources.) In addition, some of HM's extracts vary from their original sources, either due to errors in transcription or because HM revised them intentionally. The individual notes listed below by source author or title draw upon Tanselle's work and discuss HM's likely revision of his sources.

10. *Job*: HM revised "He maketh" in Job 41:32 to "Leviathan maketh."

10. *Tooke's Lucian*: HM revised the original "monsters of the deep" to "monsters of the sea," and "enormous" to "monstrous."

12. *Waller*: In his poem, Edmund Waller has "iron flail" not "modern flail." Taking this as an error in transcription, the NN editors emend the text to "iron"; however, LCRE retains "modern" as a possibly intentional revision of the source. In quoting, HM also brought two widely separated couplets together and altered "her" twice in the second couplet to "his" to make the pronouns agree in gender with those in the first couplet.

12. *Pilgrim's Progress*: HM's wording corresponds to the slightly reworded passage from John Bunyan's *The Holy War* as quoted in Cheever. In the American edition, the extract is incorrectly attributed to Bunyan's *Pilgrim's Progress*. However, it is correctly attributed to *The Holy War* in the British edition. HM may have made the correction in the proofs he sent to England, or an alert editor may have caught the mistake. The NN edition emends the attribution to *The Holy War*; however, LCRE retains *Pilgrim's Progress*, calling attention to the error here and on the text page.

12. *Paradise Lost*: In quoting from *Paradise Lost* (VII. 412–16), HM revised Milton: he gives "in the deep" instead of Milton's original "on the deep" (although this may be a typo) and "his breath spouts out a sea" instead of Milton's "his trunk spouts out a sea." Both changes, neither one corrected by British editors, may reflect HM's scorn (addressed in Ch. 55) for erroneous renderings of whales, which, of course, do not have "trunks" nor sleep "on" the deep. See note on Epigraph, p. 572.

13. *Ulloa's South America*: Building on a reference in the original source to the "insupportable smell" of a fish, HM essentially created an "extract" of his own by applying the phrase to whales.

14. *Uno Von Troil*: The source's "brim-stone" appears as "lime-stone" in both American and British editions. The NN edition emends to "brim-stone"; LCRE makes no change.

16. *Owen Chace*: The NN edition corrects the spelling of "Chace" to "Chase," as it appears in Chase's book; LCRE retains the American edition's spelling since it is a variant of the name and one HM himself used in annotating his copy of Chase's narrative. In the title cited for this extract, HM has dropped "Most Extraordinary and Distressing" as adjectives for "Shipwreck" and reduced the original "Spermaceti-Whale" to "Sperm Whale."

16. *Elizabeth Oakes Smith*: HM's quotation from Smith's "The Drowned Mariner" varies from the original in two places: He has "in the shrouds" rather than "on the shrouds" and "it floundered" rather than "he floundered." The NN edition emends "in" to "on." LCRE retains both of HM's alterations, in particular the nautically correct usage, "in the shrouds," which HM would have preferred.

17. *Thomas Beale*: HM made minor changes to his extract from Beale: he pluralized "agony," revised "sea beast" to "Sperm Whale," altered "jaw" to "jaws," added "him" to give "around him," and inserted the parenthetical phrase "(as the Sperm Whale)." The NN edition alters "jaws" back to "jaw"; LCRE retains "jaws."

19. *Newspaper Account*: In using the word "Hobomack" (with an "a") to identify the whaler *Hobomok* (with an "o") as the scene of maritime violence, HM perpetuates an error he initiated in his first book, *Typee*, where he refers to the "Hobomak" (with an "a"). In fact, no mutiny or massacre occurred on the *Hobomok*. This extract, then, is something of an invention, although HM had surely read newspaper accounts of massacres on other ships in the South Pacific. The NN edition

emends the American and British editions' spelling of "Hobomack" to "Hobomock" to bring the word closer to the ship's name, *Hobomok*; however, LCRE retains HM's original "Hobomack."

19. *Darwin's Voyage*: In the American and British editions, HM's parenthetical insertion of "(Terra Del Fuego)" gives the Portuguese "Terra" instead of the proper Spanish, "Tierra." Since HM's 1846 edition of Darwin's classic voyage of the Beagle spells the word properly, the word "Terra" is probably a typo, and LCRE corrects to "Tierra."

19. *Nantucket Song*: These lines seem to be a conflation of two renderings of a song quoted twice in different versions in Browne's *Etchings*. (See Frank, "Two Songs," in Further Reading.)

Chapter 1

22. *own brother of Jove*: Ishmael's question—intended to mean something like, Why did the Greeks make the sea a separate deity and make him Jove's brother?—is marginally grammatical. However, either HM or a British editor inserted the words "make him the" to give "make him the own brother of Jove," and thus improved the sentence. The NN edition adds the British revision to its text; LCRE makes no change.

Chapter 2

27. *dim sort of light*: HM first wrote "a dim sort of light" for the American edition, but inserted "out-hanging" on the page proofs sent to England to give the more descriptive "dim sort of out-hanging light." The NN edition includes the revision; however, LCRE makes no change.

Chapter 3

30. *you at last come to the conclusion*: Both the American and British editions print "come to the conclusion." However, the NN edition changes "come" to "came" to make the verb conform in tense with the rest of the verbs in the paragraph. LCRE retains "come," recognizing that HM may be signaling a shift in Ishmael's mind between the past in his narrative and the present tense of his coming to a conclusion while writing the narrative.

31. *like another cursed Jonah (by which name indeed they called him)*: The British version removes these words. Later in the scene, the character's name is also revised twice in the British edition to "fellow" (see p. 33). A "Jonah" is a jinx, and the usage was considered more vulgar than slang; hence, its demise.

32. *a three years' voyage*: Later, in Ch. 23, Bulkington, one of the *Grampus*'s crew, is back from a "four years'" voyage. The NN edition rectifies the inconsistency by emending "three" here in Ch. 3 to "four" to bring the length of the voyage into conformity with the reference in Ch. 23. LCRE retains the inconsistency.

33. *Jonah*: See revision narrative for p. 31.

34. ***It was fair to presume that being a harpooneer, his linen or woollen, as the case might be, would not be of the tidiest, certainly none of the finest. I began to twitch all over.*** *Besides, it was getting late, and* ***my*** *decent harpooneer ought to be home and going bed-wards.*: HM's British editor expurgated the first two sentences of this passage presumably because their reference to soiled underwear was too indelicate for Victorian readers. And since the removal made HM's sarcastic "my decent harpooneer" in the third sentence pointless, the British also revised "my decent harpooneer" to "any decent harpooneer." Both the NN edition and LCRE retain the expurgated text. But, assuming that "any" is HM's correction of the mistranscribed word "my," the NN edition emends to "any decent harpooneer." LCRE, however, retains the sarcastic "my decent harpooneer."

36. **Sall** *and me slept . . . Sal used to put*: Both American and British editions spell the wife's name inconsistently, and both spellings are found in texts of the day. The NN edition emends "Sall" to "Sal"; LCRE makes no change.

37. *I never saw such a sight in my life. I*: The British version excises this sentence and the word "I" following it, thus bringing the clauses on either side together to form a single sentence: "I went up in it to a bit of glass . . . and tore myself out of it. . . ." The excised sentence does not exhibit the kind of political, religious, or manifestly sexual content that resulted in other expurgations imposed by editors. Perhaps this excision is an error caused by a printer's "eye skip." That is, while setting type, the printer may have inadvertently skipped from the first "I" to the word following the second "I," omitting the text in between. However, the dropping of "I" altogether argues against an eye skip. Another possibility is that HM removed the line himself because he thought the sentence had become counterfactual to something he had come to write in a later chapter. That is, Ishmael has seen such a sight, and in proofreading HM corrected Ishmael's denial by removing "I never saw such a sight in my life." One speculation is that the garment in question is what Ishmael in Chapter 95 calls a "cassock," i.e., a kind of poncho made from the foreskin of a whale (Bryant, *Melville and Repose*, 189).

Chapter 4

43. *then leave me to dress afterwards,* **leaving** *the whole apartment to myself.*: In both the American and British editions, the modifier, "leaving the whole apartment to myself," is placed far enough from the word it modifies ("he," i.e. Queequeg) that it may seem to be dangling, but HM's meaning is clear. The NN edition revises "leaving" to "having," thus forcing the phrase to modify "me" (i.e. Ishmael) in "leave me to dress afterwards." LCRE retains "leaving."

Chapter 6

48. *Can Herr Alexander perform a feat like that?*: This sentence referring to the German magician known as "Herr Alexander" was omitted from the British edition, probably due to a printer's error; or, perhaps, it was assumed that British readers would not understand the American popular culture allusion.

48. *the barren refuse rocks thrown aside at creation's final day.*: The British edition revises this mildly blasphemous geological image to simply "these barren refuse rocks."

Chapter 7

51. *for stave my soul,* **Jove himself cannot.**: The British edition revises the presumably blasphemous "Jove himself cannot" to "who can do this?"

Chapter 8

53. *From thence it is* **the storm of God's** *quick wrath is first descried*: In the British edition this sentence is revised to "From thence it is that the storm's quick wrath is that first descried," more, perhaps, for stylistic than religious reasons.

Chapter 9

54. *And* **left** *me deepening down to doom. // I saw the* **opening maw** *of hell*: Father Mapple's hymn is based on Psalm 18 as found in HM's standard Dutch Reformed Church hymnal. The first line of the second stanza in the source hymn reads, "I saw the op'ning gates of hell." HM substituted "opening maw" (mouth) for "op'ning gates" in the American edition; but in the British version, "opening" (which adds a syllable to the original "op'ning") is changed, either by HM or an editor, to "open," which preserves the meter of the original hymn. (See Battenfeld and Olsen-Smith listed in Further Reading for their separate discussions of other changes.) In

the last line of the first stanza, the marginally grammatical verb "lift" is changed in the British edition to "left." The NN edition emends to "left," as does LCRE.

57. *when boxes, bales, and jars are **clattering** overboard;*: The word "clattering" is revised to "tumbling" in the British edition, probably by HM.

59. *seemed communing with **God and himself.***: The British edition revises the presumably blasphemous "God and himself" to "his God."

Chapter 12

68. *Queequeg disdained no seeming ignominy, if thereby he might **happily** gain the power of enlightening his untutored countrymen.*: The word "happily" is altered to "haply" (meaning "by chance") in the British edition. The NN edition emends the text to "haply," assuming it to be a correction. However, "happily" may have been originally intended, especially in light of the comparison of Queequeg to Czar Peter the Great. As a young man, Peter purposefully toiled *incognito* in a Dutch shipyard in order to learn techniques for the betterment of the Russian shipbuilding industry; he would have gained this enlightenment "happily," and certainly not "haply." Similarly, Queequeg's intention, stated a few lines later, is to "learn among the Christians" so that he may make his people "happier." However ill-advised, "haply" could be a revision; but, more likely, it is a typo. Whatever the case, LCRE retains "happily."

Chapter 13

71. *him **bevy** small-e fish-e*: Queequeg's "bevy" is dialect for "very." The NN edition takes "bevy" to be a typo and emends the word to "bery." LCRE makes no change.

Chapter 14

74. *he alone resides and **riots** on the sea*: The NN editors argue that "riots" does not effectively introduce the "word pattern" in the paragraph that includes the idea of "rest." They also argue that "riots" may have been a transcriber's misreading of some other word in HM's manuscript. Thus, the NN edition revises "riots" to "rests." The assumption is that HM would have intended a thesis statement encompassing the details to come in his paragraph. However, one image—that of the prairie cock—in the paragraph does, in fact, evoke riotous (that is, extravagant) behavior. And while the last words stress "rest" (in the sense of death), that fact does not argue for an emendation. LCRE retains "riots."

Chapter 15

77. ***only** three barrels of ile . . . weepons in their rooms **at night***: HM revised "only" to "ony" and "at night" to "a-night" for the British edition, in order to enhance Mrs. Hussey's dialect.

Chapter 16

78. *I never could master his **liturgies and XXXIX Articles***: The sentence appears in the British edition as "I never could master his religion," an editorial revision that amounts to a religious expurgation. The Articles of Religion are thirty-nine statements of faith, established by parliament, to which Anglican congregants and priests subscribe.

82. *if either by birth or other circumstances, he **have***: By using "have" instead of "has," HM shifts to the subjunctive, that grammatical "mood" reserved for statements regarding the hypothetical or implausible, which is fitting here for Ishmael's reflection on the kind of man the sea might attract. British editors revised "have" to "has," thereby removing the subjunctive, an editorial practice found at several other revision sites.

83. *worthy Captain* **Bildad.**: The American edition error "worthy Captain Peleg" is corrected in the British edition, probably by HM; the NN edition adopts the correction, as does LCRE.

86. ***That's he;*** *thank ye, Bildad.*: "That's he" stands in both the American and British editions. However, the NN editors (and Mansfield and Vincent before them) speculate that the words are a corruption based on a mistranscription of HM's handwriting, and since "the context makes clear" (NN 792) that HM intends Peleg to repeat himself, they change "That's he" to "Thank ye." However, the context also indicates that Peleg has asked Bildad to sharpen his quill, and may be saying "That's he" (meaning something like "That's it") upon receiving the sharpened quill from his partner. LCRE retains the American and British version.

86. *What lay does* **he** *want?*: The British edition italicizes "he" to indicate Bildad's emphasis of the word, and the NN edition also italicizes. HM certainly made this revision on the proof sheets he sent to England, either to fulfill his original intention or to add the emphasis as a new thought while proofreading. In keeping with its principle of not mixing stages of revision, LCRE retains the unitalicized original.

Chapter 17

89. *Ramadan,* ***or Fasting and Humiliation***: Ramadan is the ninth month in the Muslim calendar, and a period devoted to daytime fasting, sexual abstinence, and verbal restraint. Ishmael uses the word figuratively to mean "fasting and humiliation"; however, "humiliation" is not a part of the Islamic rituals related to Ramadan. In the British edition, "or Fasting and Humiliation" has been removed, probably by HM: the phrase is neither accurate nor in keeping with Ishmael's subsequent argument for tolerance.

90. *clapping the* **vinegar-cruet** *to one side of her nose*: Since Mrs. Hussey has just put the vinegar-cruet down and holds only a mustard-pot, she cannot, in fact, put the vinegar-cruet to her nose. The NN editors address this inconsistency by changing "vinegar-cruet" to "mustard-pot." However, this problem is not easily fixed through textual emendation, for it is just as likely that HM might have intended Mrs. Hussey to put the mustard-pot down earlier in the scene so that she would clap the more astringent vinegar-cruet to her nose. Rather than try to fix the dilemma one way or the other, LCRE leaves the text unaltered.

Chapter 18

96. *said Peleg, his partner*: The phrase, "his partner," seems unnecessary here since Bildad and Peleg have long since been established as partners. Perhaps it is a remnant of an earlier draft version of the narrative in which HM used this scene to introduce the two captains. The NN editors speculate that HM intended to write "said Peleg to his partner" and changed their text accordingly, by thereby reassigning the "partner" reference from Peleg to Bildad. LCRE retains the American reading.

96. *Quohog. his mark.*: The mark supplied in the American and British editions bears no resemblance to the "queer round figure which was tattooed" on Queequeg's arm. In the 1931 Lakeside Press edition (reprinted by Random House), illustrator Rockwell Kent revised the text by providing at this point a handwritten version of the words and a hand-drawn infinity sign for Queequeg's mark. LCRE makes no change to the American edition text. Readers can imagine a more appropriate mark for Queequeg's signature by exploring records of Pacific tattooing.

Chapter 19

99. *and nothing about his losing his leg last voyage, according to the prophecy.*: In the American edition, Elijah's statement interrupts his series of questions and seems to under-

score his instability. The British edition replaces the period after "prophecy" with a question mark. HM might have made the change to bring the sentence into conformity with the surrounding questions, or an over-attentive British copyeditor might have supplied an unwanted question mark. The NN edition adds the question mark; LCRE makes no change.

Chapter 20

101. *the heaviest* **stowage** *of the Pequod*: Probably HM, and not an editor, corrected the American edition typo, "storage," to the nautical term "stowage" for the British version. The NN edition makes the correction, as does LCRE.

102. *Peleg came* **hobbling**: The British edition reads "Peleg came running." It is unlikely that an editor would make such a change, and HM probably revised the text on the proof sheets he sent to England. The NN edition incorporates the revision into its text; LCRE does not.

Chapter 21

104. *The profoundest slumber* **slept** *upon him.*: The British edition gives "slumber was upon him," a change that removes the redundancy of slumber sleeping. HM or an editor could have made this revision.

104. *upon questioning him* **in his broken fashion,** *Queequeg*: The placement of the comma affects meaning. The British edition repositioned it after "him," thus making Queequeg speak in his own "fashion" rather than have Ishmael adopt Queequeg's manner and question him in the Polynesian's "broken" way. This revision perpetuates one grammatical problem while creating another, both related to misplaced modifiers. To begin with, HM's phrase "upon questioning him" (typical of his dangling modifiers) is positioned to modify Queequeg although it is clearly intended to modify Ishmael (who is doing the questioning), but this problem cannot be solved by comma placement. The repositioning of the comma, in fact, creates a second problem because it places the modifier "in his broken fashion" in front of "Queequeg," whereas we might expect such a phrase to come after. HM or an editor may have made this problematic revision. The NN edition adopts the British repositioning; LCRE makes no change.

Chapter 22

106. *her last* **gift**: Both American and British editions print "gift," even though the subsequent list indicates Charity comes bearing several gifts. The NN editors revised the text by pluralizing gift; LCRE retains the singular.

107. *spring I say, all of ye—***spring! Quohag!**: Quohag may be another of Peleg's comic variations on Queequeg's name (including Quohog and Hedgehog), or a misspelling of his favorite name, Quohog. The British edition gives "Quohog" which may be a correction by either HM or an editor, or itself a typo. The NN edition adopts the British version, and it also revises the first exclamation point to a comma, thus making the second "spring" refer to Queequeg and thereby bringing the command in parallel to the following similar commands. LCRE make no change.

109. **If ye touch at the islands, Mr. Flask, beware of fornication**: The British edition expurgated this sentence.

Chapter 23

110. *indefinite as* **God**: HM's British editor revised "God" to "the Almighty."

Chapter 26

117. *a tame chapter of* **sounds**: The NN editors revise "sounds" to "words" on the basis of a perceived aesthetic imbalance between "pantomime of action" and "chapter of words." According to their argument, just as "a pantomime consists of actions; [so then] a chapter consists of words (not sounds)" (NN 849). They further speculate that HM's inscription of "words" might have been misread as "sounds." While this is likely, given HM's handwriting, the idea that "chapters" are without "sounds" is debatable. LCRE retains the American reading.

118. *upon all* **mortally** *practical occasions.*: The British edition omits the word "mortally"; the deletion may be authorial or editorial.

118. *that sort of* **bravery chiefly, visible** *in some intrepid men*: Comma placement affects meaning in this passage. Here, the sense is something like "it was chiefly that sort of bravery that is visible in some men." The NN edition repositions the comma after "bravery" so that the meaning is "it was that sort of bravery that is chiefly visible." The British edition, which may reflect HM's revision or an editorial change, leaves out the comma altogether, thus allowing for either reading. LCRE makes no change.

Chapter 27

121. *by universal* **prescription**: The British edition reads "by universal consent," a revision of some consequence. In law, "prescription" is generally a laying down of rules; however, "consent" suggests an arrangement by mutual agreement. It seems unlikely that an editor would make such a change, and since the revision to "consent" underscores a democratic aspect of whaling, the revision is likely to be HM's.

121. *Ahab would* **probably** *marshal his forces*: Though both American and British versions print "probably," the NN editors revise the text so that Ahab would "presently" marshal his forces. They reason that Ahab does in fact, and not "probably," arrange his mates in the manner described; they also argue that "presently," as written in HM's hand, might easily have been mistranscribed as "probably." However, "presently" makes little sense here, for Ahab does not marshal his forces for several chapters and several days in the narrative. Moreover, HM's likely revision of "prescription" to "consent" in the preceding sentence underscores the implications of "probably," for if the assignment of mates to boats involves some discussion, the final arrangement is a probability, not a certitude prescribed or mandated exclusively by Ahab's authority. LCRE makes no change.

123. *Pip—he never did—***oh, no! he went before.** *Poor Alabama boy!*: The British edition revises this foreshadowing passage to "Pip—he never did! Poor Alabama boy!" thus removing the statement that he dies "before" the rest of the crew. In fact, Pip is one of the last to die, although his madness, resulting from his being cast away at sea, may be construed as a form of death. There is little doubt that this is HM's revision. One explanation is that he had originally intended Pip to die at sea rather than be saved and go mad, and that he had forgotten to correct this now-false foreshadowing until he was reviewing the proof sheets he sent to England. The NN edition adopts the British revision; however, LCRE notes the revision here but makes no change in the text.

Chapter 28

126. *with a* **crucifixion** *in his face*: British editors revised this phrase to "with an apparently eternal anguish in his face."

Chapter 31

132. *never speak* **quick** *to him*: Stubb's advice to Flask is essentially that one should be cautious around Ahab, but the original American text—"never speak to him, whatever he says"—does not make sense in context. Since following the advice of never speaking would be a punishable act of insolence, no sailor would offer such advice or accept it. Chances are the adverb "quick" had been dropped in the American version of the sentence and that HM restored that word on the page proofs he sent to England. Thus, the British version, "never speak quick to him," is most likely HM's correction of a mangled text, and it is adopted by both the NN edition and LCRE.

Chapter 32

133. *Rev.* **Henry T. Cheever**: The American and British texts read simply "Rev. T. Cheever" in acknowledgment of Henry T. Cheever's *The Whale and His Captors*. Presumably, "Henry" was inadvertently dropped from Cheever's name and not corrected by HM or his copyeditor. Since HM supplies the author's full name in "Extracts," and since "T. Cheever" is misleading, both the NN edition and LCRE restore "Henry."

134. *I shall not pretend . . . to much of any* **description. My object here is simply to project the draught of a** *systemization of cetology.*: In the British edition, this introductory statement has been cut to "I shall not pretend . . . to much of any [. . .] systemization of cetology." Because the removed words fit a single line of type in the American edition (with the word "a" appearing at the beginning of a second line), the deletion may have been due to an "eyeskip," in which the British typesetter, working from the proofs HM had sent to England, skipped a full line of the text he was attempting to copy. However, HM might have made the deletion because its phrasing—"the draught of a systemization"—anticipates and diminishes (perhaps) the impact of the chapter's famous, concluding line: "This whole book is but a draught—nay, but the draught of a draught."

134. *In his System of Nature, A.D.* **1776**, *Linnæus declares*: Linnaeus first published *Systema Naturae* as a pamphlet in 1735, which grew into a multivolume work in its tenth edition in 1758. His last edition, appearing in 1766–68, provided a taxonomy for animals. However, HM derived details in this chapter and his presumed quotations from Linnaeus from the *Penny Cyclopedia* article on "Whales," which cites the 1766 edition. The NN edition treats HM's "1776" as a typo and corrects to the *Penny Cyclopedia* source date, 1766. However, since "Cetology" is something of a declaration of independence from systemization, HM's 1776 may well be an intended joke. LCRE makes no change.

140. *even in* **the** *lawless seas*: In the British edition, "the" has been dropped to give "even in lawless seas." The shift has significance, for with "*the* lawless seas," all seas are lawless, while "*lawless* seas" designates only certain seas as lawless.

142. **God** *keep me*: The British revision to "Heaven keep me" eliminates the use of the Lord's name in vain.

Chapter 33

143. **the** *grand distinction*: The British revision to "one of the grand distinctions," probably by HM, moderates Ishmael's excess.

144. *highest* **honors**: The British reading, "highest honour," registers the expected shift to the *-our* spelling. However, the revision to the singular (perhaps by HM) brings the word in parallel to the singular "Such large virtue" a few lines later.

144. **direst** *swing*: The American version gives "direct swing," which makes little or no sense;

the typo was corrected, either by HM or an editor, to "direst swing" in the British edition, and that correction is adopted by the NN edition and LCRE.

Chapter 34

148. *to some hurried **order***: The British text is revised to "to some hurried method," which seems to be an incomplete revision to the more grammatical "*in* some hurried method." Chances are HM altered "order" to "method" to eliminate the repetition of "order" in the preceding line; however, the necessary revision of "to" to "in" was either not made or not registered by the printer.

148. ***its** door*: HM, rather than his British copyeditor, probably made the small alteration to "his door," a phrase that designates Dough-Boy's private space or hideout from the fearsome harpooneers.

Chapter 35

151. *Louis **the Devil***: A British editor toned down HM's political satire by revising to "Louis Napoleon." Louis Napoleon Bonaparte, Napoleon's controversial nephew, had become president of the Republic of France but was making moves to establish himself as emperor at the time HM was completing *Moby-Dick*.

152. *in **cold** weather*: Probably it was HM, not an editor, who revised "cold" to "coolish" in the British edition. The NN edition also revises to "coolish"; however, LCRE makes no change.

Chapter 36

157. *a sixteen dollar piece, men.*: The British version adds "—a doubloon" to give "a sixteen dollar piece, men,—a doubloon." Chances are HM made this addition to the proofs he sent to England. The word "doubloon" does not appear again until Ch. 99, "The Doubloon," and HM would have added the word here in Ch. 36, when Ahab first shows the coin, to provide a clear verbal link between it and Ch. 99. The NN edition adds this revision to its text; however, in keeping with its principle of not mixing versions, LCRE notes the revision here but does not make the change.

158. *he shouted with a terrific, loud, animal **sob***: Either an editor or HM altered this arresting image by revising "sob" to "shout" in the British edition. Regardless of who made the change, the clumsy revision—essentially, he shouted with a shout—seems the result of carelessness.

159. *thy silence, **then,** that voices thee.*: The British version revises "then," to "that—" to give "thy silence, that—*that* voices thee." The revision, which HM probably made, creates a dramatic repetition and intensifies Ahab's delivery.

159. *cannot oppose me **now**, without rebellion.*: The British edition removes "now," a revision that eliminates the repetition in "Starbuck now is mine" in the preceding line. Since a copyeditor might not bother with such niceties, and HM frequently did, the revision is probably his.

160. *revive **a noble** custom*: The British version reads "revive an old custom," an editorial revision reflecting uneasiness with HM's democratizing agenda.

160. *he would fain have shocked **into them** the same fiery emotion*: Ishmael characterizes Ahab as a "Leyden jar," the device used in parlor demonstrations for generating static electricity and administering harmless shocks to observers, who are usually holding hands so that all can feel the shock. In the image, Ahab contains an "interior volition," which, like the static built up

in a Leyden jar, he wants to transmit, like an electric shock, into the crew, thus animating them with his will. In "Hawthorne and His Mosses" (the review essay written during the composition of *Moby-Dick*), HM uses a similar version of the same electric image to describe Hawthorne's genius, which administered a "shock of recognition" to the rest of the world. Thus, the locution "shocked into them" carries for HM its own specialized meaning. However, the British edition changes the phrasing of "shocked into them" to "shocked them into," and thereby inverts the electric image. Here, Ahab provides a shock so that the crew, with a volition of its own, might then become as fiery as Ahab. The revision is probably editorial.

Chapter 37

162. *the solid metal; **aye, steel skull, mine; the sort that needs no helmet in the most brain-battering fight!***: The British version of this passage ends (without an exclamation point) at the words "solid metal." In the American version, HM piles metal upon metal—gold, iron, then steel—but the British revision reduces the metaphorizing by eliminating "steel" from the mix. HM probably shortened the sentence in the proof sheets he sent to England.

Chapter 39

165. *We'll drink to-night . . . / To **love,** as gay and fleeting / As bubbles*: HM takes the song from Charles Fenno Hoffman's "Sparkling and Bright"; however, Hoffman's original wording "To loves as gay and fleeting" has been changed to "To love, as gay and fleeting." The NN edition reckons that "To love," is the result of a mistranscription of HM's handwriting that he failed to correct in page proofs, and it revises the text to conform to the Hoffman original. However, the change may be an intended revision to the singular. LCRE makes no change.

Chapter 40

166. *Our captain's **commanded**—*: The American edition places a period after commanded, which gives the impression of sentence completion when, in fact, the singers are being interrupted in mid-line. The British edition corrects the error, as do the NN and LCRE editions. The third line of the folk song usually reads "For we've received orders"; however, HM's version, "Our captain's commanded," stresses Ahab's agency.

167. *Tell 'em it's the resurrection; they must kiss their last, and come to judgment.*: The British edition expurgates this mildly blasphemous line that equates the Resurrection and Judgment Day to a drunken stupor.

168. **AZORE** SAILOR: The island group off the coast of Portugal is in English variously called the Azores (pronounced AY-zorz), the Azores Islands, or the Azore Islands. The NN editors take "Azore" to be a typo and emend it to "Azores" in both iterations of "Azore Sailor." But since "Azore Islands" is found in print in the early nineteenth century, LCRE does not make a change.

168. *break the **jinglers**! . . . **Jinglers**, you say?*: The Azore Sailor urges Pip to "break the jinglers," the rattling metal disks on his tambourine, as he entertains the dancing sailors. Pip's response, "Jinglers, you say?" indicates that the word may be suggestive. "To jingle" had mild sexual connotations in some folk music, and a "jingle-boy" is a gold coin. Given the musical and sexual references in the dance scene, which celebrates Ahab's offer of a gold coin, the word is rich with suggestive meanings. However, in the British edition, "jinglers" has been changed to "jigglers" in both instances. "Jiggler" may mean dancer, as in "to jig it" or dance a jig. But according to Partridge's *Dictionary of Slang and Unconventional English*, "jiggle" is also a strong, working-class, slang expression for sexual intercourse that had

found its way into print around 1845. Although HM had known enough British sailors who might have used this word on board ship in the early 1840s, he is not likely to have revised his merely suggestive "jinglers" to the more explicitly vulgar "jigglers." Nor would his British copyeditor, who is careful elsewhere to sanitize HM's racy language, revise HM's innocent-enough "jinglers" to a clearly salacious "jigglers." (Possibly the editor might not have been aware of the new working-class expression.) Moreover, the fact that the word is revised in both places indicates that the alteration is not likely to be a random typo. Who, then, might have made this change, and how might it have occurred? One possibility is that the revision is a printer's prank. Because this chapter is printed in three different font styles as well as with both centered and justified lines of type, the compositor would have slowed down to set the type, and in doing so he might have also paid enough attention to the text to recognize the raciness of the scene. He might then have converted HM's "jinglers" to "jigglers," a new, low-class vulgarism that might not be detected in proofs by higher-class editors and proofreaders of the day.

168. *O **Christ**!*: The British version reads "O Lord!," a revision that amounts to a religious expurgation.

168. *the whole world's **a ball**, as **you** scholars have it*: In this speech, the Old Manx Sailor addresses first himself; then the other dancing sailors; then Christ (or what might be called the heavens); then himself again along with an audience including "you scholars," and finally the sailors. This progression of rhetorical poses is complicated by two changes possibly made by HM. The first involves "you scholars." Here, the old sailor facetiously refers to the readers of *Moby-Dick* as scholars, underscoring his own scholarly paraphrase of Shakespeare to come. But in the British edition, "you scholars" is changed to "your scholars," meaning simply "the scholarly tradition." The change (whether a correction or a revision) eliminates the possibility of the Manx Sailor's addressing (directly or ironically) a scholarly audience. A second change alters the Manx Sailor's Shakespearean paraphrase. Here, "the whole world's a ball" (a punning reference to Jaques's famous line, "All the world's a stage," in *As You Like It*, 2.7) is revised to "the whole world's one ball," which lessens the Shakespearean echo and creates a redundancy with "one ball-room" in the following line. The NN editors consider the first change to be a correction of a typo, and they adopt it. They also adopt the second change as an emendation of their text, but without discussion. Since the first may have been a change of mind on HM's part and hence not a correction, and since the second, may be a compositor's eye-skip, LCRE makes no change.

169. *It's the **waves**—the **snow's caps** turn to jig it*: In the previous speech, the Lascar (Indian) Sailor observes that a wind is blowing up (a sign of the coming storm): the sea (called a "high-tide Ganges") becomes transformed; it is "turned to wind," or perhaps it turns darker in facing the wind. In any case, the darkened sea has become choppy with "white-caps," the little cresting waves kicked up at sea by the wind. In the present speech, the Maltese Sailor calls them "snow's caps" (likely a neologism evoking snowcapped mountains, also found as "snow-caps" in Ch. 126), and, playing on the Lascar's idiom "turned to wind," he observes that it is these little cresting waves that now "turn to jig it," or transform themselves in order to dance. But since the exhausted sailors are coming to the end of their dancing, it is also possible that the Maltese Sailor is saying that it is now the waves' turn (opportunity) to dance. Assuming that HM intended this latter possibility, the NN editors change "waves" into the plural possessive "waves'." They also revised "snow's caps" to "snow-caps'," converting it as well to the plural possessive. Finding no compelling argument for these plural possessives, LCRE makes no change.

169. *unceasing touch and go!* **not taste, observe ye, else come satiety.**: As the men continue dancing with each other, the Sicilian observes that the physical touching should be lim-

ited to "grazings" and no "tast[ings]"; otherwise the dancing might become explicitly sexual and lead to over-indulgence. The British edition removed "not taste observe ye, else come satiety," expurgating the hint of sexual consequences.

171. *Why then, God, mad'st thou the ring?*: The Old Manx Sailor facetiously suggests that God created the world in order for men to kill their brothers, and the British Edition expurgates this cynical blasphemy.

171. *Blang-whang!* **God!** *Duck lower, Pip*: The British edition expurgates "God!"—a use of the Lord's name in vain.

Chapter 41

174. *most lively **terrors***: HM is quoting from Beale, who uses the singular "terror." Noting that HM quotes Beale precisely elsewhere in this passage, the NN editors correct HM's mis-quoted "terrors" to Beale's original "terror." However, because HM may have intended to revise Beale, LCRE makes no change.

176. *to whose dominion even the modern Christians ascribe one-half of the worlds*: The reference is to Manichaeism, a third-century doctrine derived from Persian, Gnostic, and Christian thinking that divides existence into good and evil. Augustine adopted but later renounced it in the fourth century. It became prevalent in thirteenth-century southern France, where it was brutally repressed. HM's claim that "modern Christians" subscribe to the kind of Manichean dualism projected here is arguably excessive, and the British edition removed it.

177. *ye **nobler, sadder** souls*: The British edition adds "and" to give "ye nobler, and sadder souls." HM probably made the revision, which implies that these souls are sadder *because* they are nobler.

Chapter 42

180–81. *its vast **archangel** wings . . . I peeped to secrets **which took hold of God***: HM's British editor altered Ishmael's footnote on the albatross, reducing its religious references. The word "archangel" is removed, and the words "which took hold of God" are revised to "not below the heavens."

181. *But I doubt not, that leathern tally, meant for man, was taken off in Heaven, when the white fowl flew to join the wing-folding, the invoking, and adoring cherubim!*: The image of men sending messages ("leathern tally") via the albatross is not blasphemous, but the thought that the bird might be a spiritual messenger between man and heaven, or heaven's angels ("cherubim") was not acceptable, and the British edition expurgated the entire sentence.

184. *the instinct of the knowledge of the demonism **in** the world*: The British edition alters the last prepositional phrase to "demonism of the world." The shift in prepositions—which echoes the New Testament distinction between being "in" the world but not necessarily "of" it—is significant. The original "in" suggests that demonism is one feature to be found in the world; whereas the revised "of" suggests that demonism is an inherent quality of the world. The change may have been performed by HM, an editor, or printer.

Chapter 44

189. *when all possibilities would become probabilities, and, as Ahab fondly thought, every **possibility** the next thing to a certainty.*: The NN edition finds a problem in the logic of these statements. As it stands in both the American and British editions, the idea is that, the-

oretically, when Ahab reaches a certain "set time or place," the possibility of finding Moby Dick becomes a probability, and that, in Ahab's mind, such a possibility is actually a certainty. In other words, the notion of possibility is redefined in Ahab's point of view. However, the NN editors argue that HM intended a graduated, logical progression in the statements rather than a vaulting redefinition, and they revised the word "possibility" to "probability" so that in the first clause, possibilities become probabilities, and in the second (via Ahab's mentality) "probability" becomes "the next thing to a certainty." The NN version significantly alters meaning. Whereas HM's original wording reveals an Ahab so certain of his chartings that he can make, in his mind, a near certainty out of mere possibilities, the NN revision renders Ahab's logical leap much smaller, from a probability to near certainty. Because there is no reason to think HM's original wording violates logic or requires correction, LCRE makes no change.

191. *unbidden and **unfathered** birth*: Perhaps the most laughable typo in the British edition is the alteration of "unfathered" to "unfeathered," which conjures up the image of Ahab as a plucked fowl. The absurd image could not be more poorly placed, as it ruins the serious tone of Ahab's desperate night terrors. The typo is doubly unfortunate for, despite its absurdity, the association with an unfledged or new-born bird still lacking flight feathers is plausible enough so that British readers might not recognize it as an error. Moreover, those finding it odd would not readily guess at the intended spelling, "unfathered birth," which, among mammals, is unlikely.

Chapter 45

193. *Captain **Butler** of old*: HM confuses Col. William Butler with Capt. Benjamin Church, who pursued Annawon. The NN edition revises Butler to Church. LCRE notes the confusion but makes no change.

194. *Upon one particular voyage which I made to the Pacific, among many **others,** we spoke about thirty different ships*: The American and British editions do not include the second comma, and its absence is confusing. Without this comma, "among many others" must refer to "thirty different ships," with the implication that these thirty are only a fraction of the many ships he met (or "spoke"). In turn, this lack of punctuation would mean that the total number of men reported killed came only from the thirty ships and that the many other ships reported no deaths. This reduced death rate would undercut, if not contradict, the conclusion that there is at least one drop of human blood in each gallon of whale oil. However, with the second comma included, "among many others" refers to the voyages Ishmael has made in his life, and the implication is that on this one particular voyage, he met thirty ships, each one of which reported at least one death, a fact that substantiates Ishmael's claim concerning blood and whale oil. The NN edition adds the second comma to their text, as does LCRE.

195. *Was not Saul of Tarsus converted from unbelief by a similar fright?*: Ishmael facetiously compares Saul's dramatic conversion to Christianity to the whaling captain's brush with death, and his British editor was not amused; the entire line was expurgated.

196. *head **on** a gun*: The acknowledged source for this paragraph is Wafer, and HM changes the original, lifted text in several places. According to the NN editors, one such change—head *on* a gun—"does not make sense" (NN 869), and, assuming the word "on" to be a mistranscription of Wafer's original word "over," they emend their text in conformity with Wafer to read "head *over* a gun." The point of the Wafer anecdote is that the force of the whale's impact is so great that it knocks cannons out of their carriages and men out of their hammocks; in addition, the captain sleeping in his cabin directly over the guns situated below decks is also knocked out of his room. However, the change to "head on a gun" also makes sense. One possible reading is that the buccaneer captain is sleeping with a gun under his pillow; another is

that the captain may have rested his head on a small cannon, often mounted in captains' stern quarters. Whatever the situation imagined, the change heightens the drama of the anecdote and is not misleading; and since it may be HM's intended revision. LCRE makes no change.

197. *Commodore Davis*: HM's "good authority" is the article on "Whale" in Kitto; however, the officer mentioned in that source is "Commander Davies." The NN edition revises the text to "Commander Davies"; LCRE makes no change.

Chapter 47

200. *directed by free will*: Probably HM, not an editor, revised "directed" to "modified" for the British edition. In Ishmael's extended weaving metaphor, necessity is the warp or fixed vertical threads, which only move (vibrate) when they are separated by the traversing shuttle (in this case, Ishmael's hand), which carries the woof, or thread, of free will; Queequeg's wooden sword of chance unevenly tamps down the woof into the warp. But at the same time, Ishmael concludes, necessity and free will limit the effect of chance just as warp and woof provide the restraints and conditions by which Queequeg's sword must be applied. To some extent, then, free will "directs" chance in that it gives direction to chance events. However, HM may have felt that "directed" overstates the power of free will, allowing the will to seem to control chance. By revising so that chance is merely "modified by free will," HM lessens the will's controlling power. The NN editors adopted HM's revision as the "more appropriate word" (790); however, noting the revision, LCRE makes no change.

201. *swiftly swims*: The British edition inverts the wording so that the whale "mills round, and swims swiftly off." The revision (probably HM's) puts the two verbal sets in parallel and alters the rhythm of the passage.

Chapter 48

202. *wide **black** trowsers*: The British version drops the word "black," probably to eliminate the repetition in "black cotton" in the preceding phrase and the redundancy in "same dark stuff" just below. The NN editors considered adopting this revision—and, in fact, printed only "wide trowsers" in the 1967 Norton Critical Edition of *Moby-Dick*—but for their 1988 edition, they retained "wide black trowsers." LCRE makes no change.

205. *King-Post was small and short . . . King-Post was full of **a** large and tall ambition*: The deletion of "a" in the British edition, to give "large and tall ambition," tightens the parallel structure with "small and short," sharpens the tone of mockery, and accentuates the taunting repetition of "King-Post." HM probably made the revision.

206. *But it bade **far** to outstrip them*: The NN editors assert that "far" is "undoubtedly" a typo (792), and they revise their text to read "bade fair," which gives the meaning, "it seemed likely to outstrip them." However, the original wording might also mean "it strived to outstrip them by far." LCRE makes no change.

Chapter 50

211. ***Archy's** published discovery*: In both the American and British editions, the wording reads: "Cabaco's published discovery." But as is clear from Ch. 48, it is Archy who tells Cabaco about the stowaways. Although HM was the most likely corrector of a similar confusion (of Peleg for Bildad) in Ch. 16, he apparently failed to correct this confusing inversion of names. The NN editors changed "Cabaco's" to "Archy's," as does LCRE.

Chapter 51

216. *Cape **Tormentoto***: HM clearly indicates Cape Tormentoso (Tempestuous Cape), now known as the Cape of Good Hope. The misspelling may be a typo, and the NN edition emends to "Cape Tormentoso"; however, HM's misspelling evokes the notion of "tormented" and may represent an unconscious reflex or even an intended "mistake." LCRE makes no change.

Chapter 54

223. *sail **eastward** from the eaves of this good Golden Inn*: The direction given in both the American and British editions is "eastward," a likely typo (but also a possible joke) that would put the *Town-Ho* in the Andes mountains. The NN edition and other editions emend the text to "westward"; however, LCRE makes no change.

223. *Radney, . . . a **Vineyarder***: Later in the chapter, in both the American and British versions, Radney (here called a "Vineyarder") is referred to three times as a "Nantucketer." Although Martha's Vineyard is Nantucket's neighboring island, Ishmael previously associates radically different characters with these different islands. (Flask, for instance, is a Vineyarder, and Starbuck, a Nantucketer; and each has his "different way," see Ch. 28.) Therefore, it is unlikely that HM would want to conflate the two, although in writing he might have erred here, or in the other three places, by substituting one island origin for the other. It is also possible that in the writing process HM changed his mind about Radney's origin, but failed to make his text record the change consistently, thus leaving Radney in one place a Vineyarder and in others a Nantucketer. The NN editors revise "Vineyarder" to "Nantucketer" (NN 875). But since the discrepancy might be the vestige of an incomplete revision, LCRE makes no change.

223. *"'**Lakeman!**—Buffalo! Pray, what is a Lakeman, and where is **Buffalo?**'*: "The Town-Ho's Story" is a story within a story, and Ishmael speaks to us in different modes: he introduces the place where he first told the tale and reports his interactions with his audience there as well as the dialogue of the characters at sea in the story proper. To record these narrative layers, HM adopts a complicated structure of double and single quotation marks. Because Ishmael proposes to "preserve the style in which [he] once narrated" the tale, the story in its entirety is one long quotation, indicated by double quotation marks. However, the interruptions by Don Pedro and Don Sebastian at the Golden Inn and his dialogue with them here and at the end are set off in single quotation marks, as are the speeches of such characters as Radney, Steelkilt, and the Captain in the tale itself. Also, in accordance with punctuation conventions, double quotation marks do not close a paragraph if the speaker continues in subsequent paragraphs; only the last paragraph of quoted material takes a closing double quotation mark. An exception to this rule is that paragraphs preceding an interruption by one of the Dons do take a closing double quotation mark. But these general rules are not perfectly followed in the American edition, and re-settings of the text in the prepublication version in *Harper's* magazine and in the British edition add as many errors as corrections. In addition, the NN edition makes over 80 changes to the quotation marks; some of them are corrections but most replace with double quotes the American edition's single quotes from the dialogue of the Dons. For instance, in this passage, the NN edition reading is "Lakeman! . . . Buffalo?". LCRE retains the single quotes, and makes only seventeen changes to the American edition (as listed in Variants Not Discussed).

227. *I will tell **ye***: In both *Harper's New Monthly Magazine* and the British edition, "ye" has been changed to "you." Since the versions were prepared separately, the coincidence strongly

suggests that HM instructed, on the American proof sheets he sent to both editors, that the intended revision in dialect be made. Throughout "The Town-Ho's Story," the working-class "ye" (pronounced yuh) is reserved almost exclusively for sailor dialogue, whereas Ishmael and the gentlemen Dons speak with more sophisticated diction, referring almost exclusively to each other as "you." An exception, however, is that Ishmael uses "ye" twice in conversation with the Dons, here at the beginning of the story, with "I will tell ye," and again at the end, with "the story I have told ye." Chances are, HM's strategy in revising Ishmael's "ye" to "you" was to make Ishmael speak only like the Dons in the tale's frame, and never like the sailors featured in the tale; and while he made that revision in the first instance, he failed to do so in the second. As with the Vineyarder-Nantucketer problem (see revision narrative for p. 223), the discrepancy indicates an incomplete revision.

227. *through the* **holy-of-holies** *of great forests*: HM's British editor expurgated "the holy-of-holies of" to give simply "through great forests."

228. *openly toying with his red-cheeked Cleopatra,* **ripening his apricot thigh upon the sunny deck**.: HM's line echoes the sensual description of Cleopatra's barge in *Antony and Cleopatra* (2.2); however, HM's British editor expurgated the homoerotic reference to Mark Antony's thigh, leaving him simply "openly toying with his red-cheeked Cleopatra."

229. *Captain,* **by God,** *look to yourself*: HM's British editor expurgated "by God" to remove a use of the Lord's name in vain.

232. *the ship's run for* **salvation**: The two former mutineers fear retribution from the rest of the crew and are placed in the "run," a crawl space between decks, for safekeeping. However, in the British edition, "salvation" is revised to "security." While "salvation" is a suitable word, it also suggests exoneration, and HM may have opted for the more neutral "security." By the same token, an editor might have supplied the substitution, finding the religious implications of "salvation" to be inappropriate. (However, three other instances of "salvation" in *Moby-Dick* were not expurgated.)

235. *Then I entreat* **you,** **tell** *me*: The British version reads "Then I entreat you to tell me." The addition of "to" along with the elimination of the comma corrects the sentence's comma splice but creates a repetition of "to" that HM would probably have wanted to avoid. Chances are an editor made the alteration in mechanics.

236. *I knew the* **crew;** *I have seen and talked with Steelkilt*: Ishmael's final sentence is an intense series of main clauses; it is punctuated with semi-colons; its intensity is heightened by the punctuation. In the British edition, the conjunction "and" has been inserted between the last two clauses to give "I knew the crew; and I have seen and talked with Steelkilt." The revision is purely stylistic, and it can be argued whether the insertion of "and" enhances or detracts from the power of the sentence, and whether it was made by HM or his editor.

Chapter 55

239. *Bentham's skeleton, which* **hangs for candelabra** *in the library*: The British edition revises "hangs for candelabra" to simply "is preserved." The utilitarian philosopher did in fact have his clothed skeleton placed on display for the edification of the masses, but it was never used as a candelabra. HM is not likely to have made this revision as it spoils a good joke; chances are an editor changed the text for the sake of accuracy and out of respect for Bentham's somewhat egocentric monument.

Chapter 58

248. *who have gone upon the **waters***: The British edition converts "waters" to the singular. "The waters" appears numerous times in Genesis, and HM also uses that biblical plural throughout *Moby-Dick*. Given the reference in this passage to humankind's immemorial relation to the sea, "waters" seems the more effective reading; "water" is probably a typo.

Chapter 61

254. *we **then** were voyaging*: Throughout *Moby-Dick*, HM uses time modifiers such as "then" to remind readers of Ishmael's narrative distance from the events he is relating. Here, the oddly placed adverb calls attention to itself. The British edition, however, repositions the word to give the more conventional "we were then voyaging." Either HM or an editor may have performed this stylistic nicety.

257. *"He's dead, Mr. Stubb," said **Daggoo***.: Given that Stubb and his boat crew (including his harpooneer, Tashtego) have been separated from the other boats, the context clearly calls for Native American Tashtego, not the African Daggoo, to declare the whale dead. HM did not correct this apparent error in the British edition. However, the NN edition emends the text to read "said Tashtego." LCRE makes no change.

Chapter 64

264. *the propriety **of devil-worship,** and **the** expediency of conciliating the devil*.: HM's British editor removed "of devil-worship" and "the" to give "the propriety and expediency of conciliating the devil," thus eliminating any condoning of "devil-worship" or breaking of the third commandment: "Thou shalt have no other gods before me."

264. ***Blast** me*: According to Partridge, this vulgarism meant "curse" or "damn." HM's editor changed Stubb's curse to the far more acceptable "Hang me," an expression of anger and vexation which essentially means, "I'll be hanged." (See revision narrative for p. 294.)

265. *Cook! why, **damn your eyes,** you mustn't swear*: HM's editor expurgated the blasphemous "damn your eyes" from the British edition, thus destroying the joke of having Stubb swear in telling Fleece not to swear while preaching. Rodney's use of the same expression in Ch. 54 was not cut.

267. *"Fetch him? **How? In a coach and four, as they fetched Elijah?** And fetch him where?"*: In 2 Kings 2.11, the prophet Elijah is taken to heaven in a chariot of fire. Reducing this memorable and stirring biblical image to a modern "coach and four" was irreverent enough to induce an editor to cut the reference altogether, for the British wording is merely "Fetch him—and fetch him where?"

267. *But don't you know the higher you climb, the colder it gets? Main-top eh?*: Both sentences were deleted in the British edition, probably by an editor for religious reasons.

267. *But, perhaps you expect to get into heaven by crawling through the lubber's hole, cook; but, no, no. cook, you don't get there, except you go the regular way, round by the rigging. It's a ticklish business, but must be done, or else it's no go. But none of us are in heaven yet.*: This lengthy passage was expurgated in the British edition, although the reason is not entirely clear. The "lubber's hole" allows climbers easy access to the "top," a platform at the juncture of the lower mast and topmast, typically reached by more experienced seamen along the masts' support rigging. Stubb's earthy message is nothing more than a seaman's version of the truism that you cannot get to heaven the easy way, but Stubb's seemingly careless (and obvi-

ously comic) attitude toward this "ticklish business" of salvation may have been read as irreverence; hence the expurgation.

267. *There, now **ye** may go.*: Stubb uses "ye" only one other time in this speech, in the contracted "d'ye hear," and seems to make a point of using the more formal "you" in giving his orders to Fleece. Probably HM, not an editor, revised "ye" in this final sentence to "you" to maintain the formal usage.

268. *more **of** shark dan Massa Shark hisself*: The British edition changes "more of shark" to "more a shark." The alteration is significant as it intensifies Fleece's characterization of Stubb: the first mate is a shark, not simply one who possesses a certain sharkishness. The change may be a botched correction to the possible original wording "more of a shark"; that is, this original was mistranscribed in the American edition as "more of shark" and then corrected to "more of a shark" in the proofs HM sent to England but then re-set by a printer as "more a shark" in the British edition. Or, a British editor might have made the change to "more a shark." Another possible scenario is that HM originally wrote "more of shark" and then changed his mind, revising it to "more a shark."

Chapter 65

271. ***formally** indite*: The NN editors speculate that "formally" should be "formerly," and they emended their text accordingly. Their argument—which is not based on a British variant—is that "formerly" better fits the context of the following sentence in which we learn that the Anti-Cruelty society has, "within the last month or two," switched from goose quill pens to steel. The point made clear by "formerly" is that the society once used quills but now has stopped. The editors also argue that, given HM's handwriting, "formerly" could have been misread as "formally" (NN *Moby-Dick* 792), an error that HM could have corrected in page proofs but, in fact, did not. But the American and British word "formally" fits the context equally well, if not better, as it indicates the solemn pretension of the ludicrously hypocritical society that has only recently discovered its hypocrisy. Indeed, the use of "formerly" undercuts this concluding joke by anticipating and stepping on the punch line in the last sentence. LCRE makes no change.

Chapter 66

273. *"Queequeg no care what god made him shark," said the savage, agonizingly lifting his hand up and down; "weder Fejee god or Nantucket god; but de god wat made shark must be one dam Ingin."*: The British edition expurgated Queequeg's observation for religious reasons.

Chapter 69

279. *There's orthodoxy!*: This final line in Ishmael's paragraph regarding the often immaterial sources of odd traditions and false beliefs also undermines religious codes in general, and was expurgated from the British edition.

280. *while in life the great whale's body may have been a real terror to his foes, in his death his ghost becomes a **powerful** panic to a world.*: The American reading is "powerless panic," which is plausible, but in context confusing. A "powerless panic" may be a sense of fear that results in no effective action or leaves the individual feeling helpless, and one reason HM might have intended this turn of phrase is that it may fit a contrast he seems to be constructing between the "real terror" of the living whale and what might be taken as the unreal, ineffectual, or "powerless panic" created by the ghost of the dead whale. But this apparent contrast does not fit the context of the preceding paragraph, which inveighs against the real

power that mindless orthodoxy has over all humans, not our powerlessness to oppose it. This view complements a more likely contrast found in the final phrasings of the sentence, contrasting not so much real terror versus powerless panic, but real terror for whalemen versus a real terror to other ships. In fact, given the tirade against orthodoxy in the preceding paragraph, what is expected in the sentence is that the false appearances of the dead whale excite a very "powerful" not "powerless" panic. Indeed, in the British edition, the wording has been changed to "powerful panic." While Bentley's copyeditor might have questioned "powerless," he would not presume to make such an inversion, and chances are that HM did it. Taking the change to be a correction, not a revision, LCRE also emends the text to "powerful."

Chapter 70

282. *O head! thou hast seen enough to split the planets and make an infidel of Abraham, and not one syllable is thine!*: Ahab's concluding line is expurgated in the British edition because of the irreverent suggestion that the world's horrors might induce the likes of Abraham to forsake God.

Chapter 71

284. *the **archangel** forthwith opened all his seals and vials*: The British reading revises "archangel" to "maniac." Although Ahab is referred to as "monomaniac" several times throughout the book. HM never uses the root word *maniac* by itself in the American edition, and he is not likely to have made this revision. In "The Jeroboam's Story," Gabriel calls himself an "archangel," and Ishmael repeatedly adopts the epithet in referring to Gabriel, thus lending an ironic narratorial sanction to the madman's presumption of divine prophecy. Finding this blasphemous, an editor probably made the change to "maniac." (Two similar revisions for p. 285 are discussed below.)

285. *that **the archangel** cared little*: HM's editor no doubt changed "the archangel" to "he" in the British text.

285. *his archangel nature*: HM's editor revised the phrase to "his self-styled archangel nature" to emphasize Gabriel's delusion.

286. *This **terrible** event*: Probably HM, rather than a British editor, removed "terrible" from this phrase to eliminate the redundancy it creates with "terror-stricken crew" in the previous sentence.

Chapter 72

288. *the Highland costume—a **shirt** and socks—*: The NN edition emends the American and British wording of "shirt" to "skirt," assuming that HM intended the image of Queequeg wearing a kilt. LCRE makes no change.

290. *all of us **men** in this whaling world?*: The word "men" has been deleted in the British edition. With Queequeg figured as a model man in a predominantly male industry, the word may have been considered superfluous; according to this gendered logic, "us" would be presumed to be exclusively masculine. Either HM or an editor may have made the change. Historically, women played an active role in the whaling industry, mostly behind a desk at home but also at sea as captains' wives. But the particular fictional world of *Moby-Dick* is famously male (with such exceptions as Aunt Charity, a mention of Ahab's wife, and Madame Leviathan in Ch. 87), and the possibility that HM might have removed "men" in order to make "each and all of us" include both genders is worth consideration but, finally. remote.

290. *the sort of **bitters** by which he blows back the **life** into a half-drowned man?*: The British reading, no doubt a revision by HM, is "the sort of *bellows* by which he blows back the *breath* into a half-drowned man." Both American and British readings fit the context equally well. The joke in this chapter is that after risking his life on the monkey-rope, Queequeg is offered something like ginger ale to warm him up. Ginger was a common home-remedy for indigestion, and Stubb playfully compares the steward to an apothecary (druggist), who, in the American reading, dispenses "bitters" (that is, mildly alcoholic medications for stomachache and de-worming) in order to restore "life." In the British version, however, the apothecary uses a "bellows" as a life-saving device that puts new "breath" into the half-drowned man. The NN editors follow the British version, arguing only that "breath" is the "more appropriate word" (NN *Moby-Dick*, 790). LCRE acknowledges the revision here but makes no change.

291. *only don't **hit** him again*: Either HM or an editor revised "hit" to "strike" for the British version. The revision heightens the Quaker Starbuck's diction, especially in contrast to Stubb, who uses the word *hit* repeatedly in response to Starbuck's reprimand.

Chapter 73

294. *Blast him!*: In this case, Stubb's profanity was altered to "D—n me!" in the British edition. (See revision narrative for p. 264.)

Chapter 76

303. *as though your own mouth **were** entirely under your chin*: The British edition converts the proper subjunctive "were" (used to indicate conditions contrary to fact) to the marginally grammatical "was." Similar, ill-advised conversions occur elsewhere (see, for instance, revision narrative for p. 82). While an editor might be expected to know better, such changes seem to be editorial rather than authorial.

304. *the dread goddess's veil at **Lais***: The American and British editions read "Lais," which is clearly incorrect. Ishmael refers to the myth of a youth who dies soon after lifting a veil covering a statue of Isis (representing Truth), located in Sais, Egypt. According to the NN editors, the "Lais" error may have been the result of a misreading of HM's handwriting, in which upper-case *L*'s and *S*'s look alike; however, it is also possible that HM inadvertently inscribed "Lais," confusing the place that held the veiled statue of Truth with the famous Athenian courtesan, "Lais, fairest of her kind," whom HM compared to the sculpted architecture of the Parthenon, in his late poem of that name. Mansfield and Vincent emended their Hendricks House text to "Sais," as does the NN edition; LCRE makes no change.

Chapter 79

311. *the mightiest **royal beadle** on his throne*: The British reading replaces "royal beadle" with "royalty." A beadle is a church official who keeps the peace, a kind of parish constable and bill collector. But in obsolete usage, the word also designates a herald of authority or town crier, one who announces proclamations or bears a symbolic staff of power in royal or academic processions. A beadle would not, however, sit on a throne, and HM or an editor may have made the revision to "royalty" as a correction. Since the passage has us imagine ourselves tweaking the nose of royalty, it is a wonder that HM's editor, who elsewhere censored slights against monarchy, did not strike the sentence entirely.

312. *this high and mighty **god-like** dignity*: The British edition adds a second "and" to give "high and mighty and god-like." The additional *and* signals a subtle but real aggrandizement, allowing us to recognize that the Sperm Whale's brow is both "high and mighty" as with such

dignified mortals as Shakespeare, but more: it is also "god-like." Because an editor would not have an interest in making such a subtle transition, HM is more likely to have made the revision. See also revision narrative for p. 177.

Chapter 80

313. *The whale, like all things that are mighty, wears a false **bow** to the common world.*: In this chapter, titled "The Nut," Ishmael notes that the whale's brain is so deeply embedded in the skull that the pseudoscience of phrenology (which gauges character and ability by the shape of the skull) is of no use in understanding the whale's "true brain." The skull, he remarks, is "an entire delusion" and "a false bow." A false bow is additional sheathing or structures, in wood or metal, applied to the bow of a ship to repair damage, provide reinforcement, or deceive enemies; its presence conceals a ship's true structure. However, an argument can be made that "bow" is a typo and that the intended wording is "false brow," a reading that corresponds more closely to phrenology and the word "forehead" in the previous paragraph. The NN edition emends to "brow"; LCRE makes no change.

Chapter 81

317. *I tell **ye** what it is, men*: The British edition alters Stubb's informal or working class dialect "ye" (pronounced yuh) to the formal "you." One explanation is that an editor made the change in an attempt to clean up the dialogue, but this seems unlikely because Stubb's other uses of "ye" are left unrevised. Another possibility is that HM switched to the formal usage to give Stubb's introductory "I tell you" special emphasis, as if he were in effect pointing to his listeners. For other reasons, HM made similar revisions of Ishmael's "ye" to "you" in relating "The Town-Ho's Story"; see revision narrative for p. 227.

317. *The short and **long** of it*: A second "the" was added to the British edition to give "the short and the long of it," an expression introduced into the language in Shakespeare's *The Merry Wives of Windsor* (II, ii). The insertion renders the quotation precisely, and may have been added by HM or an editor.

319. *the **sharp** barbs*: In the British edition "sharp" has been revised to "keen," probably by HM, to eliminate repetition in "sharp lance" later in the same sentence.

Chapter 82

325. *the head-waters of our **fraternity** in nothing short of the great gods themselves*: The British edition gives "paternity" instead of "fraternity." Both readings lead to the same conclusion: whalemen find their father, or affirm that they are brothers with the same father, in the gods. HM probably made the change, although a printer might also have confused the two.

325. *one of the three persons **in** the godhead of the Hindoos*: In the British edition, "in" is altered to "of"; the change in meaning is significant. The preposition "in" seems to treat "godhead" as a pantheon, that is a collection of all gods or a place wherein various orders of gods and their "incarnations" might reside. However, in this paragraph HM directs our attention from "heroes, saints, demigods, and prophets" to the "great gods themselves," and though his phrase, "the three persons *in* the godhead," may indicate that only these three inhabit the godhead (and not their incarnations or avatars), the use of *in* might seem to contradict HM's intended use of "godhead," which properly means the essence of divinity, not a place for the gods to reside. With this in mind, HM may have revised to the more precise phrasing, "the three persons *of* the godhead." Both HM and his editor would have been aware of the doctrine among many Christians of the "Godhead" as the "three-person" God of the Holy Trinity,

and either one might have opted for "of" to stress that trinitarian connection.

Chapter 84

330. *The agonized whale goes into **his** flurry*: The British reading, "its flurry," objectifies the whale, eliminating its gender and thereby reducing its potential for our sympathy. HM may have calculated this effect in making the revision; however, an editor may have made the change (although other references to the whale as "he" and "him" in the chapter and throughout the book are allowed to stand).

Chapter 85

331. *this sixteenth day of December*, A.D. ***1851***: The British and American editions appeared in October and November of 1851, so Ishmael's claim to have written Ch. 85 in December seems impossible. Either HM or a watchful editor changed "1851" to "1850" in the British edition. The variant date in the two editions creates odd and different reading experiences. Typically, in fictions of the time, references to actual dates were represented by dashes, as in "18—." But here, HM's tactic is to jar his contemporary reader into an awareness of the immediacy of Ishmael's writing experience by giving an exact and quite recent date. Of course, the apparent typo of "1851" in the American edition would, for one month, undermine that tactic because for HM's earliest American readers, Ishmael would seem to be writing this chapter, absurdly enough, a month after its publication. However, British readers (with the date changed to "1850") would find Ishmael pinpointing a date of composition more realistically almost a year in the past. The NN editors argue that "1851" is an error resulting from a misreading of HM's handwritten "1850," and they follow the British correction to "1850." But considering the possibility that HM might have intended a little joke with his 1851 date or mistimed the publication of his book, and that the British editor might have acted unilaterally, LCRE makes no change.

334. *such as Plato, Pyrrho, **the Devil**, Jupiter, Dante, and so on*: HM's British editor removed "the Devil" from Ishmael's list of "all ponderous profound beings,"

Chapter 86

336. *And whatever they may reveal of the divine love in the Son, the soft, curled, **hermaphroditical** Italian pictures*: Technically, a hermaphrodite is a plant or animal with both male and female genitals. However, the word can be used to describe anything that combines both sexual traits or, more generally, any opposing characteristics; in some instances, it is synonymous with *effeminate* or *androgynous*, that is, of ambiguous sexuality. HM was probably familiar with a specialized nautical usage, the hermaphrodite brig, a vessel combining the sails of a brig and a schooner. However, his reference to Italian Renaissance renderings of Jesus adopts the word's more daring connotation of *epicene,* indicating not only sexual ambiguity and youthful beauty, but also a lack of masculine strength or vigor. HM's editor removed "hermaphroditical" from the British edition, making Ishmael's complex negotiations, which refer to the tradition of linking Christian benevolence and passivity to androgynous depictions of Christ, more difficult to comprehend.

336. *the opposing **water***: In Ishmael's description, water is a substance that diminishes the impact of the whale's tail. But in the British edition, "water" is pluralized, adding a poetic or biblical tone to the phrase. An editor is not likely to have made the change; instead, HM may have wanted the biblical resonance and changed the word himself.

337. *the middle of **solitary** seas*: The British version reads "the solitary seas." The insertion

of "the" alters meaning significantly, for the phrase "solitary seas" in the American version indicates any sea that happens on occasion to be solitary; whereas "the solitary seas" indicates that all seas are solitary. HM probably made the addition.

337. *You would **almost** think a great gun had been discharged*: The British edition deletes "almost" to give the more certain "You would think." The deletion creates an exact parallelism with the following clause and is probably HM's revision.

337. *the highest **heaven***: In the British edition, "heaven" is pluralized. Throughout *Moby-Dick*, HM uses "heaven" five times more often than "heavens," reserving the plural (except in the commonplace "good heavens") for such expressions as "the seven-storied heavens," "the fabled heavens," "the high heavens," "the starry heavens," "the ineffable heavens," and "the frozen heavens," each preceded with "the," and each evoking a mythic potential. In keeping with that pattern, HM no doubt added an *s* to create the plural "the highest heavens."

337. *Standing at the mast-head **of my ship***: The phrase "of my ship" is odd for a number of reasons. It is superfluous unless Ishmael wants to distinguish this mast-head from that of another ship, but what ship might that be other than the *Pequod*? Elsewhere (particularly in Ch. 54, "The Town-Ho's Story"), Ishmael alludes to sailing on various cruises after the sinking of the *Pequod* and before he writes the present narrative. With this in mind, "of my ship" might lead readers to think that Ishmael is referring to an event occurring on some other vessel on which he sailed, or even mislead them to think he owned a ship. In any event, the British edition removes these considerations by removing the phrase, probably at HM's request.

338. *I **but go** skin deep*: The British edition revises this sentence to "I go but skin deep." Although the change may be a printer's inversion, the repositioning of "but" (meaning "only") creates subtle changes in tone and meaning. In the American edition, the sense of "I only go skin deep" puts limits on Ishmael's metaphoric act of understanding: he doesn't "dive" or "reach"; he only "goes." In the British edition's sense of "I go only skin deep," the adverb placement more clearly states the limit of how far Ishmael can go. As elsewhere, HM may have made this subtle grammatical revision himself.

338. *I know him not, and never **will***: The British edition alteration of "will" to "shall" may have been editorial. In formal English grammar (primarily in England), the word "shall" is reserved for future tense or the conditional; and "will" is reserved for statements of the intention to do something. Thus we have the difference between "Tomorrow I shall go whaling" (future) or "if I go whaling, I shall surely die" (conditional) and "Regardless of what you say, I will go whaling" (intention). HM uses the auxiliary verb "will" 315 times and "shall" 92 times in *Moby-Dick*; however, a cursory study indicates no consistent reliance on the traditional English rule. Nevertheless, the revision from "never will" to "never shall" demonstrates an effective use of the grammatical distinction. Ishmael cannot know the whale, and this is not a matter of what he intends or wishes: the whale is unknowable, now and forever. Thus, even if Ishmael tries to know him, he never shall.

Chapter 87

345. ***still becharmed** panic*: The NN editors argue that "the context makes clear that 'still' is not to be regarded as an adverb [modifying 'becharmed'] but is rather one of two adjectives modifying 'panic'" (803). Accordingly, they revise the text by inserting a comma after "still." However, Ishmael's boat is situated in a "sleek," or smooth-surfaced area of water, in the midst of the otherwise rough waters of the distantly circling whales, and partakes of "an enchanted calm which they say lurks at the very heart of every commotion." The context,

then, also allows for the "becharmed panic" of the small whales to reflect this peculiar combination of "enchanted calm" and "commotion" in the water. And since this "becharmed panic" has persisted throughout the experience, from its first mention in the preceding paragraph, it can be said that the whales' panic is "still becharmed," like a dog's in sniffing a stranger. Given this possibility, LCRE makes no change.

346. *We saw young Leviathan amours in the deep.*: HM's British editor expurgated the sentence for its explicit sexuality. The footnote attached to this sentence in the American edition is attached to the previous sentence in the British.

346. *it might do well with strawberries.* **When overflowing with mutual esteem, the whales salute more hominum.**: In his footnote, attached in the American edition to the sexually-loaded sentence, "We saw young Leviathan amours in the deep," HM adds to Scoresby's discussion of the richness of whale milk, the jolting idea of serving it on strawberries. HM also tinkers with Bennett's observation that whales "couple *more hominum*," that is, they have sex facing each other in the manner of humans. Instead of "couple," HM has his whales "salute," which means simply "to kiss." Nevertheless, HM's British editor saw through the euphemism and expurgated the entire sentence, including the "strawberries" reference.

Chapter 88

350. **impotent**, *repentant, admonitory stage of life*: The notion of impotency as a reason for the Ottoman's sexual restraint comically contradicts his love of virtue, which is cited as a cause in the previous clause. Probably an editor removed "impotent" from the British edition.

350. *his **amorous** errors*: The British edition changes this phrase to "his own juvenile errors," which eliminates the sexual implication.

Chapter 89

353. *by **way** of doxology*: In the British edition, "by way of doxology" is revised to "by the way of doxology." The insertion of "the" is significant. A doxology is any one of several short prayers that inculcate matters of church doctrine; the phrase "by the way of doxology" emphasizes that the defendant captain in the case has not simply resorted to some self-styled seaman's doxology or doctrine to justify his appropriation, but that he has also intoned his rights as if reading from scripture, in "the way" one recites doxologies. Since an editor is not likely to alter the conventional phrasing of "by way of," the revision is probably HM's.

353. **Erskine was on the other side; and he then supported it by saying**: HM drew the details of the "loose-fish" whaling case, in which British barrister Thomas Erskine represented the defense, from an appendix in Scoresby. The description in Scoresby also makes the comparison to the civil case in which a husband filed claims against his estranged wife. Earlier, HM makes clear that "the witty Erskine" had also represented the wife, and HM or an editor dropped the superfluous reference here, revising it to simply "He then proceeded to say."

354. *broken-backed laborers (**all sure of heaven without any of Savesoul's help**) what is that globular 100,000 but a Fast-Fish?*: HM's British editor was willing to allow the author's satire of the facetiously named Anglican archbishop of Savesoul, but expurgated the parenthetical comment, which flatly asserts that the priesthood has no role in an individual's salvation. The British edition also inserted a superfluous lower-case *l* after 100,000 to indicate British pounds.

354. *What is the principle of religious belief in **them** but a Loose-Fish?*: In the British edition, "them" (referring to "all men") has been revised, probably by an editor, to "many of us," thus eliminating HM's claim that, like liberty, belief is a universal, inalienable right.

Chapter 90

356. Is this the still militant old man, standing at the corners of the three kingdoms, on all hands coercing alms of beggars?: HM's disdain for Arthur Wellesley, England's revered Duke of Wellington, is pronounced, and the concluding question concerning the "still militant old man's" greed transgresses civility by expressing scorn for aristocracy as well. The British edition expurgated the entire sentence.

356–57. *"**Ye** tail is **ye** Queen's, that **ye** Queen's wardrobe may be supplied with **ye** whale-bone."*: Chances are that HM instructed that the *e*'s in the four *ye*'s in this quotation be raised in the British edition so that each would appear as "y^e," which denotes an archaic version of the definite article "the," and not the form of *you* spelled and pronounced "ye." The use of this ploy underscores HM's whimsical parody of "black letter," or gothic-style print, and is pure fabrication based on Blackstone's paraphrasing of Prynne, itself referring to the whimsicality of the ancient law in question. The NN editors adopt the superscripted "y^e" in their text. However, the superscripting might represent a change of mind rather than a correction; therefore, LCRE makes no change.

Chapter 91

360. *anything but **a** good humor*: In the British edition, "a" has been dropped to give simply "good humor," which effectively converts "a good humor" into a generalized or more absolute condition. The change may have been HM's decision, or a printer's error.

Chapter 93

367. ***considerations** towards oarsmen . . . is not always manifested*: The British edition alteration of "considerations" to "considerateness" corrects the faulty subject-verb agreement problem, but also modifies meaning. It is not that the whalemen have no consideration toward timid oarsmen like Pip, but that they are not always able to be considerate. Taking the British revision "considerateness" to be a "genuine improvement," not just a correction (788–89), the NN edition emends its text to "considerateness," but because the variant is a revision of meaning, LCRE makes no change.

367. *feels then uncompromised, **indifferent as his God***: The final phrase, "indifferent as his God," was removed in the British version, expurgated by an editor for its double blasphemy: that God is indifferent (or that such indifference is "Heaven's sense"), and that man can achieve this level of divine awareness.

Chapter 95

372. *boiling **out** the oil*: An editor or perhaps a printer dropped "out" from the British edition. The process HM mentions in his footnote (more fully discussed in the following chapter) is the extraction of the oil from the blubber by boiling. Thus, "out" is crucial to the meaning, and an experienced whaler like HM would not have made this erroneous deletion.

Chapter 96

374. *We were clear from the **carcase***: In the British edition, "carcase" is changed to "case." The word might be a typo, but the dropping of an entire syllable (car-) required to make

such an error would be atypical of the smaller typos found in the British version. As a revision, the word "case" is viable but also problematic. In Ch. 77, Ishmael explains that the "case" (or what he calls the Great Heidelburgh Tun) of a whale is the top portion of the head that contains a vast well of liquid spermaceti. According to Beale (HM's primary whaling source in this chapter), the whale's body is stripped first and then disposed of before the case (in the head hanging from the stern) is bailed and dropped, sinking immediately. However, HM's description of the butchering of the whale reverses Beale's sequencing, making the stripping of the carcass the final act. Thus, the American description ends with the *Pequod* getting "clear from the carcase" and makes no mention of the disposal of the head. However, in the British version, the ship gets "clear from the case"; that is, its last act is to dispose of the head, and there is no mention of the stripped carcass. Neither American or British reading adequately accounts for the full and actual whaling practice. Nevertheless, HM's possible revision to "case" underscores his earlier attention to the whale's head and its contents.

Chapter 98

378. ***and, like Shadrach, Meshach, and Abednego***: In the British edition, the comparison to the three Hebrew provincial rulers who, in the book of Daniel, survived execution unscathed in Nebuchadnezzar's fiery furnace, has been removed, and the word "how" is added to sustain the parallelism of the preceding *how*-clauses. HM's reference makes light of a memorable Bible story that depicts Jewish commitment to monotheism. This expurgation also eliminates the irreverent linking of the three heroes to "spermaceti, oil, and bone," the commercial products of the sperm whaling industry.

Chapter 99

383. *I'll get the almanack; and as **I have** heard*: The conversion of "I have" to "I've" in the British edition is almost certainly HM's revision to bring Stubb's colloquial speech in line with his other contractions.

383. *the Ram—**lecherous dog**, he begets us*: A term used freely by HM's early English sources, "lecherous" had little currency in the mid-nineteenth century among polite readers, and it may have been his own desire to tone down the lewdness of his comparison of the Ram to a "lecherous dog" that led HM himself to cut this phrase from the British edition; if not, an editor surely obliged.

383. ***and to wind up*** *with Pisces, or the Fishes, we sleep*: Given its punctuation (not altered in the British edition), the clause is slightly ambiguous. Stubb may be announcing that he is going "to wind up" his discourse and conclude that we sleep with Pisces, or the fishes; or he may be saying that he is winding up his discourse with a focus on Pisces, and our final end is that we sleep in death. The NN edition adds commas to set off "to wind up" and settles on the first reading only; LCRE makes no change.

384. *that **ghost-devil***: The British version reads "that old ghost-devil." Traditionally, in popular culture, the devil is taken to be ancient or ageless. Earlier, in Ch. 50, the demonic Fedallah is also associated with aboriginal culture. Chances are, then, that HM added "old" in the proof sheets he sent to England to sustain the association.

Chapter 100

387. *they **were** mine*: The British edition's conversion of "were" to "are" makes a significant difference with regard to Ahab's sensibility and the earlier discussion of whaling law in "Fast-

Fish and Loose-Fish" (Ch. 89). In the present chapter, Ahab identifies the harpoons stuck in Moby Dick as his; however, according to the law as explained in Ch. 89, the harpoons now belong to the whale, and then to whoever captures that whale. To say that the harpoons "were mine" suggests that Ahab acknowledges his loss; but to say that "they are mine" (as he does in the British edition) suggests that he still claims possession despite the law. Since grammar does not require a shift from "were" to "are," an editor is not likely to have made this change; however, HM, himself, may have revised to intensify Ahab's perceived claim on Moby Dick.

389. *you're a precious jolly rascal*: In the British edition, "you're" is expanded to "you are," putting added emphasis on Captain Boomer's declaration that his companion *is* quite the rascal. An editor is not likely to have bothered with such tonal modulations; chances are HM made the change.

389. *Do ye see this dent, sir*: Dr. Bunger has a more learned demeanor than his companion, Captain Boomer, and the change in the British edition of "ye" to "you" is no doubt HM's tinkering with Bunger's speech to give it more sophistication.

390. *How long since thou saw'st him last*: When Ahab first addresses Captain Boomer, he asks, "Where did'st thou see the White Whale?" And here, in the American edition, he concludes by using the same Quaker locution: "thou." However, in the British edition, HM apparently altered "thou saw'st" to the working-class form "ye saw," something Captain Boomer might say. It is not likely that an editor would make such a change, but it is not clear why HM would make this shift either.

Chapter 101

391. *Samuel and his Sons—how many, their mother only knows—*: Samuel Enderby Jr., son of Samuel, the founder of the famous British whaling firm Samuel Enderby & Sons, was married to Mary, who bore three sons, all of whom inherited the family business in 1829. Since these sons—Charles, Henry and George—remained active in their company, HM's suggestive comment (a routine joke at best) would have offended the still thriving and influential Enderby family, and other British readers. Probably to avoid libel, an editor excised the remark.

391. *to go on a tasting cruise*: HM is drawing directly from Beale's description of the British whaler *Syrene*'s "experimental voyage" to the Pacific, which is called an "experimental cruise" and "tasting cruise" in HM's paraphrase. The NN edition takes the word "tasting" for a typo and emends it to "testing cruise"; LCRE makes no change.

Chapter 102

395. *untagging the points of his hose*: A "point" is a ribbon or lace used to attach a gentleman's doublet (a vest-like jacket) to his hose (leggings); the laces are called points because of the metal tags (also "points") used to keep the tips from fraying. Here, Ishmael speaks of undressing, and the expected verb for undoing the "points of his hose" is something like "unlacing" not "untagging," which suggests removing the metal tips from the laces. In the British edition, the word has been revised to "untrussing." Well into the eighteenth century, to "untruss one's points" was a common term for untying one's clothing. HM may have misspoken in first writing "untagging the points" and realizing the error, revised to "untrussing"; or an editor might have made the correction.

395. *discoursing upon the joists and beams; the rafters, ridge-pole, sleepers, and under-pin-*

nings: In the British edition, the first *the* has been deleted to give "discoursing upon joists and beams." Removing the definite article changes "joists and beams" from individual items to a general category of roof support; what follows the semicolon, then, are the particular kinds of supports. Given this distinctive modulation, the revision may have been HM's.

396. *by that weaving **is he** deafened*: In the British edition, "is he" has been transposed to "he is." The transposition is a common enough typographical event performed, perhaps, by a printer at an inattentive moment, which, in this case, foils the more poetic tone of the inverted "is he" diction. However, HM may have had a hand in the revision. Ishmael's sentence is composed in precise iambic meter, with alternating unstressed and stressed syllables. In fact, the transposition does not mar this consistent beat, for "he is deafened" can be read with the same stress pattern as "is he deafened." The only difference is that in the American version "is" is the stressed word, while in the British, "he" (the "weaver-god") is stressed. The transposition here also puts "he is deafened" in parallel with "we . . . are deafened" in the next clause. This modification, then, may have been authorial.

397. ***Sir Clifford thinks of charging twopence for a peep at the whispering gallery in the spinal column; threepence to hear the echo in the hollow of his cerebellum; and sixpence for the unrivalled view from his forehead.***: HM's acquaintance with Sir F. Clifford Constable is entirely through Beale, who praised the gentleman's good work in bringing to the public the skeleton of a beached whale found in Yorkshire in 1825. Portraying the showman Constable as a British P. T. Barnum may or may not have been fair, but HM's British editor probably removed this sentence to avoid offense or the possibility of a libel suit.

397. *and wished **the** other parts of my body to remain a blank page*: The British edition inserts the word "all" to give "all the other parts of my body." The intensification is not grammatically required and was probably added by HM. The revision suggests not only that Ishmael is a poet, but that the poem he is writing is long enough to fill the entire (otherwise untattooed) surface of his body.

Chapter 103

398. *resembled the **hull***: On the proof sheets he sent to England, HM added the word "embryo" to give "the embryo hull," a bracing image of life amidst death, considering the skeleton being described. The NN edition adds "embryo" to its text; however, given its policy of not mixing versions, LCRE makes no change but notes the revision here.

399. *in place of the **weighty** and majestic*: The British edition changes "weighty" to "mighty." The change might be HM's revision, but "weighty," implying both heavy and significant, seems to be the better word in context, and the shift to "mighty" could also be a British printer's error. However, equally plausible is that HM intended "mighty" in manuscript and that the word was misread by his American printer as "weighty," in which case the British change might be HM's correction of "weighty" to his original "mighty."

399. *great **knobbed** blocks on a Gothic spire*: HM viewed over a dozen gothic cathedrals in his tour of England in 1849–50, and had ample opportunity to observe the characteristic spires, which, at a distance, appear to be ornamented with knobs. Up close, the knobs are tight flower buds that look like brussels sprouts. In the British edition, "knobbed" has been altered to "knobbled," which is probably not a typo. "Knobble," an archaic form of the word "knob," seems to have been regaining currency in the mid-nineteenth century, and according to the *Oxford English Dictionary*, at least one editor had made the shift from "knobbed" to "knobbled" in a standard dictionary entry on glassblowing. Here, the change also seems to be editorial.

399. *some little cannibal urchins, **the priest's children***: The British edition removes "the priest's children." Even though Polynesian and Protestant priests were not celibate, the implication of reproduction in the expression, "priest's children," added to the suggestion that such offspring might steal sacred bones to play marbles, was irreverent enough to doom the seemingly innocuous phrase.

Chapter 104

400. *a huge quarto **edition** of Johnson*: Samuel Johnson's *Dictionary of the English Language* (1755) first appeared as a folio, and was not published as a quarto until 1808. (Ishmael makes use of these bibliographic terms in his classification of whales by size in Ch. 32, "Cetology." Here, a similar joke is employed: a large-format dictionary is appropriate for the big words needed to describe Leviathan.) Because, in most cases, the size of a book is an integral part of what defines an "edition" of a work, Ishmael's phrase, "quarto edition," is redundant, and either he or (more likely) an editor dropped the word "edition" from the British version.

401. *throughout the whole universe, **not excluding its suburbs***: In the British edition, "not excluding its suburbs" is deleted, probably at HM's request. Ishmael's famous seriocomic paragraph on the writing of his narrative combines humorous exaggeration with more serious notions of the "comprehensiveness" of his ideas and the crafting of "a mighty book." In fact, so comprehensive are his thoughts that they embrace "the whole universe, not excluding its suburbs." The flippant paradox of the "whole universe" as somehow having "suburbs," is a serviceable joke in keeping with Ishmael's inveterate self-deflation. At the same time, its removal allows the sentence to end on a more serious note, one that does not detract the reader's attention from the notion of a "mighty theme" to come.

402. *Who can show a pedigree like **Leviathan***?: The word "the" has been added (probably by HM) to give "the Leviathan" in the British edition. Throughout *Moby-Dick*, HM uses "Leviathan" (both upper- and lower-case) either in reference to the biblical creature (twenty-six times), in which case the definite article is not used, or as a term referring to a specific whale or to whales in general (sixty-seven times), in which case the definite or indefinite article (or a word such as each, any, this, or that) is used. Since HM is referring to "ante-chronical" (that is, prehistoric) whales, the evolutionary ancestors of the present species, and not a biblical or mythic beast, the insertion of "the" is justified.

402. *after all **humane** ages*: In the British edition, "humane" has been altered to "human," which in context seems to be the more likely word. That is, when humankind ceases to exist, the "terrors of the whale" will continue. Hence, the alteration may be a correction, and one performed by HM or an editor. Also plausible is that HM intended "humane" to suggest that humankind's period of existence is characterized by a sense of humanity in stark contrast to the "terrors" symbolized by the whale. In this case, the word "human" may not have been a correction (or revision for that matter), but simply a typo.

Chapter 107

409. *If he **did not have** a common soul*: The change in the British edition to "If he had not a common soul" makes the dependent clause parallel with the main clause, "he had a subtle something, . . ." and it eliminates the repetition of "did" later on. Chances are that HM made the revision.

Chapter 110

418. *which alike levels all, **alike** impresses all*: In the British edition, the second *alike* has been

cut, possibly by an editor to remove the grammatically unnecessary repetition. The repetition of "alike" creates a halting rhythm that underscores the idea that every person not only dies but also has at the end a special revelation; this stressed commonality also validates Queequeg's final vision, even though he is a "savage." If HM made the cut, he might have done so because he no longer felt that the halting rhythm was effective. Another possibility is that the repetition was an error to begin with; that is, HM may have originally written "which levels all, alike impresses all," and then transposed "alike" so that it would appear before "levels," but his American printer failed to remove the original *alike*, thus creating the repetition. In this scenario, HM would have corrected the error by removing the second *alike* in the British edition.

418. *and so form the white breakers of the milky way.* ***He*** *added, that he shuddered*: In the British edition, this passage has been revised so that the two sentences are joined by a dash and the phrase "after saying this." The alteration involves a subtle clarification of who is speaking that an editor would not presume to make; therefore, HM most likely made the change. In this passage, Ishmael relates that Queequeg "called one to him" (presumably Ishmael himself) and "said" that he had observed the use of coffins for burial in Nantucket, which "was not unlike" the Polynesian custom of setting corpses adrift in canoes. In effect, Ishmael is relating Queequeg's words through indirect dialogue, and for the most part balances Queequeg's diction ("dark canoes") with his own ("starry archipelagoes"). But as he proceeds, Ishmael's idiom begins to dominate: "for not only do they believe that the stars are isles [Queequeg's idiom], but that far beyond all visible horizons, their own mild, uncontinented seas, interflow with the blue heavens; and so form the white breakers of the milky way" [Ishmael's]. HM's insertion of "after saying this" clearly assigns such Ishmaelean words as "visible horizons," "mild, uncontinented seas," and "interflow" to Queequeg, thus, in some way blending the two consciousnesses.

Chapter 111

422. *whose* ***gently*** *awful stirrings*: In the British version, the change from "gently" to "gentle" may be a typo; however, the alteration creates a significant tonal variation: "gently awful" suggests stirrings that inspire awe in a gentle way; "gentle awful" suggests stirrings that are both gentle and awe-inspiring at the same time. One version of the Anglican hymn, "Come to Our Poor Nature's Night," includes the phrase "Gentle, awful Holy Guest" in reference to the Holy Ghost as a "comforter divine," and an editor or a printer may have had this lyric in mind when he consciously or unconsciously altered "gently" to "gentle."

422. *wide-rolling* ***watery*** *prairies* ***and Potters' Fields*** *of all four continents*: The two changes in the British version of this passage may be HM's revisions. First, "watery prairies" has been altered to "water prairies." Thus, instead of an image of plains dotted with pools of water, we are given a metaphor (like the preceding image of "sea-pastures") that evokes prairie-like expanses of water. Second, "and Potters' Fields" has been removed entirely so that the final British text reads "wide-rolling water prairies of all four continents." A potter's field is a graveyard for the poor, and HM may have felt that such a social reference, although used elsewhere in *Moby-Dick*, was not appropriate for the mystical tone of the passage.

422. *zones the world's* ***whole*** *bulk about*: In the British edition, the revision of "whole" to "own," probably made by HM, creates an internal rhyme between "own" and "zones," and may have been performed to enhance the poetic quality of Ishmael's prose paean to the Pacific.

Chapter 113

428. *cluster of dark **nods** replied*: In the British edition, the word "nods" appears as "nobs." The seemingly obvious explanation is that the change is due to the common error of a printer's mixing up of the letter *b* with its mirror image *d*. However, the word "nob" was, and remains, a slang term for head, and a cluster of dark heads, rather than the nodding the heads perform, is a viable image, so that the change may be a revision.

Chapter 116

435. *thy **unnamable** imminglings*: HM probably revised "unnameable" to "nameless" on the proof sheets he sent to England. The change in meaning is significant. Watching the dying whale turn toward the sun, Ahab experiences a "wondrousness unknown before," and in the soliloquy that follows, he distinguishes the whale's vain sun worship at the end from the sea's darker truth which rocks him "with a prouder, if a darker faith." But by referring to the sea's "imminglings" (its mixtures of life and death) as "unnamable," Ahab admits that these mysteries cannot be named or known, and that he has no control over them. However, the revision to "nameless" alters this effect, suggesting that while the imminglings are presently nameless, they are nevertheless "namable," hence knowable in some way. The prideful implication is that Ahab's "darker faith" allows him a measure of control over the unknown.

Chapter 118

438. *and **the** eager mariners quickly run*: In the British edition, "the" has been dropped. Though probably a typo, the missing word may convey a significantly different meaning. Whereas "the eager mariners" implies that all the crew of the *Pequod* are eager; "eager mariners" may mean only those of the crew who are eager. Since Ahab's success depends upon the eagerness of the entire crew, the dropped "the" might suggest some dissent, an important matter in the final chapters.

438. ***Now**, in that Japanese sea*: Although in his whaling years HM traveled as far west in the Pacific as Tahiti and Hawai'i, he never approached Japan. Indeed, most of *Moby-Dick* is set in waters the author never sailed. In the proof sheets he sent to England, HM almost certainly inserted the important qualifier "sometimes" after "Now," as a hedge on his statement (personally unverifiable given his limited experience) concerning the "days in summer" in that Japanese sea. The NN edition adds this revision. LCRE makes no change, but notes the revision here.

438. *his wild face was subdued to an **earthly** passionlessness*: The British edition alteration of "earthly" to "unearthly" may be an authorial correction or revision. That is, HM may have originally intended "unearthly," but his American typesetter dropped the "un-," and HM used the British edition to correct the American typo to "unearthly." Or he may have intended "earthly" and changed his mind to "unearthly." In either event, the change is significant. The Parsee (Fedallah) is dark and racialized, hence, arguably "earthly"; however, he is also ominous and remote, hence "unearthly." In this scene, his "wild face" transforms into a "passionlessness" so that we in fact witness both his "earthly" and "unearthly" attributes. The use of any modifier (earthly or unearthly) allows for a subtle modulation of Fedallah's character and the change to "unearthly" at this point in the narrative stresses his more ethereal potential, in keeping with his prophetic role as Ahab approaches his fated end.

439. *live in the game, and **die it**!*: The oddly elliptical phrasing of "and die it" appears in both the American and British editions. Given HM's occasional Shakespeareanisms (as in "Down, dog, and kennel" in Ch. 29) and the peculiarities of Stubb's diction, the barely grammatical expression might be intended. The NN edition considers the wording to be one of many

"mistakes in typesetting" (792) and emends it to "and die in it," which is only one of several possible emendations. LCRE makes no change.

Chapter 119

443. *lofty **tri-pointed trinity** of flames*: A British editor is probably responsible for the revision of this phrase to "try-pointed flames." Removing "trinity of" eliminates the apparent redundancy of "tri-pointed trinity," but also the crucial (though no doubt sacrilegious) comparison of the glowing masts to the "Holy Trinity." In fact, HM is attempting to describe three sets of three-pointed flames, each set on a separate mast, as referenced in the "nine flames" mentioned in the subsequent stage direction, so there is no redundancy. As for the alteration of "tri-" to "try-," the latter does not appear in the *OED* as an alternative spelling for the former, nor is it likely to be HM's invention, as it would confusingly echo the many earlier references to "try-works." However, having had to compose the word "try" so often, a printer may have inadvertently made the change, thus creating a typo.

444. *thou **omnipotent***: The British version reads "thou omniscient," a likely revision by HM. In this scene, Ahab challenges the inscrutable, god-like force embodied in the electric glow from the masts; his claim to superiority is that while he knows both how he was begotten and that he has a beginning, this force he confronts does not. Moreover, it does not know what Ahab further claims: there is "some suffusing thing beyond thee," which Ahab feels he is close to grasping. Thus, when Ahab states, "I know that of me, which thou knowest not of thyself, oh, thou omnipotent," the final word is delivered sarcastically, for Ahab's point is that this god-like force is not in fact "all powerful." But since self-awareness and knowledge, not power, are at stake in Ahab's speech, the revision to "omniscient" (meaning all-knowing) is all the more ironic.

Chapter 123

449. ***oh-he-yo***: The chorus of syllables from the sea shanty "Cheerly, Men" has been changed in the British edition to *"ho-he-ho."* HM knew the song from his sailing days, and words from it, in different spellings, appear one way or another in his early works. He refers to the shanty twice in *Omoo*, once with sailors singing out simply, "Ho, cheerly men!" The song's chorus is rendered most fully in *Redburn* as *"Ho-o-he-yo, cheerily men!"* The shorter "oh-he-yo" and "ho-he-ho" found in *Moby-Dick*'s American and British editions, respectively, may be attempts to vary the sound of the chorus for aesthetic reasons.

450. *if this ship **come** to any deadly harm*: HM's proper use of the subjunctive in "if this ship come" to indicate a hypothetical possibility has been changed in the British edition to the conditional, "if this ship comes." This inconsistent removal of HM's subjunctives appears elsewhere and is probably the work of a British editor.

450. *and slowly, **stealthily,** and half sideways looking*: The British version reads "steadily" instead of "stealthily." Both readings are viable. Starbuck is contemplating what to do with the sleeping Ahab, and he considers the possibility of murder. Either he "stealthily" aims his musket, suggesting his shame in contemplating the deed; or he "steadily" aims, which suggests his resolve. "Stealthily" reinforces the "half sideways looking" that follows; however, "steadily" reinforces the word "slowly" that comes before. The change could be either a correction or a revision made by HM.

Chapter 124

453. *The yards were **braced** hard up*: The American edition reads simply "The yards were hard up"; "braced" was added in the British version. The expression is intended to indicate that

the yards have been pulled in such a way as to point the ship as straight into the wind as possible. In nautical dictionaries of the day, "hard up" used by itself is applied only to the rudder (which has no braces), and "braced hard up" is the appropriate terminology for yards. Since an editor is not likely to make such a change, and since it is almost certainly HM's correction, not a revision or change of mind, LCRE adopts the British reading, as does the NN edition.

453. *the compasses would* ***fain*** *have wrecked me*: The American reading is "feign," which was corrected to "fain" in the British edition by either HM or an editor. The two words are homonyms. The verb "feign" means to deceive or indulge in fiction; the adverb "fain" means gladly or eagerly. HM's sentence structure clearly calls for an adverb, either "feignedly" (meaning deceivingly) or "fain." Previously, in Ch. 118, Ahab destroyed his quadrant, and he continues to navigate by dead reckoning; now, as if in retaliation, the electrical storm has inverted the polarity of his compass needles. The fact that Ahab was at first deceived by the inverted compasses would argue that something like "feignedly" may have been HM's intended word. However, claiming that he "is lord over the level loadstone" (the magnetized needle), Ahab reacts to the deception with renewed defiance: the world would eagerly destroy him, but now he will just as eagerly strike back. Thus, the word "fain" is also appropriate. However, since "feigned" appears only once in *Moby-Dick*, and "feignedly" never; and given that "would fain" appears over a dozen times, HM's intended word is most likely "fain." Moreover, the British edition's change to "fain," whether by HM or an editor, corrects both the misspelling and the sentence's grammar. LCRE follows the British text and corrects to "fain."

Chapter 125

456. *to him* ***nothing's*** *happened*: The British edition alters "nothing's" to "nothing." While this may be a typo, the change also alters meaning and may, therefore, be an intentional revision. "Nothing's happened" is a contraction of the present perfect, "nothing has happened," and from the Manxman's point of view this usage seems to refer to his recognition of the series of events that Ahab has just enumerated: the crushed quadrant, the inverted needles, the lost log and line. The Manxman (whose prophetic insight is first revealed in Ch. 40) seems to accept Ahab's broader perspective, but adds to it his own pessimistic interpretation that "something seems loosening out of the middle of the world." However, the British reading— "nothing happened"—converts the present perfect to the simple past tense and seems to refer only to the most immediate, log and line incident, and not Ahab's enumerated series. The alteration to "nothing," then, effectively reduces the scope of the Manxman's insight.

456. One hundred pounds of clay reward for Pip;: The NN edition finds a "lack of sense" in Pip's call for a reward as it appears in both the American and British versions (902), and it alters the text to read: "Reward for Pip! One hundred pounds of clay—" (522). In its original form, Pip may be offering nothing but a "clay reward" for his recovery, indicating his lack of self-esteem (and furthering Stubb's reduction of him in Ch. 93 to mere cash), and evoking the biblical notion that all humans are nothing but clay. The NN reading argues that HM intended Pip to announce an unspecified reward for himself and then offer an itemized description beginning with his weight, "One hundred pounds of clay." While this emendation is reasonable, LCRE makes no change.

457. ***What's*** *this?*: In the British edition, "What's" has been changed to "Who's." The "what," in the American version, is Ahab's hand, which Pip then calls "so kind a thing"; the reference to Ahab's hand as "a thing" justifies the pronoun "what." The alteration of "what" to "who" in the British version converts the hand into a representation of Ahab. Such a recognition may hint at the crazed and alienated Pip's own return to personhood. Since "what" is grammatically preferred, it seems unlikely that an editor would have made the change; HM is the likely reviser.

Chapter 127

461. ***I will*** *be with ye again presently*: Probably HM, not an editor, altered "I will" to "I'll" in the British edition to signal Ahab's growing intimacy with Pip.

462. *get these traps out of **sight***: The British version reads "out of my sight." The insertion of "my" appropriately modifies Ahab's order: in the American version he gives the impossible command that the process of converting Queequeg's coffin into a life-buoy be concealed from everyone's view; in the British, he orders the process hidden from his view only. The revision, probably made by HM, underscores Ahab's growing anxiety.

462. *Blind and **dumb** might well be envied now*: Ahab's opening words in his soliloquy, "There's a sight! There's a sound!" set up a parallelism imperfectly matched in the subsequent line in which Ahab wishes he might be "Blind and dumb." This is a sight he does not want to see and a sound he does not want to hear; therefore, "blind and deaf" is the expected phrase. A likely cause of the error is that the phrase "blind and dumb," repeated in a scene from one of Jesus' miracles (Matthew 12.22), may have come to mind while HM was writing. The NN edition emends "dumb" to "deaf." Because the error does not seriously confuse the reader, LCRE makes no change.

462. *the dark side of **earth***: In the British edition, "the" has been inserted to give "the dark side of the earth." The change alters meaning significantly, and brings the imagery closer to a recurring pattern in HM's writing that contrasts, but also combines, the dark and bright sides of reality. In his soliloquy, Ahab refers to the planet Earth, with its night and day hemispheres. Although the world revolves through these dark and bright regions, Ahab claims he is stuck in the dark side always: for him, the bright side seems only "theoretic," and twilight (that is, light becoming darkness) is uncertainty. (In a positive inversion of this image found in his "Mosses" essay, HM likens Hawthorne, whose fiction unites bright and dark views, to an "evermoving dawn.") But, in the American edition, "earth" (not capitalized and without the definite article) may indicate soil, the substance of the material world, not the actual revolving planet. Of course, HM may have initially intended this symbolic meaning so that Ahab seems to position himself in the perpetual darkness of materiality (earth); however, "the earth" indicates an equally intentional shift in symbol to the image of the planet, and is congruent with the "twilight" imagery that concludes the sentence. Whether a correction or revision, the change was probably made by HM and not an editor.

Chapter 129

466. *the blackness of his **living** skin*: The British version deletes "living." After his nearly fatal abandonment, Pip consistently considers himself dead; here, however, he mentions his "drowned bones" and yet, incongruously, his "living skin." Chances are that HM authorized the deletion of "living" in this instance to sustain Pip's self-image as being no longer alive.

Chapter 130

468. *his wan but wondrous eyes **did plainly say***: The Bible-like phrasing "did plainly say" has been altered to the more direct, less portentous "plainly said" in the British edition. The same kind of change occurs in several places in the final chapters, indicating a pattern of revision more readily attributable to HM than to an editor. (See also the shift from "did crack" to "cracked" in Ch. 133 and "did point" to "pointed" in Ch. 134, both listed in Variants Not Discussed.)

470. *relying eye upon the chief mate, **he said***: HM's long sentence describing Ahab's reviewing of the crew consists of two main clauses combined by a semicolon. The series of introductory phrases that begins the second clause ("pausing his glance . . .," "but shunning . . .,"

and "then settling . . .") requires a subject and verb to complete the sentence; however, the American version simply reads "said," with no subject. The introductory phrases might be confused as a continuation of the first clause; but if this were the case, the sentence would require a compound verb "and said" to make sense, and there is no conjunction in the text either. Without the requisite subject (or conjunction), HM's long sentence is grammatically incorrect. A British editor or HM corrected the error by supplying the needed "he," and LCRE does the same.

Chapter 131

472. *Are **ye** ready there?*: The captain of the *Delight* speaks formally to Ahab, using such forms as "thee," "thou," and "you"; however, he uses the more familiar word "ye" when he addresses the crew. The British edition alters "ye" in this instance to "you," thus eliminating this subtle verbal distinction.

Chapter 132

475. *however **wilful and** erring*: The British edition deletes "wilful and," thus eliminating the parallelism with "to save and to bless" at the end of the sentence; the deletion also removes the notion that Ahab has been merely willful. HM may have authorized the change.

476. *better than to gaze into **sea** or sky; better than to **gaze** upon God*: The British edition shows evidence of HM's tinkering. The word "the" is inserted to give the more specific "the sea or sky," and the second *gaze* is revised to "look" to eliminate the repetition but also, perhaps, to bring the text closer to scripture: "And Moses hid his face; for he was afraid to look upon God" (Exodus 3.6).

Chapter 133

480. *not Jove**, not that great majesty Supreme**!*: The epithet ("not that great majesty Supreme") is omitted in the British edition, no doubt an editorial cut to eliminate Ishmael's mild blasphemy.

480. *the parted swell, that but once **leaving** him, then flowed so wide away*: The British edition alters "leaving" to "laving." Both words are viable. On the one hand, the "parted swell" that Moby Dick makes as he swims forward may be seen first to "leave" his side and then "flow" widely away; on the other hand, the swell may be seen to "lave" or wash the whale's side before flowing off. The NN edition argues that "laving" is the "more appropriate word" (789) and emends its text accordingly; LCRE makes no change.

480. *Ahab could **discover** no sign*: The British edition revises "discover" to "perceive," a change certainly made by HM. In this memorable scene, Ahab peers into the water and eventually sees Moby Dick rising from deep below, appearing at first as merely a "white living spot." But the birds floating on the surface have already sensed this initially invisible thing; their "vision" is "keener" than Ahab's, and in the American version Ahab cannot "discover" what they see. At the end of the next, chilling sentence, Moby Dick is seen rising from the "undiscoverable" sea floor. Since Ahab's human vision (vis à vis the birds) is at issue here, and since the "undiscoverable" sources and ocean home of Moby Dick are mentioned later, HM may have revised "discover" to "perceive" to accentuate Ahab's limited vision, distinguishing more effectively the subsequent matter of undiscoverability.

481. *wrench it from **its** gripe*: HM or perhaps an editor changed "its" to "his" in the British edition to stress Moby Dick's gender and bring the pronoun into conformity with the two other masculine pronouns referring to the whale in the paragraph and elsewhere.

483. **Moby Dick**: The consistent pattern of hyphenation in the American edition is that the book's title (*Moby-Dick*) is hyphenated while the name of the whale is not. The only exception is the one instance here, in which the whale's name appears as "Moby-Dick." The British edition hyphenates neither title nor name, and either HM or a British editor may have removed the hyphen from this one American text exception to bring the name into full conformity with the standard, unhyphenated spelling. The NN edition follows the British reading here, as does LCRE.

Chapter 134

486. *guilt and* **guiltiness**: In context, this pairing of similar rather than contrasting features is certainly an error. In the preceding lines, Ishmael demonstrates the crew's "individualities" with the initial pairing of "this man's valor, that man's fear." However, the "guilt and guiltiness" pairing of two virtually equivalent values does not parallel that contrast, and the promise of an example of the crew's "varieties" is not fulfilled. The British edition does not correct this error. To fix it, the NN edition emends "guiltiness" to "guiltlessness," arguing that the latter word was probably misread in manuscript as the former (792). But the emendation creates an inversion of the value arrangement: that is, whereas the first pair places positive before negative (valor then fear), the second as emended places negative before positive (guilt then guiltlessness). Moreover, the appearance of the word "guilt" in both features is oddly repetitious. One possibility is that "guilt" is the misread word, and that HM intended some other contrasting term, perhaps something like "purity," to be printed. Although the text is flawed, there can be no definite correction. LCRE makes no change.

489. *As with Fedallah the day before, so Ahab was now found* **grimly** *clinging*: The British edition removes the word "grimly"; HM probably made the change. On the previous day, after Moby Dick has crushed Ahab's whale boat, Fedallah is found "incuriously and mildly" eyeing Ahab while the crew clings to the wrecked stern. HM may have deleted "grimly" because it does not accurately recall Fedallah's incurious and mild demeanor.

Chapter 135

493. *Mississippies of the land* **swift** *and swerve about*: The British edition alters "swift" to "shift"; both verbs make sense. According to the *OED*, "swift" can mean "to go swiftly." Thus, "swift and swerve" is a legitimate alliterating doublet (pairing of synonyms) that parallels "turn and tack" earlier in the text. But since the Mississippi is well known for its shifting banks, it is also possible that HM revised the text to "shift."

495. *but clouds* **sweep** *between*: In the British edition, "sweep" is changed to "step." Given that Starbuck has used the words "shoots through me" and "swim before me" to describe his rush of emotions, the use of "sweep between" seems an appealing and more effective word choice than the mundane, even anthropomorphic "step between." HM might have authorized the change, but it is probably a typo.

495. *Suddenly the* **waters** *around them slowly swelled*: The word "waters" is revised to "waves" in the British edition, probably by HM. The alteration exchanges one repetition for another. Overall, "waters" seems the better word since the collective sea around the boat (including its waves) swells as Moby Dick breaches. However, "waters" also appears later in the paragraph, and HM may have revised to "waves" to reduce that repetition, even though "waves" itself is repeated twice in the preceding lines.

496. *Daggoo and* **Queequeg**: Queequeg is Starbuck's harpooneer, and since Starbuck stays on the *Pequod* while the other boat crews hunt Moby Dick, it is assumed that Queequeg would also stay behind. The NN edition therefore argues that his presence in this scene is an error (905), and it changes "Queequeg" to "Tashtego." LCRE makes no change.

497. *Almost* **simultaneously**, *with a mighty volition of ungraduated, instantaneous swiftness*: In the British edition, "simultaneously" is changed to "instantaneously," most likely the result of a printer's "eye-skip" to "instantaneous" at the end of the sentence. However, there is some logic to the change. Once harpooned, Moby Dick first writhes then immediately darts off; however, the lengthy description of the three sailors' being bumped—important because the third is Ishmael who survives to tell the tale—intervenes between these two "almost simultaneous" events, and by the time the text reaches the second event, the simultaneity of the writhing and darting off might not on second thought have seemed relevant to HM. One possibility, then, is that HM intended to substitute "instantaneously" for "simultaneously" and delete what would then become a repetitive "instantaneous" at the end of the sentence; however, while the transposition was made, the deletion of "instantaneous" was not.

498. *yet ring glasses with* **ye** . . . *Oh, oh!* **oh, oh!** *thou grinning whale*: HM probably altered Stubb's "ye" to the grammatically correct "thee" in the British edition, bringing the phrasing in parallel with "I grin at thee" three sentences earlier. In addition, the fourth *oh!* has been altered to "ho!" in the British edition. HM may have made the change to add a touch of characteristic humor to Stubb's speech. Rather than repeat the "oh oh" phrasing to render a kind of worrisome "Uh oh," HM may have Stubb modulate that worry into a more jaunty greeting to the whale itself: "oh ho."

499. *thou uncracked keel;* **and only god-bullied hull**: The second phrase suggests that only God can damage the *Pequod*, and that God is a bully; thus, "only god-bullied hull" is remarkable for the economy of its offense to the religious sensibilities of the day, and for that, it was expurgated in the British edition.

499. *with* **archangelic** *shrieks*: The revision in the British edition to "unearthly shrieks" was probably performed by a censorious editor.

Epilogue

500. *EPILOGUE*: The entire "Epilogue" was omitted from the British edition. Since it is the only evidence of Ishmael's survival, the omission caused HM undeserved embarrassment when British reviewers marveled at the ineptitude of a narrative whose narrator seems to die with the rest of the crew. The British edition also prints "Etymology" and "Extracts" (properly positioned in the front) as back matter. One explanation for the omission of the "Epilogue" and misplacement of "Etymology" and "Extracts" is that the American proofs for these elements may have been sent to England together but separately from the rest of the proofs, and that in the last-minute flurry to get the book published, the "Epilogue" was simply overlooked.

LIST OF IN-TEXT REVISION NARRATIVES

In the LCRE *Moby-Dick*, narratives explaining representative revisions to HM's text appear on the text pages near the revision sites being discussed. The following list provides the titles and page numbers for these thirty-one "in-text" revision narratives. Over three hundred other revision sites are discussed in narratives found in Making *Moby-Dick*. Readers will also find over five hundred additional revision sites too numerous to discuss in **Changes Not Discussed**.

CHANGES NOT DISCUSSED

Significant revisions to the first American edition of *Moby-Dick*—found in the *Harper's New Monthly Magazine* version of Ch. 54 (H), the first British edition (B), the Northwestern-Newberry edition (NN), and this edition (LCRE)—are discussed in the LCRE revision narratives. Thirty-one narratives appear in the text of *Moby-Dick*, near the relevant revision sites (see **List of In-Text Revision Narratives** for an index of these narratives); and over three hundred other sites are discussed in the revision narratives in Making *Moby-Dick*. Listed below are over 550 additional revision sites too numerous to be discussed in this edition. Readers may inspect these changes ("variants") in context, and devise revision narratives of their own. (A website for sharing narratives is under consideration.) In this list of changes not discussed (which includes authorial and editorial revisions as well as undiscussed NN and LCRE emendations), a vertical bar (|) separates the American edition text on the left from its variant on the right; the bracketed abbreviations following a variant indicate the variant's appearance in one or more of the versions indicated above. Dropped letters or broken type are represented with braces ({}). Accordingly, the entry **Rokovoko | Kokovoko [B, NN, LCRE]** indicates that the word "Rokovoko" in the American edition was changed to "Kokovoko" in the British, and that this variant was then adopted as an emendation by both the NN and LCRE editions.

Extracts

11.9 like | like a [B] • 11.14 *Ibid* | *Ibid.* [B, NN, LCRE] • 11.19 leach's | leech's [B] • 11.19 secure | recure [NN] • 11.21 lowly | lovely [NN] • 11.23 thro' | from [NN] • 11.28 Hosmannus | Hofmannus [NN, LCRE] • 12.32 feet | foot [NN, LCRE] • 13.4 *into* | *to* [B] • 13.6 huge | large [B] • 13.14 Shetland | Hitland [NN] • 13.21 feet | foot [NN] • 13.23 Pitferren | Pitfirren [NN, LCRE] • 13.28 *Strafford's* | *Stafford's* [NN, LCRE] • 13.33 those | these [NN] • 14.4 stuffed | stiff [B, NN] • 14.9 *Goldsmith,* | *Goldsmith's* [B] • 14.26 1778 | 1788 [NN] • 14.35 coast | coasts [NN] • 15.6 blew | flew [NN] • 15.7 fire | fires [NN, LCRE] • 15.8 Around | Amid [NN] • 15.35 instincts | instinct [NN] • 15.38 jaw. | jaw, [B, NN, LCRE] • 16.29 *Ocean.* | *Ocean."* [NN, LCRE] • 17.22 these | those [NN] • 17.40 *Cruize* | *Cruise* [B, NN] • 18.3 *Mutiny,* | *Mutiny,"* [NN, LCRE] • 18.4 *Hussey* | *Hussey,* [NN] • 18.10 *Bennett* | *Bennet* [NN, LCRE] • 18.19 *gathered* | *as gathered* [NN] • 18.24 *tke* | *the* [B, NN, LCRE] • 18.34 near | mere [NN, LCRE] • 19.15 *Fisherman* | *Fishermen* [NN] • 19.24 upon turning | turning [B]

Chapters 1–15

21.16 battery | Battery [B, NN, LCRE] • 21.19 of | on [B] • 22.5 virtue of | virtue in [B] • 23.16 about some | about [B] • 24.4 other's | others' [B] • 25.20 mid most | midmost [B, NN, LCRE] • 31.8 handle | handle, [NN] • 31.22 of | on [B] • 31.37 gulph | gulp [B] • 32.15 he | she [B] • 33.8 or whether | whether [B] • 34.11 feeling of | feeling [B] • 34.33 what | that [B] • 35.3 early | airley [B, NN] • 35.6 bamboozingly | bamboozling [B, NN, LCRE] • 36.32 wardrobe, no doubt | wardrobe no doubt, [NN] • 36.39-40 as you see the same | the same as [B] • 37.2 it of | it on [B] • 39.14 so long been | been so long [B] • 41.18 mother | stepmother [B] • 41.27 going down | going [B] • 43.26 auy | any [B, NN, LCRE] • 47.14 Tongatabooars | Tongatabooans [B, NN, LCRE] • 47.21 came | come [B] • 48.11 condition | a condition [B] • 51.9 a universal | an universal [B] • 51.17 wherefore but | wherefore [B] • 51.32 me | myself [B] • 52.23 a stairs | stairs [B] • 55.12 "And | 'And [B, NN, LCRE] • 55.13 Jonah." | Jonah.' [B, NN, LCRE] • 56.26 'Who's | "'Who's [B, NN, LCRE] • 56.38 Now | "Now [B, NN, LCRE] • 58.24 became | become [B, NN] • 58.30 of | upon [B] • 58.31 And | "And [B, NN, LCRE] • 60.24 remained kneeling | remained, kneeling [NN] • 62.9 night previous | previous night [B] • 63.8 then | there [B] • 67.3 When | While yet [B] • 68.1 Czar | the Czar [B] • 70.9 hand | hands [NN] • 70.16 & 20 Rokovoko | Kokovoko [B, NN, LCRE] • 71.13 brows | bows [B, NN, LCRE] • 73.16 extravaganzas | extravagances [B] • 73.23 there they | there [B] • 74.21 not | scarcely [B] • 75.4 & 7 Try | Twy

[B] • 76.29 fishing | fishy [B, NN, LCRE] • 76.37 this here | this [B] • 76.37 on | upon [B] • 76.40 Try | Twy [B] • 77.2 vertebra | vertebrae [B] • 77.19 herring | herrings [B]

Chapters 16–30

78.7 purposed | proposed [B] • 79.17 Beckett | Becket [B, NN, LCRE] • 79.30 over | through [B] • 79.34 its | his [B] • 80.32 Merchant | Marchant [B, NN] • 81.13 by | about [B] • 82.34 virgin voluntary | virgin, voluntary, [B, NN, LCRE] • 85.4 what | that [B] • 85.4 mighty deal | deal [B] • 85.9 *"Lay* | " *'Lay* [NN] • 85.10 moth—" | moth—'" [NN] • 85.28 "for | " 'for [NN] • 85.29 also." | also.'" [NN] • 86.23 to | a [B] • 86.39 shore | short [B] • 86.40 have | has [B] • 87.15 that | that, [B, NN, LCRE] • 91.1 knot | knob [B, NN, LCRE] • 91.4 top | the top [B] • 91.15 he | I [B, NN, LCRE] • 91.21 it's | its [B] • 94.title XVII | XVIII [B]; 18 [NN, LCRE] • 96.13 his harpoon | the harpoon [B] • 97.5 Bell | Bel [B, NN, LCRE] • 100.6 you? | you?" [B, NN, LCRE] • 101.27 storage | stowage [B, NN, LCRE] • 103.21 we | he [B] • 104.15 would | should [B] • 112.12 ships | ships' [B] • 112.30, 31 & 34 Cookes . . . Cooke . . . Cooke | Cooks . . . Cook . . . Cook [B, NN, LCRE] • 113.1 those | these [B] • 114.18 that somehow | that [B] • 114.20 fish." * | fish." [B] • 114.29 very heavens | heavens [B] • 114.38 properly | probably [B] • 117.2 on an | on [B] • 118.4 was | is [B] • 118.9 Stbub | Stubb [B, NN, LCRE] • 118.9 any other | any [B] • 120.4 crisis | crises [B] • 121.24 {}o | to [B, NN, LCRE] • 121.24 batter{}ng | battering [B, NN, LCRE] • 124.16 warranty | warranty [B, NN, LCRE] • 125.5 forenoon | afternoon [B] • 125.12 cast | cast of [B] • 125.20 say, | say. [B, NN, LCRE] • 126.10 in | into [B]

Chapters 31–45

131.21 Slid | 'Slid [NN] • 132.2 eating of | eating [B] • 132.5 'Halloa, | 'Halloa,' [B, NN, LCRE] • 133.26 Bonneterre | Bonnaterre [B, NN, LCRE] • 133.28 Olmstead | Olmsted [NN, LCRE] • 134.38 swam | swum [B] • 135.32 Lamatins | Lamantins [NN, LCRE] • 136.12 Pottsfich | Pottfisch [NN, LCRE] • 136.40 Baliene | Baleine [NN, LCRE] • 138.40 Growlands Walfish | Gronlands Walfisk [NN, LCRE] • 137.26 man-haters | men-haters [B] • 138.3 afford the basis | afforded the bases [B] • 138.9 each of these | each [B] • 138.14 has | have [B] • 139.4 Thrasher . . . Killer | *Killer . . . Thrasher* [NN] • 140.1 bill-fish | the bill-fish [B] • 140.17 bold | old [B] • 140.20 in | at [B] • 140.40 *(Duodecimo.)* | *(Duodecimo).* [N] • 141.5 i.e | *i.e.* [B, NN, LCRE] • 145.6 deep | deeps [B] • 147.15 his | this [B] • 147.17 turn | tune [B] • 148.11 to obtain | obtain [B] • 149.14 whetstone | whetstones [B, NN] • 149.30 anybody else | anybody [B] • 149.35 hereby | thereby [B] • 151.11 ever | even [B, NN] • 151.15 however | however, [NN, LCRE] • 151.28 mast-heads | masts [B] • 151.30 pleasant | pleasant—the [B, NN, LCRE] • 152.20 *crow's-nests* | *crows'-nests* [B] • 152.28 ridiculous | ridiculously [B] • 153.19 South | Southern [B, NN, LCRE] • 154.9 a harpooneer | an harpooneer [B] • 157.15 while | when [B] • 158.5 ye | you [B] • 158.19 Stubb | Stubbs [B] • 158.24 tha{} | that [B, NN, LCRE] • 159.22 man | men [B] • 159.31 unrecking | unreeking [B] • 160.32 wer't | wert [B, NN, LCRE] • 160.46 yon | you [B] • 162.4 goblet's | goblets [B] • 162.23 prophesy | prophecy [B] • 163.3 unsounded | unsound [B] • 164.17 demigorgon | demogorgon [B, NN, LCRE] • 164.24 me! | I! [B] • 165.2 Ha! ha! ha! ha! | Ha! ha! ha! [B] • 165.20 through with | through [B] • 167.36 come's | comes [B, NN, LCRE] • 169.13 TAHITAN | TAHITIAN [B, NN, LCRE] • 169.15 low veiled | low-valed [B]; low valed [NN] • 170.16 one | own [B] • 173.31 fearfnlly | fearfully [B, NN, LCRE] • 174.2 & 11 Povelson | Povelsen [NN, LCRE] • 174.38 as well | also [B] • 175.2 Strello | Strella [NN, LCRE] • 175.11 immortality | mortality [B] • 175.38 aforethought | forethought [B] • 176.28 but felt | felt [B] • 177.11 concentred | concentrated [B] • 177.41 scorched | sore [B] • 178.5-6 the one only | the only [B] • 178.6 any one | any [B] • 178.13 chiefly | that chiefly [B] • 179.18 Cæsarian, | Cæsarian [B, NN, LCRE] • 180.24 albatross, | albatross: [B, NN] • 180.37 whence | hence [B] • 180.38 funereal | funeral [B] • 181.10 revived | have revived [B] • 181.24 kin? | kin! [NN] • 181.33 our | the [B] • 182.14 much like | much [B, NN] • 183.15 seas: | seas; [B, NN, LCRE] • 184.21 distant | the distant [B] • 186.18 eat | ate [B] • 188.22 incrossing | in crossing [B, NN, LCRE] • 188.23 grounds he could | grounds [B] • 188.41 on which | in which [NN] • 189.8 or | and [B, NN] • 189.27 correctly | covertly [B, NN, LCRE] • 190.19 or | of [B] • 192.4 but the | the [B] • 192.30 previous | previously [B] • 193.22 & 24 Tom . . . Jack | Jack . . . Tom [NN, LCRE] • 193.31 Tom | Jack [B] • 194.14 that had | had [B] • 194.17 ashore | on shore [B] • 194.28 First: In | In [B] • 194.28 of | the [B] • 194.34 has | has ever [B] • 194.39 & 42 Chace . . . Chace's | Chase . . . Chase's [NN] • 195.26 Okhotsh | Okhotsk [NN, LCRE] • 195.31 just before | just [B]

Chapters 46–60

198.19 stand | stands [B, NN] • 200.9 the | a [B] • 201.22 steward! | steward!" [NN, LCRE] • 202.6 rumpled | rumbled [B] • 203.9 back!" ¶ "Never | back!—Never [B, NN, LCRE] • 203.10 sir,' | sir," [B, NN, LCRE] • 203.11 the hold | hold [B] • 203.25 ye | you [B] • 204.6 boys!") | boys!)" [NN, LCRE] • 204.19 previous | previously [B] • 204.42 whales | whale [B] • 205.1 oars | oar [B, NN, LCRE] • 205.17 on | go on [B] • 205.38 Though truly | Though, truly, [B, NN] • 206.1 his | is [B] • 206.21 eyes darted | eyes, darted [NN] • 206.24 startlingly | startingly [B] • 206.37 hearts-alive | heart's-alive [B] • 207.14-15 headsmen | headsman [B] • 207.38 sprang | sprung [B] • 209.7 worryings | worrying [B] • 211.17 comprises | compromises [B] • 211.18 a whale-boat | the whale-boat [B] • 213.7-8 planks . . . wreck | plank . . . wrecks [B] • 213.25 asked | ask [B] • 214.10 of | on [B] • 214.20 not | hardly [B] • 215.1 yawingly | yawningly [B] • 216.13 accustomed | customary [B] • 220.33 straightway | straitway [B] • 221.5 the columns | columns [B] • 222.12 particular | particular [H]; peculiar [B] • 224.9 beech | birch [NN] • 224.16 yet | yet [H]; still [B] • 225.31 nose." | nose.' [H, B, NN, LCRE] • 225.33 sailors' | sailor's [NN, LCRE] • 226.35 could but | could but [H]; could [B] • 226.40 rose | rose [H]; arose [B] • 227.17 Canallers. | Canallers." [NN, LCRE] • 227.18 ' "Canallers!' | "Canallers!" [NN]; " 'Canallers!' [LCRE] • 227.18 "We | 'We [H, NN]; 'We [LCRE] • 227.28 most thriving | most thriving [H]; thriving [B] • 227.39 vicinities | vicinities" [NN, LCRE] • 227.41 plazza | plaza [H, NN]; piazza [LCRE] • 228.1 " 'In | "In [NN]; 'In [LCRE] • 228.22 scarce | scarce [H]; scarcely [B] • 228.43 barricade." | barricade. [B, NN, LCRE] • 229.12 men?" | men?' [H, NN, LCRE] • 229.16 boy's | boys' [H, B] • 230.15 united perhaps | united perhaps [H]; united [B] • 230.18 others | others [H]; other [B] • 230.20 now? | now! [B, NN, LCRE] • 231.10 these [B] | three [H, NN, LCRE] • 231.22 try-pots | try-pots [H]; twy-pots [B] • 231.39 But | "But [H, B, NN, LCRE] • 232.18 leak | leak [H]; leek [B] • 232.35 between | beneath [NN] • 232.43 "but | 'but [H, B, NN, LCRE] • 233.19-20 there she rolls!' Jesu, what a whale! | there she rolls! Jesu, what a whale!' [NN, LCRE] • 233.20 Dick. | Dick." [NN, LCRE] • 233.29 fill up up | fill up [H, B, NN, LCRE] • 233.30 Now. | Now, [H, B, NN, LCRE] • 234.3-4 topmost | topmost [H]; topmast [B] • 234.31 cannon | cannon [H]; cannons [B] • 235.4 As | "As [NN, LCRE] • 235.6 me!' | me!" ' [NN, LCRE] • 235.21 him. | him." [NN, LCRE] • 235.27 ' "Also | "Also [NN]; " 'Also [H, LCRE] • 235.29 ' 'Is | "Is [H, NN]; " 'Is [LCRE] • 235.38 can.' | can." [NN]; can' " [LCRE] • 236.1 honor | honor, [H, LCRE]; honour, [B] • 239.6 systemized | systematized [B] • 242.37 great battles | battles [B] • 245.20 Dutch | German [B] • 245.41-42 else . . . hills, that | else— . . . hills— [B, NN] • 245.44 Soloma . . . Figuera | Solomon . . . Figueroa [NN, LCRE] • 247.7 fringing | fringy [B] • 248.8 his one | his own [B] • 250.3 awaiting | waiting [B] • 250.37 Pontoppodan | Pontoppidan [NN, LCRE] • 251.20 twenty | twelve [NN] • 252.42 contortion | contortions [B, NN, LCRE] • 253.16 prophesies | prophecies [B]

Chapters 61–75

254.29 all at once | at once [B] • 256.20 rocking | rocky [B] • 256.32 bowsman{!} | bowsman; [B, NN, LCRE] • 257.8 bowsman | bowman [B] • 258.8 uttermost | utmost [B] • 269.16 fastidions | fastidious [B, NN, LCRE] • 270.1-2 substance | substances [B] • 270.20 man | man man [B] • 272.8 two . . . hour, | two, . . . hour [B, NN, LCRE] • 272.19 her side | side [B] • 273.3 marksmen | marksman [B] • 273.18 end | end is [B] • 275.13 slicings | slices [B] • 279.16-17 vultureism | vulturism [B, NN] • 282.34 on matter | in matter [B, NN, LCRE] • 283.3 strangers'

| stranger's [B, NN] • 284.2 way ahead | ahead [B] • 284.21 the way | way [B] • 284.43 be | be in [B] • 287.13 upon | on [B] • 289.19 Nor | How [B] • 290.16 involuntarily trembling | trembling [B] • 290.39 bade | bad [B] • 293.12 fagged | flagged [B] • 294.11 get | to get [B] • 294.32 helped | helped to [B] • 295.11 let's | lets [B, NN, LCRE] • 295.15 suppose it | suppose [B] • 295.17 his | the [B] • 295.20 and | an [B] • 295.41-42 black bone | back-bone [B] • 296.3 Meantime | Meanwhile [B] • 297.24 one | see one [B] • 298.31 moment of time | time [B] • 299.39 into | in [B] • 301.12 its circular | circular [B] • 301.20 arch | reach [B]

Chapters 76–90

305.25 irrevocably | irrecoverably [B] • 306.17 fata{} | fatal [B, NN, LCRE] • 307.4 single-sheaved | shingle-sheaved [B] • 307.8 high | highly [B] • 307.26 baling | bailing [B] • 308.1 cabled | cable [B] • 308.3 to fall | fall [B] • 308.30 top | the top [B] • 309.40-310.1 undetached | detached [B] • 311.title The Praire | The Prairie [B, NN, LCRE] • 315.12 can there | can [B] • 316.20 sort of | sort of a [B] • 316.26 yaw | yawn [B] • 317.25 rivals' | rival's [B] • 317.32 Fiercely, but evenly | Fiercely but evenly, [NN] • 318.6 diagonically | diagonally [B, NN] • 318.11 yawed | yawled [B] • 318.26 and | and, [NN] • 318.30 harpooneer | harpooneers [B] • 319.4 lead-lined | lead-line [B] • 320.8 ship's | ships' [B, LCRE] • 321.7 new made | newly-made [B] • 323.6 go | goes [B] • 328.5 the whale | a whale [B] • 329.3 as such | such [B] • 330.18 minds | reminds [B] • 330.24 old Monongahela! | Monongahela! [B] • 332.8 fishermon | fishermen [B, NN, LCRE] • 332.22 necessities | necessities, [NN] • 333.21 perceived | perceive [B] • 336.3 Eckerman | Eckermann [NN, LCRE] • 336.27 descend | descends [B] • 339.13-14 spices, and silks | spices, [B] • 340.11 his | the [B] • 341.25 these | the [B] • 341.32 to | to to [B] • 342.8 had | has [B] • 342.22 flashing | fishing [B] • 342.41 for | from [B] • 344.27 overboard | over [B] • 345.20 snuffling | snuffing [B] • 345.36 scarce yet | scarce [B] • 346.6 vicisitudes | vicissitudes [B, NN, LCRE] • 349.3 times | time [B] • 350.18 fishermen | fisherman [B] • 352.15 fishermen | fisherman [B] • 353.9 seas; and when indeed | seas, [B, NN] • 353.10 they were . . . obliged | but . . . were obliged • 353.11 itself. Ultimately | itself,—Furthermore: ultimately [B] • 353.13 plaintiffs. And | plaintiffs;—Yet again:—and [B] • 353.14 plaintiffs' | plaintiff's [B] • 353.16 which | all of which [B] • 353.40 plaintiffs | defendants [B, NN, LCRE] • 356.39 (twice) Plowdon | Plowden [NN, LCRE] • 357.1 warbrobe | wardrobe [B, NN, LCRE] • 357.9 of | at [B]

Chapters 91–105

358.2 not | *that* [B, NN, LCRE] • 358.5 vapory | vapour [B] • 361.3 argued | augured [NN] • 362.10 it's | its [B] • 362.32 withont | without [B, NN, LCRE] • 364.3 the chapter | this chapter [B] • 364.27 gave forth | gave [B] • 365.9 boats' | boat's [B] • 365.12 heard of | head [B] • 366.5 effulgenees | effulgences [B, NN, LCRE] • 366.40 wont | won't [B, LCRE] • 366.43 loved | loves [NN] • 366.44 interferes | interfered [B] • 368.19 snuffed | sniffed [B] • 368.25 petulence | petulance [B, NN, LCRE] • 369.33 and a | a [B] • 369.37 the tubs | tubs [B] • 370.17 This | The [B] • 370.20 assistants' | assistant's [NN, LCRE] • 373.5 foremast | fore- [B] • 373.5 main-/mast | mainmast [B, NN]; main-mast [LCRE] • 374.11 he | he had [B] • 374.23 conflagrations | conflagration [B] • 375.30 spite of | in spite of [B] • 381.19 flows | flow [B, NN, LCRE] • 382.12 the third | a third [B] • 382.30 ol{} | old [B, NN, LCRE] • 383.10 almanack{} | almanack; [B, NN, LCRE] • 383.14 Bull and Jimimi! | Bull;—and Jimini! [B, NN]; Bull and Jimini! [LCRE] • 383.32-33 rear | the rear [B, LCRE] • 384.4 wont | won't [B, LCRE] • 384.16 it is | is it [B] • 384.33 Hark! | Hark!" [NN, LCRE] • 387.10 blubber-hook | blubber-book [B] • 387.34 the bottom | bottom [B] • 388.1 on to | on [B] • 388.23 when, when, | when, [B] • 389.14 wound | a wound [B, LCRE] • 390.5 swallow | to swallow [B, LCRE] • 391.14 1778 | 1788 [NN] • 391.16 a whale-boat | a a whale-boat [B] • 392.35 and drinking | drinking [B] • 395.25 And as | As [B] • 396.17 hair-hung | air-hung [B] • 396.21-22 with all | with [B] • 397.27 upon | on [B] • 401.11-12 & 40 antichronical | ante-chronical [B, LCRE]; antechronical [NN] • 401.21

Dauphiné | Dauphine [NN] • 401.32 skeleton of the whale | skeleton [B] • 402.5 Pharaoh's | Pharaohs' [B, NN, LCRE] • 402.24 pass it | pass by it [NN] • 402.29 This Rib (says John Leo) | This Rib [B] • 403.22 Cooke's | Cook's [B, NN, LCRE] • 403.22 Danish | Swedish [NN] • 403.23 reydan-siskur | Reydan-siskur [B]; reydar-fiskur [NN, LCRE] • 404.1 these | the [B] • 404.35 horse | horses [B] • 405.21 Harto | Horto [NN, LCRE]

Chapters 106–120

406.25 canonic | canonical [B] • 407.29 signers | singers [B] • 409.1-2 longed . . . oar; | longs . . . oar: [NN] • 409.38 had to do | had [B] • 413.23 Greek god | a Greek god [B, NN, LCRE] • 413.29 vertebra | vertebræ [B] • 415.3 into | in [B] • 418.4 but little | little [B] • 419.2 convenience | convenience' [B, LCRE] • 419.3 be | be made [B] • 419.28 hovering near | hovering [B] • 424.11 petulence | petulance [B, NN, LCRE] • 424.15 painful | painfully [B] • 425.10 iron lullaby | lullaby [B] • 432.8 down | up [NN] • 432.19 officers' | officer's [B] • 432.26 pantaloons | pantaloon [B] • 433.2 nearer | near [B] • 433.12 cursed | accursed [B] • 435.1 power? | power! [NN, LCRE] • 435.2 strivest . . . jettest | striveth . . . jetteth [NN] • 438.16 its | the [B] • 439.6 drop of | drop [B] • 440.17-18 reeling . . . tetering | reelish . . . tottering [B] • 441.5-6 ships . . . lips | ship . . . lip [B] • 441.25 Yes | "Yes [B, NN, LCRE] • 441.39 considerable | a considerable [B] • 442.21 sailors' | sailors, [B, NN, LCRE] • 442.25 Tekel | Tekel, [B, NN, LCRE] • 442.41 too look | to look [B, NN, LCRE] • 443.1 will yet be | will be [B] • 443.35 *leap lengthwise* | *leap* [B] • 444.20 t'is | It's [B] • 444.27 ran | run [B] • 446.20 theh older | the holder [B, NN, LCRE] • 447.14 skirts | shirts [B]

Chapters 121–135

448.title THUNDER AND LIGHTNING | LIGHTNING AND THUNDER [B] • 449.7 Pequod's | *Pequod* [B] • 449.12 shivered | shivering [B] • 449.25 order | orders [B] • 453.24 he issued | issued [B] • 453.29 inflexible | the inflexible [B] • 456.8 hey | eh [B] • 456.29 A hatchet! a hatchet! | A hatchet! [B] • 456.45 my | mine [B] • 457.1 intenting | intently [B, NN, LCRE] • 458.20 He | He then [B] • 459.9 long beat | beaten [B] • 459.43 wont | won't [B, LCRE] • 460.3 its undignified | it's undignified [NN, LCRE] • 461.4 *the cabin-gangway* | *cabin-gangway* [B] • 461.4 *aud* | *and* [B, NN, LCRE] • 462.1 helped | helped to [B] • 463.22 loomed up | loomed [B] • 463.24 instantly lowered | instantly [B] • 464.32 boat's | boats' [NN, LCRE] • 465.21 yaw | yawl [B] • 465.24 while all | yet all [B] • 468.6 preceding | preceding that [B] • 469.14 two only | only two [B] • 469.29 yoked | yolked [B] • 469.37 had yet | had [B] • 470.31 close round | round [B] • 470.33 Then | Now [B] • 472.3 upom | upon [B, NN, LCRE] • 475.8 morn | moon [B] • 475.35 Forty—forty—forty years | Forty—forty years [B] • 475.41 without | throughout [B] • 476.3 bread | bread, [NN] • 476.15-16 as though | and as though [B] • 476.28 child | children [B] • 476.42 cozzening | cozening [B, NN, LCRE] • 477.12 airs | air [B, NN, LCRE] • 479.38 of | off [B] • 480.3 fowels | fowls [B, NN, LCRE] • 480.15 this | that [B] • 480.22 wrenched | wretched [B] • 481.38 tilting | tilting it [B] • 482.29 prows were | prow was [B, NN, LCRE] • 482.33 did crack | cracked [B] • 483.4 circumferences | circumference [B] • 483.25 canvas | canvass [B] • 483.45 this that laughs | that that laughs [B] • 484.5 wives' | wife's [B] • 486.13 spine's | spin's [B] • 486.37 did point | pointed [B] • 488.1 those | these [B] • 488.18 rope | ropes [B] • 489.16 not stood | not not stood [B] • 489.22 inaccessible | inaccessible being [B, NN, LCRE] • 489.26 boat's | boats' [B, NN, LCRE] • 490.32 brave men, | brave, men, [B, NN, LCRE] • 490.40 the whole | all the whole [B] • 491.7 sat | set [B, NN, LCRE] • 492.14 turned | turn [B, NN, LCRE] • 492.17 Vesuvius | Vesuvius' [B] • 492.26 but had | had but [B] • 494.3 Will | Shall [B] • 496.1 Whilc | While [B, NN, LCRE] • 496.22 own straight | straight [B] • 497.24-25 inboard again | inboard [B] • 497.39 night | nigh [B] • 498.11 fit | fit. [B, NN, LCRE] • 499.27 intermixingly | intermixedly [B] • 499.36 death-gasp | death-grasp [B, NN, LCRE]

TEXTUAL EMENDATIONS

The LCRE *Moby-Dick* reprints the first American edition; however, it emends (alters) the text, in 177 places, to correct typographical errors and unintended or confusing misspellings and faulty punctuation. In the following list, all LCRE emendations appear to the left of the vertical bar (|) with the original American text indicated to the right. In almost all cases the LCRE emendations are based on corrections found in the first British edition. The abbreviations in brackets ([]) following an emendation indicate, where applicable, the earlier appearance of that variant in one or a combination of the versions listed below. Dropped letters or broken type in words found in the American and British versions are represented with braces ({}). Forty-four of the LCRE emendations appeared for the first time in the 1988 NN edition, and eight appear in LCRE without textual precedent. Most LCRE emendations are non-controversial; however, those that affect meaning are listed in boldface and are discussed in a revision narrative either in the text of *Moby-Dick* or in Making *Moby-Dick*. Accordingly, the entry **left [B, NN]** | **lift** indicates that the emended word "left" in the LCRE text, which is also found in the British edition and was adopted as an emendation in the NN edition, originally appeared as "lift" in the American edition. Because the entry is in boldface, a revision narrative discussing the word has been provided (in this case in Making *Moby-Dick*).

> H   "The Town-Ho's Story," *Harper's New Monthly Magazine* (October, 1851)
> B   First British Edition. London: Richard Bentley, 1851.
> NN   Northwestern-Newberry Edition. Evanston and Chicago: Northwestern University Press and The Newberry Library, 1988.

Extracts
5.10 Prairie [B, NN] | Praire • 8.17 **WHÆL [NN]** | **WHŒL** • 11.14 *Ibid.* [B, NN] | *Ibid* • 11.28 Hofmannus [NN] | Hosmannus • 12.32 foot [NN] | feet • 13.23 Pitfirren [NN] | Pitferren • 13.28 *Stafford's* [NN] | *Strafford's* • 15.7 fires [NN] | fire • 15.38 jaw, [B, NN] | jaw. • 16.29 *Ocean."* [NN] | *Ocean.* • 18.3 *Mutiny,"* [NN] | *Mutiny,* • 18.10 *Bennet* [NN] | *Bennett* • 18.24 the [B, NN] | tke • 18.34 mere [B, NN] | near

Chapters 1–15
21.16 Battery [B, NN] | battery • 25.20 midmost [B, NN] | mid most • 43.26 any [B, NN] | auy • 47.14 Tongataboooans [B, NN] | Tongatabooarrs • **54.17 left [B, NN]** | **lift** • 55.12 'And [B, NN] | "And • 55.13 Jonah.' [B, NN] | Jonah." • 56.26 "'Who's [B, NN] | 'Who's • 56.38 "Now [B, NN] | Now • 58.31 "And [B, NN] | And • 70.16 & 20 Kokovoko [B, NN] | Rokovoko • 71.13 bows [B, NN] | brows • 76.29 fishy [B, NN] | fishing

Chapters 16–30
79.17 Becket [B, NN] | Beckett • 82.34 virgin, voluntary, [B, NN] | virgin voluntary • **83.13 Bildad [B, NN]** | **Peleg** • 87.15 that, [B, NN] | that • 91.1 knob [B, NN] | knot • 91.15 I [B, NN] | he • 94.title 18 [B, NN] | XVII • 97.5 Bel [B, NN] | Bell • 100.6 you?" [B, NN] | you? • 101.27 stowage [B, NN] | storage • 112.30, 31 & 34 Cooks . . . Cook . . . Cook [B, NN] | Cookes . . . Cooke . . . Cooke • 118.9 Stubb [B, NN] | Stbub • 121.24 to [B, NN] | {}o • 121.24 battering [B, NN] | batter{}ng • 124.16 warranty [B, NN] | warranty • 125.20 say. [B, NN] | say,

Chapters 31–45
132.5 'Halloa,' [B, NN] | 'Halloa, • **132.22 speak quick [B, NN]** | **speak** • 133.26 Bonnaterre [NN] | Bonneterre • 133.28 Olmsted [NN] | Olmstead • **135.11 Henry T. Cheever [NN]** | **T. Cheever** • 135.32 Lamantins [NN] | Lamatins • 136.12 Pottfisch [NN] | Pottsfisch • 136.40 Baleine [B, NN] | Baliene • 138.40 Gronlands Walfisk [NN] | Growlands Walfish • 141.5 *i.e.* [B,

NN] | i.e • **144.38 direst [B, NN] | direct** • 151.15 however, [NN] | however • 151.30 pleasant— [B, NN] | pleasant • 153.19 Southern [B, NN] | South • 158.24 that [B, NN] | tha{} • 160.32 wert [B, NN] | wer't • 164.17 demogorgon [B, NN] | demigorgon • **166.5 commanded— [B] | commanded.—** • 167.36 comes [NN] | come's • 169.13 TAHITIAN [B, NN] | TAHITAN • 173.31 fearfully [B, NN] | fearfnlly • 174.2 & 11 Povelsen [NN] | Povelson • 175.2 Strella [NN] | Strello • 179.18 Cæsarian [B, NN] | Cæsarian, • 183.15 seas; [B, NN] | seas: • 188.22 in crossing [B, NN] | incrossing • 189.27 covertly [B, NN] | correctly • 193.22 & 24 Jack . . . Tom [NN] | Tom . . . Jack • **194.12 others, [NN] | others** • 195.26 Ochotsk [NN] | Ochotsh

Chapters 46–60

201.22 steward!" [NN] | steward! • 203.9 back!—Never [B, NN] | back!" ¶ "Never • 203.10 sir," [B, NN] | sir,' • 204.6 boys!)" [NN] | boys!") • 205.1 oar [B, NN] | oars • **211.28 Archy's [NN] | Cabaco's** • 225.31 nose.' [H, B, NN] | nose." • 225.33 sailor's [NN] | sailors' • 227.17 Canallers." [NN] | Canallers. • 227.18 " 'Canallers!' | ' "Canallers!' • 227.18 'We | " 'We • 227.39 vicinities" [NN] | vicinities • 227.41 piazza | plazza • 228.1 'In | " 'In • 228.43 barricade. [B, NN] | barricade." • 229.12 men?' [H, NN] | men?" • 230.20 now! [B, NN] | now? • 231.10 three [H, NN] | these • 231.39 "But [H, B, NN] | But • 232.43 'but [H, B, NN] | "but • 233.19-20 there she rolls! Jesu, what a whale!' [H, B, NN] | there she rolls!' Jesu, what a whale! • 233.20 Dick." [NN] | Dick. • 233.29 fill up [H, B, NN] | fill up up • 233.30 Now, [H, B, NN] | Now. • 235.4 "As [NN] | As • 235.6 me!" ' [NN] | me!' • 235.21 him." [NN] | him. • 235.27 " 'Also [H] | ' "Also • 235.29 " 'Is | ' "Is • 235.38 can.' " | can.' • 236.1 honor, [H, B, NN] | honor • 245.44 Solomon . . . Figueroa [NN] | Soloma . . . Figuera • 250.37 Pontoppidan [NN] | Pontoppodan • 252.42 contortions [B, NN] | contortion

Chapters 61–75

256.32 bowsman; [B, NN] | bowsman{!} • **266.5 yourselbs [B, NN] | yoursebls** • 269.16 fastidious [B, NN] | fastidions • 272.8 two, for an hour [B, NN] | two for an hour, • **280.2 powerful [B] | powerless** • 282.34 in matter [B, NN] | on matter • 283.3 stranger's [B, NN] | strangers' • 295.11 lets [B, NN] | let's

Chapters 76–90

306.17 fatal [B, NN] | fata{} • 311.title Prairie [B, NN] | Praire • 320.8 ships' [B] | ship's • 332.8 fishermen [B, NN] | fishermon • 332.8 Eckermann [NN] | Eckerman • **343.32 sc. II. [LCRE] | [not present]** • 346.6 vicissitudes [B, NN] | vicisitudes • 353.40 defendants [B, NN] | plaintiffs • 356.39 (twice) Plowden [NN] | Plowdon • 357.1 wardrobe [B, NN] | warbrobe

Chapters 91–105

358.2 *that* [B, NN] | not • 362.32 without [B, NN] | withont • 366.5 effulgences [B, NN] | effulgenees • 366.40 won't [B] | wont • 368.25 petulance [B, NN] | petulence • 370.20 assistant's [NN] | assistants' • 373.5 main-mast | main-/mast • 381.19 flow [B, NN] | flows • 382.30 old [B, NN] | ol{} • 383.10 almanack; [B, NN] | almanack{} • 383.14 Jimini [B, NN] | Jimimi • 383.32-33 the rear [B] | rear • 384.4 won't [B] | wont • 384.33 Hark!" [NN] | Hark! • 389.14 a wound [B] | wound • 390.5 to swallow [B] | swallow • 401.11-12 & 40 ante-chronical [B] | antichronical • 402.5 Pharaohs' [B, NN] | Pharaoh's • 403.22 Cook's [B, NN, LCRE] | Cooke's • 403.23 reydar-fiskur [NN] | reydan-siskur • 405.21 Horto [NN] | Harto

Chapters 106–120

413.23 a Greek [B, NN] | Greek • 419.2 convenience' [B] | convenience • 424.11 petulance [B, NN] | petulence • 435.1 power! [NN] | power? • 441.25 "Yes [B, NN] | Yes • 442.21 sailors, [B, NN] | sailors' • 442.25 Tekel, [B, NN] | Tekel • 442.41 to look [B, NN] | too look • 446.20 the holder [B, NN] | theh older

Chapters 121–135
453.20 braced hard up [B, NN] | **hard up** • **453.34 fain [B]** | **feign** • 457.1 intently [B, NN] | intenting • 459.43 won't [B] | wont • 460.3 it's undignified [NN] | its undignified • 461.4 *and* [B, NN] | *aud* • 464.32 boats' [NN] | boat's • **470.6 he said, [B]** | **said,** • 472.3 upon [B, NN] | upom • 476.42 cozening [B, NN] | cozzening • 477.12 air [B, NN] | airs • 480.3 fowls [B, NN] | fowels • 482.29 prow was [B, NN] | prows were • **483.27 Moby Dick [B, NN]** | **Moby-Dick** • 489.22 inaccessible being [B, NN] | inaccessible • 489.26 boats' [B, NN] | boat's • 490.32 brave, men [B, NN] | brave men • 491.7 set [B, NN] | sat • 492.14 turn [B, NN] | turned • 496.1 While [B, NN] | Whil*c* • 498.11 fit. [B, NN] | fit • 499.36 death-grasp [B, NN] | death-gasp

MELVILLE'S
SOURCES

Readers marvel at the amount of reading and research Melville put into the making of *Moby-Dick*. He quotes familiar and unfamiliar works, sometimes without acknowledging those sources, and sometimes revising them as he quotes. Studying Melville's sources allows us to locate scenes of intertexuality and to assess how the writer interacted with other writers and the culture.

The following list, arranged alphabetically by author and title, provides the sources Melville mentions in *Moby-Dick* and the editions he used or might have used in quoting or borrowing from those sources. Sources mentioned only by title in *Moby-Dick* are listed by that title with a cross-reference to the full citation of the author. Melville sometimes borrowed passages that appeared as quotations in other works, and we list such secondary works with cross-references to the original texts. An asterisk before an entry indicates a book Melville purchased on his trip to England and Europe just before he began writing *Moby-Dick*. (For a complete list of these purchases, see NN *Journals* 144–46.) In addition, readers will find entries for popular songs and graphic art specifically mentioned in *Moby-Dick*.

To track Melville's use of these sources, readers may also consult valuable source studies listed in **Further Reading**. These studies include Merton Sealts's 1988 *Melville's Reading*, which offers a numbered list of books that Melville owned or borrowed from libraries. Subsequent discoveries of Melville's books, transcriptions of his marginal annotations, and updates on the ownership of his books are recorded (by Steven Olsen-Smith) in *Leviathan: A Journal of Melville Studies*.

In addition, Mary K. Bercaw's *Melville's Sources* numbers sources in all of Melville's writings, indicates the work in which a source appears, and links each source to the studies of it. (Our list supplies Sealts and Bercaw numbers in brackets where appropriate.) Melville often annotated the books he read; several critical studies, also listed in **Further Reading**, provide transcriptions of his underlinings, markings, and marginal notes.

Anonymous. "The Whale and Whale Catching." *American Magazine of Useful and Entertaining Knowledge* (Sept. 1835:5–7). [Bercaw 753]

Bacon, Sir Francis. *History Naturall and Experimentall of Life and Death*. London, 1638.

———. *Of the Proficience and Advancement of Learning*. London: Pickering, 1840.

———. *The Translation of Certaine Psalmes*. London, 1625.

Bayle, Pierre. *An Historical and Critical Dictionary*. Trans. Jacob Tonson. London: Harper, 1710. [Sealts 51, Bercaw 50]

Beale, Thomas. *The Natural History of the Sperm Whale*. 2nd ed. London: Van Voorst, 1839. [Sealts 52, Bercaw 51]

°Beaumont, Francis, and John Fletcher. *Fifty Comedies and Tragedies*. London: Martyn, 1679. [Sealts 53, Bercaw 53]

Bennett, Frederick Debell. *Narrative of a Whaling Voyage round the Globe*. London: 1840. [Bercaw 60]

Bible. *The Holy Bible . . . Together with the Apocrypha*. Philadelphia: Butler, 1846. [Sealts 62, also 60–61, 63–65; Bercaw 63]

Blackstone, William. *Commentaries on the Laws of England*. Oxford, 1765.

°Boswell, James. *The Life of Samuel Johnson, LL.D.* Ed. John Wilson Croker. London: Murray, 1835. [Sealts 84, Bercaw 72]

Bradford, Alexander W. *American Antiquities and Researches into the Origins of the Red Race*. New York, 1841. [Bercaw 74]

Browne, J. Ross. *Etchings of a Whaling Cruise*. New York: Harper, 1846. [Sealts 88, Bercaw 82; see also Melville's review of Browne in NN *Piazza Tales* 205–11]

°Browne, Thomas. *Sir Thomas Browne's Works*, ed. Simon Wilkin. London: Pickering, 1835–36; and *Works*. London: Basset, 1686. [Sealts 89–90, Bercaw 83]

Bunyan, John. *The Pilgrim's Progress*. [Bercaw 93; the "Extract" attributed to "Pilgrim's Progress" is from *The Holy War*. London, 1682; as qtd. by Cheever]

Burke, Edmund. *Speech of Edmund Burke, Esq; on Moving His Resolutions for Conciliation with the Colonies, March 22, 1775*. London, 1775; as qtd. in Beale or Browne's *Etchings*.

Burton, Robert. *The Anatomy of Melancholy*. New York: Wiley, 1847. [Sealts 102, Bercaw 100].

Byron, George Gordon (Baron). *Childe Harold's Pilgrimage* (1812–18). Ed. unknown. [Sealts 107–12, Bercaw 107]

Byron, John. *The Narrative of the Honorable John Byron*. London: Baker and Leigh, 1768. [Sealts 113, Bercaw 108]

Camoens, Luis de. *The Lusiad; or Discovery of India*. Trans. William Mickle (1776). In Alexander Chalmers, *The Works of the English Poets*. Vol. 21. London, 1810. [Bercaw 111]

Carlyle, Thomas. *The French Revolution, A History* (1837). [Bercaw 115]

_____. *Sartor Resartus*. Boston, Munroe, 1840; or New York, Wiley and Putnam, 1847. [Sealts 123, Bercaw 119]

Cervantes Saavedra, Miguel de. *Don Quixote de la Mancha* (1610). Ed. unknown. [Sealts 124–25, Bercaw 122; Melville did not purchase the 1853 Jarvis trans. until 1855]

A Chapter on Whaling in Ribs and Trucks. See Weld.

Chase, Owen. *Narrative of the Most Extraordinary and Distressing Shipwreck of the Whale-Ship Essex*. New York: Gilley, 1821. [Sealts 134, Bercaw 130]

Cheever, Henry T. *The Whale and His Captors*. New York: Harper, 1849. [Bercaw 136]

Coleridge, Samuel Taylor. *Notes and Lectures upon Shakespeare*. London: Pickering, 1849. [Sealts 155, Bercaw 149]

_____. "The Rime of the Ancient Mariner" in *Lyrical Ballads* (1798). [Bercaw 150]

Colnett, James. *A Voyage to the South Atlantic and round Cape Horn*. London: Bennett, 1798. [Bercaw 154]

Comstock, William. *The Life of Samuel Comstock, the Terrible Whaleman*. Boston: James Fisher, 1840. [Bercaw 157]

Cook, James. *A Voyage to the Pacific*. 2nd ed, London: Nichol and Cadell, 1785. [Bercaw 160]

Cooper, James Fenimore. *The Pilot; A Tale of the Sea* (1824). [Bercaw 167]

_____. *The Red Rover*. Boston: Putnam, 1849. [Sealts 159, Bercaw 170; see also Melville's review in NN *Piazza Tales* 237–38]

_____. *The Sea Lions; or, The Lost Sealers*. New York: Stringer and Townsend, 1849. [Sealts 160, Bercaw 171; see also Melville's review in NN *Piazza Tales* 235–36]

Cowley, William. *Voyage round the Globe*, as qtd. in Dampier. [See also Bercaw 176]

Cowper, William. "On the Queen's Visit to London," in William Hayley, *The Life, and Posthumous Writings, of William Cowper*. London, 1803.

_____. *Poems* (1782). Ed. unknown. [Sealts 161, Bercaw 177]

Cruise in a Whale Boat. See Rhodes.

Currents and Whaling. U.S. Ex. Ex. See Wilkes.

Cuvier, Georges (Baron). *The Animal Kingdom Arranged in Conformity with Its Organization*. London: Whittaker, 1827–43. [Sealts 171, Bercaw 186]

°D'Avenant, William. "Preface to Gondibert." In *The Works of Sir William D'Avenant*. London: Herringman, 1673. [Sealts 176, Bercaw 192; for Melville's annotations see Olsen-Smith and Marnon in Further Reading]

Dampier, William. *A Collection of Voyages* (1699). London, 1729. [Bercaw 187a]

Dana, Richard Henry. *Two Years before the Mast*. New York: Harper, 1840. [Sealts 173, Bercaw 189]

Dante, Alighieri. *The Vision; or Hell, Purgatory, and Paradise*. Trans. Cary. London: Bohn, 1847. [Sealts 174, Bercaw 190]

Darwin, Charles. *Journal of Researches into the Natural History and Geology of the Countries Visited during the Voyage of H.M.S. Beagle round the World*. New York: Harper, 1846. [Sealts 175, Bercaw 191]

°De Quincey, Thomas. *Confessions of an English Opium Eater* (1822). Ed. unknown. [Sealts 180, Bercaw 204]

Denon, Vivant. *Travels in Upper and Lower Egypt*. New York, 1803. [Bercaw 201]

Dryden, John. *Annus Mirabilis*. London, 1667.

Durand-Brager, Henri. *Baleinier au Mouillage* and *Baleinier Français en Pêche*. Engravings. Paris, ca. 1844–45.

D'Wolf, John. *A Voyage to the North Pacific and a Journey through Siberia More than Half a Century Ago*. Cambridge, MA: Welch, Bigelow, 1861. [Sealts 196; D'Wolf's anecdotes did not appear in print until after *Moby-Dick*]

Eckermann, Johann. *Conversations with Goethe*. Trans. Margaret Fuller. Boston, Hilliard and Gray, 1839. [Bercaw 235]

Edge, Thomas. *Ten Voyages to Spitzbergen, in Purchass*; as qtd, in Harris.

Emerson, Ralph Waldo. *Essays*. Series and ed. unknown. [Sealts 204–5, Bercaw 249–50]

_____. *Representative Men*. Boston: Phillips, Sampson, 1850. [Sealts 206a, Bercaw 254]

"Facts and Opinions." *Literary World* 6 (June 29, 1850), 642. [Sealts 326, Bercaw 260]

Fairie Queen. See Spenser.

Falconer, William. *The Shipwreck* (1762). Ed. unknown. [Bercaw 261]

Forester, Fanny [Emily Chubbuck Judson]. *Alderbrook: A Collection of Fanny Forester's Village Sketches, Poems, Etc*. Boston, 1847.

Froissart, Jean. *Chronicles of England, France, Spain and the Adjoining Countries* (1523–25). Ed. unknown. [Bercaw 282]

Fuller, Thomas. *The Holy State, and the Profane State*, ed. James Nichols. London: Tegg, 1841. [Sealts 221, Bercaw 283]

Garneray, Ambroise Louis. *Pêche du Cachalot; Cachalot Fishery* and *Pêche de la Baleine; Whale Fishery*. Engravings. Paris, 1834, 1835.

Gillies, Robert Pearse. *Tales of a Voyager to the Arctic Ocean*. London, 1826. [Bercaw 292]

°Goethe, Johann Wolfgang von. *The Auto-Biography of Goethe*. London: Bohn, 1848–49. [Sealts 228, Bercaw 296]

_____. *Faust*. Ed. unknown. [Bercaw 299]. See also Eckermann.

Goldsmith, Oliver. *Goldsmith's Natural History*. Abridged school ed., Philadelphia, 1829; *History of the Earth and Animated Nature*. Abridged ed., London: Vernor, Hood, Sharpe, 1807. [Bercaw 306–7]

Goldsmith to Johnson; as qtd. in Boswell.

Hakluyt, Richard. *Principall Navigations, Voiages, and Discoveries of the English Nation* (1589, 1598–1600). [Bercaw 313]

Halyard, Harry. *Wharton the Whale-Killer!* Boston, 1848. [Bercaw 319a]

Hamlet. See Shakespeare.

Harris, John. *Navigantium atque Itinerantium Bibliotheca; or, a Compleat Collection of Voyages and Travels*. London, 1705. [Bercaw 323]

Hart, Joseph C. *Miriam Coffin; or, The Whale-Fishermen*. New York, 1834. [Bercaw 325]

Hawthorne, Nathaniel. *The House of the Seven Gables*. Boston: Ticknor, Reed, and Fields, 1851. [Sealts 246, Bercaw 331]

_____. *Mosses from an Old Manse*. New York: Wiley and Putnam, 1846. [Sealts 248, Bercaw 333; see also Melville's review essay of Hawthorne in NN *Piazza Tales* 239–53]

_____*Twice-Told Tales*. Boston: American Stationers, 1837. [Sealts 258, also 259–60; Bercaw 341]

Hazlitt, William. *Table Talk*; or *Original Essays on Men and Manners*. New York: Wiley and Putnam, 1845. [Sealts 266a, Bercaw 347a]

Henry, Robert. *The History of Great Britain*. London, 1774.

Herbert, Thomas. *Voyages into Asia and Africa. From Some Yeares Travels into Divers Parts of Asia and Afrique*. London, 1638, as qtd. in Harris.

Hobbes, Thomas. *The Leviathan* (1651). [Bercaw 358]

Hoffman, Charles Fenno. "Sparklling and Bright" (1830, 1842). Ed. unknown. [Bercaw 360]

Hogarth, William. *Perseus Descending*. In Lewis Theobald. *Perseus and Andromeda*. London, 1730.

Holland's Pliny; as qtd. in Richardson [Bercaw 556]

Holland's Plutarch's Morals. See Plutarch.

°Hope, Thomas. *Anastasius, or Memoirs of a Greek*. London: John Murray, 1836. [Sealts 282, Bercaw 372]

°Howitt, William. *The Aristocracy of England*. 2nd ed. London: Wilson, 1846(?). [Sealts 288, Bercaw 375]

Hunter, John. "Observations on the Structure and Oeconomy of Whales," as qtd. in Paley.

Jefferson, Thomas. *Memoir, Correspondence, and Miscellanies*, ed. Thomas Jefferson Randolph. Charlottesville, VA, 1829.

Johnson, Samuel. *A Dictionary of the English Language* (1755). [Bercaw 400]

King Henry. See Shakespeare.

"The King of the Southern Sea" [song], *Sailor's Magazine* 16 (Dec. 1843), 129. [Bercaw 417a]

Kitto, John, ed., *A Cyclopaedia of Biblical Literature*. Edinburgh, 1845; New York, 1846. [Bercaw 421]

°Knight, Charles. *London*. 6 vols. in 3. London. [Sealts 312, Bercaw 422]

Krusenstern, Adam Ivan. *Voyage round the World, in the Years 1803–1806*. London: Murray, 1813. [Bercaw 426]

Lamb, Charles. "The Triumph of the Whale," rpt. in *The Poetical Recreations of The Champion*. Ed. John Thelwall. London, 1822.

°_____. *The Works of Charles Lamb*. London: Moxon, 1848. [Sealts 316, Bercaw 431]

Langsdorff, George H. von. *Voyages and Travels in Various Parts of the World . . . 1803–1807*. London: Colburn, 1813. [Bercaw 433],

°Lavater, Johann Caspar. *Essays on Physiognomy* (1775–78; in English 1789–98). Ed. unknown. [Sealts 322, Bercaw 436]

Lay, William, and Cyrus M. Hussey. *A Narrative of the Mutiny, on Board the Ship Globe*. New London, CT: Lay & Hussey, 1828. [Sealts 323, Bercaw 437]

Le Sage, Alain-René. *The Adventures of Gil Blas of Santillane* (1715–35). Ed. unknown. [Bercaw 444a]

Linnaeus, Carolus (Carl von Linné). *Systema Naturae* (1735, 1758, 1766–68). Ed. unknown. [Bercaw 446]

Lord Bacon's Version of the Psalms and *"History of Life and Death."* See Bacon.

Lucian. "The True History," in *Lucian of Samosota from the Greek*. Trans. William Tooke. London: Longman, 1820. [Bercaw 458a]

Macy, Obed. *The History of Nantucket*. Boston: Hilliard, Gray, 1835. [Sealts 345, Bercaw 469]

°Marlowe, Christopher. *The Dramatic Works*. London: Simpkin, Marshall, Chapple, 1820(?). [Sealts 348, Bercaw 477]

Martens, Friedrich. "Voyage into Spitzbergen and Greenland" (1671). From *An Account of Several Late Voyages & Discoveries to the South and North*. Ed. Tancred Robinson. London, 1694; as qtd. in Harris.

Massachusetts calendar. See Thomas.

Maurice, Thomas. *Indian Antiquities* (1793–1800). [Bercaw 492]

Maury, Lieut. F. M. *Explanations and Sailing Directions to Accompany the Wind and Current Charts*. Washington, DC, 1851. [Bercaw 493]

Mayo, William Starbuck. *Kaloolah, or, Journeyings to the Djebel Kumri: An Autobiography of Jonathan Romer*. New York: George P. Putnam, 1849. [Bercaw 495]

McCulloch, John Ramsay. *A Dictionary, Practical, Theoretical, and Historical, of Commerce and Commercial Navigation*. London, 1832; as qtd. in Browne's *Etchings*.

Milton, John. *The Poetical Works of John Milton*. Boston: Hilliard, Gray, 1836. [Sealts 358b, Bercaw 499; for Melville's annotations, see Grey and Robillard in Further Reading]

Miriam Coffin or the Whale Fisherman [sic]. See Hart.

Missionary Journal. See Tyerman and Bennet.

Montaigne, Michel Eyquem de. "Apology for Raimond Sebond." In *The Complete Works*. Trans. Cotton; ed. William Hazlitt. London: Templeman, 1842. [Sealts 366, Bercaw 502]

Montgomery, James. *The World before the Flood* [Bercaw 503; the "Extract" attributed to *World* is from *The Pelican Island*, as qtd. in Cheever.]

Morgan, Lewis H. *League of the Ho-de-no-sau-nee or Iroquois*. Rochester, NY, 1851. [Bercaw 507; as excerpted in *Literary World* 7 (28 December 1850), 521–23]

Nantucket Song. As qtd. in Browne's *Etchings*.

"Narrative of the Globe Mutiny." See Lay and Hussey.

The New England Primer. Introd. Rev. H. Humphrey. Worcester: Howland, 183–. [Sealts 384, Bercaw 517]

Newspaper Account. [Melville's invention]

Oken, Lorenz. *Elements of Physiophilosophy*. London: Ray Society, 1847. [Sealts 387a, Bercaw 525b]

Olafssón, Eggert, and Bjarni Pálsson. *Travels in Iceland*. London: Phillips, 1805. [Bercaw 526; as qtd. in Beale]

Olassen and Povelson. See Olafssón and Pálsson.

Olmsted, Francis Allyn. *Incidents of a Whaling Voyage*. New York, 1841. [Bercaw 528]

Other or Octher's Verbal Narrative. From Henry; as qtd. in Browne's *Etchings*.

Paley, William. *Natural Theology; or Evidences of the Existence and Attributes of the Deity*. London, 1802. [Bercaw 537]

[Palgrave, Sir Francis]. "Superstition and Knowledge." *Quarterly Review*, July 1823, 440–75.

Paradise Lost. See Milton.

The Penny Cyclopaedia of the Society for the Diffusion of Useful Knowledge. London: Knight, 1833–43. [Bercaw 544]

The Pilgrim's Progress. Misattribution of *Holy War*. See Bunyan.

Plato. *Phaedon; or, A Dialogue on the Immortality of the Soul*. Trans. Dacier. New York: Gowan, 1833. [Bercaw 549]

Plutarch, *The Philosophy Commonly Called the Morals*. Trans. Philemon Holland. London, 1603, 1657. [Bercaw 559]

Poe, Edgar Allan. *The Narrative of Arthur Gordon Pym, of Nantucket*. New York: Harper & Brothers, 1838. [Copy owned by Melville's brother Gansevoort]

Pope, Alexander. *The Rape of the Lock*. London, 1714.

Psalm 18 [in "The Sermon" (Ch. 9)]. In *The Psalms and Hymns of the Reformed Protestant Dutch Church*, comp. John H. Livingston (1789, 1846). [Bercaw 569]

Purchas, Samuel. *Purchas his Pilgrimes*. London, 1625; as qtd. in Harris. [Bercaw 570]

Rabelais, François. *The Works of Rabelais*. Trans. Duchat, Ozell, et al. London: Smith, Miller, 1844(?). [Sealts 417, Bercaw 574]

Rape of the Lock. See Pope.

Reni, Guido. "Perseus and Andromeda." See D. Stephen Pepper. *Guido Reni: A Complete Catalogue of His Works, with an Introductory Text*. New York: New York UP, 1984.

Reynolds, Jeremiah N. "Mocha Dick: or the White Whale of the Pacific," *The Knickerbocker, or New-York Monthly Magazine* 13 (May 1839): 377–92. [Bercaw 582]

Rhodes, James A. *A Cruise in a Whale Boat*. New York, 1848.

Richardson, Charles. *A New Dictionary of the English Language*. London, 1836–37; Philadelphia, 1846. [Bercaw 585]

°Rousseau, Jean-Jacques. *Confessions* (1781, 1788). Ed. unknown. [Sealts 429, Bercaw 590]

°Schiller, Friedrich von. *The Poems and Ballads*. Trans. Sir Edward Bulwer Lytton. Leipzig: Tauchnitz, 1844. [Sealts 439, Bercaw 606]

Schouten, William Cornelius. *Sixth Circumnavigation*. From *The Relation of a Wonderful Voyage Made by William Cornelius Schouten of Horn*. London, 1619; as qtd. in Harris. [Bercaw 614]

Scoresby, William. *An Account of the Arctic Regions, with a History and Description of the Northern Whale Fishery*. Edinburgh: Constable, 1820. [Sealts 450, Bercaw 615]

———. *Journal of a Voyage to the Northern Whale Fishery*. Edinburgh: Constable, 1823. [Sealts 451, Bercaw 616]

Shakespeare, William. *The Dramatic Works of William Shakespeare*. Boston: Hilliard, Gray, 1837. [Sealts 460, Bercaw 634, see also NN *Journals* 144–46]

°Shelley, Mary Wollstonecraft. *Frankenstein: or, The Modern Prometheus*. London: Bentley, 1849. [Sealts 467, Bercaw 636].

Sibbald, Sir Robert. *A History, Ancient and Modern, of the Sheriffdoms of Fife and Kinross*. Cupar-Fife, 1803. [Bercaw 642]

Smith, C. Hamilton, "Whale," as qtd. in Kitto.

Smith, Elizabeth Oakes. "The Drowned Mariner," in *Poetical Writings* (New York, 1845).

"Something" unpublished. [Melville's invention, in "Extracts"]

Spenser, Edmund. *The Faerie Queen*; as qtd. in Richardson.

Stafford, Richard. "Letter from the Bermudas." From the Royal Society's *Philosophical Transactions*; as qtd. in Beale or Browne's *Etchings*.

Sterne, Laurence. *The Life and Opinions of Tristram Shandy, Gent.* (1760–67). Ed. unknown. [Sealts 490, Bercaw 670]

Stone, William Leete. *Life of Joseph Brant—Thayendanegea*. New York: Dearborn, 1838. [Sealts 491a, Bercaw 674]

Stow, John. *The Chronicles* [later *Annales*] *of England* (1580). Ed. unknown. [Bercaw 675]

Tales of a Whale Voyager. See Gillies.

Tooke's Lucian. "The True History." See Lucian.

Thomas, Isaiah. *Massachusetts, Connecticut, Rhode-Island, New-Hampshire and Vermont Almanack* (1779–1820). [Bercaw 702]

Tyerman, Daniel, and George Bennet. *Journal of Voyages and Travels*. Boston: Crocker & Brewster; New York: Leavitt, 1832. [Bercaw 724]

Ulloa, Antonio de. *A Voyage to South-America*. London, 1758. [Bercaw 725]

Vidocq, François Eugène. *Memoirs of Vidocq* (1828–29). Ed. unknown.

von Troil, Uno. *Letters on Iceland*. London, 1780.

Voyage to Greenland. See Martens.

Wafer, Lionel. *A New Voyage and Description of the Isthmus of America*. London, 1699. [Bercaw 738]

Waller, Edmund. *Poems*. London, 1664.

Ward, William. *View of the History, Literature, and Mythology of the Hindoos*. 3 vols. London, 1822.

Watts, Isaac. *Hymns and Spiritual Songs* (1707). Ed. unknown. [Bercaw 748]

Webster, Daniel. *Speeches and Forensic Arguments*. Boston, 1830.

Webster, Noah. *An American Dictionary of the English Language*. New York: Harper, 1846 (or later). [Sealts 550, Bercaw 751]

Weld, Horatio Hastings. "A Chapter on Whaling." In *Ribs and Trucks, From Davy's Locker*. Boston, 1842. [Bercaw 752b]

"The Whale and Whale Catching." See Anonymous.

Whale Song. As qtd. in Cheever. [See also Frank, "'The King of the Southern Sea,'" in Further Reading]

Wharton the Whale-Killer! See Halyard.

Wilkes, Charles. *United States Exploring Expedition*. Philadelphia: Sherman, 1844. [Sealts 532, Bercaw 759]

FURTHER READING

All primary and secondary sources that have been cited in the **Introduction**, **Explanatory Notes** and **Making *Moby-Dick*** are given full citations in one of the following five bibliographical sections. The first section lists in chronological order the historical versions of *Moby-Dick* and subsequent versions of the text based on reliable editorial principles. The second, arranged alphabetically by editor, is a selection of modern editions with important textual, literary, historical, and cultural annotations. (An item in one section could also be classified in the other: for instance, the Longman Critical Edition, featured in Versions of *Moby-Dick*, is thoroughly annotated and could also be included in Selected Annotated Editions, whereas the Hendricks House edition, listed among selected editions, was a textual standard for a decade and could also be considered a version of *Moby-Dick*.) The third section, arranged alphabetically by author, lists the major book-length biographies of Herman Melville, and the fourth provides useful reference "tools" for focused research on Melville and *Moby-Dick*. The final section is a selection of scholarly and critical works either fully or partially devoted to *Moby-Dick*. (For citations of the sources Melville refers to or used in writing *Moby-Dick*, see **Melville's Sources**.)

Versions of *Moby-Dick*

Melville, Herman. "The Town-Ho's Story," *Harper's New Monthly Magazine* (October, 1851)

_____. *The Whale; or, Moby Dick*. 3 vols. London: Bentley, 1851.

_____. *Moby-Dick; or, The Whale*. New York: Harper, 1851.

_____. *Moby-Dick*. Ed. Arthur Stedman. New York: United States Book Co., 1892.

_____. *Moby-Dick*. In *The Works of Herman Melville*, vols. 7–8. Ed. Michael Sadleir. London: Constable, 1922.

_____. *Moby-Dick or The Whale*. *The Writings of Herman Melville*. Vol. 6. Ed. Hayford, Harrison, Hershel Parker, and G. Thomas Tanselle. Evanston, IL: Northwestern UP and the Newberry Library, 1988.

_____. *Moby-Dick; or, The Whale*. Ed. John Bryant and Haskell Springer. New York: Longman, 2006.

Selected Annotated Editions of *Moby-Dick*

Beaver, Harold, ed. *Moby-Dick; or, The Whale*. Harmondsworth: Penguin English Library, 1972.

Delbanco, Andrew, introd. *Moby-Dick; or, The Whale*. Endnotes by Tom Quirk. New York: Penguin, 1992.

Feidelson, Charles, ed. *Moby-Dick or, The Whale*. Indianapolis and New York: Bobbs-Merrill, 1964.

Hayford, Harrison and Hershel Parker, eds. *Moby-Dick*. New York: Norton, 1967; 2nd ed., 2002.

Mansfield, Luther S., and Howard Vincent, eds. *Moby-Dick or, The Whale*. New York: Hendricks House, 1952.

Thorp, Willard, ed. *Moby-Dick or The Whale*. New York: Oxford UP, 1947.

Melville Biography

Arvin, Newton. *Herman Melville*. New York: Viking, 1957.

Delbanco, Andrew. *Melville: His World and Work*. New York: Knopf, 2005.

Garner, Stanton. *The Civil War World of Herman Melville*. Lawrence: UP of Kansas, 1993.

Howard, Leon, *Herman Melville: A Biography*. Berkeley: U of California P, 1951.

Metcalf, Eleanor Melville. *Herman Melville: Cycle and Epicycle*. Cambridge: Harvard UP, 1953.

Miller, Edwin Haviland. *Melville*. New York: George Braziller, 1975.

Mumford, Lewis. *Herman Melville*. New York: Literary Guild of America, 1929.

Parker, Hershel. *Herman Melville: A Biography*. 2 vols. Baltimore: Johns Hopkins UP, 1996, 2002.

Robertson-Lorant, Laurie. *Melville: A Biography*. New York: Clarkson Potter, 1996.

Sealts, Merton M. Jr. *The Early Lives of Melville*. Madison: U of Wisconsin P, 1974.

Weaver, Raymond. *Herman Melville, Mariner and Mystic*. New York: Doran, 1921.

Research Tools

Ashley, Clifford W. *The Yankee Whaler*. Boston: Houghton Mifflin, 1926; Ottawa: Algrove, 2001.

Bercaw, Mary K. *Melville's Sources*. Evanston, IL: Northwestern UP, 1987.

Bradford, Gershom. *The Mariner's Dictionary*. New York: Barre Publishers, 1952.

Bryant, John, ed. *A Companion to Melville Studies*. Westport, CT: Greenwood, 1986.

_____. *Melville Dissertations, 1924–1980*. Westport, CT: Greenwood, 1983.

Busch, Briton Cooper. *Whaling Will Never Do for Me: The American Whaleman in the Nineteenth Century*. Lexington, KY: U of Kentucky P, 1994.

Church, Albert Cook. *Whaleships and Whaling*. New York: Norton, 1938.

Coffler, Gail H. *Melville's Allusions to Religion*. Westport, CT: Greenwood, 2004.

_____. *Melville's Classical Allusions*. Westport, CT: Greenwood, 1985.

Cowen, Wilson Walker. *Melville's Marginalia*. New York: Garland, 1987.

Dana, Richard Henry, Jr. *The Seaman's Friend: Containing a Treatise on Practical Seamanship, with Plates; A Dictionary of Sea Terms*. Boston: Little and Brown, 1841.

Ellis, Richard. *Men and Whales*. New York: Knopf, 1991.

Frank, Stuart M. *Herman Melville's Picture Gallery: Sources and Types of the "Pictorial" Chapters of Moby-Dick*. Fairhaven, MA: Edward Lefkowicz, 1980.

Gidmark, Jill B. *Melville Sea Dictionary*. Westport, CT: Greenwood P, 1982.

Goode, George Brown. *The Fisheries and Fishery Industries of the United States*. Section V, Part 2. By James Templeman Brown. Washington: Government Printing Office, 1887.

Grey, Robin and Douglas Robillard (in consultation with Hershel Parker). "Melville's Milton: A Transcription of Melville's Marginalia in His Copy of *The Poetical Works of John Milton*," *Leviathan* 4.1 and 2 (March and Oct. 2002): 117–204. Rpt. as *Melville and Milton: An Edition of Melville's Annotations on Milton*, ed. Robin Grey. Pittsburgh: Duquesne UP, 2004.

Hayes, Kevin J. *The Critical Response to Herman Melville's Moby-Dick*. Westport, CT: Greenwood, 1994

Hayford, Harrison and Hershel Parker, eds. *Moby-Dick as Doubloon: Essays and Extracts, 1851–1970*. New York: Norton, 1970.

Higgins, Brian. *Herman Melville, an Annotated Bibliography, 1846–1930*. Boston: G. K. Hall, 1979.

_____. *Herman Melville: A Reference Guide, 1931–1960*. Boston: G. K. Hall, 1987.

_____, and Hershel Parker, eds. *Critical Essays on Herman Melville's Moby-Dick*. New York: G. K. Hall, 1992.

_____, eds. *Herman Melville: The Contemporary Reviews*. Cambridge: Cambridge UP, 1995.

Jeffrey, Lloyd N. "A Concordance to the Biblical Allusions in *Moby-Dick*." *Bulletin of Bibliography* 21 (May–Aug. 1956): 223–29.

Kier, Kathleen. *A Melville Encyclopedia: The Novels*. New York: Whitston Publishing, 1990, 1994.

Lackey, Kris. "Additional Biblical Allusions in *Moby-Dick*." *Melville Society Extracts* 54 (May 1983): 12.

Leavitt, John F. *The Charles W. Morgan*. Mystic, CT: Mystic Seaport, 1973.

Lever, Darcy. *The Young Sea Officer's Sheet Anchor; or A Key to the Leading of Rigging, and to Practical Seamanship*. New York: E & G. W. Blunt, 1863.

Leviathan: A Journal of Melville Studies. 1999–.

Leyda, Jay. *The Melville Log: A Documentary Life of Herman Melville, 1819–1891*. 2 vols. New York: Harcourt, Brace, 1951; enlarged ed. Gordian P, 1969.

Maury, Matthew F. *Whale Chart*. Washington, D.C.: United States Hydrographical Office, 1851.

Melville Society Extracts. Published by The Melville Society, 1969–2006. [Continued as a department in *Leviathan*]

Melville, Herman. *Billy Budd, Sailor (An Inside Narrative)*. Ed. Harrison Hayford and Merton M. Sealts Jr. Chicago: U of Chicago P, 1962.

_____. *Moby-Dick, or, The Whale*. http://etext.virginia.edu/toc/modeng/public/Mel2Mob.html.

_____. *The Poems of Herman Melville*. Ed. Douglas Robillard. Kent, OH: Kent State UP, 2000.

_____. *The Writings of Herman Melville*. Ed. Hayford, Harrison, Hershel Parker, and G. Thomas Tanselle. Evanston, IL: Northwestern UP and the Newberry Library. Vol 1,

Typee (1968); vol. 2, *Omoo* (1968); vol. 3, *Mardi* (1969); vol. 4, *Redburn* (1970); vol. 5, *White-Jacket* (1970); vol. 6, *Moby-Dick* (1988); vol. 7, *Pierre* (1971); vol. 8, *Israel Potter* (1982); vol. 9, *The Piazza Tales and Other Prose Pieces, 1839–1860* (1987); vol. 10, *The Confidence-Man* (1984); vol. 12, *Clarel*, ed. Walter E. Bezanson and Alma A. MacDougall (1991); vol. 14, *Correspondence*, ed. Lynn Horth (1993): vol. 15, *Journals*, ed. Howard C. Horsford with Lynn Horth (1989).

Olsen-Smith, Steven, and Dennis C. Marnon. "Melville's Marginalia in *The Works of Sir William D'Avenant*." *Leviathan* 6.1 (March 2004): 79–102.

_____, ed. *Melville's Marginalia Online*. http://www.boisestate.edu/melville/.

Russell, W. Clark. *Sailors' Language: A Collection of Sea-Terms and Their Definitions*. London: Sampson Low, Marston, Searle, & Rivington, 1883.

Sealts, Merton M. Jr. *Melville's Reading*. Rev. ed. Columbia: U of South Carolina P, 1988. [See also supplemental updates in *Melville Society Extracts*, Nos. 80, 90, and 95, and a cumulative supplement in *Leviathan* 6.1]

Smyth, Admiral W. H. *The Sailor's Word-Book: An Alphabetical Digest of Nautical Terms*. London: Blackie, 1867.

Tanselle, G. Thomas. *A Checklist of Editions of Moby-Dick, 1851–1976*. Evanston and Chicago: Northwestern UP and The Newberry Library, 1976.

_____. "Melville and the World of Books." In Bryant, *A Companion to Melville Studies*, 781–835.

Tryckare, Tre. *The Lore of Ships*. New York and Gothenburg: Crown/A. B. Nordbok, 1975.

Wallace, Robert K. "Melville's Prints: The E. Barton Chapin, Jr, Family Collection." *Leviathan* 2.1 (March 2000): 5–65.

Wilson, James. *The Hawthorne and Melville Friendship: An Annotated Bibliography, Biographical and Critical Essays, and Correspondence Between the Two*. Jefferson, NC: McFarland & Co., 1991.

Selected Scholarship and Criticism

Abbott, Collamer M. "Ishmael and Herr Alexander." *Melville Society Extracts* 84 (Feb. 1991): 10–11.

Adler, Joyce Sparer. *War in Melville's Imagination*. New York: New York UP, 1981.

Allen, Gay Wilson. *Melville and His World*. New York: Viking, 1971.

Anderson, Charles R. *Melville in the South Seas*. New York: Columbia UP, 1939.

Arac, Jonathan. *Commissioned Spirits: The Shaping of Social Motion in Dickens, Carlyle, Melville, and Hawthorne*. New Brunswick: Rutgers UP, 1979.

Baird, James. *Ishmael: A Study of the Symbolic Mode in Primitivism*. New York: Harper, 1960.

Barbour, James. "The Composition of *Moby-Dick*." *American Literature* 47.3 (Nov. 1975): 343–60.

Battenfeld, David H. "The Source for the Hymn in *Moby-Dick*," *American Literature* 27 (Nov. 1955): 393–96.

Baym, Nina. "Melville's Quarrel with Fiction." *PMLA* 94 (Oct. 1979): 909–23.

Bell, Millicent. "Pierre Bayle and *Moby-Dick*." *PMLA* 66 (Sept. 1951): 626–48.

Berthoff, Warner. *The Example of Melville*. Princeton, NJ: Princeton UP, 1962.

Bezanson, Walter E. "*Moby-Dick:* Document, Drama, Dream." In Bryant, *A Companion to Melville Studies*, 169–210.

_____. "*Moby-Dick*, Work of Art." In Hillway and Mansfield, *Moby-Dick Centennial Essays*, 30–58.

Blish, Sister M. "Melville and the Sea Drifters of Japan." *Melville Society Extracts* 76 (Feb. 1989): 14–16.

Bode, Rita. "'Suckled by the Sea': The Maternal in *Moby-Dick*." *Melville and Women*. Ed. Elizabeth Schultz and Haskell Springer. Kent, OH: Kent State UP, 2006.

Bowen, Merlin. *The Long Encounter: Self and Experience in the Writings of Herman Melville*. Chicago: U of Chicago P, 1960.

Braswell, William. *Melville's Religious Thought*. Durham: Duke UP, 1943.

Brodhead, Richard H. *Hawthorne, Melville, and the Novel*. Chicago: U of Chicago P, 1976.

_____, ed. *New Essays on Moby-Dick*. New York: Cambridge UP, 1986.

Brodtkorb, Paul. *Ishmael's White World: a Phenomenological Reading of Moby Dick*. New Haven, Yale UP, 1965.

Bryant, John. *Melville and Repose: The Rhetoric of Humor in the American Renaissance*. New York: Oxford UP, 1993.

_____. "Melville Essays the Romance: Comedy and Being in *Frankenstein*, 'The Big Bear of Arkansas,' and *Moby-Dick*." *Nineteenth-Century Literature* 61.3 (Dec. 2006).

_____. "*Moby-Dick* as Revolution." In Levine, *The Cambridge Companion to Herman Melville*, 65–90.

_____. "Texts and Discourse: The New *Moby-Dick*." *Resources for American Literary Study* 18.2 (1992): 179–193.

_____, Mary K. Bercaw Edwards, and Timothy Marr, eds. *Ungraspable Phantom: Essays on Moby-Dick*. Kent, OH: Kent State UP, 2006.

Cameron, Sharon. *The Corporeal Self: Allegories of the Body in Melville and Hawthorne*. Baltimore: Johns Hopkins UP, 1982.

Castronovo, Russ. *Fathering the Nation: American Genealogies of Slavery and Freedom*. Berkeley: U of California P, 1995.

Chase, Richard. *Herman Melville: A Critical Study*. New York: Macmillan, 1949.

Cohen, Hennig. "Melville's Masonic Secrets." *Melville Society Extracts* 108 (March 1997): 3–17.

Cowan, Bainard. *Exiled Waters: Moby-Dick and the Crisis of Allegory*. Baton Rouge: Louisiana State UP, 1982.

Dimock, Wai-chee. *Empire for Liberty: Melville and the Poetics of Individualism*. Princeton: Princeton UP, 1989.

Dreisinger, Batsheva. "'Behold the Hope of Him is in Vain': A Hebraic Reading of *Moby-Dick*," *Melville Society Extracts* 114 (Sept. 1998): 1–4.

Dryden, Edgar A. *Melville's Thematics of Form: The Great Art of Telling the Truth*. Baltimore: Johns Hopkins UP, 1968.

Duban, James. *Melville's Major Fiction: Politics, Theology, and Imagination*. DeKalb, IL: Northern Illinois UP, 1983.

Edinger, Edward F. *Melville's Moby-Dick: A Jungian Commentary*. New York: New Directions, 1978.

Eigner, Edwin M. *The Metaphysical Novel in England and America: Dickens, Bulwer, Melville, and Hawthorne.* Berkeley: U of California P, 1978.

Feidelson, Charles. *Symbolism and American Literature.* Chicago: U of Chicago P, 1953.

Fiedler, Leslie. *Love and Death in the American Novel.* New York: Criterion Books, 1960.

Finkelstein, Dorothee Metlitzki. *Melville's Orienda.* New Haven: Yale UP, 1961.

Frank, Stuart M. "'Cheer'ly Man': Chanteying in *Omoo* and *Moby-Dick.*" *New England Quarterly* 58 (March 1985): 68–82.

———. "'The King of the Southern Sea' and 'Captain Bunker': Two Songs in *Moby-Dick.*" *Melville Society Extracts* 63 (Sept. 1985): 4–7.

Franklin, H. Bruce. *The Wake of the Gods: Melville's Mythology.* Stanford: Stanford UP, 1963.

Fussell, Edwin S. *Frontier: American Literature and the American West.* Princeton: Princeton UP, 1965.

Gaines, Kendra. "A Consideration of an Additional Source for Melville's *Moby-Dick.*" *Melville Society Extracts* 29 (Jan. 1977): 6–12.

Gilmore, Michael T. *American Romanticism and the Marketplace.* Chicago: U of Chicago P, 1985.

Grejda, Edward S. *The Common Continent of Men: Racial Equality in the Writings of Herman Melville.* Port Washington, NY: Kennikat, 1974.

Gretchko, John M. J. "New Evidence for Melville's Use of John Harris in *Moby-Dick,*" *Studies in the American Renaissance* (1983): 303–11.

———. "William Ward, A Source for Melville's Vishnoo." *Melville Society Extracts* 88 (March 1992): 16.

Grey, Robin. *The Complicity of Imagination: The American Renaissance, Contests of Authority, and Seventeenth-Century English Culture.* New York: Cambridge UP, 1997.

Hanson, Elizabeth I. "Melville and the Polynesian-Indian." *Melville Society Extracts* 17 (Feb. 1974): 13–14.

Hayford, Harrison. "Unnecessary Duplicates: A Key to the Writing of *Moby-Dick.*" In Pullin, 128–61.

Heflin, Wilson. *Herman Melville's Whaling Years.* Ed. Mary K. Bercaw Edwards and Thomas Farel Heffernan. Nashville: Vanderbilt UP, 2004.

Heimert, Alan. "*Moby-Dick* and American Political Symbolism." *American Quarterly* 15.4 (Winter 1963): 498–534.

Herbert, T. Walter. *Moby-Dick and Calvinism: A World Dismantled.* New Brunswick, NJ: Rutgers UP, 1977.

Hillway, Tyrus, and Luther S. Mansfield, eds. *Moby-Dick Centennial Essays.* Dallas: Southern Methodist UP, 1953.

Hoffman, Daniel G. *Form and Fable in American Fiction.* New York: Oxford UP, 1961.

Howard, Leon. *The Unfolding of Moby-Dick.* Ed. James Barbour and Thomas Quirk. Glassboro, NJ: The Melville Society, 1987.

Inge, M. Thomas. "Melville in Popular Culture." In Bryant, *A Companion to Melville Studies,* 695–739.

Irwin, John T. *American Hieroglyphics: The Symbol of the Egyptian Hieroglyphics in the American Renaissance.* Baltimore, MD: Johns Hopkins UP, 1980.

Jehlen, Myra, ed. *Herman Melville: a Collection of Critical Essays*. Englewood Cliffs, NJ: Prentice Hall, 1994.

Karcher, Carolyn L. *Shadow Over the Promised Land: Slavery, Race, and Violence in Melville's America*. Baton Rouge, LA: Louisiana State UP, 1980.

Keil, James C. "Melville's '"American Goldsmith': *Moby-Dick* and Irving's *A History of New York*." *Melville Society Extracts* 102 (Sept. 1995): 13–16.

Kelley, Wyn, ed. *A Companion to Herman Melville*. Oxford: Blackwell, 2006.

Kelley, Wyn. *Lying in Various Attitudes: Staging Melville's Pip in Digital Media* http://web.mit.edu/lit/www/spotlightarticles/stagingpip.html

_____. *Melville's City: Literary and Urban Form in Nineteenth-Century New York*. New York: Cambridge UP, 1996.

Lawrence, D. H. *Studies in Classic American Literature*. New York: Thomas Seltzer, 1923.

Lee, A. Robert. "*Moby-Dick*: The Tale and the Telling." In Pullin, 86–127.

Leverenz, David. *Manhood and the American Renaissance*. Ithaca, NY: Cornell UP, 1989.

Levin, Harry. *The Power of Blackness: Hawthorne, Poe, Melville*. New York: Knopf, 1958.

Levine, Robert S., ed. *The Cambridge Companion to Herman Melville*. New York: Cambridge UP, 1998.

Levine, Robert S. *Conspiracy and Romance: Studies in Brockden Brown, Cooper, Hawthorne, and Melville*. New York: Cambridge UP, 1989.

Mailloux, Steven. *Interpretive Conventions: The Reader in the Study of American Fiction*. Ithaca, NY: Cornell UP, 1982.

Markels, Julian. *Melville and the Politics of Identity: From King Lear to Moby-Dick*. Urbana: U of Illinois P, 1993.

Martin, Robert K. *Hero, Captain, and Stranger: Male Friendship, Social Critique, and Literary Form in the Sea Novels of Herman Melville*. Chapel Hill: U of North Carolina P, 1986.

Marx, Leo. *The Machine in the Garden: Technology and the Pastoral Ideal in America*. New York: Oxford UP, 1964.

Matthiessen, F. O. *American Renaissance: Art and Expression in the Age of Emerson and Whitman*. New York: Oxford UP, 1964.

Metlitzki, Dorothee. "The Letter 'H' in Melville's Whale." *Melville Society Extracts* 47 (Sept. 1981): 9.

Milder, Robert. "The Composition of *Moby-Dick*: A Review and a Prospect." *ESQ: A Journal of the American Renaissance*, 23 (1977): 203–16.

_____. *Exiled Royalties: Melville and the Life We Imagine*. New York: Oxford UP, 2006.

Miller, James E., Jr. *A Reader's Guide to Herman Melville*. New York: Farrar Straus and Cudahy, 1962.

Miller, Perry. *The Raven and the Whale: The War of Words and Wits in the Era of Poe and Melville*. New York: Harcourt Brace, 1956.

Morrison, Toni. "Unspeakable Things Unspoken: The Afro-American Presence in American Literature." *Michigan Quarterly Review* 28 (1989): 1–34.

Murray, Henry A. "'In Nomine Diaboli.'" *The New England Quarterly* 24 (Dec. 1951): 435–52.

Olsen-Smith, Steven. "The Hymn in *Moby-Dick*: Melville's Adaptation of 'Psalm 18,'" *Leviathan* 5.1 (March 2003): 29–47.

_____. "Melville's Marginalia in Thomas Beale's *The Natural History of the Sperm Whale*: Recovering a Source of Evidence for the Composition of *Moby-Dick*." *Harvard Library Bulletin* (forthcoming).

Olson, Charles. *Call Me Ishmael*. New York: Reynall and Hitchcock, 1947.

Otter, Samuel. *Melville's Anatomies*. Berkeley: U of California P, 1999.

Parke, John. "Seven *Moby-Dicks*." *New England Quarterly* 28.3 (Sept. 1955): 319–38.

Pease, Donald E. *Visionary Compacts: American Renaissance Writings in Cultural Context*. Madison: U of Wisconsin P, 1987.

Pollin, Burton R. "Traces of Poe in Melville." *Melville Society Extracts* 109 (June 1997): 2–12.

Pommer, Henry F. *Milton and Melville*. Pittsburgh: U of Pittsburgh P, 1950.

Poole, Gordon. "Stubb Diddles the Rose-bud," *Melville Society Extracts* 92 (March 1993): 11–13.

Pullin, Faith, ed. *New Perspectives on Melville*. Kent, OH and Edinburgh: Kent State UP and Edinburgh UP, 1978.

Quirk, Tom. "The Judge Dragged to the Bar: Melville, Shaw, and the Webster Murder Trial," *Melville Society Extracts* 84 (Feb. 1991): 1–8.

Reynolds, David S. *Beneath the American Renaissance: The Subversive Imagination in the Age of Emerson and Melville*. New York: Knopf, 1988.

Reynolds, Larry J. *European Revolutions and the American Literary Renaissance*. New Haven, CT: Yale UP, 1988.

Robillard, Douglas. "Lorenz Oken and *Moby-Dick*." *Melville Society Extracts* 100 (March 1995): 8–9.

Rogin, Michael Paul. *Subversive Genealogy: The Politics and Art of Herman Melville*. New York: Knopf, 1983.

Rosenberry, Edward. *Melville and the Comic Spirit*. Cambridge: Harvard UP, 1955.

Sanborn, Geoffrey, "The Name of the Devil: Melville's Other 'Extracts' for *Moby-Dick*," *Nineteenth-Century Literature* 47.2 (Sept. 1992): 212–35.

_____. *The Sign of the Cannibal: Melville and the Making of a Postcolonial Reader*. Durham NC: Duke UP, 1998.

Scherting, Jack. "The Chaldee Allusion in *Moby-Dick*: Its Antecedent and its Implicit Skepticism." *Melville Society Extracts* 49 (Feb. 1982): 14–15.

Schleifer, Neal, "Melville as Lexicographer: Linguistics and Symbolism in *Moby-Dick*." *Melville Society Extracts* 98 (Sept. 1994): 1–6.

Schultz, Elizabeth A. *Unpainted to the Last: Moby-Dick and Twentieth-Century American Art*. Lawrence: UP of Kansas, 1995.

_____. "Melville's Environmental Vision in *Moby-Dick*." *ISLE* 7.1 (Winter 2000): 97–113.

_____. "The Sentimental Subtext of *Moby-Dick*: Melville's Response to the 'World of Woe.'" *ESQ: A Journal of the American Renaissance* 42.1 (1996): 29–51.

Sealts, Merton M. Jr. *Pursuing Melville: 1940–1980*. Madison: U of Wisconsin P, 1982.

Sheldon, Leslie E. "Messianic Power and Satanic Decay: Milton in *Moby-Dick*." In Grey, *Melville and Milton*, 25–46.

Shillingsburg, Peter. "The Three *Moby-Dicks.*" *American Literary History* 2.1 (Spring 1990): 119–30.

Slotkin, Richard. *Regeneration through Violence: The Mythology of the American Frontier, 1600–1860.* Middletown, CT: Wesleyan UP, 1973.

Smith, Henry Nash. *Democracy and the Novel: Popular Resistance to Classic American Writers.* New York: Oxford UP, 1978.

Springer, Haskell, ed. *America and the Sea: A Literary History.* Athens: U of Georgia P, 1995.

_____, ed. "Of the Monstrous Pictures of Whales" (*Moby-Dick*, Ch. 55). http://web.ku.edu/~zeke/md.

Stauffer, John. *The Black Hearts of Men: Radical Abolitionists and the Transformation of Race.* Cambridge, MA: Harvard UP, 2002.

Sten, Christopher. *Sounding the Whale.* Kent, OH: Kent State UP, 1996.

Stewart, George R. "The Two *Moby-Dicks.*" *American Literature* 25.4 (Winter 1954): 417–48.

Stuckey, Sterling. "The Tambourine in Glory: African Culture and Melville's Art." In Levine, *The Cambridge Companion to Herman Melville,* 37–64.

Sweeney, Gerard M. *Melville's Use of Classical Mythology.* Amsterdam: Rodopi, 1975.

Thompson, Lawrance. *Melville's Quarrel with God.* Princeton: Princeton UP, 1952.

Van Cromphout, Gustaaf. "*Moby-Dick*: The Transformation of the Faustian Ethos." *American Literature* 51 (March 1979): 17–32.

Vincent, Howard P. *The Trying-Out of Moby-Dick.* Carbondale, IL: Southern Illinois UP, 1949.

Wallace, Robert K. *Douglass and Melville: Anchored Together in Neighborly Style.* New Bedford, MA: Spinner Publications, 2005.

_____. *Frank Stella's Moby Dick: Words and Shapes.* Ann Arbor: U of Michigan P, 2000.

_____. *Melville and Turner: Spheres of Love and Fright.* Athens: U of Georgia P, 1992.

Ward, J. A. "The Function of the Cetological Chapters in *Moby-Dick.*" *American Literature* 28 (May 1956): 164–83.

Wendel, Thomas. "Touchstone and the Virtue of If," *Melville Society Extracts* 114 (Sept. 1998): 8–9.

Wenke, John. *Melville's Muse: Literary Creation and the Forms of Philosophical Fiction.* Kent, OH: Kent State UP, 1995.

Wright, Nathalia. *Melville's Use of the Bible.* Durham, NC: Duke UP, 1949.

Young, James D. "The Nine Gams of the Pequod." *American Literature* 15 (Jan. 1954): 449–463.

Zimmer, Carl. "The Equation of a Whale," *Discover* (April 1998).

Zoellner, Robert. *The Salt-Sea Mastodon: A Reading of Moby-Dick.* Berkeley: U of California P, 1973.

ILLUSTRATIONS

Ambrose Louis Garneray, *Pêche du Cachalot* (aquatint, 1834). Widely copied in color and black-and-white in Melville's day, and approvingly described in Ch. 56. Courtesy of the New Bedford Whaling Museum.

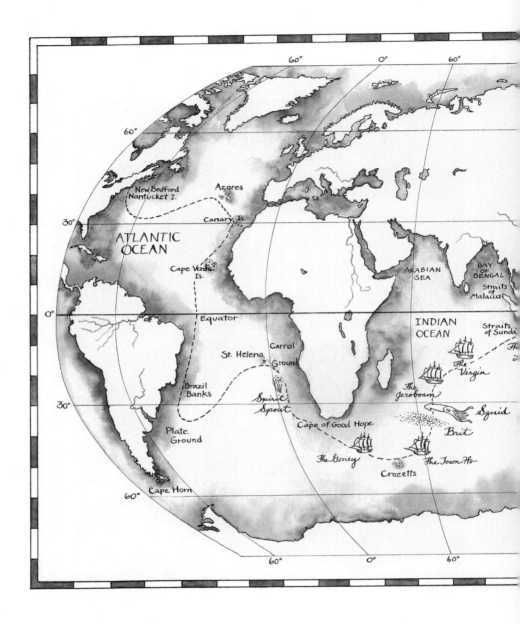

The Voyage of the **Pequod.**

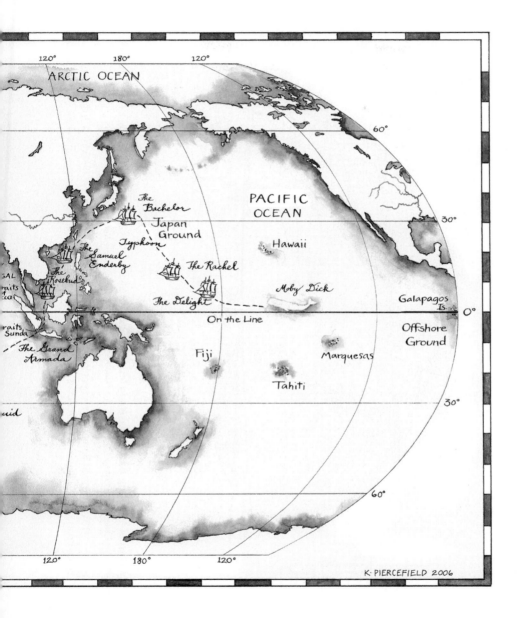

Courtesy of Kathleen Piercefield.

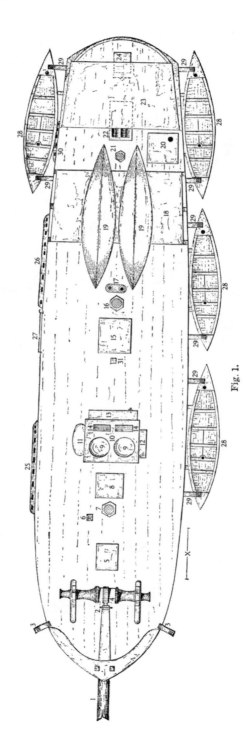

Deck Plan and Cutaway Plan of Whaling Bark *Alice Knowles*. In essential details, the plans on these two pages depict the construction of the *Pequod*. From George Brown Goode, *The Fisheries and Fishery Industries of the United States*, 1887. Courtesy of the New Bedford Whaling Museum.

Fig. 1. Deck Plan: 1) Bowsprit. 4) Windlass. 5) Forecastle companion-way. 7) Foremast. 8) Fore hatch. 9) Try-pots. 10) Try-works. 15) Main hatch. 16) Mainmast. 19) Spare boats. 20) Galley. 21) Mizzenmast. 25, 26, 30) Fore, main, and mizzen channels and chains. 28) Whaleboats ready for use. 29) Davits.

Fig. 1.

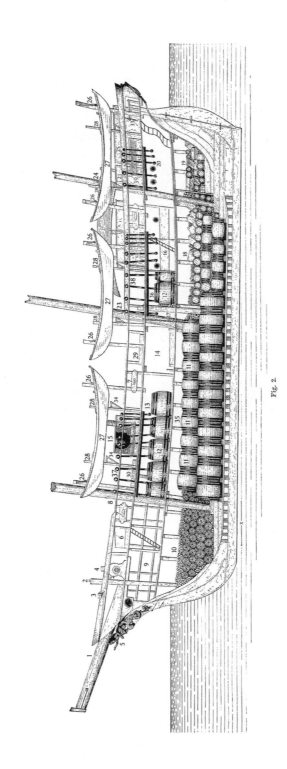

Fig. 2.

Fig. 2. Cutaway Plan: 1) Bowsprit. 4) Windlass. 6) Forecastle companion-way. 8) Foremast. 9) Forecastle. 10) Fore hold. 11 and 12) Casks for oil. 14) Blubber room. 15) Try-works. 20) Captain's cabin. 21) Galley. 22) Shears for spare boats. 23) Mainmast. 24) Mizzenmast. 26) Davits. 27) Whaleboats. 29) Main hatch. 30) Fore hatch. 34) Cranes. 37–39) Chains.

A Ship's Sails. Selected here are those most important in reading *Moby-Dick*. 2) Jib.
7) Foresail. 8) Fore topsail. 9) Fore topgallant sail. 10) Fore royal. 11) Fore skysail.
12) Mainsail. 13) Main topsail. 14) Main topgallant sail. 15) Main royal. 16) Main skysail.
17) Mizzen topsail. 18) Mizzen topgallant sail. 19) Mizzen royal. 20) Mizzen skysail.
21–27) Studdingsails. From R. H. Dana Jr., *The Seaman's Friend* (1841). Courtesy of the New Bedford Whaling Museum.

The Spars, Rigging, and Other Parts of a Ship most pertinent to reading *Moby-Dick*.

The three masts, from front to rear, are the **Foremast**, **Mainmast**, and **Mizzenmast**. Each is made of five sections. The lowest has the same name as the entire mast, while the four sections above are, in rising order, the **topmast**, **topgallant mast**, **royal mast**, and **skysail mast**. Each section is prefixed by its mast name, thus: 21) Foremast, 22) Fore topmast, 23) Fore topgallant mast, 24) Fore royal mast, 25) Fore skysail mast.

Yards are horizontal poles crossing the masts, from which the sails hang. They, too, take the same names from bottom to top; the lowest is simply called by the name of its mast, the ones above (top, topgallant, royal, and skysail) are preceded by the name of their mast, as in 53) Main yard, 54) Main topsail yard, 55) Main topgallant yard, 56) Main royal yard. (Skysail yards are omitted here.)

The rigging is of two kinds: **standing** (fixed) and **running** (adjustable). **Stays** and **Backstays** are fixed ropes supporting the masts—forward and to the rear; each is named for the section of the mast it strengthens. The fixed **Shrouds** support each mast on both sides. For example, then, the Mainmast: 87) Main stay, 88) Main topmast stay, 89) Main topgallant stay, 90) Main royal stay, 102) Main topmast backstays, 103) Main topgallant backstays, 104) Main royal backstays, 99) Main shrouds, 100) Main topmast shrouds, 101) Main topgallant shrouds. For the running rigging, **Lifts** (e.g. 73) support the yards from the tops of their masts; **Braces** (e.g. 92, 94, 96, 98) swing the yards horizontally; and **Halyards** (not shown) are used to raise and lower the yards.

See Glossary for the following parts of the ship: 1) Head, 2) Head-boards, 3) Stem, 4) Bows, 5) Forecastle, 6) Waist, 7) Quarter-deck, 10) Stern, 11) Taffrail, 12–14) Chains, 15) Bowsprit, 16) Jib-boom, 66) Jib stay, 40) Fore top, 42) Fore topmast cross-trees, 43) Main top, 45) Main topmast cross-trees, 46) Mizzen top, 48) Mizzen topmast cross-trees. From R. H. Dana Jr., *The Seaman's Friend* (1841). Courtesy of the New Bedford Whaling Museum.

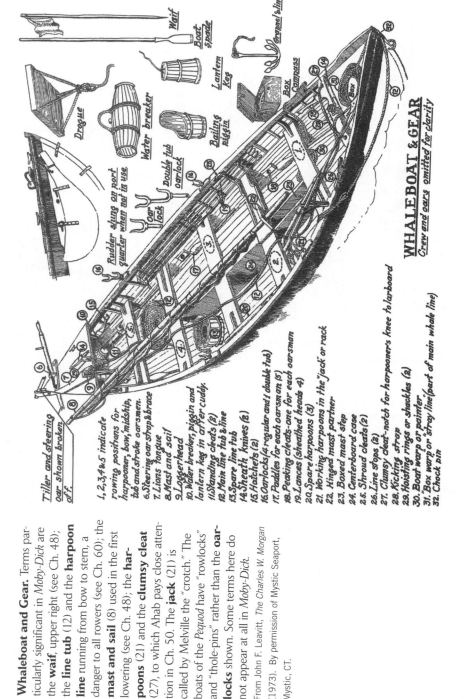

Waif

Boat Spade

Drogue

Water breaker

Grapnel & line

Lantern Keg

Bailing Piggin

Box Compass

Box

Double tub oarlock

Oar lock

Rudder slung on port quarter when not in use.

WHALEBOAT & GEAR
Crew and oars omitted for clarity

Tiller and steering oar shown broken off.

1,2,3,4&5 indicate rowing positions for harpooner, bow, midship, tub and stroke oarsmen.
6. Steering oar shop & brace
7. Lions tongue
8. Mast and sail
9. Loggerhead
10. Water breaker, piggin and lantern keg in after cuddy.
11. Standing cleats (2)
12. Main line tub & line
13. Spare line tub
14. Sheath knives (2)
15. Hatchets (2)
16. Oarlocks (4 regular and 1 double tub)
17. Paddles for each oarsman (5)
18. Peaking cleats-one for each oarsman
19. Lances (sheathed heads 4)
20. Spare harpoons (3)
21. Working harpoons in the "jack or rack
22. Hinged mast partner
23. Boxed mast step
24. Centerboard case
25. Shroud cleats (2)
26. Line stops (2)
27. Clumsy cleat—notch for harpooners knee to larboard
28. Kicking strap
29. Hoisting rings or shackles (2)
30. Boat warp or painter
31. Box warp or "stray line (part of main whale line)
32. Chock pin

Whaleboat and Gear. Terms particularly significant in *Moby-Dick* are the **waif,** upper right (see Ch. 48); the **line tub** (12) and the **harpoon line** running from bow to stern, a danger to all rowers (see Ch. 60); the **mast and sail** (8) used in the first lowering (see Ch. 48); the **harpoons** (21) and the **clumsy cleat** (27), to which Ahab pays close attention in Ch. 50. The **jack** (21) is called by Melville the "crotch." The boats of the *Pequod* have "rowlocks" and "thole-pins" rather than the **oarlocks** shown. Some terms here do not appear at all in *Moby-Dick.*

From John F. Leavitt, *The Charles W. Morgan* (1973). By permission of Mystic Seaport, Mystic, CT.

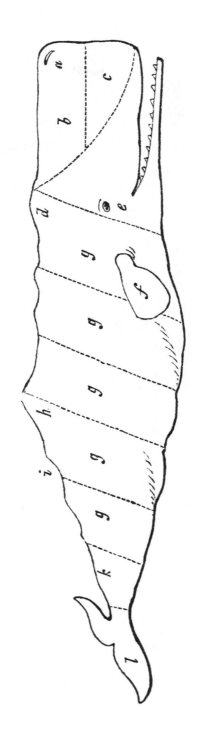

Cutting-In Diagram of a Sperm Whale. Whalers peeled off blubber following the cutting pattern shown here and described in Ch. 67. Beale labels the parts of the whale as a) the nostril or spout-hole; b) the case; c) the junk; d) the bunch of the neck; e) the eye; f) the fin; g) the spiral strips or blanket pieces; h) the hump; i) the ridge; k) the small; l) the tail or flukes. The blanket pieces are explained by Melville in Ch. 68, the junk and the case in Ch. 77.

From Thomas Beale, *The Natural History of the Sperm Whale* (1839). Courtesy of the New Bedford Whaling Museum.

Bailing the Case. A sperm whale's case, which contains the spermaceti, has been separated from the head and secured to the ship within the lowered cutting-stage. It is being bailed out by a man standing on it and using a long pole to push a bucket deep into the cavity; see Ch. 78.

From George Brown Goode, *The Fisheries and Fishery Industries of the United States* (1887). Courtesy of the New Bedford Whaling Museum.

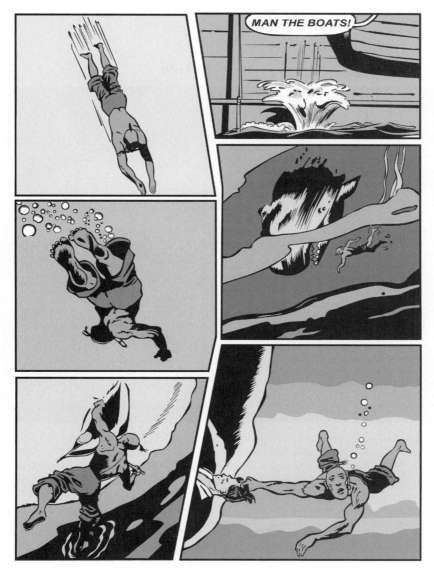

Queequeg's Delivery of Tashtego. In Ch. 78, "Cisterns and Buckets," Tashtego uses a pole and bucket to pull fluid spermaceti out of a cavity (the case) in the detached and suspended whale's head (see facing page). When Tash slips into the head, which in turn falls into the sea, Queequeg dives to the rescue. The 1945 *Classic Comics* version of *Moby-Dick* is the first to illustrate this remarkable scene. In the bottom left panel, Queequeg slices open the whale's head to find Tashtego's knee. In Melville's version, he then flips Tash over to reach his head, and, as seen in the final panel, "delivers" Tashtego as an obstetrician would a baby, performing a kind of Caesarian operation. The British edition of the novel kept this indelicate scene but censored all references to obstetrics, midwifery, and "delivery." From *Moby Dick*, Comics Classics #5 (1945), illus. Louis Zansky. © 2006 First Classics Inc. All Rights Reserved. By permission of Jack Lake Productions Inc.

Ahab as Lover. Screen idol John Barrymore starred in the 1926 (silent) and 1930 hit film versions of *Moby-Dick*. In the former, called *The Sea Beast*, Ahab pledges his love for sweetheart "Esther" (played by Barrymore's sweetheart Dolores Costello). Ahab loses a leg to Moby Dick, and Ahab's jealous, deceiving brother, Derek, drives the two lovers apart. In the end, Ahab kills the whale and gets the girl.

From *The Sea Beast* (1926), dir. Millard Webb; prod. Warner Bros. Warner Bros./Springer/Photofest. © Warner Bros. Photographer: Bert Lynch.

Revising Ahab's Death. In John Huston's 1956 film epic *Moby Dick,* screenwriter Ray Bradbury revised the ending. In the novel, Fedallah is killed on the second day of the final chase, and his corpse resurfaces the following day, lashed by harpoon lines to Moby Dick's back (Ch. 135). In the film, Fedallah does not appear at all, but his manner of dying is transferred to Ahab (Gregory Peck).

From *Moby Dick,* directed by John Huston. Courtesy Warner Bros./Photofest.

GLOSSARY

OF NAUTICAL AND WHALING TERMS

Moby-Dick is rich in nautical language, and at times Melville provides his own definitions and descriptions. Since in most cases, today's readers are not likely to know these words, or remember them while reading, the Glossary is a ready guide. Many terms have more than one meaning; this list focuses on Melville's usage in context.

Nautical and whaling terms also defined elsewhere in the Glossary appear in **bold**. Synonyms and related terms are *italicized*. The sources for this Glossary are standard dictionaries as well as nautical word lists by such sailor-authors as Dana, Falconer, Russell, Smyth, Lever, and Bradford (see Further Reading).

abaft Behind; toward the stern.

abeam At 90 degrees to a vessel's midsection.

above hatches On deck.

afoul Tangled up or dangerously in contact with; see also **foul** and **coming afoul of**.

aft Toward, to, or at the rear.

after-oar The oar in the whaleboat closest to the **stern**.

alow Below.

anchor-watch The short night watch, kept by fewer men than usual, when a whaling vessel is tethered to a whale carcass; it is named by analogy to the practice on non-whaling vessels, which keep a reduced watch while at anchor.

apeak Pointing upward. The oars' handles are placed in notches in the flooring on the opposite side of the boat, leaving the oars pointing up into a V shape; also *peaked*.

argosy Large merchant vessel.

articles Seaman's contract with the owners.

athwartships Across, crosswise; also *athwart*.

avast "Stop," or "stop that!"

away from the wind With the wind directly behind.

back Turn the **spar** holding a sail so the wind strikes the front of the sail (and slows the vessel), as in "back the **main-yard**"

backstays Strong ropes supporting a mast, leading from it, rearward, to the sides of the ship.

baleen Long, fringed plates in the mouth, with which certain whales strain their food from seawater. Also called **whalebone**; they are not bone but are made of keratin, the main component of teeth and hair.

ballast Heavy materials such as iron or stones placed in the hold of a vessel to keep it from capsizing.

bands 1) Ties fastening whaleboats to their ship. 2) Iron collars near the ends of the **yardarms**, to which the supporting **lifts** are shackled. Also meaning strips of canvas sewn across the top of a sail to strengthen it. *Reef bands* are narrow strips of strengthening canvas sewn across a sail to hold a line of *reef-points*, the short ropes with which a sail is partly tied up to reduce its area.

bank Large elevated area of the sea floor, usually rich in fish and other marine life.

barrel An inexact measure; in *Moby-Dick* there are ten barrels to the ton of sperm oil (Ch. 68), and six barrels to an oil **cask** (Ch. 98).

batten Also *batten down*. Seal tightly with canvas and *battens*, pieces of wood, as in "batten the hatches."

belay Secure a rope to a **belaying pin**. Also "stop that," *avast*.

belaying-pins Often shortened to *pins*. Tapered bars of wood or iron (but of whale ivory on the *Pequod*) in various places on deck, to which ropes of the **running rigging** are secured.

bells To mark time, a bell is struck every half-hour with one added strike for each successive half hour, over a four-hour period, after which the sequence is repeated. Thus, 12:30 a.m. is one bell; one o'clock, two bells, and so on to four a.m., or eight bells. Eight a.m., noon, four p.m., eight p.m., and midnight are also eight bells. "Eight bells there below! Tumble up!" (Ch. 40).

bible leaves Thin slices (like pages in a Bible) into which **horse-pieces** of blubber are cut with **mincing knives**.

binnacle Box at the **helm** for the two compasses. A *binnacle lamp* shines on the compass **cards**; a *binnacle watch* is a timepiece placed there.

blocks...sheaves A block houses a **sheave**, a roller or wheel; together they make a pulley.

bluff bows Rounded, full front, as in the architecture of a whaleship.

boarding-sword Long, two-handed, double-edged knife used in the work of peeling blubber from the whale and bringing it *on board*; thus the name. Also *boarding knife*.

boat hook Pole with an iron hook at the end, used for pushing off from or holding on to objects when in a boat.

boat-knife Knife kept at the bow of a whaleboat, used for cutting the whale line in an emergency. Also **line-knife**.

boat-header Commander of a whaleboat, usually a mate, who kills the harpooned whale.

boat-spade Short-handled tool usually used to cut a hole in the dead whale through which to pass a towing line.

boatswain Pronounced "bos'n." A subordinate ship's officer in charge of rigging, cables, anchors, and supplies.

bone in her mouth A fast-moving vessel creating a white bow wave is said to have a bone in her mouth.

boom 1) The heavy pole extending from the mast along the foot of a **fore-and-aft sail**. 2) A small spar rigged to extend the length of a **yard** to permit adding a small **stunsail** beside the **square sail**, thereby extending the total sail area. 3) Other booms, also attached to the masts, are used in moving cargo or bringing aboard parts of the butchered whale.

bow The front of a vessel. *The bows* signifies the entire rounded front part.

bowline Pronounced "bohlin." A fixed loop made in a line as part of a knot of that name. Also a "rope leading forward from the [vertical edge] of a square sail to keep [it extended]" (Dana).

bowsman The man who pulls the second oar, after the harpooner, and is later directly behind the mate who has come to the bow to lance the whale.

bowsprit The pole projecting from the bow of a vessel.

box-line A section of harpoon line coiled in the bow of the whaleboat. Defined in Ch. 60.

brace up Using the **braces**, sailors pull the **yards** as far as possible toward the fore-and-aft position, thereby pointing the ship as closely into the wind as it can sail. Also *brace sharp up*, *brace hard up*.

braces Long ropes attached to the ends of the **yardarms** and leading to the deck. Pulling on them, sailors change the angle of the sails to the wind.

break out Remove objects from the **hold**.

breaker Small barrel for liquids.

brig Two-masted, **square-rigged** vessel.

bright waist A broad band of white paint encircling the hull. On it black squares were sometimes painted to deceive pirates, who, from a distance, might mistake them for gun-ports and believe that the vessel was armed with cannon.

bring by the lee Unintentionally turn the vessel so the wind hits the **lee** side of its sails and may possibly cause it to capsize.

brit Tiny marine organisms, including crustaceans, the food of **baleen** whales; defined in Ch. 58.

bulkhead A partition wall below deck.

bull's eye Thick, rounded piece of glass set in the deck to let light below; also a small block of strong wood with a hole through which a rope may pass.

bulwarks Pronounced "bularks." The part of a ship's side above the deck.

Burtons Hoisting **tackles** for moving items into or out of the hold.

by the board Over the side, overboard.

Cape-Horner Large, square-rigged ship built to withstand the rigors of a Cape Horn passage.

capstan Large, upright cylindrical device, turned by men pushing on long, spoke-like bars, and used for heavy tasks, such as raising the anchor. See **windlass**, which serves the same functions, and appears twice as often in *Moby-Dick*.

capstan-head The rounded top of the capstan.

card Short for **compass card**.

carlines Carlings; fore-and-aft timbers between the deck beams, which in the cabin are ceiling beams.

cask Containers varying greatly in size used for different purposes. An oil cask contains six barrels (Ch. 98), though the term **barrel** is also inexact.

chains Combination of rigid links of chain and narrow wooden platforms called *channels*, fastened to the sides of a ship to take the strain of the rigging supporting the masts.

chock a' block 1) The situation when the two blocks of a **tackle** come together, at the limit of its use. 2) Full to the brim, said of the hold or a container.

chocks Lead-lined grooves in the **prow** of a whaleboat through which the harpoon line travels.

chronometer Exceptionally precise timepiece set to Greenwich Mean Time, and used in finding a ship's longitude.

close-reef Partially tie up a sail so that its minimum area is exposed to the wind.

clumsy cleat Brace in the **bow** of a whaleboat, in which the harpooner or the lance-throwing mate places his knee for stability.

coasting smack Fishing boat that stays close to shore.

cockpits Properly *cockpit*. Low-ceilinged space below the waterline in a man-of-war, used for treating the wounded.

coffer-dam A watertight structure within which repairs can be made below water level.

coming afoul of Coming dangerously in contact or getting tangled with.

companion-way Protected staircase between the deck and the level below.

compass-card Pivoted horizontal disk marked with the points and degrees of the compass. Also simply **card**.

cooper's club hammer Axe-like hammer used by the cooper (barrel-maker).

copper Sheathing on a wooden hull to protect it from boring worms.

copper-pump Device used to pump whale oil from one barrel to another.

cranes Hinged, triangular wooden supports that swing out to support the whaleboats when they are hanging from the ship's side.

cross-trees Light, horizontal timbers attached high up on a mast. In Ch. 35 Ishmael stands on the **t'gallant** cross-trees, on the lookout for whales.

crotch A support in the **bow** of the whaleboat for the wooden ends of the harpoons; defined in Ch. 63.

crowd sail. Raise as many sails as possible.

crown The place where the arms of an anchor join its shank.

cruising ground An area of the sea where, expecting to find whales, a whaler will slowly sail back and forth.

cutting stage Narrow platform hung over a ship's side for men to stand on while removing (**cutting in**) the whale's blubber.

cutting tackles Heavy, multiple block-and-tackle arrangement with a large hook, used in the process of stripping off the whale's blubber. See Ch. 67.

cutting-in Removing the whale's blubber.

Davy Jones *Davy Jones's Locker* at the bottom of the sea, the destination of the dead in sailor folklore.

dead reckoning "Dead" is a corruption of the abbreviation "ded.," meaning "deduced"; *dead reckoning* deduces a ship's approximate position relative to its previous one by multiplying speed by time elapsed to give distance covered, by observing the compass courses steered, and by estimating the effects of *drift* caused by winds and currents. It is much less precise than celestial navigation.

dog-vane Small flag or streamer indicating wind direction.

double-banked Two men to an oar.

douse sail Lower sails in a hurry.

down helm Push the tiller away from the wind, thereby turning the ship itself toward the wind. A wheel is turned toward the wind to achieve the same effect.

draw Require a certain depth of water in order to float; said of a vessel.

eye-splice Loop made by weaving the strands of the end of a rope back into its body.

fathom Six feet in length or depth.

fiddle-headed beak Decorative block of wood carved like the head of a violin; an economical alternative to a figurehead.

fore 1) Forward part of a vessel and the opposite of **aft**. 2) Short for foremast.

fore-and-aft sails Sails (mostly triangular) set from masts or **stays** rather than from **yards**.

"All sails which are not set to yards" (Smyth).

fore hatchway Opening in the deck above the forward hold.

forecastle Pronounced "fohcs'l." 1) The sailors' living/sleeping quarters, below decks in the **bow** of the ship. 2) Short for the *forecastle deck*.

forecastle deck That part of the deck above the sailors' quarters, forward of the foremast; sometimes also called, confusingly, the *forecastle*.

forecastle scuttle Stairway from the deck to the **forecastle** below.

foremast The first mast, closest to the **bow**.

foul 1) Entangled or dangerously touching, as in "got foul of," or "a foul line." 2) Unfavorable or contrary, as "foul weather" or "a foul breeze."

founder Sink.

from stem to stern From front to back, end to end.

furl Roll up and secure a sail on its **yard** or **boom**.

gaff Hooked tool used for moving pieces of blubber.

galliot Dutch or Flemish cargo vessel with rounded sides and flattened bottom.

gam "A social meeting of two (or more) Whale-ships" at sea. (Melville's definition, Ch. 53.)

gangway On the *Pequod*, the passageway between the deck and the stern cabin below.

give way Command to begin rowing or to row harder.

glass Telescope.

grapnel Small, anchor-like device with several arms, used for dragging the sea floor and for holding on to objects.

green-hand Inexperienced crewman.

ground-swell Long, rolling waves.

ground-tier butts Bottom layer of large oil casks in the hold.

gunwale Pronounced "gun'l"; strip of wood along the top of a vessel's side.

halyards Ropes for raising and lowering sails.

hamper 1) Spars and rigging aloft; also *top-hamper*. 2) Tangled ropes and other gear.

handspike Lever used for turning a **windlass**.

hard down Command to a helmsman to steer into the wind, bringing the vessel more or less to a stop.

harpoon Barbed spear used to fasten the whaleboat to a whale; the fishhook of whaling.

hatch Covering for a **hatchway** (also called a *hatch*), an opening in the deck of a ship.

hatchway Square or rectangular opening in the deck, giving access to the deck below or to a **hold**.

hawser Thick rope used for towing and other heavy work.

head sea Waves running directly against the course of a vessel.

headsails triangular **fore-and-aft** sails at a vessel's bow.

head-wind Wind blowing from the direction of a vessel's intended course.

headway Forward progress through the water.

heave-to Make a pause on the sea by adjusting sails to counteract one another and so keep the vessel relatively still; past tense **hove to**.

heave down Tip a vessel over on one side for repairs, careen. Also *heave out*. (Past tense, *hove down*.)

helm 1) Steering position. 2) The steering gear (wheel, tiller, rudder).

helmsman Sailor at the helm, steering the ship.

hogshead Large barrel holding at least 63 gallons.

hold Large storage compartment; a whaleship might have three.

hornpipe Lively sailor's dance.

horns Ends of the **cross-trees**.

horse-pieces Blocks of blubber about 10 inches wide and 2 feet long (Browne), so called because they were placed on a wooden bench called a "horse" to be sliced.

hove out Tipped up on one side.

hove over Leaning.

hove-to Stopped.

Indiaman Large cargo vessel trading with the East Indies (which includes Indonesia, the Philippines, Southeast Asia, and India).

jib Triangular sail rigged to the **jib-boom** and **jib-stay**.

jib-boom "A Spar supported by the **bowsprit**, and extending beyond it" (Russell).

jib-stay The support line leading from the **foremast** to the **jib-boom**, on which the triangular **jib** sail is strung.

jolly-boat A small work boat, usually carried at the stern of a vessel and sometimes called a *yawl*.

jury-mast Temporary replacement for a lost or badly damaged mast.

keel The lowest timber of a vessel, and its backbone.

keel up Capsize.

kelson Long, strong timber bolted to the ship's keel for reinforcement.

kentledge Pig iron **ballast**, laid along the **kelson**, or *keelson*.

King-Post "Short, square timber known by that name in Arctic whalers [serving]…to brace the ship against the icy concussions of those battering seas" (Melville's definition, Ch 27).

knight-heads Strong timbers coming up vertically through the deck in the bow of a vessel; they support the **bowsprit**.

lance Spear used to kill the whale by striking a vital organ.

larboard Left, or the left side when facing forward on a ship. The now-common term *port* is not used in *Moby-Dick*.

lash the helm a'lee Fasten the steering mechanism so the ship remains pointed into the wind, stopping its forward motion. Also *a-lee the helm*.

lashing Rope fastening one thing to another.

lead Lead weight attached to a marked line, used for measuring water depth beneath a vessel; also short for *lead line*, the line and weight together.

league Three nautical miles, each of which is 6,080 feet. One degree of latitude equals 60 nautical miles or 20 leagues.

lee 1) The side protected from the wind. 2) The direction opposite to that from which the wind is blowing; also **leeward**. See also **bring by the lee**.

lee coast A shore on a ship's **lee** side (to **leeward**) close enough to be a danger because the wind may blow the vessel ashore.

lee-beam At a right angle to the middle of the ship, on the **lee** side.

lee-way The distance a ship is pushed to **leeward** of its course by the wind.

leeward Pronounced "looard." Downwind.

lifts Ropes leading from each **mast-head** to its **yardarm** ends, supporting the weight of the **yards**.

line-knife See **boat-knife**.

line-of-battle ship The largest warship of the time, carrying seventy-four or more guns.

locker Storage chest or closet.

log Log book, a daily record of all navigational details and other observations.

log-line A thin line marked with attached knots and wound on a reel. At the line's end is a *chip* or *log* of wood that is thrown overboard. The line unreels for a set period of time, and the length of line that has run out by then indicates the ship's speed.

loggerhead "[A] stout sort of post rooted in the keel [of a whaleboat], and rising some two feet above the level of the stern platform" (Melville's definition, Ch. 48).

lubber Nautically ignorant, awkward person.

lubber's-hole An opening in the platform called the **top**; the scorned access to the topmast, easier than climbing the supporting ropes (**shrouds**).

luff Or *luff up*; bring the bow closer to the wind.

main brace Rope attached to an end of the **main-yard**, used to control the angle of the *mainsail* to the wind.

main-mast Of a whaleship's three masts, the center and tallest one.

main-top The platform at the top of the lower **main-mast**.

main-truck The round cap on the **main-mast**.

main-yard The lowest **yard** on the **main-mast**.

make 1) To see. 2) To arrive at. 3) *Make sail* is to set sail. 4) *Make fast* is to secure.

man-rope Safety line.

marline Pronounced "marlin." Narrow, two-stranded, tarred rope.

marling-spike Pointed metal tool used in splicing rope; also *marlinespike*.

mast-head The top of a mast.

men before the mast Those who live in the **forecastle**, forward of the foremast; non-officers.

mess Group of shipmates who eat their meals together.

middle-watch Midnight to 4 a.m.

midships "The middle part of the vessel, either with regard to her length or breadth" (Smyth); also *amidships*.

mincing knives Cutting implements over 2 feet long, with a handle at each end; used to slice blubber for the **try-pots**.

mizen shrouds The fixed rigging supporting the rearmost mast, the **mizen-mast**.

mizen-mast The third and rearmost mast; commonly spelled *mizzenmast*.

mizentop Small platform at the top of the lower **mizen-mast**, the ship's third mast.

oakum Fibers from unraveled old ropes, impregnated with tar and used to caulk seams in wooden ships.

offing 1) That distant part of the sea visible from shore. 2) A good distance out to sea at the start of a voyage.

on the quarter From the rear, at about a 45-degree angle to the ship's side.

open 1) To sight. 2) Unobscured.

orlop-deck The lowest deck; also *orlop*.

packet Vessel making regular, scheduled trips between the same ports.

pike Single-pronged pole used for moving chunks of blubber.

piled-up With all sails set.

pin Short for **belaying pin**.

plug-hole Drain hole in the bottom of a boat.

pod A school of whales; a group that travels together.

point 1/32 of a compass circle, or 11.25 degrees.

poop Raised section of the deck at the stern.

Post Captain Commanding officer of a ship who also has the naval rank of Captain.

preventer tackles Additional ropes as backup to the rudder tackles.

proa Large Malay war-vessel, propelled by oars and sails.

prow The **bow**.

quarter The side of a vessel, from the **stern** forward to the rigging supporting the **main-mast** (Lever, Dana). See **on the quarter**.

quarter-boat One of the whaleboats hanging from the ship's **quarter**.

quarter-deck The part of the deck to the rear of the **main-mast**, and special domain of the captain.

raise See and shout out for.

range Come abreast of another vessel or a whale.

razee Cut down, reduce. (Normally in reference to a ship's hull.)

reef Reduce sail area by tying up part of the sail.

reeve Pass a rope through a hole or over the wheel of a pulley.

riggers Workers hired to prepare the ship's ropes and **tackle**.

rigging A vessel's visible ropes. A sailing vessel has *standing rigging*, fixed ropes supporting the masts, and *running rigging*, pulled on to control yards and sails.

ring-bolt Large iron ring bolted through the deck.

rope walk A building in which rope was manufactured; it could be 1,000 feet long or more.

round-house Normally a cabin in the stern large enough to walk around in (thus its name), but in *Moby-Dick* also the French captain's privy (Ch. 99).

rowlocks Pronounced "rolicks"; spaces cut in a boat's **gunwale** for the oars to rest in while rowing.

royal mast The highest section of any mast; also, confusingly, the name given to the top portion of the top-gallant mast; also called in the text **t' gallant mast**.

royal mast-head The top of the **royal mast**.

royal yard The fourth **yard** from the deck, on any mast.

run A separate area below decks where a ship begins to narrow and curve upward toward the stern.

running rigging Ropes that are pulled on or otherwise adjusted while sailing.

sail Figure of speech for a sailing ship or ships.

schooner Common type of sailing vessel with two or more masts, **fore-and-aft** rigged.

scud Blowing mist or low, broken clouds.

scupper-holes Drainholes in the deck's gutters. Also *scuppers*.

scuttle 1) An opening in the deck which, in *Moby-Dick*, is always the entrance to a stairway leading below. 2) Verb meaning to sink a vessel by making or opening holes in its hull.

scuttle-butt Fresh-water cask on deck. From sailors' conversations there comes the meaning "gossip."

seas Waves, as in "sledge-hammering seas" (Ch. 135); also singular, as in "a combing sea dashed me off" (Ch. 100).

Season-on-the-Line One of the best places and times to hunt sperm whales in the Pacific was within a few degrees of the equator (*the Line*) from near the Galapagos Islands off South America to the Kingsmills Islands 90 degrees longitude to the west, and from November or December to April.

seizings Bindings of cord or rope.

seventy-four Large, 74-gun warship.

shallop Small boat.

shears Beams above the quarter-deck on some whaleships, bearing spare or disabled boats; defined in Ch. 131.

sheave See **blocks . . . sheaves**.

sheet home Spread the sail horizontally as far as possible by pulling on the **sheets**, the ropes attached to one or both lower corners of a sail.

sheets 1) Ropes controlling the lower corners or *clews* of **square sails** and the rear lower corners of **fore-and-aft sails** (also called *clews*). 2) The sheets of a **boom** hold it against the force of the wind in its sail.

ship biscuit Unsalted flour-and-water biscuit baked hard for preservation; *hardtack*.

ship keepers Crew members who work only aboard ship (not in the whaleboats).

shoal 1) Large group (usually of sea-creatures). 2) Particularly shallow place in the water.

shorten Reduce sail area by **furling** and/or **reefing** the sails set.

shrouds The fixed (*standing*) **rigging** supporting the masts.

skiff Small rowboat.

skrimshander Now called "scrimshaw": incised sperm whale teeth or items carved from whale bone (Melville's definition, Ch. 57).

sky-sail A small, light **square sail** above the **royal**, used in fair weather.

skylarking Fooling; playing tricks.

skysail-poles Detachable upper extremities of masts, rising above the **royal masts** to support the highest yards and sails, **sky-sails**.

slip the cable Let go of the anchor cable rather than raise the anchor.

sloop Sailing vessel with one mast.

sogger Meaning "soldier"; in sailor-usage, someone whose supposed hard work is only pretense.

sou'-wester Waterproof sailor's hat with an extra-wide brim at the back.

soundings Material from the sea bottom brought up by a deep-sea measuring line and lead (as used in Ch. 106); to be *on soundings* is to be in water shallow enough for the line to reach the sea floor; *off soundings* means being in water too deep to be measured by the line.

spar Wooden, sail-supporting part of a vessel. "The general term for any **mast**, **yard**, **boom**, **gaff**, &c." (Smyth).

speak: Communicate with a ship at sea.

splice 1) Make two ropes into one by weaving their strands together. 2) A joining made by weaving together. See **eye-splice**.

sprung Strained enough to injure the wood fibers.

square in Turn the **yards** so that they (and their **square sails**) are at right angles to the hull of the vessel. Also *square the yards*.

square-rigged Referring to a vessel with masts crossed by horizontal **yards** from which rectangular **square sails** hang.

square sail Four-cornered sail hung from a **yard** which is suspended at the middle from a mast.

stand away Steer a course, as in "stood away for the nearest harbor" (Ch. 54).

Star—bo-l-e-e-n-s The men in the starboard watch; from **starboard** and **bowline**.

starboard Right, or the right side when facing forward on a ship.

stave Smash in or puncture, past tense **stove**; as in "come a stove boat and stove body when they will, for stave my soul, Jove himself cannot" (Ch. 7).

stay Rope supporting a mast segment (as *main-topmast stay*, *fore-t'gallant stay*, etc.). A *forestay* leads straight forward; a *backstay* leads to the ship's side, to the rear.

stem The foremost timber in the hull of a vessel.

stern The rear of a vessel; and as a verb, to row backwards. Used in various expressions, such as *by the stern*, meaning stern-first, "[the *Pequod*] profoundly settled by the stern" (Ch. 124); *under the stern*, meaning close to the stern, "[a boat] pulled round under the stern" (Ch. 48), and also from behind, "a ship . . . bearing down under the stern" (Ch. 100).

stern sheets The space to the rear of the **thwarts** (rowing seats) in a small boat.

storm-trysail Strong triangular sail used in bad weather.

stove Also *staved*, *staven*, or *stoven*, the past tense and participle of **stave**; describing anything smashed in or punctured.

strike To lower. *Strike down* is to lower something into the hold.

stunsail Pronounced "stuns'l." Studding sail, a light sail rigged from a portable extension to a **yardarm** called a stunsail **boom**, and set in fair weather to increase speed.

sway up Lift by means of **tackles**.

sword-mat A yarn mat, named for the sword-shaped wooden slat used in weaving it.

t' gallant-mast Topgallant mast, the third section of a mast from the deck up, pronounced as Melville spelled it. The **royal-mast** is actually the top portion of this mast.

tack Change from one course to another by turning the vessel's **bow** through the wind.

tackles Pronounced "taykls." Lifting devices made of ropes and pulleys (see **blocks . . . sheaves**).

taffrail Curved deck railing at the ship's stern.

tarpaulins Waterproof hats.

thole-pins Upright pins in the **gunwale** of a boat that keep the oars in place while rowing.

thwart Rowing seat of a whaleboat.

tiller Steering lever attached to the rudder.

timber head The part of a ship's rib above the deck, to which large ropes may be tied.

top Platform at the top of a lower mast.

top-block Large single-pulley block used to raise or lower the topmasts.

top-gallant sails Pronounced "t'gallant" and sometimes spelled that way in *Moby-Dick*. The third level of sails above the deck.

top-maul Heavy hammer.

topsails Second layer of sails above the deck.

train oil Oil from right whales, large baleen whales; defined in Ch. 32.

transom A crossbeam in the stern, used as a seat.

tree-nails Pronounced "trunnels." Long hardwood pins joining together the planks and timbers as nails would do.

trick Two-hour turn at the helm (Russell).

trim dish Adjust a vessel's posture, its *trim*.

truck Small circle of wood topping a mast; metaphorically, the finishing piece.

try-pots Huge iron pots mounted in the brick **try-works** on a whaleship's deck, in which blubber is fried to extract the oil. See Ch. 96.

try-works The brick structure on deck holding the **try-pots**.

tub *Line tub* placed in the bottom of a whaleboat, in which the harpoon line is coiled.

Turk's-head Complex, turban-shaped decorative knot.

turn to! "Get to work!"

turning flukes Said of a whale in the act of diving, and thereby showing its tail flukes.

under weigh A ship is under weigh when the anchor has been raised (*weighed*). It is *under way* when it is moving through the water.

up helm Command to move the tiller toward the windward side of the vessel, which would turn it so the wind blows from astern.

waif pole "[A] pennoned pole…which, when additional game is at hand, [is] inserted upright into the floating body of a dead whale, both to mark its place on the sea, and also as token of prior possession…" (Ch. 87).

waist The midsection of the deck, between the **forecastle** and the **quarterdeck**.

watch A period of time on duty (usually four hours), and the men in that duty group. The on-duty watch is *on deck*, while those off duty are referred to as *below*.

weather side Windward side; the side struck by the wind, opposite the **lee** side.

weather-sheet Rope on the windward side of a vessel controlling a **boom** or the lower corner of a sail.

whale-pike Single-pronged pole used for moving pieces of blubber.

whalebone See **baleen**. Also *whale-bone* but not *whale bone*, which is actual bone.

whip Light **tackle** made of a single rope and single **block**.

white-bone The white water at the bow of a moving vessel or the head of a swimming whale. See also **bone in her mouth**.

windlass Horizontal cylindrical machine near the bow, turned with handles or with levers called **handspikes**, and used, as is a **capstan**, in raising the anchor and other heavy tasks.

windlass-bitts Two strong timbers protruding from the deck and supporting the ends of the **windlass**.

working Coming loose.

yard Long, heavy pole, attached at its center to a mast, from which a **square sail** is suspended. A yard is a type of **spar**.

yard-arm One of a **yard**'s two arms, from the mast to its end.

yaw Swing from one side to the other of an intended course.